# abnormal psychology

eighth edition

THOMAS F.
## OLTMANNS
Washington University in St. Louis

ROBERT E.
## EMERY
University of Virginia

## PEARSON

Boston    Columbus    Indianapolis    New York    San Francisco    Upper Saddle River
Amsterdam    Cape Town    Dubai    London    Madrid    Milan    Munich    Paris    Montréal    Toronto
Delhi    Mexico City    São Paulo    Sydney    Hong Kong    Seoul    Singapore    Taipei    Tokyo

To Gail, Josh, Sara, Billy, Presley, Riley,
and Kinley—T.F.O.

To Kimberly, Maggie, Julia, Bobby,
Lucy, and John—R.E.E.

**Editor-in-Chief:** Dickson Musslewhite
**Senior Acquisitions Editor:** Amber Chow
**Editorial Assistant:** Alex Stavrakas
**VP, Director of Marketing:** Brandy Dawson
**Senior Marketing Manager:** Jeremy Intal
**Marketing Assistant:** Frank Alarcon
**Director, Project Management Services:**
  Lisa Iarkowski
**Senior Managing Editor:** Linda Behrens
**Project Manager:** Shelly Kupperman
**Program Manager:** Annemarie Franklin

**Procurement Manager:** Mary Fischer
**Procurement Specialist:** Diane Peirano
**Interior/Cover Designer:** DeMarinis Design LLC
**Digital Media Editor:** Tom Scalzo
**Digital Media Project Manager:** Pamela Weldin
**Full-Service Project Management:** PreMediaGlobal
**Printer/Binder:** R. R. Donnelley and Sons
**Cover Printer:** Lehigh-Phoenix Color/Hagerstown
**Cover Image:** Terry Vine/Blend Images/Getty Images
**Text Font:** Adobe Garamond Pro 10.5/13

Credits and acknowledgments borrowed from other sources and reproduced, with permission, in this textbook appear on the appropriate page of appearance and on pages 561–563.

**Library of Congress Cataloging-in-Publication Data**

Oltmanns, Thomas F.
  Abnormal psychology \ Thomas F. Oltmanns, Washington University in St. Louis, Robert E. Emery, University of Virginia.—Eighth edition.
    pages cm
  ISBN 978-0-205-97074-2
1. Psychology, Pathological.   2. Mental illness.   I. Emery, Robert E.   II. Title.
RC454.O44 2014
616.89—dc23

2013037915

10 9 8 7 6 5 4 3 2 1

**Student Edition**
ISBN-10:      0-205-97074-5
ISBN-13:  978-0-205-97074-2

**Books à la Carte**
ISBN-10:      0-205-97106-7
ISBN-13:  978-0-205-97106-0

# brief contents

# contents

## 6 Anxiety Disorders and Obsessive-Compulsive Disorder   143

## 7 Acute and Posttraumatic Stress Disorders, Dissociative Disorders, and Somatic Symptom Disorders   174

# preface

Emotional suffering touches all of our lives at some point in time. Psychological problems affect many of us directly and all of us indirectly—through our loved ones, friends, and the strangers whose troubled behavior we cannot ignore. Abnormal psychology is not about "them." Abnormal psychology is about all of us.

Abnormal psychology is also about scientific inquiry. In this eighth edition of our text, once again, we bring both the science and the personal aspects of abnormal psychology to life. We answer pressing intellectual and human questions as accurately, sensitively, and completely as possible, given the pace of new discoveries. Throughout this book, we offer an engaging yet rigorous treatment of abnormal psychology, highlighting both the latest research and theory and the urgent needs of the people behind the disorders.

## Why Do You Need This New Edition?

- *DSM-5*! The eighth edition of *Abnormal Psychology* is completely updated with information from the recently published *DSM-5*. We delayed our revision for a few months, so we could do more than just add tables of *DSM-5* diagnostic criteria. You will find a great many *DSM-5* tables, of course. But you will also see a discussion of the conceptual, practical, and political debates about *DSM-5* integrated throughout the text.

- *Thinking Critically About DSM-5* is a new feature that appears in every chapter. We teach students about *DSM-5*. Then we encourage the students to *think deeply* about the pros and cons of this diagnostic system. How does *DSM-5* deal with dimensions versus categories in defining abnormal behavior? Is autism really best viewed as a spectrum disorder? What arguments lie behind *DSM-5*'s decision to include new diagnoses like binge eating disorder and hoarding disorder? Has *DSM-5* taken the descriptive approach too far, for example, grouping diagnoses like anorexia nervosa and pica together because both involve eating? What does *DSM-5* say about the causes and treatment of mental disorders?

- We include hundreds of new studies about *DSM-5* and dozens of other topics. Psychological science is dynamic, ever-changing, and ever-growing. Our textbook grows with the field, bringing to life both the exciting process of discovery and important new findings about disorders and their causes and effective treatment. This eighth edition is at the cutting edge, because we have culled the best and most important new research from thousands of studies to include hundreds of new ones here.

- How can a student new to abnormal psychology learn to think critically about such a broad, important topic? We guide you in your learning—and in critical thinking—with "The Big Picture" a set of probing questions that open each chapter. "The Big Picture" orients you to key issues and themes covered in the relevant chapter. Each chapter ends with "The Big Picture Revisited," returning to the key issues, briefly summarizing the central point, and directing you to pages where you can find a discussion of the details. You may have been asking yourself these kind of critical questions, but if in case you weren't, we show you how to keep the big picture in mind.

- We focus on the forest *and* the trees. *Abnormal Psychology* is about real people. We bring the human side of psychology problems to life with a series of new *Speaking Out* videos that we edited personally. We promise that these videos will make you think and make you feel, too. We also have included more on the human side of psychological problems with new and updated case studies, as well as updated "Getting Help" features that offer practical advice for you and your loved ones.

- You will find that *Abnormal Psychology* introduces you to new concepts from the frontiers of understanding interactions between genes and the environment. For example, are you a "dandelion" who can survive in most any environment, or instead are you a fragile "orchid" who will wither under harsh conditions but bloom gloriously in the right environment?

- You will find new and updated discussions of treatments that work. Do we at last have an effective treatment for adolescents with anorexia nervosa? Read our discussion of the "Maudsley method" in Chapter 10.

- We do not shy away from controversy, because we all can learn from facing the issues squarely. "Sexual addiction" seems to be epidemic. Is this a mental disorder? We draw you into the latest issues, research, and debates in Chapter 12. Or speaking of epidemics, what about the purported "epidemic of autism"? We not only take you through the misguided (and largely resolved) controversy about vaccines and autism, but also discuss how much current controversy about the autism "epidemic" stems from much broader criteria used to diagnose autism spectrum disorder.

## DSM-5 Is Here and Intergrated Everywhere in This Eighth Edition!

Much anticipated and at long last, *DSM-5* was published in May 2013. The new version of the Diagnostic and Statistical Manual includes many changes. A great many of the revisions incorporated into *DSM-5* are a step forward. Others, well, not so much. . . .

We eagerly awaited the final publication of the *DSM-5*, as did other mental health professionals and textbook authors. We were curious to see what much-discussed and debated changes made it into the final *DSM-5*, and what diagnoses and diagnostic criteria remained the same. Naturally, we wanted our eighth edition of *Abnormal Psychology* to include *DSM-5*, so that students and instructors could have up-to-date information on this very influential diagnostic system. Yet, we made a decision not to rush this revision. Why? We wanted to do more than just include tables with new, *DSM-5* diagnostic criteria. We wanted to integrate and evaluate *DSM-5* into the fabric of every chapter. As a result, we might not be the first textbook published to be able to proclaim that we include *DSM-5*. We think it's better to be able to say that the eighth edition of our text includes, integrates, and evaluates *DSM-5* in a thorough, careful, and critical way.

Of course, you will find a great many tables of *DSM-5* diagnostic criteria in this text. But you will find much more. The most visible addition is our brand-new feature, *Thinking Critically About DSM-5*. Appearing in every chapter, *Thinking Critically About DSM-5* asks and answers questions like these: How does the *DSM-5*'s categorical diagnostic system deal with dimensional variations in abnormal (and normal) behavior? Is autism really best viewed as a spectrum disorder? What arguments—scientific, political, and practical—lie behind *DSM-5*'s decision to include new diagnoses like binge eating disorder and temper dysregulation disorder? Has *DSM-5* taken the descriptive approach too far, too literally grouping diagnoses together based solely on appearance (such as pica and anorexia nervosa)? What does (and doesn't) *DSM-5* say about the causes and treatment of mental disorders—and why?

Our goal in writing the *Thinking Critically About DSM-5* features was, first, to teach students about the *DSM-5*, and, second, to help students *think* about *DSM-5*. We want students to understand the principles behind classification and diagnosis in general. We want them to grapple with the conceptual and empirical uncertainties concerning particular disorders. We also want students to recognize at least some of the practical and political agendas that influence what, in the context of our culture and times, we decide is or isn't a mental disorder.

These ambitious goals require more than *DSM-5* tables and new features. So, we also integrated various diagnostic and conceptual controversies about *DSM-5* throughout every chapter. Of course, we updated the text specifically for *DSM-5*. But in fact, we have highlighted the theoretical issues behind various diagnoses in every edition of our text. We are proud to note that many contemporary controversies surrounding the *DSM-5* have been highlighted in our text for a long time. To offer just one example: Should abnormal behavior be classified along dimensions or into categories? This issue has been a key theme of Oltmanns and Emery, *Abnormal Psychology*, since the first edition. Questions like this are not just about the *DSM-5*. Debates about topics like dimensions versus categories are about critical thinking in general. Consider this question: Where does an instructor set cutoffs, turning the dimension of test score averages into the category of letter grades? Now, *that's* a debate about dimensions and categories that a student can understand!

## Critical Thinking

*Abnormal Psychology* is all about critical thinking. We believe that critical thinking is essential for science, for helping those in need, and for the intellectual and personal development of our students. Today's students are overwhelmed with information from all kinds of media. Critical thinking is indispensible, so students can distinguish between information that is good, bad, or ugly (to borrow a phrase from our favorite Western movie). We want students to think critically about abnormal psychology—and everything else.

We encourage the readers of *Abnormal Psychology* to be *inquiring skeptics*. Students need to be skeptical in evaluating all kinds of claims. We help them to do so by teaching students to *think like psychological scientists*. Yet, we also want students to be inquiring, to be skeptical not cynical. Pressing human needs and fascinating psychological questions make it essential for us to seek answers, not just explode myths.

In this eighth edition of our text, we emphasize critical thinking in several ways. As noted, we include the new feature, *Thinking Critically About DSM-5*. We also refined our chapter opening feature, "The Big Picture," to link even more tightly with our chapter ending, "The Big Picture: Critical Thinking Review." "The Big Picture" draws students into each chapter by posing common yet critical questions about key substantive topics. The questions also orient the student to conceptual themes about the substance and the methods of abnormal psychology. Then, at the end of each chapter, we have a section called "The Big Picture: Critical Thinking Review," which summarizes key, big-picture questions and includes handy page references for review purposes.

We also have continued to revise and expand our "Critical Thinking Matters" discussions, which are found in every chapter. These features address some timely, often controversial, and always critically important topics, for example, the purported link between vaccines and autism (see Chapter 2). Critical thinking matters because psychological problems matter deeply to those who suffer and to their loved ones. Good research tells us—and them—which treatments work, and which ones don't, as well as what might cause mental illness, and what doesn't. Critical thinking matters because students in abnormal psychology surely will not remember all the details they learn in this course. In fact, they shouldn't focus exclusively on facts, because data will change with new scientific developments. But if students can learn to think critically about abnormal psychology, the lesson will last a lifetime and be used repeatedly, not only in understanding psychological problems, but also in every area of their lives.

Our "Critical Thinking Matters" features help students to *think* about science, about pseudo-science, and about themselves. For example, in Chapter 2 we address the mistaken belief, still promoted widely on the Internet and in the popular media, that mercury in widely used measles/mumps/rubella (MMR) vaccinations in the 1990s caused an epidemic of autism (and perhaps a host of other psychological problems for children). "Critical Thinking Matters" outlines the concerns of the frightened public, but goes on to point out (1) the failure to find support for this fear in numerous, large-scale scientific studies; (2) the scientific stance that the burden of proof lies with the proponents of any hypothesis, including speculations about MMR; (3) the widely ignored fact that 10 of the original 13 authors who raised the theoretical possibility *publicly withdrew their speculation about autism and MMR*; (4) the fact that the findings of legal actions, sadly, do not necessarily reach conclusions consistent with scientific knowledge; and (5) recent discrediting of the scientists, journal article, and legal findings that originally "supported" this false claim. As we discuss in Chapter 15, moreover, the apparent epidemic of autism very likely resulted from increased awareness of the disorder and loosened criteria for diagnosing autism, not from an actual increase in cases.

## Real People

We want students to think critically about disorders *and* to be sensitive to the struggles of individuals with psychological problems. As scientist-practitioners, we see these dual goals not only as compatible, but also as essential. One way that we underscore the personal nature of emotional problems is in our "Getting Help" features found in every chapter. In "Getting Help," we directly address the personal side of psychological disorders and try to answer the sorts of questions that students often ask us privately after a lecture or during office hours. The "Getting Help" sections give responsible, empirically sound, and concrete guidance on such personal topics as

- What treatments should I seek out for a particular disorder? (See Chapters 2, 6, 10, and 12)

- What can I do to help someone I know who has a psychological problem? (See Chapters 5, 9, 10, and 16)

- How can I find a good therapist? (See Chapters 3, 5, and 12)

- Where can I get reliable information from books, the Internet, or professionals in my community? (See Chapters 1, 5, 7, and 11)

- What self-help strategies can I try or suggest to friends? (See Chapters 6, 11, and 12)

Students can also find research-based information on the effectiveness and efficacy of various treatments in Chapter 3, "Treatment of Psychological Disorders," and in the "Treatment" headings near the end of every disorder chapter. We cover treatment generally at the beginning of the text but in detail in the context of each disorder, because different treatments are more or less effective for different psychological problems.

## "Speaking Out" Videos

One of the best ways to understand the needs of the people behind the disorders is to hear their stories in their own words. We worked in consultation with Pearson and NKP Productions to produce (and expand) a video series called ***Speaking Out: Interviews with People Who Struggle with Psychological Disorders.*** The earlier cases in the *Speaking Out* series were introduced with previous editions of our book. We have added four new cases, addressing the following problem areas: gender dysphoria, nonsuicidal self-injury, dissociative amnesia, and binge eating disorder. These interviews give students a window into the lives of people who in many ways may not be that different from anyone else, but who do struggle with various kinds of mental disorder. As before, the new video cases also include a segment called "A Day in the Life," which features interviews with friends and family members who discuss their relationships, feelings, and perspectives. We introduce students to each of these people in the appropriate chapters of our book, using their photos and a brief description of relevant issues that should be considered when viewing the video cases. The full versions of the interviews are available to instructors either on DVD or on MyPsychLab.com (www.mypsychlab.com).

We are especially proud of the *Speaking Out* videos and view them as a part of our text, not as a supplement, because we were intimately involved with their production. As with the original series, we screened the new video cases, helped to construct and guide the actual interviews, and gave detailed feedback on how to edit the films to make the disorders real for students and fit closely with the organization and themes in our eighth edition.

## New Research

The unsolved mysteries of abnormal psychology challenge all of our intellectual and personal resources. In our eighth edition, we include the latest "clues" psychological scientists have unearthed in doing the detective work of research, including references to hundreds of new studies. But the measure of a leading-edge textbook is not merely the number of new references; it is the number of new studies the authors have reviewed and evaluated before deciding which ones to include and which ones to discard. For every new reference in this edition of our text, we have read many additional papers before selecting the one gem to include. Some of the updated research and perspectives in this edition include:

- Updated discussion regarding the general definition of mental disorders, as employed in *DSM-5*, and new estimates regarding the number of mental health professionals delivering services (*Chapter 1*)

- Enhanced coverage of gene–environment interactions (including "orchids" versus "dandelions") and failures to replicate the effects of specific genes (*Chapter 2*)

- New evidence on what makes placebos "work," on disseminating evidenced-based treatments, and "3rd wave" CBT (*Chapter 3*)

- Revised discussion of the reliability of diagnosis, based on new evidence from the *DSM-5* field trials (*Chapter 4*)

- New mention of premenstrual dysphoric disorder (a category added to *DSM-5*), and new discussion of evidence regarding the increase in military suicides, which have received considerable attention in the popular media (*Chapter 5*)

- Addition of material on hoarding disorder (another new diagnostic category added to *DSM-5*) and expanded coverage of the diagnostic features and prevalence of obsessive-compulsive symptoms and spectrum disorders, which are now listed separately from anxiety disorders in *DSM-5* (*Chapter 6*)

- Further consideration of resilience in response to trauma, questions about secondary trauma, and new questions about somatoform and dissociative disorders (*Chapter 7*)

- New research on cultural differences in social support, religion, and coping, and the daily experience of pain (*Chapter 8*)

- Careful explanation of the two approaches to classification of personality disorders that are now included in *DSM-5* as well as the similarities and distinctions between them (*Chapter 9*)

- Questions and new information about binge eating disorder and obesity; latest evidence on redefining, treating (the Maudsley method), and preventing eating disorders; up-to-date consideration of women's portrayal in the media (*Chapter 10*)

- New evidence regarding the frequency of overdose deaths attributed to opioid pain-killers, which has increased dramatically in recent years as well as expanded coverage of gambling disorder, which is now listed with Substance-Related and Addictive Disorders in *DSM-5* (*Chapter 11*)

- Discussion of the revised approach to the definition and classification of paraphilic disorders (*Chapter 12*)

- Careful consideration of the proposed diagnostic construct "Attenuated Psychosis Syndrome," including its potential benefits as well as likely negative consequences (*Chapter 13*)

- Explanation of the change to neurocognitive disorders as the overall diagnostic term for this chapter as well as the deletion of the term amnestic disorder (*Chapter 14*)

- More questions about the autism spectrum, the so-called epidemic of autism, and estimates of the prevalence of autism spectrum disorder (*Chapter 15*)

- Questions about the *DSM-5*'s elimination of childhood disorders; updated discussion of adolescent depression, antidepressants, suicide risk; careful consideration of the new diagnosis and the issues behind it, disruptive mood dysregulation disorder (*Chapter 16*)

- Further consideration of "relational diagnoses," complicated grief, and psychological pain (*Chapter 17*)

- Discussion of how diagnostic thresholds are a matter of life and death in the case of intellectual disabilities; new material on advanced psychiatric directives (*Chapter 18*)

## Still the Gold Standard

We see the most exciting and promising future for abnormal psychology in the integration of theoretical approaches, professional specialties, and science and practice, not in the old, fractured competition among "paradigms," a split between psychology and psychiatry, or the division between scientists and practitioners. We view integration as the gold standard of any forward-looking abnormal psychology text, and the gold standard remains unchanged in the eighth edition of our textbook.

### Integrating Causes and Treatment

For much of the last century, abnormal psychology was dominated by theoretical paradigms, a circumstance that reminds us of the parable of the seven blind men and the elephant. One blind man grasps a tusk and concludes that an elephant is very much like a spear. Another feels a leg and decides an elephant is like a tree, and so on. Our goal from the first edition of *Abnormal Psychology* has been to show the reader the whole elephant. We do this through our unique *integrative systems approach*, in which we focus on what we know today rather than what we used to think. In every chapter, we consider the latest evidence on the *multiple* risk factors that contribute to psychological disorders, as well as the most effective psychological and biomedical treatments. Even if science cannot yet paint a picture of the whole elephant, we clearly tell the student what we know, what we don't know, and how psychologists think the pieces might fit together.

### Pedagogy: Integrated Content and Methods

We also continue to bring cohesion to abnormal psychology—and to the student—with pedagogy. Each disorder chapter unfolds in the same way, providing a *coherent* framework with a *consistent chapter outline*. We open with an Overview followed by one or two extended Case Studies. We then discuss Symptoms, Diagnosis, Frequency, Causes, and, finally, Treatment.

Abnormal psychology is not only about the latest research, but also about the methods psychologists use (and invent) in order to do scientific detective work. Unlike any other text in this field, we cover the scientific method by offering brief "Research Methods" features in every single chapter. Teaching methods in the context of content helps students appreciate the importance of scientific procedures and assumptions, makes learning research methods more manageable, and gives the text flexibility. By the end of the text, our unique approach allows us to cover research methods in *more* detail than we could reasonably cover in a single, detached chapter. Many of our students have told us that the typical research methods chapter seems dry, difficult, and—to our great disappointment—irrelevant. These problems never arise with our integrated, contextualized approach to research methods.

Abnormal psychology also is, of course, about real people with real problems. We bring the human, clinical side of abnormal psychology alive with detailed "Case Studies." The case studies take the reader along the human journey of pain, triumph, frustration, and fresh starts that is abnormal psychology. The cases help students to think more deeply about psychological disorders, much as our own clinical experience enriches our understanding. (We both have been active clinicians as well as active researchers throughout our careers.) In extended cases near the beginning of each chapter, in briefer cases later, and in first-person accounts throughout, the student sees how ordinary lives are disrupted by psychological problems—and how effective treatment can rebuild shattered lives. The case studies also make the details and complexity of the science concrete, relevant, and essential to the "real world."

Sometimes a study or problem suggests a departure from current thinking or raises side issues that deserve to be examined in detail. We cover these emerging ideas in features identified by the topic at hand. One example of an emerging issue we discuss in this way is whether the female response to stress might be to "tend and befriend" rather than fight or flight (Chapter 8). Other topics include the common elements of suicide (Chapter 5) and a system for classifying different types of rapists (Chapter 12).

## Supplements Package
## MyPsychLab for Abnormal Psychology

MyPsychLab is an online homework, tutorial, and assessment program that truly engages students in learning. It helps students better prepare for class, quizzes, and exams—resulting in better performance in the course. It provides educators a dynamic set of tools for gauging individual and class performance. To order the eighth edition with MyPsychLab, use ISBN 0205997945.

### VIRTUAL CASE STUDIES

Virtual Case Studies offers you a science-based, interactive simulation where you can learn how a number of risk factors and protective factors could impact disorder development in a virtual person. As you progress through the simulation you will not act as the character or as a clinician, but will be able to independently explore a variety of different behaviors, events, and outcomes that one who suffers from a disorder could potentially encounter. There are no right or wrong selections, as exploring the impact of both risk and protective factors in the life of the character will provide valuable insights into the experience of a disorder along a continuum. The following Virtual Case Studies are available at mypsychlab.com:

Anxiety Disorders
Mood Disorders
Eating Disorders
Substance Use Disorders

### SPEAKING OUT: INTERVIEWS WITH PEOPLE WHO STRUGGLE WITH PSYCHOLOGICAL DISORDERS

This set of video segments allows students to see firsthand accounts of patients with various disorders. The interviews were conducted by licensed clinicians and range in length from 8 to 25 minutes. Disorders include major depressive disorder, obsessive-compulsive disorder, anorexia nervosa, PTSD, alcoholism, schizophrenia, autism, ADHD, bipolar disorder, social phobia, hypochondriasis, borderline personality disorder, and adjustment to physical illness. These video segments are available on DVD or through MyPsychLab.

Volume 1: ISBN 0-13-193332-9
Volume 2: ISBN 0-13-600303-6
Volume 3: ISBN 0-13-230891-6

### INSTRUCTOR'S MANUAL (ISBN 0205979742)

A comprehensive tool for class preparation and management, each chapter includes learning objectives, a chapter outline, lecture suggestions, discussion ideas, classroom activities, discussion questions, and video resources. Available for download on the Instructor's Resource Center at www.pearsonhighered.com.

### TEST BANK (ISBN 0205979777)

The Test Bank has been rigorously developed, reviewed, and checked for accuracy, to ensure the quality of both the questions and the answers. It includes fully referenced multiple-choice, short answer, and concise essay questions. Each question is accompanied by a page reference, difficulty level, skill type (factual, conceptual, or applied), topic, a learning objective, and a correct answer. Available for download on the Instructor's Resource Center at www.pearsonhighered.com.

## MyTest (ISBN 0205982395)

A powerful assessment-generation program that helps instructors easily create and print quizzes and exams. Questions and tests can be authored online, allowing instructors ultimate flexibility and the ability to efficiently manage assessments anytime, anywhere. Instructors can easily access existing questions and edit, create, and store questions using a simple drag-and-drop technique and word-like controls. Data on each question provide information on difficulty level and the page number of corresponding text discussion. For more information, go to www.PearsonMyTest.com.

### LECTURE POWERPOINT SLIDES (ISBN 0205982409)

The PowerPoint slides provide an active format for presenting concepts from each chapter and feature relevant figures and tables from the text. Available for download on the Instructor's Resource Center at www.pearsonhighered.com.

### ENHANCED LECTURE POWERPOINT SLIDES WITH EMBEDDED VIDEOS (ISBN 0205982379)

The lecture PowerPoint slides have been embedded with select Speaking Out video pertaining to each disorder chapter, enabling instructors to show videos within the context of their lecture. No Internet connection is required to play videos.

## POWERPOINT SLIDES FOR PHOTOS, FIGURES, AND TABLES (ISBN 0205982417)

Contain only the photos, figures, and line art from the textbook. Available for download on the Instructor's Resource Center at www.pearsonhighered.com.

## CourseSmart (ISBN 0205979807)

CourseSmart textbooks online is an exciting choice for students looking to save money. As an alternative to purchasing the print textbook, students can subscribe to the same content online and save up to 60 percent off the suggested list price of the print text. With a CourseSmart eTextbook, students can search the text, make notes online, print out reading assignments that incorporate lecture notes, and bookmark important passages for later review. For more information or to subscribe to the CourseSmart eTextbook, visit www.coursesmart.com.

## Acknowledgments

Writing and revising this textbook is a never-ending task that fortunately is also a labor of love. This eighth edition is the culmination of years of effort and is the product of many people's hard work. The first people we wish to thank for their important contributions to making this text of the future, not of the past, are the following expert reviewers who have unselfishly offered us a great many helpful suggestions, both in this and in previous editions: John Dale Alden, III, Lipscomb University; John Allen, University of Arizona; Hal Arkowitz, University of Arizona; Jo Ann Armstrong, Patrick Henry Community College; Gordon Atlas, Alfred University; Deanna Barch, Washington University; Catherine Barnard, Kalamazoo Community College; Thomas G. Bowers, Pennsylvania State University, Harrisburg; Stephanie Boyd, University of South Carolina; Gail Bruce-Sanford, University of Montana; Ann Calhoun-Seals, Belmont Abbey College; Caryn L. Carlson, University of Texas at Austin; Richard Cavasina, California University of Pennsylvania; Laurie Chassin, Arizona State University; Lee H. Coleman, Miami University of Ohio; Bradley T. Conner, Temple University; Andrew Corso, University of Pennsylvania; Dean Cruess, University of Pennsylvania; Danielle Dick, Washington University; Juris G. Draguns, Pennsylvania State University; Sarah Lopez-Duran; Nicholas Eaton, Stony Brook University; William Edmonston, Jr., Colgate University; Ronald Evans, Washburn University; John Foust, Parkland College; Dan Fox, Sam Houston State University; Alan Glaros, University of Missouri, Kansas City; Ian H. Gotlib, Stanford University; Irving Gottesman, University of Virginia; Mort Harmatz, University of Massachusetts; Marjorie L. Hatch, Southern Methodist University; Jennifer A. Haythornwaite, Johns Hopkins University; Holly Hazlett-Stevens, University of Nevada, Reno; Brant P. Hasler, University of Arizona; Debra

L. Hollister, Valencia Community College; Jessica Jablonski, University of Delaware; Jennifer Jenkins, University of Toronto; Jutta Joormann, University of Miami; Pamela Keel, Florida State University; Stuart Keeley, Bowling Green State University; Lynn Kemen, Hunter College; Carolin Keutzer, University of Oregon; Robert Lawyer, Delgado Community College; Marvin Lee, Tennessee State University; Barbara Lewis, University of West Florida; Mark H. Licht, Florida State University; Freda Liu, Arizona State University; Roger Loeb, University of Michigan, Dearborn; Carol Manning, University of Virginia; Sara Martino, Richard Stockton College of New Jersey; Richard D. McAnulty, University of North Carolina–Charlotte; Richard McFall, Indiana University; John Monahan, University of Virginia School of Law; Tracy L. Morris, West Virginia University; Dan Muhwezi, Butler Community College; Christopher Murray, University of Maryland; William O'Donohue, University of Nevada–Reno; Joseph J. Palladino, University of Southern Indiana; Demetrios Papageorgis, University of British Columbia; Ronald D. Pearse, Fairmont State College; Brady Phelps, South Dakota State University; Nnamdi Pole, Smith College; Seth Pollak, University of Wisconsin; Lauren Polvere, Concordia University; Melvyn G. Preisz, Oklahoma City University; Paul Rasmussen, Furman University; Rena Repetti, University of California, Los Angeles; Amy Resch, Citrus College; Robert J. Resnick, Randolph-Macon College; Karen Clay Rhines, Northampton Community College; Jennifer Langhinrichsen-Rohling, University of South Alabama; Patricia H. Rosenberger, Colorado State University; Catherine Guthrie-Scanes, Mississippi State University; Forrest Scogin, University of Alabama; Josh Searle-White, Allegheny College; Fran Sessa, Penn State Abington; Danny Shaw, University of Pittsburgh; Heather Shaw, American Institutes of Research; Brenda Shook, National University; Robin Shusko, Universities at Shady Grove and University of Maryland; Janet Simons, Central Iowa Psychological Services; Patricia J. Slocum, College of DuPage; Darrell Smith, Tennessee State University; Randi Smith, Metropolitan State College of Denver; George Spilich, Washington College; Cheryl Spinweber, University of California, San Diego; Bonnie Spring, The Chicago Medical School; Laura Stephenson, Washburn University; Xuan Stevens, Florida International University; Eric Stice, University of Texas; Alexandra Stillman, Utah State University; Joanne Stohs, California State, Fullerton; Martha Storandt, Washington University; Milton E. Strauss, Case Western Reserve University; Amie Grills-Taquechel, University of Houston; Melissa Terlecki, Cabrini College; J. Kevin Thompson, University of South Florida; Julie Thompson, Duke University; Frances Thorndike, University of Virginia; Robert H. Tipton, Virginia Commonwealth University; David Topor, Harvard Medical School; Gaston Weisz, Adelphi University and University of Phoenix Online; Douglas Whitman, Wayne State University; Michael Wierzbicki, Marquette University; Joanna Lee Williams, University of Virginia; Ken Winters, University of Minnesota; Eleanor Webber, Johnson State College; Craig Woodsmall,

McKendree University; Robert D. Zettle, Wichita State University; Anthony Zoccolillo, Rutgers University.

We have been fortunate to work in stimulating academic environments that have fostered our interests in studying abnormal psychology and in teaching undergraduate students. We are particularly grateful to our colleagues at the University of Virginia: Eric Turkheimer, Irving Gottesman (now at the University of Minnesota), Mavis Hetherington, John Monahan, Joseph Allen, Dan Wegner, David Hill, Jim Coan, Bethany Teachman, Amori Mikami (now at the University of British Columbia), Cedric Williams, and Peter Brunjes for extended and ongoing discussions of the issues that are considered in this book. Many other colleagues at Washington University in St. Louis have added an important perspective to our views regarding important topics in this field. They include Arpana Agrawal, Deanna Barch, Ryan Bogdan, Danielle Dick (now at Virginia Commonwealth University), Bob Krueger (now at the University of Minnesota), Randy Larsen, Tom Rodebaugh, Martha Storandt and Renee Thompson. Close friends and colleagues at Indiana University have also served in this role, especially Dick McFall, Rick Viken, Mary Waldron, and Alexander Buchwald. Many undergraduate and graduate students who have taken our courses also have helped to shape the viewpoints that are expressed here. They are too numerous to identify individually, but we are grateful for the intellectual challenges and excitement that they have provided over the past several years.

Many other people have contributed to the text in important ways. Jutta Joormann provided extremely helpful suggestions with regard to Chapter 5; Bethany Teachman and members of her lab group offered many thoughtful comments for Chapter 6; Nnamdi Pole gave us extensive feedback and suggestions for Chapter 7. Pamela Keel offered a thorough, detailed, and insightful review of Chapter 10, along with dozens of excellent suggestions for change. Deanna Barch has been an ongoing source of information regarding issues discussed in Chapter 13. Kimberly Carpenter Emery did extensive legal research for Chapter 18. Danielle Dick contributed substantial expertise regarding developments in behavior genetics and gene identification methods. Martha Storandt and Carol Manning provided extensive consultation on issues related to dementia and other cognitive disorders. Jennifer Green provided important help with library research. Finally, Bailey Ocker gave us both indispensible help with research, manuscript preparation, and photo research—thank you, Bailey, we never would have finished on time or as well without you!

We also would like to express our deep appreciation to the Pearson team who share our pride and excitement about this text and who have worked long and hard to make it the very best text. Major contributors include Amber Chow, Acquisitions Editor; Jeremy Intal, Marketing Manager; Shelly Kupperman, Project Manager; Annemarie Franklin, Program Manager; Pam Weldin, Media Project Manager; Kate Cebik, Photo Researcher.

Finally, we want to express our gratitude to our families for their patience and support throughout our obsession with this text: Gail and Josh Oltmanns, and Sara, Billy, Presley, Riley, and Kinley Baber; and Kimberly, Julia, Bobby, Lucy, and John Emery and Maggie and Mike Strong. You remain our loving sources of motivation and inspiration.

—Tom Oltmanns
—Bob Emery

# about the authors

## Thomas F. OLTMANNS

is the Edgar James Swift Professor of Psychology in Arts and Sciences and professor of psychiatry at Washington University in St. Louis, where he is also director of Clinical Training in Psychology. He received his B.A. from the University of Wisconsin and his Ph.D. from Stony Brook University. Oltmanns was previously professor of psychology at the University of Virginia (1986 to 2003) and at Indiana University (1976 to 1986). His early research studies were concerned with the role of cognitive and emotional factors in schizophrenia. With grant support from NIMH, his lab is currently conducting a prospective study of the trajectory and impact of personality disorders in middle-aged and older adults. He has served on the Board of Directors of the Association for Psychological Science and was elected president of the Society for Research in Psychopathology, the Society for a Science of Clinical Psychology and the Academy of Psychological Clinical Science. Undergraduate students in psychology have selected him to receive outstanding teaching awards at Washington University and at UVA. In 2011, Oltmanns received the Toy Caldwell-Colbert Award for distinguished educator in clinical psychology from the Society for Clinical Psychology (Division 12 of APA). His other books include *Schizophrenia* (1980), written with John Neale; *Delusional Beliefs* (1988), edited with Brendan Maher; and *Case Studies in Abnormal Psychology* (9th edition, 2012), written with Michele Martin and Gerald Davison.

## Robert E. EMERY

is professor of psychology and director of the Center for Children, Families, and the Law at the University of Virginia, where he also served as director of Clinical Training for nine years. He received a B.A. from Brown University in 1974 and a Ph.D. from SUNY at Stony Brook in 1982. His research focuses on family conflict, children's mental health, and associated legal issues, particularly divorce mediation and child custody disputes. More recently, he has become involved in genetically informed research of selection into and the consequences of major changes in the family environment. Emery has authored over 150 scientific articles and book chapters. His awards include Distinguished Contributions to Family Psychology from Division 43 of the American Psychological Association, a Citation Classic from the Institute for Scientific Information, an Outstanding Research Publication Award from the American Association for Marriage and Family Therapy, the Distinguished Researcher Award from the Association of Family and Conciliation Courts, and several awards and award nominations for his three books on divorce: *Marriage, Divorce and Children's Adjustment* (2nd edition, 1998, Sage Publications); *Renegotiating Family Relationships: Divorce, Child Custody, and Mediation* (2nd edition, 2011, Guilford Press); and *The Truth About Children and Divorce: Dealing with the Emotions So You and Your Children Can Thrive* (2006, Plume). Emery currently is associate editor of *Family Court Review*, and he is principal investigator of a major grant from NICHD. In addition to teaching, research, and administration, he maintains a limited practice as a clinical psychologist and mediator.

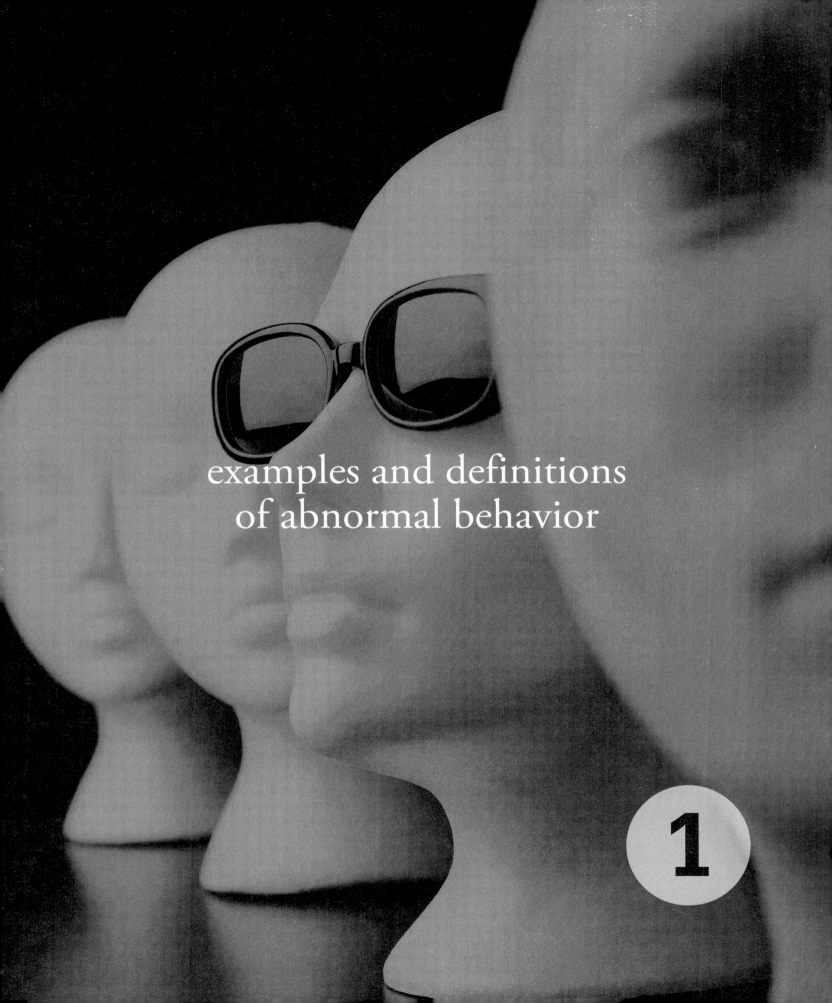

examples and definitions
of abnormal behavior

1

# The Big Picture

## learning objectives

**1.1**
What is the difference between normal and abnormal behavior?

**1.2**
How does culture influence the definition of mental disorders?

**1.3**
How does the impact of mental disorders compare to that of other health problems?

**1.4**
Who provides help for people with mental disorders?

**1.5**
Why do scientific methods play such an important role in psychology's approach to the study of mental disorders?

Mental disorders touch every realm of human experience; they are part of the human experience. They can disrupt the way we think, the way we feel, and the way we behave. They also affect relationships with other people. These problems often have a devastating impact on people's lives. In countries such as the United States, mental disorders are the second leading cause of disease-related disability and mortality, ranking slightly behind cardiovascular conditions and slightly ahead of cancer (Lopez et al., 2006). The purpose of this book is to help you become familiar with the nature of these disorders and the various ways in which psychologists and other mental health professionals are advancing knowledge of their causes and treatment.

Many of us grow up thinking that mental disorders happen to a few unfortunate people. We don't expect them to happen to us or to those we love. In fact, mental disorders are very common. At least two out of every four people will experience a serious form of abnormal behavior, such as depression, alcoholism, or schizophrenia, at some point during his or her lifetime. When you add up the numbers of people who experience these problems firsthand as well as through relatives and close friends, you realize that, like other health problems, mental disorders affect all of us. That is why, throughout this book, we will try to help you understand not only the kind of disturbed behaviors and thinking that characterize particular disorders, but also the people to whom they occur and the circumstances that can foster them.

Most importantly, this book is about all of us, not "them"— anonymous people with whom we empathize but do not identify.

Just as each of us will be affected by medical problems at some point during our lives, it is also likely that we, or someone we love, will have to cope with that aspect of the human experience known as a disorder of the mind.

## Overview

The symptoms and signs of mental disorders, including such phenomena as depressed mood, panic attacks, and bizarre beliefs, are known as **psychopathology.** Literally translated, this term means *pathology of the mind.* **Abnormal psychology** is the application of psychological science to the study of mental disorders.

In the first four chapters of this book, we will look at the field of abnormal psychology in general. We will look at the ways in which abnormal behaviors are broken down into categories of mental disorders that can be more clearly defined for diagnostic purposes, and how those behaviors are assessed. We will also discuss current ideas about the causes of these disorders and ways in which they can be treated.

This chapter will help you begin to understand the qualities that define behaviors and experiences as being abnormal. At what point does the diet that a girl follows in order to perform at her peak as a ballerina or gymnast become an eating disorder? When does grief following the end of a relationship become major depression? The line dividing normal from abnormal is not always clear. You will find that the issue is often one of degree rather than exact form or content of behavior.

The case studies in this chapter describe the experiences of two people whose behavior would be considered abnormal by mental health professionals. Our first case will introduce you to a person who suffered from one of the most obvious and disabling forms of mental disorder, known as schizophrenia. Kevin's life had been relatively unremarkable for many years. He had done well in school, was married, and held a good job. Unfortunately, over a period of several months, the fabric of his normal life began to fall apart. The transition wasn't obvious to either Kevin or his family, but it eventually became clear that he was having serious problems.

### ➡️ A Husband's Schizophrenia with Paranoid Delusions

Kevin and Joyce Warner (not their real names*) had been married for eight years when they sought help from a psychologist for their marital problems. Joyce was 34 years old, worked full time as a pediatric nurse, and was six months pregnant with her first child. Kevin, who was 35 years old, was finishing his third year working as a librarian at a local university. Joyce was extremely worried about what would happen if Kevin lost his job, especially in light of the baby's imminent arrival.

Although the Warners had come for couples therapy, the psychologist soon became concerned about certain eccentric

---

*Throughout this text we use fictitious names to protect the identities of the people involved.

aspects of Kevin's behavior. In the first session, Joyce described one recent event that had precipitated a major argument. One day, after eating lunch at work, Kevin had experienced sharp pains in his chest and had difficulty breathing. Fearful, he rushed to the emergency room at the hospital where Joyce worked. The physician who saw Kevin found nothing wrong with him, even after extensive testing. She gave Kevin a few tranquilizers and sent him home to rest. When Joyce arrived home that evening, Kevin told her that he suspected that he had been poisoned at work by his supervisor. He still held this belief.

Kevin's belief about the alleged poisoning raised serious concern in the psychologist's mind about Kevin's mental health. He decided to interview Joyce alone so that he could ask more extensive questions about Kevin's behavior. Joyce realized that the poisoning idea was "crazy." She was not willing, however, to see it as evidence that Kevin had a mental disorder. Joyce had known Kevin for 15 years. As far as she knew, he had never held any strange beliefs before this time. Joyce said that Kevin had always been "a thoughtful and unusually sensitive guy." She did not attach a great deal of significance to Kevin's unusual belief. She was more preoccupied with the couple's present financial concerns and insisted that it was time for Kevin to "face reality."

Kevin's condition deteriorated noticeably over the next few weeks. He became extremely withdrawn, frequently sitting alone in a darkened room after dinner. On several occasions, he told her that he felt as if he had "lost pieces of his thinking." It wasn't that his memory was failing, but rather he felt as though parts of his brain were shut off.

Kevin's problems at work also grew worse. His supervisor informed Kevin that his contract would definitely not be renewed. Joyce exploded when Kevin indifferently told her the bad news. His apparent lack of concern was especially annoying. She called Kevin's supervisor, who confirmed the news. He told her that Kevin was physically present at the library, but he was only completing a few hours of work each day. Kevin sometimes spent long periods of time just sitting at his desk and staring off into space and was sometimes heard mumbling softly to himself.

Kevin's speech was quite odd during the next therapy session. He would sometimes start to speak, drift off into silence, then re-establish eye contact with a bewildered smile and a shrug of his shoulders. He had apparently lost his train of thought completely. His answers to questions were often off the point, and when he did string together several sentences, their meaning was sometimes obscure. For example, at one point during the session, the psychologist asked Kevin if he planned to appeal his supervisor's decision. Kevin said, "I'm feeling pressured, like I'm lost and can't quite get here. But I need more time to explore the deeper side. Like in art. What you see on the surface is much richer when you look closely. I'm like that. An intuitive person. I can't relate in a linear way, and when people expect that from me, I get confused."

Kevin's strange belief about poisoning continued to expand. The Warners received a letter from Kevin's mother, who lived in another city 200 miles away. She had become ill after going out for dinner one night and mentioned that she must have eaten something that made her sick. After reading the letter, Kevin became convinced that his supervisor had tried to poison his mother, too.

When questioned about this new incident, Kevin launched into a long, rambling story. He said that his supervisor was a Vietnam veteran, but he had refused to talk with Kevin about his years in the service. Kevin suspected that this was because the supervisor had been a member of army intelligence. Perhaps he still was a member of some secret organization. Kevin suggested that an agent from this organization had been sent by his supervisor to poison his mother. Kevin thought that he and Joyce were in danger. Kevin also had some concerns about Asians, but he would not specify these worries in more detail.

Kevin's bizarre beliefs and his disorganized behavior convinced the psychologist that he needed to be hospitalized. Joyce reluctantly agreed that this was the most appropriate course of action. She had run out of alternatives. Arrangements were made to have Kevin admitted to a private psychiatric facility, where the psychiatrist prescribed a type of antipsychotic medication. Kevin seemed to respond positively to the drug, because he soon stopped talking about plots and poisoning—but he remained withdrawn and uncommunicative. After three weeks of treatment, Kevin's psychiatrist thought that he had improved significantly. Kevin was discharged from the hospital in time for the birth of their baby girl. Unfortunately, when the couple returned to consult with the psychologist, Kevin's adjustment was still a major concern. He did not talk with Joyce about the poisonings, but she noticed that he remained withdrawn and showed few emotions, even toward the baby.

When the psychologist questioned Kevin in detail, he admitted reluctantly that he still believed that he had been poisoned. Slowly, he revealed more of the plot. Immediately after admission to the hospital, Kevin had decided that his psychiatrist, who happened to be from Korea, could not be trusted. Kevin was sure that he, too, was working for army intelligence or perhaps for a counterintelligence operation. Kevin believed that he was being interrogated by this clever psychiatrist, so he had "played dumb." He did not discuss the suspected poisonings or the secret organization that had planned them. Whenever he could get away with it, Kevin simply pretended to take his medication. He thought that it was either poison or truth serum.

Kevin was admitted to a different psychiatric hospital soon after it became apparent that his paranoid beliefs had expanded. This time, he was given intramuscular injections of antipsychotic medication in order to be sure that the medicine was actually taken. Kevin improved considerably after several weeks in the hospital. He acknowledged that he had experienced paranoid thoughts. Although he still felt suspicious from time to time, wondering whether the plot had actually been real, he recognized that it could not really have happened, and he spent less and less time thinking about it.

## Recognizing the Presence of a Disorder

Some mental disorders are so severe that the people who suffer from them are not aware of the implausibility of their beliefs. Schizophrenia is a form of **psychosis,** a general term that refers to several types of severe mental disorders in which the person is considered to be out of contact with reality. Kevin exhibited several psychotic symptoms. For example, Kevin's firm belief that he was being poisoned by his supervisor had no basis in reality. Other disorders, however, are more subtle variations on normal experience. We will shortly consider some of the guidelines that are applied in determining abnormality.

Mental disorders are typically defined by a set of characteristic features; one symptom by itself is seldom sufficient to make a diagnosis. A group of symptoms that appear together and are assumed to represent a specific type of disorder is referred to as a **syndrome.** Kevin's unrealistic and paranoid belief that he was being poisoned, his peculiar and occasionally difficult-to-understand patterns of speech, and his oddly unemotional responses are all symptoms of schizophrenia (see Chapter 13). Each symptom is taken to be a fallible, or imperfect, indicator of the presence of the disorder. The significance of any specific feature depends on whether the person also exhibits additional behaviors that are characteristic of a particular disorder.

The duration of a person's symptoms is also important. Mental disorders are defined in terms of *persistent* maladaptive behaviors. Many unusual behaviors and inexplicable experiences are short lived; if we ignore them, they go away. Unfortunately, some forms of problematic behavior are not transient, and they eventually interfere with the person's social and occupational functioning. In Kevin's case, he had become completely preoccupied with his suspicions about poison. Joyce tried for several weeks to ignore certain aspects of Kevin's behavior, especially his delusional beliefs. She didn't want to think about the possibility that his behavior was abnormal and instead chose to explain his problems in terms of lack of maturity or lack of motivation. But as the problems accumulated, she finally decided to seek professional help. The magnitude of Kevin's problem was measured, in large part, by its persistence.

Impairment in the ability to perform social and occupational roles is another consideration in identifying the presence of a mental disorder. Delusional beliefs and disorganized speech typically lead to a profound disruption of relationships with other people. Like Kevin, people who experience these symptoms will obviously find the world to be a strange, puzzling, and perhaps alarming place. And they often elicit the same reactions in other people. Kevin's odd behavior and his inability to concentrate on his work had eventually cost him his job. His problems also had a negative impact on his relationship with his wife and his ability to help care for their daughter.

Kevin's situation raises several additional questions about abnormal behavior. One of the most difficult issues in the field

People with schizophrenia are sometimes socially withdrawn and find social relationships to be puzzling or threatening.

centers on the processes by which mental disorders are identified. Once Kevin's problems came to the attention of a mental health professional, could he have been tested in some way to confirm the presence or absence of a mental disorder?

Psychologists and other mental health professionals do not at present have laboratory tests that can be used to confirm definitively the presence of psychopathology because the processes that are responsible for mental disorders have not yet been discovered. Unlike specialists in other areas of medicine where many specific disease mechanisms have been discovered by advances in the biological sciences, psychologists and psychiatrists cannot test for the presence of a viral infection or a brain lesion or a genetic defect to confirm a diagnosis of mental disorder. Clinical psychologists must still depend on their observations of the person's behavior and descriptions of personal experience.

Is it possible to move beyond our current dependence on descriptive definitions of psychopathology? Will we someday have valid tests that can be used to establish independently the presence of a mental disorder? If we do, what form might these tests take? The answers to these questions are being sought in many kinds of research studies that will be discussed throughout this book.

Before we leave this section, we must also mention some other terms. You may be familiar with a variety of words that are commonly used in describing abnormal behavior. One term is *insanity,* which years ago referred to mental dysfunction but today is a legal term that refers to judgments about whether a person

Andy Warhol was one of the most influential painters of the 20th century. His colleague, Jean-Michel Basquiat, was also an extremely promising artist. His addiction to heroin, which led to a fatal overdose, provides one example of the destructive impact of mental disorders.

should be held responsible for criminal behavior if he or she is also mentally disturbed (see Chapter 18). If Kevin had murdered his psychiatrist, for example, based on the delusional belief that the psychiatrist was trying to harm him, a court of law might consider whether Kevin should be held to be *not guilty by reason of insanity.*

Another old-fashioned term that you may have heard is *nervous breakdown.* If we said that Kevin had "suffered a nervous breakdown," we would be indicating, in very general terms, that he had developed some sort of incapacitating but otherwise unspecified type of mental disorder. This expression does not convey any specific information about the nature of the person's problems. Some people might also say that Kevin was acting *crazy.* This is an informal, pejorative term that does not convey specific information and carries with it many unfortunate, unfounded, and negative implications. Mental health professionals refer to psychopathological conditions as mental disorders or abnormal behaviors. We will define these terms in the pages that follow.

## Defining Abnormal Behavior

Why do we consider Kevin's behavior to be abnormal? By what criteria do we decide whether a particular set of behaviors or emotional reactions should be viewed as a mental disorder? These are important questions because they determine, in many ways, how other people will respond to the person, as well as who will be responsible for providing help (if help is required). Many attempts have been made to define abnormal behavior, but none is entirely satisfactory. No one has been able to provide a consistent definition that easily accounts for all situations in which the concept is invoked (Phillips et al., 2012; Zachar & Kendler, 2007).

One approach to the definition of abnormal behavior places principal emphasis on the individual's experience of personal distress. We might say that abnormal behavior is defined in terms of subjective discomfort that leads the person to seek help from a mental health professional. However, this definition is fraught with problems. Kevin's case illustrates one of the major reasons that this approach does not work. Before his second hospitalization, Kevin was unable or unwilling to appreciate the extent of his problem or the impact his behavior had on other people. A psychologist would say that he did not have *insight* regarding his disorder. The discomfort was primarily experienced by Joyce, and she had attempted for many weeks to deny the nature of the problem. It would be useless to adopt a definition that considered Kevin's behavior to be abnormal only after he had been successfully treated.

Another approach is to define abnormal behavior in terms of statistical norms—how common or rare it is in the general population. By this definition, people with unusually high levels of anxiety or depression would be considered abnormal because their experience deviates from the expected norm. Kevin's paranoid beliefs would be defined as pathological because they are idiosyncratic. Mental disorders are, in fact, defined in terms of experiences that most people do not have.

This approach, however, does not specify *how* unusual the behavior must be before it is considered abnormal. Some conditions that are typically considered to be forms of psychopathology are extremely rare. For example, gender dysphoria, the belief that one is a member of the opposite sex trapped in the wrong body, affects less than 1 person out of every 30,000. In contrast, other mental disorders are much more common. Mood disorders affect 1 out of every 5 people at some point during their lives; alcoholism and other substance use disorders affect approximately 1 out of every 6 people (Kessler et al., 2005; Moffitt et al., 2010).

Another weakness of the statistical approach is that it does not distinguish between deviations that are harmful and those

## MyPsychLab VIDEO CASE

### Bipolar Disorder

FELIZIANO

*"Depression is the worst part. My shoulders feel weighted down, and your blood feels warmer than it is. You sink deeper and deeper."*

👁 **Watch** the **Video** *Feliziano: Bipolar Disorder* on **MyPsychLab**

As you watch the interview and the day-in-the-life segments, ask yourself what impact Feliziano's depression and hypomania seem to have on his ability to function. Are these mood states harmful?

that are not. Many rare behaviors are not pathological. Some "abnormal" qualities have relatively little impact on a person's adjustment. Examples are being extremely pragmatic or unusually talkative. Other abnormal characteristics, such as exceptional intellectual, artistic, or athletic ability, may actually confer an advantage on the individual. For these reasons, the simple fact that a behavior is statistically rare cannot be used to define psychopathology.

## Harmful Dysfunction

One useful approach to the definition of mental disorder has been proposed by Jerome Wakefield of Rutgers University (Wakefield, 2010). According to Wakefield, a condition should be considered a mental disorder if, and only if, it meets two criteria:

1. The condition results from the inability of some internal mechanism (mental or physical) to perform its natural function. In other words, something inside the person is not working properly. Examples of such mechanisms include those that regulate levels of emotion, and those that distinguish between real auditory sensations and those that are imagined.

2. The condition causes some harm to the person as judged by the standards of the person's culture. These negative consequences are measured in terms of the person's own subjective distress or difficulty performing expected social or occupational roles.

A mental disorder, therefore, is defined in terms of **harmful dysfunction.** This definition incorporates one element that is based as much as possible on an objective evaluation of performance. The natural function of cognitive and perceptual processes is to allow the person to perceive the world in ways that are shared with other people and to engage in rational thought and problem solving. The dysfunctions in mental disorders are assumed to be the product of disruptions of thought, feeling, communication, perception, and motivation.

In Kevin's case, the most apparent dysfunctions involved failures of mechanisms that are responsible for perception, thinking, and communication. Disruption of these systems was presumably responsible for his delusional beliefs and his disorganized speech. The natural function of cognitive and perceptual processes is to allow the person to perceive the world in ways that are shared with other people and to engage in rational thought and problem solving. The natural function of language abilities is to allow the person to communicate clearly with other people. Therefore, Kevin's abnormal behavior can be viewed as a pervasive dysfunction cutting across several mental mechanisms.

The harmful dysfunction view of mental disorder recognizes that every type of dysfunction does not lead to a disorder. Only dysfunctions that result in significant harm to the person are considered to be disorders. This is the second element of the definition. There are, for example, many types of physical dysfunctions, such as albinism, reversal of heart position, and fused toes, that

clearly represent a significant departure from the way that some biological process ordinarily functions. These conditions are not considered to be disorders, however, because they are not necessarily harmful to the person.

Kevin's dysfunctions were, in fact, harmful to his adjustment. They affected both his family relationships—his marriage to Joyce and his ability to function as a parent—and his performance at work. His social and occupational performances were clearly impaired. There are, of course, other types of harm that are also associated with mental disorders. These include subjective distress, such as high levels of anxiety or depression, as well as more tangible outcomes, such as suicide.

The definition of abnormal behavior employed by the official *Diagnostic and Statistical Manual of Mental Disorders,* published by the American Psychiatric Association and currently in its fifth edition—*DSM-5* (APA, 2013)—incorporates many of the factors that we have already discussed. This classification system is discussed in Chapter 4. This definition is summarized in Table 1.1, along with a number of conditions that are specifically excluded from the *DSM-5* definition of mental disorders (Stein et al., 2010).

The *DSM-5* definition places primary emphasis on the consequences of certain behavioral syndromes. Accordingly, mental disorders are defined by clusters of persistent, maladaptive behaviors that are associated with personal distress, such as anxiety or depression, or with impairment in social functioning, such as job performance or personal relationships. The official definition, therefore, recognizes the concept of dysfunction, and it spells out ways in which the harmful consequences of the disorder might be identified.

The *DSM-5* definition excludes voluntary behaviors, as well as beliefs and actions that are shared by religious, political,

---

**TABLE 1.1**
### Defining Characteristics of Mental Disorders

**Features**

1. A syndrome (groups of associated features) that is characterized by disturbance of a person's cognition, emotion regulation, or behavior.
2. The consequences of which are clinically significant distress or disability in social, occupational, or other important activities.
3. The syndrome reflects a dysfunction in the psychological, biological, or developmental processes that are associated with mental functioning.
4. Must not be merely an expectable response to common stressors and losses or a culturally sanctioned response to a particular event (e.g., trance states in religious rituals).
5. That is not primarily a result of social deviance or conflicts with society.

*Source:* Based on Stein, D. J., Phillips, K. A., Bolton, D. D., Fulford, K. M., Sadler, J. Z., & Kendler, K. S. 2010. What is a mental/psychiatric disorder? From DSM-IV to DSM-V. Psychological Medicine, 40, 1759–1765.

or sexual minority groups (e.g., gays and lesbians). In the 1960s, for example, members of the Yippie Party intentionally engaged in disruptive behaviors, such as throwing money off the balcony at a stock exchange. Their purpose was to challenge traditional values. These were, in some ways, maladaptive behaviors that could have resulted in social impairment if those involved had been legally prosecuted. But they were not dysfunctions. They were intentional political gestures. It makes sense to try to distinguish between voluntary behaviors and mental disorders, but the boundaries between these different forms of behavior are difficult to draw. Educated discussions of these issues depend on the consideration of a number of important questions (see Critical Thinking Matters on page 9).

In actual practice, abnormal behavior is defined in terms of an official diagnostic system. Mental health, like medicine, is an applied rather than a theoretical field. It draws on knowledge from research in the psychological and biological sciences in an effort to help people whose behavior is disordered. Mental disorders are, in some respects, those problems with which mental health professionals attempt to deal. As their activities and explanatory concepts expand, so does the list of abnormal behaviors. The practical boundaries of abnormal behavior are defined by the list of disorders that are included in the official *Diagnostic and Statistical Manual of Mental Disorders.* The categories in that manual are listed inside the back cover of this book. The *DSM-5* thus provides another simplistic, although practical, answer to our question as to why Kevin's behavior would be considered abnormal: He would be considered to be exhibiting abnormal behavior because his experiences fit the description of schizophrenia, which is one of the officially recognized forms of mental disorder (see Thinking Critically About *DSM-5*).

## Mental Health Versus Absence of Disorder

The process of defining abnormal behavior raises interesting questions about the way we think about the quality of our lives when mental disorders are *not* present. What is mental health? Is optimal mental health more than the absence of mental disorder? The answer is clearly "yes." If you want to know whether one of your friends is physically fit, you would need to determine more than whether he or she is sick. In the realm of psychological functioning, people who function at the highest levels can be described as *flourishing* (Fredrickson & Losada, 2005; Keyes, 2009). They are people who typically experience many positive emotions, are interested in life, and tend to be calm and peaceful. Flourishing people also hold positive attitudes about themselves and other people. They find meaning and direction in their lives and develop trusting relationships with other people. Complete mental health implies the presence of these adaptive characteristics. Therefore, comprehensive approaches to mental health in the community must be concerned both with efforts to diminish the frequency and impact of mental disorders and with activities designed to promote flourishing.

## Culture and Diagnostic Practice

The process by which the *Diagnostic and Statistical Manual* is constructed and revised is necessarily influenced by cultural considerations. **Culture** is defined in terms of the values, beliefs, and practices that are shared by a specific community or group of people. These values and beliefs have a profound influence on opinions regarding the difference between normal and abnormal behavior (Bass et al., 2012).

The impact of particular behaviors and experiences on a person's adjustment depends on the culture in which the person

## THINKING CRITICALLY about DSM-5

### Revising an Imperfect Manual

The official diagnostic manual for mental disorders is revised by the *American Psychiatric Association* on a regular basis, about once every 15 to 20 years. You might be surprised that the classification system changes so often, but these updates reflect the evolution of our understanding regarding these complex problems. Even more well-established and widely accepted classification systems change. You may remember when Pluto was removed from the list of planets, or recall that new elements have been added to the Periodic Table as a result of nuclear science. Classification systems change as knowledge expands.

The fifth and latest version, *DSM-5*[1], was published in 2013, an event surrounded by excitement as well as heated controversy.

More than a dozen workgroups concerned with specific disorders (e.g., mood disorders, psychotic disorders) were composed of expert researchers and clinicians who had been appointed to represent current knowledge in their respective areas. Each group produced a series of proposals that were subjected to public comments as well as field trials that were intended to generate data regarding the reliability of the new definitions. In the end, some experts considered the final product to be a major step forward while others viewed it as a serious step back (Kupfer & Regier, 2011; Frances & Widiger, 2012).

We have added a new feature, *Thinking Critically About DSM-5*, to each chapter in this text. These features are designed to

*Continued*

help you understand ways in which this diagnostic manual has evolved, criteria that are used to judge its progress, and issues that are most controversial following publication of its latest edition. We don't want you to accept the *DSM-5* definitions simply because they were published on the authority of the American Psychiatric Association. On the other hand, we also don't want you to reject the manual because everything in it isn't perfect. Above all else, remember that *DSM-5* is a handbook, not the Bible (Frances, 2012). There are no absolute truths to be found in the classification of mental disorders.

The debates about *DSM-5* generate considerable emotion from people on both sides because changes in the manual affect so many people's lives. Crucial economic resources are clearly at stake. Adding a diagnostic category can create or expand a market for specific treatments (e.g., medications to treat a new disorder may reap enormous profits) while also raising challenging issues about whether insurance companies must pay for those treatments, whether schools will be expected to provide special services, and whether the government must pay disability claims. There are also pressures on the other side. Deleting an existing category, or narrowing the criteria that are used to define it, can create serious hardships for individuals and families who are then unable to find or afford suitable services upon which they depend. Mental health professionals, research scientists, and patient advocacy groups all play a crucial role in these debates.

Everyone agrees that the classification system must evolve, but what principles should guide this process of change? When

DSM-IV (APA, 1994) was being produced, the process was designed to be conservative. Changes were presumably allowed only when there was substantial evidence to support a shift in the diagnostic criteria for a particular disorder. A few years later, when discussions about *DSM-5* began, the process was designed to be more open. Workgroups were encouraged to make changes that would bring the system in line with contemporary thinking, even if hard evidence was not available to indicate that the change was empirically justified. Reasonable arguments can be made for both approaches to the revision process. Ultimately, the value of these changing definitions will be judged by the outcomes. Are the new definitions meaningful? Can they be used to improve people's lives?

In the midst of public debates about the *DSM-5* process, another issue has taken center stage. What group is best positioned to manage this system? The American Psychiatric Association clearly owns *DSM*, having launched its original version in 1952. Given the fact that other mental health professions also play important roles in treating and studying mental disorders, does it make sense for this one organization to be the sole owner and manager of the classification system that governs so many aspects of our lives? Should decisions to change the system be guided, even in part, by the enormous economic benefits that have fallen to one professional organization? Some critics have argued that the classification system for mental disorders should be governed by some type of government organization, such as the National Institutes of Health, rather than a profit-making professional association. This issue will undoubtedly be debated and explored in coming years.

---

[1]Previous editions of the manual have been identified using roman numerals, e.g., DSM-III, DSM-IV. The current edition uses Arabic numerals in the hope that more frequent revisions of the text (e.g., DSM-5.1 and so on) can be produced easily and labeled clearly, much like updates to computer software packages.

---

lives. To use Jerome Wakefield's (1992) terms, "only dysfunctions that are socially disvalued are disorders" (p. 384). Consider, for example, the *DSM-5* concept of female orgasmic disorder, which is defined in terms of the absence of orgasm accompanied by subjective distress or interpersonal difficulties that result from this disturbance (see Chapter 12). A woman who grew up in a society that discouraged female sexuality might not be distressed or impaired by the absence of orgasmic responses. According to *DSM-5,* she would not be considered to have a sexual problem. Therefore, this definition of abnormal behavior is not culturally universal and might lead us to consider a particular pattern of behavior to be abnormal in one society and not in another.

There have been many instances in which groups representing particular social values have brought pressure to bear on decisions shaping the diagnostic manual. The influence of

cultural changes on psychiatric classification is perhaps nowhere better illustrated than in the case of homosexuality. In the first and second editions of the *DSM,* homosexuality was, by definition, a form of mental disorder, in spite of arguments expressed by scientists, who argued that homosexual behavior was not abnormal (see Chapter 12). Toward the end of the 1960s, as the gay and lesbian rights movement became more forceful and outspoken, its leaders challenged the assumption that homosexuality was pathological. They opposed the inclusion of homosexuality in the official diagnostic manual. After extended and sometimes heated discussions, the board of trustees of the American Psychiatric Association agreed to remove homosexuality as a form of mental illness. They were impressed by numerous indications, in personal appeals as well as the research literature, that homosexuality, per se, was not invariably associated with impaired functioning. They decided that, in order to

# CRITICAL THINKING matters

## Is Sexual Addiction a Meaningful Concept?

Stories about mental disorders appear frequently in the popular media. One topic that once again attracted a frenzy of media attention in 2010 was a concept that has been called "sexual addiction." Tiger Woods, the top-ranked golfer in the world and wealthiest professional athlete in history, confessed to having a series of illicit sexual affairs and announced that he would take an indefinite break from the professional tour. At the time, Woods was married to former Swedish model Elin Nordegren, who had given birth to their second child earlier that same year. More than a dozen women came forward to claim publicly that they had sexual relationships with Woods, and several large companies soon cancelled lucrative endorsement deals that paid him millions of dollars to endorse their products. Newspapers, magazines, and television programs sought interviews with professional psychologists who offered their opinions regarding Woods' behavior. Why would this fabulously successful, universally admired, iconic figure risk his marriage, family, and career for a seemingly endless series of casual sexual relationships?

Many experts responded by invoking the concept of mental disorder, specifically "sexual addiction" (some called it "sexual compulsion," and one called it the "Clinton syndrome" in reference to similar problems that had been discussed in the midst of President Clinton's sex scandal in 1998). The symptoms of this disorder presumably include low self-esteem, insecurity, need for reassurance, and sensation seeking, to name only a few. One expert claimed that 20 percent of highly successful men suffer from sexual addiction.

Most of the stories failed to mention that sexual addiction does not appear as an officially recognized mental disorder in *DSM-5*. That, by itself, is not an insurmountable problem. Disorders have come and gone over the years, and it's possible that this one—or some version of it—might eventually turn out to be useful. In fact, the work group that revised the list of sexual disorders for *DSM-5* did consider but ultimately rejected adding a new category called "hypersexual disorder" (Reid et al., 2012) (see Thinking Critically About DSM-5 in Chapter 12). We shouldn't ignore a new concept simply because it hasn't become part of the official classification system (or accept one on faith, simply because it has). The most important thing is that we *think critically* about the issues that are raised by invoking a concept like sexual addiction.

At the broadest possible level, we must ask ourselves "What is a mental disorder?" Is there another explanation for such thoughtless and damaging behavior? Tiger Woods received several weeks of treatment for sexual addiction at a residential mental health facility. Has that treatment been shown to be effective for this kind of behavioral problem? Is it necessary? Does the diagnosis simply provide him with a convenient excuse that might encourage the public to forgive his immoral behavior?

Another important question is whether sexual addiction is more useful than other similar concepts (Moser, 2011). For example, narcissistic personality disorder includes many of the same features (such as lack of empathy, feelings of entitlement, and a history of exploiting others). What evidence supports the value of one concept over another? In posing such questions, we are not arguing for or against a decision to include sexual addiction or hypersexual disorder as a type of mental disorder. Rather, we are encouraging you to think critically.

Students who ask these kinds of questions are engaged in a process in which judgments and decisions are based on a careful analysis of the best available evidence. In order to consider these issues, you need to put aside your own subjective feelings and impressions, such as whether you find a particular kind of behavior disgusting, confusing, or frightening. It may also be necessary to disregard opinions expressed by authorities whom you respect (politicians, journalists, and talk-show hosts). Be skeptical. Ask questions. Consider the evidence from different points of view, and remember that some kinds of evidence are better than others.

---

be considered a form of mental disorder, a condition ought to be associated with subjective distress or seriously impaired social or occupational functioning. The stage was set for these events by gradual shifts in society's attitudes toward sexual behavior (Bullough, 1976; Minton, 2002). As more and more people came to believe that reproduction was not the main purpose of sexual behavior, tolerance for greater variety in human sexuality grew. The revision of the *DSM*'s system for describing sexual disorders was, therefore, the product of several forces, cultural as well as political. These deliberations are a reflection of the practical nature of the manual and of the health-related professions.

Value judgments are an inherent part of any attempt to define "disorder" (Sedgwick, 1981).

Many people think about culture primarily in terms of exotic patterns of behavior in distant lands. The decision regarding homosexuality reminds us that the values of our own culture play an intimate role in our definition of abnormal behavior. These issues also highlight the importance of cultural change. Culture is a dynamic process; it changes continuously as a result of the actions of individuals. To the extent that our definition of abnormal behavior is determined by cultural values and beliefs, we should expect that it will continue to evolve over time.

## Who Experiences Abnormal Behavior?

Having introduced many of the issues that are involved in the definition of abnormal behavior, we now turn to another clinical example. The woman in our second case study, Mary Childress, suffered from a serious eating disorder known as *bulimia nervosa*. Her problems raise additional questions about the definition of abnormal behavior.

As you are reading the case, ask yourself about the impact of Mary's eating disorder on her subjective experience and social adjustment. In what ways are these consequences similar to those seen in Kevin Warner's case? How are they different? This case also introduces another important concept associated with the way that we think about abnormal behavior: How can we identify the boundary between normal and abnormal behavior? Is there an obvious distinction between eating patterns that are considered to be part of a mental disorder and those that are not? Or is there a gradual progression from one end of a continuum to the other, with each step fading gradually into the next?

### → A College Student's Eating Disorder

Mary Childress was, in most respects, a typical 19-year-old sophomore at a large state university. She was a good student, in spite of the fact that she spent little time studying, and was popular with other students. Everything about Mary's life was relatively normal—except for her bingeing and purging.

Mary's eating patterns were wildly erratic. She preferred to skip breakfast entirely and often missed lunch as well. By the middle of the afternoon, she could no longer ignore the hunger pangs. At that point, on two or three days out of the week, Mary would drive her car to the drive-in window of a fast-food restaurant. Her typical order included three or four double cheeseburgers, several orders of french fries, and a large milkshake (or maybe two). Then she binged, devouring all the food as she drove around town by herself. Later she would go to a private bathroom, where she wouldn't be seen by anyone, and purge the food from her stomach by vomiting. Afterward, she returned to her room, feeling angry, frustrated, and ashamed.

Mary was tall and weighed 110 pounds. She believed that her body was unattractive, especially her thighs and hips. She was extremely critical of herself and had worried about her weight for many years. Her weight fluctuated quite a bit, from a low of 97 pounds when she was a senior in high school to a high of 125 during her first year at the university. Her mother was a "full-figured" woman. Mary swore to herself at an early age that she would never let herself gain as much weight as her mother had.

Purging had originally seemed like an ideal solution to the problem of weight control. You could eat whatever you wanted and quickly get rid of it so you wouldn't get fat. Unfortunately, the vomiting became a vicious trap. Disgusted by her own behavior, Mary often promised herself that she would never binge and purge again, but she couldn't stop the cycle.

For the past year, Mary had been vomiting at least once almost every day and occasionally as many as three or four times a day. The impulse to purge was very strong. Mary felt bloated after having only a bowl of cereal and a glass of orange juice. If she ate a sandwich and drank a diet soda, she began to ruminate about what she had eaten, thinking, "I've got to get rid of that!" Usually, before long, she found a bathroom and threw up. Her excessive binges were less frequent than the vomiting. Four or five times a week she experienced an overwhelming urge to eat forbidden foods, especially fast food. Her initial reaction was usually a short-lived attempt to resist the impulse. Then she would space out or "go into a zone," becoming only vaguely aware of what she was doing and feeling. In the midst of a serious binge, Mary felt completely helpless and unable to control herself.

There weren't any obvious physical signs that would alert someone to Mary's eating problems, but the vomiting had begun to wreak havoc with her body, especially her digestive system. She had suffered severe throat infections and frequent, intense stomach pains. Her dentist had noticed problems beginning to develop with her teeth and gums, undoubtedly a consequence of constant exposure to strong stomach acids.

Mary's eating problem started to develop when she was 15 years old. She had been seriously involved in gymnastics for several years, but eventually developed a knee condition that forced her to give up the sport. She gained a few pounds in the next month or two and decided to lose weight by dieting. Buoyed by unrealistic expectations about the immediate, positive benefits of a diet that she had seen advertised on television, Mary initially adhered rigidly to its recommended regimen. Six months later, after three of these fad diets had failed, she started throwing up as a way to control her intake of food.

Mary's problems persisted after she graduated from high school and began her college education. She felt guilty and ashamed about her eating problems. She was much too embarrassed to let anyone know what she was doing and would never eat more than a few mouthfuls of food in a public place, such as the dorm cafeteria. Her roommate, Julie, was from a small town on the other side of the state. They got along reasonably well, but Mary managed to conceal her bingeing and purging, thanks in large part to the fact that she was able to bring her own car to campus. The car allowed her to drive away from campus several times a week so that she could binge.

Mary's case illustrates many of the characteristic features of bulimia nervosa. As in Kevin's case, her behavior could be considered abnormal not only because it fits the criteria for one of the categories in *DSM-5* but also because she suffered from a dysfunction (in this case, of the mechanisms that regulate appetite) that was obviously harmful. The impact of the disorder was greatest in terms of her physical health: Eating disorders can be fatal if they are not properly treated because they affect so many vital organs of the body, including the heart and kidneys. Mary's social

How thin is too thin? Does this dancer suffer from an eating disorder? Some experts maintain that the differences between abnormal and normal behavior are essentially differences in degree, that is, quantitative differences.

functioning and her academic performance were not yet seriously impaired. There are many different ways in which to measure the harmful effects of abnormal behavior.

Mary's case also illustrates the subjective pain that is associated with many types of abnormal behavior. In contrast to Kevin, Mary was acutely aware of her disorder. She was frustrated and unhappy. In an attempt to relieve this emotional distress, she entered psychological treatment. Unfortunately, painful emotions associated with mental disorders can also interfere with, or delay, the decision to look for professional help. Guilt, shame, and embarrassment often accompany psychological problems and sometimes make it difficult to confide in another person, even though the average therapist has seen such problems many times over.

## Frequency in and Impact on Community Populations

Many important decisions about mental disorders are based on data regarding the frequency with which these disorders occur. At least 3 percent of college women would meet diagnostic criteria for bulimia nervosa (see Chapter 10). These data are a source of considerable concern, especially among those who are responsible for health services on college campuses.

**Epidemiology** is the scientific study of the frequency and distribution of disorders within a population (Gordis, 2008). Epidemiologists are concerned with questions, such as whether the frequency of a disorder has increased or decreased during a particular period, whether it is more common in one geographic area than in another, and whether certain types of people—based on such factors as gender, race, and socioeconomic status—are at greater risk than other types for the development of the disorder. Health administrators often use such information to make decisions about the allocation of resources for professional training programs, treatment facilities, and research projects.

Two terms are particularly important in epidemiological research. **Incidence** refers to the number of new cases of a disorder that appear in a population during a specific period of time. **Prevalence** refers to the total number of active cases, both old and new, that are present in a population during a specific period of time (Susser et al., 2006). The *lifetime prevalence* of a disorder is the total proportion of people in a given population who have been affected by the disorder at some point during their lives. Some studies also report 12-month prevalence rates, indicating the proportion of the population that met criteria for the disorder during the year prior to the assessment. Lifetime prevalence rates are higher than 12-month prevalence rates because some people who had problems in the past and then recovered will be counted with regard to lifetime disorders but not be counted for the most recent year.

**LIFETIME PREVALENCE AND GENDER DIFFERENCES** How prevalent are the various forms of abnormal behavior? The best data regarding this question come from a large-scale study known as the *National Comorbidity Survey Replication* (NCS-R) conducted between 2001 and 2003 (Kessler et al., 2005; Kessler, Merikangas, & Wang, 2007). Members of this research team interviewed a nationally representative sample of approximately 9,000 people living in the continental United States. Questions were asked pertaining to several (but not all) forms of mental disorder. The NCS-R found that 46 percent of the people interviewed received at least one *lifetime* diagnosis, with first onset of symptoms usually occurring during childhood or adolescence. This proportion of the population is much higher than many people expect, and it underscores the point that we made at the beginning of this chapter: All of us can expect to encounter the challenges of a mental disorder—either for ourselves or for someone we love—at some point during our lives.

Figure 1.1 lists some results from this study using lifetime prevalence rates—the number of people who had experienced each disorder at some point during their lives. The most prevalent specific type of disorder was major depression (17 percent). Substance use disorders and various kinds of anxiety disorders were also relatively common. Substantially lower lifetime prevalence rates were found for schizophrenia and eating disorders (bulimia and anorexia), which affects approximately 1 percent of the population. These lifetime prevalence rates are consistent with data reported by earlier epidemiological studies of mental disorders.

Although many mental disorders are quite common, they are not always seriously debilitating, and some people who qualify for a diagnosis do not need immediate treatment. The NCS-R

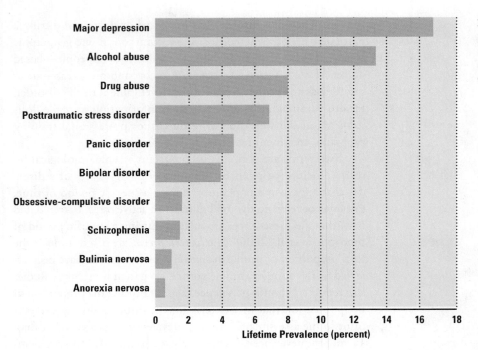

**FIGURE 1.1**

**Frequency of Mental Disorders in the Community**
Lifetime prevalence rates for various mental disorders (NCS-R data).
Courtesy of Thomas F. Oltmanns and Robert E. Emery.

investigators assigned each case a score with regard to severity, based on the severity of symptoms as well as the level of occupational and social impairment that the person experienced. Averaged across all of the disorders diagnosed in the past 12 months, 40 percent of cases were rated as "mild," 37 percent as "moderate," and only 22 percent as "severe." Mood disorders were the most likely to be rated as severe (45 percent) while anxiety disorders were less likely to be rated as severe (23 percent).

Epidemiological studies such as the NCS-R have consistently found gender differences for many types of mental disorder: Major depression, anxiety disorders, and eating disorders are more common among women; alcoholism and antisocial personality are more common among men. Some other conditions, such as bipolar disorder, appear with equal frequency in both women and men. Patterns of this sort raise interesting questions about possible causal mechanisms. What conditions would make women more vulnerable to one kind of disorder and men more vulnerable to another? There are many possibilities, including factors such as hormones, patterns of learning, and social pressures. We will discuss gender differences in more detail in subsequent chapters of this book.

Clinical psychologists perform many roles. Some provide direct clinical services. Many are involved in research, teaching, and various administrative activities.

**COMORBIDITY AND DISEASE BURDEN**  Most severe disorders are concentrated in a relatively small segment of the population. Often these are people who simultaneously qualify for more than one diagnosis, such as major depression and alcoholism. The presence of more than one condition within the same period of time is known as **comorbidity** (or co-occurrence). Six percent of the people in the NCS-R sample had three or more 12-month disorders, and 50 percent of those cases were rated as being "severe." While mental disorders occur relatively frequently, the most serious problems are concentrated in a smaller group of people who have more than one disorder. These findings have shifted the emphasis of epidemiological studies from counting the absolute number of people who have any kind of mental disorder to measuring the functional impairment associated with these problems.

Mental disorders are highly prevalent, but how do we measure the extent of their impact on people's lives? And how does that impact compare to the effects of other diseases? These are important questions when policymakers must establish priorities for various types of training, research, and health services (Eaton et al., 2012).

Epidemiologists measure disease burden by combining two factors: mortality and disability. The common measure is based on time: lost years of healthy life, which might be caused by premature death (compared to the person's standard life expectancy) or living with a disability (weighted for severity). For purposes of comparison among different forms of disease and injury, the disability produced by major depression is considered to be equivalent to that associated with blindness or paraplegia. A psychotic disorder such as schizophrenia leads to disability that is comparable to that associated with quadriplegia.

The World Health Organization (WHO) sponsored an ambitious study called the Global Burden of Disease Study, which used these measures to evaluate and compare the impact of more than 100 forms of disease and injury throughout the world (Lopez et al., 2006). Although mental disorders are responsible for only 1 percent of all deaths, they produce 47 percent of all disability in economically developed countries, such as the United States, and 28 percent of all disability worldwide. The combined index (mortality plus disability) reveals that, as a combined category, mental disorders are the second leading source of disease burden in developed countries (see Figure 1.2). Investigators in the WHO study predict that, relative to other types of health problems, the burden of mental disorders will increase by the year 2020. These surprising results strongly indicate that mental disorders are one of the world's greatest health challenges.

## Cross-Cultural Comparisons

As the evidence regarding the global burden of disease clearly documents, mental disorders affect people all over the world. That does not mean, however, that the symptoms of psychopathology and the expression of emotional distress take the same form in all cultures. Epidemiological studies comparing the frequency of

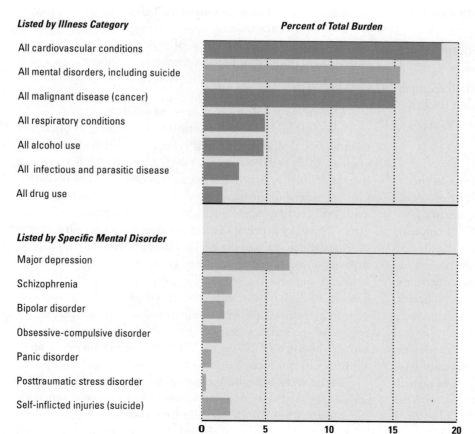

*Listed by Illness Category*

All cardiovascular conditions
All mental disorders, including suicide
All malignant disease (cancer)
All respiratory conditions
All alcohol use
All infectious and parasitic disease
All drug use

*Listed by Specific Mental Disorder*

Major depression
Schizophrenia
Bipolar disorder
Obsessive-compulsive disorder
Panic disorder
Posttraumatic stress disorder
Self-inflicted injuries (suicide)

*Percent of Total Burden*

0   5   10   15   20

**FIGURE 1.2**

**Comparison of the Impact of Mental Disorders and Other Medical Conditions on People's Lives**  Disease burden in economically developed countries measured in disability-adjusted life years (DALYs).
*Source*: Murray, CJLM, Lopez, AD, eds. 1996. The Burden of Global Disease: A comprehensive assessment of mortality and disability from diseases, injuries, and risk factors in 1990 and projected to 2020. Vol. 1. Cambridge, MA: Harvard University Press.

mental disorders in different cultures suggest that some disorders, such as schizophrenia, show important consistencies in cross-cultural comparisons. They are found in virtually every culture that social scientists have studied.

Other disorders, such as bulimia, are more specifically associated with cultural factors, as revealed by comparisons of prevalence in different parts of the world and changes in prevalence over generations. Almost 90 percent of bulimic patients are women. Within the United States, the incidence of bulimia is much higher among university women than among working women, and it is more common among younger women than among older women. The prevalence of bulimia is much higher in Western nations than in other parts of the world. Furthermore, the number of cases increased dramatically during the latter part of the twentieth century (Keel & Klump, 2003). These patterns suggest that holding particular sets of values related to eating and to women's appearance is an important ingredient in establishing risk for development of an eating disorder.

The strength and nature of the relationship between culture and psychopathology vary from one disorder to the next. Several general conclusions can be drawn from cross-cultural studies of psychopathology (Draguns & Tanaka-Matsumi, 2003), including the following points:

- All mental disorders are shaped, to some extent, by cultural factors.

- No mental disorders are entirely due to cultural or social factors.

- Psychotic disorders are less influenced by culture than are nonpsychotic disorders.

- The symptoms of certain disorders are more likely to vary across cultures than are the disorders themselves.

We will return to these points as we discuss specific disorders, such as depression, phobias, and alcoholism, throughout this book.

## The Mental Health Professions

People receive treatment for psychological problems in many different settings and from various kinds of service providers. Specialized mental health professionals, such as psychiatrists, psychologists, and social workers, treat fewer than half (40 percent) of those people who seek help for mental disorders (Kessler & Stafford, 2008). Roughly one-third (34 percent) are treated by primary care physicians, who are most likely to prescribe some form of medication. The remaining 26 percent of mental health services are delivered by social agencies and self-help groups, such as Alcoholics Anonymous.

Many forms of specialized training prepare people to provide professional assistance to those who suffer from mental disorders. Table 1.2 presents estimated numbers of different types of mental health professionals currently practicing in the United States. The overall number of professionals who provide mental health services expanded dramatically during the past two decades, with most

**TABLE 1.2**

### Estimated Number of Clinically Trained Professionals Providing Mental Health Services in the United States

| Profession | Number |
| --- | --- |
| Psychiatrists | 30,000 |
| Clinical Psychologists | 93,000 |
| Mental Health and Substance Abuse Social Workers | 115,000 |
| MH Counselors and Marriage and Family Therapists | 156,000 |
| Psychiatric Nurses | 18,000 |
| Psychosocial Rehabilitation Providers | 100,000 |

*Sources*: United States Department of Labor; Bureau of Labor Statistics.

of this growth occurring among nonphysicians (Robiner, 2006). Most of these professions require extensive clinical experience in addition to formal academic instruction. In order to provide direct services to clients, psychiatrists, psychologists, social workers, counselors, nurses, and marriage and family therapists must be licensed in their own specialties by state boards of examiners.

**Psychiatry** is the branch of medicine that is concerned with the study and treatment of mental disorders. Psychiatrists complete the normal sequence of coursework and internship training in a medical school (usually four years) before going on to receive specialized residency training (another four years) that is focused on abnormal behavior. By virtue of their medical training, psychiatrists are licensed to practice medicine and therefore are able to prescribe medication. Most psychiatrists are also trained in the use of psychosocial intervention.

**Clinical psychology** is concerned with the application of psychological science to the assessment and treatment of mental disorders. A clinical psychologist typically completes five years of graduate study in a department of psychology, as well as a one-year internship, before receiving a doctoral degree. Clinical psychologists are trained in the use of psychological assessment procedures and in the use of psychotherapy. Within clinical psychology, there are two primary types of clinical training programs. One course of study, which leads to the Ph.D. (doctor of philosophy) degree, involves a traditional sequence of graduate training with major emphasis on research methods. The other approach, which culminates in a Psy.D. (doctor of psychology) degree, places greater emphasis on practical skills of assessment and treatment and does not require an independent research project for the dissertation. One can also obtain a Ph.D. degree in counseling psychology, a more applied field that focuses on training, assessment, and therapy.

**Social work** is a third profession that is concerned with helping people to achieve an effective level of psychosocial functioning. Most practicing social workers have a master's degree in social work. In contrast to psychology and psychiatry, social work is based less on a body of scientific knowledge than on a commitment to action. Social work is practiced in a wide range of settings, from courts and prisons to schools and hospitals, as well as other social service agencies. The emphasis tends to be on social and cultural factors, such as the effects of poverty on the availability of educational and health services, rather than on individual differences in personality or psychopathology. Psychiatric social workers receive specialized training in the treatment of mental health problems.

Like social workers, professional counselors work in many different settings, ranging from schools and government agencies to mental health centers and private practice. Most are trained at the master's degree level, and the emphasis of their activity is also on providing direct service. Marriage and family therapy (MFT) is a multidisciplinary field in which professionals are trained to provide psychotherapy. Most MFTs are trained at the master's level, and many hold a degree in social work, counseling, or psychology as well. Although the theoretical orientation is focused on couples and family issues, approximately half of the people treated by MFTs are seen in individual psychotherapy. Psychiatric nursing is a rapidly growing field. Training for this profession typically involves a bachelor's degree in nursing plus graduate level training (at least a master's degree) in the treatment of mental health problems.

Another approach to mental health services that is expanding rapidly in size and influence is psychosocial rehabilitation (PSR). Professionals in this area work in crisis, residential, and case management programs for people with severe forms of disorder, such as schizophrenia. PSR workers teach people practical, day-to-day skills that are necessary for living in the community, thereby reducing the need for long-term hospitalization and minimizing the level of disability experienced by their clients. Graduate training is not required for most PSR positions; three out of four people providing PSR services have either a high school education or a bachelor's degree.

It is difficult to say with certainty what the mental health professions will be like in the future. Boundaries between professions change as a function of progress in the development of therapeutic procedures, economic pressures, legislative action, and courtroom decisions. This has been particularly true in the field of mental health, where enormous changes have taken place over the past few decades. Reform is currently being driven by the pervasive influence of managed care, which refers to the way that services are financed. For example, health insurance companies typically place restrictions on the types of services that will be reimbursed, as well as the specific professionals who can provide them. Managed care places a high priority on cost containment and the evaluation of treatment effectiveness. Legislative issues that determine the scope of clinical practice are also very important. Many psychologists are pursuing the right to prescribe medication (Fox et al., 2009). Decisions regarding this issue will also have a dramatic impact on the boundaries that separate the mental health professions. Ongoing conflicts over the increasing price of health care, priorities for treatment, and access to services suggest that debates over the rights and privileges of patients and their therapists will intensify in coming years.

One thing is certain about the future of the mental health professions: There will always be a demand for people who are trained to help those suffering from abnormal behavior. Many people experience mental disorders. Unfortunately, most of those who are in need of professional treatment do not get it (Kessler et al., 2005; Ormel et al., 2008). Several explanations have been proposed. Some people who qualify for a diagnosis may not be so impaired as to seek treatment; others, as we shall see, may not recognize their disorder. In some cases, treatment may not be available, the person may not have the time or resources to obtain treatment, or the person may have tried treatments in the past that failed (see Getting Help at the end of this chapter.)

## Psychopathology in Historical Context

Throughout history, many other societies have held very different views of the problems that we consider to be mental disorders. Before leaving this introductory chapter, we must begin to place contemporary approaches to psychopathology in historical perspective.

The search for explanations of the causes of abnormal behavior dates to ancient times, as do conflicting opinions about the etiology of emotional disorders. References to abnormal behavior have been found in ancient accounts from Chinese, Hebrew, and Egyptian societies. Many of these records explain abnormal behavior as resulting from the disfavor of the gods or the mischief of demons. In fact, abnormal behavior continues to be attributed to demons in some preliterate societies today.

### The Greek Tradition in Medicine

More earthly and less supernatural accounts of the etiology of psychopathology can be traced to the Greek physician Hippocrates (460–377 B.C.E.), who ridiculed demonological accounts of illness and insanity. Instead, Hippocrates hypothesized that abnormal behavior, like other forms of disease, had natural causes. Health depended on maintaining a natural balance within the body, specifically a balance of four body fluids (which were also known as the four humors): blood, phlegm, black bile, and yellow bile. Hippocrates argued that various types of disorders, including psychopathology, resulted from either an excess or a deficiency of one of these four fluids. The specifics of Hippocrates' theories obviously have little value today, but his systematic attempt to uncover natural, biological explanations for all types of illness represented an enormously important departure from previous ways of thinking.

The Hippocratic perspective dominated medical thought in Western countries until the middle of the nineteenth century (Golub, 1994). People trained in the Hippocratic tradition viewed "disease" as a unitary concept. In other words, physicians (and others who were given responsibility for healing people who were disturbed or suffering) did not distinguish between mental disorders and other types of illness. All problems were considered to be the result of an imbalance of body fluids, and treatment procedures were designed in an attempt to restore the ideal balance. These were often called "heroic" treatments because they were drastic (and frequently painful) attempts to quickly reverse the course of an illness. They involved bloodletting (intentionally cutting the person to reduce the amount of blood in the body) and purging (the induction of vomiting), as well as the use of heat and cold. These practices need to be part of standard medical treatments well into the nineteenth century (Starr, 1982).

## The Creation of the Asylum

In Europe during the Middle Ages, "lunatics" and "idiots," as the mentally ill and intellectually disabled were commonly called, aroused little interest and were given marginal care. Most people lived in rural settings and made their living through agricultural activities. Disturbed behavior was considered to be the responsibility of the family rather than the community or the state. Many people were kept at home by their families, and others roamed freely as beggars. Mentally disturbed people who were violent or appeared dangerous were often imprisoned with criminals. Those who could not subsist on their own were placed in almshouses for the poor.

In the 1600s and 1700s, "insane asylums" were established to house the mentally disturbed. Several factors changed the way that society viewed people with mental disorders and reinforced the relatively new belief that the community as a whole should be responsible for their care (Grob, 2011). Perhaps most important was a change in economic, demographic, and social conditions. Consider, for example, the situation in the United States at the beginning of the nineteenth century. The period between 1790 and 1850 saw rapid population growth and the rise of large cities. The increased urbanization of the American population was accompanied by a shift from an agricultural to an industrial economy. Lunatic asylums—the original mental hospitals—were created to serve heavily populated cities and to assume responsibilities that had previously been performed by individual families.

Early asylums were little more than human warehouses, but as the nineteenth century began, the moral treatment movement led to improved conditions in at least some mental hospitals. Founded on a basic respect for human dignity and the belief that humanistic care would help to relieve mental illness, moral treatment reform efforts were instituted by leading mental health professionals of the day, such as Benjamin Rush in the United States, Philippe Pinel in France, and William Tuke in England. Rather than simply confining mental patients, moral treatment offered support, care, and a degree of freedom. Belief in the importance of reason and the potential benefits of science played an important role in the moral treatment movement. In contrast to the fatalistic, supernatural explanations that had prevailed during the Middle Ages, these reformers touted an optimistic view, arguing that mental disorders could be treated successfully.

Many of the large mental institutions in the United States were built in the nineteenth century as a result of the philosophy of moral treatment. In the middle of the 1800s, the mental health

This 16th century illustration shows sick people going to the doctor who attempts to cure their problems by extracting blood from them using a leech. The rationale for such treatment procedures was to restore the proper balance of bodily fluids.

advocate Dorothea Dix was a leader in this movement. Dix argued that treating the mentally ill in hospitals was both more humane and more economical than caring for them haphazardly in their communities, and she urged that special facilities be built to house mental patients. Dix and like-minded reformers were successful in their efforts. In 1830, there were only four public mental hospitals in the United States that housed a combined total of fewer than 200 patients. By 1880, there were 75 public mental hospitals, with a total population of more than 35,000 residents (Torrey, 1988).

The creation of large institutions for the treatment of mental patients led to the development of a new profession—psychiatry. By the middle of the 1800s, superintendents of asylums for the insane were almost always physicians who had experience in the care of people with severe mental disorders. The Association of Medical Superintendents of American Institutions for the Insane (AMSAII), which later became the American Psychiatric Association (APA), was founded in 1844. The large patient populations within these institutions provided an opportunity for these men to observe various types of psychopathology over an extended period of time. They soon began to publish their ideas regarding the causes of these conditions, and they also experimented with new treatment methods (Grob, 2011).

## Worcester Lunatic Hospital: A Model Institution

In 1833, the state of Massachusetts opened a publicly supported asylum for lunatics, a term used at the time to describe people with mental disorders, in Worcester. Samuel Woodward, the asylum's first superintendent, also became the first president of the AMSAII. Woodward became very well known throughout the United States and Europe because of his claims that mental disorders could be cured just like other types of diseases. We will describe this institution and its superintendent briefly because, in many ways, it became a model for psychiatric care on which other nineteenth-century hospitals were built.

Woodward's ideas about the causes of disorders represented a combination of physical and moral considerations. Moral factors focused on the person's lifestyle. Violations of "natural" or conventional behavior could presumably cause mental disorders. Judgments regarding the nature of these violations were based on the prevailing middle class, Protestant standards that were held by Woodward and his peers, who were almost invariably well-educated, white males. After treating several hundred patients during his first 10 years at the Worcester asylum, Woodward argued that at least half of the cases could be traced to immoral behavior, improper living conditions, and exposure to unnatural stresses. Specific examples included intemperance (heavy drinking), masturbation, overwork, domestic difficulties, excessive ambition, faulty education, personal disappointment, marital problems, excessive religious enthusiasm, jealousy, and pride (Grob, 2011). The remaining cases were attributed to physical causes, such as poor health or a blow to the head.

Treatment at the Worcester Lunatic Hospital included a blend of physical and moral procedures. If mental disorders were often caused by improper behavior and difficult life circumstances, presumably they could be cured by moving the person to a more appropriate and therapeutic environment, the asylum. Moral treatment focused on efforts to reeducate the patient, fostering the development of self-control that would allow the person to return to a "healthy" lifestyle. Procedures included occupational therapy, religious exercises, and recreation. Mechanical restraints were employed only when considered necessary.

Moral treatments were combined with a mixture of physical procedures. These included standard heroic interventions, such as bleeding and purging, which the asylum superintendents had learned as part of their medical training. For example, some symptoms were thought to be produced by inflammation of the brain, and it was believed that bleeding would restore the natural balance of fluids. Woodward and his colleagues also employed various kinds of drugs. Patients who were excited, agitated, or violent were often treated with opium or morphine. Depressed patients were given laxatives.

Woodward claimed that "no disease, of equal severity, can be treated with greater success than insanity, if the remedies are applied sufficiently early." He reported that the recovery rates at the Worcester hospital varied from 82 percent to 91 percent between 1833 and 1845. His reports were embraced and endorsed by other members of the young psychiatric profession. They fueled enthusiasm for establishing more large public hospitals, thus aiding the efforts of Dorothea Dix and other advocates for public support of mental health treatment.

## Lessons from the History of Psychopathology

The invention and expansion of public mental hospitals set in motion a process of systematic observation and scientific inquiry that led directly to our current system of mental health care. The

An engraving of the Massachusetts Lunatic Asylum as it appeared in 1835.

creation of psychiatry as a professional group, committed to treating and understanding psychopathology, laid the foundation for expanded public concern and financial resources for solving the problems of mental disorders.

There are, of course, many aspects of nineteenth-century psychiatry that, in retrospect, seem to have been naive or misguided. To take only one example, it seems silly to have thought that masturbation would cause mental disorders. In fact, masturbation is now taught and encouraged as part of treatment for certain types of sexual dysfunction (see Chapter 12). The obvious cultural biases that influenced the etiological hypotheses of Woodward and his colleagues seem quite unreasonable today. But, of course, our own values and beliefs influence the ways in which we define, think about, and treat mental disorders. Mental disorders cannot be defined in a cultural vacuum or in a completely objective fashion. The best we can do is to be aware of the problem of bias and include a variety of cultural and social perspectives in thinking about and defining the issues (Mezzich et al., 2008).

The other lesson that we can learn from history involves the importance of scientific research. Viewed from the perspective of contemporary care, we can easily be skeptical of Samuel Woodward's claims regarding the phenomenal success of treatment at the Worcester asylum. No one today believes that 90 percent of seriously disturbed, psychotic patients can be cured by currently available forms of treatment. Therefore, it is preposterous to assume that such astounding success might have been achieved at the Worcester Lunatic Hospital. During the nineteenth century, physicians were not trained in scientific research methods. Their optimistic statements about treatment outcome were accepted, in large part, on the basis of their professional authority. Clearly, Woodward's enthusiastic assertions should have been evaluated with more stringent, scientific methods.

Unfortunately, the type of naive acceptance that met Woodward's idealistic claims has become a regrettable tradition. For the past 150 years, mental health professionals and the public alike have repeatedly embraced new treatment procedures that have

**TABLE 1.3**

## Somatic Treatments Introduced and Widely Employed in the 1920s and 1930s

| Name | Procedure | Original Rationale |
|------|-----------|--------------------|
| Fever therapy | Blood from people with malaria was injected into psychiatric patients so that they would develop a fever. | Observation that symptoms sometimes disappeared in patients who became ill with typhoid fever |
| Insulin coma therapy | Insulin was injected into psychiatric patients to lower the sugar content of the blood and induce a hypoglycemic state and deep coma. | Observed mental changes among some diabetic drug addicts who were treated with insulin |
| Lobotomy | A sharp knife was inserted through a hole that was bored in the patient's skull, severing nerve fibers connecting the frontal lobes to the rest of the brain. | Observation that the same surgical procedure with chimpanzees led to a reduction in the display of negative emotion during stress |

*Note:* Lack of critical evaluation of these procedures is belied by the unusual honors bestowed upon their inventors. Julius Wagner-Jauregg, an Austrian psychiatrist, was awarded the Nobel Prize in 1927 for his work in developing fever therapy. Egaz Moniz, a Portuguese psychiatrist, was awarded the Nobel Prize in 1946 for introduction of the lobotomy.

been hailed as cures for mental disorders. Perhaps most notorious was a group of somatic (bodily) treatment procedures that was introduced during the 1920s and 1930s (Valenstein, 1986). They included inducing fever, insulin comas, and lobotomy, a crude form of brain surgery (see Table 1.3). These dramatic procedures, which have subsequently proved to be ineffective, were accepted with the same enthusiasm that greeted the invention of large public institutions in nineteenth-century America. Thousands of patients were subjected to these procedures, which remained widespread until the early 1950s, when more effective pharmacological treatments were discovered. The history of psychopathology teaches us that people who claim that a new form of treatment is effective should be expected to prove it scientifically (see Research Methods on page 19).

## Methods for the Scientific Study of Mental Disorders

This book will provide you with an introduction to the scientific study of psychopathology. The application of science to questions regarding abnormal behavior carries with it the implicit assumption that these problems can be studied systematically and objectively. Such a systematic and objective study is the basis for finding order in the frequently chaotic and puzzling world of mental disorders. This order will eventually allow us to understand the processes by which abnormal behaviors are created and maintained.

Clinical scientists adopt an attitude of open-minded skepticism, tempered by an appreciation for the research methods that are used to collect empirical data. They formulate specific hypotheses, test them, and then refine them based on the results of these tests. For example, suppose you formulated the hypothesis that people who are depressed will improve if they eat more than a certain amount of chocolate every day. This hypothesis could be tested in a number of ways, using the methods discussed throughout this book. In order to get the most from this book, you may have to set aside—at least temporarily—personal beliefs that you have already

acquired about mental disorders. Try to adopt an objective, skeptical attitude. We hope to pique your curiosity and share with you the satisfaction, as well as perhaps some of the frustration, of searching for answers to questions about complex behavior problems.

## The Uses and Limitations of Case Studies

We have already presented one source of information regarding mental disorders: the **case study,** an in-depth look at the symptoms and circumstances surrounding one person's mental disturbance. For many people, our initial ideas about the nature and potential causes of abnormal behavior are shaped by personal experience with a close friend or family member who has struggled with a psychological disorder. We use a number of case studies in this book to illustrate the symptoms of psychopathology and to raise questions about their development. Therefore, we should consider the ways in which case studies can be helpful in the study of psychopathology, as well as some of their limitations.

A case study presents a description of the problems experienced by one particular person. Detailed case studies can provide an exhaustive catalog of the symptoms that the person displayed, the manner in which these symptoms emerged, the developmental and family history that preceded the onset of the disorder, and whatever response the person may have shown to treatment efforts. This material often forms the basis for hypotheses about the causes of a person's problems. For example, based on Mary's case, one might speculate that depression plays a role in eating disorders. Case studies are especially important sources of information about conditions that have not received much attention in the literature and for problems that are relatively unusual. Dissociative identity disorder and gender dysphoria are examples of disorders that are so infrequent that it is difficult to find groups of patients for the purpose of research studies. Much of what we know about these conditions is based on descriptions of individual patients.

Case studies also have several drawbacks. The most obvious limitation of case studies is that they can be viewed from many different perspectives. Any case can be interpreted in several ways, and competing explanations may be equally plausible. Consider, for example, Abraham Lincoln, who suffered through periods of profound depression throughout his adult life. Some historians have argued that Lincoln's mood disorder can be traced to the sudden death of his mother when he was 9 years old (Burlingame, 1994). The impact of this tragic experience was later intensified by several other losses, including the deaths of two of his four sons. Heredity may also have played a role in the origins of Lincoln's depression. Some of Lincoln's cousins were apparently also depressed, and neighbors recalled that Lincoln's father "often got the blues." Speculation of this sort is intriguing, particularly in the case of a man who played such an important role in the history of the United States. But we must remember that case studies are not conclusive. Lincoln's experience does not indicate conclusively whether the loss of a parent can increase a person's vulnerability to depression, and it does not prove that

## RESEARCH methods

### Who Must Provide Scientific Evidence?

Scientists have established a basic and extremely important rule for making and testing any new hypothesis: The scientist who makes a new prediction must prove it to be true. Scientists are not obligated to disprove other researchers' assertions. Until a hypothesis is supported by empirical evidence, the community of scientists assumes that the new prediction is false.

The concepts of the experimental hypothesis and the null hypothesis are central to understanding this essential rule of science. A **hypothesis** is any new prediction, such as the idea that eating chocolate can alleviate depression, made by an investigator. Researchers must adopt and state their experimental hypothesis in both correlational studies and experiments (discussed in Research Methods in Chapters 2 and 3). In all scientific research, the **null hypothesis** is the alternative to the experimental hypothesis. The null hypothesis always predicts that the experimental hypothesis is not true, for example, that eating chocolate does not make depressed people feel better. The rules of science dictate that scientists must assume that the null hypothesis holds until research contradicts it. That is, the burden of proof falls on the scientist who makes a new prediction, and offers an experimental hypothesis.

These rules of science are analogous to rules about the burden of proof that have been adopted in trial courts. In U.S. courtrooms, the law assumes that a defendant is innocent until proven guilty. Defendants do not need to prove their innocence; rather, prosecutors need to prove the defendant's guilt. Thus, the null hypothesis is analogous to the assumption of innocence, and the burden of proof in science falls on any scientist who challenges the null hypothesis, just as it falls on the prosecutor in a court trial.

These rules in science and in law serve important purposes. Both are conservative principles designed to protect the field from false assertions. Our legal philosophy is, "It is better to let 10 guilty people go free than to punish one innocent person." Scientists adopt a similar philosophy—that false "scientific evidence" is more dangerous than undetected knowledge. Because of these safeguards, we can be reasonably confident when an experimental hypothesis is supported or when a defendant is found guilty.

We can easily apply these concepts and rules to claims that were made for the effectiveness of treatment methods such as lobotomy. In this example, the experimental hypothesis is that severing the nerve fibers that connect the frontal lobes to other areas of the brain will result in a significant decrease in psychotic symptoms. The null hypothesis is that this treatment is no more effective than having no treatment at all. According to the rules of science, a clinician who claims to have discovered a new treatment must prove that it is true. Scientists are not obligated to prove that the assertion is false, because the null hypothesis holds until it is rejected.

The value of this conservative approach is obvious when we consider the needless suffering and permanent neurological dysfunction that was ultimately inflicted upon thousands of patients who were given lobotomies or subjected to fevers and comas during the 1940s (Valenstein, 1986). Had surgeons assumed that lobotomies did not work, many patients' brains would have been left intact. Similar conclusions can be drawn about less invasive procedures, such as institutionalization, medication, and psychotherapy. These treatments are also associated with costs, which range from financial considerations—certainly important in today's health care environment—to the disappointment brought about by false hopes. In all these cases, clinicians who provide mental health services should be required to demonstrate scientifically that their treatment procedures are both effective and harmless (Chambless et al., 2006; Dimidjian & Hollon, 2010).

There is one more similarity between the rules of science and the rules of the courtroom. Courtroom verdicts do not lead to a judgment that the defendant is "innocent," but only to a decision that she or he is "not guilty." In theory, the possibility remains that a defendant who is found "not guilty" did indeed commit a crime. Similarly, scientific research does not lead to the conclusion that the null hypothesis is true. Scientists never prove the null hypothesis; they only fail to reject it. The reason for this position is that the philosophy of knowledge, epistemology, tells us that it is impossible ever to prove that an experimental hypothesis is false in every circumstance.

Many people lead successful lives and make important contributions to society in spite of their struggles with mental disorder. For example, Abraham Lincoln suffered episodes of severe depression.

genetic factors are involved in the transmission of this disorder. These questions must be resolved through scientific investigation.

The other main limitation of case studies is that it is risky to draw general conclusions about a disorder from a single example. How can we know that this individual is representative of the disorder as a whole? Are his or her experiences typical for people with this disorder? Again, hypotheses generated on the basis of the single case must be tested in research with larger, more representative samples of patients.

## Clinical Research Methods

The importance of the search for new information about mental disorders has inspired us to build another special feature into this textbook. Each chapter includes a Research Methods feature that explains one particular research issue in some detail. The Research Methods feature in this chapter, for example, is concerned with the null hypothesis, the need to consider not only that your hypothesis may be true, but also that it may be false. A list of the issues addressed in Research Methods throughout this textbook appears in Table 1.4. They are arranged to progress from some of the more basic research methods and issues, such as correlational and experimental designs, toward more complex issues, such as gene identification and heritability.

We decided to discuss methodological issues in small sections throughout the book, for two primary reasons. First, the problems raised by research methods are often complex and challenging. Some students find it difficult to digest and comprehend

an entire chapter on research methods in one chunk, especially at the beginning of a book. Thus, we have broken it down into more manageable bites. Second, and perhaps more important, the methods we discuss generally make more sense and are easier to understand when they are presented in the context of a clinical question that they can help answer. Our discussions of research methods are, therefore, introduced while we are explaining contemporary views of particular clinical problems.

Research findings are not the end of the road, either. The fact that someone has managed to collect and present data on a particular topic does not mean that the data are useful. We want you to learn about the problems of designing and interpreting research studies so that you will become a more critical consumer of scientific evidence. If you do not have a background in research design or quantitative methods, the Research Methods features will familiarize you with the procedures that psychologists use to test their hypotheses. If you have already had an introductory course in methodology, they will show you how these problems are handled in research on abnormal behavior.

### TABLE 1.4
### List of Research Methods Featured in This Book

| Chapter | Topic |
|---------|-------|
| 1 | Who Must Provide Scientific Evidence? |
| 2 | Correlations: Does a Psychology Major Make You Smarter? |
| 3 | The Experimental Method: Does Therapy *Cause* Improvement? |
| 4 | Reliability: Agreement Regarding Diagnostic Decisions |
| 5 | Analogue Studies: Do Rats Get Depressed, and Why? |
| 6 | Statistical Significance: When Differences Matter |
| 7 | Retrospective Reports: Remembering the Past |
| 8 | Longitudinal Studies: Lives over Time |
| 9 | Cross-Cultural Comparisons: The Importance of Context |
| 10 | Psychotherapy Placebos: Controlling for Expectations |
| 11 | Studies of People at Risk for Disorders |
| 12 | Hypothetical Constructs: What Is Sexual Arousal? |
| 13 | Comparison Groups: What Is Normal? |
| 14 | Finding Genes That Cause Behavioral Problems |
| 15 | Central Tendency and Variability: What Do IQ Scores Mean? |
| 16 | Samples: How to Select the People We Study |
| 17 | Heritability: Genes and the Environment |
| 18 | Base Rates and Prediction: Justice Blackmun's Error |

Many students take an abnormal psychology class, in part, to understand more about their own problems or the problems of friends or family members. If you are considering whether you want to get help for yourself or for someone you know, these Getting Help sections should give you a head start in finding good therapists and effective treatments.

Of course, psychology is not just about problems. If you are wondering if you need help, if you are just curious about the problems people can have, or even if you are skeptical or disinterested, you will definitely learn more about yourself and others from this course and by studying psychology in general. That is what makes the subject so fascinating! But when the topic is abnormal psychology, you should be warned in advance about two risks.

The first is the "medical student's syndrome." As medical students learn about new illnesses, they often "develop" the symptoms of each successive disease they study. The same thing can happen when studying abnormal psychology. In fact, because many symptoms of emotional disorders share much in common with everyday experiences, students of abnormal psychology are even more likely to "discover" symptoms in themselves or others. ("Gee, I think maybe I have an anxiety disorder." "He is so self-absorbed; he has a personality disorder.") We all are frightened about experiencing illness and abnormality, and this fear can make us suggestible. So try to prepare yourself for bouts of the medical student's syndrome. And remember that it is normal to experience mild versions of many of the symptoms you will read about in this text.

Our second warning is much more serious. If you are genuinely concerned about your own problems or those of a loved one, you probably have or will consult various "self-help"

resources—books, Web sites, or perhaps groups online or offline. Do not accept uncritically the treatment programs they may suggest. You probably know that not everything you hear or read is true, and psychological advice is no exception.

Misleading, inaccurate, or simply wrong information is a particular problem in abnormal psychology for three reasons. First, to be honest, as you will learn throughout this course, psychological scientists simply do not know the causes of or absolutely effective treatments for many emotional problems. Second, people who have emotional problems, and those who have loved ones who have emotional problems, often are desperate to find a cure. Third, some well-meaning—and some unscrupulous—people will provide authoritative-sounding "answers" that really are theories, speculations, or distortions.

How can you know what information is accurate and what information is inaccurate? We have worked hard to bring you the most recent scientific information in this text. In addition to the detailed information we present in each chapter, we give you practical tips including recommended self-help books and Web sites in these Getting Help sections in each chapter. Two general resources you might want to explore now are Martin Seligman's book, *What You Can Change and What You Can't* (2007), and the homepage of the National Institute of Mental Health: www.nimh.nih.gov. But we don't want you to rely only on this book or other authorities. We want you to rely on your own critical thinking skills, especially when it comes to getting help for yourself or someone you care about. Remember this: There is an army of scientists out there trying to solve the problems of emotional disorders, because, like us, they want to help. Breakthrough treatments that really are breakthrough treatments will not be kept secret. They will be announced on the front page of newspapers, not in obscure books or remote Web sites.

# Summary

Mental disorders are quite common. At least 50 percent of all men and women will experience a serious form of abnormal behavior, such as depression, alcoholism, or schizophrenia, at some point during their lives.

Mental disorders are defined in terms of typical signs and symptoms rather than identifiable causal factors. A group of symptoms that appear together and are assumed to represent a specific type of disorder is called a **syndrome.** There are no definitive psychological or biological tests that can be used to confirm the presence of psychopathology. At present, the diagnosis of mental disorders depends on observations of the person's behavior and descriptions of personal experience.

No one has been able to provide a universally accepted definition of abnormal behavior. One useful approach defines mental disorders in terms of **harmful dysfunction.** The official classification system, *DSM-5*, defines mental disorders as a group of persistent maladaptive behaviors that result in personal distress or impaired functioning.

Various forms of voluntary social deviance and efforts to express individuality are excluded from the definition of mental disorders. Political and religious actions, and the beliefs on which they are based, are not considered to be forms of abnormal behavior, even when they seem unusual to many other people. Nevertheless, **culture** has an important influence on the process of defining psychopathology.

The scientific study of the frequency and distribution of disorders within a population is known as **epidemiology.** The global burden of mental disorders is substantial. Some severe forms of abnormal behavior, such as schizophrenia, have been observed in virtually every society that has been studied by social scientists. There are also forms of psychopathology—including eating disorders—for which substantial cross-cultural differences have been found.

Many forms of specialized training prepare people to provide professional help to those who suffer from mental disorders. A **psychiatrist** is licensed to practice medicine and is therefore able to prescribe medication. A **clinical psychologist** has received graduate training in the use of assessment procedures and psychotherapy. Most psychologists also have extensive knowledge regarding research methods, and their training prepares them for the integration of science and practice.

Throughout history, many societies have held different ideas about the problems that we consider to be mental disorders. Although the earliest asylums were little more than human warehouses, the moral treatment movement introduced improved conditions in some mental hospitals. The creation of large institutions for mental patients led to the development of psychiatry as a profession. These physicians, who served as the superintendents of asylums, developed systems for describing, classifying, and treating people with various types of mental disorders. Their efforts led to the use of scientific methods to test these new ideas.

A person who proposes a new theory about the causes of a form of psychopathology, or someone who advocates a new form of treatment, should be expected to prove these claims with scientific evidence. The burden of proof falls on the clinical scientist who offers a new prediction. In other words, the **null hypothesis** (the alternative to the **experimental hypothesis**) is assumed to be true until it is contradicted by systematic data. Individual **case studies** do not provide conclusive evidence about the causes of, or treatments for, mental disorders.

## The Big Picture

# critical thinking review

**1.1** What is the difference between normal and abnormal behavior?
While the line between normal and abnormal is not always obvious, several important considerations help to clarify the distinction . . . (see pages 5–6).

**1.2** How does culture influence the definition of mental disorders?
Social and political forces influence the extent to which certain kinds of experience are considered to be pathological . . . (see pages 7–8).

**1.3** How does the impact of mental disorders compare to that of other health problems?
Mental disorders are responsible for almost half of all disability in economically developed countries, ranking second in total disease burden behind cardiovascular disease . . . (see page 13).

**1.4** Who provides help for people with mental disorders?
Many different forms of training can prepare people for professional careers in the delivery of mental health services . . . (see page 14).

**1.5** Why do scientific methods play such an important role in psychology's approach to the study of mental disorders?
The hallmark of psychology as an academic discipline is the use of rigorous scientific methods to test the validity of alternative hypotheses regarding issues such as the causes and treatment of mental disorders . . . (see page 18).

# key terms

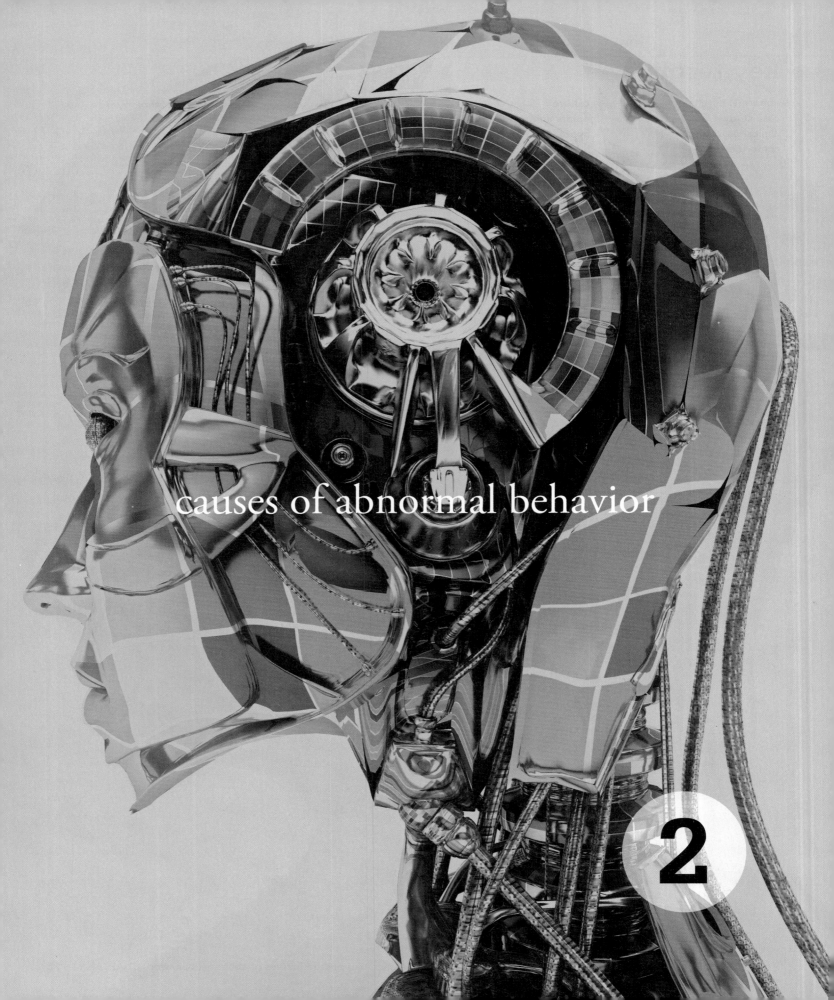

causes of abnormal behavior

2

# The Big Picture

## learning objectives

**2.1**
What is the biopsychosocial model and why do we need it?

**2.2**
What does "correlation does not mean causation" mean?

**2.3**
How is "mental illness caused by a chemical imbalance in the brain" an example of reductionism?

**2.4**
Are scientists likely to discover a gene that causes mental disorders?

**2.5**
How do social and psychological factors contribute to emotional problems?

**2.6**
Is abnormal behavior really all about labeling and role playing?

What causes abnormal behavior? We all want an answer to this question. People suffering from emotional problems, and their loved ones, may be desperate for one. Some "experts" will offer a ready response, pointing to the trauma of abuse, poor parenting, a "broken brain," or other handy explanations. Unfortunately, such simple accounts are almost certainly wrong. Trauma, upbringing, and biology all may contribute to different mental disorders, but most emotional problems appear to result from a combination of various biological, psychological, and social influences. And the truth is that we do not know the specific cause of most emotional disorders. What we have is an unsolved mystery, and psychological scientists have much detective work to do. In this chapter, we introduce you to psychology's hard evidence, working theories, and hot leads in pursuit of answers to this compelling mystery.

## Overview

You may be distressed to learn that the cause, or *etiology,* of most abnormal behavior is unknown. In fact, you may have read or heard popular accounts with headlines like, "Depression Found in the Brain!" Our reaction to such breathless stories is: We *know* depression is in the brain. Of course, it is exciting that

neuroscientists are identifying specific brain regions and chemicals involved in mental illnesses. But scientists often cannot answer basic "chicken or egg" questions like: Do chemical imbalances in the brain cause depression? Or do trying experiences cause depression—and changes in brain chemistry that reflect depression? Media accounts about what causes abnormal behavior typically are oversimplified—and often misleading. They "solve" the mystery in today's headline, but retract it on the back page the next day.

Some scientists also claim to have solved the mystery. Throughout much of the twentieth century, many psychologists vowed allegiance to one of the four broad theories of abnormal behavior—the biological, psychodynamic, cognitive-behavioral, and humanistic paradigms. A **paradigm** is a set of shared assumptions that includes both the substance of a theory and beliefs about how scientists should collect data and test hypotheses. Thus, the four paradigms disagreed not only about what causes abnormal behavior, but also about how to prove each theory.

Most psychological scientists today suspect that abnormal behavior is caused by a combination of biological, psychological, and social factors (Kendler & Prescott, 2006). Biological contributions range from brain chemistry to genetic predispositions. Psychological contributions range from troubled emotions to distorted thinking. Social and cultural contributions range from conflict in family relationships to sexual and racial bias. In short, contemporary research is guided by the **biopsychosocial model,** an effort to integrate evidence on these broad contributions to mental disorders.

In this chapter, we briefly review the four traditional paradigms and explain how integrated approaches have emerged to replace them. We also introduce a number of biological, psychological, and social processes that appear to contribute to emotional problems. In later chapters, we return to these concepts when discussing specific psychological disorders. As we do in every chapter, we begin our investigation with a case study. Most cases, including the following one, come from our own therapy files.

### → Meghan's Many Hardships

At the age of 14, Meghan B. attempted to end her life by taking approximately 20 Tylenol® capsules. Meghan took the pills after an explosive fight with her mother over Meghan's grades and a boy she was dating. Meghan was in her room when she impulsively took the pills, but shortly afterward she told her mother what she had done. Her parents rushed Meghan to the emergency room, where her vital signs were closely monitored. As the crisis was coming to an end, Meghan's parents agreed that she should be hospitalized to make sure that she was safe and to begin to treat her problems.

Meghan talked freely during the 30 days she spent on the adolescent unit of a private psychiatric hospital. Most of her complaints focused on her mother. Meghan insisted that her mother was always "in her face," telling her what to do and when and how to do it. Her father was "great," but he was too busy with his job as a chemical engineer to spend much time with her.

Meghan also had long-standing problems in school. She barely maintained a C average despite considerable efforts to do better. Meghan said she didn't care about school, and her mother's insistence that she could do much better was a major source of conflict between them. Meghan also complained that she had few friends, either in or outside of school. She described her classmates as "straight" and said she had no interest in them. Meghan was obviously angry as she described her family, school, and friends, but she also seemed sad. She often denounced herself as "stupid," and she cried about being a "reject" when discussing why no friends, including her boyfriend, came to see her at the hospital.

Mrs. B. provided details on the history of Meghan's problems. Mr. and Mrs. B. could not have children of their own, and they adopted Meghan when she was 2 years old. According to the adoption agency, Meghan's birth mother was 16 years old when she had the baby. Meghan's biological mother was a drug user, and she haphazardly left the baby in the care of friends and relatives for weeks at a time. Little was known about Meghan's biological father except that he had had some trouble with the law. Meghan's mother had known him only briefly.

After a six-month legal investigation, Meghan's mother agreed to give her up for adoption. Meghan came to live with Mr. and Mrs. B. shortly thereafter.

Mrs. B. happily doted on her daughter. She said that Mr. B. was a loving father, but agreed with Meghan that he was rarely at home. Meghan seemed fine until first grade, when teachers began to complain about her. She disrupted the classroom with her restlessness, and she did not complete her schoolwork. In second grade, a school psychologist suggested that Meghan was a "hyperactive" child who also had a learning disability. Her pediatrician recommended medication. Mrs. B. was horrified by the thought of medication or of sending Meghan to a "resource room" for part of the school day. Instead, she redoubled her efforts at parenting.

Meghan's grades and classroom behavior remained acceptable as long as Mrs. B. consulted repeatedly with the school. Mrs. B. noted with bitterness, however, that the one problem that she could not solve was Meghan's friendships. The daughters of Mrs. B.'s friends and neighbors were well behaved and excellent students. Meghan did not fit in, and she never got invited to play with the other girls.

Mrs. B. was obviously sad when discussing Meghan's past, but she became agitated and angry when discussing the present. She was very concerned about Meghan, but she wondered out loud if the suicide attempt had been manipulative. Mrs. B. said that she had had major conflicts with Meghan ever since Meghan started middle school. Meghan would no longer work with her mother on her homework for the usual two hours each night. She began arguing about everything from picking up her room to her boyfriend, an 18 year old whom Mrs. B. abhorred. Mrs. B.

complained that she did not understand what had happened to her daughter. She clearly stated, however, that whatever it was, she would fix it.

••••••••••••••••••••••••••••••••••••••••••••••••••••••••••••••••••••••••••••

What was causing Meghan's problems? Her case study suggests many possibilities. Some difficulties seem to be a reaction to a mother whose attentiveness at age 8 seems intrusive at age 14. We could also trace some of her troubles to anger over her failures in school or rejection by her peers. However, Meghan's problems seem bigger than this. Surely she was affected by the physical abuse, inconsistent love, and chaotic living arrangements during the first, critical years of her life. But could those distant events account for her current problems? What about biological contributions? Did her birth mother's drug abuse affect Meghan as a developing fetus? Was Meghan a healthy, full-term newborn? Given her biological parents' history of troubled behavior, could Meghan's problems be partly genetic? We do not have easy answers to these questions, but we can tell you how psychological scientists are seeking to answer them.

## Brief Historical Perspective

The search for explanations of the causes of abnormal behavior dates to ancient times. But it was not until the nineteenth and early twentieth centuries that three major scientific advances occurred. One was the discovery of the cause of general paresis, a severe mental disorder that eventually ends in death. The second was the work of Sigmund Freud, a thinker who had a profound influence on abnormal psychology and Western society. The third was the emergence of a new academic discipline called psychology.

### The Biological Paradigm

The discovery of the cause of *general paresis* (general paralysis) is a remarkable and historically important example of the *biological paradigm*, which looks for biological abnormalities that cause abnormal behavior, for example, brain diseases, brain injuries, or genetic disorders. General paresis is caused by *syphilis*, a sexually transmitted disease. We know this as a result of over a century of research—some good and some bad.

In 1798, John Haslam, a British physician, distinguished general paresis from other forms of "lunacy" based on its symptoms, which include delusions of grandeur, cognitive impairment (dementia), and progressive paralysis. (General paresis has an unremitting course and ends in death after many years.) The diagnosis inspired a search for the cause of the disorder, but it took scientists more than 100 years to solve the mystery.

The breakthrough began with the recognition that many people with general paresis had contracted syphilis earlier in their lives. Yet, researchers still questioned this linkage. For example, in 1894, the French syphilis expert, Jean Fournier, found that only 65 percent of patients with general paresis reported a history of syphilis. How could syphilis cause the disorder if a third

German microbiologist Paul Ehrlich (1854–1915) developed *arsphenamine*, an arsenic-based treatment for syphilis that prevented general paresis. He won the Nobel Prize for Medicine.

method involves accurate diagnosis as the first step (see Thinking Critically about DSM-5 on p. 28). The second step is identifying a specific biological cause. The third is developing treatments that prevent, eliminate, or alter the cause. Unfortunately, specific biological causes have been identified only for a few cognitive disorders (see Chapter 14) and about half of all cases of intellectual disability (see Chapter 15). Will the future bring similar discoveries for depression, bipolar disorder, schizophrenia, perhaps even substance abuse? Some scientists hope to identify specific genes and brain processes that cause these disorders. Others believe that we will never discover a single cause, because so many factors are involved in the development of psychological disorders (Kendler & Prescott, 2006).

Like most psychologists, we agree more with the second group of scientists than the first. Specific biological causes, many genetic, probably will be discovered for a small percentage of mental disorders. Yet, we expect the great majority of cases of abnormal behavior to defy simple explanation. Like heart disease and cancer, most mental disorders appear to be "lifestyle diseases" that are caused by a combination of biological, psychological, and social influences.

## The Psychodynamic Paradigm

The *psychodynamic paradigm,* an outgrowth of Sigmund Freud's (1856–1939) theories, asserts that abnormal behavior is caused by unconscious mental conflicts that have roots in early childhood experience. Freud was trained in Paris by Jean Charcot (1825–1893), a neurologist who used hypnosis to treat *hysteria*. Hysteria is characterized by unusual physical symptoms in the

of patients never contracted it? But three years later, Austrian–German psychiatrist Richard von Krafft-Ebing attempted to inoculate patients with general paresis against syphilis. No one became infected when exposed to the inoculation's mild form of the disease. There could be only one explanation: *All* of the patients had been infected with syphilis previously. Fournier's statistic, based on imperfect self-reports, was wrong.

Soon thereafter, scientists identified the type of bacteria (called a *spirochete*) that causes syphilis. Postmortem examinations revealed that the spirochete had invaded and destroyed parts of patients' brain. In 1910, Paul Ehrlich, a German microbiologist, developed an arsenic-containing chemical that destroyed the spirochete and prevented general paresis. (Unfortunately, the drug worked only if the patient was treated in the early stages of infection.) Later, scientists learned that syphilis could be cured by another new drug, *penicillin*—the first antibiotic. General paresis was virtually eliminated when antibiotics became widely available after World War II.

The dramatic discovery of the cause of general paresis promoted hopes that scientists could use similar methods to uncover biological causes for other mental disorders. Broadly, the medical

Sigmund Freud arriving in Paris with his friend, Marie Bonaparte, Princess of Greece and Denmark, and U.S. Ambassador William Bullitt.

## Diagnosis and Causes of Mental Disorders

You know that many physical illnesses are diagnosed based on their cause. Strep throat (caused by streptococcal infection) is one familiar example. Given your experience with problems like strep throat, you may be surprised to learn that most psychological problems are *not* diagnosed based on their cause.

The *DSM-5*, in fact, explicitly does not attempt to diagnose mental disorders based on what is, or might be, causing the problem. Instead, the system takes a *descriptive approach* to classifying abnormal behavior, grouping psychological problems into categories based on similarities in how people act and what they report about their inner experiences. There are many good reasons why *DSM-5* follows a descriptive approach. One reason is that experts simply do not know what causes most mental disorders, as we have discussed. (This is also true for many physical disorders: Think cancer.) A second reason is that the descriptive approach helps professionals to agree about the presence or absence of an emotional problem. Agreement is more formally known as the *reliability* of a diagnosis (see Chapter 4). In a very real sense, the descriptive approach of *DSM-5* gives mental health professionals a common language for talking about mental illness.

Does this mean that *DSM-5* reveals *nothing* about causation? No. Some diagnoses have some *etiological validity*, which simply means the diagnosis reveals something about causation (see Chapter 4). We know that there is a very strong genetic contribution to attention-deficit/hyperactivity disorder, for example, even though we do not know what genes are involved (see Chapter 16). For a few other conditions, a specific causal factor is a part of the diagnosis itself. For example, drinking too much is part of the definition of alcoholism, and you cannot have post-traumatic stress disorder without first experiencing a trauma. Finally, scientists have discovered a specific cause for a minority of psychological disorders, particularly some forms of dementia (see Chapter 14) and various intellectual disabilities (formerly called mental retardation).

The intellectual disabilities may be a model for the future diagnosis of mental disorders. A century ago, diagnosing intellectual disabilities was similar to diagnosing mental disorders today. Causation was largely unknown. But over the last 100 years, scientists have identified specific causes for about 60 percent of all cases of intellectual disability, which has a great many different causes (see Chapter 15). Future researchers similarly may identify subtypes of today's "same" *DSM-5* disorder, differentiating subtypes based on known causation (e.g., perhaps a single gene causes a small percentage of cases of depression or schizophrenia, a subtype not recognized today).

Another possibility is that future versions of the *DSM* will be structured in a completely different way from the *DSM-5*, for example, based on new knowledge about normal functioning. As we have said, the field of abnormal psychology is in the predicament of diagnosing abnormal behavior—*not* normal behavior—in the absence of a definition of "normal." Affective neuroscientist Jaak Panksepp (Panksepp & Biven, 2012) argues, for example, that the diagnosis of mental disorders should be based on knowledge about evolved, basic affects observed in the behavior of all mammals, including humans that are being confirmed in the "archaeology" of neuroscience. Along these lines, we might speculate that one such (future) diagnosis might be "fight or flight" anxiety. (Fight or flight is observed across many animals, for example, a cat confronted by a dog can either flee up a nearby tree or lash out with claws extended.) In addition to the logic of evolution and mounting evidence from neuroscience, such a classification has clinical implications not suggested by today's *DSM-5* diagnosis of anxiety disorders. Like a cat facing a barking dog, some anxious people get very angry when they feel "cornered." More generally these people seem to have an exaggerated fight or flight response, ready to run or attack, even in the face of relatively minor challenges.

We are fascinated by affective neuroscience—and think the field may well help psychology to begin to develop its "periodic table" of basic elements. We also recognize that both affective neuroscience and acceptance of its principles are in their early stages, and there are good reason for the *DSM* to move cautiously. In fact, the *DSM* once classified mental disorders based on "causation," including a long list of "neuroses" wrongly presumed to be caused by the unconscious conflicts of psychoanalytic theory. Thus, for the present and foreseeable future, we understand and support the descriptive approach of *DSM-5*. The method has many advantages, but you should know that *DSM-5* diagnoses provide little information about the specific causes of most mental disorders.

---

absence of physical impairment. For example, "hysterical blindness" is the inability to see, but the blindness is not caused by an organic dysfunction. Hysteria appears to have been common in Freud's time, although the diagnosis is controversial today (see Chapter 7).

Freud concluded that hysterical patients did not fake or consciously associate their physical symptoms with emotional distress. Instead, he suggested that their psychological conflicts were unconsciously "converted" into physical symptoms. His conclusion about the peculiar problem of hysteria led Freud to theorize that many psychological processes are unconscious. This assumption served as the impetus behind his elaborate **psychoanalytic theory,** a term that refers specifically to Freud's theorizing. The broader term *psychodynamic theory* includes not only Freudian theory but also the revisions of his followers (see Chapter 3).

Psychoanalytic theory is complicated and historically important, so we describe it in some detail here. You should know, however, that college students today are much more likely to learn about Freud's ideas in English departments than in psychology courses! Eighty-six percent of classes on psychoanalysis on U.S. campuses are taught *outside* of psychology departments (Shulman & Redmond, 2008). Why? The theory is a rich source of theorizing—and weak on science.

Psychoanalytic theory divides the mind into three parts: the id, the ego, and the superego. The **id** is present at birth and houses biological drives, such as hunger, as well as two key psychological drives: sex and aggression. In Freudian theory, the id operates according to the *pleasure principle*—the impulses of the id seek immediate gratification and create discomfort or unrest until they are satisfied. Thus, in Freud's view, sexual or aggressive urges are akin to biological urges, like hunger.

The **ego** is the part of the personality that must deal with the realities of the world as it attempts to fulfill id impulses as well as perform other functions. Thus, the ego operates on the *reality principle.* According to Freud, the ego begins to develop in the first year of life, and it continues to evolve, particularly during the preschool years. Unlike id impulses, which are primarily unconscious, much of the ego resides in conscious awareness.

The third part of the personality is the **superego,** which is roughly equivalent to your conscience. The superego contains societal standards of behavior, particularly rules that children learn in their preschool years from trying to be like their parents. Freud viewed the superego's rules as efforts to govern the id's sexual and aggressive impulses, with the ego mediating between the two. Freud called conflict between the superego and the ego *moral anxiety,* and conflict between the id and the ego *neurotic anxiety.*

Freud suggested that the ego protects itself from neurotic anxiety by utilizing various **defense mechanisms,** unconscious self-deceptions that reduce conscious anxiety by distorting anxiety-producing memories, emotions, and impulses. For example, the defense of *projection* turns the tables psychologically. When you use projection, you project your own feelings on to someone else: "I'm not mad at you. You're mad at me!" A list of some of the more familiar defenses can be found in Table 2.1. Many of these terms are now a part of everyday language, testimony to Freud's influence on Western culture.

Freud viewed early childhood experiences, especially related to forbidden topics, as shaping personality and emotional health. His theory of *psychosexual development* argued that different stages of child development are defined by sexual conflicts (see Table 2.5 on page 47). For example, Freud's *oedipal conflict* suggests that boys harbor sexual desire for their mothers. Freud argued that boys resolve this impossible impulse by becoming like their

**TABLE 2.1**
## Some Freudian Defense Mechanisms

| | |
|---|---|
| Denial | Insistence that an experience, memory, or need did not occur or does not exist. For example, you completely block a painful experience from your memory. |
| Displacement | Feelings or actions are transferred from one person or object to another that is less threatening. For example, you kick your dog when you are upset with your boss. |
| Projection | Attributing one's own feelings or thoughts to other people. For example, a husband argues that his wife is angry at him when, in fact, he is angry at her. |
| Rationalization | Intellectually justifying a feeling or event. For example, after not getting the offer, you decide that a job you applied for was not the one you really wanted. |
| Reaction formation | Converting a painful or unacceptable feeling into its opposite. For example, you "hate" a former lover, but underneath it all you still really love that person. |
| Repression | Suppressing threatening material from consciousness but without denial. For example, you "forget" about an embarrassing experience. |
| Sublimation | Diverting id impulses into constructive and acceptable outlets. For example, you study hard to get good grades rather than giving in to desires for immediate pleasure. |

mothers' lover: They *identify* with their fathers. Freud hypothesized that girls, unlike boys, do not desire their opposite gender parent sexually. Instead, girls confront the *electra complex,* yearning for something their fathers have and they are "missing"—a penis. This is the Freudian notion of "penis envy."

It is not difficult to criticize these ideas as far-fetched, overly sexualized, and sexist. We also can (and do) criticize psychoanalytic theory on scientific grounds. Still, Freud offered many innovative ideas about unconscious mental processes, conflicts between biological needs and social rules, psychological defenses, and more. Even today, some psychoanalysts insist on interpreting Freud literally. We believe that Freud would have criticized such unchanging interpretations. After all, he often revised his own ideas. In this spirit, we view Freud's theories as metaphors that are more valuable in the abstract than in their specifics.

### The Cognitive-Behavioral Paradigm

Like the biological and psychodynamic paradigms, the foundations of the *cognitive-behavioral paradigm,* which views abnormal behavior as a product of learning can be traced to the nineteenth century, specifically to 1879, when Wilhelm Wundt

(1832–1920) began the science of psychology at the University of Leipzig. Wundt's substantive contributions to psychology were limited, but he made a profound contribution by introducing the scientific study of psychological phenomena, especially learning.

Two prominent early scientists who made lasting substantive contributions to learning theory and research were the Russian physiologist Ivan Pavlov (1849–1936) and the U.S. psychologist B. F. Skinner (1904–1990). These scientists articulated the principles of classical conditioning and operant conditioning—concepts that continue to be central to psychology today.

In his famous experiment, Pavlov (1928) rang a bell when he fed meat powder to dogs. After repeated trials, the sound of the bell alone elicited salivation. This illustrates Pavlov's theory of classical conditioning. **Classical conditioning** is learning through association, and involves four key components. There is an *unconditioned stimulus* (the meat powder), the stimulus that automatically produces the *unconditioned response* (salivation). A *conditioned stimulus* (the bell) is a neutral stimulus that, when repeatedly paired with an unconditioned stimulus, comes to produce a *conditioned response* (salivation). **Extinction** gradually occurs once a conditioned stimulus no longer is paired with an unconditioned stimulus. Eventually, the conditioned stimulus no longer elicits the conditioned response.

Skinner's (1953) **operant conditioning** asserts that behavior is a function of its consequences. Specifically, behavior increases if it is rewarded, and it decreases if it is punished. In his numerous studies of rats and pigeons in his famous "Skinner box," Skinner identified four different, crucial consequences. *Positive reinforcement* is when the *onset* of a stimulus *increases* the frequency of behavior (e.g., you get paid for your work). *Negative reinforcement* is when the *cessation* of a stimulus *increases* the frequency of behavior (you give in to a nagging friend). *Punishment* is when the *onset* of a stimulus *decreases* the frequency of behavior (you are quiet after a teacher's scolding); and *response cost* is when the *cessation* of a stimulus *decreases* the frequency of behavior (you stop talking back when your parents take away your allowance). *Extinction* results from ending the association between a behavior and its consequences as in classical conditioning.

The U.S. psychologist John B. Watson (1878–1958) was an influential proponent of applying learning theory to human behavior. Watson argued for *behaviorism,* suggesting that observable behavior was the only appropriate subject matter for the science of psychology because, he argued, thoughts and emotions cannot be measured objectively. However, very important research, including therapies we discuss in Chapter 3, has shown the importance of cognitive processes in learning. Thus, "cognitive" joined "behavioral." True to their historical roots, cognitive-behavior therapists value and have promoted psychological research in many areas of abnormal psychology.

## The Humanistic Paradigm

The *humanistic paradigm* argues that human behavior is the product of *free will,* the view that we control, choose, and are responsible for our actions. This stance is a reaction against *determinism,* the scientific assumption that human behavior is caused by potentially knowable factors (a position held by the other three paradigms). Because free will, by definition, is not predictable, it is impossible to determine the causes of abnormal behavior according to the humanistic paradigm. For this reason, the approach perhaps is best considered as an alternative philosophy, not as an alternative psychological theory.

The humanistic paradigm is also distinguished by its explicitly positive view of human nature. Humanistic psychologists blame abnormal behavior on society, not on the individual, whom they see as inherently good (see Table 2.2). The term *humanistic* is appealing, but we should be clear about this: All psychologists are humanists in the sense that their ultimate goal is to improve the human condition.

## The Problem with Paradigms

The historian and philosopher Thomas Kuhn (1962) showed how paradigms can both direct and misdirect scientists. Paradigms can tell us how to find answers, but sometimes the guidance can be a hindrance. The idea that paradigms can guide or blind us is illustrated by the following enigma, written by Lord Byron:

---

**TABLE 2.2**

## Comparison of Biological, Psychodynamic, Cognitive-Behavioral, and Humanistic Paradigms

| Topic | Biological | Psychodynamic | Cognitive-Behavioral | Humanistic |
|---|---|---|---|---|
| Inborn human nature | Competitive, but some altruism | Aggressive, sexual | Neutral—a blank slate | Basic goodness |
| Cause of abnormality | Genes, neurochemistry, physical damage | Early childhood experiences | Social learning | Frustrations of society |
| Type of treatment | Medication, other somatic therapies | Psychodynamic therapy | Cognitive-behavior therapy | Nondirective therapy |
| Paradigmatic focus | Bodily functions and structures | Unconscious mind | Observable behavior | Free will |

I'm not in earth, nor the sun,
nor the moon.
You may search all the sky—
I'm not there.
In the morning and evening—
though not at noon,
You may plainly perceive me,
for like a balloon,
I am suspended in air.
Though disease may possess me,
and sickness and pain,
I am never in sorrow nor gloom;
Though in wit and wisdom
I equally reign
I am the heart of all sin and have
long lived in vain;
Yet I ne'er shall be found in the tomb.

What is this poem about? The topic is not the soul or ghosts, life or shadows, or a dozen other possibilities. The topic is the letter *i*. (Suspended in a*i*r, the heart of all s*i*n.) Why is the puzzle so difficult to solve? Because most people assume that the solution lies in the content of the poem, not its form. This illustrates how our assumptions (a paradigm) can lead us to overlook possible answers. Yet, paradigms can also open up new perspectives. Now that you have been able to adopt a new "paradigm"—to focus on the form, not the content of words—you can easily solve the following puzzle:

The beginning of eternity, the end
of time and space,
The beginning of every end, the end
of every place.

The now obvious answer is the letter *e*.

Like your initial approach to the brainteaser, the four paradigms make assumptions about the causes of abnormal psychology that can be too narrow. The biological paradigm can overemphasize the *medical model,* the analogy between physical and psychological illnesses. The psychodynamic paradigm can be unyielding in focusing on childhood experiences, unconscious conflicts, and interpreting Freud literally. The cognitive-behavioral paradigm can overlook the rich social and biological context of human behavior. Finally, the humanistic approach can be antiscientific. In short, each paradigm has weaknesses—and strengths. As with word puzzles, the trick is knowing when to use a different approach.

## Systems Theory

**Systems theory** is an integrative approach to science, one that embraces not only the importance of multiple contributions to causality but also their interdependence. Systems theory has influenced many sciences. For example, systems theory is basic to ecology, the study of the interdependence of living organisms in the natural world. Systems theory also offers an important perspective on the causes of abnormal behavior, one that we adopt throughout this text. Systems theory includes the biopsychosocial model and elements of each of the four paradigms, but it also highlights the need to understand the ecology of human behavior. Several key concepts deserve explanation.

### Holism

A central principle of systems theory is *holism,* the idea that the whole is more than the sum of its parts. Holism is a familiar but important concept. Holistic medicine, for example, focuses not just on physical illness, but on health, psychological, and social needs. Similarly, a holistic approach to abnormal behavior views mental illness in the context of the individual's personality, including their strengths, and more broadly, in the interpersonal and societal contexts.

The holistic approach contrasts with its scientific counterpoint, reductionism. **Reductionism** attempts to understand problems by focusing on smaller and smaller units, suggesting that the smallest (or most molecular) account is the "true" cause (Kagan, 2007; Valenstein, 1998). From this perspective, the Higgs boson (the "God Particle") provides the ultimate explanation in physics, and neurochemistry offers the ultimate explanation of abnormal behavior.

We value the discoveries produced by reductionist approaches, but we also want you to appreciate that there are different *levels of analysis* for understanding psychological problems (physics, biology, medicine, etc.) (Hinde, 1992). Biological, psychological, and social views of abnormal behavior each use a different "lens"; one is a microscope, another a magnifying glass, and the third a telescope. No lens is "right." They are just different. Each has value for different purposes. In fact, we can order all academic disciplines according to their level of analysis (Schwartz, 1982; see Table 2.3).

We can illustrate the importance of levels of analysis with a far-out example. Assume that three Martian scientists are sent to Earth to discover what causes those mysterious metallic vehicles to speed across the planet's landmass. A Martian ecologist reports that the vehicles (called "automobiles") move at different speeds based on the width of the black paths on which they are set, whether the paths are straight or curved, and the presence of something called "radar traps." A Martian psychologist disagrees, noting that the speed of automobiles is determined by the age, gender, and mood of the individual who sits behind the wheel. A third scientist, a reductionist, laughs at the other two. The Martian physicist notes that the speed of automobiles ultimately is caused by a chemical process that occurs inside an outdated machine, the internal combustion engine. The process involves oxygen, fuel, and heat and results in mechanical energy. The Martian example illustrates that the most reductionistic, or *molecular,* explanation is not necessarily more (or less) accurate than the most broad, or *molar,* one.

### Causality

You may be a bit frustrated by the "Russian *matreska* doll" approach of systems theory, with one explanation nested within

**TABLE 2.3**

## Ordering Academic Disciplines by Level of Analysis

| Level of Analysis | Academic Discipline |
| --- | --- |
| Beyond Earth | Astronomy |
| Supranational | Ecology, economics |
| National | Government, political science |
| Organizations | Organizational science |
| Groups | Sociology |
| Organisms | Psychology, ethology, zoology |
| Organs | Cardiology, neurology |
| Cells | Cellular biology |
| Biochemicals | Biochemistry |
| Chemicals | Chemistry, physical chemistry |
| Atoms | Physics |
| Subatomic particles | Subatomic physics |
| Abstract systems | Mathematics, philosophy |

*Source:* Based on G.E. Schwartz, 1982, "Testing the biopsychosocial model: The ultimate challenge facing behavioral medicine," *Journal of Consulting and Clinical Psychology,* 50, 1040–1053.

Like car accidents, mental illnesses have many causes, not one.

another. This is understandable. Human beings are not very patient with complicated explanations. Our orderly minds want to pinpoint a single culprit. We want to know *the* cause of cancer, *the* cause of heart disease, and *the* cause of mental illness.

But a question might help to unhinge you from this search for simplicity: What is *the* cause of automobile accidents? Car accidents have many causes: excessive speed, drunk drivers, slippery roads, and worn tires. It would be fruitless to search for *the* cause of car accidents. The same is true for most mental disorders (and cancer and heart disease).

**EQUIFINALITY AND MULTIFINALITY** Car accidents and abnormal behavior are examples of the principle of *equifinality,* which indicates that there are many routes to the same destination (or disorder). We use the term *multiple pathways* as a synonym for equifinality. The same disorder may have several different causes.

Equifinality has a mirror concept, *multifinality,* which says that the same event can lead to different outcomes. For example, not all abused children grow up with the same problems later in life. In fact, not all abused children *have* psychological problems as adults. Throughout the text, you will repeatedly see examples of equifinality and multifinality. The human psyche is indeed a very complex system.

**THE DIATHESIS-STRESS MODEL** The diathesis-stress model is a common way of summarizing multiple influences on abnormal behavior. A **diathesis** is a predisposition toward developing a disorder, for example, an inherited tendency toward depression. A **stress** is a difficult experience, for example, the loss of a loved

one through an unexpected death. The diathesis-stress model suggests that mental disorders develop when a stress is added on top of a predisposition (Zuckerman, 1999). But multiple stressors or **risk factors** may contribute to mental disorders (Belsky & Pluess, 2009). You should know, moreover, that the term *risk factor* refers to circumstances that are *correlated* with an increased likelihood of a disorder but do not necessarily cause it (see Research Methods).

**RECIPROCAL CAUSALITY** We like to think of causes as a one-way street. But a systems approach emphasizes interdependency and *reciprocal causality,* mutual influences where "cause" and "effect" sometimes is a matter of perspective. Does the experimenter cause the rat in a Skinner box to press the bar, or does the rat cause the experimenter to feed it? B. F. Skinner himself toyed with this question, as the accompanying cartoon illustrates (Skinner, 1956). As we search for explanations of mental disorders, we sometimes similarly need to shift perspectives, and ask, for example: Do troubled relationships cause mental disorders, or do trouble people make relationships difficult?

"Boy, have I got this guy conditioned! Every time I press the bar down he drops a piece of food."

© Robert E. Emery.

## RESEARCH methods

### Correlations: Does a Psychology Major Make You Smarter?

The correlational study and *the experiment* (see Chapter 3) are two basic and essential research methods. In a **correlational study,** the relation between two factors (their co-relation) is studied systematically. For example, you might hypothesize that psychology majors learn more about research methods than biology majors. To support this hypothesis, you might simply argue your point, or you could rely on case studies—"I know more about research than my roommate, and she's a biology major!"

If you were to conduct a correlational study, you would collect a large sample of both psychology and biology majors and compare them on an objective measure of knowledge of research methods. You would then use statistics to test whether research knowledge is correlated with academic major.

An important statistic for measuring how strongly two factors are related is the **correlation coefficient.** The correlation coefficient is a number that always ranges between −1 and +1. If all psychology majors got 100 percent correct on your test of research methods and all biology majors got 0 percent correct, the correlation between academic major and research knowledge would be 1. If all psychology and biology majors got 50 percent of the items correct, the correlation between major and knowledge would be zero. Two factors are more strongly correlated when a correlation coefficient has a higher absolute value, regardless of whether the sign is positive or negative.

*Positive correlations* (from 0.01 to 1) indicate that, as one factor goes up, the other factor also goes up. For example, height and weight are positively correlated, as are years of education and employment income. Taller people weigh more; educated people earn more money. *Negative correlations* (from −1 to −0.01) indicate that, as one number gets bigger, the other number gets smaller. For example, your course load and your free time are negatively correlated. The more courses you take, the less free time you have.

In this chapter, we discuss many factors that are correlated with and *might* cause psychological problems. Levels of neurotransmitters are positively correlated with some emotional problems (they are elevated in comparison to normal), and they are negatively correlated with other types of emotional problems (they are depleted in comparison to normal). However, you should always remember that *correlation does not mean causation*. This is true for the correlation between major and research knowledge and for the correlation between neurotransmitters and mental health (Kagan, 2007).

We might want to conclude that X causes Y—depleted neurotransmitters cause depression. A correlation *may* result from causation, but there are always two alternative explanations: reverse causality and third variables. **Reverse causality** indicates that causation could be operating in the opposite direction: Y could be causing X. Depression could be causing the depletion of neurotransmitters. The **third variable** problem indicates that a correlation between any two variables might be explained by their joint relation with some unmeasured factor—a third variable. For example, stress might cause both depression *and* the depletion of neurotransmitters.

So if you found that psychology majors know more about research methods, could you conclude that majoring in psychology *caused* this result? No! People who know more about research methods to begin with might become psychology majors (reverse causality). Or more intelligent people might both major in psychology and learn more about research methods (third variable).

As we discuss in Chapter 3, the experiment *does* allow scientists to determine cause and effect. However, it often is impractical or unethical to conduct experiments on psychological problems, while correlational studies can be conducted with far fewer practical or ethical concerns. Thus, the correlational method has the weakness that correlation does not mean causation, but the strength that it can be used to study many real-life circumstances.

## Developmental Psychopathology

**Developmental psychopathology** is an approach to abnormal psychology that emphasizes change over time. The approach recognizes the importance of *developmental norms*—age-graded averages—to understanding influences on (and the definition of) abnormal behavior (Cicchetti & Cohen, 1995; Rutter & Garmezy, 1983). Developmental norms tell us that a full-blown temper tantrum is normal at 2 years of age, for example, but that kicking and screaming to get your own way is abnormal at the age of 22. Development does not end at the age of 22, however, as predictable changes in both psychological and social experiences occur throughout adult life. Recognizing this, we devote an entire chapter (Chapter 17) to discussing the normal but psychologically trying changes that result from developmental transitions during adult life.

A developmental approach is also important for abnormal behavior itself. Many psychological disorders follow unique developmental patterns. Sometimes there is a characteristic **premorbid history,** a pattern of behavior that precedes the onset of the disorder. A disorder may also have a predictable course, or **prognosis,** for the future. Abnormal behavior is a moving picture of development and not just a diagnostic snapshot.

The remainder of this chapter has sections on biological, psychological, and social factors involved in the development of psychopathology. This basic material sets the stage for our more specific discussions of the causes of abnormal behavior in later chapters.

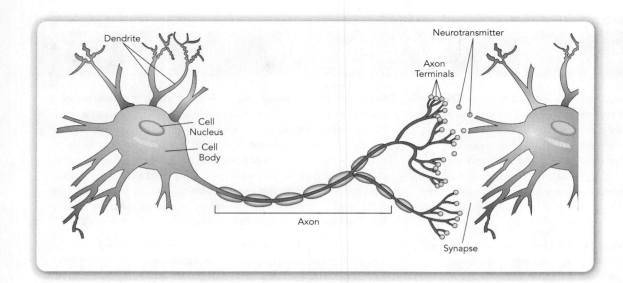

**FIGURE 2.1**

**The Neuron** The anatomic structure of the neuron, or nerve cell.
*Source:* © Pearson Education, Upper Saddle River, New Jersey.

## Biological Factors

We begin our discussion of biological factors affecting mental functioning by considering the smallest anatomic unit within the nervous system—the neuron or nerve cell. Next, we consider the major brain structures and current knowledge of their primary behavioral functions. We then turn to psychophysiology, the effect of psychological experience on the functioning of various body systems. Finally, we consider the broadest of all biological influences, the effect of genes on behavior.

In considering biological influences, it is helpful to note the distinction between the study of biological structures and biological functions. The field of *anatomy* is concerned with the study of biological structures; the field of *physiology* investigates biological functions. *Neuroanatomy* and *neurophysiology* are subspecialties within these broader fields that focus specifically on brain structures and brain functions. The study of neuroanatomy and neurophysiology is the domain of an exciting, multidisciplinary field of research called *neuroscience.*

### The Neuron and Neurotransmitters

Billions of tiny nerve cells—**neurons**—form the basic building blocks of the brain. Each neuron has four major anatomic

components: the soma or cell body, the dendrites, the axon, and the axon terminal (see Figure 2.1). The *soma*—the cell body and largest part of the neuron—is where most of the neuron's metabolism and maintenance are controlled and performed. The *dendrites* branch out from the soma; they serve the primary function of receiving messages from other cells. The *axon* is the trunk of the neuron. Messages are transmitted down the axon toward other cells. Finally, the *axon terminal* is the end of the axon, where messages are sent out to other neurons (Barondes, 1993). ⊙ **Watch** the **Video** *The Anatomy of the Neuron* on **MyPsychLab**

Within each neuron, information is transmitted as a change in electrical potential that moves from the dendrites and cell body, along the axon, toward the axon terminal. The axon terminal is separated from other cells by a **synapse,** a small gap filled with fluid. Neurons typically have synapses with thousands of other cells (see Figure 2.2).

Unlike the electrical communication within a neuron, information is transmitted chemically across a synapse to other neurons. The axon terminal contains *vesicles* containing chemical substances called **neurotransmitters,** which are released into the synapse and are received at the **receptors** on the dendrites

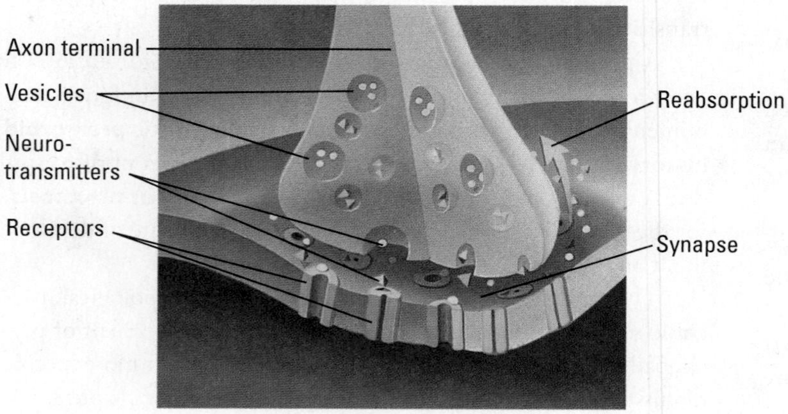

**FIGURE 2.2**

**Synaptic Transmission** When an electrical nerve impulse reaches the end of a neuron, synaptic vesicles release neurotransmitters into the synapse. The chemical transmission between cells is complete when neurotransmitters travel to receptor sites on another neuron.
*Source:* Keith Kasnot/National Geographic Stock.

or soma of another neuron. Different receptor sites are more or less responsive to particular neurotransmitters. Dozens of different chemical compounds serve as neurotransmitters in the brain. *Serotonin* and *dopamine* are two that are known to be particularly important for abnormal behavior. ⊙ **Watch** the **Video** *How Neurotransmitters Work* on **MyPsychLab**

Not all neurotransmitters cross the synapse and reach the receptors on another neuron. The process of **reuptake,** or reabsorption, captures some neurotransmitters in the synapse and returns the chemical substances to the axon terminal. The neurotransmitter then is reused in subsequent neural transmission.

In addition to the neurotransmitters, a second type of chemical affects communication in the brain. *Neuromodulators* are chemicals that can influence communication among many neurons by affecting the functioning of neurotransmitters (Ciarnello et al., 1995). Neuromodulators often affect regions of the brain that are quite distant from where they were released. This occurs, for example, when stress causes the adrenal gland to release hormones that affect many aspects of brain functioning (as we discuss shortly).

## Neurotransmitters and Psychopathology

Scientists have found neurotransmitter disruptions in some people with mental disorders. An oversupply of certain

## Mind–Body Dualism

Some people mistakenly conclude that, because brain functions are correlated with having a psychological problem, this means that there is something wrong in the brain that causes the disorder. Certain regions of the brain "light up" with depression. This means that depression is a "brain disease," right? Medications that affect brain chemistry lessen symptoms of depression. This means depression is caused by a "chemical imbalance in the brain," right? Wrong—on both counts.

Much of this misguided thinking can be traced to the logical error formally known as **dualism,** the mistaken view that the mind and body are somehow separable. This wrong-headed reasoning has a long and *un*distinguished history. Dualism dates to the French philosopher René Descartes (1596–1650), who attempted to balance the dominant religious views of his times with emerging scientific reasoning. Descartes recognized the importance of human biology, but he wanted to elevate human spirituality beyond the brain. To balance scientific and religious beliefs, he argued that many human experiences result from brain function, but higher spiritual thoughts and feelings somehow exist apart from the body.

Descartes argued for a distinction—a dualism—between mind and body. But he was wrong. No psychological experience can exist apart from biology. Just like computer software cannot run without computer hardware, *no* psychological experience runs independently from the hardware of the brain (Turkheimer, 1998; Valenstein, 1998).

Even love has a biochemical explanation, a fact that Calvin ponders in the accompanying cartoon. If you are unpersuaded by Calvin, you may be convinced by a study. Images of married women's brains show bigger responses to threat when a woman is holding a stranger's hand instead of her husband's. Brain images also show a bigger response to threat when women are holding hands with husbands to whom they are less happily married (Coan, Schaefer, & Davidson, 2006). Like depression, anxiety, and other troublesome emotions (and all our thoughts and feelings), the "software" experience of love is represented in underlying brain "hardware." Yet, love will still be love (not a brain disease) even after scientists identify the "chemical imbalance" that explains it. And as with love, depression (and other mental disorders) are not necessarily caused by a "broken brain" just because certain parts of the brain "light up" when people are depressed.

CALVIN AND HOBBES © Bill Watterson. Reprinted with permission of UNIVERSAL UCLICK. All rights reserved.

neurotransmitters is found in some cases, an undersupply in others, and disturbances in reuptake in still other cases. In addition, the density and/or sensitivity of receptors may play a role in some abnormal behavior.

Much research has investigated how drugs alter brain chemistry, and in turn, affect symptoms. For example, medications that alleviate some symptoms of schizophrenia block receptors sensitive to the neurotransmitter *dopamine*. This suggests that abnormalities in the dopamine system may be involved in schizophrenia (see Chapter 13). Evidence that effective treatments for depression inhibit the reuptake of the *serotonin* links a depletion of that neurotransmitter to mood disorders (see Chapter 5). As we discuss in the appropriate

chapters, however, several neurotransmitters are likely to be involved in these and other mental disorders. Consistent with our discussion of levels of analysis, moreover, a biochemical difference does not necessarily mean that these problems are caused by "a chemical imbalance in the brain," even though many people, including many mental health professionals, mistakenly leap to this conclusion (see box on Mind–Body Dualism on page 35).

## Major Brain Structures

Neuroanatomists broadly divide the brain into the hindbrain, the midbrain, and the forebrain (see Figure 2.3). Basic bodily functions are regulated by the structures of the *hindbrain*, which

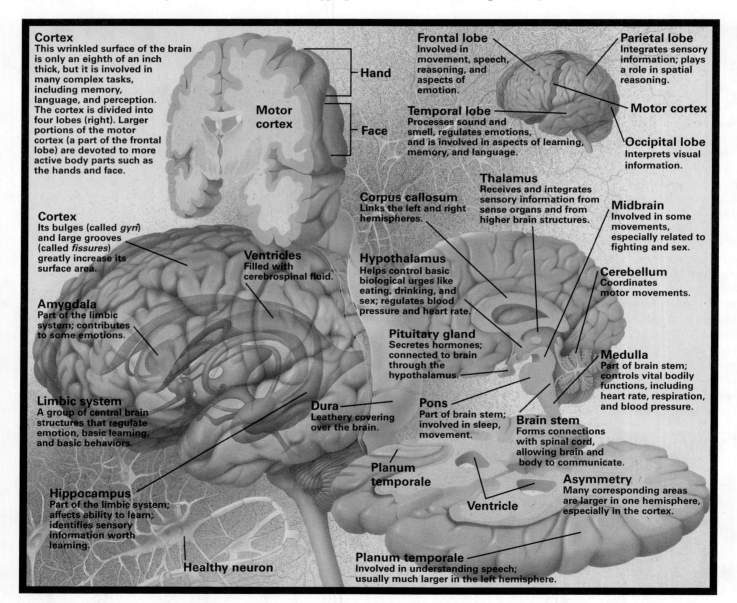

**FIGURE 2.3**

**The Healthy Brain** Scientists are only beginning to discover how the healthy brain performs its complex functions. You should view this complex figure as a rough road map that will be redrawn repeatedly. Like a roadmap, you should not try to memorize the figure, but use it as a guide. You will appreciate more and more detail as you return to examine it repeatedly. Despite the continuing mysteries, increasingly sophisticated tools have allowed researchers to identify more and more of the functions performed by different areas of the brain. For example, the four lobes of the brain's cortex play very different roles in thought, emotion, sensation, and motor movement (see top right of figure). Still, our incomplete knowledge of the healthy brain limits our understanding of brain abnormalities.

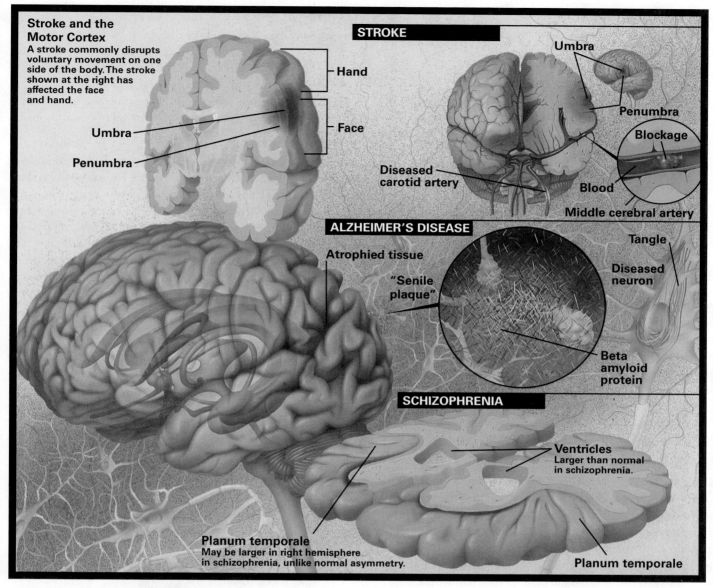

**Stroke and the Motor Cortex**
A stroke commonly disrupts voluntary movement on one side of the body. The stroke shown at the right has affected the face and hand.

Hand

Face

Umbra

Penumbra

**STROKE**

Umbra

Penumbra

Blockage

Diseased carotid artery

Blood

Middle cerebral artery

**ALZHEIMER'S DISEASE**

Atrophied tissue

"Senile plaque"

Tangle

Diseased neuron

Beta amyloid protein

**SCHIZOPHRENIA**

Ventricles
Larger than normal in schizophrenia.

Planum temporale
May be larger in right hemisphere in schizophrenia, unlike normal asymmetry.

Planum temporale

**FIGURE 2.3** (*Continued*)

**The Unhealthy Brain** Scientists have identified clear brain abnormalities only for some severe mental disorders. A stroke is caused by loss of blood supply to a region of the brain, and it kills off nearby cells (see Chapter 14). Cells die rapidly near the center of the damaged tissue, the umbra. Cells die less rapidly in the periphery, the penumbra, and may be saved by future medical advances. Alzheimer's disease is a severe cognitive disorder associated with aging (see Chapter 14) that is characterized by atrophied brain tissue, "senile plaques" (caused by clumps of beta amyloid protein), and tangles of diseased or dead neurons. Schizophrenia is a very serious psychotic illness (see Chapter 13) that remains a mystery as a brain disorder, despite some promising leads. For example, among people with schizophrenia the ventricles often are enlarged, and asymmetries in the planum temporale may be reversed.
*Source:* Keith Kasnot/National Geographic Stock.

include the medulla, pons, and cerebellum. Few forms of abnormal behavior are linked with disturbances in the hindbrain.

👁 **Watch** the **Video** *Geography of the Brain* on **MyPsychLab**

The *midbrain* is involved in the control of some motor activities, especially those related to fighting and sex. Much of the reticular activating system is located in the midbrain, although it extends into the pons and medulla as well. The *reticular activating system* regulates sleeping and waking. Damage to areas of the midbrain can cause extreme disturbances in sexual behavior, aggressiveness, and sleep, but such abnormalities typically result from specific brain traumas or tumors (Matthysse & Pope, 1986).

Most of the human brain consists of the *forebrain*. The forebrain evolved more recently and is the site of most sensory, emotional, and cognitive processes. The forebrain is linked with the midbrain and hindbrain by the **limbic system,** which is made up of several structures that regulate emotion and learning. Two important components of the limbic system are the thalamus and the hypothalamus. The *thalamus* receives and integrates sensory information from both the sense organs and higher brain structures. The **hypothalamus** controls basic biological urges, such as eating, drinking, and sexual activity. Much of the functioning of the autonomic nervous system (which we discuss shortly) is also directed by the hypothalamus.

## Cerebral Hemispheres

Most of the forebrain is composed of the two **cerebral hemispheres.** Many brain functions are **lateralized,** so that one hemisphere serves a specialized role as the site of specific cognitive and emotional activities. In general, the *left cerebral hemisphere* is involved in language and related functions, and the *right cerebral hemisphere* is involved in spatial organization and analysis.

The two cerebral hemispheres are connected by the *corpus callosum,* coordinates the different functions performed by the left and the right hemispheres. When we view a cross section of the forebrain, four connected chambers, or **ventricles,** become apparent. The ventricles are filled with cerebrospinal fluid, and they are enlarged in some psychological and neurological disorders.

The **cerebral cortex** is the uneven surface area of the forebrain that lies just underneath the skull. It is the site of the control and integration of sophisticated memory, sensory, and motor functions. The cerebral cortex is divided into four lobes (see Figure 2.3). The *frontal lobe,* located just behind the forehead, controls a number of complex functions, including reasoning, planning, emotion, speech, and movement. The *parietal lobe,* located at the top and back of the head, receives and integrates sensory information and also plays a role in spatial reasoning. The *temporal lobe,* located beneath much of the frontal and parietal lobes, processes sound and smell, regulates emotions, and is involved in some aspects of learning, memory, and language. Finally, the *occipital lobe,* located behind the temporal lobe, receives and interprets visual information.

**MAJOR BRAIN STRUCTURES AND PSYCHOPATHOLOGY**
Only the most severe mental disorders have clearly been linked to abnormalities in neuroanatomy. In most cases, brain damage is extensive. For example, during a *stroke,* blood vessels in the brain rupture, cutting off the supply of oxygen to parts of the brain and killing surrounding brain tissue. This disrupts the functioning of nearby healthy neurons because the brain cannot remove the dead tissue (see Figure 2.3). Tangles of neurons are found in patients with *Alzheimer's disease,* but the damage can be identified only during postmortem autopsies (see Figure 2.3). In patients with schizophrenia, the ventricles of the brain are enlarged, and asymmetries are also found in other brain structures (see Figure 2.3). 👁
**Watch** the **Video** *Brain Damage in Alzheimer's Disease* on **MyPsychLab**

Neuroscientists have made dramatic breakthroughs in developing instruments that allow us to observe the anatomic structure of the living brain and record broad physiological processes. These imaging procedures are being used to study psychological disorders ranging from schizophrenia to learning disabilities; they are discussed in Chapter 4, along with other methods of psychological assessment.

At present, brain imaging is more exciting technically than practically for identifying biological causes of mental disorders. However, there is every reason to hope that brain imaging techniques will greatly improve our understanding of both normal and abnormal brain structure and function.

## Psychophysiology

**Psychophysiology** is the study of changes in the functioning of the body that result from psychological experience. Some of these reactions are familiar. Psychophysiological responses include a pounding heart, a flushed face, tears, sexual excitement, and numerous other reactions. Such responses reflect a person's psychological state, particularly the degree and perhaps the type of his or her emotional arousal.

**ENDOCRINE SYSTEM**  Psychophysiological arousal results from the activity of two different communication systems within the body—the endocrine system and the nervous system. The **endocrine system** is a collection of glands found at various locations throughout the body. Its major components include the ovaries or testes and the pituitary, thyroid, and adrenal glands (see Figure 2.4). Endocrine glands produce psychophysiological responses by releasing **hormones** into the bloodstream—chemical substances that affect the functioning of distant body systems and sometimes act as neuromodulators. The endocrine system regulates some aspects of normal development, particularly physical growth and sexual development. Parts of the endocrine system, particularly the adrenal glands, are also activated by stress and help prepare the body to respond to an emergency.

Certain abnormalities in the functioning of the endocrine system are known to cause psychological symptoms. For example, in *hyperthyroidism,* also known as *Graves' disease,* the thyroid gland secretes too much of the hormone thyroxin, causing restlessness,

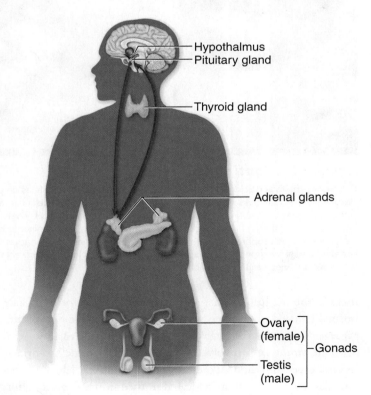

**FIGURE 2.4**

**The Endocrine System** The glands that comprise the endocrine system, which affects physical and psychophysiological responses through the release of hormones into the bloodstream.
*Source:* © Pearson Education, Upper Saddle River, New Jersey.

agitation, and anxiety. Research on depression also suggests that endocrine functioning sometimes contributes to causing this disorder.

⊙► **Simulate** the **Experiment** *The Endocrine System* in **MyPsychLab**

**AUTONOMIC NERVOUS SYSTEM** The basic system of communication within the body is the nervous system. The human nervous system is divided into the central nervous system, which includes the brain and the spinal cord, and the peripheral nervous system. The peripheral nervous system includes all connections that stem from the central nervous system and innervate the body's muscles, sensory systems, and organs.

The peripheral nervous system itself has two subdivisions. The voluntary, *somatic nervous system* governs muscular control, and the involuntary, **autonomic nervous system** regulates the functions of various body organs, such as the heart and stomach. The somatic nervous system controls intentional or voluntary actions like scratching your nose. The autonomic nervous system is responsible for psychophysiological reactions—responses that occur with little or no conscious control.

The autonomic nervous system can be subdivided into two branches, the sympathetic and parasympathetic nervous systems. In general, the *sympathetic nervous system* controls activities associated with increased arousal and energy expenditure, and the *parasympathetic nervous system* controls the slowing of arousal and energy conservation. Thus, the two branches work somewhat in opposition, which works to maintain homeostasis.

**PSYCHOPHYSIOLOGY AND PSYCHOPATHOLOGY** Psychophysiological overarousal and underarousal can contribute to abnormal behavior. For example, overactivity of the autonomic nervous system (a pounding heart and sweaty hands) has been linked to excessive anxiety. In contrast, chronic autonomic underarousal may explain some of the indifference to social rules and the failure to learn from punishment found in antisocial personality disorder. Psychophysiological assessment also can be a useful way of objectively measuring reactions to psychological events (see Chapter 4).

## Behavior Genetics

**Genes** are ultramicroscopic units of DNA that carry information about heredity. Genes are located on **chromosomes,** chainlike structures found in the nucleus of cells. Humans normally have 23 pairs of chromosomes.

*Genetics* is the study of genes and their hereditary functions, a field that often focuses at the level of molecules. **Behavior genetics** traditionally studies broad genetic influences on normal and abnormal behavior, focusing on whether genes are more or less important in development (Plomin, DeFries, McClearn, & McGuffin, 2008; Rutter et al., 2001). However, many experts in genetics and behavior genetics are working together today in the hope of identifying specific genes involved in normal and abnormal behavior (Kendler & Prescott, 2006; Kim-Cohen & Gold, 2009).

**GENOTYPES AND PHENOTYPES** A basic principle of genetics is the distinction between genotypes and phenotypes. A **genotype** is an individual's actual genetic structure. A **phenotype** is the

expression of a given genotype. Different genotypes can produce the same phenotypes. And the environment can affect a phenotype, but experience does not change a genotype.

**DOMINANT AND RECESSIVE INHERITANCE** Genes have alternative forms known as *alleles*. *Dominant/recessive inheritance* occurs when a trait is caused by a single or *autosomal* gene that has only two alleles (e.g., A and a) and only one locus, a specific location on a chromosome. Austrian monk Gregor Mendel (1822–1884) discovered this pattern in his famous studies of garden peas. (This form of genetic transmission is often called "Mendelian inheritance" in his honor.) The gene for color in Mendel's peas had only two alleles, A (yellow, dominant) and a (green, recessive). Thus, three genotypes were possible: AA, aA (or Aa), and aa. Because A is dominant over a, however, both AA and aA plants were yellow, while aa plants were green. Thus, there are three genotypes, but only two phenotypes. Figure 2.5 illustrates patterns of inheritance for dominant and recessive disorders.

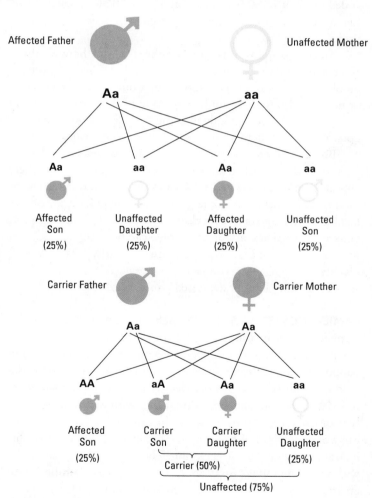

**FIGURE 2.5**

**Dominant and Recessive Genetic Disorders** Patterns of transmission from parents to children for dominant (top figure) and recessive disorders (bottom figure). Note that the single gene (autosomal) disorder is either present or absent for both patterns of inheritance.
*Source:* Based on Garone, Stephen. 1999. *Genetics of Mental Disorders: A Guide for Students, Clinicians, and Researchers.* Guilford Press.

**POLYGENIC INHERITANCE** Dominant/recessive inheritance causes some rare forms of mental retardation (Plomin et al., 2008), but most mental disorders do not appear to be caused by a single gene. Instead, they are **polygenic,** that is, they are influenced by multiple genes (Gottesman, 1991)—and by the environment.

Polygenic inheritance is critical to how we think about abnormal behavior. In contrast to the categorically different phenotypes produced by a single gene (like yellow versus green), polygenic inheritance produces characteristics that fall along a dimension (like height). In fact, the distribution of a phenotype begins to resemble the normal distribution as more genes are involved (see Figure 2.6).

The distinction between categories and dimensions might seem a bit abstract, so let's bring it down to earth with a familiar example. Test score averages are a dimension. Letter grades are different categories. We turn dimensions into categories by setting a cutoff. The cutoff can be critical, as you know if you ever ended up with an 89.9 average—and got a "B" for a letter grade. Like your professor, psychologists set cutoffs or *thresholds* for defining mental disorders.

All of this holds important implications for how we think about genes and abnormal behavior. We tend to think of emotional problems in terms of categories: A young woman is either depressed or not. We also tend to think of genes in terms of dominant and recessive inheritance: She either has the "gene for" depression or she doesn't. However, both assumptions appear to be wrong.

But as best we can tell, there is no single "gene for" depression or most any other known mental disorder. Instead, there appear to be *multiple* genes involved in the risk for different mental disorders, just as multiple genes affect height. And just like height, this means there is no clear genetic basis for drawing a line between normal and abnormal. People can be "*really* short," "not really short," "kind of short," and so on. Similarly, because mental disorders are polygenic, people can be "*really* depressed," "not really depressed," "kind of depressed," and so on.

**FAMILY INCIDENCE STUDIES** Behavior geneticists have developed several methods for studying genetic contributions to behavior, including family incidence studies, twin studies, and adoption studies. Family incidence studies ask whether diseases "run in families." Investigators identify normal and ill **probands,** or index cases, and tabulate the frequency with which other members of their families suffer from the same disorder. If a higher prevalence of illness is found in the family of an ill proband, this is consistent with genetic causation. The finding also is consistent with environmental causation, however, because families share environments as well as genes. Therefore, family incidence studies do not lead to firm conclusions about the role of genes versus the environment.

**TWIN STUDIES** Studies of twins, in contrast, can provide strong evidence about genetic and environmental contributions.

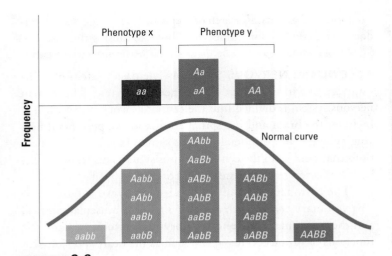

**FIGURE 2.6**

**Single Gene and Polygenetic Inheritance** Single genes produce phenotypes that differ qualitatively, as illustrated in the top panel. Multiple genes produce phenotypes that differ quantitatively. The distribution of traits approximates the normal curve as more genes are involved—as illustrated for only two genes in the bottom panel.

**Monozygotic (MZ) twins** are *identical*. One egg is fertilized by one sperm, and thus MZ twins have identical genotypes. **Dizygotic (DZ) twins** are *fraternal*. These twins are produced from two eggs and two sperm. Thus, like all siblings, DZ twins share an average of 50 percent of their genes, while MZ twins share 100 percent of their genes. Most MZ and DZ twin pairs are raised together in the same family. Thus MZ and DZ twins differ in their genetic similarity, but they are alike in their environmental experiences.

The natural experiment of comparing MZ and DZ twins can reveal genetic and environmental contributions to behavior. For mental disorders, a key is the **concordance rate** for the two sets of twins. A twin pair is *concordant* when both twins either have the same disorder or are free from the disorder, for example, both suffer from schizophrenia. The twin pair is *discordant* when one twin has the disorder but the other does not, for example, one twin has schizophrenia but the co-twin does not.

Any differences between the concordance rates for MZ and DZ twins must be caused by genetics (assuming that MZ and DZ twin pairs experience similar environments). If a disorder is purely genetic, scientists should find a concordance rate of 100 percent for MZ twins and 50 percent for DZ twins (see Table 2.4). Test yourself. You should be able to explain why.

In contrast, similar concordance rates for MZ and DZ twins indicate environmental causation. This is true whether the concordance rates are both 0 percent, both 100 percent, or both anywhere in between. However, high versus low concordance rates reveal what kind of experiences are causal. *High* concordance rates point to the influence of the **shared environment,** experiences twins share in common, for example, growing up in

TABLE **2.4**

## Twin Studies: Implications of Different Findings

| Concordance for MZs versus DZs | Supports Influence of | Perfect Case[1] |
| --- | --- | --- |
| MZ > DZ | Genes | MZ = 100%; DZ = 50% |
| MZ = DZ; both high | Shared environment | MZ = 100%; DZ = 100% |
| MZ = DZ; both low | Nonshared environment | MZ = 0%; DZ = 0% |

[1]The identified influence explains everything in the perfect case. Actual concordance rates almost always fall between these extremes, thus providing an index of the relative contributions of genes, the shared environment, and/or the nonshared environment.

poverty. If the shared environment explained all of the variance in a problem, the concordance rate would be 100 percent for both MZ and DZ twins (see Table 2.4).

What about *low* concordance rates? Low concordance rates point to the influence of the **nonshared environment,** experiences unique to one twin, for example, an abusive boyfriend or girlfriend. If the nonshared environment was entirely responsible for a problem, the concordance rate would be 0 for both MZ and DZ twins (see Table 2.4). As we have noted, however, abnormal behavior is not explained purely by genes, the shared environment, or the nonshared environment. Twin studies provide useful estimates of the importance of each influence by yielding data in between the perfect scenarios summarized in Table 2.4.

**ADOPTION STUDIES** In adoption studies, people who were adopted are compared with their biological versus their adoptive relatives (usually their parents) in terms of concordance for a disorder. If concordance is higher for biological than adoptive

Robert Emery with identical twins he interviewed for a research project at the Twins Days Festival, the world's largest gathering of twins.

relatives, then genetic factors are involved, because adopted children share their biological relatives' genes but not their environment. On the other hand, if children are more similar to their adoptive than to their biological relatives, then environment is causal, because adopted children share their adoptive relatives' environment but not their genes.

Think about the case of the adopted girl, Meghan, from the beginning of this chapter. Genetic influences are implicated if Meghan develops problems similar to her biological, but not adoptive, parents. On the other hand, environmental influences are causal if Meghan develops problems more similar to her adoptive than her biological parents.

Adoption studies have some potential problems, for example, the fact that adoption placement can be selective. Still, you can be confident in the findings of behavior genetic research when adoption and twin studies produce similar results (Kendler & Prescott, 2006; Plomin et al., 2008).

**GENETICS AND PSYCHOPATHOLOGY** Genetic influences on mental disorders are pervasive, as you will learn in subsequent chapters. But traditional twin and adoption studies do not tell us what genetic mechanism is at work. When we read that twin studies reveal that a disorder is "genetic," we may think there is "a gene for" depression, alcoholism, or hyperactivity. But such a conclusion is wrong.

Think about this: Criminal behavior is also "genetic," as is divorce and political affiliation! (Concordance rates are higher for MZ than for DZ twins for all of these complex behaviors.) But no one thinks that people have a "crime gene," a "divorce gene," or a "Republican gene." (We hope.) Behavior genetic research tells us that genes are important, but many genes appear to affect abnormal behavior, often in ways that are subtle and indirect. As we noted, geneticists and behavior geneticists are collaborating, and we may eventually identify specific genes involved in rare subtypes of certain mental disorders (as was discovered for rare intellectual disabilities; see Chapter 15). Even so, a large "multiply caused" group is likely to remain (as is also true for intellectual disabilities).

And unfortunately, people often misinterpret behavior genetic research (Dar-Nimrod & Heine, 2011; Kagan, 2007;

Rutter, Moffitt, & Caspi, 2006). One serious misinterpretation is that DNA is destiny. Genetic influences on abnormal behavior are *predispositions,* increased risks, not *predestinations*—inevitabilities (Faraone, Tsuang, & Tsuang, 1999).

It also is wrong to think that genetic characteristics cannot be modified. Even for intellectual disabilities with a known genetic cause, environmental experiences such as dietary restrictions or early intellectual stimulation can substantially increase IQ (Turkheimer, 1991). In short, the conclusion "It's genetic" does not mean "It's inevitable" or "It's hopeless."

Genetic influences on behavior are pervasive, but we want you to think critically and beyond familiar models of dominant and recessive inheritance. In fact, you should be skeptical of anyone who claims to have found "the" cause of any mental disorder (see Critical Thinking Matters).

**GENES AND THE ENVIRONMENT** Nature and nurture are not separate influences on behavior. Nature and nurture always work together (Li, 2003). You need to know two broad ways in which genes and the environment do this. The first is **gene–environment interaction,** genetic predispositions and environmental experiences combining to produce more than their separate influences. In fact, collaborating geneticists and behavior geneticists have identified specific genes that appear to produce abnormal behavior only under specific environmental circumstances, a very exciting area of research. But here is an important caution: Many studies of gene–environment interactions are not replicated in subsequent research (Risch et al., 2009). Of course, false leads are to be expected, when you combine a new field, 25,000 genes, innumerable potential experiences—and the complexity of human behavior. We know that genes and the environment work together; we are only beginning to discover how (Champagne & Mashoodh, 2009; Cole, 2009).

A second key concept is **gene–environment correlation,** the fact that our experience is correlated with our genetic makeup (Rutter et al., 2006). Anxious parents give children "anxious" genes *and* an anxious upbringing. Thrill-seeking, a genetically influenced trait, also propels people into risky experiences. In short, experience is *a* genetically random. Anxious parenting, risk taking, and probably most other experiences are correlated with our genetic makeup. This means that any link between an experience and a disorder may be explained by correlated genes, not by the experience itself (e.g., see Research Methods on page 33).

## Psychological Factors

We must begin our overview of psychological influences on abnormal behavior on a humbling note: We face the task of trying to explain abnormal behavior without a good understanding of normal behavior! Psychology does not have a widely accepted theory of *personality,* the essential traits that, taken as a whole, describe human behavior. This is a huge limitation, akin to describing circulatory diseases before agreeing about the normal structure and functions of blood, arteries, veins, and the heart! As

*Harry Potter* learned what it means to be wizard, yet psychologists do not agree about what defines normal human behavior. This makes the definition of *abnormal* (*not* normal) challenging.

a result, any listing of the psychological factors involved in mental disorders, including our own, is necessarily incomplete and perhaps controversial. Still, we can organize many psychological factors affecting mental health into six categories: (1) human nature, (2) temperament, (3) emotion, (4) learning and cognition, (5) our sense of self, and (6) human development.

### Human Nature

What is human nature—psychological motivations that we share with other animals and others that are uniquely human? As you are well aware, this is a big question. Freud's answer was that we have two basic drives, sex and aggression. In contrast, Watson suggested that we come into the world as blank slates—there is no human nature apart from experience. Today, psychologists are addressing questions about human nature in an exciting and controversial field of study called evolutionary psychology.

**EVOLUTIONARY PSYCHOLOGY Evolutionary psychology** is the application of the principles of evolution to understanding the animal and human mind (Confer et al., 2009). Evolutionary psychologists study *species-typical characteristics*—genetically influenced motivations that people share in common. Behavior

# CRITICAL THINKING matters

## Do Vaccinations Cause Autism?

In 1998, the highly reputable British journal *Lancet* published a study by Dr. Andrew Wakefield and a dozen coauthors (1998). The authors speculated that the measles/mumps/rubella (MMR) vaccination might be responsible for 12 cases of autism they diagnosed. *Autism* is a severe psychological disorder that begins very early in life and is marked by extreme problems with communication, social interaction, and stereotyped behavior (see Xavier Video Case). The researchers did not analyze any scientific data, or study children who were vaccinated but did not develop autism. In fact, a skeptical editorial was published with the article (Chen & DeStefano, 1998).

None of these limitations prevented a subsequent tsunami of fear and claims that vaccinations cause autism. Warnings spread on television, radio, in print, and especially over the Internet. The U.S. Congress held hearings. The National Institutes of Health funded new research. Many parents refused to vaccinate their children. This worried public health officials. Measles, mumps, and rubella are serious illnesses, and the MMR vaccination not only protects the vaccinated child but helps keep these highly contagious diseases from spreading (Offit, 2010).

What does science say about the vaccination hypothesis? One Danish study of *half a million* children found no differences in the rate of autism between children who did and did not receive the MMR vaccine containing the supposed autism causing agent, *thimerosal* (Hviid et al., 2003), as did a major study in the United Kingdom (Chen, Landau, & Sham, 2004) and two in Japan (Honda et al., 2005; Uchiyama et al., 2007). If this does not make you skeptical, consider this: 10 of the original 13 coauthors of the 1998 paper retracted their speculation (*New York Times*, March 4, 2004). Or consider this: In 2011, the prestigious Institute of Medicine concluded that evidence favors rejection of the hypothesis that MMR vaccine causes autism (Stratton, Ford, Rusch, & Clayton, 2011).

Misinformation, fear, and anger still abound even after public retractions and negative results for hundreds of thousands of children (versus speculations about 12). Search the Internet, and you will find many vehement assertions that MMR causes autism. With so much information on the Internet (and opinion masquerading as information), you *have* to be skeptical in evaluating all kinds of assertions—including your own! We want you to think critically in abnormal psychology and in life.

And here's another reason to think critically: Lawyers. Thousands of parents are suing a special federal compensation court that awards money for injuries caused by vaccines. The court was established in 1988 in response to fears that the diphtheria-pertussis-tetanus (DPT) vaccine causes neurological damage, fears that experts now conclude were false (Sugarman, 2007).

Still, lawyers convinced some juries otherwise, and the legal costs led most manufacturers to stop making DPT. When the last manufacturer threatened to halt production, the U.S. government created the fund, fearing devastating public health consequences if children were no longer vaccinated (Sugarman, 2007).

In 2008, the court awarded money to the parents of Hannah Poling, who was diagnosed with autism. Hannah's behavior deteriorated rapidly around the time she was vaccinated. However, she also had a rare disorder of the *mitochondria*, the energy factories of cells. Mitochondrial disorders often surface following only a severe infection. An expert witness claimed that this is what happened to Hannah as a result of her multiple vaccinations, a claim that leading vaccine scientists note has no basis in science. Vaccines, in fact, may protect people with mitochondrial disorders by warding off serious infection (Offit, 2008).

Know this: Legal rulings are *not* scientific evidence. The law is about convincing a judge or jury that some allegation is true. Scientists must prove facts publicly and repeatedly. In fact, the same federal vaccine court has now *rejected* the idea that vaccines cause autism in three specially selected test cases (*New York Times*, February 13, 2009).

And while we are on the topic of legal action, here's another one: In 2010, Britain's General Medical Council banned Dr. Andrew Wakefield from practicing medicine in his native country due to unprofessional conduct surrounding his vaccine "research" (*New York Times*, May 24, 2010). Also in 2010, *Lancet* took the highly unusual step of withdrawing Wakefield et al.'s (1998) article. Why? Wakefield failed to disclose that his anti-MMR "research" was supported financially by lawyers suing manufacturers of the MMR vaccine—or that, in 1997, he had patented a new measles vaccine that might have replaced MMR (*New York Times*, February 2, 2010). Skeptical yet?

It is far easier to create false fears than to dispel them. In November 2010, the Web site of the National Institute of Child Health and Human Development read: "There is no conclusive scientific evidence that any part of a vaccine or combination of vaccines causes autism . . ." If you are paranoid, you can focus on the "conclusive" qualification. But science can *never* prove the negative. (Prove that those Martian scientists we discussed earlier did *not* write this textbook. *You* just can't see them!) This is why the burden of proof rests upon any scientist who offers a hypothesis. If I speculate that vaccinations cause autism (or Martians write textbooks), I need to prove I am right. You do not need to prove me wrong. Skepticism is a basic rule of science. Until I show that my hypothesis is true, the community of scientists assumes it is false. Critical thinking *matters*.

geneticists, in contrast, study how genes influence *individual differences,* or what makes people different from one another. Evolutionary psychologists assume that animal and human psychology, like animal and human anatomy, evolved through natural selection and sexual selection.

*Natural selection* is the process in which successful, inherited adaptations to environmental problems become more common over successive generations. The adaptation is selected by evolution, because it increases *inclusive fitness,* the reproductive success of those who have the adaptation, their offspring, and/or their kin. For example, the large human brain, with its particularly large cerebral cortex, was selected by evolution because of the adaptations it enabled (e.g., the use of tools and weapons). Early humans with larger brains were more likely to survive and pass their adaptive genes on to more offspring.

*Sexual selection* improves inclusive fitness through increased access to mates and mating. Mating success can be increased by successful *intra*sexual competition, for example, a dominant male limits the mating opportunities of other males; or by successful *inter*sexual selection, for example, a more brightly colored bird attracts more members of the opposite sex (Gaulin & McBurney, 2001; Larsen & Buss, 2002).

Evolutionary psychology seeks to understand how evolution shaped human behavior. Psychologists do not agree about the nature of human nature, but two qualities that belong at the top of anyone's list are the need to form close relationships and the competition for dominance.

**ATTACHMENT THEORY** The writings of British psychiatrist John Bowlby (1907–1990) greatly influenced psychologists' views about the human need to form close relationships. The heart of Bowlby's theory was the observation that infants form **attachments** early in life—special, selective bonds with their caregivers.

Bowlby based his approach, known as *attachment theory,* on findings from *ethology,* the study of animal behavior. Ethologists documented that close relationships develop between infants and caregivers in many species of animals. Human infants develop selective bonds to caregivers more slowly during the first year of life. These bonds, together with displays of distress when separated, keep infant and parent in close proximity. You can readily observe the result: Ducklings swim in line behind their mother; toddlers explore the world in an irregular orbit around a parent. From an evolutionary standpoint, proximity has survival value, because parents protect their offspring from danger. Attachment behavior is an inborn characteristic, a product of natural selection.

Attachment theory has generated much psychological research (Cassidy & Shaver, 2008). Particularly relevant to abnormal behavior are studies of *insecure* or *anxious attachments*, parent–child relationships that are a product of inconsistent and unresponsive parenting during the first year of life (Ainsworth et al., 1978). Anxious attachments can make children mistrustful, dependent, and/or rejecting in subsequent relationships, patterns that may continue into adult life. Attachment difficulties can be

Mammals form strong bonds between infants and caregivers. Disruptions in human attachments can contribute to abnormal behavior.

overcome (Rutter & Rutter, 1993), and research shows that supportive relationships promote mental health throughout the life span, not just early in life (Dykas & Cassidy, 2011).

**DOMINANCE** The development of attachments, or more generally of affiliation with other members of the same species, is one of the two broad categories of social behaviors studied by ethologists. The second is **dominance,** the hierarchical ordering of a social group into more and less privileged members (Sloman, Gardner, & Price, 1989). Dominance hierarchies are easily observed in human as well as other animal social groups. Dominance competition is basic to sexual selection, and therefore a prime candidate on our short list of species-typical human qualities (Buss, 2009). Exciting, recent theorizing suggests that dominance motivation play a role in antisocial behavior, narcissism, and mania (Johnson, Leedom, & Muhtadie, 2012).

Additional motivations surely belong on psychology's "periodic table" of human elements (Kenrick et al., 2010). Still, we are confident that attachment and dominance will rank high on the final list. Freud might agree. We view Freud's basic drives, sex and aggression, as metaphors for the broader motivations of affiliation and dominance.

## Temperament

A key area of research on personality is the study of **temperament,** characteristic styles of relating to the world. Researchers generally

*"It's not you—it's natural selection."*

The cartoon pokes fun at evolution and perhaps suggests a new break up line.
© Carolita Johnson/The New Yorker Collection/www.cartoonbank.com

agree that temperament consists of five dimensions (McAdams & Pals, 2006; Zuckerman, 1991). The "big five" are (1) openness to experience—imaginative and curious versus shallow and imperceptive; (2) conscientiousness—organized and reliable versus careless and negligent; (3) extraversion—active and talkative versus passive and reserved; (4) agreeableness—trusting and kind versus hostile and selfish; and (5) neuroticism—nervous and moody versus calm and pleasant. The acronym OCEAN (the first letter of each term) will help you to remember "the big five." Individual differences in temperament are basic to understanding personality disorders (Chapter 9).

## Emotions

**Emotions,** internal feeling states, are essential to human experience and to our understanding of mental disorders. We have hundreds of words for different feelings in the English language. What emotions are most essential? Researchers have used statistical analysis to reduce our lexicon of feelings to six basic emotions:

- Love
- Joy
- Surprise
- Anger
- Sadness
- Fear

This list can be pared further into two categories, positive emotions (the left column) and negative emotions (the right column). Of course, negative emotions are most relevant to abnormal psychology, but differentiating between negative emotions is also a key. One recent study found that, among people who experienced intense negative emotions, those who could better describe their feelings consumed less alcohol than others who could only talk generally about being upset or feeling bad (Kashdan et al., 2010).

Emotions come to us without intention, effort, or desire. Emotions are controlled primarily by subcortical brain structures

Evolution shapes behavior in animals and humans. Do humans compete for dominance, perhaps in more subtle ways than these stags compete?

that are older in evolutionary terms and more similar to brain structures found in other animals (who do not have humans' large cortex). Thus, our feelings are more "basic" or primitive than our thoughts, which are controlled by the cerebral cortex, a more recent product of evolution (Shariff & Tracy, 2011). Cognition can regulate emotion, but we cannot wholly control our feelings intellectually (Panksepp & Biven, 2012). This fact often becomes an issue in treating abnormal behavior, as people may want to but cannot easily change their emotions.

## Learning and Cognition

Motivations, temperament, and emotions can be modified, at least to some degree, by learning. Earlier, we discussed classical and operant conditioning, two modes of learning that are essential to the development of normal and abnormal behavior. We know, for example, that classical conditioning can create new fears, and antisocial behavior can be maintained by positive reinforcement.

A third learning mechanism described by the U.S. psychologist Albert Bandura of Stanford University (Bandura & Walters, 1963) is **modeling,** or learning through imitation, a process that you surely have observed many times. A particular concern for abnormal behavior is when parents or other important adults model dysfunctional behavior for children, for example, excessive drinking.

Cognitive psychologists study other, more complex learning mechanisms such as attention, information processing, and memory. In doing so, cognitive psychologists often draw analogies between human thinking and computers, but the "human computer" apparently is programmed to make decision making more efficient but less objective (Kahneman, 2003). We routinely make cognitive errors not because we reason wrongly, but because we use shorthand calculations (*heuristics*) that require little effort and typically are accurate enough—but sometimes may be way off the mark.

Cognitive psychology has profoundly affected theorizing about the cause of mental disorders, as has the parallel field of *social cognition*—the study of how humans process information about the social world. The important concept of attribution

*"Surely you can tell me your secret identity."*
© Charles Barsotti/The New Yorker Collection/www.cartoonbank.com.

illustrates this approach. **Attributions** are perceived causes, people's *beliefs* about cause–effect relations. We are "intuitive scientists." We routinely draw shorthand conclusions about causality instead of examining things scientifically. If your boyfriend gets mad at you for "ditching" him at a party, for example, you are unlikely to examine his feelings objectively. Instead, you attribute his anger to some reasonable cause, perhaps his tendency to cling to you. Intuitive judgments are efficient because they require little cognitive effort, but research shows that attributions often are inaccurate (Nisbett & Wilson, 1977; Wilson, 2002).

One cognitive theory suggests that automatic and distorted perceptions of reality cause people to become depressed (Beck et al., 1979). For example, people prone to depression may conclude that they are inadequate based on a single unpleasant experience. A successful treatment based on this theory encourages depressed people to be more scientific and less intuitive in evaluating conclusions about themselves (see Chapter 5). One controversy, however, is whether depressed people actually see the world all too accurately. Perhaps nondepressed people are the ones who make routine cognitive errors by seeing the world, and themselves, in an unrealistically *positive* light (Taylor et al., 2003).

## The Sense of Self

We share emotions and motivations with other animals, and we share some information-processing strategies with computers. Perhaps our sense of self is uniquely human. The exact definition of self can be elusive, however, both in psychological theory and personally.

One influential idea is Erik Erikson's (1968) concept of **identity,** an integrated sense of self. Erikson viewed identity as the product of the adolescent's struggle to answer the question, "Who am I?" As we discuss in Chapter 17, Erikson urged young people to take some time and try new values and roles before adopting a single, enduring identity.

Other theorists argue that we do not have one identity but many "selves." The psychologist George Kelly (1905–1967), for example, emphasized the identities linked with the different roles that people play in life. These include obvious roles such as being a daughter, a student, and a friend, as well as less obvious roles, such as being a "caretaker," a "jock," or "the quiet one." Kelly

argued that people develop many different role identities, various senses of self corresponding with actual life roles. A related, contemporary theory is that people have multiple *relational selves,* unique actions and identities linked with different significant relationships (Chen, Boucher, & Tapias, 2006).

**Self-control**—internal rules for guiding appropriate behavior—is another important part of the internal self. Self-control is learned through the process of *socialization,* where parents, teachers, and peers use discipline, praise, and their own example to teach children prosocial behavior and set limits on their antisocial behavior. Over time, these standards are *internalized*—that is, the external rules become internal regulations. The result is self-control (Maccoby & Mnookin, 1992).

*Self-esteem,* valuing one's abilities, is another important and sometimes controversial aspect of our sense of self. The concept of self-esteem has been derided recently, partly in reaction to misguided school programs that urged raising children's self-esteem as a cure to everything from school dropout to teen pregnancy (Swann, Chang-Schneider, & McClarty, 2007). High self-esteem appears to be as much a product of success as a cause of it; raising children's self-esteem in isolation from actual achievement produces little benefit (Baumeister et al., 2003). Similarly, low self-esteem can result from psychological problems as well as cause them.

One final note: Our sense of self may be uniquely human, but there is still no dualism between mind and body. Like all psychological experiences, our sense of self is represented in the brain. In fact, the human sense of self may be localized in the frontal lobe. A terrible form of degenerative brain disease rapidly damages the front lobe, and causes patients to lose much self-reflection and self-control (Levenson & Miller, 2007).

## Stages of Development

How people grow and change is of basic importance to normal and abnormal psychology. A key developmental concept is that psychological growth can be divided into **developmental stages**—periods of time marked by age and/or social tasks during which children or adults face common social and emotional challenges.

Two prominent theories of developmental stages are Freud's theory of psycho*sexual* development and Erikson's theory of

Intimate relationships can be a source of great social support or emotional distress.

psycho*social* development. Freud highlighted the child's internal struggles with sexuality as marking the various stages of development. In contrast, Erikson emphasized social tasks and the conflicts involved in meeting the demands of the external world. Erikson also suggested that development does not end with adolescence; rather, he proposed that development continues throughout the life span.

The key tasks, ages, and defining events of these two stage theories are summarized in Table 2.5. Note the differences between the theories, but also note that both theorists used similar ages to mark the beginning and end of different stages. Other theorists also have suggested that key developmental transitions occur around the ages of 1, 6, and 12. These are critical times of change for children.

*Developmental transitions* mark the end of one developmental stage and the beginning of a new one—for example, the end of childhood and the beginning of adolescence. Developmental

**TABLE 2.5**
## Freud's and Erikson's Stage Theories of Development

| AGE[1] | 0–1½ | 1–3 | 2–6 | 5–12 | 11–20 | 18–30 | 25–70 | 65 On |
|---|---|---|---|---|---|---|---|---|
| **Freud** | **Oral** | **Anal** | **Phallic** | **Latency** | **Genital** | | | |
| | Oral gratification through breastfeeding. Meeting one's own needs. | Learning control over environment and inner needs through toilet training. | Sexual rivalry with opposite-gender parent. Oedipal conflicts, penis envy, identification. | Not a stage, as psychosexual development is dormant during these ages. | Mature sexuality and formation of mutual heterosexual relationships. | | | |
| **Erikson** | **Basic Trust vs. Basic Mistrust** | **Autonomy vs. Shame and Doubt** | **Initiative vs. Guilt** | **Industry vs. Inferiority** | **Identity vs. Role Confusion** | **Intimacy vs. Self-absorption** | **Generativity vs. Stagnation** | **Integrity vs. Despair** |
| | Developing basic trust in self and others through feeding and care-taking. | Gaining a sense of competence through success in toileting and mastering environment. | Gaining parental approval for initiative rather than guilt over inadequacy. | Curiosity and eagerness to learn leads to a sense of competence or inadequacy. | Identity crisis is a struggle to answer question, "Who am I?" | Aloneness of young adult resolved by forming friendships and a lasting intimate relationship. | Success in work but especially in raising the next generation, or failure to be productive. | Satisfaction with the life one lived rather than despair over lost opportunities. |

[1]Ages are approximate, as indicated by overlap in age ranges

transitions are often a time of turmoil. As we are forced to learn new ways of thinking, feeling, and acting, stressful developmental transitions may worsen or contribute to abnormal behavior. They can also be extremely challenging psychologically, as we discuss in detail in Chapter 17.

## Social Factors

At a broader level of analysis, abnormal behavior can be understood in terms of *social roles,* behavior that, like a role in a play, is shaped by social "scripts." In fact, *labeling theory* asserts that emotional disorders themselves are enactments of prescribed social roles (Rosenhan, 1973). Labeling theory suggests that people's actions conform to the expectations created by the label, a process termed the *self-fulfilling prophesy* (Rosenthal, 1966).

There is little doubt that expectations affect behavior, but labeling alone offers a limited understanding of much abnormal behavior. For example, how could labeling someone "schizophrenic" cause severe hallucinations, delusions, and life disruptions? (On the other hand, labeling a child a "troublemaker" may play a key role in the development of antisocial behavior.) The roles we play in life—including roles shaped by gender, race, social class, and culture—help to shape who we become. But psychopathology is much more than a social role.

Potential social influences on abnormal behavior are numerous, including interpersonal relationships, social institutions, and cultural values. We can offer a few key examples here, including close relationships, gender roles, ethnicity, prejudice, and poverty.

### Close Relationships

Researchers consistently find that relationship problems, particularly conflict and anger in close relationships, are associated with various emotional disorders (Beach et al., 2006; Miklowitz, Otto, & Frank, 2007). Do troubled relationships cause abnormal behavior, or do an individual's psychological problems cause relationship difficulties?

**MARITAL STATUS AND PSYCHOPATHOLOGY** The association between marital status and psychopathology is a good example of the cause–effect dilemma. The demographics of the U.S. family have changed greatly over the last few decades. Cohabitation before marriage is frequent, many children are born outside of marriage, and almost half of all marriages end in divorce (Bramlett & Mosher, 2001). In part because of the uncertainty created by these rapid changes, researchers have carefully studied the psychological consequences of alternative family structures for children and adults.

Marital status and psychological problems clearly are *correlated.* Children and adults from divorced or never-married families have somewhat more psychological problems than people from always-married families (Amato, 2010; Emery, Shim, & Horn, 2012; Waite & Gallagher, 2000; Whisman, Sheldon, & Goering, 2000). But does marital status cause these problems?

In order to better address the question of causality, researchers are now comparing twins (or their children) who *differ* in terms of some major life experience (Rutter, 2007). If we find that MZ twins who divorce have more psychological problems than their married co-twins, we know that the difference is *not* due to genes. We also know that the difference is *not* caused by childrearing or other experiences that twins share. Why? Identical twins have identical genes and grow up in the same families. Any difference between them therefore must be caused by the nonshared environment, their unique experiences, one of which is divorce in the present example. In fact, twin research suggests that divorce does cause some psychological problems both in children (D'Onofrio et al., 2007) and adults (Horn et al., in press; South & Krueger, 2008).

**SOCIAL RELATIONSHIPS** Research also shows that a good relationship with someone *outside* of the family is associated with better mental health among children (Landis, Gaylord-Harden, & Malinowski, 2007; Werner & Smith, 1992) and adults (Birditt & Antonucci, 2007; Reis, Collins, & Berscheid, 2000). A few things are critical about this **social support**—the emotional and practical assistance received from others. Significantly, one close relationship can provide as much support as many relationships. The greatest risk comes from having *no* social support. In addition, it is much worse to be actively rejected than to be neglected. Especially among children, it is far worse to be "liked least" than not to be "liked most" by your peers (Coie & Kupersmidt, 1983). Finally, neuroscience and psychological evidence shows the depression and anger that come from being ostracized, ignored, or excluded (Williams & Nida, 2011).

Once again, the association between abnormal behavior and the relationship troubles may have several causes. For some, peer rejection may cause emotional difficulties. In other cases, the lack of a close relationship may be a consequence of abnormal behavior. Finally, social support may help some people to cope more successfully with preexisting emotional problems.

### Gender and Gender Roles

Gender and **gender roles,** expectations regarding the appropriate behavior of males or females, can dramatically affect our behavior. Some gender differences are determined by genetics and hormones, but socially prescribed gender roles also exert a strong influence on our behavior (Maccoby, 1998).

Gender roles may influence the development, expression, or stigma of psychopathology. Some theorists suggest, for example, that women's traditional roles foster dependency and helplessness, which accounts for the considerably higher rates of depression among women (Nolen-Hoeksema, 1990). Others argue that gender roles may not cause abnormal behavior, but influence how psychopathology is expressed. For example, social expectations may allow women to become depressed when confronted with adversity, whereas men's roles dictate that they "carry on" or perhaps sooth their inner turmoil with alcohol or drugs. Finally, recent research shows that more stigma is attached to gender-typical emotional problems. People view depression in women and alcohol abuse in men as more controllable than the converse (depression in men,

Socially prescribed gender roles exert a strong influence on our behavior and perhaps on the development, expression, and consequences of psychopathology.

alcohol abuse in women), and as a result, they are less sympathetic and less inclined to offer help (Wirth & Bodenhausen, 2009).

Some believe that *androgyny*—the possession of both "female" and "male" gender-role characteristics—is the answer to the problems associated with being either overly "feminine" or overly "masculine." Others embrace traditional gender roles. We do not address this value conflict in this text, although we do consider gender differences in the prevalence of various psychological disorders. When appropriate, we also interpret gender differences in terms of the roles played by men and women.

## Prejudice, Poverty, and Society

Prejudice and poverty are broad social influences on psychological well-being in the United States today (Cox, Abramson, Devine, & Hollon, 2012). We consider these two factors together because they are so commonly linked in American life. In 2009, 9.3 percent of white families were living below the poverty level, compared with 22.7 percent of black, 22.7 percent of Latino, and 9.4 percent of Asian families. Race and poverty are also closely linked to marital status. Among African Americans, 8.6 percent of married families lived in poverty compared to 36.7 percent of families headed by single women. Among whites, the comparable rates were 5.4 percent married versus 27.3 percent single women; 16.0 percent versus 38.8 percent for Hispanics; and 7.9 versus 16.9 for Asians (U.S. Census Bureau, 2012).

Poverty affects a disproportionate number of African Americans, but the experiences of American blacks and whites differ in many ways. African Americans have endured a history of slavery and discrimination, and racial prejudices undermine physical and mental health (Clark et al., 1999). Of course, African Americans are not the only targets of prejudice. For example, extensive evidence links the prejudice experienced by gays and lesbians to an increased risk for mental health problems (Meyer, 2003).

Poverty is linked with many stressors (Evans & Kim, 2012), including exposure to gruesome traumas. One researcher found that 12 percent of school–aged children living in a Washington, DC, neighborhood reported seeing a dead body in the streets outside their homes (Richters, 1993). Poverty also increases exposure to chemical toxins, such as the lead found in old, chipped paint and automotive exhaust fumes (Evans, 2004). When ingested at toxic levels, lead can damage the central nervous system.

We recognize that society and culture influence abnormal behavior even more broadly. Our lives, our education, and even our science are embedded within our culture. Societal practices, beliefs, and values help to shape the definition of abnormal behavior and the scientific enterprise that attempts to uncover its roots.

## MyPsychLab VIDEO CASE

### Autism

XAVIER

*"He is now talking, which was a blessing."*

⊙ **Watch** the **Video** *Xavier: Autism* on **MyPsychLab**

As you watch the video, observe Xavier's communication struggles and odd behavior, and keep in mind that he is functioning pretty well in comparison to many children with autism.

The problems that you study in abnormal psychology can touch your life in a very personal way. At one time or another, you, someone in your family, or one of your close friends will likely experience a psychological problem. If so, we hope you will seek and find meaningful help. What can you do if you think you may want to get help?

A good place to start is to talk frankly with someone you trust—a friend, a family member, a mental health professional, maybe a professor. Taking this step can be difficult, but you will surely be relieved once you have opened up a little. In fact, this may be the end of your search. With the aid of a little perspective, you may be reassured that what you thought were "crazy" feelings or concerns are pretty normal.

Normal? Yes. We mean it when we say that there is not a high wall dividing normal from abnormal behavior. Negative emotions are part of everyday life. Most of us experience mild to moderate levels of anxiety, sadness, and anger fairly often. In fact, these emotions are often adaptive. These feelings can energize us to cope with the challenges in our lives. So, maybe all you really need is the understanding and perspective of a caring friend or relative, or of an objective third party.

Recognizing where you are in your life may also help you to achieve a little perspective. The late teens and early twenties—the age of many people taking this class—are frequently at a time of uncertainty and self-doubt. It is quite common for young people to question their goals, beliefs, values, friendships, sexuality, family relationships, and almost everything else. If this sounds like you, you may want to read ahead in Chapter 17, which discusses many of the challenges of the transition to adult life. You also may want to look at Chapter 17 if you are a nontraditional student, because we also discuss many other common but trying developmental transitions throughout the adult life span. Times of change and challenge can be very exciting, but they also can be very distressing and lonely.

What should you do if you do not feel better after talking with someone you trust? We suggest that you consider consulting a mental health professional. This is a good next step whether you think you are suffering from a psychological problem, are not sure, or simply want help with some normal but distressing life experience. We know that there can be a stigma about seeing a therapist, but we strongly believe that the stigma is wrong. Mental health problems are incredibly common, and a therapist, or maybe your family doctor, can offer you an informed perspective and some good treatment alternatives. We give suggestions about how to go about finding a reliable mental health professional in the Getting Help section of Chapter 3.

# Summary

The **biological**, **psychodynamic**, **cognitive-behavioral**, and **humanistic** approaches to understanding the causes of abnormal behavior are alternative **paradigms**, and not just alternative theories. Biological approaches emphasize causes "within the skin." Psychodynamic theory highlights unconscious processes. Cognitive-behavioral viewpoints focus on observable, learned behavior. The humanistic paradigm argues that behavior is a product of free will.

Abnormal behavior is best understood in terms of the **biopsychosocial model**, the combination of different biological, psychological, and social factors. **Systems theory** is a way of integrating different contributions to abnormal behavior. Its central principle is **holism**, the idea that the whole is more than the sum of its parts.

Biological factors in abnormal behavior begin with the **neuron**, or nerve cell. Communication between neurons occurs when the axon terminals release chemical substances called **neurotransmitters** into the synapse between nerve cells. Disrupted communication among neurons, particularly disruptions in the functioning of various neurotransmitters, is involved in several types of abnormal behavior, although you should be cautioned against mind–body dualism.

The brain is divided into three subdivisions: the hindbrain, the midbrain, and the forebrain. Because of the rudimentary state of our knowledge about the brain, only the most severe mental disorders have been clearly linked with abnormalities in neuroanatomy.

**Psychophysiology** involves changes in the functioning of the body that result from psychological experiences. Psychophysiological arousal is caused by the **endocrine system** and the nervous system. Endocrine glands release **hormones** into the bloodstream that regulate some aspects of normal development as well as some responses to stress. The autonomic nervous system is the part of the central nervous system that is responsible for psychophysiological reactions.

Most forms of abnormal behavior are **polygenic**—that is, caused by more than one **gene**. While genes are involved in most mental illnesses, the fact that a psychological disorder has a genetic component does not mean that it is inevitable.

Psychology has not developed a list of its core components. Some promise toward this goal is offered by **evolutionary psychology**, the application of the principles of evolution to our understanding of the animal and human minds. Two basic psychological motivations seen in humans and other animals are the formation of **attachments** and competition for **dominance**.

**Temperament** is an individual's characteristic style of relating to the world, and researchers agree on the "big five" dimensions of temperament.

**Emotions** are internal feeling states that come to us without intention, effort, or desire. Emotional disruptions are at the core of many mental disorders.

Learning mechanisms include **classical conditioning**, **operant conditioning**, **modeling**, and human cognition and contribute to both normal and abnormal behavior.

The sense of self is a uniquely human quality that may also play a role in causing emotional problems.

The idea of **developmental stages** not only charts the course of normal development, against which abnormal behavior must be compared, but it also highlights the important issue of developmental transitions.

**Social support** from people other than family members can be an important buffer against stress. **Gender roles** may influence the development, expression, or consequences of psychopathology. Race and poverty are also broad social influences on psychological well-being.

## The Big Picture

## critical thinking review

**2.1** What is the biopsychosocial model and why do we need it?
Paradigms can tell us how to find answers, but sometimes the guidance can be a hindrance . . . (see page 30).

**2.2** What does "correlation does not mean causation" mean?
A correlation *may* result from causation, but there are always two alternative explanations: reverse causality and third variables . . . (see page 33).

**2.3** How is "mental illness caused by a chemical imbalance in the brain" an example of reductionism?
This means depression is caused by a "chemical imbalance in the brain," right? Wrong . . . (see page 35).

**2.4** Are scientists likely to discover a gene that causes mental disorders?
. . . there is no single "gene for" depression or most any other known mental disorder . . . (see page 40).

**2.5** How do social and psychological factors contribute to emotional problems?
. . . any listing of the psychological factors involved in mental disorders, including our own, is necessarily incomplete and likely to be controversial . . . (see page 42).

**2.6** Is abnormal behavior really all about labeling and role playing?
The roles we play in life—including roles shaped by gender, race, social class, and culture—help to shape who we become. But psychopathology is much more than a social role . . . (see page 48).

## key terms

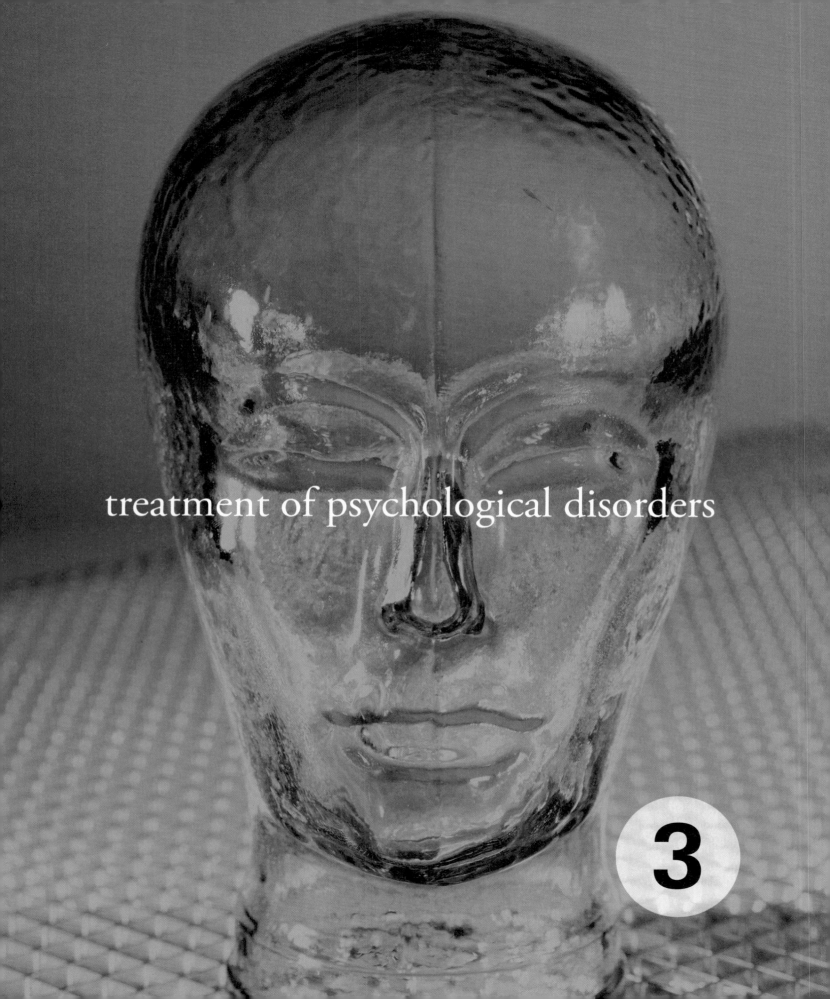

treatment of psychological disorders

3

# The Big Picture

## learning objectives

**3.1**
What do treatments for psychological problems look like?

**3.2**
How did Freud influence psychotherapy?

**3.3**
What is cognitive-behavior therapy?

**3.4**
Does psychotherapy work?

**3.5**
What is the placebo effect? How do placebos work?

**3.6**
Is it important to "click" with your therapist?

Many people seek psychological help when battling bulimia, depression, anxiety, or other psychological problems. Others consult a professional when struggling with relationships, or searching for a happier, more meaningful life. Can treatment help? Does it matter if you see a psychiatrist, clinical psychologist, social worker, or counselor? Should you look for someone who specializes in your particular problem? Should you try medication? What should you expect a therapist to do and say? How can "talking" help?

## Overview

What can help? Few questions in abnormal psychology are more important than this one. We use psychological science to explore answers to this essential question in this chapter. However, we continue to ask, "What helps?" throughout the text, because research shows that different treatments work better for different disorders (Barlow, 2008; Nathan & Gorman, 2007).

One treatment that can help is **psychotherapy,** the use of psychological techniques and the therapist–client relationship to produce emotional, cognitive, and behavior change. We can define psychotherapy generally, but it can be a challenge to be more specific. One complication is that adherents to different paradigms offer very different treatments (Prochaska & Norcross, 2006). Mental health professionals often ask one another, "What is your

theoretical orientation?" The answer is supposed to be "biological," "psychodynamic," "cognitive-behavioral," or "humanistic," an indication of the therapist's preferred treatment approach.

Today, most mental health professionals describe themselves as *eclectic*, meaning they use different treatments for different disorders (Bechtoldt et al., 2001). We embrace the eclectic approach, as long as clinicians use research to select the most effective treatment (Baker, McFall, & Shoham, 2008; Chambless & Ollendick, 2000). That is, the practice of psychotherapy must be *evidenced-based*. Research may support alternative treatments, based on either therapy *outcome*, how well a treatment works, or therapy *process*, what makes therapy work (Kazdin, 2008).

Evidence-based treatment is the scientific—and practical—approach to therapy. Unfortunately, some therapists fail to educate their clients about evidence-based treatments. Yet, there is an even bigger problem: Most people with psychological problems do not get *any* help. Over one in 10 people in the United States get some kind of mental health treatment, and rates of receiving help have increased in recent decades. Yet, two-thirds of people with a diagnosable mental disorder still do *not* receive treatment (Kessler et al., 2005).

We introduce treatment with the following case study. As you read, ponder what you think might be wrong with this young woman and what might help her. After the case, we discuss how different therapists might treat her using a biological, psychodynamic, cognitive-behavioral, or humanistic approach.

### → Why Is Frances Depressed?

Frances was a 23-year-old woman when she first sought treatment. She had been depressed for almost three years, with periods of relative happiness or deeper despair. When she came into therapy, her depression was severe. She had little appetite, had lost 10 pounds over the previous six weeks, and her erratic sleeping patterns were worse than usual. She awoke around 2 or 3 A.M. every night, tossed in bed for several hours, and finally fell asleep again near dawn.

Frances reported feeling profoundly depressed about herself, her new marriage, and life in general. She admitted to occasional thoughts of suicide, but she could never commit the act. She felt that she "lacked the courage" to take her own life. Frances also said that she lacked motivation. She withdrew from her husband and the few friends she had, and she frequently called in sick at work. Frances's reported symptoms were consistent with her careless dress, frequent bouts of crying, and slowed speech and body movements.

Frances said she had a happy childhood. She had not known depression until the current episode began in her last year in college. At first, she convinced herself that she was only suffering from "senior year syndrome." She wasn't sure what to do with her life. Secretly, she longed to move to New York and finally break out and do something exciting. But when she told her parents about her plans, her mother begged Frances to return home. She insisted that the two of them needed to have fun together again after four long years with Frances away at school. Frances returned home.

Shortly after moving home, Frances realized that her difficulties were much more serious than she had thought. She found herself intermittently screaming at her doting mother and being "super-nice" after feeling guilty about losing her temper. Frances thought that her erratic behavior toward her mother was all her fault. She described her mother as "a saint." Her mother apparently agreed. In both their minds, Frances was a failure as a daughter.

Frances described her mother as giving, but some of her comments about her were far from glowing. She said she was her mother's best friend. When asked if her mother was her best friend, Frances began to cry.

She felt like her mother's infant, her parent, or even her husband, but not her friend and certainly not like her grown daughter.

Frances had little to say about her father. She pictured him drinking beer, eating meals, and falling asleep in front of the television.

Throughout the time she lived at home, Frances's depression only deepened. After a year of living with her parents, she married her high school sweetheart. Frances felt pressured to get married. Both her future husband and her mother insisted that it was time for her to settle down and start a family. Frances had hoped that marriage might be the solution to her problems. The excitement of the wedding added to this hope. But after the marriage, Frances said that things were worse—if that were possible.

Frances's husband was a young accountant who reminded Frances of her father. He didn't drink but spent most of his brief time at home working or reading in his study. She said they had little communication, and she felt no warmth in her marriage. Her husband often was angry and sullen, but Frances said she couldn't blame him for feeling that way. His problem was being married to

her. She wanted to love him, but she never had. She was a failure as a wife. She was a failure in life.

The theme of self-blame pervaded Frances's descriptions of her family. She repeatedly noted that, despite their flaws, her parents and her husband were good and loving people. She was the one with the problem. She had everything that she could hope for, yet she was unhappy. One reason she wanted to die was to ease the burden on them. How could they be happy when they had to put up with her foul moods? When she talked about these things, however, Frances's tone of voice often sounded more angry than depressed.

## Four Views of Frances

How might Frances's problems be viewed through the lens of the four paradigms? Biological, psychodynamic, cognitive-behavioral, and humanistic therapists all would note her depressed mood, self-blame, and troubled relationships. However, therapists working within these different paradigms would evaluate Frances and approach treatment in very different ways (see Table 3.1).

Biological therapies approach mental illness by drawing an analogy with physical illness. Thus, a biologically oriented psychiatrist or psychologist would focus first on making a diagnosis of Frances's problems. This would not be difficult because Frances's symptoms paint a clear picture of depression. The therapist also would take note of Frances's description of her father, who seems chronically depressed. Perhaps a genetic predisposition runs in her family.

A biologically oriented therapist would sympathize with Frances's interpersonal problems but would not blame either Frances or her family for their troubles. Rather, the therapist would blame something that neither Frances nor her family members could control: depression. It is exhausting to deal with someone who is constantly agitated and depressed. In the end,

---

**TABLE 3.1**

## Comparison of Biological, Psychodynamic, Cognitive-Behavioral, and Humanistic Treatments

| Topic | Biological | Psychodynamic | Cognitive-Behavioral | Humanistic |
|---|---|---|---|---|
| Goal of treatment | Alter biology to relieve psychological distress | Gain insight into defenses/unconscious motivations | Learn more adaptive behaviors/cognitions | Increase emotional awareness |
| Primary method | Diagnosis, medication | Interpretation of defenses | Instruction, guided learning, homework | Empathy, support, exploring emotions |
| Role of therapist | Active, directive, diagnostician | Passive, nondirective, interpreter (may be aloof) | Active, directive, nonjudgmental, teacher | Passive, nondirective, warm, supporter |
| Length of treatment | Brief, with occasional follow-up visits | Usually long term; some new short-term treatments | Short term, with later "booster" sessions | Varies; length not typically structured |

the therapist might explain that depression is caused by a chemical imbalance in the brain, recommend medication, and schedule follow-up appointments to monitor the effects of the medication on Frances's mood.

A psychodynamic therapist would also note Frances's depression but likely would focus on her *defensive style*. The therapist might view Frances's justification of her parents' and husband's behavior as a form of *rationalization*. The therapist would also see a pattern of *denial* in Frances's refusal to acknowledge the imperfections of her loved ones and their failure to fulfill her needs. When Frances says that she is a burden on her family, a psychodynamic therapist might wonder if she was *projecting* onto them her own feelings of being burdened by her mother's demands and her husband's indifference.

A psychodynamic therapist probably would not challenge Frances's defenses early in therapy but instead begin by exploring her past. The goal would be to illuminate patterns in Frances's internal conflicts, unconscious motivations, and defenses. Sooner or later, the psychodynamic therapist would confront Frances's defenses in order to help her gain *insight* into her hidden resentment toward her mother, longing for a relationship with her father, and unfulfilled fantasies about marriage.

A cognitive-behavior therapist might note many of the same issues in Frances's life. Rather than focusing on defense mechanisms and the past, however, the therapist would hone in on Frances's cognitive and behavioral patterns now. Frances's self-blame—her pattern of attributing all of her interpersonal difficulties to herself—would be seen as a cognitive error. Her withdrawal from pleasing activities and unassertiveness also might be seen as contributing to her depression. In comparison to a psychodynamic therapist, a cognitive-behavior therapist would be far more directive in discussing these topics. For example, he or she would tell Frances that her thinking was distorted and causing her depression.

The therapist also would make direct suggestions to teach Frances new ways of thinking, acting, and feeling. The therapist might encourage Frances to blame others appropriately, not just herself, for relationship problems and urge her to try out new ways of relating to her mother, father, and husband. The therapist would want Frances to play an active role in this process by completing *homework*—activities outside the therapy, for example, writing about her anger or actually confronting her mother and husband. A cognitive-behavior therapist would expect Frances's depressed mood to begin to lift once she learned to assert herself and no longer blame herself for everything that went wrong.

A humanistic therapist would also note Frances's depression, self-blame, and unsatisfactory relationships. A more prominent focus, however, would be her lack of emotional genuineness—her inability to "be herself" with other people and within herself. The therapist would explore Frances's tendency to bury her true feelings. The goal would be to help Frances recognize how she *really* feels.

In therapy, the humanistic therapist would be nondirective about discussion but would continually focus on underlying emotions. Initially, the therapist might simply empathize with Frances's feelings of sadness, loneliness, and isolation. Over time, he or she might suggest that Frances had other feelings that she did not express, including frustration and guilt over her mother's controlling yet dependent style, and anger at her husband's and father's self-centeredness. The humanistic therapist might tell Frances that all of her conflicting feelings were legitimate and encourage Frances to "own" them. The therapist would not directly encourage Frances to act differently. Instead, Frances might make changes in her life as a result of her increased emotional awareness.

These approaches to treating Frances are very different, but you may wonder if a therapist could use the best aspects of each one (see Thinking Critically About *DSM-5* on p. 56). In fact, psychologists often integrate elements of different approaches when working to find more effective treatments. One straightforward example is when psychotherapy is combined with medication, although most people who take antidepressants do not get therapy—and the number who do is declining (Olfson & Marcus, 2009). Before considering how approaches can be integrated, however, we first need to elaborate on their differences.

# Biological Treatments

The history of the discovery of the cause and cure of general paresis illustrates the hope and the methods of the medical model (see Chapter 2). First, a diagnosis is developed and refined. Second, clues are put together like pieces of a puzzle that eventually fit together to identify a specific cause. Third, scientists experiment with ways to prevent or eliminate the specific cause until they find an effective treatment. These are not simple steps. It took a century to diagnose general paresis, discover that syphilis caused it, and develop antibiotics to cure syphilis and prevent general paresis.

Today, scientists often search for biological treatments without knowing a disorder's specific cause. These treatments focus on *symptom alleviation*, reducing the dysfunctional symptoms of a disorder but not eliminating its root cause (Valenstein, 1998). Happily, numerous medications have been discovered since the 1950s, and particularly since the 1980s, that offer effective symptom alleviation.

## Psychopharmacology

**Psychopharmacology** is the use of medications to treat psychological disturbances. There are many *psychotropic medications*, chemical substances that affect psychological state, used to treat various mental disorders (see Table 3.2 on p. 57). Some medications, for example, antianxiety drugs, produce rapid changes in thinking, mood, and behavior. Others, such as antidepressants, have more subtle influences that build up gradually over time. Still other psychotropic drugs affect people with mental disorders very

## Diagnosis and Treatment

DSM-5 is the official list of mental disorders. What does the manual say about how various disorders should be treated? Nothing. In fact, developers of the manual explicitly did *not* attempt to detail the best treatments for various mental disorders. The Web site describing the development of the new diagnostic system says, "DSM-5 is intended to be a manual for assessment and diagnosis of mental disorders and will not include information or guidelines for treatment for any disorder."

Why does the *DSM-5* not contain information about treatment? There are two broad reasons. First, as we detail in Chapter 4, the developers of the manual are primarily concerned with the *reliability* of the *DSM-5*, the extent to which different mental health experts reach the same diagnosis, not the manual's *validity* or value for different purposes, including its value for identifying the best treatments. Second, considerable controversy exists about the best treatments for various mental disorders. Is a given mental disorder best treated with medication or psychotherapy, and if the answer is therapy, what form of psychotherapy is most effective?

The American Psychiatric Association, which publishes the *DSM-5*, also develops and publishes "Clinical Practice Guidelines" for various mental disorders. At the time we were writing this, guidelines for 14 disorders were published on the organization's Web site, http://www.psych.org/practice/clinical-practice-guidelines. The American Psychiatric Association developed these guidelines by appointing panels of experts who reviewed the literature, reached various conclusions about treatment, and eventually published the guidelines after seeking extensive feedback from researchers, practitioners, and others. Even more rigorous methods will be used to develop future guidelines, for example, formal surveys will be used to obtain feedback on the conclusions and recommendations reached by panels of experts.

A group of psychologists has taken a different approach to listing the most effective therapies for mental disorders, by identifying "empirically supported treatments" for different disorders.

As we were writing this, the Web site of the clinical psychology division of the American Psychological Association listed empirically supported treatments for 11 different mental disorders http://www.apa.org/divisions/div12/cppi.html. The Web site identifies a single committee as developing all of these 11 lists, although various experts have published different versions of the lists using the same name, "empirically supported treatments" (Woody, Weisz, & McClean, 2005).

So where is the controversy? Pretty much everywhere. For example, even though the list of empirically supported treatments is published by its clinical psychology division, a resolution adopted by the entire American Psychological Association offers a set of statements touting the general effectiveness of psychotherapy (while indicating that practice guidelines will be developed in the future). http://www.apa.org/about/policy/resolution-psychotherapy.aspx This statement defines psychotherapy and the disorders for which psychotherapy is effective very broadly, whereas the list of empirically supported therapies is very specific to given disorders and dominated by cognitive-behavior therapies. The American Psychiatric Association's guidelines tend to emphasize medication, while the American Psychological Association's statement claims that psychotherapy is more effective than medication in the long run. (Recall that psychiatrists can prescribe medication, while clinical psychologists generally cannot.)

Mental health professionals need to do a better job of reaching consensus about the most effective treatments for different disorders by working together across professions and truly striving for objectivity. And people seeking mental health care—and students in Abnormal Psychology classes—need to be smart consumers who think critically about the (differing) conclusions reached by experts. We help you hone your critically think skills throughout the text. In particular, we take you through the pros and cons of different treatments for different disorders in every chapter.

---

differently from the way they affect someone who is functioning normally. Antipsychotic medications help to eliminate delusions and hallucinations among people suffering from schizophrenia, but the same medications would disorient most people and send them into a long, groggy sleep.

Psychopharmacology has grown dramatically in recent decades, too much, perhaps. In the United States, prescriptions for psychostimulants, used to treat inattentive and hyperactive behavior, tripled for preschoolers during the 1990s (Zito et al., 2000).

Today, one in 20 children takes medication for mental health issues (Glied & Frank, 2009). Prescriptions for antidepressants doubled in the last decade (Olfson & Marcus, 2009). In fact, antidepressants are prescribed more often than *any* medication (passing drugs that lower blood pressure in 2005) (Cherry et al., 2007). A leading U.S. managed care organization for prescription drugs reported that 21 percent of adult women were taking an antidepressant, as were almost half as many men (Medico, 2011). Even antipsychotics are used with surprising frequency.

## TABLE 3.2
## Major Categories of Medications for Treating Psychological Disorders

| Therapeutic Use | Chemical Structure or Psychopharmacologic Action | Example | |
|---|---|---|---|
| | | Generic Name | Trade Name |
| Antipsychotics (also called major tranquilizers or neuroleptics) | Phenothiazines<br>Thioxanthenes<br>Butyrophenones<br>Rauwolfia alkaloids<br>Atypical neuroleptics | Chlorpromazine<br>Thiothixene<br>Haloperidol<br>Reserpine<br>Clozapine | Thorazine<br>Navane<br>Haldol<br>Sandril<br>Clozaril |
| Antidepressants | Tricyclic antidepressants (TCAs)<br>Monoamine oxidase inhibitors (MAOIs)<br>Selective serotonin reuptake inhibitors (SSRIs)<br>Atypical antidepressants | Amitriptyline<br>Phenelzine<br><br>Fluoxetine<br><br>Bupropion | Elavil<br>Nardil<br><br>Prozac<br><br>Wellbutrin |
| Psychomotor stimulants | Amphetamines<br>Other | Dextroamphetamine<br>Methylphenidate | Dexedrine<br>Ritalin |
| Antimanic | Metallic element<br>Anticonvulsants | Lithium carbonate<br>Carbamazepine | Eskalith<br>Tegretol |
| Antianxiety (also called minor tranquillizers) | Benzodiazepines<br>Triazolobenzodiazepine | Diazepam<br>Alprazolam | Valium<br>Xanax |
| Sedative hypnotic | Barbiturates<br>Benzodiazepines | Phenobarbital<br>Triazolam | <br>Halcion |
| Antipanic | Benzodiazepines<br>SSRIs | Alprazolam<br>Paroxetine | Xanax<br>Paxil |
| Antiobsessional | TCA<br>SSRIs | Clomipramine<br>Fluvoxamine | Anafranil<br>Luvox |

Two antipsychotic medications, Abilify and Seroquel, were the fifth and sixth most prescribed medications in 2011—often used for the questionable purpose of treating anxiety or depression (*New York Times,* September 25, 2012).

We review different psychotropic medications in relevant chapters later in the text. For now, you should note a few general points. First, medication often is an effective and safe treatment. Second, psychotropic medications do not cure underlying causes, but symptom alleviation still is extremely important. Where would we be without pain relievers, which offer only symptom relief? Third, many psychotropic drugs must be taken for a long time. Because the medications do not produce a cure, patients may need to keep taking the drug—for months, years, or sometimes for a lifetime. Fourth, all medications have side effects, some of which are very unpleasant. Partly for this reason, many patients do not take their medication as prescribed, and they may experience a relapse as a result. Fifth, most psychotropic medications are prescribed by primary care physicians, not psychiatrists (Mojtabai & Olfson, 2008). Finally, we worry, despite the benefits of psychopharmacology, that Americans are perhaps too eager to find a pill to solve all their problems (Barber, 2008).

## Electroconvulsive Therapy

Medication is the most common biological treatment, but it is not the only one. **Electroconvulsive therapy (ECT)** involves deliberately inducing a seizure by passing electricity through the brain. In 1938, the technique was discovered by Italian physicians Ugo Cerletti and Lucio Bini, seeking to cure schizophrenia. At the time, schizophrenia was erroneously thought to be rare among people who had epilepsy. Could epileptic seizures somehow prevent the disorder? A bizarre source gave Cerletti and Bini an idea about how to test this hypothesis. When visiting a slaughterhouse, they observed electric current being passed through the brains of animals, producing a convulsion (and unconsciousness for slaughter). With this inspiration, the two physicians developed a modified electroconvulsive technique as an experimental treatment for schizophrenia. ECT failed in this goal, but today ECT can be effective for severe depressions that do not respond to other treatments (UK ECT Review Group, 2003).

Typically, ECT involves a series of 6 to 12 sessions over the course of a few weeks. Approximately 100 volts of electric current is passed through a patient's brain in order to cause a convulsion. In *bilateral ECT,* electrodes are placed on the left and right temples, and the current passes through both brain hemispheres. In *unilateral ECT*, the current is passed through only one side of the brain, the nondominant hemisphere.

Unilateral ECT produces less *retrograde amnesia*—loss of memory of past events, a disturbing side effect of ECT (Lisanby et al., 2000). Unfortunately, unilateral ECT is less effective than bilateral ECT. Similarly, low-dose ECT (just enough current to produce a seizure) is less effective but causes fewer memory impairments than high-dose ECT (2.5 or more times the minimal current) (Sackheim, Prudic, & Devanand, 2000; UK ECT Review Group, 2003). Thus, effectiveness must be weighed against increased side effects.

Books and movies such as *One Flew over the Cuckoo's Nest* highlight past misuses of ECT. Today, however, ECT is employed infrequently and cautiously. Side effects can be serious and can include memory loss and even death in rare cases. Still, ECT can be very useful in treating severe depressions, especially when patients do not respond to other treatments.

## Psychosurgery

*Psychosurgery*, the surgical destruction of specific regions of the brain, is another biological treatment with a checkered history. Egas Moniz (1874–1955), a Portuguese neurologist, introduced psychosurgery in 1935. He performed a procedure called *prefrontal lobotomy*, irrevocably severing the frontal lobes of the brain. In 1949, Moniz won the Nobel Prize for his work. But his treatment was subsequently discredited because of its limited benefits and frequent, often severe, side effects, including excessive tranquility, emotional unresponsiveness, and even death.

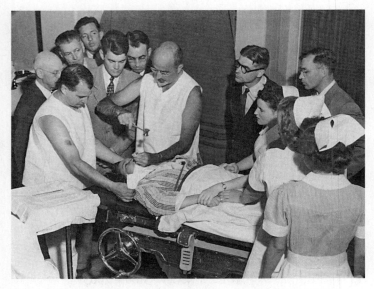

American neurologist Walter Freeman performed almost 3,500 lobotomies, often severing the frontal lobes by knocking an instrument through the back of the eye socket. Today, lobotomy is completely discredited, but refined neurosurgery may play a role in treating severe disorders that do not respond to other treatments.

Moniz himself was shot and paralyzed by one of his lobotomized patients, a sad testament to the unpredictable outcome of the procedure.

Prefrontal lobotomies are a thing of the past, but as the popular movie *Shutter Island* reminded viewers, thousands of prefrontal lobotomies were performed around the world—between 10,000 and 20,000 in the United States alone. Today, very precise psychosurgeries may be used to treat severe affective or anxiety disorders—when all other treatments have failed. For example, *cingulotomy*, lesioning pinpointed regions of the cingulate cortex, may help very severe cases of obsessive–compulsive disorder (Mashour, Walker, & Martuza, 2005). Still, the irreversibility of brain damage makes psychosurgery a very rarely used procedure. Perhaps the future will bring effective refinements (Dougherty & Rauch, 2007).

# Psychodynamic Psychotherapies

Psychodynamic psychotherapies seek to uncover inner conflicts and bring them into conscious awareness. All are an outgrowth of Freudian theory, which emphasizes the importance of gaining insight into complex, unconscious conflicts.

## Freudian Psychoanalysis

An early influence on Freud's "talking cure" was Joseph Breuer (1842–1925), who used hypnosis to induce troubled patients to talk freely about problems in their lives. Upon awakening from a hypnotic trance, many patients reported relief from their symptoms. Breuer assumed that pent-up emotion was responsible for his patients' psychological problems, and he attributed their improvement to *catharsis*, the release of previously unexpressed feelings.

Freud collaborated with Breuer early in his career, and he temporarily adopted the hypnotic method. But Freud soon concluded that hypnosis was unnecessary to encourage open expression. Instead, Freud simply told his patients to speak freely about whatever thoughts crossed their mind. This method, called *free association*, became a cornerstone of Freud's famous treatment, **psychoanalysis.**

Unlike Breuer, Freud did not see catharsis as an end in itself. The true benefit of free association was that it revealed aspects of the unconscious mind. Freud found clues to his patients' unconscious desires in their unedited speech. Freud also believed that information about the unconscious revealed in dreams, when defenses presumably are weak, and by slips of the tongue (now called "Freudian slips," for example, saying "sin" when you meant to say "sex"). Thus, free association, dreams, and slips of the tongue are all Freudian "windows into the unconscious."

**PSYCHOANALYTIC TECHNIQUES** Freud saw the psychoanalyst's first task as discovering the unconscious conflicts that cause

*"You've got to want to connect the dots, Mr. Michaelson."*

© Danny Shanahan/The New Yorker Collection/www.cartoonbank.com.

psychological difficulties. In order to overcome their problems, however, patients must come to share the psychoanalyst's understanding. They must achieve what Freud called **insight,** bringing formerly unconscious material into conscious awareness. Freud asserted that insight is sufficient for curing psychological disorders.

The analyst's main tool for promoting insight is **interpretation.** In offering an interpretation, the analyst suggests hidden meanings to patients' accounts of their life. Typically, interpretations relate to past experiences, especially experiences with loved ones. Recall from Chapter 2, however, that Freud viewed the defense mechanisms as keeping intrapsychic conflicts from conscious awareness. Thus, psychoanalysts must overcome defenses like reaction formation as patients resist their interpretations. ("Hate my mother? My mother is a *saint!*")

Timing is everything in overcoming such *resistance.* The patient must be on the verge of discovering the hidden meaning himself or herself; otherwise, the interpretation will be rejected. For example, consider the dilemma of convincing Frances (from the earlier case study) that deep resentment lies beneath her professed love for her mother. Given her long history of subjugating her own needs to those of her mother, Frances would be unlikely to accept such an interpretation if it were made too early in treatment.

According to Freud, one essential element in probing the unconscious mind is *therapeutic neutrality*, maintaining a distant stance toward the patient in order to minimize the therapist's personal influence. The classical psychoanalyst "sits behind the patient where the patient cannot see him. He tries to create, as far as possible, a controlled laboratory situation in which the individual peculiarities of the analyst shall play as little role as possible in stimulating the patient's reactions" (Alexander & French, 1946, p. 83).

The analyst's distant stance is thought to encourage *transference*, the process whereby patients transfer their feelings about some key figure in their life onto the shadowy figure. For psychoanalysis to succeed, the analyst must not respond to transference in a manner that the patient views as critical or threatening. Analysts also must avoid reacting to their patients in the same way as key figures in their life, for example, by responding to Frances's helplessness by becoming overprotective (like her mother). Finally, psychoanalysts must guard against *countertransference*, or letting their own feelings influence their responses to their patients. Instead, the analyst's job is to maintain therapeutic neutrality and offer interpretations that will promote insight. For example, "You seem frustrated that I won't tell you what to do. I wonder if you have come to expect authority figures to solve your problems for you."

Insight into the transference relationship presumably helps patients understand how and why they are relating to the analyst in the same dysfunctional manner in which they are related to a loved one. This awareness creates a new understanding both of past relationships and of unconscious motivations in present relationships. For example, Frances might have trouble accepting a therapeutic relationship in which she was receiving care instead of giving it. She might, therefore, try to get the analyst to reveal personal problems. The therapist's polite refusal of Frances's attempts at caretaking might cause Frances to feel hurt, rejected, and eventually, angry. As therapy proceeded, these actions could be interpreted as reflecting Frances's style of relating to her mother and her tendency to deny her own needs.

A common misconception about psychoanalysis is that the ultimate goal of insight is to rid the patient of all defenses. This is not the case. According to Freud, defenses are essential for the functioning of a healthy personality. Thus, rather than ridding the patient of defenses, one goal of psychoanalysis is to replace them. Defenses such as denial and projection are confronted because they distort reality dramatically, whereas "healthier" defenses, such as rationalization and sublimation, are left unchallenged. A second goal of psychoanalysis is to help patients become more aware of their basic needs so that they may find appropriate outlets for them.

**THE DECLINE OF FREUDIAN PSYCHOANALYSIS** In traditional psychoanalysis, patients meet with their analyst for an hour several times each week. These sessions often go on for years. Because psychoanalysis requires substantial time, expense, and self-exploration, it is accessible only to people who are functioning well, introspective, and financially secure. Also, little research has been conducted on its effectiveness. You should view psychoanalysis more as a process for people seeking self-understanding than as a treatment for emotional disorders.

Psychoanalysis has declined greatly, but the approach has spawned numerous variations broadly referred to as **psychodynamic psychotherapy.** Psychodynamic psychotherapists often are more engaged and directive, and treatment may be relatively brief in comparison to psychoanalysis.

## Ego Analysis

Several notable psychoanalysts developed variations on Freud's theories that emphasizes the role of the ego over that of the id. One major function of the ego is to mediate between the conflicting impulses of the id and the superego (see Chapter 2). Of equal importance to ego analysts is the ego's role in dealing with reality. *Ego analysts*, therefore, are concerned not only with unconscious motivations, but also with the patient's dealings with the external world.

Past and present relationships are of greatest importance according to Harry Stack Sullivan (1892–1949), an influential ego analyst, who suggested that personality characteristics can be conceptualized in interpersonal terms. Sullivan saw two basic dimensions of relationships. Interpersonal power ranges from dominance to submission. Interpersonal closeness ranges from love to hate. In looking at Frances's relationships, Sullivan might say that she was both overly submissive and perhaps unloved, since she busily met others' needs while ignoring her own.

Other influential ego analysts include Erik Erikson (1902–1994) and Karen Horney (1885–1952). Horney's (1939) lasting contribution was her view that people have conflicting ego needs: to move toward, against, and away from others. Essentially, Horney argued that there are competing human needs for closeness, for dominance, and for autonomy. In her view, the key to a healthy personality is finding a balance among the three styles of relating to others. Pause and consider these three needs in relation to Frances. You should be able to identify her conflicts between Horney's three needs.

We introduced Erikson's stage theory of development in Chapter 2. As with other ego analysts, Erikson focused on the interpersonal context, as evident in his emphasis on the psycho*social* stages of development. Importantly, Erikson also argued that an individual's personality is not fixed by early experience but develops as a result of predictable psychosocial conflicts throughout the life span. John Bowlby's (1907–1990) *attachment theory* perhaps has had the greatest effect on contemporary thought about interpersonal influences on psychopathology (see Chapter 2). Unlike Freud, Bowlby elevated the need for close relationships to a primary human characteristic. From an attachment theory perspective, people are inherently social beings. Our hunger to form close relationships is not so different from our hunger for food, as both reflect a basic human need.

## Psychodynamic Psychotherapy

Various approaches to psychotherapy are based on the theories of Sullivan, Horney, Erikson, Bowlby, and other ego analysts. All seek to uncover hidden motivations, and all emphasize the importance of insight (Shedler, 2010). However, psychodynamic psychotherapists are much more actively involved with their patients than are psychoanalysts. They are more ready to direct the patient's recollections, to focus on current life circumstances, and to offer interpretations quickly and directly. Most psychodynamic psychotherapists are also much more "human" in conducting therapy. They may be distant and reflective at times, but they also are willing to offer appropriate emotional support.

*Short-term psychodynamic psychotherapy* is a form of treatment that uses many psychoanalytic techniques. Therapeutic neutrality is typically maintained, and transference remains a central issue. But therapy focuses on a particular emotional issue rather than relying on free association. The short-term approach has gained attention because it typically is limited to 25 or fewer sessions and is less expensive and more amenable to research (Luborsky, Barber, & Beutler, 1993).

Psychodynamic therapy has not been studied extensively. Some recent reviews concluded that evidence supports the treatment's effectiveness (Leichsenring & Rabung, 2008; Shedler, 2010), but that view is controversial. We believe that more, high quality research is needed before psychodynamic therapy can be said to have empirical support equal to other, evidence-based treatments.

One outgrowth of psychodynamic therapy that does have solid research support is **interpersonal therapy (IPT),** an evidenced-based treatment that focuses on changing emotions and styles of interacting in close relationships. IPT views parent–child and other close relationships as teaching patterns, or characteristic styles, in relating to others. Certain patterns (e.g., dependency), in turn, can create psychological problems in some relationships (e.g., depression following rejection) or during certain life transitions (e.g., a divorce). IPT therapists help clients to recognize their characteristic patterns of relating—as well as associated emotional upheavals. But IPT shares two key features in common with our next topic: a focus on making changes in the present and solid research support (see Chapter 5) (Bleiberg & Markowitz, 2008).

## Cognitive-Behavior Therapy

**Cognitive-behavior therapy (CBT)** uses various research-based techniques to help troubled clients learn new ways of thinking, acting, and feeling. The approach contrasts sharply with psychodynamic therapy. CBT encourages collaborative therapist–client relationships, a focus on the present, direct efforts to change problems, and the use of different, empirically supported treatments.

The beginnings of CBT can be traced to John B. Watson's (1878–1958) *behaviorism,* the view that the appropriate focus of psychological study is observable behavior. Watson viewed the therapist as a teacher and the goal of treatment as providing new, more appropriate learning experiences. Early behavior therapists relied heavily on animal learning principles, particularly Pavlov's classical conditioning and Skinner's operant conditioning. Today, CBT incorporates many learning principles based on cognitive psychology. Thus, the term *cognitive-behavior therapy* has largely replaced the older term *behavior therapy.*

Unlike psychoanalysis, CBT is not based on an elaborate theory about human personality. Rather, CBT is a practical approach oriented to changing behavior rather than trying to understand the dynamics of personality. One of the most important aspects of CBT is its embrace of empirical evaluation. Cognitive-behavior therapists have asked, "What works?" in hundreds of treatment outcome studies that use the *experimental method* (see Research Methods, page 62). The answers include a variety of different treatments for different problems.

## Systematic Desensitization

Joseph Wolpe (1915–1997), a South African psychiatrist, developed **systematic desensitization,** a technique for eliminating fears that has three key elements. The first is relaxation training using *progressive muscle relaxation*, a method of inducing a calm state by tightening and then relaxing all the major muscle groups. The second is constructing a *hierarchy of fears* ranging from very mild to very intense, a ranking that allows clients to confront their fears gradually. The third part is the *learning process*, maintaining

The fear is genuine, yet cognitive-behavior therapy shows that gradually confronting anxiety and phobias (exposure) is the key to effective treatment.

relaxation while confronting ever-increasing fears. Wolpe had his clients confront fears in their imagination. Thus, systematic desensitization involves imagining increasingly fearful events while simultaneously maintaining a state of relaxation.

Systematic desensitization has been studied extensively; in fact, the technique can be credited with spurring both cognitive behavior therapy and psychotherapy outcome research in general. Evidence shows that it can be an effective treatment for fears and phobias.

## Other Exposure Therapies

Many factors contribute to effective systematic desensitization, but most investigators agree that *exposure* ultimately is the key to fear reduction: In order to conquer your fears, you must confront them (Barlow, Raffa, & Cohen, 2002). Other exposure therapies include *in vivo desensitization*, gradually confronting fears in real life while simultaneously maintaining a state of relaxation. *Flooding*, in contrast, involves confronting fears at full intensity. Someone who was afraid of heights might be brought to the top of the CN Tower in Toronto (the world's tallest free-standing structure) in a quick and dramatic attempt to extinguish fear.

## Aversion Therapy

The goal in *aversion therapy* is to create, not eliminate, an unpleasant response. The technique is used primarily in treating substance use disorders, such as alcoholism and cigarette smoking. For example, one form of aversion therapy pairs the sight, smell, and taste of alcohol with severe nausea produced artificially by a drug.

Aversion therapy is controversial precisely because of its aversive nature. Moreover, it is not clear whether aversion therapy is effective (Finney & Moos, 2002). Aversion treatments often achieve short-term success, but relapse rates are high. Everyday life offers the substance abuser the opportunity, and perhaps the motivation, to desensitize himself or herself to the classically conditioned responses learned in aversion therapy.

## Contingency Management

*Contingency management* directly changes rewards and punishments for identified behaviors. A *contingency* is the relationship between a behavior and its consequences; contingency management involves changing this relationship. The goal of contingency management is to reward desirable behavior systematically and to extinguish or punish undesirable behavior. In order to achieve this goal, the therapist must control relevant rewards and punishments. Thus, contingency management is used primarily in circumstances where the therapist has considerable direct or indirect control over the environment, such as in institutional settings or when children are brought for treatment by their parents.

Research shows that contingency management successfully changes behavior for diverse problems such as institutionalized

## The Experiment: Does Treatment *Cause* Improvement?

How can researchers discover whether treatment *causes* improved psychological functioning? They must use an **experiment,** the only research method that allows researchers to determine cause and effect. The experiment has four essential features.

The first is a **hypothesis**—the experimenter's prediction about cause and effect. For example, a researcher might predict that in comparison to no treatment at all, cognitive-behavior therapy will reduce symptoms of depression.

The second feature of the experiment is the **independent variable,** a variable controlled and carefully manipulated by the experimenter. The independent variable might be whether patients receive therapy or no treatment at all. People who receive an active treatment belong to the **experimental group.** Those who receive no treatment belong to the **control group.**

The third feature is **random assignment,** ensuring that each participant has a statistically equal chance of receiving different levels of the independent variable. Flipping a coin is one of many ways of randomly assigning participants to experimental or control groups. Random assignment ensures that the members of the experimental and control groups did not differ *before* they began the experiment. If people could choose whether they receive psychotherapy or nontreatment, for example, researchers could not know whether any differences obtained between the groups were caused by the treatment or by characteristics that led people to pick one treatment or no treatment. Random assignment guards against such possibilities.

The fourth feature is the measurement of the **dependent variable,** the outcome that is hypothesized to vary according to manipulations in the independent variable. The outcome *depends* on the experimental manipulation—thus the term *dependent variable.* Symptoms are commonly measured dependent variables in psychotherapy outcome research.

Statistical tests establish whether the independent variable has reliably changed the dependent variable, or whether the outcomes are a result of chance. A finding is considered to be **statistically significant** if it occurs by chance in fewer than 1 out of 20 experiments. That is, the probability of a chance outcome is less than 5 percent, a specification that is often written as $p < 0.05$. A statistically significant **result** is not the same as a *clinically significant* finding. A treatment may cause statistically significant changes in symptoms, but the changes may be too small to be clinically significant, to make a meaningful difference in the patient's life.

Treatments can be studied in experiments, because researchers can randomly assign patients to different therapies. However, completely controlling the independent variable—treatment—is a challenge. Some people drop out of treatment, and others seek additional help outside of the experiment. Therapists might individualize psychotherapy instead of treating everyone the same, or patients might not take a medication being studied. These are only a few of the many ways in which the independent variable can be *confounded* with other factors. Confounds threaten the *internal validity* of an experiment, whether the experiment accurately links changes in the dependent variable to changes in the independent variable. If the independent variable is confounded with other factors, we can no longer accurately determine cause and effect. The confound, not the independent variable, may have changed the dependent variable.

*External validity* refers to whether the findings of an experiment generalize to other circumstances. Experiments require a degree of artificiality in order to maximize internal validity. For example, therapy might last for exactly 10 sessions, and therapists might follow a prescribed script. These rules help protect against confounds, but they can compromise external validity. In the real world, the length and nature of treatment often are tailored to the individual client's needs. Scientists and practitioners can, and often do, raise questions about the external validity of psychotherapy outcome research—whether the findings generalize to the real world.

The ability to demonstrate causation is the powerful, major strength of the experiment. (Recall that in Chapter 2 we introduced the *correlational method* but concluded that correlation does not mean causation.) The major limitation, however, is that many important variables cannot be manipulated practically or ethically in real life. Researchers can randomly assign clients to different treatments, but we cannot, for example, randomly assign children to live with abusive parents to test hypotheses about the consequences of abuse! This is why you must understand the strengths and the limitations of both the correlational and the experimental methods. Psychologists seek to understand cause and effect, but ethical and practical concerns often prohibit researchers from using experiments.

clients with schizophrenia (Paul & Lentz, 1977) and juvenile offenders in group homes (Phillips et al., 1973). However, improvements often do not generalize to real-life situations. A psychologist can set up clear contingencies for a juvenile living in a group home, but it may be impossible to alter the rewards and punishments the teenager encounters when he or she returns to live with a chaotic family or delinquent peers (Emery & Marholin, 1977). Sadly, in the real world a troubled adolescent's positive behavior may be ignored, his undesirable behavior may be rewarded, and punishment can be inconsistent or long delayed.

## Social Skills Training

The goal of *social skills training* is to teach clients new ways of behaving that are both desirable and likely to be rewarded in everyday life. Two commonly taught skills are assertiveness and social problem solving.

The goal of *assertiveness training* is to teach clients to be direct about their feelings and wishes. The training may involve different levels of detail, from learning to make eye contact to asking a boss for a raise. In teaching assertiveness, therapists frequently use *role playing*, an improvisational acting technique that allows clients to rehearse new social skills. Clients try out new ways of acting as the therapist assumes the role of some person in their life. For example, a cognitive-behavior therapist might assume the role of Frances's mother and ask Frances to express some of her frustration to her "mother" during a role play.

*Social problem solving* is a multistep process that has been used to teach children and adults ways to go about solving a variety of life's problems. The first step involves defining the problem in detail, breaking a complex difficulty into smaller, more manageable pieces. "Brainstorming" is the second step. In order to encourage creativity, therapists ask clients to come up with as many alternative solutions as they can imagine—even wild and crazy options—without evaluating these alternatives. The third step involves carefully evaluating these options. Finally, the best solution is chosen and implemented, and its success is evaluated objectively. If the option does not work, the entire process can be repeated until an effective solution is found.

It is difficult to draw general conclusions about the effectiveness of social skills training because the technique has been applied to many specific problems with varying degrees of success. Clients can learn new social skills in therapy, but it is less clear whether these skills are used effectively in real life (Mueser & Bellack, 2007).

## Cognitive Techniques

All the techniques we have discussed so far have foundations in either classical or operant conditioning. Other methods are rooted in cognitive psychology. One example is *attribution retraining*, based on the idea that people are "intuitive scientists" who are constantly drawing conclusions about the causes of events in their lives. These perceived causes, which may or may not be objectively accurate, are called *attributions*. Attribution retraining involves changing attributions, often by asking clients to abandon intuitive strategies. Instead, clients are instructed in more scientific methods, such as objectively testing hypotheses about themselves and others. For example, first-year college students often attribute their "blues" to their own failings. If they carefully observe the reactions of other first-year students, however, they may be persuaded to adopt a more accurate causal explanation: The first year of college can be trying, lonely, and stressful (Wilson & Linville, 1982).

*Self-instruction training* is another cognitive technique that is often used with children. In Meichenbaum's (1977) self-instruction training, the adult first models an appropriate behavior while saying

the self-instruction aloud. Next, the child is asked to repeat the action and also to say the self-instruction aloud. Following this, the child repeats the task while whispering the self-instructions. Finally, the child does the task while repeating the instructions silently. This procedure is designed as a structured way of developing *internalization*, helping children to learn internal controls over their behavior.

## Beck's Cognitive Therapy

CBT has been strongly influenced by the clinical work of Aaron Beck (1976). Beck's **cognitive therapy** was developed specifically as a treatment for depression (Beck et al., 1979). Beck suggested that depression is caused by errors in thinking. These distortions lead depressed people to draw incorrect, negative conclusions about themselves, conclusions that create and maintain depression. Simply put, Beck hypothesized that depressed people see the world through gray-colored glasses (as opposed to the rose-colored variety). According to his analysis, this negative filter makes the world appear much bleaker than it really is.

Beck's cognitive therapy challenges cognitive errors, often by having clients analyze their thoughts more carefully (Beck et al., 1979). For example, a cognitive therapist might ask Frances to keep a record of her various family conflicts, including a brief description of the dispute, her thoughts in the moment, and her feelings that followed. The cognitive therapist might help Frances use this information to challenge her tendency to engage in "black-and-white" (all bad or all good) thinking about her relationships. "Yes, your mother got angry, but does the fact that you didn't meet her expectations really mean that she *hates* you and you are a complete failure and totally worthless?"

## Rational–Emotive Therapy

Albert Ellis's (1913–2007) *rational–emotive therapy (RET)* is also designed to challenge cognitive distortions. According to Ellis (1962), emotional disorders are caused by *irrational beliefs*, absolute, unrealistic views of the world, such as "Everyone must love me all the time." The rational–emotive therapist searches for a client's irrational beliefs, points out the impossibility of fulfilling them, and uses any and every opportunity to persuade the client to adopt more realistic beliefs. Rational–emotive therapy shares concepts and techniques in common with Beck's approach. A major difference, however, is that rational–emotive therapists directly challenge the client's beliefs during therapy (Ellis, 1962). For example, a rational–emotive therapist might strongly challenge Frances's desire to make her mother happy with a sharp comment like, "That's impossible! That's irrational!"

### "Third-Wave" CBT

Recent years have witnessed a "third wave" of CBT, following the first wave (based on operant and classical conditioning), and the second (cognitive therapies; Hayes, 2004). Third-wave CBT treatments focus on broad, abstract principles such as acceptance, mindfulness, values, and relationships (Herbert & Forman, 2011). For example, *dialectical behavior therapy*, a treatment for borderline personality disorder (see Chapter 9), includes an emphasis on "mindfulness," increased awareness of your feelings, thoughts, and motivations (Linehan, 1993). *Acceptance and commitment therapy*, a values-oriented approach used in treating a variety of disorders and problems, encourages accepting oneself, not just on making changes (Hayes, 2004). Empirical support is not as strong for third-wave CBT as it is for other forms of CBT, but importantly, the treatments are being evaluated systematically (Öst, 2008).

## Humanistic Therapies

**Humanistic psychotherapy** developed as a "third force" in psychotherapy, a counterpoint to both psychodynamic and cognitive-behavior therapy. Humanistic psychologists see both approaches as ignoring what is most essential about being human: making choices and shaping our own future. To be human is to be responsible for your own life—and for finding meaning in it. From this perspective, therapy cannot solve problems for you. Therapy can help you to solve only your own problems, to make better choices in your life (Rogers, 1951).

The key to making better choices is increased *emotional awareness*. Humanistic therapists encourage people to recognize and experience their true feelings. Like psychodynamic therapy, this involves "uncovering" hidden emotions; thus, both treatments strive to promote insight. Yet, humanistic therapists are more concerned with how people feel rather than why they are feeling that way. And like CBT, humanistic therapy focuses on the present.

Humanistic therapy is also distinguished by its emphasis on the therapist–client relationship. CBT and psychodynamic therapy see the therapy relationship as important to making the real treatment—insight or behavior change—more effective. In humanistic therapy, the relationship *is* the treatment.

### Client-Centered Therapy

Carl Rogers (1902–1987) and his **client-centered therapy** epitomize this focus on the therapy relationship. Rogers (1951) took a strong stand and argued that three qualities were *necessary and sufficient* for therapeutic change: warmth, genuineness, and particularly **empathy,** emotional understanding. Empathy involves putting yourself in someone else's shoes and conveying your understanding of that person's feelings and perspectives. Therapists show empathy by reflecting their client's feelings and, at a deeper level, by anticipating emotions their clients have not yet expressed.

Rogers also encouraged appropriate therapist *self-disclosure*, revealing some personal feelings and experiences as a way of helping clients to better understand themselves. And because emotional understanding can grow out of many life experiences, Rogers felt that client-centered therapists need not always be professionals. They could be ordinary people who had faced life difficulties similar to those of their clients.

Client-centered therapists demonstrate *unconditional positive regard*, valuing clients for who they are and not judging them. Client-centered therapists also are *nondirective*. Rogers believed that, if clients can experience and accept themselves, they will be able to resolve their own problems.

### A Means, Not an End?

Few *outcome* research studies address whether humanistic therapy effectively changes abnormal behavior. Still, Rogers and his colleagues were committed to psychotherapy *process* research. Process research shows that the **therapeutic alliance** or bond between a therapist and client is crucial to the success of therapy (Baldwin, Wampold, & Imel, 2007). A therapist's caring, concern, and respect for the individual are important to the success of *all* psychological (and medical) treatments. As for humanistic therapy alone, the approach is perhaps best viewed as a way to gain emotional understanding, not as a treatment for specific mental disorders (Pascual-Leone & Greenberg, 2007).

Social support is vital in all kinds of relationships, including feeling supported by your therapist.

**TABLE 3.3**

## Therapies That May Harm

| Name | Brief Description | Potential Harm |
|---|---|---|
| Critical incident stress debriefing | "Processing" trauma soon after the experience | Increased risk for posttraumatic stress symptoms |
| Scared straight | Seasoned inmates scare youth about consequences of criminality | Increased conduct problems |
| Facilitated communication | Facillitator helps impaired individual type on keyboard | False accusations of child abuse |
| Rebirthing therapy | Wrapped tightly in sheets while group resists struggle to be "reborn" | Physical injury, death |
| Recovered memories | Encouragement to "recover" memories of trauma | Creation of false memories |
| Boot camps | Delinquent youth sent to military style camp | Increased conduct problems |
| DARE programs | Preadolescent children educated about danger of drugs | Increased substance use |

*Source*: Adapted from S. O. Lilionfeld, 2007, "Psychological Treatments That Cause Harm," *Perspectives on Psychological Science, 2*, 53–70.

## Research on Psychotherapy

Some people claim not to "believe" in psychotherapy. Is their skepticism well founded? Does psychotherapy work? And if therapy is helpful, what approach works best?

Researchers sometimes disagree, perhaps vehemently, about the answers to these questions. Based on the evidence we discuss in the following sections, however, we reach four major conclusions about psychotherapy. First, psychotherapy *does* work—for many but not all people and problems. Second, successful psychotherapies share key "active ingredients," for example, a strong therapeutic alliance. Third, different treatments are more or less effective for different disorders. Fourth, some "treatments" are complete shams that not only do not help but may well harm (Castonguay et al., 2010; see Critical Thinking Matters on page 66 and Table 3.3).

### Does Psychotherapy Work?

*Psychotherapy outcome research* examines the outcome, or result, of psychotherapy—its effectiveness for relieving symptoms,

eliminating disorders, and/or improving life functioning. Hundreds of studies have compared the outcome of psychotherapy with alternative treatments or with no treatment at all. In order to summarize findings across all of these studies, psychologists often use a statistical technique called **meta-analysis,** a statistical procedure that allows researchers to combine the results from different studies in a standardized way. Meta-analysis creates a common currency for research findings, similar to converting euros, yen, rubles, yuan, and so on into dollar amounts.

Meta-analysis indicates that the average benefit of psychotherapy is 0.85 standard deviation units (Smith & Glass, 1977). We describe the mathematical meaning of the *standard deviation* in Research Methods in Chapter 15. For now, you should know that the statistic means that the average therapy client is better off than 80 percent of untreated people (see Figure 3.1). By comparison, nine months of reading instruction leads to a 0.67 standard deviation unit increase in reading achievement among elementary schoolchildren. Chemotherapy has about a 0.10 effect size in reducing mortality following breast cancer (Lipsey & Wilson, 1993).

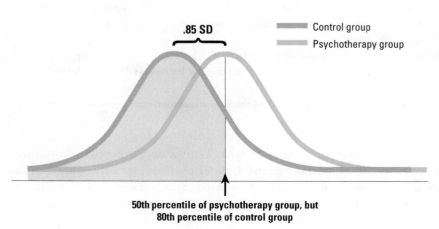

.85 SD

Control group
Psychotherapy group

50th percentile of psychotherapy group, but
80th percentile of control group

**FIGURE 3.1**

On average, psychotherapy produces .85 standard deviation units of change. This means that the average client who receives therapy (vertical line) functions better than 80 percent of untreated controls (shaded area).
*Source*: Adapted from M. L. Smith, G. V. Glass, and T. I. Miller, 1980, *The Benefits of Psychotherapy*, Baltimore: Johns Hopkins University Press.

# CRITICAL THINKING matters

## Are All Therapies Created Equal?

Research demonstrates that, in general, psychotherapy "works." Evidence also shows that different approaches to therapy share "active ingredients" that contribute to their success. Does this mean that all therapies are equally effective? No way!

Contemporary research shows that specific treatments are more or less effective for specific disorders (DeRubeis, Brotman, & Gibbons, 2005; Nathan & Gorman, 2007). Because of this, we strongly believe that therapists are ethically obligated to inform their clients about the effectiveness of alternative treatments. We also believe that there is a long list of "therapies" that professionals should *never* offer as a treatment for *any* emotional problem.

Many so-called treatments are, to be blunt, hoaxes. The list of phony therapies has grown in recent years, as susceptible members of the public seem to have lost faith in science and instead placed their hopes in "alternative" therapies. The problem has led several scientifically minded psychologists to debunk various fake therapies (e.g., Lilienfeld, Lynn, & Lohr, 2003; Singer & Lalich, 1996). Among the most dubious of treatments are:

- "Rebirthing therapy," a technique that purports to free people from deep-seated emotional problems by teaching them to breathe using their diaphragm instead of their chest.
- "Primal therapy," where patients overcome the trauma of their own birth by learning the appropriate way to scream and thereby release destructive emotions.
- "Attunement-enhancing, shame-reducing, attachment therapy," which involves holding a child firmly and encouraging her rage and despair, as a way of getting the child to talk about trauma.
- "Alien abduction therapy," which helps people to cope with the various mental disorders caused by being abducted by aliens. (We're not making this up!)
- "Facilitated communication," a technique in which a facilitator helps someone with impaired communication to speak by "assisting" his or her typing on a keyboard.

We hope that these treatments strike you as completely outlandish. They are. To see just how far some "experts" are willing to go with their outrageous claims, you might do a Web search on these and other "alternative" therapies.

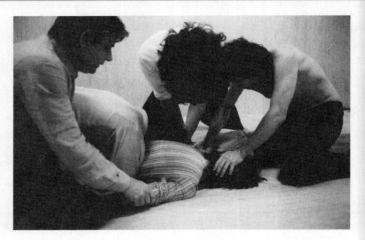

A primal therapy session, one of many "treatments" debunked by psychological scientis

The treatments may seem silly, but they have a very serious effect. The desperation of people suffering from mental disorders, and their loved ones, can lead them to be duped into trying sham treatments—and to perhaps miss out on legitimate ones. For example, facilitated communication was so widely promoted as a treatment for autism in the 1990s that legitimate scientists, and a panel of experts appointed by the American Psychological Association, had to spend valuable time proving that the technique does *not* work. We detail this troubling story in Chapter 15, but here's a hint how it works: Ever heard of the Ouija board?

Scientists cannot debunk every hare-brained idea offered by misguided or deceptive "therapists," nor should they have to. The burden of proof in science falls on the shoulders of anyone who claims that alien abductions cause mental disorders (or any other hypothesis). Until a hypothesis is proven true, scientists are skeptics. And proof requires objective, replicable evidence—not testimonials.

Outlandish therapies—and seemingly legitimate but ineffective treatments—would cause fewer problems if two things happened. First, mental health professions need to take a strong stand and endorse clear standards of care for treating various mental disorders. Second, the public—you—need to think critically. Hone your inquiring skepticism. Don't be duped by self-anointed experts or sensational media stories, however believable they may seem.

---

**IMPROVEMENT WITHOUT TREATMENT?** Another widely accepted statistic is that about two-thirds of clients improve as a result of psychotherapy. This statistic raises two questions. First, how many people would change anyway without treatment? Second, what can we do for people who do not respond to therapy? In later chapters, we offer different answers to the second question. Some disorders respond better to therapy, some to medication; others are difficult to treat with any known approach. But we need to answer the first question now.

Some skeptics have suggested that a high percentage of emotional disorders show *spontaneous remission*, they improve without any treatment at all. British psychologist Hans Eysenck (1916–1997) famously concluded that psychotherapy was totally ineffective for this very reason. Eysenck (1952/1992) agreed that therapy helps about two out of three people. The problem, he claimed, is that two-thirds of people also improve *without* treatment.

Was Eysenck right? This simple question turns out to be not so easy to answer. Consider a basic experiment. Clients seeking therapy are randomly assigned to receive either psychotherapy or no treatment at all. People in the *no-treatment control group* might be put on a waiting list, with the promise that they will receive therapy in the future. But people on a waiting list are likely to seek counseling and advice from family members, friends, religious leaders, or maybe a different professional. If we find their problems improved six months later, is this spontaneous remission or a result of *informal* psychological help?

Informal counseling often is helpful, as you surely know from your own life experiences. In fact, researchers have found that as many as one-half of people seeking psychotherapy improve as a result of simply having unstructured conversations with a professional (Lambert & Bergin, 1994). Thus, some experts argue that so-called no-treatment controls actually receive some form of treatment. Others assert that "just talking" is hardly psychotherapy. Should we consider informal counseling to be part of psychotherapy, or is "just talking" merely a placebo?

**THE PLACEBO EFFECT** In medicine, *placebos* are pills that are pharmacologically inert; they have no medicinal value. More broadly, placebos are any treatment that contains no known active ingredients. But the absence of active ingredients does not prevent placebos from healing. The **placebo effect,** the powerful healing produced by inert treatments, has been documented widely in psychotherapy, psychopharmacology, dentistry, optometry, cardiovascular disease, cancer treatment, and even surgery (Baskin et al., 2003). The recipient's belief in a treatment, and expectation of improvement, is responsible for much of what works in psychological—and physical—treatments. Consider this: About half of internal medicine physicians report prescribing placebos (usually vitamins or over-the-counter pain relievers) regularly to their patients (Tilburt et al., 2008). A recent study found that full-price placebos (costing $2.50 per pill) produced significantly more pain relief than "discount" placebos (costing 10¢ per pill) (Waber et al., 2008).

Some view the placebo effect as a mere nuisance. This is understandable, because our goal is to identify *active ingredients*—treatments that are more than placebos (Baskin et al., 2003). But we can also view the placebo effect as a treatment—one that

heals psychologically. Of course, psychotherapy also heals psychologically. Viewed in this light, the placebo effect is something to study, not dismiss. Ironically, psychotherapy research must identify the "active ingredients" in placebos! In fact, a recent study showed that the passage of time (spontaneous remission), a healing ritual (acupuncture in this study), and the therapist–client relationship all contributed to heightening the placebo effect. The most effective placebo contained all three "active ingredients" (Kaptchuk et al., 2008). Neuroscientists have found that placebos actually decrease the brain's response to pain; the placebo effect produces real changes in experience, not just decreased reporting of pain (Wager, 2005). We need to understand the placebo effect, as well as devise treatments to surpass it.

**PLACEBO CONTROL GROUPS** In order to identify active ingredients *beyond* the placebo effect, medical investigators routinely include placebo control groups in their studies—patients intentionally are given treatments that contain no active ingredients, for example, sugar pills. But there is another complication: The doctor's expectations also can influence a treatment's effectiveness. To control for this second effect, scientists use *double-blind studies*, investigations where neither the physician nor the patient knows whether the pill is real or a placebo.

Unfortunately, there is no way to construct a double-blind study of psychotherapy. You can disguise a pill, but you cannot disguise psychotherapy. Therapists know when a treatment is the real thing or a placebo—"just talk." Does this matter? Yes. Research shows that a therapist's "allegiance" to one form of therapy or another has a powerful influence on whether it is effective (see The Allegiance Effect on p. 68).

Because it is impossible to conduct double-blind studies, more and more psychotherapy research is involving competitions between rival "teams" of therapists, each believing in their own, unique treatment (Klein, 1999). This does not eliminate the placebo effect, but it hopefully makes the placebo effect similar for the rival treatments.

After all of these considerations, what is our "bottom line" about improvement without treatment? Our best estimate is that about one-third of people improve without treatment. Thus, psychotherapy does, indeed, work.

**EFFICACY AND EFFECTIVENESS** Tightly controlled experiments provide important information about the *efficacy* of psychotherapy, that is, whether the treatment *can* work under prescribed circumstances. However, such studies provide little information about the *effectiveness* of the treatment— whether the therapy *does* work in the real world. In the real world, therapies are not assigned at random; therapists vary the type and length of treatment, and clients commonly have multiple problems (Weston, Novotny, & Thompson-Brenner, 2004). How does psychotherapy fare under these circumstances?

## The Allegiance Effect

The **allegiance effect** is the tendency of researchers to find that their favorite treatment—the one to which they hold allegiance—is most effective (Luborsky et al., 1999). In comparing psychodynamic therapy and cognitive-behavior therapy, for example, researchers allied with cognitive-behavior therapy tend to find *that* treatment to be more effective. In contrast, researchers allied with psychodynamic therapy, tend to find *that* treatment to be more effective. In fact, one meta-analysis of 29 studies (Luborsky et al., 1999) found that 69 percent of the variance in the effectiveness of one treatment over another was explained by allegiance effects.

What causes allegiance effects? In discussing the double-blind study, we already suggested one influence: a therapist's expectations contribute to a treatment's effectiveness. Other, less subtle influences also contribute to the allegiance effect (Luborsky et al., 1999). When designing a study, researchers probably pick a weak alternative treatment. This may or may not be intentional, but investigators, of course, want their preferred approach to "win."

Another contribution may be that investigators are more likely to publish research papers when their findings are consistent with their hypotheses (Luborsky et al., 1999). For example, a researcher allied with psychodynamic therapy might quickly publish findings demonstrating the superiority of that treatment but be more reluctant to publish results favoring cognitive-behavior therapy! This is called the *file drawer problem*. We know the results of published studies; we can only guess about the results of research sitting in someone's file drawer. The file drawer problem is not necessarily deliberate. Instead, researchers may be genuinely puzzled by, or just not believe, results that contradict their hypotheses.

Finally, sometimes allegiance may not *cause* biased results, but instead be an *effect* of convincing findings (Leykin & DeRubeis, 2009). Researchers may ally with the treatment they find to be most effective! We would be delighted if this circumstance fully explained the allegiance effect, but we doubt that this is so.

---

Studies on the effectiveness of psychotherapy attempt to answer this question. For example, the magazine *Consumer Reports* (1995, November) surveyed nearly 3,000 readers who had seen a mental health professional in the past three years, and the respondents generally rated psychotherapy highly. Among the major findings:

- Of the 426 people who were feeling "very poor" at the beginning of treatment, 87 percent reported feeling "very good," "good," or at least "so-so" when they were surveyed.

- Clients of psychologists, psychiatrists, and social workers reported no differences in treatment outcome, but all three professions were rated more effective than marriage counselors.

- People who received psychotherapy alone reported no more or less improvement than people who received psychotherapy plus medication (Seligman, 1995).

Because the *Consumer Reports* study was correlational, we cannot draw conclusions about causation. For example, perhaps people who had good experiences in therapy were more likely to complete the survey than were people who had bad experiences. Still, like other research, the *Consumer Reports* study suggests that psychotherapy helps many people in the real world, not just in the laboratory.

**WHEN DOES PSYCHOTHERAPY WORK?** What predicts when psychotherapy is more or less likely to be effective? The most important predictor is the nature of a client's problems—the diagnosis. For this reason, we discuss research on specific treatments for specific disorders in every chapter throughout the text. Here, we consider two of the many other predictors of treatment outcome: the length of treatment and the client's background characteristics.

If therapy is going to be effective, it usually works pretty fast. As Figure 3.2 indicates, improvement is greatest in the first several months of treatment (Howard et al., 1986). Improvement continues with long-term therapy, but at a notably slower rate (Baldwin et al., 2009). Unfortunately, the average client sees a therapist for only about five sessions, because so many people drop out of treatment early (Hansen, Lambert, & Forman, 2002). Also unfortunately, many benefits of psychotherapy diminish in the year or two after treatment ends (Westen & Bradley, 2005). These findings suggest that we may need a new, "family doctor" model of therapy where brief, intensive treatment is followed up by expected returns for treatment as needed.

Clients' background characteristics also predict outcome in psychotherapy. The acronym YAVIS was coined to indicate that clients improve more in psychotherapy when they are "young, attractive, verbal, intelligent, and successful." This finding has caused considerable concern, for it seems to indicate that psychotherapy works best for the most advantaged members of our society. Another concern is that men are considerably less likely than women to seek therapy. The masculine role seems to discourage appropriate help seeking (Addis & Mahalik, 2003).

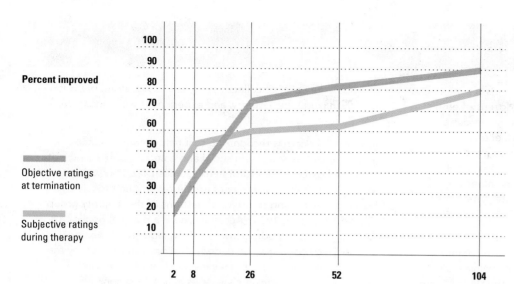

**FIGURE 3.2**

**Improvement as a Function of Number of Psychotherapy Sessions** Most improvement occurs early in psychotherapy, suggesting that relatively short-term treatments are effective and cost effective, too.

*Source:* From K. J. Howard, S. M. Kopta, M. S. Krause, and D. E. Orlinsky, 1986, "The Dose-Effect Relationship in Psychotherapy," *American Psychologist, 41*, 159–164. Copyright © 1986 by American Psychological Association. Reprinted by permission.

## Psychotherapy Process Research

How does psychotherapy work? This is the question asked by *psychotherapy process research*, an approach that examines what aspects of the therapist–client interaction account for better outcomes (Doss, 2004; Kazdin, 2008; Norcross & Hill, 2004).

**COMMON FACTORS** Some important process research has compared psychodynamic, cognitive-behavioral, and humanistic psychotherapy. Do these different psychotherapies share *common factors* that help make them effective?

Yes, according to a classic study by Sloane and colleagues (1975). Ninety patients with moderate anxiety, depression, or similar problems were assigned at random to either psychodynamic psychotherapy, behavior therapy, or no treatment. The study used six therapists, all highly experienced in their preferred form of treatment. Both treatments lasted for an average of 14 sessions. To ensure that the treatments were offered as planned, the differences between the two therapies were clearly defined (see Table 3.4), and tape recordings of the fifth sessions were coded so the actual treatments could be compared.

The two therapies clearly differed. Behavior therapists talked about as often as their clients, gave specific advice, and directed much of the therapy. Psychodynamic therapists talked only one-third as often as their clients, refused to answer specific questions, and followed their clients' lead. Psychodynamic therapists focused on feelings, their underlying causes, and techniques such

---

**TABLE 3.4**
## Definitions of Psychotherapy and Behavior Therapy

| Technique | Psychotherapy | Behavior Therapy |
|---|---|---|
| Specific advice | Given infrequently | Given frequently |
| Transference interpretation | May be given | Avoided |
| Resistance interpretation | Used | Not used |
| Dreams | Interested and encouraged | Disinterested |
| Level of anxiety | Maintained when possible | Diminished when possible |
| Relaxation training | Only indirect | Directly undertaken |
| Desensitization | Only indirect | Directly undertaken |
| Assertion training | Indirectly encouraged | Directly encouraged |
| Report of symptoms | Discouraged | Encouraged |
| Childhood memories | Explored | Historical interest only |

*Source:* "Differences in Technique in Behavior Therapy and Psychotherapy," as adapted from R. B. Sloane, F. R. Staples, A. H. Cristo, N. J. Yorkston, and K. Whipple, 1975, *Psychotherapy versus Behavior Therapy*, Cambridge, MA: Harvard University Press, 237–240.

Treating people from diverse backgrounds is a major challenge for psychologists. Among the dozens of ethnic groups in the United States, the most numerous are African Americans, Latinos, Asian Americans, and Native Americans. In fact, over 25 percent of Americans today are ethnic minorities, and minorities will outnumber whites by the middle of the twenty-first century. Despite the numbers, mainstream psychotherapy does not adequately meet their needs (Lopez, Barrio, Kopelowicz, & Vega, 2012; Snowden, 2012; Sue, Cheng, Saad, & Chu, 2012).

Mental health professionals must recognize both commonalities and diversity in the values and experiences of ethnic minorities. For example, most immigrants came to the United States voluntarily; Native Americans, however, were driven from their homeland and confined to reservations. African Americans share a common history of racism but differ widely based on socioeconomic status, religion, and region of upbringing. Latinos share the Spanish language but may be black or white and have diverse origins in Mexico, the Caribbean, and Central and South America. Asian Americans share some cultural traditions, for example, the value of collectivism over individualism, but differ greatly in language, country, and experiences with industrialization (Surgeon General, 2001).

A second concern is recognizing that many problems faced by ethnic minorities stem from social and cultural experiences, not individual psychological problems (Comas-Diaz, 2000). All ethnic minorities face the challenge of acculturation, the process of learning or adopting the cultural patterns of the majority group (Casas, 1995; Sue, 1998). Acculturation is a political goal of the American "melting pot." However, language, ethnic values, and social customs may be undermined or even derided by the majority culture. African Americans and Native Americans have faced particularly difficult challenges in acculturation.

Acculturation challenges *ethnic identity*, minority members' understanding of self in terms of their own culture. Atkinson, Morten, and Sue (1993) proposed a five-stage model of the development of ethnic identity: (1) conformity, a time of self-deprecation and discrimination; (2) dissonance, a period of conflict between self-deprecation and appreciation of one's ethnicity; (3) resistance and immersion, a stage of self-appreciation and ethnocentrism, accompanied by depreciation of the majority group; (4) introspection, a phase of questioning the basis of self-appreciation, as well as the basis for depreciation of the majority group; and (5) synergetic articulation and awareness, including both self-appreciation and appreciation of the basis for majority group values.

Researchers have infrequently studied this model of ethnic identity development, but it provides a helpful framework for understanding struggles with acculturation (Casas, 1995).

Some evidence suggests that psychotherapy may be more effective when client and therapist share a similar cultural background and when the treatment is tailored to the specific culture (Hwang, 2006; Leong, 2007). Therapy also may be more effective when therapists are trained to be sensitive to minority issues (Hall, 2001; Parks, 2003). What is most clear, however, is the need to adapt psychotherapy to meet the unique needs of ethnic minority group members.

Therapy may be more effective when the client and therapist share a similar cultural background.

as free association. Behavior therapists focused on specific behaviors, ways of changing them, and techniques such as systematic desensitization.

Did the very different treatments share anything in common? Perhaps more than you would expect. For example, behavior therapists and psychodynamic therapists offered the same number of interpretations. Clients' ratings of therapist warmth, empathy, and genuineness predicted successful outcome in both treatments. Clients rated the therapy relationship as the single most important aspect of both therapies (Sloane et al., 1975). Plus, this classic study is *not* dated. A recent, major study also concluded that common factors—improved self-understanding and coping skills—account for much change in both CBT and psychodynamic therapy (Gibbons et al., 2009). Much of the effectiveness of different psychotherapies is explained by common factors (Baardseth et al.,

2013; Wampold, 2007). Consider this analogy: Basketball and soccer differ greatly, but participating in some sport, any sport, is more important for your health than the particular activity. The common factor? Exercise.

*Motivational interviewing* is a contemporary example of the importance of common factors. Now viewed as an evidence-based treatment, motivational interviewing originally was designed as a placebo to compare against a theoretically "real" treatment for alcohol abuse (behavior therapy). But the therapeutic relationship proved to be a far better predictor of reduced, future drinking for both treatments. Initial and subsequent research showed that the motivational interviewing "placebo" was an effective treatment! In fact, the "placebo" contains active ingredients including empathy, instilling interpersonal spirit, and eliciting promises of change (Miller & Rose, 2009).

**THERAPY AS SOCIAL SUPPORT** A positive therapist–client relationship predicts positive outcomes across approaches to treatment (Baldwin et al., 2007; see Table 3.5). Yet, a supportive relationship is not defined simply by a therapist's behavior but by a therapist's behavior in relation to a particular client. Some people, perhaps most, feel understood when a therapist makes empathic statements; others are more comfortable with a more reserved therapist. In fact, members of different ethnic and cultural groups may be more comfortable with less emotional expressiveness. Asians and Asian Americans, for example, often feel *more* supported when asked to disclose less distress (Kim et al., 2008). Social support is a key ingredient in therapy, but warmth, empathy, and genuineness are more subtle than saying, "I feel your pain."

**THERAPY AS SOCIAL INFLUENCE** Psychotherapy is a process of social influence, as well as social support. Even Carl Rogers, the advocate of nondirective therapy, directed his clients. Audiotapes indicate that Rogers empathized more with certain types of statements (Truax & Carkhuff, 1967). He responded to his clients conditionally and thereby directed therapy subtly.

Jerome Frank (1909–2005), an American trained both in psychology and psychiatry, argued that, in fact, psychotherapy is a process of persuasion—persuading clients to make beneficial changes in their emotional life. Frank (1973) highlighted a gentle aspect of persuasion in therapy—instilling hope. People seek professional help when they have been unable to solve their own problems, when they have lost hope. Frank saw therapy as a chance to instill hope and help people to make the changes they have been struggling to make (Frank, 1973).

Process research demonstrates other aspects of the therapist's influence. For example, clients tend to adopt beliefs similar to those of their therapists. In fact, treatment is more effective when this happens (Beutler et al., 1991; Kelly, 1990). Positive outcomes are more likely when the new beliefs relate directly to psychotherapy, not personal values—for example, it is important to express emotions (Beutler, Machado, & Neufeldt, 1994).

Still, recognition of therapists' influence raises questions about values in psychotherapy. Psychotherapy is not value free. There are values inherent in the nature of therapy itself—for example, talking is good. Moreover, the values of individual therapists about such topics as love, marriage, work, and family can influence clients. Psychotherapists cannot transcend their own beliefs and values. All we can do is recognize our biases and inform our clients about them.

**PAIN RELIEF?** The desire for pain relief—relief from psychological pain—motivates many people to seek psychological

---

**TABLE 3.5**
## Common Factors in Effective Brief Psychotherapies

1. Treatment is offered soon after the problem is identified.

2. Assessment of the problem is rapid and occurs early in treatment.

3. A therapeutic alliance is established quickly, and it is used to encourage change in the client.

4. Therapy is designed to be time limited, and the therapist uses this to encourage rapid progress.

5. The goals of therapy are limited to a few specified areas.

6. The therapist is directive in managing the treatment sessions.

7. Therapy is focused on a specific theme.

8. The client is encouraged to express strong emotions or troubling experiences.

9. A flexible approach is taken in the choice of treatment techniques.

*Source:* Adapted from M. P. Koss and J. M. Butcher, 1986, "Research on Brief Psychotherapy," in S. L. Garfield and A. E. Bergin, Eds., *Handbook of Psychotherapy and Behavior Change*, 3rd ed, New York: Wiley, 627–670.

*"You haven't a clue what I'm talking about, do you?"*

© Jack Ziegler/The New Yorker Collection/www.cartoonbank.com

help. In our language, we regularly draw analogies between emotional and physical pain. We talk about "hurt feelings" or "the stabbing wound of rejection." Neuroscience research increasingly shows that such references are more than an analogy. The same regions of the brain are involved in the experience of both physical and psychological pain (MacDonald & Leary, 2005; Panksepp, 2005). Oral pain relievers—acetaminophen—reduce these neural responses (DeWall et al., 2010). We expect that common factors such as empathy also relieve psychological pain, a central benefit across different approaches to psychotherapy. Of course, we also know psychotherapy is more effective when it contains "active ingredients" for treating a specific disorder, especially when the problem is severe (Stevens, Hynan, & Allen, 2000).

## Couple, Family, and Group Therapy

Medication and psychotherapy treat problems by changing the individual. Consistent with a systems perspective, professionals also can treat individual problems by changing social circumstances, particularly for children (Kazak et al., 2010). Consider the case of Frances. Medication or therapy might improve her troubled family relationships, but improving her relationships with her parents and husband also might alleviate Frances's depression. Some would argue, in fact, that Frances became depressed precisely because of the roles women play in families and in society. We briefly consider treatments for couples and families, group therapy, and efforts at preventing emotional disorders through social change.

### Couple Therapy

**Couple therapy** involves seeing intimate partners together in therapy. This approach is sometimes called *marital therapy* or *marriage counseling*, but a range of partners may seek treatment together. Dating pairs, prospective mates, live-in partners, and gay and lesbian couples (who cannot marry in some places) also may seek couple therapy.

The goal of couple therapy typically is to improve the relationship, not the individual. In treating relationships, all couple therapists focus on resolving conflicts and promoting mutual satisfaction. Couple therapists do not tell their clients what compromises they should accept or how they should change their relationship. Instead, they typically help partners improve their *communication* and *negotiation* skills (Emery, 2011; Gurman & Jacobson, 2002; Jacobson & Christensen, 1996).

How does this work? A couple therapist might suggest that Frances had a problem with "mind reading" in her marriage. Without ever telling him, Frances might expect her husband to know what she wants. She might want more attention, but she never asks for it—she wants him to "figure it out for himself." A couple therapist would point out that no one can read another person's mind; instead, partners need to communicate their wishes directly (Gottman, 1997). This may sound simple, but learning to be direct can be tricky for many people. Frances may feel selfish when making requests, or perhaps she wants to be "surprised" with her husband's attention. She may think that his attention is less meaningful if she asks for it.

Another component of most couple therapies is negotiation or *conflict resolution*. Negotiation is the art of give and take. Effective negotiation defines problems clearly, considers a wide range of solutions, uncovers hidden agendas (unstated concerns), and experiments with alternative solutions. These strategies are similar to the social problem-solving model discussed earlier, an approach that has been effectively applied to couples (Emery, 2011). Politeness also is an essential component of effective negotiation, and setting clear ground rules can facilitate polite communication. Examples of ground rules include not raising your voice, not interrupting the other person, and speaking about your *own* feelings—not telling your partner how he or she feels (Emery, 2011; Gottman et al., 1976).

Research shows that couple therapy can improve satisfaction in marriages (Baucom & Epstein, 1990; Gurman & Jacobson, 2002). However, questions remain about the long-term effectiveness of couple therapy, the efficacy of alternative approaches, and the values of couple therapy for gender, marriages, individuals, and society (Alexander, Holtzworth-Munroe, & Jameson, 1994).

Couple therapy also may be used in treating specific disorders, including depression, anxiety, substance abuse, and child behavior problems. Couple therapy in these circumstances is typically either a supplement or an alternative to individual therapy. Couple therapy, alone or combined with individual treatment, often is more effective than individual therapy alone (Beach,

Family therapists attempt to improve mental health by altering family relationships.

Sandeen, & O'Leary, 1990; Jacobson, Holtzworth-Munroe, & Schmaling, 1989).

## Family Therapy

**Family therapy** might include two, three, or more family members in a treatment designed to improve communication, negotiate conflicts, and perhaps change relationships and roles. Like couple therapy, family therapy has the goal of improving relationships. Some forms of family therapy also focus on resolving specific conflicts, such as disputes between adolescents and their parents. *Parent management training* is an approach that teaches parents new skills for rearing troubled children (Patterson, 1982). Other types of family therapy are designed to educate families about how best to cope with the serious psychopathology of one family member.

There are many different styles of family therapy, but most share an emphasis on systems theory, viewing the individual within the family system (Gurman & Jacobson, 2002). For example, a family therapists may call attention to the pattern of *alliances* among family members. In well-functioning families, the primary alliance is between the two parents, even when the parents do not live together. In contrast, dysfunctional families often have alliances that cross generations—"teams" that include one parent and some or all of the children opposing the other parent or another child. Like a poorly organized business, families function inadequately when their leaders fail to cooperate. Thus, a common goal in family therapy is to strengthen the alliance between the parents, to get parents to work together and not against each other (Emery, 1992).

## Group Therapy

**Group therapy** involves treating several people facing similar emotional problems or life issues. Therapy groups may be as small as three or four people or as large as 20 or more. Group therapy has numerous variations and targets for treatment, and here we can highlight only a few facets of the group approach.

*Psychoeducational groups* teach specific psychological information or life skills. The term *psychoeducational* aptly conveys that teaching is the primary mode of treatment. Of course, the content of the "course" is psychological. For example, group might teach assertiveness to shy people, or how to cope with threats to body image to at risk college students.

There are two basic reasons for offering therapy in groups: less expense and social support. Many people with psychological problems feel isolated, alone, and "weird." Learning that you are not alone can be a powerful experience that is one of the unique "active ingredients" in group therapy.

In *experiential group therapy*, relationships are the primary mode of treatment. Group members might be encouraged to look beyond one another's "façades"—to reveal secrets about themselves or otherwise to break down the barriers that we all erect in relationships. Experiential groups typically include members who are well functioning and who view the group as an opportunity for personal growth. Little research has been conducted on their effectiveness.

*Self-help groups* bring together people who face a common problem and who seek to help themselves and each other by sharing information and experiences. Self-help groups are very popular—including Internet-based groups (Taylor & Luce,

Can suicide be prevented? Telephone hotlines, crisis centers, and public education are intended to help prevent psychological problems and their sometimes tragic consequences.

2003). The potential organizing topics are as numerous as the problems life throws at us. Technically, self-help groups are not therapy groups, because a professional does not lead them. If there is a leader, it may be someone who already has faced the particular problem, perhaps a former group member.

## Prevention

Social influences on psychopathology extend far beyond interpersonal relationships. Social institutions, school, and work environments are important contributors to mental health, as are such broad societal concerns as poverty, racism, and sexism. *Community psychology* is one approach within clinical psychology that attempts to improve individual well-being by promoting social change (Wandersman & Florin, 2003).

The concept of prevention is an important consideration in promoting social change. Community psychologists often distinguish among three levels. *Primary prevention* tries to improve the environment in order to prevent new cases of a mental disorder from developing. The goal is to promote wellness, not just treat illness. Efforts range from offering prenatal care to pregnant women to teaching schoolchildren about the dangers of drug abuse.

*Secondary prevention* focuses on the early detection of emotional problems in the hope of preventing them from becoming more serious. The screening of "at-risk" schoolchildren is one

example. Crisis centers and hotlines are other attempts to detect and treat problems before they become more serious.

Finally, *tertiary prevention* may involve any of the treatments discussed in this chapter, because the intervention occurs after the illness has been identified. In addition to providing treatment, however, tertiary prevention also addresses some of the adverse, indirect consequences of mental illness. Helping the chronically mentally ill to find adequate housing and employment is an example of tertiary prevention.

No one can doubt the importance of prevention, whether directed toward biological, psychological, or social causes of abnormal behavior. Unfortunately, many prevention efforts face an insurmountable obstacle: We simply do not know the specific cause of most psychological disorders. Prevention efforts directed at broader social change face another obstacle that also seems insurmountable at times. Social problems like poverty, racism, and sexism defy easy remedies.

## Specific Treatments for Specific Disorders

Psychotherapy began with treatments based solely in theory and case studies. It progressed as researchers documented the superiority of psychotherapy over no treatment at all. Contemporary researchers are advancing knowledge by studying factors common to all therapies. The ultimate goal, however, is to identify therapies that have specific active ingredients for treating specific disorders (Nathan & Gorman, 2007). Consistent with this goal, in subsequent chapters we discuss only treatments that either are promising or have proved to be effective for alleviating the symptoms of the disorder at hand.

We strongly believe that mental health professionals must inform their clients about evidence on alternative treatments for their problem. If a therapist is not skilled in offering the most effective approach, he or she should offer to refer the client to someone with specialized training (McHugh & Barlow, 2010). A client's problems, not a therapist's "theoretical orientation," should determine the choice of treatment.

Researchers have not yet identified a clear treatment of choice for some emotional problems, but this does not mean "anything goes." Experimental therapies must be acknowledged as experimental, and the rationale for the approach must be clear to both the therapist and the client.

The identification of effective treatments for specific disorders is necessary if clinical psychology is to fulfill its scientific promise (Baker et al., 2008). Even as we explore evidence-based treatments, however, we must remember the central importance of a human relationship in psychotherapy. Individual people, not diagnostic categories, seek treatment for psychological disorders.

How can you find the right therapist for yourself, a friend, or a family member? First, be a good consumer. Find out more about the psychological problem and about treatments that work for it. You will find much useful information in later chapters on treatments for specific disorders, including the Getting Help sections, where we make many practical suggestions.

As a good consumer, you also should think carefully about what type of treatment you think you prefer and whom you prefer to see. A good "fit" between you and your therapist is an important part of effective therapy. For example, you may be more comfortable seeing a man or a woman. If you are not comfortable with a particular therapist, you should feel free to "shop around" until you find one who not only offers well-supported treatments, but who also seems to understand you. In fact, you may want to consult briefly with a few professionals before starting therapy, so you can pick the one who seems best for you.

People from a lot of different professional backgrounds offer psychotherapy. The person usually is more important than the profession, but we generally recommend that you seek a professional from one of the three major mental health professions—a clinical psychologist, a psychiatrist, or a clinical social worker.

If you feel you may need medication, your family physician should be willing to prescribe antidepressants or other commonly used medications. You will need to talk to a psychiatrist, a physician specializing in mental illnesses, if your family physician is uncomfortable prescribing psychotropic medication or if you would prefer to talk with a physician who is a specialist.

If you are considering psychotherapy, read about different types, particularly those that research shows to be more helpful for certain disorders. In addition to the Getting Help and treatment sections of Chapters 5 through 17, you might also want to explore some self-help books or resources on the Internet. You will need to be a good consumer when consulting these sources, however, as there is a lot of conflicting and inaccurate information about psychological problems and their treatment. A good starting point is the Web site of the National Institute of Mental Health, which contains much useful, up-to-date information on disorders and treatments.

# 3 Summary

Unique treatments come out of the *biological paradigm*, especially **psychopharmacology**, medications that have psychological effects; the *psychodynamic paradigm* including Freudian **psychoanalysis, psychodynamic psychotherapy**, and **interpersonal therapy**, all of which encourage the exploration of past relationships in order to obtain **insight** to current motivations; the *cognitive-behavioral paradigm*, where **cognitive-behavior therapy** focuses on the present and teaching more adaptive thoughts, behaviors, and feelings; the *humanistic paradigm*, where **humanistic**

**psychotherapy** focuses on empathy and heightening emotional awareness.

Different therapies "work" and include both common factors important across treatments and "active ingredients" for specific disorders. The text focuses on specific treatments for specific disorders, yet for empirical and humanistic reasons, we must recognize the universal importance of the therapist–client relationship.

The **placebo effect** produces change through expectations about a treatment's effectiveness. This makes placebos important both as controls for common factors and to study as an "active ingredient," since placebos produce change psychologically.

Traditional treatments focus on the individual, but couple therapy, family therapy, and group therapy all produce individual change by changing relationships. Some prevention efforts attempt to change dysfunctional aspects of society.

## The Big Picture

# critical thinking review

**3.1** What do treatments for psychological problems look like?
How might Frances's problems be viewed through the lens of the four paradigms? . . . (see page 54).

**3.2** How did Freud influence psychotherapy?
Freud simply told his patients to speak freely about whatever thoughts crossed their mind. This method, called *free association*, became a cornerstone of Freud's famous treatment, *psychoanalysis* . . . (see page 58).

**3.3** What is cognitive-behavior therapy?
Cognitive-behavior therapy (CBT) uses various research-based techniques to help troubled clients learn new ways of thinking, acting, and feeling . . . (see page 60).

**3.4** Does psychotherapy work?
. . . we reach four major conclusions about psychotherapy. First, psychotherapy *does* work—for many people and for many problems . . . (see page 65).

**3.5** What is the placebo effect? How do placebos work?
. . . placebos are any treatment that contains no known active ingredients. But the absence of active ingredients does not prevent placebos from healing . . . (see page 67).

**3.6** Is it important to "click" with your therapist?
A positive therapist–client relationship predicts positive outcomes across approaches to treatment . . . (see page 71).

# key terms

classification and assessment
of abnormal behavior

4

# The Big Picture

## learning objectives

**4.1**
Why do we need a system to classify abnormal behavior?

**4.2**
Should disorders that are unique to our own culture be considered cultural concepts of distress?

**4.3**
What is the difference between reliability and validity?

**4.4**
How could the DSM-5 classification system be improved?

**4.5**
Why do clinical interviews sometimes provide limited or distorted results?

**4.6**
Why is the MMPI-2 sometimes called an objective personality test?

**4.7**
Why are brain imaging procedures not used for the diagnosis of mental disorders?

Imagine that you are a therapist who has begun to interview a new patient. She tells you that she has had trouble falling asleep for the past few weeks. She has become increasingly frustrated and depressed, in part because she is always so tired when she goes to work in the morning. Your job is to figure out how to help this woman. How serious is her problem? What else do you need to know? What questions should you ask and how should you collect the information? The process of gathering this information is called **assessment.** You will want to use data from your assessment to compare her experiences with those of other patients whom you have treated (or read about). Are there any similarities that might help you know what to expect in terms of the likely origins of her problems, how long they will last, and the kinds of treatment that might be most helpful? In order to make those comparisons, you will need a kind of psychological road map to guide your search for additional information. This road map is known as a *classification system*—a list of various types of problems and their associated symptoms. This chapter will describe the classification system that has been developed to describe various forms of abnormal behavior. It will also summarize the different kinds of assessment tools that psychologists use.

## Overview

One important part of the assessment process is making a diagnostic decision based on the categories in the official classification system that describes mental disorders. **Diagnosis** refers to the identification or recognition of a disorder on the basis of its characteristic symptoms. In the field of mental health, a clinician assigns a diagnosis if the person's behavior meets the specific criteria for a particular type of disorder, such as schizophrenia or major depressive disorder. This decision is important because it tells the clinician that the person's problems are similar to those that have been experienced by some other people. The diagnosis enables the clinician to refer to the base of knowledge that has accumulated with regard to the disorder. For example, it will provide clues about associated symptoms and treatments that are most likely to be effective. To formulate a comprehensive treatment plan, the clinician utilizes the person's diagnosis plus many other types of information that we will discuss in this chapter.

In some fields, diagnosis refers to *causal* analysis. If your car doesn't start, you expect that your mechanic's "diagnosis" will explain the origins of the problem. Has the battery lost its charge? Is the fuel line blocked? Is the ignition switch dead? In this situation, the "diagnosis" leads directly to the problem's solution. In the field of psychopathology, assigning a diagnosis does not mean that we understand the etiology of the person's problem (see Chapter 2). Specific causes have not been identified for mental disorders. Psychologists can't "look under the hood" in the same way that a mechanic can examine a car. In the case of a mental disorder, assigning a diagnostic label simply identifies the nature of the problem without implying exactly how the problem came into existence.

Our consideration of the assessment enterprise and diagnostic issues will begin with an example from our own clinical experience. In the following pages we will describe Michael, a young man who found himself thinking and acting in ways that he could not seem to control. This case study illustrates the kinds of decisions that psychologists have to make about ways to collect and interpret information used in diagnosis and assessment.

### → Obsessions, Compulsions, and Other Unusual Behaviors

Michael was an only child who lived with his mother and father. He was 16 years old, a little younger than most of the other boys in the eleventh grade, and he looked even younger. From an academic point of view, Michael was an average student, but he was not a typical teenager in terms of social behavior. He felt alienated from other boys, and he was extremely anxious when he talked to girls. He despised everything about school. His life at home was also unpleasant. Michael and his parents argued frequently, especially Michael and his father.

One awful incident summed up Michael's bitter feelings about school. As a sophomore, he decided to join the track team. Michael was clumsy and not athletic. When he worked out with the other long-distance runners, he soon became the brunt of their jokes. One day, a belligerent teammate forced Michael to take off his clothes and run naked to a shelter in the park. When he got there, Michael found an old pair of shorts, which he put on and wore back to the locker room. The experience was humiliating. Later that night, Michael started to worry about those shorts. Who had left them in the park? Were they dirty? Had he been exposed to some horrible disease? Michael quit the track team the next day, but he couldn't put the experience out of his mind.

In the following year, Michael became more and more consumed by anxiety. He was obsessed about "contamination," which he imagined to be spreading from his books and school clothes to the furniture and other objects in his house. When the clothes that he had worn to school rubbed against a chair or a wall at home, he felt as though that spot had become contaminated. He didn't believe this was literally true; it was more like a reminder by association. When he touched something that he had used at school, he was more likely to think of school. That triggered unpleasant thoughts and the negative emotions with which they were associated (anger, fear, sadness).

Michael tried in various ways to minimize the spread of contamination. For example, he took a shower and changed his clothes every evening at 6 o'clock immediately after he finished his homework. After this "cleansing ritual," he was careful to avoid touching his books or dirty clothes as well as anything that they had touched.

If he bumped into one of the contaminated objects by accident, he went into the bathroom and washed his hands. Michael washed his hands 10 or 15 times in a typical evening. He paced back and forth watching television without sitting down so that he would not touch contaminated furniture.

Whenever he was not in school, Michael preferred to be alone at home, playing games on his computer. He did not enjoy sports, music, or outdoor activities. The only literature that interested him was fantasy and science fiction. *Dungeons & Dragons* was the only game that held his attention. He read extensively about the magical powers of fantastic characters and spent hours dreaming up new variations on themes described in books about this imaginary realm. When Michael talked about the *Dungeons & Dragons* characters and their adventures, his speech would sometimes become vague and difficult to follow. Other students at Michael's school shared his interest in *Dungeons & Dragons,* but he didn't want to play the game with them. Michael said he was different from the other students. He expressed contempt for other teenagers as well as for the city in which he lived.

Michael and his parents had been working with a family therapist for more than two years. Although the level of interpersonal conflict in the family had been reduced, Michael's anxiety seemed to be getting worse. He had become even more isolated from other boys his own age and had become quite suspicious about their motives. He often felt that they were talking about him, and that they were planning to do something else in order to humiliate him.

His worries about contamination had become almost unbearable to his parents, who were deeply confused and frustrated by his behavior. They knew that he was socially isolated and extremely unhappy. They believed that he would never be able to resume a more normal pattern of development until he gave up these "silly" ideas. Michael's fears disrupted his parents' own activities in several ways. They weren't allowed to touch him or his things after being in certain rooms of the house. His peculiar movements and persistent washing were troublesome to them. Michael's father usually worked at home, and he and Michael quarreled frequently, especially when Michael ran water in the bathroom next to his father's study.

Michael and his mother had always been very close. He was quite dependent on her, and she was devoted to him. They spent a lot of time together while his father was working. His mother had begun to find it difficult to be close to Michael. He shunned physical contact. When she touched him, he sometimes cringed and withdrew. Once in a while he would shriek, reminding her that she was contaminated by her contact with chairs and other objects like his laundry. Recently, Michael had also become aloof intellectually. His mother felt that he was shutting her out, as he seemed to withdraw further into his fantasy world of *Dungeons & Dragons* and his obsessive thoughts about contamination.

After learning about Michael's problems, his worries about contamination, his efforts to avoid contamination, and his fear of being with other people, his therapist would be faced with several important decisions. One involves the level of analysis at which she should think about the problem. Is this primarily Michael's problem, or should she consider this problem in terms of all members of the family? One possibility is that Michael has a psychological disorder that is disrupting the life of his family. It may be the other way around, however. Perhaps the family system as a whole is dysfunctional, and Michael's problems are only one symptom of this dysfunction. *DSM-5* defines mental disorders in terms of the individual rather than relationships or family systems.

Another set of choices involves the type of data that his therapist will use to describe Michael's behavior. What kinds of information should be collected? The therapist can consider several sources of data. One is Michael's own report, which can be obtained in an interview or through the use of questionnaires. Another is the report of his parents. The therapist may also decide to employ psychological tests.

In conducting an assessment and arriving at a diagnosis, one question the therapist must ask is whether Michael's abnormal behavior is similar to problems that have been exhibited by other people. She would want to know if Michael's symptoms fall into a pattern that has been documented by many other mental health professionals. Rather than reinventing the wheel each time a new patient walks into her office, the therapist can use a classification system to streamline the diagnostic process. The classification system serves as a common language among therapists, giving them a form of professional "shorthand" that enables them to discuss issues with colleagues. Because different disorders sometimes respond to different forms of treatment, the distinctions can be very important. In the next section we will review the development and modification of classification systems for abnormal behavior.

## Basic Issues in Classification

A **classification system** is used to subdivide or organize a set of objects. The objects of classification can be inanimate things, such as songs, rocks, or books; living organisms, such as plants, insects, or primates; or abstract concepts, such as numbers, religions, or historical periods. Formal classification systems are essential for the collection and communication of knowledge in all sciences and professions.

There are many ways to subdivide any given class of objects. Classification systems can be based on different principles (Bowker & Star, 1999). Some systems are based on descriptive similarities. For example, both a diamond and a ruby may be considered jewels because they are valuable stones. Other systems are based on less obvious characteristics, such as structural similarities. A diamond and a piece of coal, for example, may belong together because they both are made of carbon.

The point is simple: Classification systems can be based on various principles, and their value will depend primarily on the purpose for which they were developed. Different classification systems are not necessarily right or wrong; they are simply more or less useful. In the following section we will consider several fundamental principles that affect all attempts to develop a useful classification or typology of human behavior.

### Categories Versus Dimensions

Classification is often based on "yes or no" decisions. After a category has been defined, an object is either a member of the category or it is not. A **categorical approach to classification** assumes that distinctions among members of different categories are qualitative. In other words, the differences reflect a difference in kind (quality) rather than a difference in amount (quantity). In the classification of living organisms, for example, we usually consider species to be qualitatively distinct; they are different kinds of living organisms. Human beings are different from other primates; an organism is either human or it is not. Many medical conditions are categorical. Infection is one clear example. A person is either infected with a particular virus, or she is not. It doesn't make sense to talk about whether someone is partially infected or almost infected.

Although categorical classification systems are often useful, they are not the only kind of system that can be used to organize information systematically. As an alternative, scientists often employ a **dimensional approach to classification**—that is, one that describes the objects of classification in terms of continuous dimensions. Rather than assuming that an object either has or does not have a particular property, it may be useful to focus on a specific characteristic and determine *how much* of that characteristic the object exhibits. This kind of system is based on an ordered sequence or on quantitative measurements rather than on qualitative judgments (Kraemer, 2008).

For example, in the case of intellectual ability, psychologists have developed sophisticated measurement procedures. Rather than asking whether a particular person is intelligent (a "yes or no" judgment), the psychologist sets out to determine how much intelligence the person exhibits on a particular set of tasks. This process allows scientists to record subtle distinctions that would be lost if they were forced to make "all-or-none" decisions.

### From Description to Theory

The development of scientific classification systems typically proceeds in an orderly fashion over a period of many decades. The initial stages, which focused on simple descriptions or observations, are followed by more advanced theoretical stages. At the latter point, greater emphasis is placed on scientific concepts that explain causal relationships among objects. In the study of many medical disorders, this progression begins with an emphasis on the description of specific symptoms that cluster together and follow a predictable course over time. The systematic collection of more information regarding this syndrome may then lead to the discovery of causal factors.

Taxonomy is the science of arranging living organisms into groups. Humans and dolphins belong to the same "class" (mammals) because they share certain characteristics (are warm-blooded, nourish their young, and have body hair).

Clinical scientists hope that similar progress will be made in the field of psychopathology (Murphy, 2006). Mental disorders are currently classified on the basis of their descriptive features or symptoms because specific causal mechanisms have not yet been discovered. While we may eventually develop a more sophisticated, theoretical understanding of certain disorders, this does not necessarily mean we will ever know the precise causes of disorders or that it will be possible to develop a classification system based entirely on causal explanations (Kendler et al., 2011). In fact, the most likely explanations for mental disorders involve complex interactions of psychological, biological, and social systems (see Chapter 2).

## Classifying Abnormal Behavior

We need a classification system for abnormal behavior for two primary reasons. First, a classification system is useful to clinicians, who must match their clients' problems with the form of intervention that is most likely to be effective. Second, a classification system must be used in the search for new knowledge. The history of medicine is filled with examples of problems that were recognized long before they could be treated successfully. The classification of a specific set of symptoms has often laid the foundation for research that eventually identified a cure or a way of preventing the disorder.

Modern classification systems in psychiatry were introduced shortly after World War II. During the 1950s and 1960s, psychiatric classification was widely criticized. One major criticism focused on the lack of consistency in diagnostic decisions (Nathan & Langenbucher, 2003). Independent clinicians frequently disagreed with one another about the use of diagnostic categories. Objections were also raised from philosophical, sociological, and political points of view. For example, some critics charged that diagnostic categories in psychiatry would be more appropriately viewed as "problems in living" than as medical disorders (Szasz, 1963). Others were concerned about the negative impact of using diagnostic labels. In other words, once a psychiatric diagnosis is assigned, the person so labeled might experience discrimination of various kinds and also find it more difficult to establish and maintain relationships with other people (see Labels and Stigma on page 82). These are all serious problems that continue to be the topic of important, ongoing discussions involving mental health professionals as well as patients and their families. Debates regarding these issues did fuel important improvements in the diagnosis of mental disorders, including emphasis on the use of detailed criteria sets for each disorder.

Currently, two diagnostic systems for mental disorders are widely recognized. One—the *Diagnostic and Statistical Manual* (DSM)—is published by the American Psychiatric Association. The other—the *International Classification of Diseases* (ICD)—is published by the World Health Organization. Both systems were first developed shortly after World War II, and both have been revised several times. Because the American diagnostic manual is now in its fifth edition, it is called *DSM-5*. The World Health Organization's manual is in its tenth edition and is therefore known as *ICD-10*. The two manuals are quite similar in most respects. Most of the categories listed in the manuals are identical, and the criteria for specific disorders are usually similar.

### The DSM-5 System

More than 200 specific diagnostic categories are described in *DSM-5*. These are arranged under 22 primary headings. A complete list appears inside the back cover of this book. Disorders that present similar kinds of symptoms are grouped together. For example, conditions that include a prominent display of anxiety are listed under "Anxiety Disorders," and conditions that involve a depressed mood are listed under "Depressive Disorders."

The manual lists specific criteria for each diagnostic category. We can illustrate the ways in which these criteria are used by examining the diagnostic decisions that would be considered in Michael's case. The criteria for obsessive–compulsive disorder (OCD) are listed in *DSM-5: Criteria for Obsessive-Compulsive Disorder* (see page 83). Michael would meet all of the criteria in "A" for both obsessions and compulsions. His repetitive hand-washing rituals were performed in response to obsessive thoughts regarding contamination. Consistent with criterion "B," Michael's compulsive behaviors were time consuming and interfered with his family's routine. His relationships with friends were severely limited because he refused to invite them to his house, fearing that they would spread contamination.

For various types of disorders, the duration of the problem is considered as well as the clinical picture. For example, criterion "B" for OCD specifies that the patient's compulsive rituals must take more than one hour each day to perform.

In addition to the inclusion criteria, symptoms that must be present, many disorders are also defined in terms of certain exclusion criteria. In other words, the diagnosis can be ruled out if certain conditions prevail. For example, in the case of OCD, the diagnosis would not be made if the symptoms were the product of using drugs or the presence of another medical condition (criterion "C"). Finally, OCD would not be considered as the diagnosis if the symptoms were part of another mental disorder, such as a seriously depressed person being preoccupied with guilty ruminations (criterion "D").

Clinical disorders are defined largely in terms of symptomatic behaviors. Most diagnoses, such as OCD, schizophrenia, and depressive disorders, are characterized by episodic periods of psychological turmoil. A person can be assigned more than one diagnosis if he or she meets criteria for more than one disorder.

Michael would receive a primary diagnosis of obsessive–compulsive disorder. His obsessions and compulsions were, in fact, his most obvious symptoms. Michael would also be

## Labels and Stigma

What does it mean to be labeled with a psychiatric diagnosis? Labeling theory is a perspective on mental disorders that is primarily concerned with the negative consequences of assigning a diagnostic label, especially the impact that diagnosis has on ways in which people think about themselves and the ways in which other people react to the designated patient (Link & Phelan, 2010). It assigns relatively little importance to specific behaviors as symptoms of a disorder that resides within the person. Labeling theory is primarily concerned with social factors that determine whether a person will be given a psychiatric diagnosis rather than the psychological or biological reasons for the abnormal behaviors. In other words, it is concerned with events that take place after a person has behaved in an unusual way rather than with factors that might explain the original appearance of the behavior itself.

According to contemporary versions of labeling theory, public attitudes toward mental illness shape a person's reaction to being assigned a diagnosis. Influenced by negative beliefs about people with mental disorders (such as "they are less competent," or "they are dangerous"), the person may try to avoid rejection by withdrawing from interactions with other people. Unfortunately, this withdrawal can lead to further isolation and diminished levels of social support (Kroska & Harkness, 2006).

The probability that a person will receive a diagnosis is presumably determined by several factors, including the severity of the unusual behavior. Beyond the nature of the disorder itself, however, the social context in which the problem occurs and the tolerance level of the community are also important. The labeling theory perspective places considerable emphasis on the social status of the person who exhibits abnormal behavior and the social distance between that person and mental health professionals. People from disadvantaged groups, such as racial and sexual minorities and women, are presumably more likely to be labeled than are white males.

The merits and limitations of labeling theory have been debated extensively. The theory has inspired research on a number of important questions. Some studies have found that people from lower status groups, including racial minorities, are indeed more likely to be assigned severe diagnoses (Phelan & Link, 1999). On the other hand, it would also be an exaggeration to say that the social status of the patient is the most important factor influencing the diagnostic process. In fact, clinicians' diagnostic decisions are determined primarily by the form and severity of the patient's symptoms rather

Demonstrators rally outside the U.S. capitol to combat stigma and support a bill that would require health insurance companies to provide equal coverage for mental health and addiction treatment.

than by such factors as gender, race, and social class (Ruscio, 2004).

Another focus of the debate regarding labeling theory is the issue of **stigma** and the negative effects of labeling. Stigma refers to a stamp or label that sets the person apart from others, connects the person to undesirable features, and leads others to reject the person. Labeling theory notes that negative attitudes toward mental disorders prevent patients from obtaining jobs, finding housing, and forming new relationships. Various kinds of empirical evidence support the conclusion that a psychiatric label can have a harmful impact on a person's life. Negative attitudes are associated with many types of mental disorders, such as alcoholism, schizophrenia, and sexual disorders. When people become psychiatric patients, many expect to be devalued and discriminated against (Couture & Penn, 2003; Yang et al., 2007). These expectations could cause the person to behave in strained and defensive ways, which may in turn lead others to reject him or her.

Labeling theory has drawn needed attention to several important problems associated with the classification of mental disorders. Of course, it does not provide a complete explanation for abnormal behavior. Many factors other than the reactions of other people contribute to the development and maintenance of abnormal behavior. It is also important to realize that a diagnosis of mental illness can have positive consequences, such as encouraging access to effective treatment. Many patients and their family members are relieved to learn that their problems are similar to those experienced by other people and that help may be available. The effects of diagnostic labeling are not always harmful.

A. Presence of obsessions, compulsions, or both.
Obsessions are defined by (1) and (2):

1. Recurrent and persistent thoughts, urges, or images that are experienced, at some time during the disturbance, as intrusive and unwanted, and that in most individuals cause marked anxiety or distress.

2. The individual attempts to ignore or suppress such thoughts, urges, or images, or to neutralize them with some other thought or action (i.e., by performing a compulsion).

Compulsions are defined by (1) and (2):

1. Repetitive behaviors (e.g., hand washing, ordering, checking) or mental acts (e.g., praying, counting, repeating words silently) that the individual feels driven to perform in response to an obsession or according to rules that must be applied rigidly.

2. The behaviors or mental acts are aimed at preventing or reducing anxiety or distress, or preventing some dreaded event or situation; however, these behaviors or mental acts are not connected in a realistic way with what they are designed to neutralize or prevent, or are clearly excessive.

**Note**: Young children may not be able to articulate the aims of these behaviors or mental acts.

B. The obsessions or compulsions are time-consuming (e.g., take more than 1 hour per day) or cause clinically significant distress or impairment in social, occupational, or other important areas of functioning.

C. The obsessive-compulsive symptoms are not attributable to the physiological effects of a substance (e.g., a drug of abuse, a medication) or another medical condition.

D. The disturbance is not better explained by the symptoms of another mental disorder (e.g., excessive worries, as in generalized anxiety disorder; preoccupation with appearance, as in body dysmorphic disorder; difficulty discarding or parting with possessions, as in hoarding disorder; hair pulling, as in trichotillomania [hair-pulling disorder]; skin picking, as in excoriation [skin-picking] disorder; stereotypies, as in stereotypic movement disorder; ritualized eating behavior, as in eating disorders; preoccupation with substances or gambling, as in substance-related and addictive disorders; preoccupation with having an illness, as in illness anxiety disorder; sexual urges or fantasies, as in paraphilic disorders; impulses, as in disruptive, impulse-control, and conduct disorders; guilty ruminations, as in major depressive disorder; thought insertion or delusional preoccupations, as in schizophrenia spectrum and other psychotic disorders; or repetitive patterns of behavior, as in autism spectrum disorder).

coded as meeting criteria for schizotypal personality disorder (see Chapter 9). This judgment depends on a consideration of his long-standing, relatively rigid patterns of interacting with other people and his inability to adjust to the changing requirements of different people and situations. For example, he was suspicious of other people's motives, he did not have any close friends in whom he could confide, and he was very anxious in social situations because he was afraid that other people might take advantage of him. These are important considerations for a therapist who wants to plan a treatment program for Michael, but they are relatively subtle considerations in comparison to the obsessions and compulsions, which were currently the primary source of conflict with his parents.

## Culture and Classification

*DSM-5* addresses the relation between cultural issues and the diagnosis of psychopathology in two principal ways. First, the manual encourages clinicians to consider the influence of cultural factors in both the expression and recognition of symptoms of mental disorders. People express extreme emotions in ways that are shaped by the traditions of their families and other social groups to which they belong. Intense, public displays of anger or grief might be expected in one culture but considered signs of disturbance in another. Interpretations of emotional distress and other symptoms of disorder are influenced by the explanations that a person's culture assigns to such experiences. Religious beliefs, social roles, and sexual identities all play an important part in constructing meanings that are assigned to these phenomena (Hwang et al., 2008). The accuracy and utility of a clinical diagnosis depend on more than a simple count of the symptoms that appear to be present. They also hinge on the clinician's ability to consider the cultural context in which the problem appeared. This is a particularly challenging task when the clinician and the person with the problem do not share the same cultural background.

The diagnostic manual also attempts to sensitize clinicians to cultural issues by including a discussion of **cultural concepts of distress.** These are patterns of erratic or unusual thinking and behavior that have been identified in diverse societies around the world and do not fit easily into the other diagnostic categories that are listed in the main body of *DSM-5*. They are considered to be unique to particular societies, particularly in non-Western or developing countries. Their appearance is easily recognized and understood to be a form of abnormal behavior by members of certain cultures, but they do not conform to typical patterns of mental disorders seen in the United States or Europe. The cultural concepts of distress have also been called *culture-bound syndromes* or *idioms of distress.* In other words, they represent a manner of expressing negative emotion that is unique to a particular culture and cannot be easily translated or understood in terms of its individual parts.

One concept or syndrome of this type is known as *ataques de nervios*, which has been observed most extensively among people from Puerto Rico and other Caribbean countries (Lewis-Fernández et al., 2002; San Miguel et al., 2006). Descriptions of this experience include four dimensions, in which the essential theme is loss of control—an inability to interrupt the dramatic sequence of emotion and behavior. These dimensions include emotional expressions (an explosion of screaming and crying, coupled with overwhelming feelings of anxiety, depression, and anger), bodily sensations (including trembling, heart palpitations, weakness, fatigue, headache, and convulsions), actions and behaviors (dramatic, forceful gestures that include aggression toward others, suicidal thoughts or gestures, and trouble eating or sleeping), and alterations in consciousness (marked feelings of "not being one's usual self," accompanied by fainting, loss of consciousness, dizziness, and feelings of being outside of one's body).

*Ataques* are typically provoked by situations that disrupt or threaten the person's social world, especially the family. Many *ataques* occur shortly after the person learns unexpectedly that a close family member has died. Others result from an imminent divorce or after a serious conflict with a child. Women are primarily responsible for maintaining the integrity of the family in this culture, and they are also more likely than men to experience *ataques de nervios.* Puerto Rican women from poor and working-class families define themselves largely in terms of their success in building and maintaining a cohesive family life. When this social role is threatened, an *ataque* may result. This response to threat or conflict—an outburst of powerful, uncontrolled negative emotion—expresses suffering while simultaneously providing a means for coping with the threat. It serves to signal the woman's distress to important other people and to rally needed sources of social support.

What is the relation between cultural concepts of distress and the formal categories listed in *DSM-5?* The answer is unclear and also varies from one syndrome to the next. Are they similar problems that are simply given different names in other cultures? Probably not, at least not in most instances (Guarnaccia & Pincay, 2008). In some cases, people who exhibit behavior that would fit the definition of a cultural concepts of distress would also qualify for a *DSM-5* diagnosis, if they were diagnosed by a clinician trained in the use of that manual (Tolin et al., 2007). But everyone who displays the cultural concepts of distress would not meet criteria for a *DSM-5* disorder, and of those who do, not all would receive the same *DSM-5* diagnosis.

The discussion of cultural concepts of distress has been praised as a significant advance toward integrating cultural considerations into the classification system (Lopez & Guarnaccia, 2000). It has also been criticized for its ambiguity. The most difficult conceptual issue involves the boundary between these syndromes and categories found elsewhere in the diagnostic manual. Some critics have argued that they should be fully integrated, without trying to establish a distinction (Hughes, 1998). Others have noted that if culturally unique disorders must be listed separately from other, "mainstream" conditions, then certain disorders now listed in the main body of the manual—especially eating disorders, such as bulimia—should actually be listed as cultural concepts of distress. Like *ataques de nervios,* bulimia nervosa is a condition that is found primarily among a limited number of cultures (Keel & Klump, 2003). The difference is that bulimia is found in *our* culture—people living in Western or developed countries—rather than in other cultures. Dissociative amnesia—the inability to recall important personal information regarding a traumatic event—also resembles cultural concepts of distress because it appears to be experienced only by people living in modern, developed cultures (Pope et al., 2007).

Thinking about this distinction helps to place the more familiar diagnostic categories in perspective and shows how our own culture has shaped our views of abnormal behavior. We must not be misled into thinking that culture shapes only conditions that appear to be exotic in faraway lands; culture shapes various facets of all disorders. Though it is imperfect, the consideration of cultural concepts of distress does serve to make clinicians more aware of the extent to which their own views of what is normal and abnormal have been shaped by the values and experiences of their own culture (Mezzich, Berganza, & Ruiperez, 2001).

Just as judges sometimes disagree in their assessment of evidence presented during a trial, psychologists and psychiatrists do not always agree on how various disorders should be diagnosed. Of course, both judges and mental health professionals attempt to be reliable (consistent) in their judgments.

## Evaluating Classification Systems

One of the most important things to understand about the classification of mental disorders is that the official diagnostic manual is revised on a regular basis. That process is guided by research on mental disorders, and the evidence takes many forms. How can we evaluate a system like *DSM-5*? Is it a useful classification system? Utility can be measured in terms of two principal criteria: reliability and validity.

### Reliability

**Reliability** refers to the consistency of measurements, including diagnostic decisions. If a diagnosis is to be useful, it will have to be made consistently. One important form of reliability, known as "interrater reliability," refers to agreement between clinicians who are provided with exactly the same information.

Suppose, for example, that two psychologists watch the same video recording of an interview with a patient and that each psychologist independently assigns a diagnosis using *DSM-5*. If both psychologists decide that the patient fits the criteria for a major depressive disorder, they have used the definition of that category consistently. A more difficult challenge involves "test–retest reliability." This situation may yield lower levels of consistency because the patient's condition could change between the two assessments (and both clinicians would not have exactly the same information). Of course, one or two cases would not provide a sufficient test of the reliability of a diagnostic category. The real question is whether the clinicians would agree with each other over a large series of patients. The process of collecting and interpreting information regarding the reliability of diagnosing mental disorders is discussed in Research Methods below.

## RESEARCH methods

### Reliability: Agreement Regarding Diagnostic Decisions

Several formal procedures have been developed to evaluate diagnostic reliability. Most studies of psychiatric diagnosis employ an index known as kappa. Instead of measuring the simple proportion of agreement between clinicians, kappa indicates the proportion of agreement that occurred above and beyond that which would have occurred by chance. Negative values of kappa indicate that the rate of agreement was less than that which would have been expected by chance in this particular sample of people. Thus, kappa of zero indicates chance agreement, and a kappa of 1.0 indicates perfect agreement between raters.

How should we interpret the kappa statistic? There is no easy answer to this question (Kraemer et al., 2012). It would be unrealistic to expect perfect consistency, especially in view of the relatively modest reliability of some other types of diagnostic decisions that are made in medical practice (Garb, Klein, & Grove, 2002; Meyer et al., 2001). On the other hand, it isn't very encouraging simply to find that the level of agreement among clinicians is a bit better than chance. We should expect more than that from a diagnostic system, especially when it is used as a basis for treatment decisions. One traditional convention suggests that kappa values of .70 or higher indicate relatively good agreement, but that is a standard that is seldom met outside of highly controlled research situations, using specially trained raters, structured diagnostic interviews, and highly selected patient samples. Values of kappa below .40 are often interpreted as indicating questionable or poor agreement.

The reliability of many diagnostic categories is better than it was many years ago, in part, because clinicians use more detailed diagnostic criteria to define specific disorders. Still, most studies also indicate that there is considerable room for improvement.

The reliability of some diagnostic categories remains open to serious question. Consider, for example, evidence from field trials that were conducted by the American Psychiatric Association when DSM-5 was being prepared (Regier et al., 2013). Data were collected by a large number of mental health professionals at several large medical centers, using representative samples of patients from each center. The field trials followed a test–retest design. Each patient was interviewed by a clinician, who recorded a diagnosis. A second clinician then independently conducted a second interview with the same patient, and that person also recorded a diagnosis. The follow-up interviews occurred at least four hours and not more than two weeks after the initial interview in order to minimize the chance that the patient's clinical condition changed between the assessments (either spontaneous recovery or the onset of a new disorder). Structured diagnostic interviews were not employed because they are seldom used in standard clinical practice. This design provided a fair estimate of the reliability of the DSM-5 diagnostic criteria as they would be used in actual clinical practice.

Kappa values for several diagnostic categories are presented in Figure 4.1. The data are presented separately for a few representative adult and childhood diagnoses, and they are organized on the basis of levels of agreement. Relatively few diagnostic categories showed "very good" agreement, defined in terms of kappa higher than .60. The diagnostic reliability for several categories was "good," if we take values of kappa between .40 and .60 as the criterion for that judgment. It should also be noted that quite a few categories demonstrated "questionable" levels of reliability, including major depressive disorder and generalized anxiety disorder (two of the most frequently employed diagnostic categories in DSM-5). This pattern of results is clearly mixed; it is reassuring for some disorders and somewhat alarming for others.

*Continued*

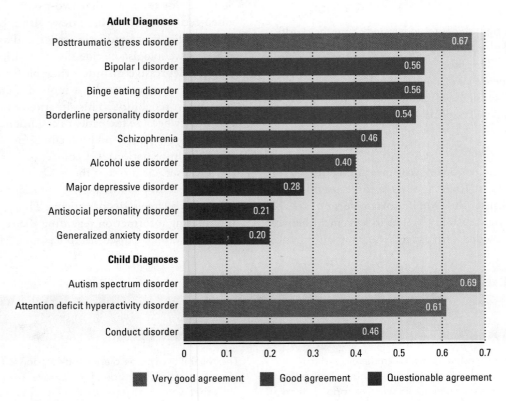

**Adult Diagnoses**

| | |
|---|---|
| Posttraumatic stress disorder | 0.67 |
| Bipolar I disorder | 0.56 |
| Binge eating disorder | 0.56 |
| Borderline personality disorder | 0.54 |
| Schizophrenia | 0.46 |
| Alcohol use disorder | 0.40 |
| Major depressive disorder | 0.28 |
| Antisocial personality disorder | 0.21 |
| Generalized anxiety disorder | 0.20 |

**Child Diagnoses**

| | |
|---|---|
| Autism spectrum disorder | 0.69 |
| Attention deficit hyperactivity disorder | 0.61 |
| Conduct disorder | 0.46 |

0   0.1   0.2   0.3   0.4   0.5   0.6   0.7

■ Very good agreement    ■ Good agreement    ■ Questionable agreement

**FIGURE 4.1**

**Test–retest Reliability of Diagnoses from the *DSM-5* Field Trials**

*Source:* From R. Freedman, D. A. Lewis, R. Michels, D. S. Pine, S. K. Schultz, C. A. Tamminga,. . . . & J. Yager, 2013, *"The initial field trials of DSM-5: New Blooms and old thorns,"* American Journal of Psychiatry, 170, 1–5

This evidence from the *DSM-5* field trials suggests that we should not accept uncritically the assumption that the diagnostic categories in *DSM-5* can be used reliably (Jones, 2012). Cautious skepticism is clearly warranted when clinicians use these terms to organize information and communicate with each other and with their patients about the nature of mental health problems. On the other hand, we should also welcome the efforts that were made to evaluate and describe levels of diagnostic reliability that might be expected for the revised diagnostic manual. And finally, we should keep in mind the fact that, in actual clinical practice, mental disorders are seldom diagnosed on the basis of a single interview. It is important for clinicians to consider a wide range of information for each person, including the results of various assessment procedures and consultation with more than one source (e.g., other family members).

## Validity

The most important issue in the evaluation of a diagnostic category is whether it is *useful* (Kendell & Jablensky, 2003). By knowing that a person fits into a particular group or class, do we learn anything meaningful about that person? For example, if a person fits the diagnostic criteria for schizophrenia, is that person likely to improve when he or she is given antipsychotic medication? Or is that person likely to have a less satisfactory level of social adjustment in five years than a person who meets diagnostic criteria for bipolar disorder? Does the diagnosis tell us anything about the factors or circumstances that might have contributed to the onset of this problem? These questions are concerned with the validity of the diagnostic category. The term **validity** refers to the meaning or importance of a measurement—in this case, a diagnostic decision (Kraemer, 2010). Importance is not an "all-or-none" phenomenon; it is a quantitative issue. Diagnostic categories are more or less useful, and their validity (or utility) can be determined in several ways.

Validity is, in a sense, a reflection of the success that has been achieved in understanding the nature of a disorder. Have important facts been discovered? Systematic studies aimed at establishing the validity of a disorder may proceed in a sequence of phases (Robins & Guze, 1989), such as those listed in Table 4.1. After a clinical description has been established, diagnostic categories are refined and validated through this process of scientific exploration. It should be emphasized, however, that the sequence listed in

Table 4.1 represents an ideal scenario. Relatively few, if any, of the disorders listed in *DSM-5* are supported by an extensive set of research evidence supporting all these points. Clinical scientists have not identified "points of rarity" between related syndromes (McGuffin & Farmer, 2005). For most disorders, the evidence regarding long-term outcome and treatment response varies considerably from one person to the next. You should not assume that the types of studies listed in Table 4.1 have all provided unequivocal support for the validity of the disorders listed in *DSM-5*.

It may be helpful to think of different forms of validity in terms of their relationship in time with the appearance of symptoms of the disorder. *Etiological validity* is concerned with factors that cause or contribute to the onset of the disorder. These are things that have happened in the past. Was the disorder regularly triggered by a specific set of events or circumstances? Did it run in families? The ultimate question with regard to etiological validity is whether there are any specific causal factors that are regularly, and perhaps uniquely, associated with this disorder. If we know that a person exhibits the symptoms of the disorder, do we in turn learn anything about the circumstances that originally led to the onset of the problem?

*Concurrent validity* is concerned with the present time and with correlations between the disorder and other symptoms, circumstances, and test procedures. Is the disorder currently associated with any other types of behaviors, such as performance on psychological tests? Do precise measures of biological variables, such as brain structure and function, distinguish reliably between

people who have the disorder and those who do not? Clinical studies that are aimed at developing a more precise description of a disorder also fall into this type of validity.

*Predictive validity* is concerned with the future and with the stability of the problem over time. Will it be persistent? If it is short-lived, how long will an episode last? Will the disorder have a predictable outcome? Do people with this problem typically improve if they are given a specific type of medication or a particular form of psychotherapy? The overall validity of a diagnostic category depends on the body of evidence that accumulates as scientists seek answers to these questions.

The list of categories included in *DSM-5* is based on the results of research studies as well as clinical experience. Some disorders are based on a much more extensive foundation of evidence than others. Each time the manual is revised, new categories are added and old categories are dropped, presumably because they are not sufficiently useful. Up to the present time, clinicians have been more willing to include new categories than to drop old ones. It is difficult to know when we would decide that a particular diagnostic category is not valid. At what point in the accumulation of knowledge are clinical scientists willing to conclude that a category is of no use and to recommend that the search for more information should be abandoned? This is a difficult question that the authors of each revision of the diagnostic manual must confront. The situation regarding validity and psychiatric diagnosis is an evolving process, with more evidence being added on a regular basis.

## THINKING CRITICALLY about DSM-5

### Scientific Progress or Diagnostic Fads?

Everyone agrees that the official diagnostic manual needs to be updated periodically to bring it into closer alignment with current knowledge and practice. But what principles and standards should guide that process? When *DSM-III* was revised to produce *DSM-IV*, the workgroups were instructed to follow a rather conservative principle: "Don't make changes unless there is clear scientific evidence to support the change." The authors of *DSM-5* set out with a more expansive and open-minded

view of their task (Kupfer, First, & Regier, 2002). They recognized that larger changes might be needed in order to "transcend the limitations of the DSM paradigm," and they wanted to "encourage thinking beyond the *DSM-IV* framework." Workgroups were told that "there are no preset limitations on the number of changes that may occur" (Kupfer, Regier, & Kuhl, 2008). This shift in emphasis generated quite a bit of controversy as the revision unfolded (Frances & Widiger, 2012).

*Continued*

New disorders are considered for inclusion in the diagnostic manual every time that it is revised. Changes were particularly evident this time around, given the less conservative tone that was set at the outset of the process. In the end, some of the proposals for new disorders were accepted, and others were not. New disorders include binge eating disorder, disruptive mood regulation disorder, and premenstrual dysphoric disorder. They are controversial, in part, because they are likely to be among the most frequently diagnosed conditions in the manual, expanding substantially the overall prevalence of mental disorders in the general population. It is also reasonable to wonder if these new diagnostic categories provide the best possible explanation for the adjustment problems that they describe (see Critical Thinking Matters in Chapter 1). Strong fluctuations in mood and struggles with impulse control may be part of normal human experience rather than manifestations of disorder.

Among those new disorders that were considered and ultimately rejected, some were included in Section III of *DSM-5*, which is an appendix that describes "Emerging Measures and Models." These are disorders that require further study, and they may eventually be moved into the main body of the manual. Several controversial forms of behavioral problems are included in Section III, including: attenuated psychosis syndrome (see Thinking Critically About DSM-5 in Chapter 13), Internet gaming disorder, and persistent complex bereavement disorder. These proposals for new diagnostic categories all include behavioral issues, emotional distress, and adjustment difficulties that affect large numbers of people. Many of these people seek professional help,

and mental health professionals would like to have a way to categorize these forms of distress. On the other hand, it is also reasonable to wonder if the creation of a new, formal diagnostic category is the best way to handle the situation. What is the downside to this wholesale expansion of the diagnostic manual? One persuasive critique of *DSM-5* argued, "Fads punctuate what has become a basic background of overdiagnosis. Normality is an endangered species" (Frances & Widiger, 2012).

In the absence of a universally accepted definition of mental disorder (see Chapter 1), a definition that would identify an obvious boundary between normal and abnormal behavior, decisions about which problems are included in the diagnostic manual will necessarily be made on the basis of social processes. These include pressures from patients' advocates, mental health professionals, insurance companies, and the pharmaceutical industry. All of these groups express, in one way or another, the understandable desire to identify and explain psychological problems that are a source of distress or social impairment. Research evidence is certainly considered when the diagnostic manual is revised, but these data do not represent huge scientific breakthroughs that identify major causal pathways responsible for the etiology of these conditions. Rather, this evidence tends to be concerned with the efficiency and utility of various options for describing each disorder, the connections between diagnostic procedures and efficacy of treatment procedures, and so on. The bottom line is that the new categories included in *DSM-5* probably reflect diagnostic fads more than scientific breakthroughs. But we shouldn't really expect more than that. It's still a useful manual.

## Problems and Limitations of the DSM-5 System

Many experts believe that *DSM-5* is an improvement over earlier versions of APA's classification system, but the manual has already been criticized extensively, often with good reason. One fundamental question that applies to every disorder involves the boundary between normal and abnormal behavior. This is a longstanding problem in the classification of mental disorders. The definitions that are included in the manual are often vague with regard to this threshold (Frances & Widiger, 2012). *DSM-5* is based on a categorical approach to classification, but most of the symptoms that define the disorders are actually dimensional in nature. Depressed mood, for example, can vary continuously from the complete absence of depression to moderate levels of depression on up to severe levels of depression. The same thing can be said with regard to symptoms of anxiety disorders, eating disorders, and substance use disorders. These are all continuously distributed phenomena, and there is not a bright line that divides people with problems from those who do not have problems.

The absence of a specific definition of social impairment is another practical issue that plagued previous versions of the diagnostic manual. Most disorders in *DSM-5* include the requirement

that a particular set of symptoms causes "clinically significant distress or impairment in social or occupational functioning." No specific measurement procedures are provided to make this determination. Mental health professionals must rely on their own subjective judgment to decide how distressed or how impaired a person must be by his or her symptoms in order to qualify for a diagnosis. There is an important need for more specific definitions of these concepts, and better measurement tools are needed for their assessment.

Criticisms of the current classification system have also emphasized broad conceptual issues. Some clinicians and investigators have argued that the syndromes defined in *DSM-5* do not represent the most useful ways to think about psychological problems, either in terms of planning current treatments or in terms of designing programs of research. For example, it might be better to focus on more homogeneous dimensions of dysfunction, such as anxiety or angry hostility, rather than on syndromes (groups of symptoms) (Smith & Combs, 2010).

Critics pose questions such as: Should we design treatments for people who exhibit distorted, negative ways of thinking about themselves, regardless of whether their symptoms happen to

This warning system for fire danger is an example of a dimensional classification system. It conveys information about "how much danger" is present rather than simply indicating that the situation is either dangerous or not dangerous.

involve a mixture of depression, anxiety, or some other pattern of negative emotion or interpersonal conflict? The answer is: We don't know. It would certainly be premature to cut off consideration of these alternatives just because they address problems in a way that deviates from the official diagnostic manual. In our current state of uncertainty, diversity of opinion should be encouraged, particularly if it is grounded in cautious skepticism and supported by rigorous scientific inquiry.

From an empirical point of view, *DSM-5* is hampered by a number of problems that suggest that it does not classify clinical problems into syndromes in the simplest and most beneficial way (Helzer, Kraemer, & Krueger, 2006). One of the thorniest issues involves **comorbidity,** which is defined as the simultaneous appearance of two or more disorders in the same person. Comorbidity rates are very high for mental disorders as they are defined in the DSM system (Eaton, South, & Krueger, 2010). For example, in the National Comorbidity Survey, among those people who qualified for at least one diagnosis at some point during their lifetime, 56 percent met the criteria for two or more disorders. A small subgroup, 14 percent of the sample, actually met the diagnostic criteria for three or more lifetime disorders. That group of people accounted for almost 90 percent of the severe disorders in the study.

There are several ways to interpret comorbidity (Krueger, 2002). Some people may independently develop two separate conditions. In other cases, the presence of one disorder may lead to the onset of another. Unsuccessful attempts to struggle with prolonged alcohol dependence, for example, might lead a person to become depressed. Neither of these alternatives creates conceptual problems for *DSM-5.* Unfortunately, the very high rate of comorbidity suggests that these explanations account for a small proportion of overlap between categories.

The real problem associated with comorbidity arises when a person with a mixed pattern of symptoms, usually of a severe nature, simultaneously meets the criteria for more than one disorder. Consider, for example, a client who was treated by one of the authors of this text. This man experienced a large number of diffuse problems associated with anxiety, depression, and interpersonal difficulties. According to the *DSM-5* system, he would have met the criteria for major depressive disorder, generalized anxiety disorder, and obsessive–compulsive disorder, as well as three types of personality disorders. It might be said, therefore, that he suffered from at least six types of mental disorders. But is that really helpful? Is it the best way to think about his problems? Would it be more accurate to say that he had a complicated set of interrelated problems that were associated with worrying, rumination, and the regulation of high levels of negative emotion and that these problems constituted one complex and severe type of disorder?

The comorbidity issue is related to another limitation of *DSM-5:* the failure to make better use of information regarding the course of mental disorders over time. More than 100 years ago, when schizophrenia and bipolar mood disorder were originally described, the distinction between them was based heavily on observations regarding their long-term course. Unfortunately, most disorders listed in *DSM-5* are defined largely in terms of snapshots of symptoms at particular points in time. Diagnostic decisions are seldom based on a comprehensive analysis of the way that a person's problems evolve over time. If someone meets the criteria for more than one disorder, does it matter which one came first? Is there a predictable pattern in which certain disorders follow the onset of others? What is the nature of the connection between childhood disorders and adult problems? Our knowledge of mental disorders would be greatly enriched if greater emphasis were placed on questions regarding life span development (Buka & Gilman, 2002; Oltmanns & Balsis, 2011).

These issues will be debated by mental health experts for many years to come. It seems unlikely that they will be solved in the near future. Attempts to provide solutions to these problems and limitations will ensure that the classification system will continue to be revised. As before, these changes will be driven by the interaction of clinical experience and empirical evidence. Students, clinicians, and research investigators should all remain skeptical when using this classification system and its successors.

## Basic Issues in Assessment

Up to this point, we have discussed the development and use of classification systems. But we haven't talked about the way in which a psychologist might collect the information that is necessary to arrive at a diagnostic decision. Furthermore, we have looked at the problem only in relatively general terms. The diagnostic decision is one useful piece of information. It is not, however, a systematic picture of the specific person's situation. It is only a starting point. In the following section we extend our discussion to consider methods of collecting information. In so doing, we discuss a broad range of data that may be useful in understanding psychopathological behavior.

### Purposes of Clinical Assessment

To appreciate the importance and complexity of assessment procedures, let's go back to the example of Michael. When Michael and his parents initially approached the psychologist, they were clearly upset. But the nature of the problem, in terms of Michael's behavior and the family as a whole, was not clearly defined. Before he could attempt to help this family, the psychologist had to collect more information. He needed to know more about the range and frequency of Michael's obsessions and compulsions, including when they began, how often he experienced these problems, and the factors that made them better or worse. He also needed to know whether there were other problems, such as depression or delusional beliefs that might either explain these responses or interfere with their treatment. In addition, he had to learn how Michael got along with classmates, how he was doing in school, and how his parents responded when he behaved strangely. Was his behavior, at least in part, a response to environmental circumstances? How would the family support (or interfere with) the

Diagnostic interviews provide an opportunity to make detailed inquiries about a person's subjective experience while also observing his or her behavior.

therapist's attempts to help him change? The psychologist needed to address Michael's current situation in terms of several different facets of his behavior.

Psychological assessment is the process of collecting and interpreting information that will be used to understand another person. Numerous data-gathering techniques can be used in this process. Several of these procedures are described in the following pages. We must remember, however, not to confuse the process of assessment with this list of techniques. Assessment procedures are tools that can be used in many ways. They cannot be used in an intellectual vacuum. The person who conducts the assessment must adopt a theoretical perspective regarding the nature of the disorders that are being considered and the causal processes that are involved in their origins (see Chapter 2). Interviews can be used to collect all sorts of information for all sorts of reasons. Psychological tests can be interpreted in many different ways. The value of assessment procedures can be determined only in the context of a specific purpose (McFall, 2005).

Assessment procedures can be used for several purposes. Perhaps most obvious is the need to describe the nature of the person's principal problem. This goal typically involves making a diagnosis. The clinician must collect information to support the diagnostic decision and to rule out alternative explanations for the symptoms. Assessment procedures are also used for making predictions, planning treatments, and evaluating treatments. The practical importance of predictions should be obvious: Many crucial decisions are based on psychologists' attempts to determine the probability of future events. Will a person engage in violent behavior? Can a person make rational decisions? Is a parent able to care for his or her children? Assessment is also commonly used to evaluate the likelihood that a particular form of treatment will be helpful for a specific patient and to provide guideposts by which the effectiveness of treatment programs can be measured. Different assessment procedures are likely to be employed for different purposes. Those that are useful in one situation may not be helpful in another.

## Assumptions About Consistency of Behavior

Assessment involves the collection of specific samples of a person's behavior. These samples may include things that the person says during an interview, responses that the person makes on a psychological test, or things that the person does while being observed. None of these would be important if we assumed that they were isolated events. They are useful to the extent that they represent examples of the ways in which the person will feel or behave in other situations. Psychologists, therefore, must be concerned about the consistency of behavior across time and situations. They want to know if they can *generalize,* or draw inferences about the person's behavior in the natural environment on the basis of the samples of behavior that are obtained in their assessment. If the client is depressed at this moment, how did she feel one week ago, and how will she feel tomorrow? In other words, is this a persistent phenomenon, or is it a temporary state? If a child is anxious and unable to pay attention in the psychologist's office, will he also exhibit these problems in his classroom? And how will he behave on the playground?

Psychologists typically seek out more than one source of information when conducting a formal assessment. Because we are trying to compose a broad, integrated picture of the person's adjustment, we must collect information from several sources and then attempt to integrate these data. Each piece of information may be considered to be one sample of the person's behavior. One way of evaluating the possible meaning or importance of this information is to consider the consistency across sources. Do the conclusions drawn on the basis of a diagnostic interview agree with those that are suggested by a psychological test? Do the psychologist's observations of the client's behavior and the client's self-report agree with observations that are reported by parents or teachers?

## Evaluating the Usefulness of Assessment Procedures

The same criteria that are used to evaluate diagnostic categories are used to evaluate the usefulness of assessment procedures: reliability and validity. In the case of assessment procedures, reliability can refer to various types of consistency. For example, the consistency of measurements over time is known as test–retest reliability. Will a person receive the same score if an assessment procedure is repeated at two different points in time? The internal consistency of items within a test is known as split-half reliability. If a test with many items measures a specific trait or ability, and if the items are divided in half, will the person's scores on the two halves agree with each other? Assessment procedures must be reliable if they are to be useful in either clinical practice or research.

The validity of an assessment procedure refers to its meaning or importance (Meyer et al., 2001; Strauss & Smith, 2009). Is the person's score on this test or procedure actually a reflection of the trait or ability that the test was designed to measure? And does the score tell us anything useful about the person's behavior in other

Every assessment device has its own strengths and weaknesses. Each presents a somewhat different (and perhaps limited or distorted) perspective on the person.

situations? Knowing that the person has achieved a particular score on this evaluation, can we make meaningful predictions about the person's responses to other tests or about his or her behavior in future situations? These are all questions about the validity of an assessment procedure. In general, the more consistent the information provided by different assessment procedures, the more valid each procedure is considered to be (see Critical Thinking Matters).

Cultural differences present an important challenge to the validity of assessment procedures. It is often difficult to understand the thoughts and behaviors of people from a cultural background that is different from our own. Measurement procedures that were constructed for one group may be misleading when they are applied to people from another culture. Language, religion, gender roles, beliefs about health and illness, and attitudes toward the family can all have an important impact on the ways in which psychological problems are experienced and expressed. These factors must be taken into consideration when psychologists collect information about the nature of a specific person's

## CRITICAL THINKING matters

problems. Interviews, observational procedures, and personality tests must be carefully evaluated for cross-cultural validity (Padilla, 2001). Unfortunately, this issue has often been overlooked in treatment planning and in psychopathology research. We should not assume that a questionnaire developed in one culture will necessarily be useful in another. Investigators must demonstrate empirically that it measures the same thing in both groups.

## Psychological Assessment Procedures

Our purpose in the rest of this chapter is to outline a range of assessment procedures. This is a selective sampling of measures rather than an exhaustive review. We begin our discussion with psychological assessment procedures, ranging from interviews to various kinds of psychological tests. The last section of this chapter is concerned with biological assessment procedures that tap neurological and biochemical events that are associated with mental disorders.

"Person variables" are typically the first things that come to mind when we think about the assessment of psychopathology. What did the person do or say? How does the person feel about his or her current situation? What skills and abilities does the person possess, and are there any important cognitive or social

deficits that should be taken into consideration? These questions about the individual person can be addressed through a number of procedures, including interviews, observations, and various types of self-report instruments and psychological tests.

### Interviews

Often, the best way to find out about someone is to talk with that person directly. The clinical interview is the most commonly used procedure in psychological assessment. Most of the categories that are defined in *DSM-5* are based on information that can be collected in an interview. These data are typically supplemented by information that is obtained from official records (previous hospital or clinic admissions, school reports, court files) and interviews with other informants (e.g., family members), but the clients' own direct descriptions of their problems are the primary basis for diagnostic decisions. Except for decisions regarding intellectual disability, none of the diagnostic categories in *DSM-5* is defined in terms of psychological or biological tests.

Interviews provide an opportunity to ask people for their own descriptions of their problems. Many of the symptoms of psychopathology are subjective, and an interview can provide a detailed analysis of these problems. Consider, for example, Michael's problems with anxiety. The unrelenting fear and revulsion that

## Depression/Deliberate Self-Harm

SARAH

*"I would be asked later 'well how did these cuts get here' and I would know that I had done it, but I wouldn't remember how I had done it or with what."*

👁 **Watch** the **Video** *Sarah: Depression/Deliberate Self-Harm* on **MyPsychLab**

Notice how the interviewer uses a flexible sequence of questions to elicit a compelling description of the subjective experiences associated with Sarah's cutting behavior.

he experienced at school were the central features of his problem. His obsessive thoughts of contamination were private events that could only be known to the psychologist on the basis of Michael's self-report, which was quite compelling. His family could observe Michael's peculiar habits with regard to arranging his schoolbooks, changing his clothes, and washing his hands, but the significance of these behaviors to Michael was not immediately apparent without the knowledge that they were based on an attempt to control or neutralize his anxiety-provoking images of taunting classmates.

Interviews also allow clinicians to observe important features of a person's appearance and nonverbal behavior. In Michael's case, the psychologist noticed during the initial interview that the skin on Michael's hands and lower arms was red and chafed from excessive scrubbing. He was neatly dressed but seemed especially self-conscious about his hair and glasses, which he adjusted repeatedly. Michael was reluctant to make eye contact, and his speech was soft and hesitant. His obvious discomfort in this social situation was consistent with his own descriptions of the anxiety that he felt during interactions with peers. It was also interesting to note that Michael became visibly agitated when discussing particular subjects, such as the incident with his track team. At these points in the interview, he would fidget restlessly in his seat and clasp his arms closely around his sides. These nonverbal aspects of Michael's behavior provided useful information about the nature of his distress.

**STRUCTURED INTERVIEWS** Assessment interviews vary with regard to the amount of structure that is imposed by the clinician. Some are relatively open-ended, or nondirective. In this type of interview, the clinician follows the train of thought supplied by the client. One goal of nondirective interviews is to help people clarify their subjective feelings and to provide general empathic support for whatever they may decide to do about their problems. In contrast to this open-ended style, some interviews follow a more specific question-and-answer format. Structured interviews, in which the clinician must ask each patient a specific list of detailed questions, are frequently employed for collecting information that will be used to make diagnostic decisions and to rate the extent to which a person is impaired by psychopathology.

Several different structured interviews have been developed for the purpose of making psychiatric diagnoses in large-scale epidemiological and cross-national studies (Segal et al., 2010). Investigators reasoned that the reliability of their diagnostic decisions would improve if they could ensure that clinicians always made a consistent effort to ask the same questions when they interviewed patients. Other forms of structured diagnostic interviews have been designed for use in the diagnosis of specific types of problems, such as personality disorders, anxiety disorders, dissociative disorders, and the behavior problems of children.

Structured interviews list a series of specific questions that lead to a detailed description of the person's behavior and experiences. As an example, consider the Structured Interview for DSM-IV Personality Disorders (SIDP-IV; Pfohl, Blum, & Zimmerman, 1995), which could have been used as part of the assessment process in Michael's situation. The SIDP-IV is a widely used interview that covers all of the personality disorder categories. Selected questions from the SIDP-IV are presented in Table 4.2. We have included in this table some of the questions that are specifically relevant to a diagnosis of schizotypal personality disorder.

Structured interview schedules provide a systematic framework for the collection of important diagnostic information, but they don't eliminate the need for an experienced clinician. If the interviewer is not able to establish a comfortable rapport with the client, then the interview might not elicit useful information. Furthermore, it is difficult to specify in advance all the questions that should be asked in a diagnostic interview. The client's responses to questions may require clarification. The interviewer must determine when it is necessary to probe further and in what ways to probe. Having lists of specific questions and clear definitions of diagnostic criteria will make the clinician's job easier, but clinical judgment remains an important ingredient in the diagnostic interview.

**ADVANTAGES** The clinical interview is the primary tool employed by clinical psychologists in the assessment of psychopathology. Several features of interviews account for this popularity, including the following issues:

1. The interviewer can control the interaction and can probe further when necessary.

2. By observing the patient's nonverbal behavior, the interviewer can try to detect areas of resistance. In that sense, the validity of the information may be enhanced.

3. An interview can provide a lot of information in a short period of time. It can cover past events and many different settings.

---

**TABLE 4.2**

# Sample Interview Questions for the Assessment of Schizotypal Personality Disorder

**Social Relationships**

This set of questions concerns the way you think and act in situations that involve other people. Remember that I'm interested in the way you are when you are your usual self.

**DSM Diagnostic Criterion:** Excessive social anxiety that does not diminish with familiarity and tends to be associated with paranoid fears rather than negative judgments about self.

Question: "Do you generally feel nervous or anxious around people?"

(IF YES, ask follow-up questions): "How bad does it get?" "Do you get nervous around people because you worry about what they might be up to?" "Are you less nervous after you get to know people better?"

**Perception of Others**

The questions in this section ask about experiences you may have had with other people.

**DSM Diagnostic Criterion:** Suspects, without sufficient basis, that others are exploiting, harming, or deceiving him or her

Question: "Have you had experiences where people who pretended to be your friends took advantage of you?"

(IF YES, follow-up questions): "What happened?" "How often has this happened?"

Question: "Are you good at spotting someone who is trying to deceive or con you?"

(IF YES, follow-up questions): "Can you give me some examples?"

**DSM Diagnostic Criterion:** Ideas of reference (the belief that irrelevant or harmless events refer to the person directly or have special personal significance for him or her)

Question: "Have you ever found that people around you seem to be talking in general, but then you realize their comments are really meant for you?"

(IF YES, follow-up question): "How do you know they're talking about you?"

Question: "Have you felt like someone in charge changed the rules specifically because of you, but they wouldn't admit it?"

Question: "Do you sometimes feel like strangers on the street are looking at you and talking about you?"

(IF YES, follow-up question): "Why do you think they notice you in particular?"

---

*Source:* Bruce, M.D. Pfohl, Nancee Blum and Mark Zimmerman. 1997. Structured Interview for DSM-IV Personality. American Psychiatric Association. Reprinted with permission from the Structured Interview for DSM-IV; Personality (SIDP-IV) (Copyright © 1997). American Psychiatric Association. All Rights Reserved.

*Note:* The DSM-5 diagnostic criteria for types of personality disorders are identical to those in DSM-IV.

*LIMITATIONS* Several limitations in the use of clinical interviews as part of the assessment process must be kept in mind. These include the following considerations:

1. Some patients may be unable or unwilling to provide a rational account of their problems. This may be particularly true of young children, who have not developed verbal skills, as well as some psychotic and demented patients who are unable to speak coherently.

2. People may be reluctant to admit experiences that are embarrassing or frightening. They may feel that they should report to the interviewer only those feelings and behaviors that are socially desirable.

3. Information provided by the client is necessarily filtered through the client's eyes. It is a subjective account and may be influenced or distorted by errors in memory and by selective perception.

4. Interviewers can influence their clients' accounts by the ways in which they phrase their questions and respond to the clients' responses.

## Observational Procedures

In addition to the information that we gain from what people are willing to tell us during interviews, we can also learn a lot by watching their behavior. Observational skills play an important part in most assessment procedures. Sometimes the things that we observe confirm the person's self-report, and at other times the person's overt behavior appears to be at odds with what he or she says. A juvenile delinquent might express in words his regret at having injured a classmate, but his smile and the twinkle in his eye may raise doubts about the sincerity of his statement. In situations such as this, we must reconcile information that is obtained from different sources. The picture that emerges of another person's adjustment is greatly enriched when data collected from interviews are supplemented by observations of the person's behavior.

Observational procedures may be either informal or formal. Informal observations are primarily qualitative. The clinician observes the person's behavior and the environment in which it occurs without attempting to record the frequency or intensity of specific responses. Michael's case illustrates the value of informal observations in the natural environment. When the therapist

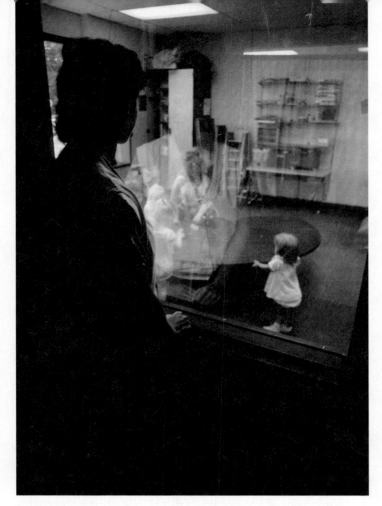

Direct observation can provide one of the most useful sources of information about a person's behavior. In this case, the children and their teacher are being observed from behind a one-way mirror in order to minimize reactivity, the effect that the observer's presence might have on their behavior.

environment. These artificial situations may also allow for more careful measurements of the person's problem than could be accomplished in a more complex situation.

In the case of obsessive–compulsive behavior, this approach might involve asking the person deliberately to touch an object that would ordinarily trigger ritualistic behaviors. The therapist might collect a set of objects that Michael would not want to touch, such as a schoolbook, a pair of old track shorts, and the knob of a door leading to the laundry room. It would be useful to know specifically which objects he would touch, the degree of discomfort that he experienced when touching them, and the length of time that he was able to wait before washing his hands after touching these objects. This information could also be used as an index of change as treatment progressed.

**RATING SCALES** Various types of procedures can be used to provide quantitative assessments of a person's behavior that are based on observations. One alternative is to use a **rating scale** in which the observer is asked to make judgments that place the person somewhere along a dimension. For example, a clinician might observe a person's behavior for an extended period of time and then complete a set of ratings that are concerned with dimensions such as the extent to which the person exhibits compulsive ritualistic behaviors.

Ratings can also be made on the basis of information collected during an interview. The Yale-Brown Obsessive Compulsive Scale (Y-BOCS; Goodman et al., 1989; Woody, Steketee, & Chambless, 1995) is an example of an interview-based rating scale that is used extensively in the evaluation of people with problems like Michael's. The interviewer asks the person a series of specific questions about the nature of his or her experience with obsessive thoughts and compulsive behaviors. For example, "How much of your time is occupied by obsessive thoughts?" Using a scale that ranges from 0 (none) to 4 (extreme), the interviewer then assigns a rating on several dimensions such as "time spent occupied by obsessive thoughts," "interference due to obsessive thoughts," "distress associated with obsessive thoughts," and "resistance against obsessions." The composite rating—the total across all the items in the scale—can be used as an index of the severity of the disorder.

Rating scales provide abstract descriptions of a person's behavior rather than a specific record of exactly what the person has done. They require social judgments on the part of the observer, who must compare this person's behavior with an ideal view of other people. How does this person compare to someone who has never experienced any difficulties in this particular area? How does the person compare to the most severely disturbed patients? The value of these judgments depends on the experience of the person who makes the ratings. They are useful to the extent that the observer is able to synthesize accurately the information that has been collected and then rate the frequency or severity of the problem relative to the behavior of other people.

visited Michael and his parents at their home, he learned that his ritualistic behaviors were more extreme than Michael had originally described. This was useful, but not particularly surprising, as patients with OCD are often reluctant to describe in an interview the full extent of their compulsive behavior. The therapist also learned that the parents themselves were quite concerned with rules and order. Everything in their home was highly polished and in its place. This observation helped the therapist understand the extent to which Michael's parents might contribute to, or reinforce, his rigid adherence to a strict set of rules.

Although observations are often conducted in the natural environment, there are times when it is useful to observe the person's behavior in a situation that the psychologist can arrange and control. Sometimes it isn't possible to observe the person's behavior in the natural environment because the behavior in question occurs infrequently or at times when an observer cannot be present; at other times the environment is inaccessible; and sometimes the behavior that is of interest is inherently a private act. In these cases, the psychologist may arrange to observe the person's behavior in a situation that in some ways approximates the real

**BEHAVIORAL CODING SYSTEMS** Another approach to quantifying observational data depends on recording the person's actual activities. Rather than making judgments about where the person falls on a particular dimension, behavioral coding systems focus on the frequency of specific behavioral events (Furr & Funder, 2007). This type of observation, therefore, requires fewer inferences on the part of the observer. Because they require extensive time and training, behavioral coding systems are used more frequently in research studies than in clinical settings. Coding systems can be used with observations that are made in the person's natural environment as well as with those that are performed in artificial, or contrived, situations that are specifically designed to elicit the problem behavior under circumstances in which it can be observed precisely. In some cases, the observations are made directly by a therapist, and at other times the information is provided by people who have a better opportunity to see the person's behavior in the natural environment, including teachers, parents, spouse, and peers.

Some approaches to systematic observation can be relatively simple. Consider, once again, the case of Michael. After the psychologist had conducted several interviews with Michael and his family, he asked Michael's mother to participate in the assessment process by making detailed observations of his hand washing over a period of several nights. The mother was given a set of forms—one for each day—that could be used to record each incident, the time at which it occurred, and the circumstances that preceded the washing. The day was divided into 30-minute intervals starting at 6:30 a.m., when Michael got out of bed, and ending at 10:30 p.m., when he usually went to sleep. On each line (one for each time interval), his mother indicated whether he had washed his hands, what had been going on just prior to washing, and how anxious (on a scale from 1 to 100) Michael felt at the time that he washed.

Some adult clients are able to complete this kind of record by keeping track of their own behavior—a procedure known as *self-monitoring*. In this case, Michael's mother was asked to help because she was considered a more accurate observer than Michael and because Michael did not want to touch the form that would be used to record these observations. He believed that it was contaminated because it had touched his school clothes, which he wore to the therapy session.

Two weeks of observations were examined prior to the start of Michael's treatment. They indicated several things, including the times of the day when Michael was most active with his washing rituals (between 6 and 9 p.m.) and those specific objects and areas in the house that were most likely to trigger a washing incident. This information helped the therapist plan the treatment procedure, which would depend on approaching Michael's problem at the level that could most easily be handled and moving toward those situations that were the most difficult for him. The observations provided by Michael's mother were also used to mark his progress after treatment began.

**ADVANTAGES** Observational measures, including rating scales and behavioral coding systems, can provide a useful supplement to information that is typically collected in an interview format. Their advantage lies primarily in the fact that clinicians observe behavior directly rather than relying on patients' self-reports. Specific types of observational measures have distinct advantages:

1. Rating scales are primarily useful as an overall index of symptom severity or functional impairment.

2. Behavioral coding systems provide detailed information about the person's behavior in a particular situation.

**LIMITATIONS** Observations are sometimes considered to be similar to photographs: They provide a more direct or realistic view of behavior than do people's recollections of their actions and feelings. But just as the quality of a photograph is influenced by the quality of the camera, the value of observational data depends on the procedures that are used to collect them. Thus, observations have a number of limitations:

1. Observational procedures can be time-consuming and therefore expensive. Raters usually require extensive training before they can use a detailed behavioral coding system.

2. Observers can make errors. Their perception may be biased, just as the inferences of an interviewer may be biased. The reliability of ratings as well as behavioral coding must be monitored.

3. People may alter their behavior, either intentionally or unintentionally, when they know that they are being observed—a phenomenon known as **reactivity.** For example, a person who is asked to count the number of times that he washes his hands may wash less frequently than he does when he is not keeping track.

4. Observational measures tell us only about the particular situation that was selected to be observed. We don't know if the person will behave in a similar way elsewhere or at a different time, unless we extend the scope of our observations.

5. There are some aspects of psychopathology that cannot be observed by anyone other than the person who has the problem. This is especially true for subjective experiences, such as guilt or low self-esteem.

## Personality Tests and Self-Report Inventories

Personality tests are another important source of information about an individual's adjustment. Tests provide an opportunity to collect samples of a person's behavior in a standardized situation. The person who is being tested is presented with some kind of standard stimuli, usually specific questions that can be answered true or false. Exactly the same stimuli are used every time that the test is given. In that way, the clinician can be sure that differences in performance can be interpreted as differences in abilities or traits rather than differences in the testing situation.

**Personality inventories** consist of a series of straightforward statements; the person being tested is typically required to indicate whether each statement is true or false in relation to himself or herself. Several types of personality inventories are widely used. Some are designed to identify personality traits in a normal population, and others focus more specifically on psychological problems. We have chosen to focus on the most extensively used personality inventory—the *Minnesota Multiphasic Personality Inventory* (MMPI)—to illustrate the characteristics of these tests as assessment devices.

The original version of the MMPI was developed in the 1940s at the University of Minnesota. For the past 60 years, it has been the most widely used psychological test. Thousands of research articles have been published on the MMPI. The inventory was revised several years ago, and it is currently known as the MMPI-2 (Butcher, 2006).

The MMPI-2 is based on a series of more than 500 statements that cover topics ranging from physical complaints and psychological states to occupational preferences and social attitudes. Examples are statements such as, "I sometimes keep on at a thing until others lose their patience with me"; "My feelings are easily hurt"; and "There are persons who are trying to steal my thoughts and ideas." After reading each statement, the person is instructed to indicate whether it is true or false. Scoring of the MMPI-2 is objective. After the responses to all questions are totaled, the person receives a numerical score on each of 10 clinical scales as well as four validity scales.

Before considering the possible clinical significance of a person's MMPI-2 profile, the psychologist will examine a number of validity scales, which reflect the patient's attitude toward the test and the openness and consistency with which the questions were answered. The L (Lie) Scale is sensitive to unsophisticated attempts to avoid answering in a frank and honest manner. For example, one statement on this scale says, "At times I feel like swearing." Although this is perhaps not an admirable trait, virtually all normal subjects indicate that the item is true. Subjects who indicate that the item is false (does not apply to them) receive 1 point on the L scale.

Several responses of this sort would result in an elevated score on the scale and would indicate that the person's overall test results should not be interpreted as a true reflection of his or her feelings. Other validity scales reflect tendencies to exaggerate problems, carelessness in completing the questions, and unusual defensiveness.

If the profile is considered valid, the process of interpretation will be directed toward the 10 clinical scales, which are described in Table 4.3. Some of these scales carry rather obvious meaning, whereas others are associated with a more general or mixed pattern of symptoms. For example, Scale 2 (Depression) is a relatively straightforward index of degree of depression. Scale 7 (Psychasthenia), in contrast, is more complex and is based on items that measure anxiety, insecurity, and excessive doubt. There are many different ways to obtain an elevated score on any of the clinical scales, because each scale is composed of many items. Even the more obvious scales can indicate several different types of problems. Therefore, the pattern of scale scores is more important than the elevation of any particular scale.

Rather than depending only on their own experience and clinical judgment, which may be subject to various sorts of bias and inconsistency, many clinicians analyze the results of a specific test on the basis of an explicit set of rules that are derived from empirical research (Greene, 2006). This is known as an **actuarial interpretation.** We can illustrate this process using Michael's profile. The profile is first described in terms of the pattern of scale scores, beginning with the highest and proceeding to the lowest. Those that are elevated above a scale score of 70 are most important, and interpretations are sometimes based on the "high-point pair."

---

**TABLE 4.3**
## Clinical Scales for the MMPI-2

| Scale Number | Scale Name | Interpretation of High Scores |
|---|---|---|
| 1 | Hypochondriasis | Excessive bodily concern; somatic symptoms |
| 2 | Depression | Depressed; pessimistic; irritable; demanding |
| 3 | Hysteria | Physical symptoms that cannot be traced to a medical illness; self-centered; demands attention |
| 4 | Psychopathic Deviate | Asocial or antisocial; rebellious; impulsive, poor judgment |
| 5 | Masculinity-Femininity | For men: aesthetic interests<br>For women: assertive; competitive; self-confident |
| 6 | Paranoia | Suspicious, sensitive; resentful; rigid; may be frankly psychotic |
| 7 | Psychasthenia | Anxious; worried; obsessive; lacks self-confidence; problems in decision making |
| 8 | Schizophrenia | May have thinking disturbance, withdrawn; feels alienated and unaccepted |
| 9 | Hypomania | Excessive activity; lacks direction; low frustration tolerance; friendly |
| 0 | Social-Introversion | Socially introverted; shy; sensitive; overcontrolled; conforming |

Following this procedure, Michael's profile could be coded as a 2–0; that is, his highest scores were on Scales 2 and 0. The clinician then looks up this specific configuration of scores in a kind of MMPI-2 "cookbook" to see what sort of descriptive characteristics apply. One cookbook offers the following statement about adolescents (mostly 14 and 15 years old) who fit the 2–0/0–2 code type:

> Eighty-seven percent of the 2–0/0–2s express feelings of inferiority to their therapists. They say that they are not good-looking, that they are afraid to speak up in class, and that they feel awkward when they meet people or try to make a date (91 percent of high 2–0/0–2s). Their therapists see the 2–0/0–2s as anxious, fearful, timid, withdrawn, and inhibited. They are depressed, and very vulnerable to threat. The 2–0/0–2 adolescents are overcontrolled; they cannot let go, even when it would be appropriate for them to do so. They are afraid of emotional involvement with others and, in fact, seem to have little need for such affiliation. These adolescents are viewed by their psychotherapists as schizoid; they think and associate in unusual ways and spend a good deal of time in personal fantasy and daydreaming. They are serious young people who tend to anticipate problems and difficulties. Indeed, they are prone toward obsessional thinking and are compulsively meticulous.
>
> (Marks, Seeman, & Haller, 1974, p. 201)

Several comments must be made about this statement. First, nothing is certain. Actuarial descriptions are probability statements. They indicate that a certain proportion of the people who produce this pattern of scores will be associated with a certain characteristic or behavior. If 87 percent of the

adolescents who produce this code type express feelings of inferiority, 13 percent do not. Many aspects of this description apply to Michael's current adjustment, but they don't all fit. The MMPI-2 must be used in conjunction with other assessment procedures. The accuracy of actuarial statements can be verified through interviews with the person or through direct observations of his or her behavior.

**ADVANTAGES** The MMPI-2 has several advantages in comparison to interviews and observational procedures. In clinical practice, it is seldom used by itself, but, for the following reasons, it can serve as a useful supplement to other methods of collecting information.

1. The MMPI-2 provides information about the person's test-taking attitude, which alerts the clinician to the possibility that clients are careless, defensive, or exaggerating their problems.

2. The MMPI-2 covers a wide range of problems in a direct and efficient manner. It would take a clinician several hours to go over all these topics using an interview format.

3. Because the MMPI-2 is scored objectively, the test's description of the person's adjustment is not influenced by the clinician's subjective impression of the client.

4. The MMPI-2 can be interpreted in an actuarial fashion, using extensive banks of information regarding people who respond to items in a particular way.

**LIMITATIONS** The MMPI-2 also has some limitations. Some of its limitations derive from the fact that it has been used for many years, and the ways in which different forms of psychopathology are viewed have changed over time.

1. The utility of the traditional clinical scales (see Table 4.3) has been questioned, especially with regard to their ability to discriminate between different types of mental disorders. Restructured clinical scales have been developed in order to address these problems, but the new scales remain controversial (Nichols, 2006).

2. The test depends on the person's ability to read and respond to written statements. Some people cannot complete the rather extensive list of questions. These include many people who are acutely psychotic, intellectually impaired, or poorly educated.

3. Specific data are not always available for a particular profile. Many patients' test results do not meet criteria for a particular code type with which extensive data are associated. Therefore, actuarial interpretation is not really possible for these profiles.

4. Some studies have found that profile types are not stable over time. It is not clear whether this instability should be interpreted as lack of reliability or as sensitivity to change in the person's level of adjustment.

*"Here they come—act infantile."*

## Projective Personality Tests

In **projective tests,** the person is presented with a series of ambiguous stimuli. The best known projective test, introduced in 1921 by Hermann Rorschach (1884–1922), a Swiss psychiatrist, is based on the use of inkblots. The Rorschach test consists of a series of 10 inkblots. Five contain various shades of gray on a white background, and five contain elements of color. The person is asked to look at each card and indicate what it looks like or what it appears to be. There are, of course, no correct answers. The instructions are intentionally vague in order to avoid influencing the person's responses through subtle suggestions.

Projective techniques such as the Rorschach test were originally based on psychodynamic assumptions about the nature of personality and psychopathology. Considerable emphasis was placed on the importance of unconscious motivations—conflicts and impulses of which the person is largely unaware. In other words, people being tested presumably project hidden desires and conflicts when they try to describe or explain the cards. In so doing, they may reveal things about themselves of which they are not consciously aware or that they might not be willing to admit if they were asked directly. The cards are not designed or chosen to be realistic or representational; they presumably look like whatever the person wants them to look like.

Michael did not actually complete any projective personality tests. We can illustrate the way in which these tests might have been used in his case, however, by considering a man who had been given a diagnosis of obsessive–compulsive disorder as well as showing evidence of two types of personality disorders—dependent and schizotypal features. This patient was 22 years old, unemployed, and living with his mother. His father had died in an accident four years earlier. Like Michael, this man was bothered by intrusive thoughts of contamination, and he frequently engaged in compulsive washing (Hurt, Reznikoff, & Clarkin, 1991). His responses to the cards on the Rorschach

Projective tests require a person to respond to ambiguous stimuli. Here, a woman is taking the Thematic Apperception Test (TAT), in which she will be asked to make up a story about a series of drawings of people.

frequently mentioned emotional distress ("a man screaming"), interpersonal conflict ("two women fighting over something"), and war ("two mushrooms of a nuclear bomb cloud"). He did not incorporate color into any of his responses to the cards.

The original procedures for scoring the Rorschach were largely impressionistic and placed considerable emphasis on the content of the person's response. Responses given in the example above might be taken to suggest a number of important themes. Aggression and violence are obvious possibilities. Perhaps the man was repressing feelings of hostility, as indicated by his frequent references to war and conflict. These themes were coupled with a guarded approach to emotional reactions, which is presumably reflected by his avoidance of color. The psychologist might have wondered whether the man felt guilty about something, such as his father's death. This kind of interpretation, which depends heavily on symbolism and clinical inference, provides intriguing material for the clinician to puzzle over. Unfortunately, the reliability and validity of this intuitive type of scoring procedure are very low (Garb et al., 2005).

When we ponder the utility of these interpretations, we should also keep in mind the relative efficiency of projective testing procedures. Did the test tell us anything that we didn't already know or that we couldn't have learned in a more straightforward manner? The clinician might learn about a client's feelings of anger or guilt by using a clinical interview, which is often a more direct and efficient way of collecting information.

More recent approaches to the use of projective tests view the person's descriptions of the cards as a sample of his or her perceptual and cognitive styles (Meyer & Viglione, 2008). The Comprehensive System, an objective scoring procedure for the Rorschach, is based primarily on the form rather than the content of the subject's responses. According to this system, interpretation of the test depends on the way in which the descriptions take into account the shapes and colors on the cards. Does the person see movement in the card? Does she focus on tiny details, or does she base her descriptions on global impressions of the entire form of the inkblot? These and many other considerations contribute to the overall interpretation of the Rorschach test. The reliability of this scoring system is much better than would be achieved by informal, impressionistic procedures. Research evidence supports the validity of some of these scales, especially those concerned with cognitive and perceptual processes (Mihura et al., 2013), but the validity of other scores remains open to question (Wood et al., 2003).

There are many different types of projective tests. Some employ stimuli that are somewhat less ambiguous than the inkblots in the Rorschach. The Thematic Apperception Test (TAT), for example, consists of a series of drawings that depict human figures in various ambiguous situations. Most of the cards portray more than one person. The figures and their poses tend to elicit stories with themes of sadness and violence. The person is asked to describe the identities of the people in the cards and to make up a story about what is happening. These stories presumably reflect the person's own ways of perceiving reality.

**ADVANTAGES** The advantages of projective tests center on the fact that the tests are interesting to give and interpret, and they sometimes provide a way to talk to people who are otherwise reluctant or unable to discuss their problems. Projective tests are more appealing to psychologists who adopt a psychodynamic view of personality and psychopathology because such tests are believed to reflect unconscious conflicts and motivations. Some specific advantages are listed as follows:

1. Some people may feel more comfortable talking in an unstructured situation than they would if they were required to participate in a structured interview or to complete the lengthy MMPI.

2. Projective tests can provide an interesting source of information regarding the person's unique view of the world, and they can be a useful supplement to information obtained with other assessment tools (Weiner & Meyer, 2009).

3. To whatever extent a person's relationships with other people are governed by unconscious cognitive and emotional events, projective tests may provide information that cannot be obtained through direct interviewing methods or observational procedures (Meyer & Archer, 2001; Stricker & Gold, 1999).

**LIMITATIONS** There are many serious problems with the use of projective tests. The popularity of projective tests has declined considerably since the 1970s, even in clinical settings, primarily because research studies have found relatively little evidence to support their reliability and validity (Garb et al., 2005).

1. Lack of standardization in administration and scoring was a serious problem, but the Comprehensive System for scoring the Rorschach has made improvements in that regard.

2. Little information is available on which to base comparisons to normal adults or children.

3. Some projective procedures, such as the Rorschach, can be very time consuming, particularly if the person's responses are scored with a standardized procedure such as the Comprehensive System.

4. Information regarding the reliability and validity of projective tests is mixed, with many scales showing little systematic value.

## Biological Assessment Procedures

Clinicians have developed a number of techniques for measuring the association between biological systems and abnormal behavior. These techniques are seldom used in clinical practice (at least for the diagnosis of psychopathology), but they have been employed extensively in research settings, and it seems possible that they will one day become an important source of information on individual patients.

### Brain Imaging Techniques

The past three decades have seen a tremendous explosion of information and technology in the neurosciences. We now understand in considerable detail how neurons in the central nervous system communicate with one another, and scientists have invented sophisticated methods to create images of the living human brain (Bremner, 2005; Lagopoulos, 2010). Some of these procedures provide static pictures of various brain structures at rest, just as an X-ray provides a photographic image of a bone

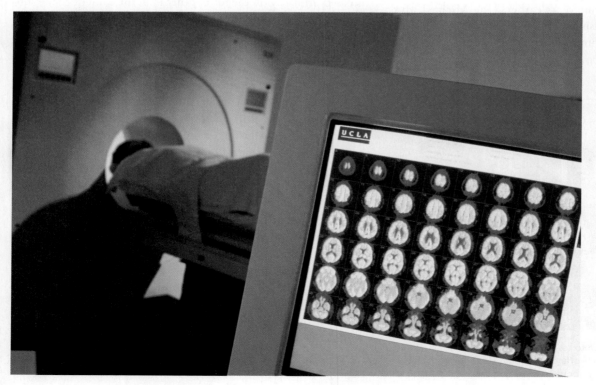

Positron emission tomography (PET scan) can provide useful images of dynamic brain functions. Areas that appear red or yellow indicate areas of the brain that are active (consuming the labeled glucose molecules), whereas those that are blue or green are relatively inactive. Different areas of the brain become active depending on whether the person is at rest or engaged in particular activities when the image is created.

or some other organ of the body. Studies of this type are typically concerned with the size of various parts of the brain. For example, many studies have compared the average size of the lateral ventricles—large chambers filled with cerebrospinal fluid—in groups of patients with schizophrenia and normal comparison groups. Other methods can be used to create dynamic images of brain functions—reflecting the rate of activity in various parts of the brain—while a person is performing different tasks. These functional images allow scientists to examine which parts of the brain are involved in various kinds of events, such as perception, memory, language, and emotional experience. They may also allow us to learn whether specific areas or pathways in the brain are uniquely associated with specific types of mental disorders.

Precise measures of brain structure can be obtained with *magnetic resonance imaging* (MRI). In MRI, images are generated using a strong magnetic field rather than X-rays (Posner & Di-Girolamo, 2000). A large magnet in the scanner causes chemical elements in specific brain regions to emit distinctive radio signals. Both computed tomography (CT) scanning and MRI can provide a static image of specific brain structures. MRI provides more detailed images than CT scans and is able to identify smaller parts of the brain. For this reason, and because it lends itself more easily to the creation of three-dimensional pictures of the brain, MRI has replaced CT scanning in most research facilities.

In addition to structural MRI, which provides a static view of brain structures, advances in the neurosciences have also produced techniques that create images of brain functions (Brown & Thompson, 2010; Raichle, 2005). *Positron emission tomography* (PET) is one scanning technique that can be used to create functional brain images (Wahl, 2002). This procedure is much more expensive than the other imaging techniques because it requires a nuclear cyclotron to produce special radioactive elements. PET scans are capable of providing relatively detailed images of the brain. In addition, they can reflect changes in brain activity as the person responds to the demands of various tasks.

The newest and most exciting method of imaging brain functions involves *functional MRI* (fMRI). When neurons are activated, their metabolism increases and they require increased blood flow to supply them with oxygen. The magnetic properties of blood change as a function of the level of oxygen that it is carrying. In fMRI, a series of images is acquired in rapid succession. Small differences in signal intensity from one image to the next provide a measure of moment-to-moment changes in the amount of oxygen in blood flowing to specific areas of the brain. While other functional imaging procedures such as PET are only able to measure activities that are sustained over a period of several minutes, fMRI is able to identify changes in brain activity that lasts less than a second (Huettel, Song, & McCarthy, 2004).

Functional brain imaging procedures have been used extensively to study possible neurological underpinnings of various types of mental disorders. For example, in the case of obsessive-compulsive disorder (OCD), studies using PET and fMRI have suggested that symptoms of OCD are associated with multiple brain regions, including the caudate nucleus, the orbital prefrontal cortex, and the anterior cingulate cortex (located on the medial surface of the frontal lobe). These pathways are illustrated in Figure 4.2. They seem to be overly active in people with OCD, especially when the person is confronted with stimuli that provoke his or her obsessions (Husted, Shapira, & Goodman, 2006; Menzies et al., 2008).

These results are intriguing because they suggest that certain regions and circuits in the brain may somehow be associated with the presence of obsessive–compulsive symptoms. We must emphasize, however, that the results of such imaging procedures are not useful diagnostically with regard to an individual person. In other words, some people with OCD do not exhibit increased metabolism rates in the caudate or the anterior cingulate cortex, and some people who do not have OCD do show increased levels of activity in these brain regions.

**ADVANTAGES** Brain imaging techniques provide detailed information regarding the structure of brain areas and activity levels in the brain that are associated with the performance of particular tasks. They have important uses, primarily as research tools:

1. In clinical practice, imaging techniques can be used to rule out various neurological conditions that might explain behavioral or cognitive deficits. These include such conditions as brain tumors and vascular disease.

2. Procedures such as fMRI and PET can help research investigators explore the relation between brain functions and specific mental disorders. This type of information will be considered in several chapters later in this book.

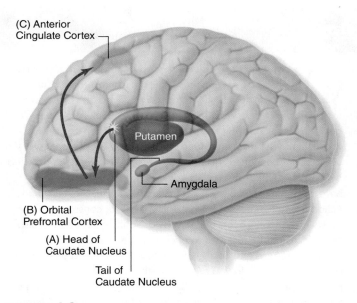

**FIGURE 4.2**

**Brain Regions Associated with OCD** When a person with OCD experiences symptoms, an increase in neural activity is seen in the caudate (A), which triggers the urge to "do something," through the orbital prefrontal cortex (B), which gives the feeling that "something is wrong," and back through the anterior cingulated cortex (C), which keeps attention fixed on the feeling of unease.

This view of Earth from space shows hot spots on the Earth's surface at night, an indication of areas of heavier population. Imaging techniques like fMRI offer views of the brain that are similarly fascinating—and similarly lacking in resolution, detail, and meaning.

**LIMITATIONS** Brain imaging procedures are used extensively in the study and assessment of neurological disorders. In the field of psychopathology, they are currently research tools and have little clinical importance outside the assessment and treatment of disorders such as Alzheimer's disease (see Chapter 14). Some of the major limitations are listed here:

1. Norms have not been established for any of these measures. It is not possible to use brain imaging procedures for diagnostic purposes.

2. These procedures are relatively expensive—especially PET scans and fMRI—and some procedures must be used cautiously because the patient may be exposed to radioactive substances.

3. We should not assume that all cognitive processes, emotional experiences, or mental disorders are necessarily linked to activity (or the absence of activity) in a specific area of the brain. Scientists are still debating the extent to which these experiences are localized within the brain (Uttal, 2001).

## getting HELP

Only one in five people who need treatment actually gets it. There are several reasons for this unfortunate state of events. One is lack of information. If you don't recognize the presence of a serious problem, you won't seek help. You will get care more promptly and make better treatment choices if you understand your problems. One consideration is the extent to which your experiences resemble the formal diagnostic terms used by mental health professionals. Allen Frances and Michael First have written a useful book called *Your Mental Health: A Layman's Guide to the Psychiatrist's Bible.* This primer for consumers of mental health services covers many types of adult and childhood disorders. Each chapter includes a concise, readable description of the typical symptoms and course of the disorder, followed by a discussion designed to help you decide whether your problems warrant professional help ("Am I okay?"). Finally, the authors review treatment options and where to go for help for each of the problems.

Even after they recognize the presence of a serious problem, some people are reluctant to seek help; they fear there is a stigma attached to "mental problems" despite the fact that seeking therapy is now commonplace. Negative stereotypes regarding mental disorders persist. We hope that you will not allow these distorted views to delay or interfere with efforts to improve your life. If you have concerns about this issue, it may help to read about stigma and mental health, a problem that has been addressed by Rosalynn Carter, a leading advocate on behalf of people with mental disorders and wife of former president Jimmy Carter. Her book, *Helping Someone with Mental Illness,* contains an excellent discussion of these issues. The Carter Center is actively involved in issues that affect public policies regarding mental disorders. The URL for its Web page is www.cartercenter.org. It also contains information relevant to the struggle to correct biased and inaccurate views of people with mental disorders.

We all can help eliminate discrimination against those who suffer from (or have recovered from) mental disorders. Advice for positive action is presented on several Web sites, including the National Mental Health America's home page. People will find it easier to seek help when they no longer need to worry about the potential effects of distorted, negative views of their problems.

# 4 Summary

Formal classification systems for mental disorders have been developed in order to facilitate communication, research, and treatment planning. Clinicians assign a diagnosis if the person's behavior meets the specific criteria for a particular type of disorder, such as schizophrenia or major depressive disorder.

The current official system published by the American Psychiatric Association is the fifth edition of the *Diagnostic and Statistical Manual of Mental Disorders,* or *DSM-5.* It is based on a **categorical approach to classification** and typically employs specific inclusion and exclusion criteria to define each disorder. The categories that are defined in *DSM-5* are based primarily on descriptive principles rather than on theoretical knowledge regarding the etiology of the disorders.

Scientists may also use a **dimensional approach to classification**— that is, one that describes the objects of classification in terms of continuous dimensions. In fact, most features of mental disorders, such as anxiety and depressed mood, are dimensional in nature.

Cultural factors play an important role in both the expression and recognition of symptoms of mental disorders. The accuracy and utility of a clinical diagnosis depend on the clinician's ability to consider the cultural context in which the problem appeared. *DSM-5* includes a glossary of cultural concepts of distress, such as *ataques de nervios.*

The usefulness of a classification system depends on several criteria, especially **reliability** and **validity.** The reliability of many categories in DSM-5 is good, but other disorders are more problematic in this regard. The validity of most categories remains under active investigation.

The general process of collecting and interpreting information is called **assessment.** Interviews, observations, and tests are among the most frequently used assessment procedures. It is never possible to learn everything about a particular person. Choices have to be made, and some information must be excluded from the analysis.

Structured diagnostic interviews are used extensively in conjunction with the *DSM-5* classification system. The main advantage of interviews is their flexibility. Their primary limitation lies in the inability or unwillingness of some clients to provide a rational description of their own problems, as well as the subjective factors that influence the clinician's interpretation of data collected in an interview.

**Personality inventories,** like the MMPI-2, offer several advantages as assessment devices. They can be scored objectively, they often contain validity scales that reflect the person's attitude and test-taking set, and they can be interpreted in reference to well-established standards for people with and without specific types of adjustment problems.

Some psychologists use **projective personality tests,** like the Rorschach, to acquire information that might not be obtained from direct interviews or observations. Research studies have found mixed evidence to support the validity of projective tests, and their continued use is controversial.

Biological assessment procedures are used primarily in research studies. These include brain imaging techniques, such as fMRI and PET scans, as well as psychophysiological recording procedures. Biological assessment procedures do not yet have diagnostic value in clinical situations, except for the purpose of ruling out certain conditions, such as brain tumors and vascular disease.

## The Big Picture

## critical thinking review

**4.1 Why do we need a system to classify abnormal behavior?**
Classification systems provide a way for scientists and clinicians to organize information and communicate with each other and with patients regarding the nature of mental disorders . . . (see page 78).

**4.2 Should disorders that are unique to our own culture be considered cultural concepts of distress?**
In the same way that *ataques de nervios* is a behavioral phenomenon associated with the culture of Puerto Rico, bulimia seems to be uniquely associated with Western culture and is closely linked to its values regarding beauty . . . (see page 84).

**4.3 What is the difference between reliability and validity?**
The fact that two people agree on assigning a specific diagnosis does not necessarily imply that it is meaningful . . . (see pages 85–86).

**4.4 How could the DSM-5 classification system be improved?**
Many experts agree that the classification system should pay greater attention to the dimensional nature of abnormal behaviors while attempting to clarify the boundaries between mental disorders and normal behavior . . . (see pages 88–90).

**4.5** Why do clinical interviews sometimes provide limited or distorted results?

Some people are either unwilling or unable to provide an accurate account of their problems . . . (see page 94).

**4.6** Why is the MMPI-2 sometimes called an objective personality test?

The person's responses to test items are scored according to an explicit set of rules that are based on empirical research and interpreted using actuarial predictions . . . (see page 97).

**4.7** Why are brain imaging procedures not used for the diagnosis of mental disorders?

They are currently best seen as research tools. No unique patterns of brain structure or function have been found that consistently and accurately identify people with specific mental disorders . . . (see page 102).

# key terms

actuarial
   interpretation   97
assessment   78
categorical approach to
   classification   80
classification system   80
comorbidity   89
cultural concepts of
   distress   84
diagnosis   78
dimensional approach to
   classification   80
personality inventory   97
projective tests   99
rating scale   95
reactivity   96
reliability   85
stigma   82
validity   86

# mood disorders and suicide

**5**

# The Big Picture

## learning objectives

**5.1**
What is the difference between clinical depression and a low mood?

**5.2**
Are there different kinds of depression?

**5.3**
How do depressive and bipolar disorders differ?

**5.4**
Are we more likely to experience depression as we get older?

**5.5**
Why do some people become depressed after stressful life events while others do not?

**5.6**
Is psychological treatment as effective as medication in treating depression?

**5.7**
Why do some people want to end their own lives?

Sadness may be the price that we pay for attachments to other people. Losses are inevitable, and we all endure the pain that comes with them. Beyond relatively short-lived feelings of grief and sorrow, prolonged sadness can grow into something much more debilitating. Everyone's life contains the potential for despair. Some people are able to work their way through it, but others become overwhelmed. When it reaches higher levels of intensity and begins to interfere with a person's ability to function and enjoy life, a low mood is known as clinical depression. In this chapter we will consider emotional disorders that involve prolonged periods of severe depression.

## Overview

If one measures disability in terms of years lived with severe impairments, major depression is the leading cause of disability worldwide (Moussavi et al., 2007). The magnitude of the problem is truly staggering. Depression accounts for almost 10 percent of all disability (see Table 5.1). Experts predict that it will become an even greater problem by the year 2020. Younger generations are experiencing higher rates of depression than their predecessors, and those who become depressed are doing so at an early age.

Psychopathologists use several terms to describe problems that are associated with emotional response systems. This language can become confusing because most of us already use these words in our everyday vocabulary. Thus, we must define these terms as they are used in psychopathology so that our discussion will be clear. *Emotion* refers to a state of arousal that is defined by subjective states of feeling, such as sadness, anger, and disgust. Emotions are often accompanied by physiological changes, such as changes in heart rate and respiration rate. **Affect** refers to the pattern of observable behaviors, such as facial expression, that are associated with these subjective feelings. People also express affect through the pitch of their voices and with their hand and body movements. **Mood** refers to a pervasive and sustained emotional response that, in its extreme form, can color the person's perception of the world (APA, 2013). The disorders discussed in this chapter are primarily associated with two specific moods: depression and elation.

Depression can refer either to a mood or to a *clinical syndrome,* a combination of emotional, cognitive, and behavioral symptoms. The feelings associated with a **depressed mood** often include disappointment and despair. Although sadness is a universal experience, profound depression is not. No one has been able to identify the exact point at which "feeling down or blue" crosses a line and becomes depression. One experience shades gradually into the next. The transition has been described by

**TABLE 5.1**

## Leading Causes of Disability Worldwide as Measured by Years of Life Lived with a Disability

| All Causes | Proportion of Total Years Lived with Disability |
|---|---|
| 1. Depression | 9.4 |
| 2. Hearing loss | 5.5 |
| 3. Cataracts | 5.2 |
| 4. Osteoarthritis | 3.2 |
| 5. Vision disorders | 3.1 |
| 6. Cerebrovascular disease | 2.7 |
| 7. Dementia | 2.6 |
| 8. Perinatal conditions | 2.5 |
| 9. Alcohol-use disorders | 2.5 |
| 10. Chronic obstructive pulmonary disease | 2.1 |

*Source:* Andrews, Gavin. Depression is very disabling. The Lancet. 2007 September 8; 370(9590).

Andrew Solomon (2001) in *The Noonday Demon,* an eloquent book in which he documents his own struggles with depression:

> Depression starts out insipid, fogs the days into a dull color, weakens ordinary actions until their clear shapes are obscured by the effort they require, leaves you tired and bored and self-obsessed—but you get through all that. Not happily, perhaps, but you can get through. No one has ever been able to define the collapse point that marks major depression, but when you get there, there's not much mistaking it. (p. 17)

People who are in a severely depressed mood describe the feeling as overwhelming, suffocating, or numbing. In the syndrome of depression, which is also called **clinical depression,** a depressed mood is accompanied by several other symptoms, such as fatigue, loss of energy, difficulty in sleeping, and changes in appetite. Clinical depression also involves a variety of changes in thinking and overt behavior. The person may experience cognitive symptoms, such as extreme guilt, feelings of worthlessness, concentration problems, and thoughts of suicide. Behavioral symptoms may range from constant pacing and fidgeting to extreme inactivity. Throughout the rest of this chapter, we will use the term depression to refer to the clinical syndrome rather than the mood.

**Mania,** the flip side of depression, also involves a disturbance in mood that is accompanied by additional symptoms. **Euphoria,** or elated mood, is the opposite emotional state from a depressed mood. It is characterized by an exaggerated feeling of physical and emotional well-being (APA, 2013). Manic symptoms that frequently accompany an elated mood include inflated self-esteem, decreased need for sleep, distractibility, pressure to keep talking, and the subjective feeling of thoughts racing through the person's head faster than they can be spoken. Mania is, therefore, a syndrome in the same sense that clinical depression is a syndrome.

**Mood disorders** are defined in terms of *episodes*—discrete periods of time in which the person's behavior is dominated by either a depressed or manic mood. Unfortunately, most people with a mood disorder experience more than one episode. The following case studies illustrate the way that numerous symptoms combine to form syndromes that are used to define mood disorders. They also provide examples of the two primary types of mood disorders: (1) those in which the person experiences only episodes of depression, known as **depressive disorders;** and (2) those in which the person experiences episodes of mania as well as depression, known as **bipolar disorder.** Episodes of depression are defined by the same symptoms, regardless of whether the person's disorder is depressive or bipolar in nature. A small number of patients have only manic episodes with no evidence of depression; they are included in the bipolar category. Years ago, bipolar disorder was known as *manic–depressive disorder.* Although this term has been replaced in the official diagnostic manual, some clinicians still prefer to use it because it offers a more direct description of the patient's experience.

## → An Attorney's Major Depressive Episode

Cathy was a 31-year-old attorney who had been promoted to the rank of partner the previous year and was considered one of the brightest, most promising young members of her firm. In spite of her apparent success, she was plagued by doubts about her own abilities and was convinced that she was unworthy of her promotion. Cathy decided to seek treatment because she was profoundly miserable. Beyond being depressed, she felt numb. She had been feeling unusually fatigued and irritable for several months, but her mood took a serious swing for the worse after one of the firm's clients, for whom Cathy was primarily responsible, decided to switch to another firm. Although the decision was clearly based on factors that were beyond her control, Cathy blamed herself. She interpreted this event as a reflection of her professional incompetence, in spite of the fact that virtually all of her other clients had praised her work and the senior partners in her firm had given her consistently positive reviews.

Cathy had always looked forward to going to the office, and she truly enjoyed her work. After she lost this client, however, going to work had seemed like an overwhelming burden. She found it impossible to concentrate and instead brooded about her own incompetence. Soon she started calling in sick. She began to spend her time sitting in bed staring at the television screen, without paying attention to any program, and she never left her apartment. She felt lethargic all the time, but she wasn't sleeping well. Her appetite disappeared. Her best friend tried repeatedly to get in touch with her, but Cathy wouldn't return her calls. She listened passively as her friend left messages on the answering machine. She just didn't feel like doing anything or talking to anyone. "Life has lost its interest and meaning. I've failed at my job and failed in my relationships. I deserve to be alone."

Cathy considered her social life to be a disaster, and it didn't seem to be getting any better. She had been separated from her husband for five years, and her most recent boyfriend had started dating another woman. She had tried desperately for several weeks to force herself to be active, but eventually she stopped caring. The situation seemed completely hopeless. Although she had often gone to parties with other members of her law firm, she usually felt as though she didn't fit in. Everyone else seemed to be part of a couple, and Cathy was usually on her own. Other people didn't appreciate the depth of her loneliness. Sometimes it seemed to Cathy that she would be better off dead. She spent a good deal of time brooding about suicide, but she feared that if she tried to harm herself she might make things worse than they already were.

Cathy's problems would be classified as a depressive disorder because she had experienced at least one episode of major depression and she had never had a manic episode. Her experience provides a framework in which we can discuss the difference between normal sadness and clinical depression.

| TABLE 5.2 |
|:---|
| **Important Considerations in Distinguishing Clinical Depression from Normal Sadness** |

1. The mood change is pervasive across situations and persistent over time. The person's mood does not improve, even temporarily, when he or she engages in activities that are usually experienced as pleasant.
2. The mood change may occur in the absence of any precipitating events, or it may be completely out of proportion to the person's circumstances.
3. The depressed mood is accompanied by impaired ability to function in usual social and occupational roles. Even simple activities become overwhelmingly difficult.
4. The change in mood is accompanied by a cluster of additional signs and symptoms, including cognitive, somatic, and behavioral features.
5. The nature or quality of the mood change may be different from that associated with normal sadness. It may feel "strange," like being engulfed by a black cloud or sunk in a dark hole.

Some important considerations regarding this distinction are listed in Table 5.2. They include the extent to which the low mood remains consistent over an extended period of time as well as the inability to occasionally enjoy activities that would otherwise provide some relief from feeling down or blue. Distractions such as watching television or talking on the phone with a friend had lost their ability to make Cathy feel any better. Her mood had deteriorated shortly after one of her clients switched to another firm. The intensity of her depression was clearly way out of proportion to the event that seemed to trigger it (departure of a client to another firm). She had withdrawn from other people and was no longer able to work or to participate in any kind of social activity. The onset of her depression was accompanied by a number of other symptoms, including feelings of guilt, lack of energy, and difficulty sleeping. Finally, the quality of her mood was more than just a feeling of sadness; she was so profoundly miserable that she felt numb. For all of these reasons, Cathy's problems would fit the description of major depression.

Our next case illustrates the symptoms of mania, which often appear after a person has already experienced at least one episode of depression. People who experience episodes of both depression and mania are given a diagnosis of bipolar disorder. The symptoms of a full-blown manic episode are not subtle. People who are manic typically have terrible judgment and may get into considerable trouble as a result of their disorder. The central feature of mania is a persistently elevated or irritable mood that lasts for at least one week.

### → Debbie's Manic Episode

Debbie, a 21-year-old single woman, was admitted to a psychiatric hospital in the midst of a manic episode. She had been in psychotherapy for depression for several months while she was in high school but had not received any type of treatment since then. After she completed two semesters at a community college, Debbie found a good-paying job in the advertising office of a local newspaper, where she had been working for two years.

Debbie's manic episode could be traced to experiences that began three or four months prior to her admission to the hospital. Debbie had been feeling unusually good for several weeks. At first she didn't think anything was wrong. In fact, her impression was quite the opposite. Everything seemed to be going right for her. Her energy level was up, and she felt a renewed confidence in herself and her relationships with other people, especially with her boyfriend, who had recently moved to a distant city. Debbie initially welcomed these feelings, especially because she had been so lethargic and also tended to be reserved with people.

One day when she was feeling particularly exhilarated, Debbie impulsively quit her job and went to visit her boyfriend. Giving up her job without careful consideration and with no prospect for alternative employment was the first indication that Debbie's judgment was becoming impaired. Although she left home with only enough money to pay for her airplane ticket, she stayed for several weeks, mostly engaged in leisure activities. It was during this time that she started having trouble sleeping. The quality of her mood also began to change. It was often less cheerful and frequently irritable. She was extremely impatient and would become furious if her boyfriend disagreed with her. On one occasion, they had a loud and heated argument in the parking lot of his apartment complex. She took off her blouse and angrily refused to put it on again in spite of his demands and the presence of several interested bystanders. Shortly after the fight, she packed her clothes and hitchhiked back home.

After returning to her parents' home, Debbie argued with them almost continuously for several days. Her moods shifted constantly. One moment she would be bubbling with enthusiasm, gleefully throwing herself into new and exciting activities. If her plans were thwarted, she would fly into a rage. She phoned an exclusive tennis club to arrange for private lessons, which she obviously could not afford, especially now that she was unemployed. Her mother interrupted the call and canceled the lessons. Debbie left the house in a fury and set off to hitch a ride to the tennis club. She was picked up by two unknown men, who persuaded her to accompany them to a party rather than go to the club. By the time they arrived at the party, her mood was once again euphoric. She stayed at the party all night and had intercourse with three men whom she had never met before.

The following day, Debbie borrowed money from a friend and took a train home. Another argument ensued when she arrived at home. Debbie struck her father and took the family car. Angry and frightened by her apparently irrational behavior, her parents phoned the police, who found her and brought her home. When another argument broke out, even more hostile than the first, the police took Debbie to their precinct office, where she was interviewed by a psychiatrist. Her attitude was flippant, and her language was abusive and obscene. On the basis of her clearly irrational and violent mood, as well as her marked impairment in judgment, the psychiatrist arranged for her to be committed to a psychiatric hospital.

Debbie's behavior on the ward was belligerent, provocative, and demanding. Although she hadn't slept a total of more than four hours in the previous three days, she claimed to be bursting with energy. She behaved seductively toward some of the male patients, sitting on their laps, kissing them, and occasionally unfastening her clothing. Although her speech was coherent, it was rapid and pressured. She expressed several grandiose ideas, including the boast that she was an Olympic swimmer and that she was a premed student in college. She had no insight into the severity of her mental condition. Failing to recognize that her judgment was impaired, she insisted that she had been brought to the ward so that she could help the other patients.

"I am a psychic therapist, filled with the healing powers of the universe. I see things so clearly and deeply, and I must share this knowledge with everyone else."

## Symptoms

The cases of Cathy and Debbie illustrate many of the most important symptoms and signs of mood disorders, which can be divided into four general areas: emotional symptoms, cognitive symptoms, somatic symptoms, and behavioral symptoms. Episodes of major depression and mania typically involve all four kinds of symptoms.

### Emotional Symptoms

We all experience negative emotions, such as sadness, fear, and anger. These reactions usually last only a few moments, and they serve a useful purpose in our lives, particularly in our relationships with other people. Emotional reactions serve as signals to other people about our current feelings and needs. They also coordinate our responses to changes in the immediate environment.

Depressed, or **dysphoric** (unpleasant), mood is the most common and obvious symptom of depression. Most people who are depressed describe themselves as feeling utterly gloomy,

The quality of a depressed mood is often different from the sadness that might arise from an event such as the loss of a loved one. Some depressed people say that they feel like they are drowning or suffocating.

dejected, or despondent. The severity of a depressed mood can reach painful and overwhelming proportions. Andrew Solomon (2001) has described the progression from sadness to severe depression in the following ways:

> I returned, not long ago, to a wood in which I had played as a child and saw an oak, a hundred years dignified, in whose shade I used to play with my brother. In twenty years, a huge vine had attached itself to this confident tree and had nearly smothered it. It was hard to say where the tree left off and the vine began. The vine had twisted itself so entirely around the scaffolding of tree branches that its leaves seemed from a distance to be the leaves of the tree; only up close could you see how few living oak branches were left. I empathized with that tree. My depression had grown on me as that vine had conquered the oak; it had been a sucking thing that had wrapped itself around me, ugly and more alive than I. (p. 18)

In contrast to the unpleasant feelings associated with clinical depression, manic patients like Debbie experience periods of inexplicable and unbounded joy known as euphoria. Debbie felt extremely optimistic and cheerful—"on top of the world"—in spite of the fact that her inappropriate behavior had made a shambles of her current life circumstances. In bipolar disorders, periods of elated mood tend to alternate with phases of depression.

Kay Jamison, professor of psychiatry at Johns Hopkins University School of Medicine, has written an eloquent and moving description of her own experiences with mania and depression.

> My manias, at least in their early and mild forms, were absolutely intoxicating states that gave rise to great personal pleasure, an incomparable flow of thoughts, and a ceaseless energy that allowed the translation of new ideas into papers and projects. (1995, pp. 5–6)

Unfortunately, as these feelings become more intense and prolonged, they can become ruinous. It may not be clear when the person's experience crosses the unmarked boundary between being productive and energetic to being out of control and self-destructive. Jamison described this subtle transition in the following way:

There is a particular kind of pain, elation, loneliness, and terror involved in this kind of madness. When you're high it's tremendous. The ideas and feelings are fast and frequent like shooting stars, and you follow them until you find better and brighter ones. Shyness goes, the right words and gestures are suddenly there, the power to captivate others a felt certainty. There are interests found in uninteresting people. Sensuality is pervasive, and the desire to seduce and be seduced irresistible. Feelings of ease, intensity, power, well-being, financial omnipotence, and euphoria pervade one's marrow. But, somewhere, this changes. The fast ideas are far too fast, and there are far too many; overwhelming confusion replaces clarity. Memory goes. Humor and absorption on friends' faces are replaced by fear and concern. Everything previously moving with the grain is now against—you are irritable, angry, frightened, uncontrollable, and enmeshed totally in the blackest caves of the mind. (p. 67)

Many depressed and manic patients are irritable. Their anger may be directed either at themselves or at others, and frequently at both. Even when they are cheerful, people in a manic episode, like Debbie, are easily provoked to anger. Debbie became extremely argumentative and abusive, particularly when people challenged her grandiose statements about herself and her inappropriate judgment.

Anxiety is also common among people with mood disorders, just as depression is a common feature of some anxiety disorders (see Chapter 6). People who are depressed are sometimes apprehensive, fearing that matters will become worse than they already are or that others will discover their inadequacy. They sometimes report that they are chronically tense and unable to relax.

## Cognitive Symptoms

In addition to changes in the way people feel, mood disorders also involve changes in the way people think about themselves and their surroundings. People who are clinically depressed frequently note that their thinking is slowed down, that they have trouble concentrating, and that they are easily distracted. Cathy's ability to concentrate was so disturbed that she became unable to work. She had extreme difficulty making even the simplest decisions. After she started staying home, she sat in front of the television set but was unable to pay attention to the content of even the simplest programs.

Guilt and worthlessness are common preoccupations. Depressed patients blame themselves for things that have gone wrong, regardless of whether they are in fact responsible. They focus considerable attention on the most negative features of themselves, their environments, and the future—a combination known as the "depressive triad" (Beck, 1967).

Manic episodes are associated with euphoria as well as boundless energy and enthusiasm.

In contrast to the cognitive slowness associated with depression, manic patients commonly report that their thoughts are speeded up. Ideas flash through their minds faster than they can articulate their thoughts. Manic patients can also be easily distracted, responding to seemingly random stimuli in a completely uninterpretable and incoherent fashion. Grandiosity and inflated self-esteem are also characteristic features of mania.

Many people experience self-destructive ideas and impulses when they are depressed. Interest in suicide usually develops gradually and may begin with the vague sense that life is not worth living. Such feelings may follow directly from the overwhelming fatigue and loss of pleasure that typically accompany a seriously depressed mood. In addition, feelings of guilt and failure can lead depressed people to consider killing themselves. Over a period of time, depressed people may come to believe that they would be better off dead or that their family would function more successfully and happily without them. Preoccupation with such thoughts then leads to specific plans and may culminate in a suicide attempt.

## Somatic Symptoms

The **somatic symptoms** of mood disorders are related to basic physiological or bodily functions. They include fatigue, aches and pains, and serious changes in appetite and sleep patterns. People, like Cathy, who are clinically depressed often report feeling tired all the time. The simplest tasks, which she had previously taken for granted, seemed to require an overwhelming effort. Taking a shower, brushing her teeth, and getting dressed in the morning became virtually impossible.

Sleeping problems are also common, particularly trouble getting to sleep. This disturbance frequently goes hand in hand with cognitive difficulties mentioned earlier. Worried about her endless problems and unable to relax, Cathy found that she would toss and turn for hours before finally falling asleep. Some people also report having difficulty staying asleep throughout the night, and they awaken two or more hours before the usual time.

Early-morning waking is often associated with particularly severe depression. A less common symptom is for a depressed individual to spend more time sleeping than usual.

In the midst of a manic episode, a person is likely to experience a drastic reduction in the need for sleep. Some patients report that reduced sleep is one of the earliest signs of the onset of an episode. Although depressed patients typically feel exhausted when they cannot sleep, a person in a manic episode will probably be bursting with energy in spite of the lack of rest.

Depressed people frequently experience a change in appetite. Although some patients report that they eat more than usual, most reduce the amount that they eat; some may eat next to nothing. Food just doesn't taste good any more. Depressed people can also lose a great deal of weight, even without trying to diet.

People who are severely depressed commonly lose their interest in various types of activities that are otherwise sources of pleasure and fulfillment. One common example is a loss of sexual desire. Depressed people are less likely to initiate sexual activity, and they are less likely to enjoy sex if their partners can persuade them to participate.

Various ill-defined somatic complaints can also accompany mood disorders. Some patients complain of frequent headaches and muscular aches and pains. These concerns may develop into a preoccupation with bodily functions and fear of disease.

## Behavioral Symptoms

The symptoms of mood disorders also include changes in the things that people do and the rate at which they do them. The term **psychomotor retardation** refers to several features of behavior that may accompany the onset of serious depression. The most obvious behavioral symptom of depression is slowed movement. Patients may walk and talk as if they are in slow motion. Others become completely immobile and may stop speaking altogether. Some depressed patients pause for very extended periods, perhaps several minutes, before answering a question.

In marked contrast to periods when they are depressed, manic patients are typically gregarious and energetic. Debbie's behavior provided many examples, even after her admission to the psychiatric hospital. Her flirtatious and provocative behavior on the ward was clearly inappropriate. She found it impossible to sit still for more than a moment or two. Virtually everything was interesting to her, and she was easily distracted, flitting from one idea or project to the next. Like other manic patients, Debbie was full of plans that were pursued in a rather indiscriminate fashion. Excessive pursuit of life goals is frequently associated with the onset of manic episodes.

## Other Problems Commonly Associated with Depression

Many people with mood disorders suffer from some clinical problems that are not typically considered symptoms of depression. Within the field of psychopathology, the simultaneous manifestation of a mood disorder and other syndromes is referred to as comorbidity, suggesting that the person exhibits symptoms of more than one underlying disorder. The greatest overlap is with anxiety disorders. Among people who meet the diagnostic criteria for major depression at some point during their lives, 60 percent also qualify for a diagnosis of at least one anxiety disorder (Kessler, Merikangas, & Wang, 2007).

Alcoholism and depression are also closely related phenomena. Many people who are depressed also drink heavily, and many people who are dependent on alcohol—approximately 40 percent—have experienced major depression at some point during their lives (Swendsen & Merikangas, 2000). The order of onset for the depression and alcoholism varies from one person to the next. Some people become depressed after they develop a drinking problem; others begin drinking after being depressed.

## Diagnosis

Many alternative approaches have been proposed for the diagnosis of mood disorders over the past 100 years. Two primary issues have been central in debates about these systems. First, should mood disorders be defined in a broad or a narrow fashion? A narrow approach to the definition of depression would focus on the most severely disturbed people—those whose depressed mood seems to be completely unrelated to any precipitating events, is entirely pervasive, and is completely debilitating. A broader approach to the definition would include milder forms of depression. Some recent critics have argued that the current diagnostic system has expanded the definition of depression to include normal sadness because it does not exclude reactions to a wide array of negative events, such as betrayal by a romantic partner or failing to reach an important life goal (Horwitz & Wakefield, 2007). This issue is, of course, a question about the validity of this diagnostic category (see Chapter 4). Is depression necessarily "normal" if it follows a stressful event? The resolution of this debate depends on several issues, including the consideration of research evidence (see Thinking Critically About *DSM-5*).

The second issue regarding the diagnosis of mood disorders concerns heterogeneity. All depressed patients do not have exactly the same set of symptoms, the same pattern of onset, or the same course over time. Some patients have manic episodes, whereas others experience only depression. Some exhibit psychotic symptoms, such as delusions and hallucinations, in addition to their symptoms of mood disorder; others do not. In some cases, the person's depression is apparently a reaction to specific life events, whereas in others the mood disorder seems to come out of nowhere. Are these qualitatively distinct forms of mood disorder, or are they different expressions of the same underlying problem? Is the distinction among the different types simply one of severity?

The *DSM-5* approach to classifying mood disorders recognizes two distinct types: depressive disorders and bipolar disorders. The manual also lists additional forms of depressive and bipolar disorder under each of those major headings.

## Depression or Grief Following a Major Loss?

Depression often begins after a person goes through a negative life event. These experiences can take many forms, such as breaking up with a romantic partner, loss of a job, or onset of a life-threatening illness. In *DSM-IV*, the diagnostic criteria for an episode of major depression provided an exception for one specific type of event. People who had recently experienced the death of a close relative or friend could not qualify for a diagnosis of depression until two months after the loss. This "bereavement exclusion" was eliminated for *DSM-5*, and the change ignited a firestorm of controversy.

Critics of the change argue that it will turn normal grief into a form of illness, expanding even farther the boundaries of mental disorders (Frances, 2013; Wakefield, 2011). People who are grieving the loss of a loved one may indeed show symptoms of depression, and their sadness can become intense. Many experience sleep problems, loss of interest in other activities, and trouble concentrating. These symptoms are usually transient, and most people who are recovering from the loss of a loved one do not think of themselves as having a mental disorder. Of course, some people do develop a full-blown episode of depression following a loss, and treatment becomes an important option for them. The bereavement exclusion was developed in order to distinguish between these cases and those for whom symptoms are only temporary. Its purpose was to minimize the number of "false positives," that is, normally grieving people who would have been assigned a diagnosis of depression if not for the bereavement exclusion.

What's wrong with waiting two months to assign a diagnosis of depression? At a practical level, it could delay access to much-needed treatment. At a more conceptual level, the bereavement exclusion is arbitrary and illogical. All kinds of stressful and traumatic events can lead to the onset of major depression. Divorce, sudden financial hardships, and the need to assume unexpected family responsibilities (e.g., caring for a family member who suddenly becomes ill) are obvious example of events that can be devastating. Why aren't people who experience those events also excluded from a diagnosis of depression until two months after the event? In order to be consistent, the diagnostic manual would either need to expand the exclusion to cover all stressful life events or eliminate the bereavement exclusion. The

workgroup for mood disorders chose the latter option. That was one reason for the change in *DSM-5*.

The decision also hinged on research evidence regarding depression following loss of a partner or other close relative. Is their depression somehow different from other forms of depression? Several research studies have addressed this issue, comparing two groups of people: (1) those who meet criteria for major depression and are *not* bereaved and (2) those who meet criteria for major depression and *are* bereaved (and who would otherwise be excluded from the diagnosis using the grief rule-out). Arguments in favor of the exclusion depend on finding that the two groups are different in important ways. For example, it might be expected that the grieving people would have a later age of onset, fewer previous episodes, a shorter duration of episodes, or fewer recurrent episodes in the future. None of those differences have been found (Kendler, Myers, & Zisook, 2008). In other words, depression following loss of a loved one is not different from other forms of depression. Therefore, it seems illogical to subdivide cases on this basis.

Public outcry about elimination of the grief exclusion has made some exaggerated claims, such as the notion that people who are grieving will now be exposed to unnecessary treatments, including antidepressant medication. Some fear that bereavement will be stigmatized. In fact, most grieving people do not meet diagnostic criteria for major depression. That is not to say that they do not experience sadness or loneliness that is extremely difficult to endure. But there are several important features of major depression that make it distinct from these other forms of emotional distress (see Table 5.2).

Finally, it is clearly left to the discretion of mental health professionals to decide, on the basis of their own judgment and clinical experience, whether to initiate some form of treatment for a person who qualifies for the diagnosis of major depression. Recognizing that a patient is grieving might lead the clinician to wait and see how things progress. But in the face of, for example, serious suicidal thoughts, a more active intervention might be pursued. Treatment remains an option that should be pursued by joint agreement of the therapist and the patient.

**DEPRESSIVE DISORDERS** Depressive disorders include three main types among adults: major depressive disorder, persistent depressive disorder (also known as dysthymia), and premenstrual dysphoric disorder. A fourth type of depressive disorder, known as disruptive mood dysregulation disorder, was added with the publication of *DSM-5*. It is intended to describe children with chronic, severe irritability (see Chapter 16).

In order to meet the criteria for major depressive disorder, a person must experience at least one major depressive episode in the absence of any history of manic episodes. *DSM5: Criteria for Major Depressive Episode* lists the *DSM-5* criteria for major depressive episode. Although some people experience a single, isolated episode of major depression followed by complete recovery, most cases of depression follow an intermittent course with repeated episodes.

**Persistent depressive disorder (dysthymia)** differs from major depression in terms of both severity and duration. Persistent depressive disorder represents a chronic mild depressive condition that has been present for many years. In order to fulfill

Most people who are grieving the loss of a loved one do not become clinically depressed, but some do. The "bereavement exclusion" was dropped from DSM-5, in part, because this is only one of many types of stressful life events can lead to the onset of an episode of depression.

*DSM-5* criteria for this disorder, the person must, over a period of at least two years, exhibit a depressed mood for most of the day on more days than not. Two or more of the following symptoms must also be present:

1. Poor appetite or overeating
2. Insomnia or hypersomnia
3. Low energy or fatigue
4. Low self-esteem
5. Poor concentration or difficulty making decisions
6. Feelings of hopelessness

These symptoms must not be absent for more than two months at a time during the two-year period. If, at any time during the initial two years, the person met criteria for a major depressive episode, the diagnosis would be major depression rather than persistent depressive disorder. As in the case of major

## criteria for
## Major Depressive Episode
### DSM-5

**A.** Five (or more) of the following symptoms have been present during the same 2-week period and represent a change from previous functioning; at least one of the symptoms is either (1) depressed mood or (2) loss of interest or pleasure. **Note:** Do not include symptoms that are clearly attributable to another medical condition.

1. Depressed mood most of the day, nearly every day, as indicated by either subjective report (e.g., feels sad, empty, hopeless) or observation made by others (e.g., appears tearful). (Note: In children and adolescents, can be irritable mood.)
2. Markedly diminished interest or pleasure in all, or almost all, activities most of the day, nearly every day (as indicated by either subjective account or observation).
3. Significant weight loss when not dieting or weight gain (e.g., a change of more than 5% of body weight in a month), or decrease or increase in appetite nearly every day. (Note: In children, consider failure to make expected weight gain.)
4. Insomnia or hypersomnia nearly every day.
5. Psychomotor agitation or retardation nearly every day (observable by others; not merely subjective feelings of restlessness or being slowed down).
6. Fatigue or loss of energy nearly every day.
7. Feelings of worthlessness or excessive or inappropriate guilt (which may be delusional) nearly every day (not merely self-reproach or guilt about being sick).
8. Diminished ability to think or concentrate, or indecisiveness, nearly every day (either by subjective account or as observed by others).
9. Recurrent thoughts of death (not just fear of dying), recurrent suicidal ideation without a specific plan, or a suicide attempt or a specific plan for committing suicide.

**B.** The symptoms cause clinically significant distress or impairment in social, occupational, or other important areas of functioning.

**C.** The episode is not attributable to the physiological effects of a substance or another medical condition.

**Note:** Criteria A–C represent a major depressive episode.

**Note:** Responses to a significant loss (e.g., bereavement, financial ruin, losses from a natural disaster, a serious medical illness or disability) may include the feelings of intense sadness, rumination about the loss, insomnia, poor appetite, and weight loss noted in Criterion A, which may resemble a depressive episode. Although such symptoms may be understandable or considered appropriate to the loss, the presence of a major depressive episode in addition to the normal response to a significant loss should also be carefully considered. This decision inevitably requires the exercise of clinical judgment based on the individual's history and the cultural norms for the expression of distress in the context of loss.[1]

**D.** The occurrence of the major depressive episode is not better explained by schizoaffective disorder, schizophrenia, schizophreniform disorder, delusional disorder, or other specified and unspecified schizophrenia spectrum and other psychotic disorders.

**E.** There has never been a manic episode or a hypomanic episode.

**Note:** This exclusion does not apply if all of the manic-like or hypomanic-like episodes are substance-induced or are attributable to the physiological effects of another medical condition.

Reprinted with permission from the *Diagnostic and Statistical Manual of Mental Disorders*, Fifth Edition, (Copyright 2013). American Psychiatric Association.

depressive disorder, the presence of a manic episode would rule out a diagnosis of persistent depressive disorder.

The distinction between major depressive disorder and persistent depressive disorder is somewhat artificial because both sets of symptoms are frequently seen in the same person. In such cases, rather than thinking of them as separate disorders, it is more appropriate to consider them as two aspects of the same disorder, which waxes and wanes over time. Some experts have argued that chronic depression is a single, broadly conceived disorder that can be expressed in many different combinations of symptoms over time (McCullough et al., 2003).

Premenstrual dysphoric disorder (PMDD) was added as a new diagnostic category in *DSM-5*. Previous versions of the diagnostic manual had listed this category in the appendix, under "disorders provided for further study." Members of the *DSM-5* workgroup for mood disorders decided that sufficient evidence had been accumulated to justify its inclusion as a formal diagnostic category (Epperson et al., 2012). Women commonly experience premenstrual symptoms that center around emotional and physical complaints, but they are typically mild. A few experience these symptoms in greater numbers and with increased severity, to the extent that they are associated with obvious social and occupational impairment. These are the people for whom PMDD may be an appropriate diagnosis (Cunningham et al., 2009). It should be noted, however, that this category remains controversial, with questions being raised about the validity of its diagnostic criteria (Callaghan et al., 2009).

PMDD is defined in terms of various mood-related symptoms that occur repeatedly during the premenstrual phase of the cycle and are then diminished at the onset or shortly after menses. Symptoms include mood lability, irritability, dysphoria, and anxiety as well as cognitive (difficulty concentrating, feeling of being overwhelmed or out of control), and somatic symptoms (e.g., lethargy, changes in appetite, sleep problems, joint or muscle pain, a sensation of bloating, etc.). In order to meet the diagnostic criteria for this disorder, a woman must exhibit at least five of these symptoms, and at least one of those symptoms must involve a disturbance in mood (e.g., mood swings or marked irritability). The symptoms must have been present for most of the woman's menstrual cycles in the past year, and they must be associated with clinically significant distress or interference with social or occupational functioning (Hartlage et al., 2012).

**BIPOLAR DISORDERS** All three types of bipolar disorders involve manic or hypomanic episodes. *DSM5: Criteria for Diagnosis of Manic Episode* lists the *DSM-5* criteria for a manic episode. The mood disturbance must be severe enough to interfere with occupational or social functioning. A person who has experienced at least one manic episode would be assigned a diagnosis of *bipolar I disorder*. The vast majority of patients with this disorder have episodes of major depression in addition to manic episodes.

Some patients experience episodes of increased energy that are not sufficiently severe to qualify as full-blown mania. These episodes are called **hypomania.** A person who has experienced at least one major depressive episode, at least one hypomanic episode, and no full-blown manic episodes would be assigned a

---

**criteria for**
## Diagnosis of Manic Episode

### DSM-5

**A.** A distinct period of abnormally and persistently elevated, expansive, or irritable mood and abnormally and persistently increased goal-directed activity or energy, lasting at least 1 week and present most of the day, nearly every day (or any duration if hospitalization is necessary).

**B.** During the period of mood disturbance and increased energy or activity, three (or more) of the following symptoms (four if the mood is only irritable) are present to a significant degree and represent a noticeable change from usual behavior:
1. Inflated self-esteem or grandiosity.
2. Decreased need for sleep (e.g., feels rested after only 3 hours of sleep).
3. More talkative than usual or pressure to keep talking.
4. Flight of ideas or subjective experience that thoughts are racing.
5. Distractibility (i.e., attention too easily drawn to unimportant or irrelevant external stimuli), as reported or observed.

6. Increase in goal-directed activity (either socially, at work or school, or sexually) or psychomotor agitation (i.e., purposeless nongoal-directed activity).
7. Excessive involvement in activities that have a high potential for painful consequences (e.g., engaging in unrestrained buying sprees, sexual indiscretions, or foolish business investments).

**C.** The mood disturbance is sufficiently severe to cause marked impairment in social or occupational functioning or to necessitate hospitalization to prevent harm to self or others, or there are psychotic features.

**D.** The episode is not attributable to the physiological effects of a substance (e.g., a drug of abuse, a medication, other treatment) or to another medical condition.
**Note:** A full manic episode that emerges during antidepressant treatment (e.g., medication, electroconvulsive therapy) but persists at a fully syndromal level beyond the physiological effect of that treatment is sufficient evidence for a manic episode and, therefore, a bipolar I diagnosis.

ANN

*"I felt very tense, like my mind was racing; that I was making unusual connections; that I couldn't sleep at night."*

👁 **Watch** the **Video** *Ann: Bipolar Disorder* on **MyPsychLab**

Although Ann's manic episodes were associated with increased productivity, they also led to serious occupational and social problems.

---

diagnosis of *bipolar II disorder.* The symptoms used in *DSM-5* to identify a hypomanic episode are the same as those used for manic episode (at least three of the seven symptoms listed in *DSM5: Criteria for Diagnosis of Manic Episode*). The differences between manic and hypomanic episodes involve duration and severity. The symptoms need to be present for a minimum of only four days to meet the threshold for a hypomanic episode (as opposed to one week for a manic episode). The mood change in a hypomanic episode must be noticeable to others, but the disturbance must not be severe enough to impair social or occupational functioning or to require hospitalization.

**Cyclothymia** is considered by *DSM-5* to be a chronic but less severe form of bipolar disorder. It is, therefore, the bipolar equivalent of persistent depressive disorder. In order to meet criteria for cyclothymia, the person must experience several periods of time with hypomanic symptoms and frequent periods of depression (or loss of interest or pleasure) during a period of two years. There must be no history of major depressive episodes and no clear evidence of a manic episode during the first two years of the disturbance.

**FURTHER DESCRIPTIONS AND SUBTYPE** *DSM-5* includes several additional ways of describing subtypes of the mood disorders. These are based on two considerations: (1) more specific descriptions of symptoms that were present during the most recent episode of depression (known as *episode specifiers*) and (2) more extensive descriptions of the pattern that the disorder follows over time (known as *course specifiers*). These distinctions may provide a useful way to subdivide depressed patients, who certainly present a heterogeneous set of problems. On the other hand, the validity of these subtypes is open to question, especially those based on episode specifiers. Long-term follow-up studies suggest that a patient's subtype diagnosis is likely to change over repeated episodes (Angst, Sellaro, & Merikangas, 2000).

One episode specifier allows the clinician to describe a major depressive episode as having melancholic features. **Melancholia** is a term that is used to describe a particularly severe type of depression. Some experts believe that melancholia represents a subtype of depression that is caused by different factors than those that are responsible for other forms of depression (Parker et al., 2010). The presence of melancholic features may also indicate that the person is likely to have a good response to biological forms of treatment, such as antidepressant medication and electroconvulsive therapy (Taylor & Fink, 2008).

In order to meet the *DSM-5* criteria for melancholic features, a depressed patient must either (1) lose the feeling of pleasure associated with all, or almost all, activities or (2) lose the capacity to feel better—even temporarily—when something good happens. The person must also exhibit at least three of the following: (1) The depressed mood feels distinctly different from the depression a person would feel after the death of a loved one; (2) the depression is most often worst in the morning; (3) the person awakens early, at least two hours before usual; (4) marked psychomotor retardation or agitation; (5) significant loss of appetite or weight loss; and (6) excessive or inappropriate guilt.

Another episode specifier allows the clinician to indicate the presence of *psychotic features*—hallucinations or delusions—during the most recent episode of depression or mania. The psychotic features can be either consistent or inconsistent with the patient's mood. For example, if a depressed man reports hearing voices that tell him he is a worthless human being who deserves to suffer for his sins, the hallucinations would be considered "mood congruent psychotic features." Depressed patients who exhibit psychotic features are more likely to require hospitalization and treatment with a combination of antidepressant and antipsychotic medication (Parker et al., 1997).

Another episode specifier applies to women who become depressed or manic following pregnancy. A major depressive or manic episode can be specified as having a *postpartum onset* if it begins within four weeks after childbirth. Because the woman must meet the full criteria for an episode of major depression or mania, this category does not include minor periods of postpartum "blues," which are relatively common (Seyfried & Marcus, 2003).

The *DSM-5* course specifiers for mood disorders allow clinicians to describe further the pattern and sequence of episodes, as well as the person's adjustment between episodes. For example, the course of a bipolar disorder can be specified as *rapid cycling* if the person experiences at least four episodes of major depression, mania, or hypomania within a 12-month period. Patients whose disorder follows this problematic course are likely to show a poor response to treatment and are at greater risk than other types of bipolar patients to attempt suicide (Coryell et al., 2003).

A mood disorder (either depressive or bipolar) is described as following a seasonal pattern if, over a period of time, there is a regular relationship between the onset of a person's episodes and particular times of the year. The most typical seasonal pattern is one in which the person becomes depressed in the fall or winter, followed by a full recovery in the following spring or summer.

Many new mothers experience transient symptoms of the "baby blues" (e.g., trouble sleeping, tearfulness, feeling overwhelmed), but postpartum depression is more than that. The person meets full diagnostic criteria for depression.

Researchers refer to a mood disorder in which the onset of episodes is regularly associated with changes in seasons as **seasonal affective disorder.**[1] The episodes most commonly occur in winter, presumably in response to fewer hours of sunlight. Seasonal depression is usually characterized by somatic symptoms, such as overeating, carbohydrate craving, weight gain, fatigue, and sleeping more than usual. Among outpatients who have a history of at least three major depressive episodes, approximately one out of six will meet criteria for the seasonal pattern (Westrin & Lam, 2007). Most patients with seasonal affective disorder have a depressive disorder.

## Course and Outcome

To describe the typical sequence over time and outcome of mood disorders, it is useful to consider depressive and bipolar disorders separately. Most studies point to clear-cut differences between these two conditions in terms of age of onset and prognosis.

---

[1]"Affect" and "mood" are sometimes used interchangeably in psychiatric terminology. Depression and mania were called "affective disorders" in *DSM-III*.

## Depressive Disorders

People with depressive mood disorders typically have their first episode in their early thirties; the average age of onset is 32 (Kessler et al., 2007). The length of episodes varies widely. *DSM-5* sets the minimum duration at two weeks, but they can last much longer. Most depressive patients will have at least two depressive episodes. The mean number of lifetime episodes is five or six.

The results of long-term follow-up studies of treated patients indicate that major depressive disorder is frequently a chronic and recurrent condition in which episodes of severe symptoms may alternate with periods of full or partial recovery (Thase, 2003). When a person's symptoms are diminished or improved, the disorder is considered to be in **remission,** or a period of recovery. **Relapse** is a return of active symptoms in a person who has recovered from a previous episode. These phases of the disorder are represented schematically in Figure 5.1.

Approximately half of all depressive patients recover within six months of the beginning of an episode. After recovery from an episode of major depression, the risk of relapse goes down as the period of remission increases. In other words, the longer the person remains free of depression, the better his or her chance of avoiding relapse (Hart, Craighead, & Craighead, 2001).

## Bipolar Disorders

Onset of bipolar disorders usually occurs between the ages of 18 and 22 years, which is younger than the average age of onset for depressive disorders. The first episode is just as likely to be manic as depressive. The average duration of a manic episode runs between two and three months. The onset of a manic episode is not always sudden. Jamison noted, for example:

> I did not wake up one day to find myself mad. Life should be so simple. Rather, I gradually became aware that my life and mind were going at an ever faster and faster clip until finally, over the course of my first summer on the faculty, they both had spun wildly and absolutely out of control. But the acceleration from quick thought to chaos was a slow and beautifully seductive one. (1995, p. 68)

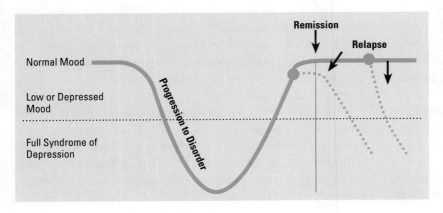

**FIGURE 5.1**

**The Course of an Episode of Major Depression** The phases leading into (and out of) an episode of depression. *Source:* Frank E, Swartz HA, Kupfer DJ. Interpersonal and social rhythm therapy: managing the chaos of bipolar disorder. Biological Psychiatry. 2000 Sep 15;48(6):593–604.

The long-term course of bipolar disorders is most often intermittent (Cuellar, Johnson, & Winters, 2005). Most patients have more than one episode, and bipolar patients tend to have more episodes than depressive patients. The length of intervals between episodes is difficult to predict. The long-term prognosis is mixed for patients with bipolar disorder. Although some patients recover and function very well, others experience continued impairment. Several studies that have followed bipolar patients over periods of up to 10 years have found that approximately half of the people are able to achieve a sustained recovery from the disorder. On the other hand, many patients remain chronically disabled. **◉ Watch** the **Video** *Feliziano: Living with Bipolar Disorder* on **MyPsychLab**

## Frequency

Several studies provide detailed information regarding the frequency of mood disorders in various countries around the world (Kessler, Merikangas, & Wang, 2007). Some are based on information collected from nonclinical samples of men and women by investigators using structured diagnostic interviews. In other words, the people who participated in these studies did not have to be in treatment at a hospital or clinic in order to be identified as being depressed. These studies are particularly important because large numbers of people experience serious depression without wanting or being able to seek professional help. Data based exclusively on treatment records would underestimate the magnitude of the problem.

### Incidence and Prevalence

Depression is one of the most common forms of psychopathology. In a representative sample of more than 9,000 people who were interviewed for the National Comorbidity Survey Replication (NCS-R), approximately 16 percent suffered from major depressive disorder at some point during their lives. Lifetime risk for persistent depressive disorder (dysthymia) was approximately 3 percent. The lifetime risk

for bipolar I and II disorders combined was close to 4 percent. Taken together, depressive disorders are much more common than bipolar disorders. The ratio of depressive to bipolar disorders is at least 5:1 (Kessler & Wang, 2008).

Evidence regarding the prevalence of premenstrual dysphoric disorder is, of course, preliminary because it has been added recently to the diagnostic manual. It has not been included as a category in any of the large-scale epidemiological studies in the United States. As many as 8 percent of women experience moderate to severe symptoms of premenstrual dysphoric disorder, and one study reported that 3 percent meet the diagnostic criteria for this disorder (Cunningham et al., 2009; Tschudin et al. 2010).

Because the NCS-R study identified a representative sample of community residents rather than patients already in treatment, it provides some insight regarding the proportion of depressed people who seek professional help for their problems. Slightly more than 20 percent of those people who met diagnostic criteria for a mood disorder in the past 12 months had received adequate treatment during that same time period. These data indicate that a substantial proportion of people who are clinically depressed do not receive professional treatment for their disorders. Finding ways to help these people represents an important challenge for psychologists and psychiatrists who treat mood disorders.

### Risk for Mood Disorders Across the Life Span

Age is an important consideration in the epidemiology of mood disorders. Some readers might expect that the prevalence of depression would be higher among older people than among younger people. This was, in fact, what many clinicians expected prior to large-scale epidemiological investigations, such as the NCS-R. This belief may stem from the casual observation that many older people experience brief episodic states of acute unhappiness, often precipitated by changes in status (e.g., retirement, relocation) and loss of significant others (e.g., children

Contrary to popular views, older people are actually less likely to be depressed than are younger people. Some subgroups of elderly people, however, are at high risk for depression.

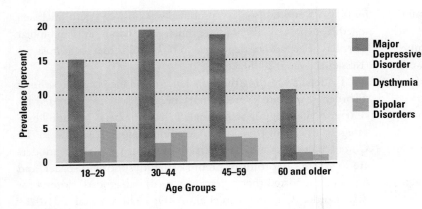

**FIGURE 5.2**

**Lifetime Prevalence of Mood Disorders by Age (NCS-R data)** Lifetime prevalence of major depression, persistent depressive disorder (dysthymia), and bipolar disorder in a representative community sample.

*Source:* Based on Kessler et al. Lifetime Prevalence and Age-of-Onset Distributions of DSM-IV Disorders in the National Comorbidity Survey Replication. Archives of General Psychiatry. 2005; 62.

moving away, deaths of friends and relatives). But brief episodes of sadness and grief are not the same thing as clinical depression.

Although many people mistakenly identify depression with the elderly, data from the NCS-R project suggest that mood disorders are most frequent among young and middle-aged adults. These data are illustrated in Figure 5.2. Prevalence rates for major depressive disorder, persistent depressive disorder, and bipolar disorder were all significantly lower for people over the age of 60.

Several explanations have been offered for this pattern. One interpretation is based on the fact that elderly people are more likely to experience memory impairments (see Chapter 14). People who are in their sixties and seventies may have more trouble remembering, and therefore may fail to report, episodes of depression that occurred several months or years before the research interview is conducted. Also, because mood disorders are associated with increased mortality (e.g., suicide), many severely depressed people might not have survived into old age. These are plausible hypotheses that may have influenced the results of the NCS-R study. Nevertheless, the same pattern has been observed in several studies, and most investigators now believe that the effect is genuine: Clinical depression is less common among elderly people than it is among younger adults (Blazer, 2004).

The findings on age and depression also raise another important question: Has the frequency of depression increased in recent years? The answer is apparently yes. People born after World War II seem to be more likely to develop mood disorders than were people from previous generations. In fact, several studies have reported a consistent trend toward higher lifetime rates of depression in successively younger generations. The average age of onset for clinical depression also seems to be lower in people who were born more recently (Kessler et al., 2005).

## Gender Differences

Women are two or three times more vulnerable to depression than men are (Kessler, 2006; Van de Velde et al., 2010). This pattern has been reported in study after study, using samples of treated patients as well as community surveys, and regardless of the assessment procedures employed. The increased prevalence of depression among women is apparently limited to depressive disorders. Gender differences are not typically observed for bipolar disorders.

Some observers have suggested that the high rates for depression in women reflect shortcomings in the data collection process. Women simply might be more likely than men to seek treatment or to be labeled as being depressed. Another argument holds that culturally determined sanctions make it more difficult for men to admit to subjective feelings of distress, such as hopelessness and despair. None of these alternatives has been substantiated by empirical evidence. Research studies clearly indicate that the higher prevalence of depression among women is genuine. Possible explanations for this gender difference have focused on a variety of factors, including sex hormones, stressful life events, and childhood adversity as well as response styles that are associated with gender roles (Hankin & Abramson, 2001; Kuehner, 2003). These issues are discussed later in this chapter.

## Cross-Cultural Differences

Comparisons of emotional expression and emotional disorder across cultural boundaries encounter a number of methodological problems (see Research Methods in Chapter 9). One problem involves vocabulary. Each culture has its own ways of interpreting reality, including different styles of expressing or communicating symptoms of physical and emotional disorder. Words and concepts that are used to describe illness behaviors in one culture might not exist in other cultures. For example, some African cultures have

## MyPsychLab VIDEO CASE

### Major Depression

**EVERETT**

*"You feel absolute worthlessness. You feel there is no hope for the future."*

👁 **Watch** the **Video** *Everett: Major Depression* on **MyPsychLab**

Watch the video "Major Depression: Everett" on MyPsychLab. Notice the importance and persistence of the negative way in which he views himself and his abilities.

only one word for both anger and sadness. Interesting adaptations are, therefore, required to translate questions that are supposed to tap experiences, such as anxiety and depression. One investigation, which employed a British interview schedule that had been translated into Yoruba—a language spoken in Nigeria—used the phrase "the heart goes weak" to represent depression (Leff, 1988). Our own diagnostic categories have been developed within a specific cultural setting; they are not culture-free and are not necessarily any more reasonable than the ways in which other cultures describe and categorize their own behavioral and emotional disorders (Lavender, Khodoker, & Jones, 2006).

Cross-cultural differences have been confirmed by a number of research projects that have examined cultural variations in symptoms among depressed patients in different countries. These studies report comparable overall frequencies of mood disorders in various parts of the world, but the specific type of symptom expressed by the patients varies from one culture to the next. In Chinese patients, depression is more likely to be described in terms of somatic symptoms, such as sleeping problems, headaches, and loss of energy (Kleinman, 2004). Depressed patients in Europe and North America are more likely to express feelings of guilt and suicidal ideas (Kirmayer, 2001).

These cross-cultural comparisons suggest that, at its most basic level, clinical depression is a universal phenomenon that is not limited to Western or urban societies. They also indicate that a person's cultural experiences, including linguistic, educational, and social factors, may play an important role in shaping the manner in which he or she expresses and copes with the anguish of depression. Cross-cultural variations should also be kept in mind when clinicians attempt to identify central or defining features of depression. We will return to this point later in the chapter when we discuss the rationale behind studies that rely on animal models of depression.

## Causes

In the next few pages we turn our attention to current speculation and knowledge about causes of mood disorders. Discussions of this topic must keep in mind the relatively high prevalence of these problems. Major depression is a severely disabling condition that affects at least 16 percent of the population, usually appearing during young adulthood when the person would be expected to be most active and productive. Why hasn't this problem been eliminated through the process of natural selection? Evolutionary theorists suggest that it is because, in addition to being painful and disruptive to a person's life, mild to moderate symptoms of depression may serve a useful purpose (Gilbert, 2006; Price, Gardner, & Erickson, 2004). This argument is focused on those situations in which depression represents a temporary response to circumstances in the person's environment. As we will see, many episodes of depression do seem to be triggered by stressful life events and harsh social circumstances. An evolutionary perspective would hold that the symptoms of depression—slowing down, loss of motivation, withdrawal from

other people—may represent a response system that helps the person disengage from a situation that is not going well (Nesse, 1999; Taylor et al., 2011). For example, someone who is involved in an unsuccessful marriage may eventually become depressed, withdrawn, and reconsider the long-term benefits of investing further time and resources in a relationship that is likely to remain unrewarding. At low levels and over brief periods of time, depressed mood may help us refocus our motivations, and it may help us to conserve and redirect our energy in response to experiences of loss and defeat.

Psychological explanations for mood disorders focus on individual differences, and they are primarily concerned with the most severe and disabling forms of depression. Following difficult and challenging experiences, why do some people develop major depression and others do not? What factors are responsible for a relatively drastic failure of the psychological and biological systems that regulate mood? A disorder that is as common as depression must have many causes rather than one.

Our consideration of cause is organized around different levels of analysis. We will consider social, psychological, and biological mechanisms that are involved in the onset and maintenance of mood disorders. This organization should help you appreciate the complementary nature of these analyses. After we have considered the impact of stressful life events on mood, we will discuss psychological factors, such as cognitive biases, that shape a person's response to stress. Then we will review what is known about hormones and brain activities that coordinate our responses to environmental stressors.

### Social Factors

It should not be surprising that much of the literature on mood disorders is focused on interpersonal loss and separation. From birth to death, our lives are intertwined with those of other people. We are fundamentally social organisms, and we feel sad when someone close to us dies or a relationship ends. Similar feelings occasionally follow major disappointments, such as failure to win acceptance to the school of our choice or being fired from a job. In these cases, rather than losing other people, some clinicians have suggested that we may be losing "social roles" or ways in which we think about ourselves. Clues to the causes of depression may be found in studying these experiences of normal sadness. The onset and maintenance of clinical depression clearly involve a disruption or failure of the normal mechanisms that regulate the negative emotions following major losses.

#### STRESSFUL LIFE EVENTS AND DEPRESSIVE DISORDERS
Several investigations have explored the relationships between stressful life events and the development of depressive disorders. Do people who become clinically depressed actually experience an increased number of stressful life events? The answer is yes. The experience of stressful life events is associated with an increased probability that a person will become depressed. This correlation has been demonstrated many times (Hammen, 2005; Monroe & Reid, 2009).

Investigators have faced difficult methodological issues in order to interpret the strong relationship between stressful life events and the onset of depression. One particularly troublesome problem involves the direction of the relationship between life events and mood disorders. For example, being fired from a job might lead a person to become depressed. On the other hand, the onset of a depressive episode, with its associated difficulties in energy and concentration, could easily affect the person's job performance and lead to being fired. Therefore, if depressed people experience more stressful events, what is the direction of effect? Does failure lead to depression, or does depression lead to failure?

By using prospective research designs, in which subjects are followed over time, investigators have been able to address the question of cause and effect (see Research Methods in Chapter 8). Prospective studies have found that stressful life events are useful in predicting the subsequent onset of depression (Brown, 2002; Monroe & Harkness, 2005). This evidence supports the argument that, in many cases, stressful life events contribute to (and are not merely consequences of) the onset of mood disorders.

Although many kinds of negative events are associated with depression, a special class of circumstances—those involving major losses of important people or roles—seems to play a crucial role in precipitating major depression, especially a person's first lifetime episode. This conclusion is based, in large part, on a series of studies that have compared the living circumstances and life experiences of depressed and nondepressed women (Brown & Harris, 1978). *Severe* events—those that are particularly threatening and have long-term consequences for the woman's adjustment—increase the probability that a woman will become depressed. On the other hand, the ordinary hassles and difficulties of everyday living (events that are not severe) do not seem to lead to the onset of depression (Stroud et al., 2010).

A series of studies comparing the life experiences of women in six communities—including Harare, Zimbabwe—found that the greater the frequency of severe events, the higher the prevalence of depression.

Severe events increase the probability of depression, but most women who experience a severe event do not become depressed. What is the difference between the circumstances of women who become depressed after a severe event and those who do not? Some evidence suggests that depression is more likely to occur when severe life events are associated with feelings of humiliation, entrapment, and defeat (Brown, 2002; Nanni et al., 2012). An example of a humiliating event would be a woman learning unexpectedly of her husband's long-standing infidelity. An example of an event fitting the entrapment theme would be a woman receiving official notification that her application to move out of appalling housing conditions had been denied. These data point to a particularly powerful relationship between the onset of depression and certain kinds of stressful life events. The likelihood that a woman will become depressed is especially high if she experiences a severe event that would be expected to lead to a sense of being devalued as a person or trapped with no way toward a brighter future (Kendler et al., 2003).

In fact, the relationship between stressful life events and depression actually runs in both directions. Some depressed people create difficult circumstances that increase the level of stress in their lives. Examples include breaking up with a romantic partner or being fired from a job. This phenomenon is known as *stress generation*. In comparison to people who are not depressed, depressed people generate higher levels of stress, especially in the context of interpersonal relationships (Hammen, 2005; Harkness & Stewart, 2009). Maladaptive tactics for coping with marital distress are important factors in this process. For example, when involved in a serious disagreement with a spouse, a depressed person might express escalating complaints and hostile, provocative comments rather than trying to work toward a solution to the conflict. This dynamic process leads to an escalation of stress.

Gender differences in the frequency and nature of stressful life events may help to explain gender differences in the prevalence of major depression. Some research evidence indicates that women who are depressed are more likely than men to report that they experienced a severe life event in the months prior to the onset of their mood disorder (Harkness et al., 2010). Furthermore, it is specifically negative interpersonal stress that seems to have a particularly detrimental impact in the lives of young women (Cyranowski & Frank, 2006; Shih & Eberhart, 2010). Women may be more likely to generate interpersonal stress and to suffer from its consequences because they are more likely than men to invest in, and base their evaluations of themselves upon, the importance of relationships with other people. Men, on the other hand, are more likely to focus on the importance of individual accomplishments related to school, work, and sports (Crick & Zahn-Waxler, 2003).

**SOCIAL FACTORS AND BIPOLAR DISORDERS** Most investigations of stressful life events have been concerned with depressive disorders. Less attention has been paid to bipolar disorders, but some have found that the weeks preceding the onset of a manic episode are marked by an increased frequency of stressful life

events (Bender & Alloy, 2011; Miklowitz & Johnson, 2009). The kinds of events that precede the onset of mania tend to be different from those that lead to depression. While the latter include primarily negative experiences involving loss and low self-esteem, the former include schedule-disrupting events (such as loss of sleep) as well as goal attainment events. Some patients experience an increase in manic symptoms after they have achieved a significant goal toward which they had been working (Johnson et al., 2009). Examples of this kind of goal attainment event would be a major job promotion, being accepted to a competitive professional school program, or the blossoming of a new romantic relationship. These exhilarating experiences, coupled with the person's ongoing problems with emotion regulation, may contribute to a spiral of positive emotion and excess activity that culminates in a full-blown manic episode.

Aversive patterns of emotional expression and communication within the family can also have a negative impact on the adjustment of people with bipolar disorders. Longitudinal studies of bipolar patients have focused on the relation between frequency of relapse and the emotional climate within their families. Patients living with family members who are hostile toward or critical of the patient are more likely to relapse shortly after being discharged from the hospital (Miklowitz, 2007). Furthermore, bipolar patients who have less social support are more likely to relapse and recover more slowly than patients with higher levels of social support (Cohen et al., 2004). This evidence indicates that the course of bipolar disorder can be influenced by the social environment in which the person is living.

## Psychological Factors

Severe events are clearly related to the onset of depression, but they do not provide a complete account of who will become depressed. Many people who do not become depressed also experience severe events. Presumably, those who become depressed are somehow more vulnerable to the effects of stress. Several psychological factors may contribute to a person's vulnerability to

stressful life events. In the following pages, we will consider two principal areas that have received attention in the research literature: cognitive factors and social skills.

**COGNITIVE VULNERABILITY** Cognitive theories concerning the origins of depression are based on the recognition that humans are not only social organisms, they are also thinking organisms, and the ways in which people perceive, think about, and remember events in their world can have an important influence on the way that they feel. Two people may react very differently to the same event, in large part because they may interpret the event differently. Cognitive theories about vulnerability to depression have focused on the ways in which people attend to, think about, and recall information from their environment. Most often, this involves cognitive activity related to experiences involving loss, failure, and disappointment. According to the cognitive perspective, pervasive and persistent negative thoughts about the self and pessimistic views of the environment play a central role in the onset and subsequent maintenance of depression after these thoughts are activated by the experience of a negative life event (Gotlib & Joormann, 2010; Mathews & MacLeod, 2005).

Various types of distortions, errors, and biases are characteristic of the thinking of depressed people. One is the tendency to assign global, personal meaning to experiences of failure. An example might be a person who has been turned down after he tried out for a competitive sports team and says to himself, "This proves that I am a failure" rather than acknowledging that many talented people were being considered, that only a few people could be retained, and difficult decisions had to be made by the coach. Another cognitive distortion associated with depression is the tendency to overgeneralize conclusions about the self based on negative experiences. Following the example raised earlier, the person might also say to himself, "The fact that I was cut from the team shows that I am also going to fail at everything else." A third type of cognitive error involves drawing arbitrary inferences about the self in the absence of supporting evidence (often in spite of contradictory evidence). In this regard, consider a player who is a member of an athletic team. If the team loses a game and the coach is upset, the player might arbitrarily decide that the loss was his fault and the coach doesn't like him, even though nothing about his performance was particularly instrumental with regard to the team's performance in the game. The final type of cognitive bias related to depression is the tendency to recall selectively events with negative consequences and to exaggerate the importance of negative events while simultaneously discounting the significance of positive events. For example, suppose that an athlete is looking back over her experiences during the course of an entire season. She would be more likely to feel depressed about her performance if she tends to dwell on the mistakes that she made and the games that the team lost rather than emphasizing the positive contributions that she made and the successes that she shared with her teammates.

How do these self-defeating biases lead to the onset of depression? One cognitive approach to depression is focused on the importance of *maladaptive schemas,* which are general patterns of thought that guide the ways in which people perceive and interpret events in their environment. Schemas are enduring and highly organized representations of prior experience. Although schemas may be latent—that is, not prominently represented in the person's conscious awareness at any given point in time—they are presumably reactivated when the person experiences a similar event. Depressive schemas increase the probability that the person will overreact to similar stressful events in the future (Eberhart et al., 2011).

A similar view of cognitive vulnerability to depression has been described in terms of hopelessness (Alloy et al., 2009). Hopelessness refers to the person's negative expectations about future events and the associated belief that these events cannot be controlled. According to this view, depression is associated with the expectation that desirable events probably will not occur or that aversive events probably will occur regardless of what the person does. Following a negative life event, the probability that the person will become depressed is a function of the explanations and importance that the person ascribes to these events. These explanations are known as *causal attributions.*

Some people tend to explain negative events in terms of internal, stable, global factors. This pattern has been called a depressogenic attributional style. For example, after failing an important exam, someone who uses this cognitive style would probably think that her poor performance was the result of her own inadequacies (internal), which she has recognized for a long time and which will persist into the future (stable), and which also are responsible for her failure in many other important tasks, both academic and otherwise (global). As in other cognitive views of depression, this kind of attributional style is not considered to be a sufficient cause of depression. It does represent an important predisposition to depression, however, to the extent that people who use it are more likely to develop hopelessness if they experience a negative life event.

The importance of biased cognitive processing in risk for depression has been demonstrated persuasively in many laboratory studies (Gotlib & Joormann, 2010). The cognitive problems that depressed people experience seem to reflect primarily problems in the control of attention to, and memory for, negative emotional material. If depressed people begin to think unpleasant thoughts, they have difficulty inhibiting or disengaging from them (Joormann, 2010). For most people, adaptive strategies for mood regulation include the ability to change the content of their working memory and shift their thoughts away from distressing ruminations. Depressed people experience special problems in this regard. This perspective helps to explain why encounters with stressful life events may have a more lasting and detrimental impact on people who are vulnerable to depression.

Problems with the inhibition of negative thoughts have also been used to explain further the observation of gender differences in the prevalence of depression (Nolen-Hoeksema et al., 2008). The manner in which a person responds to the onset of a depressed mood can influence the duration and severity of the mood (Nolen-Hoeksema, 1994, 2000). Two different response styles have been emphasized in this work. Some people respond to feelings of depression by turning their attention inward, contemplating the causes and implications of their sadness. This is called a *ruminative style.* Writing in a diary or talking extensively with a friend about how one feels is an indication of a ruminative style. Other people employ a *distracting style* to divert themselves from their unpleasant mood. They work on hobbies, play sports, or otherwise become involved in activities that draw their attention away from symptoms of depression.

The first hypothesis of this model is that people who engage in ruminative responses have longer and more severe episodes of depression than do people who engage in distracting responses. The second hypothesis is that women are more likely to employ a ruminative style in response to depression, whereas men are more likely to employ a distracting style. Because the ruminative style leads to episodes of greater duration and intensity, women are more susceptible to depression than are men.

**INTEGRATION OF COGNITIVE AND SOCIAL FACTORS** The factors that we have considered in the preceding pages almost certainly work in combination rather than individually. We do not need to decide whether cognitive vulnerabilities are somehow more or less important than stressful life events because they undoubtedly work in combination. The development of depression must be understood in terms of several stages: vulnerability, onset, and maintenance. Life events and cognitive factors play an important role within each stage (Alloy et al., 2006; Gotlib & Hammen, 1992).

Vulnerability to depression is influenced by experiences during childhood, including events such as being repeatedly neglected or harshly criticized by parents. Negative ways of thinking about the world and dysfunctional interpersonal skills are presumably learned early in life (Ingram & Ritter, 2000). As the child grows up, the combination of biased cognitive schemas and deficits in interpersonal skills then affects his or her social environment in several ways: It increases the likelihood that the person will enter problematic relationships; it diminishes the person's ability to resolve conflict after it occurs; and it minimizes the person's ability to solicit support and assistance from other people (Hammen & Garber, 2001).

The onset of depression is most often triggered by life events and circumstances. The stressful life events that precipitate an episode frequently grow out of difficult personal and family relationships. The impact of these experiences depends on the meanings that people assign to them. People become depressed when they interpret events in a way that diminishes their sense of self-worth. Persistent interpersonal and cognitive problems also serve to maintain a depressed mood over an extended period of time and help it escalate to clinical proportions.

## Biological Factors

We have considered a number of social and psychological factors that contribute to the etiology of mood disorders. Biological factors are also influential in the regulation of mood. Various studies suggest that genetic factors are somehow involved in both depression and bipolar disorder, that hormonal abnormalities are regularly associated with depression, and that depression is associated with abnormalities in the activation of specific regions of the brain.

**GENETICS** Genetic factors are clearly involved in the transmission of mood disorders (Lau & Eley, 2010). Studies that support this conclusion also suggest that bipolar disorders are much more heritable than depressive disorders.

**TWIN STUDIES** The comparison of monozygotic (MZ) and dizygotic (DZ) twin pairs provides one test of the possible influence of genetic factors (see Chapter 2). Several twin studies of mood disorders have reported higher concordance rates among MZ than among DZ twins (Kendler & Prescott, 2006).

One classic study used national twin and psychiatric registers in Denmark to identify 110 pairs of same-sex twins in which at least one member was diagnosed as having a mood disorder

Separation from a spouse during a war can be extremely stressful. Whether the person becomes depressed is influenced by cognitive events as well as interpersonal skills that are used to cope with this difficult situation.

(Bertelson, Harvald, & Hause, 1977). The concordance rates for bipolar disorders in MZ and DZ twins were .69 and .19, respectively. For depressive disorders, concordance rates for MZ and DZ twins were .54 and .24, respectively. The fact that the concordance rates were significantly higher for MZ than for DZ twins indicates that genetic factors are involved in the transmission of both bipolar and depressive mood disorders. The fact that the difference between the MZ and DZ rate was somewhat higher for bipolar than for depressive disorders may suggest that genes play a more important role in bipolar disorders than in depressive disorders. Similar patterns of MZ and DZ concordance rates have been reported subsequently from twin studies of mood disorders conducted in Norway (Nes et al., 2007; Rekhborn-Kjennerud et al., 2010) and in England (McGuffin et al., 1996).

Twin studies also tell us that environmental factors influence the expression of a genetically determined vulnerability to depression. The best evidence for the influence of nongenetic factors is the concordance rates in MZ twins, which consistently fall short of 100 percent. If genes told the whole story, MZ twins would always be concordant. Mathematical analyses have been used to estimate the relative contributions of genetic and environmental events to the etiology of mood disorders. The results of these analyses are expressed in terms of *heritability,* which can range from 0 percent (meaning that genetic factors are not involved) to 100 percent (meaning that genetic factors alone are responsible for the development of the trait in question) (see Research Methods in Chapter 17). These analyses indicate that genetic factors are particularly influential in bipolar disorders, for which the heritability estimate is 80 percent. Genes and environment contribute about equally to the etiology of major depressive disorder, in which the heritability estimate is close to 50 percent (McGuffin et al., 2003).

**SEARCHING FOR SPECIFIC GENES** The family and twin studies indicate that genetic factors play an important role in the development of mood disorders. They have not, however, established exactly how that happens. It is difficult to identify specific genes involved in complex behavioral disorders because there is no straightforward pattern of inheritance. All of the evidence indicates that mood disorders are polygenic—that is, they are influenced by many different genes rather than a single gene—and each of these genes on its own only changes risk for the disorder by a small amount (Christoforou et al., 2011; Lewis et al., 2010; Shyn et al., 2011).

Several research strategies can be used to find evidence of a link between specific genes and the development of mood disorders (see Research Methods in Chapter 14). Various linkage and association studies have focused on both bipolar and depressive mood disorders. With the introduction of new gene-mapping techniques, our knowledge in this area is expanding dramatically, but the results remain inconclusive. Many findings have been reported, but specific genes and genetic risk factors have not been confirmed (Gershon et al. 2011). Preliminary reports regarding specific genes have often failed to replicate when they were tested by investigators in different laboratories.

The possibility of identifying specific genes that are involved in the development of mood disorders is very exciting. This knowledge might eventually enable mental health professionals to identify people who are vulnerable to a disorder before the onset of overt symptoms. At the same time, however, two important cautions must be kept in mind regarding the complexity of the search for causes of mood disorders. One problem involves genetic heterogeneity. Within the general population, there may be more than one locus that contributes to the development of depression. Mood disorders may be linked to one marker within a certain extended family and to an entirely different marker in another family (Detera-Wadleigh & McMahon, 2004). Second, we also know that the environment plays an important role in the development of mood disorders. The onset of a mood disorder is determined by a combination of genetic and environmental risk factors that the individual experiences.

### GENETIC RISK AND SENSITIVITY TO STRESS

How do genetic factors and stressful life events interact to bring about depression? One demonstration of this effect was based on new genetic techniques that allow investigators to identify specific genes (Caspi et al., 2003). This investigation focused on the serotonin transporter (5-HTT) gene, which has been studied because several drugs that are used to treat depression have a direct impact on this particular neurotransmitter (see page 128). There are two alleles (long and short) for one particular region of the 5-HTT gene: The short allele ("s") is associated with reduced efficiency of neural transmission in serotonin pathways. People who are homozygous for the "s" allele of the 5-HTT gene are at a particularly high risk for becoming clinically depressed if they experience stressful life events (see Figure 5.3). In the absence of increased stress, the presence of this gene does not increase the person's risk for depression. Both factors seem to be necessary. The effects of the environment and genetic factors are not independent. Genetic factors apparently control the person's sensitivity to environmental events (Caspi et al., 2010; Karg et al., 2011).

**THE NEUROENDOCRINE SYSTEM** Various kinds of central nervous system events are associated with the connection between stressful life events and major depression. In the following sections, we will consider evidence regarding hormones and specific regions of the brain. These are the biological phenomena that are closely associated with the social and psychological factors that we have described thus far. Cognitive and emotional events are implemented in these events (Miller & Keller, 2000). They are part of the process by which the brain communicates with the rest of the body and mobilizes activities in response to changes in the external environment.

The endocrine system plays an important role in regulating a person's response to stress. Endocrine glands, such as the pituitary, thyroid, and adrenal glands, are located at various sites throughout the body (see Figure 2.4). In response to signals from the brain, these glands secrete hormones into the bloodstream. One important pathway in the endocrine system that may be closely related to the etiology of mood disorders is called the *hypothalamic–pituitary–adrenal (HPA) axis*. When the person detects a threat in the environment, the hypothalamus signals the pituitary gland to secrete a hormone called ACTH, which in turn modulates secretion of hormones, such as cortisol, from the adrenal glands into the bloodstream. Increased levels of cortisol help the person to prepare to respond to the threat by increasing alertness and delivering more fuel to muscles while also decreasing interest in other activities that might interfere with self-protection (such as sleeping and eating). This system is illustrated in Figure 5.4.

An association between the HPA axis and depression is indicated by evidence regarding the *dexamethasone suppression test* (DST), which has been used extensively to study endocrine dysfunction in patients with mood disorders (Nemeroff, 1998a). Dexamethasone is a potent synthetic hormone. People who have taken a test dose of dexamethasone normally show a suppression of cortisol secretion because the hypothalamus is fooled into thinking that there is already enough cortisol circulating in the system. Some depressed people show a different response: Approximately half of depressed patients show a failure of suppression in response to the DST. After their symptoms have improved, most of these patients exhibit a normal response on the DST. This pattern is consistent with the hypothesis that a dysfunction of the HPA axis may be involved in the development or maintenance of clinical depression, at least for some people (Stone, Lin, & Quarermain, 2008; Whybrow, 1997).

In what ways might endocrine problems be related to other causal factors? Several possibilities exist. In terms of the specific link between the endocrine system and the central nervous system, overproduction of cortisol may lead to changes in brain structure and function. At a more general level, hormone regulation may

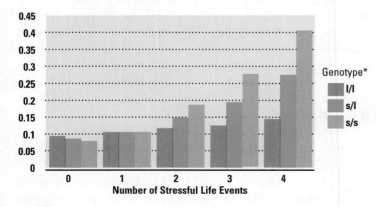

## FIGURE 5.3

**Combined Effects of Stress and Genetic Vulnerability on Risk for Depression**   Probability of onset of major depressive episode as a function of genotype for the serotonin transporter gene.

*The short ("s") allele is associated with lower efficiency compared to the long ("l") allele. *Source:* Caspi et. al. Influence of Life Stress on Depression: Moderation by a Polymorphism in the 5-HTT Gene. Science. 2003 July 18, 2003; 18.

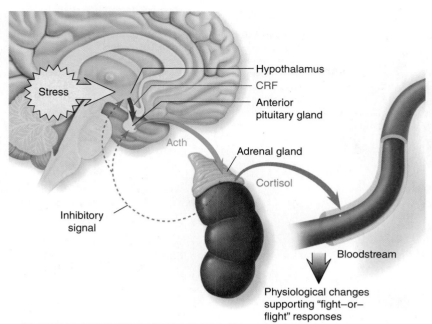

**FIGURE 5.4**

**Hormonal System Known as the Hypothalamic–Pituitary–Adrenal (HPA) Axis** The hypothalamic-pituitary-adrenal axis is activated in response to stress. ⊙ **Watch** the **Video** *The Hypothalamic-Pituitary-Adrenal (HPA) Axis* on **MyPsychLab** *Source:* Based on Nemeroff, C. The Neurobiology of Depression. Scientific American. 1998; 278: 28–35.

| Effects of CRF application to brain in animals | |
|---|---|
| Decreased | Increased |
| Eating<br>Sleeping<br>Reproductive activity | Restless activity in familiar environments<br>Withdrawal in unfamiliar environments |

provide a process through which stressful life events interact with a genetically determined predisposition to mood disorder. Stress causes the release of adrenal steroids, such as cortisol, and steroid hormones play an active role in regulating the expression of genes (Gotlib et al., 2008).

**BRAIN IMAGING STUDIES** The newest tools in the search for biological underpinnings of mood disorders are those that allow scientists to create detailed images of brain structures and to monitor ongoing brain functions in living patients (see Chapter 4 for a description of these procedures). The brain circuits that are involved in the experience and control of emotion are complex, centering primarily on the limbic system and its connections to the prefrontal cortex and the anterior cingulate cortex. Brain imaging studies indicate that severe depression is often associated with abnormal patterns of activity as well as structural changes in various brain regions (Davidson et al., 2002; Gotlib & Hamilton, 2008). Some of these areas of the brain are illustrated in Figure 5.5. See Figure 2.3 for illustrations of the amygdala, hippocampus, and other structures involved in the limbic system.

Abnormal patterns of activation in regions of the prefrontal cortex (PFC) are often found in association with depression. This evidence has been collected using functional brain imaging procedures, such as PET and fMRI. Some areas show *decreased activity,* especially the dorsolateral prefrontal cortex on the left side of the brain. This area of the PFC is involved in planning that is guided by the anticipation of emotion. A person who has a deficit of this type might have motivational problems, such as an inability to work toward a pleasurable goal. Other areas of the PFC have been found to show *abnormally elevated* levels of activity in depressed people. These include the orbital PFC and the ventromedial PFC, areas of the brain that are important for determining a person's responses to reward and punishment. More specifically, the orbital PFC inhibits inappropriate behaviors and helps the person ignore immediate rewards while working toward long-term goals. The ventromedial PFC is involved in the experience of emotion and the process of assigning meaning to perceptions. Overactivity in these regions of the brain might be associated with the prolonged experience of negative emotion.

The anterior cingulate cortex (ACC) provides a connection between the functions of attention and emotion. It allows us to focus on subjective feelings and to consider the relation between our emotions and our behavior. For example, the ACC is activated when a person has been frustrated in the pursuit of a goal, or when he or she experiences an emotion, such as sadness, in a situation where it was not expected. People suffering from major depressive disorder typically show decreased activation of the ACC (Davidson et al., 2002). A reduction in ACC activity might be reflected in a failure to appreciate the maladaptive nature of prolonged negative emotions and a reduced ability to engage in more adaptive behaviors that might help to resolve the person's problems.

The amygdala (see Figure 5.5), almond-sized nuclei near the tip of the hippocampus on each side of the brain, appear to be an

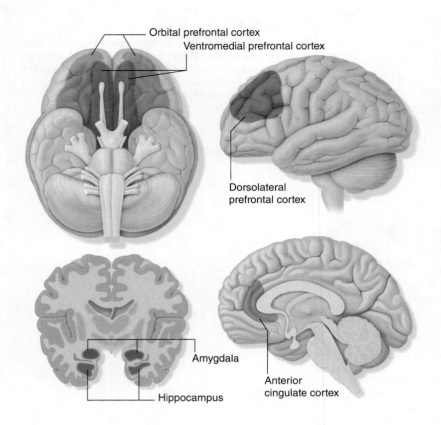

**FIGURE 5.5**

**Areas of the Brain Involved in Depression** Brain regions involved in emotion and mood disorders.
*Source:* Davidson, Richard J., Diego Pizzagalli, Jack B. Nitschke, and Katherine Putnam. DEPRESSION: Perspectives from Affective Neuroscience. Annual Review of Psychology. 2002. 53:545–74.
Copyright (c) 2002 by Annual Reviews. All rights reserved.

important part of the neural circuit involved in emotion (Canli, 2009). They are extensively connected to the hypothalamus. This system is responsible for monitoring the emotional significance of information that is processed by the brain and regulating social interactions. Functional imaging studies have identified elevated levels of resting blood flow and glucose metabolism in the amygdala among patients with major depressive disorder and bipolar disorder (Drevets, 2002). Higher metabolism rates are associated with more severe levels of depression. Patients who respond positively to treatment show a normalization of amygdala metabolism.

It is tempting to infer from this pattern that the increased activity reflected in images of the amygdala represents, at the neurochemical level of analysis, a reflection of the distorted cognitive functions that have been described by clinical psychologists in association with depression (Gotlib & Hamilton, 2008). Of course, this kind of speculation will need to be tested using more detailed research strategies in which specific cognitive processes are measured while brain activities are recorded in depressed and nondepressed people.

**NEUROTRANSMITTERS** Communication and coordination of information within and between areas of the brain depend on neurotransmitters, chemicals that bridge the gaps between individual neurons (see Chapter 2). Over the past several decades, scientists have gathered a great deal of information concerning the neurochemical underpinnings of depression and mania (Delgado &

Moreno, 2006). Our knowledge in this area began with the accidental discovery, during the 1950s, of several drugs that have the ability to alter people's moods. The development of antidepressant drugs stimulated research on several specific neurotransmitters that have been shown to be responsible for their effects. Most notable among these are serotonin, norepinephrine, and dopamine. Each neurotransmitter works in a broad set of pathways connecting fairly specific brain locations.

Serotonin is the chemical messenger that is enhanced by medications, such as Prozac. It has a profound effect on a person's mood, with higher levels being associated with feelings of serenity and optimism. Serotonin also plays an important role in areas of the brain that regulate sleep and appetite. Serotonin pathways include connections involving the amygdala, the hypothalamus, and areas of the cortex. The beneficial effects of drugs such as Prozac (see the section on treatment of depression) provide the most convincing evidence for the argument that some type of malfunction in serotonin pathways is involved in the etiology of depression.

We know that the relation between neurotransmitters and depression is complex, and the specific mechanisms are not well understood. There may be more than 100 different neurotransmitters in the central nervous system, and each neurotransmitter is associated with several types of postsynaptic receptors. It seems unlikely that a heterogeneous disorder such as depression, which involves a dysregulation of many cognitive and emotional functions, will be linked to only one type of chemical messenger or only one loop in the brain's circuitry. Current theories tend to emphasize the interactive effects of several neurotransmitter systems, including serotonin, norepinephrine, dopamine, and neuropeptides (short chains of amino acids that exist in the brain and appear to modulate the activity of the classic neurotransmitters) (Stockmeier, 2003; Thase, Ripu, & Howland, 2002).

## Integration of Social, Psychological, and Biological Factors

We have considered a variety of social, psychological, and biological factors that appear to be related to the causes of mood disorders. How can these factors be combined or integrated? One type of research that illustrates this point has employed an animal model of depression (see Research Methods). When laboratory animals are exposed to uncontrollable stress (such as a 15-minute forced swim in cold water from which they cannot escape), they frequently exhibit behavioral symptoms that are similar to

(yet obviously not the same as) those seen in depressed humans (Lanfumey, Mongeau, & Cohen-Salmon, 2008). The animals develop deficits in motor activity, sleep, and eating behaviors. This type of stress-induced depression in laboratory rats produces various temporary effects on neurotransmitters, including changes in the concentration of norepinephrine, serotonin, and dopamine in the specific regions of the limbic system and the frontal cortex. Rats that show these neurochemical consequences following exposure to stress exhibit signs of depression. If the neurotransmitters are not depleted, the rats do not appear to be depressed. Furthermore, administering antidepressant drugs to these animals has been shown to reverse or prevent the behavioral effects of uncontrollable stress. Selective breeding experiments have been able to produce subtypes of rats that differ in their response to behavioral challenges (such as the forced swim test), as well as in their response to antidepressant medication (Ressler & Mayberg, 2007).

## RESEARCH methods

### Analogue Studies: Do Rats Get Depressed, and Why?

Many questions about the causes of psychopathology cannot be addressed using highly controlled laboratory studies with human subjects. For example, does prolonged exposure to uncontrollable stress cause anxiety disorders? This kind of issue has been addressed using correlational studies with people who have the disorders in question, but experiments on these issues cannot be done with human subjects. For important ethical reasons, investigators cannot randomly assign people to endure conditions that are hypothesized to produce full-blown disorders, such as clinical depression. The best alternative is often to study a condition that is similar, or analogous, to the clinical disorder in question. Investigations of this type are called **analogue studies** because they focus on behaviors that resemble mental disorders—or isolated features of mental disorders—that appear in the natural environment.

Many analogue studies depend on the use of animal models of psychopathology, which have provided important insights regarding the etiology of conditions such as anxiety, depression, and schizophrenia (Fernando & Robbins, 2010). In the 1960s, Harry Harlow's research demonstrated that rhesus monkey infants develop despair responses after separation from their mothers. The somatic symptoms exhibited by these monkeys—facial and vocal displays of sadness and dismay, social withdrawal, changes in appetite and sleep, and psychomotor retardation—were remarkably similar to many symptoms of clinical depression in humans.

This social separation model of depression has been used to explore several important variables that may be involved in mood disorders. For example, infant monkeys who have extensive experience with peers and other adults are less likely to become depressed following separation from their mothers. The skills

that they learn through social exploration apparently allow them to cope more successfully with stress. The social separation model has also been used to explore neurochemical factors and mood disorders. Drug companies have used the model to evaluate the antidepressant effects of new drugs.

Some clinicians have argued that mental disorders, such as depression, cannot be modeled in a laboratory setting, especially using animals as subjects. Cognitive symptoms—such as Beck's depressive triad—cannot be measured with animals. Do monkeys feel guilty? Can rats experience hopelessness or suicidal ideas? But these symptoms are not necessarily the most central features of the disorder. Cross-cultural studies have shown that in some non-Western societies somatic symptoms are the most prominent symptoms of depression. Many of these aspects of mood disorder are seen in animals. The value of any analogue study hinges, in large part, on the extent to which the analogue condition is similar to the actual clinical disorder. Some models are more compelling than others.

Analogue studies have one important advantage over other types of research design in psychopathology: They can employ an experimental procedure. Therefore, the investigator can draw strong inferences about cause and effect. The main disadvantage of analogue studies involves the extent to which the results of a particular investigation can be generalized to situations outside the laboratory. If a particular set of circumstances produced a set of maladaptive behaviors in the laboratory, is it reasonable to assume that similar mechanisms produce the actual clinical disorder in the natural environment? In actual practice, questions about the etiology of disorders, such as depression, will probably depend on converging evidence generated from the use of many different research designs.

This animal model illustrates the need to consider the interaction between biological and psychological phenomena. The data on stress-induced depression in rats suggest that neurochemical processes may be reactions to environmental events, such as uncontrollable stress in rats or severe life events in people. Psychological and biological explanations of depression are complementary views of the same process, differing primarily in terms of their level of analysis.

## Treatment

Several procedures, both psychosocial and biological, have proved to be useful in the treatment of mood disorders. In the following pages we will examine some of the more prominent contemporary approaches to the treatment of major depression and bipolar disorder, as well as the research evidence on their usefulness.

### Depressive Disorders

Most psychological approaches to the treatment of depression owe some debt to psychodynamic procedures and Freud's emphasis on the importance of interpersonal relationships. According to Freud's view, the primary goal of therapy should be to help the patient understand and express the hostility and frustration that are being directed against the self. These negative emotions are presumably rooted in dysfunctional relationships with other people. Freud also placed considerable emphasis on the apparently irrational beliefs that depressed people hold about themselves and their world. These cognitive factors are also emphasized by cognitive therapists.

### Cognitive Therapy

The cognitive model assumes that emotional dysfunction is influenced by the negative ways in which people interpret events in their environments and the things that they say to themselves about those experiences. Based on the assumption that depression will be relieved if these maladaptive schemas are changed, cognitive therapists focus on helping their patients replace self-defeating thoughts with more rational self-statements (Dobson, 2008; Garratt et al., 2007).

A specific example may help illustrate this process. Consider the case of Cathy, the depressed attorney whom we introduced at the beginning of the chapter. Cathy focused a great deal of attention on relatively minor negative events at work, blaming herself for anything other than a perfect performance. Her therapist helped her to recognize that she was engaging in a pattern of cognitive distortion that has been labeled "selective abstraction." Taking a detail out of context, she would invariably ignore those aspects of her performance that refuted the conclusion that she was professionally incompetent. Her therapist helped her overcome these tendencies by teaching her to question her conclusions and to develop more objective ways of evaluating her experiences.

Cathy also tended to think about herself in absolute and unvarying terms. During the course of therapy, she learned to recognize this pattern and to substitute more flexible self-statements. Instead of saying to herself, "I am a hopeless introvert and will never be able to change," she learned to substitute, "I am less comfortable in social situations than some other people, but I can learn to be more confident."

The cognitive approach to treatment shares many features with behavioral approaches to intervention. Cognitive therapists are active and directive in their interactions with clients, and they focus most of their attention on their clients' current experience. They also assume that people have conscious access to cognitive events: Our thinking may not always be rational, but we can discuss private thoughts and feelings. Another important aspect of the cognitive approach to treatment, and a characteristic that it shares with the behavioral perspective, is a serious commitment to the empirical evaluation of the efficacy of treatment programs. Several studies have found that cognitive therapy is effective in the treatment of nonpsychotic depression (Hollon, Stewart, & Strunk, 2006).

**INTERPERSONAL THERAPY** Interpersonal therapy is another contemporary approach to the psychological treatment of depression (Bleiberg & Markowitz, 2008; Weissman, Markowitz, & Klerman, 2000). It is focused primarily on current relationships, especially those involving family members. The therapist helps the patient develop a better understanding of the interpersonal problems that presumably give rise to depression and attempts to improve the patient's relationships with other people by building communication and problem-solving skills. Therapy sessions often include nondirective discussions of social difficulties and unexpressed or unacknowledged negative emotions, as well as role-playing to practice specific social skills.

**ANTIDEPRESSANT MEDICATIONS** The types of medications that are used most frequently in the treatment of depressive mood disorders fall into four general categories: selective serotonin reuptake inhibitors (SSRIs), tricyclic antidepressants (TCAs), monoamine oxidase inhibitors (MAOIs), and "other," more recently developed drugs. Among patients who respond positively to antidepressant medication, improvement is typically evident within four to six weeks, and the current episode is often resolved within 12 weeks (DePaulo & Horvitz, 2002). Medication is usually continued for at least six to 12 months after the patient has entered remission in order to reduce the chance of relapse.

***SELECTIVE SEROTONIN REUPTAKE INHIBITORS*** The **selective serotonin reuptake inhibitors (SSRIs)** were developed in the early 1980s and are now the most frequently used form of antidepressant medication, accounting for more than 80 percent of all prescriptions written for that purpose (Hirschfeld, 2001). Unlike the original forms of antidepressant medication, which were discovered by accident, SSRIs were synthesized in the laboratories of pharmaceutical companies on the basis of theoretical speculation regarding the role of serotonin in the etiology of mood disorders.

## TABLE 5.3
## Medications for Depressive Mood Disorders

| Drug Class | Generic Name (Trade Name) | Mode of Action |
|---|---|---|
| Selective serotonin reuptake inhibitors (SSRIs) | Fluoxetine (Prozac) | Block 5-HT reuptake |
| | Paroxetine (Paxil) | |
| | Sertraline (Zoloft) | |
| | Citalopram (Celexa) | |
| | Fluvoxamine (Luvox) | |
| Tricyclic antidepressants (TCAs) | Amitriptyline (Elavil) | Block reuptake of 5-HT and norepinephrine |
| | Clomipramine (Anafranil) | |
| | Imipramine (Tofranil) | |
| Monoamine oxidase inhibitors (MAOIs) | Phenelzine (Nardil) | Deactivate enzyme that breaks down monoamines |
| Other antidepressants | Trazodone (Desyrel) | Block 5-HT reuptake and block 5-HT receptors |
| | Bupropion (Wellbutrin) | Block norepinephrine and dopamine reuptake |
| | Venlafaxine (Effexor) | Block reuptake of 5-HT and norepinephrine |

Note: 5-HT is serotonin.

There are many specific types of SSRIs (see Table 5.3). Controlled outcome studies indicate that Prozac and other SSRIs are about as effective as traditional forms of antidepressant medication (von Wolff et al., 2013).

The SSRIs inhibit the reuptake of serotonin into the presynaptic nerve ending and thus promote neurotransmission in serotonin pathways by increasing the amount of serotonin in the synaptic cleft. They are called "selective" because they seem to have little if any effect on the uptake of norepinephrine and dopamine. Nevertheless, the SSRIs are not entirely selective, in the sense that some of them do block reuptake of other neurotransmitters. They also vary in the potency with which they block serotonin reuptake. Their effectiveness in treating depression does not seem to be directly related to either the extent to which a particular SSRI is selective with regard to serotonin or its potency in blocking serotonin reuptake (Pallanti & Sandner, 2007).

The SSRIs are typically considered to be easier to use than other antidepressant drugs. They also have fewer side effects (such as constipation and drowsiness), and they are less dangerous in the event of an overdose. This does not mean, of course, that they are completely without side effects (see Critical Thinking Matters on page 131). Some patients experience nausea, headaches, and sleep disturbances, but these symptoms are usually mild and short term. The most troublesome side effects associated with SSRIs are sexual dysfunction and weight gain. The rate of decreased sexual desire and orgasmic dysfunction may be as high as 50 percent among both men and women taking SSRIs. Weight changes in response to SSRIs vary in relation to length of treatment. Many patients experience an initial weight loss, but most regain this weight after six months. Those who continue to take the medication may gain an average of 20 pounds.

**TRICYCLICS** The **tricyclics antidepressants (TCAs),** such as imipramine (Tofranil) and amitriptyline (Elavil), have been in relatively widespread use since the 1950s, but their use has declined since the introduction of the SSRIs because they have more side effects. Common reactions include blurred vision, constipation, drowsiness, and a drop in blood pressure. The TCAs affect brain functions by blocking the uptake of neurotransmitters (especially norepinephrine) from the synapse. Several controlled double-blind studies indicate that TCAs benefit many depressed patients, although improvements might not be evident until two or three weeks after the beginning of treatment (Thase, 2006). The several different kinds of tricyclic medication vary in potency and side effects, but they are generally equal in terms of effectiveness. Comparisons of TCAs and SSRIs indicate that they are approximately equal in terms of success rates, with positive responses being shown by 50 to 60 percent of depressed patients (Schulberg et al., 1999).

**MONOAMINE OXIDASE INHIBITORS** The antidepressant effects of **monoamine oxidase inhibitors (MAOIs),** such as phenelzine (Nardil), were discovered at about the same time as those of the tricyclic drugs. These drugs have not been used as extensively as tricyclics, however, primarily for two reasons. First, patients who use MAOIs and also consume foods containing large amounts of the compound tyramine, such as cheese and chocolate, often develop high blood pressure. Second, some early empirical evaluations of antidepressant medications suggest that MAOIs are not as effective as tricyclics.

More recent studies have shown that MAO inhibitors are indeed useful in the treatment of depressed patients (Thase, 2006). They can be used safely when the patient avoids foods such as

*"I think the dosage needs adjusting. I'm not nearly as happy as the people in the ads."*

© Barbara Smaller/The New Yorker Collection/www.cartoonbank.com

cheese, beer, and red wine. In addition, MAOIs are now widely used in the treatment of certain anxiety disorders, especially agoraphobia and panic attacks (see Chapter 6).

### THE EFFICACY OF PSYCHOTHERAPY AND MEDICATION

Considerable time and energy have been devoted to the evaluation of psychological and pharmacological treatments for depression. The bottom line in this lengthy debate—based on extensive reviews of the research literature—is that both cognitive therapy and antidepressant medication are effective forms of treatment for people who suffer from depression (Hollon, Thase, & Markowitz, 2002). This is true for people with major depressive disorder as well as persistent depressive disorder. In actual practice, many experts recommend treatment with a combination of psychotherapy and medication (Kupfer & Frank, 2001; Simon et al., 2006).

Carefully controlled treatment outcome studies indicate that medication and psychotherapy are approximately equivalent in the treatment of people who are chronically depressed. Either form of treatment is a reasonable choice for people suffering from depression. Recent evidence indicates that the combination of psychotherapy and antidepressant medication often leads more quickly to a remission of symptoms than either form of treatment alone (Cuijpers et al., 2012).

### Bipolar Disorders

Treatment of bipolar disorders has also focused on the combined use of medication and psychotherapy. A variety of mood-stabilizing drugs are employed with bipolar patients. They are used to help people recover from episodes of mania and depression and also on a long-term maintenance basis to reduce the frequency of future episodes (Geddes et al., 2004). Antidepressant medications are sometimes used, usually in combination with a mood stabilizer, for the treatment of bipolar patients (Fountoulakis et al., 2008). Clinicians must be cautious, however, because antidepressants can sometimes trigger a switch from depression into a hypomanic or manic episode.

**LITHIUM** An extensive literature indicates that the salt *lithium carbonate* is an effective form of treatment in the alleviation of manic episodes, and it remains the first choice for treating bipolar disorders. It is also useful in the treatment of bipolar patients who are experiencing a depressive episode. Perhaps most importantly, bipolar patients who continue to take lithium between episodes are significantly less likely to experience a relapse (Bauer & Mitchner, 2004).

Unfortunately, there are also some limitations associated with the use of lithium. Many bipolar patients, perhaps 40 percent, do not improve when they take lithium (Mendlewicz, Souery, & Rivelli, 1999). Nonresponse is particularly common among rapid cycling patients, those who exhibit a mixture of manic and depressed symptoms, and those with comorbid alcohol abuse. Compliance with medication is also a frequent problem; at least half the people for whom lithium is prescribed either fail to take it regularly or stop taking it against their psychiatrist's advice. The main reasons that patients give for discontinuing lithium involve its negative side effects, including nausea, memory problems, weight gain, and impaired coordination.

**ANTICONVULSANT MEDICATIONS** Often, bipolar patients who do not respond to lithium are prescribed anticonvulsant drugs, particularly carbamazepine (Tegretol) or valproic acid (Depakene) (Reinares et al., 2013). Outcome data suggest that slightly more than 50 percent of bipolar patients respond positively to these drugs. Like lithium, carbamazepine and valproic acid can be useful in reducing the frequency and severity of relapse, and they can be used to treat acute manic episodes. Valproic acid may be more effective than lithium for the treatment of rapid cycling bipolar patients and those with mixed symptoms of mania and depression in a single episode (Gadde & Krishman, 1997). Common side effects include gastrointestinal distress (nausea, vomiting, and diarrhea) and sedation.

**PSYCHOTHERAPY** Although medication is the most important method of treatment for bipolar disorders, psychotherapy can be an effective supplement to biological intervention. Both cognitive therapy and interpersonal therapy have been adapted for use with bipolar disorders. Cognitive therapy can address the patient's reactions to stressful life events as well as his or her reservations about taking medication (Craighead & Miklowitz, 2000).

A variation on interpersonal therapy, known as interpersonal and social rhythm therapy has been developed for use with

# CRITICAL THINKING matters

## Do Antidepressant Drugs Cause Violent Behavior?

Extensive media attention has been devoted to the suggestion that some of the SSRIs can increase the risk of violent and suicidal behavior. Several dramatic cases have been discussed at great length. One example is Chris Pittman, who was found guilty in 2005 of killing his paternal grandparents with a shotgun when he was 12 years old. No one questioned the basic facts of the case. Pittman admitted that he blasted his grandparents with a shotgun while they were sleeping. He then set their house on fire and fled the area. After he was caught, his defense team mounted what some court observers called the Zoloft defense, claiming that the murders were triggered by the boy's reaction to antidepressant medication that he had been taking for several days before the murders (see Chapter 18 for a discussion of the insanity defense). Prosecutors argued, on the other hand, that he killed his grandparents because he was angry after they disciplined him for fighting with a younger student on the school bus earlier that day. In other words, his motivation did not involve a mental disorder or a reaction to medication. Pittman was tried as an adult, convicted by a jury, and sentenced to 30 years in prison.

Tragic public cases such as this one generate strong opinions on both sides. Magazines and Web sites are filled with warnings about the dangers of treating children and adolescents with SSRIs, some more extreme than others. Many psychiatrists have responded by noting the beneficial effects that antidepressant medication can have for young people. Clearly, parents should be warned about negative side effects that are sometimes associated with drugs such as Zoloft, but should they be frightened to the point that they avoid using one of the most effective forms of treatment for mood disorders? Critical thinking must prevail.

One important issue in this ongoing debate is the need for empirical evidence. Do SSRIs cause a significant increase in the risk of violence and suicide? Millions of people take antidepressant medication. Many depressed people commit suicide, in spite of the best efforts to treat their condition. The fact that one person committed suicide or any other violent crime while taking a specific drug does not provide convincing evidence that the drug caused the person to engage in that behavior. The question is whether people taking Zoloft are more likely to be suicidal or violent than other (similarly) depressed people who are being given another form of treatment. The data suggest that SSRI treatment does not increase risk of suicidal behavior, but the issue has not been closed entirely (Breggin, 2004; Gibbons et al., 2007). In the absence of better evidence, the U.S. Food and Drug Administration (FDA) requires that a warning be printed on the label when Zoloft (and some other SSRIs) is prescribed for children, including the following statement:

> Families and caregivers of pediatric patients being treated with antidepressants . . . should be alerted about the need to monitor patients for the emergence of agitation, irritability, unusual changes in behavior, and the other symptoms described above, as well as the emergence of suicidality.

The legal implications of these findings remain ambiguous. Most forms of antidepressant medication are capable of triggering manic episodes in people who are depressed (Goldberg & Truman, 2003), and the symptoms of mania sometimes include hostility and aggression. Does that mean that SSRIs can cause someone to become homicidal or suicidal? When people come out of a period of depression and their mood is lifting, they also experience an increase in energy. For many years, experts have recognized that this period of time can be especially dangerous for people who have harbored serious thoughts of violence. If they decide to act on those impulses, is it the pill's fault? Is the person no longer responsible for his or her behavior?

While the public does need to be warned about side effects that can be associated with medication, it is also irresponsible to exaggerate or distort that evidence. People who are frightened do not make well-informed decisions. In fact, the risks of medication side effects must be balanced against the risks associated with failing to treat a potentially lethal condition such as depression (Brent, 2004).

---

bipolar patients (Frank, 2005). It is based on the recognition that a repeated episode of either mania or depression is often precipitated by one of the following factors: stressful life events, disruptions in social rhythms (the times of day in which the person works, sleeps, and so on), and failure to take medication. Special emphasis is placed on monitoring the interaction between symptoms (especially the onset of hypomanic or manic episodes) and social interactions. Therapists help patients learn to lead more orderly lives, especially with regard to sleep–wake cycles, and to resolve interpersonal problems effectively. Regulation of sleep and work patterns is also important. This therapy program is employed in combination with the long-term use of mood stabilizing medication.

Current evidence indicates that the combination of psychotherapy and medication for the treatment of bipolar disorder is more beneficial than medication alone (Miklowitz et al., 2007). There is an obvious need for more extensive research on the effectiveness of various types of psychosocial treatment for bipolar disorders.

## Electroconvulsive Therapy

The procedure known as electroconvulsive therapy (or ECT) has proved beneficial for many patients suffering from mood disorders (see Chapter 3 for a review of the background of ECT). Electroconvulsive therapy is typically administered in an inpatient setting and consists of a series of treatments given three times a week for two to seven weeks (Abrams, 2002). Many patients show a dramatic improvement after six to eight sessions, but some require more. In current clinical practice, muscle relaxants are always administered before a patient receives ECT. This procedure has eliminated bone fractures and dislocations that were unfortunate side effects of techniques used many years ago. The electrodes can be placed either bilaterally (on both sides of the head) or unilaterally (at the front and back of the skull on one side of the patient's head). Unilateral placement on the nondominant hemisphere (the right side of the head for right-handed people) may minimize the amount of post-seizure memory impairment, but it may also be less effective.

Although how ECT works remains largely a mystery, empirical studies have demonstrated that it is an effective form of treatment for severely depressed patients (Khalid et al., 2008). Reservations regarding the use of ECT center around widely publicized, although infrequent, cases of pervasive and persistent memory loss. Reviews of the research evidence indicate that ECT-induced changes in memory and other cognitive functions are almost always short-lived, and ECT does not induce loss of neurons or other changes in brain structure (Lisanby, 2007).

No one denies that ECT is an invasive procedure that should usually be reserved for patients who have been resistant to other forms of intervention, such as medication

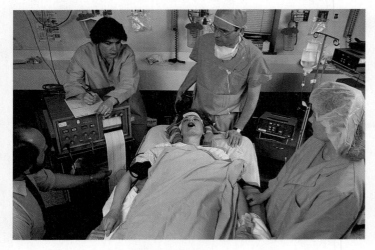

Electroconvulsive therapy is an effective form of treatment for severely depressed patients. It should be considered for people who do not improve with psychotherapy or antidepressant medication.

and cognitive therapy. Nevertheless, it remains a viable and legitimate alternative for some severely depressed patients, especially those who are so suicidal that they require constant supervision to prevent them from harming themselves. As always, the risks of treatment must be carefully weighed against those associated with allowing the disorder to follow its natural course.

## Seasonal Mood Disorders

The observation that changes in seasons can help bring on episodes of mood disorder leads to the relatively obvious implication that some patients might respond to manipulations of the natural environment. For centuries, physicians have prescribed changes in climate for their depressed clients (Wehr, 1989). The prominent French psychiatrist Jean Esquirol (1772–1840) reportedly advised a patient whose depression appeared when the days grew shorter to move from Belgium to Italy during the winter.

Modern light therapy was introduced in the 1980s. Typical treatment involves exposure to bright (2,500 lux), broad-spectrum light for one to two hours every day. Some patients also respond positively to shorter periods (30 minutes) of high-intensity (10,000 lux) light. This high-intensity light is roughly equivalent to the amount of light that would be generated by a 750-watt spotlight focused on a surface 1 square meter in area. The light source—most often a rectangular box containing fluorescent ceiling fixtures—must be placed close to the patient at eye level. Improvement in the person's mood is often seen within two to five days (Golden et al., 2005).

Outcome studies have found that light therapy is an effective form of treatment for seasonal affective disorder, with outcome being roughly equivalent to the use of standard antidepressant medication (Lam et al., 2006). The combination of light therapy with cognitive therapy may be more effective than either form of treatment alone (Rohan et al., 2007). Many patients with seasonal affective disorders do respond well to light therapy, and it is considered by many clinicians to be a useful approach to this disorder. It is not exactly clear why or how light therapy works, but the process may help the body to normalize circadian rhythms, which regulate processes such as hormone secretion (Whybrow, 1997).

## Suicide

### → An Admiral's Suicide

Admiral Jeremy (Mike) Boorda was the highest ranking officer in the U.S. Navy when, at the age of 56, he committed suicide (Thomas, 1996). He was married and the father of four children. Boorda was the first person in the history of the Navy to rise from the enlisted ranks to become chief of naval operations. Although his record of leadership was widely admired by both fellow

This man is receiving light therapy for the treatment of seasonal affective disorder.

officers and prominent politicians, he had recently been the subject of journalistic scrutiny. Questions had been raised about whether Boorda had legitimately earned two medals that he displayed on his uniform for several years (small Vs that are awarded to people who have shown valor in combat). These public symbols of heroism are a source of considerable status, especially among professional military people. Boorda had stopped wearing the medals after the issue was initially raised, but some members of the media had decided to pursue the issue further. On the morning of his death, Boorda was told that reporters from *Newsweek* magazine wanted to ask him some more questions about his justification for wearing these medals. He never met with them. Telling other officers that he was going home for lunch, Boorda went home and shot himself in the chest with a .38 revolver.

Why would such a successful person choose to end his own life? Suicide is an extremely personal, private, and complicated act. We will never know exactly why Admiral Boorda killed himself, but the circumstances surrounding his death are consistent with a number of facts about suicide. The highest rate of suicide in the United States is found among white males over the age of 50. Within this group, men who have been occupationally successful are more likely to commit suicide, especially if that success is threatened or lost. Notes that the admiral left for his wife and for Navy personnel indicated that he could no longer face the public dishonor that might result from *Newsweek*'s investigation. Escape from psychological suffering is often a significant motive in suicide. Did Boorda commit suicide primarily to end his own subjective distress? Or was his death intended to avoid bringing disgrace to the Navy, which had been plagued by other scandals in recent years? When he was appointed chief of naval operations, several months before his death, it had been hoped that he would

restore morale and improve public confidence in the Navy. The *Newsweek* probe threatened to negate all of those efforts. Did his death represent a personal sacrifice for the military service that he loved and to which he had devoted 40 years of his life? These difficult questions illustrate the challenges faced by clinicians, who must try to understand suicide so that they can more effectively prevent it.

Aides said that Admiral Boorda did not show any signs of being depressed, even on the morning that he died. Nor were there any indications of substance abuse or other mental disorders. In this respect, Boorda's situation was unusual. Although many people who commit suicide do not appear to be depressed, and psychopathology doesn't explain all suicidal behavior, there is undoubtedly a strong relationship between depression and self-destructive acts. The available evidence suggests that at least 50 percent of all suicides occur as a result of, or in the context of, a primary mood disorder (Nock et al., 2012). Moreover, the risk of completed suicide is much higher among people who are clinically depressed than it is among people in the general population. Follow-up studies consistently indicate that 15 to 20 percent of all patients with mood disorders will eventually kill themselves (Hawton et al., 2013). Thus, it seems reasonable to conclude that there is a relatively close link between suicide and depression.

## Classification of Suicide

Common sense tells us that suicide takes many forms. *DSM-5* does not address this issue; rather, it lists suicidal ideation (thoughts of suicide) only as a symptom of mood disorders. Clinicians and social scientists have proposed a number of systems for classifying subtypes of suicide, based on speculation regarding different motives for ending one's own life. Therefore, in contrast to the principles that were followed in creating *DSM-5,* classification systems for suicide are based on causal theories rather than descriptive factors.

The most influential system for classifying suicide was originally proposed in 1897 by Émile Durkheim (1858–1917), a French sociologist who is one of the most important figures in the history of sociology (Coser, 1977). In order to appreciate the nature of this system, you must understand Durkheim's approach to studying social problems. Durkheim was interested in "social facts," such as religious groups and political parties, rather than the psychological or biological features of particular individuals. His scientific studies were aimed at clarifying the social context in which human problems appear, and they were based on the assumption that human passions and ambition are controlled by the moral and social structures of society. One of his most important scientific endeavors was a comparison of suicide rates among various religious and occupational groups.

Distinctions among Durkheim's types of suicide can be difficult to make. Do the motives of suicide bombers reflect a breakdown of social order? Or does their violent behavior represent a personal sacrifice for the sake of their society?

In his book *Suicide,* Durkheim (1897/1951) argued that the rate of suicide within a group or a society would increase if levels of social integration and regulation are either excessively low or excessively high. He identified four different types of suicide, which are distinguished by the social circumstances in which the person is living:

- Egoistic suicide (diminished integration) occurs when people become relatively detached from society and when they feel that their existence is meaningless (Maimon & Kuhl, 2008). Egoistic suicide is presumably more common among groups such as people who have been divorced and people who are suffering from mental disorders. The predominant emotions associated with egoistic suicide are depression and apathy.

- Altruistic suicide (excessive integration) occurs when the rules of the social group dictate that the person must sacrifice his or her own life for the sake of others. One example is the former practice in some Native American tribes of elderly persons voluntarily going off by themselves to die after they felt they had become a burden to others.

- Anomic suicide (diminished regulation) occurs following a sudden breakdown in social order or a disruption of the norms that govern people's behavior. Anomic suicide explains increased suicide rates that occur following an economic or political crisis or among people who are adjusting to the unexpected loss of a social or occupational role. The typical feelings associated with *anomie* (a term coined by Durkheim, which literally means "without a name") are anger, disappointment, and exasperation.

- Fatalistic suicide (excessive regulation) occurs when the circumstances under which a person lives become unbearable. A slave, for example, might choose to commit suicide in order to escape from the horrible nature of his

or her existence. This type of suicide was mentioned only briefly by Durkheim, who thought that it was extremely uncommon.

Durkheim believed that egoistic and anomic suicide were the most common types of suicide in Western industrial societies. Although he distinguished between these two dominant forms, he recognized that they were interconnected and could operate together. Some people may become victims of both diminished integration and ineffective regulation.

Durkheim's system for classifying types of suicide has remained influential, but it does have some limitations (Leenaars, 2004; Stack, 2004). For example, it does not explain why one person commits suicide while other members of the same group do not. All the people in the group are subject to the same social structures. Another problem with Durkheim's system is that the different types of suicide overlap and may, in some cases, be difficult to distinguish. If the system is used to describe individual cases of suicide, such as that of Admiral Boorda, would clinicians be likely to agree on these subtypes? We are not aware of any attempts to evaluate the reliability of such judgments, but it might be quite low.

**NONSUICIDAL SELF-INJURY** Some people deliberately harm themselves without trying to end their own lives. The most frequent forms of nonsuicidal self-injurious behaviors involve cutting, burning, or scratching the skin, usually in a place where the wounds and resulting scars can easily be concealed from others (Levenkron, 2006). Nonsuicidal self-injury must be distinguished from fashion trends, such as piercing and tattooing. People get tattoos and pierce various parts of their bodies with ornaments and jewelry because the effect on their appearance is considered stylish or distinctive. These activities are accomplished

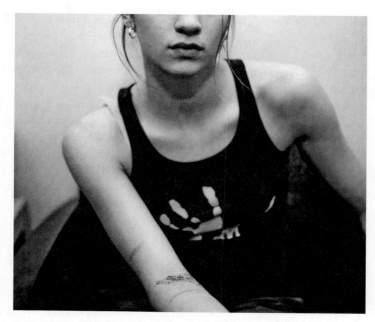

Self-injury is often a maladaptive way to regulate intense, negative emotions.

in spite of the initial pain that the person must endure. In contrast, people who engage in nonsuicidal self-injury do it because the pain serves a useful purpose for them regardless of its impact on their appearance. ⊙ **Watch** the **Video** *Mary: Non-Suicidal Self Injury* on **MyPsychLab**

This problem can take many different forms and be associated with various kinds of mental disorders. Deliberate self-harm is listed in *DSM-5* as one of the symptoms of borderline personality disorder (see Chapter 9), but it also occurs among people suffering from other disorders, especially substance use disorders, eating disorders, depression, and posttraumatic stress disorder. Approximately 4 percent of people in the general population report that they have engaged in nonsuicidal self-injurious behaviors, and many of them would not qualify for the diagnosis of any specific disorder (Klonsky, Oltmanns, & Turkheimer, 2003; Nock & Kessler, 2006). Sometimes, deliberate self-harm is itself the primary problem.

Why do some people deliberately hurt themselves, often disfiguring their own bodies? Several different explanations have been reported (Klonsky, 2007). For some people, cutting is a way to punish the self and is a reflection of frustration and anger. In other cases, the person uses self-inflicted pain in an effort to combat extended periods of dissociation and feelings of emptiness that accompany the absence of family members and friends. But the most commonly reported mechanism suggests that self-injury becomes a maladaptive way to regulate intense, negative emotional states. Episodes of self-injurious behavior are typically preceded by strong feelings of anxiety, anger, frustration, or sadness. These emotions are quickly diminished once the cutting has begun, and the person experiences relief. The final phase of the sequence involves the experience of shame or guilt when the episode is completed and the person reflects on what they have done.

## Frequency of Suicide

In the United States and Canada, the annual rate of completed suicide across all age groups has averaged approximately 12 people per 100,000 population for many years (Goldsmith, 2001). More than 35,000 people in the United States kill themselves every year. In 2010, more people died by suicide than in car accidents (Center for Disease Control and Prevention, 2013). Suicide rates vary as a function of many factors, including age, gender, and socioeconomic status. The suicide rate increased among adolescents from the 1970s through the mid 1990s, corresponding to an increase in the prevalence of depression and a decrease in the average age of onset for depression. More recently, suicide rates have increased by nearly 30 percent among middle-aged Americans (see Figure 5.6). Rates among other age groups either fell or remained steady. Suicide has become the third leading cause of death for people between the ages of 15 and 24, and it is the eighth leading cause of death in the general population (Kochanek et al., 2004).

Suicide attempts are much more common than are completed suicides. The ratio of attempts to completed suicides in the general population is approximately 10 to 1; among adolescents, the ratio

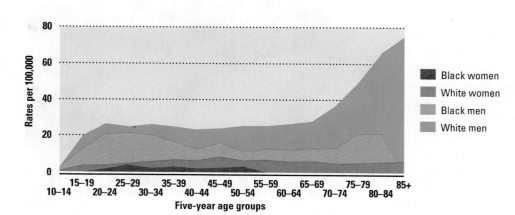

### FIGURE **5.6**

**Suicide Rates Across the Lifespan**   Suicide rates per 100,000 population by five-year group, race, and gender, United States, 1991. *Source:* Moscicki, E. K. (1995), "Epidemiology of Suicidal Behavior." *Suicide and Life-Threatening Behavior,* 25: 22–35. Copyright © 1995 The American Association for Suicidology. Reprinted by permission of John Wiley & Sons, Inc.

is closer to 100 to 1 (Hendin, 1995). There are important gender differences in rates of attempted suicide versus rates of completed suicide. Females aged 15 to 19 years make three times as many suicide attempts as males. Completion rates, however, are four times higher among males (Spirito & Esposito-Smythers, 2006). The difference in fatalities may be due, in part, to the methods employed. Men and boys are more likely to use violent and lethal methods such as firearms and hanging, whereas women and girls are more likely to take an overdose of drugs, which may allow time for discovery and interventions by other people.

The risk of completed suicide is highest among older people. Suicide rates have increased among middle-aged adults in recent years, but the highest rates are still found among older people, especially older white men. Although suicide attempts are most common among younger people, with most being made by those younger than 30, the proportion of suicide attempts that end in death is particularly high among the elderly. It is not clear whether this pattern should be attributed to a difference in method or to decreased physical resilience.

Suicides in the U.S. military increased dramatically after more than a decade of combat in Iraq and Afghanistan (Kuehn, 2010). In 2012, the number of active duty and reserve troops who committed suicide exceeded the number of American combat deaths in Afghanistan. Many of these deaths reflect the enormous stress associated with life in a combat zone, but a significant proportion of the people who took their own lives had not been deployed. The challenges faced by military personnel obviously include depression, posttraumatic stress, and substance use disorders, all of which are associated with an increase in suicide rates. But they also extend to problems associated with long-term separations from family members, financial problems, and the challenges associated with return to civilian life (Black et al., 2011).

## Causes of Suicide

Many factors contribute to suicidal behavior. In the following discussion, we consider some of the variables that operate at the level of the individual person—psychological and biological considerations—and are associated with suicidal behavior. We also summarize some contemporary research on social factors that are related to suicide.

**PSYCHOLOGICAL FACTORS** Many experts have argued that psychological events lie at the core of suicidal behavior (Joiner, 2005). Social factors may set the stage for self-destructive acts, but events taking place within the person's mind are most immediately responsible for determining whether a particular individual will attempt to end his or her own life. Prominent among these events are intense emotional distress and hopelessness. An outline of several psychological variables that are commonly associated with suicide is presented in Common Elements of Suicide.

The interpersonal-psychological theory of suicidal behavior maintains that suicidal behavior represents an attempt to escape from unbearable psychological pain (Joiner, 2005; Schneidman,

1996). According to this perspective, psychological pain is produced by prolonged frustration of psychological needs. Most important are the needs for affiliation and competence. People who view themselves as having failed in these domains—those who are low in belongingness or high in burdensomeness—will experience intense negative emotional states, such as shame, guilt, anger, and grief. For some people, suicide appears to offer a solution or a way to end their intolerable distress.

The desire to die is linked closely to social isolation and the belief that one has become a burden to others. But most people who experience these problems do not go on to attempt suicide. That action requires that the desire to end one's own life must be accompanied by the ability to enact lethal self-injury. Fear of death is one of our strongest emotions, and self-preservation is a powerful motive. Fortunately, these instincts protect most people in their worst emotional moments. The second component of the interpersonal-psychological theory holds that people who make lethal suicide attempts often work their way up to the act gradually (Joiner, 2005). This process may involve repeated nonsuicidal self-injurious behaviors, which allow the person to habituate to pain and fear of death. Previous suicide attempts, those that do not result in death, may also set the stage for a final lethal attempt. The interpersonal-psychological theory holds that death by suicide requires a combination of both the desire to die and the ability to inflict lethal harm to the self, which is frequently acquired through previous experience. Research evidence provides considerable support for this proposal (Van Orden et al., 2008).

**BIOLOGICAL FACTORS** Studies of the connection between neurotransmitters and suicide have focused primarily on reduced levels of serotonin, which might be related to poor impulse control as well as increased levels of violent and aggressive behavior

Brain injuries may increase the risk of suicide, particularly among military combat veterans and athletes in violent sports. Junior Seau, one of the most honored football players of his generation, retired from the NFL in 2009. He committed suicide in 2012 at the age of 43. An autopsy showed that he suffered from chronic traumatic encephalopathy.

## Common Elements of Suicide

Most people who kill themselves are suffering from some form of mental disorder, such as depression, post-traumatic stress disorder, a substance use disorder, or schizophrenia (Jamison, 1999). No single explanation can account for all self-destructive behavior, but the following list includes features that are frequently associated with completed suicide (Schneidman, 1996).

1. The common purpose of suicide is to seek a solution. Suicide is not a pointless or random act. To people who think about ending their own lives, suicide represents an answer to an otherwise insoluble problem or a way out of some unbearable dilemma. It is a choice that is somehow preferable to another set of dreaded circumstances, emotional distress, or disability, which the person fears more than death. Attraction to suicide as a potential solution may be increased by a family history of similar behavior. If someone else whom the person admired or cared for has committed suicide, then the person is more likely to do so.

2. The common goal of suicide is cessation of consciousness. People who commit suicide seek the end of conscious experience, which to them has become an endless stream of distressing thoughts with which they are preoccupied.

3. The common stimulus (or information input) in suicide is unbearable psychological pain. Excruciating negative emotions—including shame, guilt, anger, fear, and sadness—frequently serve as the foundation for self-destructive behavior.

4. The common stressor in suicide is frustrated psychological needs. People with high standards and expectations are especially vulnerable to ideas of suicide when progress toward these goals is suddenly frustrated. People who attribute failure or disappointment to their own shortcomings may come to view themselves as worthless, incompetent, or unlovable. Family turmoil is an especially important source of frustration to adolescents. Occupational and interpersonal difficulties frequently precipitate suicide among adults.

5. The common emotion in suicide is hopelessness–helplessness. A pervasive sense of hopelessness, defined in terms of pessimistic expectations about the future, is even more important than other forms of negative emotion, such as anger and depression, in predicting suicidal behavior. The suicidal person is convinced that absolutely nothing can be done to improve his or her situation; no one can help.

6. The common cognitive state in suicide is ambivalence. Most people who contemplate suicide, including those who eventually kill themselves, have ambivalent feelings about this decision. They are sincere in their desire to die, but they simultaneously wish that they could find another way out of their dilemma.

7. The common perceptual state in suicide is constriction. Suicidal thoughts and plans are frequently associated with a rigid and narrow pattern of cognitive activity that is analogous to tunnel vision. The suicidal person is temporarily unable or unwilling to engage in effective problem-solving behaviors and may see his or her options in extreme, all-or-nothing terms.

8. The common action in suicide is escape. Suicide provides a definitive way to escape from intolerable circumstances, which include painful self-awareness (Baumeister, 1990).

9. The common interpersonal act in suicide is communication of intention. One of the most harmful myths about suicide is the notion that people who really want to kill themselves don't talk about it. Most people who commit suicide have told other people about their plans. Many have made previous suicidal gestures.

10. The common pattern in suicide is consistency of lifelong styles. During crises that precipitate suicidal thoughts, people generally employ the same coping responses that they have used throughout their lives. For example, people who have refused to ask for help in the past are likely to persist in that pattern, increasing their sense of isolation.

---

(Currier & Mann, 2008; Joiner, Brown, & Wingate, 2005). Analogue studies with animals have found that lesions resulting in serotonin dysfunction lead to increases in aggression and failure to inhibit responses that were previously punished. Difficulty in regulating serotonin systems has been found among people who attempted suicide, and it has also been found among people who have shown other types of violent and aggressive behavior.

Twin studies and adoption studies have found that genetic factors are involved in the transmission of mood disorders. Do genes contribute to the risk for suicide indirectly by increasing the risk for mental disorders, such as depression, schizophrenia, and substance abuse? Or is there a more direct contribution of genetic factors to self-destructive behavior? The answer appears to be yes.

Genes associated with various neurotransmitter systems, especially serotonin, influence the development of impulsive personality traits, and suicide appears to be an especially likely outcome when a person inherits a predisposition to both psychopathology and impulsive or violent behavior. Genetic factors moderate the impact of environmental factors, such as stressful life events and childhood abuse, on suicidal behavior (Brezo, Klempan, & Turecki, 2008).

**SOCIAL FACTORS** Durkheim (1897/1951) believed that suicide rates had increased during the nineteenth century because of an erosion of the influence of traditional sources of social integration and regulation, such as the church and the family. Social structures do represent one important consideration with regard to suicide

(Stockard & O'Brien, 2002). For example, religious affiliation is significantly related to suicide rates. The active social networks encouraged by some church communities can become an important source of emotional support during difficult times, protecting the person from the potential influence of self-destructive impulses.

Social policies regulating access to firearms, especially handguns, also have an effect on suicide rates. Guns are a particularly lethal method of suicide, accounting for more than 60 percent of the 35,000 to 40,000 deaths that occur in the United States each year (Hendin, 1995). In states and countries with restrictive gun laws, the suicide rate usually drops, particularly among adolescents (Brent & Bridge, 2003; Kapusta et al., 2007). Of course, people who have definitely decided to end their own lives inevitably find a way to accomplish that goal, but many people who attempt suicide are ambivalent in their intent. Many attempts are made impulsively. Ready access to guns increases the chance that a person who does engage in an impulsive suicide attempt will die, because gunshot wounds are very likely to be fatal.

## Treatment of Suicidal People

Efforts to avoid the tragic consequences of suicidal behavior can be organized at several levels. One approach would focus on social structures that affect an entire society. Durkheim's theory of suicide, for example, indicates that the social structure of a society influences suicide rates. The social factors that we have just considered suggest some changes that could be made in contemporary Western societies in an effort to reduce the frequency of suicide. For example, more restrictive gun control laws might minimize access to the most lethal method of self-destruction. More cautious reporting by the media of suicidal deaths might reduce the probability of cluster suicides. These are, of course, controversial decisions, in which many other considerations play an important role. The media, for example, are motivated to report stories in a way that will maximize their popularity with the public. And many people oppose gun control legislation for reasons that have nothing to do with suicide rates. Therefore, it may be unrealistic to hope that these measures, aimed broadly at the level of an entire population, would be implemented widely. Most treatment programs that are concerned with suicidal behavior have been directed toward individual persons and their families.

**CRISIS CENTERS AND HOTLINES** Many communities have established crisis centers and telephone hotlines to provide support for people who are distraught and contemplating suicide. The purpose of these programs is typically viewed in terms of suicide prevention. Sponsored by various agencies, including community mental health centers, hospitals, and religious groups, these services are often staffed by nonprofessionals, frequently volunteers. They offer 24-hour-a-day access to people who have been trained to provide verbal support for those who are in the midst of a crisis and who may have nowhere else to turn. Rather than provide ongoing treatment, most crisis centers and hotlines help the person through the immediate crisis and then refer him or her to mental health professionals.

Public and professional enthusiasm for suicide prevention centers peaked during the 1960s and 1970s. Unfortunately, data that were reported in the 1970s and 1980s did not support optimistic claims that these centers were "saving lives." Empirical studies showed that suicide rates do not differ in comparisons of similar communities that either have or do not have suicide prevention programs. Availability of crisis centers and hotlines does not seem to reduce suicide rates in communities (Brown et al., 2007; Lester, 2002).

Why don't hotlines reduce suicide rates? The challenges faced by these programs are enormous. Think about the characteristics of people who are driven to contemplate suicide. They are often socially isolated, feeling hopeless, and unable to consider alternative solutions. Many people with the most lethal suicidal ideation will not call a hotline or visit a drop-in crisis center. In fact, most clients of suicide prevention centers are young women; most suicides are committed by elderly men. The primary problem faced by suicide prevention programs is this: The people who they are trying to serve are, by definition, very difficult to reach.

It might be hard to justify the continued existence of crisis centers and hotlines if they are viewed solely in terms of suicide prevention. Only a small proportion of people who call hotlines are seriously suicidal. Most are people who are experiencing serious difficulties and who need to talk to someone about those problems. The value of contact with these individuals should not be underestimated. Crisis centers and hotlines provide support and assistance to very large numbers of people in distress. These services are undoubtedly valuable in their own right, even if serious questions remain about their impact on suicide rates.

**PSYCHOTHERAPY** Psychological interventions with people who are suicidal can take many forms. These include all the standard approaches to psychotherapy. The research evidence indicates that cognitive behavior therapy does lead to a significant reduction in suicidal behavior, at least over short- and medium-term follow-up periods (Tarrier, Taylor, & Gooding, 2008). Psychological treatments can address underlying problems that set the stage for the person's current problems. Additional treatment guidelines are also dictated by the threat of suicide. The following recommendations cover special considerations that are particularly important when clients have expressed a serious intent to harm themselves (adapted from Berman & Jobes, 1994):

1. Reduce lethality. The most important task is to reduce the person's experience of psychological pain from which the person is seeking escape. At a more concrete level, this also involves reducing access to means that could be used to commit suicide, such as guns and pills.

2. Negotiate agreements. Therapists frequently ask clients who have threatened to kill themselves to sign a contract, in which

the client agrees to postpone self-destructive behavior for at least a short period of time. Of course, these agreements can be broken, but they may provide brakes to inhibit impulsive actions.

3. Provide support. It is often useful to make concrete arrangements for social support during a suicidal crisis. Friends and family members are alerted and asked to be available so that the person is not alone.

4. Replace tunnel vision with a broader perspective. People who are seriously contemplating suicide are typically unable to consider alternative solutions to their problems. The therapist must help potential suicide victims develop or recover a more flexible and adaptive pattern of problem solving.

**MEDICATION**  Treatment of mental disorders, especially depression, anxiety, and schizophrenia, is usually the most important element of intervention with suicidal clients. The use of various types of medication is often an important part of these treatment efforts. Antidepressant drugs are frequently given to patients who are clinically depressed, and antipsychotic medication is useful with those who meet the diagnostic criteria for schizophrenia (see Chapter 13).

Considerable attention has been devoted recently to the use of selective serotonin reuptake inhibitors (SSRIs), such as fluvoxamine (Luvox) and fluoxetine (Prozac), because of the link between suicide and serotonin disregulation. Extensive clinical reports suggest that the use of SSRIs in treating depression actually lowers suicide rates (Gibbons et al., 2007). It should also be noted, however, that placebo-controlled outcome studies have not addressed this specific question. Furthermore, cases have been reported in which treatment with SSRIs has been followed by the development of new suicidal ideation (King, Segman, & Anderson, 1994). This pattern suggests that the relation between serotonin and suicide is neither direct nor simple and that caution is warranted in the use of SSRIs in treating suicidal clients (see Critical Thinking Matters on page 131).

**INVOLUNTARY HOSPITALIZATION**  People who appear to be on the brink of committing suicide are often hospitalized, either with their permission or involuntarily (see Chapter 18 for a discussion of the legal issues involved in this process). The primary consideration in such cases is safety. In many cases, commitment to a hospital may be the best way to prevent people from harming themselves. The person's behavior can be monitored continuously, access to methods of harming oneself can be minimized (although perhaps not entirely eliminated), and various types of treatment can be provided by the hospital's professional staff.

## getting HELP

The distinction between severe depression and the ups and downs of everyday life provides an important guide to the need for treatment. If you have been seriously depressed for several weeks and if depression is interfering with your ability to function, you should seek professional help. Fortunately, you have already taken the first step toward improvement. By reading this chapter, you can learn to recognize the symptoms of mood disorders.

Several effective forms of treatment are available for mood disorders. The first step in getting help is to find someone with whom you can talk. This might be your family physician, someone at your school's counseling center, or a therapist in private practice. It is important that you feel comfortable with the person you choose and with the form of treatment that she or he will provide.

Depression is not uncommon, but people who are depressed often feel lonely and alienated. A number of good books may help make it easier for you to find the right treatment for yourself. Various forms of treatment, including antidepressant medication, are described in *Understanding Depression: What We Know and What You Can Do About It*, by Raymond DePaulo. Self-help books may be useful to people whose depression has not reached severe proportions. The cognitive approach to therapy is described with exceptional clarity in *Feeling Good: The New Mood Therapy*, by David Burns. Helpful information regarding bipolar disorder can be found in *The Bipolar Disorder Survival Guide*, by David Miklowitz.

People who are depressed need support and encouragement to seek treatment. Families and friends of depressed people find themselves in a very difficult and challenging situation. Mood disorders interfere with the person's ability to get along with other people and deplete his or her energy and motivation for seeking treatment. If the person doesn't follow through with therapy or make noticeable improvements after several sessions, friends can easily become discouraged or frustrated. Don't feel guilty if your efforts appear to go unrewarded. And don't blame the depressed person if he or she doesn't get better right away. Mood disorders are serious problems that require professional help. More detailed advice for families and friends can be found in a useful book entitled *How You Can Survive When They're Depressed: Living and Coping with Depression Fallout*, by Anne Sheffield.

# 5 Summary

**Mood disorders** are defined in terms of emotional, cognitive, behavioral, and **somatic symptoms**. In addition to a feeling of pervasive despair or gloom, people experiencing an episode of major **depression** are likely to show a variety of symptoms, such as diminished interest in normal activities, changes in appetite and sleep, fatigue, and problems in concentration.

A person in a manic episode feels elated and energetic. Manic patients also exhibit related symptoms, such as inflated self-esteem, rapid speech, and poor judgment.

*DSM-5* lists two major categories of mood disorders. People with **depressive disorders** experience only episodes of depression. People with **bipolar disorders** experience episodes of **mania**, which are most often interspersed with episodes of depression. There are several specific types of depressive disorders in *DSM-5*. Major depressive disorder is diagnosed if the person has experienced at least one episode of major depression without any periods of mania. **Persistent depressive disorder (dysthymia)** is a less severe, chronic form of depression in which the person has been depressed for at least two years without a major depressive episode.

A person who has experienced at least one manic episode would receive a diagnosis of bipolar I disorder, regardless of whether he or she has ever had an episode of depression. One episode of major depression combined with evidence of at least one period of **hypomania** would qualify for a diagnosis of bipolar II disorder. **Cyclothymia** is a less severe, chronic form of bipolar disorder in which the person has experienced numerous periods of hypomania interspersed with periods of depressed mood.

Mood disorders are among the most common forms of psychopathology. Epidemiological studies have found that the lifetime risk for major depressive disorder is approximately 16 percent and the lifetime risk for persistent depressive disorder is approximately 3 percent. Rates for both of these disorders are two or three times higher among women than among men. The lifetime risk for bipolar I and II disorders combined is close to 4 percent.

The causes of mood disorders can be traced to the combined effects of social, psychological, and biological factors. Social factors include primarily the influence of stressful life events, especially severe losses that are associated with significant people or significant roles.

Cognitive theories are primarily concerned with the way in which depressed people experience a severe event.

Interpersonal theories focus on the ways in which individuals respond to people and events in their environments. Depressed people behave in ways that have a negative impact on other people. In this way they contribute to the stressful nature of their social environment.

Twin studies indicate that genetic factors play an important role in the etiology of both depressive and bipolar disorders. They also indicate that genetic factors may play a stronger role in the development of bipolar than depressive disorders. Genes may contribute to the development of depression directly through an effect on the central nervous system and indirectly by influencing the person's sensitivity to environmental events, such as severe stress.

Neurochemical messengers in the brain also play a role in the regulation of mood and the development of mood disorders. Current thinking is focused on serotonin, norepinephrine, and dopamine, although many other neurotransmitter substances may also be involved in depression.

Several types of psychological and biological treatments have been shown to be effective for mood disorders. Two types of psychotherapy, cognitive therapy and interpersonal therapy, are beneficial for depressive and dysthymic patients. Three types of antidepressant medications are also useful in the treatment of major depressive disorder: selective serotonin reuptake inhibitors, tricyclic antidepressants, and monoamine oxidase inhibitors. Medication and psychotherapy are frequently used together. Outcome studies do not consistently favor either psychological or psychopharmacologic treatment.

Three other types of biological treatments are beneficial for specific types of mood disorders. Lithium carbonate and certain anticonvulsant drugs are useful for patients with bipolar disorders. Electroconvulsive therapy has been shown to be effective in the treatment of certain depressed patients, and it may be especially useful for patients who are severely suicidal or have failed to respond to other types of treatments. Light therapy seems to be effective for managing seasonal affective disorders.

People commit suicide for many different reasons. Most people who kill themselves are suffering from some form of mental disorder, such as depression, substance abuse, or schizophrenia. For some people, suicide represents an escape from unbearable negative emotions, which are often associated with social isolation and the perception of being a burden to others.

## The Big Picture

# critical thinking review

**5.1** What is the difference between clinical depression and a low mood?

There is not an obvious marker to identify when sadness crosses over to serious depression, but several considerations help clinicians identify the disorder. These include duration of the depressed mood, presence of associated symptoms, and an inability to occasionally enjoy activities that would otherwise provide some relief from feeling down or blue . . . (see page 108).

**5.2** Are there different kinds of depression?

The easy (and short) answer is "yes." Many systems have been proposed to identify meaningful subtypes of depressive disorders. In addition to recognizing differences between major depression and persistent depressive disorder, DSM-5 uses episode specifiers and course specifiers to describe this heterogeneous set of problems . . . (see page 115).

**5.3** How do depressive and bipolar disorders differ?

The age of onset and course of these disorders vary from one person to the next, but—on average—bipolar disorders have an earlier age of onset and bipolar patients typically experience more episodes over their lifetime . . . (see pages 116–117).

**5.4** Are we more likely to experience depression as we get older?

Although many people mistakenly identify depression with the elderly, epidemiological studies have shown that mood disorders actually are most frequent among young and middle-aged adults . . . (see page 118).

**5.5** Why do some people become depressed after stressful life events while others do not?

Part of the answer depends on how a person interprets the event. Does he or she exaggerate the importance of the negative event, blowing it out of proportion? . . . (see page 121).

**5.6** Is psychological treatment as effective as medication in treating depression?

The bottom line is that medication and psychotherapy are approximately equivalent in the treatment of people who are chronically depressed . . . (see page 130).

**5.7** Why do some people want to end their own lives?

The desire to die is linked closely to social isolation and the belief that one has become a burden to others . . . (see page 137).

# key terms

affect   106
analogue studies   127
bipolar disorders   107
clinical depression   107
cyclothymia   115
depressed mood   106
depressive disorders   107

dysphoric   109
euphoria   107
hypomania   114
mania   107
melancholia   115
monoamine oxidase inhibitors
   (MAOIs)   129

mood   106
mood disorders   107
persistent depressive
   disorder (dysthymia)   112
psychomotor retardation   111
relapse   116
remission   116

seasonal affective
   disorder   116
selective serotonin reuptake
   inhibitors (SSRIs)   128
somatic symptoms   110
tricyclics antidepressants
   (TCAs)   129

# Virtual Case Studies

Virtual Case Studies offers you a science-based, interactive simulation where you can learn how a number of risk factors and protective factors could impact disorder development in a virtual person. As you progress through the simulation you will not act as the character or as a clinician, but will be able to independently explore a variety of different behaviors, events, and outcomes that one who suffers from a disorder could potentially encounter. You can access the Virtual Case Study on *Mood Disorders* at **mypsychlab.com**

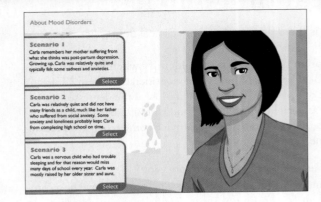

About Mood Disorders

**Scenario 1**
Carla remembers her mother suffering from what she thinks was post-partum depression. Growing up, Carla was relatively quite and typically felt some sadness and anxieties.
Select

**Scenario 2**
Carla was relatively quiet and did not have many friends as a child, much like her father who suffered from social anxiety. Some anxiety and loneliness probably kept Carla from completing high school on time.
Select

**Scenario 3**
Carla was a nervous child who had trouble sleeping and for that reason would miss many days of school every year. Carla was mostly raised by her older sister and aunt.
Select

# anxiety disorders and obsessive-compulsive disorder

6

# 6

## The Big Picture

### learning objectives

**6.1**
Why is a panic attack sometimes calleda "false alarm?"

**6.2**
What is the expected long-term outcome for people with anxiety disorders?

**6.3**
Is there a unique causal pathway for each type of anxiety disorder?

**6.4**
If phobias are learned quickly and easily, why are they so hard to extinguish?

**6.5**
Do psychological treatments have any advantages over medication for treatment of anxiety?

**6.6**
What is the difference between obsessions and normal intrusive thoughts?

**6.7**
Why is response prevention coupled with exposure in the treatment of OCD?

Fear and anxiety play important roles in all of our lives. Fear helps us avoid danger in our immediate environment. Have you ever jumped out of the street to avoid a car that was unexpectedly rushing toward you? Or run away from an animal with a menacing growl? The sudden burst of fear that you experienced allowed you to react immediately. Anxiety is focused on the future rather than the immediate present. It helps us anticipate and prepare for important events. Remember when you called someone for the first time, performed at a musical recital, or spoke up in class? If you felt anxious in the time leading up to this event, you may have also noticed that your heart was pounding, your mouth was dry, and you were breathing faster. These are some of the physical signs of anxiety. Anxiety may be unpleasant, but it is often adaptive; we would have trouble organizing our lives if it were eliminated completely. Unfortunately, anxiety can also disrupt our lives. There are many ways in which anxiety can become maladaptive. It is often a question of degree rather than kind. We can worry too much, feel anxious too often, or be afraid at inappropriate times. In this chapter we will explore many of the important distinctions that psychologists make among phenomena such as fear, anxiety, worry, and panic. We will discuss the ways in which these experiences can become maladaptive and the ways in which the problems can be treated.

A related set of disorders involves various forms of persistent, intrusive thoughts and troublesome habitual behaviors. We will discuss obsessive-compulsive disorder (OCD) and some of its related disorders, such as trichotillomania (hair-pulling disorder), in the latter half of this chapter. OCD was formerly grouped together with anxiety disorders, but it has been moved to its own chapter and separated from the anxiety disorders in *DSM-5*.

## Overview

Taken together, the various forms of anxiety disorders—including phobias, panic attacks, social anxiety, and extreme worry—represent the most common type of abnormal behavior. The National Comorbidity Survey Replication (NCS-R) found that 18 percent of adults in the U.S. population have at least one type of anxiety disorder in any given year (Kessler et al., 2009). This figure was higher than the one-year prevalence rates that were observed for mood disorders (10 percent) and substance use disorders (4 percent). Anxiety disorders lead to significant social and occupational impairment and a reduced quality of life (Tolin et al., 2010).

Anxiety disorders share several important similarities with mood disorders. From a descriptive point of view, both categories are defined in terms of negative emotional responses. Feelings such as guilt, worry, and anger frequently accompany anxiety and depression. Many patients who are anxious are also depressed, and, similarly, many patients who are depressed are also anxious (Kessler et al., 2008; Shankman & Klein, 2003). The order in which these problems emerge in the person's life can vary, but usually anxiety precedes the onset of depression.

The close relationship between symptoms of anxiety and those for depression suggests that these disorders may share common causal features. In fact, stressful life events seem to play a role in the onset of both depression and anxiety. Cognitive factors are also important in both types of problems. From a biological point of view, certain brain regions and a number of neurotransmitters are involved in the etiology of anxiety disorders as well as mood disorders (Ressler & Mayberg, 2007).

The following case study illustrates the kinds of symptoms that are included under the heading of anxiety disorders. You should notice the overlap among different features of anxiety disorders, including panic, worry, avoidance, and a variety of alarming physical sensations. This narrative was written by Johanna Schneller (1988), a freelance writer who has been treated for panic disorder. *Agoraphobia* refers to an exaggerated fear of being in situations from which escape might be difficult, such as being caught in a traffic jam on a bridge or in a tunnel.

#### ⟶ A Writer's Panic Disorder with Agoraphobia

Three years have passed since my first panic attack struck, but even now I can close my eyes and see the small supermarket where it happened. I can feel the shoppers in their heavy coats jostling me with their plastic baskets, and once again my stomach starts to drop away.

"It was November. I had just moved to New York City and completed a long search for a job and an apartment. The air felt close in that checkout line, and black fuzz crept into the corners of my vision. Afraid of fainting, I began to count the number of shoppers ahead of me, then the number of purchases they had. The overhead lights seemed to grow brighter. The cash register made pinging sounds that hurt my ears. Even the edges of the checkout counter looked cold and sharp. Suddenly I became nauseated, dizzy. My vertigo intensified, separating me from everyone else in the store, as if I were looking up from underwater. And then I got hot, the kind of hot you feel when the blood seems to rush to your cheeks and drain from your head at the same time.

"My heart was really pounding now, and I felt short of breath, as if wheels were rolling across my chest. I was terrified of what was happening to me. Would I be able to get home? I tried to talk myself down, to convince myself that if I could just stay in line and act as if nothing was happening, these symptoms would go away. Then I decided I wasn't going to faint—I was going to start screaming. The distance to the door looked vast and the seconds were crawling by, but somehow I managed to stay in the checkout line, pay for my bag of groceries, and get outside, where I sat on a bench, gulping air. The whole episode had taken ten minutes. I was exhausted.

"At home, I tried to analyze what had happened to me. The experience had been terrifying, but because I felt safe in my kitchen, I tried to laugh the whole thing off—really, it seemed ridiculous, freaking out in a supermarket. I decided it was an isolated incident; I was all right, and I was going to forget it ever happened.

"Two weeks later, as I sat in a movie theater, the uncomfortable buzz began to envelop me again. But the symptoms set in faster this time. I mumbled something to my friends about feeling sick as I clambered over them. It was minutes before I caught my breath, hours before I calmed down completely.

"A month full of scattered attacks passed before they started rolling in like Sunday evenings, at least once a week. I tried to find a pattern: They always hit in crowded places, places difficult to escape. My whole body felt threatened, primed to run during an attack. Ironically, my attacks were invisible to anyone near me unless they knew what to look for—clenched neck muscles, restless eyes, a shifting from foot to foot—and I was afraid to talk to anyone about them, to perhaps hear something I wouldn't want to hear. What if I had a brain tumor? And I was embarrassed, as if it were my fault that I felt out of control. But then one night I had an attack alone in my bed—the only place I had felt safe. I gave in and called a doctor.

"As the weeks passed and the attacks wore on, I began to think maybe I was crazy. I was having attacks in public so often I became afraid to leave my house. I had one on the subway while traveling to work almost every morning but, luckily, never panicked on the job. Instead, I usually lost control in situations where I most wanted to relax: on weekend trips, or while visiting friends.

I felt responsible for ruining other people's good time. One attack occurred while I was in a tiny boat deep sea fishing with my family; another hit when I was on a weekend canoe trip with my boyfriend. I also suffered a terrifying attack while on my way to see friends, stuck in traffic, merging into a tunnel near Boston's Logan Airport, with no exit ramp or emergency lane in sight.

"I began declining offers I wanted to accept: All I could think was, 'What if I panic in the middle of nowhere?' The times I did force myself to go out, I sat near the doors of restaurants, in aisle seats at movie theaters, near the bathroom at parties. For some reason, I always felt safe in bathrooms, as if whatever happened to me there would at least be easy to clean up.

"On days when I didn't have an actual attack, I could feel one looming like a shadow over my shoulder; this impending panic was almost worse than the real thing. By remembering old episodes, I brought on new ones, and each seemed to pull me closer to a vision I had of my mind snapping cleanly in half, like a stalk of celery."

Johanna's description of her problems raises a number of interesting questions, to which we will return later in the chapter. Was it just a coincidence that her first attack occurred shortly after the difficult experience of moving to a new city, starting a new job, and finding a new apartment? Could the stress of those experiences have contributed to the onset of her disorder? Was there a pattern to her attacks? Why did she feel safe in some situations and not in others? She mentions feeling out of control, as if she were responsible for her attacks. Could she really bring on another attack by remembering one from the past?

## Symptoms of Anxiety Disorders

People with anxiety disorders share a preoccupation with, or persistent avoidance of, thoughts or situations that provoke fear or anxiety. Anxiety disorders frequently have a negative impact on various aspects of a person's life. Johanna found that anxiety and its associated problems constrained both her ability to work and her social relationships. Most people who knew Johanna probably did not know that she suffered from a mental disorder. In spite of the private terrors that she endured, she was able to carry on most aspects of her life.

In addition to these general considerations, the diagnosis of anxiety disorders depends on several specific types of symptoms, which we discuss in the following sections. We begin with the nature of anxiety, which should be distinguished from more discrete emotional responses, like fear and panic.

### Anxiety

Like depression, the term *anxiety* can refer to either a mood or a syndrome. Here, we use the term to refer to a mood. Specific syndromes associated with anxiety disorders are discussed later in the chapter.

Anxious mood is often defined in contrast to the specific emotion of fear, which is more easily understood. **Fear** is experienced in the face of real, immediate danger. It usually builds quickly in intensity and helps organize the person's behavioral responses to threats from the environment (escaping or fighting back). Classic studies of fear among normal adults have often focused on people in combat situations, such as airplane crews during bombing missions over Germany in World War II (Rachman, 1991). In contrast to fear, **anxiety** involves a more general or diffuse emotional reaction—beyond simple fear—that is out of proportion to threats from the environment (Barlow, 2004). Rather than being directed toward the person's present circumstances, anxiety is associated with the anticipation of future problems.

Anxiety can be adaptive at low levels, because it serves as a signal that the person must prepare for an upcoming event. When you think about final exams, for example, you may become somewhat anxious. That emotional response may help to initiate and sustain your efforts to study. In contrast, high levels of anxiety become incapacitating by disrupting concentration and performance.

A pervasively anxious mood is often associated with pessimistic thoughts and feelings ("If something bad happens, I probably won't be able to control it"). The person's attention turns inward, focusing on negative emotions and self-evaluation ("Now I'm so upset that I'll never be able to concentrate during the exam!") rather than on the organization or rehearsal of adaptive responses that might be useful in coping with negative events. Taken together, these factors can be used to define *anxious apprehension,* which consists of (1) high levels of diffuse negative emotion, (2) a sense of uncontrollability, and (3) a shift in attention to a primary self-focus or a state of self-preoccupation (Barlow, 2004).

## Excessive Worry

Worrying is a cognitive activity that is associated with anxiety. In recent years psychologists have studied this phenomenon carefully because they consider it to be critical in the subclassification of anxiety disorders (*DSM-5*). **Worry** can be defined as a relatively uncontrollable sequence of negative, emotional thoughts that are concerned with possible future threats or danger. This sequence of worrisome thoughts is usually self-initiated or provoked by a specific experience or ongoing difficulties in the person's daily life. When excessive worriers are asked to describe their thoughts, they emphasize the predominance of verbal, linguistic material rather than images (Borkovec, Alcaine, & Behar, 2004). In other words, worriers are preoccupied with "self-talk" rather than unpleasant visual images.

Because everyone worries at least a little, you might wonder whether it is possible to distinguish between pathological and normal worry. The answer is yes, but there is not a clear line that divides the two kinds of experiences. The distinction hinges on quantity—how often the person worries and about how many different topics the person worries. It also depends on the quality of worrisome thought. Excessive worriers are more likely than other people to report that the content of their thoughts is negative, that they have less control over the content and direction of their thoughts, and that in comparison to other adults, their worries are less realistic (Newman & Llera, 2010).

Fear is a response to immediate danger, while anxiety is concerned with events that might happen in the future.

### Generalized Anxiety Disorder

PHILIP

*"I worry a lot, I just analyze, analyze, until I'm paralyzed."*

👁 **Watch** the **Video** *Philip: Generalized Anxiety Disorder* on **MyPsychLab**

CHRISTY

*"It's impacted a lot of my close relationships, or potential to bond with others."*

👁 **Watch** the **Video** *Christy: Generalized Anxiety Disorder with Insomnia* on **MyPsychLab**

Watch both interviews and ask yourself what symptoms these two people have in common. Then ask yourself how they are different. People with GAD share some important similarities, but they are not identical.

## Panic Attacks

A **panic attack** is a sudden, overwhelming experience of terror or fright, like the attack that was experienced by Johanna as she waited in the checkout line. Whereas anxiety involves a blend of several negative emotions, panic is more focused. Some clinicians think of panic as a normal fear response that is triggered at an inappropriate time (Barlow, Brown, & Craske, 1994). In that sense, panic is a "false alarm." Descriptively, panic can be distinguished from anxiety in two other respects: It is more intense, and it has a sudden onset.

Panic attacks are defined largely in terms of a list of somatic or physical sensations, ranging from heart palpitations, sweating, and trembling to nausea, dizziness, and chills. *DSM5: Diagnostic Criteria for Panic Disorder* lists the *DSM-5* criteria for panic disorder, and the criteria for a panic attack appear at the beginning of that definition. A person must experience at least four of these 13 symptoms in order for the experience to qualify as a full-blown panic attack. The symptoms develop suddenly, and they usually reach a peak intensity within 10 minutes. The actual numbers and combinations of panic symptoms vary from one person to the next, and they may also change over time within the same person.

People undergoing a panic attack also report a number of cognitive symptoms. They may feel as though they are about to die, lose control, or go crazy. Some clinicians believe that the misinterpretation of bodily sensations lies at the core of panic disorder. Patients may interpret heart palpitations as evidence of an impending heart attack or racing thoughts as evidence that they are about to lose their minds.

Panic attacks are further described in terms of the situations in which they occur, as well as the person's expectations about their occurrence. An attack is said to be expected, or *cued,* if it occurs only in the presence of a particular stimulus. For example, someone who is afraid of public speaking might have a cued panic attack if forced to give a speech in front of a large group of people. Unexpected panic attacks, like Johanna's experience in the grocery checkout line, appear without warning or expectation, as if "out of the blue."

### Phobias

In contrast to both diffuse anxiety, which represents a blend of negative emotions, and panic attacks, which are frequently unexpected, **phobias** are persistent, irrational, narrowly defined fears that are associated with a specific object or situation. Avoidance is an important component of the definition of phobias. A fear is not considered phobic unless the person avoids contact with the source of the fear or experiences intense anxiety in the presence of the stimulus. Phobias are also irrational or unreasonable. Avoiding only snakes that are poisonous or only guns that are loaded would not be considered phobic.

The most straightforward type of phobia involves fear of specific objects or situations. Different types of specific phobias have traditionally been named according to the Greek words for these objects. Examples of typical specific phobias include fear of heights (acrophobia), fear of enclosed spaces (claustrophobia), fear of small animals (zoophobia), fear of blood (hemophobia), fear of flying on airplanes (aerophobia), and fear of being in places from which escape might be difficult (agoraphobia).

## Diagnosis of Anxiety Disorders

The *DSM-5* (APA, 2013) approach to classifying anxiety disorders is based primarily on descriptive features and recognizes several specific subtypes. They include specific phobia, social anxiety disorder (social phobia), panic disorder, agoraphobia, and generalized anxiety disorder. The manual also describes problems with anxiety that appear in children, specifically separation anxiety disorder and selective mutism. These problems will be discussed in Chapter 16.

Some other conditions that are often associated with the experience of anxiety should also be mentioned. Obsessive-compulsive and related disorders are described in a separate chapter in *DSM-5;* they will be discussed in the second part of this chapter. Post-traumatic stress disorder (PTSD) and acute stress disorder are also closely associated with anxiety disorders. We will discuss PTSD and acute stress disorder in Chapter 7.

**A.** Recurrent unexpected panic attacks. A panic attack is an abrupt surge of intense fear or intense discomfort that reaches a peak within minutes, and during which time four (or more) of the following symptoms occur:

**Note:** The abrupt surge can occur from a calm state or an anxious state.

1. Palpitations, pounding heart, or accelerated heart rate.
2. Sweating.
3. Trembling or shaking.
4. Sensations of shortness of breath or smothering.
5. Feelings of choking.
6. Chest pain or discomfort.
7. Nausea or abdominal distress.
8. Feeling dizzy, unsteady, light-headed, or faint.
9. Chills or heat sensations.
10. Paresthesias (numbness or tingling sensations).
11. Derealization (feelings of unreality) or depersonalization (being detached from oneself).
12. Fear of losing control or "going crazy."
13. Fear of dying.

**Note:** Culture-specific symptoms (e.g., tinnitus, neck soreness, headache, uncontrollable screaming or crying) may be seen. Such symptoms should not count as one of the four required symptoms.

**B.** At least one of the attacks has been followed by 1 month (or more) of one or both of the following:
1. Persistent concern or worry about additional panic attacks or their consequences (e.g. losing control, having a heart attack, "going crazy").
2. A significant maladaptive change in behavior related to the attacks (e.g., behaviors designed to avoid having panic attacks, such as avoidance of exercise or unfamiliar situations).

**C.** The disturbance is not attributable to the physiological effects of a substance (e.g., a drug of abuse, a medication) or another medical condition (e.g., hyperthyroidism, cardiopulmonary disorders).

**D.** The disturbance is not better explained by another mental disorder (e.g., the panic attacks do not occur only in response to feared social situations, as in social anxiety disorder; in response to circumscribed phobic objects or situations, as in specific phobia; in response to obsessions, as in obsessive-compulsive disorder; in response to reminders of traumatic events, as in posttraumatic stress disorder; or in response to separation from attachment figures, as in separation anxiety disorder).

**SPECIFIC PHOBIA** A **specific phobia** is defined in *DSM-5* as "a marked fear or anxiety about a specific object or situation that almost always provokes immediate fear or anxiety" (APA, 2013, p. 197). This object or situation is actively avoided (or endured with intense fear or anxiety) and the fear or anxiety is out of proportion to the actual danger posed by the object or situation. Frequently observed types of specific phobias include fear of heights, small animals (such as spiders, bugs, mice, snakes, or bats), and being in a closed place (such as a very small room). Exposure to the phobic stimulus must be followed by an immediate fear response. *DSM-5* also provides a severity threshold: The avoidance or distress associated with the phobia must interfere significantly with the person's normal activities or relationships with others, and it must be persistent (typically lasting six months or more).

**SOCIAL ANXIETY DISORDER (SOCIAL PHOBIA)** The *DSM-5* definition of **social anxiety disorder** is almost identical to that for specific phobia, but it is focused on social situations in which the person may closely observed or evaluated by other people. People with social anxiety disorder are afraid of (and avoid) social situations in which they may be scrutinized. These situations fall into two broad headings: doing something in front of unfamiliar people (performance anxiety) and interpersonal interactions (such as dating and parties). Fear of being humiliated or embarrassed presumably lies at the heart of the person's discomfort. Some people have a circumscribed form of social anxiety that is focused on one particular type of situation. Examples include giving a speech, playing a musical instrument, urinating in a public rest room, or eating in a restaurant. For these people, the feared task could be completed easily if they were able to do it privately. In other cases, the fear is more generalized, and the person is intensely anxious in almost any situation that involves social interaction. This type of person might be described as being extremely shy.

**AGORAPHOBIA** The least circumscribed form of phobia is **agoraphobia**, which literally means "fear of the marketplace (or places of assembly)" and is usually described as fear of public spaces. It is often associated with a pervasive avoidance of many

## Splitting Up the Anxiety Disorders

Experts who classify mental disorders can be described informally as belonging to one of two groups: "lumpers" and "splitters" (Rousseau, 2009; Wittchen, Schuster, & Lieb, 2001). Lumpers would argue that anxiety is a generalized condition or set of symptoms without any special subdivisions. Splitters would distinguish among a number of more specific conditions, each of which is presumed to have its own unique causes and perhaps respond best to a particular form of treatment. The popularity of these approaches tends to swing back and forth over the years. Throughout most of the twentieth century, psychiatrists tended to adopt a generalized position with regard to anxiety disorders (see Jablensky, 1985). In other words, they lumped together all kinds of problems under a very broad title of anxiety disorders.

Beginning with DSM-III (APA, 1980), the pendulum swung back in the opposite direction (toward splitting and away from lumping). That approach—dividing the anxiety disorders into smaller, distinct types—has become increasingly popular over the past 30 years. Now DSM-5 has taken splitting to a new level. Two disorders that were previously listed as types of anxiety disorders—OCD and PTSD—have been removed from the group of anxiety disorders to create their own chapters (or headings), with other descriptively similar conditions being organized under these new umbrella terms. The rationale for this fairly dramatic change is grounded in the desire to group together conditions that are descriptively most similar. For example, the problems listed under "Obsessive-Compulsive and Related Disorders" share prominent features that involve intrusive thoughts and habitual behaviors. Problems listed under "Trauma- and Stress-Related Disorders" all involve exposure to a traumatic or stressful event as one required criterion for their diagnosis. The net effect of these changes is that the problems formerly known as anxiety disorders now cover three separate chapters in DSM-5.

The impact of this shift in the classification of anxiety disorders is clearly increased precision. The essential features and diagnostic boundaries of these conditions have been clarified. In that sense, the change is helpful and not particularly controversial. On the other hand, you should not be misled into thinking that the new organizational structure for these disorders reflects a major shift in our understanding of the causes of these disorders or a dramatic improvement in the efficacy of treatment methods aimed at specific types of disorder. It does not. The text in DSM-5 says that the separate chapters were created to "reflect the increasing evidence of these disorders' relatedness to one another in terms of a range of diagnostic validators as well as the clinical utility of grouping these disorders in the same chapter." That's psychobabble for "we think they look alike."

At the same time that OCD and PTSD are being listed separately from other disorders that involve high levels of anxiety, the field has also begun to embrace a more integrated and unified perspective with regard to anxiety disorders and mood disorders (Brown & Barlow, 2009; Kendler et al., 2011; Krueger & Markon, 2006). In other words, there is also a swing back in the direction of lumping, and it is reflected in the organizational sequence of chapters in DSM-5 (i.e., bipolar disorders, depressive disorders, anxiety disorders, obsessive-compulsive related disorders, trauma-related disorders, and dissociative disorders in that order). This part of the discussion regarding classification is focused on using a conceptual scheme that organizes various forms of psychopathology using two broad dimensions or spectra: internalizing and externalizing disorders. Mood disorders, anxiety, OCD-related disorders, and trauma-related disorders fall into the internalizing domain because they are all characterized by symptoms that involve high levels of negative emotion and internal distress. Externalizing disorders (such as antisocial personality disorder and substance use disorders) are more concerned with failure to inhibit problematic behaviors (Andrews et al., 2009). In some ways, DSM-5 demonstrates the influence of both lumping and splitting.

Arguments about the relative merits of lumping and splitting in the classification of mental disorders are fundamentally questions about the validity of diagnostic categories (see Chapter 4). Decisions regarding the breadth or specificity of anxiety disorders and various related conditions will ultimately depend on evidence from many areas. Do phobias and obsessive-compulsive disorder show distinct, separate patterns in family studies? Do they respond to different types of treatment? Can we distinguish between them in terms of typical patterns of onset and course? Definitive answers are not yet available. Future research efforts are needed to address these issues.

---

different kinds of situations, rather than one specific feared object or situation (as in other phobias). The case of Johanna at the beginning of this chapter provides a brief description of the types of problems experienced by a person suffering from agoraphobia. Typical situations that are feared include crowded streets and shops, enclosed places like theaters and churches, traveling on public transportation, and driving an automobile on bridges, in tunnels, or on crowded expressways. In any of these situations, the presence of a trusted friend may help the person with agoraphobia feel more comfortable. In the most extreme form of the disorder, agoraphobic patients are unable to venture away from their own homes.

Specific phobias are irrational fears associated with specific situations that the person avoids. Acrophobia is the name given to fear of heights (which this climber clearly does not have).

## MyPsychLab VIDEO CASE

### Social Anxiety Disorder

STEVE

*"I imagine that people are watching me. They are watching me stumble in my efforts. . . ."*

**⊙ Watch** the **Video** *Steve: Social Anxiety Disorder (Social Phobia)* on **MyPsychLab**

What is his worst fear when he is talking to another person at a party?

---

*DSM-5* defines agoraphobia in terms of anxiety about being in situations from which escape might be either difficult or embarrassing. Avoidance and distress are important elements of the definition. In order to meet the *DSM-5* criteria, the person must either avoid agoraphobic situations, such as traveling away from his or her own home; endure the experience with great distress; or insist on being accompanied by another person who can provide some comfort or security. In most cases, the person avoids a wide variety of situations rather than just one specific type of situation.

**PANIC DISORDER** To meet the diagnostic criteria for **panic disorder**, a person must experience recurrent, unexpected panic attacks (see *DSM5: Diagnostic Criteria for Panic Disorder*). At least one of the attacks must have been followed by a period of one month or more in which the person has either persistent concern about having additional attacks, or a significant maladaptive change in behavior related to the attacks (such as avoidance of exercise or unfamiliar situations).

**GENERALIZED ANXIETY DISORDER** Excessive anxiety and worry are the primary symptoms of **generalized anxiety disorder (GAD)**. The person must have trouble controlling these worries, and the worries must lead to significant distress or impairment in occupational or social functioning. The worry must occur more days than not for a period of at least six months, and it must be about a number of different events or activities. In order to distinguish GAD from other forms of anxiety disorder, *DSM-5* notes that the person's worries should *not* be focused on having a panic attack (as in panic disorder), being embarrassed in public (as in social anxiety disorder), or being contaminated (as in obsessive-compulsive disorder). Finally, the person's worries and free-floating anxiety must be accompanied by at least three of the following symptoms: (1) restlessness or feeling keyed up or on edge, (2) being easily fatigued, (3) difficulty concentrating or mind going blank, (4) irritability, (5) muscle tension, and (6) sleep disturbance.

### Course and Outcome

Anxiety disorders are often chronic conditions. Long-term follow-up studies focused on clinical populations indicate that many people continue to experience symptoms of anxiety and associated social and occupational impairment many years after their problems are initially recognized. On the other hand, some people do recover completely. The most general conclusion, therefore, is that the long-term outcome for anxiety disorders is mixed and somewhat unpredictable (Ramsawh et al., 2009).

Most people with these disorders continue to have significant problems for many years (Beesdo-Baum et al., 2012; Rubio & Lopez-Ibor, 2007). The frequency and intensity of panic attacks tend to decrease as people reach middle age, but agoraphobic avoidance typically remains stable. The nature of the most prominent symptoms may also evolve over time. In patients with GAD, worries may be replaced by complaints about physical symptoms. Worse outcomes tend to be associated with a younger age of onset and lack of appropriate treatment.

## Frequency of Anxiety Disorders

Some epidemiological studies focus exclusively on treated cases of a disorder, but that strategy can provide a distorted view of the distribution of the disorder within the general population. Many factors can influence whether a person decides to seek treatment. Some cases are less severe than others. Some people treat themselves without consulting a mental health professional. Some people are suspicious of medical facilities, and others are concerned about what people will think of them if they are treated for a mental disorder. Of course, people with agoraphobia are extremely reluctant to leave their homes for any reason. This issue has been a special problem in epidemiological studies of anxiety disorders. Only about 25 percent of people who qualify for a diagnosis of anxiety disorder ever seek psychological treatment. Therefore, our estimates of the frequency and severity of these problems must be based on community surveys.

### Prevalence

The National Comorbidity Survey Replication (NCS-R), which included approximately 9,000 people aged 18 and older throughout the United States, found that anxiety disorders are more common than any other form of mental disorder (Kessler et al., 2005). Specific phobias are the most common type of anxiety disorder, with a one-year prevalence of about 9 percent of the adult population (men and women combined). Social anxiety disorder is almost as common, with a one-year prevalence of 7 percent. Panic disorder and GAD both affect approximately 3 percent of the population. Another 1 percent of the population meets criteria for agoraphobia.

### Comorbidity

The symptoms of various anxiety disorders overlap considerably. For example, many people who experience panic attacks develop phobic avoidance. More than 50 percent of people who meet the criteria for one anxiety disorder also met the criteria for at least one other form of anxiety disorder or mood disorder (Klein et al., 2012).

Both anxiety and depression are based on emotional distress, so it is not surprising that considerable overlap also exists between anxiety disorders and mood disorders (Kessler et al., 2008). Approximately 60 percent of people who receive a primary diagnosis of major depression also qualify for a secondary diagnosis of some type of anxiety disorder. The average of age of onset for anxiety disorders is much younger than the average age of onset for depression, so when they are both present in the same person's life, the usual pattern is for anxiety to appear first (Kessler et al., 2007).

This extensive overlap between anxiety and depression raises interesting questions about the relation between these general diagnostic categories. Do people who meet the criteria for both depression and an anxiety disorder really suffer from two distinct syndromes? Or should we think about the existence of three types of disorders: "pure" anxiety disorders, "pure" mood disorders, and a third type of disorder that represents a mixture of anxiety and depression? Reasonable arguments have been made on both sides of this debate, which remains unresolved (Batelaan et al., 2012; Das-Munshi et al., 2008).

Substance dependence is another problem that is frequently associated with anxiety disorders. People who have an anxiety disorder are about three times more likely to have an alcohol use disorder than are people without an anxiety disorder (Grant et al., 2004). In situations such as these, questions of cause and effect are not clear. Did the person use alcohol in an attempt to reduce heightened anxiety, or did he or she become anxious after drinking excessively? Prospective studies conclude that it works both ways (Kushner, Sher, & Erickson, 1999).

### Gender Differences

There are significant gender differences in lifetime prevalence for several types of anxiety disorders. Furthermore, among people who suffer from an anxiety disorder, relapse rates are higher for women than for men. The gender difference in prevalence is particularly large for specific phobias, where women are three times as likely as men to experience the disorder. Women are about twice as likely as men to experience panic disorder, agoraphobia (without panic disorder), and generalized anxiety disorder. Social anxiety disorder is also more common among women than among men, but the difference is not as striking as it is for other types of phobias.

The significant gender differences in the prevalence and course of anxiety disorders must be interpreted in the light of causal theories, which are considered in the next section. Several explanations remain plausible. Psychological speculation has focused on such factors as gender differences in child-rearing practices or differences in the way in which men and women respond to stressful life events. Gender differences in hormone functions or neurotransmitter activities in the brain may also be responsible (Altemus, 2006).

### Anxiety Disorders Across the Life Span

Prevalence rates for anxiety disorders have been found to be lower when people over the age of 60 are compared to younger adults (Kessler et al., 2005). On the other hand, the gradual reduction in anxiety that has been observed among middle-aged adults may reverse itself later in life. Anxiety may increase as people move into their 70s and 80s (O'Connor, 2006; Teachman, 2006). Increased anxiety among the elderly may be due to problems associated with loneliness, increased dependency, declining physical and cognitive capacities, and changes in social and economic conditions.

Most elderly people with an anxiety disorder have had the symptoms for many years. It is relatively unusual for a person to develop a new case of panic disorder, specific phobia, or social anxiety at an advanced age. The only type of anxiety disorder that begins with any noticeable frequency in late life is agoraphobia (Barlow et al., 2003).

Heavy drinkers are more likely than other people to develop anxiety disorders, and people who are highly anxious are more likely to start to drink heavily.

The diagnosis of anxiety disorders among elderly people is complicated by the need to consider factors such as medical illnesses and other physical impairments and limitations (Carmin & Ownby, 2010). Respiratory and cardiovascular problems may resemble the physiological symptoms of a panic attack. Hearing losses may lead to anxiety in interpersonal interactions. Subsequent avoidance might be inappropriately attributed to the onset of social anxiety disorder. A frail elderly person who falls down on the street may become afraid to leave home alone, but this may be a reasonable concern rather than a symptom of agoraphobia. For reasons such as these, the diagnosis of anxiety disorders must be done with extra caution in elderly men and women.

## Cross-Cultural Comparisons

People in different cultures express anxiety in different ways (see the description of *ataques de nervios* in Chapter 4 on page 84). As in the case of depression, people in nonwestern cultures are more likely to communicate their anxiety in the form of somatic complaints, such as "My chest hurts," "I can't breathe," or "I'm tired and restless all the time" (Halbreich et al., 2007; Hoge et al., 2006). The primary focus of anxiety complaints also varies considerably across cultural boundaries. In other words, we need to consider the kinds of situations that provoke intense anxiety as well as the ways in which we recognize that a person is anxious. People in Western societies often experience anxiety in relation to their work performance, whereas in other societies people may be more concerned with family issues or religious experiences. In the Yoruba culture of Nigeria, for example, anxiety is frequently associated with fertility and the health of family members (Good & Kleinman, 1985).

Anxiety disorders have been observed in preliterate as well as Westernized cultures. Of course, the same descriptive and diagnostic terms are not used in every culture, but the basic psychological phenomena appear to be similar (Draguns & Tanaka-Matsumi,

2003). Cultural anthropologists have recognized many different cultural concepts of distress that, in some cases, bear striking resemblance to anxiety disorders listed in *DSM-5*.

Very few epidemiological studies have attempted to collect cross-cultural data using standardized interviews and specific diagnostic criteria. One such study was conducted to evaluate specific drugs for the treatment of panic attacks (Cross-National Collaborative Panic Study, 1992). More than 1,000 patients were treated in 14 different countries in North America, Latin America, and Europe. Several interesting findings emerged from this study. Most important was the fact that panic disorder occurred in all the countries that were included in the study. The most prominent symptoms—choking or smothering, fear of dying, phobic avoidance—varied from one region to the next, but the overall prevalence rate appeared to be about the same.

## Causes of Anxiety Disorders

Now that we have discussed the various symptoms associated with anxiety disorders and their distribution within the population, we can consider the origins of these disorders. How do these problems develop? Going back to the case that was presented at the beginning of the chapter, what might account for the onset of Johanna's panic attacks?

### Adaptive and Maladaptive Fears

Current theories regarding the causes of anxiety disorders often focus on the evolutionary significance of anxiety and fear. These emotional response systems are clearly adaptive in many situations. They mobilize responses that help the person survive in the face of both immediate dangers and long-range threats. An evolutionary perspective helps to explain why human beings are vulnerable to anxiety disorders, which can be viewed as problems that arise in the regulation of these necessary response systems (Hofer, 2010). The important question is not why we experience anxiety, but why it occasionally becomes maladaptive. When anxiety becomes excessive, or when intense fear is triggered at an inappropriate time or place, these response systems can become more harmful than helpful. In order to understand the development of anxiety disorders, we must consider a variety of psychological and biological systems that have evolved for the purpose of triggering and controlling these alarm responses.

Should we expect to find unique causal pathways associated with each of the types of anxiety disorder listed in *DSM-5*? This seems unlikely, particularly in light of the extensive overlap among the various subtypes. Should we expect that all the different types of anxiety disorders are produced by the same causes? This also seems unlikely, and an evolutionary perspective suggests that a middle ground between these two extremes may provide the most useful explanation (Marks & Nesse, 1994). Generalized forms of anxiety probably evolved to help the person prepare for threats that could not be identified clearly. More specific forms of anxiety and fear probably evolved to provide more effective responses to certain types of danger. For example, fear of heights is associated with a freezing of muscles rather than running away, which could lead to a fall. Social threats are more likely to provoke responses such as shyness and embarrassment that may increase acceptance by other people by making the individual seem less threatening. Each type of anxiety disorder can be viewed as the dysregulation of a mechanism that evolved to deal with a particular kind of danger. This model leads us to expect that the etiological pathways leading to various forms of anxiety disorders may be partially distinct but not completely independent.

## Social Factors

Stressful life events, particularly those involving danger and interpersonal conflict, can trigger the onset of certain kinds of anxiety disorders. For example, various aspects of parent–child relationships may leave some people more vulnerable to the development of anxiety disorders when they become adults. Taken together, the evidence bearing on these issues helps explain the relationship between, and the overlap among, anxiety disorders and mood disorders.

**STRESSFUL LIFE EVENTS** Common sense suggests that people who experience high stress levels are likely to develop negative emotional reactions, which can range from feeling "on edge" to the onset of full-blown panic attacks. In Chapter 5 we reviewed the literature concerning stressful life events and depression. Several investigations suggest that stressful life events can influence the onset of anxiety disorders as well as depression. Patients with anxiety disorders are more likely than other people to report having experienced a negative event in the months preceding the initial development of their symptoms (Kendler et al., 2003).

Why do some negative life events lead to depression while others lead to anxiety? The nature of the event may be an important factor in determining the type of mental disorder that appears (McLaughlin & Hatzenbuehler, 2009; Updegraff & Taylor, 2000). People who develop an anxiety disorder are much more likely to have experienced an event involving danger, insecurity, or family discord, whereas people who are depressed are more likely to have experienced a severe loss (lack of hope). Different types of environmental stress lead to different types of emotional symptoms.

**CHILDHOOD ADVERSITY** If recent dangers and conflicts can precipitate the full-blown symptoms of an anxiety disorder, do past experiences—those that took place years ago—set the stage for this experience? Several research studies indicate that they can (Harkness & Wildes, 2002). Studies of these phenomena focus on measures of childhood adversity. This concept includes experiences such as maternal prenatal stress, multiple maternal partner changes, parental indifference (being neglected by parents),

Japanese women react with fear as rescue workers check for radiation contamination following a massive earthquake that damaged a nuclear reactor.

and physical abuse (being physically beaten or threatened with violence). Children who are exposed to higher levels of adversity are more likely to develop anxiety disorders later in their lives (Moffitt et al., 2007; Phillips et al., 2005).

Evidence regarding childhood adversity and the development of psychopathology points, once again, to similarities between depression and anxiety. Keep in mind that there is substantial overlap in these disorders; people who meet criteria for anxiety disorders also frequently meet criteria for major depression. Those who are exposed to parental abuse, neglect, and violence are more vulnerable to the development of both anxiety disorders and major depression (Kessler et al., 2008; Lara & Klein, 1999). There does not seem to be a direct connection between particular forms of adverse environmental events and specific types of mental disorders.

**ATTACHMENT RELATIONSHIPS AND SEPARATION ANXIETY** The evidence regarding childhood adversity is similar to another perspective on the origins of anxiety disorders that has been concerned with the infant's attachment relationship with caretakers. Attachment theory (see Chapter 2) integrates the psychodynamic perspective with field observations of primate behavior and with laboratory research with human infants. According to the British psychiatrist John Bowlby (1973, 1980), anxiety is an innate response to separation, or the threat of separation, from the caretaker. Those infants who are insecurely attached to their parents are presumably more likely to develop anxiety disorders, especially agoraphobia, when they become adults.

Several studies have found that people with a variety of anxiety disorders are more likely to have had attachment problems as children (Cassidy & Mohr, 2001; Dozier et al., 2008; Lewinsohn et al., 2008). Anxious attachment as infants may make these individuals more vulnerable, once they are adults, to the threats that are contained in interpersonal conflict, for example, loss of a loved one if a marriage dissolves. This hypothesis fits nicely with the observation that interpersonal conflict is a relatively frequent triggering event for the onset of agoraphobic symptoms. There is also an interesting connection between attachment styles and childhood adversity. People who report childhood adversities involving interpersonal trauma (assault, abuse, neglect) are more likely to be insecurely attached, and they are also more vulnerable to depression and anxiety (Mickelson, Kessler, & Shaver, 1997).

## Psychological Factors

Research suggests that stressful life events and childhood adversity contribute to the development of anxiety disorders. But what are the specific mechanisms that link these experiences to emotional difficulties, such as intense fears, panic attacks, and excessive worry? This question brings our discussion of causes to a different level of analysis. A number of psychological mechanisms undoubtedly play important roles in helping to shape the development and maintenance of anxiety disorders. They include learning processes and cognitive events.

**LEARNING PROCESSES** Since the 1920s, experimental psychologists working in laboratory settings have been interested in the possibility that specific fears might be learned through classical (or Pavlovian) conditioning (Ayres, 1998). The central mechanism in the classical conditioning process is the association between an unconditioned stimulus (US) and a conditioned stimulus (CS). The US is able to elicit a strong unconditioned emotional response (UR), such as fear. Examples of potential USs are painfully loud and unexpected noises, the sight of dangerous animals, and sudden, intense pain. According to psychologists' original views of the classical conditioning process, the CS could be any neutral stimulus that happened to be present when an intense fear reaction was provoked. Through the process of association, the CS would subsequently elicit a conditioned response (CR), which was similar in quality to the original UR (see Chapter 2). This explanation for the development of specific phobias fits easily with common sense as well as with clinical experience. Many intense, persistent, irrational fears seem to develop after the person has experienced a traumatic event (Merckelbach, Muris, & Schouten, 1996).

Current views on the process by which fears are learned suggest that the process is guided by a *module,* or specialized circuit in the brain, that has been shaped by evolutionary pressures (Öhman & Mineka, 2001). Some psychologists have argued that the mind includes a very large number of prepared modules (specialized neural circuits) that serve particular adaptive functions, such as the recognition of faces and the perception of language (Pinker, 1997). These modules are designed to operate at maximal speed, are activated automatically, and perform without

conscious awareness. They are also highly selective, in the sense that the module is particularly responsive to a narrow range of stimuli. Human beings seem to be prepared to develop intense, persistent fears only to a select set of objects or situations. Fear of these stimuli may have conferred a selective advantage upon those people—hundreds of thousands of years ago—who were able to develop fears and consequently avoid certain kinds of dangerous stimuli, such as heights, snakes, and storms. This is not to say that the fears are innate or present at birth, but rather that they can be learned and maintained very easily.

Many investigations have been conducted to test various facets of this **preparedness model** (Mineka & Oehlberg, 2008). The results of these studies support many features of the theory. For example, conditioned responses to fear-relevant stimuli (such as spiders and snakes) are more resistant to extinction than are those to fear-irrelevant stimuli (such as flowers). Furthermore, it is possible to develop conditioned fear responses after only one trial of learning.

The process of prepared conditioning may play an important role in the development of both specific phobias and social anxiety disorder. In specific phobias, the prepared stimuli are things like snakes, heights, storms, and small enclosed places. The prepared stimulus in social anxiety disorder might involve other people's faces. We are prepared to fear faces that appear angry, critical, or rejecting if they are directed toward us (Öhman, 1996). This process is presumably an evolutionary remnant of factors involved in establishing dominance hierarchies, which maintain social order among primates. Animals that are defeated in a dominance conflict are often allowed to remain as part of the group if they behave submissively. The responses of people with social anxiety disorder may be somewhat analogous, in the sense that they are afraid of directly facing, or being evaluated by, other people. When a performer makes eye contact with his or her audience, an association may develop very quickly between fear and angry or critical facial expressions.

We all learn many behaviors through imitation. Albert Bandura's early work on modeling, for example, demonstrated that children who observe a model hitting a doll are more likely to behave aggressively themselves when given the opportunity (see Chapter 2). Similar processes may also affect the development of intense fear, because some phobias develop in the absence of any direct experience with the feared object. People apparently learn to avoid certain stimuli if they observe other people showing a strong fear response to those stimuli (Poulton & Menzies, 2002). In other words, the traumatic event does not have to happen to you; it may be enough for you to witness a traumatic event happening to someone else or to watch someone else behave fearfully.

**COGNITIVE FACTORS** Up to this point, we have talked about the importance of life events and specific learning experiences—variables that can be measured outside the organism. But cognitive events also play an important role as mediators between experience and response. Perceptions, memory, and attention all influence the ways that we react to events in our environments. It is now widely accepted that these cognitive factors play a crucial role in the development and maintenance of various types of anxiety disorders. We will focus on three aspects of this literature: perception of controllability and predictability, catastrophic misinterpretation (panic attacks), and attentional biases and shifts in the focus of attention.

**PERCEPTION OF CONTROL** There is an important relationship between anxiety and the perception of control. People who believe that they are able to control events in their environment are less likely to show symptoms of anxiety than are people who believe that they are helpless. This is, of course, part of the reason that the events of September 11, 2001 were so terrifying. The attack on the World Trade Center in New York City was beyond the control of its victims, who were going about their everyday activities.

An extensive body of evidence supports the conclusion that people who believe that they are less able to control events in their environment are more likely to develop global forms of anxiety (Andrews, 1996), as well as various specific types of anxiety disorders (Mineka & Zinbarg, 1998). Laboratory research indicates that feelings of lack of control contribute to the onset of panic attacks among patients with panic disorder. The perception of uncontrollability has also been linked to the submissive behavior frequently seen among people with social anxiety disorder as well as the chronic worries of people with generalized anxiety disorder.

**CATASTROPHIC MISINTERPRETATION** A somewhat different type of cognitive dysfunction has been discussed extensively with relation to the development of panic disorder. According to this view, panic disorder may be caused by the *catastrophic misinterpretation* of bodily sensations or perceived threat (D. M. Clark, 1986; L. A. Clark, 1999). Although panic attacks can be precipitated by external stimuli, they are usually triggered by internal stimuli, such as bodily sensations, thoughts, or images. On the basis of past experience, these stimuli initiate an anxious mood, which leads to a variety of physiological sensations that typically accompany negative emotional reactions (changes in heart rate, respiration rate, dizziness, and so on). Anxious mood is accompanied by a narrowing of the person's attentional focus and an increased awareness of bodily sensations.

The crucial stage comes next, when the person misinterprets the bodily sensation as a catastrophic event. For example, a person who believes that there is something wrong with his heart might misinterpret a slight acceleration in heart rate as being a sign that he is about to have a heart attack. He might say to himself, "My heart will stop and I'll die!" This reaction ensures the continued operation of this feedback loop, with the misinterpretation

enhancing the person's sense of threat, and so on, until the process spirals out of control. Thus, both cognitive misinterpretation and biological reactions associated with the perception of threat are necessary for a panic attack to occur.

The person's automatic, negative thoughts may also lead him to engage in behaviors that are expected to increase his safety, when in fact they are counterproductive. For example, some people believe that they should take deep breaths or monitor their heart rate if they become aroused. This is actually incorrect information, and the alleged safety behaviors can further exaggerate the person's fear response.

Many research studies have found that the subjective experience of body sensations is, in fact, closely associated with maladaptive or catastrophic thoughts among patients with panic disorder (McNally, 1994). This connection by itself does not provide strong evidence for a *causal* link between catastrophic thoughts and the onset of panic attacks because catastrophic thoughts (such as fear of losing control and fear of dying) are, in fact, part of the definition of a panic attack (see *DSM5: Diagnostic Criteria for Panic Disorder*). The theory is difficult to test (cannot be disproven) if there is no way to separate the measurement of catastrophic thoughts and the panic attack itself (Roth, Wilhelm, & Pettit, 2005).

Catastrophic misinterpretations cannot account for all instances of panic attacks. For example, patients with panic disorder sometimes experience panic attacks in their sleep (Craske & Rowe, 1997). How could that happen if the escalation to panic requires catastrophic misinterpretation of physical sensations, which presumably involves conscious cognitive processes? Clearly, other factors are also involved. One alternative explanation involves classical conditioning. The experience of an initial panic attack might lead to conditioned anxiety to cues associated with the first attack. These could be either internal bodily sensations or external stimuli. The conditioned anxiety might lower the person's threshold for subsequent panic attacks (Bouton, Mineka, & Barlow, 2001).

**ATTENTION TO THREAT AND BIASED INFORMATION PROCESSING** Earlier in this chapter we mentioned that anxiety involves negative thoughts and images anticipating some possible future danger. In recent years, several lines of research have converged to clarify the basic cognitive mechanisms involved in generalized anxiety disorder as well as panic disorder. Experts now believe that attention plays a crucial role in the onset of this process. People who are prone to excessive worrying and panic are unusually sensitive to cues that signal the existence of future threats (MacLeod et al., 2002; Teachman, Smith-Janik, & Saporito, 2007). They attend vigilantly to even fleeting signs of danger, especially when they are under stress. At such times, the recognition of danger cues triggers a maladaptive, self-perpetuating cycle of cognitive processes that can quickly spin out of control.

The threatening information that is generated in this process is presumably encoded in memory in the form of elaborate schemas, which are easily reactivated. The threat schemas of anxious people contain a high proportion of "what-if" questions, such as "What am I going to do if I don't do well in school this semester?" Once attention has been drawn to threatening cues, the performance of adaptive, problem-solving behaviors is disrupted, and the worrying cycle launches into a repetitive sequence in which the person rehearses anticipated events and searches for ways to avoid them. This process activates an additional series of "what-if" questions that quickly leads to a dramatic increase in negative affect (McLaughlin, Borovec, & Sibrava, 2007).

If worriers are preoccupied with the perception of threat cues and the rehearsal of dangerous scenarios but are unable to reach satisfactory solutions to their problems, why do they continue to engage in this vicious, maladaptive cycle? Two considerations are particularly important in explaining the self-perpetuating nature of worry: (1) Worry is an experience that is made up of "self-talk"—things that people say to themselves rather than visual images ("I'll never get all this work done!"). (2) Worry serves the function of avoiding unpleasant somatic activation through the suppression of imagery (Borkovec, Alcaine, & Behar, 2004). In other words, some people apparently continue to worry, even though it is not productive, because worrying is reinforced by an immediate (though temporary) reduction in uncomfortable physiological sensations.

Attentional mechanisms also seem to be involved in the etiology and maintenance of social anxiety disorder. People who are capable of performing a particular task when they are alone (in practice) cannot perform it in front of an audience. This deterioration in skill may be caused by anxious apprehension, which is similar to the cognitive processes involved in worrying (Barlow, 2004). The cycle is illustrated in Figure 6.1. An increase in negative affect presumably triggers a shift toward self-focused attention ("Oh, no, I'm getting really upset") and activates cognitive biases and threat schemas ("What if I make a mistake?"). The person becomes distracted by these thoughts, and performance deteriorates. In a sense, the person's fearful expectations become a self-fulfilling prophesy (Heerey & Kring, 2007).

## Biological Factors

Several pieces of evidence indicate that biological events play an important role in the development and maintenance of anxiety disorders. In the following pages we review the role of genetic factors, the connection between anxiety symptoms and specific regions in the brain, and the use of chemicals to induce symptoms of panic. These factors undoubtedly interact with the social and psychological variables that we have considered in the preceding sections.

**GENETIC FACTORS** Some of the most useful information about the validity of anxiety disorders comes from studies aimed at identifying the influence of genetic factors. These data address the overlap, as well as the distinctions, among various types of anxiety disorders. They also shed additional light on the relationship between anxiety and depression.

One particularly influential study, known as the "Virginia Adult Twin Study," has examined anxiety disorders—as well as

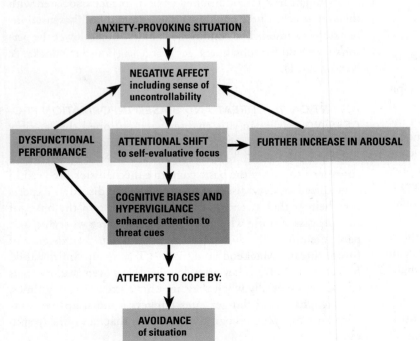

**FIGURE 6.1**

**Anxious Apprehension and Social Phobia** Processes involved in the generation of social anxiety.
*Source:* Based on Barlow, David. 2004. Anxiety and Its Disorders: The Nature and Treatment of Anxiety and Panic. Guilford Press.

many other forms of psychopathology—in a large sample of twins (Kendler & Prescott, 2006). The people who participated in this study were not psychiatric patients; they were living in the community and were identified through a statewide registry of twins born in Virginia. For each specific type of anxiety disorder, concordance rates were significantly higher for monozygotic (MZ) twins than for dizygotic (DZ) twins. Nevertheless, the MZ concordance rates were also relatively low (in comparison to MZ concordance rates for bipolar disorders, for example). Anxiety disorders appear to be modestly heritable, with genetic factors accounting for between 20 and 30 percent of the variance in the transmission of GAD. (See Research Methods in Chapter 16 for a discussion of heritability.) These results led the investigators to several important conclusions:

1. Genetic risk factors for these disorders are neither highly specific (a different set of genes being associated with each disorder) nor highly nonspecific (one common set of genes causing vulnerability for all disorders).

2. Two genetic factors have been identified: one associated with GAD, panic disorder, and agoraphobia, and the other with specific phobias.

3. Environmental risk factors that would be *unique* to individuals also play an important role in the etiology of all anxiety disorders. Environmental factors that would be *shared* by all members of a family do not seem to play an important role for many people.

**NEUROBIOLOGY** Laboratory studies of fear conditioning in animals have identified specific pathways in the brain that are responsible for detecting and organizing a response to danger (LeDoux, 2000; Öhman & Mineka, 2003). The amygdala plays a central role in these circuits, which represent the biological underpinnings of the evolved fear module that we discussed earlier in connection with classical conditioning and phobias (see pages 154–155). Scientists have discovered these pathways by monitoring and manipulating brain activities in animals that are participating in studies using classical conditioning to pair an originally neutral stimulus (the CS) with an aversive stimulus (the US). The results of these studies tell us *where* emotional responses, such as fear and panic, are located in terms of brain regions. They also begin to explain *how* they are produced. That knowledge, coupled with data regarding social and psychological factors, will help us understand *why* people experience problems such as irrational fears and panic attacks.

The brain circuits involved in fear conditioning are illustrated in Figure 6.2. This drawing uses the example of a person who has seen a dangerous snake (Carter, 1999). Sensory information is projected to the thalamus, and from there it is directed to other brain areas for processing. Emotional stimuli follow two primary pathways, both of which lead to the amygdala. The first pathway (the red arrow) might be called a "shortcut" and represents the

evolved fear module for conditioned fear. The message follows a direct connection between the thalamus and the amygdala, which is connected to the hypothalamus. Behavioral responses (such as the "fight-or-flight" response) are then activated and coordinated through projections from the hypothalamus to endocrine glands and the autonomic nervous system (see Chapter 2, as well as the discussion of the HPA axis in Chapter 5). Notice that this first pathway does not involve connections to cortical areas of the brain that might involve higher-level cognitive functions such as conscious memory or decision making. The amygdala does store unconscious, emotional memories—the kind that are generated through prepared learning.

A second, complementary path from the thalamus (the purple arrow) leads to the cortex and provides for a detailed, and comparatively slower, analysis of the information that has been detected. Using the example in Figure 6.2, information about the snake would be sent to the visual cortex. Once the pattern is recognized as a snake, the data would be integrated with additional information from memory about its emotional significance ("potentially dangerous"). This message would then be sent to the amygdala, which could, in turn, trigger an organized response to threat. This second pathway is longer and more complex than the first, and it will take longer to generate a response. The first pathway has presumably evolved because it is adaptive; it provides the organism with an alarm system that can be used to avoid immediate dangers in the environment. The fact that information can follow either path is consistent with the idea that some fear responses are "hardwired" (easily learned, difficult to extinguish, and mediated by unconscious processes) while others are dependent on higher-level analyses that involved thinking and reasoning.

A word of caution must be added when we consider the functions of these specific neural pathways. The fact that they are involved in processing fearful reactions does not mean that the amygdala and associated structures are exclusively dedicated to this particular purpose. Studies with animals have shown that artificial stimulation of the amygdala can produce different effects, depending in large part on the environmental context in which the animal is stimulated (Kagan, 1998). Anger, disgust, and sexual arousal are all emotional states that are associated with activity in pathways connecting the thalamus, the amygdala, and their projections to other brain areas. Fear responses are, therefore, only one of the many kinds of behavior associated with these circuits.

The brain regions that have been identified in studies of fear conditioning play an important role in phobic disorders and panic disorder (Etkin & Wager, 2007; Ninan & Dunlop, 2005). In the case of panic disorder, the fear module may be triggered at an inappropriate time. The sensitivity of this pathway is not the same in all people, and it is presumably influenced by genetic factors as well as hormone levels. Social and psychological factors that affect the threshold of the fear module include stressful life events and the development of separation anxiety during

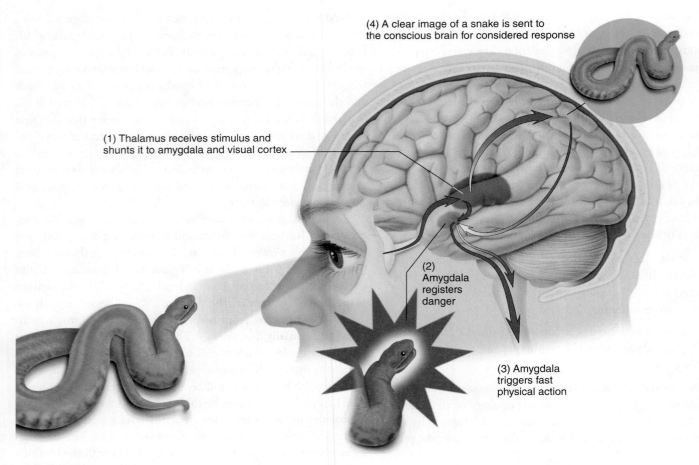

(4) A clear image of a snake is sent to the conscious brain for considered response

(1) Thalamus receives stimulus and shunts it to amygdala and visual cortex

(2) Amygdala registers danger

(3) Amygdala triggers fast physical action

**FIGURE 6.2**

**Two Pathways in the Brain That Detect Danger and Trigger Fear Responses** (1) Evolved fear module, and (2) slower, indirect route through cortical processing areas.

*Source:* Based on Carter, Rita. 1998. Mapping the Mind. Berkeley: University of California Press.

childhood (which increases the rate of panic disorder when these children become adults). The subcortical pathway between the thalamus and the amygdala may be responsible for the misinterpretation of sensory information, which then triggers the hypothalamus and activates a variety of autonomic processes (dramatic increases in respiration rate, heart rate, and so on). Some investigators have also speculated that this brain circuit may be associated with the biased attention to threat cues that has been demonstrated in patients with various types of anxiety disorders (Bishop, 2007).

Several different neurotransmitters are responsible for communication in the brain regions that regulate emotion. Their role in the development and maintenance of anxiety disorders has been examined in studies of animal models of anxiety (Pohl et al., 2007) as well as in studies of the impact of medications on human behavior (Kalueff & Nutt, 2007). Perhaps most important with regard to the anxiety disorders are serotonin, norepinephrine, gamma-aminobutyric acid (GABA), and dopamine. Serotonin

and GABA are inhibitory neurotransmitters that function to dampen stress responses. Pharmacological and environmental challenges that increase their availability lead to decreased levels of anxiety. Conversely, experiences that reduce levels of serotonin and GABA can provoke increases in fear and anxiety.

## Treatment of Anxiety Disorders

Anxiety disorders are one of the areas of psychopathology in which clinical psychologists and psychiatrists are best prepared to improve the level of their clients' functioning (see Getting Help).

### Psychological Interventions

Psychoanalytic psychotherapy has been used to treat patients with anxiety disorders since Freud published his seminal papers at the turn of the twentieth century. The emphasis in this type of treatment is on fostering insight regarding the unconscious motives that presumably lie at the heart of the patient's symptoms. Although

Exposure treatments can be administered in imagination, in the person's natural environment, or using virtual reality designs. This man is being treated for fear of flying in a computerized flight simulator.

many therapists continue to employ this general strategy, it has not been shown to be effective in controlled outcome studies.

### SYSTEMATIC DESENSITIZATION AND INTEROCEPTIVE EXPOSURE

Like psychoanalysis, behavior therapy was initially developed for the purpose of treating anxiety disorders, especially specific phobias. The first widely adopted procedure was known as systematic desensitization (see Chapter 3). In desensitization, the client is first taught progressive muscle relaxation. Then the therapist constructs a hierarchy of feared stimuli, beginning with those items that provoke only small amounts of fear and progressing through items that are most frightening. Then, while the client is in a relaxed state, he or she imagines the lowest item on the hierarchy. The item is presented repeatedly until the person no longer experiences an increase in anxiety when thinking about the object or situation. This process is repeated several times as the client moves systematically up the hierarchy, sequentially confronting images of stimuli that were originally rated as being more frightening.

In the years since systematic desensitization was originally proposed, many different variations on this procedure have been employed. The crucial feature of the treatment involves systematic maintained exposure to the feared stimulus (McNally, 2007; Rachman, 2002). Positive outcomes have been reported, regardless of the specific manner in which exposure is accomplished. Some evidence indicates that direct ("in vivo") exposure works better than imaginal exposure. A few prolonged exposures can be as effective as a larger sequence of brief exposures. Another variation on exposure procedures, known as flooding, begins with the most frightening stimuli rather than working up gradually from the bottom of the hierarchy. All of these variations on the basic procedure have been shown to be effective in the treatment of phobic disorders (Barlow, Raffa, & Cohen, 2002).

The treatment of panic disorder often includes two specific forms of exposure. One, *situational exposure,* is used to treat agoraphobic avoidance (Hahlweg et al., 2001). In this procedure, the person repeatedly confronts the situations that have previously been avoided. These often include crowded public places, such as shopping malls and theaters, as well as certain forms of transportation, such as buses and trains.

*Interoceptive exposure,* the other form of exposure, is aimed at reducing the person's fear of internal, bodily sensations that are frequently associated with the onset of a panic attack, such as increased heart and respiration rate and dizziness. The process is accomplished by having the person engage in standardized exercises that are known to produce such physical sensations. These may include spinning in a swivel chair, running in place, breathing through a narrow straw, or voluntary hyperventilation, depending on the type of sensation that the person fears and avoids. Outcome studies indicate that interoceptive exposure is one of the most important ingredients in the psychological treatment of panic disorder (Barlow et al., 2002; Meuret et al., 2005).

**RELAXATION AND BREATHING RETRAINING** Behavior therapists have used relaxation procedures for many years. Relaxation training usually involves teaching the client alternately to tense and relax specific muscle groups while breathing slowly and deeply. This process is often described to the client as an active coping skill that can be learned through consistent practice and used to control anxiety and worry.

Outcome studies indicate that relaxation is a useful form of treatment for various forms of anxiety disorder (Arntz, 2003; Siev & Chambless, 2007). For example, applied relaxation and cognitive behavior therapy have been compared to nondirective psychotherapy for the treatment of patients with generalized anxiety disorder. Patients who received relaxation training and those who received cognitive therapy were more improved at the end of treatment than those who received only nondirective therapy (Borkovec et al., 2002).

*Breathing retraining* is a procedure that involves education about the physiological effects of hyperventilation and practice in slow breathing techniques. It is often incorporated in treatments used for panic disorder (Hazlett-Stevens & Craske, 2009). This process is similar to relaxation in the sense that relaxation exercises also include instructions in breathing control. The person learns to control his or her breathing through repeated practice using the muscles of the diaphragm, rather than the chest, to take slow, deep breaths. Although breathing retraining appears to be a useful element in the treatment of panic disorder, the mechanisms involved are not entirely clear. A simple reduction in the frequency of hyperventilation is apparently not the main effect of breathing retraining. Some clinicians believe that the process works by enhancing relaxation or increasing the person's perception of control.

**COGNITIVE THERAPY** Cognitive therapy is used extensively in the treatment of anxiety disorders. Cognitive treatment procedures for anxiety disorders are similar to those employed in the treatment of depression. Therapists help clients identify cognitions that are relevant to their problem; recognize the relation between these thoughts and maladaptive emotional responses (such as prolonged anxiety); examine the evidence that supports or contradicts these beliefs; and teach clients more useful ways of interpreting events in their environment (Schuyler, 1991).

In the case of anxiety disorders, cognitive therapy is usually accompanied by additional behavior therapy procedures. Barlow's approach to the treatment of panic disorder, for example, includes a cognitive component in addition to applied relaxation and exposure (Barlow, 1997). One aspect of the cognitive component involves an analysis of errors in the ways in which people think about situations in their lives. Typical examples of faulty logic include jumping to conclusions before considering all of the evidence, overgeneralizing ("That C in biology shows I'll never be a doctor"), "all-or-none" thinking (assuming that one mistake means total failure), and so on.

A second aspect of Barlow's cognitive component for panic patients is called *decatastrophizing*. In this procedure, the therapist asks the client to imagine what would happen if his or her worst-case scenario actually happened. The same principles that are used in examining faulty logic are then applied to this situation. The therapist might say, "I don't think that you will fail the exam. But what would happen if you did fail the exam?" The client's initial reaction might be catastrophic ("I would die." "My parents would kill me." "I would flunk out of school."). Upon more careful analysis, however, the client might agree that these negative predictions actually represent gross exaggerations that are based on cognitive errors. Discussions in the therapy session are followed by extensive practice and homework assignments during the week. As one way of evaluating the accuracy of their own hypotheses, clients are encouraged to write down predictions that they make about specific situations and then keep track of the actual outcomes.

Several controlled outcome studies attest to the efficacy of cognitive therapy in the treatment of various types of anxiety disorders, including panic disorder, agoraphobia, social anxiety disorder, and generalized anxiety disorder (Hofmann et al., 2012). Most of these patients experience clinically important benefits (see Research Methods). Improvement in symptoms over time seems to be preceded by changes in cognitive processing. This observation provides support for the hypothesis that cognitive factors do play an important role in maintenance of these disorders (Teachman, Marker, & Smith-Janik, 2009).

## Biological Interventions

Medication is the most effective and most commonly used biological approach to the treatment of anxiety disorders. Several types of drugs have been discovered to be useful. They are often used in conjunction with psychological treatment (Otto, Smits, & Reese, 2004; Vanin, 2008).

**ANTIANXIETY MEDICATIONS** The most frequently used types of minor tranquilizers are from the class of drugs known as benzodiazepines, which includes diazepam (Valium) and alprazolam (Xanax). These drugs reduce many symptoms of anxiety, especially vigilance and subjective somatic sensations, such as increased muscle tension, palpitations, increased perspiration, and gastrointestinal distress. They have relatively less effect on a person's tendency toward worry and rumination. Benzodiazepines were the most widely prescribed form of psychiatric medication until the 1990s.

Benzodiazepines bind to specific receptor sites in the brain that are ordinarily associated with a neurotransmitter known as GABA. Benzodiazepines, which enhance the activity of GABA neurons, are of two types, based on their rate of absorption and elimination from the body. Some, such as alprazolam and lorazepam (Ativan), are absorbed and eliminated quickly, whereas others, such as diazepam, are absorbed and eliminated slowly.

## Statistical Significance: When Differences Matter

Let's say that an outcome study reveals a statistical difference in the effectiveness of one form of treatment versus another form (or no treatment at all). Does this automatically mean that the difference is clinically significant? The answer is no. We can explain this point by using a hypothetical example. Imagine that you want to know whether exposure and response prevention are effective in the treatment of OCD. You could conduct a study, using an experimental design, in which 50 patients with OCD are randomly assigned to receive exposure and response prevention and another 50 patients—the control group—are not. The latter group might receive a placebo pill or nondirective supportive psychotherapy for purposes of comparison. Measures of obsessions and compulsions are collected before and after treatment for patients in both groups. Your hypothesis is that exposure treatment will lead to more improvement than will placebo or nondirective therapy. In contrast, the null hypothesis (see Research Methods in Chapter 1) holds that the two forms of treatment are not truly different. To conclude that exposure and response prevention are effective, you must reject the null hypothesis.

After collecting your data, you can use statistical tests to help you decide whether you can reject the null hypothesis. These tests assign a probability to that result, indicating how often we would find that result if there are not really differences between the two treatments. Psychologists have adopted the .05 level, meaning that if a difference occurs only by chance, you would find this difference less than five times out of every 100 times you repeated this experiment. Differences that exceed the .05 level, therefore, are assumed to reflect real differences between the variables rather than mere chance. Such results are said to be *statistically significant*.

Statistical significance should not be equated with clinical importance (Jacobson & Truax, 1991; Lambert, Hansen, & Bauer, 2008). It is possible for an investigator to find statistically significant differences between groups (and therefore reject the null hypothesis) on the basis of relatively trivial changes in the patients' adjustment. Consider the hypothetical example outlined above

and suppose that you measured outcome in terms of a questionnaire for obsessions and compulsions whose scores could range from 0 (no symptoms) to 100 (highest score possible). Let's also assume that the average person without OCD gets a score of 50 on this questionnaire and that a score of 70 or higher is typically considered to indicate the presence of problems that are associated with a disruption of the person's social and occupational functioning. Both groups have a mean rating of 90 on the scale prior to treatment. At the end of treatment, the mean rating for the exposure group has dropped to 75, and the mean for the control group is now 85. If you have included enough subjects, and depending on the amount of variation among scores within each group, this difference might reach statistical significance. But is it clinically important? Probably not. The average patient in the exposure group still has a score above the cutoff for identifying meaningful levels of psychopathology and 25 points above the average for adults in the general population.

Clinical importance is sometimes measured in terms of the proportion of people in the treatment group whose outcome scores fall below a certain threshold of severity or within the range of scores that are produced by people without the disorder in question. In the case of OCD, people treated with exposure and response prevention do show levels of change that are considered clinically important as well as statistically significant (Abramowitz, 1998).

Clinical investigators should also consider the *kind* of changes that they expect to find as well as the *amount* of change. In addition to looking at changes in particular symptoms, such as a reduction in the frequency of compulsive behaviors, some clinical investigators also ask questions about the patient's quality of life (Gladis et al., 1999). These include an interest in the person's overall satisfaction as well as his or her ability to perform various social roles, at work, at school, or with friends and family. Therapists obviously hope that their patients will experience improvements in their overall quality of life and level of social adjustment when they are able to achieve a reduction in the severity of symptoms of mental disorders.

---

Benzodiazepines have been shown to be effective in the treatment of generalized anxiety disorders and social anxiety disorder (Ballenger, 2001; Benitez et al., 2008). Drug effects are most consistently evident early in treatment. The long-term effects of benzodiazepines (beyond six months of treatment) are not well established (Mahe & Balogh, 2000). They are not typically beneficial for patients with specific phobias. Certain high-potency benzodiazepines are also useful for treating panic disorder (Spiegel & Bruce, 1997). Alprazolam (Xanax) is considered by

some psychiatrists to be the drug of choice for patients with this condition because it produces clinical improvement more quickly than antidepressants.

Many patients with panic disorder and agoraphobia relapse if they discontinue taking medication (Marks et al., 1993). Exposure may be a preferable form of treatment for patients with a diagnosis of panic disorder with agoraphobia because of high relapse rates that have been observed after alprazolam is withdrawn.

Common side effects of benzodiazepines include sedation accompanied by mild psychomotor and cognitive impairments. These drugs can, for example, increase the risk of automobile accidents, because they interfere with motor skills. They can also lead to problems in attention and memory, especially among elderly patients.

The most serious adverse effect of benzodiazepines is their potential for addiction. Approximately 40 percent of people who use benzodiazepines for six months or more will exhibit symptoms of withdrawal if the medication is discontinued (Michelini et al., 1996). Withdrawal reactions include the reappearance of anxiety, somatic complaints, concentration problems, and sleep difficulties. They are most severe among patients who abruptly discontinue the use of benzodiazepines that are cleared quickly from the system, such as alprazolam.

Another class of antianxiety medication, known as the azapirones, includes drugs that work on entirely different neural pathways than the benzodiazepines (Cadieux, 1996). Rather than inhibiting the activity of GABA neurons, azapirones act on serotonin transmission. The azapirone that is used most frequently in clinical use is known as buspirone (BuSpar). Placebo-controlled outcome studies indicate that buspirone is effective in the treatment of generalized anxiety disorder (Davidson et al., 1999). Some clinicians believe that buspirone is preferable to the benzodiazepines because it does not cause drowsiness and does not interact with the effects of alcohol. The disadvantage is that patients do not experience relief from severe anxiety symptoms as quickly with buspirone as they do with benzodiazepines.

**ANTIDEPRESSANT MEDICATIONS** The selective serotonin reuptake inhibitors (SSRIs), discussed in Chapter 5, have become the preferred form of medication for treating almost all forms of anxiety disorder. These include drugs such as fluoxetine (Prozac), fluvoxamine (Luvox), sertraline (Zoloft), and paroxetine (Paxil). Reviews of controlled outcome studies indicate that they are at least as effective as other, more traditional forms of antidepressants in reducing symptoms of various anxiety disorders (Anderson, 2006; Roy-Byrne & Cowley, 2002). They also have fewer unpleasant side effects, they are safer to use, and withdrawal reactions are less prominent when they are discontinued. Therefore, the SSRIs are now considered the first-line medication for treating panic disorder and social anxiety.

Imipramine (Tofranil), a tricyclic antidepressant medication, has been used for more than 40 years in the treatment of patients with panic disorder. A large number of double-blind, placebo-controlled studies indicate that it produces beneficial results (Jefferson, 1997; Mavissakalian & Ryan, 1998). Psychiatrists often prefer imipramine to antianxiety drugs for the treatment of panic disorder because patients are less likely to become dependent on the drug than they are to high-potency benzodiazepines like alprazolam.

The tricyclic antidepressants are used less frequently than the SSRIs because they produce several unpleasant side effects, including weight gain, dry mouth, and overstimulation (sometimes referred to as an "amphetamine-like" response). Some of the side effects (like feeling jittery, nervous, lightheaded, and having trouble sleeping) are upsetting to patients because they resemble symptoms of anxiety. Side effects often lead patients to discontinue treatment prematurely.

In actual practice, anxiety disorders are often treated with a combination of psychological and biological procedures. The selection of specific treatment components depends on the specific group of symptoms that the person exhibits. The potential benefits and costs of combined treatment with medication and psychological procedures should be studied more carefully. Current evidence suggests that patients who receive both medication and psychotherapy may do better in the short run, but patients who receive only cognitive behavior therapy may do better in the long run because of difficulties that can be encountered when medication is discontinued (Otto et al., 2005).

## Obsessive-Compulsive and Related Disorders

Obsessive-compulsive disorder (OCD) is one of the most debilitating disorders in the world, including all kinds of medical disorder (see Figure 1.2 on page 13). OCD was listed as a form of anxiety disorder in previous editions of the diagnostic manual (see Thinking Critically about DSM-5 on page 149). Now it is listed separately. *DSM-5* devotes a separate chapter to obsessive-compulsive and related disorders. All of these disorders are defined by the presence of unwanted intrusive thoughts and/or habitual behaviors. In the following pages, we will discuss OCD, hoarding disorder, trichotillomania, and excoriation (skin-picking) disorder. Body dysmorphic disorder is discussed in Chapter 7.

OBSESSIVE-COMPULSIVE SQUARE DANCE

*"Spin your partner round and round, then spin your partner round again, spin her round six more times, now touch the light switch near the door."*

© Joe Dator/The New Yorker Collection/www.cartoonbank.com

## Symptoms of OCD

**Obsessions** are repetitive, unwanted, intrusive cognitive events that may take the form of thoughts or images or urges. They intrude suddenly into consciousness and lead to an increase in subjective anxiety. Obsessive thinking can be distinguished from worry in two primary ways: (1) Obsessions are usually experienced by the person as being nonsensical, whereas worries are often triggered by problems in everyday living; and (2) the content of obsessions most often involves themes that are perceived as being socially unacceptable or horrific, such as sex, violence, and disease/contamination, whereas the content of worries tends to center around more acceptable, commonplace concerns, such as money and work (de Silva & Rachman, 2004). 👁 **Watch** the **Video** *Dave: Obsessive Compulsive Disorder (OCD)* on **MyPsychLab**

**Compulsions** are repetitive behaviors or mental acts that are used to reduce anxiety. Examples include checking many times to be sure that a door is locked or repeating a silent prayer over and over again. These actions are typically considered by the person who performs them to be senseless or irrational. The person attempts to resist performing the compulsion but cannot. The following case study illustrates many of the most common features of obsessions and compulsions.

#### ➡ Ed's Obsessive-Compulsive Disorder

Ed, a 38-year-old lawyer, lived with his wife, Phyllis. Most aspects of Ed's life were going well, except for the anxiety-provoking thoughts that lurked beneath his relatively easygoing exterior. One focus of Ed's anxiety was handwriting. He became so tense that his eyes hurt whenever he was forced to write. Feeling exhausted and overwhelmed, Ed avoided writing whenever possible. The problem seemed utterly ridiculous to him, but he couldn't rid himself of his obsessive thoughts.

Sinister meanings had somehow become linked in Ed's imagination to the way in which letters and numbers were formed. The worst letters were *P* and *T* (the first letters in "Phyllis" and in "Tim," his younger brother's name). "Improperly" formed letters reminded Ed of violent acts, especially decapitation and strangulation. If the parts of a letter, such as the two lines in the letter *T*, were not connected, an image of a head that was not attached to its body might pop into his mind.

Closed loops reminded him of suffocation, like a person whose throat had been clamped shut. These images were associated with people whose names began with the malformed letter. As a result of these concerns, Ed's handwriting had become extremely awkward and difficult to read.

These writing problems made it very difficult for Ed to complete his work, especially when he was under time pressure. In one particularly upsetting incident, Ed was responsible for completing an important official form that had to be mailed that day. He came to a section in which he needed to write a capital *P* and became concerned that he hadn't done it properly. The loop seemed to be closed, which meant that Phyllis might be strangled! He tore up the first copy and filled it out again. When it was finally done to his satisfaction, Ed sealed the form in an envelope and put it in the box for outgoing mail. After returning to his desk, he was suddenly overwhelmed by the feeling that he had indeed made a mistake with that *P*. If he allowed the form to be mailed, the evil image would be associated forever with his wife. Consumed by fear, Ed rushed back to the mailbox, tore up the envelope, and started a new form. Twenty minutes later, he had the form filled out and back in the mailbox. Then the cycle repeated itself. Each time, Ed became more distraught and frustrated, until he eventually felt that he was going to lose his mind.

In addition to his problems with writing, Ed was also afraid of axes. He would not touch an ax, or even get close to one. Any situation in which he could possibly encounter an ax made him extremely uncomfortable. He refused to shop in hardware stores because they sell axes, and he would not visit museums because their exhibits often contain artifacts such as medieval armor. His fear of axes was quite specific. Ed wasn't afraid of knives, guns, or swords.

One frightening experience seemed to trigger the pervasive anxiety that had plagued Ed for 20 years. When he was 17 years old, some friends persuaded Ed to try smoking marijuana. They told him that it would make him feel high—relaxed, sociable, and perhaps a bit giddy. Unfortunately, Ed didn't react to the drug in the same way that the others had. The physical effects seemed to be the same, but his psychological reaction was entirely different. After sharing two joints with his friends, Ed began to feel lightheaded. Then things around him began to seem unreal, as though he were watching himself and his friends in a movie. The intensity of these feelings escalated rapidly, and panic took over. Frightening thoughts raced through his head. Was he losing his mind? When would it stop? This experience lasted about two hours.

The marijuana incident had an immediate and lasting impact. Ed became preoccupied with a fear of accidentally ingesting any kind of mind-altering drug, especially LSD. Every spot on his skin

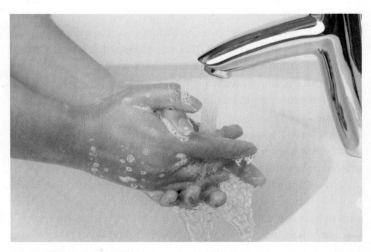

Obsessive thoughts about germs and contamination can trigger frequent ritualistic hand washing that can take hours out of the day and lead to serious skin problems

or clothing seemed as though it might be a microscopic quantity of this hallucinogen. He felt compelled to clean his hands and clothes repeatedly to avoid contamination. Intellectually, Ed knew that these concerns were silly. How could a tiny spot on his hand be LSD? It didn't make any sense, but he couldn't keep the thought out of his mind.

The most horrifying aspect of the drug experience was the sensation of being totally out of control of his actions and emotions. The fear of returning to that state haunted Ed. He struggled to resist urges that he had never noticed before, such as the temptation to shout obscenities aloud in church. He also began to worry that he might hurt his younger brother. He resisted these urges with all his might. He never acted on them, but they pervaded his consciousness and absorbed his mental energy.

The thoughts were so persistent and unshakable that Ed began to wonder if he might, in fact, be a pathological killer. Could he be as deranged and evil as Richard Speck, who had brutally murdered eight nurses in a Chicago apartment building in 1966? Ed spent many hours reading articles about Speck and other mass murderers. The number 8 came to have special meaning to him because of the number of Speck's victims. Over time, Ed's fears and worries became focused on numbers and letters. The violent images and impulses became a less prominent part of his everyday life, but the writing difficulties escalated proportionately.

Ed's thoughts about violence and death illustrate the anxiety-provoking nature of obsessions. It is not just the intrusive quality of the thought, but also the unwanted nature of the thought that makes it an obsession. Some scientists and artists, for example, have reported experiencing intrusive thoughts or inspirational ideas that appear in an unexpected, involuntary way, but these thoughts are not unwanted. Obsessions are unwelcome, anxiety-provoking thoughts. They are also nonsensical; they may seem silly or "crazy." In spite of the recognition that these thoughts do not make sense, the person with full-blown obsessions is unable to ignore or dismiss them.

Examples of typical obsessive thoughts include the following: "Did I kill the old lady?" "Christ was a bastard!" "Am I a sexual pervert?" Examples of obsessive urges include "I might expose my genitals in public," "I am about to shout obscenities in public," "I feel I might strangle a child." Obsessional images might include mutilated corpses, decomposing fetuses, or a family member being involved in a serious car accident. Although obsessive urges are accompanied by a compelling sense of reality, obsessive people seldom act upon these urges.

Most normal people report having had some intrusive, unacceptable thoughts or urges that are similar in many ways to those experienced by patients being treated for obsessive-compulsive disorder (Rachman & de Silva, 1978; Salkovskis & Harrison, 1984). These include urges to hurt other people, urges to do something dangerous, and thoughts of accidents or disease. In contrast to these normal experiences, obsessions described by

clinical patients occur more frequently, last longer, and are associated with higher levels of discomfort. Clinical obsessions are also resisted more strongly, and patients report more difficulty dismissing their unwanted thoughts and urges. Someone who experiences clinical obsessions is also prone to interpret them as meaning that he is a terrible person, someone who might actually act on the urge to harm another person. Research evidence suggests that intrusive thoughts are relatively common, and clinical obsessions differ from them in degree rather than in nature.

Ed's constricted style of forming letters and his habitual pattern of going back to check and correct his writing illustrate the way in which compulsions are used to reduce anxiety. If he did not engage in these ritualistic behaviors, he would become extremely uncomfortable. His concern about someone being strangled or decapitated if the letters were not properly formed was not delusional, because he readily acknowledged that this was a "silly" idea. Nevertheless, he couldn't shake the obsessive idea that some dreadful event would occur if he was not excruciatingly careful about his writing. He felt as though he had to act, even though he knew that his obsessive thought was irrational. This paradox is extremely frustrating to obsessive-compulsive patients, and it is one of the most common and interesting aspects of the disorder.

Compulsions reduce anxiety, but they do not produce pleasure. Thus, some behaviors, such as gambling and drug use, that people describe as being "compulsive" are not considered true compulsions according to this definition.

Although some clinicians have argued that compulsive rituals are associated with a complete loss of voluntary control, it is more accurate to view the problem in terms of *diminished* control. For example, Ed could occasionally manage to resist the urge to write in his compulsive style; the behavior was not totally automatic. But whenever he did not engage in this ritualistic behavior, his subjective level of distress increased dramatically, and within a short period of time he returned to the compulsive writing style.

Two common forms of compulsive behavior are checking and cleaning. The case of Michael, presented in Chapter 4, provides an example of a person with compulsive cleaning rituals. Compulsive cleaning is often associated with an irrational fear of contamination, and in that respect it bears a strong resemblance to certain phobias. There are passive as well as active features of compulsive cleaning. Compulsive cleaners, like Michael, go out of their way to avoid contact with dirt, germs, and other sources of contamination. Then, when they believe that they have come into contact with a source of contamination, they engage in ritualistic cleaning behavior, such as washing their hands, taking showers, cleaning kitchen counters, and so on. These rituals typically involve a large number of repetitions. Some people may wash their hands 50 times a day, taking several minutes to scrub their hands up to the elbow with industrial-strength cleanser. Others take showers that last two or three hours in which they wash each part of their body in a fixed order, needing to repeat the scrubbing motion an exact number of times.

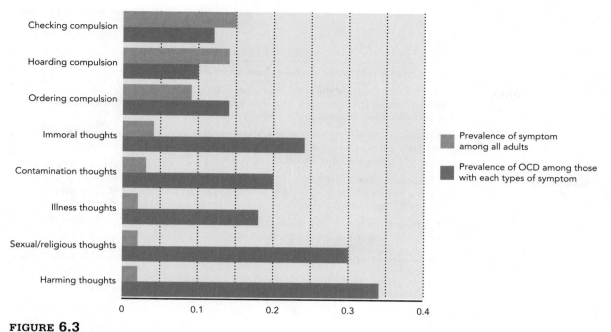

**FIGURE 6.3**

Lifetime prevalence of specific types of obsessions and compulsions, and prevalence of OCD diagnosis given presence of specific symptoms.
*Source:* A. M. Ruscio, D. J. Stein, W. T. Chiu, and R. C. Kessler, 2010, "The epidemiology of obsessive-compulsive disorder in the National Comorbidity Survey Replication." *Molecular Psychiatry, 15,* 53–63.

Compulsive checking frequently represents an attempt to ensure the person's safety or the safety and health of a friend or family member. The person checks things, such as the stove or the lock on a door, over and over in an attempt to prevent the occurrence of an imagined unpleasant or disastrous event (e.g., an accident, a burglary, or an assault).

The most common forms of obsessions include immoral thoughts, thoughts about being contaminated or being exposed to illness, unwanted sexual and religious thoughts, and thoughts about harming other people. Data regarding these symptoms are presented in Figure 6.3. Participants in the large epidemiological survey known as the NCS-R were asked to indicate whether they had experienced certain kinds of obsessions ("unpleasant thought, images or impulses") and compulsions ("repeated behaviors or mental acts that you felt compelled to do"). In order to be counted as present, the symptoms had to be present most days for at least a period of two weeks. Almost 30 percent of the people reported having experienced either obsessions or compulsions at some point during their lives, but most of these people did not qualify for a diagnosis of OCD.

### Diagnosis of OCD and Related Disorders

*DSM-5* defines OCD in terms of the presence of either obsessions or compulsions. Most people who meet the criteria for this disorder actually exhibit both of these symptoms. The person must attempt to ignore, suppress, or neutralize the unwanted thoughts or impulses, and they must be time-consuming (take more than one hour per day) or cause significant subjective distress or social impairment. The diagnostic manual specifies further that these

thoughts must not be simply excessive worries about real problems. Intrusive thoughts about overdue bills, for example, would not qualify as obsessions. Finally, *DSM-5* provides for a specification of the person's level of insight regarding beliefs that are associated with OCD symptoms. The condition can be described as being present: (1) with good or fair insight (i.e., understands that the beliefs are either definitely or probably not true); (2) with poor insight (the person thinks that OCD beliefs are probably true); or (3) with absent insight/delusional beliefs (the person is completely convinced that the OCD beliefs are true).

The line of demarcation between compulsive rituals and normal behavior is often difficult to define. How many times should a person wash her hands in a day? How long should a shower last? Is it reasonable to check more than one time to be sure that the door is locked or the alarm clock is set? *DSM-5* has established an arbitrary threshold that holds that rituals become compulsive if they cause marked distress, take more than an hour per day to perform, or interfere with normal occupational and social functioning.

Additional OCD-related disorders are listed in Table 6.1. Hoarding disorder was added to *DSM-5* as a new form of mental disorder. In the previous version of the diagnostic manual, hoarding had been listed as one potential symptom of obsessive-compulsive personality disorder ("Unable to discard worn-out or worthless objects even when they have no sentimental value." See Chapter 9). It has also been considered a subtype of OCD, presumably because the person's fear of losing important belongings might be viewed as an obsessive thought (increasing anxiety). Distress associated with allowing other people to touch or move these belongings also bears some resemblance to concerns about symmetry and ordering

| TABLE 6.1 | |
|---|---|
| **Obsessive-Compulsive Related Disorders in _DSM-5_** | |
| **All must be associated with subjective distress or social impairment in order for the person to qualify for a diagnosis.** | |
| Body Dysmorphic Disorder | Preoccupation with perceived defects in personal appearance. The person believes that these flaws are unsightly or abnormal. The perceived defects are not noticeable, or appear to be completely insignificant, to other people. |
| Hoarding Disorder | Persistent difficulties in getting rid of possessions, regardless of their real value. The reluctance to discard property is due to perceived need to save the items, and it results in accumulation of possessions that obstruct active areas of the person's home. |
| Trichotillomania (Hair-Pulling Disorder) | Recurrent pulling out one's own hair, in spite of many attempts to decrease or stop this behavior. The hair may be pulled from any area of the body, with the most common sites being scalp, eyebrows, and eyelids. |
| Excoriation (Skin-Picking) Disorder | Persistent picking at one's own skin, most often on the person's face, arms, and hands. This picking leads to skin lesions and is not the result of another medical condition, and it is resistant to the person's frequent attempts to stop the skin picking or decrease its frequency. |

compulsions (Frost, Steketee, & Tolin, 2012). Research studies concerned with hoarding as a distinct form of psychopathology began to appear in the mid 1990s, and interest in this problem has subsequently exploded. In fact, there are at least two popular reality TV programs that are devoted exclusively to the description of people who suffer from clinically significant hoarding.

The core element of hoarding disorder, as it is defined in _DSM-5,_ is unrelenting trouble associated with getting rid of personal belongings. In order to meet the criteria for this disorder, the person must feel a strong need to save these possessions. Throwing the items away leads to a sharp increase in strong negative emotions. As a result, living areas in the person's home become completely cluttered to the point that they are unusable.

The impairment associated with hoarding is obvious and can become extremely disruptive to the person's life. Congestion caused by accumulating possessions can lead to major safety risks and health hazards. Fire is one obvious danger. In rare, extreme cases, people have been crushed by piles of heavy belongings that crashed after being stacked to the ceiling.

The symptoms of hoarding are, in many important ways, quite different from symptoms of OCD (Frost, Steketee, & Tolin, 2012; Pertusa et al., 2010).

People with hoarding disorder save things that most other people would consider worthless. The accumulated clutter interferes with use of living and work spaces and can become quite dangerous.

1. Unlike obsessions, thoughts associated with hoarding are not necessarily intrusive or unwanted. People who engage in hoarding find it pleasant to think about their possessions.

2. The distress associated with hoarding follows as a result of congestion of the person's home (including problems with relatives and sometimes authorities who object to the mess) rather than thoughts about possessions or hoarding behaviors themselves.

3. The experience of obsessions leads to an increase in anxiety, but hoarding behaviors are associated with positive emotion. Anxiety is increased when the person is forced to get rid of the possessions.

In fact, a substantial proportion of people who meet the *DSM-5* criteria for hoarding disorder do not qualify for a diagnosis of OCD (Hall et al., 2013). For all of these reasons, it does make sense to consider hoarding as a distinct form of mental disorder.

Trichotillomania is defined in terms of recurrent hair-pulling. People who meet the criteria for this disorder pull out their own hair and, as a result, experience serious hair loss (Duke et al., 2010). The hair is usually pulled from the scalp, eyebrows, or eyelids, but it can be from any area of the body. As in the case of compulsive behaviors, the person attempts unsuccessfully to resist or stop the hair pulling. The extent of hair loss varies in extent and visibility from one person to the next. Some people with this disorder conceal the loss of hair by wearing wigs, hats, or scarves.

Excoriation disorder is defined by repeated skin picking which produces skin lesions. As with other disorders related to OCD, these recurrent skin picking behaviors are resisted unsuccessfully. Most people with this disorder pick at skin on the face, arms, or hands. The following brief case study describes the experience of one young woman who was treated by one of the authors.

### ➜ Amber's Skin-picking

Amber was a 24-year-old graduate student when she came to the clinic, seeking help to stop herself from scratching at her face with her fingernails. She was a strikingly attractive woman, but her face was covered with rough scars, which looked as though they might have been vestiges of serious acne. For the past three or four years, she had experienced intermittent episodes of scratching that would last anywhere from a few minutes to more than two hours. Sometimes these episodes happened two or three times a week, with the longest interval between episodes being one month. Amber was usually standing in front of a mirror in her bathroom when she started to scratch her face. It often started when she noticed a small blemish or other irregularity on her face. She would lean closer to the mirror and begin to press or pick at the spot with a fingernail. As she ran her finger across her face, she would gradually "zone out" or begin to lapse into what might be called an "out of body experience," otherwise known as dissociation (see Chapter 7). Her thoughts typically wandered to many other topics, and she was usually not at all aware of what she was doing. During the episode, she scratched and poked and picked

at her face. Eventually, and without warning, she would suddenly become aware of herself standing in front of the mirror again, with her face bleeding openly. At that point, she would become aware of pain from the deep scratches, but her mood in the aftermath of an episode was typically calm.

Amber was not aware of any particular feelings or situations that were likely to trigger an episode. In an effort to prevent face scratching, she had tried covering all of the mirrors in her apartment with newspaper, but it didn't work. She would eventually find herself in front of the mirror bleeding, after pulling off enough of the paper to create a spot large enough to see her face in the mirror. Unable to control the scratching on her own, she sought professional treatment in an effort to break what she considered to be a terrible habit.

........................................................................

Hair-pulling and skin-picking disorders are quite similar in several ways (Snorrason, Belleau, & Woods, 2012). One is that people with these problems often report certain kinds of negative emotional experiences before episodes, ranging from boredom to anxiety, and a subsequent reduction in these feelings after the problem behavior has stopped. This pattern suggests that the picking and pulling behaviors may serve the purpose of regulating negative emotional states. The connection with negative emotions is also less direct, however, than it is in OCD. In OCD, the experience of an obsession (a specific, intrusive thought) leads to a sharp rise in anxiety. The compulsive behavior is specifically designed to reduce that anxiety (e.g., cleaning compulsions following contamination or illness thoughts). Skin-picking and hair-pulling seem to regulate negative emotional states, but they are not specifically triggered by intrusive, unwanted thoughts and impulses.

Another distinction between OCD and these other disorders involves the automaticity of the behavior (Snorrason et al., 2012). A substantial percentage of people with skin-picking and hair-pulling also describe themselves as being in a trance-like state (or feeling hypnotized) while they are engaging in the problem behavior. Many patients report that they are not aware of the picking or pulling when they are doing it. Patients with OCD, on the other hand, are typically acutely aware of what they are doing when they engage in compulsive rituals.

## Course and Outcome of OCD

The long-term course of obsessive-compulsive disorder typically follows a pattern of improvement mixed with some persistent symptoms. One remarkable study has reported outcome information for a sample of 144 patients with severe OCD who were assessed at two follow-up intervals: first about five years after they were initially treated at a psychiatric hospital and then again more than 40 years later (Skoog & Skoog, 1999). The data are interesting both because of the very long follow-up interval and because the patients were initially treated between 1947 and 1953, well before the introduction of modern pharmacological and psychological treatments for the disorder. Slightly less than 30 percent of the patients were rated as being recovered at the first follow-up interval. By the time of the 40-year follow-up, almost 50 percent of the patients were considered to show either full recovery or recovery with subclinical symptoms. More than 80 percent of the patients showed improved levels of functioning if we also count people who continued to exhibit some clinical symptoms. Nevertheless, half of the patients in this sample exhibited symptoms of OCD for more than 30 years. This study shows that although many patients do improve, OCD is a chronic disorder for many people.

Much less information is available regarding the course and outcome of the OCD-related disorders. Most evidence suggests that hoarding tends to be a long-term, chronic condition (Tolin et al., 2010). Skin-picking and trichotillomania also seem to be chronic problems that following a waxing and waning course over time (Snorrason et al., 2012).

## Frequency of OCD and Related Disorders

Approximately two percent of the U.S. population meets diagnostic criteria for OCD at some point during their lives, and the 12-month prevalence rate for OCD is 1.2 percent (Ruscio et al., 2010). Similar rates have been reported in other countries (Subramaniam et al., 2012). All of the evidence suggests that OCD is less common than most of the anxiety disorders and major depression. Also unlike the anxiety and depressive disorders, OCD does not appear to show a significant gender difference; men and women are equally likely to be affected (Adam et al., 2012; Torres et al., 2006).

The 12-month prevalence of other OCD-related disorders is illustrated in Figure 6.4. These data should be considered tentative because none of these disorders has been included in large-scale epidemiological studies using structured interviews and *DSM-5* criteria. Nevertheless, it does seem clear that hoarding disorder and excoriation (skin-picking) disorder are both more common than the other kinds of problems. Hoarding disorder is much more common than OCD, affecting almost 6 percent of community residents, with no differences in frequency between

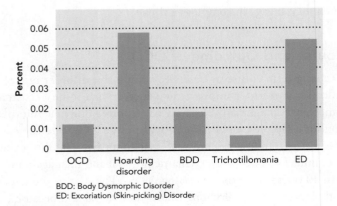

**FIGURE 6.4**

12-month prevalence of OCD and OCD-related disorders.

men and women (Timpano et al., 2011). Excoriation disorder appears to be much more common than trichotillomania, though there is some overlap between these disorders (Hayes, Storch, & Berlanga, 2009). The current prevalence of body dysmorphic disorder is approximately 2 percent (Buhlmann et al., 2010).

## Causes of OCD

The cognitive model of worry or anxious apprehension places primary emphasis on the role of attentional processes. Worrying is unproductive and self-defeating in large part because it is associated with a focus on self-evaluation (fear of failure) and negative emotional responses rather than on external aspects of the problem and active coping behaviors. We may be consciously aware of these processes and simultaneously be unable to inhibit them. The struggle to control our thoughts often leads to a process known as *thought suppression,* an active attempt to stop thinking about something.

It seems simple to say, "Stop worrying," but it is virtually impossible for some people to do so. In fact, recent evidence suggests that trying to rid one's mind of a distressing or unwanted thought can have the unintended effect of making the thought more intrusive (Wegner, 1994). Thought suppression might actually increase, rather than decrease, the strong emotions associated with those thoughts. The bond between a thought and its associated emotion allows activation of one to result in the reinstatement of the other, a kind of dual pathway.

Obsessive-compulsive disorder may be related, in part, to the maladaptive consequences of attempts to suppress unwanted or threatening thoughts that the person has learned to see as being dangerous or forbidden (Abramowitz, Tolin, & Street, 2001; Purdon, 2004). Remember that obsessive thoughts are a common experience in the general population. They resemble "abnormal" obsessions in form and content. However, the obsessions of those in treatment for OCD are more intense and, perhaps most importantly, are more often strongly resisted and more difficult to dismiss. This resistance may be a key component in the association between emotional sensitivity and the development of troublesome obsessive thoughts. People who are vulnerable to the development of OCD apparently react strongly to events that trigger an emotional response. These individuals become aware of their exaggerated reactivity and find it unpleasant. In an effort to control their reaction, they attempt to resist or suppress the emotion (Campbell-Sills et al., 2006).

As a result of an individual's attempt to suppress strong emotion, a rebound effect may occur, culminating in a vicious cycle. Thoughts that are present during the instigation of such a cycle become robustly associated with the emotion and may become the content of an obsessive thought. This model may help to explain the episodic nature of obsessive-compulsive symptoms; relapse may be triggered by intense emotional episodes.

There are also biological perspectives regarding causal mechanisms associated with OCD. Some are based on the broad foundation of research regarding attention and emotion regulation. The neurological foundations of OCD seem to involve regions of the brain that are different than those involved in other types of anxiety disorders (Bartz & Hollander, 2006). As we discussed in Chapter 4, obsessions and compulsions are associated with multiple brain regions, including the basal ganglia (a system that includes the caudate nucleus and the putamen), the orbital prefrontal cortex, and the anterior cingulate cortex (see Figure 4.2 on page 101). These circuits are overly active in people with OCD, especially when the person is confronted with stimuli that provoke his or her obsessions (Husted et al., 2006; Menzies et al., 2008).

By moving OCD to its own chapter, the authors of *DSM-5* will probably draw even more research attention to this serious mental disorder. Studies aimed at understanding the origins of OCD will continue to be inspired by observations of clinical patients and the ideas that they generate. New hypotheses will need to be evaluated using rigorous research methods (see Critical Thinking Matters).

## Treatment of OCD

A variety of psychological and biological forms of treatment have been shown to be effective with people suffering from OCD. We begin our discussion of this literature by describing procedures that were used in an effort to help Ed, the person with obsessive-compulsive disorder whose problems were described at the beginning of this section of the chapter.

### ⟶ Ed's Treatment

Ed's psychiatrist gave him a prescription for clomipramine (Anafranil), an antidepressant drug that is also used to treat

## CRITICAL THINKING matters

### Can a Strep Infection Trigger OCD in Children?

New hypotheses about the causes of mental disorders are usually based on clinical observations. These ideas are then evaluated in research studies designed to test their validity. Sometimes the data support the new idea, and sometimes they don't. During this period of evaluation, clinicians and scientists find themselves in a period of uncertainty, with some people embracing what they consider to be an important advance in knowledge while others provide skeptical criticism. Both groups need to think critically about relevant evidence.

This state of affairs is currently illustrated by a controversial proposal regarding the development of OCD in children. Clinical scientists at the National Institute of Mental Health suggested that, in some cases, symptoms of OCD develop suddenly following a strep infection. According to their hypothesis, antibodies that are triggered by the infection attack nerve cells in the basal ganglia of the brain (see Figure 4.1 on page 86). The investigators created a new term to use in diagnosing children with OCD who have a sudden onset and also test positive for a strep infection. They call the disorder pediatric autoimmune neuropsychiatric disorders associated with streptococcal infection, or PANDAS (Swedo & Grant, 2005). They recommend that a throat culture be given to any child who shows a sudden onset of symptoms of OCD. Children who test positive for strep are put on long-term antibiotics that are claimed, in some cases, to produce "miraculous results" (Anderson, 1996).

Does the recognition of PANDAS represent a breakthrough discovery? Is it a valid diagnostic concept? Or is it a mistaken hypothesis with potentially risky treatment implications? Reasonable people have taken both sides. The empirical evidence is incomplete (da Rocha, Correa, & Teixeira, 2008; Leckman et al., 2011), and some say it is weak (Gilbert & Kurlan, 2009). Many cases have been described that fit this clinical profile. One paper described 109 cases in which the parents described a rapid onset of OCD symptoms (Swedo et al., 1998). Among these, 50 tested positive for strep. That leaves 59 rapid-onset cases that must have been triggered by some other, unknown factor. But even in the cases that did test positive, the existence of a strep infection does not prove that it was causally related to the OCD.

> If 100 kids fall out of a tree and break their arms and we test them for strep, there's going to be a very high percentage of children who have evidence of recent infection. That doesn't mean strep is the reason they fell out of a tree. (Shulman, quoted in Belkin, 2005)

Skeptics argue that, until more conclusive evidence is available to support the theory, we should assume that children who experience obsessions and compulsions are suffering from OCD, nothing more or less (Kurlan & Kaplan, 2004). Undue emphasis on the use of antibiotic treatment may lead parents to ignore more conventional treatments for the disorder. In fact, the combination of cognitive behavior therapy and SSRI medications has been shown to be effective for children with PANDAS-related OCD (Storch et al., 2006). Clinicians should also consider potential problems associated with the use of antibiotics as a form of treatment for children with OCD. Risks include the possibility of developing drug allergies and the promotion of antibiotic resistance.

While PANDAS is an intriguing hypothesis, remember that the burden of proof lies with those who propose new diagnostic categories or causal theories. Until it has been supported by strong empirical evidence, which is not yet the case with regard to PANDAS, the community of scientists assumes that the new hypothesis is false.

people with severe obsessions. Weekly psychotherapy sessions continued as the dose was gradually increased. The medication had a beneficial impact after four weeks. Ed said that he had begun to feel as though he was trapped at the bottom of a well. After the medication, he no longer felt buried. His situation still wasn't great, but it no longer seemed hopeless or unbearable. He was also less intensely preoccupied by his obsessive violent images. They were still there, but they weren't as pressing. The drug had several annoying, though tolerable, side effects. His mouth felt dry, and he was occasionally a bit dizzy. He also noticed that he became tired more easily. Although Ed was no longer feeling seriously depressed, and the intensity of his obsessions was diminished, they had not disappeared, and he was now avoiding writing altogether.

Because the obsessions were still a problem, Ed's psychiatrist referred him to a psychologist who specialized in behavior therapy for anxiety disorders. He continued seeing the psychiatrist every other week for checks on his medication, which he continued to take. The new therapist told Ed that his fears of particular letters and numbers would be maintained as long as he avoided writing. Ed agreed to begin writing short essays every day, for a period of at least 30 minutes. The content could vary from day to day—anything that Ed felt like writing about—but he was encouraged to include the names of his wife and brother as often as possible. Furthermore, he was instructed to avoid his compulsive writing style, intentionally allowing the parts of letters to be separated or loops to be closed. At the beginning and end of each essay, Ed was required to record his anxiety level so that the therapist could monitor changes in his subjective discomfort. Over a period of 8 to 10 weeks, Ed's handwriting began to change. It was less of a struggle to get himself to write, and his handwriting became more legible.

The final aspect of behavioral treatment was concerned with his fear of axes. Ed and his therapist drew up a list of objects and situations related to axes, arranging them from those that were the least anxiety-provoking through those that were most frightening. They began with the least frightening. In their first exposure session, Ed agreed to meet with the psychologist while a relatively dull, wood-splitting maul was located in the adjoining room. Ed was initially quite anxious and distracted, but his anxiety diminished considerably before the end of their two-hour meeting. Once that had been accomplished, the therapist helped him to confront progressively more difficult situations. These sessions were challenging and uncomfortable for Ed, but they allowed him to master his fears in an orderly fashion. By the end of the twelfth session of exposure, he was able to hold a sharp ax without fear.

**EXPOSURE AND RESPONSE PREVENTION** The most effective form of psychological treatment for obsessive-compulsive disorder combines prolonged exposure to the situation that increases the person's anxiety with prevention of the person's typical compulsive response (Abramowitz, 2006; Franklin & Foa, 2002). Neither component is effective by itself. The combination of exposure and response prevention is necessary because of the way in which people with obsessive-compulsive disorder use their compulsive rituals to reduce anxiety that is typically stimulated by the sudden appearance of an obsession. If the compulsive behavior is performed, exposure is effectively cut short.

Consider, for example, the treatment program employed with Ed. His obsessive thoughts and images, which centered around violence, were associated with handwriting. They were likely to pop into his mind when he noticed letters that were poorly formed. In an effort to control these thoughts, Ed wrote very carefully, and he corrected any letter that seemed a bit irregular. By the time he entered behavior therapy, Ed had avoided writing altogether for several months. The therapist arranged for him to begin writing short essays on a daily basis to be sure that he was exposed, for at least 30 minutes each day, to the situation that was most anxiety-provoking. He encouraged Ed to deliberately write letters that did not conform to his compulsive style. In their sessions, for example, Ed was also required to write long sequences of the letter $T$ in which he deliberately failed to connect the two lines. He was not allowed to go back and correct this "mistake." The combination represents prolonged exposure to an anxiety-provoking stimulus and response prevention.

Controlled outcome studies indicate that this approach is effective with most OCD patients (Allen, 2006). After a few weeks of treatment with exposure and response prevention, most patients show improvements that are clinically important. On the other hand, some patients (perhaps as many as 20 percent) do not respond positively to this form of treatment and many continue to exhibit mild symptoms of the disorder after they have been successfully treated.

**BIOLOGICAL TREATMENTS** Medication is also beneficial for many patients with OCD. Selective serotonin reuptake inhibitors are used most frequently. Specific SSRIs used with OCD patients include fluoxetine (Prozac), fluvoxamine (Luvox), and sertraline (Zoloft). Controlled studies indicate that these drugs can be quite effective in the treatment of OCD (Dell'Osso et al., 2006). The SSRIs are often preferred to other forms of medication because they have fewer side effects.

Clomipramine (Anafranil), another tricyclic antidepressant, has been used extensively in treating obsessive-compulsive disorder. Several placebo-controlled studies have shown clomipramine to be effective in treating OCD (Abramowitz, 1997; Kozak, Liebowitz, & Foa, 2000). One study found that more than 50 percent of the patients who received clomipramine improved to a level of normal functioning over a period of 10 weeks, compared to only 5 percent of the patients in a placebo group (Katz, DeVeaugh-Geiss, & Landau, 1990). Patients who continue to take the drug maintain the improvement, but relapse is common if medication is discontinued.

## getting HELP

Most people suffering from anxiety disorders can be treated successfully. Several forms of intervention are beneficial, primarily behavior therapy, cognitive therapy, and medication. If you plan to work with a professional therapist, do some research before you begin working with a specific service provider. Read about treatments that have been evaluated empirically. One terrific source of information is a Web site on research-supported psychological treatments that is maintained by the Society of Clinical Psychology. The address is: www.psychologicaltreatment.org.

Some other excellent Internet sites may help you find the best therapist for you, hopefully someone who uses one of the procedures that has been shown to be effective. Patient-run organizations have established support groups in many communities and share information about treatment alternatives. One outstanding example is the Anxiety Disorders Association of America. The URL for its website is www.adaa.org. It includes a consumer's guide to treatment alternatives that is organized by specific types of anxiety disorders. More detailed information about obsessive-compulsive disorder and related problems can be obtained from the Obsessive Compulsive Foundation, a not-for-profit organization composed of people with OCD, their families, and professionals. Its Web address is www.ocfoundation.org.

Some people may be able to make improvements on their own with the advice of a useful self-help book. There are a lot of good alternatives to choose from in the area of anxiety disorders. We recommend two books that describe a combination of cognitive and behavioral approaches to treatment. *Triumph over Fear*, by Jerilyn Ross and Rosalynn Carter, describes the successful experiences of people who have recovered from various types of anxiety disorders, including phobias, panic disorder, and generalized anxiety disorder. Practical, self-help strategies are also summarized in *Overcoming Panic, Anxiety, and Phobias: New Strategies to Free Yourself from Worry and Fear*, written by Shirley Babior and Carol Goldman. This book includes simple instructions in progressive muscle relaxation, cognitive techniques to master anxiety, and exposure procedures for overcoming avoidance. Finally, more specific information about dealing with obsessive-compulsive disorder can be found in *Stop Obsessing: How to Overcome Your Obsessions and Compulsions*, by Edna Foa and Reid Wilson.

# 6 Summary

Anxiety disorders are defined in terms of a preoccupation with, or persistent avoidance of, thoughts or situations that provoke **fear** or anxiety. **Anxiety** involves a diffuse emotional reaction that is associated with the anticipation of future problems and is out of proportion to threats from the environment.

A **panic attack** is a sudden, overwhelming experience of terror or fright. Panic attacks are defined largely in terms of a list of somatic sensations, ranging from heart palpitations, sweating, and trembling to nausea, dizziness, and chills.

**Phobias** are persistent and irrational narrowly defined fears that are associated with avoidance of a specific object or situation. The most complex type of phobic disorder is **agoraphobia**, which is usually described as fear of public spaces.

*DSM-5* recognizes several specific subtypes of anxiety disorders: **panic disorder,** specific phobia, social anxiety, agoraphobia, and generalized anxiety disorder.

Anxiety disorders are the most common type of mental disorder. Specific phobias have a one-year prevalence of about 9 percent among adults, followed by social anxiety disorder (7 percent), generalized anxiety disorder (3 percent), and panic disorder (3 percent).

Severe life events, particularly those involving danger, insecurity, or family conflict, can lead to the development of anxiety symptoms. Various kinds of childhood adversity, including parental neglect and abuse, increase a person's risk for the later onset of an anxiety disorder.

The learning model explained the development of phobic disorders in terms of classical conditioning. A modified learning view, known as the **preparedness model,** is based on recognition that there are biological constraints in this process. We may be prepared to develop intense, persistent fears only to a select set of objects or situations.

Cognitive theorists have argued that panic disorder is caused by the catastrophic misinterpretation of bodily sensations or perceived threat.

People who are prone to excessive **worrying** are unusually sensitive to cues that signal the existence of future threats. The recognition of danger cues triggers a maladaptive, self-perpetuating cycle of cognitive processes that can quickly spin out of control.

Twin studies indicate that genetic factors are involved in the etiology of several types of anxiety disorders, including panic disorder, generalized anxiety disorder, and social anxiety disorder. The influence of environmental events seems to be greatest in specific phobias.

Studies of fear conditioning in animals have identified specific pathways in the brain that are responsible for detecting and organizing a response to danger. The amygdala plays a central role in these circuits. Several other areas of the brain are also associated with anxiety and the symptoms of anxiety disorders.

Serotonin, norepinephrine, GABA, and dopamine are some of the neurotransmitters that are involved in the production of panic attacks. Many interacting neurotransmitter systems play a role in the etiology of anxiety disorders, and they are largely the same ones that are also involved in major depression.

Several psychological approaches to the treatment of anxiety disorders have been shown to be effective. These include the use of exposure and flooding in the treatment of phobic disorders, prolonged exposure and response prevention in the treatment of obsessive-compulsive disorders, and cognitive therapy in the treatment of panic disorder and GAD. Various types of medication are also effective treatments for anxiety disorders.

**Obsessions** are repetitive, unwanted, intrusive cognitive events that may take the form of thoughts or images or urges. They intrude suddenly into consciousness and lead to an increase in subjective anxiety. **Compulsions** are repetitive behaviors that reduce the anxiety associated with obsessions.

## The Big Picture

# critical thinking review

**6.1** Why is a panic attack sometimes calleda "false alarm?"
Panic attacks resemble normal fear responses, but they are triggered at an inappropriate time (when the person is not confronted by an immediate source of danger) . . . (see page 147).

**6.2** What is the expected long-term outcome for people with anxiety disorders?
Some people recover, but they are most often chronic conditions . . . (see page 151).

**6.3** Is there a unique causal pathway for each type of anxiety disorder?
Probably not. Studies of environmental events, genetic factors, and neurobiological mechanisms suggest that pathways leading to different types of anxiety disorders overlap to a considerable extent . . . (see page 153).

**6.4** If phobias are learned quickly and easily, why are they so hard to extinguish?
Because their development is guided by a "prepared module," which is presumably efficient, highly selective, and operating outside conscious awareness . . . (see page 154).

**6.5** Do psychological treatments have any advantages over medication for treatment of anxiety?
Yes. Problems with medication include various side effects, the potential for addiction (benzodiazepines), and increased risk of relapse following their discontinuation . . . (see page 162).

**6.6** What is the difference between obsessions and normal intrusive thoughts?
Their content is similar (such as impulses to hurt other people). The differences hinge on duration, frequency, and the extent to which the person struggles against the obsessive thought . . . (see page 164).

**6.7** Why is response prevention coupled with exposure in the treatment of OCD?
If the therapist did not prevent compulsive behaviors, a patient with OCD would use them to reduce anxiety that is stimulated by exposure to the obsession and the process would not be effective . . . (see page 170).

# key terms

| | | | |
|---|---|---|---|
| **agoraphobia** 148 | **generalized anxiety disorder (GAD)** 150 | **panic disorder** 150 | **specific phobia** 148 |
| **anxiety** 146 | **obsessions** 163 | **phobias** 147 | **worry** 146 |
| **compulsions** 163 | **panic attack** 147 | **preparedness model** 154 | |
| **fear** 146 | | **social anxiety disorder** 148 | |

# Virtual Case Studies

**V**irtual Case Studies offers you a science-based, interactive simulation where you can learn how a number of risk factors and protective factors could impact disorder development in a virtual person. As you progress through the simulation you will not act as the character or as a clinician, but will be able to independently explore a variety of different behaviors, events, and outcomes that one who suffers from a disorder could potentially encounter. You can access the Virtual Case Study on *Anxiety Disorders* at mypsychlab.com.

acute and posttraumatic stress disorders, dissociative disorders, and somatic symptom disorders

7

# The Big Picture

## learning objectives

**7.1**
How does *DSM-5* define trauma?

**7.2**
Does trauma always lead to PTSD?

**7.3**
Can the unconscious mind cause mental disorders?

**7.4**
What are recovered memories?

**7.5**
Is multiple personality disorder real?

**7.6**
Were conversion disorders common in Freud's time?

A soldier experiences a flashback and prepares for combat—as a civilian at home. A young woman's personality transforms completely, almost as if an alien has taken control of her body. A middle-aged man claims his leg is paralyzed with weakness, yet neurological tests show normal strength. To the extent they can be believed, each example involves the dramatic transformation of stress or trauma into strange psychological symptoms. Such unusual problems defy ready explanation and raise profound questions about the nature and power of *unconscious mental processes*, information processing outside of conscious awareness. Can the unconscious mind really affect people in such mysterious ways?

## Overview

We repeatedly ask this question in this chapter in the context of discussing traumatic stress disorders, dissociative disorders, and somatic symptom disorders. These psychological problems look very different, but they share an important similarity: **dissociation**—the disruption of the normally integrated mental processes involved in memory, consciousness, identity, or perception. You should know from the outset that we are entering controversial territory in this chapter. Some psychologists view the unconscious mind as all-powerful. Others doubt its existence. We approach the topic with both skepticism and curiosity. Especially

given limited research, we are skeptical about problems that can be overdramatized. At the same time, we are captivated by unusual case studies that raise fascinating questions about their origin—and about how the mind works. We begin by considering the least controversial and most studied problem, traumatic stress disorders.

## Acute and Posttraumatic Stress Disorders

Stress is an inevitable, and in many ways a desirable, part of everyday life. Some stressors, however, are so catastrophic and horrifying that they can cause serious psychological harm. **Traumatic stress** is defined in *DSM-5* as an event that involves actual or threatened death, serious injury, or sexual violence to self, or witnessing others experience trauma, learning that loved ones have been traumatized, or repeatedly being exposed to details of trauma. Trauma includes rape, military combat, bombings, airplane crashes, earthquakes, major fires, and devastating automobile wrecks. In recent years, we know trauma all too well as a result of the September 11, 2001 terrorist attacks, sexual assaults, combat in Iraq and Afghanistan, and school shootings like the dreadful massacre at Sandy Hook Elementary School.

It is normal for survivors, witnesses, and loved ones to be greatly distressed by trauma. For some, however, the disturbance continues long after the trauma has ended. **Acute stress disorder (ASD)** occurs within a month after exposure to traumatic stress. **Posttraumatic stress disorder (PTSD)** lasts longer than one month and sometimes has a delayed onset. Although *DSM-5* describes them somewhat differently, both ASD and PTSD involve essentially the same symptoms: intrusive reexperiencing of the event, avoidance of reminders of the trauma, negative mood or thoughts, exaggerated arousal or reactivity, and often, dissociation. The following case study describes the enduring trauma of sexual assault.

An impromptu memorial for victims of the Sandy Hook School shootings.

## The Enduring Trauma of Sexual Assault

One spring evening, Stephanie Cason, a bright, attractive, and well-adjusted 27-year-old graduate student, ran outside to investigate a fire in another building in her apartment complex. While watching the firemen, Stephanie chatted with a man who she assumed was a neighbor. After talking with a few other people, she returned to her apartment. The fire had caused a power outage, but Stephanie found her way upstairs and changed into her nightclothes. When she came back downstairs, she was startled by the man she had met outside. Without saying a word, he raised a tire iron and struck Stephanie across the top of her head—repeatedly—until she fell to the floor and stopped screaming. Stephanie was cut deeply and stunned by the vicious blows, but she attempted to resist as the man began to grab at her breasts and rip at her clothes. He began to mutter obscenities and told Stephanie he wanted to have sex with her. Stephanie thought, "He's going to kill me."

Somehow Stephanie managed to think clearly despite the blood pouring from her head. She "agreed" to have sex with her assailant but told him that she needed to "freshen up" first. Eventually, he let her go to clean up. When Stephanie reached her bedroom, she shoved a bureau in front of the door and screamed frantically out the window for help. Her screams frightened her attacker, who tried to flee. But one of the firefighters tackled and captured him as he attempted to run away.

Stephanie saved herself from being raped, but she could not protect herself from the emotional fallout of her sexual assault. For days, eventually weeks and months, she felt intermittently terrified, dazed, and grateful to be alive. She replayed the horror of the evening in her mind repeatedly, and when she managed to fall asleep, she often was awakened by frightening nightmares. Stephanie was terrified to be alone, especially at night, but also at many times during the day. She relied on the unwavering support of her boyfriend and friends to stay nearby and help her cope.

Shortly after the assault, Stephanie sought help from a skilled clinical psychologist, but she fell into a depression despite the therapy. Antidepressant medication helped somewhat with her mood and lethargy, but for months she was hypervigilant—constantly on the lookout for new threats. She had difficulty concentrating and experienced intermittent feelings of numbness or unreality. In addition, she frequently reexperienced the images and emotions surrounding the dreaded event. She was able to resume her studies after about three months, and within six or eight months she was working fairly regularly but with considerably less confidence and concentration than before. As the anniversary of her assault approached, Stephanie grew increasingly upset. The spring weather, usually a welcome change, reminded her of the terror of the previous year. Her feelings of unreality returned. She had more flashbacks, reliving the dreaded night. The nightmares and fears of being alone reappeared. As the dreaded date passed, her reactions eased slowly. After about two or three months, she was able to resume her normal life—as normal as her life could be.

Stephanie found it painful but also helpful to talk about her assault with friends and, over time, more publicly. After the passing of the one-year anniversary, she actually began to lecture about her experiences to classes and to women's groups. Lecturing gave her some relief, and more importantly, it gave her a sense that some good might come from her trauma. Stephanie also testified at the trial of her assailant, who was convicted and sent to prison for 20 years. Although she appeared strong in the courtroom, the trial renewed many of Stephanie's symptoms. She again relived the terror of the assault, avoided being alone at night, and became fearful and hypervigilant about dangers in her world.

Once her assailant was imprisoned, Stephanie felt a degree of resolution. Still, she could not fully banish the demons. She again experienced intensely distressing episodes near the second and third anniversaries of the assault. Even at other times, Stephanie could unexpectedly fall victim to terror. For example, more than three years after the assault, her boyfriend (now her husband) silently entered her room after returning home unexpectedly one night. Frightened by his sudden appearance, Stephanie first screamed in terror, then sobbed in uncontrollable fear, and felt numb and unreal for several days afterwards.

Stephanie showed amazing bravery during her assault, throughout the trial, and in her public discussions of her trauma. But despite her strength, Stephanie could not prevent or control the recurrent terror of PTSD brought on by a violent sexual assault.

## Symptoms of ASD and PTSD

The essential difference between ASD and PTSD is duration. ASD lasts no longer than a month, while PTSD continues or sometimes begins at least a month after the trauma. The symptoms of ASD and PTSD are basically the same, even though *DSM-5* defines them somewhat differently (as you will see and perhaps be confused by). Both problems include (1) intrusive reexperiencing, (2) avoidance of reminders of the trauma, (3) increased arousal or reactivity, (4) negative mood or thoughts, and often (5) dissociation.

**INTRUSIVE REEXPERIENCING** Survivors often experience intrusive symptoms following trauma, symptoms sometimes called *reexperiencing*. Some people experience repeated, distressing memories of the incident. Others relive the trauma in horrifying dreams. Many people have repeated and intrusive **flashbacks**, sudden memories during which the trauma is replayed in images or thoughts—often at full emotional intensity. In rare cases, reexperiencing occurs as a *dissociative state*, where the person feels and acts as if the trauma actually were recurring in the moment. A combat veteran might act as if he were back in **battle**, and he may even take dangerous actions like gathering weapons or barricading himself in his residence. Typically, dissociative states are of short duration, but in unusual cases they can last for days.

Following trauma, many people have intrusive flashbacks, sudden memories during which the trauma is replayed in images and thoughts often at full emotional intensity.

**AVOIDANCE** Persistent avoidance of stimuli associated with the trauma is another symptom of ASD and PTSD. Trauma victims may attempt to avoid thoughts or feelings related to the event, or, like Stephanie, they may avoid people, places, or activities that remind them of the trauma. Avoidance also may include refusal to discuss the events or the feelings resulting from trauma. Avoidance of terrifying feelings makes complete sense, especially in the short run. Yet the road to longer term healing often involves facing feelings, memories, and perhaps some of the circumstances surrounding trauma.

**INCREASED AROUSAL OR REACTIVITY** People suffering from ASD and PTSD often experience increased arousal following the trauma, a symptom that, when it is more severe, predicts a worse prognosis (Schell, Marshall, Jaycox, 2004). Stephanie's hypervigilance in searching for danger is a classic example of hyperarousal, as was her *exaggerated startle response*, excessive fear in reaction to the unexpected. ASD and PTSD were previously classified as anxiety disorders because of the hyperarousal symptoms. However, *DSM-5* moved the disorders into a new category, in part, because heightened reactivity can take other forms. Instead of showing increased anxiety, some people become irritable and prone to angry outbursts. Others have trouble concentrating or sleeping.

**NEGATIVE MOOD OR THOUGHTS** People may experience a range of negative feelings in ASD and PTSD. These may include the inability to experience positive emotions, persistent fear, anger, or guilt, or feelings of detachment from others. In some cases, there is a general *numbing of responsiveness* or *emotional anesthesia*, a term that well captures the emotional dampening. Other people's negativity is more cognitive. They may blame themselves, repeatedly question what they might have done differently, or see the world in an unrealistically negative way.

**DISSOCIATIVE SYMPTOMS** Though not required for a diagnosis of either ASD or PTSD, dissociative symptoms are common following trauma. Many people feel dazed, and act "spaced out." Others experience *depersonalization*, feeling cut off from themselves or their environment. They might feel like "a robot," or as if they were sleepwalking. Others experience *derealization*, a marked sense of unreality. Immediately after 9/11, many people awoke wondering if the terrorist attacks had been only a nightmare—a sense of unreality that continued for days or longer. Some people experience *dissociative amnesia*—they are unable to remember aspects of the trauma events (Harvey, Bryant, & Dang, 1998).

### Diagnosis of ASD and PTSD

*DSM-5* no longer considers ASD and PTSD to be anxiety disorders (see Chapter 6) and instead created a new diagnostic grouping called *Trauma- and stressor-related disorders*. This new category includes *adjustment disorders*, difficulties coping with normal challenges in life, which we discuss in Chapter 17, and a few adjustment problems found among children. In essence, ASD and PTSD are now in their own diagnostic category.

**POSTTRAUMATIC STRESS DISORDER** Formally, the *DSM-5* diagnosis of PTSD requires only four of the symptoms we have discussed, while a subtype is defined by the presence of dissociative symptoms, depersonalization or derealization (see "DSM-5: Criteria for Posttraumatic Stress Disorder" on p. 178). This organization partially reflects controversy about the role of dissociation in PTSD. Some experts have suggested that ASD and PTSD really are dissociative disorders (van der Kolk & McFarlane, 1996). We do *not* view PTSD as a dissociative disorder, but discuss both problems in this chapter because they raise similar issues about unconscious mental processes. As you look through the *DSM-5* diagnostic criteria in "DSM-5: Posttraumatic Stress Disorder," note that dissociation is involved in many PTSD symptoms, not just the explicit dissociative symptoms.

Historically, maladaptive reactions to trauma have been of particular interest to the military, where "normal" performance is expected in the face of the trauma of combat. Military concern initially focused on battle dropout, that is, men who leave the field of action as a result of what has been called *shell shock* or *combat neurosis* (Jones, Thomas, & Ironside, 2007). During the Vietnam War, however, battle dropout was less frequent than in earlier wars, but delayed reactions to combat were much more common (Figley, 1978). This prompted much interest in PTSD, a condition first listed in the *DSM* in 1980. PTSD lasts longer than a month or emerges after that amount of time has passed following a trauma.

A. Exposure to actual or threatened death, serious injury, or sexual violence in one (or more) of the following ways:
   1. Directly experiencing the traumatic event(s).
   2. Witnessing, in person, the event(s) as it occurred to others.
   3. Learning that the traumatic event(s) occurred to a close family member or close friend. In cases of actual or threatened death of a family member or friend, the event(s) must have been violent or accidental.
   4. Experiencing repeated or extreme exposure to aversive details of the traumatic event(s) (e.g., first responders collecting human remains; police officers repeatedly exposed to details of child abuse).

   **Note:** Criterion A4 does not apply to exposure through electronic media, television, movies, or pictures, unless this exposure is work related.

B. Presence of one (or more) of the following intrusion symptoms associated with the traumatic event(s), beginning after the traumatic event(s) occurred:
   1. Recurrent, involuntary, and intrusive distressing memories of the traumatic event(s).

   **Note:** In children older than 6 years, repetitive play may occur in which themes or aspects of the traumatic event(s) are expressed.

   2. Recurrent distressing dreams in which the content and/or affect of the dream are related to the traumatic event(s).

   **Note:** In children, there may be frightening dreams without recognizable content.

   3. Dissociative reactions (e.g., flashbacks) in which the individual feels or acts as if the traumatic event(s) were recurring. (Such reactions may occur on a continuum, with the most extreme expression being a complete loss of awareness of present surroundings.)

   **Note:** In children, trauma-specific reenactment may occur in play.

   4. Intense or prolonged psychological distress at exposure to internal or external cues that symbolize or resemble an aspect of the traumatic event(s).
   5. Marked physiological reactions to internal or external cues that symbolize or resemble an aspect of the traumatic event(s).

C. Persistent avoidance of stimuli associated with the traumatic event(s), beginning after the traumatic event(s) occurred, as evidenced by one or both of the following:
   1. Avoidance of or efforts to avoid distressing memories, thoughts, or feelings about or closely associated with the traumatic event(s).

   2. Avoidance of or efforts to avoid external reminders (people, places, conversations, activities, objects, situations) that arouse distressing memories, thoughts, or feelings about or closely associated with the traumatic event(s).

D. Negative alterations in cognitions and mood associated with the traumatic event(s), beginning or worsening after the traumatic event(s) occurred, as evidenced by two (or more) of the following:
   1. Inability to remember an important aspect of the traumatic event(s) (typically due to dissociative amnesia and not to other factors such as head injury, alcohol, or drugs).
   2. Persistent and exaggerated negative beliefs or expectations about oneself, others, or the world (e.g., "I am bad," "No one can be trusted," "The world is completely dangerous," "My whole nervous system is permanently ruined").
   3. Persistent, distorted cognitions about the cause or consequences of the traumatic event(s) that lead the individual to blame himself/herself or others.
   4. Persistent negative emotional state (e.g., fear, horror, anger, guilt, or shame).
   5. Markedly diminished interest or participation in significant activities.
   6. Feelings of detachment or estrangement from others.
   7. Persistent inability to experience positive emotions (e.g., inability to experience happiness, satisfaction, or loving feelings).

E. Marked alterations in arousal and reactivity associated with the traumatic event(s), beginning or worsening after the traumatic event(s) occurred, as evidenced by two (or more) of the following:
   1. Irritable behavior and angry outbursts (with little or no provocation) typically expressed as verbal or physical aggression toward people or objects.
   2. Reckless or self-destructive behavior.
   3. Hypervigilance.
   4. Exaggerated startle response.
   5. Problems with concentration.
   6. Sleep disturbance (e.g., difficulty falling or staying asleep or restless sleep).

F. Duration of the disturbance (Criteria B, C, D, and E) is more than 1 month.

G. The disturbance causes clinically significant distress or impairment in social, occupational, or other important areas of functioning.

H. The disturbance is not attributable to the physiological effects of a substance (e.g., medication, alcohol) or another medical condition.

**A.** Exposure to actual or threatened death, serious injury, or sexual violation in one (or more) of the following ways:

1. Directly experiencing the traumatic event(s).
2. Witnessing, in person, the event(s) as it occurred to others.
3. Learning that the event(s) occurred to a close family member or close friend. **Note:** In cases of actual or threatened death of a family member or friend, the event(s) must have been violent or accidental.
4. Experiencing repeated or extreme exposure to aversive details of the traumatic event(s) (e.g., first responders collecting human remains, police officers repeatedly exposed to details of child abuse).

   **Note:** This does not apply to exposure through electronic media, television, movies, or pictures, unless this exposure is work related.

**B.** Presence of nine (or more) of the following symptoms from any of the five categories of intrusion, negative mood, dissociation, avoidance, and arousal, beginning or worsening after the traumatic event(s) occurred:

**Intrusion Symptoms**

1. Recurrent, involuntary, and intrusive distressing memories of the traumatic event(s). **Note:** In children, repetitive play may occur in which themes or aspects of the traumatic event(s) are expressed.
2. Recurrent distressing dreams in which the content and/or affect of the dream are related to the event(s). Note: In children, there may be frightening dreams without recognizable content.
3. Dissociative reactions (e.g., flashbacks) in which the individual feels or acts as if the traumatic event(s) were recurring. (Such reactions may occur in a continuum, with the most extreme expression being a complete loss of awareness of present surroundings.) **Note:** In children, trauma-specific reenactment may occur in play.
4. Intense or prolonged psychological distress or marked physiological reactions in response to internal or external cues that symbolize or resemble an aspect of the traumatic events(s).

**Negative Mood**

5. Persistent inability to experience positive emotions (e.g., inability to experience happiness, satisfaction, or loving feelings).

**Dissociative Symptoms**

6. An altered sense of the reality of one's surroundings or oneself (e.g., seeing oneself from another's perspective, being in a daze, time slowing).
7. Inability to remember an important aspect of the traumatic event(s) (typically due to dissociative amnesia and not to other factors such as head injury, alcohol, or drugs).

**Avoidance Symptoms**

8. Efforts to avoid distressing memories, thoughts, or feelings about or closely associated with the traumatic event(s).
9. Efforts to avoid external reminders (people, places, conversations, activities, objects, situations) that arouse distressing memories, thoughts, or feelings about or closely associated with the traumatic event(s).

**Arousal Symptoms**

10. Sleep disturbance (e.g., difficulty falling or staying asleep, restless sleep).
11. Irritable behavior and angry outbursts (with little or no provocation), typically expressed as verbal or physical aggression toward people or objects.
12. Hypervigilance.
13. Problems with concentration.
14. Exaggerated startle response.

**C.** Duration of the disturbance (symptoms in Criterion B) is 3 days to 1 month after trauma exposure.

   **Note:** Symptoms typically begin immediately after the trauma, but persistence for at least 3 days and up to a month is needed to meet disorder criteria.

**D.** The disturbance causes clinically significant distress or impairment in social, occupational, or other important areas of functioning.

**E.** The disturbance is not attributable to the physiological effects of a substance (e.g., medication or alcohol) or another medical condition (e.g., mild traumatic brain injury) and is not better explained by brief psychotic disorder.

**ACUTE STRESS DISORDER** Except that ASD lasts for less than a month, the diagnostic criteria for ASD and PTSD are the same conceptually. Frustratingly, however, the details of the *DSM-5* diagnostic criteria differ somewhat for ASD (see "DSM-5: Acute Stress Disorder"). We know of no good empirical or conceptual reason for this. The *DSM-5* does not explain why the required symptoms differ, why symptoms are expected to change a month and a day following trauma, or how many people who meet diagnostic criteria for the nine required symptoms of ASD also meet criteria for the six required symptoms of PTSD (see "DSM-5: Posttraumatic Stress Disorder" and "DSM-5: Acute Stress Disorder").

## The Trauma of Sexual Assault

Like many other traumas, sexual assault is all too common. Almost 10 percent of women report having been raped at least once in their lifetime, according to national surveys, and 12 percent report having been sexually molested (Kessler et al., 1995). Other evidence suggests a notably higher prevalence when the data include *acquaintance rapes*, assaults committed by people known to the victim (Goodman, Koss, & Russo, 1993).

Rape can be devastating physically, socially, and emotionally. Thirty-nine percent of rape victims are physically injured on parts of their bodies other than the genitals. A significant proportion of rape victims are infected with sexually transmitted diseases, and about 5 percent of rapes result in pregnancy (Goodman et al., 1993). Socially, sexual assault can undermine women's work, as well as their intimate relationships (Byrne et al., 1999).

Most victims of sexual assault show the symptoms of PTSD. Victims may reexperience the horrors of the assault; they may feel numbed in reacting to others, particularly sexual partners; they may avoid any potentially threatening situation; and they may maintain both autonomic hyperarousal and hypervigilance against possible victimization. Depression is also common. Sadness, crying, and withdrawal from others often are coupled with sleep and appetite disturbances. Loss of interest in sex, insecurities about sexual identity, sexual dysfunction, and negative feelings toward men also are common (Goodman et al., 1993).

Many victims of sexual assault also blame themselves. Women may wonder if they unwittingly encouraged their assailant or chastise themselves for not being more cautious in avoiding dangerous circumstances. This irrational self-blame is abetted by cultural myths that women provoke rape or actually enjoy it. *Secondary victimization* is a growing concern, as insensitive legal, medical, and even mental health professionals can add to a rape victim's emotional burden. In fact, victims of acquaintance rape show increased symptoms of PTSD when they encounter victim-blaming behaviors from professionals who are supposed to help them (Campbell, 2008). Such findings may help explain why as many as two-thirds of stranger rapes and four-fifths of acquaintance rapes are not reported to authorities.

---

These discrepancies are surprising as well as frustrating, because ASD was added to the DSM (in 1994) in the hope that early intervention would prevent the development of PTSD (Frances et al., 1995). In fact, the presence of ASD symptoms predicts PTSD better than the full diagnosis (Bryant et al., 2010). Interventions with ASD do reduce the number of expected cases of PTSD (Bryant et al., 2010).

Some experts wonder whether ASD really describes *normal* reactions to trauma and suggest that the reaction should not be called a mental disorder (Bryant et al., 2010). Many experts raise similar questions about PTSD, a diagnosis that may be handed out too easily, particularly to combat veterans returning from Iraq and Afghanistan. Many normal reactions to combat and to readjustment to civilian life are being called PTSD, in part because mental health resources and veterans' benefits are tied to the diagnosis (Dobbs, 2009).

**WHAT DEFINES TRAUMA** *DSM-5* defines trauma as an exposure to actual or threatened death, serious injury, or sexual violation either (1) directly, (2) as a witness, (3) learning of violence to a loved one, or (4) through repeated exposure to details of trauma. Sexual violation is a new part of the definition, reflecting both the frequency and the intensity of this trauma, especially for women. The definition of exposure also is more explicit. This is a result of controversy about whether PTSD can be caused by indirect exposure, such as seeing horrible scenes of 9/11 on television (Neria & Galea, 2007). Media exposure does not qualify as traumatic stress (Bryant et al., 2010). Secondary exposure is limited to learning about violence to a loved one, or repeated, extreme exposure, for example, first responders collecting human remains.

Any trauma is horrific, but different events have unique psychological consequences. Thus, researchers study both common and unique reactions to traumatic events including combat (Monson et al., 2006), terrorism (Hobfoll, Canetli-Nisim, & Johnson, 2006), child sexual abuse (McDonagh et al., 2005), spouse abuse (Taft et al., 2005), children's coping with residential fires (Jones & Ollendick, 2002), and torture (Basoglu et al., 1997). We discuss some unique aspects of sexual assault in The Trauma of Sexual Assault box.

One trauma of particular concern is exposure to disasters, which commonly involve large numbers of people. A random telephone survey of 1,008 residents living south of 110th Street in Manhattan on September 11, 2001, found that, regardless of whether they directly witnessed the World Trade Center (WTC) attacks, 7.5 percent—67,000 people—suffered from PTSD one month later (Galea et al., 2002). This obviously is a huge public health issue, yet there are reasons for optimism, too. Four months after the attacks, the prevalence of PTSD in the same area dropped to 1.7 and to 0.6 percent after six months (Galea et al., 2003). What protected the New Yorkers? We cannot know for certain, but key influences surely include the outpouring of support (McNally, Bryant, & Ehlers, 2003) and underestimated human resilience (Bonanno, Westphal, & Mancini, 2011).

Firefighters, police, and paramedics must remain calm during a disaster, but this does not make them immune to

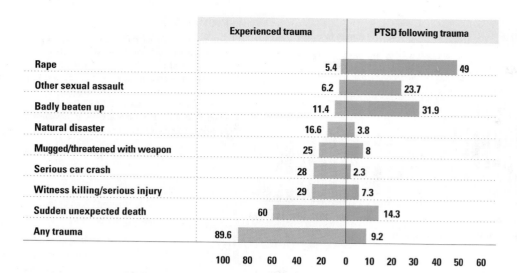

**FIGURE 7.1**

Bars to the left of center indicate the percentage of adults who had experienced each trauma among a representative sample of 2,181 adults aged 18 to 45 and living in the Detroit area. Bars to the right of center indicate the percentage of adults who developed PTSD after exposure to the particular trauma. *Note:* The prevalence of rape as reported in this study was lower than that reported in other studies. We assume that this statistic reflects only more violent rapes. *Source:* Based on data from "Traumatic and Posttraumatic Stress Disorder in the Community: The 1996 Detroit Area Survey of Trauma" by N. Breslau, R. C. Kessler, H. D. Chilcoat, L.R. Schultz, G. C. Davis, and P. Andreski, Archives of General Psychiatry, (1998), 55, pp. 626–632. Copyright © 1998. This material can be found at: http://archpsyc.ama-assn.org/cgi/content/abstract/55/7/626. Reprinted by permission of American Medical Association.

aftereffects. Five months after Hurricane Katrina in 2005, 22 percent of responding firefighters in New Orleans suffered from PTSD (CDC, 2006). In general, however, emergency workers are less than half as likely to develop PTSD as victims (Neria & Galea, 2007). Emergency workers are protected by their training, preparation, and sense of purpose. More generally, *hardiness*, a sense of commitment, control, and challenge in facing stress, predicts lower risk for PTSD (Sutker et al., 1995). Still, emergency workers need education about the psychological effects of trauma on *them*, opportunities to express troubling emotions, and, in some cases, specialized psychological help.

**COMORBIDITY** Many people with PTSD also suffer from another mental disorder, particularly depression, anxiety disorders, and substance abuse (Brady, Back, & Coffey, 2004). Other comorbid problems include disturbing nightmares, physical symptoms like headaches and gastrointestinal problems, grief, and relationship difficulties (Cook et al., 2004). Anger—at others or at oneself—had been noted as another prominent issue (Orth & Wieland, 2006), which is why negative thoughts and emotions became a part of the new *DSM-5* definition (Grant et al., 2008). Increased suicide risk also is notable. One study found that 33 percent of rape survivors had thoughts of suicide, and 13 percent actually made a suicide attempt (Kilpatrick, Edmunds, & Seymour, 1992).

## Frequency of Trauma, PTSD, and ASD

DSM once defined trauma as an event "outside the range of usual human experience." Unfortunately, it is not. A random sample of 2,181 adults living in the Detroit area found that almost 90 percent had experienced at least one trauma in their lifetime. About 9 percent developed PTSD (Breslau et al., 1998; see Figure 7.1). A national study found that 6.8 percent of the people in the United States suffered from PTSD at some point (Kessler et al., 2005). Similar rates of trauma and PTSD also are found in Mexico (Norris et al., 2003). Rape and assault clearly are among

the very worst traumas, and they pose an especially high risk for PTSD (see Figure 7.1).

Women are more likely than men to develop PTSD following trauma (Tolin & Foa, 2006). Sexual violence is a particular risk for women, while combat exposure is for men (Kessler et al., 1995; Prigerson, Maciejewski, & Rosenbeck, 2002). Children are especially vulnerable to trauma, with 20 to 40 percent developing PTSD (Neria & Galea, 2007). Minority group members are more likely to experience PTSD, in large part because of their more difficult living conditions (Pole, Gone, & Kulkarni, 2008). PTSD also is common among crime victims (Kilpatrick & Acierno, 2003).

**TRAUMA IS NOT RANDOM** Whether people get caught in events like the Virginia Tech shootings is a matter of luck. Many traumas, however, do not occur at random. Because they engage in more risky behavior, men, young people, those with a history of conduct disorders, and extroverts all are more likely to experience trauma. People who are anxious or who have a family history of mental illness also experience more trauma, but the reasons why are less clear.

The development of PTSD following a trauma also is not random. Those who are anxious and easily upset are more likely to develop PTSD after a trauma, as are people with a family or personal history of mental disorder (Breslau et al., 1998). In fact, a recent prospective study found that over 90 percent of those who developed PTSD following trauma exposure met criteria for some other diagnosis earlier in their life (Koenen et al., 2008). People who developed PTSD following an earlier trauma also are at greater risk following a second trauma (Breslau, Peterson, & Schultz, 2008). Despite the risks, *resilience*, successful psychological coping, is the most common human response to trauma (Bonanno et al., 2011).

**COURSE AND OUTCOME** People who suffer from ASD symptoms are more likely to develop PTSD (Bryant et al., 2010). Three symptoms—numbing, depersonalization, and a sense of reliving the experience—are the best predictors of future PTSD (Bryant & Harvey, 2000).

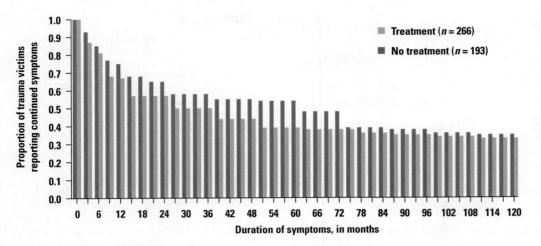

**FIGURE 7.2**

The symptoms of PTSD decline over time but persist for 10 years among one-third of people. Treatment appears to hasten recovery, but this correlational finding may not mean causation.

*Source:* Based on Kessler et al. 1995. Posttraumatic Stress Disorder in the National Comorbidity Survey. Archives of General Psychiatry; 52: 1057.

The symptoms of PTSD generally diminish with time. Symptoms improve fairly rapidly during the first year, but more gradually thereafter (see Figure 7.2). Symptoms diminish faster among people who receive treatment. Despite improvements, over one-third of people still report symptoms 10 years after the trauma, regardless of whether they were treated (Kessler et al., 1995).

PTSD can persist even longer. One study found symptoms among World War II prisoners of war—*40 years* after confinement. Only 30 percent of POWs who had suffered from PTSD were fully recovered; 10 percent either showed no recovery or had a deteriorating course (Kluznik et al., 1986). Many victims of the Holocaust also show PTSD symptoms decades later. Still, even following exposure to the unbelievable horrors of the Holocaust, remarkable resilience is the most common outcome (Barel et al., 2010).

## Causes of PTSD and ASD

By definition, trauma causes ASD and PTSD. Because not every traumatized person develops a disorder, however, trauma is a necessary but not a sufficient cause. What increases risk or resilience in the face of trauma?

## MyPsychLab VIDEO CASE

### Posttraumatic Stress Disorder

BONNIE

*"I basically resigned myself to the fact that I was going to die."*

👁 **Watch** the **Video** *Bonnie: Posttraumatic Stress Disorder (PTSD)* on **MyPsychLab**

As you watch the video, consider the terrible events Bonnie witnessed on 9/11. Her PTSD symptoms make sense. What treatments might help her recover?

**SOCIAL FACTORS** Research on social factors and the risk for PTSD focuses primarily on (1) the nature of the trauma and the individual's level of exposure to it and (2) the availability of social support following the trauma. Victims of trauma are more likely to develop PTSD when the trauma is more intense, life-threatening, and involves greater exposure (Neria & Galea, 2007). For example, victims of attempted rape are more likely to develop PTSD if the rape is completed, if they are physically injured during the assault, and if they perceive the sexual assault as life-threatening (Kilpatrick et al., 1989). Similarly, PTSD is more prevalent in Vietnam veterans who were wounded, who were involved in the deaths of noncombatants, or who witnessed atrocities (Koenen et al., 2003; Oei, Lim, & Hennessy, 1990). A study of PTSD following September 11 terror attack found a greater prevalence among people who lived south of Canal Street, close to the World Trade Center (Galea et al., 2002).

As with less severe stressors, social support after a trauma can play a crucial role in alleviating long-term psychological damage. A lack of social support is thought to have contributed to the high prevalence of PTSD found among Vietnam veterans (Oei et al., 1990). Rather than being praised as heroes, returning veterans often were treated with disdain. This made it difficult for many veterans to find meaning in their sacrifices and likely increased their risk for PTSD. People who had little social support also were more likely to develop PTSD following September 11 (Galea et al., 2002).

A study of identical twins strongly supports the role of the environment in PTSD. Among 715 monozygotic (MZ) twin pairs who were discordant for military service in Southeast Asia during the Vietnam War era, the prevalence of PTSD was *nine times* higher for co-twins who served in Vietnam and experienced high levels of combat in comparison to their identical twins who did not serve (Goldberg et al., 1990).

**BIOLOGICAL FACTORS** The same twin study also strongly points to biological factors in PTSD. In an analysis of more than 4,000 twin pairs, MZ twins had a higher concordance rate for exposure to combat than dizygotic (DZ) twins. Following exposure, identical twins also had higher concordance rates

Police and participants react to the Boston Marathon bomb explosion. The *DSM-5* defines trauma as an event that involves actual or threatened death, serious injury, or sexual violence to self, or witnessing others experience trauma, learning that loved ones have been traumatized, or repeatedly being exposed to details of trauma.

for PTSD symptoms than fraternal twins (True et al., 1993). Importantly, genetic contributions differed across symptoms. Genes contributed most strongly to arousal symptoms and least strongly to reexperiencing. Conversely, level of combat exposure predicted reexperiencing and avoidance but not arousal (True et al., 1993).

Does exposure to trauma have biological consequences as well as biological causes? People with PTSD show differences in the functioning, and perhaps the structure, of the amygdala and hippocampus. These findings are consistent with the experience of heightened fear reactivity and intrusive memories (Kolassa & Elbert, 2007). Other evidence links PTSD with general psychophysiological arousal, for example, an increased resting heart rate (Pole, 2007). This suggests that the sympathetic nervous system is aroused and the fear response is sensitized in PTSD.

Does this mean that trauma damages the brain? A study of identical twins—one Vietnam veteran with PTSD and his co-twin who neither served in Vietnam nor suffered from PTSD—found smaller than average hippocampus volume in *both* twins (Gilbertson et al., 2002). Twin research shows that preexisting differences account for IQ deficits that have been mistakenly attributed to brain damage due to trauma (Gilbertson et al., 2006). Differences between people with and without PTSD are *correlations*—correlations apparently due to preexisting differences, not due to brain damage caused by trauma.

**PSYCHOLOGICAL FACTORS** Some theories suggested that dissociation is an unconscious defense that helps victims to cope with trauma (Oei et al., 1990). However, dissociation predicts more, not less PTSD (Ehlers, Mayou, & Bryant, 1998; Griffin, Resick, & Mechanic, 1997; Harvey et al., 1998). Among a sample of Israeli war trauma victims, for example, more dissociation reported within one week following trauma predicted *more* severe PTSD six months later (Shalev et al., 1996).

Preparedness, purpose, and the absence of blame can aid coping with trauma. Pilots cope more successfully with helicopter crashes if they have training than if they have none, underscoring the importance of preparedness and control (Shalev, 1996). The value of purpose is supported by evidence that, despite greater physical suffering, political activists develop fewer psychological symptoms than non-activists following torture (Basoglu et al., 1997). On the other hand, negative appraisals—the rape victim who blames herself, or the driver who thinks he could have avoided an accident—are strongly tied to an increased risk for PTSD (Bonanno et al., 2011; Bryant & Guthrie, 2005; Halligan et al., 2003; McNally et al., 2003).

Over time, victims of trauma must find a balance between gradually facing their painful emotions while not being overwhelmed by them. New York City college students had lower rates of PTSD following the September 11 terrorist attack if they were better at enhancing *and* suppressing emotional expression (Bonanno et al., 2004). This illustrates what psychologist Edna Foa, a leading PTSD researcher, calls *emotional processing*, which involves three key steps. First, victims must engage emotionally with their traumatic memories. Second, victims need to find a way to articulate and organize their chaotic experience. Third, victims must come to believe that, despite the trauma, the world is not a terrible place (Cahill & Foa, 2007; Foa & Street, 2001).

This last step is similar to what other psychologists call *meaning making*—eventually finding some value or reason for having endured trauma (Ehlers & Clark, 2000). Meaning making is very personal and may involve religion, a renewed appreciation for life, or public service. Importantly, the *search* for meaning is associated with *more* PTSD symptoms, whereas *finding* meaning is linked to better adjustment (Park, 2010). Stephanie found meaning in her efforts to make others more aware of sexual assault.

In the long run, many people actually report that trauma leads to growth (Tedeschi & McNally, 2011). *Posttraumatic growth*, positive changes resulting from trauma, is linked with less depression and more positive well-being, but also with more intrusive and avoidant thoughts (Helgeson, Reynolds, & Tomich, 2006). Finding meaning in trauma does not mean forgetting about it.

**INTEGRATION AND ALTERNATIVE PATHWAYS** There are multiple pathways to developing ASD and PTSD. Anyone might develop ASD or PTSD if exposed to a trauma of sufficient intensity. In other cases, trauma exacerbates or reveals a preexisting disorder. In most cases, ASD and PTSD develop as a result of a combination of factors, including trauma, personality characteristics that predate the trauma, exposure during the trauma, and emotional processing and social support afterwards (Ozer et al., 2003; Ozer & Weiss, 2004). We note again, however, that resilience is the most common outcome following trauma exposure (Bonanno et al., 2011).

## Prevention and Treatment of ASD and PTSD

We know that trauma precedes ASD and PTSD. This leads to a very important question: Can we prevent the disorders with early intervention?

**EMERGENCY HELP FOR TRAUMA VICTIMS** Many experts hope that prevention is possible. In fact, the U.S. Federal Emergency Management Agency (FEMA) provides special funding to community mental health centers during disasters. Emergency treatments range from intensive individual counseling sessions with hurricane victims to group discussions with children following school violence (Litz, 2004). Approaches differ greatly, but offering immediate support to trauma victims is a common goal (McNally et al., 2003; Raphael et al., 1996).

Perhaps the most widely used early intervention is *critical incident stress debriefing (CISD)*, a single one- to five-hour group meeting offered one to three days following a disaster. CISD involves several phases where participants share their experiences and reactions, and group leaders offer education, assessment, and referral if necessary (Mitchell, 1982; Mitchell & Dyregrov, 1993).

CISD is difficult to evaluate, since it is conducted in the midst of a crisis (Tuckey, 2007). Still, research provides *no* evidence that CISD prevents future PTSD (Bryant & Harvey, 2000; McNally et al., 2003), and some studies find that CISD is actually harmful (Lilienfeld, 2007). CISD may provoke too much emotion too soon after trauma. Another problem is the CISD is unnatural. It is not offered by people who are a part of the victims' world. CISD generally is provided by outsiders to groups of individuals who have no relationship to one another.

More naturalistic interventions show more promise. Since World War I, interventions with soldiers who drop out of combat have been based on the three principles of offering: (1) immediate treatment in the (2) proximity of the battlefield with the (3) expectation of return to the front lines upon recovery (Jones et al., 2007). The effectiveness of these principles was not studied systematically until a 1982 evaluation of the Israeli army during

Students gather for a vigil following the Virginia Tech shootings. For many, shared grief and support eases the pain of trauma and reduces the risk for PTSD.

the Lebanon war. Results indicated that 60 percent of soldiers treated near the front recovered sufficiently to return to battle within 72 hours. Soldiers who expected to return to the front experienced lower rates of PTSD than did those who did not. Soldiers who were treated on the front lines also were less likely to develop PTSD subsequently compared to soldiers who were treated away from the battlefield (Oei et al., 1990).

Former Mayor Rudolph Giuliani intuitively followed similar principles when, in the immediate aftermath of September 11, he regularly encouraged New Yorkers to grieve but also to go back to work, to go out, and to go on despite the horrors of the World Trade Center attacks. Such community-based efforts are more appealing, and perhaps more effective, than artificial debriefings. Consider this: Government agencies allocated over $150 million to pay for psychotherapy for New Yorkers in the wake of September 11, but $90 million remained unspent two years later (McNally et al., 2003).

A study of veterans returning from a year-long deployment in Iraq shows the promise of more naturalistic interventions in preventing PTSD symptoms (Adler et al., 2009). Soldiers were randomly assigned to (1) the army's "treatment as usual," stress education in groups of about 100, (2) battlemind debriefing, discussions in groups of 20 to 32 that included some review of combat experiences but focused on the transition home and building peer support, and (3) battlemind training, focused on finding inner strength in combat, teaching skills to help unit members, and reframing redeployment difficulties as normal problems that require adapting occupational coping skills. Battlemind training was offered both in small (18 to 45 individuals) and large (126 to 225 individuals) groups to control for the potential confound of group size. As portrayed in Figure 7.3, all three experimental

conditions produced a significant reduction on the PTSD Checklist (PCL), but only among soldiers exposed to a large number of combat events (Adler et al., 2009).

**COGNITIVE BEHAVIOR THERAPY FOR PTSD** While great sensitivity is required, the most effective treatment for PTSD is therapeutic reexposure to trauma (Foa, Gillihan, & Bryant, 2013). One of the first studies of *prolonged exposure* asked rape victims to relive the trauma repeatedly over nine therapy sessions. While surely painful, exposure reduced PTSD symptoms more, over the long term, than three randomized alternatives, including relaxation/stress management, supportive counseling, and a wait list control group (Foa et al., 1991). Among other trauma, prolonged exposure has now been successfully used for PTSD following combat (Monson et al., 2006), childhood sex abuse (McDonagh et al., 2005), and assault (Foa et al., 2005).

Depending on the client, the therapist, and the circumstances of the trauma, prolonged exposure might involve confronting feared situations in real life, in one's imagination, or by recounting events in therapy (Foa et al., 2013). One treatment, *imagery rehearsal therapy*, successfully reduces recurrent nightmares, a troubling problem frequently associated with PTSD. The exposure involves reliving nightmares while awake, but rewriting the nightmare script in any way the client wishes (Krakow et al., 2001).

Across studies, approximately 50 percent of patients still meet diagnostic criteria after treatment with prolonged exposure (Resick et al., 2007), as do about 20 percent at 5- to 10-year follow-up (Resnick et al., 2013). Prolonged exposure is the most strongly supported treatment for PTSD (Foa et al., 2013), but perhaps treatment is the beginning, not the end, of the healing

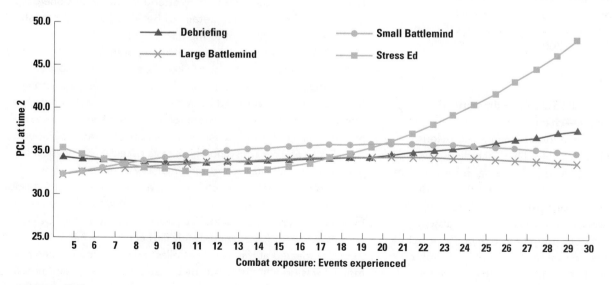

## FIGURE 7.3

**PTSD Symptoms among Soldiers Returning from Iraq: Effects of Four Prevention Programs** Battlemind debriefing and battlemind training (in small and large groups) significantly reduced symptoms measured on the PTSD Checklist (PCL) when compared to stress education, but only among soldiers exposed to high levels of combat. These results support the benefits of more naturalistic prevention efforts directed toward groups most at risk.

*Source:* A. B. Adler, et al., "Battlemind debriefing and battlemind training as early interventions with soldiers returning from Iraq: Randomized by platoon." Journal of Consulting and Clinical Psychology, 77, 937. Copyright © 2009, American Psychological Association.

process. Meaning making is ultimately a reframing and reinterpretation of the experience of trauma. Perhaps this is more than what can be expected from any therapy.

**EMDR** One treatment for PTSD, *eye movement desensitization and reprocessing (EMDR)*, is a technique that has been greeted with considerable enthusiasm—and skepticism. Psychologist Francine Shapiro (1995) "discovered" that rapid back-and-forth eye movements reduced her own anxiety, so she tried the technique on her clients, who appeared to benefit from it. Why should this work? No one has a good theory why, which is the heart of the controversy (Keane, Marshall, & Taft, 2006). Still, Shapiro and other proponents use EMDR as a relaxation technique, while clients with PTSD simultaneously relive vivid images of trauma. A recent meta-analysis concluded that EMDR may be effective (Bisson et al., 2007); however, prolonged exposure, not eye movements, appears to be the "active ingredient" (Foa et al., 2013).

**TREATMENT OF ASD** Research shows that structured interventions with ASD can lead to the prevention of future PTSD (Bryant et al., 2010). Unlike CISD, these treatments last longer and target the select group of trauma victims who meet ASD diagnostic criteria. The evidence based ASD treatments use principles of cognitive behavior therapy, although they are briefer, typically involving five 90-minute sessions (Bryant et al., 2006; Bryant, Moulds, & Nixon, 2003).

**ANTIDEPRESSANT MEDICATION** Numerous practice guidelines recommend antidepressants (SSRIs) as a treatment for PTSD (Friedman & Davidson, 2007). The effectiveness of SSRIs is likely at least partially due to the high comorbidity between PTSD and depression (Newport & Nemeroff, 2000). While antidepressants are helpful, only about 30 percent of treated patients recover fully from PTSD symptoms (Friedman, Resick, & Keane, 2007). Traditional antianxiety medications are *not* effective for PTSD (Golier, Legge, & Yehuda, 2007).

## Dissociative Disorders

While dissociation in ASD and PTSD can be dramatic, the symptoms of **dissociative disorders**—characterized by persistent, maladaptive disruptions in the integration of memory, consciousness, or identity—verge on the unbelievable. They include psychologically produced amnesia, confused travel of long distances from home (perhaps under a new identity), and the existence of two or more separate personalities in one person. Are these symptoms real? The answer is controversial. Some experts think dissociative disorders are phony, examples of nothing more than the power of suggestion. Others view them as real but rare problems. Still others believe dissociative disorders are misunderstood, overlooked, and prevalent. This controversy is about much more than dissociative disorders. It concerns the very nature of the human psyche.

Dissociative disorders sometimes are of more interest to novelists than to scientists. You may be familiar with dramatic portrayals of *multiple personality disorder*, an old name for a dissociative disorder, in *Sybil*[1] or *The Three Faces of Eve*, both of which were widely read books that became popular motion pictures. In recent years, psychological scientists have grown more interested in unconscious mental processes (Bargh & Morsella, 2008). Partially as a result, interest in dissociative disorders also has grown—without resolving basic controversies. We introduce these problems, and the debate, in the following case study.

### ⟶ Dissociative Fugue—Dallae's Journey

Dallae disappeared mysteriously in the middle of final exams during her junior year at a California university. Her roommate last saw her studying for her organic chemistry exam. Dallae had been agitated that night. She kept bothering her roommate, who was cramming for the same exam, and left her room repeatedly. Dallae did not take the exam the next day. When she missed two more finals, her roommate contacted the authorities.

At first, the police suspected foul play, because it seemed unlikely that Dallae would leave college on her own. None of her personal possessions was missing; even her eyeglasses were still sitting on her desk. However, bank records indicated that Dallae withdrew all of her money from her bank account the day before the exam. Investigators also discovered that Dallae had told her parents that she had an A in organic chemistry. In fact, she was failing the course.

When the local police failed to locate Dallae, they contacted the FBI. After a four-week investigation, they found Dallae in a college town on the East Coast. She had been brought to a hospital emergency room after she was found wandering the streets. She appeared confused and disoriented. She told the emergency room (ER) physician that her name was Dawn and that she had been living on the streets and sleeping in dormitory lounges. She said that she had just moved from the West Coast and had come to the town because she hoped to attend the university. She gave a vague account of other details of her life. For example, she could not say how she got to the East Coast.

Dallae allowed herself to be voluntarily admitted to the hospital's psychiatric unit. There she talked little and spent most of her time watching television. She told the staff that she was Vietnamese and had been adopted by American parents, but her stories remained vague and inconsistent. She said that she could not remember many things, but she was not upset by her impairment. A CAT scan and neuropsychological tests detected no physical abnormalities or deficits in short-term memory or motor functioning.

A hospital social worker contacted the local police about the disoriented young patient, and the police were able to identify Dallae from a missing persons report. The social worker contacted Dallae's parents, and her mother immediately flew east to see her. When her mother appeared at the hospital, Dallae did not recognize her. Her mother was greatly distressed by Dallae's indifference and noted other oddities and inconsistencies. For one thing, Dallae was not Vietnamese, and she was not adopted. She had grown up with her married parents, who were Korean immigrants. Her mother also noted

---

[1]A review of tapes of a few of Sybil's sessions concluded that her "alters" were implanted by her therapist. Sybil reportedly confessed that she created her alters to please her therapist (Rieber, 2006).

that although Dallae was right-handed, she used her left hand to write a note at the hospital. Dallae's consistent use of her left hand was confirmed by the staff and by the neuropsychologist who had tested her.

Two nights after her mother arrived, Dallae's memories apparently returned. That night, she attempted suicide by slashing her wrists, but she was discovered by a hospital staff member, who quickly stopped the bleeding. Dallae was intermittently depressed and extremely agitated for the next several days, especially after seeing her mother. Although she would not talk at length, her conversation indicated that much of her memory was now intact, and she began using her right hand again.

During the next two weeks, Dallae gradually related details about her life to the psychologist who was treating her. Dallae had been a quiet and obedient girl all through her childhood. Her parents worked very hard and had high ambitions for their three children. Dallae's older brother had an M.B.A. and was a successful young executive. Her older sister currently was editor of the law review at a prestigious law school. Throughout her life, her parents had told friends and relatives that Dallae would be a doctor one day.

During discussions with her therapist, Dallae began to talk more freely. She noted that she had been terrified to tell her parents, especially her father, about her grades and her lack of interest in medicine. She cried at length when relating how he had struck her across the face during the previous Thanksgiving break, when she tried to tell him that she no longer wanted to study medicine.

After six weeks in the hospital, Dallae returned to California with her parents. Her memory was intact at the time of the discharge, except that she continued to have no recollection of her trip across the country or many of her days living on the streets. She was uncertain why she thought her name was Dawn. She did mention being vaguely influenced by a television show about a Vietnamese child who had been adopted. At the time of Dallae's discharge, her depression had abated, and she was no longer actively suicidal. She reported being relieved at having told her mother about her feelings about medical school, but she remained very anxious about facing her father.

..........

Dallae suffered from *dissociative fugue*, which is characterized by sudden, unplanned travel, the inability to remember details about the past, and confusion about identity or the assumption of a new identity. The travel is purposeful. Despite her confusion and memory impairments, Dallae knew where she was going and provided at least a vague explanation about why. Dissociative fugue typically follows a traumatic event. It perhaps is most commonly observed among soldiers following a particularly gruesome battle.

Purposeful travel is the distinguishing symptom, but the core questions about fugue—and about all dissociative disorders—concern the split between conscious and unconscious psychological experience. How could Dallae be aware of the present but be unaware of her past? Why didn't all her memories return after she saw her mother? Could she be faking part or all of her "illness"? Key figures in the history of abnormal psychology have tried to answer such perplexing questions.

## Hysteria and the Unconscious

Historically, dissociative disorders (and some somatic symptom disorders, which we discuss shortly) were viewed as forms of hysteria. In Greek, *hystera* means "uterus," and the term **hysteria** reflects the ancient view that frustrated sexual desires, particularly a woman's desire to have a baby, cause the unusual symptoms. Ancient beliefs held that the uterus detached and moved about the body, causing a problem wherever it eventually lodged. This strange belief lived well into the late nineteenth century, when many experts argued that hysteria occurred only among women (Showalter, 1997).

**CHARCOT, FREUD, AND JANET** In the latter half of the nineteenth century, French neurologist Jean-Martin Charcot used hypnosis both to induce and treat hysteria. Charcot greatly influenced Sigmund Freud, who observed Charcot's hypnotic treatments early in his training. Charcot also strongly influenced Freud's contemporary and rival, Pierre Janet (1859–1947). Janet was a French philosophy professor who conducted psychological experiments on dissociation and who later trained as a physician in Charcot's clinic.

Both Janet and Freud were eager to explain hysteria, and both developed theories of unconscious mental processes to do so. Their theories differed sharply, however. Janet saw dissociation as an abnormal process. To him, detachment from conscious awareness occurred only as a part of psychopathology. In contrast, Freud considered dissociation to be normal, a routine means for the ego to defend itself against unacceptable unconscious thoughts. Freud saw dissociation and repression similarly. In fact, he often used the two terms interchangeably (Erdelyi, 1990). Thus, Freud viewed hysteria merely as one expression of unconscious conflict.

The two theorists criticized each other frequently. Janet thought that Freud greatly overstated the importance of the unconscious; Freud thought that Janet greatly underestimated it. However, Janet's work became increasingly obscure over time, as Freudian theory dominated throughout much of the twentieth century. As Freudian influences have declined, scholars have rediscovered Janet's contributions and his more narrow conception of dissociation and unconscious mental processes.

The French neurologist Jean Charcot (1825–1893) demonstrating a case of hysteria at the Salpêtrière, a famous hospital in Paris.

# CRITICAL THINKING matters

## Recovered Memories?

In 1990, George Franklin was convicted of the brutal murder of an eight-year-old girl. The crime occurred over 20 years earlier. The major evidence was the "recovered memory" of Franklin's daughter Eileen. Eileen claimed she had witnessed her father commit a rape and murder, but dissociation pushed the memory into her unconscious mind. Twenty years later, according to the daughter, the memory returned.

Eileen provided both verifiable and inconsistent accounts of the horrifying event. She recalled a smashed ring on her friend's finger as she raised her hand to protect herself from a blow with a rock. Records corroborated the incident. On the other hand, Eileen changed her story about the time of day and whether her sister also was with them. Based solely on his daughter's testimony, George Franklin was convicted. However, his conviction was overturned in 1995, and he was released from prison. A U.S. District Court judge ruled that the lower court erred in excluding evidence that Eileen could have learned details of the 1969 murder from newspaper articles. The prosecutor decided not to retry the case when Eileen's sister revealed they both were hypnotized before the first trial—a fact Eileen lied about. Eileen also had accused her father of a second murder, but DNA evidence cleared him.

Was Eileen's memory fact or fiction? Our concern about so-called recovered memories extends well beyond the Franklin case. In the 1990s, as many as 25 percent of therapists said that recovering memories, particularly of sexual abuse, was an important part of their therapy with female clients (Poole et al., 1995). Popular books also have encouraged people to search for (create?) memories. For example, in *The Courage to Heal*, the authors stated:

Where were you when the World Trade Center towers collapsed? Researchers find that even powerful "flashbulb" memories of dramatic events often grow inaccurate over time.

To say "I was abused," you don't need the kind of recall that would stand up in a court of law. . . . Often the knowledge that you were abused starts with a tiny feeling, an intuition. It's important to trust that inner voice and work from there. Assume your feelings are valid. So far, no one we've talked to thought she might have been abused and then later discovered that she hadn't been. (Bass & Davis, 1988, p. 22)

Could such suggestions lead some people to create memories about events that never happened? Faced with accusations of past abuse, many parents say that misguided therapists have created false memories. In fact, the term, *false memory syndrome*, was coined to account for the implanting of false beliefs (Kihlstrom, 1998a).

Research shows that memories, even of highly dramatic events, can be inaccurate (Loftus, 2003, 2004). In one study, researchers interviewed people the day after the space shuttle Challenger exploded and detailed how participants learned of the tragedy. Three years later, they asked the same people to remember what they were doing. About one-third reported vivid and grossly inaccurate memories (Neisser & Harsch, 1992). In another study, researchers created false memories of "sliming" a first- or second-grade teacher (putting slime in the teacher's desk)—among 65 percent of the participants! The key to the deception was using actual school photos to help participants to "remember" (Lindsay et al., 2004). Such research does not prove that recovered memories of trauma are false (Gleaves et al., 2004). In fact, recent experimental research shows that laboratory-induced interference and subsequent cuing can produce forgetting and remembering, respectively (Smith & Moynan, 2008). Still, the malleability of memory suggests many reasons for skepticism.

There certainly are good reasons to question the validity of "recovered memories" from early in life, since few people can report *any* accurate memories before age three or four (Loftus, 2003, 2004). The fact that people are especially likely to remember emotionally intense events is another reason to think critically about claims of recovered memories. Some documented victims of sexual abuse do not recall the experience many years later (Williams, 1994), but most do remember what happened (Goodman et al., 2003). And, of course, documented cases of forgetting do not prove that undocumented cases of remembering are accurate.

Are some claims of recovered memories more accurate than others? A recent study found that memories that returned outside of therapy were more likely to be corroborated than memories "recovered" in therapy (Geraerts et al., 2007). Sadly, some patients with recovered memories apparently are victims of their therapists, not of abuse.

Hypnotized college students reacting to the suggestion that they are on a beach in Hawaii. Performance hypnotists produce such dramatic effects by selecting only highly suggestible subjects for their demonstrations.

**HYPNOSIS: ALTERED STATE OR SOCIAL ROLE?** A topic of historical importance and contemporary debate about the unconscious mind is the nature of **hypnosis**, in which subjects experience loss of control over their actions in response to suggestions from the hypnotist. All agree that demonstrations of the power of hypnotic suggestion are impressive, and that different people are more or less susceptible to hypnosis. However, some experts assert that hypnosis is a dissociative experience, an altered state of consciousness. Others argue that hypnosis is merely a social role, a subject voluntarily complying with suggestions due to social expectations (Barnier, 2002; Kihlstrom, 1998b; Kirsch & Lynn, 1998; Woody & Sadler, 1998). Beware of concluding that hypnosis must be real and powerful because you have seen it at work in a group demonstration. Hypnotists select highly susceptible (or highly compliant!) participants from a large group for demonstration purposes. How? They usually give a small suggestion to the entire group, like closing your eyes and imagining that a helium balloon is tied to your hand. If your arm flies in the air, you're a candidate for coming on stage.

**PSYCHOLOGICAL SCIENCE AND THE UNCONSCIOUS** Most psychological scientists today agree that unconscious mental processes play a role in both normal and abnormal emotion and cognition (Bargh & Morsella, 2008). We remember a phone number, for example, without knowing how we accessed the memory. However, scientists debate the importance of unconscious processing. Some cognitive scientists call the unconscious mind "dumb," not "smart" (Loftus & Klinger, 1992), that is, of limited importance. Others propose elaborate models of unconscious mental processes—for example, that we have two systems of information processing (Epstein, 1994). The *rational system* uses abstract, logical knowledge to solve complex problems over time. The *experiential system* uses intuitive knowledge to respond to problems immediately without the delay of thought. The unconscious experiential system is hypothesized to be emotional, powerful, and often illogical (Epstein, 1994). Rationally, we might know that airplanes are safer than automobiles, for example, but emotionally, we are more likely to fear flying.

Contemporary scientists also have developed new methods to study unconscious processes. Consider the distinction between explicit and implicit memory. *Explicit memory* is conscious recollection. *Implicit memory* is unconscious and evident only because past experience can change behavior (Schacter, 1987). For example, the *implicit association test* reveals implicit memories by comparing response times to cues. Black and good versus white and good would be an example. Quicker responses reflect established associations in memory. We respond automatically and quickly to associations that implicitly "make sense." Evidence shows that implicit attitudes about delicate subjects like racial prejudice differ considerably from explicitly reported beliefs (Ratliff & Nosek, 2010).

Exciting new methods like the implicit association test allow psychological scientists to go beyond making assertions about the unconscious mind and to actually study it. Unfortunately, available methods are too limited to truly test bold assertions about the unconscious that we consider in this chapter, like the true nature of hypnosis and dissociative disorders.

## Symptoms of Dissociative Disorders

The extraordinary symptoms of dissociative disorders apparently involve mental processing outside of conscious awareness. Extreme cases of dissociation include a split in the functioning of the individual's entire sense of self. In *dissociative identity disorder (DID)*, two or more personalities coexist within a single individual. Unless we assume that the symptom is feigned, dissociative identity disorder demonstrates that the mind can function on multiple levels of consciousness.

*Depersonalization* is a less dramatic symptom where people feel detached from themselves. One example is an out-of-body experience, such as the sensation of floating outside yourself and watching your actions as if you were another person. *Derealization* is a related symptom that involves feelings of unreality or detachment from the environment, such as experiencing the world as being more dreamlike than real.

Another dramatic example is *dissociative amnesia*—the partial or complete loss of recall for particular events or for a particular period of time. Brain injury or disease can cause amnesia, but dissociative amnesia results from trauma or severe emotional distress. Dissociative amnesia may occur alone or in conjunction with other dissociative experiences. For example, in dissociative identity disorder one personality may report that it does not remember the actions, or even the existence, of another (Spiegel & Cardena, 1991). Recent laboratory evidence calls self-reports of amnesia into question, however, as DID patients show transfer of memories between identities on experimental tasks (Kong, Allen, & Glisky, 2008).

**TRAUMA AND DISSOCIATIVE SYMPTOMS** Dissociative amnesia is widely viewed as being caused by trauma, as is the dissociative fugue that sometime accompanies it. The trauma usually is clear and sudden, and after a time, psychological functioning rapidly returns to normal in most cases. Much more controversial is the role of trauma in DID. Some argue that DID is linked with past, not present, trauma, particularly with chronic physical or sexual child abuse (Gleaves, 1996). Many psychological scientists are skeptical about this assertion, however, because information about childhood trauma is based solely on clients' reports—reports that may be distorted by many factors, including a therapist's expectations (Kihlstrom, 2005). A related controversy concerns so-called *recovered memories*, dramatic recollections of long-ago traumatic experiences supposedly blocked from the conscious mind by dissociation (see Critical Thinking Matters box).

## Diagnosis of Dissociative Disorders

*DSM-5* lists three types of dissociative disorders: dissociative amnesia, depersonalization disorder, and dissociative identity disorder. **Dissociative amnesia** involves a sudden inability to recall extensive and important personal information that exceeds normal forgetfulness. Patients typically suffer from *selective amnesia*—they do not lose all of their memory but instead cannot remember selected events and information, often related to a traumatic experience. The memory loss is not attributable to substance abuse, head trauma, or a cognitive disorder, such as Alzheimer's disease. A subtype of dissociative amnesia involves **dissociative fugue**, sudden and unexpected travel, associated with amnesia about identity or other important information. Dissociative amnesia and fugue typically have a sudden onset following trauma or extreme stress and an equally sudden recovery of memory. The following case study provides one dramatic account, based on an article written by David Grann for the *New York Times* (January 13, 2002). ⊙ **Watch** the **Video** *Sharon: Dissociative Amnesia* on **MyPsychLab**

→ **Amnesia for September 11**

Kevin Shea, a firefighter for the Fire Department of New York, was one of the very few survivors rescued from the wreckage of the World Trade Center. On the evening of September 11, Shea was found buried under a pile of rubble, his thumb severed and his neck broken in three places. Fortunately, Shea was not paralyzed by his spinal injury, but, like his neck, Shea's memory was badly fractured.

Shea could remember his past and a few events from early on the day of September 11. For example, he could remember volunteering to help, even though he was off duty, and jumping on his firehouse's Engine 40 to rush downtown. As the engine approached the scene, he remembered seeing people falling from high floors of the towers. After this, however, Shea had no real memory of September 11, not until after he was hospitalized late in the day. For example, he had no memory of either tower collapsing, even though he was there at the horrifying, chaotic scene.

Shea lost every member of his engine in the WTC rescue attempt. He became desperate to learn that he survived despite trying to save others and not because he instead focused on saving himself. Through diligent efforts in the months after September 11, he was able to piece together some evidence about what happened to him. Some details brought back fragments of his memory. For example, when another

Kevin Shea, a firefighter for the FDNY, received numerous injuries, including a broken vertebrae, working as a rescue worker during the World Trade Center attacks. Shea also suffered from amnesia, perhaps as a result of a blow to the head or perhaps from emotional causes.

firefighter reminded him that they had embraced in the command center of the South Tower shortly before it collapsed, Shea remembered the event. However, no memories returned when Shea met another firefighter who himself was injured while trying to rescue Shea.

It is unclear whether Shea suffered from dissociative amnesia due to the emotional trauma of the day, or whether his memory loss was caused by a blow to his head. Although by all accounts Kevin Shea was a hero, he had trouble convincing himself of the truth of this assessment, because he could not remember his own actions on September 11.

∙∙∙∙∙∙∙∙∙∙∙∙∙∙∙∙∙∙∙∙∙∙∙∙∙∙∙∙∙∙∙∙∙∙∙∙∙∙∙∙∙∙∙∙∙∙∙∙∙∙∙∙∙∙∙∙∙∙∙∙∙∙∙∙∙∙∙∙

**Depersonalization/derealization disorder** is characterized by feelings of being detached from oneself or the world around you. Occasional experiences of depersonalization or derealization, such as feelings of *déjà vu*, are normal and are reported by about half the population. In depersonalization/derealization disorder, the symptoms are persistent or recurrent and cause marked personal distress. The onset of the disorder commonly follows a new or disturbing event, such as drug use. All depersonalization and derealization experiences are "as-if" feelings, not delusional beliefs. You *feel* as if you are a robot; you don't really believe it. In fact, some experts question whether the problem should be considered a dissociative disorder, because it involves only limited splitting between conscious and unconscious mental processes, and no memory loss occurs (Spiegel & Cardena, 1991).

To many people, the most fascinating dissociative disorder is **dissociative identity disorder (DID)**, a condition formerly known as **multiple personality disorder**. This extremely unusual problem is characterized by the existence of two or more distinct personalities in a single individual. Two or more of these personalities repeatedly take control of the person's behavior, with alterations in mood, behavior, and at least some loss of recall between the personalities. The original personality especially is likely to have amnesia for subsequent personalities, which may or may not be aware of other "alters" (Aldridge-Morris, 1989). Recent case studies claim to have identified more and more alters. The case of "Eve," published in 1957, identified three; "Sybil" was reported to have 16 in a 1973 best-seller (the veracity of which has been questioned; Nathan, 2012); and some more recent case studies have "discovered" 100, even 1,000, alters. Not surprisingly, such claims have generated more debate about a controversial diagnosis.

### The Three Faces of Eve

A famous case study of multiple personality disorder is Thigpen and Cleckley's book (1957) that was adapted into *The Three Faces of Eve*, a motion picture. Thigpen and Cleckley, two psychiatrists who treated the young woman, described Eve White as a young mother with a troubled marriage who sought psychotherapy for severe headaches, feelings of inertia, and "blackouts." Eve White was seen for several therapy sessions and was hypnotized during this time as a treatment for her amnesia. Then, during what proved to be a remarkable session, Eve White became agitated and complained of hearing an imaginary voice. As Thigpen and Cleckley wrote, "After a tense moment of silence, her hands dropped. There was a quick, reckless smile and, in a bright voice that sparkled, she said, 'Hi there, Doc!'" (p. 137). Eve Black had emerged—a carefree and flirtatious personality who insisted upon being called "Miss" and who scorned Eve White, the wife and mother.

Therapy with Eve White, Eve Black, and a third, more calm and mature personality, Jane, lasted over two-and-a-half years. Thigpen used hypnosis to bring out the different personalities in an attempt to understand and reconcile them with one another. He eventually adopted the goal of fading out the two Eves and allowing Jane to take control. Therapy appeared to be successful. According to the psychiatrists' account, treatment ended with one integrated personality in control. This personality was much like Jane, but she decided to call herself "Mrs. Evelyn White."

But the end of therapy with Thigpen and Cleckley was not the end of therapy for "Eve." Eve, whose real name is Chris Sizemore, claims to have had a total of 22 different personalities, some of which developed before her treatment with Thigpen and Cleckley and some of which developed afterward. The personalities always occurred in groups of three, and they always included a wife/mother image, a party girl, and a more normal,

Chris Sizemore is "Eve" from the book and the movie *The Three Faces of Eve*, based on her psychiatrists' account of her life and treatment for multiple personality disorder. Sizemore is now cured and is an advocate for the mentally ill.

intellectual personality (Sizemore & Pittillo, 1977). Sizemore has written several books about her life, and, as a well-functioning, unified personality, she has become a spokesperson for mental health concerns. In her book *A Mind of Her Own*, she offers the following observations on her personalities:

> Among these twenty-two alters, ten were poets, seven were artists, and one had taught tailoring. Today, I paint and write, but I cannot sew. Yet these alters were not moods or the result of role-playing. They were entities that were totally separate from the personality I was born to be, and am today. They were so different that their tones of voice changed. What's more, their facial expressions, appetites, tastes in clothes, handwritings, skills, and IQs were all different, too (Sizemore, 1989, p. 9).

The case of Chris Sizemore dramatically illustrates the characteristics of DID. Sizemore's words also foreshadow controversies about the condition. Some professionals argue that DID is nothing more than role playing; others assert that multiple personalities are very real and very common. While controversy centers on DID, skepticism abounds

This new study shows that 5 out of 4 people have a multiple personality disorder.

© GABRIEL UTASI
06·23·07

© Gabriel Utasi

about all dissociative disorders. Little evidence supports the validity of dissociative amnesia (McNally, 2003). As in the case of Kevin Shea, dissociative amnesia and fugue may be attributable to neurological conditions (Kihlstrom, 2005). Finally, very little research has been completed on the seemingly less controversial problem of depersonalization disorder (Geisbrecht et al., 2008).

## Frequency of Dissociative Disorders

These controversies contribute to widely varying estimates of the prevalence of dissociative disorders. Most experts consider the problems to be extremely rare. Only about 200 case histories of DID were reported in the entire world literature prior to 1980 (Greaves, 1980). Surely as a result of *Sybil* influences, the estimated number skyrocketed to about 40,000 in the next two decades (Pintar & Lynn, 2008). A small but vocal group of professionals has argued that many patients suffering from dissociative disorders are misdiagnosed as having schizophrenia, borderline personality disorder, depression, panic disorder, or substance abuse (Gleaves, 1996; Ross, 2009). One study claimed that over 10 percent of the general adult population suffers from a dissociative disorder—including 3 percent of adults with DID (Ross, 1991). The same author claimed that 40 percent of hospitalized psychiatric patients met earlier DSM criteria for the diagnosis of a dissociative disorder (Ross, Duffy, & Ellason, 2002). These estimates are stunning—so stunning as to be unbelievable. Perhaps even more stunning is that *DSM-5* includes an estimated prevalence of DID of 1.5 percent, while offering the disclaimer that the number is based on a "small study" (*DSM-5*, 2013; see Thinking Critically about DSM-5).

Clearly, experts either missed tens of thousands of cases of dissociative disorders for decades, or some advocates have been overzealous in defining dissociative disorders. Research suggests

## THINKING CRITICALLY about DSM-5

### More on Diagnostic Fads

Fads come and go. Hula hoops. Pet rocks. Platform shoes. iPods. Piercing various body parts. Tattoos. When we look back on them, fads can be embarrassing. You should see pictures of our long hair during our hippie days. But perspective is hard to obtain in the middle of a fad craze. Right now, DSM–5 diagnoses are "in."

Do fads really develop for psychological diagnoses? Doesn't science make the field immune? The short answers are "yes" and "no."

Allen Frances, the psychiatrist who was in charge of the fourth revision of the DSM, has one big worry about *DSM-5* fads. We are diagnosing *everything*, turning normal quirks, disappointments, and stress into mental disorders. In his book, *Saving Normal*, Frances (2013) critiques many of *DSM-5*'s specific changes. More broadly, he worries that the faddish rise in diagnosing mental disorders is stigmatizing far too many people, helping the pharmaceutical industry promote drugs for all kinds of normal life problems, and helping to break family and national budgets with health care expenditures. Frances is intensely critical,

sometimes over the top. *DSM-5 is* embracing science. The goal *is* to help more people, and help them better, by crafting clearer and more accurate diagnoses. But Frances also has a point. The diagnosis of mental disorders is exploding, and that is not always or necessarily a good thing—even though we can have a hard time seeing or admitting to problems when a fad is "hot."

Two topics that we discuss in this chapter were "hot" in the 1990s: Dissociative disorders and recovered memories. As you have read, the recovered memory movement has been largely discredited. But a 1995 study found that 25 percent of therapists said that recovering memories, particularly of sexual abuse, was an important part of their therapy with female clients (Poole et al., 1995). Not a problem? Read about the Franklin case in *Critical Thinking Matters*. And a 1991 study claimed that 3 percent of adults suffered from dissociative identity disorder (Ross, 1991), when only about 200 case histories of multiple personality were reported in the entire world literature prior to 1980 (Greaves, 1980). Some work has been published on dissociative identity disorders since the 1990s, but almost all cases can be attributed to a small group of clinicians, there are almost no other documented cases, and laboratory simulations of DID are almost indistinguishable from identified cases (Boysen & VanBergen, 2013). A small group of mental health professionals are still captivated by the DID diagnosis, but the fad is over. In a combined 60-plus years of practice, we have observed a total of one, legitimate case of DID. Why did *DSM-5* include an estimated community prevalence of 1.5 percent of DID based on an unidentified "small study?" We think that's a good question.

In more recent years, diagnostic fads have focused on mental disorders in children. As we discuss in Chapter 15, The estimated prevalence of autism spectrum disorder increased by a factor of 50 between 1994 and today (Blumberg et al., 2013). That is not a typo. Fifty times as many children are said to suffer

from this disorder in 2013 as in 1994. Only slightly less dramatic is the increase in the diagnosis of bipolar disorders in children. Between 1994 and 2003, the diagnosis increased by a factor of 40 (Moreno et al., 2007). And as we discuss in Chapter 16, the children apparently did not suffer from bipolar disorder. In fact, *DSM-5* created a whole new diagnosis to deal with this particular fad.

We do not know what consequences today's diagnostic fads will bring, good or bad. We do know how easy it is to get caught up in a fad, and how difficult it can be to say, "Wait a minute!" But science is a wait-a-minute approach to knowledge. Sometimes we need to slow down, admit what we do not know, and focus on trying to solve problems one small step at a time.

---

many reasons to disbelieve claims that dissociative disorders are prevalent and overlooked (Kihlstrom, 2005; Piper & Merskey, 2004a, 2004b):

- Most cases of dissociative disorders are diagnosed by a handful of ardent advocates.

- The frequency of the diagnosis of dissociative disorders in general, and DID in particular, increased rapidly after release of the very popular book and movie *Sybil*.

- The number of personalities claimed to exist in cases of DID grew rapidly, from a handful to 100 or more.

- Interest in dissociative disorders declined beginning in the middle of 1990s (after *Sybil*), as specialized treatment units closed and professionals withdrew from organizations and journals devoted to the topic.

- Dissociative disorders are rarely diagnosed outside of the United States and Canada; for example, only one unequivocal case of DID has been reported in Great Britain in the last 25 years (Casey, 2001).

- The symptoms of dissociation in the most commonly used instruments like the Dissociative Experiences Questionnaire are far less dramatic than those found in dissociative disorders (Geisbrecht et al., 2008; see Table 7.1).

**DISORDER OR ROLE ENACTMENT?** Some experts even doubt the very existence of DID, arguing that DID is created by the power of suggestion (Piper & Mersky, 2004a, 2004b). The Canadian psychologist Nicholas Spanos (1942–1994) was a particularly outspoken critic. He argued that multiple personalities are caused by role playing. Influenced by their own and their therapists' expectations, Spanos (1994) argued that, like an actor who loses all perspective, patients come to believe that the role is real.

To test his theory, Spanos and his colleagues conducted analogue experiments inspired by the case of Kenneth Bianchi, the infamous "Hillside Strangler." In 1979, Bianchi was charged with murdering two college women and was implicated in several

other rape-murder cases where victims were left naked on the hillsides of Los Angeles. Considerable evidence supported Bianchi's guilt, but he reported frequent episodes of "blanking out," including an inability to remember events from the night that the murders were committed. At the request of his attorney, Bianchi was seen by a mental health expert, who hypnotized Bianchi and suggested to him, "I've talked a bit to Ken, but I think that perhaps there might be another part of Ken that I haven't talked to, another part that maybe feels somewhat differently from the part I've talked to. And I would like to communicate with that other part" (Watkins, 1984). Bianchi responded that he was not Ken, but Steve. Steve knew of Ken, and he hated him. Steve also confessed to strangling "all of these girls."

Numerous experts who interviewed Bianchi disagreed about whether his apparent DID was real or feigned. One was

---

**TABLE 7.1**

## Sample Items from the Dissociative Experiences Questionnaire

- Some people find that sometimes they are listening to someone talk and they suddenly realize that they did not hear part or all of what was said.

- Some people have the experience of being in a familiar place but finding it strange and unfamiliar.

- Some people have the experience of finding themselves dressed in clothes that they don't remember putting on.

- Some people are told that they sometimes do not recognize friends or family members.

- Some people have the experience of feeling that their body does not seem to belong to them.

- Some people find that in one situation they may act so differently compared with another situation that they feel almost as if they were two different people.

*Source:* Data from Bernstein, E.M., & Putnam, F.W. 1986. Development, reliability, and validity of a dissociation scale. Journal of Nervous and Mental Disease, 174(12), 727–735.

the psychologist and psychiatrist Martin Orne (1927–2000), an internationally recognized authority on hypnosis. Orne tested Bianchi by suggesting new symptoms to him. If Bianchi was faking, he might further the deception by developing the new symptoms. Orne suggested, for example, that if Bianchi really had DID, he should have a third personality. Sure enough, a third personality, Billy, "emerged" when Bianchi was hypnotized (Orne, Dingers, & Orne, 1984). While hypnotized, Bianchi also followed Orne's suggestion to hallucinate that his attorney was in the room. Bianchi actually shook hands with the supposed hallucination—a very unusual behavior for someone under hypnosis. Orne concluded that Bianchi was indeed faking and actually suffered from antisocial personality disorder (see Chapter 9). Bianchi's insanity defense failed, and he was found guilty of murder.

In testing his role theory, Spanos simulated procedures from the Bianchi case. In one study, undergraduate students played the role of the accused murderer and were randomly assigned to one of three conditions. In the "Bianchi" condition, the subjects were hypnotized, and the interviewer asked to communicate with their other part, just as Bianchi's interviewer had asked. Subjects assigned to the second "hidden part" condition also were hypnotized, but this time it was suggested that hypnosis could get behind the "wall" that hid inner thoughts and feelings from awareness. In the final condition, there was no hypnosis, and subjects simply were told that personality included "walls" between hidden thoughts and feelings.

When subsequently asked, "Who are you?" in the mock murder case, 81 percent of the subjects in the Bianchi condition gave a name different from the one assigned to them in the role play, as did 70 percent of the subjects in the hidden part condition. In contrast, only 31 percent of the subjects in the no-hypnosis condition gave a new name (Spanos, Weekes, & Bertrand, 1985). In a subsequent study, hypnotized subjects also provided more "information" on exactly when in the past their alternate personalities had first emerged (Spanos et al., 1986).

These findings certainly raise the caution that the "symptoms" of DID can be induced by role playing and hypnosis (Lilienfeld et al., 1999). Moreover, accumulating evidence indicates that fantasy proneness and suggestibility play a key role in the development of dissociative disorders (Geisbrecht et al., 2008). Still, analogue studies cannot prove that role playing causes real cases of multiple personality (Gleaves, 1996).

Given the limited research, our inquiring skepticism causes us to reach some cautious conclusions. True dissociative disorders appear to be rare. Although some cases no doubt are misdiagnosed, a much greater problem is the creation of the diagnosis in the minds of clinicians and clients (Piper & Mersky, 2004a, 2004b). At the same time, we remain curious about the dramatic cases and theoretical issues posed by accounts of dissociative disorders.

## Causes of Dissociative Disorders

Little systematic research has been conducted on the cause of dissociative disorders. Thus, theory and outright speculation dominate this field.

**PSYCHOLOGICAL FACTORS** There is little controversy that dissociative amnesia and fugue usually are precipitated by trauma. What about DID? Many case studies suggest that DID develops in response to trauma, particularly the trauma of child abuse. In fact, some researchers have compiled large numbers of case studies from surveys of practitioners that support this view (Ross, 2009; see Table 7.2).

### TABLE 7.2
### Correlates of Dissociative Identity Disorder in Two Surveys of Clinicians

| Item | Ross[1] N = 236 | Putnam[2] N = 100 |
|---|---|---|
| Average age | 30.8 | 35.8 |
| Percentage of females | 87.7% | 92.0% |
| Average years of treatment before diagnosis | 6.7 | 6.8 |
| Average number of personalities | 15.7 | 13.3 |
| Opposite-sex personality present | 62.6% | 53.0% |
| Amnesia between personalities | 94.9% | 98.0% |
| Past suicide attempt | 72.0% | 71.0% |
| History of child physical abuse | 74.9% | 75.0% |
| History of child sexual abuse | 79.2% | 83.9% |

[1]Based on data from C. A. Ross, G. R. Norton, and K. Wozney. 1989. Multiple Personality Disorder: An Analysis of 236 Cases. Canadian Journal of Psychiatry; 34: 413–418.

[2]Based on data from F. W. Putnam, J. J. Curoff, et al. 1986. The Clinical Phenomenology of Multiple Personality Disorder: Review of 100 Recent Cases. Journal of Clinical Psychiatry; 47: 285–293.

## Retrospective Reports: Remembering the Past

Psychologists have long been skeptical about the accuracy of people's reports about the past. The concern is about the reliability and validity of *retrospective reports*—current recollections of past experiences, for example, events that occurred during childhood. Problems with retrospective reports are one of several reasons why investigators prefer prospective, longitudinal studies over retrospective research designs (see the Research Methods box in Chapter 8).

Concerns about retrospective reports focus on three particular issues. First, normal memory often is inaccurate, particularly memory for events that occurred long ago and early in life. Second, memories of people with emotional problems may be particularly unreliable. Third, abnormal behavior may systematically bias memory; for example, memory processes may be "mood congruent." Depressed people may tend to remember sad experiences, anxious people may better recall fearful events, and so on.

Brewin, Andrews, and Gotlib (1993) revisited many of these concerns, but concluded that retrospective memories may be less flawed than some have suggested. The reviewers agreed that retrospective reports are often inaccurate. For example, only moderate correlations are found between children's and parents'

reports about their past relationships, and, on average, children report more negative memories. At the same time, agreement between parents and children increases to an acceptable level for reports of specific, factual aspects of the past. Thus, memory for specific, important events in the family may be fairly reliable and valid, but people may "rewrite" their histories with regard to more global and subjective experiences.

Brewin and colleagues (1993) also questioned the blanket assumption that psychopathology impairs memory. They found many flaws in research that supposedly demonstrated memory impairments for various psychological problems and concluded that, except for serious mental illness, there is no evidence for memory impairments associated with anxiety or depression. In particular, depressed people do not erroneously recall more than their share of negative events about the past.

Brewin and colleagues (1993) urge that retrospective reports should not be dismissed out of hand. Psychologists have many reasons to prefer prospective, longitudinal research over retrospective methods, but longitudinal research is expensive. Retrospective reports of specific events may be sufficiently reliable and valid to justify using them as an initial, less-expensive research method.

---

When interpreting these findings, however, you should note that studies of the long-term consequences of child physical or sexual abuse find little evidence of dissociation or, indeed, of any consistent forms of psychopathology (Clancy, 2010; Emery & Laumann-Billings, 1998; Rind, Tromovitch, & Bauserman, 1998). And case studies are based on patients' memories and clinicians' evaluations. They are not objective assessments of the past. Researchers have many concerns about the validity of such *retrospective reports*—evaluations of the past from the vantage point of the present (see Research Methods). Memories may be selectively recalled, distorted, or even created to conform to a clinician's expectations (Geisbrecht et al., 2008; Kihlstrom, 2005).

If trauma is involved, how might it lead to the development of multiple personalities? One theory invokes *state-dependent learning*, a process where learning that takes place in one state of affect or consciousness is best recalled in the same state of affect or consciousness (Bower, 1990). For example, when you are sad rather than happy, you more easily remember what happened when you were sad in the past. By extension, experiences that occur during a dissociated state may be most easily recalled within the same state of consciousness. Perhaps through the repeated experience of trauma, dissociation, and state-dependent learning, more complete and autonomous memories develop—ultimately leading to independent personalities (Braun, 1989).

Even if trauma contributes to dissociative disorders—and we are skeptical about trauma and DID, it clearly is not a sufficient cause. As we saw with ASD and PTSD, the vast majority of people who experience trauma do *not* develop a dissociative disorder. Thus, other factors must contribute to their development.

**BIOLOGICAL FACTORS** Little research addresses the contribution of biological factors to dissociative disorders (Kihlstrom, 2005). A recent proposal suggests that a fragmented sleep-wake cycle helps explain dissociative symptoms (van der Kloet et al., 2012). In support of this novel view, research finds a relation between sleep disturbance and dissociation, experimental deprivation of sleep increases dissociative experiences, and improved sleep decreases dissociation (Lynn et al., 2012; van der Kloet et al., 2012).

**SOCIAL FACTORS** Perhaps the most important theory about social contributions to dissociative disorders is that they are caused by **iatrogenesis**, the manufacture of a disorder by its treatment. Mersky (1992) reviewed classic case studies of DID and concluded that many "cases" were created by the expectations of therapists. Mersky does not doubt the pain experienced by the patients in these cases. He argues, however, that the patients developed multiple personalities in response to their therapists'

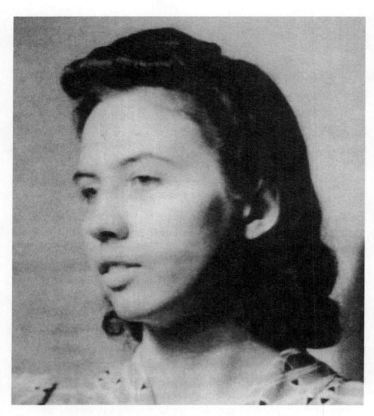

Shirley Mason Ardell, the real "Sybil." Her case spurred an explosion in the diagnosis of dissociative identity disorder, and in the number of diagnosed "alters," but actual therapy tapes suggest that her therapist may have implanted Sybil's 16 personalities.

The ultimate goal in treating DID is not to have one personality triumph over the others. Rather, the objective is to integrate the different personalities into a whole (Coons & Bowman, 2001). Integration is not unlike the task we all face in reconciling our different roles in life into a coherent sense of self. Dallae, for example, needed to reconcile her role as a daughter, including her parents' expectations, together with her role as an independent young woman with her own desires, abilities, and acculturation experiences.

At this time, no systematic research has been conducted on the effectiveness of any treatment for dissociative disorders, let alone on the comparison of alternative treatments (Kihlstrom, 2005; Maldonado, Butler, & Spiegel, 2001). Antianxiety, antidepressant, and antipsychotic medications sometimes are used, but at best these medications reduce distress. They do not cure the disorder. Advances in treatment await a better understanding of the disorders and, more generally, of conscious and unconscious mental processes. In the meantime, you should view treatments championed for dissociative disorders—and the accuracy of the diagnosis itself—with a healthy dose of skepticism.

## Somatic Symptom Disorders

In addition to dissociative disorders, hysteria included *conversion disorder*, problems with motor or sensory function occurring in the absence of a known physical illness. "Hysterical blindness" and "hysterical paralysis" are two old names and examples of these problems, symptoms that greatly influenced Freud's and Janet's theorizing, and perhaps were more common during their lifetimes. We consider conversion disorder in the same chapter with dissociative disorders because of their historical connection and because conversion disorder appears to involve dissociation. However, *DSM-5* now treats conversion disorder as a **somatic symptom disorders**—problems where physical symptoms are prominent and are accompanied by impairing psychological distress. We discuss several somatic symptom disorders in this section, and continue with the topic in the next chapter on stress and health.

### Symptoms of Somatic Symptom Disorders

All somatic symptom disorders discussed in this chapter involve complaints about physical symptoms that create psychological distress either out of proportion to actual physical problems or in the absence of a diagnosable physical illness. The symptoms are not feigned or intentionally exaggerated. The physical problem is very real in the mind, though evidently not the body, of the sufferer.

The physical symptoms can take a number of forms. In dramatic cases, the symptom involves substantial impairment, particularly in the sensory or muscular system. The patient will be unable to see, for example, or will report paralysis in one arm. In other cases, patients experience one or perhaps several more minor physical symptoms such as pain, upset stomach, dizziness, or some vague complaint that is misinterpreted as a sign of a serious

leading questions. Like Spanos (1994), Mersky argues that DID is a social role. Because of their susceptibility to suggestion, perhaps highly hypnotizable people are especially likely to suffer from iatrogenic effects (Kihlstrom, Glisky, & Angiulo, 1994).

We believe that iatrogenesis is the explanation for the explosion of DID cases diagnosed in the United States, especially in the wake of *Sybil's* popularity. However, we also believe that DID is a real if rare problem. DID has been diagnosed in the general population in Turkey, where there is no public awareness of the disorder (Akyuz et al., 1999). And suggestibility alone does not appear to explain dissociation (Dalenberg et al., 2012).

### Treatment of Dissociative Disorders

Dating from the time of Janet and Freud, most treatments of dissociative disorders have focused on uncovering and recounting traumatic memories. Presumably, the need for dissociation disappears if the trauma can be expressed and accepted (Horevitz & Loewenstein, 1994). Many clinicians use hypnosis to help patients explore and relive traumatic events. However, no research supports the effectiveness of either *abreaction*, the emotional reliving of a past traumatic experiences, or hypnosis as a treatment for dissociative disorders (Horevitz & Loewenstein, 1994). Skeptics worry, in fact, that hypnosis may create dissociative symptoms or false memories of abuse (Casey, 2001).

illness like cancer. Anxiety persists despite negative medical tests and clear reassurance by a physician.

**UNNECESSARY MEDICAL TREATMENT** People with somatic symptom disorders typically do not bring their problems to the attention of a mental health professional. Instead, they repeatedly consult their physicians about their "physical" problems (Bass, Peveler, & House, 2001; Looper & Kirmayer, 2002). This often leads to unnecessary medical treatment. In one study, patients with one of these somatic symptom disorders had seen a healthcare provider more than six times, on average, during the previous six months. One-fourth of patients had been hospitalized in the past year, compared with 12 percent of the general population (Swartz et al., 1987).

Patients often complain about realistic physical symptoms that are difficult to evaluate objectively. Thus, physicians frequently do not recognize the psychological nature of the patients' problems, and they sometimes perform unnecessary medical procedures. These patients have surgery twice as often as people in the general population (Zoccolillo & Cloninger, 1986). In fact, some common surgical procedures are performed with startling frequency on patients with these somatic symptom disorders. One research group concluded that, after discounting cancer surgeries, 27 percent of women undergoing a hysterectomy suffered from this psychological problem (Martin, Roberts, & Clayton, 1980).

Such data are distressing not only because of the risk to the patient but also because of the costs of unnecessary medical treatment. Estimates indicate that anywhere from 20 percent to 84 percent of patients who consult physicians do so for problems for which no organic cause can be found (Miller & Swartz, 1990). Such visits may account for as much as half of all ambulatory healthcare costs (Kellner, 1985). A variety of emotional problems can motivate people to consult their physicians, including the experience of trauma (Green et al., 1997). For example, patients with one of these somatic symptom disorders are three times more likely to consult physicians than are depressed patients (Morrison & Herbstein, 1988; Zoccolillo & Cloninger, 1986). Health care expenditures are nine times the average annual per capita cost of medical treatment (Smith, Monson, & Ray, 1986).

## Diagnosis of Somatic Symptom Disorders

*DSM-5* lists five major somatic symptom disorders: (1) conversion disorder, (2) somatic symptom disorder, (3) illness anxiety disorder, (4) factitious disorder, and (5) psychological factors affecting other medical conditions. The last diagnosis is different. The physical illness is undoubtedly real, and emotional reactions surrounding the illness are not exaggerated. Instead, psychological factors affecting other medical conditions are diagnosed for stress-involved physical illnesses (see Chapter 8). We briefly describe the other four somatic symptom disorders along with body dysmorphic disorder, which *DSM-5* decided to list with obsessive–compulsive disorders (see Chapter 6).

**FIGURE 7.4**

**Conversion disorder symptoms may make no anatomical sense.** As illustrated in this figure, pain insensitivity may be limited to one side of the face, but the nerves involved in pain sensation do not divide the face neatly in half.

*Source:* Adapted from D. M. Kaufman, 1985, *Clinical Neurology for Psychiatrists,* 2nd ed., p. 28. Copyright © 2007 Elsevier. Reprinted by permission.

**CONVERSION DISORDER** The dramatic symptoms of **conversion disorder** include altered motor or sensory function that typically mimic neurological problems with one exception: Conversion symptoms make no anatomic sense. A patient may complain about anesthesia (or pain) in a way that does not correspond with the innervation of the body. In some facial anesthesias, for example, numbness ends at the middle of the face. But the nerves involved in sensation do not divide the face into equal halves (see Figure 7.4).

The term *conversion disorder* accurately conveys the central assumption of the diagnosis—the idea that psychological conflicts are converted into physical symptoms. This idea captivated Charcot, Freud, and Janet and led them to develop theories about dissociation and unconscious mental processes. The following case from Janet's writings illustrates his view of hysteria.

### ⟶ Janet's Hysterical Patient

A girl of 19 years of age suffered, at the time of her monthly period, convulsive and delirious attacks which lasted several days. Menstruation began normally, but a few hours after the commencement of the flow the patient complained of feeling very cold and had a characteristic shivering; menstruation was immediately arrested and delirium ensued. In the interval of these attacks the patient had paroxysms of terror with the hallucination of blood spreading out before her and also showed various permanent stigmata, among others, anesthesia of the left side of the face with amaurosis of the left eye.

During a careful study of this patient's history, and particularly of the memories she had conserved of various experiences of her life, certain pertinent facts were ascertained. At the age of 13 she had attempted to arrest menstruation by plunging into a tub of cold water with resulting shivering and delirium; menstruation was immediately arrested and did not recur for several years; when it did reappear the disturbance I have just cited took place. Later on she had been terrified by seeing an old woman fall on the stairs and deluge the steps with her blood. At another time, when she was about 9 years old, she had been obliged to sleep with a child whose face, on the left side, was covered with scabs, and during the whole night she had experienced a feeling of intense disgust and horror (Janet, 1914/1915, pp. 3–4).

........................................................................

This case describes symptoms that are consistent with conversion disorder. The numbness on the left side of the face and loss of vision (amaurosis) are clear examples of conversion symptoms. At the same time, we wonder about other aspects of this classic case. The frightening hallucinations of blood might suggest another diagnosis, perhaps psychotic depression or schizophrenia. Differential diagnosis was poor during the time of Charcot, Janet, and Freud, and we think that this might explain why conversion disorders were thought to be prevalent then but are rare today (Shorter, 1992). Many problems would be accurately identified today probably were misdiagnosed as conversion disorders a century ago. Concerns about misdiagnosing undetected but real physical problems as being "psychological" still apply to the diagnosis today, as we discuss shortly, In fact, this is one reason why these problems were relabeled "somatic symptom disorders" (Stone et al., 2010).

**SOMATIC SYMPTOM DISORDER** **Somatic symptom disorder** (singular) is one of several somatic symptom disorder*s* (plural) and is characterized by at least one and usually several somatic complaints accompanied by excessive concern about the symptoms. Chronic pain may or may not be a part of the presentation. Similar to what was formerly called "somatization disorder," patients with somatic symptom disorder sometimes present their symptoms in a *histrionic* manner—a vague but dramatic, self-centered, and seductive style. Patients also may exhibit *la belle indifference* (the beautiful indifference), a flippant lack of concern about their symptoms. For example, a patient may list a long series of somatic complaints in an offhanded and cheerful manner. Although some experts view a histrionic style and la belle indifference as defining characteristics of somatic symptom disorder, they are found in only a minority of cases (Brown, 2004; Lipowski, 1988).

In contrast to stereotypes, somatic symptom disorder is *not* more common among the aged, who consult healthcare professionals frequently because of chronic and real physical illnesses (National Institute of Mental Health, 1990). In fact, somatic symptom disorder often begins in adolescence. The problem sometimes has been called *Briquet's syndrome*, in recognition of the French physician Pierre Briquet, who was among the first to call attention to the multiple somatic complaints found in some "hysterias" (National Institute of Mental Health, 1990).

**ILLNESS ANXIETY DISORDER** Illness anxiety disorder is characterized by a fear or belief that one is suffering from a physical illness, but physical symptoms are either absent or minor. Aspects of this disorder are familiar to you. Formerly called *hypochondriasis*, the term was changed in *DSM-5*, since it had become a demeaning part of everyday language. We all worry about our health, and even unrealistic worries sometimes are normal. For example, medical students often fear that they have contracted each new disease they encounter. We should warn you: Many students in abnormal psychology suffer from a similar problem.

Illness anxiety disorder is much more serious than these normal and fleeting worries. The disorder is preoccupying, enduring, and often leads to substantial impairment in life functioning (see "DSM-5: Illness Anxiety Disorder"). Even a thorough medical evaluation does not alleviate fears. The person still worries that the illness may be emerging or that a test was overlooked. But the patient is not delusional. Someone may worry excessively about contracting AIDS, for example, and repeatedly go for blood tests. When faced with negative results, the person does not delusionally believe that he actually has contracted the illness. Instead, he persistently worries that the test was wrong or was taken too soon to detect the disease. ⊙ **Watch** the **Video** *Henry: Illness Anxiety Disorder* on **MyPsychLab**

---

**criteria for**
## Illness Anxiety Disorder

**A.** Preoccupation with having or acquiring a serious illness.

**B.** Somatic symptoms are not present or, if present, are only mild in intensity. If another medical condition is present or there is a high risk for developing a medical condition (e.g., strong family history is present), the preoccupation is clearly excessive or disproportionate.

**C.** There is a high level of anxiety about health, and the individual is easily alarmed about personal health status.

**D.** The individual performs excessive health-related behaviors (e.g., repeatedly checks his or her body for signs of illness) or exhibits maladaptive avoidance (e.g., avoids doctor appointments and hospitals).

**E.** Illness preoccupation has been present for at least 6 months, but the specific illness that is feared may change over that period of time.

**F.** The illness-related preoccupation is not better explained by another mental disorder, such as somatic symptom disorder, panic disorder, generalized anxiety disorder, body dysmorphic disorder, obsessive-compulsive disorder, or delusional disorder, somatic type.

**BODY DYSMORPHIC DISORDER** **Body dysmorphic disorder**, now considered an obsessive-compulsive disorder, is similar to somatic symptom disorders, because the problem involves preoccupation with some imagined defect in appearance. The preoccupation typically focuses on some facial feature, such as the nose or mouth, and in some cases may lead to repeated visits to a plastic surgeon. Preoccupation with the body part far exceeds normal worries about physical imperfections. The endless worry causes significant distress, and in extreme cases, it may interfere with work or social relationships.

U.S. researchers are only beginning to study body dysmorphic disorder (Phillips et al., 2010). The problem has received somewhat more attention in Japan and Korea, where it is classified as a type of social phobia (Phillips et al., 2010). The following brief case history illustrates this problem.

#### → Body Dysmorphic Disorder

A 28-year-old single white man became preoccupied at the age of 18 with his minimally thinning hair. Despite reassurance from others that his hair loss was not noticeable, he worried about it for hours a day, becoming "deeply depressed," socially withdrawn, and unable to attend classes or do his schoolwork. Although he could acknowledge the excessiveness of his preoccupation, he was unable to stop it. He saw four dermatologists but was not comforted by their reassurances that his hair loss was minor and that treatment was unnecessary. The patient's preoccupation and subsequent depression have persisted for 10 years and have continued to interfere with his social life and work, to the extent that he avoids most social events and has been able to work only part-time as a baker. He only recently sought psychiatric referral, at the insistence of his girlfriend, who said his symptoms were ruining their relationship (Phillips, 1991, pp. 1138–1139).

**MALINGERING AND FACTITIOUS DISORDER** Somatic symptom disorders are real *psychological* problems, even though the physical symptoms are not always real. This distinguishes them from **malingering**, pretending to have a physical illness in order to achieve some external gain, such as a disability payment. Because there is no objective test for somatic symptom disorders, detecting malingering is extremely difficult. Besides searching for an obvious reason for feigning an illness, one clue to malingering can be when a patient presents symptoms that are more, not less, dramatic than is typical.

A related diagnostic concern is **factitious disorder**, a feigned condition that, unlike malingering, is motivated primarily by a desire to assume the sick role rather than by a desire for external gain. *DSM-5* lists factitious disorder as one of the somatic symptom disorders. People with factitious disorder pretend to be ill or make themselves appear to be ill, for example, by taking drugs to produce a rapid heart rate. They will undergo extensive and often painful medical procedures in order to garner attention from health care professionals. A rare, repetitive pattern of factitious disorder is sometimes called *Munchausen syndrome*, named after Baron Karl Friedrich Hieronymus von Munchausen, an eighteenth-century writer known for his tendency to embellish the details of his life.

### Frequency of Somatic Symptom Disorders

No one knows how prevalent conversion disorders were during the time of Charcot, Janet, and Freud, but the literature of the period suggests that they were common (Shorter, 1992). Today, conversion disorders are rare, perhaps as infrequent as 50 cases per 100,000 population (Akagi & House, 2001). Ironically, the unusual disorders treated by Freud and Janet have been less enduring than the theories developed to explain them. The lower prevalence today may be a result of improved diagnostic practices—cases now are correctly diagnosed as real physical or psychological illnesses, or perhaps of Western society's greater acceptance of the expression of feelings (Shorter, 1992). A very different—and controversial—viewpoint is that conversion disorders *are* prevalent today, but they take the form of conditions like chronic fatigue syndrome, fibromyalgia, irritable bowel syndrome, and similar puzzling maladies (Johnson, 2008; Showalter, 1997).

Other somatic symptom disorders are more common. *DSM-5* estimates that about 5 percent to 7 percent of the population suffers from somatic symptom disorder, while 1 percent to 10 percent suffer from illness anxiety disorder. The estimates are imprecise, because *DSM-5* changed the diagnostic criteria, making past research difficult to apply. One study found a 0.7 percent prevalence of body dysmorphic disorder (Otto et al., 2001). The prevalence of factitious disorder and malingering are impossible to pinpoint, of course, because the problems involve deliberate deception.

Children often describe their anxiety in somatic terms, "My stomach hurts!" Cultural and historical differences in somatoform disorders sometimes are attributed to a similar lack of insight into emotion.

**GENDER, SES, AND CULTURE** Somatic symptom disorders are more common among women than men (Swartz et al., 1990). Why women? Some feminist writers attribute women's hysteria during the time of Freud and Janet to the sexual repression of the Victorian era. Today's disproportionate prevalence among women often is blamed on widespread sexual abuse. Feminist Elaine Showalter (1997) criticizes both of these views. Instead, she argues, "Women still suffer from hysterical symptoms not because we are essentially irrational or because we're all victims of abuse but because, like men, we are human beings who will convert feelings into symptoms when we are unable to speak" (p. 207).

Socioeconomic status and culture also are thought to contribute to the frequency of somatic symptom disorders. In the United States, they are more common among lower socioeconomic groups, people with less than a high school education, and African Americans. The prevalence also is considerably higher in Puerto Rico than on the U.S. mainland (Canino et al., 1987). However, expected differences between industrialized and nonindustrialized countries were not found in a study sponsored by the World Health Organization. The one notable cultural difference was the high prevalence of somatization in Latin America (Gureje et al., 1997). Some speculate that this is due to a Latin view of emotional expression as a sign of weakness, while others hypothesize that it is due to the stigma associated with mental illness.

In addition to affecting prevalence, culture can influence when and how somatic symptoms are experienced. An example is *hwa-byung*, a Korean folk syndrome that is attributed to unexpressed anger. (The open expression of anger is frowned upon in Korea.) The symptoms of hwa-byung include fatigue, insomnia, indigestion, and various aches and pains.

**COMORBIDITY** Somatic symptom disorders typically occur with other psychological problems, particularly depression and anxiety (Creed & Barsky, 2004; Otto et al., 2001; Smith et al., 2005). The link with depression has several possible explanations. Either condition may cause the other, or both could be caused by a third variable, such as life stress. One possibility that primary care physicians must consider carefully is that some patients may express depression indirectly through their somatic complaints (Lipowski, 1988).

There also are several possible explanations for the comorbidity with anxiety, including the fact that anxiety often is experienced physically and may be misreported in terms of physical symptoms (upset stomach, dizziness, weakness, sweating, dry mouth). A particular concern is the accurate, differential diagnosis of panic disorder. Some symptoms of panic, such as dizziness, numbness, and fears about dying, may be dismissed by physicians, or misdiagnosed as either illness anxiety disorder or somatic symptom disorder (Lipowski, 1988).

Finally, somatic symptom disorder has frequently been linked with *antisocial personality disorder*, a lifelong pattern of irresponsible behavior that involves habitual violations of social rules. The two disorders do not typically co-occur in the same individual, but they often are found in different members of the same family (Lilienfeld, 1992). Because antisocial personality disorder is far more common among men, while somatic symptom disorder has the opposite pattern, some have speculated that the two problems are flip sides of the same coin. Antisocial personality disorder may be the male expression of high negative emotion and the absence of inhibition, whereas somatic symptom disorder is the female expression of the same characteristics (Lilienfeld, 1992).

## Causes of Somatic Symptom Disorders

Despite their historical and medical significance, surprisingly little systematic research has been conducted on somatic symptom disorders. We integrate emerging findings with some theoretical considerations in the context of the biopsychosocial model.

**BIOLOGICAL FACTORS—THE PERILS OF DIAGNOSIS BY EXCLUSION** An obvious—and potentially critical—biological consideration in somatic symptom disorders is the possibility of misdiagnosis. A patient may be incorrectly diagnosed as suffering from a psychological problem when, in fact, he or she actually has a real physical illness, one that is undetected or is perhaps unknown. The diagnosis of a conversion disorder requires that there is no *known* organic cause of the symptom. This is very different from the positive identification of a psychological cause of the symptom.

The identification of somatic symptom disorders often involves a process called *diagnosis by exclusion*. The physical complaint is assumed to be a psychological disorder after various known physical causes are ruled out. Indeed, experts increasingly refer to somatic symptom disorders as *medically unexplained syndromes* (Johnson, 2008; Smith et al., 2005). The possibility always remains that an incipient somatic disease has

Diagnosis by exclusion is like identifying a criminal by ruling out other suspects. "It isn't the guy in the flowered shirt, he didn't have a mustache, and the two guys on the left are too stocky. It must be the guy on the right." But the real criminal might not be in the lineup, and the real disease might go undetected when using diagnosis by exclusion.

been overlooked. Some of the problems with diagnosis by exclusion can be appreciated by way of analogy. Consider the difference in certainty between two police lineups, one in which a victim positively identifies a criminal—"That's him!"—versus a second where the identification is made by ruling out alternatives—"It isn't him or him or him, so I guess it must be that one."

The possibility of misdiagnosis is more than a theoretical concern. Follow-up studies of patients diagnosed as suffering from conversion disorders show that somatic illnesses are later detected in some cases (Escobar et al., in press; Kroenke et al., 2007). Typically, a neurological disease such as epilepsy or multiple sclerosis is the eventual diagnosis. In one classic study, a *quarter* of patients diagnosed as having a conversion symptom later developed a neurological disease (Slater, 1965). Fortunately, recent research has found a much smaller percentage (5 percent or less) of undetected physical illnesses when following up cases of somatic symptom disorders several years later (Crimlisk et al., 1998; Schuepbach, Adler, & Sabbioni, 2002). We attribute the new findings to the improved detection of real physical illnesses, and again wonder how many of the hysterias treated by Charcot, Freud, and Janet would be diagnosed correctly as real physical conditions today.

Consider the case presented in the November 11, 2009, Diagnosis column of the *New York Times Magazine*. A 46-year-old woman suffered from a variety of mysterious physical symptoms. Over the years, she received multiple diagnoses, including that her problems were psychological. At the age of 23, she developed intermittent attacks of abdominal pain, fever, and vomiting that continued to the present day. Recently, her hands and feet had become numb, so much so that she could barely hold a pen or walk without stumbling. The woman was hospitalized dozens of times and had 13 surgeries, including the removal of her appendix, ovaries, and most of her colon.

Classic conversion disorder? Janet may have thought so, and at least some contemporary physicians reached that conclusion using diagnosis by exclusion. Yet, a neurologist finally diagnosed the very rare condition, *porphyria*, a genetically transmitted disease of the nervous system that affects red blood cells. Porphyria causes multiple physical and mental symptoms, sometimes including hallucinations and paranoia. The disease cannot be cured, but it at least can be understood and managed.

To avoid problems with diagnosis by exclusion, some experts recommend limiting the diagnosis of *functional neurological symptoms* (a proposed replacement term for conversion disorders) to cases where neurological tests clearly show inconsistent results (Friedman & LaFrance, 2010). An example would be when a patient has a "seizure," but an EEG indicates normal brain activity (APA, 2010). Perhaps the use of such a more circumspect definition of conversion disorder will help us to better understand how psychological stress can cause physical symptoms—and avoid telling patients with real physical illnesses that the problem is "all in your head."

**PSYCHOLOGICAL FACTORS—IMAGINED OR REAL TRAUMA** Initially, both Freud and Janet assumed that conversion disorders were caused by a trauma, particularly sexual abuse. However, Freud later questioned the accuracy of his patients' reports. Instead, he decided that their sexual memories were fantasized, not real. This led him to develop his theory of childhood sexuality (Freud, 1924/1962). He came to view dissociation as protecting people from unacceptable sexual impulses, not from intolerable memories (Freud, 1924/1962). Sadly, we now know that childhood sexual abuse is all too common. Freud's initial position may have been the accurate one.

Somatization at least sometimes can be triggered by traumatic stress. A study of 358 people who worked in the mortuary during the first Gulf War found an increase in somatic symptoms as a result of the experience. Symptoms included faintness, pain in the chest, nausea, trouble breathing, hot or cold spells, numbness, and feeling weak. Importantly, the before-to-after increase occurred more among workers with greater exposure to death. Symptoms increased more among workers who actually handled bodies compared to those who only observed bodies. Symptoms did not increase among workers with no exposure (McCarroll et al., 2002). Likely contributors to why trauma leads to somatization include the somatic consequences of stress, an increased awareness of one's own body, and the expression of psychological distress through somatic complaints.

Freud also suggested that the *primary gain* of hysterical symptoms was the expression of unconscious conflicts. He also indicated that conversion could produce *secondary gain*, for example, avoiding work or gaining attention. This latter view has more support than Freud's ideas about primary gain, although cognitive behavior therapists call this *reinforcement*. In addition to positive reinforcement (extra attention) or negative reinforcement (avoidance of work), *learning the sick role* through modeling may contribute to somatic symptom disorders (Lipowski, 1988). Cognitive factors also may play a role, especially (1) a tendency to amplify somatic symptoms (Brown, 2004; Kirmayer, Robbins, & Paris, 1994); (2) *alexithymia*—a deficit in one's capacity to recognize and express the emotions signaled by physiological arousal (Bankier, Aigner, & Bach, 2001); (3) the misattribution of normal somatic symptoms (Brown, 2004; Rief, Hiller, & Margraf, 1998); and (4) memory biases (Pauli & Alpers, 2002). Figure 7.5 summarizes how these and other factors may contribute to the development of somatic symptom disorders.

**SOCIAL FACTORS** A widely held social theory of somatic symptom disorders argues that when people in certain cultures experience psychological distress, they describe and experience their emotions as physical symptoms. Why? The theory assumes that some cultures do not teach or allow open emotional expression. A simple analogy for this theory is a child who complains about an upset stomach, not fear of failure, before giving a piano recital. Presumably, increasing psychological awareness explains both a decline in somatic symptom disorders over time and a lower

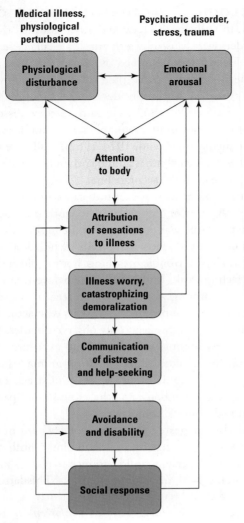

Medical illness,
physiological
perturbations

Psychiatric disorder,
stress, trauma

**Physiological
disturbance**

**Emotional
arousal**

**Attention
to body**

**Attribution
of sensations
to illness**

**Illness worry,
catastrophizing
demoralization**

**Communication
of distress
and help-seeking**

**Avoidance
and disability**

**Social response**

**FIGURE 7.5**

Minor physical symptoms may develop into a somatoform disorder when combined with emotional arousal, excessive attention to physical symptoms, misattributions, and other psychological tendencies and social reactions.

*Source:* Copyright © 2002, American Psychological Association.

prevalence in the West compared to other cultures today (Shorter, 1992). As noted earlier, however, unusual physical illnesses may have been misdiagnosed 100 years ago, and the disorders do *not* appear to be more prevalent in nonindustrialized than industrialized countries today. In fact, many suggest that contemporary, Western psychological "awareness" has become more than a little overdone. The Western focus on emotion may have moved beyond "open" into the realm of "obsessed."

## Treatment of Somatic Symptom Disorders

Charcot, Janet, and Freud encouraged their patients to recall and recount psychologically painful events as a way of treating conversion disorders. In the century or more since they refined their techniques, however, no systematic research was conducted on any *cathartic* therapies for conversion disorders, or for that matter,

on any treatment. While research is still limited, accumulating evidence indicates that cognitive behavior therapy can reduce physical symptoms in somatic symptom disorder (Woolfolk, Allen, & Tiu, 2007), illness anxiety disorder (Clark et al., 1998; McManus et al., 2012), and body dysmorphic disorder (Rosen, Reiter, & Orosan, 1995).

The most extensive studies focus on pain management. Cognitive behavioral approaches to chronic pain alter contingencies that reward *pain behavior* and the sick role. The goal is to reward successful coping and life adaptation instead (Kroenke, 2007). Cognitive behavior therapy also uses cognitive restructuring to address the emotional and cognitive components of pain. Research demonstrates the effectiveness of both approaches in treating chronic lower back pain (Blanchard, 1994).

Antidepressants also may be helpful in treating somatic symptom disorders, although less research has been conducted on their effectiveness (Kroenke, 2007). SSRIs produce more improvement in comparison to placebo for body dysmorphic disorder (Phillips, Albertini, & Rasmussen, 2002) and pain (Fishbain et al., 1998). Both medication and cognitive behavior therapy may be

"Anna O," a pseudonym for Bertha Pappenheim and the subject of a famous case study by Sigmund Freud, actually was treated by Josef Breuer. Anna O suffered from multiple "conversion" symptoms and was "successfully" treated with free association. Historical records indicate that treatment failed and suggest a neurological basis for her symptoms.

effective, in part, because the treatments alleviate the depression and anxiety that often are comorbid with somatic symptom disorders (Looper & Kirmayer, 2002; Simon, 2002). However, a recent study of mindfulness-based cognitive therapy found that the approach reduced illness anxiety beyond usual treatment *without* reducing comorbid anxiety or depression. Of interest, the mindfulness approach encourages more, not less, awareness of physical symptoms. Consistent with its roots in Eastern meditation, however, mindfulness encourages *acceptance* of symptoms as passing events, a contrast to Western approach to control and change them (McManus et al., 2012).

One reason for the limited psychological research is that primary care physicians treat most somatic symptom disorders (Bass et al., 2001). Patients typically consult physicians about their ailments, and they often insist that their problems are physical despite negative test results. Such patients are likely to refuse a referral to a mental health professional. As a result, primary care physicians often must learn how to manage the problems in a medical setting.

This can be difficult. The absence of a clear physical problem can frustrate primary care physicians, who may be unsympathetic toward "hypochondriacs" when they have so many patients with "real" problems. Not surprisingly, such reactions weaken the physician–patient relationship, and this can intensify the problem. In fact, the major recommendation for the medical management of patients with somatic symptom disorders is to establish a strong and consistent physician–patient relationship. Physicians are urged to schedule routine appointments with these patients every month or two and to conduct brief medical exams during this time (Allen et al., 2002). This approach not only provides consistent emotional support and medical reassurance but also helps to reduce unnecessary medical care. Patients who feel misunderstood are likely to recruit a new, more understanding physician (Allen et al., 2002). On the other hand, a physician who knows the patient can recognize the psychological origin of the physical complaints and order fewer unnecessary medical tests or treatments.

## getting HELP

The disorders discussed in this chapter are fascinating, and the controversies about them are intellectually exciting—unless you or someone you know is suffering from PTSD or a dissociative or somatic symptom disorder. In this case, the unusual symptoms can be extremely frightening, the lack of acceptance can be isolating, and the controversy surrounding the disorders can seem callous.

The controversies and limited scientific information make it difficult to make clear recommendations for getting help. However, you can review the treatment sections of the three disorders to get some specifics on the best approaches based on current research. These treatments generally involve some type of cognitive behavior therapy and/or antidepressant medication.

We also can readily offer a strong suggestion: If you have been the victim of trauma, for example, rape, abuse, or disaster, or a victim or witness of some other form of violence, talk to someone about it. You may find it difficult to trust anyone, but trying to "forget about it" is exactly the wrong thing to do. Confronting fear, embarrassment, or others' lack of understanding is far better than keeping it all inside. If you are not willing to consider therapy, start by confiding in a friend, a family member, even a stranger.

We are particularly concerned about the trauma of rape, including acquaintance rape, an all-too-frequent occurrence among college students. If you or someone you know has been raped, the first step may be to get to a hospital emergency room or to call the police. You also may want to contact a rape crisis center in your area. The Rape Abuse and Incest Network National hotline, (800)-656-4673, can provide you with the telephone number of the rape crisis center closest to you. You also may want to visit its Web site: http://www.rainn.org. A good self-help book on rape is *Free of the Shadows: Recovering from Sexual Violence*, by Caren Adams and Jennifer Fay.

There are many other resources available for victims of rape, disasters, and other traumas. If you are surfing the Web for information, we suggest that you begin your Internet exploration with the National Institute of Mental Health (NIMH). You will find much helpful information there, as well as links to other useful websites.

Another reason why we recommend that you begin with the NIMH website is that you need to be extremely cautious about information on PTSD and dissociative and somatic symptom disorders. The controversies discussed in this chapter are not just theoretical ones. There are many self-help resources—and professionals—who claim that one side or the other of a given controversy is fact, not theory or opinion. We urge you to be wary if a professional or resource fails to acknowledge the uncertain state of scientific information and the range of opinion about such things as the long-term consequences of childhood trauma, the prevalence of multiple personality disorder, or the nature of recovered memories. A dramatic illustration of the havoc that can be created by those who are supposed to help can be found in the book, *Remembering Satan*, Lawrence Wright's journalistic account of the consequences of one episode of false "recovered memories" of satanic ritual abuse.

# 7 Summary

**Dissociation** is the disruption of the normally integrated mental processes involved in memory or consciousness.

**Traumatic stress** is an event that involves actual or threatened death, serious injury, or sexual violence to self, or witnessing others experience trauma, learning that loved ones have been traumatized, or repeatedly being exposed to details of trauma.

**Acute stress disorder (ASD)** is a reaction to trauma that lasts less than one month and is characterized by symptoms of (1) intrusive reexperiencing, (2) avoidance of reminders of the trauma, (3) increased arousal or reactivity, (4) negative mood or thoughts, and often (5) dissociation.

**Posttraumatic stress disorder (PTSD)** is characterized by very similar symptoms as ASD, even though *DSM-5* lists them somewhat differently, but the symptoms either last for longer than one month or have a delayed onset.

Trauma is distressingly common and often leads to PTSD, especially rape for women and combat exposure for men.

Trauma is the central cause of PTSD, but other factors contribute to its development, including level of exposure, social support, genetics, pretrauma personality, avoidance, and emotional processing.

Targeted and naturalistic early intervention can prevent future PTSD, but some interventions like *critical incident stress debriefing* may actually increase risk.

Resilience is the most common response to trauma, although perhaps one-third of cases of PTSD become chronic.

**Dissociative disorders** are persistent, maladaptive disruptions in the integration of memory, consciousness, or identity.

**Somatic symptom disorders** involve complaints about physical symptoms that create psychological distress either out of proportion to actual physical problems or in the absence of a diagnosable physical illness

**Dissociative identity disorder (DID),** also known as **multiple personality disorder,** is a dramatic problem characterized by the existence of two or more distinct personalities in a single individual, but the diagnosis is rare and very controversial.

The term **conversion disorder** accurately conveys the central assumption of the diagnosis—the idea that psychological conflicts are converted into physical symptoms. The disorder involves *diagnosis by exclusion*, raising important concerns that some real but rare physical illness has been overlooked.

## The Big Picture

## critical thinking review

**7.1** How does *DSM-5* define trauma?
*DSM-5* defines trauma as exposure to actual or threatened death, serious injury, or sexual violation. . . (see page 180).

**7.2** Does trauma always lead to PTSD?
Because not every traumatized person develops a disorder, trauma is a necessary but not a sufficient cause. What increases risk or resilience in the face of trauma? . . . (see page 182).

**7.3** Can the unconscious mind cause mental disorders?
Both Janet and Freud were eager to explain hysteria, and both developed theories of unconscious mental processes to do so. . . (see page 187).

**7.4** What are recovered memories?
Our concern about so-called recovered memories extends well beyond the Franklin case . . . (see page 188).

**7.5** Is multiple personality disorder real?
Some experts even doubt the very existence of DID, arguing that DID is created by the power of suggestion. . . (see page 193).

**7.6** Were conversion disorders common in Freud's time?
No one knows how prevalent conversion disorders were during the time of Charcot, Janet, and Freud, but the literature of the period suggests that they were common . . . (see page 199).

# key terms

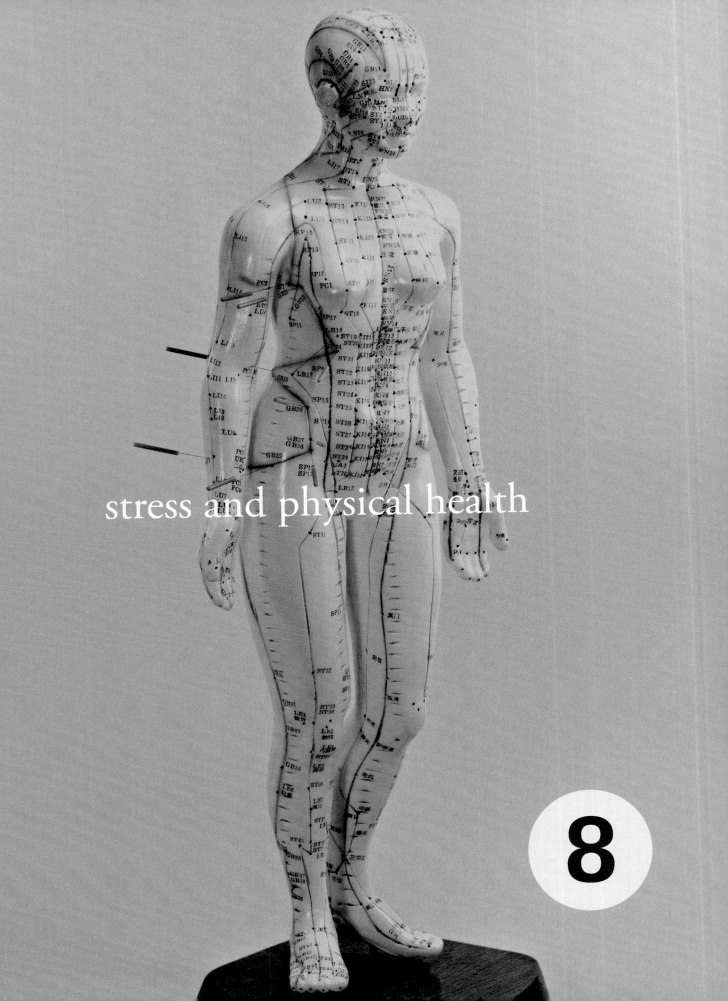

stress and physical health

8

# The Big Picture

## learning objectives

**8.1**
How can stress make you physically ill?

**8.2**
What are some good ways of coping with stress?

**8.3**
What does it mean to say people are resilient?

**8.4**
Does stress really play a role in diseases like cancer and AIDS?

**8.5**
What is a "lifestyle disease"?

**8.6**
What is "Type A" behavior? Can it really cause heart attacks?

How do you feel when you are "stressed out"? Different people feel jittery, tired, down, preoccupied, vigilant, defeated, angry, sick, or just plain lousy. How do you cope? Some people try to eliminate stress by solving the problem; others calm themselves by writing or talking about the stress; and still other people distract themselves in healthy ways like exercising or unhealthy ones like smoking or drinking. Can stress *really* make you sick? How? What physical illnesses are caused by stress? And, actually, what is stress anyway?

## Overview

Scientists define *stress* as any challenging event that requires physiological, cognitive, or behavioral adaptation. Stress may involve minor, daily hassles, like taking an exam, or major events, such as going through a divorce. The most common daily stressors involve interpersonal arguments and tensions (Almeida, 2005). As we saw in Chapter 7, *traumatic stress* involves exposure to actual or threatened death, serious injury, or sexual violence. This chapter is about normal stress, how we cope with it, and how stress affects our physical health.

Scientists once thought that stress contributed to only a few physical diseases. Ulcers, migraine headaches, hypertension (high blood pressure), asthma, and a few other illnesses were thought

to be *psychosomatic disorders*,[1] a product of both the *psyche* (mind) and the *soma* (body) (Harrington, 2008). Today, the term is outdated. Medical scientists now view *every* physical illness—from colds to cancer to AIDS—as a product of the interaction between the mind and body. Thus, there is no list of psychosomatic disorders in the *DSM-5* or elsewhere.

This holistic view of health and disease has brought about major changes in medicine. **Behavioral medicine** is a multidisciplinary field that includes both medical and mental health professionals who focus on psychological influences on the symptoms, cause, and treatment of physical illnesses. Psychologists who specialize in behavioral medicine often are called *health psychologists*.

Learning more adaptive ways of dealing with stress can limit the recurrence or improve the course of many physical illnesses (Lazarus, 2000; Snyder, 1999). In order to promote health, specialists in behavioral medicine therefore encourage healthy coping through stress management, proper diet, regular exercise, and avoidance of tobacco use. In treating diseases, behavioral medicine includes interventions such as educating parents of chronically ill children, teaching strategies for coping with chronic pain, and running support groups for people with terminal cancer.

In this chapter, we discuss innovations in behavioral medicine and review evidence on the link between stress and some major physical illnesses. In order to illustrate the challenges in studying stress, we also include an extended discussion of the number one killer in the United States today, cardiovascular disease. We begin with a case study.

### ➜ Bob Carter's Heart Attack

One Thursday afternoon, Bob Carter, a salesman for a beer and liquor wholesaler, was completing his route, calling on customers. Throughout the morning, he had felt a familiar discomfort in his chest and left arm. As had happened on occasion for at least a year, that morning he experienced a few fleeting but sharp pains in the center and left side of his chest. This was followed by a dull ache in his chest and left shoulder and a feeling of congestion in the same areas. Breathing deeply made the pain worse, but Bob could manage it as long as he took shallow breaths. He continued on his route, alternately vowing to see a doctor soon and cursing his aging body.

After grabbing a hamburger for lunch, Bob called on a customer who was behind in his payments. At first, Bob shared a cigarette with the customer and chatted with him in a friendly way. He was a salesman, after all. Soon it was time to pressure him about the bill. As Bob raised his voice in anger, a crushing pain returned to his chest and radiated down his left arm. This was much worse than anything he had experienced before. The pain was so intense that Bob was unable to continue speaking. He slumped forward against the table, but with his right arm he waved away any attempt to help him. After sitting still for about 10 minutes, Bob dragged himself to his car and drove to his home 30 miles away. When his wife saw

[1]In everyday language, we sometimes use the term *psychosomatic* to imply that an illness is imagined or not real. But unlike conversion disorders (Chapter 7), psychosomatic disorders involve very real physical damage or dysfunction.

him shuffle into the house looking haggard and in obvious pain, she called for an ambulance. The Carters soon discovered that Bob had suffered a *myocardial infarction* (a heart attack).

Bob was 49 years old. His home life was happy, but it also put a lot of pressure on him. His 24-year-old daughter was living at home while her husband was serving in combat overseas. Naturally, the entire family was anxious about the son-in-law's well-being. More stress came from Bob's 21-year-old daughter, who had just graduated from college and was getting married in three weeks. Finally, Bob's 19-year-old son was home from his first year of college, full of ideas that challenged Bob's authority.

Bob also put plenty of stress on himself at work. A former high school athlete, he had always been competitive and hard-driving. He wanted to be the best at whatever he did, and right now his goal was to be the best salesman in his company. Bob used his charm, humor, and some not-so-gentle pressure to sell his products, and it worked. But once he had become the best salesman in his company, Bob wanted to be the best salesman for the producers whose products he sold. No matter what he accomplished, Bob drove himself to meet a new goal.

Bob maintained his drive and competitiveness from his youthful days as a star athlete, but he had not maintained his physical condition. The only exercise he got was playing golf, and he usually rode in a cart instead of walking the course. He was at least 30 pounds overweight, smoked a pack and a half of cigarettes a day, ate a lot of fatty red meat, and drank heavily. Bob was a good candidate for a heart attack.

Bob recuperated quickly in the hospital. He was tired and in considerable pain for a couple of days, but he was telling jokes before the end of a week. His cardiologist explained what had happened and gave Bob a stern lecture about changing his lifestyle. He wanted Bob to quit smoking, lose weight, cut down on his drinking, and gradually work himself back into shape. He urged Bob to slow down at work and told him to quit worrying about his children—they were old enough to take care of themselves.

To underscore these messages, the cardiologist asked a psychologist from the hospital's behavioral medicine unit to consult with Bob. The psychologist reviewed information on coronary risk and gave Bob several pamphlets to read. The psychologist also explained that the hospital ran several programs that might interest Bob, including workshops on stress management, weight reduction, and exercise. Fees were minimal, because the hospital offered them as a community service. The psychologist also offered to talk to Bob, because cardiac patients and their families sometimes have trouble adjusting to the sudden reminder of the patient's mortality. But Bob waved off the offer of assistance much as he had waved off help in the middle of his heart attack.

Bob was discharged from the hospital five days after being admitted. Against his doctor's advice, he walked his daughter down the aisle at her wedding the following weekend, and he was back to work within a month. At his six-week checkup, Bob admitted that he was smoking again. His weight was unchanged, and his exercise and drinking were only a "little better." When the cardiologist chastised Bob, he promised to renew his efforts. However, he thought to himself that giving up these small pleasures would not make him live any longer. It would just seem that way.

The case of Bob Carter illustrates how stress can contribute to coronary heart disease, but it also raises a number of questions. What is the physiological mechanism that transforms psychological stress into coronary risk? Is stress the problem, or is the real culprit the unhealthy behaviors that result from stress—smoking, drinking, and overeating? What is the role of personality in stress? Can someone like Bob change his lifestyle, and, if so, does this lower the risk for future heart attacks? We consider these and related questions in this chapter. First, though, we need to consider more carefully exactly what we mean by "stress."

## Defining Stress

We define **stress** as a challenging event that requires physiological, cognitive, or behavioral adaptation. However, we need to examine this definition closely. Is stress the event itself? Some

Stress is a part of life, whether you are taking the SAT exam or even celebrating life-changing, positive events like getting married.

people would relax after becoming the top salesman, but Bob Carter viewed this achievement as another challenge. Perhaps stress should be defined in terms of the individual's reactions to an event. But if we define stress in terms of the reactions it causes, is it merely circular logic to say stress has unwanted effects? In fact, scientists continue to debate whether stress is best defined as a life event itself or the event plus the individual's reaction to it.

### Stress as a Life Event

Researchers often define stress as a life event—a difficult circumstance regardless of the individual's reaction to it. A measure that contributed greatly to the development of stress research, and still widely used, is Holmes and Rahe's (1967) Social Readjustment Rating Scale (SRRS), a scale that assigns stress values to life events based on the judgments of a large group of normal adults. The SRRS views stressors that produce more *life change units* as causing more stress (see Table 8.1).

Ratings on the SRRS and similar instruments are correlated with a variety of physical illnesses (Dohrenwend, 2006; Miller, 1989). Critics note, however, that stress checklists (1) rely on retrospective reports; (2) contain stressors that do not apply to people of different ages and ethnic backgrounds (Contrada et al., 2001) (Is the SRRS a good measure of college student stress?); (3) treat both positive and negative events as stressors (Would you equate getting married with getting fired?); (4) fail to distinguish between short-lived and chronic stressors; and most importantly, (5) treat the same event as causing the same amount of stress for everyone (Is getting pregnant just as stressful for an unwed teenager as it is for a married couple who want a baby?).

Dohrenwend and colleagues (1990) demonstrated the importance of this last point. They found, for example, that an assault caused a *large* change for nearly 20 percent of respondents, but it caused *no* change for the same percentage of people (see Table 8.2 on p. 210).

### TABLE 8.1
## Change Caused by Different Life Events

| Life Event | Life Change Units | Life Event | Life Change Units |
|---|---|---|---|
| Death of one's spouse | 100 | Son or daughter leaving home | 29 |
| Divorce | 73 | Trouble with in-laws | 29 |
| Marital separation | 65 | Outstanding personal achievement | 28 |
| Jail term | 63 | Wife beginning or stopping work | 26 |
| Death of a close family member | 63 | Beginning or ending school | 26 |
| Personal injury or illness | 53 | Change in living conditions | 25 |
| Marriage | 50 | Revision of personal habits | 24 |
| Being fired at work | 47 | Trouble with one's boss | 23 |
| Marital reconciliation | 45 | Change in work hours or conditions | 20 |
| Retirement | 45 | Change in residence | 20 |
| Change in the health of a family member | 44 | Change in schools | 20 |
| Pregnancy | 40 | Change in recreation | 19 |
| Sex difficulties | 39 | Change in church activities | 19 |
| Gain of a new family member | 39 | Change in social activities | 18 |
| Business readjustment | 39 | Mortgage or loan of less than $10,000 | 17 |
| Change in one's financial state | 38 | Change in sleeping habits | 16 |
| Death of a close friend | 37 | Change in number of family get-togethers | 15 |
| Change to a different line of work | 36 | Change in eating habits | 15 |
| Change in number of arguments with one's spouse | 35 | Vacation | 13 |
| Mortgage over $10,000 | 31 | Christmas | 12 |
| Foreclosure of a mortgage or loan | 30 | Minor violations of the law | 11 |
| Change in responsibilities at work | 29 | | |

The SRRS rates different stressors as causing more or less life change for people. More difficult stressors have a higher number of "life change units."

*Source:* Based on Holmes, TH and RH Rahe. The Social Readjustment Scale. Journal of Psychosomatic Research. 1967; 11(2): 213–218.

**TABLE 8.2**

## Different Reactions to the Same Life Event

| Type of Event | Percentage of Subjects Reporting Each Amount of Change | | | |
| --- | --- | --- | --- | --- |
| | Large | Moderate | Little | None |
| Serious physical illness | 47.2% | 27.8% | 8.3% | 16.7% |
| Relations with mate got worse | 41.2 | 47.1 | 0.0 | 11.8 |
| Relative died (not child/spouse) | 8.3 | 8.3 | 29.2 | 54.2 |
| Close friend died | 5.3 | 15.8 | 29.8 | 49.1 |
| Financial loss (not work related) | 16.3 | 44.2 | 18.6 | 20.9 |
| Assaulted | 18.5 | 22.2 | 40.7 | 18.5 |
| Broke up with a friend | 0.0 | 26.1 | 37.0 | 37.0 |
| Laid off | 13.3 | 63.3 | 13.3 | 10.0 |
| Had trouble with a boss | 17.5 | 35.0 | 32.5 | 15.0 |
| Got involved in a court case | 9.5 | 9.5 | 28.6 | 52.4 |

Large percentages of people rate the same life event as causing large, moderate, little, or no change in their lives. This illustrates a key problem with assigning a set level of stress to any given life event, and more generally, of defining stress in terms of a stimulus alone.

*Source:* Based on Wong, Paul. Measuring Life Events: The Problem with Variability within Event Categories. Stress Medicine. July/September 1990. 6(3); 171–255.

## Stress as Appraisal of Life Events

Because of this variability, many experts define stress as the combination of an event plus each individual's reaction to it. Richard Lazarus (1966) defined stress as the individual's *appraisal* of a challenging life event. An impending exam is stressful when you feel inadequately prepared, but less so when you are confident. Lazarus also distinguished between people's *primary appraisal*, our evaluation of the challenge, threat, or harm posed by an event, and people's *secondary appraisal*, our assessment of our abilities and resources for coping with that event (Lazarus & Folkman, 1984). Thus, even if you feel unprepared, the impending exam causes less stress if you have the time and the ability to study.

The appraisal approach recognizes that the same event is more or less stressful for different people but runs the risk of circular reasoning. What is stress? An event that causes us to feel threatened and overwhelmed. What causes us to feel threatened and overwhelmed? Stress. Logically, such a definition would be a *tautology*, a redundant statement that means nothing. Because of the potential tautology, researchers must carefully distinguish independent variables (stressors) from hypothesized dependent variables (adverse outcomes).

## Symptoms of Stress

Stress is an *adaptive* response to many aspects of living. If you had no stress response, you would not jump out of the way of a cement truck barreling down on you, let alone study for your exams!

The fight or flight response (in the cat, not the dog!).

## Tend and Befriend: The Female Stress Response?

Health psychologist Shelly Taylor and her colleagues (2006) suggest that fight-or-flight may be a particularly *male* response to stress. Females, particularly primate females, may **tend and befriend** instead. *Tending* involves caring for offspring, especially protecting them from harm. *Befriending* involves social affiliation, finding safety in numbers, and sharing resources.

Theoretically, tend and befriend, like fight-or-flight, is a product of evolution. Inclusive fitness may be increased by caretaking and blending into the environment in response to threat. Attachment is the mechanism hypothesized to underlie tending and befriending, but Taylor (2006) focuses on the benefits for the caretaker rather than the infant. She argues that evolution selected for caretaking tendencies in adult females.

Taylor and her colleagues (2000) suggested that, unlike male aggression, female aggression is activated less by sympathetic nervous system arousal (due to the lack of *testosterone*, the male sex hormone). This limits the female's fight response. Flight tendencies, in turn, are countered by *oxytocin* released by the pituitary and by the female sex hormone, *estrogen*. Theoretically, the result is the activation of the parasympathetic nervous system, which has a calming effect.

Tend and befriend is a speculative hypothesis, but it focuses attention on important issues, for example, including more females in studies of stress. Prior to 1995, males made up 83 percent of the participants in laboratory studies of stress. Moreover, evidence repeatedly shows major differences between women and men in response to stress, susceptibility to different diseases, and longevity, as women outlive men by five to 10 years in industrialized countries (Kajantie, 2008). Critics might see sexism in Taylor's assertions about female–male sex differences, but Taylor carefully acknowledges cultural influences on gender roles. And under the right conditions, or through learning, males may also respond to stress by tending and befriending.

---

The renowned American physiologist Walter Cannon (1871–1945), one of the first and foremost stress researchers, recognized the adaptive, evolutionary aspects of stress. Cannon (1935) viewed stress as the activation of the **fight-or-flight response**,[2] the reaction you witness when a cat is surprised by a barking dog. The cat can either scratch at the dog or flee to safety. The fight-or-flight response has obvious survival value. Cannon observed, however, that fight-or-flight is a *maladaptive* reaction to much stress in the modern world. Fight-or-flight is not an adaptive response to being reprimanded by your boss or giving a speech before a large audience. In other words, the human environment may have evolved more rapidly than our physiological reactions to it. (Some psychologists think that fight-or-flight is a *male* reaction to stress; see Tend and Befriend.)

### Psychophysiological Responses to Stress

Physiologically, the fight-or-flight response activates the *sympathetic nervous system:* Your heart and respiration rates increase, your blood pressure rises, your pupils dilate, your blood sugar levels elevate, and your blood flow is redirected in preparation for muscular activity (Baum et al., 1987; Koranyi, 1989). These physiological reactions heighten attention, provide energy for quick action, and prepare the body for injury (Sapolsky, 2003). This physiological reaction presumably was an adaptive response to many threats over the course of human evolution. But when your boss is yelling—or you worry that your boss *might* yell—the response only leaves your body racing and you feeling nervous and agitated.

**ADRENAL HORMONES** How does the stress response work physiologically? When a perceived threat registers in the cortex, it signals the *amygdala*, the brain structure primarily responsible for activating the stress response, which secretes *corticotrophin-releasing factor (CRF)*. CRF stimulates the brainstem to activate the sympathetic nervous system. In response to the sympathetic arousal, the *adrenal glands* release two key hormones. One is *epinephrine* (commonly known as *adrenaline*), which acts as a neuromodulator and leads to the release of *norepinephrine* and more *epinephrine* into the bloodstream (see Figure 8.1 on p. 212). This familiar "rush of adrenaline" further activates the sympathetic nervous system.

The second key adrenal hormone is **cortisol**, often called the "stress hormone" because its release is so closely linked with stress. Cortisol has a less rapid action than adrenaline, yet it functions quickly to help the body make repairs in response to injury or infection. One function of cortisol is "containment" of pathogens in the body—the same function performed by the steroids that you may take for inflammation and skin irritation. Like externally administered steroids, however, cortisol can promote healing in

---

[2]Ethologists now view mammals' responses to threat as more nuanced: freeze-flight-fight-fright. Mammals' first response to threat is to freeze (hide); if that fails, they flee; fighting is the third option. Fright or *tonic immobility*, also known as "playing dead," is the final option when a threat is imminent and mortal (Bracha et al., 2004). Stress research is beginning to incorporate freeze-flight-fight-fright (Roelofs et al., 2010), but we use the fight-or-flight dichotomy, which dominates in current efforts.

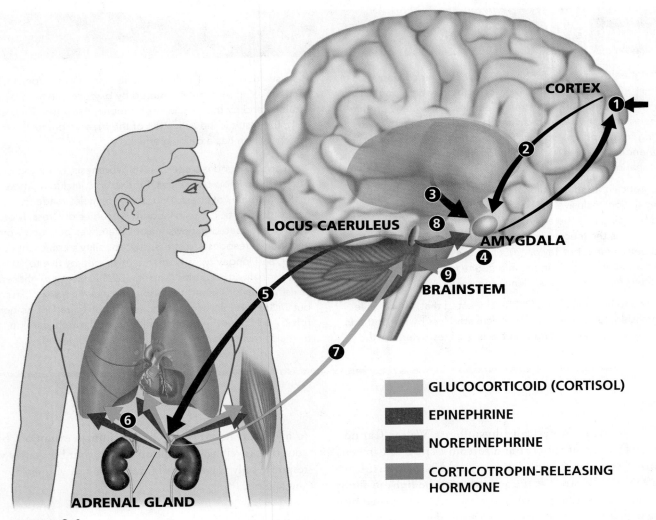

**CORTEX**

**LOCUS CAERULEUS**

**AMYGDALA**

**BRAINSTEM**

**ADRENAL GLAND**

GLUCOCORTICOID (CORTISOL)

EPINEPHRINE

NOREPINEPHRINE

CORTICOTROPIN-RELEASING HORMONE

**FIGURE 8.1**

Stress pathways are diverse and involve many regions of the brain in feedback loops that can sometimes greatly amplify a response. The process—simplified somewhat in this diagram—begins when an actual or perceived threat activates the sensory and higher reasoning centers in the cortex (1). The cortex then sends a message to the amygdala, the principal mediator of the stress response (2). Separately, a preconscious signal may precipitate activity in the amygdala (3). The amygdala releases corticotropin-releasing hormone, which stimulates the brain-stem (4) to activate the sympathetic nervous system via the spinal cord (5). In response, the adrenal glands produce the stress hormone epinephrine; a different pathway simultaneously triggers the adrenals to release glucocorticoids. The two types of hormones act on the muscle, heart, and lungs to prepare the body for "fight or flight" (6). If the stress becomes chronic, glucocorticoids induce the locus caeruleus (7) to release norepinephrine that communicates with the amygdala (8), leading to the production of more CRH (9)—and to ongoing reactivation of stress pathways.

*Source:* © Pearson Education, Upper Saddle River, New Jersey.

the short run, but an excess of cortisol can harm the hippocampus, cause muscular atrophy, and produce hypertension (Song & Leonard, 2000; Yehuda, 2002). 👁 **Watch** the **Video** *Hormonal Pathways* on **MyPsychLab**

**IMMUNE SYSTEM RESPONSES** The release of cortisol and CRF also cause *immunosuppression*, the decreased production of immune agents. Stress affects *T cells*, white blood cells that fight off *antigens*—foreign substances like bacteria that invade the body. This makes the body more susceptible to infectious diseases. The field of **psychoneuroimmunology (PNI)** investigates the relation between stress and immune function (Adler, 2001; Song & Leonard, 2000).

Why would stress inhibit immune function? From an evolutionary perspective, *heightened* immune functioning might seem

A white blood cell called a *macrophage* (colored yellow) attacks bacteria (blue).

to better prepare the body for the infection that may follow injury. However, the immune response creates inflammation, maintains fever, and intensifies pain—all of which impair immediate action (Maier, Watkins, & Fleshner, 1994). Thus, immunosuppression may actually be an adaptive short-term reaction to stress.

Current evidence suggests a response to stress that is more nuanced than blanket immunosuppression. Short-term stressors and physical threats *enhance* immune responses that are quick, require little energy, and contain infection due to an injury. However, stress *impairs* immune responses that drain energy from the fight-or-flight response. Chronic stressors and losses (as opposed to threats) also create immunosuppression (Segerstrom, 2007; Segerstrom & Miller, 2004), perhaps permanently altering immune functioning in a way to explain associations between childhood stress and diseases of aging (Miller, Chen, & Parker, 2011). Of interest, causality can work in the opposite direction: Immunosuppression can cause behavior change. Recently ill study participants are more vigilant in avoiding people who appear to be at risk for carrying infection (Miller & Maner, 2011).

**ILLNESS AND CHRONIC STRESS** Repeated stress can leave you susceptible to illness. Cannon (1935) hypothesized that this occurs because intense or chronic stress overwhelms the body's **homeostasis** (a term he coined), the tendency to return to a steady state of normal functioning. He suggested that prolonged arousal of the sympathetic nervous system eventually damages the body, because it no longer returns to its normal resting state.

Canadian physiologist Hans Selye (1907–1982), another very influential stress researcher, offered a different hypothesis based on his concept of the **general adaptation syndrome (GAS)**, which consists of three stages: alarm, resistance, and

exhaustion. The first stage of *alarm* involves the mobilization of the body in reaction to threat. The next stage, *resistance*, is a period of time when the body is physiologically activated and prepared to respond to the threat. *Exhaustion* occurs if the body's resources are depleted by chronic stress. Selye viewed the exhaustion as how stress causes physical illness. The body is damaged by continuous, failed attempts to reactivate the GAS (Selye, 1956).

Selye's theory differs from Cannon's in important ways. An analogy for Cannon's theory is a car in which the engine continues to race instead of idling down after running fast. An analogy for Selye's is a car that has run out of gas and is damaged because stress keeps turning the key, trying repeatedly to restart the engine. A third mechanism also may be at work. The stress response may use so much energy that the body cannot do routine upkeep like storing energy or repairing injuries (Sapolsky, 1992). An analogy for this third theory is a car running at such high speeds that the cooling and lubricant systems cannot keep up, making a breakdown likely.

## Coping

People cope with stress in many ways, good and bad. Two basic strategies are problem-focused and emotion-focused coping (Lazarus & Folkman, 1984). **Problem-focused coping** involves attempts to change a stressor. If your job is stressful, you look for a new one. **Emotion-focused coping** is an attempt to alter internal distress. Before taking a big exam, you sit quietly and breathe deeply to calm yourself.

We all face a big problem in deciding how to cope: What will work? What if you are stressed out by poor grades in a difficult class? Should you redouble your efforts, drop the course, or accept that this is not your best subject? Culturally, Americans prefer change over acceptance. Asian cultures, in contrast, emphasize acceptance over change. What works best? We think that flexibility is the key. There is much truth in Reinhold Niebuhr's "Serenity Prayer":

> God, give me the serenity to accept the things I cannot change;
> The courage to change the things I cannot accept;
> And the wisdom to know the difference.

**PREDICTABILITY AND CONTROL** Events are less stressful when we are better prepared to cope with them. Studies of animals and humans show that *predictability* and *control* both dramatically reduce stress. For example, when a flash of light signals an impending shock, rats show a smaller stress response than when the shock is unsignaled (Sapolsky, 1992). The predictability allows animals (and humans, too) to begin to cope even before the onset of a stressor.

Animal research also shows the benefits of control. When they can stop a shock by pressing a bar, rats have a smaller stress response than when they have no control (Sapolsky, 1992). Even the *illusion* of control can help to alleviate stress. However, the perception of control *increases* stress when people believe they could have exercised control but failed to do so, or when they lose control over a formerly controllable stressor (Mineka & Kihlstrom, 1978). Control lessens stress when we have it, even when it is illusory, but failed attempts at control intensify stress.

**OUTLETS FOR FRUSTRATION** Physical activity also reduces physiological reactions to stress, even when the effort does not include problem-focused coping. For example, rats secrete less cortisol following an electric shock if they can attack another rat or run on a running wheel (Sapolsky, 1992). Sounds like you at the gym—or dumping on your roommates? Having *outlets for frustration* does reduce stress.

**REPRESSION** *Repression*, keeping feelings bottled up, is a maladaptive form of emotion-focused coping (Cramer, 2000; Somerfield & McCrae, 2000). People who report positive mental health but whom clinicians judge to have emotional problems (so-called "defensive deniers") show greater psychophysiological reactions to stress (Shedler, Mayman, & Manis, 1993). On the flip side, stress is reduced when people talk about their stressful experiences, especially when stress is uncontrollable, you are comfortable talking about your emotions, and close others are supportive (Stanton & Low, 2012).

**OPTIMISM** *Optimism* is a healthy coping style. Pessimists are defeated from the outset. Optimists have a positive attitude about dealing with stress, even when they cannot control it. Positive thinking is linked with better health habits and less illness

(Carver & Scheier, 1999; Kubzansky et al., 2001). Optimism about school predicts better immune functioning among law students (Segerstrom & Sephton, 2010). Stress is taxing, but less so if we approach it as a challenge instead of as an obstacle.

**RELIGION** Surprisingly, psychologists have only recently begun to study the health benefits of religious coping (Hill & Pargament, 2003). Evidence demonstrates that mortality risk is lower among those who attend church services, probably as a result of improved health behavior (Powell, Shahabi, & Thoresen, 2003; Schnall et al., 2008). Forgiveness, a religious and philosophical virtue, apparently also offers earthly benefits; it improves health (Witvliet, Ludwig, & Vander Laan, 2001).

Forgiveness can be healthful, as can finding meaning in life either through or outside of religion (Yanez et al., 2009). Other research shatters some misconceptions about religious coping, which often is thought to only promote acceptance of God's will. A study of 200 Latinos with arthritis found that religion encouraged *active*, not passive, coping—and led to less pain, less depression, and improved psychological well-being (Abraído-Lanza, Vásquez, & Echeverría, 2004). Religious beliefs can help sufferers to gain control *with* God, not just to accept control *by* God (Pargament & Park, 1995). This distinction is critical, since passive religious coping may worsen health while active religious coping enhances it (Edwards et al., 2009; see Critical Thinking Matters).

## Health Behavior

Stress can affect health directly, but stress also contributes to illness *indirectly* by disrupting health behavior (Cohen & Williamson, 1991; see Figure 8.3). **Health behavior** is any action that promotes

## CRITICAL THINKING matters

### Resilience

Popular culture, and much psychological research, tells us that stress is bad, something to be avoided. Stress will make us tense, irritable, and unhappy. Stress makes us sick.

Stress *can* make us more susceptible to illness, but a little critical thinking leads us to ask: Are we really so vulnerable to stress? After all, humans evolved in stressful, often dangerous environments. Evolution *must* have selected for successful strategies for coping with stress, not crumbling in the face of it. And stress is a part of everyday life, often a good part—a challenge. We typically expect to rise to the challenge of a sporting event, a difficult class, even a crisis in our lives. Does it make sense that humans are fragile in the face of stress?

The answer is "No" according to proponents of *positive psychology*, an approach that highlights human psychological strengths (Linley & Joseph, 2005). Positive psychologists instead

see pervasive human **resilience**, the ability to cope successfully with the challenges of life, including very stressful ones. Most people overcome not only normal stress but traumatic stress too. For example, most people do *not* develop PTSD following trauma; most people who lose a loved one are *not* overcome by depression in their grief (Bonanno, 2004).

Not only are most people resilient, but some people grow—they get stronger—as a result of stress (Linley & Joseph, 2005). For example, J.K. Rowling was divorced, depressed, and nearly broke before she wrote the *Harry Potter* series. In fact, research shows a U-shaped relationship between adversity and many measures of well-being. Too much stress can be harmful but so can too little (Seery, 2011; see Figure 8.2)

Resilience lies partly within the individual—for example, positive affect is related to many indices of health (Cohen &

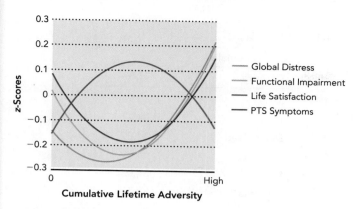

**FIGURE 8.2**

**Life Adversity and Well-Being** Too much stress—or too little stress—can be unhealthy. Moderate challenges help us to "exercise" coping skills.

*Source:* Based on Seery, MD. Resilience: A silver lining to experiencing adverse life events? Current Directions in Psychological Science. 2011; 20: 390–394.

Pressman, 2006). Resilience also is partly attributable to social support and other aspects of environments (Roisman, 2005). One fascinating theory suggests that individual traits and environmental characteristics interact in important ways. According to this perspective, some people are "dandelions," while others are "orchids." Dandelions may not be beautiful, but they are the epitome of resilience. Dandelions grow everywhere, even when you try to kill them. Orchids can die, even when tended carefully. But in just the right environment, orchids explode with beauty (Ellis & Boyce, 2008). Although largely untested, the analogy offers a new, challenging perspective on resilience.

Whatever resilience is, it is a quality that most people possess in most circumstances. Stress can make us weaker, or it can make us stronger. While chronic, uncontrollable stress can break us down, most people find the strength they need to cope when confronted by stress.

good health. It includes healthy habits like a balanced diet, regular sleep, and exercise, as well as avoiding unhealthy activities like cigarette smoking, excessive alcohol consumption, and drug use. Poor health habits, not stress per se, may be responsible for much of the relation between stress and illness (Bogg & Roberts, 2004).

Behavior is critical to health, and health behavior is influenced by cultural as well as individual characteristics. The prestigious National Research Council (NRC) (2013) recently reported that life expectancy in the United States lags behind other high-income countries (see Table 8.3). The NRC (2013) blamed the discrepancy primarily on behavioral issues: (1) poor health

behavior like excessive smoking, drinking, and eating; (2) poverty due to large income disparities in the U.S.; (3) physical environments that depend more on driving and less on exercise; and (4) health care systems that limit access to primary care.

**MEDICAL ADVICE** One very important health behavior is following medical advice, something that as many as 93 percent of all patients *fail* to do fully (Taylor, 1990). This is a particular problem for illnesses like hypertension (high blood pressure) that usually have no obvious symptoms. Patients may discontinue their medication, for example, because it offers no noticeable

The real-life Patch Adams inspired the film in which Robin Williams played the title role. Adams was a rebellious medical student in the 1960s who wanted to provide holistic care and instill optimism in his patients.

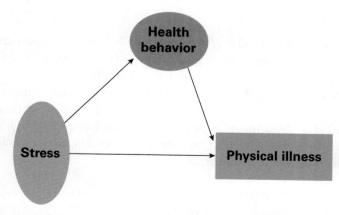

**FIGURE 8.3**

**Direct and Indirect Effects of Stress on Physical Illness** Stress may cause illness directly, for example, through suppression of immune functioning. Stress also may cause illness indirectly by causing poor health behavior.

## TABLE 8.3
## Life Expectancy in Seventeen High-Income Countries

| | Males | | | Females | |
|---|---|---|---|---|---|
| Rank | Country | LE | Rank | Country | LE |
| 1 | Switzerland | 79.33 | 1 | Japan | 85.98 |
| 2 | Australia | 79.27 | 2 | France | 84.43 |
| 3 | Japan | 79.20 | 3 | Switzerland | 84.09 |
| 4 | Sweden | 78.92 | 3 | Italy | 84.09 |
| 5 | Italy | 78.82 | 5 | Spain | 84.03 |
| 6 | Canada | 78.35 | 6 | Australia | 83.78 |
| 7 | Norway | 78.25 | 7 | Canada | 82.95 |
| 8 | Netherlands | 78.01 | 7 | Sweden | 82.95 |
| 9 | Spain | 77.62 | 9 | Austria | 82.86 |
| 10 | United Kingdom | 77.43 | 10 | Finland | 82.86 |
| 11 | France | 77.41 | 11 | Norway | 82.68 |
| 12 | Austria | 77.33 | 12 | Germany | 82.44 |
| 13 | Germany | 77.11 | 13 | Netherlands | 82.31 |
| 14 | Denmark | 76.13 | 14 | Portugal | 82.19 |
| 15 | Portugal | 75.87 | 15 | United Kingdom | 81.68 |
| 16 | Finland | 75.86 | 16 | United States | 80.78 |
| 17 | United States | 75.64 | 17 | Denmark | 80.53 |

The United States has the lowest life expectancy among major high-income countries largely due to behavioral issues including poor health behavior, poverty, physical environments that discourage exercise and limited access to primary care.

*Source*: Courtesy of Thomas F. Oltmanns and Robert E. Emery.

relief, even though it may control a dangerous underlying condition. Stress also can interfere with treatments that *do* affect symptoms. For example, family conflict makes children with insulin-dependent diabetes less likely to adhere to medical advice about exercise, diet, and testing blood sugars (Miller-Johnson et al., 1994).

**ILLNESS BEHAVIOR** *Illness behavior*—behaving as if you are sick—also is stress related. Increased stress is correlated with such illness behaviors as making more frequent office visits to physicians or allowing chronic pain to interfere with everyday activities (Taylor, 1990). Effective coping is partly a matter of perception, including ignoring of some physical discomfort and living life as normally as possible, particularly when coping with chronic illness (Petrie & Weinman, 2012).

**SOCIAL SUPPORT** *Social support* both encourages positive health behavior and has direct, physical benefits (Uchino, 2009). Even stressed monkeys exhibit less immunosuppression when they interact more with other monkeys (Cohen et al., 1992). Stressed rabbits develop clogged arteries more slowly if they affiliate with other rabbits (McCabe et al., 2002). Increased social

support in humans predicts improved immune, cardiovascular, and endocrine functioning (Schneiderman, Ironson, & Siegel, 2004).

People seek social support in different ways. Cultural differences can be important. For example, Asians and Asian Americans benefit from *implicit* social support such as focusing on valued social groups. *Explicit* social support such as seeking advice and emotional solace does not buffer stress for Asians, but it does for European Americans (Taylor et al., 2007). And it sometimes is better to give than to receive. *Providing* social support promotes good health at least as much as receiving it does (Brown et al., 2003).

Of all potential sources of social support, a good marriage can be critical (Kiecolt-Glaser & Newton, 2001). One fascinating study admitted 90 newlyweds to a hospital research ward where the couples discussed marital problems for 30 minutes. Partners who were hostile or negative had more immunosuppression over the next 24 hours, and their blood pressure remained elevated, too (Kiecolt-Glaser et al., 1993). And a follow-up study found that epinephrine levels were 34 percent higher for couples who got divorced in the next 10 years (Kiecolt-Glaser et al., 2003). A conflicted marriage is bad for your health, and too much stress is bad for your marriage!

## Illness as a Cause of Stress

Stress can cause illness, but illness also causes stress. For example, consider the effects of the diagnosis of insulin-dependent diabetes on a 10-year-old boy and his family. In order to maintain a normal range of blood sugar, the child and his parents must frequently test his blood, adjust to giving and receiving one, two, or three injections of insulin daily, and carefully monitor exercise and diet because of their effects on blood sugar. In addition, the child and his family must somehow cope with the stigma of being "different." Finally, they have to learn to cope with the possibility of him suffering long-term side effects from hyperglycemia (high blood sugar), including kidney dysfunction or blindness. As this example suggests, helping children, adults, and families cope with the stress of chronic illness is an important part of behavioral medicine (Martire & Schulz, 2007).

## Diagnosis of Stress and Physical Illness

The *DSM-5* classifies stress related to physical illness as *Psychological Factors Affecting Other Medical Conditions*. This diagnosis is a part of a new *DSM-5* category called *Somatic Symptom and Other Disorders*, which also includes problems like *conversion disorder*, where psychological issues are prominent but the physical symptoms often are medically unexplained (and may involve symptoms that make no medical sense) (see Chapter 7). *DSM-5* grouped stress-related physical illnesses together with other somatic symptom disorders for the obvious reason that they all include physical symptoms and often are treated as medical settings. The new category, somatic symptom disorders, may have practical benefits for medical practitioners, but we question its conceptual basis (see Thinking Critically About *DSM-5*).

## THINKING CRITICALLY about DSM-5

### Is the Descriptive Approach Too Literal Sometimes?

*DSM-5* takes a descriptive approach to classification, basing a diagnosis on similar, observed symptoms. The descriptive approach has advantages, as we discussed in Chapter 4. Perhaps the foremost advantage is reliability. Different clinicians are more likely to agree about a diagnosis that is based on observable symptoms.

The *DSM-5* also follows a descriptive approach when grouping diagnoses into broader categories. For example, the new diagnostic category, somatic symptom disorders, combines psychological factors affecting other medical conditions together with conversion disorder and other problems that involve somatic symptoms (reviewed in Chapter 7). It is hard to argue with the practical reason *DSM-5* made this change: Somatic symptom disorders all involve physical symptoms and are usually treated in medical settings by medical practitioners.

Yet, we do not want you to follow *DSM-5* slavishly or uncritically. Diagnostic classifications can be based on many grounds. We decided, for example, to discuss dissociative disorders and conversion disorder together in Chapter 7 because of their historical ("hysteria") and conceptual (unconscious processes) association. (We did place psychological factors affecting other medical conditions adjacent to other *DSM-5* somatic symptom disorders to help you understand and appreciate *DSM-5*'s approach.)

When we teach abnormal psychology, we do a class demonstration to make the point that classifications can be based on many, different criteria. We bring a couple of dozen items from our desk, and ask students to sort them into categories. All of the items can be grouped together as desk materials. But we can also group them based on their function: pens, pencils, a computer keyboard; staples, paper clips, scotch tape; scissors, a wood letter opener. Or we can group them based on the main material in the object: pencils, letter opener (wood); staples, paper clips, scissors (metal); computer keyboard, pens, scotch tape (plastic). Or we can group them according to psychoanalytic theory: pens, pencils, scissors, letter opener; everything else. (What's the theory? Phallic symbols!)

We question *DSM-5*'s descriptive approach to a number of problems (and we want you to question *DSM-5* too). To offer another example, *pica*, eating nonfood substances (e.g., paper) is now classified as an eating disorder. Sure, pica involves eating issues, as do anorexia nervosa and bulimia nervosa (see Chapter 10). But anorexia and bulimia have a lot in common. They both include major issues with body image, often have an onset in adolescence, are much more common among women, are influenced by cultural standards of beauty, and so on. Pica typically occurs among very young children, particularly children with intellectual disabilities or autism spectrum disorders (see Chapter 15). Is *DSM-5* being too literal in grouping these problems together based on their appearance? We think so. It is a bit like you saying that staples, paper clips, and scissors *have* to go together. They are all shiny and sliver!

Critical thinking requires much more than memorization. Of course, we want you to learn about the *DSM-5* diagnoses, but we also want you to understand and evaluate the diagnostic system. Our goal is not to criticize *DSM-5*. Our goal is to help you think more deeply about the *DSM-5* and all kinds of scientific classifications. Is Pluto a planet? Why is plasma different from gas?

Who knows? Maybe *you* will help to create a new, improved version of the DSM one day. For now, just remember this: Classifying symptoms and disorders together based on their description is a reasonable approach at this point in the evolution of the diagnosis of mental disorders. Yet, the descriptive approach is not necessarily the best way to classify psychological problems. And it certainly is not the only way.

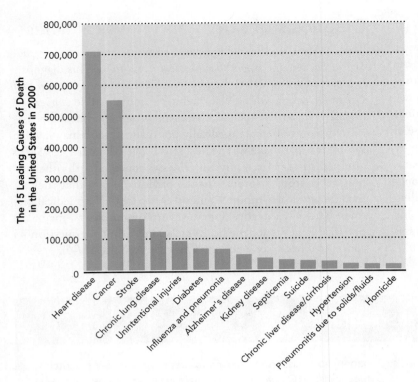

FIGURE **8.4**

Stress and health behavior play a central role in most of the major causes of death in the United States today.

## Psychological Factors and Some Familiar Illnesses

Psychological Factors Affecting Other Medical Conditions may involve any physical illness. There is no subset of "psychosomatic" disorders. The psychological factors may include distress, interaction patterns, coping styles, or maladaptive health behaviors, not necessarily a mental disorder (see "DSM-5: Psychological Factors Affecting Other Medical Conditions").

At the beginning of the twentieth century, infectious diseases, specifically influenza, pneumonia, and tuberculosis, were the most common causes of death in the United States (Taylor, 1995). Thanks to advances in medical science, and especially in public health, far fewer people die of infectious diseases now. Today, most of the leading causes of death are *lifestyle diseases* that are affected by stress and health behavior (Human Capital Initiative, 1996; see Figure 8.4).

In the following sections we briefly review evidence on stress and lifestyle in the cause, course, and treatment of cancer, HIV infection, chronic pain, and sleep disorders. After this, we consider in some detail the relation between stress and today's number one killer, cardiovascular disease.

### Cancer

Cancer is the second leading cause of mortality in the United States today, accounting for 23 percent of all deaths. At first glance, cancer may seem to be a purely biological illness, but the

---

**criteria for**
**Psychological Factors Affecting Other Medical Conditions**　　　**DSM-5**

**A.** A general medical symptom or condition (other than a mental disorder) is present.

**B.** Psychological or behavioral factors adversely affect the medical condition in one of the following ways:

1. The factors have influenced the course of the medical condition as shown by a close temporal association between the psychological factors and the development or exacerbation of, or delayed recovery from, the medical condition.

2. The factors interfere with the treatment of the general medical condition (e.g., poor adherence).

3. The factors constitute additional well-established health risks for the individual.

4. The factors influence the underlying pathophysiology, precipitating or exacerbating symptoms or necessitating medical attention.

Reprinted with permission from the *Diagnostic and Statistical Manual of Mental Disorders, Fifth Edition,* (Copyright © 2013). American Psychiatric Association.

Social support helps cancer patients cope with uncomfortable treatments and side effects, while improving their quality of life.

importance of psychological factors quickly becomes apparent. For example, health behavior such as cigarette smoking contributes to exposure to various *carcinogens*, cancer-causing agents.

Psychological factors also are at least modestly associated with the course of cancer (McKenna et al., 1999). Not surprisingly, cancer patients often are anxious or depressed, and commonly suffer "cancer-related fatigue," a condition attributable to both emotional factors and the physical side effects of cancer treatments like chemotherapy (Kangas et al., 2008). Negative emotions can lead to increases in poor health behavior such as alcohol consumption and decreases in positive health behavior such as exercise. PTSD among cancer patients also is quite common (Kangas, Henry, & Bryant, 2005).

The absence of social support also can undermine compliance with unpleasant but vitally important medical treatments (Anderson, Kiecolt-Glaser, & Glaser, 1994). Cancer patients who are more emotionally expressive miss fewer medical appointments, report a better quality of life, and maintain a better health status (Stanton et al., 2000). And in facing the specter of cancer, the encouragement and physical assistance of family and friends can boost patients' resolve to bear side effects such as hair loss and intense nausea. Of course, a diagnosis of cancer is a source of considerable emotional distress to loved ones, as well as to victims (Hagedoorn et al., 2008). For example, partners' reactions to breast cancer predict relationship quality a year later (Wimberly et al., 2005).

Stress also may directly affect the course of cancer. In animal studies, rats exposed to inescapable shock are less able to reject implanted cancer tumors than rats exposed to escapable shock or no stress at all (Visintainer, Seligman, & Volpicelli, 1982). Immunity plays an important role in limiting the spread of cancerous tumors, and immunosuppression due to stress may disrupt this protective function (Anderson, Kiecolt-Glaser, & Glaser, 1994).

Can psychological treatment alter the course of cancer? One early study found that, six years after treatment, significantly fewer patients who participated in a support group died (9 percent) in comparison to patients who received no psychosocial treatment (29 percent) (Fawzy et al., 1993). Sadly, hopes have been dashed by repeated failures to replicate this optimistic result (Coyne et al., 2009). Still, the benefits of support groups for quality of life, if not longevity, are important, and include less social disruption, greater well-being, and more positive affect (Antoni et al., 2006; Brothers et al., 2011).

## Acquired Immune Deficiency Syndrome (AIDS)

**Acquired immune deficiency syndrome (AIDS)** is caused by the **human immunodeficiency virus (HIV)**, which attacks the immune system and leaves the patient susceptible to infection, neurological complications, and cancers that rarely affect people with normal immune function. HIV-positive patients vary widely in how rapidly they develop AIDS. Some develop AIDS within months; others remain symptom-free for 10 years or more.

In 1981, AIDS was diagnosed for the first time; in 1996, it was the eighth leading cause of death in the United States (Peters, Kochanek, & Murphy, 1998). HIV and AIDS also reached epidemic proportions in other parts of the world, with a notably high prevalence in Africa. In the United States, over 1 million cases of HIV/AIDS have been reported to the Centers for Disease Control and Prevention (CDC) (CDC, 2008). Fortunately, death due to AIDS has declined rapidly since the middle of the 1990s due to treatments that do not cure the illness but do promote a longer, healthier life. As a result, AIDS no longer is among the 15 leading causes of death in the United States (Minino & Smith, 2001).

Behavioral factors play a critical role in the transmission of HIV. Scientists have yet to determine precisely how HIV is transmitted, but researchers have isolated a number of high-risk behaviors. Contact with bodily fluids, particularly blood and semen, is very risky. The CDC reports that the highest incidence of new cases of HIV are among men who have unprotected sex with men and individuals who participate in high-risk heterosexual sexual intercourse, such as unprotected anal and vaginal intercourse

Basketball superstar Ervin (Magic) Johnson became a spokesman for increasing awareness of HIV and AIDS after he tested HIV positive.

(CDC, 2008). The use of condoms greatly reduces the risk of the sexual transmission of HIV. Other factors that increase the risk for HIV infection include intravenous drug use and mothers infected with HIV who transmit the infection to their unborn children (U.S. Department of Health and Human Services, 1993). A tricky problem for HIV-positive mothers is telling growing children about their HIV status. Fortunately, recent evidence shows that focused psychological intervention encourages disclosure—with benefits for both mothers and school-aged children (Murphy et al., 2011).

Scientists and policymakers have launched large-scale media campaigns to educate the public about HIV and AIDS and to change risky behavior. Are they effective? Evidence indicates that prevention efforts produce significant but small changes in behavior (for example, condom use). Knowledge and attitudes change more, and more rapidly, than behavior (Albarracín, Durantini, & Earl, 2006). The most effective programs focus on changing specific behaviors and attitudes; the least effective programs use fear tactics (Albarracín et al., 2005). Unfortunately, but perhaps not surprisingly, the people most interested in participating in HIV change programs are the ones already engaged in less risky behavior (Earl et al., 2009).

Stress is linked with a more rapid progression of HIV, while social support is associated with a more gradual onset of symptoms (Evans et al., 1997; Leserman et al., 1999). Support groups lower distress among treated patients, but no benefits for longevity have been found. Broader social support also is extremely important to the AIDS patient's social and psychological well-being. Unfortunately, misunderstanding and fear cause many people, including many health professionals, to distance themselves from AIDS rather than offering understanding and support.

## Pain Disorder

Pain is adaptive. Pain signals that something is wrong, and it motivates people to seek treatment for acute injuries and illnesses. But pain is not always useful. In many cases, pain is *not* a sign of an underlying condition that can be treated. Examples of maladaptive pain include recurrent acute problems like headaches or chronic ones like lower back problems. In such circumstances, the *DSM-5* diagnosis of *Somatic Symptom Disorder* (with predominant pain) may apply.

Pain can take a huge toll on the sufferer, family members, and financial resources. In a typical day, 28.8 percent of American men and 26.6 percent of women report feeling some pain (Krueger & Stone, 2008; see Figure 8.5). The past year prevalence of chronic neck or back pain is 19 percent of the U.S. population (Von Korff et al., 2005). Perhaps 50 million Americans experience some type of dysfunctional pain, costing society $70 billion in annual health care (Gatchel et al., 2007).

Pain is subjective. This makes pain difficult to evaluate, particularly when there is no identifiable injury or illness, as is common with headaches and lower back pain. Reports of greater pain

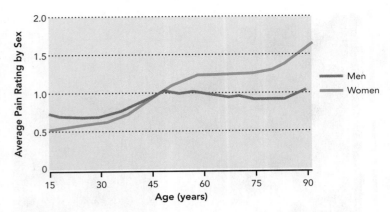

**FIGURE 8.5**

Reports of routine pain intensity increase with age but are not strongly associated with gender in this nationally representative U.S. sample. 0 = no pain and 2 = slight pain.

are associated with depression and anxiety (Gatchel et al., 2007), and, conversely, higher levels of positive affect predict lower levels of reported pain (Zautra, Johnson, & Davis, 2005). People who are anxious or depressed may be more sensitive to pain, less able to cope with it, and simply more willing to complain (Pincus & Morley, 2001).

Many experts view insight-focused psychotherapy as counterproductive and potentially damaging in treating pain (Keefe et al., 2001). More direct treatments include relaxation training and cognitive therapy. Each approach has some research support, but pain reduction typically is modest (Patterson, 2004). Most efforts therefore focus on the *pain management*, not pain reduction. The goal of pain management is to help people to cope with pain in a way that minimizes its impact on their lives, even if the pain cannot be eliminated or controlled entirely. Programs typically include education about pain and its consequences, pain control methods such as relaxation or exercise, attempts to change maladaptive expectations about pain, and interventions with families or support groups.

Pain management programs can help with a wide variety of problems, including headaches, lower back pain, and facial pain. Following treatment, patients report greater satisfaction with their life and relationships, improved employment status, and less reliance on medication. Once they are better able to function in their lives, patients also often say that their pain has lessened (Gatchel et al., 2007). Improved life functioning may alter patients' awareness of discomfort, but emerging research suggests that treatment may directly alter the experience of pain. Techniques like distraction, relaxation, and reappraisal (e.g., labeling a shot as pressure instead of pain) not only lead to reduced reports of pain but also to less activation of pain processing circuitry in the brain (Edwards et al., 2009).

## Sleep-Wake Disorders

Historically, sleep disturbances were of concern to mental health professionals only secondarily, as a symptom of a mental disorder such as depression or anxiety. However, *DSM-5* includes a variety

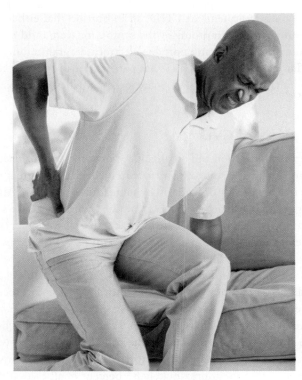

Estimates indicate that fifty million people in the United States experience some form of dysfunctional pain.

of **Sleep-Wake Disorders** where sleep is the primary complaint. The manual includes 10 categories of sleep-wake disorders.

*Insomnia disorder* is characterized by problems with sleep quantity or quality and may include problems in initiating or maintaining sleep. Insomnia disorder must occur three nights a week for three months and cause significant distress or impairment in functioning. Insomnia is a common problem, although people with insomnia often overestimate how long it takes to fall asleep and underestimate their total sleep due to misperception, worry, and brief awakenings (Harvey & Tang, 2012). Effective treatments include stimulus control techniques (only staying in bed during sleep) and resetting circadian rhythms (going to bed and getting up at set times), as well as not napping, regardless of the length of sleep (Morin et al., 2006). Internet-based programs can help alleviate insomnia (Ritterband et al., 2010).

*Hypersomnolence disorder* is excessive sleepiness despite at least getting at least seven hours' sleep. Sleepiness leads to prolonged sleep (more than nine hours), lapses into sleep during the day, or difficulty becoming fully awake. A similar problem is *narcolepsy*, irresistible periods of need to sleep that are accompanied by specific physical symptoms such as brief, sudden loss of muscle tone precipitated by laughter (APA, 2013).

*Breathing-related sleep disorders* involve the disruption in sleep due to breathing problems. An example is "obstructive sleep apnea hypopnea," the temporary obstruction of the respiratory airway that causes loud snoring or breathing pauses, making sleep unrefreshing and causing sleepiness. Not surprisingly, sleep apnea disrupts both the patient's sleep and the sleep of others in their

vicinity. *Circadian rhythm sleep disorder* is a mismatch between the patients' 24-hour sleeping patterns and their 24-hour life demands. The disorder is found more commonly among adolescents and people who work night shifts (APA, 2013).

"Parasomnias" are characterized by abnormal events that occur during sleep, and include five types of sleep-wake disorders. *Non-rapid eye movement sleep arousal disorders* are characterized by incomplete awakening and either sleepwalking or sleep terrors, recurrent episodes of screaming or other signs of great fear. The patient has no memory of these episodes, which usually occur during the first third of sleep, and may quickly fall back into sleep. *Nightmare disorder*, another parasomnia, is characterized by frequent awakening by terrifying dreams. Unlike sleep terrors, patients remember nightmares and quickly orient to being awake. *Rapid eye movement sleep behavior disorder*, a third parasomnia, involves arousal during sleep associated with vocalization or complex motor behaviors, but unlike sleepwalking, the individual quickly awakens. A fourth parasomnia, *restless legs syndrome*, involves an urge to move the legs that disturbs sleep at least three times a week for three months and causes significant distress or impairment in functioning. The last parasomnia is *substance/medication-induced sleep disorder* which involves severe sleep disturbances apparently caused by intoxication or medication.

## Cardiovascular Disease

We focus on cardiovascular disease as a more detailed example of stress research and treatment. **Cardiovascular disease (CVD)** is a group of disorders that affect the heart and circulatory system. The most important of these illnesses are *hypertension* (high blood pressure) and **coronary heart disease (CHD)**. The most deadly

Cardiovascular disorders, including myocardial infarction (heart attack), are the leading cause of death in the United States and most industrialized countries.

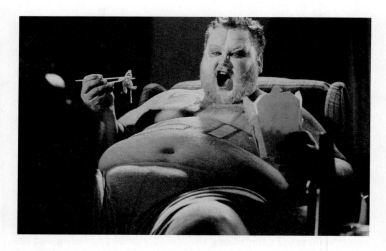

Over half of all victims of sudden death following myocardial infarction (heart attack) have no previous history of treatment for CHD.

and well-known form of CHD is *myocardial infarction (MI),* commonly called a heart attack. Hypertension increases the risk for CHD, as well as for other serious disorders, such as strokes.

Cardiovascular disorders are the leading cause of mortality not only in the United States, where they account for over one-third of all deaths (Minino & Smith, 2001), but also in most industrialized countries. Mortality due to CHD is of particular concern because victims of the disease tend to be relatively young. About half of all Americans with CHD and about a quarter of all stroke victims are under the age of 65 (Jenkins, 1988). Risk for CVD is associated with health behavior, including weight, diet, exercise, and cigarette smoking. Personality styles, behavior patterns, and emotional expression also can contribute to CVD (Rozanski, Blumenthal, & Kaplan, 1999).

## Symptoms of CVD

Hypertension is often referred to as the "silent killer" because it produces no obvious symptoms. For this reason, high blood pressure often goes undetected, and routine blood pressure monitoring is extremely important. *Systolic* blood pressure is the highest pressure that the blood exerts against the arteries. This occurs when the heart is pumping blood. *Diastolic* blood pressure is the lowest amount of pressure that the blood creates against the arteries. This occurs between heartbeats. Generally, hypertension is defined by a systolic reading above 140 and/or a diastolic reading above 90 when measured while the patient is in a relaxed state.

The most notable symptom of CHD is chest pain. Typically, the pain is centralized in the middle of the chest, and it often extends through the left shoulder and down the left arm. In less severe forms of the disorder, the pain is mild, or it may be sharp but brief. The pain of myocardial infarction typically is so intense, however, that it is crippling. Two-thirds of all deaths from CHD occur within 24 hours of a coronary event (Kamarck & Jennings, 1991). In over half of these sudden deaths, the victim received

no previous treatment for CHD, an indication that either there were no warning symptoms or the symptoms were mild enough to ignore. Research using portable electrocardiogram monitoring and diary recordings indicates that patients are unaware of many episodes (Krantz et al., 1993; Schneiderman, Chesney, & Krantz, 1989).

## Diagnosis of CVD

Myocardial infarction and angina pectoris are the two major forms of coronary heart disease. *Angina pectoris* involves intermittent chest pains that are usually brought on by some form of exertion. Attacks of angina do not damage the heart, but the chest pain can be a sign of underlying pathology. MI (heart attack) does involve damage to the heart, and it often causes *sudden cardiac death,* which is usually defined as death within 24 hours of a coronary episode.

*Secondary hypertension* results from a known problem such as a diagnosed kidney or endocrine disorder. It is called secondary because the high blood pressure is a consequence of another physical disorder. Primary or *essential hypertension* is diagnosed when the high blood pressure is the principal or only disorder. There is no single, identifiable cause of essential hypertension, which accounts for approximately 85 percent of all cases of high blood pressure. Instead, multiple physical and behavioral risk factors contribute to the elevated blood pressure.

## Frequency of CVD

Cardiovascular disease has been the leading killer in the United States since the 1920s, but the death rate due to CVD has declined by 25 percent or more in the United States, Japan, and many Western European countries. At the same time, mortality rates attributed to CVD have increased in many eastern European countries. Some but not all of these trends are attributable to changes in diet, cigarette smoking, and blood pressure (Jenkins, 1988). Another part of the explanation may be increased awareness of the negative effects of stress in the West—and the increased industrialization and increased stress in Eastern Europe.

## Causes of CVD

**BIOLOGICAL FACTORS** The immediate cause of CHD is the deprivation of oxygen to the heart muscle. No permanent damage is caused by the temporary oxygen deprivation (*myocardial ischemia*) that accompanies angina pectoris, but part of the heart muscle dies in cases of heart attack (*myocardial infarction*). Oxygen deprivation can be caused by temporarily increased oxygen demands on the heart, for example, as a result of exercise. More problematic is when atherosclerosis causes the gradual deprivation of the flow of blood (and the oxygen it carries) to the heart. *Atherosclerosis* is the thickening of the coronary artery wall that occurs as a result of the accumulation of blood lipids (fats) with age, and which also may be caused by inflammation resulting from stress (Black & Garbutt, 2002). The most dangerous circumstance is when oxygen deprivation is sudden, as occurs in a *coronary occlusion*. Coronary occlusions result either from arteries that are completely blocked by fatty deposits or from blood clots that make their way to the heart muscle.

The immediate biological causes of hypertension are less well understood, as are the more distant biological causes of both hypertension and CHD. A positive family history is a risk factor for both hypertension and CHD, and most experts interpret this as a genetic contribution. However, research using animal models of CVD suggests a gene-environment interaction. For example, rats prone to develop hypertension do so only when exposed to salty diets or environmental stress (Schneiderman et al., 1989).

**PSYCHOLOGICAL FACTORS IN CVD**  Psychological influences on CVD include (1) health behavior, (2) immediate and more chronic stress, (3) personality, especially Type A behavior, and (4) depression and anxiety.

*Health Behavior*  Several health behaviors are linked to CVD and especially CHD, which is why it is called a "lifestyle disease." Hypertension increases the risk for CHD by a factor of two to four. The risk for CHD also is two to three times greater among those who smoke a pack or more of cigarettes a day. Obesity, a fatty diet, elevated serum cholesterol levels, heavy alcohol consumption, and lack of exercise also increase the risk for CHD. Weight, diet, cholesterol,

Employed women with children are more likely to suffer from heart disease than employed women without children or homemakers. Job strain includes conflict between work and family life.

## RESEARCH methods

### Longitudinal Studies: Lives over Time

A **longitudinal study** involves studying people repeatedly over time. The approach contrasts with the **cross-sectional study** in which people are studied at only one time point. A common goal of a longitudinal study is to determine whether hypothesized causes come before their assumed effects. We know that causes must precede effects in time. The bat is swung before the ball flies over the fence. If we demonstrate that stress precedes heart disease in longitudinal research, this helps scientists rule out the alternative interpretation (reverse causality) that the illness caused the stress.

Longitudinal studies cost more. It is much less expensive to study stress and heart disease at one point in time than to assess stress now and CHD as it develops over the next 10 years. One way around the expense is to use a *retrospective study* (sometimes called "a follow-back study"). In this design, scientists look backward in time either by asking people to recall past events or by examining records from the past. The retrospective method is less expensive, but it is of limited value because of distorted memories and limited records (see the Research Methods in Chapter 7).

The *prospective design* (sometimes called a *follow-forward study*) is a more effective but more expensive alternative.

In prospective research, supposed causes are assessed in the present, and subjects are followed longitudinally to see if the hypothesized effects develop over time. Using the follow-up method, scientists can assess a range of predictions more thoroughly and more objectively than in follow-back studies.

Researchers use both methods in studying health and illness (and abnormal psychology generally). When a finding is supported in prospective longitudinal research, you can have greater confidence in an investigator's causal hypothesis than in cross-sectional research. However, correlation does not mean causation, even in a longitudinal study. The supposed "cause" and the "effect" could both result from some third variable. For example, a researcher might find that Type A behavior measured at one point in time predicts CHD several years later. But chronic job stress may cause both Type A behavior and later heart disease. Scientists need many studies using many different research methods to establish causation. And you need to understand the strengths and weaknesses of research methods in order to be an informed consumer of scientific information.

alcohol consumption, and exercise all are highly correlated, but each appears to contribute independently to the disease (Jenkins, 1988).

**Stress**  Stress contributes to CVD in at least two ways. First, over the long run, the heart may be damaged by constant stress. Second, stress immediately taxes the cardiovascular system, increasing the heart rate and blood pressure, which can precipitate sudden symptoms or even an MI. A dramatic example of the immediate effects of stress was observed during the Los Angeles earthquake of 1994. Cardiac deaths on the day of the earthquake rose to 24 from an average of 4.6 the preceding week (Leor, Poole, & Kloner, 1996).

Increased blood pressure and heart rate are normal reactions to stress, but researchers have long observed that different people exhibit different *cardiovascular reactivity to stress*, greater or lesser increases in blood pressure and heart rate when exposed to stress in the laboratory. Are people who show greater cardiovascular reactivity to stress more likely to develop CVD?

Yes. In a study of patients with coronary artery disease, patients who reacted to mental stress in the laboratory with greater myocardial ischemia (oxygen deprivation to the heart) had a higher rate of fatal and nonfatal cardiac events over the next five years in comparison to their less reactive counterparts. In fact, mental stress was a better predictor of subsequent cardiac events than was physical stress (exercise testing) (Jiang et al., 1996).

Chronic stress increases the risk for CVD and CHD (Krantz et al., 1988; Schneiderman et al., 2004). For example, increased rates of CHD are found among people with high-stress occupations. What appears to be most damaging is *job strain*, a situation that pairs high psychological demands with a low degree of decisional control (Karasek et al., 1982). A waitress has relatively high demands and low control, for instance, whereas a forest ranger has relatively few demands and a high degree of control. Figure 8.6 portrays a number of occupations and how they vary in terms of psychological demands and decisional control.

Several studies have found a relationship between job strain and CHD (Krantz et al., 1988; Rozanski et al., 1999). For example, the risk for CHD was one and one-half times higher among women who had high job strain based on objective evaluations of their occupations in the Framingham Heart Study, a major *longitudinal study* of the development of coronary heart disease (see Research Methods). The risk was three times higher among women whose self-reports indicated high job strain (LaCroix & Haynes, 1987).

Work strain is not limited to employment but also includes work that is performed in other life roles. In an earlier analysis of the Framingham study, women who were employed for more than half of their adult lives were no more likely to develop CHD than were homemakers. However, employed women with children were more likely to suffer from heart disease. In fact, the risk increased with the number of children for employed women but not for homemakers (Haynes & Feinleib, 1980). Women (and men) encounter strain not only in their occupations, but also in the competition between their various life roles.

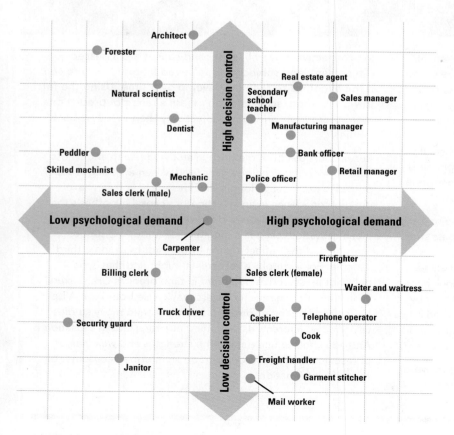

**FIGURE 8.6**

Occupations classified according to the degree of demand and control that are associated with them. Jobs with low control and high demands cause more job strain and increased cardiovascular risk.
*Source:* Kranz, DS. Environmental stress and biobehavioral antecedents of coronary heart disease. . ." Journal of Consulting and Clinical Psychology. June 1988; 56(3): 333–341.

***Type A Behavior and Hostility*** Personality may also increase the risk for CVD, particularly the **Type A behavior pattern**—a competitive, hostile, time urgent, impatient, and achievement-striving style of responding to challenge. As originally identified by cardiologists Meyer Friedman and Ray Rosenman (1959), the Type A individual is a "superachiever" who, like Bob Carter, knows no obstacle to success and who may sacrifice everything for the sake of achievement (Jenkins, 1988). Type B individuals, in contrast, are more calm and content.

In 1981, the National Blood, Heart, and Lung Institute concluded that Type A behavior was a risk factor for CHD, independent of other risks such as diet. This official sanction stimulated a great deal of additional research, but many studies conducted since 1980 failed to support earlier findings (Rozanski et al., 1999). Increasingly it appears that *hostility* predicts future CHD better than other aspects of Type A behavior (Miller et al., 1996; Smith & Ruiz, 2002). A Finnish investigation found that three items reliably predicted death among men who had a history of CHD or hypertension: ease with which anger was aroused, argumentativeness, and irritability (Koskenvuo et al., 1988).

***Depression and Anxiety*** Depression is three times more common among patients with CHD than in the general population, and depression doubles the risk for future cardiac events (Frasure-Smith & Lespèrance, 2005). Is depression a reaction to heart disease? Or does depression increase CHD, and if so, how? A study of over 2,400 depressed or isolated heart attack patients supports the first interpretation. A major randomized trial of cognitive behavior therapy, sometimes combined with antidepressant medication, alleviated depression somewhat, but the treatment group had no better coronary outcome than untreated controls (ENRICHD, 2003).

Anxiety seems to be associated with one crucial aspect of CHD: sudden cardiac death (Rozanski et al., 1999). *Heart-focused anxiety*, preoccupation with heart and chest sensations, is another important concern (Eifert, Zvolensky, & Lejuez, 2000).

**SOCIAL FACTORS IN CVD** Social factors can influence the risk for CVD in many ways. Friends and family members can encourage a healthy—or an unhealthy—lifestyle. Interpersonal conflict can create anger and hostility, which increase the risk for coronary heart disease. Economic resources, being married, and/or having a close confidant all are related to a more positive prognosis (Williams et al., 1992). In fact, a *spouse's* confidence in coping with heart disease predicts a *patient's* increased survival over four years (Rohrbaugh et al., 2004). In one study, the more the well spouse used the pronoun "we" when talking about his or her loved one's health, the more the heart failure patient improved in the next six months (Rohrbaugh et al., 2008). More broadly, societal values

*"Once upon a time, there was a frozen pizza, and inside the pizza some very bad monsters lived. Their names were refined white flour, reconstituted tomato, and processed cheese. But the worst monster of all was called pepperoni!"*

(for example, about smoking) and cultural norms (for example, about job stress) also can affect the risk for CVD.

Recognizing the importance of interpersonal and societal influences, many efforts have been directed toward structuring the *social ecology*—the interrelations between the individual and the social world—to promote health (Stokols, 1992). As a child, you were exposed to many of these efforts, such as antismoking campaigns or the awards given in school for physical fitness. Good health is commonly promoted in the media, and more employers also are encouraging positive health behavior. Do these broad-scale efforts work? We address this question shortly.

**INTEGRATION AND ALTERNATIVE PATHWAYS** CVD is an excellent example of the value of the systems approach. To illustrate this, we return to our automotive analogy. Some cars are built for high performance, some for economy. Some are defective when they leave the factory. Whatever its original condition, a car's state of repair is affected by how it is driven and how it is maintained. Similarly, CVD is caused by a combination of genetic makeup, an occasional structural defect, maintenance in the form of health behavior, and how hard the heart is driven by stress, depression, coping, and societal standards.

Much progress has been made in identifying biological, psychological, and social risk factors for CVD. An important goal for future research is to integrate knowledge across risk factors (Kop, 1999). Numerous questions need to be addressed. For example, how do we distinguish the effects of stress as an immediate, precipitating cause of CHD from its cumulative effects on health over long periods of time? To what extent are the risks associated with stress caused by poor health behavior and not by stress itself? What protects those individuals who do not become ill, even when they are exposed to multiple risk factors?

## Prevention and Treatment of CVD

Several medications known as *antihypertensives* are effective treatments for reducing high blood pressure. Other drugs, called *beta blockers*, reduce the risk of myocardial infarction or sudden coronary death following a cardiac episode (Johnston, 1989). Still other biomedical interventions reduce the risk factors associated with CVD. For example, serum cholesterol can be lowered with medication, and this reduces CVD and mortality (Taylor et al., 2011). It also may be possible to lower the risk for heart disease with psychological interventions.

**PRIMARY PREVENTION** Numerous efforts attempt to prevent CVD by encouraging people to quit smoking, eat well, exercise, monitor their blood pressure, and otherwise improve their health behavior. Many of these familiar efforts have not been evaluated, but researchers have conducted a handful of careful studies. One of the most important took place in three small California communities near Stanford University (Farquhar et al., 1977). Media campaigns designed to improve knowledge and change behavior were offered in two towns that formed the experimental groups, whereas no intervention was given in one town that was used as a control group. The media campaigns were supplemented with face-to-face interviews in one of the two towns receiving the intervention.

Findings indicated that the media campaigns increased the public's knowledge about CHD, particularly in the community where face-to-face interviews took place. Did this increased knowledge lead to changes in behavior? The answer appears to be yes—up to a point. People in the experimental communities improved their diet and lowered their serum cholesterol, but they made only minor changes in smoking (Farquhar et al., 1977). The study could not determine whether the interventions helped reduce the incidence of heart disease. Recall, however, that the rates of CVD have declined in Western countries as health behavior has improved. Increasing public awareness can slowly improve health behavior and eventually may lower the risk of heart disease.

**SECONDARY PREVENTION** The treatment of essential hypertension is one of the most important attempts at the secondary prevention of CHD. Treatments of hypertension fall into two categories. One focuses on improving health behavior, and the other emphasizes *stress management*, attempts to teach more effective coping skills.

Weight reduction, decreased alcohol consumption, and reduced intake of dietary salt all can help lower blood pressure. For many patients these behavioral changes eliminate the need for taking antihypertensive medication (Johnston, 1989). But can experts help people make the necessary lifestyle changes? Many efforts are only minimally effective, in part because they are weak or poorly constructed. For example, a physician may simply encourage a patient to lose weight or give him educational pamphlets to read. More intensive treatments appear to be more effective (Dusseldorp et al., 1999).

The major form of stress management used to treat hypertension is behavior therapy, particularly relaxation training and

A graphic health warning on a pack of cigarettes sold in Canada. In 2000, the Canadian government approved such warnings, the first country in the world to take such an aggressive anti-smoking stance.

biofeedback. **Biofeedback** uses laboratory equipment to monitor physiological processes that generally occur outside conscious awareness and to provide the patient with conscious feedback about these processes. Blood pressure may be displayed on a video screen, for example, so that increases or decreases are readily apparent to the patient. The patient can then experiment with various coping strategies, for example, imagining lying on a beach, to see whether the technique reduces his or her blood pressure.

Biofeedback produces reliable reductions in blood pressure, as does relaxation training. Unfortunately, the reductions are small, often temporary, and considerably less than those produced by antihypertensive medications (Andrews et al., 1984). Overall, stress management appears to improve quality of life but has little effect on disease (Claar & Blumenthal, 2003). Biofeedback is a particularly dubious treatment for hypertension, one that some well-respected investigators suggest should be abandoned (Johnston, 1989).

The Trials of Hypertension Prevention (TOHP) is an important study of whether stress management and health behavior interventions can lower high blood pressure (TOHP Collaborative Research Group, 1992). More than 2,000 women and men with hypertension were randomly assigned to one of seven different treatments, three lifestyle interventions—weight reduction, sodium (salt) reduction, and stress management—plus four nutritional supplement conditions. Group meetings were held over several weeks for the three lifestyle interventions. In the nutrition conditions, the patient's ordinary diet was supplemented with dietary agents hypothesized to lower blood pressure: calcium, magnesium, potassium, or fish oil. Results from Phase I of the study indicated that only the weight reduction and the salt reduction programs lowered blood pressure over a follow-up period of up to

Exercise and maintaining a healthy weight can help prevent heart disease and also lower the risk for recurrence.

one and one-half years. Neither stress management nor any of the dietary supplements produced benefits. Findings from Phase II of the TOHP underscored the importance of weight loss. Even a modest reduction in weight produced clinically significant reductions in blood pressure (Stevens et al., 2001).

The Multiple Risk Factor Intervention Trial (MRFIT), another major investigation, included over 12,000 men at risk for CHD. Participants were assigned at random to intervention programs, including both education and social support. Treatment caused improved health behavior, specifically reduced smoking and lower serum cholesterol. However, the treatment groups did not have a lower incidence of heart disease than controls seven years later (MRFIT, 1982). An encouraging interpretation of this discouraging outcome is that men in the control group also

*"Is there anyone here who specializes in stress management?"*
© Edward Koren/The New Yorker Collection/www.cartoonbank.com

improved their health behavior. The control group had a lower disease rate than expected based on their risk indicators, and the study was conducted during a time when the public's concern with health increased dramatically.

**TERTIARY PREVENTION** Tertiary prevention of CHD targets patients who have already had a cardiac event, typically a myocardial infarction. The hope is to reduce the incidence of recurrence of the illness. Exercise programs are probably the most common treatment recommended for cardiac patients, but evidence of their effectiveness is limited (Johnston, 1989). The most effective programs are both structured and individualized for each patient (Blanchard, 1992; Frasure-Smith & Prince, 1985). One patient may benefit from a smoking reduction program, a second by a stress reduction workshop, and a third by exercise classes. Handing out pamphlets or delivering stern lectures does little to alter health behavior.

More optimistic evidence on preventing the recurrence of CHD comes from efforts to alter the Type A behavior pattern (Friedman et al., 1986), a somewhat surprising circumstance given the controversies about Type A. Successful intervention is multifaceted. For example, it includes *role playing*—improvisational play acting—to teach patients how to respond to stressful interactions with reduced hostility. The cardiac patient might act out his usual response to a bothersome subordinate, for example. In subsequent role plays, the patient tries out a new, less hostile

way of responding. Cognitive therapy designed to alter faulty thought patterns also is a part of these interventions (Thoresen & Powell, 1992). For example, Bob Carter believed that he must be the best at everything. Cognitive therapy helps patients like Bob to develop beliefs and goals that are more realistic—and healthy.

Type A behavior can be modified, and this may reduce the subsequent risk for CHD (Nunes, Frank, & Kornfeld, 1987; Thoresen & Powell, 1992). One study of nearly 600 patients found that stress management training reduced the annual incidence of cardiac events by almost 50 percent in comparison to 300 patients who received standard medical care (Friedman et al., 1986). Importantly, subjects who showed the greatest reduction in Type A behavior were four times less likely to experience a myocardial infarction during the following two years.

Finally, we should note that some treatments focus on the effects of heart disease on life stress rather than the other way around. These treatments teach cardiac patients and their families to cope more effectively with the psychological consequences of having a heart attack, including depression, anxiety, and changes in sexuality, marriage, and family relationships (Johnston, 1985). Since depression is a risk factor for future cardiac illness (Carney et al., 1995), such interventions may, in turn, help improve the patient's physical health. The link between stress and physical health clearly is a reciprocal one.

## getting HELP

Stressed out? We all are at times—when we face exams, have to deal with difficult relationships, or just have too much to do and not enough time to do it.

If there is too much stress in your life, a helpful first step is to analyze it. One great way to begin is to write about the situations that stress you out, your responses, and your attempts at coping. You could start a journal; you could write someone a letter (that you may or may not mail); or you could just jot down a few notes. Writing can help you get some things off your chest—and off your mind. Writing can also help you to sort things out. Writing takes thoughts and feelings from inside your head and puts them out there, where you can look at them. Sometimes just putting your thoughts down on paper can help: "Whew! I don't have to think about that anymore!" Another benefit is that you can go back and read what you wrote and correct and organize your thoughts and feelings. An engaging, research-based account of the benefits of writing is James Pennebaker's *Opening Up: The Healing Power of Expressing Emotions*.

Another way to analyze stress in your life is to complete some stress-rating forms. You can find one commonly used form in

Table 8.1 (page 209), or you can complete a stress rating measure online. A quick Internet search will pull up several sites that allow you to complete stress rating measures. Some are designed specifically for college students.

What about coping with stress? If your usual strategies aren't working, a useful resource about relaxation is Herbert Benson's book *The Relaxation Response*. Exercise is another healthy coping technique. If you have troubling physical symptoms linked with stress, you should consult your family physician. A mental health professional may be more appropriate to contact if your problems with stress are emotional.

Finally, if you are suffering from the stress of having a physical illness and want to know about the latest research, the place to start online is the homepage of the National Institutes of Health (NIH). If your illness is chronic, particularly difficult, or rare, you might find it helpful to communicate online with others who suffer from the same disease. Because there are so many resources on the Internet, most search engines contain a category specifically for "health." As you browse, remember to be skeptical and cautious in evaluating information.

# 8 Summary

Scientists now view every physical illness as a product of the interaction between the psyche and *soma*, mind and body.

**Behavioral medicine** is a multidisciplinary field that investigates psychological factors in physical illness.

**Stress** is a challenging event that requires physiological, cognitive, or behavioral adaptation.

Stress activates the **fight-or-flight response,** an evolved reaction to threat that leads to the intense arousal of the sympathetic nervous system.

In response to stress, the *adrenal glands* release two key hormones, epinephrine (adrenaline), which leads to the familiar "rush of adrenaline," and **cortisol** (the "stress hormone"), which helps the body make repairs similar to steroids.

**Psychoneuroimmunology (PNI)** is the study of how stress also impairs immune functioning.

**Problem-focused coping** is an attempt to change the stressor, while **emotion-focused coping** involves altering internal distress.

**Health behavior** includes positive actions like exercise and negative ones like cigarette smoking.

Lifestyle is central to the top causes of death in the United States today.

The number one killer is **cardiovascular disease (CVD),** disorders that affect the heart and circulatory system. Psychological factors contributing to CVD include health behavior, cardiovascular reactivity, chronic stressors like job strain, the hostility that is part of the **Type A behavior pattern,** and depression and anxiety.

The primary prevention of CHD includes efforts to improve health behavior. Treating hypertension by encouraging improved health behavior and stress management are efforts at the secondary prevention of CHD. Tertiary prevention of CHD targets patients who have already had a cardiac event, for example, attempting to modify their Type A behavior.

## The Big Picture

## critical thinking review

**8.1  How can stress make you physically ill?**
Cannon observed . . . that fight or flight is a *maladaptive* reaction to much stress in the modern world . . . (see page 211).

**8.2  What are some good ways of coping with stress?**
People cope with stress in many ways, good and bad. Two basic strategies are problem-focused and emotion-focused coping . . . (see page 213).

**8.3  What does it mean to say people are resilient?**
Positive psychologists . . . see pervasive human **resilience**, the ability to cope successfully with the challenges of life, including very stressful ones . . . (see page 214).

**8.4  Does stress really play a role in diseases like cancer and AIDS?**
At first glance, cancer may seem to be a purely biological illness, but the importance of psychological factors quickly becomes apparent.

For example, health behavior such as cigarette smoking contributes to exposure to various *carcinogens*, cancer-causing agents . . . (see page 218).

**8.5  What is a "lifestyle disease"?**
Several health behaviors are linked to CVD . . . which is why it is called a "lifestyle disease." . . . Obesity, a fatty diet, elevated serum cholesterol levels, heavy alcohol consumption, and lack of exercise . . . increase the risk for CHD . . . (see page 223).

**8.6  What is "Type A" behavior? Can it really cause heart attacks?**
Characteristic styles of responding to stress may also increase the risk for CVD, particularly the Type A behavior pattern—a competitive, hostile, time-urgent, impatient, and achievement-striving style of responding to challenge . . . (see page 224).

# key terms

# personality disorders

**9**

# The Big Picture

## learning objectives

**9.1**
What is the difference between being eccentric and having a personality disorder?

**9.2**
In what ways are borderline and narcissistic personality disorders similar?

**9.3**
What are the advantages of a dimensional approach that would describe personality problems as variations on maladaptive personality traits?

**9.4**
Which personality disorders are least likely to change as a person gets older?

**9.5**
Why are personality disorders so difficult to treat?

**9.6**
What is the difference between antisocial personality disorder and psychopathy?

People are social organisms. Reproduction and survival depend on successful, cooperative interactions with other people. We form social alliances for many purposes, such as raising families, doing our jobs, and living in a community. We also compete with others, and in some cases we have to protect ourselves from others. These relationships are governed by a variety of psychological mechanisms that, taken together, constitute our personalities. **Personality** refers to enduring patterns of thinking and behavior that define the person and distinguish him or her from other people. Included in these patterns are ways of expressing emotion as well as patterns of thinking about ourselves and other people. For the most part, personality serves as the glue that anchors and facilitates interactions with other people. But it can also go awry. When enduring patterns of behavior and emotion bring the person into repeated conflict with others, and when they prevent the person from maintaining close relationships with others, an individual's personality may be considered disordered.

Of course, the dividing line between eccentricity and personality pathology is difficult to define. We all have our quirks and idiosyncrasies, and there are many different ways to manage relationships with other people. For example, it is often helpful to be skeptical of the things that other people do and say. When does a tendency to be suspicious of other people's motives cross the line into paranoia? Self-confidence is another admirable quality, but it can lead to problems if it escalates into full-blown grandiosity. In many ways, the distinctions among healthy traits, eccentricity, and personality pathology depend on the person's ability to adapt to the demands of different situations. Variety and flexibility in interpersonal behavior are undoubtedly helpful. People with personality disorders can make their own social problems worse (often unwittingly) by persistently responding in ways that do not suit the social challenges that they face.

## Overview

All of the personality disorders are based on exaggerated personality traits that are frequently disturbing or annoying to other people. For example, in the first case study of this chapter, you will meet a young man whose consistently impulsive and deceitful behavior brought him into repeated conflicts with other people and with legal authorities.

In order to qualify for a personality disorder diagnosis in *DSM-5*, a person must fit the *general definition* of personality disorder (which applies to all 10 subtypes) and must also meet the *specific criteria* for a particular type of personality disorder. The specific criteria consist of a list of symptoms and behaviors that characterize the disorder. The general definition of **personality disorder (PD)** presented in *DSM-5* emphasizes the duration of the pattern and the social impairment associated with the symptoms in question. The problems must be part of "an enduring pattern of inner experience and behavior that deviates markedly from the expectations of the individual's culture" (APA, 2013). The pattern must be evident in two or more of the following domains: cognition (such as ways of thinking about the self and other people), emotional responses, interpersonal functioning, or impulse control. This pattern of maladaptive experience and behavior must also be

- Inflexible and pervasive across a broad range of personal and social situations.

- The source of clinically significant distress or impairment in social, occupational, or other important areas of functioning.

- Stable and of long duration, with an onset that can be traced back at least to adolescence or early adulthood.

The concept of social dysfunction plays an important role in the definition of personality disorders. It provides a large part of the justification for defining these problems as mental disorders. If the personality characteristics identified in *DSM-5* criteria sets typically interfere with the person's ability to get along with other people and perform social roles, they become more than just a collection of eccentric behaviors or peculiar habits. They can then be viewed as a form of harmful dysfunction (Wakefield, 1999). In fact, most of the clusters of pathological personality characteristics that are described in *DSM-5* do lead to impaired social functioning or occupational impairment (Ro & Clark, 2010; Skodol et al., 2007).

Personality disorders are among the most controversial categories in the diagnostic system for mental disorders (Tyrer, 2012; Verheul, 2012). They are difficult to identify reliably, they show high levels of comorbidity among themselves and with other mental disorders, and their definition has not been well-grounded in scientific knowledge regarding basic elements of personality. For all of these reasons, you should think critically about the validity of these categories.

Although they are difficult to define and measure, personality disorders are also crucial concepts in the field of psychopathology. Several observations support this argument. First, personality disorders are associated with significant social and occupational impairment. They disrupt interpersonal relationships, including those involving friends and coworkers. Personality disorders also play an important role in many cases of marital discord and violence (Weinstein, Gleason, & Oltmanns, 2012; Whisman, Tolejko, & Chatav, 2007). Second, the presence of pathological personality traits during adolescence is associated with an increased risk for the subsequent development of other mental disorders (Cohen et al., 2007). Negative emotionality (high neuroticism) often predicts the later onset of major depression or an anxiety disorder. Impulsivity and antisocial personality increase the person's risk for alcoholism. Third, in some cases, personality disorders actually represent the beginning stages of the onset of a more serious form of psychopathology. Paranoid and schizoid personality disorders, for example, sometimes precede the onset of schizophrenic disorders. Finally, the presence of a comorbid personality disorder can interfere with the treatment of a disorder such as depression (Fournier et al., 2008).

The following cases illustrate several of the most important features of personality disorders. Our first case is an example of antisocial personality disorder, which is defined in terms of a pervasive and persistent disregard for, and frequent violation of, the rights of other people. This 21-year-old man was described by Hervey Cleckley (1976) in his classic treatise on this topic. The man had been referred to Cleckley by his parents and his lawyer after his most recent arrest for stealing. The parents hoped that their son might avoid a long prison sentence if Cleckley decided that he was suffering from a mental disorder.

### ⟶ A Car Thief's Antisocial Personality Disorder

Tom looks and is in robust physical health. His manner and appearance are pleasing. In his face a prospective employer would be likely to see strong indications of character as well as high incentive and ability. He is well-informed, alert, and entirely at ease, exhibiting a confidence in himself that the observer is likely to consider amply justified. This does not look like the sort of man who will fail or flounder about in the tasks of life, but like someone incompatible with all such thoughts.

[In childhood, Tom] appeared to be a reliable and manly fellow but could never be counted upon to keep at any task or to give a straight account of any situation. He was frequently truant from school. No advice or persuasion [deterred] him [from] his acts, despite his excellent response in all discussions. Though

he was generously provided for, he stole some of his father's chickens from time to time, selling them at stores downtown. Pieces of table silver would be missed. These were sometimes recovered from those to whom he had sold them for a pittance or swapped them for odds and ends, which seemed to hold no particular interest or value for him. He resented and seemed eager to avoid punishment, but no modification in his behavior resulted from it. He did not seem wild or particularly impulsive, a victim of high temper or uncontrollable drives. There was nothing to indicate he was subject to unusually strong temptations, lured by definite plans for high adventure and exciting revolt.

He lied so plausibly and with such utter equanimity, devised such ingenious alibis, or simply denied all responsibility with such convincing appearances of candor that for many years his real career was poorly estimated.

Among typical exploits with which he is credited stand these: prankish defecation into the stringed intricacies of the school piano, the removal from his uncle's automobile of a carburetor for which he got 75 cents, and the selling of his father's overcoat to a passing buyer of scrap materials.

At 14 or 15 years of age, having learned to drive, Tom began to steal automobiles with some regularity. Often his intention seemed less that of theft than of heedless misappropriation. A neighbor or friend of the family, going to the garage or to where the car was parked outside an office building, would find it missing. Sometimes the patient would leave the stolen vehicle within a few blocks or miles of the owner, sometimes out on the road where the gasoline had given out. After he had tried to sell a stolen car, his father consulted advisors and, on the theory that he might have some specific craving for automobiles, bought one for him as a therapeutic measure. On one occasion while out driving, he deliberately parked his own car and, leaving it, stole an inferior model which he left slightly damaged on the outskirts of a village some miles away.

Private physicians, scoutmasters, and social workers were consulted. They talked and worked with him, but to no avail. Listing the deeds for which he became ever more notable does not give an adequate picture of the situation. He did not every day or every week bring attention to himself by major acts of mischief or destructiveness. He was usually polite, often considerate in small, appealing ways, and always seemed to have learned his lesson after detection and punishment. He was clever and learned easily. During intervals in which his attendance was regular, he impressed his teachers as outstanding in ability. Some charm and apparent modesty, as well as his very convincing way of seeming sincere and to have taken resolutions that would count, kept not only the parents but all who encountered him clinging to hope. Teachers, scoutmasters, the school principal, and others recognized that in some very important respects he differed from the ordinary bad or wayward youth. (They) made special efforts to help him and to give him new opportunities to reform or readjust.

When he drove a stolen automobile across a state line, he came in contact with federal authorities. In view of his youth and the wonderful impression he made, he was put on probation. Soon afterward he took another automobile and again left it in the adjoining state. It was a very obvious situation. The consequences could not have been entirely overlooked by a person of his excellent shrewdness. He admitted that the considerable risks of getting caught had occurred to him but felt he had a chance to avoid detection and would take it. No unusual and powerful motive or any special aim could be brought out as an explanation.

Tom was sent to a federal institution in a distant state where a well-organized program of rehabilitation and guidance was available. He soon impressed authorities at this place with his attitude and in the way he discussed his past mistakes and plans for a different future. He seemed to merit parole status precociously and this was awarded him. It was not long before he began stealing again and thereby lost his freedom (Cleckley, 1976, pp. 64–67).

Notice that the fundamental features of Tom's problems were clearly evident by early adolescence, and they were exhibited consistently over an extended period of time. The stable, long-standing nature of personality disorders is one of their most characteristic features. In this way, they are distinguished from many other forms of abnormal behavior that are episodic in nature.

This case is an excellent example of the senseless nature of the illegal and immoral acts committed by people who meet the diagnostic criteria for antisocial personality disorder. Another puzzling feature of this disorder is the person's apparent lack of remorse and the inability to learn from experience that accompanies such a history of delinquent behavior. It is difficult to understand why someone would behave in this manner. Mental health professionals appeal to the notion of personality disorder to help them understand these irrational behaviors.

The case of Tom also illustrates some other important features of personality disorders. Most other forms of mental disorder, such as anxiety disorders and mood disorders, are *ego-dystonic*; that is, people with these disorders are distressed by their symptoms and uncomfortable with their situations. Personality disorders are usually *ego-syntonic*—the ideas or impulses with which they are associated are acceptable to the person. People with personality disorders frequently do not see themselves as being disturbed. We might also say that they do not have insight into the nature of their own problems. Tom did not believe that his repeated antisocial behavior represented a problem. The other people for whom he created problems were suffering, but he was not. Many forms of personality disorder are defined primarily in terms of the problems that these people create for others rather than in terms of their own subjective distress (Oltmanns & Powers, 2012).

The ego-syntonic nature of many forms of personality disorder raises important questions about the limitations of self-report measures—interviews and questionnaires—for their assessment. Many people with personality disorders are unable to view themselves realistically and are unaware of the effect that their behavior has on others. Therefore, assessments based exclusively on self-report may have limited validity (Oltmanns & Turkheimer, 2009). They may underestimate the frequency and severity of certain

aspects of personality pathology, particularly those problems associated with narcissism. The development of alternative assessment methods, such as collecting information from peers, family members, or mental health professionals, remains an important challenge for future research studies (Clark, 2007).

## Symptoms

The specific symptoms that are used to define personality disorders represent maladaptive variations in several of the building blocks of personality (see Chapter 2). These include motives, cognitive perspectives regarding the self and others, temperament, and personality traits. We have organized our description of typical symptoms around these issues, which run through the broad mixture of specific symptoms that define the 10 types of personality disorder included in *DSM-5*.

### Social Motivation

The concept of a motive refers to a person's desires and goals (Emmons, 1997). Motives (either conscious or unconscious) describe the way that the person would like things to be, and they help to explain *why* people behave in a particular fashion. For example, a man might have neglected to return a telephone call because he wanted to be alone (rather than because he forgot that someone had called). Two of the most important motives in understanding human personality are *affiliation*—the desire for close relationships with other people—and *power*—the desire for impact, prestige, or dominance (Winter et al., 1998). Individual differences with regard to these motives have an important influence on a person's health and adjustment.

Many of the symptoms of personality disorders can be described in terms of maladaptive variations with regard to needs for affiliation and power. One particularly important issue is the absence of motivation for affiliation. While most people enjoy spending time with other people and want to develop intimate

*"You want only happiness, Douglas. I want wealth, power, fame, and happiness."*

relationships with friends and family members, some people do not. They prefer isolation. Severely diminished or absent motivation for social relationships is one pervasive theme that serves to define certain kinds of personality disorder.

Exaggerated motivation for power (and achievement) also contributes to the picture that describes personality disorders. For example, some people are preoccupied with a need for admiration and the praise of others. They think of themselves as privileged people and insist on special treatment. In some cases, excessive devotion to work and professional accomplishment can lead a person to ignore friends and family members as well as the pursuit of leisure activities. This lack of balance can have a serious disruptive effect on the person's social adjustment.

## Cognitive Perspectives Regarding Self and Others

Our social world also depends on mental processes that determine knowledge of ourselves and other people (Baumeister, 1997; Kihlstrom & Hastie, 1997). Distortions of these mechanisms are associated with personality disorders. For example, one central issue involves our image of ourselves. When you are able to maintain a realistic and stable image of yourself, you can plan, negotiate, and evaluate your relationships with other people. Knowing (and having confidence in) your own values and opinions is a necessary prerequisite for making independent decisions without the assistance or reassurance of others. Self-image is also intimately connected to mood states. If you vacillate back and forth between unrealistically positive and negative views of yourself, your mood will swing dramatically. You may also need constant reassurance from others and be too dependent on their opinions as a means of maintaining your own self-esteem. We have to be able to evaluate our own importance. Of course, it's useful to think of yourself in positive terms (and many maintain a positive "halo"), but extreme grandiosity can be disruptive. Perhaps even more damaging is a pattern in which people see themselves as socially inept or inferior to other people.

When we misperceive the intentions and motives and abilities of other people, our relationships can be severely disturbed. Paranoid beliefs are one example. Some people believe, without good reason, that other people are exploiting, deceiving, or otherwise trying to harm them. Unreasonable fears of being abandoned, criticized, or rejected are also examples of distorted perception of others' intentions. Working effectively in a group of people also requires realistic appraisal of the talents and abilities of others. In order to cooperate with other people, we must be able to appreciate their competence. People with personality disorders run into problems because they misperceive other people in many different ways (as being either threatening, or uncaring, or incompetent).

Many elements of social interaction also depend on being able to evaluate the nature of our relationships with other people and then to make accurate judgments about appropriate and inappropriate behaviors. A successful relationship with a sexual partner involves knowing when intimacy is expected and when it should be avoided. Some people with personality disorders experience persistent problems in social distance (either becoming too intimate or maintaining too much distance from others). Finally, another important element of interpersonal perception is the ability to empathize with others—to anticipate and decipher their emotional reactions and use that knowledge to guide our own behavior. Deficits in the ability to understand the emotions of other people represent one of the core features of personality disorders.

## Temperament and Personality Traits

If motivation helps to explain *why* people behave in certain ways, temperament and personality traits describe *how* they behave. *Temperament* refers to a person's most basic, characteristic styles of relating to the world, especially those styles that are evident during the first year of life (Caspi & Shiner, 2008; Mervielde et al., 2005). Definitions of temperament typically include dimensions such as activity level and emotional reactivity (see Chapter 2). These factors vary considerably in level or degree from one infant to the next and have important implications for later development, such as social and academic adjustment when the child eventually enters school. For example, children who demonstrate a lack of control when they are very young are much more likely than their peers to experience problems with hyperactivity, distractibility, and conduct disorder when they are adolescents (Caspi et al., 1995). Young children who are extremely shy are more likely to be anxious and socially inhibited in subsequent years (Eisenberg et al., 1998; see Chapter 16).

Experts disagree about the basic dimensions of temperament and personality. Some theories are relatively simple, using only three or four dimensions. Others are more complicated and consider as many as 30 or 40 traits. One point of view that has come to be widely accepted is known as the five-factor model (FFM) of personality (McCrae & Costa, 2013). The basic traits (also known as domains) included in this model have already been summarized in Chapter 2. They are neuroticism, extraversion, openness to experience, agreeableness, and conscientiousness. Each of the five principal domains can be subdivided into six

Individual differences in childhood temperament, such as emotional reactivity and self-regulation, predict personality characteristics in adulthood.

more specific elements or facets (see Table 9.1). Taken as a whole, the five-factor model provides a relatively comprehensive description of any person's behavior.

Many personality disorders are defined in terms of maladaptive variations on the kinds of traits listed in Table 9.1 (Widiger, Costa, & McCrae, 2013). Problems may arise in association with extreme variations in either direction (high or low). Dramatically elevated levels of anger–hostility, impulsiveness, and excitement seeking are particularly important, as are extremely low levels of trust, compliance, and tender-mindedness. Although some forms of personality

---

**TABLE 9.1**
## Domains and Facets of the Five-Factor Model of Personality

| | People with High Scores Are | People with Low Scores Are |
|---|---|---|
| **Neuroticism** | | |
| Anxiety | extremely nervous | lacking appropriate anxiety |
| Anger–Hostility | hypersensitive; easily angered | unable to express anger |
| Depression | continually depressed | unable to appreciate losses |
| Self-consciousness | very easily embarrassed | indifferent to opinions of others |
| Impulsiveness | extremely impulsive | restrained or restricted; dull |
| Vulnerability | easily overwhelmed by stress | oblivious to danger |
| **Extraversion** | | |
| Warmth | inappropriately affectionate | unable to develop intimate relations |
| Gregariousness | unable to tolerate being alone | socially isolated |
| Assertiveness | domineering, pushy | resigned and ineffective |
| Activity | driven, frantic, distractible | sedentary and passive |
| Excitement-seeking | reckless, careless | dull, monotonous |
| Positive Emotions | giddy, lose control of emotions | solemn, unable to enjoy things |
| **Openness to Experience** | | |
| Fantasy | preoccupied with daydreams | unimaginative |
| Aesthetics | obsessed with unusual interests | don't appreciate culture or art |
| Feelings | governed by strong emotionality | seldom have strong feelings |
| Actions | unpredictable | avoid change, stick to routine |
| Ideas | preoccupied with strange ideas | reject new ideas |
| Values | lack guiding belief systems | dogmatic and closed-minded |
| **Agreeableness** | | |
| Trust | gullible | paranoid and suspicious |
| Straightforwardness | too self-disclosing | dishonest and manipulative |
| Altruism | often exploited or victimized | lacking regard for rights of others |
| Compliance | acquiescent, docile, submissive | argumentative, defiant |
| Modesty | meek and self-denigrating | conceited, arrogant, pompous |
| Tender-mindedness | overwhelmed by others' pain | callous, coldhearted, ruthless |
| **Conscientiousness** | | |
| Competence | overly perfectionistic | lax, incapable of work |
| Order | preoccupied with rules, order | disorganized, sloppy |
| Dutifulness | places duty above morality | not dependable, unreliable |
| Achievement-striving | workaholic | aimless, no clear goals |
| Self-discipline | single-minded pursuit of goals | hedonistic, self-indulgent |
| Deliberation | ruminate to excess | careless making decisions |

*Source:* Adapted from T.A. Widiger, P.T. Costa, Jr., and R.R. McCrae, 2002, "A proposal for Axis II: Diagnosing Personality Disorders Using teh Five-Factor Model," in P.T. Costa, Jr., and T.A. Widiger, Eds., Personality Disorders and the Five-Factor Model of Personality, 2nd ed, pp. 431-456. Washington, DC: American Psychological Association.

disorder are associated with high levels of anxiousness and vulnerability, people with antisocial personality disorder frequently exhibit unusually low levels of anxiety and concern about danger. We return to these dimensions in the next section of this chapter.

## Context and Personality

Two important qualifications must be made about the development and persistence of individual differences in temperament and personality. First, these differences may not be evident in all situations. Some important personality features may be expressed only under certain challenging circumstances that require or facilitate a particular response (Eaton, South, & Krueger, 2009). For example, Tom did not always appear to be impulsive and irresponsible. He was usually polite when he was with adults, and he went through intervals in which he followed rules and attended school regularly.

The second qualification involves the consequences of exhibiting particular traits. Social circumstances frequently determine whether a specific pattern of behavior will be assigned a positive or negative meaning by other people. Difficult temperament, for example, may serve an adaptive function when it is beneficial for an infant to be demanding and highly visible—for example, during a famine or while living in a large institution. On the other hand, in some circumstances, difficult temperament can be associated with an increased risk for certain psychiatric and learning disorders.

Consider the traits that Tom exhibited, especially impulsivity and lack of fear. These characteristics might be maladaptive under normal circumstances, but they could be useful—indeed, admirable—in certain extraordinary settings. War is one extreme example. People in combat situations have to act quickly and decisively, often at great risk to their own physical health. A disregard for personal safety might be adaptive under these circumstances. Tom's ability to lie in a calm and convincing fashion was another interesting trait. Again, this might have been a valuable adaptive skill if Tom had been an espionage agent. The meanings that are assigned to particular traits depend on the environment in which they are observed.

## Diagnosis

*DSM-5* includes two different approaches to the classification of personality disorders. The main body of the manual describes the traditional, categorical approach. Each of 10 specific types of personality disorder is defined by a set of characteristic symptoms. People who meet the general criteria for a personality disorder and who also exhibit enough symptoms to pass the diagnostic threshold for a specific type of disorder would qualify for a diagnosis. Those who do not meet this somewhat arbitrary threshold do not have a disorder, according to this perspective. We will refer to this approach as the *categorical definition of personality disorders*.

The workgroup charged with revising the classification of personality disorders proposed a dramatic change for *DSM-5*. Their proposal emphasized the description of maladaptive personality traits using a set of 25 dimensional scales. We will refer to this approach as the *dimensional definition of personality disorders*, and it will be described later in this chapter. The new dimensional definition was ultimately rejected, but it is included in Section III of the manual, along with other conditions that require further consideration (see Thinking Critically about *DSM-5* on page 243). For now, the categorical model remains the official *DSM-5* approach to defining personality disorders.

The *DSM-5* categorical system for personality disorders includes 10 types that are organized into three clusters on the basis of broadly defined characteristics. Specific disorders in each cluster are listed in Table 9.2. In the following pages we give brief descriptions of these personality disorder types. These

---

**TABLE 9.2**
## Personality Disorders Listed in *DSM-5*

| Cluster A Includes People Who Often Appear Odd or Eccentric | |
| --- | --- |
| Paranoid | Distrust and suspiciousness of others. |
| Schizoid | Detachment from social relationships and restricted range of expression of emotions. |
| Schizotypal | Discomfort with close relationships, cognitive and perceptual distortions, eccentricities of behavior. |

| Cluster B Includes People Who Often Appear Dramatic, Emotional, or Erratic | |
| --- | --- |
| Antisocial | Disregard for and frequent violation of the rights of others. |
| Borderline | Instability of interpersonal relationships, self-image, emotions, and control over impulses. |
| Histrionic | Excessive emotionality and attention seeking. |
| Narcissistic | Grandiosity, need for admiration, and lack of empathy. |

| Cluster C Includes People Who Often Appear Anxious or Fearful | |
| --- | --- |
| Avoidant | Social inhibition, feelings of inadequacy, and hypersensitivity to negative evaluation. |
| Dependent | Excessive need to be taken care of, leading to submissive and clinging behavior. |
| Obsessive–Compulsive | Preoccupation with orderliness and perfectionism at the expense of flexibility. |

*Source:* Courtesy of Thomas F. Oltmanns and Robert E. Emery, based on the DSM-5.

descriptions provide an overview that will be useful when we review the epidemiology of personality disorders. Later in the chapter we describe in considerably more detail three disorders that are clinically important and have been studied most extensively: schizotypal, borderline, and antisocial personality disorders.

## Cluster A: Paranoid, Schizoid, and Schizotypal Personality Disorders

Cluster A includes three disorders: paranoid, schizoid, and schizotypal forms of personality disorder. The behavior of people who fit the subtypes in this cluster is typically odd, eccentric, or asocial. All three types share similarity with the symptoms of schizophrenia (see Chapter 13). One implicit assumption in the *DSM-5* system is that these types of personality disorders may represent behavioral traits or interpersonal styles that precede the onset of full-blown psychosis. Because of their close association with schizophrenia, they are sometimes called *schizophrenia spectrum disorders.*

**Paranoid personality disorder** is characterized by the pervasive tendency to be inappropriately suspicious of other people's motives and behaviors. People who fit the description for this disorder are constantly on guard. They expect that other people are trying to harm them, and they take extraordinary precautions to avoid being exploited or injured. Although we can all benefit from being cautious and skeptical, paranoid thinking is much more than that. The pattern is so stable and wide-ranging that it interferes with the person's social and occupational adjustment. People who are paranoid are completely inflexible in the way that they view the motives of other people, and they are unable to choose situations in which they can trust other people (see Critical Thinking Matters).

Because paranoid people do not trust anyone, they have trouble maintaining relationships with friends and family members. They frequently overreact in response to minor or ambiguous events to which they attribute hidden meaning. When they overreact, people with paranoid personality disorder often behave aggressively or antagonistically. These actions can easily create

## CRITICAL THINKING matters

### Can Personality Disorders Be Adaptive?

Andrew Grove, former chairman of the board of Intel Corporation, has written a popular book about business management titled Only the Paranoid Survive. He argues that successful corporate leaders must be vigilant; they have to anticipate negative events in the business world as well as future problems with their competitors. Grove's title raises an interesting point about the nature of personality disorders. Their definition does reflect a tension between adaptive personality traits and more extreme, maladaptive ways of thinking about oneself and other people. It can be useful to be suspicious, vigilant, skeptical, or even jealous (in some circumstances), but we should not confuse these traits with paranoid thought. By promoting an informal and misleading use of the word paranoia, Grove's title does the field of psychopathology a disservice. In order to make progress toward understanding the nature of mental disorders, we have to be precise in our use of terms.

How can we distinguish between a cautious approach to the motives of other people and pathological paranoia? The difference depends, in part, on emotional reactions—such as irritability and hostility—that are associated with chronic suspicion and vigilance (Frances et al., 1995). Because they believe that others are causing problems for them, paranoid people are angry (Clifton, Turkheimer, & Oltmanns, 2004). Paranoid people can also become anxious and withdrawn. Their fear is based on the conviction that others intend to cause them harm, and they try to protect themselves by avoiding other people. The

exaggerated negative emotions that accompany paranoid thinking are not likely to foster survival in the business world or in other social circumstances.

Another way to distinguish between normal suspicions and paranoia involves the amount of time that the person spends thinking about threats posed by other people. While most people become suspicious from time to time, paranoid people are preoccupied with the notion that others are out to get them. They are unable to think otherwise (Shapiro, 1965). Paranoid people are also impaired in their ability to consider information from another person's point of view. Most of us are able to seek and consider another person's perception or interpretation of uncertain events; paranoid people cannot. For all of these reasons, paranoia will promote failure rather than survival in the business world.

One of the most important elements of critical thinking involves the careful definition of terms. Sloppy talk leads to sloppy thinking. People who suggest that "a little paranoia can be useful" or "only the paranoid survive" are engaging in a misleading use of terms. It is clearly useful to be skeptical and cautious when considering the motives of other people. But the rigid and maladaptive patterns of thought that are characteristic of paranoid personality disorder are clearly pathological. The failure to appreciate the complexity and extent of these phenomena represents a distraction from, rather than a contribution to, serious scholarship.

a self-fulfilling prophesy. In other words, thinking (incorrectly) that he or she is being attacked by others, the paranoid person strikes. The other person is, naturally, surprised, annoyed, and perhaps frightened by this behavior and begins to treat the paranoid person with concern and caution. This response serves to confirm the original suspicions of the paranoid individual, who does not comprehend how his or her own behavior affects others.

Paranoid personality disorder must be distinguished from psychotic disorders, such as schizophrenia and delusional disorder. The pervasive suspicions of people with paranoid personality disorder do not reach delusional proportions. In other words, they are not sufficiently severe to be considered obviously false and clearly preposterous. In actual practice, this distinction is sometimes quite subtle and difficult to make.

**Schizoid personality disorder** is defined in terms of a pervasive pattern of indifference to other people, coupled with a diminished range of emotional experience and expression. These people are loners; they prefer social isolation to interactions with friends or family. Other people see them as being cold and aloof. By their own report, they do not experience strong subjective emotions, such as sadness, anger, or happiness.

**Schizotypal personality disorder** centers around peculiar patterns of behavior rather than on the emotional restriction and social withdrawal that are associated with schizoid personality disorder. Many of these peculiar behaviors take the form of perceptual and cognitive disturbance. People with this disorder may report bizarre fantasies and unusual perceptual experiences. Their speech may be slightly difficult to follow because they use words in an odd way or because they express themselves in a vague or disjointed manner. Their affective expressions may be constricted in range, as in schizoid personality disorder, or they may be silly and inappropriate.

In spite of their odd or unusual behaviors, people with schizotypal personality disorder are not psychotic or out of touch with reality. Their bizarre fantasies are not delusional, and their unusual perceptual experiences are not sufficiently real or compelling to be considered hallucinations.

## MyPsychLab VIDEO CASE

### Borderline Personality Disorder

LIZ

*"I have problems with anger management. In the past it has meant suicide attempts."*

👁 **Watch** the **Video** *Liz: Borderline Personality Disorder* on **MyPsychLab**

Pay careful attention to the description of her thoughts immediately prior to her suicide attempt.

## Cluster B: Antisocial, Borderline, Histrionic, and Narcissistic Personality Disorders

Cluster B includes antisocial, borderline, histrionic, and narcissistic personality disorders. According to *DSM-5*, these disorders are characterized by dramatic, emotional, or erratic behavior, and all are associated with marked difficulty in sustaining interpersonal relationships. The rationale for grouping these disorders together is less compelling than that for Cluster A. In particular, antisocial personality disorder clearly involves something more than just a dramatic style or erratic behavior.

**Antisocial personality disorder** is defined in terms of a persistent pattern of irresponsible and antisocial behavior that begins during childhood or adolescence and continues into the adult years. The case study of Tom, with which we opened this chapter, illustrates this pattern of behavior. The *DSM-5* definition is based on features that, beginning in childhood, indicate a pervasive pattern of disregard for, and violation of, the rights of others. Once the person has become an adult, these difficulties include persistent failure to perform responsibilities that are associated with occupational and family roles. Conflict with others, including physical fights, is also common. These people are irritable and aggressive with their spouses and children as well as with people outside the home. They are impulsive, reckless, and irresponsible.

We have all read newspaper accounts of famous examples of antisocial personality disorder. These often include people who have committed horrendous acts of violence against other people, including genocidal war crimes and serial murders. You

Ted Bundy was executed in 1989 for killing at least 22 women. He was charming, intelligent, and self-assured.

should not be misled, however, into thinking that only serious criminals meet the criteria for this disorder. Many other forms of persistently callous and exploitative behavior could lead to this diagnosis.

**Borderline personality disorder** is a diffuse category whose essential feature is a pervasive pattern of instability in mood and interpersonal relationships. People with this disorder find it very difficult to be alone. They form intense, unstable relationships with other people and are often seen by others as being manipulative. Their mood may shift rapidly and inexplicably from depression to anger to anxiety over a pattern of several hours. Intense anger is common and may be accompanied by temper tantrums, physical assault, or suicidal threats and gestures.

Many clinicians consider identity disturbance to be the diagnostic hallmark of borderline personality disorder. People with this disturbance presumably have great difficulty maintaining an integrated image of themselves that simultaneously incorporates their positive and negative features. Therefore, they alternate between thinking of themselves in unrealistically positive terms and then unrealistically negative terms at different moments in time. When they are focused on their own negative features, they have a deflated view of themselves and may become seriously depressed. They frequently express uncertainty about such issues as personal values, sexual preferences, and career alternatives. Chronic feelings of emptiness and boredom may also be present.

### → Borderline Personality Disorder

A single woman of 35 had worked with four (therapists) over a period of 11 years, before the last of these referred her to me. Since Beatrice had graduated from college at age 22, she had seemed to circulate in a holding pattern. She saw herself as an executive-to-be in the corporate world but in actuality had held just a few entry-level jobs, and those only briefly. Once or twice she quit in a huff because the job, as she said, was "not interesting enough" or because "they weren't promoting me fast enough." She had no distinct career goals, nor had she taken any special courses to prepare herself for some particular path. The work problem did not pose a threat to her well-being, since she lived off a large trust fund that her family had set up for her.

On the relational side her situation was not much better. Beatrice had never been "serious" with anyone and had little interest in men apart from their ability to pay compliments on her appearance. Her self-image was contradictory: She alternated between seeing herself as "model pretty" or else ugly. While buying an ice cream, she would feel devastated if the counterman did not make eyes at her; if he did, she would feel "insulted."

She had no hobbies or sustaining interests and found evenings with nothing to do intolerable. On such evenings she would usually engage her mother in long phone conversations (her parents lived in a different city), demanding that her mother come and visit. If this were not possible, she would slam the phone down, only to then call her mother back half an hour later to apologize.

During the time I worked with Beatrice, her most noticeable personality traits were those of anger, argumentativeness, scornfulness, irritability, and vanity. Her intensity and demandingness made her troublesome in her family; her parents and siblings were mostly good-natured and got on well when she was not in their midst (Stone, 1993, pp. 250–251).

**Histrionic personality disorder** is characterized by a pervasive pattern of excessive emotionality and attention seeking behavior. People with this disorder thrive on being the center of attention. They want the spotlight on them at all times. They are self-centered, vain, and demanding, and they constantly seek approval from others. When interacting with other people, their behavior is often inappropriately sexually seductive or provocative. Their emotions tend to be shallow and may vacillate erratically. They frequently react to situations with inappropriate exaggeration.

The concept of histrionic personality disorder overlaps extensively with other types of personality disorders, especially borderline personality disorder. People with both disorders are intensely emotional and manipulative. Unlike people with borderline personality disorder, however, people with histrionic personality disorder have an essentially intact sense of their own identity and a better capacity for stable relationships with other people.

The essential feature of **narcissistic personality disorder** is a pervasive pattern of grandiosity, need for admiration, and inability to empathize with other people. Narcissistic people have

Since 1981, this successful artist has painted more than 1,500 self-portraits. He says he will never paint anything other than his own image because it is the only subject that holds his interest. Self-absorption is one central feature of narcissistic personality disorder.

a greatly exaggerated sense of their own importance. They are preoccupied with their own achievements and abilities. Because they consider themselves to be very special, they cannot empathize with the feelings of other people and are often seen as being arrogant or haughty.

There is a considerable amount of overlap between narcissistic personality disorder and borderline personality disorder. Both types of people feel that other people should recognize their needs and do special favors for them. They may also react with anger if they are criticized. The distinction between these disorders hinges on the inflated sense of self-importance that is found in narcissistic personality disorder and the deflated or devalued sense of self found in borderline personality disorder (Ronningstam & Gunderson, 1991).

## Cluster C: Avoidant, Dependent, and Obsessive–Compulsive Personality Disorders

Cluster C includes avoidant, dependent, and obsessive–compulsive personality disorders. The common element in all three disorders is presumably anxiety or fearfulness. This description fits most easily with the avoidant and dependent types. In contrast, obsessive–compulsive personality disorder is more accurately described in terms of preoccupation with rules and with lack of emotional warmth than in terms of anxiety.

**Avoidant personality disorder** is characterized by a pervasive pattern of social discomfort, fear of negative evaluation, and timidity. People with this disorder tend to be socially isolated when outside their own family circle because they are afraid of criticism. Unlike people with schizoid personality disorder, they want to be liked by others, but they are extremely shy—easily hurt by even minimal signs of disapproval from other people. Thus they avoid social and occupational activities that require significant contact with other people.

Avoidant personality disorder is often indistinguishable from social anxiety disorder (see Chapter 6). In fact, some experts have argued that they are probably two different ways of defining the same condition (Frances et al., 1995). Others have argued that people with avoidant personality disorder have more trouble than people with social anxiety disorder in relating to other people (Millon & Martinez, 1995; Rodebaugh et al., 2010). People with avoidant personality disorder are presumably more socially withdrawn and have very few close relationships because they are so shy. People with social anxiety disorder may have a lot of friends, but they are afraid of performing in front of them or being judged by them. This distinction is relatively clear when social anxiety is defined narrowly in terms of a particular kind of situation, such as public speaking. It is much more difficult to make if the person's social anxiety becomes more generalized.

The essential feature of **dependent personality disorder** is a pervasive pattern of submissive and clinging behavior. People with this disorder are afraid of separating from other people on whom they are dependent for advice and reassurance. Often unable to make everyday decisions on their own, they feel anxious and helpless when they are alone. Like people with avoidant personality disorder, they are easily hurt by criticism, extremely sensitive to disapproval, and lacking in self-confidence. One difference between avoidant and dependent personality disorders involves the point in a relationship at which they experience the most difficulty. People who are avoidant have trouble initiating a relationship (because they are fearful). People who are dependent have trouble being alone or separating from other people with whom they already have a close relationship. For example, a person with dependent personality disorder might be extremely reluctant to leave home in order to attend college.

**Obsessive–compulsive personality disorder (OCPD)** is defined by a pervasive pattern of orderliness, perfectionism, and mental and interpersonal control, at the expense of flexibility, openness, and efficiency. People with this disorder set ambitious standards for their own performance that frequently are so high as to be unattainable. Many would be described as *workaholics*. In other words, they are so devoted to work that they ignore friends, family members, and leisure activities. They are so preoccupied with details and rules that they lose sight of the main point of an activity or project. Intellectual endeavors are favored over feelings and emotional experience. These people are excessively conscientious, moralistic, and judgmental, and they tend to be intolerant of emotional behavior in other people.

The central features of this disorder may involve a marked need for control and lack of tolerance for uncertainty (Gibbs, South, & Oltmanns, 2003). At modest levels, these traits can represent an adaptive coping style, particularly in the face of the demands of our complex, technological society. Very high levels of these characteristics begin to interfere with a person's social and occupational adjustment. For example, people with OCPD find it difficult to delegate responsibilities to others, and their perfectionism makes it extremely difficult for them to finish projects within established deadlines.

Obsessive–compulsive personality disorder should not be confused with obsessive–compulsive disorder (OCD) (see Chapter 6). A pattern of intrusive, unwanted thoughts accompanied by ritualistic behaviors is used to define OCD. The definition of obsessive–compulsive personality disorder, in contrast, is concerned with personality traits, such as excessively high levels of conscientiousness.

## A Dimensional Perspective on Personality Disorders

The diagnostic manual has always treated personality disorders as discrete categories, and it has assumed that there are sharp boundaries between normal and abnormal personalities. In fact, there are a lot of people with serious personality problems who do not fit the traditional diagnostic types. The categorical approach to diagnosis forces clinicians to employ an arbitrary threshold

Anger and hostility are frequently associated with several forms of personality disorder, including paranoid, antisocial, borderline, and narcissistic PDs.

that has been set to distinguish between normal and abnormal personality types.

Another frequent complaint about the description of personality disorders is the considerable overlap among categories. Many patients meet the criteria for more than one type (Grant et al., 2005). It is cumbersome to list multiple diagnoses, especially when the clinician is already asked to consider such a broad range of other mental disorders. In fact, many clinicians are reluctant to diagnose more than one personality disorder; consequently, much information is frequently left out.

For these reasons, many experts have long favored the development of an alternative classification system for PDs, one that would be based on a dimensional view of personality pathology and also grounded in extensive research on the basic elements of personality (Widiger, Costa, & McCrae, 2013). A dimensional system based on specific personality traits could provide a more complete description of each person, and it would be more useful with patients who fall on the boundaries between, or present combinations of, different types of personality disorders.

The workgroup that was charged with revising the classification of personality disorders for *DSM-5* proposed a model that represents a substantial change from the system that was included in DSM-IV (Skodol et al., 2011). Their proposal, which we call the dimensional PD model, was ultimately rejected in favor of retaining the traditional categorical model (see Thinking Critically About DSM-5). Nevertheless, the dimensional PD model is listed in Section III of *DSM-5*, and many experts believe that it will eventually replace the categorical PD model, after it has been studied more extensively.

According to the PD workgroup's proposal, the diagnosis of personality disorders is based on a two-part process. First, the clinician is asked to make a judgment regarding impairment in personality functioning as defined by problems with the person's view of self and others (identity and self-direction) as well as difficulties with maintaining interpersonal relationships (empathy

and intimacy). Problems identified in these areas serve as general markers for the presence of a personality *disorder*; it is the key decision point in deciding whether to assign a diagnosis. This judgment replaces the categorical model's general criteria for PDs, which are often ignored and have been criticized for being vague and unreliable. In fact, many experts have argued that the most important consideration regarding assessment of personality pathology is overall level of severity rather than specific types of PDs (Tyrer et al., 2011). The dimensional system for rating level of personality functioning is relatively straightforward, and it might be efficient and effective in that role.

The second step in the proposed dimensional process specifies the nature or form of the disorder using ratings of pathological personality traits. What *kind* of personality problem does the person exhibit? The organization of these traits generally follows the FFM, but the broad domains are labeled in a way that emphasizes the maladaptive nature of characteristics associated with PDs (Krueger et al., 2011). For example, the domain known as agreeableness in the FFM is called antagonism in the new model. More specific facets are included under each of these domains (e.g., manipulativeness, deceitfulness, grandiosity, callousness, and hostility are listed under antagonism). These traits are listed in Table 9.3 on page 244. Altogether, the proposed system includes consideration of 25 core traits. You may find it useful to compare the list of FFM traits in Table 9.1 with the maladaptive traits for *DSM-5* in Table 9.3. Some of the traits in Table 9.3 are taken directly from the FFM (e.g., depressivity, anxiousness, and hostility). For others, the workgroup used a trait or personality dimension from the FFM and changed its name to emphasize the maladaptive end of the continuum (e.g., trust becomes suspiciousness, gregariousness becomes withdrawal, and modesty becomes grandiosity). The traits listed under psychoticism (e.g., perceptual dysregulation) are less clearly derived from the FFM and were added to the new dimensional system to provide coverage for schizotypal PD. The clinician's task involves selecting and rating the traits in this list that best describe the nature of the personality problems that are related to the person's impaired personal and social functioning.

The dimensional model places primary emphasis on ratings of the maladaptive traits, but it also retains six of the 10 specific types of PD from the categorical model. These types are listed in Table 9.3, which also identifies specific traits that are associated with each of them. Traits replace diagnostic criteria for each PD in the categorical system. By including some of the types, the dimensional system retains some continuity with the categorical system, which mental health professionals already know. The types may provide a useful shorthand in communicating with other professionals and in conceptualizing certain kinds of problems because they bring to mind familiar or prototypical combinations of several maladaptive traits.

Other forms of PD will be identified in the dimensional system using a new diagnosis called Personality Disorder Trait Specified (PDTS). In order to qualify for this diagnosis, the person

## Is a Dimensional Model Too Complicated?

All of the workgroups that produced sections of *DSM-5* were encouraged to think beyond the framework of the previous version of the manual. None of the workgroups pushed the limits of the system harder than the committee that tackled personality disorders. They proposed a dramatically different approach to the classification of personality disorder. Some considered their efforts heroic. After years of debate about the relative merits of categorical and dimensional approaches to personality disorders, the field remains divided. In the end, the Board of Trustees of the American Psychiatric Associated rejected the new proposal, voting to keep the categorical approach as the official system in *DSM-5*. They also placed the new dimensional system in Section III of the manual where it could receive further consideration. This is the only set of disorders in *DSM-5* where two different approaches to classification are both included (though one is clearly given priority over the other). If scientific data cannot resolve an issue, politics still matter in the world of psychopathology.

The dimensional system offers many attractive features, including the fact that it explicitly recognizes the continuous nature of these phenomena and resolves problems of excessive comorbidity. Who would object to such careful a thoughtful plan? Almost everyone! In fact, the proposal received criticism from every conceivable direction. Some people thought it went too far, placing less emphasis on traditional diagnostic constructs, especially borderline PD, and losing contact with years of knowledge gained in scientific research and clinical experience with patients who meet the criteria for these disorders (Gunderson, 2010). Others thought it didn't go far enough. One leading member of the workgroup resigned, taking the radical position that there is no evidence to support the validity of the PD types (Livesley, 2012). Another resigned because adequate scientific support was not yet available to justify discarding the traditional categorical approach

(Verheul, 2012), and several influential experts agreed with him (Zimmerman, 2012).

Almost everyone believed that the proposal was too complex. One of the practical problems with dimensional systems is that they can be hard to use. That impression is even stronger if you are already familiar with a different system. For example, after reading our description of the 10 PD types, which are often labeled with familiar terms such as paranoid, narcissistic, and dependent, you may find the material in Table 9.3 rather complicated. Many of the terms used to describe the maladaptive traits are less familiar, and that is especially true for clinicians who have already been trained to use the categorical approach. Furthermore, the intellectual appeal of the dimensional approach may be somewhat misleading when we consider the way in which such a system must be used in clinical practice. Therapists ultimately need to make certain important decisions that are fundamentally categorical in nature, such as whether or not a person needs treatment and whether or not that treatment should be reimbursed financially.

Is it a serious problem to have two competing systems for the classification of personality disorders? Not really, as long as one is recognized as the official system for use in clinical practice. Both have advantages and disadvantages, and both will continue to be evaluated empirically. As we pointed out in Chapter 2, classification systems are not right or wrong; they are simply more or less useful. The controversy surrounding categorical and dimensional approaches to defining PDs provides a good example of the rationale for switching from Roman numerals to Arabic numbers to label *DSM-5*. Presumably, the manual will be revised more frequently than in the past, with new editions being numbered like new apps for your phone (DSM-5.1, DSM-5.2, and so on). Many leading experts hope that research will soon favor a formal switch, with the dimensional model being moved into the main body of the manual. Time will tell.

---

must exhibit significant impairment in self or interpersonal functioning as well as one or more pathological personality traits. This system replaces four of the categorical types with simplified trait ratings. Paranoid PD, for example, would be described by a high rating on suspiciousness, histrionic PD would be described by a high rating on attention seeking, and dependent PD would be described by a high rating on submissiveness. This system makes it easier to describe problems exhibited by people with a variety of maladaptive traits because it avoids the need to assign more than one type of PD diagnosis. Furthermore, people who exhibit a few symptoms that would be below the diagnostic threshold in the categorical system are easily described with one set of ratings.

Notice that the trait descriptors actually help explain the overlap or co-morbidity that has been observed for many of the PD types. One example involves borderline and antisocial PD. Many people qualify for a diagnosis of both disorders using the categorical system. Table 9.3 shows clearly that the borderline and antisocial types share several maladaptive traits involving antagonism (e.g., hostility) and disinhibition (impulsivity). It also shows, however, that borderline and antisocial PD types are most clearly distinguished by the fact that people with borderline PD are also high on traits involving negative affectivity (e.g., emotional lability, anxiousness, and depressivity). Again, the relative simplicity of the trait-based approach offers an advantage over the categorical approach.

## TABLE 9.3
## Maladaptive Personality Traits in the *DSM-5* Dimensional Model of Personality Disorders.

| TRAITS | TYPES OF PERSONALITY DISORDER | | | | | |
|---|---|---|---|---|---|---|
| | Schizotypal | Borderline | Antisocial | Narcissistic | Avoidant | OCPD |
| **NEGATIVE AFFECTIVITY** | | | | | | |
| Emotional lability | | × | | | | |
| Anxiousness | | × | | | × | |
| Separation insecurity | | × | | | | |
| Submissiveness* | | | | | | |
| Perseveration | | | | | | × |
| Depressivity | | × | | | | |
| **DETACHMENT** | | | | | | |
| Withdrawal | × | | | | × | |
| Intimacy avoidance | | | | | × | × |
| Anhedonia | | | | | × | |
| Restricted affectivity | × | | | | | × |
| Suspiciousness | × | | | | | |
| **ANTAGONISM** | | | | | | |
| Manipulativeness | | | × | | | |
| Deceitfulness | | | × | | | |
| Grandiosity | | | | × | | |
| Attention seeking | | | | × | | |
| Callousness | | | × | | | |
| Hostility | | × | × | | | |
| **DISINHIBITION** | | | | | | |
| Irresponsibility | | | × | | | |
| Impulsivity | | × | × | | | |
| Distractibility | | | | | | |
| Risk taking | | × | × | | | |
| Rigid perfectionism (lack of) | | | | | | × |
| **PSYCHOTICISM** | | | | | | |
| Unusual beliefs and experiences | × | | | | | |
| Eccentricity | × | | | | | |
| Cognitive and perceptual dysregulation | × | | | | | |

*Dependent PD, from DSM-IV, is not included as a PD type in the DSM-5 dimensional model. It is replaced by the trait "Submissiveness," which is not associated with any of the other 6 PD types in that model.
*Source:* Courtesy of Thomas F. Oltmanns and Robert E. Emery, based on the DSM-5.

An example of a description of a personality disorder based on the dimensional approach to PDs is provided in the following brief case study.

### → Narcissism from the Perspective of DSM-5

Patricia was a 41-year-old married woman who presented at an outpatient mental health clinic complaining of interpersonal difficulties at work and recurring bouts of depression. [She] reported a long history of banking jobs in which she had experienced interpersonal discord. Shortly before her entrance into treatment, Patricia was demoted from a supervisory capacity at her current job because of her inability to interact effectively with those she was supposed to supervise. She described herself as always feeling out of place with her coworkers and indicated that most of them failed to adequately appreciate her skill or the amount of time she put in at work. She reported that she was beginning to think that perhaps she had something to do with their apparent dislike of her. However, even during the initial treatment sessions, her descriptions of her past and current job situations quickly and inevitably reverted to defensive statements concerning others' mistreatment and lack of appreciation of her. Despite her stated goal of changing her own behavior to be better liked, it quickly became clear that her actual wish was to cause her coworkers and supervisors to realize her superiority and to treat her accordingly.

Patricia often made condescending remarks about coworkers working under her, indicating that they were inferior to her in intelligence and abilities and thus had little or nothing to offer her. Patricia pretended to have a back injury as an excuse to avoid sales work, thus forcing the other employees to do this less pleasant job while she was given more prestigious loan accounts. [She] also reported one incident in which a friend had agreed to meet her for dinner but was late because her child was ill. Patricia was highly offended and irritated by what she referred to as her friend's "lack of consideration" in being late. She felt no compassion for her friend or the child.

Patricia's tendency toward suspiciousness was exemplified by her belief that others did not like her and conspired against her to make her job harder (e.g., by "purposely" failing to get necessary paperwork to her on time). Finally, her uncooperativeness was illustrated by her tendency not to follow instructions at work and to refuse to cooperate with her husband at home. For example, although her boss had asked Patricia not to stay at the bank after hours because of security considerations, she often stayed late to work, saying that the boss's request was "stupid and restrictive."

Patricia described herself as both depressed and anxious. She also tended to become enraged when criticized or "treated badly." Although Patricia denied feelings of humiliation and insecurity, when criticized [she] would blush and either defensively make excuses for her behavior or negate the criticism ("She's just envious of me because I'm smarter than she is").

Other people seldom called or visited with her to talk about their problems; when they did, she responded with intellectual advice usually delivered in a condescending manner, such as, "When you're older, you'll understand better how things are." Her solitary nature in having few friends and keeping to herself at work may in fact have resulted in part from actual rebuffs from others in response to her antagonistic behavior.

Finally, Patricia perceived herself as accomplished, persistent, and strongly committed to the highest standards of conduct. These impressions may indicate a classic narcissistic inflation of self-image, especially given that she was, even by her own report, having considerable difficulties at work (Corbitt, 2002, pp. 294–297).

........................................................

The dimensional approach to diagnosing PDs would begin with a consideration of level of personality functioning. In terms of impairment in self functioning, Patricia demonstrated excessive reliance on others for self-definition and regulation of her self-esteem. She desperately wanted others to recognize her superiority. She also suffered from clear impairment in interpersonal functioning, including an inability to empathize with the problems of her coworkers. Based on these observations, she would qualify for a diagnosis of personality disorder.

The more specific nature of her personality disorder would then be described in terms of a combination of traits related to antagonism (grandiosity, hostility, and manipulativeness), high negative affectivity (anxiousness, depressivity, and suspiciousness), detachment (withdrawal and restricted affectivity), and rigid perfectionism. If we used the *DSM-5* categorical approach for diagnosis, she would meet the criteria for narcissistic personality disorder. But that approach would also require that the clinician note the presence of some features of paranoid PD (such as unjustified doubts about the loyalty of coworkers; reacting with rage to perceived attacks on her character or reputation) and obsessive–compulsive PD (excessive devotion to work to the exclusion of leisure activities and friendships), even though she did not exhibit enough features of these other disorders to meet their diagnostic threshold. In several ways, the new dimensional approach offers a more straightforward and comprehensive description of Patricia's personality pathology.

## Frequency

Personality disorders are generally considered to be among the most common forms of psychopathology, when they are considered as a general category. Several epidemiological studies in the United States and in Europe have used structured diagnostic interviews to assess personality disorders in samples of people living in the community.

### Prevalence in Community and Clinical Samples

How many people in the general population would meet the criteria for at least one personality disorder if they were given a diagnostic interview? In studies that have examined community-based samples of adults, the overall lifetime prevalence for having at least one personality disorder (any type) is approximately 10 percent (Lenzenweger et al., 2007; Trull et al., 2010). While this figure tends to be relatively consistent from one study to the next, prevalence rates for specific types of personality disorders vary quite a bit. The highest prevalence rates are usually found to be associated with obsessive–compulsive personality disorder, antisocial personality disorder, and avoidant personality disorder, which may affect 3 or 4 percent of adults.

The most precise information that is available regarding the prevalence of personality disorders in community samples is concerned specifically with the antisocial type. In two large-scale epidemiological studies of mental disorders, structured interviews were conducted with several thousand participants.

The overall lifetime prevalence rate for antisocial personality disorder (men and women combined) was 3 percent in both studies (Kessler et al., 1994; Robins & Regier, 1991). The prevalence rates for other specific types tend to be approximately 1 or 2 percent of the population. The most obvious exception is narcissistic personality disorder, which appears to be the least common form, affecting much less than 1 percent of the population.

One final issue regarding prevalence rates involves comorbidity. There is considerable overlap among categories in the personality disorders. At least 50 percent of people who meet the diagnostic criteria for one personality disorder also meet the criteria for another disorder (Coid et al., 2006). To some extent, this overlap is due to the fact that similar symptoms are used to define more than one disorder. For example, impulsive and reckless behaviors are part of the definition of both antisocial and borderline PDs. Social withdrawal is used to define schizoid, schizotypal, and avoidant PD.

There is also extensive overlap between personality disorders and other kinds of mental disorder. Approximately 75 percent of people who qualify for a personality disorder diagnosis also meet criteria for a syndrome such as major depression, substance dependence, or an anxiety disorder (Dolan-Sewell, Krueger, & Shea, 2001). This overlap may also be viewed from the other direction: Many people who are treated for another type of mental disorder, such as depression or alcoholism, would also meet the criteria for a personality disorder (Thomas, Melchert, & Banken, 1999). Borderline personality disorder appears to be the most common personality disorder among patients treated at mental health facilities (both inpatient and outpatient settings). Averaged across studies, the evidence suggests that this disorder is found among slightly more than 30 percent of all patients who are treated for psychological disorders (Lyons, 1995).

## Gender Differences

The overall prevalence of personality disorders is approximately equal in men and women (Lenzenweger, 2007). There are, however, consistent gender differences with regard to at least one specific disorder: Antisocial personality disorders is unquestionably much more common among men than among women, with rates of approximately 5 percent reported for men and 2 percent for women (Trull et al., 2010). Thus, antisocial personality disorder is actually an alarmingly common problem among adult males in the United States.

Epidemiological evidence regarding gender differences for the other types of personality disorders is much more ambiguous. Borderline personality disorder and dependent personality disorder may be somewhat more prevalent among women than men, but the evidence is not strong (Skodol & Bender, 2003). There has been some speculation that paranoid and obsessive–compulsive personality disorders may be somewhat more common among men than women (Coid et al., 2006).

Vivien Leigh won an Academy Award for her performance as Blanche DuBois in A Streetcar Named Desire (1951). She also won for her performance as Scarlett O'Hara in Gone with the Wind (1939). Both characters exhibit blends of histrionic and narcissistic PD features.

## Stability of Personality Disorders over Time

Temporal stability is one of the most important assumptions about personality disorders. Evidence for the assumption that personality disorders appear during adolescence and persist into adulthood has, until recently, been limited primarily to antisocial personality disorder. One classic follow-up study (Robins, 1966) began with a large set of records describing young children treated for adjustment problems at a clinic during the 1920s. The investigator was able to locate and interview almost all of these people, who by then were adults. The best predictor of an adult diagnosis of antisocial personality was conduct disorder in childhood. The people who were most likely to be considered antisocial as adults were boys who had been referred to the clinic on the basis of serious theft or aggressive behavior; who exhibited such behaviors across a variety of situations; and whose antisocial behaviors created conflict with adults outside their own homes. More than half of the boys who exhibited these characteristics were given a diagnosis of antisocial personality disorder as adults.

Another longitudinal study has collected information regarding the prevalence and stability of personality disorders among adolescents (Cohen et al., 2005). This investigation is particularly important because it did not depend solely on subjects who had been referred for psychological treatment and because it was concerned with the full range of personality disorders. The rate of personality disorders was relatively high in this sample: Seventeen percent of the adolescents received a diagnosis of at least one personality disorder. Categorically defined diagnoses were not particularly stable; fewer than half of the adolescents who originally qualified for a personality disorder diagnosis met the same criteria two years later. Nevertheless, many of the study participants continued to exhibit similar problems over the next 20 years. Viewed from a dimensional perspective, the maladaptive traits that represent the core features of the disorders remained relatively stable between adolescence and young adulthood (Crawford, Cohen, & Brook, 2001).

Several studies have examined the stability of personality disorders among people who have received professional treatment for their problems, especially those who have been hospitalized for schizotypal or borderline disorders. Many patients who have been treated for these problems are still significantly impaired several years later, but the disorders are not uniformly stable (Paris, 2003; Skodol et al., 2008). Recovery rates are relatively high among patients with a diagnosis of borderline personality disorder. If patients who were initially treated during their early twenties are followed up when they are in their forties and fifties, only about one person in four would still qualify for a diagnosis of borderline personality disorder (Zanarini et al., 2006). The long-term prognosis is less optimistic for schizotypal and schizoid personality disorders. People with these diagnoses are likely to remain socially isolated and occupationally impaired.

## Culture and Personality

In *DSM-5*, personality disorders are defined in terms of behavior that "deviates markedly from the expectations of the individual's culture." In setting this guideline, the authors of *DSM-5* recognized that judgments regarding appropriate behavior vary considerably from one society to the next. Some cultures encourage restrained or subtle displays of emotion, whereas others promote visible, public displays of anger, grief, and other emotional responses. Behavior that seems highly dramatic or extraverted (histrionic) in the former cultures might create a very different impression in the latter cultures. Cultures also differ in the extent to which they value individualism (the pursuit of personal goals) as opposed to collectivism (sharing and self-sacrifice for the good of the group; Triandis, 1994). Someone who seems exceedingly self-centered and egotistical in a collectivist society, such as Japan, might appear to be normal in an individualistic society like the United States.

The personality disorders may be more closely tied to cultural expectations than any other kind of mental disorder (Alarcon, 2005). Some studies have compared the prevalence and symptoms of personality disorders in different countries, and the data suggest that similar problems do exist in cultures outside the United States and Western Europe (Pinto et al., 2000; Yang et al., 2000). Nevertheless, much more information is needed before we can be confident that the *DSM-5* system for describing personality disorders is valid in other societies. Two questions are particularly important:

1. In other cultures, what are the personality traits that lead to marked interpersonal difficulties and social or occupational impairment? Are they different from those that have been identified for our own culture?

2. Are the diagnostic criteria that are used to define personality disorder syndromes in *DSM-5* (and ICD-10) meaningful in other cultures?

Cross-cultural studies that are designed to address these issues must confront a number of difficult methodological problems (see Research Methods).

Within a particular society, the experiences of people from cultural and ethnic minorities should also be considered carefully before diagnostic decisions are made. Phenomena associated with paranoid personality disorder, including strong feelings of suspicion, alienation, and distrust, illustrate this issue. People who belong to minority groups (and those who are recent immigrants from a different culture) are more likely

Is this young Afghan woman more extraverted than the others? Is she a risk-taker? It is impossible to make these personality judgments without more knowledge of the culture in which she lives. She may be unveiled because she is younger than the other women, or because she is not married.

than members of the majority or dominant culture to hold realistic concerns about potential victimization and exploitation. For example, black Americans may develop and express mild paranoid tendencies as a way of adapting to ongoing experiences of oppression (Whaley, 2001). Clinicians may erroneously diagnose these conditions as paranoid personality disorder if they do not recognize or understand the cultural experiences in which they are formed. In this particular case, it is obviously important for the clinician to consider the person's attitudes and beliefs regarding members of his or her own family or peer group, as well as the person's feelings about the community as a whole.

## RESEARCH methods

### Cross-Cultural Comparisons: The Importance of Context

Over the past 40 years, psychologists have begun to adopt a broader focus in their consideration of human behavior, including mental disorders. This means paying more attention to cultural diversity in the samples used in research studies.

At the broadest level, culture is a system of meanings that determines the ways in which people think about themselves and their environments. It shapes their most basic view of reality. Consider, for example, the process of bereavement following the death of a close relative. In some Native American cultures, people learn to expect to hear the spirit of the dead person calling to them from the afterworld (Kleinman, 1988). This is a common experience for people in these cultures. It resembles auditory hallucinations (perceptual experiences in the absence of external stimulation) that are seen in people with psychotic disorders. But among some Native American peoples, hearing voices from the dead is a "normative" or common response; it is not a sign of dysfunction. Perhaps most importantly, this type of experience is not regularly associated with social or occupational impairment. It would be a mistake, therefore, to consider these experiences to be symptoms of a mental disorder.

**Cross-cultural psychology** is the scientific study of ways that human behavior and mental processes are influenced by social and cultural factors (Berry et al., 2002). This field includes the study of ethnic differences (among cultural groups living in close proximity within a single nation). Comparison is a fundamental element of any cross-cultural study. Cross-cultural psychologists examine ways in which human behaviors are different, as well as ways in which they are similar, from one culture to the next.

Cross-cultural comparisons are relevant to the study of psychopathology in many ways (Draguns & Tanaka-Matsumi, 2003; Kirmayer, 2006). One way involves epidemiology—comparisons of the prevalence of disorders across cultures. Investigations aimed at etiological mechanisms, including biological, psychological, and social variables, can also be extremely informative when viewed in cross-cultural perspective. For example, we know that negative patterns of thinking are correlated with depressed mood in middle-class Americans. Is the same relationship found among people living in rural China? Virtually any study of psychopathology would provide useful information if it were replicated in different cultures.

The valuable process of making cross-cultural comparisons can actually be quite difficult (Draguns, 2006; Ratner & Hui, 2003). Several complex issues must be faced by investigators who want to study psychopathology in cross-cultural perspective:

1. *Identifying meaningful groups:* The first step in making cross-cultural comparisons is the selection of participants who are representative members of different cultures. This might be a relatively straightforward process if the comparison is to be made between two small, homogeneous groups such as two isolated rural villages in two very different countries (say, Peru and Zimbabwe). The situation becomes much more complex if the investigator's goal is to compare ethnic groups within a large, multicultural society such as the United States. Hispanic Americans, for example, include people whose cultural backgrounds can be traced to many different Spanish-speaking homelands with very different cultural traditions, such as Puerto Rico, Mexico, and Cuba. Even greater cultural diversity is found among various Native American peoples. How do we determine which people share a common culture? What is the "cultural unit," and how do we find its boundaries?

2. *Selecting equivalent measurement procedures:* Comparison between groups can be valid only if equivalent measurement procedures are used in both cultures (or in all groups). Participants in different cultures often speak different languages (or different dialects). Questionnaires and psychological tests must be cross-validated to ensure that they measure the same concepts in different cultures.

3. *Considering causal explanations:* Suppose that investigators identify a reliable difference between people in two different cultures. They must now decide how to interpret this difference. Is it, in fact, due to cultural variables? Or would the differences disappear if other variables, such as poverty, education, and age, were held constant between the two groups?

4. *Avoiding culturally biased interpretations:* Investigators, who are often middle class and white, must interpret the results of cross-cultural research cautiously. In particular, scientists must not interpret differences between cultures or ethnic groups as being indicative of deficits in minority groups or non-Western cultures. Some cross-cultural psychologists have suggested that it is more important to study developmental processes within cultures or ethnic groups than to compare outcomes between groups.

## Schizotypal Personality Disorder (SPD)

Now that we have reviewed some of the important general issues for the entire set of personality disorders, we consider three specific types of disorders in more detail. We focus on schizotypal, borderline, and antisocial types because they have been the subject of extended research and debate in the scientific literature.

We begin each of the three sections with a brief case study. We have chosen cases that are prototypes for each disorder. In other words, these are people who exhibit most, if not all, of the features of the disorder. You should not infer from these descriptions that everyone who meets the criteria for these disorders would represent this type of typical case. Remember, also, that many people simultaneously meet the criteria for more than one personality disorder; these cases are relatively simple examples. The following case illustrates some of the most important features of schizotypal personality disorder (SPD).

The concept of schizotypal personality disorder is closely tied to the history of schizophrenia as a diagnostic entity (Gottesman, 1987). The term was originally coined as an abbreviation for *schizophrenic phenotype*. These maladaptive personality traits are presumably seen among people who possess the genotype that makes them vulnerable to schizophrenia. The symptoms of schizotypal personality disorder represent early manifestations of the predisposition to develop the full-blown disorder. It has been recognized for many years that a fairly large proportion of the family members of schizophrenic patients exhibit strange or unusual behaviors that are similar to, but milder in form than, the disturbance shown by the patient.

### ⟶ Schizotypal Personality Disorder

Sandra, when she first came for treatment at the age of 27, presented with marked anxiety in social situations and in getting along with coworkers, eccentric behavior, and paranoid ideas. She had no close female friends and only one male friend, and though the latter was a sexual relationship, she revealed almost nothing to him about her past. She had many strange beliefs involving astrology, foods, and medicines.

Sandra had only one friend during her adolescence: someone who shared her faddishness about foods and her beliefs in astrology. Girls excluded her from their school clubs. She never understood why they rejected her, though it is probable that they considered her "weird" because of her inability to make small talk, and her voice pattern: a flat, high-pitched, stilted-sounding monotone that made her come across as mannered and insincere. Added to this peculiarity of speech was her tendency to skip from topic to topic abruptly, giving equal emphasis to each, such that it was difficult to distinguish the trivial from the important. From a therapeutic standpoint, this was particularly bedeviling, since it strained one's intuitive capacities to the uttermost just to figure out what was really bothering her or what was the "main theme" on any particular day.

Her empathic skills were very limited, leading her to comment at times that she found people and their motives completely puzzling: "I can't connect up with them. If they invite me to lunch with them, I can't seem to join in the conversation or else I say the wrong thing, so after a while they don't invite me anymore and I eat by myself." If a teaching supervisor wore a dour expression walking down the hall, Sandra assumed the supervisor was dissatisfied with her work, even though it might be a person who was not even assigned to her department. She tended to be surly and "superior" sounding when asking for vacation requests and the like—and often didn't get what she wanted because of having alienated the people whose favor she needed. This reinforced her notion that the world was pretty much against her.

Although considered a knowledgeable teacher, she had no charm or patience with the children and was eventually given a semi-administrative job where little interaction with others was necessary. With boyfriends, she was comfortable about having sex but made such fussy and endless-seeming preparations (such as doing her fingernails in the bathroom for half an hour) that the men lost the mood and usually ended the relationship after a few months.

More striking than her empathic difficulties was a curious inability to grasp what one might call the statistics of everyday life. Travel was a great burden, since she felt it necessary to plan for all possible contingencies. She once went to (France) on an August vacation packing her winter overcoat, because, as she reminded me, "There was a cold spell there in the '50s and it could happen again." Furthermore, she sent a packet of clothes on ahead to the hotel because, "What if my baggage got stolen?" She had great difficulty, in other words, aligning her behavior in harmony with the expectable, in contrast with the remotely possible—all thinkable events being in her mind equally probable (Stone, 1993, pp. 179–180).

### Symptoms

The *DSM-5* criteria for schizotypal personality disorder are listed in "DSM-5: Schizotypal Personality Disorder." These criteria represent a blend of those characteristics that have been reported among the relatives of schizophrenic patients and those symptoms that seem to characterize nonpsychotic patients with schizophrenic-like disorders (Esterberg, Goulding, & Walker, 2010). In addition to social detachment, emphasis is placed on eccentricity and cognitive or perceptual distortions.

People who meet the criteria for schizotypal personality disorder frequently meet the criteria for additional disorders. There is considerable overlap between schizotypal personality disorder and other personality disorders in Cluster A (paranoid and schizoid), as well as with avoidant personality disorder.

**A.** A pervasive pattern of social and interpersonal deficits marked by acute discomfort with, and reduced capacity for, close relationships as well as by cognitive or perceptual distortions and eccentricities of behavior, beginning by early adulthood and present in a variety of contexts, as indicated by five (or more) of the following:

1. Ideas of reference (excluding delusions of reference).
2. Odd beliefs or magical thinking that influences behavior and is inconsistent with subcultural norms (such as superstitiousness, belief in clairvoyance, telepathy, or "sixth sense"; in children and adolescents, bizarre fantasies or preoccupations).
3. Unusual perceptual experiences, including bodily illusions.
4. Odd thinking and speech (such as vague, circumstantial, metaphorical, overelaborate, or stereotyped).
5. Suspiciousness or paranoid ideation.
6. Inappropriate or constricted affect.*
7. Behavior or appearance that is odd, eccentric, or peculiar.
8. Lack of close friends or confidants other than first-degree relatives.
9. Excessive social anxiety that does not diminish with familiarity and tends to be associated with paranoid fears rather than with negative judgments about self.

**B.** Does not occur exclusively during the course of schizophrenia, a bipolar disorder or depressive disorder with psychotic features, another psychotic disorder, or autism spectrum disorder.

Reprinted with permission from the *Diagnostic and Statistical Manual of Mental Disorders*, Fifth Edition, (Copyright © 2013). American Psychiatric Association.

*Inappropriate affect refers to emotional responses that appear to be inconsistent with the social context—for example, uncontrollable giggling at a wake or funeral. Constricted affect refers to the absence of emotional responsiveness, such as lack of facial expressions. See Chapter 13 for a more detailed discussion.

This finding is not particularly surprising, given the conceptual origins of the schizotypal category. There is also quite a bit of overlap between schizotypal personality disorder and borderline personality disorder.

## Causes

Most of the interest in the etiology of schizotypal personality disorder has focused on the importance of genetic factors. Is schizotypal personality disorder genetically related to schizophrenia? Family and adoption studies indicate that the answer is *yes?* (Reichborn-Kjennerud, 2010). Twin studies have examined genetic contributions to schizotypal personality disorder from a dimensional perspective in which schizotypal personality traits are measured with questionnaires. This evidence also points to a significant genetic contribution (Linney et al., 2003).

The first-degree relatives of schizophrenic patients are considerably more likely than people in the general population to exhibit symptoms of schizotypal personality disorder. Several studies have examined the prevalence of schizotypal personality disorder among the parents and siblings of patients being treated for schizophrenia (Tienari et al., 2003). The most striking and consistent finding has been an increased prevalence of schizotypal personality disorder among the relatives of the schizophrenic patients. Prevalence rates for paranoid and avoidant personality disorder also tend to be higher among the relatives of the schizophrenic patients. These types of personality disorders are not more prevalent among the relatives of people with major depression. Results from these studies are consistent with the conclusion that schizotypal personality disorder is genetically related to schizophrenia.

## Treatment

Two important considerations complicate the treatment of people with personality disorders in general and SPD in particular and make it difficult to evaluate the effectiveness of various forms of intervention. One consideration involves the ego-syntonic nature of many personality disorders (discussed earlier). Many people with these disorders do not seek treatment for their problems because they do not see their own behavior as being the source of distress. A related difficulty involves premature termination: A relatively high proportion of personality disorder patients drop out of treatment before it is completed.

When people with personality disorders appear at hospitals or clinics, it is often because they are also suffering from another type of mental disorder, such as depression or a substance use disorder. This comorbidity is the second consideration that complicates treatment. "Pure forms" of personality disorder are relatively rare. There is tremendous overlap between specific personality disorder categories and other forms of abnormal behavior. Treatment is seldom aimed at problem behaviors that are associated with only one type of personality disorder, and the efficacy of treatment is, therefore, difficult to evaluate.

The literature regarding treatment of schizotypal personality disorder, like that dealing with its causes, mirrors efforts aimed at schizophrenia. A few studies have focused on the possible treatment value of antipsychotic drugs, which are effective with many schizophrenic patients. Some studies have found that low doses of antipsychotic medication are beneficial in alleviating cognitive problems and social anxiety in patients who have received a diagnosis of schizotypal personality disorder

(Koenigsberg et al., 2003). There is also some indication that patients with schizotypal personality disorder may respond positively to antidepressant medications, including SSRIs. In general, the therapeutic effects of medication are positive, but they tend to be modest.

Clinical experience suggests that these patients do not respond well to insight–oriented psychotherapy, in part because they do not see themselves as having psychological problems and also because they are so uncomfortable with close personal relationships. Some clinicians have suggested that a supportive, educational approach that is focused on fostering basic social skills may be beneficial if the goals of treatment are modest (Crits-Christoph, 1998; Gabbard, 2000). Unfortunately, controlled studies of psychological forms of treatment with schizotypal personality disorder have not been reported.

## Borderline Personality Disorder (BPD)

Borderline personality disorder is one of the most perplexing, most disabling, and most frequently treated forms of personality disorder. Because of the severity of their problems, people with BPD are more likely to come into clinics seeking treatment. The following case illustrates many of the features associated with borderline personality disorder.

### ⟶ Borderline Personality Disorder

Barbara, single woman of 24, sought treatment with me shortly after discharge from a hospital, where she had spent three weeks because of depression, panic attacks, and a suicide gesture. This had been her seventh hospitalization—all of them brief, and all for similar symptoms—since age 17. Cheerful and cooperative as a young girl, she underwent a radical change of personality at the time of her menarche. Thereafter, she became irascible, rebellious, moody, and demanding.

For a time she was anorexic; later on, bulimic (maintaining her normal weight by vomiting). Schoolwork deteriorated, and she took up with a wild crowd, abusing marijuana and other drugs and engaging in promiscuous sex. At one point she ran away from home with a boyfriend and didn't return for three months.

She quit high school with one year to go. Her life became even more chaotic; she scratched her wrists on a number of occasions, and consorted with abusive men who would use her sexually and then beat her up.

By the time I began working with Barbara, she had been abusing alcohol for about a year and had also become addicted to benzodiazepines. Her proneness to panic-level anxiety now took the form of agoraphobia, necessitating her being accompanied by a parent to her therapy sessions. Premenstrually, her irritability rose to fever pitch: she would strike her parents with her fists, sometimes necessitating help from the police. She would then threaten to kill herself.

Lacking any hobbies or interests, apart from dancing, she was bored to distraction at home, yet afraid to venture out. Nothing gave her any pleasure except glitzy clothes (which her agoraphobia rendered irrelevant).

For a few weeks Barbara dated a man from her neighborhood, and although she was able to leave the house if she were with him, she used the opportunity in a self-destructive way, going to wild nightclubs and provoking him with demands to the point where he drove her only halfway home, pushing her out of the car, so that she had to hitchhike home at 2 A.M. This precipitated a suicide attempt with a variety of medications (Stone, 1993, pp. 248–249).

The intellectual heritage of BPD is quite diverse and more difficult to trace than that of schizotypal personality disorder. One influential perspective on these problems developed from psychodynamic theory (Kernberg, 1967, 1975). According to this view, borderline personality is not a specific syndrome. Rather, it refers to a set of personality features that can be found in individuals with various disorders. The common feature of people with borderline personality is *splitting*—the tendency to see people and events alternately as entirely good or entirely bad. Thus, a man might perceive his wife as almost perfect at some times and as highly flawed at other times. The tendency toward splitting helps explain the broad mood swings and unstable relationships associated with borderline personality. Viewed from this perspective, borderline personality can encompass many types of abnormal behavior, including paranoid and schizoid personality disorders, impulse control disorders (see Impulse Control Disorders), substance use disorders, and various types of depression. Psychodynamic views regarding personality organization were eventually transformed into a definition of borderline personality disorder (Gunderson, 1984, 1994).

Some people with borderline personality disorder engage in recurrent suicidal gestures of self-mutilating behavior.

Failure to control harmful impulses is associated with several of the disorders listed in *DSM-5*. People who meet the criteria for borderline personality disorder and antisocial personality disorder engage in various types of impulsive, maladaptive behaviors (most often self-mutilation in the case of BPD, and theft and aggression in the case of ASPD). People in the midst of a manic episode frequently become excessively involved in pleasurable activities that can have painful consequences, such as unrestrained buying or sexual indiscretions. These are examples of impulse control problems that appear as part of a more broadly defined syndrome or mental disorder.

*DSM-5* includes several additional problems under a heading called **impulse control disorders** (Hollander & Stein, 2006). Relatively little is known about these problems. They are defined in terms of persistent, clinically significant impulsive behaviors that are not better explained by other disorders in *DSM-5*. They include the following:

- *Intermittent explosive disorder:* Aggressive behaviors resulting in serious assaultive acts or destruction of property (Coccaro, Posternak, & Zimmerman, 2005; Olvera, 2002). The level of aggression is grossly out of proportion to any precipitating psychosocial stressors.
- *Kleptomania:* Stealing objects that are not needed for personal use or for their financial value. The theft is not motivated by anger or vengeance (Presta et al., 2002).
- *Pyromania:* Deliberate and purposeful setting of fires, accompanied by fascination with or attraction to fire and things that are associated with it. The behavior is not motivated by financial considerations (as in arson), social or political ideology, anger, vengeance, or delusional beliefs (Lejoyeux, McLoughlin, & Ades, 2006).

This broad diagnostic group also used to include pathological gambling, but that problem has been moved to the *DSM-5* section on Substance Use Disorders (see Chapter 11).

In most cases, the impulsive behavior is preceded by increasing tension and followed by a feeling of pleasure, gratification, or relief. The motivation for these impulsive behaviors is, therefore, somewhat different than the motivation for compulsive behavior (see Chapter 6). Impulsive and compulsive behaviors can be difficult to distinguish, as both are repetitious and difficult to resist. The primary difference is that the original goal for impulsive behavior is to experience pleasure, and the original goal for compulsive behavior is to avoid anxiety (Frances, et al., 1995; Grant & Potenza, 2006).

The impulse control disorders occupy an interesting and controversial niche in *DSM-5*. The implication of impulse control disorders is that people who repeatedly engage in dangerous, illegal, or destructive behaviors must have a mental disorder. If they do not, why do they do these things? Unfortunately, this reasoning quickly becomes circular. Why does he set fires recklessly? Because he has a mental disorder. How do you know he has a mental disorder? Because he sets fires recklessly. This logical dilemma is particularly evident in the case of impulse control disorders when the problem behaviors do not appear as part of a broader syndrome in which other symptoms of disorder are also present. In other words, the problem behavior is the disorder. Until we can step outside this loop, validating the utility of the diagnostic concept by reference to other psychological or biological response systems, we are left with an unsatisfying approach to the definition of these problems.

## Symptoms

The *DSM-5* criteria for borderline personality disorder are presented in "DSM-5: Borderline Personality Disorder". The overriding characteristic of borderline personality disorder is a pervasive pattern of instability in self-image, in interpersonal relationships, and in mood.

> To be borderline means to lack grounding emotionally and to exist from moment to moment without any sense of continuity, predictability, or meaning. Life is experienced in fragments, more like a series of snapshots than a moving picture. It is a series of discrete points of experience that fail to flow together smoothly or to create an integrated whole.
>
> (Moskovitz, 1996, pp. 5–6)

Borderline personality disorder overlaps with several other PD categories, including the histrionic, narcissistic, paranoid, dependent, and avoidant types. There is also a significant amount of overlap between borderline personality disorder and major depression (Trull, Stepp, & Solhan, 2006). Many patients with other types of impulse control problems, such as substance dependence and eating disorders, also qualify for a diagnosis of borderline personality disorder.

Follow-up studies suggest many similarities between borderline personality disorder and depressive disorders. In many cases, the symptoms of BPD are evident before the onset of major depression. For example, one study focused on a group of 100 outpatients with a diagnosis of borderline personality disorder (Akiskal, 1992). During follow-up, 29 percent of the sample developed severe depression. Another longitudinal study of patients who were discharged from a private psychiatric hospital is also interesting in this regard. In a sample of patients with a pure diagnosis of borderline personality disorder (that is, those who were not diagnosed with any additional mental disorders), 23 percent developed major depressive episodes during the course of the 15-year follow-up (McGlashan, 1986).

## Causes

Genetic factors are clearly involved in the etiology of borderline personality disorder when it is viewed in terms of the syndrome that is defined in *DSM-5* (Distel et al., 2010). Furthermore, the fundamental personality traits that serve to define the disorder, such as neuroticism and impulsivity, are also influenced by genetic factors (Livesley, 2008). The most important question is how a genetic predisposition toward certain personality characteristics can interact with various types of detrimental environmental events to produce the problems in emotional regulation and attachment relationships that are seen among patients with borderline personality disorder.

Some investigators have argued that borderline patients suffer from the negative consequences of parental loss, neglect, and mistreatment during childhood (Fonagy & Bateman, 2008). This model is supported by studies of the families of borderline patients and by comparisons with the literature on social development in monkeys that examined the effects of separating infants from their mothers. Studies of patients with borderline personality disorder do point toward the influence of widespread problematic relationships with their parents. Adolescent girls with borderline personality disorder report pervasive lack of supervision, frequent witnessing of domestic violence, and being subjected to inappropriate behavior by their parents and other adults, including verbal, physical, and sexual abuse (Helgeland & Torgersen, 2004; Pally, 2002). The extent and severity of abuse vary widely across individuals. Many patients describe multiple forms of abuse by more than one person.

The association between borderline personality disorder and the patients' recollections of childhood maltreatment raises an important question about the direction of this relationship: Does childhood abuse lead to borderline personality disorder? Or are people with borderline personality disorder simply more likely to remember that they were abused by their parents, due to biased reporting?

Longitudinal data from a study of adolescents in upstate New York provide important evidence on this point (Johnson et al., 1999). Rather than relying exclusively on self-report measures, the investigators obtained data on child maltreatment from the New York State Central Registry for Child Abuse. Maltreatment included documented cases of physical abuse, sexual abuse, and childhood neglect. People with documented evidence of childhood abuse and neglect were four times more likely than those who had not been mistreated to develop symptoms of personality disorders as young adults. Strongest connections were found for Cluster B disorders (see Figure 9.1). Physical abuse was most closely associated with subsequent antisocial personality disorder; sexual abuse with borderline personality disorder; and childhood neglect with antisocial, borderline, narcissistic, and avoidant

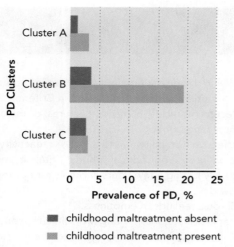

## FIGURE 9.1

**Family Environment and Risk for Personality Disorders** Associations between childhood maltreatment and risk for early adulthood personality disorders.

*Source:* Based on Cohen et al. Childhood Maltreatment Increases Risk for Personality Disorders during Early Adulthood. Archives of General Psychiatry 1999; 56.

personality disorder. These data support the argument that maladaptive patterns of parenting and family relationships increase the probability that a person will develop certain types of personality disorder.

## Treatment

Given that the concept of borderline personality disorder is rooted in psychodynamic theory, it should not be surprising that many clinicians have advocated the use of psychotherapy for the treatment of these conditions. In psychodynamic therapy, the *transference relationship*, defined as the way in which the patient behaves toward the therapist and that is believed to reflect early primary relationships, is used to increase patients' ability to experience themselves and other people in a more realistic and integrated way (Clarkin et al., 2001; Gabbard, 2000).

As we have said, personality disorders have traditionally been considered to be hard to treat from a psychological perspective, and borderline conditions are among the most difficult. Close personal relationships form the foundation of psychological intervention, and it is specifically in the area of establishing and maintaining such relationships that borderline patients experience their greatest difficulty (see Getting Help). Their persistent alternation between idealization and devaluation leads to frequent rage toward the therapist and can become a significant deterrent to progress in therapy. Not surprisingly, between one-half and two-thirds of all patients with borderline personality disorder discontinue treatment, against their therapists' advice, within the first several weeks of treatment (Kelly et al., 1992).

One effective approach to psychotherapy with borderline patients, called *dialectical behavior therapy* (DBT), has been

developed and evaluated by Marsha Linehan (Linehan, Cochran, & Kehrer, 2001), a clinical psychologist at the University of Washington. This procedure combines the use of broadly based behavioral strategies with the more general principles of supportive psychotherapy. In philosophy, the term *dialectics* refers to a process of reasoning that places opposite or contradictory ideas side by side. In Linehan's approach to treatment, the term refers to strategies that are employed by the therapist in order to help the person appreciate and balance apparently contradictory needs to accept things as they are (such as intense negative emotions) and to work toward changing patterns of thinking and behavior that contribute to problems in the regulation of emotions. Emphasis is placed on learning to be more comfortable with strong emotions, such as anger, sadness, and fear, and learning to think in a more integrated way that accepts both good and bad features of the self and other people. Traditional behavioral and cognitive techniques, such as skill training, exposure, and problem solving, are also employed to help the patient improve interpersonal relationships, tolerate distress, and regulate emotional responses. Finally, considerable emphasis is placed on the therapist's acceptance of patients, including their frequently demanding, manipulative, and contradictory behaviors. This factor is important, because borderline patients are extremely sensitive to even the most subtle signs of criticism or rejection by other people.

One controlled study of dialectical behavior therapy produced encouraging results with regard to some aspects of the patients' behavior (Linehan et al., 1994, 1999). All of the patients in this study were women who met diagnostic criteria for BPD and also had a previous history of suicide attempts or deliberate self-harm. Patients were randomly assigned to receive either DBT or treatment as usual, which was essentially any form of treatment that was available within the community. The adjustment of patients in both groups was measured after one year of treatment and over a one-year period following termination. One of the most important results involved the dropout rate. Almost 60 percent of the patients in the treatment as usual group terminated prematurely, whereas the rate in the DBT group was only 17 percent. The patients who received DBT also showed a significant reduction in the frequency and severity of suicide attempts, spent fewer days in psychiatric hospitals over the course of the study, and rated themselves higher on a measure of social adjustment. The groups did not differ, however, on other important measures, such as level of depression and hopelessness.

Positive results have also been reported in more recent studies in which women with BPD were randomly assigned to either dialectical behavior therapy or treatment as usual. Outcome measures indicated that women who were treated with dialectical behavior therapy experienced more improvement than women in the control groups with regard to symptoms such as depression and hopelessness (Bohus et al., 2004; Koons et al., 2001; Verheul et al., 2003).

Psychotropic medication is also used frequently in the treatment of borderline patients. Unfortunately, no disorder-specific drug has been found. Psychiatrists employ the entire spectrum of psychoactive medication with borderline patients, from antipsychotics and antidepressants to lithium and anticonvulsants (Koenigsberg, Woo-Ming, & Siever, 2002; Zanarini & Frankenburg, 2001). Different types of drugs are recommended to treat individual symptoms, such as impulsive aggression, emotional instability, and transient paranoid thinking, but there is no systematic proof that a specific drug is effective for any of the borderline features.

## Antisocial Personality Disorder (ASPD)

Antisocial personality disorder (ASPD) has been studied more thoroughly and for a longer period of time than any of the other personality disorders (Blashfield, 2000). One case study involving this disorder was presented at the beginning of this chapter. Tom, the man in that case, illustrated the pattern of repeated antisocial behavior that is associated with the disorder. Emotional and interpersonal problems also play an important role in the definition of antisocial personality disorder. The following case illustrates the egocentricity that is a central feature of the disorder. It also demonstrates the stunning lack of concern that such people have for the impact of their behavior on other people, especially those who are close to them.

### ⟶ Antisocial Personality Disorder

Terry is 21, the second of three boys born into a wealthy and highly respected family. His older brother is a doctor, and his younger brother is a scholarship student in his second year of college. Terry is a first-time offender, serving two years for a series of robberies committed a year ago.

By all accounts, his family life was stable, his parents were warm and loving, and his opportunities for success were enormous. His brothers were honest and hardworking, whereas he simply "floated through life, taking whatever was offered." His parents' hopes and expectations were less important to him than having a good time. Still, they supported him emotionally and financially through an adolescence marked by wildness, testing the limits, and repeated brushes with the law—speeding, reckless driving, drunkenness—but no formal convictions. By age 20 he had fathered two children and was heavily involved in gambling and drugs. When he could no longer obtain money from his family, he turned to robbing banks, and he was soon caught and sent to prison. "I wouldn't be here if my parents had come across when I needed them," he said. "What kind of parents would let their son rot in a place like this?" Asked about his children, he replied, "I've never seen them. I think they were given up for adoption. How the hell should I know!" (Hare, 1993, p. 167).

Bernard Madoff, former U.S. stockbroker and investment counselor, is now serving a 150-year prison sentence for running a massive Ponzi scheme that cheated thousands of people out of their life savings. Grandiosity, deceit, manipulativeness, and lack of remorse are traits associated with the "white-collar psychopath."

The contrast between Terry's willingness to blame his problems on his parents and his apparent inability to accept responsibility for his own children is striking. It illustrates clearly the callous indifference and shallow emotional experience of the person with antisocial personality disorder.

Current views of antisocial personality disorder have been greatly influenced by two specific books. These books have inspired two different approaches to the definition of the disorder itself. The first book, *The Mask of Sanity*, was written by Hervey Cleckley (1976), a psychiatrist at the University of Georgia, and was originally published in 1941. It includes numerous case examples of impulsive, self-centered, pleasure-seeking people who seemed to be completely lacking in certain primary emotions, such as anxiety, shame, and guilt. Cleckley used the term **psychopathy** to describe this disorder. According to Cleckley's definition, the psychopath is a person who is intelligent and superficially charming but is also chronically deceitful, unreliable, and incapable of learning from experience. This diagnostic approach places principal emphasis on emotional deficits and personality traits. Unfortunately, Cleckley's definition was difficult to use reliably because it contained such elusive features as "incapacity for love" and "failure to learn from experience."

The second book that influenced the concept of antisocial personality disorder was a report by Lee Robins of her followup study of children who had been treated many years earlier at a child guidance clinic. The book, *Deviant Children Grown Up* (1966), demonstrated that certain forms of conduct disorder that were evident during childhood, especially among boys, were reliable predictors of other forms of antisocial behavior when these same people became adults. The diagnostic approach inspired by this research study was adopted for use in DSM-III, and it is still the model included in *DSM-5* (APA, 2013). It places principal emphasis on observable behaviors and repeated conflict with, including failure to conform to, social norms with respect to lawful behavior. This approach can be used with greater reliability than psychopathy because it is focused on concrete consequences of the disorder, which are often documented by legal records, rather than subjectively defined emotional deficits, such as lack of empathy.

Psychopathy and ASPD are two different attempts to define the same disorder. Yet they are sufficiently different that they certainly do not identify the same people, and they are no longer used interchangeably (Lynam & Vachon, 2012). Critics argue that DSM blurs the distinction between antisocial personality and criminality. Cleckley's approach had been relatively clear on this point; all criminals are not psychopaths, and all psychopaths are not criminals. The DSM definition makes it difficult to diagnose antisocial personality disorder in a person who does not already have a criminal record, such as an egocentric, manipulative, and callous businessperson. It also includes a much larger proportion of criminals within the boundaries of antisocial personality disorder (Hart & Hare, 1997). The true meaning of the concept may be sacrificed in *DSM-5* for the sake of improved reliability.

## Symptoms

The diagnostic criteria for antisocial personality disorder are listed in "DSM-5: Antisocial Personality Disorder." One prominent feature in this definition is the required presence of symptoms of conduct disorder (see Chapter 16) prior to the age of 15. The definition also requires the presence of at least three out of seven signs of irresponsible and antisocial behavior after the age of 15. One of these criteria, *lack of remorse*, was one of Cleckley's original criteria.

Some investigators and clinicians prefer the concept of psychopathy to the *DSM-5* definition of antisocial personality. Robert Hare has developed a systematic approach to the assessment of psychopathy, known as the Psychopathy Checklist (PCL), that is based largely on Cleckley's original description of the disorder. The PCL includes two major factors (groups of symptoms): (1) emotional/interpersonal traits and (2) social deviance associated with an unstable or antisocial lifestyle. Key symptoms for both factors are summarized in Table 9.4. The major difference between this definition of psychopathy and the *DSM-5* definition of antisocial personality disorder involves the list of emotional and interpersonal traits (although *DSM-5* does include being deceitful and failure to experience remorse). Extensive research with the PCL indicates that, contrary to previous experience with Cleckley's criteria, the emotional and interpersonal traits can be used reliably (Hart & Hare, 1997).

The ultimate resolution of this prolonged dispute over the best definition of antisocial personality disorder will depend on systematic comparisons of the two approaches (Lilienfeld, 1994; Widiger, 2006). This situation is another classic example of studying the validity of a diagnostic concept (see Chapter 4). How different are these definitions? Which definition is most useful in predicting events such as repeated antisocial behavior following release from prison?

---

## criteria for
## Antisocial Personality Disorder                                           DSM-5

**A.** A pervasive pattern of disregard for and violation of the rights of others, occurring since age 15 years, as indicated by three (or more) of the following:

1. Failure to conform to social norms with respect to lawful behaviors, as indicated by repeatedly performing acts that are grounds for arrest.
2. Deceitfulness, as indicated by repeated lying, use of aliases, or conning others for personal profit or pleasure.
3. Impulsivity or failure to plan ahead.
4. Irritability and aggressiveness, as indicated by repeated physical fights or assaults.
5. Reckless disregard for safety of self or others.
6. Consistent irresponsibility, as indicated by repeated failure to sustain consistent work behavior or honor financial obligations.
7. Lack of remorse, as indicated by being indifferent to or rationalizing having hurt, mistreated, or stolen from another.

**B.** The individual is at least age 18 years.

**C.** There is evidence of conduct disorder with onset before age 15 years.

**D.** The occurrence of antisocial behavior is not exclusively during the course of schizophrenia or bipolar disorder.

Reprinted with permission from the *Diagnostic and Statistical Manual of Mental Disorders*, Fifth Edition, (Copyright 2013). American Psychiatric Association.

## TABLE 9.4
## Key Symptoms of Psychopathy

| Emotional/Interpersonal Traits | Social Deviance (Antisocial Lifestyle) |
| --- | --- |
| Glib and superficial | Impulsive |
| Egocentric and grandiose | Poor behavior controls |
| Lack of remorse or guilt | Need for excitement |
| Lack of empathy | Lack of responsibility |
| Deceitful and manipulative | Early behavior problems |
| Shallow emotions | Adult antisocial behavior |

Source: Based on Hare, R. D. 1998. Without Conscience: The Disturbing World of the Psychopaths Among Us. New York: Guilford Press.

**ANTISOCIAL BEHAVIOR OVER THE LIFE SPAN** Not everyone who engages in antisocial behavior does so consistently throughout his or her lifetime. Terrie Moffitt, a clinical psychologist at Duke University, has proposed that there are two primary forms of antisocial behavior: transient and nontransient. Moffitt (1993, 2007) considers adolescence-limited antisocial behavior to be a common form of social behavior that is often adaptive and that disappears by the time the person reaches adulthood. This type presumably accounts for most antisocial behavior, and it is unrelated to antisocial personality disorder.

A small proportion of antisocial individuals, mostly males, engage in antisocial behavior at all ages. Moffitt calls this type life-course-persistent antisocial behavior. The specific form of these problems may vary from one age level to the next:

> Biting and hitting at age 4, shoplifting and truancy at age 10, selling drugs and stealing cars at age 16, robbery and rape at age 22, and fraud and child abuse at age 30. The underlying disposition remains the same, but its expression changes form as new social opportunities arise at different points in development.
>
> (Moffitt, 1993, p. 679)

Follow-up studies suggest that in some ways psychopaths tend to "burn out" when they reach 40 or 45 years of age. These changes are most evident for the impulsive, socially deviant kinds of behavior that are represented in the second factor on Hare's Psychopathy Checklist (Harpur & Hare, 1994). Indeed, older psychopaths are less likely to exhibit a pathological "need for excitement" or to engage in impulsive, criminal behaviors. In contrast to this pattern, personality traits associated with the emotional–interpersonal factor on the PCL, such as deceitfulness, callousness, and lack of empathy, do not become less conspicuous over time. These are apparently more stable features of the disorder.

It is not clear whether the age-related decline in social deviance represents a change in personality structure (improved impulse control and diminished risk taking). Moffitt's theory suggests that, as psychopaths grow older, they may find new outlets for their aggression, impulsive behavior, and callous disregard for others. For example, they might resort to fraud or child abuse, for which they are less likely to get caught.

## Causes

Psychologists have studied etiological factors associated with psychopathy and antisocial personality disorder more extensively than for any of the other personality disorders. Research studies on this topic fall into three general areas. One is concerned with the biological underpinnings of the disorder, especially the possible influence of genetic factors. The second focus of investigation is social factors. The relationship between familial conflict and the development of antisocial behavior in children falls under this general heading. The third group of studies has addressed the nature of the psychological factors that might explain the apparent inability of people with antisocial personality disorder to learn from experience.

**BIOLOGICAL FACTORS** Several investigators have used twin and adoption methods to study the contributions of genetic and environmental factors to the development of antisocial personality disorder and of criminal behavior more generally. The adoption strategy is based on the study of adoptees: people who were separated from their biological parents at an early age and raised by adoptive families (see Chapter 2). Several adoption studies have found that the development of antisocial behavior is determined by an interaction between genetic factors and adverse environmental circumstances (Waldman & Rhee, 2006). In other words, both types of influence are important. The highest rates of conduct disorder and antisocial behavior are found among the offspring of antisocial biological parents who are raised in an adverse adoptive environment.

Consider, for example, results from one particularly informative study (Cadoret et al., 1995; Yates, Cadoret, & Troughton, 1999). The investigators studied men and women who had been separated at birth from biological parents with antisocial personality disorder. This target group was compared to a control group of people who had been separated at birth from biological parents with no history of psychopathology. The offspring and their adoptive parents were interviewed to assess symptoms of conduct disorder, aggression, and antisocial behavior in the offspring. The adversity of the adoptive home environment was measured in terms of the total number of problems that were present, including severe marital difficulties, drug abuse, or criminal activity. People who were raised in more difficult adoptive homes were more likely to engage in various types of aggressive and antisocial behavior as children and as adults. Furthermore, the harmful effects of an unfavorable environment were more pronounced in the target group than in the control group. In other words, offspring of antisocial parents were much more likely to exhibit symptoms of conduct disorder (truancy, school expulsion, lying, and stealing) as children and exaggerated aggressive behavior as adolescents if they were raised in an adverse adoptive home environment. Being raised in an adverse home environment did not significantly increase the probability of conduct disorder, aggression, or antisocial behavior among offspring in the control group. Thus, antisocial behavior appeared to result from the interaction of genetic and environmental factors.

**SOCIAL FACTORS** Adoption studies indicate that genetic factors interact with environmental events to produce patterns of antisocial and criminal behavior. The combination of a genetic predisposition toward antisocial behavior and environmental adversity is particularly harmful. What kinds of events might be involved in this process? Obvious candidates include physical abuse and childhood neglect, as indicated by the longitudinal study of adolescents and their families (Farrington, 2006; Johnson et al., 1999).

How can the interaction between genetic factors and family processes be explained? Moffitt's explanation for the etiology of life-course-persistent antisocial behavior depends on the influence of multiple, interacting systems. One pathway involves the concept of children's temperament and the effect that their characteristic response styles may have on parental behavior. Children with a "difficult" temperament—that is, those whose response style is characterized by high levels of negative emotion or excessive activity—may be especially irritating to their parents and caretakers (Bates, Wachs, & Emde, 1994). They may be clumsy, overactive, inattentive, irritable, or impulsive. Their resistance to disciplinary efforts may discourage adults from maintaining persistent strategies in this regard. This type of child may be most likely to evoke maladaptive reactions from parents who are poorly equipped to deal with the challenges presented by this kind of behavior. Parents may be driven either to use unusually harsh punishments or to abandon any attempt at discipline. This interaction between the child and the social environment fosters the development of poorly controlled behavior. Antisocial behavior is perpetuated when the person selects friends who share similar antisocial interests and problems.

Antisocial behavior can be perpetuated when the person selects friends who share similar antisocial interests and problems.

After a pattern of antisocial behavior has been established during childhood, many factors lock the person into further antisocial activities. Moffitt's theory emphasizes two sources of continuity. The first is a limited range of behavioral skills. The person does not learn social skills that would allow him or her to pursue more appropriate responses than behaviors such as lying, cheating, and stealing. Once the opportunity to develop these skills is lost during childhood, they may never be learned. The second source of continuity involves the results of antisocial behavior during childhood and adolescence. The person becomes progressively ensnared by the aftermath of earlier choices. Many possible consequences of antisocial behavior, including being addicted to drugs, becoming a teenaged parent, dropping out of school, and having a criminal record, can narrow the person's options.

**PSYCHOLOGICAL FACTORS** Adoption, twin, and family studies provide clues to the causes of antisocial personality disorder. Another series of studies, beginning in the 1950s and extending to the present, has been concerned with the psychological mechanisms that may mediate this type of behavior. These investigations have attempted to explain several characteristic features of psychopathy—such as lack of anxiety, impulsivity, and failure to learn from experience—using various types of laboratory tasks (Fowles & Dindo, 2006).

Subjects in the laboratory tasks are typically asked to learn a sequence of responses in order either to receive a reward or avoid an aversive consequence, such as electric shock or loss of money. Although the overall accuracy of psychopaths' performance on these tasks is generally equivalent to that of non-psychopathic subjects, their behavior sometimes appears to be unaffected by the anticipation of punishment.

Two primary hypotheses have been advanced to explain the poor performance of psychopaths on these tasks. One point of view is based on Cleckley's argument that psychopaths are emotionally impoverished. Their lack of anxiety and fear is particularly striking. Research support for this hypothesis is based in large part on an examination of physiological responses while subjects are performing laboratory tasks. One particularly compelling line of investigation involves the examination of the eye blink startle reflex. People blink their eyes involuntarily when they are startled by a loud, unexpected burst of noise. For most people, the magnitude of this response is increased if, at the time they are startled, they are engaged in an ongoing task that elicits fear or some other negative emotional state (such as viewing frightening or disgusting stimuli). The magnitude of the startle response is decreased if the person is engaged in a task that elicits positive emotion. Psychopaths' startle responses follow a pattern different from those observed in normal subjects (Herpertz et al., 2001; Patrick & Zempolich, 1998); they do not show the exaggerated startle response that is indicative of fear in the presence of aversive stimuli. This emotional deficit may explain why psychopaths are relatively insensitive to, or able to ignore, the effects of punishment.

The other hypothesis holds that psychopaths have difficulty shifting or reallocating their attention to consider the possible negative consequences of their behavior. Evidence for this explanation is based in large part on the observation that psychopaths respond normally to punishment in some situations, but not in others. This is especially evident in mixed-incentive situations, in which the person's behavior might be either rewarded or punished. Psychopaths are preoccupied with the potential for a successful outcome. They will continue gambling when the stakes are high, even when the odds are badly against them. And they will pursue a potential sexual encounter, even when the other person is trying to discourage their interest. They fail to inhibit inappropriate behavior because they are less able than other people to stop and consider the meaning of important signals that their behavior might lead to punishment (Hiatt & Newman, 2006; Patterson & Newman, 1993).

Critics of this line of research have noted some problems with existing psychological explanations for the psychopath's behavior. One limitation is the implicit assumption that most people conform to social regulations and ethical principles because of anxiety or fear of punishment. The heart of this criticism seems to lie in a disagreement regarding the relative importance of Cleckley's criteria for psychopathy. It might be argued that the most crucial

features are not low anxiety and failure to learn from experience, but lack of shame and pathological egocentricity. According to this perspective, the psychopath is simply a person who has chosen, for whatever reason, to behave in a persistently selfish manner that ignores the feelings and rights of other people. "Rather than moral judgment being driven by anxiety, anxiety is driven by moral judgment" (Levenson, 1992).

## Treatment

People with antisocial personalities seldom seek professional mental health services unless they are forced into treatment by the legal system. When they do seek treatment, the general consensus among clinicians is that it is seldom effective. This widely held impression is based, in part, on the traits that are used to define the disorder; like people with borderline personality disorder, people with antisocial personality disorder are typically unable to establish intimate, trusting relationships, which obviously form the basis for any treatment program.

The research literature regarding the treatment of antisocial personality disorder is sparse (Harris & Rice, 2006). Very few studies have identified cases using official diagnostic criteria for antisocial personality disorder. Most of the programs that have been evaluated have focused on juvenile delinquents, adults who have been imprisoned, or people otherwise referred by the criminal justice system. Outcome is often measured in terms of the frequency of repeated criminal offenses rather than in terms of changes in behaviors more directly linked to the personality traits that define the core of antisocial personality. The high rate of alcoholism and other forms of substance dependence in this population is another problem that complicates planning and evaluating treatment programs aimed specifically at the personality disorder itself.

Although no form of intervention has proved to be effective for antisocial personality disorder, psychological interventions that are directed toward specific features of the disorder might be useful (Wallace & Newman, 2004). Examples are behavioral procedures that were originally designed for anger management and deviant sexual behaviors. Behavioral treatments can apparently produce temporary changes in behavior while the person is closely supervised, but they may not generalize to other settings.

## getting HELP

As we mention in this chapter, many people who would meet the diagnostic criteria for a personality disorder do not enter treatment, at least not voluntarily. Although their interpersonal problems are pervasive and deeply ingrained, they are reluctant or completely unable to see the active role that they play in maintaining their own misfortunes (regardless of their origins). The pejorative way in which personality

disorders are sometimes portrayed may make some people reluctant to acknowledge that they have a personality disorder. We prefer to discuss these problems in terms of personality limitations or maladaptive response styles. No one is perfect. Being able to recognize your own weaknesses is a sign that you are open-minded and willing to change. This is the first important step toward improvement.

*Continued*

It also helps to have a little compassion for yourself, along with the determination to work toward a lasting change in the way you relate to the people and events of your life. *Lost in the Mirror: An Inside Look at Borderline Personality Disorder* by Richard Moskovitz, provides an insightful and sympathetic guide to the painful emotional experiences associated with borderline personality disorder. It also illustrates ways in which these symptoms affect the lives of patients, their families, and their friends.

If you are interested in help because you have to deal with someone who you think may have a personality disorder, you probably feel confused, frustrated, and angry. You may also feel extremely guilty if you blame yourself for problems in the relationship or for the other person's unhappiness. This may be especially true if you are involved in a romantic relationship or must work closely with someone who might meet the criteria for a PD. Fortunately, it is often possible to adapt to such interactions. Several self-help guides provide advice about getting along with difficult people. One good example is *Fatal Flaws: Navigating Destructive Relationships with People with Disorders of Personality and Character* (Yudofsky, 2005). Most recommend that you begin by learning about the predictable nature of the

other person's style. Recognize the presence of personality weaknesses and learn how to adapt to them. You must also accept the limits of your own ability to control the other person or to get him or her to change.

Sometimes the only solution is to end the relationship. At their most extreme, people with personality disorders cannot form reciprocal, mutually satisfying relationships with other people. This is particularly true in the case of antisocial personality disorder. Some unscrupulous people repeatedly abuse, exploit, and cheat others. We all may run across such people from time to time, and we need to learn how to protect ourselves. Robert Hare, an expert on psychopathy, concludes his book *Without Conscience* with a brief "survival guide" that may help you minimize your risk. He notes, for example, that we should be aware of the symptoms and interpersonal characteristics of psychopathy. We should be cautious in high-risk situations and know our own weaknesses. Hare's advice may be extremely helpful to someone who finds himself or herself trapped in a relationship with someone who is a psychopath. In fact, you may want to speak to a therapist or counselor to figure out why you have become involved in such an unequal, nonreciprocal relationship.

# 9 Summary

Personality disorders are defined in terms of rigid, inflexible, maladaptive ways of perceiving and responding to oneself and one's environment that lead to social or occupational problems or subjective distress. This pattern must be pervasive across a broad range of situations, and it must be stable and of long duration.

Personality disorders are controversial for a number of reasons, including their low diagnostic reliability and the tremendous overlap among specific personality disorder categories.

Many systems have been proposed to describe the fundamental dimensions of human personality. One popular alternative is the five-factor model, which includes the basic traits of neuroticism, extraversion, openness to experience, agreeableness, and conscientiousness. Extreme variations in any of these traits—being either pathologically high or low—can be associated with personality disorders.

*DSM-5* lists 10 types of personality disorder, arranged in three clusters. There is considerable overlap among and between these

types. Cluster A includes **paranoid, schizoid,** and **schizotypal personality disorders.** These categories generally refer to people who are seen as being odd or eccentric. Cluster B includes **antisocial, borderline, histrionic,** and **narcissistic personality disorders.** People who fit into this cluster are generally seen as being dramatic, unpredictable, and overly emotional. Cluster C includes **avoidant, dependent,** and **obsessive–compulsive personality disorders.** The common element in these disorders is presumably anxiety or fearfulness.

*DSM-5* also includes a dimensional approach to the description of personality disorders. This proposal was developed by the workgroup for *DSM-5*. After considerable debate, it was rejected in favor of retaining the traditional categorical approach. The dimensional approach includes two steps: an assessment of level of personality functioning followed by ratings on 25 maladaptive personality traits. This system offers the advantage of being better able to account for similarities and differences among people with various combinations of personality traits. It is included in Section III of *DSM-5*, along with other conditions that require further study.

The overall prevalence of personality disorders among adults in the general population (i.e., the percentage who qualify for the diagnosis of at least one type) is approximately 10 percent. The highest prevalence rates for specific types of personality disorders are usually found for obsessive–compulsive, antisocial, and avoidant personality disorders, which may affect 3 or 4 percent of adults. Prevalence rates for other specific types tend to be approximately 1 or 2 percent of the population (or less).

The disorders listed in Cluster A, especially schizoid and schizotypal personality disorders, have been viewed as possible antecedents or subclinical forms of schizophrenia. They are defined largely in terms of minor symptoms that resemble the hallucinations and delusions seen in the full-blown disorder, as well as peculiar behaviors that have been observed among the first-degree relatives of schizophrenic patients.

The most important features of borderline personality disorder revolve around a pervasive pattern of instability in self-image, in interpersonal relationships, and in mood. Research regarding the causes of borderline personality disorder has focused on two primary areas. One involves the impact of chaotic and abusive families. The other is concerned with the premature separation of children from their parents. Both sets of factors presumably can lead to problems in emotional regulation.

**Psychopathy** and antisocial personality disorder are two different attempts to define the same disorder. The *DSM-5* definition of ASPD places primary emphasis on social deviance in adulthood (repeated lying, physical assaults, reckless and irresponsible behavior). The concept of psychopathy places greater emphasis on emotional and interpersonal deficits, such as lack of remorse, lack of empathy, and shallow emotions.

Treatment for schizotypal and borderline personality disorders often involves the use of antipsychotic medication or antidepressant medication. Various types of psychological interventions, including dialectical behavior therapy, are frequently employed with borderline patients. People with antisocial personality disorder seldom seek treatment voluntarily. When they do, the general consensus among clinicians is that it is seldom effective.

## The Big Picture

## critical thinking review

**9.1** What is the difference between being eccentric and having a personality disorder?

People who are unconventional are not necessarily disagreeable or difficult interpersonally. The concept of personality disorder, on the other hand, carries the assumption that the characteristic features by which they are defined are also associated with subjective distress or social impairment . . . (see pages 232–233).

**9.2** In what ways are borderline and narcissistic personality disorders similar?

People in both groups can be hypersensitive and self-centered, thinking that others should be especially concerned with their needs and interests. When these expectations are not met, they may react with intense anger . . . (see page 241).

**9.3** What are the advantages of a dimensional approach that would describe personality problems as variations on maladaptive personality traits?

This alternative perspective would minimize problems associated with comorbidity (a person meeting criteria for more than one diagnostic category) and arbitrary cut-off points between normal and abnormal personality . . . (see pages 242–243).

**9.4** Which personality disorders are least likely to change as a person gets older?

Schizoid and schizotypal personality disorders are relatively intractable problems and are associated with enduring social isolation and occupational difficulties . . . (see page 247).

**9.5** Why are personality disorders so difficult to treat?

Many people with personality disorders are unable to recognize the nature of their problems. They may also be uncomfortable with the type of close, personal relationship that must be formed with a therapist if psychological treatment is going to be successful . . . (see pages 250–251).

**9.6** What is the difference between antisocial personality disorder and psychopathy?

The DSM-IV definition of antisocial personality disorder is focused largely on repeated conflict with authorities and failure to conform to social norms, while the definition of psychopathy places greater importance on emotional deficits (lack of remorse, shallow emotions) and personality traits (impulsivity, grandiosity, lack of responsibility) . . . (see pages 255–256).

## key terms

antisocial personality
    disorder   239
avoidant personality
    disorder   241
borderline personality
    disorder   240
cross-cultural psychology   248

dependent personality
    disorder   241
histrionic personality
    disorder   240
impulse control disorders   252
narcissistic personality
    disorder   240

obsessive–compulsive
    personality disorder
    (OCPD)   241
personality   232
personality disorder (PD)   232
paranoid personality
    disorder   238

psychopathy   255
schizoid personality
    disorder   239
schizotypal personality
    disorder   239

feeding and eating disorders

10

# The Big Picture

## learning objectives

**10.1**
How can you tell if someone has an eating disorder?

**10.2**
How do images of women in the media contribute to eating disorders?

**10.3**
Do men suffer from eating disorders?

**10.4**
What is binge-eating disorder?

**10.5**
Why do some girls and women develop eating disorders when others do not?

**10.6**
What treatments work for anorexia and bulimia?

**10.7**
Can eating disorders be prevented?

Popular culture in the United States is obsessed with physical appearance. We are told that "beauty is only skin deep," but the entertainment, cosmetic, fashion, and diet industries are eager to convince young people that "looks are everything." Perfect men are handsome, muscular, and successful. Perfect women are beautiful and thin—extremely thin. In fact, women's thinness is equated with beauty, fitness, success, and ultimately with happiness. Given our national obsession with appearance, diet, and weight, is it surprising that many people, especially young women, become obsessed to the point of developing eating disorders?

## Overview

The *DSM-5* lists six major types of disturbances in a new diagnostic category called *feeding and eating disorders,* but we think *DSM-5* was being too literal in grouping these problems together. Yes, they all involve eating, but . . . Three disorders—pica, rumination disorder, and avoidant/restrictive food intake disorder—typically begin in infancy or childhood, often among children with intellectual disabilities. A fourth, *binge-eating disorder* is a

The images of women portrayed in advertising and the popular media contribute to the development of eating disorders.

new diagnosis closely connected to the controversial question of whether *obesity* is a mental disorder. (*DSM-5* says obesity is not a mental disorder.)

In this chapter, we briefly discuss other feeding and eating disorders but focus on *anorexia nervosa* and *bulimia nervosa,* two problems that traditionally have been called *eating disorders.* Some experts suggest that "dieting disorder" is a more accurate description. An undue emphasis on weight and shape is central to both of these problems, which typically affect adolescent and young adult women.

The most obvious characteristic of **anorexia nervosa** is extreme emaciation. The term *anorexia* literally means "loss of appetite," but this is a misnomer. People with anorexia nervosa *are* hungry, yet they starve themselves nevertheless. Some unfortunate victims literally starve themselves to death.

**Bulimia nervosa** is characterized by repeated episodes of binge eating, followed by inappropriate compensatory behaviors such as self-induced vomiting, misuse of laxatives, or excessive exercise. Weight is in the normal range. *Bulimia* literally means "ox appetite" (hungry enough to eat an ox), but people with bulimia nervosa have an average appetite. Paradoxically, the problem may result from trying to maintain a weight below the body's natural set point, an effort that results in a yo-yo struggle with binge eating and compensation. Most sufferers view binge eating as a failure of control, but it really is their body's natural reaction to unnatural weight suppression (Keel et al., 2007).

Both anorexia and bulimia are about 10 times more common among females than males, and they develop most commonly among women in their teens and early twenties. The increased incidence among young people reflects the contemporary, intense focus on young women's physical appearance and the difficulties many adolescent girls have in adjusting to the rapid changes in body shape and weight that begin with puberty (Field & Kitos, 2010). While isolated cases of anorexia and bulimia have been reported throughout history, the problems received scientific attention only in recent decades (Fairburn & Brownell, 2002; Striegel-Moore & Smolak, 2001). In fact, the term *anorexia nervosa* was coined in 1874, while *bulimia nervosa* was used for the first time only in 1979 (Heaner & Walsh, 2013).

According to the National Centers for Disease Control and Prevention, at any point in time, 44 percent of high school females are attempting to lose weight compared with 15 percent of males (Serdula et al., 1993). Many adolescent boys want to *gain* weight in order to look bigger and stronger (see Eating Disorders in Males on p. xxx). Almost half of American women have a negative body image, particularly concerning their waist, hips, and/or thighs (Cash & Henry, 1995; see Figure 10.1). European American and Latina women report higher rates of body dissatisfaction than African Americans (Bay-Cheng et al., 2002; Grabe & Shibley-Hyde, 2006). Dissatisfaction increased from the 1980s to the 1990s among white women, but fortunately, levels of body dissatisfaction declined between the 1990s and 2000s for both white and black women (Cash et al., 2004). Perhaps fewer young women are falling victim to the popular media's culture of thinness.

## Eating Disorders in Males

Our culture clearly values different body types for males than for females. Adolescent boys often want to be bigger and stronger, not slimmer. Women rate themselves as being thin only when they are below 90 percent of their expected body weight. In contrast, men see themselves as thin even when they weigh as much as 105 percent of their expected weight (Anderson, 2002). Surveys indicate that the majority of females want to lose weight, but males are about equally divided between those who want to lose weight and those who want to gain weight.

Some experts argue that pressures to be strong and muscular have created a new eating disorder among males. The problem, sometimes called *reverse anorexia* or the *Adonis complex*, is characterized by excessive emphasis on extreme muscularity and often accompanied by the abuse of anabolic steroids (Anderson, 2002; Ricciardelli & McCabe, 2004). You may recall that baseball slugger Mark McGwire was taking androstenedione ("andro," an over-the-counter steroid hormone) when he broke the record for most home runs in a single season. McGwire's popularity and success apparently contributed to growing steroid use among young males in the United States, where 3 percent to 12 percent of teenage boys have tried steroids (Ricciardelli & McCabe, 2004).

More realistic expectations about thinness surely contribute to the lower prevalence of anorexia and bulimia among males. However, men with these eating disorders are less likely to seek treatment than are women, perhaps because they are less likely to recognize the problem or feel more stigmatized because of it (Woodside et al., 2001). Men with anorexia or bulimia deviate far from male norms, and this can lead to rejection and stigmatization by other men, therapists, and even females with eating disorders. The stigma of being a man with an eating disorder also alters one common symptom of anorexia nervosa. Females with anorexia nervosa typically view their appearance positively, perhaps even with a degree of pride. In contrast, anorexia nervosa can negatively affect the self-esteem of men, because weight and/or eating struggles are "unmanly" (Andersen, 1995).

Anorexia and bulimia are more common among certain subgroups of males. Male wrestlers have a particularly high prevalence of bulimia, a result of the intense pressure to "make weight"—to weigh below the weight cutoffs used to group competitors in a wrestling match. Eating disorders also are more common among gay men, who place more emphasis on appearance (Carlat, Camargo, & Herzog, 1997; Russell & Keel, 2002) and also endure minority stress (Kimmel & Mahalik, 2005).

Whether the ideal image is unrealistically thin or unrealistically muscular, cultural stereotypes about appearance can be risky for both males and females who internalize them.

Mark McGwire took androstenedione ("andro"), an over-the-counter steroid hormone, when he broke the single season home run record. Many teenage boys take steroids to build their bodies, a trend some consider to be a new eating disorder.

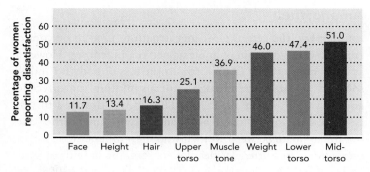

**FIGURE 10.1**

Percentage of females reporting that they were "very or mostly dissatisfied" with specific physical attributes in a national sample of women aged 18 to 70.
*Source:* Cash, Thomas and Patricia Henry. 1995. Women's Body Images: The Results of a National Survey in the U.S.A. Sex Roles; 33: 19–28.

In this chapter, we discuss the symptoms of anorexia nervosa separately from those of bulimia nervosa, because they differ considerably. We combine the two disorders when reviewing diagnosis, frequency, and causes, however, because they share many developmental similarities. For example, many people with anorexia nervosa also binge and purge on occasion; many people with bulimia nervosa have a history of anorexia nervosa. When considering treatment, we again discuss the two disorders separately, reflecting the important differences in the focus and effectiveness of therapy for each disorder. We begin with a case study.

### → Serrita's Anorexia

Serrita was an attractive, well-dressed, and polite 15-year-old high school sophomore. An excellent student, her mother described Serrita as a "sweet girl who never gave me an ounce of worry—until now." When she was first seen by a clinical psychologist for the treatment of anorexia nervosa, Serrita was 5 feet 2 inches tall and weighed 81 pounds. Serrita's gaunt appearance was painfully obvious to anyone who looked at her. Despite her constant scrutiny of her own body, however, Serrita firmly denied that she was too thin. Instead, she insisted that she looked "almost right." She was still on a diet, and every day she carefully inspected her stomach, thighs, hips, arms, and face for any signs of fat. Serrita remained deathly afraid of gaining weight. She could recite every item of food she had consumed recently and discuss its caloric and fat content.

Serrita began her diet nine months earlier after visiting her family doctor, who told her that she could stand to lose a pound or two. Her diet began normally enough. She quickly lost the 6 pounds she wanted to lose, and without really planning to do so, she simply continued her diet. Her friends' and family's compliments soon turned into worried warnings, but privately Serrita was exhilarated. To her, the concerned remarks only proved that her diet was working. Secretly, she hoped that having a "great

body" would compensate for her perceived inadequacies. She wanted to look like the women in her favorite magazines, but she felt that she wasn't a "cute, all-American girl"—she saw herself as too short, too dark, and her features as too sharp.

Serrita's breakfast consisted of one slice of dry wheat toast and a small glass of orange juice. Lunch was either an apple or a small salad without dressing. In between meals, Serrita drank several diet colas, which helped control her constant, gnawing appetite. Dinner typically was a family meal. Serrita picked at whatever she was served. Sometimes her parents would plead with her to eat more, and Serrita would eat a bit to appease them. On occasion, perhaps once a week, Serrita forced herself to vomit after dinner, because she felt that her parents made her eat too much.

Serrita's parents became so concerned that they made her go to see her family physician. The physician also was very worried about Serrita's low weight, and she discovered that Serrita had not menstruated in over six months. The physician said that Serrita was suffering from anorexia nervosa. She immediately made a referral to a psychologist as well as to a nutritionist, who, the physician hoped, would correct Serrita's extreme views about dieting.

In talking with the psychologist, Serrita agreed that she understood why everyone was concerned about her health. She knew about anorexia nervosa, which she realized was a serious problem. Serrita even hinted that she knew that she was suffering from anorexia nervosa. Nevertheless, she steadfastly denied that she needed to gain weight. Although she was happy to talk with the psychologist, she was not prepared to change her eating habits. Serrita was deathly afraid that eating even a little more would cause her to "turn into a blimp." She was proud of her mastery of her hunger. She was not about to give up the control she had fought so hard to gain.

## Symptoms of Anorexia

Serrita showed all the classic symptoms of anorexia nervosa: emaciation, a disturbed view of her body, and an intense fear of gaining weight. She also had problems commonly associated with anorexia nervosa but not defining symptoms including the cessation of menstruation, obsessive preoccupation with food, occasional purging, and a "successful" struggle for control over persistent hunger. Additional difficulties sometimes associated with anorexia nervosa include mood disturbance, sexual problems, a lack of impulse control, and medical issues.

### Significantly Low Weight

The most obvious and most dangerous symptom of anorexia nervosa is a *significantly low weight.* Anorexia nervosa often begins with a diet gone awry, as it did with Serrita. Weight falls below normal and may plummet dangerously.

*DSM-5* contains no formal cutoff as to how thin is too thin, but suggests a *body mass index (BMI)*[1] under 18.5 is a useful

---

[1]To calculate the body mass index: (1) Multiply weight in pounds by 700; (2) divide this number by height in inches; (3) divide this second number by height in inches. BMI percentiles by age are available for children and adolescents, whose low weight may be due to failure to make expected gains rather than weight loss.

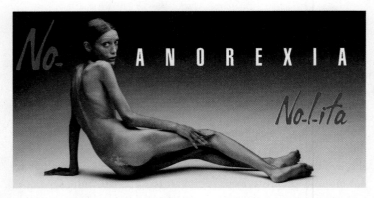

Isabelle Caro was a French model and actress who allowed her emaciated image to be used in an Italian advertising campaign against anorexia. She died on November 17, 2010, due to complications associated with her eating disorder.

indicator in adults. The average victim is far more emaciated, 25 to 30 percent below normal body weight. Many anorexics are not treated until their weight loss becomes life threatening. In fact, about 5 percent of people with anorexia nervosa die of starvation, suicide, or medical complications stemming from their extreme weight loss (Steinhausen, 2002).

## Fear of Gaining Weight

An intense fear of gaining weight or becoming fat is the second defining characteristic of anorexia. The fear of gaining weight presents particular problems for treatment. A therapist's encouragement to eat more can terrify someone who fears that relaxing control, even just a little, will lead to a total loss of control. Ironically, the fear of gaining weight is not soothed by weight loss. In fact, the fear may grow more intense as the individual loses more weight (APA, 2013).

## Disturbance in Experiencing Weight or Shape

The third and final defining symptom of anorexia nervosa involves a disturbance in how weight or shape is experienced. People with anorexia nervosa usually do not recognize their emaciation for what it is. Many steadfastly deny problems with their weight. Even when confronted with their own withered image in a mirror, some people with anorexia nervosa insist that their weight is not a problem. Sometimes this may include a *distorted body image*, an inaccurate perception of body size and shape. The following excerpt, which we received anonymously from a student, illustrates the disturbance in experiencing weight or shape.

> I'll try to explain how a person with an eating disorder sees a distorted image of herself. It's almost like she sees herself as bloated—of course she sees herself, she recognizes herself, but as bigger than usual. Also, the skinnier she gets, the more she notices fat deposits around the waist, under the arms, etc., because the more fat is lost, the more attention is drawn to the little bit of fat that still exists. Also, it's the point of reference in the background that may sometimes be distorted. She looks in the bathroom mirror and thinks, "Did I take up that much space against this wall yesterday?"

## Amenorrhea

*Amenorrhea,* the cessation of menstruation, used to be considered as a core symptom of anorexia nervosa in females. However, amenorrhea typically is a *reaction* to the loss of body fat and associated physiological changes, not a symptom that precedes anorexia (Pinheiro et al., 2007). The *DSM-5* dropped this diagnostic criterion for this reason, and because amenorrhea does not differentiate between women who meet other criteria for anorexia. Menstrual irregularities also are common in bulimia (Attia & Roberto, 2009; Pinheiro et al., 2007; Wilfley et al., 2008).

## Medical Complications

Anorexia nervosa can cause a number of medical complications. People with anorexia commonly complain about constipation, abdominal pain, intolerance to cold, and lethargy. Some complaints stem from the effects of semistarvation on blood pressure and body temperature, both of which may fall below normal. In addition, the skin can become dry and cracked, and some people develop *lanugo,* a fine, downy hair, on their face or trunk of their body. Other medical difficulties may include anemia, infertility, impaired kidney functioning, cardiovascular problems, dental erosion, and bone loss (Mitchell & Crow, 2010). A particularly dangerous medication complication is an *electrolyte imbalance,* a disturbance in the levels of potassium, sodium, calcium, and other vital elements found in bodily fluids. Electrolyte imbalance can lead to cardiac arrest or kidney failure. Anorexia nervosa may begin with the seemingly harmless desire to be a bit thinner, but the eating disorder can lead to serious health problems, including death.

## Struggle for Control

Some people with anorexia act impulsively, but more are conforming and controlling. Some theorists speculate that the disorder actually develops out of a sense of having no control. Excessively compliant "good girls" may find that obsessively regulating their diet allows them to be in charge of at least one area of their lives (Bruch, 1982). Certainly, many young people with anorexia nervosa take great pride in their self-denial, feeling like masters of control.

## Comorbid Psychological Disorders

Anorexia nervosa is associated with other psychological problems, including obsessive–compulsive disorder and obsessive–compulsive personality disorder (Halmi, 2010). People with anorexia nervosa are obsessed with food and diet, and they often follow compulsive eating rituals. However, a unique study found that such behavior can result from starvation. In this study, 32 World War II conscientious objectors fulfilled their military obligation by voluntarily undergoing semistarvation for 24 weeks. (The researchers wanted to learn about the effects of starvation on military personnel in the field.) As the men lost more and more weight, they developed extensive obsessions about food and compulsive eating rituals. For many, the obsessions and compulsions continued long after they returned to their normal weight (Keys et al., 1950). This suggests that obsessive–compulsive

Conscientious objectors participating in a study of semistarvation during World War II. Many starving men developed obsessions about food similar to those sometimes found in anorexia nervosa.

behavior may be a reaction to starvation, not a risk factor for anorexia.

Most people with anorexia nervosa also show symptoms of depression, such as sad mood, irritability, insomnia, social withdrawal, and diminished interest in sex (Halmi, 2010). Like obsessive–compulsive behavior, however, depression can either be a cause of or a reaction to the eating disorder (Vögele & Gibson, 2010).

Finally, anorexia often co-occurs with the symptoms of bulimia. In some cases, purging follows episodes of binge eating. In other cases, purging may be a means of further controlling eating that already is dramatically restricted. People with anorexia nervosa who do *not* binge eat or purge generally are better adjusted on measures of their mental health—for example, they have lower rates of depression (Braun, Sunday, & Halmi, 1994).

## Symptoms of Bulimia

Bulimia nervosa and anorexia nervosa, although different, share many similarities. One connection is that people with bulimia nervosa have often a history of anorexia nervosa, as in the following case study.

### ⟶ Michelle's Secret

Michelle was a sophomore at a state university when she first sought help for a humiliating problem. Once or twice a week, she fell into an episode of uncontrollable binge eating followed by self-induced vomiting. When Michelle was alone and feeling bad, she would buy a half-gallon of ice cream and perhaps a bag of cookies and bring the food back to her room, where she secretly gorged herself. The binge brought Michelle some comfort at first, but by the time she was finished, she felt physically uncomfortable, sickened by her lack of control, and terrified of gaining weight. To compensate, she would walk across the street to an empty bathroom in the psychology department. There, she forced herself to vomit by sticking her finger down her throat.

The vomiting brought relief from the physical discomfort, but it did not relieve her shame. Michelle was disgusted by her actions, but she could not stop herself. In fact, the pattern of binge eating and purging had been going on for most of the school year. Michelle decided to seek treatment only when a friend from her psychology class discovered her purging in the bathroom. The friend also had a history of bulimia nervosa, but she had gotten her eating under control. She convinced Michelle to try therapy.

Michelle's eating problems began when she was in high school. She had studied ballet since she was eight years old, and with the stern encouragement of her instructor, she had struggled to maintain her willowy figure as she became an adolescent. At first she dieted openly, but her parents constantly criticized her inadequate eating. To appease them, Michelle occasionally would eat a more normal meal, but she often forced herself to vomit shortly afterward. When she was a junior in high school, Michelle's parents took her to a psychologist, who treated her for anorexia nervosa. She was 5 feet 6 inches tall, but she weighed only 95 pounds. Michelle was furious and refused to talk in any depth with the therapist. She allowed herself to gain a few pounds—to about 105—only to convince her parents that she did not need treatment.

Michelle's weight eventually stabilized around 105 pounds. Even though she was very thin, Michelle continued to count every calorie at every meal every day. Throughout college, she starved herself all week so she could eat normally on dates during the weekend. Occasionally, she forced herself to vomit after eating too much, but she did not see this as a big problem. Until the previous summer, she had maintained her weight near her goal of 105 pounds. Over the summer, however, Michelle relaxed her diet as she "partied" with old friends. She gained about 15 pounds, a healthy but still quite thin weight for her height and body type. When she returned to college, however, Michelle grew disgusted with her appearance and fearful of gaining even more weight.

Michelle tried to lose weight, but she met with little success. She started to purge more frequently in a desperate attempt to "diet," but she soon found herself binge eating more frequently, too. Michelle was extremely frustrated by her "lack of self-control." Although she now recognized her past problems with anorexia nervosa, Michelle openly longed for the discipline she had once achieved over her hunger and diet.

Michelle was a bright, attractive, and successful young woman, but she felt like a failure and a "fake." She longed to have a boyfriend but never found one despite many casual dates. She was intensely, if privately, competitive with her girlfriends. She wanted to be more beautiful and intelligent than other girls, but she inevitably felt inferior to one classmate or another. She was determined at least to be thinner than her girlfriends, but she felt that she had lost all control over this goal. Michelle pretended to be happy and normal, but secretly, she was miserable.

Michelle's frequent struggles with binge eating, her self-induced vomiting and purging, and her undue focus on her weight and figure are the core symptoms that define bulimia nervosa. Depression also is commonly associated with the disorder, along with possible medical complications. Unlike anorexia, weight is in the normal range in bulimia nervosa.

## Binge Eating

The DSM-5 defines **binge eating** as consuming an amount of food that is clearly larger than most people would eat under similar circumstances in a fixed period of time, for example, less than two hours. There have been some attempts to define a binge more objectively, such as eating more than 1,000 calories, or subjectively, such as based on the individual's appraisal. Variations in normal eating complicate these alternative definitions, however. Eating a very large number of calories may be normal under certain circumstances (think: Thanksgiving). Others may consider eating two cookies to be a "binge." Thus, the *DSM-5* ultimately relies on clinical judgment.

Sadly, many inappropriate eating behaviors border on being statistically normal—and clearly unhealthy—in our food- and weight-obsessed society. Over 35 percent of people report occasional binge eating. Large numbers of people also report that they fast (29 percent) and use self-induced vomiting (8 percent) or laxatives (over 5 percent) in an attempt to compensate for their eating (Fairburn & Beglin, 1990).

Binges may be planned in advance, or they may begin spontaneously. In either case, binges typically are secret. Most people with bulimia nervosa are ashamed and go to elaborate efforts to conceal their binge eating. During a binge, the individual typically eats very rapidly and soon feels uncomfortably full. The person often selects binge foods they would not ordinarily eat. Foods also may be selected for smooth texture to make vomiting easier, one reason why ice cream is a popular binge food.

Binge eating is commonly triggered by an unhappy mood, which may begin with an interpersonal conflict, self-criticism about weight or appearance, or intense hunger following a period of fasting. The binge initially may alleviate some unhappy feelings, but physical discomfort, shame, and fear of gaining weight quickly return (Berg, Crosby, Cao, Peterson, Engel, Mitchell, and Wonderlich, 2013).

A key diagnostic feature is a sense of lack of control during a binge. Some individuals experience a binge as a "feeding frenzy," where they lose all control, eating compulsively and rapidly. Others describe a dissociative experience, as if they were watching themselves gorge. But the lack of control is not absolute. For example, people with bulimia can stop a binge if they are interrupted unexpectedly. In fact, as the disorder progresses, some people feel more in control during a binge but unable to stop the broader cycle of binge eating and compensatory behavior.

## Inappropriate Compensatory Behavior

Most people with bulimia nervosa engage in **purging,** designed to eliminate consumed food from the body. The most common form of purging is self-induced vomiting (APA, 2013). Other inappropriate compensatory behaviors include the misuse of laxatives, diuretics (which increase the frequency of urination), and, most rarely, enemas. Ironically, purging has only limited effectiveness in reducing caloric intake. Vomiting prevents the absorption of only about half the calories consumed during a binge, and laxatives, diuretics, and enemas have few lasting effects on calories or weight (Kaye et al., 1993).

Other inappropriate compensatory behaviors include extreme exercise or rigid fasting. The extent to which these actions actually compensate for binge eating also is questionable, given what we know about the body's biological regulation of weight (Brownell & Fairburn, 1995). *DSM-5* indicates that binge eating and compensatory behavior must occur once a week, on average, for at least three months.

## Excessive Emphasis on Weight and Shape

Self-evaluation is unduly influenced by body shape and weight in bulimia nervosa, a symptom shared with anorexia nervosa (see Table 10.1). Self-esteem, and daily routines, can center

---

**TABLE 10.1**
### Anorexia Nervosa and Bulimia Nervosa: Key Differences and Similarities

| Issue | Anorexia Nervosa | Bulimia Nervosa |
|---|---|---|
| | **Differences** | |
| Eating/weight | Extreme diet; below minimally normal weight | Binge eating/compensatory behavior; normal weight |
| View of disorder | Denial of anorexia; proud of "diet" | Aware of problem; secretive/ashamed of bulimia |
| Feelings of control | Comforted by rigid self-control | Distressed by lack of control |
| | **Similarities** | |
| Self-evaluation | Unduly influenced by body weight/shape | Unduly influenced by body weight/shape |
| Comorbidity of AN/BN | Some cases of AN also binge and purge | Many cases of BN have history of AN |
| SES, age, gender | Prevalent among high SES, young, female | Prevalent among high SES, young, female |

around weight and diet. Some people are exhilarated by positive comments or interest in their appearance, but self-esteem plummets if a negative comment is made or if someone else draws more attention. Others constantly criticize their appearance, and the struggle with bulimia only adds to self-denigration. In all cases, the individual's sense of self is linked too closely to appearance instead of personality, relationships, or achievements.

## Comorbid Psychological Disorders

Depression is common among individuals with bulimia nervosa. Some individuals become depressed prior to developing the eating disorder, and the bulimia may be a reaction to the depression. In many instances, however, depression begins at the same time as or follows the onset of bulimia nervosa (Braun, Sunday, & Halmi, 1994). In such circumstances, the depression is likely to be a reaction to the bulimia. In fact, depression often lifts following successful treatment (Mitchell et al., 1990). Whether depression is an effect or cause of bulimia, eating disturbances are more severe and social impairment is greater when the two problems are comorbid (Stice & Fairburn, 2003).

Other disorders that may co-occur with bulimia nervosa include anxiety disorders, personality disorders (particularly borderline personality disorder), and substance abuse, particularly excessive use of alcohol and/or stimulants. Although each of these psychological difficulties presents special challenges in treating bulimia, the comorbidity with depression is most common and most significant (Halmi, 2010).

## Medical Complications

A number of medical complications can result from bulimia nervosa. Repeated vomiting can erode dental enamel, particularly on the front teeth. In severe cases, teeth can become chipped and ragged looking. Another possible medical complication is the enlargement of the salivary glands, a consequence that has the ironic effect of making the sufferer's face appear puffy. As in anorexia nervosa, potentially serious medical complications can result from electrolyte imbalances. Finally, rupture of the esophagus or stomach has been reported in rare cases, sometimes leading to death (Mitchell & Crow, 2010).

## Diagnosis of Feeding and Eating Disorders

As noted, *DSM-5* lists six types of feeding and eating disorders. *Pica* is the eating of nonnutritive substances like paper or dirt, and is found commonly among children with intellectual disabilities. *Rumination disorder* involves repeated regurgitation of food, sometimes with rechewing, and often occurs in infants, sometimes in the context of neglect and/or intellectual disabilities. *Avoidant/restrictive food intake disorder* also occurs mostly in infants and is characterized by an apparent lack of interest in food. All of these problems appear to be relatively rare and not well understood.

**Binge-eating disorder,** episodes of binge eating without compensatory behavior, is a new diagnosis in *DSM-5*. Binge eating is associated with a number of psychological and physical difficulties, including **obesity,** often defined as a BMI greater than 30 (Marcus & Wildes, 2009). The new diagnosis is controversial in part because of its link with obesity (see Thinking Critically about DSM-5).

Anorexia nervosa is defined by the three symptoms described earlier (see DSM-5 criteria for Anorexia Nervosa on p. xx). *DSM-5* also includes two subtypes of anorexia nervosa. The *restricting type*

## THINKING CRITICALLY about DSM-5

### Is Binge Eating a Mental Disorder? Is Obesity?

DSM-5 includes the new diagnosis, *binge-eating disorder*. The disorder is defined by binge eating just like in bulimia (and, like bulimia, occurring once a week on average for 3 months), except without compensatory behavior. In addition, the binges must involve three of five symptoms: rapid eating, feeling uncomfortably full afterward, binge eating when not hungry, feeling embarrassed while eating, or feeling disgusted afterward. Yes. People with bulimia often report these subjective symptoms too, but unlike binge eating, they do not have to be present to make the diagnosis.

The inclusion of binge-eating disorder in *DSM-5* has been criticized by some. Allen Frances, the psychiatrist who chaired the previous DSM revision and vocal *DSM-5* critic wrote in his blog: "Excessive eating 12 times in three months is no longer just a manifestation of gluttony and the easy availability of really great tasting food. *DSM 5* has instead turned it into a psychiatric illness . . ." However, most experts seem to have embraced the new diagnosis, along with *DSM-5*.

In contrast to binge-eating disorder, *DSM-5* decided that obesity is *not* a mental disorder. Why? Obesity clearly is harmful. Obesity is a risk factor for heart disease, diabetes, kidney disease, sleep apneas, several kinds of cancer, and early mortality. Obesity accounts for over 9% of health expenses and is expected to consume 16% by 2030. Obesity also is linked with an increased risk for mood disorders, anxiety disorders, eating

*Continued*

disorders, and personality disorders, although it is not clear what is cause and what is effect (Marcus & Wildes, 2009).

But calling obesity a mental disorder is controversial. Suddenly, 32.2% of adults and 17.1% of children in the United States would have a mental disorder (Ogden, Carroll, Curtin, McDowell, Tabak, & Flegal, 2006). (These people would then become eligible for medical insurance reimbursement. Hmmm. Maybe DSM *would* like them to have "mental disorder.") Others question our society's castigation of obese people. Why further stigmatize overweight people by saying they have a mental disorder?

We think these are good points, but let's circle back to binge-eating disorder. *DSM-5* notes that binge-eating disorder "may also be associated with an increased risk for weight gain" (p. 352). Well, yes. Up to half of people seeking weight loss treatment report binge eating, and a recent study found that "clinically meaningful" (twice a week or more) binge eating occurred among 78.2 of 45,477 obese (BMI> 30) veterans (Higgins et al., in press). This leads us to wonder: Do the other 21.8% engage in some other problematic eating behavior? Will this become a mental disorder in future

versions of the DSM? In fact, *DSM-5* includes "night eating syndrome" in its list of "Other specified feeding or eating disorders."

The *DSM-5* tries to distinguish binge-eating disorder from obesity in other ways. The manual says that people with binge-eating disorder are more focused on weight and have more psychological problems than obese individuals. But weight concerns and emotional struggles are common among most overweight people too. *DSM-5* also says that binge eating responds to treatment, while obesity is hard to change. True, but should the manual drop anorexia as a mental disorder because it is hard to treat?

All of this leads us to wonder: Is binge-eating disorder a way of letting obesity in through DSM-5's backdoor?

Postscript: The very day that we wrote this, the American Medical Association officially recognized obesity as a disease. Among the issues involved in this decision were whether obesity is a matter of self control, whether the disease label would stigmatize—or destigmatize—obesity, labeling large numbers of people as sick, and, ahem, eligible for insurance reimbursement (*New York Times*, June 18, 2013).

includes people who have not engaged in binge eating or purging in the last three months. In contrast, the *binge eating/purging type* is defined by regular binge eating and purging. The *DSM-5* kept this distinction, even though the validity of the subtypes is questionable: They do not differ in terms of comorbidity, recovery, relapse, or mortality (Wonderlich et al., 2007). Moreover, an eight-year longitudinal study found that 62 percent of the former restrictors met diagnostic criteria for binge eating/purging, and only 12 percent of the restrictors had never regularly engaged in binge eating or purging (Eddy et al., 2002).

Bulimia nervosa is defined by the four symptoms described earlier (see "DSM-5: Bulimia Nervosa""). Previous subtypes of bulimia based on the presence or absence of purging were not

## criteria for
## Anorexia Nervosa

### DSM-5

A. Restriction of energy intake relative to requirements, leading to a significantly low body weight in the context of age, sex, developmental trajectory, and physical health. *Significantly low weight* is defined as a weight that is less than minimally normal or, for children and adolescents, less than that minimally expected.

B. Intense fear of gaining weight or of becoming fat, or persistent behavior that interferes with weight gain, even though at a significantly low weight.

C. Disturbance in the way in which one's body weight or shape is experienced, undue influence of body weight or shape on self-evaluation, or persistent lack of

recognition of the seriousness of the current low body weight.

**(F50.01) Restricting type:** During the last 3 months, the individual has not engaged in recurrent episodes of binge eating or purging behavior (i.e., self-induced vomiting or the misuse of laxatives, diuretics, or enemas). This subtype describes presentations in which weight loss is accomplished primarily through dieting, fasting, and/or excessive exercise.

**(F50.02) Binge-eating/purging type:** During the last 3 months, the individual has engaged in recurrent episodes of binge eating or purging (i.e., self-induced vomiting or the misuse of laxatives, diuretics, or enem as).

**A.** Recurrent episodes of binge eating. An episode of binge eating is characterized by both of the following:

1. Eating, in a discrete period of time (e.g., within any 2-hour period), an amount of food that is definitely larger than what most individuals would eat in a similar period of time under similar circumstances.

2. A sense of lack of control over eating during the episode (e.g., a feeling that one cannot stop eating or control what or how much one is eating).

**B.** Recurrent inappropriate compensatory behaviors in order to prevent weight gain, such as self-induced vomiting; misuse of laxatives, diuretics, or other medications; fasting; or excessive exercise.

**C.** The binge eating and inappropriate compensatory behaviors both occur, on average, at least once a week for 3 months.

**D.** Self-evaluation is unduly influenced by body shape and weight.

**E.** The disturbance does not occur exclusively during episodes of anorexia nervosa.

supported by research (Wilfley et al., 2008), so *DSM-5* dropped this categorization.

## Frequency of Anorexia and Bulimia

Estimates of the frequency of anorexia and bulimia vary, but both disorders appear to have increased since the 1960s and 1970s. Figure 10.2 illustrates the surge in new cases of anorexia nervosa based on a compilation of evidence from Northern Europe (Hoek & van Hoeken, 2003). The annual *incidence,* the number of new cases each year, of anorexia nervosa rose from 1 case per million people in 1930–1940 to 54 cases per million people in 1995–1996. Figure 10.2 also shows that anorexia nervosa is rare in the general population with the annual incidence stabilizing in recent decades. Anorexia is far more common among certain groups, however, particularly young women, where the incidence still may be increasing (Keel, 2010). *DSM-5* indicates that 12 month prevalence of anorexia nervosa is 0.4 among females, similar to a 0.9 estimate based on a recent U.S. national survey (Hudson et al., 2007). Anorexia nervosa also occurs among males, but the disorder is about 10 times more common among women than men. Establishing the exact prevalence in males is difficult, because only a few cases are identified even in large national surveys (Hudson et al., 2007).

### MyPsychLab VIDEO CASE

#### Bulimia Nervosa

JESSICA

*"It started out with a diet for me . . ."*

👁 **Watch** the **Video** *Stacy: Binge Eating Disorder* on **MyPsychLab**

As you watch the video, listen for Jessica's struggles with appearance and weight and how they were magnified—sometimes very directly—by her efforts to pursue a career in the performing arts.

Recent decades have also witnessed a torrent of new cases of bulimia nervosa. Changes in the frequency of bulimia nervosa are difficult to document, however, because the diagnostic term was introduced only in 1979. Instead, investigators have examined cohort effects in prevalence rates. A **cohort** is a group that shares some features in common, for example, year of birth; thus, **cohort effects** are differences that distinguish one cohort from another.

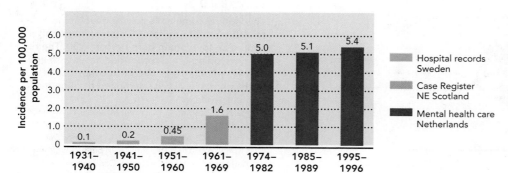

**FIGURE 10.2**

**Annual Incidence of Anorexia Nervosa in Northern Europe from 1931 to 1996**
Anorexia nervosa increased dramatically in the 1960s and 1970s, as the ideal media image of women grew thinner. Considerably higher rates are found among population subgroups, particularly young women.
*Source:* Hoek, W.H. 2003. The Distribution of Eating Disorders. In Eating Disorders and Obesity: A Comprehensive Handbook. Guilford Press.

Actress Jessica Biel was *Esquire* magazine's "sexiest woman alive." She is athletic, shapely, and fit, but not abnormally thin.

Figure 10.3 portrays birth cohort effects in lifetime prevalence rates of bulimia nervosa among a large sample of American women who were born either before 1950, between 1950 and 1959, or in 1960 or after. The figure clearly indicates substantial cohort effects. The lifetime prevalence of bulimia nervosa was far greater among the women born after 1960 than it was for those born before 1950. The risk for women born between 1950 and 1959 was intermediate between the two (Kendler et al., 1991). Figure 10.3 also shows that the risk of developing bulimia declines with increasing age, at least among older cohorts. A recent study of a national U.S. sample also found this declining risk with age and replicated the cohort effects (Hudson et al., 2007). Thus, the surge in bulimia nervosa—some say an epidemic—is due to dramatic increases among women born in more recent years. Not coincidentally, cultural standards of beauty changed for this generation of women.

Bulimia nervosa has a lifetime prevalence of 1.5 percent among U.S. women according to both *DSM-5* and national surveys (Hudson et al., 2007). Like anorexia, bulimia is about 10 times more common in women than men. Binge-eating disorder and occasional binge eating are even more common, with a respective lifetime prevalence of 3.5 percent and 4.9 percent among women and 2.0 percent and 4.0 percent among men (Hudson et al., 2007). Some evidence suggests that bulimia may be decreasing, but evidence is variable, with declines perhaps linked to changing cultural standards of beauty (Keel, 2010). Finally, we should note again the overlap between anorexia nervosa and bulimia nervosa. About 50 percent of all people with anorexia nervosa engage in episodes of binge eating and purging (Garfinkel et al., 1995), and many cases of bulimia nervosa have a history of anorexia nervosa (Wonderlich et al., 2007).

## Standards of Beauty

Many scientists believe that this huge difference in the prevalence of eating disorders between men and women is explained by gender roles (Field & Kitos, 2010). Popular attitudes about women in the United States tell us that "looks are everything," and thinness is essential to good looks. In contrast, young men are valued as much for their achievements as for their appearance, and the ideal body type for men is considerably larger and more muscular than for women (see Critical Thinking Matters). In fact, women are much more likely than men to have a negative body image, and that disparity has been growing over time (Feingold & Mazzella, 1998).

The surge in eating disorders among women appears to be partially explained by changing standards of beauty. *Playboy* centerfolds and Miss America Beauty Pageant contestants—cultural icons but dubious role models for young women—provide the statistics. Between 1959 and 1988, their ratio of weight to height declined dramatically. In fact, 69 percent of *Playboy* centerfolds and 60 percent of Miss America contestants weigh at least 15 percent below expected weight for their height (Garner et al., 1980; Wiseman et al., 1992). Marilyn Monroe, the movie idol of the 1950s, is chunky according to today's "culture of thinness."

Standards of beauty are relative, not absolute. Today, eating disorders are much more common in North America, Western

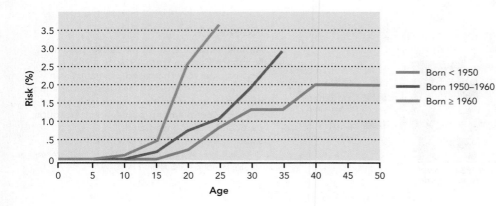

### FIGURE 10.3

The lifetime cumulative risk for developing bulimia nervosa is far greater for women born after 1960 than for women born before 1950. The risk for developing the disorder decreases with age, at least among the earlier birth cohort. Later birth cohorts have not yet moved through the entire age of risk.
*Source:* K. S. Kendler, C. MacLean, M. Neale, R. Kessler, A. Heath, and L. Eaves. The Genetic Epidemiology of Bulimia Nervosa. American Journal of Psychiatry. Dec 1991; 148: 1627–1637. Reprinted with permission from the American Journal of Psychiatry (Copyright © 1991). American Psychiatric Association. All Rights Reserved.

# CRITICAL THINKING matters

## The Pressure to Be Thin

Critical thinking matters in the classroom—and in everyday life. Consider how young women (and men) embrace standards of beauty based on images in the media, and, in turn, apply fashion model standards to themselves and others.

The images are everywhere. Super-thin models routinely grace the cover and inside of fashion magazines. The average fashion model is 5'11" and 117 pounds; the average woman in the United States is 5'4" and 140 pounds. Television and movie actresses are not only talented and beautiful, but also exceptionally thin. Advertisements in all kinds of media for all kinds of products use images of sexy, beautiful, and very thin women, images that often are altered not only to erase blemishes, but also to lengthen legs or otherwise distort body shape. Even girls' dolls are unrealistically thin and beautiful. The ubiquitous Barbie doll has a shape that translates into a 39–18–33 figure in human equivalents. (In 1994, Dolly Parton claimed that she measured 40–20–36.) And real-life GI Joe would have a 55" chest and a 27" bicep. (At his bodybuilding peak, Arnold Schwarzenegger had a 57" chest and 22" biceps.)

In 1994, Dolly Parton claimed that she measured 40-20-36.

The pressure to be thin greatly affects women who make their careers as actresses, models, and singers. The Brazilian model Ana Carolina Reston died of complications due to anorexia in 2006. (In the same year, the Spanish government banned too-thin models from a popular fashion show.) The dubious "who's who" of women in the popular media who have *publicly admitted* to having an eating disorder (often in an attempt to encourage healthier body images among the girls and women who admire them) includes actresses Mary-Kate Olsen, Demi Lovato, and Kate Winslet; fashion model Carre Otis; singers Lady Gaga, Ashlee Simpson, Paula Abdul, and Victoria Beckham (Posh Spice of the Spice Girls); and Oprah Winfrey.

Psychological studies repeatedly show that exposure to images of super-thin women increases body image dissatisfaction among girls and young women (Halliwell & Dittmar, 2004). Yet, young women face contradictory messages when told, "Beauty is only skin deep." For one, both extensive psychological research and everyday experience repeatedly tell us that attractiveness *does* matter, not only to romantic attraction (although men prefer a more curvaceous figure than women *think* they like), but also appearance matters in the evaluations of same-gender peers, teachers, employers, and on and on. And even as some public health advocates battle the culture of thinness, others tell young people—rightly—to be careful about what you eat, to not eat too much, and to try to lose weight. Obesity is a much more common public health problem than eating disorders.

So where does critical thinking come in? Critical thinking is about thinking independently. Appearance does matter, but few of us, female or male, can hope to look like models or movie stars. After all, these professionals literally are one in a million (or a billion). The stars of popular media devote much of their life to their appearance, and they *still* need the help of makeup, camera angles, creative fashions, and electronic "corrections." Health matters, too, and exercise is a great way to promote health, maintain an attractive physical appearance, and remember that your body is good for something other than being looked at. And in the end, most people are more impressed by who you are than what you look like. This is a useful reminder when we start to think critically—instead of using critical thinking—in evaluating our own weight and shape.

Europe, and industrialized Asian countries; bulimia may be completely culture bound (Keel & Klump, 2003). In other cultures, women who are more rounded are considered to be more beautiful. In Third World countries, where food is scarce, being larger is a symbol of beauty and success. In industrialized nations, the opposite is true. As the saying goes, "You can never be too rich or too thin."

## Age of Onset

Both anorexia and bulimia nervosa typically begin in adolescence or early adulthood (Hudson et al., 2007). The adolescent onset has provoked much past speculation about their cause, including hormonal changes (Garfinkel & Garner, 1982), autonomy struggles (Minuchin, Rosman, & Baker, 1978), and various sexual problems (Coovert, Kinder, & Thompson, 1989). A more simple explanation is the natural and normal changes in adolescent body shape and weight. Weight gain is normal during adolescence, but the addition of a few pounds can trouble a young woman focused on the numbers on her scale. Breast and hip development not only change body shape, but they also affect self-image, social interaction, and the fit of familiar clothes. Early pubertal timing is a risk factor for anorexia, supporting the importance of self-evaluation and social comparison as girls' shape develops normally in early adolescence (Jacobi & Fittig, 2010).

Weight and dieting become less of a concern, and disordered eating declines, as adolescent girls become women. Changes are particularly sharp following marriage and parenthood (Keel et al., 2007). Men, however, become *more* concerned with weight as they age. As men's metabolism slows with increasing age, losing weight becomes more of a worry than gaining weight.

## Causes of Anorexia and Bulimia

The culture of thinness clearly contributes to the high rate of eating disorders today. However, other social, psychological, and biological risk factors must play a role, because not every young woman suffers from these problems.

### Social Factors

Standards of beauty and the premium placed on young women's appearance contribute to causing eating disorders. This conclusion is supported by the following epidemiological evidence and other research:

- Eating disorders are far more common among young women than young men (Hoek & van Hoeken, 2003). As Striegel-Moore and Bulik (2007) recently summarized, "The single best predictor of risk for developing an eating disorder is being female..." (p. 182).
- The prevalence of eating disorders has risen, as the image of the ideal woman has increasingly emphasized extreme thinness (Hoek & van Hoeken, 2003; Wiseman et al., 1992).

Marilyn Monroe, the 1950s movie idol, was the iconic image of the curvy figure that defined beauty in that era.

- Eating disorders are even more common among young women working in fields that emphasize weight and appearance, such as models, ballet dancers, and gymnasts (Bryne, 2002).
- Young women are particularly likely to develop eating disorders during adolescence and young adult life, an age during which our culture places a particular emphasis on appearance, beauty, and thinness (Hoek, 2002).
- Eating disturbances are more common among young women who report greater exposure to popular media, endorse more gender-role stereotypes, or internalize societal standards about appearance (Grabe, Ward, & Hyde, 2008).
- Eating disorders are more common among white women, who are more likely to equate thinness with beauty, versus African American women. Eating disorders also may be increasing among well-to-do African Americans, who increasingly hold the thinness ideal (Field & Kitos, 2010; Wildes, Emery, and Simons, 2001).
- Eating disorders are far more prevalent in industrialized societies, where thinness is the ideal, than in nonindustrialized societies, where a more rounded body type is preferred (Keel & Klump, 2003).
- The prevalence of eating disorders is higher among Arab and Asian women living or studying in Western countries than among women living in their native country (Hoek, 2002).

These facts make it clear that adolescent girls and young women are at risk for developing eating disorders, in part because they attempt to shape themselves, quite literally, to fit the image of the ideally proportioned, thin woman. We should note, however, that the culture of thinness plays a stronger role in the development of bulimia than anorexia. Cases of anorexia nervosa are found in the historical literature, occur in non-Western cultures, and appear to have increased less than cases of bulimia nervosa in response to cultural ideals of thinness (Keel & Klump, 2003).

Of course, not every woman in the United States develops an eating disorder, so other factors must interact with culture to produce eating disorders (Striegel-Moore & Bulik, 2007). One basic influence is the individual's *internalization* of the ideal of thinness (Cafri et al., 2005). Same-gender peers can influence internalization (Field & Kitos, 2010; Keel, Forney, Brown, Heatherton, 2013), and so can popular media. In one study, ninth- and tenth-grade high school girls randomly received a free subscription to *Seventeen* magazine. One year later, those who received the magazine reported increased negative affect, but only if their body image was negative and they felt pressure to be thin when the study began (Stice, Spangler, & Agras, 2001). These girls apparently were more vulnerable to the media's "thin" message.

**TROUBLED FAMILY RELATIONSHIPS** Troubled family relationships may also increase vulnerability to the culture of thinness (Jacobi et al., 2004). Young people with bulimia nervosa report

Twiggy became a popular fashion model in the 1960s. Beginning her career at the age of 16, Twiggy's stick figure helped to usher in the "culture of thinness."

considerable conflict and rejection in their families, difficulties that also may contribute to their depression. In contrast, young people with anorexia generally perceive their families as cohesive and nonconflictual (Fornari et al., 1999; Vandereycken, 1995).

Although the families of young people with anorexia nervosa appear to be well functioning, some theorists see them as being too close—as *enmeshed families,* families whose members are overly involved in one another's lives. According to the enmeshment hypothesis, young people with anorexia nervosa are obsessed with controlling their eating, because eating is the *only* thing they can control in their intrusive families (Minuchin, Rosman, Baker, , 1978). However, intrusive parental concern is probably an effect, not a cause, of anorexia. Parents of an anorexic adolescent may well become "enmeshed" as a worried reaction to their daughter's emaciation.

Child sexual abuse also is a risk factor for eating disorders (Jacobi & Fittig, 2010). However, sexual abuse may not pose a specific risk. Women with eating disorders report experiencing child sexual abuse more often than normal controls but not more often than women suffering from other psychological problems (Palmer, 1995; Welch & Fairburn, 1996). Sexual abuse increases the risk for a variety of psychological problems, including, but not limited to, eating disorders.

Finally, we should note that many parents struggle with diet and thinness themselves. They are models of preoccupation for their children. Other parents directly encourage their children to be extra thin as a part of the general push to compete with their peers (Field & Kitos, 2010; Vandereycken, 2002).

## Psychological Factors

Researchers have hypothesized about many psychological factors contributing to eating disorders. Here we highlight four of the most important: control issues, depression/dysphoria, body image dissatisfaction, and reactions to dietary restraint.

**A STRUGGLE FOR PERFECTION AND CONTROL** One of the first and most prolific clinical observers of eating disorders was Hilde Bruch (1904–1984), a physician who fled her native Germany in 1933 and studied psychiatry in the United States. Bruch viewed a struggle for control as the central psychological issue in the development of eating disorders (Bruch, 1982). Bruch observed that girls with eating disorders seem overly conforming and eager to please. She suggested that they give up too much of the normal adolescent struggle for autonomy. Bruch viewed obsessive efforts to control eating and weight as a way that these overly compliant "good girls" control themselves further. At the same time, Bruch also saw their dieting as an attempt to wrest at least a little control from their parents—control over what they eat. In this *struggle for control,* young people with anorexia nervosa (at least the restricting subtype) "succeed" and take pride in their extreme self-control.

*Perfectionism* is another part of the endless pursuit of control. Perfectionists set unrealistically high standards, are self-critical, and demand a nearly flawless performance from themselves. Young women with eating disorders endorse perfectionist goals both about eating and weight and about general expectations for themselves (Bastiani et al., 1995; Jacobi & Fittig, 2010).

Young people with eating disorders may also try to control their own emotions excessively (Bruch, 1982). They may lack *interoceptive awareness*—recognition of internal cues, including hunger and various emotional states. One large study found that lack of interoceptive awareness predicted the development of eating disorders two years in the future (Leon et al., 1993, 1995). People with eating disorders appear to be more tuned in to how they look than how they feel—sad, angry, happy, or hungry (Viken et al., 2002).

**DEPRESSION, LOW SELF-ESTEEM, AND DYSPHORIA** Depression is often comorbid with eating disorders, particularly bulimia nervosa (Halmi, 2010). Antidepressant medications reduce some symptoms of bulimia nervosa, suggesting that, in some cases, bulimia is a reaction to depression (Mitchell, Raymond, & Specker, 1993). In other cases, depression may instead be a reaction to an eating disorder (Polivy & Herman, 2002). Depression improves markedly following successful group psychotherapy for bulimia (Mitchell et al., 1990). And a study of anorexia nervosa found considerable depression at the time of the original diagnosis but not at a six-year follow-up (Rastam, Gillberg, & Gillberg, 1995).

Depressive symptoms, and not necessarily clinical depression, also may play a role in eating disorders. Low self-esteem is a particular concern (Fairburn et al., 1997). In particular, women with eating disorders may be preoccupied with their *social self,* how they present themselves in public and how other people perceive and evaluate them (Striegel-Moore, Silberstein, & Rodin, 1993). Women with bulimia nervosa or a negative body image report more public self-consciousness, social anxiety, and perceived fraudulence (Striegel-Moore et al., 1993). They also show increases in self-criticism and deterioration in mood following negative social interactions (Vögele & Gibson, 2010). In short, people with eating disorders often depend on others for self-esteem.

Depressive symptoms also can play a role in maintaining problematic eating behaviors. Dysphoria or negative mood states commonly trigger episodes of binge eating (Vögele & Gibson, 2010). The dysphoria may be brought on by social criticism or conflict, dissatisfaction with eating and diet, or an ongoing depressive episode. In summary, clinical depression can either be a cause or a reaction to eating disorders, while depressed moods, low self-esteem, and dysphoria may contribute to the onset or maintenance of symptoms.

**NEGATIVE BODY IMAGE** A negative **body image**, a highly critical evaluation of one's weight and shape, is widely thought to contribute to the development of eating disorders (Polivy & Herman, 2002). One way to assess a negative body image is to compare people's ratings of their current and ideal size by asking them to pick from the schematics in Figure 10.4. Several longitudinal studies have found negative evaluations of weight, shape, and appearance to predict the subsequent development of disordered eating (Jacobi & Fittig, 2010). A negative body image may be a particular problem when combined with other risk factors, including perfectionism and low self-esteem (Field & Kitos, 2010).

**DIETARY RESTRAINT** Some symptoms of eating disorders may be effects of *dietary restraint,* that is, direct consequences of overly restrictive eating (Heatherton & Polivy, 1992). Ironically, many of the "out-of-control" symptoms of eating disorders are caused by inappropriate efforts to "control" eating. These symptoms include binge eating, preoccupation with food, and perhaps out-of-control feelings of hunger.

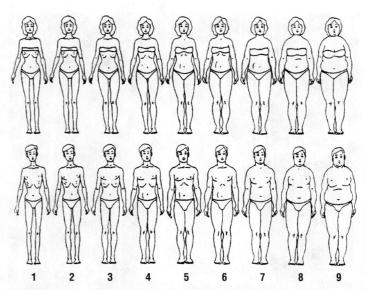

**FIGURE 10.4**

These figures are often used as one way to assess body image. People pick figures representing their current and ideal shape. The discrepancy between the ratings is a measure of negative body image.

*Source:* From p. 79 in "Assessing Body Image Disturbance: Measures, Methodology, and Implementation" by J. Kevin Thompson, in Body Image, Eating Disorders and Obesity, Ed. by J. K. Thompson. American Psychological Association, Washington, DC, Copyright © 1996.

Consistent with the dietary restraint hypothesis, adolescent girls who try to lose weight by fasting for 24 hours or more engage in more binge eating and develop bulimia more often five years later (Stice et al., 2008). Similarly, *weight suppression*— defined as highest adult weight minus current weight–predicts the maintenance and onset of bulimia 10 years later (Keel & Heatherton, 2010). An overly restrictive diet increases hunger, frustration, and lack of attention to internal cues, all of which make binge eating more likely. And "quick fix" diets rarely work, leaving dieters with a sense of failure, disappointment, and self-criticism, negative emotions that lower self-esteem and lead to more binge eating.

Dietary restraint also may directly cause some of the symptoms of anorexia nervosa. The military studies of semi-starvation conducted during World War II found that, during refeeding, many men felt intense, uncontrollable hunger, even after eating a considerable amount of food (Keys et al., 1950). Perhaps a similar reaction explains some of the intense fear of losing control and gaining weight found in anorexia nervosa.

While extreme restriction and quick-fix diets are unhealthy, sensible dieting is not. Normal weight women randomly assigned to a low-calorie diet lose weight and decrease binge eating 18 weeks later in comparison to women assigned to no diet (Presnell & Stice, 2003). As with so many things, finding a balanced middle ground is the key.

Beyonce is a gorgeous example of a bigger but ideal body type.

## Biological Factors

Our bodies, in fact, seek a middle ground. Physiologically, weight is maintained around **weight set points,** fixed weights or small ranges of weight. Weight regulation around set points results from the interplay between behavior (e.g., exercise, eating), peripheral physiological activity (e.g., digestion, metabolism), and central physiological activity (e.g., neurotransmitter release; Blundell, 1995). The process is very much like the way a thermostat regulates heating and cooling to maintain air temperature at a given setting. Thus, if weight declines, hunger increases and food consumption goes up (Keesey, 1995). There is a slowing of the *metabolic rate,* the rate at which the body expends energy, and movement toward *hyperlipogenesis,* the storage of abnormally large amounts of fat in fat cells throughout the body (Brownell & Fairburn, 1995). All these reactions have obvious survival value and are likely products of evolution. The body does not distinguish between intentional attempts to lose weight and potential starvation.

Genetic factors also contribute to eating disorders. An early twin study of bulimia nervosa found a concordance rate of 23 percent for MZ twins and 9 percent for DZ twins (Kendler et al., 1991). Higher MZ than DZ concordance rates for anorexia nervosa (Bulik et al., 2006) and for dysfunctional eating attitudes have also been reported (Klump, McGue, & Iacono, 2000). Genetic factors also contributed substantially to various symptoms of disordered eating in the only adoption study completed to date (Klump et al., 2009).

Genetic contributions to eating disorders could be explained by several different mechanisms. Eating disorders are unlikely to be directly inherited. Rather, genes may influence personality characteristics such as anxiety that, in turn, increase the risk for an eating disorder (Klump & Culbert, 2007). Or a certain body type may be inherited. Genetics contribute substantially to BMI (Wade, 2010). Inheriting a thin body type may increase the risk for anorexia—when combined with the culture of thinness, internalization of the standard, and perfectionism. Similarly, a more rounded body type may increase the risk for bulimia—when combined with social pressures to maintain a weight below one's natural set point.

Consistent with these hypotheses, recent evidence shows that genes influence eating pathology *after* puberty but not before (Culbert et al., 2009). Genetic influences also are stronger among women who engage in dietary restraint (Racine et al., 2011). Genes clearly affect weight and body type, but we cannot mindlessly conclude that eating disorders are genetic without carefully considering genetic mechanisms and gene-environment interactions.

In extremely rare cases, eating disorders have been linked with a specific biological abnormality, such as a hormonal disturbance or a lesion in the *hypothalamus,* the area of the brain that regulates routine biological functions, including appetite. But in most cases, the problem appears to be the result of an interaction of biological, psychological, and social risk factors.

## Integration and Alternative Pathways

Social and cultural values that emphasize thinness, beauty, and appearance over agency are the starting point in understanding eating disorders, particularly among young women. Risk factors that combine with cultural attitudes to produce eating disorders include direct familial and social pressures to be thin, a negative body image, dietary restraint, and genetic influences on body weight and shape (Jacobi et al., 2004; Stice, 2001, 2002). Less obvious risk factors include preoccupation with external evaluation, lack of interoceptive awareness, and excessive conformity and self-control.

The etiology of eating disorders underscores the importance of *equifinality*—there are many pathways to developing an eating disorder (Halmi, 1997). Some women are naturally thin, but their perfectionism drives them to become even thinner. Other women may have a more rounded body type determined by genetics, and they struggle, and repeatedly fail, to mold their body into something it was never meant to be. For some people, an eating disorder is an expression of depression. Others may develop an eating disorder because they focus on outward appearances instead of internal values. Finding the middle ground of a healthy weight can be very difficult, particularly when the culture of thinness sets unrealistic standards of beauty, especially for young women.

## Treatment of Anorexia

The treatments for anorexia nervosa and bulimia nervosa differ in approach and effectiveness; therefore, we consider them separately. The treatment of anorexia nervosa usually focuses on two goals. The first is to help the patient gain at least a minimal amount of weight. If weight loss is severe, the patient may be treated in an inpatient setting. Hospitalized patients may receive forced or intravenous feeding, or participate in strict behavior therapy programs that make rewards contingent on weight gain. Hospitalization also may be needed to prevent suicide, to address severe depression or medical complications, or to remove the patient temporarily from a dysfunctional social circumstance (Garner & Needleman, 1996).

The second goal in treating anorexia nervosa is to address the broader eating difficulties. Many different treatments have been tried, but accumulating evidence indicates that family therapy is more effective than individual treatment, especially for children and adolescents (Lock et al., 2010; Le Grange & Hoste, 2010). The most carefully studied family therapy is the *Maudsley method* (named after Maudsley Hospital in London where the treatment was developed). In the Maudsley method, parents take complete control over the anorexic child's eating, planning meals, preparing food, and monitoring eating. Parents do not blame the adolescent for her problems, but emphasize the uncontrollable nature of anorexia and the importance of taking her "medicine"—food—in order to get better. Age-appropriate autonomy is returned to the teenager as eating and weight improve (Lock et al., 2010; Loeb et al., 2007). Growing evidence supports the effectiveness of the Maudsley method in treating anorexia and perhaps bulimia too (Le Grange & Hoste, 2010).

Many individual therapies also have been tried, including (1) Bruch's (1982) modified psychodynamic therapy designed to increase interoceptive awareness and correct distorted perceptions of self; (2) *feminist therapies,* which encourage young women to pursue their own values rather than blindly adopting prescribed social roles (Fallon, Katzman, & Wooley, 1994); and (3) various cognitive behavioral approaches. Unfortunately, little evidence supports the effectiveness of any individual treatment (Wilson, 2010). Even worse, medication (antidepressants often are prescribed) and nutritional counseling not only offer little benefit, but patients also routinely drop out of these treatments (McElroy et al., 2010; Walsh et al., 2006; Wilson, Grilo, & Vitousek, 2007). Clearly, finding effective treatments for anorexia nervosa should be a research and public health priority.

### Course and Outcome of Anorexia Nervosa

Evidence on the course and outcome of anorexia nervosa further shows the limited effectiveness of contemporary treatments. At 10- to 20-year follow-up, nearly half of patients have a weight within the normal range, 20 percent remain significantly below their healthy body weight, and the remainder are intermediate in weight (Steinhausen, 2002). Perhaps 5 percent of patients starve themselves to death or die of related complications, including suicide.

Although important, weight gain is not the only measure of the course of anorexia nervosa. In fact, more than half the women with a history of anorexia nervosa continue to be preoccupied with diet, weight, and body shape, notwithstanding gains in weight. Moreover, people may also develop new problems with social life, depression, or bulimia, as a result of their perfectionism, reliance on external evaluation, or continued struggles with body image (Keel, 2010). Predictors of a better prognosis include an early age of onset, conflict-free parent–child relationships, early treatment, less weight loss, and the absence of binge eating and purging (Steinhausen, 2002). The following account, written by a young woman after her long and, finally, successful

Brazilian model Ana Carolina Reston died in 2006 as a result of complications due to anorexia nervosa. Bans on super-thin models have been considered in order to protect both the models and their fans.

struggle with anorexia nervosa, illustrates some of the continuing problems:

> I do not have a story that ends with a miraculous recovery, and I would be suspicious of anyone who claimed that they had completely gotten over an eating disorder. I continue to struggle with worries about food and my body. I exercise every day without fail. I am prone to stress fractures and will most likely encounter early osteoporosis due to the irreversible effects of starvation on my bones. I am lucky that I will be able to have children someday, though many long-term anorexics are never able to. Despite these lingering effects of the disorder, they pale in comparison to what I consider to be the most detrimental of all. When I look back on those six or so years, it sickens me to realize how much of life I missed. I allowed my obsession with my weight to take over my life (Zorn, 1998, p. 21).

## Treatment of Bulimia

Researchers have developed several approaches to treating bulimia nervosa. The most effective include cognitive behavior therapy, interpersonal psychotherapy, and antidepressant medication.

### Cognitive Behavior Therapy

The most thoroughly researched psychotherapy for bulimia nervosa is cognitive behavior therapy (Wilson, Grilo, & Vitousek, 2007). As developed by the British psychiatrist Christopher Fairburn, the cognitive behavioral approach views bulimia as stemming from several maladaptive tendencies, including an excessive emphasis on weight and shape; perfectionism; and dichotomous "black or white" thinking (Fairburn, 1996). Fairburn's cognitive behavioral treatment includes three stages. First, the therapist uses education and behavioral strategies to normalize eating patterns. The goal is to end the cycle where extreme dietary restraint leads to binge eating and, in turn, to purging. Second, the therapist addresses the client's broader, dysfunctional beliefs about self, appearance, and dieting. Techniques include a variation of Beck's cognitive therapy to address perfectionism or depression. Individual problems such as poor impulse control or troubled relationships also may be addressed at this stage. Third, the therapist attempts to consolidate gains and prepare the client for expected relapses in the future. Key goals at this final stage of treatment are to develop realistic expectations about eating, weight concerns, and binge eating, as well as clear strategies for coping with relapses in advance (Fairburn, 2002).

Overall, cognitive behavior therapy leads to a 70 percent to 80 percent reduction in binge eating and purging. Between one-third and one-half of all clients are able to cease the bulimic pattern completely, and the majority of individuals maintain these gains at six-month to one-year follow-up (Agras et al., 2000; Fairburn et al., 1993). Cognitive behavior therapy also may be effective in group (Mitchell et al., 1990) and self-help formats (Carter

& Fairburn, 1998), although individual therapy is more effective (Thompson-Brenner, Glass, & Westen, 2003).

### Interpersonal Psychotherapy

Interpersonal psychotherapy also can be an effective treatment for bulimia nervosa. This is surprising because interpersonal therapy does not address eating disorders directly but instead focuses on difficulties in close relationships. In fact, interpersonal therapy for bulimia initially was studied as a *placebo* treatment. Fairburn and colleagues (1991, 1993) wanted to evaluate whether cognitive behavior therapy had specific effects beyond the general benefits of psychotherapy. They chose interpersonal therapy as a credible placebo, because interpersonal problems often are associated with bulimia nervosa. But they hypothesized that cognitive behavior therapy would outperform the interpersonal approach.

When Fairburn and colleagues (1991) evaluated outcomes shortly after treatment, they found that cognitive behavior therapy was more effective than interpersonal therapy in changing dieting behavior, self-induced vomiting, and attitudes about weight and shape. Cognitive behavior therapy also was more effective than a third condition, behavior therapy alone, in terms of attitude change. However, the results of the two behavioral treatments were similar in other respects.

A very different picture emerged at 12-month follow-up. The behavior therapy group alone deteriorated over time, and a large number of patients dropped out. The cognitive behavior therapy group maintained fairly stable improvements. But the interpersonal therapy group *continued to improve*. At one-year follow-up, in fact, interpersonal therapy equaled cognitive behavior therapy and outdistanced the behavior therapy alone (Fairburn et al., 1993).

The continued improvement for interpersonal therapy was surprising and impressive, for at least two reasons. First, the interpersonal treatments explicitly excluded direct discussions of eating, diet, and related topics. Second, the investigators had lower expectations for interpersonal therapy, and the *allegiance effect* often influences treatment outcome (see Research Methods on p. xxx). A larger study replicated these results, although cognitive behavior therapy again produced more rapid change (Agras et al., 2000).

### Antidepressant Medications

All classes of antidepressant medications are somewhat effective in treating bulimia nervosa; however, medication alone is *not* the treatment of choice. Binge eating and compensatory behavior improve only among a minority of people treated with antidepressants, and relapse is common when medication is stopped (McElroy et al., 2010). Most importantly, research shows that cognitive behavior therapy is more effective (Hay & Claudino, 2010; Walsh et al., 1997; Wilson et al., 1999). One exception may be treating bulimia in a primary care setting, where most

## Psychotherapy Placebos

A placebo is a treatment that contains no active ingredients for the disorder being treated. A *placebo control group* receives only a placebo treatment. Scientists must include placebo control groups in treatment outcome research, because the mere expectation of change can produce benefits. New treatments work, in part, because the client and the therapist expect them to work.

Medication placebos are easily administered. Physicians give patients a pill that looks like the real medication but contains no active chemical ingredients. Psychotherapy placebos are much more challenging. How can we create a psychological treatment that contains no active ingredients but increases the client's expectations for change just as much as the real treatment?

One approach is to offer an established, alternative therapy, but one not designed to treat the disorder being studied. In their study of bulimia nervosa, Fairburn et al. (1993) thought interpersonal therapy was a good placebo. The investigators believed that interpersonal therapy contained no "active ingredients" for treating bulimia nervosa, but thought clients would view it as legitimate.

But getting clients to believe does not fully resolve the psychotherapy placebo problem. Researchers "believe" in their treatment too—otherwise they would not be studying it. The *allegiance effect* shows us that a *therapist's* beliefs also help to make treatment work. The allegiance effect tells us that cognitive behavior therapy should have been more successful in the Fairburn and colleagues (1993) study, for example, because the investigators were cognitive behavior therapists. In fact, we are particularly impressed by the results for interpersonal therapy, because it overcame the allegiance effect.

What research method controls for the experimenter's expectations? In drug research, scientists use the *double-blind study*, where neither the patient nor the therapist knows whether the patient is receiving an active treatment or a placebo. But even double-blind studies are not always easy to interpret. Medications are more effective when they produce more side effects (Greenberg et al., 1994). Side effects may increase the patient's expectations for change, because the drug seems powerful. Or side effects may allow clinicians to determine whether patients are receiving the real medication.

In any case, "real" and placebo psychotherapies are transparent to therapists, making it impossible to conduct double-blind studies of psychotherapy. Another way of addressing the allegiance effect in psychotherapy outcome research is to have investigators who hold *opposing allegiances* participate in the same study. Cognitive behavior therapy is offered by cognitive behavior therapists, interpersonal therapists deliver interpersonal therapy, and so on. This overcomes the allegiance effect but creates a new problem: Because the same therapists cannot deliver the different treatments, effects due to the individual therapists are uncontrolled.

Two conclusions seem clear. First, we must recognize that the expectations of clients, therapists, and experimenters can influence the findings of therapy outcome research. Second, we are particularly impressed when, contrary to expectations, a placebo psychotherapy is as effective as the "real thing."

---

patients fail to complete self-help cognitive behavior therapy programs but are more likely to follow through with antidepressant medication (Walsh et al., 2004). Overall, cognitive behavior therapy is the first-line treatment for bulimia, antidepressant medication may be a useful supplement, and interpersonal therapy is a slower acting alternative (Wilson, 2010).

### Course and Outcome of Bulimia Nervosa

Bulimia nervosa has a more favorable course than anorexia nervosa, especially with treatment (Thomson-Brenner et al., 2003). About five years following diagnosis, 70 percent of patients are free of symptoms, 20 percent show improvement but continue to struggle, and one in 10 are chronically ill (Keel, 2010). In contrast to anorexia, mortality has been thought to be rare for bulimia, but a recent study found elevated rates, particularly for suicide (Crow et al., 2009). Comorbid psychological disorders also tend to

improve with improvements in bulimia nervosa (Keel & Mitchell, 1997). Predictors of continued binge eating include a longer duration, greater emphasis on shape and weight, childhood obesity, poorer social adjustment, persistent compensatory behavior, and comorbid alcohol abuse (Fairburn et al., 2003; Keel, 2010).

## Prevention of Eating Disorders

Can eating disorders be prevented? This question is of huge importance, especially given the pervasive body dissatisfaction and disordered eating found among women today. Until recently, the results of prevention research were discouraging. Few, if any, benefits were produced by first-generation prevention efforts, which focused on education about the adverse effects of eating disorders, or by second-generation initiatives offering education about resisting the culture of thinness. However, a third

The fashion industry is making occasional efforts to portray beautiful women in a more realistic form, as illustrated by these plus size Swedish mannequins.

Karlie Kloss. Even up-and-coming fashion models continue to be extremely thin.

generation of more subtle prevention efforts is promising (Stice & Shaw, 2004).

More successful prevention efforts attack the thinness ideal *indirectly,* or promote healthy eating rather than stopping unhealthy habits (Stice et al., 2006). For example, "dissonance interventions" ask participants to complete tasks inconsistent with the thinness ideal, for example, discussing how to help younger girls from becoming obsessed with their appearance. The healthy approach emphasizes the benefits of eating well and exercising. Of 481 adolescent girls randomly assigned to one of these three-hour programs versus an assessment-only or placebo (writing about emotional issues) control group, the prevention conditions led to improvements in body dissatisfaction, internalization of the thin ideal, dieting, and binge eating/purging (Stice et al., 2006). Figure 10.5 shows the results for binge eating.

The results for the dissonance intervention have been replicated in a "real-world" setting (Stice et al., 2009), and an Internet-based program also shows promising results (Stice et al., 2012). Moreover, peer-led dissonance groups in sororities also show positive effects (Becker et al., 2008). Psychologists and society clearly have a long way to go to help women, and men, find the right balance between eating too little and too much, being obsessed with appearance, and being lax about health. Still, prevention research is an encouraging step in the right direction.

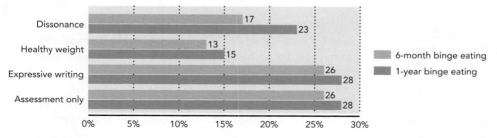

## FIGURE 10.5

Binge eating 6 and 12 months after either dissonance, healthy weight, or control interventions. At both times, the healthy weight program produced significantly less binge eating than control conditions. Differences for dissonance training approached significance at 6 months.

*Source:* Stice, Eric, Heather Shaw, Emily Burton and Emily Wade. Dissonance and healthy weight eating disorder prevention programs: A randomized efficacy trial. Journal of Consulting and Clinical Psychology. Apr 2006; 74(2): 263–275.

Eating disorders are very common, so it is likely that you or someone close to you may be struggling with eating issues. What can help?

One step is to get more information, but you need to be careful. Some self-help books and websites on eating disorders offer misleading information. And please beware of "pro-ana" and "pro-mia" websites that actually *encourage* eating disorders. One website that we recommend is the homepage of the National Eating Disorders Awareness Association, a nonprofit organization dedicated to increasing awareness and prevention of eating disorders. The Web page of the National Institute of Mental Health also contains helpful information about eating disorders. An excellent self-help book is *Overcoming Binge Eating*, by Christopher Fairburn, whose treatment research is discussed in this chapter. *Wasted* by Marya Hornbacher is a no-nonsense memoir about struggles with anorexia and bulimia. For parents, we recommend *Help Your Teenager Beat an Eating Disorder* by James Lock and Daniel Le Grange, whose promising family therapy techniques are also discussed in this chapter.

If you are seriously concerned about your own eating, weight, or body shape, you should talk with a professional. Colleges and universities often have special resources for eating disorders. Call your student health service for information. Another option is to talk with your family physician. You should have a physical exam to explore possible medical complications, and your physician also should know of mental health professionals who specialize in eating disorders. As indicated by the research we review in this chapter, some of treatments you should consider are cognitive behavior therapy, the most strongly supported treatment; interpersonal therapy; family therapy; and antidepressant medication. Hospitalization may be another option, but only for very severe weight loss.

If you are concerned about a friend's eating, you should make a plan and talk to her or him. Bring some information on local resources for treating eating disorders. And be prepared to listen as well as to talk! Your friend probably has not confided about her problems with many people. If your friend denies a problem, there is no point in arguing. You have done your job by raising the issue. It will be up to her to admit to the problem and get help. A good resource before and after talking with a friend is *Surviving an Eating Disorder: Strategies for Friends and Families*, by Michele Siegel, Judith Brisman, and Margot Weinshel.

# 10 Summary

The defining symptoms of **anorexia nervosa** include extreme emaciation, a disturbed perception of one's body, and an intense fear of gaining weight.

The defining symptoms of **bulimia nervosa** are **binge eating** and compensatory behavior (**purging** or excessive exercise), and undue focus on weight and shape.

**Binge-eating disorder** is included in the **DSM-5**, but **obesity** is not.

The prevalence of both anorexia nervosa and bulimia nervosa has increased dramatically in recent decades, particularly among young women.

Our society's gender roles, standards of beauty, and pubertal changes in body shape and weight all contribute to the onset of eating disorders in young women.

Four psychological factors in the development of eating disorders are issues of control and perfectionism, dysphoria combined with a lack of interoceptive awareness, body image dissatisfaction, and reactions to dietary restraint.

Biological contributions to eating disorders include the body's attempts to maintain **weight set points** and genetic influences on body weight and shape.

There is no clearly effective treatment for anorexia nervosa, which may require inpatient treatment, although a new form of family therapy shows promise among adolescents.

Cognitive behavior therapy is an effective first line treatment for bulimia, while interpersonal psychotherapy and antidepressant medication also can be effective secondary treatments.

Anorexia and to a lesser extent, bulimia, can be chronic, with a continuation of eating dysfunction even when some symptoms improve.

Recent research provides hope for the prevention of disordered eating, especially efforts focused on maintaining healthy weight or creating dissonance about the culture of thinness.

# The Big Picture

## critical thinking review

**10.1** How can you tell if someone has an eating disorder?
The most obvious and most dangerous symptom of anorexia nervosa is a *significantly low weight*. . . (see page 265).

**10.2** How do images of women in the media contribute to eating disorders?
Popular attitudes about women in the United States tell us that "looks are everything," and thinness is essential to good looks . . . (see page 272).

**10.3** Do men suffer from eating disorders?
. . . some experts argue that pressures to be strong and muscular have created a new eating disorder among males . . . (see page 264).

**10.4** What is binge-eating disorder?
Binge-eating disorder, episodes of binge eating without compensatory behavior, is a new diagnosis in *DSM-5*. (see page 269).

**10.5** Why do some girls and women develop eating disorders when others do not?
. . . not every woman in the United States develops an eating disorder, so other factors must interact with culture to produce eating disorders . . . (see page 274).

**10.6** What treatments work for anorexia and bulimia?
The treatments for anorexia nervosa and bulimia nervosa differ in approach and effectiveness . . . (see page 278).

**10.7** Can eating disorders be prevented?
This question is of huge importance, especially given the pervasive body dissatisfaction and disordered eating found among women today . . . (see page 280).

## key terms

anorexia nervosa  263
binge eating  268
binge-eating disorder  269

body image  276
bulimia nervosa  263
cohort  271

cohort effects  271
obesity  269

purging  268
weight set points  277

## Virtual Case Studies

Virtual Case Studies offers you a science-based, interactive simulation where you can learn how a number of risk factors and protective factors could impact disorder development in a virtual person. As you progress through the simulation you will not act as the character or as a clinician, but will be able to independently explore a variety of different behaviors, events, and outcomes that one who suffers from a disorder could potentially encounter. You can access the Virtual Case Study on *Eating Disorders* at mypsychlab.com.

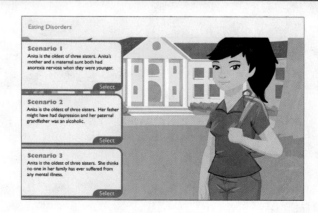

substance-related and addictive disorders

11

# The Big Picture

## learning objectives

**11.1**
What evidence is needed to show that a drug is addictive?

**11.2**
What are the long-term consequences of abusing psychomotor stimulants?

**11.3**
Where is the boundary between substance use disorders and recreational drug use?

**11.4**
In what ways are drug problems different among the elderly?

**11.5**
What are the most important risk factors for alcoholism?

**11.6**
How does AA differ from other approaches to treating alcoholism?

**11.7**
What factors predict better long-term outcome for treatment of alcoholism?

The abuse of alcohol and other drugs is one of the most serious problems facing our society today. It is likely that you or someone close to you will be affected by the substance use issues outlined in this chapter. Alcohol and drug problems receive a great deal of attention in the popular media, as illustrated by actress Lindsay Lohan's repeated struggles with alcohol and the drug-related suicide of Kurt Cobain, leader of the rock group Nirvana. Research efforts, treatment priorities, and national publicity have all helped transform national attitudes about the abuse of chemical substances. The picture of the drug addict as a homeless derelict whose personality defects and lack of motivation are largely responsible for the problem has been replaced by a new view in which substance use disorders are seen as chronic mental disorders that affect people from all walks of life.

## Overview

The costs associated with substance use disorders are astronomical. According to the World Health Organization, alcohol use was responsible for 5 percent of the total burden of disease and

disability worldwide in 2004 (Rehm et al., 2009). Cirrhosis of the liver, which is frequently the result of chronic alcoholism, is a leading cause of death in the United States. In addition, alcohol plays a prominent role in many suicides, homicides, and motor vehicle accidents. The rate of deaths attributable to the use of tobacco is growing rapidly, particularly in developing countries, where 50 percent of adult men are regular smokers. By the year 2020, tobacco is expected to kill between 8 million and 9 million people annually worldwide, more than any single disease, including AIDS (Lopez et al., 2006).

*DSM-5* defines **substance use disorders** in terms of a maladaptive pattern of behaviors that are related to the continued use of drugs, in spite of the fact that their use creates a set of significant problems for the person. These include inability to control use of the drug, risky use of the drug, social impairment following repeated use, and pharmacological consequences. The latter include tolerance (the need for increased amounts of the drug to achieve intoxication) and withdrawal (unpleasant physical and psychological effects that the person experiences when he or she tries to stop taking the drug).

Some other terms have also been used to describe substance use disorders. In previous versions of the diagnostic manual, *substance dependence* was a term that described substance use disorders that were at least moderate in severity (e.g., those with pharmacological consequences). *Addiction* is another term that is often used to describe problems such as alcoholism. Throughout this chapter, we will use the terms dependent and addiction to refer to relatively severe substance use problems.

The term addiction is being used more frequently in recent years, partly because the field has become increasingly interested in similarities and distinctions between substance use disorders and other kinds of impulsive behavior problems that involve loss of control or craving in one form or another. These include addiction-like problems such as pathological gambling, excessive use of the Internet, and hypersexual behavior (see the section on Impulse Control Disorders in Chapter 9 on page 252).

Drugs that are taken in excess, sometimes called *psychoactive substances,* are chemicals that alter a person's mood, level of perception, or brain functioning (Schuckit, 2010). All drugs of abuse can be used to increase a person's psychological comfort level (make one feel "high") or to alter levels of consciousness. The list of chemicals on which people can become dependent is long and seems to be growing longer. It includes drugs that are legally available, whether over the counter or by prescription only, as well as many that are illegal.

Depressants of the central nervous system (CNS) include alcohol as well as types of medications that are used to help people sleep, called *hypnotics,* and those for relieving anxiety, known as *sedatives* or *anxiolytics.* The CNS stimulants include illegal drugs like amphetamine and cocaine, as well as nicotine and caffeine. The opiates, also called *narcotic analgesics,* can be used clinically to decrease pain. The *cannabinoids,* such as marijuana, produce euphoria and an altered sense of time. At higher doses, they may produce hallucinations. People with a substance use disorder frequently abuse several types of drugs; this condition is known as *polysubstance abuse.*

One basic question we must address is whether we should view each type of addiction as a unique problem. Experts who answer "yes" to this question point out that each class of abused substance seems to affect the body in distinct ways. For example, when taken orally, some opiates can be used for long periods of time without leading to significant organ damage (Jaffe & Jaffe, 1999). Chronic use of alcohol and tobacco, on the other hand, can have a devastating impact on a person's physical health.

Despite these differences, the various forms of substance use disorder share many common elements. All represent an inherent conflict between immediate pleasure and longer-term harmful consequences. The psychological and biochemical effects on the user are often similar, as are the negative consequences for both social and occupational behaviors. The reasons for initial experimentation with a drug, the factors that influence the transition to addiction, and the processes that lead to relapse after initial efforts to change are all similar in many respects. For these reasons, many clinicians and researchers have adopted a view of substance use disorders that emphasizes common causes, behaviors, and consequences (Lesch et al., 2011). In fact, *DSM-5* employs a set of diagnostic criteria for substance use disorder that is relatively consistent for all drugs.

The variety of problems associated with substance use disorders can be illustrated using a case study of alcohol use disorder. Ernest Hemingway (1899–1961), a Nobel Prize–winning writer, was severely dependent on alcohol for many years. The following paragraphs, quoted from an article by Paul Johnson (1989), describe the progression of Hemingway's drinking and the problems that it created. They illustrate many typical features of substance use disorders, as well as the devastating impact that alcohol can have on various organs of the body. Johnson's description also raises a number of interesting questions about the causes of this disorder. Most men and women consume alcoholic beverages at some point during their lives. Why do some people become dependent on alcohol while others do not? What factors influence the transition from social drinking to abuse?

### → Ernest Hemingway's Alcohol Use Disorder

Hemingway began to drink as a teenager, the local blacksmith secretly supplying him with strong cider. His mother noted his habit and always feared he would become an alcoholic. In Italy he progressed to wine, then had his first hard liquor at the officers' club in Milan. His wound [from World War I] and an unhappy love affair provoked heavy drinking: In the hospital, his wardrobe was found to be full of empty cognac bottles, an ominous sign. In Paris in the 1920s, he bought Beaune by the gallon at a wine cooperative and would and did drink five or six bottles of red at a meal. He taught Scott Fitzgerald to drink wine direct from the bottle, which, he said, was like "a girl going swimming without her swimming suit." In New York, after signing his contract for *The Sun*

*Also Rises,* he was "cockeyed," he said, for "several days," probably his first prolonged bout.

Hemingway particularly liked to drink with women, as this seemed to him, vicariously, to signify his mother's approval. Hadley [the first of his four wives] drank a lot with him, and wrote: "I still cherish, you know, the remark you made that you almost worshipped me as a drinker." The same disastrous role was played by his pretty 1930s companion in Havana, Jane Mason, with whom he drank gin followed by champagne chasers and huge jars of iced daiquiris; it was indeed in Cuba in this decade that his drinking first got completely out of hand. One bartender there said he could "drink more martinis than any man I have ever seen." On safari, he was seen sneaking out of his tent at 5 A.M. to get a drink. His brother Leicester said that, by the end of the 1930s, at Key West, he was drinking 17 scotch-and-sodas a day and often taking a bottle of champagne to bed with him at night.

At this period, his liver for the first time began to cause him acute pain. He was told by his doctor to give up alcohol completely, and indeed he tried to limit his consumption to three whiskeys before dinner. But that did not last. During World War II his drinking mounted steadily and by the mid-1940s he was reportedly pouring gin into his tea at breakfast. A. E. Hotchner, interviewing him for *Cosmopolitan* in 1948, said he dispatched seven double-size Papa Doubles (the Havana drink named after him, a mixture of rum, grapefruit, and maraschino), and when he left for dinner took an eighth with him for the drive. And on top of all, there was constant whiskey: His son Patrick said his father got through a quart of whiskey a day for the last 20 years of his life.

Hemingway's ability to hold his liquor was remarkable. Lillian Ross, who wrote his profile for the *New Yorker*, does not seem to have noticed he was drunk a lot of the time he talked to her. Denis Zaphior said of his last safari: "I suppose he was drunk the whole time but seldom showed it." He also demonstrated an unusual ability to cut down his drinking or even to eliminate it altogether for brief periods, and this, in addition to his strong physique, enabled him to survive.

But despite his physique, his alcoholism had a direct impact on his health, beginning with his damaged liver in the late 1930s. By 1959, following his last big drinking bout in Spain, he was experiencing both kidney and liver trouble and possibly hemochromatosis (cirrhosis, bronzed skin, diabetes), edema of the ankles, cramps, chronic insomnia, blood-clotting and high blood uremia, as well as his skin complaints. He was impotent and prematurely aged. Even so, he was still on his feet, still alive; and the thought had become unbearable to him. His father had committed suicide because of his fear of mortal illness. Hemingway feared that his illnesses were not mortal: On July 2, 1961, after various unsuccessful treatments for depression and paranoia, he got hold of his best English double-barreled shotgun, put two canisters in it, and blew away his entire cranial vault.

Why did Hemingway long for death [and why did he drink]? He felt he was failing his art. Hemingway had many grievous faults, but there was one thing he did not lack: artistic integrity. It shines like a beacon through his whole life. He set himself the task of creating a new way of writing English, and fiction, and he succeeded. It was one of the salient events in the history of our language and is now an inescapable part of it. He devoted to this task immense resources of creative skill, energy, and patience. That in itself was difficult. But far more difficult, as he discovered, was to maintain the high creative standards he had set himself. This became apparent to him in the mid-1930s and added to his habitual depression. From then on his few successful stories were aberrations in a long downward slide.

If Hemingway had been less of an artist, it might not have mattered to him as a man. He would simply have written and published inferior novels, as many writers do. But he knew when he wrote below his best, and the knowledge was intolerable to him. He sought the help of alcohol, even in working hours. He was first observed with a drink, a "Rum St. James," in front of him while writing in the 1920s. This custom, rare at first, became intermittent, then invariable. By the 1940s, he was said to wake at 4:30 A.M. [He] "usually starts drinking right away and writes standing up, with a pencil in one hand and a drink in another." The effect on his work was exactly as might be expected, disastrous. Hemingway began to produce large quantities of unpublishable material, or material he felt did not reach the minimum standard he set himself. Some was published nonetheless and was seen to be inferior, even a parody of his earlier work. There were one or two exceptions, notably *The Old Man and the Sea* (1952), which won him the Nobel Prize, though there was an element of self-parody in that, too. But the general level was low, and falling, and Hemingway's awareness of his inability to recapture his genius, let alone develop it, accelerated the spinning circle of depression and drink (Johnson, 1989, pp. 58–59).

## Symptoms

Substance use disorders are associated with a host of problems, many of which are illustrated in the life of Ernest Hemingway. Nevertheless, they are difficult to define. Alcoholism is one important example. George Vaillant (1995), a psychiatrist at Harvard Medical School and the author of an important longitudinal study of alcoholic men, noted that it is difficult to say that one specific problem or set of problems represents the core features of this disorder:

Not only is there no single symptom that defines alcoholism, but often it is not who is drinking but who is watching that defines a symptom. A drinker may worry that he has an alcohol problem because of his impotence. His wife may drag him to an alcohol clinic because he slapped her during a blackout. Once he is at the clinic, the doctor calls him an alcoholic because of his abnormal liver-function tests. Later society labels him a drunk because of a second episode of driving while intoxicated. (p. 24)

The number of problems that a person encounters seems to provide the most useful distinction between people who are addicted to a substance and those who are not. These problems can be sorted loosely into two general areas: (1) patterns of pathological consumption, including impaired control over use of the drug and continued use in spite of mounting problems; and (2) consequences that follow a prolonged pattern of abuse, including social and occupational impairments, disruption of important interpersonal relationships, and deteriorating medical condition. Some of the physiological consequences may include the onset of tolerance and withdrawal.

It might seem that the actual amount of a drug of abuse that a person consumes would be the best indication of the existence of a problem. Hemingway, for example, clearly consumed enormous quantities of alcohol over a period of many years. The average person with an alcohol use disorder does drink more frequently and in larger quantities than the average person without an alcohol use disorder (Keyes et al., 2009). Nevertheless, the amount of a drug that a specific person consumes is not a good way to define substance use disorders, because people vary significantly in the amount of any given drug they can consume. Factors such as age, gender, activity level, and overall physical health influence a person's ability to metabolize various kinds of drugs. For example, some people can drink a lot without developing problems; others drink relatively little and have difficulties.

Many psychological features or problems are associated with the problematic use of chemical substances. One such feature involves *craving*. This word is frequently used to describe a forceful urge to use drugs, but the relationship between craving and drug use is actually very complex (Eliason & Amodia, 2007; Sayette et al., 2000). People who are dependent on drugs often say that they take the drug to control how they are feeling. They need it to relieve negative mood states or to avoid withdrawal symptoms from previous episodes. They may feel compelled to take the drug as a way to prepare for certain activities, such as public speaking, writing, or sex. Some clinicians refer to this condition as psychological dependence.

One useful index of craving is the amount of time that the person spends planning to take the drug. Is access to drugs or alcohol a constant preoccupation? If the person is invited to a party or is planning to eat at a restaurant, does he or she always inquire about the availability of alcoholic drinks? If the person is going to spend a few days at the beach in a neighboring state, will he or she worry more about whether liquor stores will be closed on weekends or holidays than about having enough food, clothes, or recreational equipment?

As the problem progresses, it is not unusual for the person who abuses drugs to try to stop. In the case of alcoholism, for example, it is possible for even heavy drinkers to abstain for at least short periods of time. Most clinicians and researchers agree that diminished control over drinking is a crucial feature of the disorder. Some experts have described this issue as "freedom of choice." When a person first experiments with the use of alcohol, his or her behavior is clearly voluntary; the person is not compelled to drink. After drinking heavily for a long period of time, most people with a drinking disorder try to stop. Unfortunately, efforts at self-control are typically short-lived and usually fail.

Two particularly important features of substance use disorders are the phenomena known as tolerance and withdrawal. **Tolerance** refers to the process through which the nervous system becomes less sensitive to the effects of alcohol or any other drug of abuse. For example, a person who has been regularly exposed to alcohol will need to drink increased quantities to achieve the same subjective effect ("buzz," "high," or level of intoxication).

The development of drug tolerance seems to be the result of three separate mechanisms (Julien, Advokat, & Comaty, 2010). Two are pharmacological and the third is behavioral. *Metabolic tolerance* develops when repeated exposure to a drug causes the person's liver to produce more enzymes that are used to metabolize, that is, break down, the drug. The drug, therefore, is metabolized more quickly and the person has to take increasingly larger doses in order to maintain the same level in his or her body. *Pharmacodynamic tolerance* occurs when receptors in the brain (see Figure 2.2 on page 34) adapt to continued presence of the drug. The neuron may adapt by reducing the number of receptors or by reducing their sensitivity to the drug. This process is known as *down regulation.* The third process involved in drug tolerance involves *behavioral conditioning mechanisms* (Siegel, 2005). Cues that are regularly associated with the administration of a drug begin to function as conditioned stimuli and elicit a conditioned response that is opposite in direction to the natural effect of the drug. As this compensatory response increases in strength, it competes with the drug response so that larger amounts of the drug must be taken to achieve the same effect.

Some drugs are much more likely than others to produce a buildup of tolerance (APA, 2013). The most substantial tolerance effects are found among heavy users of opioids, such as heroin, and CNS stimulants, such as amphetamine and cocaine. Pronounced tolerance is also found among people who use alcohol and nicotine. The evidence is unclear regarding tolerance effects and prolonged use of marijuana and hashish. Most people who use cannabinoids are not aware of tolerance effects, but these effects have been demonstrated in animal studies. Hallucinogens (LSD and PCP) may not lead to the development of tolerance.

**Withdrawal** refers to the symptoms experienced when a person stops using a drug. The symptoms can go on for several days. For example, alcohol is a CNS depressant, and the heavy drinker's system becomes accustomed to functioning in a chronically depressed state. When the person stops drinking, the system begins to rebound within several hours, producing many unpleasant side effects—hand tremors, sweating, nausea, anxiety, and insomnia. The most serious forms of withdrawal include convulsions and visual, tactile, or auditory hallucinations. Some people develop delirium, a sudden disturbance of consciousness that is accompanied by changes in cognitive processes such as lack of awareness of the environment or inability to sustain attention

(see Chapter 14). This syndrome is called *alcohol withdrawal delirium* in *DSM-5* if it is induced by withdrawal from alcohol.

The symptoms of withdrawal vary considerably for different kinds of substances. Unpleasant reactions are most evident during withdrawal from alcohol, opioids, and the general class of sedatives, hypnotics, and anxiolytics (such as Valium and Xanax). Withdrawal symptoms are also associated with stimulants, such as amphetamine, cocaine, and nicotine, although they are sometimes less pronounced than those associated with alcohol and opioids. Withdrawal symptoms are not often seen after repeated use of hallucinogens, and they have not been demonstrated with phencyclidine (PCP). Caffeine is the most widely used psychoactive substance in the world. We all know people who crave coffee, especially in the morning. And some heavy coffee users experience severe headaches when they stop drinking caffeine (James & Keane, 2007).

All these problems serve to emphasize the fact that symptoms of substance use disorders fall along a continuum. It is convenient to consider these problems in terms of qualitative distinctions: people who can control their drinking and those who cannot; people who crave alcohol and those who do not; people who have developed a tolerance to the drug and those who have not; and so on. In fact, there are no clear dividing lines on any of these dimensions. Drug use disorders lie on a continuum of severity (Helzer et al., 2008). For this reason it is difficult to define the nature of substance use disorders.

People can become dependent on many different kinds of drugs. Although patterns of dependence are similar in some ways for all drugs, each type of drug also has some unique features. Table 11.1 provides a list of the different classes of drugs that are associated with the diagnosis of substance use disorders in *DSM-5.* This table provides a very brief overview of some of the similarities and differences among these drugs. We will return to this table later in this chapter, when we describe the *DSM-5* approach to diagnosis of substance-related disorder.

In the next few pages, we briefly review some of the most important classes of drugs. For each group, we will describe short-term effects on physiology and behavior, as well as the consequences of long-term abuse. Unless otherwise specified, these

## MyPsychLab VIDEO CASE

### Alcoholism

CHRIS

*"The toughest thing I ever did was admitting that I had a problem."*

👁 **Watch** the **Video** *Chris: Alcohol Use Disorder* on **MyPsychLab**

How was Chris's pattern of drinking different from that of his friends?

**TABLE 11.1**

## Comparison of Various Types of Substances and Possible Consequences of Their Use

| | Substance Use Disorder | Intoxication | Withdrawal | Sleep Disorders | Sexual Dysfunction | Delirium | Dementia |
|---|---|---|---|---|---|---|---|
| Alcohol | yes | yes | yes | yes | yes | yes | yes |
| Caffeine | no | yes | yes | yes | no | no | no |
| Cannabis | yes | yes | yes | yes | no | yes | no |
| Hallucinogens* | yes | yes | no | no | no | yes | no |
| Inhalants | yes | yes | no | no | no | yes | yes |
| Opioids | yes | yes | yes | yes | yes | yes | no |
| Sedatives, hypnotics | yes | yes | yes | yes | yes | yes | yes |
| Stimulants** | yes | yes | yes | yes | yes | yes | no |
| Tobacco | yes | no | yes | yes | no | no | no |

*Note:* Columns 1–3 indicate whether *DSM-5* provides a set of criteria for assigning a diagnosis of substance use disorder, intoxication, or withdrawal for each type of drug. Columns 4–7 indicate some (but not all) of the other forms of mental disorder that can be observed during either intoxication or withdrawal from persistent use of the drug.
* includes phencyclidine and other hallucinogens
** includes amphetamines, cocaine, and other stimulants
*Source:* Based on data from the Diagnostic and Statistical Manual of Mental Disorders, Fifth Edition, (Copyright 2013). American Psychiatric Association.

descriptions are based on information presented by William McKim (2006) in his textbook on drugs and behavior.

## Alcohol

Alcohol affects virtually every organ and system in the body. After alcohol has been ingested, it is absorbed through membranes in the stomach, small intestine, and colon. The rate at which it is absorbed is influenced by many variables, including the concentration of alcohol in the beverage (for example, distilled spirits are absorbed more rapidly than beer or wine), the volume and rate of consumption, and the presence of food in the digestive system. After it is absorbed, alcohol is distributed to all the body's organ systems. Almost all the alcohol that a person consumes is eventually broken down or metabolized in the liver. The rate at which alcohol is metabolized varies from person to person, but the average person can metabolize about 1 ounce of 90-proof liquor or 12 ounces of beer per hour (Nathan, 1993). If the person's consumption rate exceeds this metabolic limit, then blood alcohol levels will rise.

**SHORT-TERM EFFECTS** Blood alcohol levels are measured in terms of the amount of alcohol per unit of blood. A "drink" is considered to be 12 ounces of beer, 4 ounces of wine, or 1 ounce of 86-proof whiskey. The average 160-pound man who consumes five drinks in one hour will have a blood alcohol level of 100 milligrams (mg) per 100 milliliters (ml) of blood, or 100 mg percent (Kowalski, 1998). There is a strong correlation between blood alcohol levels and CNS intoxicating effects. According to *DSM-5,* the symptoms of alcohol intoxication include slurred speech, lack of coordination, an unsteady gait, nystagmus (involuntary to-and-fro movement of the eyeballs induced when the person looks upward or to the side), impaired attention or memory, and stupor or coma.

In most states, the legal limit of alcohol concentration for driving is 80 mg percent because slowed reaction times and interference with other driving skills become particularly evident as blood alcohol levels exceed this level. People with levels of 150 to 300 mg percent will almost always act intoxicated. Neurological and respiration complications begin to appear at higher levels. There is an extreme risk of coma leading to toxic death when blood alcohol levels go above 400 mg percent.

**LONG-TERM CONSEQUENCES** The prolonged use and abuse of alcohol can have a devastating impact on many areas of a person's life. The disruption of relationships with family and friends can be especially painful. The impact of Hemingway's drinking on his writing career and his family life is clearly evident. Most critics agree that

The negative consequences of alcohol use disorder typically include a devastating impact on social relationships and work performance.

his literary accomplishments were confined primarily to the early stages of his career, before his alcoholism began to interfere with his ability to write. Drinking also took its toll on his marriages, which were characterized by frequent and occasionally furious conflict in public and by repeated episodes of verbal and physical abuse in private (Johnson, 1989). Also, the heavy use of alcohol by a pregnant woman can cause damage to her fetus (see Chapter 15).

Many people who abuse alcohol experience blackouts. In some cases, abusers may continue to function without passing out, but they will be unable to remember their behavior. An example is the person who drives home drunk from a party and in the morning finds a dent in the car bumper but can't remember how it got there. Sometimes problem drinkers will be told by a friend about how they behaved at the previous night's party, but they cannot remember what they did.

Regular heavy use of alcohol is also likely to interfere with job performance. Coworkers and supervisors may complain. Attendance at work may become sporadic. Eventually, the heavy drinker may be suspended or fired. Related to job performance is the problem of financial difficulties. Losing one's job is clearly detrimental to one's financial stability, as are the costs of divorce, healthcare, liquor, and so on.

Many heavy drinkers encounter problems with legal authorities. These problems may include arrests for drunken driving and public intoxication, as well as charges of spouse and child abuse. Many forms of violent behavior are more likely to be committed when a person has been drinking.

On a biological level, prolonged exposure to high levels of alcohol can disrupt the functions of several important organ systems, especially the liver, pancreas, gastrointestinal system, cardiovascular system, and endocrine system. The symptoms of alcoholism include many secondary health problems, such as cirrhosis of the liver, heart problems (in part, the result of being overweight), and various forms of cancer, as well as severe and persistent forms of neurocognitive disorder (see Chapter 14). Alcoholism is also associated with nutritional disturbances of many types, because chronic abusers often drink instead of eating balanced meals. In fact, over an extended period of time, alcohol dependence has more negative health consequences than does abuse of any other drug, with the exception of nicotine.

The misuse of alcohol leads to an enormous number of severe injuries and premature deaths in every region of the world (Cornelius et al., 2008). The specific impact of alcohol varies among geographic regions, in part because of differences in the age structure of different populations. Deaths that result from alcohol-related injuries are much more common among young men, while deaths from alcohol-related diseases are responsible for more deaths among older men (Murray & Lopez, 1997; see Figure 11.1).

## Tobacco

Nicotine is the active ingredient in tobacco, which is its only natural source. Nicotine is almost never taken in its pure form because it can be toxic. Very high doses have extremely unpleasant effects. Controlled doses are easier to achieve by smoking or chewing tobacco, which provides a diluted concentration of nicotine. Another way of ingesting nicotine is to inhale snuff (powdered tobacco) into the nostrils. When tobacco smoke is inhaled, nicotine is absorbed into the blood through the mucous membranes of the lungs. This route of administration results in the highest concentrations of nicotine because it is carried directly from the lungs to the heart and from there to the brain.

**SHORT-TERM EFFECTS** The effects of nicotine on the peripheral nervous system (see Chapter 2) include increases in heart rate and blood pressure. In the central nervous system, nicotine has pervasive effects on a number of neurotransmitter systems (Houezec, 1998). It stimulates the release of norepinephrine from several sites, producing CNS arousal. Nicotine also causes the release of dopamine and norepinephrine in the mesolimbic dopamine pathway, also known as the reward system of the brain. The serotonin system, which also mediates the effects of antidepressant medication, is influenced by nicotine. In fact, some people have suggested that nicotine mimics the effects of antidepressant drugs.

Nicotine has a complex influence on subjective mood states. Many people say that they smoke because it makes them feel more relaxed. Some believe that it helps them control their subjective response to stress. This phenomenon is somewhat paradoxical in light of the fact that nicotine leads to increased arousal of the sympathetic nervous system. Various explanations may account for this apparent inconsistency. One involves

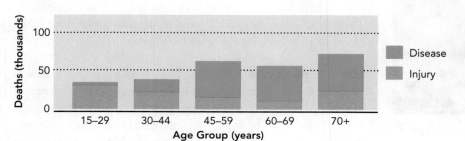

**FIGURE 11.1**

**Male Deaths Caused by Alcohol Use in Established Market Economies**  Young men are more likely to be killed by alcohol-related injuries, while older men often die as a result of alcohol-related disease.
*Source:* Based on Murray and Lopez. 1997. Global Mortality, Disability, and the Contribution of Risk Factors: Global Burden of Disease Study. Lancet; 349.

differences in dosage levels; low doses of nicotine may lead to increased arousal while higher doses lead to relaxation. Another alternative involves withdrawal. Regular smokers may feel relaxed when they smoke a cigarette because it relieves unpleasant symptoms of withdrawal.

**LONG-TERM CONSEQUENCES** Nicotine is one of the most harmful and deadly addictive drugs. Considerable evidence points to the development of both tolerance and withdrawal symptoms among people who regularly smoke or chew tobacco. The physiological symptoms of withdrawal from nicotine include drowsiness, lightheadedness, headache, muscle tremors, and nausea. People who are attempting to quit smoking typically experience sleeping problems, weight gain, concentration difficulties, and mood swings ranging from anxiety to anger and depression (Hughes, 2007b). From a psychological point of view, withdrawal from nicotine is just as difficult as withdrawal from heroin. Many people report that these symptoms disappear after a few months, but some have serious cravings for several years after they quit.

People who smoke tobacco increase their risk of developing many fatal diseases, including heart disease, lung disease (bronchitis and emphysema), and various types of cancer (Kozlowski, Henningfield, & Brigham, 2001). Eighty percent of all deaths caused by lung cancer can be attributed to smoking tobacco. More than 3.5 million people in the world die prematurely each year as a result of tobacco. Women who smoke are also more likely to experience fertility problems. Babies born to mothers who smoked during pregnancy are also likely to weigh less than those born to mothers who do not smoke, and they may be more vulnerable to certain types of birth defects.

## Amphetamine and Cocaine

Members of the class of drugs known as **psychomotor stimulants** produce their effects by simulating the actions of certain neurotransmitters, specifically epinephrine, norepinephrine, dopamine, and serotonin (as discussed later in this chapter). Cocaine is a naturally occurring stimulant drug that is extracted from the leaf of a small tree that grows at high elevations, as in the Andes Mountains. The amphetamines (such as dexedrine and methamphetamine) are produced synthetically.

The stimulants can be taken orally, injected, or inhaled. It is easier to maintain a constant blood level when the drugs are taken orally. They are absorbed more slowly through the digestive system, and their effects are less potent. More dramatic effects are achieved by injecting the drug or sniffing it. Cocaine can also be smoked, using various procedures that have been popularized in the past several years. Some people employ a particularly dangerous procedure called "freebasing," in which the drug is heated and its vapors are inhaled. Many people have been seriously burned when these highly combustible chemicals are accidentally ignited.

**SHORT-TERM EFFECTS** Cocaine and amphetamines are called stimulants because they activate the sympathetic nervous system (Constable, 2004). They increase heart rate and blood pressure and dilate the blood vessels and the air passages of the lungs. Stimulants also suppress the appetite and prevent sleep. These effects have been among the reasons for the popularity and frequent abuse of stimulants. They have been used, for example, by truck drivers who want to stay awake on long trips and by students who want to stay awake to study for exams. Unfortunately, in addition to their addicting properties, large doses of amphetamines can also lead to dizziness, confusion, and panic states, which clearly interfere with activities such as driving and studying.

Many people use (and abuse) stimulants because they induce a positive mood state. When they are injected, amphetamines and cocaine produce similar subjective effects, but the effects of cocaine do not last as long. Low doses of amphetamines make people feel more confident, friendly, and energetic. At higher doses, the person is likely to experience a brief, intense feeling of euphoria. The rushes associated with snorting or injecting cocaine are frequently described in sexual terms. Although many people believe that cocaine enhances sexual arousal and pleasure, most of the evidence suggests that prolonged use leads to sexual dysfunction (Jaffe, 1995). Tolerance develops quickly to the euphoric effects of stimulant drugs. The feelings of exhilaration and well-being are typically followed, several hours later, by the onset of lethargy and a mildly depressed or irritable mood.

Acute overdoses of stimulant drugs can result in irregular heartbeat, convulsions, coma, and death. The highly publicized overdose deaths of several prominent athletes, such as that of All-American basketball star Len Bias in 1986, indicate that the intense cardiovascular effects of cocaine can be fatal, even among people who are otherwise strong and healthy. Individual differences in sensitivity to the subjective effects of cocaine may play a role in cocaine-related deaths. In other words, people who are resistant to cocaine-induced euphoria may consume unusually large quantities of the drug while trying to achieve the rush that others have described.

**LONG-TERM CONSEQUENCES** High doses of amphetamines and cocaine can lead to the onset of psychosis. The risk of a psychotic reaction seems to increase with repeated exposure to the drug (Bolla, Cadet, & London, 1998). This syndrome can appear in people who have no prior history of mental disorder, and it usually disappears a few days after the drug has been cleared. Stimulants can also increase the severity of symptoms among people who had already developed some type of psychotic condition. The symptoms of amphetamine psychosis include auditory and visual hallucinations, as well as delusions of persecution and grandeur.

As with other forms of addiction, the most devastating effects of stimulant drugs frequently center around the disruption of occupational and social roles. The compulsion to continue taking cocaine can lead to physical exhaustion and financial ruin. People who are dependent on cocaine must spend enormous amounts of money to support their habit. They may have to sell important assets, such as their homes and cars, in order to finance extended binges. Some people become involved in a variety of criminal activities in order to raise enough money to purchase drugs.

Prolonged use of amphetamines has also been linked to an increase in violent behavior, but it is not clear whether this phenomenon is due to the drug itself or to the lifestyles with which it is frequently associated. Some violence might be related to a drug-induced increase in paranoia and hostility. Statistics concerning drugs and violent crime are very difficult to interpret. The direct effects of the drug on human behavior are confounded with various economic and social factors that are associated with buying, selling, and using an expensive, illegal drug like cocaine.

People who discontinue taking stimulant drugs do not typically experience severe withdrawal symptoms. The most common reaction is depression. Long-term exposure to high doses of amphetamine can lead to a profound state of clinical depression, which is often accompanied by ideas of suicide.

## Opiates

The **opiates** are drugs that have properties similar to those of opium. The natural source of opium is a poppy with a white flower. The main active ingredients in opium are morphine and codeine, both of which are widely used in medicine, particularly to relieve pain. They are available legally only by prescription in the United States. In Canada, small quantities of codeine are available without a prescription in over-the-counter painkillers and cough medicines. "Opioids" are synthetic versions of opium, and they are often used to reduce pain. Oxycodone (OxyContin) and hydrocodone (Vicodin) are examples of opioids. Their medical use has increased dramatically over the past 20 years, and they are also widely misused. Heroin is a synthetic opiate that is made by modifying the morphine molecule. It was originally marketed as an alternative to morphine when physicians believed, erroneously, that heroin is not addictive.

The positive, emotional effects of opiates do not last. They are soon replaced by long-term negative changes in mood and emotion.

The opiates can be taken orally, injected, or inhaled. Opium is sometimes eaten or smoked. When morphine is used as a painkiller, it is taken orally so that it is absorbed slowly through the digestive system. People who use morphine for subjective effects most often inject the drug because it leads more quickly to high concentrations in brain tissue. Heroin can be injected, inhaled through the nose in the form of snuff, or smoked and inhaled through a pipe or tube.

**SHORT-TERM EFFECTS** The opiates can induce a state of dreamlike euphoria, which may be accompanied by increased sensitivity in hearing and vision. People who inject morphine or heroin also experience a rush—a brief, intense feeling of pleasure that is sometimes described as being like an orgasm in the entire body.

Laboratory studies of mood indicate that the positive, emotional effects of opiates do not last. They are soon replaced by long-term negative changes in mood and emotion. These unpleasant experiences are relieved for 30 to 60 minutes after each new injection of the drug, but they eventually color most of the rest of the person's waking experience.

The opiates can induce nausea and vomiting among novice users, constrict the pupils of the eye, and disrupt the coordination of the digestive system. Continued use of opiates decreases the level of sex hormones in both women and men, resulting in reduced sex drive and impaired fertility.

Some people mix cocaine and opiates into a mixture known as a *speedball* to enhance these subjective feelings. The following brief case describes the preparation of this combination of drugs and one heroin addict's immediate reaction to the injection of a speedball.

### → Feelings After Injecting Heroin

He pushes the plunger on the syringe, squirting water into the heroin powder, then strikes a match and waves it just under the metal lid. The liquid bubbles and the heroin quickly dissolves with very little heat required. *That's good*, he thinks. Sometimes the dope is so good it needs hardly any fire to dissolve it. Next, he shakes in a couple of small rocks of cocaine from the foil wrapper and is impressed that they vanish immediately in the solution. He swirls the liquid around, rips open the filter from one of his Marlboros, and uses the white fibers as a strainer through which to draw the liquid speedball into the syringe. He carefully places the loaded syringe between his teeth. He rolls up his sleeve, removes his belt with one hand, and takes a seat on the edge of the toilet. He wraps the belt tight around his right arm and hopes he can get a clean hit on one of the veins he watches come up. *There, I'll go there.*

The needle point feels sharp going in, which is good; it means he's got an unused needle. When he pulls back on the plunger a little stream of blood slithers up into the syringe, discoloring the slightly yellow liquid. He loosens the belt, careful not to dislodge the needle from the vein, takes a breath, and slowly pushes the liquid into his arm. He pulls the needle out and dabs with his finger at the drop of blood left behind on his arm. As he does this, he feels the freeze in his arm from the cocaine. His arm feels numb. Then it reaches his stomach and mouth. His heart races. He tastes the medicinal flavor just as the first wave of rushes is reaching his brain. His stomach heaves. His scalp tingles and he gets a little scared at first—the wave of sensation is stronger than usual. He fights the urge to vomit, the heroin kicks in and the nausea retreats as the warm, heroin heat replaces the heart-thumping freeze caused by the cocaine. His heart starts to slow down, or so it seems. A quiet, hollow siren rages in his head. The familiar beads of perspiration crowd each other on his forehead, and one drops onto his arm when he bends over to begin cleaning everything up. He puts away his paraphernalia, threads his belt into his pants, and sits down again. *Good stuff, very good,* he thinks as he nods for a second.

Back on Houston Street now, he decides to have a cup of espresso in a little coffee shop he comes upon. Sitting back at a table with a view of the street, he savors the thick hot coffee, lights a cigarette, and blows the smoke to the ceiling. *Nothing hurts,* he thinks. The lousy job that he needs to hold onto, the flak he catches from his wife, the fact that he is turning 40 and doesn't have anything to show for his life—none of it fazes him, but he still thinks about it. A spotty work history, no college, and rent that is three weeks late don't matter right now. He feels warm, loose, and sexy. Was the waitress's smile a flirt or was she smiling because she caught him nodding? Doesn't matter. He smiles back and thinks maybe he can buy his wife a gold-plated necklace instead of the real one. It will look just like the one she pointed out anyway.

And that was what he did (Fernandez, 1998, pp. 72–73).

High doses of opiates can lead to a comatose state, severely depressed breathing, and convulsions. The number of people admitted to hospital emergency rooms for treatment of heroin overdoses increased substantially during the 1990s and has remained relatively stable since that time (see Figure 11.2). Accidental deaths due to drug overdoses have increased in the United States in recent years, primarily because more people are misusing opioid painkillers (Jones, Mack, & Paulozzi, 2013).

**LONG-TERM CONSEQUENCES** The effects of opiates on occupational performance and health depend in large part on the amount of drugs that the person takes. At high doses, people who are addicted to opiates become chronically lethargic and lose their motivation to remain productive. At low doses, some people who use opiates for an extended period of time can remain healthy and work productively in spite of their addiction. This functioning is, of course, dependent on the person's having easy and relatively inexpensive access to opiates. One possibility is being maintained by a physician on methadone, a synthetic opiate that is sometimes used therapeutically as an alternative to heroin.

People who are addicted to opiates become preoccupied with finding and using the drug, in order to experience the rush and to avoid withdrawal symptoms. Tolerance develops rather quickly, and the person's daily dose increases regularly until it eventually levels off and remains steady. Many of the severe health consequences of opiate use are the result of the lifestyle of the addict rather than the drug itself. The enormous expenses and difficulties associated with obtaining illegal opiates almost invariably consume all the person's resources. The person typically neglects housing, nutrition, and health care in the search for another fix. Heroin addicts are much more likely than other people in the general population to die from AIDS, violence, and suicide.

## Sedatives, Hypnotics, and Anxiolytics

The families of drugs known as barbiturates and benzodiazepines are also known informally as tranquilizers, hypnotics, and sedatives. *Tranquilizers* are used to decrease anxiety or agitation. *Hypnotics* are used to help people sleep. *Sedative* is a more general term that describes drugs that calm people or reduce excitement (other than the relief of anxiety). The **barbiturates,** such as phenobarbital (Nembutal) and amobarbital (Amytal), were used for a variety of purposes, including the treatment of chronic anxiety. The **benzodiazepines,** which include diazepam (Valium) and alprazolam (Xanax), have replaced the barbiturates in the treatment

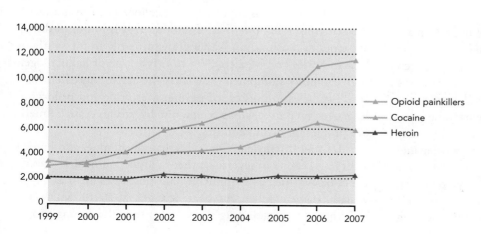

**FIGURE 11.2**

**Unintentional Drug Overdose Deaths by Major Types of Drugs, United States, 1999–2007** In 2007, the number of deaths attributed to opioid pain killers was almost double the number from cocaine and more than five times higher than those involving heroin.
*Source:* Courtesy of the Centers for Disease Control.

of anxiety disorders, in large part because of their lower potential for producing a lethal overdose.

**SHORT-TERM EFFECTS** Sedatives and hypnotics can lead to a state of intoxication that is identical to that associated with alcohol. It is characterized by impaired judgment, slowness of speech, lack of coordination, a narrowed range of attention, and disinhibition of sexual and aggressive impulses. Intravenous use of barbiturates can lead quickly to a pleasant, warm, drowsy feeling that is similar to the experience achieved when taking opiates. The benzodiazepines can sometimes lead to an increase in hostile and aggressive behavior. Some clinicians call this a "rage reaction" or aggressive dyscontrol.

**LONG-TERM CONSEQUENCES** People who abruptly stop taking high doses of benzodiazepines may experience symptoms that are sometimes called a *discontinuance syndrome.* These symptoms can include a return—and, in some cases, a worsening—of the original anxiety symptoms, if the medication was being used to treat an anxiety disorder. The person may also develop new symptoms that are directly associated with drug withdrawal. These include irritability, paranoia, sleep disturbance, agitation, muscle tension, restlessness, and perceptual disturbances. Withdrawal symptoms are less likely to occur if the medication is discontinued gradually rather than abruptly.

## Cannabis

Marijuana and hashish are derived from the hemp plant, *Cannabis sativa.* The most common active ingredient in cannabis is a compound called delta-9-tetrahydrocannabinol (THC). Because every part of the plant contains THC, cannabis can be prepared for consumption in several ways. **Marijuana** refers to the dried leaves and flowers, which can be smoked in a cigarette or pipe. It can also be baked in brownies and ingested orally. **Hashish** refers to the dried resin from the top of the female cannabis plant. It can be smoked or eaten after being baked in cookies or brownies.

Oral administration of cannabis material leads to slow and incomplete absorption. Therefore, the dose must be two or three times larger to achieve the same subjective effect as when it is smoked. Most of the drug is metabolized in the liver.

**SHORT-TERM EFFECTS** The subjective effects of marijuana are almost always pleasant. "Getting high" on marijuana refers to a pervasive sense of well-being and happiness. Laboratory research has shown that marijuana can have variable effects on a person's mood. Many people begin to feel happy, but some become anxious and paranoid. The mood of other people seems to be especially important. After smoking marijuana, a person's mood may become more easily influenced by how other people are behaving.

Cannabis intoxication is often accompanied by *temporal disintegration,* a condition in which people have trouble retaining and organizing information, even over relatively short periods of time. Conversations may become disjointed because the drug

interferes with the people's ability to recall what they have said or planned to say. Lapses in attention and concentration problems are frequent.

**LONG-TERM CONSEQUENCES** The issue of the addictive properties of cannabis remains controversial (Budney & Lile, 2009; Hall & Pacula, 2003). Some tolerance effects to THC have been observed in laboratory animals. Tolerance effects in humans remain ambiguous. Most evidence suggests that people do not develop tolerance to THC unless they are exposed to high doses over an extended period of time. Some people actually report that they become more sensitive (rather than less sensitive) to the effects of marijuana after repeated use. This phenomenon is called *reverse tolerance.* Although reverse tolerance has been reported casually by frequent users, it has not been demonstrated in a laboratory situation, where dosage levels can be carefully controlled.

Withdrawal symptoms are unlikely to develop among occasional smokers of marijuana. People who have been exposed to continuous, high doses of THC may experience withdrawal symptoms, such as irritability, restlessness, and insomnia.

Prolonged heavy use of marijuana may lead to certain types of performance deficits on neuropsychological tests, especially those involving sustained attention, learning, and decision making. Follow-up studies of adults who used cannabis heavily over a period of several years have found some evidence of cognitive decline associated with the drug (Crean , Crane, & Mason, 2011; Pope & Yurgelun-Todd, 2004).

## Hallucinogens and Related Drugs

Drugs that are called **hallucinogens** cause people to experience hallucinations. Although many other types of drugs can lead to hallucinations at toxic levels, hallucinogens cause hallucinations at relatively low doses. There are many different types of hallucinogens, and they have very different neurophysiological effects. The molecular structure of many hallucinogens is similar to the molecular structure of various neurotransmitters, such as serotonin and norepinephrine. The most common hallucinogen is a synthetic drug called *LSD* (d-lysergic acid diethylamide), which bears a strong chemical resemblance to serotonin. It achieves its effect by interacting with certain types of serotonin receptors in the brain. *Psilocybin* is another type of hallucinogen whose chemical structure resembles that of serotonin. It is found in different types of mushrooms, which grow primarily in the southern United States and Mexico. *Mescaline* is a type of hallucinogen that resembles norepinephrine. It is the active ingredient in a small, spineless cactus called peyote. Mescaline and psilocybin have been used in religious ceremonies by various Native American peoples for many centuries.

*MDMA* (Methylene-Dioxy-Methamphetamine, also known as Ecstasy) is one of several synthetic amphetamine derivates. It could be classified as a stimulant, but most texts list it as a type of hallucinogen (Julien, Advokat, & Comaty, 2010). MDMA is also known as a "club drug" because it is popular among people

MDMA is known as a "club drug" because it is popular among people who attend "raves" and dance clubs. It causes changes in perceptual experiences, such as distortions in the sense of time and space, as well as increased sensory awareness.

who attend "raves" and dance clubs (LSD and methamphetamine are also known as club drugs). MDMA is usually taken as a tablet, but the powder form can be inhaled or injected. Within half an hour of ingesting MDMA orally, the person begins to experience an enhanced mood state and a feeling of well-being that often lasts several hours. Although it does not produce vivid hallucinations, MDMA does lead to changes in perceptual experiences, such as distortions in the sense of time and space, as well as increased sensory awareness. It also produces changes in blood pressure and can interfere with the body's ability to regulate its temperature.

*Phencyclidine (PCP)* is another synthetic drug that is often classified with the hallucinogens, although its effects are very different than those associated with LSD and mescaline. It was originally developed as a painkiller. Small doses of PCP lead to relaxation, warmth, and numbness. At higher doses, PCP can induce psychotic behavior, including delusional thinking, catatonic motor behavior, manic excitement, and sudden mood changes. The drug is typically sold in a crystallized form that can be sprinkled on leaves, such as tobacco, marijuana, or parsley, and then smoked. Some people snort it or inject it after dissolving the crystals in water.

**SHORT-TERM EFFECTS** The effects of hallucinogenic drugs are difficult to study empirically because they are based primarily in subjective experience. They typically induce vivid, and occasionally spectacular, visual images. During the early phase of this drug experience, the images often take the form of colorful geometric patterns. The later phase is more likely to be filled with meaningful images of people, animals, and places. The images may change rapidly, and they sometimes follow an explosive pattern of movement.

Although these hallucinatory experiences are usually pleasant, they are occasionally frightening. "Bad trips" are a decidedly unpleasant experience that can lead to panic attacks and the fear of losing one's mind. People can usually be talked through

this process by constantly reminding them that the experience is drug-induced and will be over soon.

Most hallucinogens are not particularly toxic. People do not die from taking an overdose of LSD, psilocybin, or mescaline. However, PCP is much more toxic. High doses can lead to coma, convulsions, respiratory arrest, and brain hemorrhage. MDMA (Ecstasy) can damage serotonin neurons on a permanent basis, and it has been associated with some fatalities (Gold, Tabrah, & Frost-Pineda, 2001).

**LONG-TERM CONSEQUENCES** The use of hallucinogens follows a different pattern than that associated with most other drugs. Hallucinogens, with the possible exception of PCP, are used sporadically and on special occasions rather than continuously. If these drugs are taken repeatedly, within two or three days, their effects disappear. Most people do not increase their use of hallucinogens over time. People who stop taking hallucinogens after continued use do not experience problems; there seem to be no withdrawal symptoms associated with the hallucinogens that resemble serotonin and norepinephrine. The perceptual effects of hallucinogenic drugs almost always wear off after several hours. There are cases, however, in which these drugs have induced persistent psychotic behavior. Most experts interpret these examples as an indication that the drug experience can trigger the onset of psychosis in people who were already vulnerable to that type of disorder. As genes involved in the predisposition toward psychosis are identified, it will become possible to test this hypothesis.

Some people who have taken hallucinogens experience *flashbacks*—brief visual aftereffects that can occur at unpredictable intervals long after the drug has been cleared from the person's body. Scientists do not understand the mechanisms that are responsible for flashbacks. Flashbacks may be more likely to occur when the person is under stress or after the person has used another drug, such as marijuana.

## Diagnosis

The problems that we have reviewed indicate that substance use disorders represent an extremely diverse set of problems. Everyone—clinicians and researchers, as well as drug abusers and their families—seems to recognize the existence of a serious type of psychological disorder. But do these problems have a core? What is the best way to define them? In the following pages we briefly review some of the ways in which alcoholism and drug abuse have been defined. We must begin with the recognition that alcoholism and other types of addictions have not always been viewed as medical conditions that require treatment (Walters, 1999).

### Brief History of Legal and Illegal Substances

One of the most widely recognized facts about alcohol consumption is that drinking patterns vary tremendously from one culture to the next and, within the same culture, from one point in time

During the Prohibition era in the United States (1922–1933), it was illegal to manufacture, transport, or sell alcoholic beverages. Nevertheless, alcohol continued to be widely available from illegal sources, and the law was eventually changed. Similar efforts to control access to addicting drugs have failed in other countries.

to another. Public attitudes toward the consumption of alcohol have changed dramatically during the course of U.S. history. For example, heavy drinking was not generally considered to be a serious problem in colonial times (Levine, 1978). In fact, it seemed to be an integral part of daily life. The average amount of alcohol consumed per person each year was much higher in those days than it is today. A typical American in the eighteenth century drank approximately 4 gallons of alcohol a year; the corresponding figure for our own society is about 2.5 gallons (Fingarette, 1988). Drunkenness was not considered to be either socially deviant or symptomatic of medical illness.

Public attitudes toward alcohol changed dramatically in the United States during the first half of the nineteenth century. Members of the temperance movement preached against the consumption of alcohol in any form. Temperance workers ardently believed that anyone who drank alcohol would become a drunkard. Their arguments were largely moral and religious rather than medical or scientific, and many of their publications included essays on the personality weaknesses that were associated with

such morally reprehensible behaviors (Okrent, 2010). The temperance movement was, in fact, able to persuade many thousands of people to abandon the consumption of alcohol.

The movement finally succeeded in banning the manufacture and sale of alcoholic beverages when Congress approved the Eighteenth Amendment to the Constitution in 1919. During the following years, known as the Prohibition era, the average consumption of alcohol fell substantially, and the incidence of associated medical illnesses, such as cirrhosis of the liver, also declined. Nevertheless, these laws were extremely difficult to enforce, and Prohibition was repealed in 1933.

## DSM-5

The diagnostic manual provides definitions of substance-related disorders for 9 different classes of drugs (see Table 11.1). There are two broad types of disorder listed under this broad heading: substance use disorders and substance-induced disorders. Substance use disorders refer to the kinds of problems that come to mind for most of us when we think of someone being addicted to a drug (e.g., alcoholism). The problems that *DSM-5* calls "substance-induced disorders" include primarily the immediate impact of taking a drug (intoxication) or discontinuing its repeated use (withdrawal). *DSM-5* provides separate sets of diagnostic criteria for each different class of substances and for each type of problem under these classes. For example, with regard to alcohol, *DSM-5* lists diagnostic criteria for alcohol use disorder, alcohol intoxication, and alcohol withdrawal. For the sake of efficiency, we will focus on the diagnostic criteria for substance use disorders, and we will not describe the sets of diagnostic criteria for intoxication and withdrawal. You should note, however, that there are some variations across disorders. Caffeine is the only substance listed in *DSM-5* for which the manual does not provide a definition of substance use disorder; it only defines caffeine intoxication and caffeine withdrawal.

The workgroup that prepared the definition of substance use disorders for *DSM-5* collapsed what used to be called *substance dependence* and *substance abuse* into a single definition of substance use disorder with a continuous range of severity. In the case of alcohol, this disorder is called **alcohol use disorder**. The specific features included in the list of criteria are essentially a combination of those formerly used to identify dependence and abuse, with at least two of the total features being required to reach threshold for a diagnosis. The rationale for this change is based on research evidence showing that dependence and abuse are not clearly distinct forms of disorder (Harford, Yi, & Grant, 2010).

The *DSM-5* criteria for alcohol use disorder are presented in "DSM-5: Alcohol Use Disorder." The person has to exhibit at least two of the eleven criteria within a 12-month period of time for a diagnosis of alcohol use disorder to be made. The severity of the disorder is also noted, based on the number of symptoms that are present: mild (2–3 symptoms), moderate (4–5 symptoms), or severe (6 or more symptoms). The first four symptoms listed in "DSM-5: Alcohol Use Disorder" can be described as indicating the person's *impaired control* over use of alcohol. These include persistent and unsuccessful efforts to quit drinking as well as craving for alcohol. The next three symptoms address forms of *social impairment* that follow problematic drinking. Criteria 8 and 9 refer to patterns of *risky use,* such as drinking while driving or continuing to drink in spite of the onset of serious psychological or medical complications. Tolerance and withdrawal, which might be called the *pharmacological criteria,* are the last two symptoms included in the definition of alcohol use disorder. People with a history of tolerance and withdrawal following repeated use of alcohol report more severe drug-related problems, greater intensity of exposure to drugs, and more comorbid conditions such as anxiety and depression (Schuckit, 2010).

*DSM-5* provides separate definitions of substance use disorder for each type of substance. Previous editions of the manual had employed generic definitions of substance dependence and substance abuse that were applied across different drugs, but that approach tended to conceal differences between the kinds of problems that are associated with various classes of drugs (Frances, First, & Pincus, 1995). For example, problematic use of opiates almost always involves pharmacological symptoms of tolerance and withdrawal, whereas repeated use of hallucinogens seldom does. In fact, most of the definitions of substance use disorder are virtually identical.

## Course and Outcome

It is impossible to specify a typical course for substance use disorders, especially alcoholism. Age of onset varies widely, ranging from childhood and early adolescence throughout the life span. Although we can roughly identify stages that intervene between initial exposure

to a drug and the eventual onset of impaired control, evidence of social impairment, and onset of pharmacological symptoms, the timing with which a person moves through these phases can vary enormously. The best available information regarding the course of substance use disorders comes from the study of alcoholism. The specific course of this problem varies considerably from one person to the next. The only thing that seems to be certain is that periods of heavy use alternate with periods of relative abstinence, however short-lived they may be (Schuckit & Smith, 2011).

One influential study regarding the natural history of alcoholism examined the lives of 456 inner-city adolescents from Boston and 268 former undergraduate students from Harvard University (Vaillant, 2003). Initial information was collected in 1940, when the participants were adolescents. Follow-up information was collected every other year by questionnaire and every fifth year by physical examination. The college group has been followed until 70 years of age, and the core city group has been followed to age 60. At some point during their lives, 21 percent of the college men and 35 percent of the core city men met diagnostic criteria for alcohol abuse, which the investigators defined as the presence of four or more problems in such areas as employer complaints, marital and family difficulties, medical complications, and legal problems. As expected, the mortality rate was higher among men who abused alcohol than among those who did not. Heart disease and cancer were twice as common among the alcohol abusers, perhaps in part because they were also more likely to be heavy cigarette smokers.

Most of the alcoholic men went through repeated cycles of abstinence followed by relapse. The life course of alcohol abuse

---

| criteria for Alcohol Use Disorder | DSM-5 |
|---|---|

**A.** A problematic pattern of alcohol use leading to clinically significant impairment or distress, as manifested by at least two of the following, occurring within a 12-month period:

1. Alcohol is often taken in larger amounts or over a longer period than was intended.
2. There is a persistent desire or unsuccessful efforts to cut down or control alcohol use.
3. A great deal of time is spent in activities necessary to obtain alcohol, use alcohol, or recover from its effects.
4. Craving, or a strong desire or urge to use alcohol.
5. Recurrent alcohol use resulting in a failure to fulfill major role obligations at work, school, or home.
6. Continued alcohol use despite having persistent or recurrent social or interpersonal problems caused or exacerbated by the effects of alcohol.
7. Important social, occupational, or recreational activities are given up or reduced because of alcohol use.

8. Recurrent alcohol use in situations in which it is physically hazardous.
9. Alcohol use is continued despite knowledge of having a persistent or recurrent physical or psychological problem that is likely to have been caused or exacerbated by alcohol.
10. Tolerance, as defined by either of the following:
    a. A need for markedly increased amounts of alcohol to achieve intoxication or desired effect.
    b. A markedly diminished effect with continued use of the same amount of alcohol.
11. Withdrawal, as manifested by either of the following:
    a. The characteristic withdrawal syndrome for alcohol (refer to Criteria A and B of the criteria set for alcohol withdrawal, pp. 499–500).
    b. Alcohol (or a closely related substance, such as a benzodiazepine) is taken to relieve or avoid withdrawal symptoms.

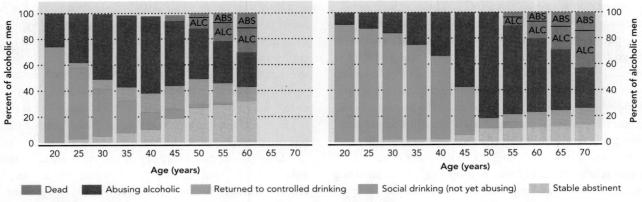

**FIGURE 11.3**

**Drinking Status of Alcoholic Men at Five-Year Intervals**
Results of a long-term follow-up study of two groups of alcoholics: 121 core city men (top) and 46 college men (bottom). The core city men began abusing alcohol at a younger age and were more likely to achieve stable abstinence by age 60.
*Source:* Based on Valliant. 1996. A Long-term Follow-up of Male Alcohol Abuse. Archives of General Psychiatry; 53: 243–249.

could be charted most clearly for 121 of the core city men who abused alcohol and remained in the study until age 60 and 46 college men who abused alcohol and remained in the study until age 70. These data are illustrated in Figure 11.3. In the graphs in Figure 11.3, abstinence is defined as less than one drink per month for more than a year. Social drinking refers to problem-free drinking for 10 years or more. Controlled drinking is more than one drink per month for at least two years with no reported problem. The main differences between the groups were that the core city men began abusing alcohol at an earlier age, and they were also more likely than the college men eventually to achieve stable abstinence. The average age of onset of alcohol abuse was 40 years for the college men and 29 years for the core city men.

Many men spent the previous 20 years alternating between periods of controlled drinking and alcohol abuse. The proportion of men who continued to abuse alcohol went down after the age of 40. The proportion of alcoholic men in both groups who became completely abstinent went up slowly, but consistently during the follow-up period. The longer a man remained abstinent, the greater the probability that he would continue to be abstinent. These data indicate that relapse to alcohol abuse was unlikely among men who were able to remain abstinent for at least six years.

Many important questions remain to be answered about the relapse process. Is there a "safe point" that separates a period of high risk for relapse from a period of more stable change? Data from the study of men in Boston suggest that the six-year mark may be important for men who abuse alcohol. Will this suggestion be replicated in other studies? And does it generalize to other drugs? Do relapse rates stabilize over time? Is an addicted person more likely to succeed on a later attempt to quit than on an early attempt? Answers to these questions will be useful in the development of more effective treatment programs.

## Other Disorders Commonly Associated with Addictions

People with substance use disorders often exhibit other forms of mental disorder as well. Most prominent among these are antisocial personality disorder (ASPD), mood disorders, and anxiety disorders. Conduct disorder (the childhood manifestation of ASPD) is strongly related to concurrent alcohol use in adolescence and the subsequent development of alcohol dependence (McGue & Iacono, 2008). ASPD and alcohol/drug dependence frequently co-occur, and there is evidence to suggest that they represent alternative manifestations of a general predisposition toward behavioral disinhibition (Kendler et al., 2003).

The complexity of the association between substance use disorders and mood/anxiety disorders makes them difficult to untangle (Grant et al., 2006). In some cases, prolonged heavy drinking or use of psychoactive drugs can result in feelings of depression and anxiety. The more the person drinks or uses drugs, the more guilty the person feels about his or her inability to control the problem. In addition, continued use of alcohol and drugs often leads to greater conflict with family members, coworkers, and other people. Sometimes the depression and anxiety precede the onset of the substance use problem. In fact, some people seem to use alcohol and drugs initially in a futile attempt to self-medicate for these other conditions. Ultimately, the drugs make things worse.

## Frequency

Drug-related problems are found in most countries. There are interesting variations, however, in patterns of use for specific types of drugs. The use of specific drugs is determined, in part, by their availability. For example, opium is used most heavily in

Southeast Asia and in some Middle Eastern countries, where the opium poppy is cultivated. Cocaine is used frequently in certain countries of South America where coca trees grow; it is also imported into North America, particularly the United States. Use of cannabis is widespread around the world, in part because the plants can grow in many different climates. In contrast, in Japan, where the amount of land available for cultivation is severely limited, the largest drug problem involves amphetamine, a synthetic drug.

The fact that people in some regions are frequent drug users does not necessarily imply that a particular population will have a high rate of substance dependence. Culture shapes people's choices about the use of drugs and the ways in which they are used. It influences such factors as the amount of a drug that is typically ingested, the route of administration, and the person's beliefs about drug effects (Room, 2007). These considerations, in turn, influence the probability that serious problems will develop. Consider, for example, the Indians of South America who produce coca for market. They have traditionally used the leaves as medicines and in religious ceremonies. They also roll the leaves into a ball that can be tucked in the cheek and sucked for an extended period of time. This form of use relieves cold, hunger, and thirst. It does not produce the severe problems that are associated with the use of refined cocaine, a much more potent drug that can be sniffed or injected.

When we consider the frequency of drug addiction, we must keep in mind the distinction between using a drug and becoming addicted to it. Many people who use drugs do not become dependent on them. Nevertheless, people have to use the drug before they can become dependent, and the age at which they *begin* to use drugs is an important risk factor. For example, the prevalence rate for alcoholism among males who began drinking alcohol before the age of 14 is double than found among males who began drinking at age 18 (McGue et al., 2001). The same pattern is found among women; those who begin to use alcohol at an earlier age have a much higher risk of becoming addicted. It is not clear whether earlier initiation leads directly to increased risk of alcohol use disorder or whether people who are already predisposed toward the development of drinking problems simply start using earlier.

Most people who occasionally use alcohol and illicit drugs do not become addicted. More serious problems almost always develop slowly after extended exposure to a drug. The average time between initial use of illicit drugs and the onset of symptoms of a substance use disorder is between two and three years (Anthony & Helzer, 1991). The distinction between people who eventually become addicted and those who use drugs without becoming addicted is an important consideration in the study of psychopathology.

## Prevalence of Alcohol Use Disorder

Approximately two out of every three males in Western countries drink alcohol regularly, at least on a social basis; less than

Actor Robert Downey Jr. suffered through several years of serious drug-related problems. His successful recovery, which has lasted more than 10 years, offers hope to others who have struggled with similarly challenging additions.

25 percent abstain from drinking completely. Among all men and women who have ever used alcohol, roughly 20 percent will develop serious problems at some point in their lives as a consequence of prolonged alcohol consumption (Anthony, Warner, & Kessler, 1994).

The National Epidemiologic Survey on Alcohol and Related Conditions (NESARC) collected information on substance use disorders and related mental health problems in a nationally representative sample of more than 43,000 adults (Grant et al., 2006). This study provides the most recent, comprehensive evidence regarding the prevalence of alcoholism in the United States. Results from the NESARC study indicate a lifetime prevalence rate of 30 percent for some form of alcohol use disorder (combining the previous categories of alcohol abuse and alcohol dependence from DSM-IV). Alcohol-related disorders are clearly among the most common forms of mental disorder in the United States. These problems most often went untreated; only 24 percent of the men and women who were assigned a diagnosis of alcohol dependence had ever received treatment for these problems.

**GENDER DIFFERENCES** Approximately 60 percent of women in the United States drink alcohol at least occasionally, but, in comparison to men, fewer develop alcoholism. Among people who chronically abuse or become dependent upon alcohol, men outnumber women by a ratio of approximately two to one. Figure 11.4 presents evidence regarding the 12-month prevalence of alcohol use disorder, as defined in *DSM-5,* among men and women who participated in the NESARC study (Agrawal, Heath, & Lynskey, 2011). Notice that, for all age groups, men are much more likely than women to qualify for the diagnosis.

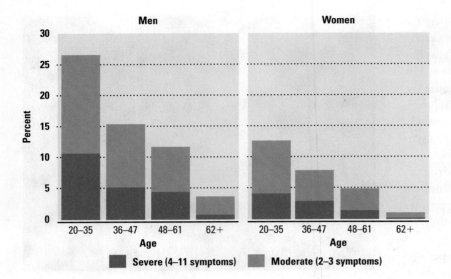

Men

Women

**FIGURE 11.4**

**Gender Differences in Substance Use Disorders**   Lifetime prevalence of substance use disorders in the United States. *Source:* Based on Agrawal, A., Heath, A. C., & Lynskey, M. T. 2011. DSM-IV to DSM-5: The impact of proposed revisions on diagnosis of alcohol use disorders. Addiction; 106: 1935–1943.

Although the rate of alcoholism among younger women has increased, prevalence is still higher in men, and the rates do not seem likely to converge (Grant & Weissman, 2007; Grucza et al., 2008). Persistent differences can probably be attributed to social and biological variables. American culture traditionally has held a negative view of intoxication among women. Social disapproval probably explains why women are more likely than men to drink in the privacy of their own homes, either alone or with another person. Women, therefore, may be less likely than men to drink heavily because the range of situations in which they are expected to drink, or in which they can drink without eliciting social disapproval, is narrower.

Biologically, there are also important gender differences in alcohol metabolism. A single standard dose of alcohol, measured in proportion to total body weight, will produce a higher peak blood alcohol level in women than in men. One explanation for this difference lies in the fact that men have a higher average content of body water than women do. A standard dose of alcohol will be less diluted in women because alcohol is distributed in total body water. This may help to explain the fact that women who drink heavily for many years are more vulnerable to liver disorders than are male drinkers.

## Prevalence of Drug and Nicotine Use Disorders

The National Epidemiologic Survey on Alcohol and Related Conditions (NESARC) also reported the frequency of problems associated with other kinds of drugs (Compton et al., 2007). The combined lifetime prevalence for abuse of or dependence on any type of controlled substance (those that are illegal or available only by prescription) was 10.3 percent. This is approximately one-third the rate for alcohol abuse and dependence. As in the case of alcohol-related disorders, drug abuse and dependence were significantly more common among men than women. Lifetime prevalence rates generated by this study for substance use disorders associated with specific types of drugs are listed in Figure 11.5. Remember that DSM-IV (the diagnostic system used when these data were compiled) recognized two types of addiction, with substance dependence being the most severe and substance abuse being less severe.

The lifetime prevalence of nicotine dependence was reported to be 24 percent in the National Comorbidity Survey (Kessler et al., 1994). The percentage of adults in the United States who smoke tobacco has actually declined since 1964, when the U.S. Surgeon General's Report announced it had found a definite link between smoking and cancer and other

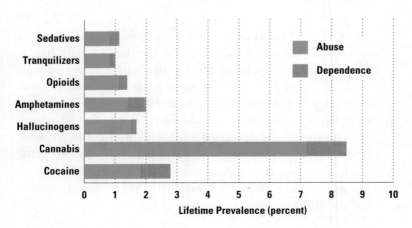

**FIGURE 11.5**

**Frequency of Drug Use Disorders**   Lifetime prevalence of problems associated with specific types of drugs in the United States (using DSM-IV definitions of abuse and dependence). *Source:* Based on data from W. M. Compton, et al. 2007. Prevalence, Correlates, Disabilities, and Comorbidities of DSM-IV Drug Abuse and Dependence in the United States. Archives of General Psychiatry; 64: 566–576.

diseases (see Critical Thinking Matters). The rate of decline has been greatest among men, who traditionally have smoked more than women. Among people between the ages of 18 and 25, however, smoking rates increased during the 1990s (Chaloupka, 2005). Furthermore, although overall tobacco consumption has declined in industrialized countries, it has increased dramatically in the developing countries, where people may be less educated about the health risks associated with smoking (McKim, 2000).

## Risk for Addiction Across the Life Span

Older people do not drink as much alcohol as younger people. The proportion of people who abstain from drinking alcohol is only 22 percent for people in their thirties, goes up to 47 percent for people in their sixties, and is approximately 80 percent for people over 80 years of age. Figure 11.4 illustrates 12-month prevalence rates for *DSM-5* alcohol use disorder in the United States among different age groups. Prevalence rates are substantially higher among young adults and lowest

among the elderly (Hasin et al., 2007). Most elderly alcohol abusers are people who have had drinking problems for many years.

The use of illegal drugs is relatively infrequent among the elderly, but there is a problem associated with their abuse of, and dependence on, prescription drugs and over-the-counter medications, especially hypnotics, sedatives, anxiolytics, and painkillers. The elderly use more legal drugs than do people in any other age group. One estimate suggested that 25 percent of all people over the age of 55 use psychoactive drugs of one kind or another (Beynon, McVeigh, & Roe, 2007). The risk for substance use disorders among the elderly is increased by frequent use of multiple psychoactive drugs combined with enhanced sensitivity to drug toxicity (caused by slowed metabolic breakdown of alcohol and other drugs).

The following case illustrates several issues that are associated with substance use disorders among the elderly, including the abuse of alcohol together with abuse of prescription medications, the presence of prominent symptoms of anxiety and

## CRITICAL THINKING matters

### Should Tobacco Products Be Illegal?

In 1996, the U.S. Food and Drug Administration (FDA) issued a regulation prohibiting the sale and distribution of tobacco products to children and adolescents. They remain legally available to adults. Previous efforts to limit smoking had focused more narrowly on restricting smoking in public places, eliminating cigarette advertisements on television, and increasing sales taxes. The new rule asserted that, as a drug, nicotine should be controlled by the government. The decisions behind this regulation raise a number of critical thinking issues with regard to substance use disorders. How does the FDA decide whether a product is a drug? Should the government control people's access to addicting drugs? If so, what is the best way to control access?

The FDA conducted an extensive investigation to examine the effects of tobacco products and to determine whether they were designed by their manufacturers to deliver nicotine to consumers. Independent research studies as well as documents from the tobacco industry's own laboratories pointed to the conclusion that *nicotine is addictive* (Dreyfuss, 1996). People who use tobacco products clearly develop symptoms of dependence, including tolerance, withdrawal, and a pattern of compulsive use. In fact, nicotine is one of the most addicting drugs, viewed in terms of the high proportion of people who become dependent if they use the drug for some period of time.

After officially recognizing that nicotine is an addicting drug, the FDA could have banned tobacco products entirely (because they are not safe for human consumption). Another option would have been to require a complete elimination of nicotine from cigarettes.

The FDA did not consider these options to be practical or politically viable. Because so many adults are already addicted to nicotine, extensive black markets would spring up immediately, similar to those involved with other illegal drugs. An outright ban on nicotine would fail, just as efforts to ban other drugs have failed (Husak, 2002; MacCoun, Reuter, & Wolf, 2001).

The FDA decided instead to approach the nicotine problem by invoking its authority to regulate medical devices (and treating cigarettes as a type of drug-delivery system). The tobacco regulations imposed by the FDA are *prevention* efforts designed to break the cycle of addiction to nicotine. They prohibit the sale of tobacco products to anyone under 18 years old and also severely restrict advertising (Cooper, 1994). Nicotine addiction almost always begins during adolescence. The FDA regulations are intended to reduce the rate at which young people are recruited to become new smokers and to minimize future health casualties from tobacco use.

This policy represents a moderate and thoughtful approach to the problem of nicotine dependence. It is a compromise between two extreme alternatives: allowing completely open access to a dangerous drug or attempting to ban it completely. Preliminary evidence suggests that the FDA regulations regarding tobacco products have been modestly successful. Between 1997 and 2004, prevalence rates for current smoking among adults in the United States dropped from 25 percent to 21 percent (Schiller et al., 2005). Public policy will not be able to eliminate completely the use of harmful drugs by adults in our society. It can reduce the risk of dependence, however, by minimizing their use at an early age.

depression, and the tendency to deny the extent of their use or abuse of drugs.

### → Ms. E's Drinking

Ms. E is an 80-year-old woman who was brought in for an evaluation by her daughters because they noticed depressive symptoms, appetite disturbance, and memory deficits. She denied all problems related to her daughters' concerns. She had a depressed affect, mild psychomotor agitation, and decrements of recent and remote memory. She was disoriented to time. She verbalized statements of guilt and self-deprecation. She denied ever drinking alcohol, which was corroborated by the daughter with whom she lived but was refuted by her other daughter, who stated that Ms. E drank one or two glasses of brandy almost every day. She had been taking various barbiturates for "nerves" for over 30 years. The dosage she ingested gradually increased over the years, and she frequently took more medications than were prescribed. Because it was unclear if her symptoms were related to her barbiturate use, she reluctantly agreed to be slowly and gradually detoxified. She refused a dementia work-up. Once detoxification was complete, her affect and appetite were improved, but her cognitive deficits were unchanged. Several months later, she and her family dropped out of treatment. She was reportedly drinking brandy, wine, and "hard liquor" every afternoon and evening, with her hired caregiver mixing the drinks (Solomon et al., 1993).

Diagnostic criteria for substance use disorders are sometimes difficult to apply to the elderly, primarily because drug use has somewhat different consequences in their lives. Tolerance to many drugs is reduced among the elderly, and the symptoms of withdrawal may be more severe and prolonged. They are less likely to suffer occupational impairment because they are less frequently employed than younger people. The probability of social impairment may be reduced because elderly people are more likely to live apart from their families.

## Causes

Our discussion of causal factors will focus primarily on alcohol use disorder. We have chosen this approach because clinical scientists know more about alcohol and its abuse than about any of the other drugs. Twin studies also suggest that alcohol dependence and other forms of drug dependence share a common etiology (Kendler & Prescott, 2006). Research on alcohol use disorder illustrates factors that are also important in the etiology of other forms of addiction.

Most contemporary investigators approach the development of alcoholism in terms of multiple systems (Sher, Grekin, & Williams, 2005). Biological factors obviously play an important role. The addicting properties of certain drugs are crucial: People become addicted to drugs like heroin, nicotine, and alcohol, but they do not become addicted to drugs like the antidepressants or to food additives like Nutrasweet. We must, therefore,

understand how addicting drugs affect the brain in order to understand the process of dependence. At the same time, we need to understand the social and cultural factors that influence how and under what circumstances an individual first acquires and uses drugs. Our expectations about the effects of drugs are shaped by our parents, our peers, and the media. These are also important etiological considerations.

The causes of alcoholism are best viewed within a developmental framework that views the problem in terms of various stages: (1) initiation and continuation, (2) escalation and transition to abuse, and (3) development of tolerance and withdrawal (Leonard et al., 2000; Tarter, Vanyukov, & Kirisci, 2008). In the following pages we review some of the social, psychological, and biological factors that explain why people begin to drink, how their drinking behaviors are reinforced, and how they develop tolerance after prolonged exposure.

## Social Factors

People who don't drink obviously won't develop alcoholism, and culture can influence that decision. Some cultures prohibit or actively discourage alcohol consumption. Many Muslims, for example, believe that drinking alcohol is sinful. Other religions encourage the use of small amounts of alcohol in religious ceremonies—such as Jewish people drinking wine at Passover seders—while also showing disdain for those who drink to the point of intoxication (Johnson, 2007). This type of cultural constraint can decrease rates of alcohol use disorder. In one large epidemiological study, for example, Jews had significantly lower rates of alcoholism than Catholics and Protestants (Yeung & Greenwald, 1992).

*Source:* www.cartoonbank.com

Among those young people who choose to drink alcohol (or smoke cigarettes, or consume other addictive substances), which ones will eventually develop problems? The development of addiction requires continued use, and it is influenced by the manner in which the drug is consumed. In other words, with regard to alcohol, will the person's initial reaction to the drug be pleasant, or will he or she become sick and avoid alcoholic beverages in the future? If the person continues drinking, will he or she choose strong or weak drinks, with or without food, with others or alone, and so on?

Several studies have examined social factors that predict substance use among adolescents. Initial experimentation with drugs is most likely to occur among those individuals who are rebellious and extroverted and whose parents and peers model or encourage use (Chassin et al., 2003). The relative influence of parents and friends varies according to the gender and age of the adolescent as well as the drug in question.

Parents can influence their children's drinking behaviors in many ways. They can serve as models for using drugs to cope with stressful circumstances. They may also help promote attitudes and expectations regarding the benefits of drug consumption, or they may simply provide access to licit or illicit drugs (Kirisci et al., 2007). Adolescents with alcoholic parents are more likely to drink alcohol than those whose parents do not abuse alcohol. This increased risk seems to be due to several factors, including the fact that alcoholic parents monitor their children's behavior less closely, thereby providing more opportunities for illicit drinking. Parental monitoring and discipline have an important impact on adolescent substance use; higher parental monitoring is associated with reduced risk of tobacco and alcohol use (Latendresse et al., 2008).

The level of negative affect is also relatively high in the families of alcoholic parents. This unpleasant emotional climate,

The circumstances in which an adolescent is initially exposed to alcohol can influence the person's pattern of drinking. Drinking small amounts of wine with meals or during religious ceremonies may be less likely to lead to alcohol dependence than the sporadic consumption of hard liquor for the purpose of becoming intoxicated.

coupled with reduced parental monitoring, increases the probability that an adolescent will affiliate with peers who use drugs (Chassin & Handley, 2006). Peer and sibling substance use are robust predictors of adolescent alcohol and drug use, even more than parental alcohol use. The impact of friends' alcohol use is greater among adolescent girls than adolescent boys.

## Biological Factors

Initial physiological reactions to alcohol can have a dramatic negative influence on a person's early drinking experiences. For example, millions of people are unable to tolerate even small amounts of alcohol. These people develop flushed skin, sometimes after only a single drink. They may also feel nauseated, and some experience an abnormal heartbeat. This phenomenon is most common among people of Asian ancestry and may affect 30 to 50 percent of this population. The adverse reaction is due to genetic variants in the ADH and ALDH genes, which are involved in the metabolism of alcohol, and are much more common in Asian populations than in other races (Dick & Foroud, 2003). Not coincidentally, the prevalence of alcoholism is unusually low among Asian populations. Research studies indicate a link between these two phenomena. For example, Japanese Americans who experience the fast-flushing response tend to drink less than those who do not flush (Chen & Yin, 2008). The basic evidence suggests that in addition to looking for factors that make some individuals especially vulnerable to the addicting effects of alcohol, it may also be important to identify protective factors that reduce the probability of substance dependence.

A person's initial use of addictive drugs is obviously one important step toward the development of substance dependence, but the fact remains that most people who drink alcohol do not develop alcoholism. What accounts for the next important phase of the disorder? Why do some people abuse the drug while others do not? In the following pages, we outline several additional biological variables. We begin by examining genetic factors, and then we consider the neurochemical effects of the drugs themselves.

**GENETICS OF ALCOHOLISM** An extensive literature attests to the fact that patterns of alcohol consumption, as well as psychological and social problems associated with alcohol abuse, tend to run in families. The lifetime prevalence of alcoholism among the parents, siblings, and children of people with alcoholism is at least three to five times higher than the rate in the general population (MacKillop, McGeary, & Ray, 2010). Of course, this elevated risk among first-degree relatives could reflect the influence of either genetic or environmental factors, because families share both types of influences. Therefore, we must look to the results of twin and adoption studies in an effort to disentangle these variables.

Several twin studies have examined twin concordance rates when the proband meets diagnostic criteria for substance dependence. Concordance rates are higher among MZ than among DZ twin pairs. For example, one study analyzed data from a large sample of twins in Australia. The investigators found concordance rates for alcohol dependence of 56 percent in male MZ twins and 33 percent in male DZ twins (Heath et al., 1997). Corresponding figures for MZ and DZ female twin pairs were 30 percent and 17 percent, respectively. Differences between MZ and DZ concordance rates were significant for both genders. The fact that concordance rates were higher for men than for women reflects the much higher prevalence rate for alcoholism among men. Heritability estimates were the same for both men and women, with approximately two-thirds of the variance in risk for alcoholism being produced by genetic factors.

The strategy followed in an adoption study (see Chapter 2) allows the investigator to separate relatively clearly the influence of genetic and environmental factors. Probands in this type of study are individuals who meet two criteria: (1) They had a biological parent who was alcoholic, and (2) they were adopted from their biological parents at an early age and raised by adoptive parents. Investigators then locate these individuals when they have become adults and determine the frequency of alcoholism as a function of both biological and environmental background. The results of adoption studies are consistent with the data from twin studies and point toward the influence of genetic factors in the etiology of alcohol use disorder (Agrawal & Lynskey, 2008). The offspring of alcoholic parents who are reared by nonalcoholic adoptive parents are more likely than people in the general population to develop drinking problems of their own. Thus, the familial nature of alcoholism is at least partially determined by genes. Being reared by an alcoholic parent, in the absence of other etiological factors, does not appear to be a critical consideration in the development of the disorder.

What exactly is inherited as the predisposition toward alcohol dependence? Some of the genes that influence the risk of developing alcohol dependence are genes involved in the metabolism of alcohol, such as the ADH and ALDH genes (discussed earlier and related to the skin flushing response). Other genes that alter the risk for alcohol dependence may be genes involved in personality traits (Dick, 2007; Spanagel et al., 2010). For example, to the extent that genes influence novelty seeking and sensation seeking, these genes may also increase the person's risk for alcohol dependence because the person is more likely to participate in dangerous patterns of consumption (such as drinking several shots of liquor in rapid succession rather than sipping beer or wine).

**NEUROANATOMY AND NEUROCHEMISTRY** All of the addicting drugs produce changes in the chemical processes by which messages are transmitted in the brain, including systems that involve catecholamines (for example, dopamine, norepinephrine, and serotonin), as well as the neuropeptides. In the following sections, we will outline some of the ways in which psychoactive drugs influence neural transmission and the areas of the brain in which these effects are most pronounced.

***DOPAMINE AND REWARD PATHWAYS*** Scientists who study the biological basis of addiction have devoted a considerable amount of their attention to understanding the rewarding or reinforcing properties of drugs (Koob, 2006; Self & Tamminga, 2004). People may become dependent on psychoactive drugs because they stimulate areas of the brain that are known as "reward pathways" (see Figure 11.6). One primary circuit in this pathway is the medial forebrain bundle, which connects the ventral tegmental area to the nucleus accumbens. Connections

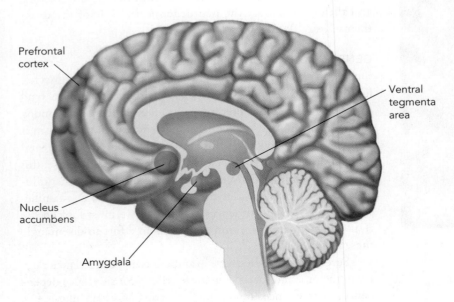

Prefrontal cortex

Ventral tegmenta area

Nucleus accumbens

Amygdala

**FIGURE 11.6**

**Reward Pathways in the Brain** Dopamine neurons in the ventral tegmental area communicate with the nucleus accumbens, which also connects to the prefrontal cortex, an area involved in planning and judgment. This pathway also involves connections to the amygdala, which play an important role in processing emotional reactions.
*Source:* © Pearson Education, Upper Saddle River, New Jersey.

from these structures to the frontal and prefrontal cortex as well as areas of the limbic system, such as the amygdala, also moderate the influence of reward. For many years, scientists have known electrical stimulation of the medial forebrain bundle can serve as a powerful source of positive reinforcement for animals as they perform an operant learning task. Natural rewards, such as food and sex, increase dopamine levels in certain crucial sections of this pathway, which is also known as the *mesolimbic dopamine pathway.*

Drugs of abuse have a dramatic effect on brain reward pathways. Some points at which different drugs influence the dopamine pathway between the ventral tegmental area and the nucleus accumbens are illustrated in Figure 11.7. For example, stimulants such as amphetamine and cocaine affect reward pathways by inhibiting the reuptake of dopamine into nerve terminals. Brain imaging studies with human participants have found that the administration of cocaine increases dopamine concentrations in limbic areas of the brain as well as the medial prefrontal cortex (Tomkins & Sellers, 2001). Furthermore, when people who are dependent on cocaine are exposed to cues that have previously signaled drug use, their medial prefrontal cortex becomes activated, suggesting that this area of the brain is involved in feelings of drug craving. ⊙ **Watch** the **Video** *The Brain's Reward System* on **MyPsychLab**

The effects of alcohol on reward pathways in the brain are more complex and less clearly understood than the effects of many other drugs (Durazzo et al., 2010). Alcohol clearly affects several different types of neurotransmitters. It may stimulate the mesolimbic dopamine pathway directly, or it may act indirectly by decreasing the activity of GABA neurons (which normally inhibit dopamine neurons). Interesting findings from genetic studies support the latter possibility. Several genes that affect GABA reception have been identified as influencing the risk for alcohol dependence (Covault et al., 2004; Radel et al., 2005).

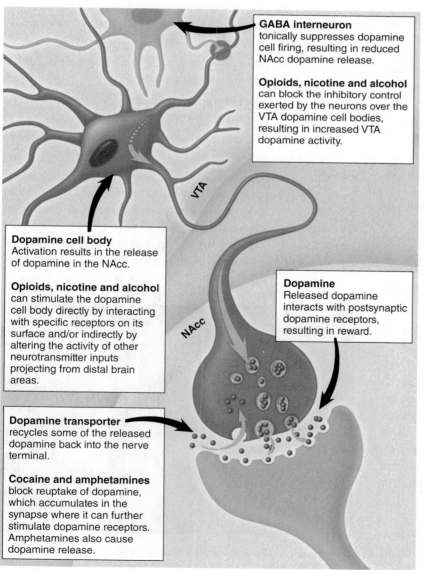

**GABA interneuron**
tonically suppresses dopamine cell firing, resulting in reduced NAcc dopamine release.

**Opioids, nicotine and alcohol**
can block the inhibitory control exerted by the neurons over the VTA dopamine cell bodies, resulting in increased VTA dopamine activity.

**Dopamine cell body**
Activation results in the release of dopamine in the NAcc.

**Opioids, nicotine and alcohol**
can stimulate the dopamine cell body directly by interacting with specific receptors on its surface and/or indirectly by altering the activity of other neurotransmitter inputs projecting from distal brain areas.

**Dopamine**
Released dopamine interacts with postsynaptic dopamine receptors, resulting in reward.

**Dopamine transporter**
recycles some of the released dopamine back into the nerve terminal.

**Cocaine and amphetamines**
block reuptake of dopamine, which accumulates in the synapse where it can further stimulate dopamine receptors. Amphetamines also cause dopamine release.

**FIGURE 11.7**

**Neurochemical Mechanisms of Drug Action**  Effects of psychoactive drugs on dopamine activity in reward pathway from the ventral tegmental area (VTA) to the nucleus accumbens (NAcc).

*Source*: Based on D. M. Tomkins and E. M. Sellers. 2001. Addiction and the Brain: The Role of Neurotransmitters in the Cause and Treatment of Drug Dependence. Canadian Medical Association Journal; 164: 817–821.

***ENDOGENOUS OPIOID PEPTIDES*** One of the most interesting and important advances in neuroscience research was the discovery of the endogenous opioids known as **endorphins** and enkephalins. These relatively short chains of amino acids, or *neuropeptides,* are naturally synthesized in the brain and are closely related to morphine in their pharmacological properties. Opioid peptides possess a chemical affinity for specific receptor sites, in the same way that a key fits into a specific lock. Several types of opioid peptides are distributed widely throughout the brain. They appear to be especially important in the activities associated with systems that control pain, emotion, stress, and reward, as well as such biological functions as feeding and growth (Froehlich, 1997).

Research studies have demonstrated many interesting features of the endorphins. Laboratory animals can develop tolerance to injections of endorphins, just as they develop tolerance to addicting drugs like morphine, and they also exhibit symptoms of withdrawal if the injections are suddenly discontinued. These studies confirm the pharmacological similarity between endogenous and exogenous opioids.

Some theorists associate alcoholism with exaggerated activation of the endogenous opioid system in response to alcohol stimulation (Gianoulakis, DeWaele, & Thavundayil, 1996). Several lines of evidence support this hypothesis. One is that opioid receptor antagonists (drugs that block the effects of opioid peptides) produce a decrease in alcohol self-administration in laboratory animals. Another important bit of information comes from drug trials with human participants: When alcoholic patients take naltrexone, an antagonist of endogenous opioids, they drink less alcohol and report that the subjective "high" associated with drinking is noticeably diminished (see the section on treatment with medication, later in this chapter). Finally, in both rodents and humans, a genetic predisposition toward increased consumption of alcohol is associated with high levels of opioid system response to the ingestion of alcohol (Froehlich, 1997). For all of these reasons, it seems likely that endogenous opioid peptides are somehow involved in mediating alcohol dependence.

## Psychological Factors

Genetic factors and neurochemistry undoubtedly account for many of the problems associated with addictive drugs, but as the systems perspective indicates, biological explanations are not incompatible with psychological ones. In fact, extensive research over the past several decades has found that the progression of substance use disorders depends on an interaction between psychological and biological factors. Drug effects interact with the person's beliefs and attitudes, as well as with the social context in which the drugs are taken.

**EXPECTATIONS ABOUT DRUG EFFECTS** Placebo effects demonstrate that expectations are an important factor in any study of drug effects (see Chapter 3). This is certainly true in the case of alcohol. Expectations account for many effects that are sometimes assumed to be products of the drug itself (Moss & Albery, 2009). For example, subjects who believed that they had ingested alcohol but who had actually consumed only tonic water display exaggerated aggression and report enhanced feelings of sexual arousal (Testa et al., 2006). Much less is known about expectancies for drugs other than alcohol, but there is good reason to believe that these cognitive factors also influence the ways in which people respond to cannabis, nicotine, stimulants, anxiolytics, and sedatives.

Many studies have examined the specific nature of alcohol expectancies (Nicolai et al., 2010). Investigators asked people, Why do you drink? What do you expect to happen after you have consumed a few beers or a couple of glasses of wine? Subjects' answers to these questions fit into six primary categories:

1. Alcohol transforms experiences in a positive way (for example: Drinking makes the future seem brighter).

2. Alcohol enhances social and physical pleasure (for example: Having a few drinks is a nice way to celebrate special occasions).

3. Alcohol enhances sexual performance and experience (for example: After a few drinks, I am more sexually responsive).

4. Alcohol increases power and aggression (for example: After a few drinks, it is easier to pick a fight).

5. Alcohol increases social assertiveness (for example: Having a few drinks makes it easier to talk to people).

6. Alcohol reduces tension (for example: Alcohol enables me to fall asleep more easily).

These expectations may constitute one of the primary reasons for continued and increasingly heavy consumption of alcoholic beverages. In fact, expectancy patterns can help predict drinking behaviors. Longitudinal studies have found that adolescents who are just beginning to experiment with alcohol and who initially have the most positive expectations about the

Common expectations about the effects of drinking alcohol include the notion that it enhances sexual arousal and experience.

effects of alcohol go on to consume greater amounts of alcoholic beverages (Smith et al., 1995). This type of demonstration is important because it indicates that, in many cases, the expectations appear before the person begins to drink heavily. Therefore, expectations may play a role in the onset of the problem rather than being consequences of heavy drinking (see Research Methods).

Where do these expectations come from, and when do they develop? In some cases they may arise from personal experiences with alcohol, but they can also be learned indirectly. Many adolescents hold strong beliefs about the effects of alcohol long before they take their first drink. These expectations are influenced by a variety of environmental factors, including parental and peer attitudes as well as the portrayal of alcohol in the mass media (Agrawal & Lynskey, 2008). Follow-up studies have demonstrated that adolescents' expectations about the effects of alcohol are useful in predicting which individuals will later develop drinking problems (Jones, Corbin, & Fromme, 2001). Positive expectancies about alcohol, which are likely to encourage people to drink, are especially influential. Negative expectancies are associated with diminished use but seem to be less powerful.

## Integrated Systems

Alcoholism and other forms of addiction clearly result from an interaction among several types of systems. Various social, psychological, and biological factors influence the person's behavior at each stage in the cycle, from initial use of the drug through the eventual onset of tolerance and withdrawal.

## RESEARCH methods

### Studies of People at Risk for Disorders

We have used the term *risk* informally throughout this book to refer to a hazard—the possibility of suffering harm. In scientific research, a risk is a statement about the probability that a certain outcome will occur. For example, the NCS found that the risk that a person in the United States will develop alcoholism at some point in his or her life is about 14 in 100. The combined risk for all types of illegal and controlled substances (such as cannabis, cocaine, heroin, and barbiturates) is about 8 in 100. The concept of risk implies only probability, not certainty. Someone who is "at risk" may or may not suffer harm, depending on many other events and circumstances. For example, men are at greater risk than women for the development of alcoholism, but that does not mean that all men will become alcoholics.

*Risk factors* are variables that are associated with a higher probability of developing a disorder. Notice that this use of the term risk implies association, not causality. The concept of risk simply reflects a correlation between the risk factor and the disorder. Some risk factors are demographic variables, such as gender and race. Others are biological and psychological variables. In the case of alcoholism, and many other types of psychopathology, family history of the disorder is an important risk factor. Expectancies about the effects of drugs represent another important risk factor for alcoholism. People who expect that alcohol will reduce tension or transform experiences in a positive way are more likely to drink frequently and heavily than those who have negative expectancies about the effects of alcohol.

In order to determine whether certain risk factors might play a *causal* role in the development of the disorder, it is often necessary to conduct longitudinal studies (see Research Methods in Chapter 8). The investigator collects information about each person before the onset of the disorder. He or she can therefore determine whether the risk factor is present before or only after the onset of symptoms. In other words, do people believe that alcohol reduces tension before they start to drink heavily, or do they develop this belief after they have been drinking heavily for some time? Longitudinal studies can be extremely expensive, and often they take several years to complete. They also require large numbers of participants because everyone in the study will not go on to develop the disorder in question.

Some of these shortcomings of longitudinal studies are especially relevant to research on substance abuse disorders. The risk for developing such disorders is quite low in the general population. For example, even though alcoholism is one of the most prevalent forms of mental disorder, a longitudinal study that follows the development of 100 randomly selected people from childhood to middle age will find only about 14 alcoholic adults (based on NCS data). Thus, to collect a useful amount of data, researchers need to study a large sample, which can be very expensive.

Recognition of this problem led scientists to develop special methods to increase the productivity of longitudinal research. One important technique is the **high-risk research design**. In high-risk research, subjects are selected from the general population based on a well-documented risk factor (Knop et al., 2003; Tarter & Vanyukov, 2001). A number of risk factors might be used to select subjects: positive family history for a given disorder, the presence of certain psychological characteristics, or perhaps a set of demographic variables such as age, gender, and/or race. High-risk research studies are designed to follow their participants over time, beginning before the onset of serious disorders. They hope to identify factors that increase or decrease the probability that people who are vulnerable to a disorder will eventually develop its active symptoms.

Furthermore, it appears that different influences are important at different stages of use. The process seems to progress in the following way. Initial experimentation with drugs is influenced by the environment—the person's family, peers, school, and neighborhood (Rhee et al., 2003). Other people also influence the person's attitudes and expectations about the effects of drugs. Access to drugs, in addition to the patterns in which they are originally consumed, is determined, in part, by cultural factors.

For many people, drinking alcohol leads to short-term positive effects that reinforce continued consumption. The exact psychological mechanisms that are responsible for reinforcing heavy drinking may take several different forms. They may involve diminished self-awareness, stress reduction, or improved mood. These effects of alcohol on behavior and subjective experience are determined, in part, by the person's expectations about the way in which the drug will influence his or her feelings and behavior (Baer, 2002).

Genetic factors play an important role in the etiology of alcoholism. After the person has begun to use alcohol, genetic factors become increasingly important in shaping patterns of use (Dick et al., 2007). There are most likely several different types of genetic influences. Genes interact strongly with environmental events for certain types of the disorders. A genetic predisposition to alcohol dependence probably causes the person to react to alcohol in an abnormal fashion. It is not clear whether those who are vulnerable to alcoholism are initially more or less sensitive than other people to the reinforcing effects of alcohol. Research studies have demonstrated both patterns of response (Sher, Grekin, & Williams, 2005).

The biological mechanisms responsible for abnormal reactions to alcohol seem to involve several interrelated neurotransmitter systems (Hyman & Malenka, 2001). Dopamine activity in the brain's reward pathway is stimulated by alcohol as well as other drugs of abuse. Another important consideration may be a deficiency in serotonin activity in certain areas of the limbic system. Drinking alcohol initially corrects this problem and increases serotonin activity, but the person eventually begins to feel worse after tolerance develops.

Drinking gradually becomes heavier and more frequent. The person becomes tolerant to the effects of alcohol and must drink larger quantities to achieve the same reinforcing effects. After he or she becomes addicted to alcohol, attempts to quit drinking are accompanied by painful withdrawal symptoms. Prolonged abuse can lead to permanent neurological impairment, as well as the disruption of many other organ systems.

## Treatment

The treatment of alcoholism and other types of substance use disorders is an especially difficult task. Many people with substance use disorders do not acknowledge their difficulties, and only a relatively small number seek professional help. When they do enter treatment, it is typically with reluctance or on the insistence of friends, family members, or legal authorities. Compliance with treatment recommendations is often low, and dropout rates are high. The high rate of comorbidity with other forms of mental disorder presents an additional challenge, complicating the formulation of a treatment plan. Treatment outcome is likely to be least successful with those people who have comorbid conditions.

The goals of treatment for substance use disorders are a matter of controversy. Some clinicians believe that the only acceptable goal is total abstinence from drinking or drug use. Others have argued that, for some people, a more reasonable goal is the moderate use of legal drugs. Important questions have also been raised about the scope of improvements that might be expected from a successful treatment program. Is the goal simply to minimize or eliminate drug use, or should we expect that treatment will also address the social, occupational, and medical problems that are typically associated with drug problems? Getting Help at the end of this chapter offers additional resources for those seeking help and information on recovering from substance abuse.

## Detoxification

Alcoholism and related forms of drug abuse are chronic conditions. Treatment is typically accomplished in a sequence of stages, beginning with a brief period of **detoxification**—the removal of a drug on which a person has become dependent—for three to six weeks (Coombs, Howatt, & Coombs, 2005). This process is often extremely difficult, as the person experiences marked symptoms of withdrawal and gradually adjusts to the absence of the drug. For many types of CNS depressants, such as alcohol, hypnotics, and sedatives, detoxification is accomplished gradually. Stimulant drugs, in contrast, can be stopped abruptly (Schuckit, 2005). Although detoxification usually takes place in a hospital, some evidence indicates that it can be accomplished with close supervision on an outpatient basis.

People who are going through alcohol detoxification are often given various types of medications, including benzodiazepines and anticonvulsants, primarily as a way of minimizing withdrawal symptoms (O'Brien & McKay, 2007). This practice is controversial, in part because many people believe that it is illogical to use one form of drug, especially one that can be abused itself, to help someone recover from dependence on another drug.

## Medications During Remission

Following the process of detoxification, treatment efforts are aimed at helping the person maintain a state of remission. The best outcomes are associated with stable, long-term abstinence from drinking. Several forms of medication are used to help the person achieve this goal.

Disulfiram (Antabuse) is a drug that can block the chemical breakdown of alcohol. It was introduced as a treatment for alcoholism in Europe in 1948 and is still used fairly extensively (Fuller & Gordis, 2004). If a person who is taking disulfiram consumes even a small amount of alcohol, he or she will become violently ill. The symptoms include nausea, vomiting, profuse sweating, and increased heart rate and respiration rate. People who are taking disulfiram will stop drinking alcohol in order to avoid this extremely unpleasant reaction. Unfortunately, voluntary compliance with this form of treatment is poor. Many patients discontinue taking disulfiram, usually because they want to resume drinking or because they believe that they can manage their problems without the drug.

Naltrexone (Revia) is an antagonist of endogenous opioids that has been found to be useful in the treatment of alcohol dependence following detoxification. Research studies have demonstrated that patients who received naltrexone and psychotherapy are less likely to relapse than patients who receive psychotherapy plus a placebo (Carmen et al., 2004). Some clinical patients report that, if they drink while also taking naltrexone, they do not feel as "high" as they would without naltrexone. Naltrexone may dampen the person's craving by blocking alcohol's ability to stimulate the opioid system. In other words, it works by reducing the rewarding effects of alcohol rather than by inducing illness if the person drinks.

Another promising medication for treating alcoholism is acamprosate (Campral). An extensive body of evidence indicates that people taking acamprosate are able to reduce their average number of drinking days by 30 percent to 50 percent (Mann, Lehert, & Morgan, 2004). It also increases the proportion of people who are able to achieve total abstinence (approximately 22 percent among people taking acamprosate and 12 percent taking placebo after 12 months of treatment). Like naltrexone, acamprosate is intended to be used in conjunction with a psychological treatment program. The dropout rate is very high without these added features (Hart, McCance-Katz, & Kosten, 2001; Malcolm, 2003).

Psychiatrists also use SSRIs, such as fluoxetine, for the long-term treatment of alcoholic patients. Outcome studies suggest that SSRIs have small and inconsistent effects in reducing drinking among those patients who are not also depressed. They do seem to be effective, however, for the treatment of people with a dual diagnosis of alcohol dependence and major depression (O'Brien & McKay, 2002).

## Self-Help Groups: Alcoholics Anonymous

One of the most widely accepted forms of treatment for alcoholism is Alcoholics Anonymous (AA). Organized in 1935, this self-help program is maintained by alcohol abusers for the sole purpose of helping other people who abuse alcohol become and remain sober. Because it is established and active in virtually all communities in North America and Europe, as well as

Group therapy is an important part of most inpatient treatment programs. It offers an opportunity for patients to acknowledge and confront openly the severity of their problems.

in many other parts of the world, AA is generally considered to be "the first line of attack against alcoholism" (Nathan, 1993). Many members of AA are also involved in other forms of treatment offered by various types of mental health professionals, but AA is not officially associated with any other form of treatment or professional organization. Similar self-help programs have been developed for people who are dependent on other drugs, such as opioids (Narcotics Anonymous) and cocaine (Cocaine Anonymous).

The viewpoint espoused by AA is fundamentally spiritual in nature (Kaskutas et al., 2003). AA is the original 12-step program. In the first step, the person must acknowledge that he or she is powerless over alcohol and unable to manage his or her drinking. The remaining steps involve spiritual and interpersonal matters such as accepting "a Power greater than ourselves" that can provide the person with direction; recognizing and accepting personal weaknesses; and making amends for previous errors, especially instances in which the person's drinking caused hardships for other people. One principal assumption is that people cannot recover on their own (Emrick, 1999).

The process of working through the 12 steps to recovery is facilitated by regular attendance at AA meetings, as often as every day of the first 90 days after the person stops drinking. Most people choose to attend less frequently if they are able to remain sober throughout this initial period. Meetings provide chronic alcohol abusers with an opportunity to meet and talk with other people who have similar problems, as well as something to do instead of having a drink. New members are encouraged to call more experienced members for help at any time if they experience an urge to drink. There is enormous variability in the format and membership of local AA meetings (Montgomery, Miller, & Tonigan, 1993).

It is difficult to evaluate the effectiveness of AA, for a number of reasons. Long-term follow-up is difficult, and it is generally impossible to employ some of the traditional methods of outcome research, such as random assignment to groups and placebo controls. Early dropout rates are relatively high: About half of all the people who initially join AA leave in less than three months. On the other hand, survival rates (defined in terms of continued sobriety) are much higher for those people who remain in AA. About 80 percent of AA members who have remained sober for between two and five years will remain sober in the next year (Tonigan, Connors, & Miller, 2003).

## Cognitive Behavior Therapy

Psychological approaches to substance use disorders have often focused on cognitive and behavioral responses that trigger episodes of drug abuse. In the case of alcoholism, heavy drinking has been viewed as a learned, maladaptive response that some people use to cope with difficult problems or to reduce anxiety. Cognitive behavior therapy teaches people to identify and respond more appropriately to circumstances that regularly precipitate drug abuse (Finney & Moos, 2002).

**COPING SKILLS TRAINING** One element of cognitive behavior therapy involves training in the use of social skills, which might be used to resist pressures to drink heavily. It also includes problem-solving procedures, which can help the person both to identify situations that lead to heavy drinking and to formulate alternative courses of action. Anger management is one example. Some people drink in response to frustration. Through careful instruction and practice, people can learn to express negative emotions in constructive ways that will be understood by others. The focus in this type of treatment is on factors that initiate and maintain problem drinking rather than the act of drinking itself.

Cognitive events also play an important part in this approach to treatment. Expectations about the effects of alcohol are challenged, and more adaptive thoughts are rehearsed. Negative patterns of thinking about the self and events in the person's environment are also addressed because they are linked to unpleasant emotions that trigger problem drinking.

**RELAPSE PREVENTION** Most people who have been addicted to a drug will say that quitting is the easy part of treatment. The more difficult challenge is to maintain this change after it has been accomplished. Unfortunately, most people will slip up and return to drinking soon after they stop. The same thing can be said for people who stop smoking or using any other drug of abuse. These slips often lead to a full-scale return to excessive and uncontrolled use of the drug. Successful treatment, therefore, depends on making preparations for such incidents.

Relapse prevention is a cognitive behavioral approach to treatment view that has been applied to all forms of substance use disorder, ranging from alcoholism to nicotine addiction (Marlatt, Blume, & Parks, 2001; Shiffman et al., 1996; Witkiewitz, Marlatt, & Walker, 2005). It has also been applied to other disorders associated with impulsive behavior, such as bulimia and inappropriate sexual behaviors (see Chapters 10 and 12). It places principal emphasis on events that take place after detoxification and is aimed at helping the addict to deal with the challenges of life without drugs. The therapist helps patients learn more adaptive coping responses, such as applied relaxation and social skills, that can be used in situations that formerly might have triggered drug use.

One important feature of the relapse prevention model is concerned with the *abstinence violation effect,* which refers to the guilt and perceived loss of control that the person feels whenever he or she slips and finds himself or herself having a drink (or a cigarette or whatever drug is involved) after an extended period of abstinence. People typically blame themselves for failing to live up to their promise to quit. They also interpret the first drink or use of the drug as a signal that further efforts to control their drinking will be useless. The following brief case study describes one man's thoughts and feelings, shortly after he returned to the use of heroin. Just prior to this relapse, he had been actively involved in a treatment program and had stayed "clean" for several months.

### ⟶ Relapse to Heroin Use

It was like goin' home," he tells me later, "and mom's got your favorite dish on the stove, and you smell it, to the back of your tongue, way back. That's the rush of the dope. It's right there, and for like two, three minutes I'm floating. I get up and lay down in my bed, put on the (music) again."

He slams his fist on his knee. "I can't believe how bad I (screwed) up," Mike wails through his tears. "Damn! I know what happened ain't nobody's fault but mine, and I'm eating myself up over it. I'm scared out of my mind. I mean, it's like I'm afraid of myself. So where do I go with that if they kick me out? How do I stay off the dope if I'm alone again?"

## MyPsychLab VIDEO CASE

### Compulsive Gambling

Ed

*"My mother was on her deathbed. Her words to me were, 'You've got to stop gambling. It's ruining your life. You'll lose everything.' She died the following day, and I spent the next year of my life proving her right. I did lose everything."*

👁 **Watch** the **Video** *Ed: Gambling Disorder* on **MyPsychLab**

As you watch the interview and the day-in-the-life segments, ask yourself what purpose Ed's gambling seemed to play in his life. How was his preoccupation with gambling different from a serious commitment to a career or a hobby?

Mike looks up, his eyes wide, wet with tears.

"Maybe what they say is true, I'm already a junkie again. It's too late. But I did just one hit, that's all. And I can't be doing more dope, I know that. If I go on a real run of heroin this time, I won't come back, ever. I've seen it now—I can blow it, I *can* relapse, I *can* die. Damn! This is the time I need help more than ever, and this is when they're going to kick me out" (Shavelson, 2001, pp. 161 and 166)

......................................................................................

Relapse prevention programs are aimed at exactly this type of conflict. They teach patients to expect that they may slip occasionally and to interpret these behaviors as a temporary "lapse" rather than a total "relapse."

**SHORT-TERM MOTIVATIONAL THERAPY** Many people with substance use disorders do not seek or take full advantage of treatment opportunities because they fail to recognize the severity of their problems. Motivational interviewing is a nonconfrontational procedure that can be used to help people resolve their ambivalence about using drugs and make a definite commitment to change their behavior (Miller, 1995). It is based on the notion that in order to make a meaningful change, people must begin by recognizing the inconsistency between their current behavior and their long-term goals. For example, chronic heavy drinking is not compatible with academic or occupational success.

Motivational interviewing begins with a discussion of problems—issues reported by the patient as well as concerns that have been expressed by others such as friends and family members. The person is asked to reflect on feedback that is provided in a nonthreatening way. Rather than confronting the person, arguing about the reasons for drinking, or demanding action, the therapist responds empathically in an effort to avoid or minimize defensive reactions that will interfere with attempts to change.

The primary goal of this process is to increase the person's awareness of the nature of his or her substance use problems. Central features of motivational interviewing include a comprehensive assessment of the situation and personalized feedback. Emphasis is placed on ways in which the person sees his or her problems rather than assigning diagnostic labels, such as "alcoholism." Various options for creating change are discussed. The therapist and the patient work together to select the most appropriate method to follow. This stage of the interaction is designed to encourage the person's belief in his or her own ability to accomplish positive change.

Motivational interviewing may be most helpful to people whose substance abuse problems are not yet severe or chronic. It can be used as a stand-alone intervention or in combination with other approaches to treatment. If the person is not ready to abstain completely, short-term motivational therapy can be used to help the person reduce the frequency or intensity of alcohol consumption (Roberts & Marlatt, 1999).

## Outcome Results and General Conclusions

Although many studies have evaluated the effects of alcohol treatment programs, two deserve special attention because of their large sample sizes and the rigorous methods that the investigators employed. One is known as Project MATCH because it was designed to test the potential value of matching certain kinds of clients to specific forms of treatment (Babor & Del Boca, 2003). In other words, would the outcomes associated with different forms of intervention be related to certain characteristics of the patients (such as the presence or absence of antisocial personality traits)?

The study evaluated three forms of psychological treatment: cognitive behavior therapy (12 sessions focused on coping skills and relapse prevention), 12-step facilitation therapy (12 sessions designed to help patients become engaged in AA), and motivational enhancement therapy (four sessions over 12 weeks designed to increase commitment to change). Most of the people in all three groups attended at least some AA meetings in addition to their assigned form of treatment. More than 1,700 patients were randomly assigned to one of these three conditions. Outcome measures were collected for three years after the end of treatment.

Results indicated that all three forms of treatment led to major improvements in amount of drinking as well as other areas of life functioning (Miller & Longabaugh, 2003). Before treatment, patients in this study averaged 25 drinking days per month. After treatment, they averaged fewer than six days per month (across all forms of treatment). Very few differences were found between the different treatment methods. The one exception favored 12-step facilitation therapy, in which 24 percent of patients were completely abstinent one year after treatment, compared to approximately 15 percent in the other two groups. Analyses that focused on the characteristics of individual clients suggested that there is relatively little reason to try to match certain kinds of patients to specific forms of treatment.

The second study involved a naturalistic evaluation of substance abuse treatment programs administered at 15 sites by the Department of Veterans Affairs (VA) (Finney, Moos, & Humphreys, 1999; Moos et al., 1999). The VA study compared programs that emphasized three approaches to the treatment of substance use disorders: 12-step programs, cognitive behavior therapy, and "eclectic therapy" (a combination of several approaches). The study included more than 3,000 patients. Most of these people had a diagnosis of alcohol dependence, but many also abused other types of drugs. Unlike Project MATCH, they were not randomly assigned to treatments. Despite these differences in methodology, results of the VA study were very similar to those obtained in Project MATCH. Patients in all three groups made significant improvements with regard to both patterns of substance use and levels of social and occupational functioning. People who participated in more treatment sessions had better outcomes than people who received less treatment. When differences were found between different forms of treatment, they tended to favor the 12-step programs. No support was found for the assumption that certain types of patients would do better in one form of treatment than in another.

Comprehensive reviews of these studies and the rest of the research literature regarding treatment of alcoholism and drug abuse point to several general conclusions (Amato et al., 2011; Glasner-Edwards & Rawson, 2010):

- People who enter treatment for various types of substance abuse and dependence typically show improvement in terms of reduced drug use that is likely to persist for several months following the end of treatment. Unfortunately, relapse is also relatively common.

- There is little evidence to suggest that one form of treatment (inpatient or outpatient, professional or self-help, individual or group) is more effective than another. When differences have been found, they tend to favor self-help groups, such as AA, particularly in terms of success in achieving abstinence.

- There is only limited support for the assumption that certain kinds of patients do better in one kind of treatment than another (the matching hypothesis).

- Increased amount of treatment and greater frequency of attendance in self-help meetings and aftercare counseling are associated with better outcomes.

- Among those people who are able to reduce their consumption of drugs, or abstain altogether, improvements following

treatment are usually not limited to drug use alone but extend to the person's health in general as well as his or her social and occupational functioning.

Long-term outcome for the treatment of alcoholism is best predicted by the person's coping resources (social skills and problem-solving abilities), the availability of social support, and the level of stress in the environment. These considerations appear to be more important than the specific type of intervention that people receive. Those individuals who are in less stressful life situations, whose families are more cohesive and less supportive of continued drinking, and who are themselves better equipped with active coping skills are most likely to sustain their improvement over several years.

## Gambling Disorder

While no one doubts that pathological gambling can be an extremely debilitating condition, the classification of this disorder has been somewhat confusing and inconsistent. In DSM-IV, it was included with impulse control disorders. The authors of *DSM-5* moved it to the chapter on substance-related and addictive disorders (see Thinking Critically about DSM-5) based in part on the observation that people with serious gambling problems frequently suffer from various substance use disorders as well (Lorains, Cowlishaw, Thomas, 2011; Milosevic & Ledgerwood, 2010). Some of the

## THINKING CRITICALLY about DSM-5

### Is Pathological Gambling an Addiction?

Many forms of psychopathology entail excessive behaviors. The persistent, harmful use of drugs is one obvious example. Mental health professionals are also concerned about an even more heterogeneous class of problems that is defined by excessive behaviors, ranging from binge eating (see Chapter 10) to hoarding and hair-pulling (see Chapter 6) and pathological gambling. At various times, all of these problems have been described informally as *behavioral addictions*. That terminology became official in *DSM-5*, where pathological gambling is now listed in the chapter on "Substance-Related and Addictive Disorders." This is an important and controversial development. The fact that one type of behavioral addiction appears in *DSM-5* will almost certainly open the door for the inclusion of others as the manual is revised. Serious consideration has already been given to excessive Internet gaming, sexual behavior, shopping, and exercise as possible forms of mental disorder. Should this expansion of the diagnostic manual be welcomed or encouraged? We think not, for several important reasons (Petry, 2006; Stein, 2008; Wilson, 2010).

One issue should be obvious. Substance use disorders involve repeated exposure of the brain to toxic chemicals, and behavioral

addictions do not. Substance use disorders frequently involve physiological mechanisms known as tolerance and withdrawal. It is less clear that these effects play an important role in the progression of pathological gambling and other behavioral addictions. Over the course of time, chronic abuse of drugs must surely involve some unique problems that will distinguish substance use disorders from other forms of excessive behavior.

Second, it is important to be careful about the meaning of specific terms in describing symptoms of psychopathology. Lumping these problems together may have the opposite effect. Some clinicians refer to *compulsive* gambling. Others talk about gambling *addiction*. And the previous version of the diagnostic manual listed pathological gambling as a type of *impulse control* disorder. These terms have all become part of our everyday language, and the vague ways in which they are used can make it hard for us to think precisely about the nature of these problems. All of the terms imply a generic loss of control over behavior as well as some kind of failure to anticipate or avoid the negative consequences of self-damaging behaviors. But the mechanisms that presumably maintain the problem behavior vary from one concept to the next. Compulsions are repetitive

*"'GameBoy: A Memoir of Addiction,' by Ronald Markowitz."*

Source: Ronald Markowitz/The New Yorker Collection/www.cartoonbank.com

behaviors that serve to *reduce anxiety* (typically anxiety caused by obsessions). Impulsive behaviors, on the other hand, typically imply failure to *resist temptation* to engage in a behavior that is pleasurable, such as eating or having sex. Compulsive behaviors are not associated with pleasure. Addictions are often performed in an effort to *relieve signs of withdrawal*, which are typically unpleasant physiological symptoms. It is not clear that behavioral addictions are associated with physiological symptoms of withdrawal. Using these terms as if they are interchangeable can lead to confusion.

You may be asking yourself, "What difference does it make?" At this stage of our science, these models imply different ways to study this set of problems as well as different avenues for treatment. The rationale presented in *DSM-5* for the inclusion of gambling disorder with substance use disorders is that these behaviors all activate reward pathways in the brain (see Figure 11.7). That's obviously an important consideration, but it's also premature to assume that our understanding of neural reward pathways provides a complete or precise guide to the nature of these problems.

Perhaps more to the point, the term "addiction" implies an absence of responsibility for one's behavior. This makes sense in the case of chemical addictions, although some would not call alcohol and drug abuse addictions for this reason. One persuasive argument suggests that alcoholism is best viewed as a *central activity*, in other words, a set of interests and patterns of behavior that motivate the person's identity, behavior, and life choices. "Heavy drinkers are people who have over time made a long and complex series of decisions, judgments, and choices of commission and omission that have coalesced into a central activity. . . . Instead of viewing heavy drinkers as the helpless victims of a disease, we come to see their drinking as a meaningful, however destructive, part of their struggle to live their lives (Fingarette, 1988, pp. 102–103).

Gambling, eating, sex, shopping, and many other behaviors surely are problematic when taken to extremes. Does this make them addictions? Are some people truly not responsible for these actions? We think this is a philosophical question more than a scientific one, a decision that is better made by law and society than by the DSM (Young, 2013). Yet, our real question is: What do you think?

symptoms of gambling disorder are also shared with problems such as alcoholism, including preoccupation with activities related to gambling and frequent, unsuccessful attempts to quit.

Most gambling is not associated with a mental disorder. Social gambling is a form of recreation that is accepted in most cultures. Professional gambling is an occupation pursued by people whose gambling is highly disciplined. Pathological gambling, in contrast, is out of control, takes over the person's life, and leads to horrendous financial and interpersonal consequences.

## Symptoms

Like various kinds of substance use disorders, the central features of gambling disorder center around impaired control of gambling activities, social impairment that follows from gambling (such as loss of jobs or relationships), and continued problem behavior in spite of the accumulation of harmful consequences.

One feature that is unique to gambling disorder, in comparison to substance use disorders, is *chasing losses*. This expression refers to the process of trying to win back money that has already been lost. Many people who gamble socially begin by setting a financial limit for themselves; if they lose that money, they quit. In pathological gambling, people frequently follow initial losses by betting even greater amounts of money (while telling themselves and others that they will quit as soon as they win big). Needless to say, this process is almost always futile and results in even greater losses.

Experiences that are similar to tolerance and withdrawal have been reported among people with serious gambling problems. Some report, for example, that they felt compelled to gamble with increased stakes in order to achieve the same emotional effects. It is important to note, however, that chasing losses could be somewhat difficult to distinguish from tolerance effects.

Investigators have also reported that withdrawal-like symptoms are sometimes experienced by people when they try to stop or cut back on their gambling. Approximately half of the people in one study reported a range of emotional consequences, including restlessness and irritability as well as feelings of anger, guilt, and depression (Cunningham-Williams et al., 2009). It remains to be seen whether the analogy with symptoms of alcohol withdrawal is useful. The latter include physiological symptoms (sweating, increased heart rate, hand tremor), nausea and vomiting, and transient hallucinations. The similarity between symptoms of gambling disorder and substance use disorders is strongest with regard to loss of control of behavior and weakest with regard to the possible development of physiological aspects of tolerance and withdrawal.

People who suffer from gambling disorder tend to be intelligent, well-educated, competitive people who enjoy the challenges and risks involved in betting. The following brief case study describes one highly publicized example of the enormous personal costs that can be associated with a serious gambling problem.

## ⟶ Art Schlichter's Gambling Disorder

The tragic life of Art Schlichter provides a vivid illustration of the devastating impact that persistent, uncontrolled gambling can have on a person and his family (Keteyian, 1986; Valente, 1996). Schlichter, an All-American quarterback at Ohio State University, was the first player drafted by the National Football League in 1982. He had been gambling since high school, but the problem became worse after he started playing professional football. His career was disappointing. As the pressures mounted, so did his gambling debts, which eventually reached $1 million. He was cut from several teams in the National Football League and the Canadian Football League and was ultimately banned from the NFL for betting on professional games. He entered treatment for his compulsive gambling on several occasions, but the results were unsuccessful and his repeated promises to stop gambling went unfulfilled. Schlichter's promising football career was ruined, and his young family was torn apart by his uncontrolled gambling.

Schlichter has been arrested and jailed on several occasions for charges that include forgery, theft, and bank fraud. In 2001, he was sentenced to six years in prison for violating the terms of his probation. Sadly, his problems continued unabated following his release from prison in 2006, in spite of the fact that he founded a non-profit organization for the purpose of teaching others about pathological gambling. In 2010, he was sentenced to another 10 years in prison after being convicted of participating in a million-dollar ticket scam. The court decided to increase the length of his prison term after learning that he tested positive for use of cocaine while he was under house arrest while the most recent case was being investigated.

## Diagnosis

DSM-5 includes nine features in its definition of gambling disorder, and the person must exhibit at least four of them in order to meet the threshold for a diagnosis. Five of these symptoms bear a strong resemblance to diagnostic criteria for alcohol use disorder (compare with "DSM-5: Alcohol Use Disorder"): gambling with increasingly larger amounts of money to experience the same level of stimulation (similar to tolerance); becoming agitated or easily annoyed when trying to stop gambling (similar to withdrawal); repeated failed efforts to quit gambling; preoccupation with gambling; and impaired social or occupational functioning as a result of gambling. The other diagnostic criteria for gambling disorder are less similar to criteria for alcohol use disorder. They are: chasing losses; frequent gambling when experiencing emotional distress; lying to other people in order to cover up the extent of gambling; and depending on financial help from others to cope with losses from gambling.

There are two noteworthy differences between this definition and the definition of gambling disorder that appeared in the previous version of the manual (*DSM-IV*). First, one diagnostic criterion—illegal acts—was dropped from the previous list. That feature stipulated that the person "has committed illegal acts such as forgery, fraud, theft, or embezzlement to finance gambling." Research studies demonstrated that the illegal acts criterion was rarely endorsed, was only associated with the most severe cases, and was not useful in distinguishing between people who do and who do not seek treatment for gambling disorder (Denis, Fatséas, Auriacombe, 2012). Second, the threshold for a diagnosis was dropped from five features to four. Empirical data support the validity of this change (Petry et al., 2012).

## Frequency

Evidence regarding the frequency of various levels of gambling problems has become increasingly available in recent years (Black, McCormick, Losch, Shaw, Lutz, Allen, 2012). Of course, these estimates vary as a function of several important factors, including the methods used to collect the data (interviews versus questionnaires), the definitions that were employed to identify gambling problems, the age of the people who were surveyed, and the country in which the data were collected (including the availability and legal status of various gambling options).

The lifetime prevalence of pathological gambling in the United States and European countries is approximately 2 percent of the population and may be increasing with the spread of legalized gambling (Sassen, Kraus, & Buhringer, 2011; Welte, Barnes, Tidwell, Hoffman, 2008). Men are more likely than women to become pathological gamblers.

If you have been looking for help in the area of substance dependence, you have probably noticed two things: (1) There are so many different sources of advice and information that the situation can quickly become quite confusing, and (2) the field is sharply divided on a number of crucial issues. Whose advice should you follow? Among all of the self-help books dealing with drugs and alcohol, one stands out on the basis of its strong link to the research literature as well as the extensive clinical experience of the author. Marc Schuckit's book *Educating Yourself About Alcohol and Drugs: A People's Primer* provides sensible answers to the questions asked by people who are wondering about their own, or someone else's, substance use problems.

Denial is a prominent feature of most substance use disorders. It is usually easier to dismiss suggestions that you have begun to use alcohol or drugs in a self-destructive pattern than it is to face the problem directly. Schuckit's book includes a perceptive chapter titled "Is there really a problem?" The bottom line is this: "If you repeatedly have returned to substance use even though that substance has caused a disruption in your life, you do have a problem." Subsequent chapters in Schuckit's book provide thoughtful and practical guidance on topics such as the symptoms of withdrawal, the process of detoxification, the relative merits of self-help groups, outpatient therapy, and hospitalization, and how to find a specific treatment program in your area.

The Internet also provides an enormous amount of information regarding substance use disorders. For information about problems associated with the use of alcohol and drugs, you might want to visit Web pages maintained by the National Institute on Alcohol Abuse and Alcoholism (www.niaaa.nih.gov) and the National Institute on Drug Abuse (www.nida.nih.gov). These Web sites are primarily concerned with information about federally funded research programs, but they also include answers to frequently asked questions, as well as treatment referral information.

Most people who enter treatment for substance use problems become involved, at least temporarily, with self-help groups such as Alcoholics Anonymous (AA) and Narcotics Anonymous (NA). Related groups, like Alanon and Alateen, are designed for the families and children of people who are dependent on alcohol. You can contact these groups through the Internet. The URL for Alcoholics Anonymous is www.alcoholics-anonymous.org. Many people believe, often passionately, that AA is the most beneficial program for helping people to recover from alcoholism. Others disagree. If you want to consider alternative points of view, visit the Web site maintained by Stanton Peele, who is one of AA's most persistent, enthusiastic, and articulate critics. The URL for his homepage is www.peele.net. Peele challenges the biological reductionism that often dominates current views of alcoholism, and he promotes approaches to treatment that do not rely exclusively on total abstinence from drinking.

Evidence regarding the long-term outcome of serious substance use disorders can be discouraging, but it is important to remember that a substantial minority of people with these problems do manage to achieve an extended, stable recovery. The research literature does not point to one form of treatment as being clearly superior to another. Therefore, you should consider several alternatives to treatment and select the one that makes most sense in terms of your own life and your own view of the world.

# 11 Summary

A drug of abuse—sometimes called a *psychoactive substance*—is a chemical substance that alters a person's mood, level of perception, or brain functioning. Although patterns of substance use disorder are similar in some ways for all drugs, each type of drug also has some unique features.

Two particularly important features of substance use disorders are known as tolerance and withdrawal. Tolerance refers to the process through which the nervous system becomes less sensitive to the effects of alcohol or any other drug of abuse. Withdrawal refers to the symptoms experienced when a person stops using a drug.

Prolonged abuse of alcohol and other drugs of abuse can have a devastating impact on social relationships and occupational functioning while disrupting the functions of several important organ systems. Alcohol use disorder has more negative health consequences than does abuse of almost any drug, with the possible exception of nicotine.

**Nicotine** is one of the most harmful addicting drugs. Recognizing the serious long-term health consequences of exposure to nicotine, the U.S. Food and Drug Administration has prohibited the sale and distribution of tobacco products to children and adolescents. This policy attempts to prevent the development of nicotine addiction rather than trying to ban use of the drug completely.

The **psychomotor stimulants**, such as amphetamine and cocaine, activate the sympathetic nervous system and induce a positive mood state. High doses of amphetamines and cocaine can lead to the onset of psychosis.

**Opiates** have properties similar to those of opium and can induce a state of dreamlike euphoria. Tolerance develops quickly to opiates. After repeated use, their positive emotional effects are replaced by long-term negative changes in mood and emotion.

**Sedatives, Hypnotics, and Anxiolytics** can be used, as prescribed by a physician, to decrease anxiety (tranquilizers) or help people sleep (hypnotics). People who abruptly stop taking high doses of these drugs may experience withdrawal symptoms, including a return of anxiety symptoms.

**Marijuana** and **hashish** can induce a pervasive sense of well-being and happiness. People do not seem to develop tolerance to THC (the active ingredient in marijuana and hashish) unless they are exposed to high doses over an extended period of time.

**Hallucinogens** induce vivid visual images that are usually pleasant but occasionally frightening. Unlike other drugs of abuse, hallucinogens are used sporadically rather than continuously. Most people do not increase their use of hallucinogens over time, and withdrawal symptoms are not observed.

*DSM-5* defines **alcohol use disorder** in terms of a set of 11 features that include signs of impaired control over use of alcohol, social impairment resulting from chronic drinking, risk use of alcohol, and pharmacological criteria. The person has to exhibit at least two of these criteria within a 12-month period of time for a diagnosis of alcohol use disorder to be made. The severity of the disorder is also noted, based on the number of symptoms that are present: mild (2–3 symptoms), moderate (4–5 symptoms), or severe (6 or more symptoms).

Alcohol use disorder is one of the most common forms of mental disorder, with a lifetime prevalence of 30 percent in the NESARC study. Among people with alcohol use disorders, men outnumber women by a ratio of approximately two to one.

Research on the causes of alcoholism illustrates the ways in which various systems interact to produce and maintain drug dependence. There are several pathways to alcoholism. Social factors are particularly influential in the early phases of substance use. The culture in which a person lives influences the types of drugs that are used, the purposes for which they are used, and the expectations that people hold for the ways in which drugs will affect their experiences and behavior.

Twin studies indicate that genetic factors influence patterns of social drinking as well as the onset of alcohol use disorder. Adoption studies indicate that the offspring of alcoholic parents who are raised by nonalcoholic parents are more likely than people in the general population to develop drinking problems of their own.

All of the psychoactive drugs cause increased dopamine activity in the reward pathways of the brain. Alcohol may stimulate the mesolimbic dopamine pathway directly, or it may act indirectly by inhibiting GABA neurons. Another focus of neurochemical research has been the role of endogenous opioids known as **endorphins**. Some theorists have argued that alcoholism is associated with excessive production of endorphins.

Expectations about drug effects have an important influence on the ways in which people respond to alcohol and other drugs. People who believe that alcohol enhances pleasure, reduces tension, and increases social performance are more likely than other people to drink frequently and heavily.

Treatment of substance use disorders is an especially challenging and difficult task, in light of the fact that many people with these problems do not recognize or acknowledge their own difficulties. Recovery begins with a process of detoxification. Self-help programs, such as Alcoholics Anonymous, are the most widely used and probably one of the most beneficial forms of treatment.

Defining features of gambling disorder include impaired control of gambling activities, social impairment that follows from gambling (such as loss of jobs or relationships), and continued problem behavior in spite of the accumulation of harmful consequences. One feature that is unique to gambling disorder, in comparison to substance use disorders, is *chasing losses*.

# The Big Picture

# critical thinking review

**11.1** What evidence is needed to show that a drug is addictive?

If repeated use of a drug is associated with the development of tolerance and withdrawal, or if it leads to a pathological pattern of use, then it is considered to be addictive . . . (see pages 287–288).

**11.2** What are the long-term consequences of abusing psychomotor stimulants?

Prolonged use of amphetamines and cocaine increases the person's risk for having a psychotic episode, but the most common and devastating

effects of stimulant drugs are the serious disruption of occupational and social roles . . . (see page 291).

**11.3** Where is the boundary between substance use disorders and recreational drug use?

The transition from recreational use to the onset of a disorder can be subtle and is not easily recognized, especially by the person who is using drugs. The distinction hinges on the pattern of use, which must be persistent over time and lead to maladaptive consequences before this diagnosis would be considered . . . (see page 296).

**11.4  In what ways are drug problems different among the elderly?**
Tolerance to many drugs is reduced among the elderly, and the symptoms of withdrawal may be more severe and prolonged . . . (see pages 301–302).

**11.5  What are the most important risk factors for alcoholism?**
Increased risk is associated with both genetic and environmental factors. Some of the genes that influence risk of alcohol dependence have an impact on the metabolism of alcohol. Others may influence personality traits which increase the tendency to participate in dangerous patterns of consumption . . . (see pages 307–308).

**11.6  How does AA differ from other approaches to treating alcoholism?**
Alcoholics Anonymous is a self-help program and is not officially associated with any other form of treatment. Its viewpoint is fundamentally spiritual in nature . . . (see page 309).

**11.7  What factors predict better long-term outcome for treatment of alcoholism?**
Long-term outcome is best predicted by the person's coping resources (social skills and problem-solving abilities), the availability of social support, and the level of stress in the environment . . . (see pages 311–312).

# key terms

**alcohol use disorder**  296
**barbiturates**  293
**benzodiazepines**  293
**detoxification**  308

**endorphins**  306
**hallucinogens**  294
**hashish**  294
**high-risk research design**  307

**marijuana**  294
**opiates**  292
**psychomotor stimulants**  291
**substance use disorder**  285

**tolerance**  288
**withdrawal**  288

## Virtual Case Studies

Virtual Case Studies offer you a science-based, interactive simulation where you can learn how a number of risk factors and protective factors could impact disorder development in a virtual person. As you progress through the simulation you will not act as the character or as a clinician, but will be able to independently explore a variety of different behaviors, events, and outcomes that one who suffers from a disorder could potentially encounter. You can access the Virtual Case Study on *Substance Abuse Disorders* at mypsychlab.com.

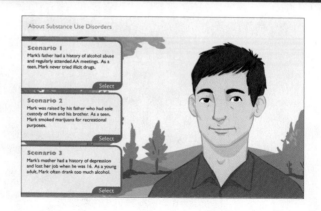

# sexual dysfunctions, paraphilic disorders, and gender dysphoria

**12**

# The Big Picture

## learning objectives

### 12.1
Should sexual problems be defined primarily in terms of difficulty reaching orgasm?

### 12.2
What role to mental scripts play in sexual arousal?

### 12.3
What are the primary targets of psychological approaches to treating sexual dysfunctions?

### 12.4
How have changing attitudes toward sexuality influenced the definition of paraphilias?

### 12.5
Should excessive sexual behavior be considered a disorder in its own right?

### 12.6
Does deviant sexual arousal ever play a role in sexual assaults?

Sex is often a perplexing area of our lives. Sexual experience can be a source of extreme pleasure, while also providing for the development and expression of intimacy with one's partner. From an evolutionary point of view, reproduction is the key to our survival. Sexual behavior also provides fertile ground for intense feelings of fear and guilt.

When something interferes with our ability to function sexually, it can be devastating both to the person who is affected and to the person's partner. Sometimes a person's inability to enjoy sexual experiences becomes so pervasive or so personally distressing that the person seeks professional help—alone or, more often, with his or her partner. In other instances, a person may enjoy sex but his or her sexual interest may be triggered by unusual stimuli, or it may involve nonconsenting partners or the pain and suffering of the self or others. The point at which occasional sexual difficulties become a "sexual dysfunction" is quite subjective and may say as much about sexual norms and expectations as anything else. Similarly, the definition of sexual conduct that is considered deviant has also changed over time. This chapter explores the mix of factors that influence what it means to be a man or a woman and the ways in which we engage in sexual relationships. It also offers a

picture of the shifting ground that surrounds what mental health professionals consider to be normal and abnormal sexual practices.

## Overview

Any discussion of sexual disorders requires some frank consideration of normal sexuality. Such openness has been encouraged and promoted by mental health professionals who specialize in the study and treatment of sexual behavior.

William Masters (1915–2001) and Virginia Johnson (1925–2013) were undoubtedly the best-known sex therapists and researchers in the United States during the second half of the twentieth century. Their first book, *Human Sexual Response,* published in 1966, was based on their studies of nearly 700 normal men and women. Observations and physiological recordings were made in a laboratory setting while these individuals engaged in sexual activities, including masturbation and intercourse. Masters and Johnson's research received widespread attention in the popular media and helped make laboratory studies of sexual behavior acceptable (Maier, 2009).

On the basis of their data, Masters and Johnson described the human sexual response cycle in terms of a sequence of overlapping phases: excitement, orgasm, and resolution. Analogous processes occur in both men and women, but the timing may differ. Many of the physiological mechanisms involved in this cycle are now understood more clearly, and progression from one phase to the next is not always strictly linear, but the general outline described by Masters and Johnson is still useful (Hayes, 2011; Levin, 2008). There are, of course, individual differences in virtually all aspects of this cycle. Variations from the most common pattern may not indicate a problem unless the person is concerned about the response.

Sexual *excitement* increases continuously from initial stimulation up to the point of orgasm. It may last anywhere from a few minutes to several hours. Among the most dramatic physiological changes during sexual excitement are those associated with *vasocongestion*—engorgement of the blood vessels of various

Sexual dysfunctions are best defined in terms of the couple rather than individual persons. They are frequently associated with marital distress.

organs, especially the genitals. The male and female genitalia become swollen, reddened, and warmed. Sexual excitement also increases muscular tension, heart rate, and respiration rate. These physiological responses are accompanied by subjective feelings of arousal, especially at more advanced stages of excitement.

The experience of *orgasm* is usually distinct from the gradual buildup of sexual excitement that precedes it. This sudden release of tension is almost always experienced as being intensely pleasurable, but the specific nature of the experience varies from one person to the next. The female orgasm occurs in three stages, beginning with a "sensation of suspension or stoppage," which is associated with strong genital sensations. The second stage involves a feeling of warmth spreading throughout the pelvic area. The third stage is characterized by sensations of throbbing or pulsating, which are tied to rhythmic contractions of the vagina, the uterus, and the rectal sphincter muscle.

The male orgasm occurs in two stages, beginning with a sensation of ejaculatory inevitability. This is triggered by the movement of seminal fluid toward the urethra. In the second stage, regular contractions propel semen through the urethra, and it is expelled through the urinary opening.

During the *resolution* phase, which may last 30 minutes or longer, the person's body returns to its resting state. Men are typically unresponsive to further sexual stimulation for a variable period of time after reaching orgasm. This is known as the refractory period. Women, on the other hand, may be able to respond to further stimulation almost immediately. They are capable of experiencing a series of distinct orgasmic responses that are not separated by a period of noticeably lowered excitement.

Sexual dysfunctions can involve a disruption of any stage of the sexual response cycle. The following case study, written by Barry McCarthy, a psychologist at American University, is concerned with a man who had difficulty controlling the rate at which he progressed from excitement to orgasm.

### ⟶ Margaret and Bill's Sexual Communication

Margaret and Bill, both in their late twenties, had been married for two years, and they had intercourse frequently. Margaret seldom reached orgasm during these experiences, but she was orgasmic during masturbation. The central feature of their problem was the fact that Bill was unable to delay ejaculation for more than a few seconds after insertion.

Unbeknownst to Margaret, Bill had attempted a "do-it-yourself" technique to gain better control [of ejaculation]. He had bought a desensitizing cream he'd read about in a men's magazine and applied it to the glans of his penis 20 minutes before initiating sex. He also masturbated the day before the couple had sex.

During intercourse he tried to keep his leg muscles tense and think about sports as a way of keeping his arousal in check. Bill was unaware that Margaret felt emotionally shut out during the sex. Bill was becoming more sensitized to his arousal cycle and was worrying about erection. He was not achieving better ejaculatory control, and he was enjoying sex less. The sexual

relationship was heading downhill, and miscommunication and frustration were growing.

Margaret had two secrets that she had never shared with Bill. Although she found it easier to be orgasmic with manual stimulation, she had been orgasmic during intercourse with a married man she'd had an affair with a year before meeting Bill. Margaret expressed ambivalent feelings about that relationship. She felt that the man was a very sophisticated lover, and she had been highly aroused and orgasmic with him. Yet the relationship had been a manipulative one. He'd been emotionally abusive to Margaret, and the relationship had ended when he accused Margaret of giving him herpes and berated her. In fact, it was probably he who gave Margaret the herpes. Margaret was only experiencing herpes outbreaks two or three times a year, but when they did occur, she was flooded with negative feelings about herself, sexuality, and relationships. She initially saw Bill as a loving, stable man who would help rid her of negative feelings concerning sexuality. Instead, he continually disappointed her with the early ejaculation. Bill knew about the herpes but not about her sexual history and strong negative feelings.

Bill was terribly embarrassed about his secret concerning masturbation, which he engaged in on a twice-daily basis. From adolescence on, Bill had used masturbation as his primary means of stress reduction. For him, masturbation was a humiliating secret (he believed married men should not masturbate). The manner in which he masturbated undoubtedly contributed to the early ejaculation pattern. Bill focused only on his penis, using rapid strokes with the goal of ejaculating as quickly as he could. This was both to prevent himself from being discovered and from a desire to "get it over with" as soon as he could and forget about it.

When it came to his personal and sexual life, Bill was inhibited, unsure of himself, and had particularly low sexual self-esteem. As an adolescent, Bill remembered being very interested sexually, but very unsure around girls. Bill's first intercourse at 19 was perceived as a failure because he ejaculated before he could insert his penis in the woman's vagina. He then tried desperately to insert because the young woman urged him to, but he was in the refractory period (a phenomenon Bill did not understand), and so he did not get a firm erection and felt doubly humiliated (McCarthy, 1989, pp. 151–159).

The case of Bill and Margaret illustrates several important points. First, many sexual problems are best defined in terms of the couple rather than each partner individually. Second, although problems in sexual behavior clearly involve basic physiological responses and behavioral skills, each person's thoughts about the meaning of sexual behavior are also extremely important. Sexual behavior usually takes place in the context of a close, personal relationship. Current views of the sexual response cycle have expanded beyond a simple focus on the mechanisms related to excitement and orgasm (Basson, Brotto, Laan, Redmond, Utian, 2005). They begin at a point of sexual neutrality and consider factors that influence whether the person will seek or be receptive to stimuli that might lead to arousal. They also extend beyond the experience of arousal and orgasm to consider feelings of emotional and physical satisfaction, which ultimately serve to build intimacy.

The classification of sexual disorders was revised dramatically in the United States and Western Europe during the twentieth century. This process reflects important changes in the way that our culture views various aspects of sexual behavior. Before describing the disorders that are included in DSM-5, we outline briefly some of the clinical and scientific perspectives on sexuality that laid the foundation for our current system.

## Brief Historical Perspective

Over the course of the late twentieth century and into the twenty-first, there has been a trend toward greater tolerance of sexual variation among consenting adult partners and toward increased concern about impairments in sexual performance and experience. Several leading intellectuals influenced public and professional opinions regarding sexual behavior during the first half of the twentieth century. The work of Alfred Kinsey (1894–1956), a biologist at Indiana University, was especially significant. In keeping with his adherence to scientific methods, Kinsey adopted a behavioral stance, focusing specifically on those experiences that resulted in orgasm. In their efforts to describe human sexual behavior, Kinsey and his colleagues interviewed 18,000 men and women between 1938 and 1956 (Jones, 1997). They asked each participant a standard series of questions such as, "How old were you the first time that you had intercourse with another person?" Or, "How many times a week do you masturbate?"

The incredible diversity of experiences reported by his subjects led Kinsey to reject the distinction between normal and abnormal sexual behavior (Robinson, 1976). He argued that differences among people are quantitative rather than qualitative. For example, Kinsey suggested that the distinction between heterosexual and homosexual persons was essentially arbitrary and fundamentally meaningless. This argument was later used in support of the decision to drop homosexuality from DSM-III (see Chapter 1) and to cease regarding homosexuality as a form of abnormal behavior. Kinsey's comments regarding sexual dysfunction reflected a similar view. He believed that low sexual desire was simply a reflection of individual differences in erotic capacity rather than a reflection of psychopathology (Kinsey, Pomeroy, & Martin, 1948).

## Sexual Dysfunctions

Sexuality represents a complex behavioral process that can easily be upset. Inhibitions of sexual desire and interference with the physiological responses leading to orgasm are called **sexual dysfunctions.** Problems can arise anywhere, from the earliest stages of interest and desire through the climactic release of orgasm. Some people also experience pain during sexual intercourse.

### Symptoms

How do people evaluate the quality of their sexual relationships? Subjective judgments obviously have an important impact on each person's commitment to a partnership. Dissatisfaction sometimes leads the couple to seek help from a mental health professional. It is useful, therefore, to know something about the ways

Satisfaction in a sexual relationship is influenced by feelings of intimacy and successful communication as well as by the experience of orgasm.

in which normal couples evaluate their own sexual activities before we consider specific symptoms of sexual dysfunction.

One important set of data regarding normal sexual behavior and satisfaction was collected by the National Health and Social Life Survey (NHSLS), the first large-scale follow-up to the Kinsey reports (Laumann, Paik, & Rosen, 1994). The NHSLS research team conducted detailed, face-to-face interviews with nearly 3,500 men and women between the ages of 18 and 59 throughout the United States. Their questionnaire asked about masturbation and four basic sexual techniques involving partners: vaginal intercourse, fellatio, cunnilingus, and anal intercourse. The results indicate that masturbation is relatively common among both men and women. Virtually all of the men (95 percent) and women (97 percent) had experienced vaginal intercourse at some time during their lives. The investigators concluded that the vast majority of heterosexual encounters focus on vaginal intercourse. Most of the men (75 percent) and women (65 percent) also reported that they had engaged in oral sexual activities (as both the person giving and receiving oral-genital stimulation). Most sexual activity occurs in the context of monogamous relationships. Most of these conclusions regarding rates and types of sexual behaviors have been confirmed by a more recent survey conducted by investigators from the Kinsey Institute at Indiana University (Herbenick, Reece, Schick, Sanders, Dodge, Fortenberry, 2010).

One of the most interesting aspects of the NHSLS results involves the ways in which the participants described the *quality* of their experiences during sexual activity. Figure 12.1 illustrates the proportion of people who said that they always had an orgasm during sexual activity with their primary partner during the past year. Several aspects of these data are worth mentioning. First, there is a very large difference between men and women with

regard to the experience of orgasm. Only 29 percent of women reported that they always have an orgasm with a specific partner, compared to 75 percent of men. Second, notice that 44 percent of men reported that their partners always had orgasms during sex. This figure is much higher than the rate reported by women themselves. There are several plausible explanations for this discrepancy. Because female orgasm is sometimes less clearly defined than male orgasm, men may misinterpret some events as signs that their partners have had an orgasm. It may also be the case that women sometimes mislead their partners into thinking that they have reached orgasm so that their partners will feel better about their own sexual prowess (Wiederman, 1997).

Figure 12.2 depicts data on participants' ratings of physical and emotional satisfaction. Here the differences between men and women are less marked. You might expect that physical and emotional satisfaction in a sexual relationship would be influenced by the experience of orgasm, but the relations among these variables are complex. A relationship may be considered intimate and satisfying simply because sexual activity occurs, regardless of whether it always results in orgasm. In fact, a large proportion of both men and women indicated that they were extremely satisfied with their partners, on both the physical and emotional dimensions. Notice in particular that, although only 29 percent of women indicated that they always have an orgasm with their partner, 41 percent of women said that they were extremely physically satisfied with their partners. This pattern suggests that the experience of orgasm is only one aspect of sexual satisfaction, especially for women. Other aspects of the relationship, including tenderness, intimacy, and affection, are also critically important (Mitchell & Graham, 2008; Tiefer, 2001).

Strong negative emotions, such as anger, fear, and resentment, are often associated with sexual dissatisfaction. In some

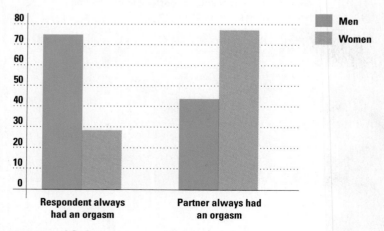

**FIGURE 12.1**

**Sexual Response in Primary Partnership During Previous Year** This graph illustrates the frequency of orgasmic response as well as differences in perception by men and women in their partners' responses.
*Source:* Based on Laumann, Edward O., John H. Gagnon, Robert T. Michael and Stuart Michaels. 1994. The Social Organization of Sexuality: Sexual Practices in the United States. University of Chicago Press.

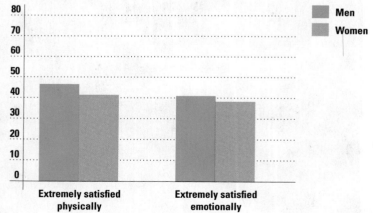

**FIGURE 12.2**

**Sexual Satisfaction in Primary Partnership During the Previous Year** This graph illustrates the physical and emotional satisfaction reported by men and women in their primary partnerships.
*Source:* Based on Laumann, Edward O., John H. Gagnon, Robert T. Michael and Stuart Michaels. 1994. The Social Organization of Sexuality: Sexual Practices in the United States. University of Chicago Press.

cases, these emotional states appear before the onset of the sexual problem, and sometimes they develop later. Given the connection that many cultures make between virile sexual performance and "manhood," it is not surprising that men with erectile difficulties are often embarrassed and ashamed. Their humiliation can lead to secondary problems, such as anxiety and depression. Similar feelings frequently accompany early ejaculation and the recognition that a partner's sexual expectations have not been fulfilled. Women who have trouble becoming aroused or reaching orgasm also frequently experience profound frustration and disappointment. The emotional consequences of sexual problems can be devastating for both partners.

## Diagnosis

*DSM-5* subdivides sexual dysfunctions into several types (see Table 12.1). The diagnostic criteria for these problems are much less specific than those used to define other kinds of disorders in *DSM-5*. Much is left to the judgment of the individual clinician. Failure to reach orgasm is not considered a disorder unless it is persistent or recurrent and results in marked distress or interpersonal difficulty. The *DSM-5* criteria also require that the sexual dysfunction is not better explained by another mental disorder (such as major depression) and is not the direct result of a chemical substance (such as alcohol) or a general medical condition.

Two diagnostic criteria that are required for all forms of sexual dysfunction defined in *DSM-5* are that: (1) the symptoms have persisted for at least six months, and (2) the symptoms lead to marked distress in the person who experiences them (Segraves, Balon, & Clayton, 2007). In other words, someone who is not interested in sex or who experiences problems in sexual responsiveness would not qualify for a diagnosis of sexual dysfunction until the problems have been evident for six months and unless this circumstance is upsetting to him or her.

Low sexual desire can reflect the impact of many factors ranging from unhappiness (including anger and worry) to poor physical health.

Sexual problems typically occur in the context of an intimate relationship. Problems in that relationship and the feelings of the person's partner are obviously important, but we must be cautious in weighing their diagnostic importance. A panel of leading experts on women's reproductive health recommended that the only consideration should be personal distress experienced by the woman (Basson, Berman, Burnett, Derogatis, Ferguson, Fourcroy, 2000). The satisfaction and concerns of her partner is an important consideration in terms of their relationship itself, but it should not be grounds for assigning to the woman a diagnosis of sexual dysfunction unless she is personally dissatisfied with her own sexual experience.

**MALE HYPOACTIVE SEXUAL DESIRE DISORDER** Sexual desire sets the stage for sexual arousal and orgasm. Some clinicians refer to sexual desire as the person's willingness to approach or engage in those experiences that will lead to sexual arousal.

---

**TABLE 12.1**
## Sexual Dysfunctions Listed in *DSM-5*

**Male Hypoactive Sexual Desire Disorder:** Persistent or recurrent lack of desire for sex and deficient/absent erotic thoughts or fantasies regarding sexual activities.

**Erectile Disorder:** Repeated failure to obtain or maintain erections during partnered sexual activities.

**Female Sexual Interest/Arousal Disorder:** Absence or reduced frequency or intensity of several indicators of interest in or response to sexual cues.

**Female Orgasmic Disorder:** Difficulty in experiencing orgasm and/or markedly reduced intensity of orgasmic sensations.

**Delayed Ejaculation:** Marked delay in or inability to achieve ejaculation.

**Premature (Early) Ejaculation:** Ejaculation occurs prior to or shortly after vaginal penetration.

**Genito-Pelvic Pain/Penetration Disorder:** Refers to a set of frequently overlapping symptoms involving having difficulty with intercourse, genito-pelvic pain, fear of pain or vaginal penetration, and tension of the pelvic floor muscles.

*Source:* Reprinted with permission from the *Diagnostic and Statistical Manual of Mental Disorders*, Fifth Edition. Copyright © 2013 by the American Psychiatric Association.

**Hypoactive sexual desire** is defined in terms of subjective experiences, such as lack of sexual fantasies and lack of interest in sexual experiences. The absence of interest in sex must be both persistent and pervasive to be considered a clinical problem (Carvalheira, Brotto, & Leal, 2010).

The absolute frequency with which a person engages in sex cannot be used as a measure of inhibited sexual desire because the central issue is *interest*—actively seeking out sexual experiences—rather than participation (Warnock, 2002). For example, some people acquiesce to their partners' demands, even though they would not choose to engage in sexual activities if it were left up to them. In the absence of any specific standard, the identification of hypoactive sexual desire must depend on a clinician's subjective evaluation of the level of desire that is expected given the person's age, gender, marital status, and many other relevant considerations.

Almost everyone recognizes that sexual desire fluctuates in intensity over time, sometimes dramatically and frequently, for reasons that we do not understand. The fact that hypoactive sexual desire is listed in *DSM-5* as a type of disorder should not lead us to believe that it is a unitary condition with a simple explanation. It is, in fact, a collection of many different kinds of problems. People who suffer from low levels of sexual desire frequently experience other mental and medical disorders. Most men seeking treatment for hypoactive sexual desire report other forms of sexual dysfunction, such as problems with arousal or genital pain. Men and women with low sexual desire also have high rates of mood disorders. The mood disorder typically appears before the onset of low sexual desire. It appears likely, therefore, that many cases of low sexual desire develop after the person has experienced other forms of psychological distress.

**ERECTILE DISORDER** Many men experience difficulties either in obtaining an erection that is sufficient to accomplish intercourse or maintaining an erection long enough to satisfy themselves and their partners during intercourse. Both problems are examples of **erectile dysfunction.** Men with this problem may report feeling subjectively aroused, but the vascular reflex mechanism fails, and sufficient blood is not pumped to the penis to make it erect (Wylie & Machin, 2007). These difficulties can appear at any time prior to orgasm. Some men have trouble achieving an erection during sexual foreplay, whereas others lose their erection around the time of insertion or during intercourse. This phenomenon used to be called *impotence,* but the term has been dropped because of its negative implications.

Erectile dysfunctions can be relatively transient, or they can be more chronic. Occasional experiences of this type are not considered unusual. When they persist and become a serious source of distress to the couple, however, erectile difficulties can lead to serious problems. Consider, for example, the feelings expressed by the man and woman in our next case study, who were treated by Bernie Zilbergeld, an expert in the treatment of sexual dysfunction.

### → Erectile Disorder

Norm and Linda are both 44 and have been married 15 years. Individually, they are very different. Linda is attractive, vivacious, and very critical. Norm seemed generally timid and reluctant to express his feelings. (They) had a serviceable relationship in many ways. The only problem, as far as they were concerned, was sex. When they first met, Linda was far more sexually experienced than Norm. But he tried to be a good student and they enjoyed frequent lovemaking at the beginning, although not as frequent or as passionate as she would have liked.

Over the years, however, Norm gradually lost interest in sex and developed erection problems. Either he wouldn't get an erection or he would lose it before or during insertion. Linda appeared to be hurt and angry in my individual session with her. "I know you're sympathetic toward men with erection problems. But what about me? How can I feel loved or desirable when he can't get it up for me? It's obvious he doesn't want me, doesn't desire me. I feel (awful)."

In my session with Norm, he repeated that he loved Linda and wanted to stay with her. When I asked if he found her sexually attractive, he hesitated and then said yes. I asked how he felt when he was first dating her. He began by saying how beautiful he found her and how surprised he was that a woman like her would take an interest "in a nerd like me." When I asked what else he felt at that time, he answered, "To tell the truth, I was frightened by her experience and sexual openness. It was like I was in kindergarten and she was a professor. I'm not sure I've ever gotten over that. I've always felt at least a little inadequate. And things really got bad after I started having trouble with erections." (Zilbergeld, 1995, pp. 315–316).

Norm and Linda experienced the frustrations and anxiety that often accompany sexual arousal difficulties. Their relationship also illustrates the marital distress that can develop when people begin to have problems with self-esteem and doubts about the affection of their partner.

**FEMALE SEXUAL INTEREST/AROUSAL DISORDER** Low sexual interest and reduced sexual arousal are combined in one diagnostic category for women. Impaired sexual arousal in women is somewhat more difficult to describe and identify than is erectile dysfunction in men. Put simply, a woman is said to experience **inhibited sexual arousal** if she cannot either achieve or maintain genital responses, such as lubrication and swelling, that are necessary to complete sexual intercourse. Low sexual desire may reflect either insensitivity to cues that would be expected to stimulate sexual interest or enhanced activity of mechanisms that inhibit sexual interest (Bloemers, van Rooij , Poels, Goldstein, Everaerd, Koppeschaar, Chivers, Gerritsen, van Ham, Olivier, Tuiten, 2013).

## Hypothetical Constructs: What Is Sexual Arousal?

The term *sexual arousal* refers to the state that precedes orgasm. It is defined in terms of two factors: physiological responses, such as vascular engorgement of the genitals, and subjective feelings of pleasure and excitement. Psychologists refer to sexual arousal as a **hypothetical construct**. Many of the concepts that we have discussed in this book are hypothetical constructs: anxiety, depression, psychopathy, and schizophrenia. Hypothetical constructs are theoretical devices. In the field of psychopathology, they refer to events or states that reside within the person and are proposed to help us understand or explain a person's behavior.

Constructs cannot be observed directly, but in order to be scientifically meaningful they must be defined in terms of observable responses (Cronbach & Meehl, 1955; Kimble, 1989). These responses are all associated with the construct, but they are not perfectly related, and the construct is not exhaustively defined by them. For example, an erect penis is not always accompanied by subjective feelings of sexual excitement, and subjective feelings of arousal are not always associated with physiological responses. In other words, the construct of sexual arousal is anchored by feelings and responses that can be measured directly, but it is more than the sum of these parts.

An **operational definition** is a procedure that is used to measure a theoretical construct. Such a definition usually includes measures of the different components of the construct. For men, one obvious component of sexual arousal is penile erection. The most widely accepted procedure for measuring male sexual arousal uses a device called a *penile plethysmograph* (Rosen, Weigel, & Gendrano, 2007). In this procedure, the man places a thin elastic strain gauge around his penis, underneath his clothing. The rubber loop is filled with a column of mercury that changes in its electrical conductance as the circumference of the penis changes. The wire extending from the strain gauge is connected to a plethysmograph, which amplifies the electrical signal passing through the strain gauge and produces a record reflecting changes in penile tumescence.

The *vaginal photometer*, a device shaped like a tampon and inserted into the vagina, is used to measure female sexual arousal. Like the penile strain gauge, the photometer can be placed in position in private and worn underneath clothing during the assessment procedure. As the woman becomes sexually aroused, the walls of the vagina become congested with blood. Vasocongestion causes changes in the amount of red light that can be transmitted through the tissue. The photometer is sensitive to subtle changes in vaginal tissue and is probably most useful in measuring moderate to low levels of sexual arousal (Janssen, 2002; Prouse & Heiman, 2009).

Clinical scientists must always think carefully about the meaning of their operational definitions. Although the penile strain gauge and the vaginal photometer measure physiological events that are directly related to sexual arousal, the responses that they measure are not the same thing as sexual arousal. They are reflections of the construct, which has many dimensions (Berman, Berman, Werbin, Flaherty, Leahy, Goldstein, 1999). One important goal of scientific studies is to determine more specifically how (and when) these physiological measures are related to the other observable referents of sexual arousal. This process will determine the **construct validity** of the penile strain gauge and the vaginal photometer—that is, the extent to which these specific measures produce results that are consistent with the theoretical construct.

---

The capacity for intercourse is less obvious and more difficult to measure for a woman than for a man, whose erect penis usually serves as a signal of readiness (see Research Methods box). Investigators who have studied sexual responses in normal women have reported low correlations between self-reports of subjective arousal and physiological measures, such as the amount of vaginal lubrication or vasocongestion (Meston, Rellini & McCall, 2010). Among women who experience sexual difficulties, the problem may more often be decreased subjective arousal rather than impaired physiological responses. The distinction between desire and subjective arousal is difficult to make. That is why hypoactive sexual desire and sexual arousal disorder were combined into one diagnostic category for women in *DSM-5* (Basson & Brotto, 2009; Giraldi, Rellini, Pfaus, Laan, 2013).

**FEMALE ORGASMIC DISORDER** Some women are unable to reach orgasm even though they apparently experience uninhibited sexual arousal. Women who experience orgasmic difficulties may have a strong desire to engage in sexual relations; they may find great pleasure in sexual foreplay and may show all the signs of sexual arousal. Nevertheless, they cannot reach the peak erotic experience of orgasm. Women whose orgasmic impairment is *generalized* have never experienced orgasm by any means. *Situational orgasmic* difficulties occur when the woman is able to reach orgasm in some situations, but not in others. That might mean that she is orgasmic during masturbation but not during intercourse, or perhaps she is orgasmic with one partner but not with another (Basson, 2002).

**Orgasmic disorder** in women is somewhat difficult to define in relation to inhibited sexual arousal because the various components of female sexual response are more difficult to measure than are erection and ejaculation in the male. One experienced researcher described this issue in the following way:

> In my experience, many women who have never reached orgasm present the following set of symptoms: They report that when engaging in intercourse they do not have difficulty lubricating and experience no pain. However, they report no genital sensations (hence the term *genital anesthesia*) and do not appear to know what sexual arousal is. Typically they do not masturbate and often have never masturbated. They do not experience the phenomenon that a sexually functional woman would call sexual desire. Most of these women seek therapy because they have heard from others or have read that they are missing something, rather than because they themselves feel frustrated. (Morokoff, 1989, p. 74)

**PREMATURE (EARLY) EJACULATION** Many men experience problems with the control of ejaculation. They are unable to prolong the period of sexual excitement long enough to complete intercourse. This problem is known as **premature ejaculation,** but most experts now prefer the term early ejaculation because it is less pejorative. Once they become intensely sexually aroused, they reach orgasm very quickly (Metz & Pryor, 2000). Almost all the literature on this topic is concerned with men, but some women are also bothered by reaching orgasm too quickly. Therefore, some clinicians have suggested that "early orgasm" might be a more appropriate description of the problem.

There have been many attempts to establish specific, quantitative criteria for premature ejaculation (Broderick, 2006). None of the attempts has been entirely satisfactory, but certain boundaries identify conditions that can be problematic. If the man ejaculates before or immediately upon insertion, or after only three or four thrusts, almost all clinicians will identify his response as premature ejaculation. Among men suffering from lifelong premature ejaculation, 90 percent routinely ejaculate within one minute after insertion of the penis in the vagina (Waldinger, 2009).

Another way to think about premature ejaculation places emphasis on subjective control and the couple's satisfaction rather than on the amount of time required to reach orgasm. The *DSM-5* definition defines the problem in terms of recurrent ejaculation shortly after penetration and before the person wishes it. If progression to orgasm is beyond the man's voluntary control once he reaches an intense level of sexual arousal, he has a problem with premature ejaculation (Symonds, Roblin, Hart, Althof, 2003).

**DELAYED EJACULATION** The central feature of this disorder, which has also been called male orgasmic disorder and ejaculatory inhibition, involves a marked delay in ejaculation, or an inability to accomplish ejaculation (Foley, 2009). The problem is defined in terms of sexual behavior with a partner. It must be experienced in most sexual encounters (at least 75% of the time), and it must not be the result of voluntary efforts by the man to delay orgasm.

In order to assign the diagnosis, the clinician must determine that the person shows a normal interest in and response to sexual stimuli and has then engaged in activity that would otherwise be considered sufficient to lead to an orgasmic response for other men.

**GENITO-PELVIC PAIN/PENETRATION DISORDER** This diagnostic category is used to describe four types of problems that often occur together: genito-pelvic pain, fear of pain or vaginal penetration, tension of the pelvic floor muscles, and trouble having intercourse. Some people experience persistent genital pain during or after sexual intercourse, which is known as *dyspareunia*. The problem can occur in either men or women, although it is considered to be much more common in women (Davis & Reissing, 2007). The severity of the discomfort can range from mild irritation following sexual activity to searing pain during insertion of the penis or intercourse. The pains may be sharp and intense, or they may take the form of a dull, aching sensation; they may be experienced as coming from a superficial area near the barrel of the vagina or as being located deep in the lower abdominal area; they may be intermittent or persistent. The experience of severe genital pain is often associated with other forms of sexual dysfunction. Not surprisingly, many women with dyspareunia develop a lack of interest in, or an aversion toward, sexual activity.

The following first-person account was written by a 40-year-old woman who had been experiencing vaginal pain for several months. She had consulted several different health professionals about the problem, and none of their treatments had relieved her discomfort. This passage describes her experience one night when she and the man with whom she had been living seemed to be on the brink of enjoying a renewed interest in their sexual relationship.

### ⟶ Genital Pain

We went to bed. For a while it was nice—more than nice. It was novel and thrilling, as if we had just met. We hadn't approached each other in more than a month. I was surprised by how wonderful I could feel. I was used to feeling lousy most of the time. The sensations of excitement were overwhelming. I'd forgotten about that. Then he pushed himself into me and it was horrible.

First I felt as if I were being torn or sliced. As he settled into a rhythm, I felt that something was scraping me over and over in the same raw spot, until the rawness and soreness were all I could feel. He didn't notice. He was intent on what he was doing. I decided to let him get on with it, but the pain was really bothering me. I pulled away inside myself, so that the events on the bed were far from where "I" was, and the pain was far away also. That worked, but I didn't like doing it. There was something nasty about it. I had the thought, People who don't like sex must feel this way. Then I realized that now I was somebody who didn't like sex (Kaysen, 2001, pp. 60–61).

Access to the vagina is controlled by the muscles surrounding its entrance. Some women find that whenever penetration of the vagina is attempted, these muscles snap tightly shut, preventing insertion of any object. This involuntary muscular spasm, known as *vaginismus,* prevents sexual intercourse as well as other activities, such as vaginal examinations and the insertion of tampons. Women with vaginismus may be completely sexually responsive in other respects, fully capable of arousal and orgasm through manual stimulation of the clitoris. Women who seek therapy for this condition often report that they are afraid of intercourse and vaginal penetration (Reissing, Binik, Khalife, Cohen, Amsel, 2004). The problem can be severe or partial in nature. Some couples report that a mild form of vaginismus occurs from time to time, making intercourse difficult and sometimes painful.

The definition of genito-pelvic pain/penetration disorder in *DSM-5* is more broadly conceived than the approach to these problems that was represented in previous versions of the diagnostic manual. Many women experience genital pain during sexual stimulation other than intercourse. Traditional definitions of dyspareunia and vaginismus focus exclusively on problems that occur during sexual intercourse. Some experts have suggested that these problems should be viewed as genital pain disorders (similar to pain disorders, such as back pain) that interfere with intercourse rather than as forms of sexual dysfunction (Binik, 2005).

## Frequency

Surveys conducted among the general population indicate that some forms of sexual dysfunction are relatively common (Christensen, Grønbæk, Osler, Pedersen, Graugaard, Frisch, 2011). We must keep in mind, however, that this impression is based on self-report questionnaires and judgments made by laypersons, which are less precise than those made by experts. Diagnoses made by experienced therapists would take into account the person's age, the context of the person's life, and whether the person had experienced stimulation that would ordinarily be expected to lead to sustained arousal and orgasm. Clinicians would also consider the amount of distress and interpersonal difficulty associated with the problem before arriving at a diagnosis of sexual dysfunction. Therefore, we must be cautious in our interpretations of survey data (Hayes, Dennerstein, Bennett, Fairleyl, 2008).

The most extensive set of information regarding sexual problems among people living in the community comes from the National Health and Social Life Survey (NHSLS). Each participant was asked whether during the past 12 months he or she had experienced "a period of *several months or more* when you lacked interest in having sex; had trouble achieving or maintaining an erection or (for women) had trouble lubricating; were unable to come to a climax; came to a climax too quickly; or experienced physical pain during intercourse." For each item, the person was asked for a simple yes or no response. Figure 12.3 indicates the overall percentage of men and women who indicated that they had experienced each of these specific problems. There are

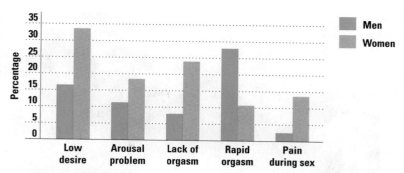

**FIGURE 12.3**

**Prevalence of Sexual Dysfunctions**  This graph shows the percentage of NHSLS respondents who reported having sexual difficulties at some time during the previous 12 months. Note the differences in the problems reported by men and women.
*Source*: Based on Laumann, Edward O., John H. Gagnon, Robert T. Michael and Stuart Michaels. 1994. The Social Organization of Sexuality: Sexual Practices in the United States. University of Chicago Press.

obviously significant gender differences in the prevalence of all types of problems. Premature ejaculation is the most frequent form of male sexual dysfunction, affecting almost one out of every three adult men. All the other forms of sexual dysfunction are reported more often by women. One-third of women said that they lacked interest in sex, and almost one-quarter indicated that they experienced a period of several months during which they were unable to reach orgasm (Laumann, Paik, & Rosen, 1999).

**SEXUAL BEHAVIOR ACROSS THE LIFE SPAN**  Sexual behavior changes with age. Masters and Johnson devoted considerable attention to this topic in their original studies. Their data challenged the myth that older adults are not interested in, or capable of performing, sexual behaviors. The NHSLS data also indicate that many people remain sexually active later in life. Gender differences become marked in the late fifties, when rates of inactivity increase dramatically for women. Between ages 70 and 74, 65 percent of men are still sexually active, compared to only 30 percent of women. These differences may be, at least partly, the result of differential mortality rates (men die earlier, so many women lose their partners) as well as biological factors that are part of the aging process. They may also reflect the influence of a cultural prejudice against sexual activity among older women.

Differences between younger and older people are mostly a matter of degree. As men get older, they tend to achieve erections more slowly, but they can often maintain erections for longer periods of time. Older men find it more difficult to regain an erection if it is lost before orgasm. As women get older, vaginal lubrication may occur at a slower rate, but the response of the clitoris remains essentially unchanged. The intensity of the subjective experience of orgasm is decreased for older men and women. For both men and women, healthy sexual responsiveness is most likely to be maintained among those who have been sexually active as younger adults (Herbenick et al., 2010).

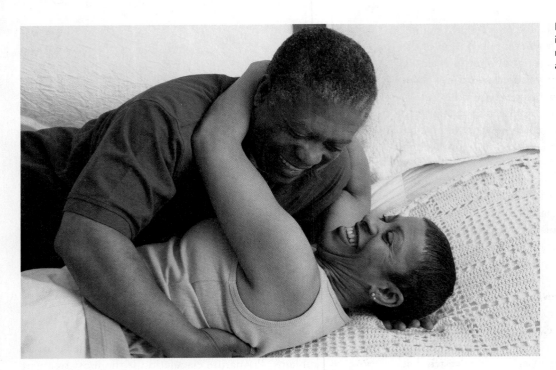

Many people remain sexually active later in life. Differences in sexual responsiveness between younger and older people are mostly a matter of degree.

The prevalence of certain types of sexual dysfunctions increases among the elderly, particularly among men (DeRogatis & Burnett, 2008). In the NHSLS, for example, the proportion of men reporting erectile problems increased from 6 percent in the 18–24 age range to 20 percent in the 55–59 age range. In contrast, several types of sexual problems actually declined in frequency among older women. Women in the 55–59 age range were less likely than women between the ages of 18 and 24 to report pain during sex or inability to reach orgasm, although they did report a slight increase in trouble with lubrication during sexual activity.

The relation between sexual experience and aging is closely related to other health problems that increase with age. People who rate their health as being excellent have many fewer sexual problems than people who rate their health as being only fair or poor (Laumann, Das, & Waite, 2008).

**CROSS-CULTURAL COMPARISONS** Patients with sexual disorders seek treatment at clinics all over the world (Steggall, Gann, & Chinegwundoh, 2004). Therefore, these problems are not unique to any particular culture. Cultural and ethnic differences have been reported for sexual practices, beliefs about sexuality, and patterns of sexual decision making. For example, Asians are more conservative than Caucasians in many regards, such as the prevalence and frequency of masturbation (Meston, Trapnell, & Gorzalka, 1996). It is not clear whether variations in sexual behavior are accompanied by cultural differences in the frequency and form of sexual dysfunctions. Cross-cultural studies of prevalence rates for specific sexual dysfunctions have not been reported. This kind of investigation may be difficult to perform because the *DSM-5* definitions of sexual dysfunctions may not be well suited to describing the sexual experiences and satisfaction of people living in non-Western cultures (Ghanem & El-Sakka, 2007).

## Causes

At each stage of the sexual response cycle, a person's behavior is determined by the interaction of many biological and psychological factors, ranging from vasocongestion in the genitals to complex cognitive events involving the perception of sexual stimuli and the interpretation of sexual meanings. Interference with this system at any point can result in serious problems. In the following pages, we review some of the factors that contribute to the etiology of various types of sexual dysfunctions.

**BIOLOGICAL FACTORS** The experience of sexual desire is partly controlled by biological factors. Sexual desire is influenced by sex hormones for both men and women (LeVay & Valente, 2003). Testosterone is particularly important for male sexual desire. Studies of men with inadequate levels of sex hormones show an inhibited response to sexual fantasies, but they are still able to have erections in response to viewing explicit erotic films. The influence of male sex hormones on sexual behavior is, therefore, thought to be on sexual appetite rather than on sexual performance. This process probably involves a threshold level of circulating testosterone (Schiavi & Segraves, 1995). In other words, sexual appetite is impaired if the level of testosterone falls below a particular point (close to the bottom of the laboratory normal range), but above that threshold, fluctuations in testosterone levels will not be associated with changes in sexual desire. The reduction of male sex hormones over the life span probably explains, at least in part, the apparent decline in sexual desire among elderly males.

Many cases of erectile dysfunction can be attributed to vascular, neurological, or hormonal impairment (Goldstein, 2004). Erection is the direct result of a threefold increase in blood flow to the penis. Thus, it is not surprising that vascular diseases, which may affect the amount of blood reaching the penis, are likely to result in erectile difficulties. Neurological diseases, such as epilepsy and multiple sclerosis, can also produce erectile difficulties, because erection depends on spinal reflexes. Diabetes may be the most common neurologically based cause of impaired erectile responsiveness.

Various kinds of drugs can also influence a man's erectile response (Clayton & West, 2003). One interesting set of results indicates that men who smoke cigarettes are more likely to experience erectile difficulties than are men in the general population. Many other drugs, including alcohol and marijuana, may have negative effects on sexual arousal.

A number of biological factors can impair a woman's ability to become sexually aroused (Clayton, 2007). Various types of neurological disorders, pelvic disease, and hormonal dysfunction can interfere with the process of vaginal swelling and lubrication. Although relatively little research has been conducted on sexual arousal in women, there is evidence to suggest that genetic factors influence the frequency with which women are able to experience orgasm (Dawood, Kirk, Bailey, Andrews, Martin, 2005).

Inhibited orgasm, in both men and women, is sometimes caused by the abuse of alcohol and other drugs. The problem may improve if the person is able to stop drinking and maintain a stable period of sobriety (Schiavi & Segraves, 1995). Orgasm problems can also be associated with the use of prescribed forms of medication. For example, as we discussed in Chapter 5, many people who take SSRIs such as fluoxetine (Prozac) for the treatment of depression have difficulty achieving orgasm as a side effect (Werneke, Northey, & Bhugra, 2006).

**PSYCHOLOGICAL FACTORS** Although sexual desire is rooted in a strong biological foundation, psychological variables also play an important role in the determination of which stimuli a person will find arousing. Sexual desire and arousal are determined, in part, by mental scripts that we learn throughout childhood and adolescence (Middleton, Kuffel, & Heiman, 2008; Wiegel, Scepkowski, & Barlow, 2007). These scripts provide structure or context to the otherwise confusing array of potential partners who might become the object of our desires. In other words, there are certain kinds of people to whom we may be sexually attracted, and there are certain circumstances in which sexual behavior is considered appropriate. According to this perspective, the personal meaning of an event is of paramount importance in releasing the biological process of sexual arousal. Both members of the potential couple must recognize similar cues, defining the situation as potentially sexual in nature, before anything is likely to happen.

Beliefs and attitudes toward sexuality, as well as the quality of interpersonal relationships, have an important influence on the development of low sexual desire, especially among women (Nobre & Pinto-Gouveia, 2006). Women seeking treatment for low interest in sex report negative perceptions of their parents' attitudes regarding sexual behavior and the demonstration of affection. In comparison to other women, they also indicate that they feel less close to their husbands, have fewer romantic feelings, and are less attracted to their husbands. The quality of the relationship is an important factor to consider with regard to low sexual desire (Metz & Epstein, 2002).

Culturally determined attitudes toward sexual feelings and behaviors can also have a dramatic impact on women's ability to become sexually aroused (Al-Sawaf & Al-Issa, 2000). Some societies openly encourage female sexuality; others foster a more repressive atmosphere. Within U.S. culture, there are tremendous variations with regard to women's ability to experience and express their sexuality. For example, many women feel guilty about having sexual fantasies, in spite of the fact that such fantasies are extremely common. Women who feel guilty about fantasizing while they are having intercourse are more likely to be sexually dissatisfied and to encounter sexual problems. The most important factors contributing to failure to reach orgasm involve negative attitudes, feelings of guilt, and failure to communicate effectively (Kelly, Strassberg, & Turner, 2004).

Couples that experience communication problems, power conflicts, and an absence of intimacy and trust are more likely than others to experience sexual problems. Lack of assertiveness and lack of comfort in talking about sexual activities and pleasures are associated with various types of female sexual dysfunctions (Rosen & Leiblum, 1995). The following brief case study provides one example of serious relationship difficulties that were experienced by one couple in which the woman, a married, 34-year-old lawyer, was being treated for long-standing vaginismus as well as alcohol dependence.

### → Penetration Difficulty and Alcohol Dependence

Gina speculated that living with Paul exacerbated her sexual anxieties, and she became increasingly dependent on alcohol to "loosen her up" sexually. Paul was sexually naive and did not press Gina to have intercourse, especially when she so visibly panicked at the approach of his penis. He, too, was sexually anxious and was afraid of inflicting pain on her. Sexually, they depended on drinking to disinhibit them, and they developed a sexual script that relied on manual stimulation and oral sex. Although sexual contact was relatively infrequent, both were reasonably content.

This state of affairs continued for many years. It was not without its costs, though. Gina felt inadequate and deficient as a woman and avoided gynecological examinations. Paul would occasionally become enraged at a seemingly small provocation and verbally attack Gina. Internally, he reported feeling humiliated, emasculated, and ashamed about the non-consummation of their marriage. When his coworkers teased and joked about "getting it on" sexually, he felt alone in the private knowledge that he had never penetrated his wife despite 13 years of living and sleeping together.

Eventually, as Gina's drinking escalated, the marital conflict grew intolerable. When Gina was drunk, she would verbally berate and abuse Paul. Her attacks and complaints about his passivity and lack of assistance with housework and her disparagement of his passion for sports undermined the earlier closeness they had experienced. Although he would usually tolerate her drunken tirades silently, he began to blow up more readily (Leiblum, 1995, p. 256).

Previous harmful or traumatic experiences can also have an important effect on various aspects of sexual interests and arousal. A previous history of sexual abuse can cause aversion to sexual stimuli, and it can interfere with a woman's ability to become sexually aroused (Najman, Dunne, Purdie, Boyle, Coxeter, 2005). Premature ejaculation and low sexual desire in men have also been linked to various kinds of long-lasting, adverse relationships with adults during childhood (Loeb, Williams, Carmona, Rivkin, Wyatt, Chin, 2002). For example, boys who grow up in a home in which their father is physically abusive may learn to associate sex with violence and become convinced that they do not want to function—sexually or interpersonally—as their father had.

Performance anxiety and fear of failure are among the most important psychological factors contributing to impaired sexual arousal. People who have experienced inhibited sexual arousal on one or two occasions may be likely to have further problems to the degree that these difficulties make them more self-conscious or apprehensive regarding their ability to become aroused in future sexual encounters. Several prominent and experienced sex therapists have assumed that anxiety and sexual arousal are incompatible emotional states. People who are anxious will presumably be less responsive to sexual stimuli. And men who have sexual arousal disorders are more likely to report feeling high levels of performance anxiety (McCabe, 2005).

Anxiety disrupts sexual performance to the extent that it alters certain cognitive processes. Several studies have compared the responses of sexually dysfunctional men with those of control subjects in laboratory settings. Dysfunctional men experience more negative emotions in the presence of erotic stimuli, and they are also more likely to shift their attention from the arousing properties of sexual stimuli to the threatening consequences of potential failures in sexual performance (Bach, Brown, & Barlow, 1999). In comparison to men without erectile disorder, men with sexual dysfunction rate negative sexual events as being more important and then are more likely to attribute the problem to something about themselves rather than external considerations (Scepkowski, Wiegel, Bach, Weisberg, Brown, Barlow, 2004).

## Treatment

Masters and Johnson (1970) were pioneers in developing and popularizing a short-term, skills-based approach to the treatment of sexual dysfunctions. Hundreds of couples who visited their clinic in St. Louis went through a two-week course of assessment and therapy in which they became more familiar with their bodies, learned to communicate more effectively with their partners, and received training in procedures designed to help them diminish their fears about sexuality. The results of this treatment program were very positive and quickly spawned a burgeoning industry of psychosocial treatment for sexual dysfunction. Getting Help at the end of this chapter discusses some of the options and resources available to anyone experiencing problems in sexual functioning or health.

**PSYCHOLOGICAL PROCEDURES** Psychological treatments for sexual dysfunction address several of the causes discussed earlier, especially negative attitudes toward sexuality, failure to engage in effective sexual behaviors, and deficits in communication skills. Sex therapy centers around three primary types of activities: sensate focus and scheduling; education and cognitive restructuring; and communication training (Meston & Rellini, 2008; Wincze, Bach, & Barlow, 2008).

The cornerstone of sex therapy is known as **sensate focus,** a series of simple exercises in which the couple spends time in a quiet, relaxed setting, learning to touch each other. They may start with tasks as simple as holding hands or giving each other back rubs. The rationale for sensate focus hinges on the recognition that people with sexual problems must learn to focus on erotic sensations rather than on performance demands. The goal is to help them become more comfortable with this kind of physical sharing and intimacy, to learn to relax and enjoy it, and to talk to each other about what feels good and what does not.

Another facet of psychological approaches to treating sexual dysfunction involves *scheduling.* This is, in fact, closely related to sensate focus because the technique of sensate focus requires that people schedule time for sex. Couples need a quiet, relaxed, and private environment in order to engage in pleasurable and satisfying sexual behavior.

Sensate focus exercises help people become aware of physical sensations that are associated with touching and being touched while minimizing demands for sexual performance.

A third aspect of sex therapy involves education and cognitive restructuring—changing the way in which people think about sex. In many cases, the therapist needs to help the couple correct mistaken beliefs and attitudes about sexual behavior. Examples are the belief that intercourse is the only true form of sex, that foreplay is an adolescent interest that most adults can ignore, and that simultaneous orgasm is the ultimate goal of intercourse. Providing information about sexual behaviors in the general population can often help alleviate people's guilt and anxiety surrounding their own experiences. Some people are relieved to know that they are not the only ones who fantasize about various kinds of sexual experiences, or that the fact that they fantasize about these things does not mean that they are going to be compelled to behave in deviant ways.

The final element of psychological treatment for sexual dysfunction is communication training. Many different studies have indicated that people with sexual dysfunction often have deficits in communication skills. They find it difficult to talk to their partners about matters involving sex, and they are especially impaired in the ability to tell their partners what kinds of things they find sexually arousing and what kinds of things turn them off. Therefore, sex therapists often employ structured training procedures aimed at improving the ways in which couples talk to each other.

The outcome results of psychological treatment programs for sexual disorders have generally been considered to be positive (Dutere, Segraves, & Althof, 2007). Early reports from Masters and Johnson's clinic were especially glowing. One summary of their results reported an overall success rate of 85 percent for male patients and 78 percent for female patients. Unfortunately, more recent studies have reported less positive results. Serious questions have been raised about the adequacy of the research methods employed in several outcome studies. Interventions have not been standardized, sample sizes have been relatively small, and long-term follow-up data are often lacking. Therefore, although psychological treatments for sexual dysfunction are frequently successful, empirical support for the efficacy of these procedures is not strong (Heiman, 2002; O'Donohue, Swingen, Dopke, Regev, 1999). Better studies are clearly needed.

Important questions have also been raised about the utility of these procedures for clients in other cultures. Clinics in India, Iran, Japan, Saudi Arabia, and South Africa report that men and women from many different backgrounds seek help for sexual dysfunctions (Verma, Khaitan, & Singh, 1998). Culture dictates the ways in which sexual issues may be discussed, and beliefs about sexuality and reproduction influence decisions about acceptable sexual behaviors. These beliefs vary extensively across cultures. For example, people in some Asian cultures believe that a man's health can be damaged through unnecessary loss of semen (Davis & Herdt, 1997). Such concerns may prohibit use of masturbation as a therapeutic exercise. Implicit rules governing communication patterns between partners are also determined by

culture. Some societies value and encourage sharp differences in gender roles, with men being expected to make decisions about the timing and type of sexual activity (Quadagno, Sly, Harrison, Eberstein, Soler, 1998). Therefore, communication training must be tailored to meet the expectations that each couple holds regarding the nature of their relationship. Mental health professionals must give careful consideration to their clients' cultural background when they conduct an assessment and design a treatment program.

**BIOLOGICAL TREATMENTS** Biological treatments—primarily medications—are also useful in the treatment of sexual dysfunctions. This is especially true for erectile disorder, the most frequent sexual problem for which men seek professional help. Sildenafil citrate (Viagra) was approved by the FDA in 1998 for the treatment of erectile dysfunction and quickly became one of the most popular drugs on the market. Competing pharmaceutical companies soon developed and began vigorously promoting similar drugs known as tadalafil (Cialis) and vardenafil (Levitra). All three drugs are phosphodiesterase-5 (PDE-5)[1] inhibitors that facilitate erection by increasing blood flow to certain areas of the penis. They increase the man's ability to respond to stimuli that he would ordinarily find sexually arousing, but they do not influence overall sexual desire (Edwards, Hackett, Collins, Curram, 2006).

Double-blind, placebo-controlled studies have evaluated the use of Viagra in men with erectile problems associated with various conditions, including hypertension, diabetes, and coronary artery disease. It is effective, increasing the number of erections for approximately two-thirds of men with severe erectile dysfunction (Fink, MacDonald, Rutks, Nelson, Wilt, 2002). Unfortunately, some men experience negative side effects, such as headache, facial flushing, nasal congestion, and altered vision. Perhaps most important, Viagra can lead to sudden drops in blood pressure if taken with various forms of medication known as "nitrates," which are used in the treatment of heart disease. Some deaths were reported after Viagra was introduced because of this misuse. The research evidence indicates that Viagra and other PDE-5 inhibitors should be used in combination with psychological treatments for sexual dysfunction (see Critical Thinking Matters).

*"It's a shame there isn't a pill to stimulate conversation."*
© Alex Gregory/The New Yorker Collection/
www.cartoonbank.com

---

[1]PDE-5 is an enzyme that metabolizes nitric oxide, which triggers sexual arousal.

## Does Medication Cure Sexual Dysfunction?

Can you remember watching a sporting event on television without seeing an advertisement for Cialis or Levitra? Attractive men and women cuddle and smile as they talk enthusiastically about the satisfaction that can be achieved with pharmacologically induced *strong, lasting erections*. It's difficult to imagine a new form of treatment for a psychological disorder that has been promoted more aggressively, or achieved a more dramatic impact on public awareness, than the PDE-5 inhibitors. In a few short years, they have generated a market that is estimated to approach $2 billion per year. They've become very popular, but do these pills offer a quick fix for all people suffering from arousal disorders?

Viagra and similar medications are clearly an important option for men with erectile problems. Countless men and their partners are grateful for their beneficial effects. Unfortunately, in many other cases, they are not a complete solution to sexual dysfunction in the absence of additional treatment. Couples that have experienced sexual problems have often struggled with a number of difficult issues for several years. Increasing the man's capacity for erection will address only one part of the problem. As one expert puts it, "Viagra can increase blood flow to the penis, but it doesn't create intimacy, love, or desire" (Morgentaler, 2003). Most experts recommend

a treatment approach that combines the use of medication with cognitive behavior therapy. Therapists need to work with couples to improve intimacy and communication while also helping them to overcome frustrations and anxiety that have accumulated over years (McCarthy, 2004; Rosen, 2000).

A related product for women, which the media have nicknamed the *female Viagra,* may be available soon. Intrinsa, a patch that delivers testosterone through the skin, is being developed to address low desire, the most frequent sexual problem reported by women (see Figure 12.3). Small doses of testosterone can increase sexual desire in some women who have had their ovaries removed, but it seems unlikely that they will be effective with women who have lost interest in sex because of relationship difficulties or other motivational and cognitive factors. Problems with fatigue, scheduling difficulties, anxiety, and low self-esteem are all issues that don't go away simply because testosterone levels increase. Medication may facilitate some of the biological functions that are necessary prerequisites for healthy sexual behaviors, but it cannot guarantee that people will find their partners appealing or that sex will be pleasurable. Consumers and medical professionals all need to think critically about the complex factors that contribute to sexual dysfunction. We should not expect to find a magic bullet that will cure them all at once.

---

Pharmaceutical companies are also developing and evaluating medications that might be used to treat sexual dysfunction in women (Korda, Goldstein, & Goldstein, 2010; van der Made, Bloemers, Yassem, Kleiverda, Everaerd, van Ham, . . . Tuiten, 2009). One product, known as Intrinsa, is a patch that delivers testosterone through the skin and could serve to increase sexual desire, especially in post-menopausal women and those who have had their ovaries removed. The FDA decided in 2004 to delay approval for Intrinsa because it did not have enough information about its long-term safety, particularly regarding increased risk for cancer and cardiovascular disease. The use of testosterone could also lead to other side effects, such as facial hair growth, deepening of the voice, and the development of other masculine features in women.

Another less frequently used procedure for the treatment of erectile dysfunction involves surgically inserting a penile implant (or prosthesis), which can be used to make the penis rigid during intercourse (Melman & Tiefer, 1992; Schwartz, Covino, Morgenstaler, DeWolf, 2000). Several devices have been used. One option is a semi-rigid silicone rod that the man can bend into position for intercourse. Another device is hydraulic and can be inflated for the purpose of sexual activity. The man squeezes a small pump, which forces fluid into the inflatable cylinder and produces an erection. The inflatable device is preferred by

partners, but it is also more expensive and can lead to more frequent postsurgical complications, such as infection.

The various forms of treatment that are available for the treatment of sexual dysfunction are certainly promising. They offer several constructive options for people who are experiencing distress as a consequence of problems in sexual desire or performance. That is the good news with regard to sexual disorders. The bad news is concerned with another set of problems, which are known collectively as paraphilic disorders. They are less well understood, in comparison to the sexual dysfunctions, and they are also more difficult to treat. The next section of this chapter reviews the current state of our knowledge regarding these difficult problems.

## Paraphilic Disorders

For some people, sexual arousal is strongly associated with unusual activities and targets, such as inanimate objects, sexual contact with children, exhibiting their genitals to strangers, or inflicting pain on another person. These conditions are known as paraphilias. Literally translated, paraphilia means "love" (*philia*) "beyond the usual" (*para*). This term refers to conditions that were formerly called perversions or sexual deviations. The central features of all paraphilias are persistent sexual urges and fantasies that are associated with (1) nonhuman objects, (2) suffering or humiliation of oneself or one's partner, or (3) children or other nonconsenting persons. According to *DSM-5,* there is an important distinction between a paraphilia and a paraphilic disorder. **Paraphilia** is a term that describes "any intense and persistent sexual interest other than sexual interest in genital stimulation or preparatory fondling with a phenotypically normal, physically mature, consenting human partner" (APA, 2013, p. 685). **Paraphilic disorder** is a term that describes a paraphilia that either leads to subjective distress or social impairment for the person or that causes harm to, or threatens, other people (Blanchard, 2010). This distinction indicates that some forms of nonnormative sexual behaviors, such as fetishism and sexual masochism, are not necessarily pathological if they are practiced voluntarily by consenting adults (Wright, 2010).

In the following pages, we summarize a few of the most common paraphilic disorders, and we consider some of the factors that might influence the development of unusual sexual preferences.

## Symptoms

One hundred years ago, many psychiatrists considered any type of sexual behavior other than heterosexual intercourse to be pathological. Contemporary researchers and clinicians have expanded the boundaries of normal behavior to include a much broader range of sexual behavior. A large proportion of men and women engage in sexual fantasies and mutually consenting behaviors such as oral sex. These experiences enhance their relationships without causing problems (Herbenick, Reece, Schick, Sanders, Dodge, Fortenberry, 2010). Problems with sexual appetites arise when a pattern develops involving a long-standing, unusual erotic preoccupation that is highly arousing, coupled with a pressure to act on the erotic fantasy.

It is actually somewhat misleading, or imprecise, to say that paraphilic disorders are defined solely in terms of reactions to unusual stimuli. The central problem is that sexual arousal is dependent on images that are detached from reciprocal, loving relationships with another adult (Levine, Risen, & Althof, 1990). Themes of aggression, violence, and hostility are common in paraphilic fantasies, as are impulses involving strangers or unwilling partners. Rather than focusing on whether the stimuli are common or uncommon, some experts place principal emphasis on the lack of human intimacy that is associated with many forms of paraphilias (Moser, 2001).

Compulsion and lack of flexibility are also important features of paraphilic behaviors. Paraphilias may take up a lot of time and consume much of the person's energy. In that sense, they are similar to the addictions. People with paraphilic disorders are not simply aroused by unusual images or fantasies. They feel *compelled* to engage in certain acts that may be personally degrading or harmful to others, in spite of the fact that these actions are often repulsive to others and are sometimes illegal. The following case describes some of the central features of paraphilic disorders.

## ⟶ Paraphilic Disorder

For the past 40 years, Jon has masturbated to images of barely clad women violently wrestling each other. Periodically throughout his marriage, he has tried to involve his wife in wrestling matches with her friends and, eventually, with their adolescent daughter. When Jon was drunk, he occasionally embarrassed his wife by trying to pick fights between her and other women. On summer vacations, he sometimes jokingly suggested the women wrestle. During much of his sober life, however, his daydreams of women wrestling were private experiences that preoccupied only him. He amassed a collection of magazines and videotapes depicting women wrestling, to which he would resort when driven by the need for excitement.

Jon presented for help with his inability to maintain his erection with his wife for intercourse. With the exception of procreational sex, he was not able to consummate his long marriage. He was able to (become) erect if his wife described herself wrestling other women while he stimulated his penis in front of her, but he always lost his erection when intercourse was attempted (Levine, Risen, & Althof, 1990).

This case illustrates the way in which paraphilic disorders can interfere with a person's life, especially relationships with other people. Jon's preoccupation with fantasies of women wrestling led him to say and do things that disrupted his marriage and his friendships with other people. Many people with paraphilic disorders experience sexual dysfunction involving desire, arousal, or orgasm during conventional sexual behavior with a partner. The wives of men with paraphilic disorders frequently protest that their husbands are not interested in their sexual relationship. In fact, the husband may be actively engaged in frequent masturbation to paraphilic fantasies. Cases of this sort present an interesting diagnostic challenge to the clinician, who must distinguish a paraphilia from what might otherwise appear to be low sexual desire.

## Diagnosis

*DSM-5* requires that the erotic preoccupation must have lasted at least six months before the person would meet diagnostic criteria for a paraphilic disorder. Furthermore, the diagnosis of paraphilic disorder is made only if the person's paraphilic urges lead to clinically significant distress or impairment. The person would be considered to be impaired if the urges have become compulsory, if they produce sexual dysfunction, if they require the participation of nonconsenting persons, if they lead to legal problems, or if they interfere with social relationships. For several specific types of paraphilic disorders, the person would qualify for a diagnosis if he acted on the urge (Hilliard & Spitzer, 2002). These include pedophilic, exhibitionistic, voyeuristic, and frotteuristic disorders (see descriptions in the following pages). For sexual sadism, acting on the urge would qualify the person for a diagnosis only if the partner had not consented to the activity. Acting on the other

## TABLE 12.2
## Paraphilic Disorders Listed in *DSM-5*

| ANOMALOUS ACTIVITY PREFERENCES | |
|---|---|
| **Courtship Disorders** | **Focus of sexual interest** |
| Voyeuristic Disorder | spying on others in private activities |
| Exhibitionistic Disorder | exposing genitals to non-consenting others |
| Frotteuristic Disorder | touching or rubbing against non-consenting others |
| **Sexual Arousal Associated with Pain** | |
| Sexual Sadism Disorder | inflicting humiliation, bondage, or suffering |
| Sexual Masochism Disorder | undergoing humiliation, bondage, or suffering |
| **ANOMALOUS TARGET PREFERENCES** | |
| **Directed at other humans** | **Focus of sexual interest** |
| Pedophilic Disorder | pre-pubescent children |
| **Directed elsewhere** | |
| Fetishistic Disorder | non-living objects or highly specific focus on non-genital body parts |
| Transvestic Disorder | cross-dressing |

*Source:* Courtesy of Thomas F. Oltmanns and Robert E. Emery.

forms of paraphilic urges (masochism, fetishism, and transvestic fetishism) would not be sufficient for a diagnosis unless the urges of fantasies lead to significant personal distress or interfere with the person's ability to function.

Although they are listed as distinct disorders, it might be more useful to think of the paraphilic disorders as one diagnostic category, with the specific forms listed in *DSM-5* representing subtypes of this single disorder (Fedoroff, 2003). Differences among them are based on the focus of sexual interest (see Table 12.2). The primary types of paraphilic disorder described in the following pages are the ones most often seen in clinics that specialize in the treatment of sexual disorders. Not surprisingly, they are also the ones that frequently lead to a person being arrested. Other types of paraphilias are listed in Table 12.3.

## TABLE 12.3
## Other Types of Paraphilias

| Name | Focus of Sexual Urges and Fantasies |
|---|---|
| Telephone scatologia | Obscene phone calls |
| Necrophilia | Corpses |
| Partialism | One specific part of the body |
| Zoophilia | Animals |
| Coprophilia | Feces |
| Klismaphilia | Enemas |
| Urophilia | Urine |
| Stigmatophilia | Piercing; marking body; tattoos |

**FETISHISTIC DISORDER** Anthropologists use the word *fetish* to describe an object that is believed to have magical powers to protect or help its owner. In psychopathology, **fetishistic disorder** is defined in terms of the association of sexual arousal with nonliving objects. The range of objects that can become associated with sexual arousal is virtually unlimited, but fetishism most often involves women's underwear, shoes and boots, or products made out of rubber or leather (Darcangelo, 2008). The person may go to great lengths, including burglary, to obtain certain kinds of fetish objects.

People who fit the description of fetishism typically masturbate while holding, rubbing, or smelling the fetish object.

Many men find women's clothing attractive or sexy, but for a man with a fetish, sexual arousal is focused *exclusively* on the object. The partner is largely irrelevant.

Particular sensory qualities of the object—texture, visual appearance, and smell—can be very important in determining whether the person finds it arousing. In addition to holding or rubbing the object, the person may wear, or ask his sexual partner to wear, the object during sexual activity. The person may be unable to become sexually aroused in the absence of the fetish object.

**TRANSVESTIC DISORDER** A *transvestite* is a person who dresses in the clothing of the other gender. In *DSM-5*, **transvestic disorder** is defined as cross-dressing for the purpose of sexual arousal. It has been described primarily among heterosexual men and should not be confused with the behavior of some gay men known as *drag queens* (for whom cross-dressing has a very different purpose and meaning).

People who meet criteria for transvestic disorder usually keep a collection of female clothes that are used to cross-dress. Some wear only a single article of women's clothing, such as female underwear, covered by male clothing. Others dress completely as women, including makeup, jewelry, and accessories. Cross-dressing may be done in public or only in private. The person

Some gay men who dress in women's clothes refer to themselves as "drag queens." This is different from transvestic fetishism, which applies only to heterosexual men whose cross-dressing is associated with intense, sexually arousing fantasies or urges.

masturbates while he is cross-dressed, often imagining himself to be a male as well as the female object of his own sexual fantasy. Aside from their interest in cross-dressing, men with transvestic disorder are unremarkably masculine in their interests, occupations, and other behaviors. Most of these men get married and have children (Schott, 1995). For some men, transvestism may eventually lead to feelings of dissatisfaction with being male (Zucker & Blanchard, 1997). They may develop persistent discomfort with their gender role or identity and may eventually want to live permanently as women.

**SEXUAL MASOCHISM DISORDER** People who become sexually aroused when they are subjected to pain or embarrassment are called masochists. *DSM-5* defines **sexual masochism disorder** in terms of recurrent, intense sexually arousing fantasies, urges, or impulses involving being humiliated, beaten, bound, or otherwise made to suffer (Hucker, 2008; Krueger, 2010). People who qualify for this diagnosis may act on these impulses by themselves or with a partner. In some large cities, clubs cater to the sexual interests of masochistic men and women, who pay people to inflict pain on them.

The person may become aroused by being bound, blindfolded, spanked, pinched, whipped, verbally abused, forced to crawl and bark like a dog, or in some other way made to experience pain or feelings of shame and disgrace. One relatively common masochistic fantasy takes the form of being forced to display one's naked body to other people. Masochists desire certain types of pain (which are carefully controlled to remain within specified limits, usually unpleasant but not agonizing), but they also go to great lengths to avoid injury during their contrived, often ritualized experiences (Stoller, 1991). They do not enjoy, and are not immune to, painful experiences that lie outside these limited areas of their lives.

The following first-person account was written by Daphne Merkin (1996), an accomplished writer whose fascinating and controversial essay on masochism appeared in *The New Yorker*.

### → Sexual Masochism Disorder

The fact is that I cannot remember a time when I didn't think about being spanked as a sexually gratifying act, didn't fantasize about being reduced to a craven object of desire by a firm male hand. Depending on my mood, these daydreams were marked by an atmosphere of greater or lesser ravishment, but all of them featured similar ingredients. Most important among them was a heightened—and deeply pleasurable—sense of exposure, brought about by the fact that enormous attention was being paid to my bottom, and by the fact that there was an aspect of helpless display attached to this particular body part. This scenario, in which my normally alert self was reduced to a condition of wordless compliance via a specific ritual of chastisement, exerted a grip that was the more strong because I felt it to be so at odds with the intellectually weighty, morally upright part of me. (p. 99)

These fantasies and urges made Merkin feel uncomfortable, and she kept them to herself for many years. Being cautious and somewhat inhibited—certainly not prone to illicit sexual adventures—she worried about the boundaries of her masochistic desires. If she ever acted on them, where would she stop? And how would her partner respond? After many years of privately harboring masochistic sexual fantasies, Merkin finally described her fascination with spanking to a man whom she had been dating for several months. She was in her late twenties at the time, and eventually married this man. The following paragraph describes what happened after her admission:

> He appeared delighted at the prospect of implementing my wishes, and so it was that I found myself in the position I had been dreaming of for years: thrust over a man's knee, being soundly spanked for some concocted misdeed. The sheer tactile stimulation of it—the chastening sting—would have been enough to arouse me, but there was also, at last, the heady sense of emotional release: I was and was not a child; was and was not being reduced; was and was not being forced into letting go; was and was not the one in control. I had fantasized about this event for so long that in the back of my mind there had always lurked the fear that its gratification would prove disappointing. I needn't have worried; the reality of spanking, at least initially, was as good as the dream. (pp. 112–113)

Merkin tired of the spankings after she gave birth to her daughter, but the fantasies and urges returned several years later, after she had been separated from her husband. She eventually became involved in a relationship with another man that she described as "a fairly conventional romance that included some light (sadism and masochism)." After their mutual interests and consenting activities had escalated, Merkin found the relationship disturbing:

> It occurred to me that underneath my own limited participation in this world I felt enormous resentment; I was following the steps in a dance I couldn't control. Spanking and its accoutrements may have helped to subdue my simmering rage toward men—as well as theirs toward me—but it also demonstrated how far I was from healthy intimacy, from the real give-and-take that makes a relationship viable. (p. 114)

This case illustrates the compelling and often contradictory nature of the fantasies that are associated with paraphilias. This successful and independent woman, who did not believe in using corporal punishment with her own daughter, found great pleasure associated with fantasies of being spanked by a man. Merkin would not have qualified for a diagnosis of sexual masochism, even after she had acted on her fantasies, unless she experienced subjective distress or social impairment as a result.

## MyPsychLab VIDEO CASE

### Exploring Sexual Sadism and Masochism

JOCELYN

*"I really wanted to feel what it was like to be overpowered."*

◉ Watch the Video *Jocelyn: Exploring Sadism and Masochism* on MyPsychLab

Do you think that voluntary sexual activities performed with a consenting partner should be considered symptoms of a disorder? In what ways could these behaviors be considered harmful to the person's life (other than the experience of pain)?

Like Daphne Merkin, many people who engage in masochistic sexual practices are highly educated and occupationally successful. Masochists tend to be disproportionately represented among the privileged groups in society. This pattern leads to the suggestion that masochism may be motivated by an attempt to escape temporarily from the otherwise constant burden of maintaining personal control and pursuing self-esteem (Baumeister & Butler, 1997).

**SEXUAL SADISM DISORDER** Someone who derives pleasure by inflicting physical or mental pain on other people is called a *sadist*. The term is based on the writings of the Marquis de Sade, whose novels describe the use of torture and cruelty for erotic purposes. *DSM-5* defines **sexual sadism disorder** in terms of intense, sexually arousing fantasies, urges, or behaviors that involve the psychological or physical suffering of a victim. Sadistic fantasies often involve asserting dominance over the victim; the experience of power and control may be as important as inflicting pain (Hucker, 1997). Some people engage in sadistic sexual rituals with a consenting partner (who may be a sexual masochist) who willingly suffers pain or humiliation. Others act on sadistic sexual urges with nonconsenting partners. In some cases, the severity of the sadistic behaviors escalates over time.

**EXHIBITIONISTIC DISORDER** *DSM-5* defines **exhibitionistic disorder** in terms of the following criteria: "(1) Over a period of at least six months, recurrent and intense sexual arousal from the exposure of one's genitals to an unsuspecting person, as manifested by fantasies, urges, or behaviors. (2) The individual has acted on these sexual urges with a nonconsenting person, or the sexual urges or fantasies cause clinically significant distress or impairment in social, occupational, or other important areas of functioning" (APA, 2013, p. 689). This behavior is also known as *indecent exposure.* Many different patterns of behavior fit into this category. About half of these men have erections while exposing themselves, and some masturbate at the time. The others usually masturbate shortly after the experience while fantasizing about the victim's reaction. Their intent usually involves a desire to shock the observer, but sometimes they harbor fantasies that the involuntary observer will become sexually aroused. They rarely attempt to touch or otherwise molest their victims, who are usually women or children (Murphy & Page, 2008).

Exhibitionistic disorder is almost exclusively a male disorder. Most exhibitionists begin to expose themselves when they are teenagers or in their early twenties. As adults, most are either married or living with a sexual partner. Exhibitionism is seldom an isolated behavior; men who engage in this type of behavior tend to do it frequently (Abel & Osborn, 1992).

**VOYEURISTIC DISORDER** The focus of sexual arousal in **voyeuristic disorder** is the act of observing an unsuspecting person, usually a stranger, who is naked, in the process of disrobing, or engaging in sexual activity (Metzl, 2004). Many people, especially men, are sexually aroused by the sight of people who are partially clad or naked. Voyeurs are not aroused by watching people who know that they are being observed. The process of looking ("peeping") is arousing in its own right. The person might fantasize about having a sexual relationship with the people who are being observed, but direct contact is seldom sought. In fact, the secret nature of the observation and the risk of discovery may contribute in an important way to the arousing nature of the situation. The voyeur reaches orgasm by masturbating during observation or later while remembering what he saw. Most keep their distance from the victim and are not dangerous, but there are exceptions to this rule (Långström, 2010).

**FROTTEURISTIC DISORDER** In **frotteuristic disorder,** a person who is fully clothed becomes sexually aroused by touching or rubbing his genitals against other, nonconsenting people.

To protect women from frotteurs, some railway companies in Japan set aside special women-only cars during peak hours and late at night. This sign in a Tokyo subway station says, "Beware of men who fondle women on crowded trains."

The frotteur usually chooses crowded places, such as sidewalks and public transportation, so that he can easily escape arrest. He either rubs his genitals against the victim's thighs and buttocks or fondles her genitalia or breasts (Horley, 2001; Lussier & Piché, 2008).

Like exhibitionism, frotteurism is a high-frequency form of paraphilic disorder; interviews with people being treated for frotteurism indicate that they may engage in hundreds of individual paraphilic acts. People who engage in frotteurism seek to escape as quickly as possible after touching or rubbing against the other person. They do not want further sexual contact.

**PEDOPHILIC DISORDER** People who persistently engage in sexual activities with children exhibit what is undoubtedly the most alarming and objectionable form of paraphilic behavior: pedophilia. Every year, more than 100,000 children in the United States are referred to child protective services because of suspected child abuse (see Chapter 18). The effects of child abuse on victims have been the subject of intense debate in recent years. Some victims later engage in excessive and risky sexual activities that lead to additional problems (Browning & Laumann, 1997). One controversial review concluded that negative consequences are neither pervasive nor typically intense (Rind, Tromovitch, & Bauserman, 1998). We must be cautious, however, about accepting the null hypothesis (see Research Methods in Chapter 1). Failure to detect significant differences between victims of abuse and other people may indicate that investigators have not examined the appropriate dependent measures. Harmful consequences of sexual abuse may take many forms, including the disruption of future relationships and discomfort with sexual activity (Emery & Laumann-Billings, 1998). Other forms of mental disorder, such as PTSD and eating disorders, can also be the product of prior sexual abuse (see Chapters 7 and 10).

**Pedophilic disorder** entails recurrent, intense, sexually arousing fantasies, sexual urges, or behaviors involving sexual activity with a prepubescent child (generally age 13 years or younger). In order to qualify for a diagnosis of pedophilia in *DSM-5*, the person must be at least 16 years of age and at least five years older than the child. The terms *pedophile* and *child molester* are sometimes used interchangeably, but this practice confuses legal definitions with psychopathology. A child molester is a person who has committed a sexual offense against a child victim. Therefore, the term depends on legal definitions of "sexual offense" and "child victim," which can vary from one state or country to another. In many locations, a child might be anyone under the age of consent, even if that person has reached puberty. All child molesters are not pedophiles. Furthermore, some pedophiles may not have molested children, because the diagnosis can be made on the basis of recurrent fantasies in the absence of actual behavior, if those fantasies cause marked distress or interpersonal difficulty (Barbaree & Seto, 1997).

Pedophilia includes a great variety of behaviors and sexual preferences (Cohen & Galynker, 2002; Fagan, Wise, Schmidt,

Berlin, 2002). Some pedophiles are attracted only to children, whereas others are sometimes attracted to adults. Most pedophiles are heterosexual, and the victims of pedophilia are more often girls than boys. Some offenders are attracted to both girls and boys. Sexual contact with children typically involves caressing and genital fondling. Vaginal, oral, and anal penetration are less common, and physical violence is relatively rare. In many cases, the child willingly and naively complies with the adult's intentions. In most cases, the child knows the person who molests him or her. More than half of all offenses occur in the home of either the child or the offender.

Incestuous relationships, in which the pedophile molests his own children, should perhaps be distinguished from those in which the offender is only casually acquainted with the victim. Incest refers to sexual activity between close blood relatives, such as father–daughter, mother–son, or between siblings. The definition may also be expanded to include stepchildren and their stepparents in reconstituted families. Most reported cases of incest involve fathers and stepfathers sexually abusing daughters and stepdaughters (Cole, 1992).

Many incest perpetrators would not be considered pedophiles, either because their victims are postpubescent adolescents or because they are also young themselves (such as male adolescents molesting their younger sisters). Perhaps as many as half of the men who commit incest have also engaged in sexual activity with children outside their own families (Abel & Osborn, 1992). This subgroup of pedophilic incest perpetrators may be the most harmful and the most difficult to treat. Their personality style is typically passive and dependent. They are unable to empathize with the plight of their victims, perhaps in part because they were absent or uninvolved in early childcare responsibilities (Williams & Finkelhor, 1990).

**RAPE AND SEXUAL ASSAULT** The legal definition of rape includes "acts involving nonconsensual sexual penetration obtained by physical force, by threat of bodily harm, or when the victim is incapable of giving consent by virtue of mental illness, mental retardation, or intoxication" (Goodman, Koss, & Russo, 1993). One conservative estimate of rape prevalence based on a national survey indicated that 14 percent of adult women had been raped (National Victim Center, 1992). The actual rate is probably higher, perhaps in the vicinity of 20 percent (Watts & Zimmerman, 2002). The impact of sexual assault on the victim is described in Chapter 7.

The frequency of coercive sex was studied as part of the NHSLS (Laumann, Gagnon, Michael, Michaels, 1994). The 3,500 participants were asked whether they had ever been forced to do something sexually that they did not want to do. The question was focused broadly and did not necessarily focus only on acts involving penetration or threats of violence. Slightly more than one out of every five women in the sample reported that they had been forced by a man to engage in some kind of sexual activity against their will. Among those women who had experienced

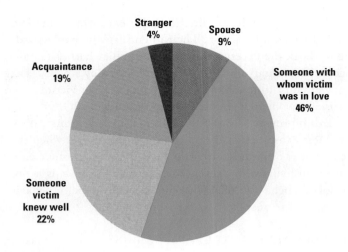

**FIGURE 12.4**

**Forced Sex: Relationship of Perpetrator to Victim**   As this chart shows, most NHSLS respondents who were forced into sexual activity knew the person who coerced them.
*Source*: Based on Laumann, Edward O., John H. Gagnon, Robert T. Michael and Stuart Michaels. 1994. The Social Organization of Sexuality: Sexual Practices in the United States. University of Chicago Press.

forced sex, 30 percent said that they had been forced sexually by more than one person.

Some rapes are committed by strangers, but many others—known as *acquaintance rapes*—are committed by men who know their victims. Most female victims know the person who raped them (Wiehe & Richards, 1995). Consider, for example, evidence from women in the NHSLS who had been victims of forced sex. Their relationship to the people who forced them to have sex is illustrated in Figure 12.4. Most reported that the person was either someone with whom they were in love or their spouse. Only 4 percent were forced to do something sexual by a stranger.

Rapes are committed by many different kinds of people for many different reasons (Bachar & Koss, 2001). The feminist perspective on rape emphasizes male aggression and violence. The traditional clinical perspective has been concerned with sexual deviance. The authors of *DSM-5* considered including rape as a type of paraphilia, but the proposal was rejected (see Thinking Critically About *DSM-5*). Nevertheless, the behavior of some rapists does include essential features of paraphilias: recurrent, intense sexually arousing fantasies and urges that involve the suffering of nonconsenting persons.

Efforts to classify sexual offenders have attempted to distinguish between those for whom deviant sexual arousal contributes to the act and those whose behavior is motivated primarily by anger or violent impulses. One interesting set of results was produced by studying convicted rapists who were imprisoned at an institution for sexually dangerous persons (Knight & Guay, 2006). Four different types of rapists were identified. Two categories include men whose motivation for sexual assault is primarily sexual in nature. *Sadistic rapists* exhibit features that are close to the generic *DSM-5* definition of a paraphilic disorder. Their

## Two Sexual Problems That Did Not Become New Mental Disorders

When we evaluate *DSM-5* critically, it's important to consider disorders that are *not* included in the manual as well as those that are. Both domains help us appreciate the thinking that shaped *DSM-5*. The popular media are fascinated by wild ideas about various kinds of behavior that someone considers to be abnormal and therefore a sign of mental disorder. Many proposals for new disorders were developed and evaluated by *DSM-5* workgroups. A few were added to the new manual, and several were ultimately rejected. Two involved sexual behaviors: hypersexual disorder and paraphilic coercion disorder.

*DSM-5* includes unusually low sexual desire as a male sexual dysfunction, but it does not mention unusually *high* sexual desire. Symptoms associated with this condition presumably include behaviors such as seeking new sexual encounters out of boredom with old ones and frequent use of pornography. Additional features include obsessive thoughts about sexual encounters, guilt resulting from problematic sexual behavior, and rationalization for continued reckless sexual behavior. Reckless and uncontrolled sexual activity can obviously disrupt a person's life and cause significant personal distress. Some experts wanted hypersexual behavior to be added to *DSM-5* (Kafka, 2010). They view uncontrolled sexual behavior as being similar to an addiction (Bancroft & Vukadinovic, 2004).

There are several good reasons to be skeptical of this concept. Perhaps most important is the heterogeneous nature of excessive or uncontrolled sexual behavior. Failure to control sexual impulses can be associated with several other disorders, including paraphilic disorders, impulse control disorders, and bipolar disorder (Levine, 2010). Many people who admit to compulsive sexual behavior also suffer from major depression, anxiety disorders, and substance use disorders (Black, Kehrberg, Flumerfelt, Schlosser, 1997; Guiliano, 2009). The concept obviously includes a diverse set of behavioral problems. It also suffers from conceptual problems that have been raised with regard to *impulse control disorders* (see page 252 in Chapter 9) and behavioral addictions (see Thinking Critically About *DSM-5* in Chapter 11). For all of these reasons, the proposal for recognizing hypersexual disorder as a new diagnosis in *DSM-5* was rejected.

The *DSM-5* workgroup also tackled a long-standing controversy regarding mental disorders and sexual assault. Do rapists suffer from a paraphilic disorder? The workgroup considered a new diagnostic category to be called paraphilic coercive disorder or PCD (Thornton, 2010). This proposal was grounded in the recognition that, for most men, sexual arousal is *inhibited* by obvious clues that their partner is feeling coerced. The new diagnosis would have applied to the minority of men for whom the opposite pattern is observed and coercion actually leads to increased sexual arousal. Sexual predator laws allow for involuntary commitment of those people who are judged to have a mental abnormality that would lead them to commit further offenses. PCD would be one option for this diagnostic decision.

Several problems are associated with the diagnosis of PCD (Wakefield, 2012). One is that paraphilic disorders are defined in terms of recurrent, intense sexually arousing *fantasies* or sexual *urges* focused on non-normative activities or targets, in this case sexual coercion. Fantasies and urges are obviously private experiences. In a criminal setting, alleged perpetrators may refuse to cooperate with assessments aimed at the identification of these subjective signs. It would then be tempting to diagnose paraphilic coercion disorder on the basis of the man's behavior (e.g., he raped several people, so he must be aroused by sexual coercion). But there would be no way to differentiate true cases of PCD from men who rape for other reasons, and the former outnumber the latter by a large margin. Furthermore, it is not clear that this syndrome can be distinguished reliably from more general sadistic urges and fantasies (Knight, 2010). For all of these reasons, the proposal to add PCD to *DSM-5* was rejected. As one critique noted: "Rape is a crime, and prison is the proper placement for rapists" (Tucker & Brakel, 2012).

Why were these proposals rejected while others were accepted? Maybe it's because they are problems that affect primarily men rather than women (cf. binge eating, premenstrual dysphoria), but we doubt it. You could also wonder if it's because both problems may be relatively rare, and the new diagnostic categories would not create huge new markets for the pharmaceutical industry. We also doubt that. We think the proposals were rejected because experts considered the evidence carefully and reached the correct decision in both cases.

Public criticism of *DSM-5* has often focused on expansion of the manual to include new diagnostic categories. Reviewers have argued that "normality is threatened" because so many people may now qualify for a diagnosis. There is certainly some merit to these arguments, but the cases of hypersexual disorder and paraphilic coercive disorder put the other additions in perspective. The workgroups did, in fact, reject a number of proposals, and their decisions were based on thoughtful consideration of the relevant evidence.

behavior is determined by a combination of sexual and aggressive impulses. The *nonsadistic* category also includes men who are preoccupied with sexual fantasies, but these fantasies are not blended with images of violence and aggression. The sexual aggression of these men may result, in part, from serious deficits in the ability to process social cues, such as the intentions of women.

The other two categories describe men whose primary motivation for rape is not sexual. *Vindictive* rapists seem intent on violence directed exclusively toward women. Their aggression is not erotically motivated, as with sadistic rapists. *Opportunistic* rapists are men with an extensive history of impulsive behavior in many kinds of settings and who might be considered psychopaths (see Chapter 9). Their sexual behavior is governed largely by immediate environmental cues. They will use whatever force is necessary to ensure compliance, but they express anger only in response to the victim's resistance. This research program confirms the impression that sex offenders are, in fact, an extremely heterogeneous group (McCabe & Wauchope, 2005).

## Frequency

There is very little evidence regarding the frequency of various types of unconventional sexual behavior. This is especially true for victimless or noncoercive forms of paraphilia, such as fetishism, transvestism, and sexual masochism, because most of these people seldom seek treatment or come to the attention of law enforcement officials. Furthermore, the fact that these forms of behavior are considered deviant or perverse makes it unlikely that people who engage in them will readily divulge their secret urges and fantasies.

With the exception of sexual masochism, paraphilias are almost always male behaviors. Some 95 percent of the people who seek treatment for paraphilic disorders are men. Paraphilias are seldom isolated phenomena. People who exhibit one type of paraphilia often exhibit others (Marshall, 2007). Gosselin and Wilson (1980) surveyed men who belonged to private clubs that cater to fetishists, sadomasochists, and transvestites, and they found that the members of different clubs often shared the same interests. This pattern has been called *crossing* of paraphilic behaviors. There is obviously a considerable amount of crossover among paraphilias.

## Causes

The high rate of overlap among paraphilias indicates that the etiology of these interests and behaviors might be most appropriately viewed in terms of common factors rather than in terms of distinct pathways that lead exclusively to one form of paraphilia or another. Those experiences and conditions that predispose an individual to one form of paraphilic disorder are apparently also likely to lead to another. In the following pages, we review a number of proposals regarding the etiology of paraphilic disorders. Some of these have been associated with specific types of paraphilias. For the most part, however, they are concerned more generally with many forms of paraphilias.

**BIOLOGICAL FACTORS** Most of the research regarding the role of biological factors in the etiology of paraphilic disorders has focused on the endocrine system (see Figure 2.4 on page 38), the collection of glands that regulate sexual responses through the release of hormones. Some studies of convicted sexually violent offenders have found evidence of elevated levels of testosterone

(Langevin, 1992). These reports must be viewed with some skepticism, however, for two reasons. First, the participants in these studies are invariably convicted sexual offenders. Thus, it is not clear that the findings can be generalized to all people with paraphilic disorders. Second, there is a high rate of alcoholism and drug abuse among men convicted of sexual crimes. For that reason, we do not know whether the biological abnormalities observed in these men are causes of their deviant sexual behavior or consequences of prolonged substance abuse.

Neurological abnormalities may also be involved in the development of paraphilic disorders. Structures located in the temporal lobes of the brain, especially the amygdala and the hippocampus, appear to play an important role in the control of both aggression and sexual behavior. These limbic structures, in conjunction with the hypothalamus, form a circuit that regulates biologically significant behaviors that sometimes are whimsically called the four Fs—feeding, fighting, fleeing, and [fornication] (Valenstein, 1973). In 1937, two scientists reported that after extensive bilateral damage to their temporal lobes, rhesus monkeys showed a dramatic increase in sexual activity, as well as a number of related behavioral and perceptual abnormalities. The monkeys apparently tried to copulate with a variety of inappropriate partners, including the investigators. This pattern has subsequently been called the Klüver–Bucy syndrome, named after the scientists who made the original observation.

Inspired by the suggestion that damage to the temporal lobe can lead to unusual patterns of sexual behavior, clinical scientists have studied a number of neurological and neuropsychological factors in convicted sex offenders. Some reports indicate that men with pedophilic disorder and exhibitionistic disorder show subtle forms of left temporal lobe dysfunction, as evidenced by abnormal patterns of electrophysiological response and impaired performance on neuropsychological tests (Bradford, 2001; Murphy, 1997).

**SOCIAL FACTORS** Some types of paraphilias seem to be distortions of the normal mating process when viewed in a broad, evolutionary context. For male primates, sexual behavior involves a sequence of steps: location and appraisal of potential partners; exchange of signals in which partners communicate mutual interest; and tactile interactions that set the stage for sexual intercourse. Voyeurism, exhibitionism, and frotteurism may represent aberrant versions of these social processes. Therefore, some types of paraphilic disorder have been described as "courtship disorders" (Freund & Blanchard, 1993; Freund & Seto, 1998). Something has apparently gone wrong, disrupting whatever mechanisms facilitate the identification of a sexual partner and govern behaviors used to attract a partner.

If people with some forms of paraphilic disorder have somehow failed to learn more adaptive forms of courtship behavior, what sort of childhood experiences might have produced such unexpected results? Several background factors have been observed repeatedly among people who engage in atypical sexual behaviors (Seto & Barbaree, 2000; Wincze, 1989). These include the following:

- Early crossing of normative sexual boundaries through a direct experience (for example, sexual abuse by an adult) or an indirect experience (hearing about a father's atypical sexual behavior)
- Lack of a consistent parental environment in which normative sexual behavior and values were modeled
- Lack of self-esteem
- Lack of confidence and ability in social interactions
- Ignorance and poor understanding of human sexuality

All these factors may increase the probability that a person might experiment with unusual types of sexual stimulation or employ maladaptive sexual behaviors.

Although the most notable feature of paraphilias is sexual arousal, ultimately the paraphilic disorders are problems in social relationships. Interpersonal skills may, therefore, play as important a role as sexual arousal. The core feature of unusual sexual behavior may be a failure to achieve intimacy in relationships with other adults (Marshall, 1989; Seidman, Marshall, Hudson, Robertson, 1994). According to this perspective, people with paraphilic disorders are lonely, insecure, and isolated and have significant deficits in social skills. Offensive sexual behaviors, such as those observed in pedophilic disorders, are maladaptive attempts to achieve intimacy through sex. These efforts are invariably unsuccessful and self-defeating in the sense that they serve to isolate the person further from the rest of the community. Paradoxically, the pattern may become deeply ingrained because it results in the momentary pleasure associated with orgasm and because it offers the illusory hope of eventually achieving intimacy with another person.

**PSYCHOLOGICAL FACTORS** Another influential perspective on the development of paraphilias has used a geographic metaphor known as a *lovemap* (Money, 2002). A lovemap is a mental picture representing a person's ideal sexual relationship. It might also be viewed as the software that encodes his or her sexual fantasies and preferred sexual practices. These "programs" are written early in life, and they are quite persistent. Children learn their lovemaps during sexual play, by imitation of their parents and other adults, and through messages that they digest from the popular media. According to this theory, when optimal conditions prevail, the child develops a lovemap that includes intercourse as a preferred form of sexual expression. The child learns that love—romantic attachment to another adult—and lust—erotic attraction—can be directed toward the same person.

The lovemap can be distorted, according to this metaphor, if the child learns that romantic attachment and sexual desire are incompatible—that these feelings cannot be directed toward the same person. The inability to integrate these aspects of the lovemap lies at the heart of this explanation for paraphilias. One

solution to this dilemma would be to avoid or deny sexual expression altogether. That might explain the development of lack of sexual desire. Sexual impulses are powerful, however, and they are not easily denied. In some cases, they are rerouted rather than being shut off completely. Various types of paraphilias represent alternative strategies through which the person finds it possible to express sexual feelings outside an intimate, loving relationship with another adult. Exhibitionism, voyeurism, and fetishism, therefore, are partial solutions to the perceived incompatibility of love and lust.

## Treatment

The treatment of paraphilic disorders is different from the treatment of sexual dysfunctions in several ways. Perhaps most important is the fact that most people with paraphilic disorders do not enter treatment voluntarily. They are often referred to a therapist by the criminal justice system after they have been arrested for exposing themselves, peeping through windows, or engaging in sexual behaviors with children. Their motivation to change is, therefore, open to question. Participation in treatment may help them receive reduced sentences or avoid other legal penalties. In many cases, they are being asked to abandon highly reinforcing behaviors in which they have engaged for many years. Their families and other members of society may be much more concerned about change than they are. We mention this issue at the beginning of our discussion because the results of outcome studies in this area are typically less positive than are those concerning the treatment of sexual dysfunctions (McConaghy, 1999; Prentky, Lee, Knight, Cerce, 1997).

**AVERSION THERAPY** For several decades, the most commonly used form of treatment for paraphilic disorders was aversion therapy. In this procedure, the therapist repeatedly presents the stimulus that elicits inappropriate sexual arousal—such as slides of nude children—in association with an aversive stimulus, such as repulsive smells, electric shock, or chemically induced nausea. Revolting cognitive images are sometimes used instead of tangible aversive stimuli. Whatever the exact procedure, the rationale is to create a new association with the inappropriate stimulus so that the stimulus will no longer elicit sexual arousal. Some studies suggested that aversion therapy produces positive effects (Kilmann, Sabalis, Gearing II, Bukstel, Scovern, 1982). This treatment eventually fell into disfavor, however, because the studies that were used to evaluate it suffered from design flaws.

**COGNITIVE BEHAVIORAL TREATMENT** Behavioral treatment programs for paraphilic disorders reflect a broader view of the etiology of these conditions. There is considerable reason to believe that paraphilic disorders are based on a variety of cognitive and social deficits. Marshall, Eccles, and Barbaree (1991) compared two approaches to the treatment of exhibitionists. One was based on aversion therapy and the other employed cognitive restructuring, social skills training, and stress management procedures. The men who received the second type of treatment were much less likely to return to their deviant forms of sexual behavior than were the men who received aversion therapy. Treatment with aversion therapy was no more effective than was treatment with a placebo. These data suggest that broad-based cognitive and social treatment procedures may be most useful in the treatment of paraphilic disorders (Marshall, Bryce, Hudson, Ward, Moth, 1996).

Unfortunately, research results regarding the effectiveness of psychological treatment for sexual offenders are discouraging. The only large-scale evaluation of such programs that has employed random assignment to treatment conditions is California's Sex Offender Treatment and Evaluation Project (SOTEP; Marques, Day, Nelson, West, 1993), which was designed for men convicted of either rape or child molestation. Men selected for this comprehensive treatment program were transferred to a special hospital unit, where they remained for several months. They received education in human sexuality as well as cognitive behavior therapy, including applied relaxation and social skills training and stress and anger management. Treatment also included a relapse prevention component that was based on procedures used in the treatment of alcoholism (see Chapter 11). Relapse prevention procedures helped the men confront personal, social, and sexual difficulties that may increase their risk of relapse after they were released from prison.

The men in the treatment group were compared to those in two control groups. Outcome was measured in several ways, but the most important consideration was being arrested again for similar crimes. Figure 12.5 illustrates some of the results from this study, highlighting the comparison between 138 men who completed the treatment and 184 men who had originally volunteered to participate in the program but were assigned to a no-treatment control group (Marques, 1999). Within four years after their release from prison, the percentage of men who were arrested for another sexual offense was essentially identical to that of the men who had been treated and of those in the control group (13 percent). The rate of arrest for subsequent violent offenses was somewhat lower for the treatment group than for the controls, but the difference was not significant.

Results were somewhat more encouraging with men convicted of rape than with those who had molested children. Nevertheless, the data from this study are discouraging. They suggest that a broadly based behavioral program focused on education, social skills, and relapse prevention procedures does not lead to obviously better outcomes than a routine period of incarceration (Maletzky, 2002).

**HORMONES AND MEDICATION** Another approach to the treatment of paraphilic disorders involves the use of drugs that reduce levels of testosterone, on the assumption that male hormones control the sexual appetite (Hill, Briken, Kraus, Strohm, Berner, 2003). One study reported that treatment of paraphilic men with cyproterone acetate, a drug that blocks the effects of testosterone, produced a significant reduction in some aspects of sexual behavior, especially sexual fantasies (Bradford & Pawlak, 1993). Among men with pedophilic disorder, the study found a greater reduction of sexual fantasies of children than of images of sex between consenting adults. Positive results have also been reported for use of triptorelin, which reduces testosterone secretion by inhibiting pituitary–gonadal function. In an uncontrolled trial, 30 male patients (25 with pedophilia) received monthly injections of triptorelin as well as supportive psychotherapy. All of the patients showed a reduction in deviant fantasies and in the number of incidents of paraphilic behaviors (Rosler & Witztum, 1998). We must remember, however, that the absence of double-blind, placebo-controlled studies leaves the efficacy of these drugs in doubt. One review of this literature concludes that treatment programs should never rely exclusively on the use of medications that reduce levels of testosterone (Prentky, 1997).

Antidepressants and antianxiety drugs have also been used to treat paraphilic disorders. Some outcome studies indicate that the SSRIs can have beneficial effects for some male patients (Thibaut, De LaBarra, Gordon, Cosyns, Bradford, 2010). The process by which these drugs manage to alter sexual behavior is open to question. For example, medication may work directly by decreasing deviant sexual interests without affecting other forms of sexual arousal. On the other hand, SSRIs may work by reducing social anxiety, which interferes with the ability to enjoy an intimate sexual relationship with another adult.

**LEGAL ISSUES** The U.S. Congress and all 50 states have passed laws that are intended to protect society from people who have

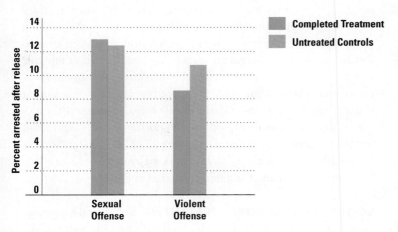

**FIGURE 12.5**

**Outcome of Psychological Treatment for Sex Offenders** Repeat arrest rates among male sex offenders (4 years after treatment).
*Source:* Based on Marques. J.K. How to Answer the Question: Does Sex Offender Treatment Work? *Journal of Interpersonal Violence.* 1999; 14: 437–451.

Sex Offender Tracker
Description
As Seen On: Mashable, Huffington Post, CNET, PC World, Perez Hilton and more!

Site web de BeenVerified.com ›    Assistance de Sex Offender Tracker ›

U.S. sex offenders can now be tracked on a radar-like app for the iPhone as glowing red dots in the Sex Offender Tracker. Under American law sex offenders must register in their local neighborhoods, and they will now be even more visible as tiny dots on a green screen. The military style radar app will, according to its makers, track sex-offenders in real-time as well as reveal detailed information of their location.

been convicted of violent or repeated sexual offenses. These laws fall into two categories. The first includes *community notification laws* (such as "Megan's Law"), which require the distribution of information to the public regarding the presence of child molesters and sexually violent offenders when they are released from prison or placed on parole. These laws are based on two assumptions: (1) Notification will reduce the offender's opportunities to commit further crimes, and (2) citizens are better able to protect themselves and their children if they know that a dangerous person lives in their neighborhood. Critics of community notification laws argue that they violate the former offender's constitutional rights by imposing an additional, unfair penalty after his sentence has been served. These laws are popular, but their impact has not been evaluated. It is not clear that people are actually better able to protect themselves after they have been notified. Furthermore, we do not know whether relapse rates are lower among sexual offenders who live in communities where such laws are strictly enforced (Edwards & Hensley, 2001; Younglove & Vitello, 2003).

The second category includes *sexual predator laws*, which are designed to keep some criminals in custody indefinitely. For example, a Kansas law passed in 1994 and later upheld by the U.S. Supreme Court permits authorities to commit certain sex offenders to a mental hospital after their prison terms are over. Each case is evaluated in a series of steps that end with a civil trial. The person can be hospitalized involuntarily and for an indefinite period of time if the jury decides the person has a "mental abnormality" that will lead him to commit further sexual offenses. Involuntary civil commitment is an infrequent outcome of this law (Fabian, 2011). When it does occur, however, serious questions are raised about the need to balance public safety against the protection of the offender's constitutional rights (see the discussion of civil commitment in Chapter 18).

# Gender Dysphoria

Our sense of ourselves as being either male or female is known as **gender identity.** Gender identity almost always reflects the child's physical anatomy: Toddlers who possess a penis learn that they are boys, and those with a vagina learn that they are girls. Gender identity is usually fixed by the time a child reaches two or three years of age (Clemans, DeRose, Graber, Brooks-Gunn, 2010).

Gender identity must be distinguished from *sex roles,* which are characteristics, behaviors, and skills that are defined within a specific culture as being either masculine or feminine. For example, certain aspects of appearance and behavior are more often associated with men than with women. These are considered to be masculine. Those behaviors and appearances that are more often associated with women are considered feminine. In our own culture, masculine and feminine sex roles have changed considerably in recent years, and they overlap to a degree (Sczesny, Bosak, Diekman, Twenge, 2008).

## Symptoms

Some people are firmly convinced that their anatomy and their gender identity do not match up. In males, this means that they feel strongly that they are women trapped in a man's body. For females, the opposite pattern holds. *DSM-5* categorizes this sense of discomfort with one's anatomical sex as **gender dysphoria.** It has also been called *transsexualism.* People with gender dysphoria do not literally believe that they are members of the other gender. Rather, they feel that, with the exception of their physical anatomy, they are more like the other gender (Becker & Johnson, 2009).

Most transsexuals report that they were aware of these feelings very early in childhood. Many report that they dressed in

Caster Semenya, a track star from South Africa, was subjected to gender testing after she won the 800 meter world championship. Her body has external female characteristics and internal male characteristics, resulting in high levels of testosterone. She was later cleared to compete as a female in the Olympic Games. Her case illustrates the important point that no single indicator—genes, hormones, or external appearance—can be used as an absolute indicator to distinguish between the sexes.

clothing and adopted sex-role behaviors of the other gender during childhood and adolescence. The intensity of the person's discomfort varies from one individual to the next. Invariably, it becomes more intense during adolescence, when the person develops secondary sexual characteristics, such as breasts and wider hips for girls, and facial hair, voice changes, and increased muscle mass for boys. These characteristics make it more difficult for a person to pass for the other gender. Many transsexuals become preoccupied with the desire to change their anatomical sex through surgical procedures (Paap, Kreukels, Cohen-Kettenis, Richter-Appelt, de Cuypere, Haraldsen, 2011).

Gender dysphoria should be distinguished from transvestic disorder, discussed earlier, which is a form of paraphilia in which a man dresses in the clothing of the other gender in order to achieve sexual arousal. These are, in fact, very different conditions. Transvestites do not consider themselves to be women, and transsexuals are not sexually aroused by cross-dressing. They dress as women to feel more comfortable about themselves.

The relation between gender dysphoria and sexual orientation has been a matter of some controversy. Some clinicians have suggested that transsexuals are homosexuals who claim to be members of the other gender as a way to avoid cultural and moral sanctions that discourage sexual relationships with members of their own sex. This proposal doesn't make sense for two reasons. First, lesbians and gay men are not uncomfortable with their own gender identity. This observation suggests that transsexuals are not simply escaping the stigma of homosexuality. Second, laboratory studies suggest that transsexual and homosexual subjects exhibit different patterns of sexual arousal in response to erotic stimuli.

## Frequency

Gender dysphoria is rare in comparison to most of the other disorders that we have considered in this book. Male-to-female transsexuals are apparently more common than female-to-male transsexuals, at least based on the numbers of people who seek treatment at clinics. Some studies estimate the prevalence to be approximately one person with gender dysphoria for every 12,000 males and 30,000 females (Olsson & Moller, 2003).

Deeply ingrained cross-gender behaviors and attitudes among children occur infrequently in the general population. Mild forms of cross-gender behavior, such as dressing up in the clothes of the other gender or expressing a desire to be a member of the other sex, are relatively common during the preschool years. Extreme forms of these behaviors are relatively rare, however, especially among boys (Zucker, 2009).

## Causes

Very little is known about the origins of gender identity in normal men and women, so it is not surprising that the etiology of

gender dysphoria is also poorly understood (Richmond, Carroll, & Denboske, 2010). There is some reason to believe that gender identity is strongly influenced by sex hormones, especially during the prenatal period (Diamond, 2009). Much of the research in this area has been done with animals, but an interesting set of data comes from studies of people with a condition that is sometimes called *pseudohermaphroditism*. Individuals with this condition are genetically male, but they are unable to produce a hormone that is responsible for shaping the penis and scrotum in the fetus. Therefore, the child is born with external genitalia that are ambiguous in appearance—thus the term *pseudohermaphrodite*.[2]

Many of these children are raised as girls by their families. When they reach puberty, a sudden increase in testosterone leads to dramatic changes in the appearance of the adolescent's genitals. The organ that had previously looked more like a clitoris becomes enlarged and turns into a penis, and testicles descend into a scrotum. The child's voice becomes deeper, muscle mass increases, and the child quickly begins to consider himself to be a man. The speed and apparent ease with which people with these conditions

Jazz was a 6-year-old male-to-female transgender child when he and his family appeared on the television news program 20/20. When Jazz was 2 years old, if his parents praised him as a "good boy," he would correct them, saying he was a good girl.

---

[2] A hermaphrodite has both male and female reproductive organs.

## MyPsychLab Video Case

adopt a masculine gender identity suggest that their brains had been prenatally programmed for this alternative (Hines, 2004).

### Treatment

There are two obvious solutions to problems of gender dysphoria: Change the person's identity to match his or her anatomy, or change the anatomy to match the person's gender identity. Various forms of psychotherapy have been used in an effort to alter gender identity, but the results have been fairly negative.

One alternative to psychological treatment is *sex-reassignment surgery*, in which the person's genitals are changed to match the gender identity (Sohn & Bosinski, 2007). Medical science can construct artificial male and female genitalia. The artificial penis is not capable of becoming erect in response to sexual stimulation, but structural implants can be used to obtain rigidity. These surgical procedures have been used with thousands of patients over the past 50 or 60 years. Clinics that perform these operations employ stringent selection procedures, and patients are typically required to live for several months as a member of the other gender before they can undergo the surgical procedure.

The results of sex-reassignment surgery have generally been positive (Johansson, Sundbom, Höjerback, Bodlund , 2010). Interviews with patients who have undergone surgery indicate that most are satisfied with the results, and the vast majority believe that they do not have trouble passing as a member of their newly assumed gender. Psychological tests obtained from patients who have completed surgery indicate reduced levels of anxiety and depression.

## getting HELP

Many sexual problems can be traced to the absence of information regarding the nature of sexual attitudes, feelings, preferences, and behaviors. Fortunately, access to these data, as well as public attitudes toward their discussion, has improved dramatically in recent years. The Sexuality Information and Education Council of the United States (SIECUS) collects and disseminates information and promotes education about sexuality. The council's Internet homepage (www.siecus.org) contains an extensive list of resources, including books and links to other websites, dealing with topics that range from reproduction, women's health, gender identity, and sexual orientation to sexually transmitted diseases and various types of sexual disorders.

If you have been troubled by problems with sexual arousal, inhibited orgasm, or premature orgasm, behavioral procedures can be helpful. Many of these problems can be treated successfully using behavioral and cognitive therapies. Before you seek professional therapy, you may want to try some self-help techniques that have developed from this treatment tradition. Two exceptionally well-written and practical books describe how these procedures can be used by people who want to enhance the pleasure that they experience in their sexual relationships. They are *Becoming Orgasmic: A Sexual and Personal Growth Program for Women,* by Julia Heiman and Joseph LoPiccolo, and *The New Male Sexuality,* by Bernie Zilbergeld.

If you are still experiencing problems after trying self-help procedures, you should seek treatment with a professional sex therapist. The person's professional background is less important than her or his training for treatment of these specific problems. When you contact potential therapists, ask them whether their treatment methods are similar to those developed by Masters and Johnson. Information regarding counseling, therapy, medical attention, and other sexuality resources for people with sexual problems is available from the Center for Disease Control and Prevention (their sexual health web page). Concise, readable descriptions of various forms of sexual dysfunction and treatments used to address them can be found at MedLine Plus, a service of the U.S. National Library of Medicine. These sites can help you increase your knowledge of sexuality, ways in which its expression can be inhibited, and procedures that can be used to improve sexual performance and experience.

Anyone who is interested in additional information regarding gender dysphoria will find help in a book called *True Selves: Understanding Transsexualism—for Families, Friends, Coworkers and Helping Professionals* (Brown & Rounsley, 2003). The authors use extended interviews with patients and families to provide valuable insights regarding important issues encountered by people who struggle with these conditions.

# 12 Summary

**Sexual dysfunctions** involve an inhibition of sexual desire or disruption of the physiological responses leading to orgasm.

**Paraphilias** are defined in terms of intense and persistent unusual sexual interests, in which sexual arousal is associated with atypical activities (such as exposing one's genitals to strangers) or targets (inanimate objects or prepubescent children). A **paraphilic disorder** can be diagnosed when a paraphilia causes distress or social impairment for the person or threatens harm to another person.

Sexual dysfunctions are subdivided into several types. These include problems related to sexual desire, sexual arousal, and orgasm. Related difficulties include **premature ejaculation**, genito-pelvic pain, and interference with vaginal penetration.

Sexual behavior is dependent on a complex interaction among biological, psychological, and social factors. These factors include cognitive events related to the perception of sexual stimuli, social factors that influence sexual meanings or intentions, and physiological responses that cause vasocongestion of the genitals during sexual arousal.

Biological factors that contribute to sexual dysfunction include inadequate levels of sex hormones as well as a variety of medical disorders. The effects of alcohol, illicit drugs, and some forms of medication can also contribute to **erectile dysfunction** in men and to **orgasmic disorder** in both men and women.

Several psychological factors are involved in the etiology of sexual dysfunction. Prominent among these are performance anxiety and guilt. Communication deficits can also contribute to sexual dysfunction. Previous experiences, including sexual abuse, play an important role in some cases of sexual dysfunction.

Psychological treatments for sexual dysfunction are quite successful. They focus primarily on negative attitudes toward sexuality, failure to engage in effective sexual behaviors, and deficits in communication skills.

Common characteristics of paraphilic disorders include lack of human intimacy and urges toward sexual behaviors that the person feels compelled to perform. The diversity and range of paraphilias are enormous. *DSM-5* describes a few of the most prominent forms of paraphilic disorder, such as **exhibitionistic, fetishism, frotteuristic, pedophilic, sexual masochism, sexual sadism, transvestic,** and **voyeuristic disorders**.

Treatment outcome is generally less successful with paraphilic disorders than with sexual dysfunctions. Currently, the most promising approaches to the treatment of paraphilic disorders address a broad range of issues, including deficits in social skills and stress and anger management, as well as knowledge and attitudes regarding sexuality.

**Gender dysphoria** is a disturbance in the person's sense of being either a man or a woman. People with this problem, which is also known as *transsexualism*, have developed a **gender identity** that is inconsistent with their physical anatomy. These disorders are extremely rare, and very little is known about their etiology. Treatment of gender dysphoria may involve sex-reassignment surgery.

# The Big Picture

## critical thinking review

**12.1** Should sexual problems be defined primarily in terms of difficulty reaching orgasm?

It's important to most people, but it's not the only purpose of sexual activity. The person's satisfaction with intimate relationships is also an important consideration . . . (see page 322).

**12.2** What role to mental scripts play in sexual arousal?

Scripts provide a perceptual structure, helping the person to recognize a situation as being potentially sexual in nature . . . (see page 329).

**12.3** What are the primary targets of psychological approaches to treating sexual dysfunctions?

They focus on negative attitudes toward sexuality, failure to engage in effective sexual behaviors, and deficits in communication between partners . . . (see pages 330–331).

**12.4** How have changing attitudes toward sexuality influenced the definition of paraphilias?

A wider range of sexual behaviors is now considered to be normal when these activities occur in the context of an adult, mutually consenting, reciprocal relationship . . . (see page 333).

**12.5** Should excessive sexual behavior be considered a disorder in its own right? Or is it a symptom of other mental disorders?

One problem with the concept of hypersexual disorder is the heterogeneous nature of poorly regulated sexual behavior, which can be associated with many different forms of mental disorder . . . (see page 339).

**12.6** Does deviant sexual arousal ever play a role in sexual assaults?

Although rapes are often motivated by aggressive and violent impulses, some rapists are preoccupied by a sadistic blend of sexual and aggressive impulses that resembles qualities of other paraphilias . . . (see page 340).

**12.7** Why are paraphilic disorders sometimes called "courtship disorders"?

An evolutionary perspective suggests that some forms of paraphilia, such as voyeurism and exhibitionism, may represent maladaptive distortions of normal mating behaviors . . . (see page 340).

**12.8** What is the difference between gender identity and sex roles?

The answer hinges on the distinction between a belief about "who you are" versus "what you do." Gender identity is the fundamental sense of being either male or female. Sex roles are characteristics and behaviors that are considered to be either masculine or feminine . . . (see page 343).

# key terms

schizophrenia spectrum and other
psychotic disorders

13

# The Big Picture

## learning objectives

**13.1**
Why do clinical scientists say that schizophrenia is a "heterogeneous" disorder?

**13.2**
How should long-term outcome be measured in schizophrenia?

**13.3**
Why are some personality disorders considered to be schizophrenia spectrum disorders?

**13.4**
Why can't we use brain imaging to diagnose schizophrenia?

**13.5**
What characteristics would define a useful marker of vulnerability to schizophrenia?

**13.6**
What aspects of schizophrenia are addressed most directly by psychosocial treatments?

**Schizophrenia** is a severe form of abnormal behavior that encompasses what most of us have come to know as "madness." People with schizophrenia exhibit many different kinds of psychotic symptoms, indicating that they have lost touch with reality. They may hear voices that aren't there or make comments that are difficult, if not impossible, to understand. Their behavior may be guided by absurd ideas and beliefs. For example, a person might believe that spaceships from another planet are beaming thoughts into his brain and controlling his behavior. Some people with schizophrenia recover fairly quickly, whereas others deteriorate progressively after the initial onset of symptoms. It is a disorder with "many different faces" (Andreasen, 2001). Because of the diversity of symptoms and outcomes shown by these patients, many clinicians believe that schizophrenia, or "the group of schizophrenias," may actually include several forms of disorder that have different causes. Others contend that schizophrenia is a single pathological process and that variations from one patient to the next in symptoms and course of the disorder reflect differences in the expression or severity of this process.

## Overview

Many of the disorders that we have discussed in this book strike us as being familiar, at least in form if not in severity. For example, depression and anxiety are experiences with which we can easily empathize. Short-lived versions of these emotions help to shape our responses to daily events. Some clinical scientists speculate that mood and anxiety disorders may be viewed as evolved adaptations or mechanisms that can serve a useful purpose, but the symptoms of schizophrenia represent a different kind of problem. It is much harder for us to understand when someone hears voices that aren't there or speaks sentences that are meaningless. These symptoms seem to stem from a fundamental breakdown in basic cognitive functions that govern the way the person perceives and thinks about the social world (Burns, 2006).

The most common symptoms of schizophrenia include changes in the way a person thinks, feels, and relates to other people and the outside environment. No single symptom or specific set of symptoms is characteristic of all schizophrenic patients. All the individual symptoms of schizophrenia can also be associated with other psychological and medical conditions. Schizophrenia is officially defined by various combinations of psychotic symptoms in the absence of other forms of disturbance, such as mood disorders (especially manic episodes), substance use disorders, and neurocognitive disorders (delirium and dementia, see Chapter 14).

Schizophrenia is a devastating disorder for both the patients and their families (Bowie et al., 2010). It can disrupt many aspects of the person's life, well beyond the experience of psychotic symptoms. The impact of this disorder is felt in many different ways. For people who develop schizophrenia, it often has a dramatic and lasting impact on their quality of life, both in terms of their own subjective satisfaction and their ability to complete an education, hold a job, and develop social relationships with other people. Approximately 10 percent of schizophrenic patients commit suicide (Heisel, 2008).

For family members of patients with schizophrenia, the consequences can also be cruel. They must come to grips with the fact that their son or daughter, or brother or sister, has developed a severe disorder that may change his or her life forever. One woman whose daughter, then in her mid-thirties, had exhibited symptoms of schizophrenia for 17 years, described her feelings in the following way: "Nothing in (our daughter's) growing up years could have prepared us for the shock and devastation of seeing this normal, happy child become totally incapacitated by schizophrenia" (Smith, 1991, p. 691).

Schizophrenia also has an enormous impact on society (Behan, Kennelly, & O'Callaghan, 2008). Among mental disorders, it is the second leading cause of disease burden (see Figure 1.2 on page 13). Most people who develop the disorder do not recover completely, and many become homeless because long-term institutional care is not available (see Chapter 18). Above and beyond the direct costs of providing treatment to patients and their families, substantial indirect costs are associated with loss of productivity and unemployment. In the United States the financial costs associated with schizophrenia were approximately $63 billion in 2002 (Wu, et al., 2005).

In the following case studies we describe the experiences of two people who exhibited symptoms of schizophrenia. The symptoms of schizophrenia take many forms. Our first case illustrates one relatively common pattern in which the person is preoccupied by paranoid delusions and becomes socially withdrawn.

### ⟶ A New Mother's Paranoid Delusions

Ann was 21 years old the first time that she was admitted to a psychiatric hospital. She had completed business college and had worked as a receptionist until she became pregnant with her son, who was born six months prior to her admission. She and her husband lived in a small apartment with his five-year-old daughter from a previous marriage. This was her first psychotic episode.

The first signs of Ann's disturbance appeared during her pregnancy, when she accused her husband of having an affair with her sister. The accusation was based on a conversation that Ann had overheard on a bus. Two women (who were neighbors in Ann's apartment building) had been discussing an affair that some woman's husband was having. Ann believed that this might have been their way of telling her about her husband's infidelity. Although her husband and her sister denied any romantic interest in each other, Ann clung to her suspicions and began to monitor her husband's activities closely. She also avoided talking with her neighbors and friends.

Before this period of time, Ann had been an outgoing and energetic person. Now she seemed listless and apathetic and would often spend days without leaving their apartment. Her husband at first attributed this change in her behavior to the pregnancy, believing that she would "snap out of it" after the baby was born. Unfortunately, Ann became even more socially isolated following the birth of her son. She seldom left her bedroom and would spend hours alone, mumbling softly to herself.

Ann's behavior deteriorated markedly two weeks prior to her hospital admission, when she noticed that some photographs of herself and her baby were missing. She told her husband that they had been stolen and were being used to cast a voodoo spell on her. Ann became increasingly preoccupied with this belief in subsequent days. She called her mother repeatedly, insisting that something would have to be done to recover the missing photographs. Her friends and family tried to reassure Ann that the photographs had probably been misplaced or accidentally discarded, but she was totally unwilling to consider alternative explanations.

Ann finally announced to everyone who would listen that someone was trying to kill her and the children. Believing that all the food in the house had been poisoned, she refused to eat and would not feed the children.

She became increasingly suspicious, hostile, and combative. Her husband and parents found it impossible to reason with her. She was no longer able to care for herself or the children. The family sought advice from their family physician, who recommended

that they contact a psychiatrist. After meeting with Ann briefly, the psychiatrist recommended that she be hospitalized for a short period of time.

After admission, Ann argued heatedly with the hospital staff, denying that she was mentally disturbed and insisting that she must be released so that she could protect her children from the conspiracy. She had no insight into the nature of her problems.

．．．．．．．．．．．．．．．．．．．．．．．．．．．．．．．．．．．．．．．．．．．．．．．．．．．

The onset of schizophrenia typically occurs during adolescence or early adulthood. The period of risk for the development of a first episode is considered to be between the ages of 15 and 35. The number of new cases drops off slowly after that, with very few people experiencing an initial episode after the age of 55 (Thompson, Pogue-Geile, & Grace, 2004).

The problems of most patients can be divided into three phases of variable and unpredictable duration: prodromal, active, and residual. Symptoms such as hallucinations, delusions, and disorganized speech are characteristic of the active phase of the disorder. The **prodromal phase** precedes the active phase and is marked by an obvious deterioration in role functioning as a student, employee, or homemaker. The person's friends and relatives often view the beginning of the prodromal phase as a change in his or her personality. Prodromal signs and symptoms are similar to those associated with schizotypal personality disorder (see Chapter 9). They include peculiar behaviors (such as talking to one's self in public), unusual perceptual experiences, outbursts of anger, increased tension, and restlessness. Social withdrawal,

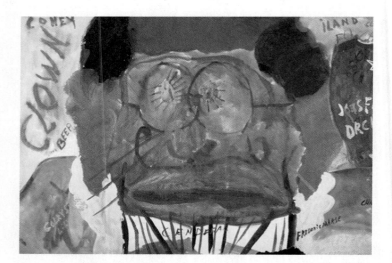

Painting by a young schizophrenic patient, illustrating his hallucinations. He saw monsters, like the one painted here, crawling on the floor. He also believed that the chairs next to his bed had turned into devils. Patient's description of the picture: "I was very sick at the time I painted this picture. The head represents my fragmented personality and a feeling of being helpless, hopeless, and off balance and of being in a cocoon of unreality. The bright colored rain and outlines represent the level of intensity of myself. The bright colors provided insulation and protected me. The colors felt like microwaves passing through my control center."

indecisiveness, and lack of willpower are often seen during the prodromal phase (Woods, et al., 2009).

The *residual phase* follows the active phase of the disorder and is defined by signs and symptoms that are similar in many respects to those seen during the prodromal phase. At this point, the most dramatic symptoms of psychosis have improved, but the person continues to be impaired in various ways. Negative symptoms, such as impoverished expression of emotions, may remain pronounced during the residual phase (McGlashan, 1998).

After the onset of schizophrenia, many people do not return to expected levels of social and occupational adjustment. Some prefer social isolation and avoid contact with other people. The man in our second case illustrates this pattern. He is also an example of the disorganized type of schizophrenia. Patients who fit criteria for this category say things that are difficult to understand, behave in a disorganized way, and fail to express expected emotions.

→ **Edward's Hallucinations and Disorganized Speech**

Edward was 39 years old and had lived at home with his parents since dropping out of school after the tenth grade. Edward worked on and off as a helper in his father's roofing business prior to his first psychotic episode at the age of 26. After that time, he was socially isolated and unable to hold any kind of job. He was hospitalized in psychiatric facilities 10 times in the next 14 years. When he was not in the hospital, most of his time at home was spent watching television or sitting alone in his room.

The tenth episode of psychosis became evident when Edward told his mother that he had seen people arguing violently on the sidewalk in front of their house. He believed that this incident was the beginning of World War II. His mother tried to persuade him that he had witnessed an ordinary, though perhaps heated, disagreement between two neighbors, but Edward could not be convinced. He continued to mumble about the fight and became increasingly agitated over the next few days. When he wasn't pacing back and forth from his bedroom to the living room, he could usually be found staring out the front window. Several days after witnessing the argument, he took curtains from several windows in the house and burned them in the street at 2 A.M. A neighbor happened to see what Edward was doing and called the police. When they arrived, they found Edward wandering in a snow-covered vacant lot, talking incoherently to himself. Recognizing that Edward was psychotic, the police took him to the psychiatric hospital.

Although his appearance was somewhat disheveled, Edward was alert and cooperative. He knew the current date and recognized that he was in a psychiatric hospital. Some of his speech was incoherent, and his answers to questions posed by the hospital staff were frequently irrelevant. For example, the following exchange occurred during a structured diagnostic interview. The psychologist asked Edward whether he had any special powers or abilities that other people do not have. He responded by saying that he didn't know because he didn't date women. Puzzled by this tangential response, the psychologist asked him to explain what he meant. Edward responded by asking his own question, "If you had a star in the middle of your head, would you swallow marbles?"

Edward's expressive gestures were severely restricted, and he sat in a relatively motionless position. Although he said that he was frightened by the recent events that he reported to his mother, his face did not betray any signs of emotion. He mumbled slowly in a monotonous tone of voice that was difficult to understand. He said that he could hear God's voice telling him that his father was "the master of the universe" and he claimed that he had "seen the shadow of the master."

Other voices seemed to argue with one another about Edward's special calling and whether he was worthy of this divine power. The voices told him to prepare for God's return to earth. At times Edward said that he was a Nazi soldier and that he was born in Germany in 1886. He also spoke incoherently about corpses frozen in Greenland and maintained that he was "only half a person."

## Symptoms

In this section, we describe in greater detail various types of symptoms that are commonly observed among schizophrenic patients and that are currently emphasized by official diagnostic systems, such as *DSM-5*. All of these symptoms can fluctuate in severity over time. Some patients exhibit persistent psychotic symptoms. Others experience symptoms during acute episodes and are better adjusted between episodes.

The symptoms of schizophrenia can be divided into three dimensions: positive symptoms, negative symptoms, and disorganization (Lenzenweger, 1999). **Positive symptoms,** also called *psychotic symptoms,* include hallucinations and delusions. In contrast, **negative symptoms** include characteristics such as lack of initiative, social withdrawal, and deficits in emotional responding. Some additional symptoms of schizophrenia, such as incoherent

Many of the symptoms of schizophrenia, including hallucinations and delusions, can be extremely distressing.

or disorganized speech, do not fit easily into either the positive or negative types. Verbal communication problems and bizarre behavior represent this third dimension, which is sometimes called *disorganization.* These symptom dimensions overlap and combine in various ways within individual patients. In the following pages, we will describe the most obvious features of these symptoms. It should also be noted, however, that attenuated versions of these symptoms occur relatively frequently in people who are not psychotic (Dominguez, et al., 2010). Like other features of psychopathology, these symptoms are not all-or-nothing phenomena; they are best viewed as falling along a continuous dimension of severity.

## Positive Symptoms

The term *positive symptoms* of schizophrenia does not imply that these symptoms are beneficial or adaptive. Rather, it suggests that they are characterized by the presence of an aberrant response (such as hearing a voice that is not really there). Negative symptoms, on the other hand, are characterized by the absence of a particular response (such as emotion, speech, or willpower).

**HALLUCINATIONS** Our senses provide us with basic information that is vital to our notions of who we are, what we are doing, and what others think of us. Many people with schizophrenia experience perplexing and often frightening changes in perception. The most obvious perceptual symptoms are **hallucinations,** or sensory experiences that are not caused by actual external stimuli. Although hallucinations can occur in any of the senses, those experienced by schizophrenic patients are most often auditory. Many patients hear voices that comment on their behavior or give them instructions. Others hear voices that seem to argue with one another. Edward heard the voice of God talking to him. Like Edward, most patients find such voices to be frightening. In some cases, however, hallucinations can be comforting or pleasing to the patient.

Hallucinations should be distinguished from the transient mistaken perceptions that most people experience from time to time (Brébion, et al., 2008). Have you ever turned around after thinking you heard someone call your name, to find that no one was there? You probably dismissed the experience as "just your imagination." Hallucinations, in contrast, strike the person as being real, in spite of the fact that they have no basis in reality. They can vary in terms of both duration and severity. Patients who experience more severe auditory hallucinations hear the voice (or voices) speaking to them throughout the day and for many days at a time.

**DELUSIONAL BELIEFS** Many schizophrenic patients express **delusions,** or idiosyncratic beliefs that are rigidly held in spite of their preposterous nature (Maher, 2001). Delusions have sometimes been defined as false beliefs based on incorrect inferences about reality. This definition has a number of problems, including the difficulty of establishing the ultimate truth of many situations.

Ann's accusation that her husband was having an affair, for example, could easily become a choice between her word and his. This suspicion would not, on its own, be considered a delusion. The judgment that her beliefs were delusional depended to a large extent on their expansion to more absurd concerns about stolen photographs, voodoo spells, and alleged plots to kill her children.

Several additional characteristics are important in identifying delusions (Lincoln et al., 2007). In the most severe cases, delusional patients express and defend their beliefs with utmost conviction, even when presented with contradictory evidence. For example, Ann's belief that the stolen photographs were being used to cast a spell on her was totally fixed and resistant to contradiction or reconsideration. Preoccupation is another defining characteristic of delusional beliefs. During periods of acute psychosis, many patients like Ann find it difficult, if not impossible, to avoid thinking or talking about these beliefs. Finally, delusional patients may be unable to consider the perspective that other people hold with regard to their beliefs. Ann, for example, was unable to appreciate the fact that other people considered her paranoid beliefs to be ridiculous. Taken together, these characteristics describe ways of identifying the severity of delusional beliefs.

Although delusional beliefs can take many forms, they are typically personal. They are not shared by other members of the person's family or cultural group. Common delusions include the belief that thoughts are being inserted into the patient's head, that other people are reading the patient's thoughts, or that the patient is being controlled by mysterious, external forces (Gutierrez-Lobos et al., 2001). Many delusions focus on grandiose or paranoid content. For example, Edward expressed the grandiose belief that his father was the Master of the universe. Ann clung persistently to the paranoid belief that someone was trying to kill her and her children.

In actual clinical practice, delusions are complex and difficult to define (Lesser & O'Donohue, 1999; Oltmanns, 1988). Their content is sometimes bizarre and confusing, as in the case of Edward's insistence that he had witnessed the beginning of World War II. Delusions are often fragmented, especially among

## MyPsychLab VIDEO CASE

### Schizophrenia

LARRY

*"My voices had gotten the most of me. . . ."*

Watch the Video *Larry: Schizophrenia* on MyPsychLab

Pay attention to the nonverbal aspects of Larry's behavior during the interview (lack of expression in face and voice). Notice that, in spite of his symptoms, he does express satisfaction with his life.

severely disturbed patients. In other words, delusions are not always coherent belief systems that are consistently expressed by the patient. At various times, for example, Edward talked about being a Nazi soldier and half a person. Connections among these fragmented ideas are difficult to understand.

The subjective experiences of people who struggle with schizophrenia are an important source of knowledge about this disorder, particularly delusional beliefs. Some of the most fundamental elements of psychosis involve private events that cannot be observed directly by others. Fortunately, many articulate patients have provided compelling accounts of their own internal struggles. The box below is a first person account by a patient who is being treated for schizophrenia. She describes experiences that are part of an elaborate delusional belief system.

## Negative Symptoms

Negative symptoms of schizophrenia are defined in terms of responses or functions that appear to be missing from the person's behavior. In that sense, they may initially be more subtle or difficult to recognize than the positive symptoms of this disorder. Negative symptoms tend to be more stable over time than positive symptoms, which fluctuate in severity as the person moves in and out of active phases of psychosis (Buchanan, 2007; Stahl & Buckley, 2007).

**AFFECTIVE AND EMOTIONAL DISTURBANCES** One of the most common symptoms of schizophrenia involves a flattening or restriction of the person's nonverbal display of emotional responses. This symptom, called **diminished emotional expression,** or *blunted affect,* was clearly present in Edward's case. Patients with this symptom fail to exhibit signs of emotion or feeling. They are neither happy nor sad, and they appear to be completely indifferent to their surroundings. Their faces are apathetic and expressionless. Their voices lack the typical fluctuations in volume and pitch that other people use to signal changes in their mood. Events in their environment hold little consequence for them. They may demonstrate a complete lack of concern for themselves and for others (Blanchard, Cohen, & Carreño, 2007).

## First-Person Account of Delusional Beliefs

At the beginning of my last year at (the university), "feelings" began to descend on me. I felt distinctly different from my usual self. I would sit for hours on end staring at nothing, and I became fascinated with drawing weird, disconnected monsters. I carefully hid my drawings, because I was certain I was being watched. Eventually, I became aware of a magical force outside myself that was compelling me in certain directions. The force gained power as time went on, and soon it made me take long walks at 2 or 3 o'clock in the morning down dark alleys in my high-crime neighborhood. I had no power to disobey the force. During my walks I felt as though I was in a different, magical, four-dimensional universe. I understood that the force wanted me to take those walks so that I might be killed.

I do not clearly understand the relationship between the force and the Alien Beings (alas, such a name!), but my universe soon became populated with them. The Alien Beings were from outer space, and of all the people in the world, only I was aware of them. The Alien Beings soon took over my body and removed me from it. They took me to a faraway place of beaches and sunlight and placed an Alien in my body to act like me. At this point, I had the distinct impression that I did not really exist, because I could not make contact with my kidnapped self. I also saw that the Aliens were starting to take over other people as well, removing them from their bodies and putting Aliens in their place. Of course, the other people were unaware of what was happening; I was the only person in the world who had the power to know it. At this point, I determined that the Aliens were involved in a huge conspiracy against the world.

The Alien Beings were gaining strength and had given me a complex set of rules. The rules were very specific and governed every aspect of my behavior. One of the rules was that I could not tell anyone else about the Aliens or the rules, or else the Aliens would kill me. Another of the rules was that I had to become utterly, completely mad. So now I was living in a world of great fear.

I had a number of other symptoms as well. I felt as though I had been pushed deep within myself, and I had little or no reaction to events or emotions around me. Almost daily the world became unreal to me. Everything outside of me seemed to fade into the distance; everything was miles away from me. I came to feel that I had the power to influence the behavior of animals; that I could, for instance, make dogs bark simply by hooking up rays of thought from my mind to theirs. Conversely, I felt that certain people had the capacity to read my mind. I became very frightened of those people and tried my best to avoid them. Whenever I saw a group of two or three people, I was sure they were talking about me. Paranoia is a very painful emotion! But when I saw crowds of people (as in a shopping mall), I felt an acute longing to wander among them, singing hymns and nursery rhymes (Payne, 1992, pp. 726–727).

Another type of emotional deficit is called **anhedonia,** which refers to the inability to experience pleasure. Whereas diminished emotional expression refers to the lack of outward expression, anhedonia is a lack of positive subjective feelings. People who experience anhedonia typically lose interest in recreational activities and social relationships, which they do not find enjoyable. They may also be unable to experience pleasure from physical sensations, such as taste and touch.

Longitudinal studies indicate that anhedonia associated with both social and physical experiences is an enduring feature of the disorder for many people with schizophrenia (Herbener & Harrow, 2002). For some people, it may also be an early marker, signaling the onset of the prodromal phase of the disorder (Kwapil, 1998). Like other symptoms of schizophrenia, anhedonia is not unique to this disorder; it is also found among people who are severely depressed.

**AVOLITION AND ALOGIA** One of the most important and seriously debilitating aspects of schizophrenia is a malfunction of interpersonal relationships (Meehl, 1993). Many people with schizophrenia become socially withdrawn. In many cases, social isolation develops before the onset of symptoms, such as hallucinations and delusions. It can be one of the earliest signs that something is wrong. This was certainly true in Ann's case. She became socially isolated from her family and friends many weeks before she started to talk openly about the stolen pictures and the plot to kill her children. Social withdrawal appears to be both a symptom of the disorder and a strategy that is actively employed by some patients to deal with their other symptoms. They may, for example, attempt to minimize interactions with other people in order to reduce levels of stimulation that can exacerbate perceptual and cognitive disorganization (Walker, Davis, & Baum, 1993).

The withdrawal seen among many schizophrenic patients is accompanied by indecisiveness, ambivalence, and a loss of willpower. This symptom is known as **avolition** (lack of volition or will). A person who suffers from avolition becomes apathetic and ceases to work toward personal goals or to function independently. He or she might sit listlessly in a chair all day, not washing or combing his or her hair for weeks.

Another negative symptom involves a form of speech disturbance called *alogia,* which refers to impoverished thinking. Literally translated, it means "speechlessness." In one form of alogia, known as *poverty of speech,* patients show remarkable reductions in the amount of speech. They simply don't have anything to say. In another form, referred to as thought blocking, the patient's train of speech is interrupted before a thought or idea has been completed.

## Disorganization

Some symptoms of schizophrenia do not fit easily into either the positive or negative type. Thinking disturbances and bizarre behavior represent a third symptom dimension, which is sometimes called disorganization (Rietkerk, et al., 2008).

**THINKING DISTURBANCES** One important set of schizophrenic symptoms, known as **disorganized speech,** involves the tendency of some patients to say things that don't make sense. Signs of disorganized speech include making irrelevant responses to questions, expressing disconnected ideas, and using words in peculiar ways (Berenbaum & Barch, 1995). This symptom is also called *thought disorder,* because clinicians have assumed that the failure to communicate successfully reflects a disturbance in the thought patterns that govern verbal discourse. The woman described in the following case exhibited signs of disorganized speech.

### ⟶ Marsha's Disorganized Speech and Catatonic Behavior

Marsha was a 32-year-old graduate student in political science. She had never been treated for psychological problems.

Marsha called Dr. Higgins, a clinical psychologist who taught at the university, to ask if she could speak with him about her twin sister's experience with schizophrenia. When she arrived at his office, she was neatly dressed and had a Bible tucked tightly under her arm. The next three hours were filled with a rambling discussion of Marsha's experiences during the past 10 years. She talked about her education, her experience as a high school teacher before returning to graduate school, her relationships with her parents, and most of all her concern for her identical twin sister, Alice, who had spent six of the last 10 years in psychiatric hospitals.

Marsha's emotional expression vacillated dramatically throughout the course of this conversation, which was punctuated by silly giggles and heavy sighs. Her voice would be loud and emphatic one moment as she talked about her stimulating ideas and special talents. At other moments, she would whisper in a barely audible voice or sob quietly as she described the desperation, fear, and frustration that she had experienced watching the progression of her sister's disorder. She said that she had been feeling very uptight in recent months, afraid that she might be "going crazy" like her sister. She had been scared to death to go home because her parents might sense that something was wrong with her. Her behavior was frequently inconsistent with the content of her speech. As she described her intense fears, for example, Marsha occasionally giggled uncontrollably.

Dr. Higgins also found Marsha's train of thought difficult to follow. Her speech rambled illogically from one topic to the next, and her answers to his questions were frequently tangential. For example, when Dr. Higgins asked what she meant by her repeated use of the phrase "the ideal can become real," Marsha replied, "Well, after serving the Word of Christ in California for three years, making a public spectacle of myself, someone apparently called my parents and said I had a problem. I said I can't take this anymore and went home. I perceived that Mom was just unbelievably nice to me. I began to think that my face was changing. Something about my forehead resembled the pain of Christ. I served Christ, but my power was not lasting."

At the end of this three-hour interview, Dr. Higgins was convinced that Marsha should be referred to the mental health center for outpatient treatment. He explained his concerns to Marsha, but she refused to follow his advice, insisting that she did not want to receive the medication with which her sister had been treated. She agreed to return to Dr. Higgins's office in three days for another interview, but she did not keep that appointment.

Two weeks later, Marsha called Dr. Higgins to ask if he would talk with her immediately. It was very difficult to understand what she was saying, but she seemed to be repeating in a shrill voice "I'm losing my mind." The door to his office was closed when she arrived, but he could hear her shuffling awkwardly down the hallway, breathing heavily. He opened his door and found Marsha standing in a rigid posture, arms stiffly at her sides. Her eyes were opened wide, and she was staring vacantly at the nameplate on his door. In contrast to her prim and neat appearance at their first meeting, Marsha's hair and clothes were now in disarray. She walked stiffly into the office without bending her knees and sat, with some difficulty, in the chair next to Dr. Higgins's desk. Her facial expression was rigidly fixed. Although her eyes were open and she appeared to hear his voice, Marsha did not respond to any of Dr. Higgins's questions. Recognizing that Marsha was experiencing an acute psychotic episode, Dr. Higgins and one of the secretaries took her to the emergency room at the local hospital.

..........................................................................

Marsha's speech provides one typical example of disorganized speech. She was not entirely incoherent, but parts of her speech were difficult to follow. Connections between sentences were sometimes arbitrary, and her answers to the interviewer's questions were occasionally irrelevant.

Several types of verbal communication disruption contribute to clinical judgments about disorganized speech (Docherty, DeRosa, & Andreasen, 1996; Kerns & Berenbaum, 2002). Common features of disorganized speech in schizophrenia include shifting topics too abruptly, called *loose associations* or *derailment;* replying to a question with an irrelevant response, called *tangentiality;* or persistently repeating the same word or phrase over and over again, called *perseveration.* We all say things from time to time that fit these descriptions. It is not the occasional presence of a single feature but, rather, the accumulation of a large number of such features that defines the presence of disorganized speech.

**ABNORMAL MOTOR BEHAVIOR** Schizophrenic patients may exhibit various forms of unusual motor behavior, such as the rigidity displayed by Marsha when she appeared for her second interview with Dr. Higgins. *Catatonic behavior* refers to an obvious reduction in reactivity to external stimuli. It most often refers to immobility and marked muscular rigidity, but it can also refer to excitement and overactivity. For example, some patients engage in apparently purposeless pacing or repetitive movements, such as rubbing their hands together in a special pattern for hours at a time. Many catatonic patients exhibit reduced or awkward spontaneous movements. In more extreme forms, patients may assume unusual postures or remain in rigid standing or sitting positions for long periods of time. For example, some patients will lie flat on their backs in a stiff position with their heads raised slightly off the floor as though they were resting on a pillow. Catatonic patients typically resist attempts to alter their position, even though maintaining their awkward postures would normally be extremely uncomfortable or painful.

Catatonic posturing is often associated with a *stuporous state,* or generally reduced responsiveness. The person seems to be unaware of his or her surroundings. For example, during her acute psychotic episode, Marsha refused to answer questions or to make eye contact with others. Unlike people with other stuporous conditions, however, catatonic patients seem to maintain a clear state of consciousness, and it is likely that Marsha could hear and understand everything that Dr. Higgins said to her. Many patients report after the end of a catatonic episode that they were perfectly aware of events that were taking place around them, in spite of their failure to respond appropriately.

Another kind of bizarre behavior involves affective responses that are obviously inconsistent with the person's situation. This symptom is particularly difficult to describe in words. The most remarkable features of *inappropriate affect* are incongruity and lack of adaptability in emotional expression. For example, when Marsha described the private terror that she felt in the presence of her family, she giggled in a silly fashion. The content of Marsha's speech was inconsistent with her facial expression, her gestures, and her voice quality.

## Diagnosis

The broad array of symptoms outlined in the previous section has all been described as being part of schizophrenic disorders. The specific organization of symptoms has been a matter of some controversy for many years, and schizophrenic disorders have been defined in many different ways. One popular misconception should be mentioned at the outset. The term *schizophrenia* was coined in 1911 by Eugen Bleuler, a Swiss psychiatrist. This term referred to the *splitting of mental associations,* which Bleuler believed to be the fundamental disturbance in schizophrenia. One unfortunate consequence of this choice of terms has been that laypeople frequently confuse schizophrenia with dissociative identity disorder (also known as multiple personality). The latter is a severe form of dissociative disorder (see Chapter 7), and it has little in common with schizophrenia.

### DSM-5

Several specific criteria for schizophrenia are listed in *DSM-5* (see "DSM-5: Schizophrenia"). The first requirement (Criterion A) is that the patient must exhibit two (or more) active symptoms for at least one month. Negative symptoms, such as diminished

**A.** Two (or more) of the following, each present for a significant portion of time during a 1-month period (or less if successfully treated). At least one of these must be (1), (2), or (3):

1. Delusions.
2. Hallucinations.
3. Disorganized speech (e.g., frequent derailment or incoherence).
4. Grossly disorganized or catatonic behavior.
5. Negative symptoms (i.e., diminished emotional expression or avolition).

**B.** For a significant portion of the time since the onset of the disturbance, level of functioning in one or more major areas, such as work, interpersonal relations, or self-care, is markedly below the level achieved prior to the onset (or when the onset is in childhood or adolescence, there is failure to achieve expected level of interpersonal, academic, or occupational functioning).

**C.** Continuous signs of the disturbance persist for at least 6 months. This 6-month period must include at least 1 month of symptoms (or less if successfully treated) that meet Criterion A (i.e., active-phase symptoms) and may include periods of prodromal or residual symptoms.

During these prodromal or residual periods, the signs of the disturbance may be manifested by only negative symptoms or by two or more symptoms listed in Criterion A present in an attenuated form (e.g., odd beliefs, unusual perceptual experiences).

**D.** Schizoaffective disorder and depressive or bipolar disorder with psychotic features have been ruled out because either 1) no major depressive or manic episodes have occured concurrently with the active-phase symptoms, or 2) if mood episodes have occured during active-phase symptoms, they have been present for a minority of the total duration of the active and residual periods of the illness.

**E.** The disturbance is not attributable to the physiological effects of a substance (e.g., a drug of abuse, a medication) or another medical condition.

**F.** If there is a history of autism spectrum disorder or a communication disorder of childhood onset, the additional diagnosis of schizophrenia is made only if prominent delusions or hallucinations, in addition to the other required symptoms of schizophrenia, are also present for at least 1 month (or less if successfully treated).

Reprinted with permission from the *Diagnostic and Statistical Manual of Mental Disorders*, Fifth Edition, (Copyright 2013). American Psychiatric Association.

emotional expression and avolition, also play a relatively prominent role in the *DSM-5* definition of schizophrenia.

The *DSM-5* definition takes into account the person's level of functioning as well as the duration of the disorder (Criteria B and C). It requires evidence of a decline in the person's social or occupational functioning as well as the presence of disturbed behavior over a continuous period of at least six months. Active phase symptoms do not need to be present for this entire period. The total duration of disturbance is determined by adding together continuous time during which the person has exhibited prodromal, active, and residual symptoms of schizophrenia. If the person displays psychotic symptoms for at least one month but less than six months, the diagnosis would be *schizophreniform disorder*. The diagnosis would be changed to schizophrenic disorder if the person's problems persisted beyond the six-month limit.

The final consideration in arriving at a diagnosis of schizophrenia involves the exclusion of related conditions, especially mood disorders. According to *DSM-5*, active phase symptoms of schizophrenia must appear in the absence of a major depressive or manic episode. If symptoms of depression or mania are present, their duration must be brief relative to the duration of the active and residual symptoms of schizophrenia.

## Subtypes

Schizophrenia is a heterogeneous disorder with many different clinical manifestations and levels of severity. The title of Bleuler's classic text referred to "the group of schizophrenias" in an effort to draw attention to the varied presentations of the disorder. It is not clear, however, how best to think about the different forms of schizophrenia. Many clinicians and investigators believe that schizophrenia is a general term for a group of disorders, each of which may be caused by a completely different set of factors. Other clinicians believe that the numerous symptoms of schizophrenia are most likely varying manifestations of the same underlying condition (Gottesman, 1991). Given the current state of evidence, it is not possible to choose between these conceptual options. Nevertheless, most investigators agree that we should at least consider the possibility that there are distinct forms.

Previous versions of the diagnostic manual, tracing back to DSM-I, have recognized several official subtypes of schizophrenia. These included the paranoid, disorganized, catatonic, and undifferentiated subtypes, with the latter being used to identify patients who meet criteria for several subtypes of schizophrenia at the same time. The subtypes were used to describe the most prominent symptoms exhibited by the patient during the most

# CRITICAL THINKING matters

## Why Were the Symptom-Based Subtypes of Schizophrenia Dropped from *DSM-5*?

The validity of the traditional subtypes was debated for many years. The evidence on which they are based was weak. Clinicians who favored continued use of subtype diagnoses claimed that these categories are *moderately* stable over time (Fenton, 2000). There is also some evidence indicating that patients who fit descriptions of the catatonic and paranoid subtypes have a somewhat better prognosis, whereas those in the disorganized subtype may have—on average—a worse prognosis (McGlashan & Fenton, 1991). If we think critically, this was *not* strong support for the inclusion of these subtypes in the official diagnostic manual.

Critics pointed to a number of serious problems. Traditional subtypes do not strongly predict either the course of the disorder or response to treatment. The subtypes also have relatively poor diagnostic reliability and are frequently unstable over time. Patients who fit a traditional subcategory during one psychotic episode frequently qualified for a different subtype diagnosis during a subsequent episode. Based on this evidence, it became reasonable to ask: "How does it help the clinician or the patient to assign a subtype diagnosis such as disorganized type or undifferentiated type?"

Perhaps the most important consideration with regard to the validity of subtypes involves the genetic evidence. Studies of extended families suggest that the subtypes are not etiologically distinct syndromes (Cardno et al., 1998; Linscott et al., 2010). If several members of a family—or two members of a monozygotic twin pair—have developed symptoms of schizophrenia, they will not necessarily exhibit symptoms of the same subtype. That fact argues strongly against the notion that the subtypes are qualitatively different disorders.

This is perhaps the greatest irony in research on schizophrenia. For more than 100 years, clinicians and investigators have agreed that the disorder is extremely heterogenous. The diagnostic category that we now recognize as schizophrenia may well be composed of many different kinds of mental disorders. This common opinion stands in contrast to the harsh fact that no one has been able to identify truly meaningful subtypes. At best, the diagnostic subtypes for schizophrenia were placeholders, serving primarily to remind us that the disorder is heterogeneous in nature. For all of the reasons mentioned above, the *DSM-5* workgroup for schizophrenia decided that it was finally time to drop the symptom-based subtypes from the diagnostic manual. We desperately need more knowledge in this area. We need better research that will help us find truly meaningful subtypes based on sophisticated measurement procedures that may involve genetic factors, cognitive performance, treatment response, or some other facet of the disorder that has not yet been studied. One thing that does seem to be clear is that it has not been particularly useful to focus on symptoms as the basis for reducing the heterogeneity of the complex disorder.

---

recent episode. *DSM-5* has eliminated these symptom-based subtypes because the research evidence that accumulated over a period of many years indicated clearly that they were not valid (see Critical Thinking Matters).

## Related Psychotic Disorders

The schizophrenia spectrum disorders that are listed in *DSM-5* include several additional disorders that are characterized by prominent psychotic symptoms. The manual also notes that schizotypal personality disorder (see Chapter 9) should be recognized as part of the schizophrenia spectrum.

People with **delusional disorder** do not meet the full symptomatic criteria for schizophrenia, but they are preoccupied for at least one month with delusions that are not bizarre. These are beliefs about situations that could occur in real life, such as being followed or poisoned. Ann's delusion, for example, might have fit this description. She believed that someone was trying to kill her and her children and that someone was trying to cast a voodoo spell on them. Ann would not be assigned a diagnosis of delusional disorder, however, because she also displayed negative symptoms, such as avolition. The presence of hallucinations, disorganized speech, catatonic behavior, or negative symptoms rules out a diagnosis of delusional disorder. The definition of delusional disorder also holds that the person's behavior is not bizarre and that social and occupational functioning are not impaired except for those areas that are directly affected by the delusional belief.

**Brief psychotic disorder** is a category that includes those people who exhibit psychotic symptoms—delusions, hallucinations, disorganized speech, or grossly disorganized or catatonic behavior—for at least one day but no more than one month. An episode of this sort is typically accompanied by confusion and emotional turmoil, often (but not necessarily) following a markedly stressful event. After the symptoms are resolved, the person returns to the same level of functioning that had been achieved prior to the psychotic episode. The long-term outcome is good for most patients who experience a brief episode of psychosis (Susser, et al., 1998). This diagnosis is not assigned if the symptoms are better explained by a mood disorder, schizophrenia, or substance abuse.

Elyn Saks, a professor at the University of Southern California and recipient of a MacArthur Foundation "genius award," has written eloquently about her experience with schizophrenia in her autobiography, *The Center Cannot Hold: My Journey Through Madness*. In her TED talk, she argues persuasively that "there's a tremendous need to implode the myths of mental illness, to put a face on it, to show people that a diagnosis does not have to lead to a painful and oblique life."

## MyPsychLab VIDEO CASE

### Schizoaffective Disorder

JOSH

*"When I was first in the hospital, I thought I was in the middle of a massacre . . ."*

👁 **Watch** the **Video** *Josh: Schizoaffective Disorder* on **MyPsychLab**

In addition to describing bizarre delusional beliefs, Josh has also experienced several symptoms of bipolar mood disorder, such as racing thoughts and grandiosity.

The diagnostic criteria for *schizophreniform disorder* are exactly the same as those for schizophrenia (in Criterion A). The difference between them is based on the duration of symptoms. Total duration for schizophreniform disorder is more than one month but less than six months. If the person does not recover after six months, the diagnosis would be changed to schizophrenia. In terms of duration, schizophreniform disorder falls between brief psychotic disorder (which lasts at least one day but less than one month) and schizophrenia.

**Schizoaffective disorder** is an ambiguous and somewhat controversial category (Averill, et al., 2004; Lake & Hurwitz, 2007). It describes the symptoms of patients who fall on the boundary between schizophrenia and mood disorder with psychotic features. This diagnosis applies only to the description of a particular episode of disturbance; it does not describe the overall lifetime course of the person's disorder. Schizoaffective disorder is defined by an episode in which the symptoms of schizophrenia partially overlap with a major depressive episode or a manic episode. The key to making this diagnosis is the presence of delusions or hallucinations for at least two weeks in the absence of prominent mood symptoms. If the delusions and hallucinations are present only during a depressive episode, for example, the diagnosis would be major depressive episode with psychotic features.

## Course and Outcome

Schizophrenia is a severe, progressive disorder that most often begins in adolescence and typically has a poor outcome. In fact, classic descriptions of the disorder considered the deteriorating course to be one of the principal defining features. Current evidence suggests that this view may be unnecessarily pessimistic (Hafner, et al., 2003; Perkins, Miller-Anderson, & Lieberman, 2006). Many patients experience a more favorable outcome in the sense that their symptoms are improved. For example, Manfred Bleuler (1978) studied a sample of 208 schizophrenic patients who had been admitted to his hospital in Switzerland during 1942 and 1943. After a follow-up period of 23 years, 53 percent of the patients were either recovered or significantly improved. More recent evidence indicates that, while some patients do have a positive outcome, relatively few are able to achieve successful aging (Lang, et al., 2013).

Follow-up studies of schizophrenic patients have found that the description of outcome is a complicated process (Harvey et al., 2009). Many factors must be taken into consideration other than whether the person is still in the hospital. Is the person still exhibiting symptoms of the disorder? Does he or she have any other problems, such as depression or anxiety? Is the person employed? Does she have any friends? How does he get along with other people? The evidence indicates that different dimensions of outcome, such as social adjustment, occupational functioning, and symptom severity are only loosely correlated. As in most situations where psychologists attempt to predict future behavior, the outcome data regarding schizophrenia suggest that the best predictor of future social adjustment is previous social adjustment. Similarly, the best predictor of symptom severity at follow-up is severity of psychotic symptoms at initial assessment (Bromet, et al., 2005).

## Frequency

One of the most informative ways of examining the frequency of schizophrenia is to consider the lifetime prevalence—that is, the proportion of a specific population that will be affected by the disorder at some time during their lives. Most studies in Europe and the United States have reported lifetime prevalence figures of approximately 1.0 percent if they include people who meet diagnostic criteria for schizophrenia as well as related psychotic disorders (Kessler et al., 2005; Saha, Chant, & McGrath, 2008). In other words, approximately one out of every 100 people will experience or display symptoms of schizophrenia at some time during their lives. Of course, prevalence rates depend on the diagnostic criteria that are used to define schizophrenia in any particular study, as well as the methods that are used to identify cases in the general population. Investigators who have employed more narrow or restrictive criteria for the disorder report lower prevalence rates (Messias, Chen, & Eaton, 2007).

### Gender Differences

Although experts believed for many years that men and women are equally likely to develop schizophrenia, this conclusion has been challenged by several recent studies. Current evidence suggests that men are 30 to 40 percent more likely to develop schizophrenia than women (Seeman, 2008).

There are some interesting and widely recognized differences between male and female patients with regard to patterns of onset, symptoms, and course of the disorder. For example, the average age at which schizophrenic males begin to exhibit overt symptoms is younger by about four or five years than the average age at which schizophrenic women first experience problems. A summary of reported gender differences in schizophrenia is presented in Table 13.1 on page 360. Male patients are more likely than female patients to exhibit negative symptoms, and they are also more likely to follow a chronic, deteriorating course (Atalay & Atalay, 2006; Moriarty, et al., 2001).

Gender differences in the age of onset and symptomatic expression of schizophrenia can be interpreted in several ways. The alternatives fall into two types of hypotheses. One approach assumes that schizophrenia is a single disorder and that its expression varies in men and women. A common, genetically determined vulnerability to schizophrenia might be expressed differently in men than in women. Mediating factors that might account for this difference could be biological differences between men and women—perhaps involving certain hormones—or different environmental demands, such as the timing and form of stresses associated with typical male and female sex roles. An alternative approach suggests that there are two qualitatively distinct subtypes of schizophrenia: one with an early onset that affects men more often than women, and another with a later onset that affects women more often than men. Both approaches assume a combination of genetically determined predisposition to disorder with the onset of symptoms being triggered by environmental events. The available evidence does not allow us to favor one of these explanations over the other (Haefner et al., 1998; Taylor & Langdon, 2006).

*"He could be psychotic or he could be appealing to his base."*
© Barbara Smaller/www.cartoonbank.com

**TABLE 13.1**
## Typical Gender Differences in Schizophrenia

| Variable | Men | Women |
|---|---|---|
| Age of onset | Earlier (18–25) | Later (25–35) |
| Premorbid functioning; adjustment | Poor social functioning; more schizotypal traits | Good social functioning; fewer schizotypal traits |
| Typical symptoms | More negative symptoms; more withdrawn and passive | More hallucinations and paranoia; more emotional and impulsive |
| Course | More often chronic; poorer response to treatment | Less often chronic; better response to treatment |

*Source:* Based on J. M. Goldstein. 1995. The Impact of Gender on Understanding the Epidemiology of Schizophrenia. In M.V. Seeman, Ed., Gender and Psychopathology. Washington, DC: American Psychiatric Press: 159–199.

## Cross-Cultural Comparisons

Schizophrenia has been observed in virtually every culture that has been subjected to careful analysis. Although it is a universal disorder, the frequency of schizophrenia is not constant around the world. The annual incidence of schizophrenia—that is, the number of *new* cases appearing in any given year—varies from one country to the next. Reported estimates range from 8 to 43 cases per 100,000 people (McGrath, 2005). Urban populations have higher rates than rural areas, but incidence is not related to a country's economic status (Saha et al., 2006). As epidemiologists attempt to unravel these differences and explain them, we will learn more about the causes of the disorder.

Substantial cross-cultural differences have also been found with regard to the course of schizophrenia. Two large-scale epidemiological studies, conducted by teams of scientists working for the World Health Organization (WHO), have drawn considerable attention to differences in short- and long-term outcome for schizophrenia in the third world and industrialized countries (Sartorius, 2007). The International Pilot Study of Schizophrenia (IPSS) began in the 1960s and was conducted in nine countries in Europe, North America, South America, Africa, and Asia. It included 1,200 patients who were followed for 15 to 25 years after their initial hospitalization. The Collaborative Study on the Determinants of Outcome of Severe Mental Disorders (DOS) was begun a few years later in six of the same countries that participated in the IPSS, plus four others. The DOS study included more than 1,500 patients. Both the IPSS and DOS projects examined rural and urban areas in both Western and non-Western countries. For purposes of cultural comparison, the countries were divided into those that were "developing" and those that were already "developed" on the basis of prevailing socioeconomic conditions. All the interviewers were trained in the use of a single, standardized interview schedule, and all employed the same sets of diagnostic criteria.

The IPSS results indicated that patients who exhibited characteristic signs and symptoms of schizophrenia were found in all of the study sites. Comparisons of patients across research centers revealed more similarities than differences in clinical symptoms at the time of entry into the study, which was always an active phase of disorder that required psychiatric treatment. The IPSS investigators found that clinical and social outcomes were significantly better for schizophrenic patients in developing countries than in developed countries, such as the United States, England, and Russia. The DOS study confirmed those results (Hopper, et al., 2007).

The WHO studies provide compelling support for the conclusion that, although the frequency of schizophrenia varies around the world, it is expressed in terms of similar symptoms in different cultures. Most experts believe that the more favorable clinical outcome that was observed in India and Nigeria is a product of the greater tolerance and acceptance extended to people with psychotic symptoms in developing countries. This conclusion is consistent with evidence regarding the relationship between frequency of relapse and patterns of family communication, which we consider later in this chapter in the section on expressed emotion. These cross-cultural data certainly testify to the important influence of culture in shaping the experience and expression of psychotic symptoms (Thakker & Ward, 1998; Whaley & Hall, 2009).

## Causes

Having considered the defining characteristics of schizophrenia, ways in which it has been classified, and some basic information regarding its distribution within the general population, we now review the evidence regarding factors that might contribute to the development of the disorder, as well as its course and outcome.

### Biological Factors

Many of the early investigators who defined schizophrenia at the beginning of the twentieth century believed that the disorder was the product of a biological dysfunction. At that time very little was known about human genetics or the biochemistry of the brain. Research in the areas of molecular genetics and the neurosciences has progressed at an explosive rate in the past decade. Much of what we know today about the biological substrates of schizophrenia has emerged from advances that have taken place in other sciences.

**GENETICS** The role of genetic factors has been studied more extensively with regard to schizophrenia than with any other type of mental disorder. The existing data are based on sophisticated methods that have been refined over many years. The cumulative weight of this evidence points clearly toward some type of genetic influence in the transmission of this disorder (Pogue-Geile & Gottesman, 2007).

*FAMILY STUDIES* Figure 13.1 illustrates the lifetime risk for schizophrenia for various types of relatives of a person with schizophrenia. This figure was created by pooling data from 40 European studies that were published between 1920 and 1987 (Gottesman, 1991). All of the studies employed conservative diagnostic criteria for the disorder.

Consider the data for first-degree relatives and second-degree relatives. On average, siblings and children share 50 percent of their genes with the schizophrenic proband; nieces, nephews, and cousins share only 25 percent. The lifetime morbid risk for schizophrenia is much greater among first-degree relatives than it is among second-degree relatives. The risk in the second-degree relatives is greater than the 1 percent figure that is typically reported for people in the general population. As the degree of genetic similarity increases between an individual and a schizophrenic patient, the risk to that person increases. The family history data are consistent with the hypothesis that the transmission of schizophrenia is influenced by genetic factors (Goldstein,

et al., 2010). They do not prove the point, however, because family studies do not separate genetic and environmental events (see Chapter 2).

*TWIN STUDIES* Several twin studies have examined concordance rates for schizophrenia. The results of these studies are also summarized in Figure 13.1. The average concordance rate for MZ twins is 48 percent, whereas the comparable figure for DZ twins is 17 percent. One study from Finland found a concordance rate of 46 percent among MZ twins and only 9 percent among DZ twins (Cannon, et al., 1998). Although the specific rates vary somewhat from study to study, all of the published reports have found that MZ twins are significantly more likely than DZ twins to be concordant for schizophrenia. This pattern suggests strongly that genetic factors play an important role in the development of the disorder.

It should also be pointed out, however, that none of the twin studies of schizophrenia has found a concordance rate that even approaches 100 percent, which would be expected if genetic factors were entirely responsible for schizophrenia. Thus, the twin studies also provide compelling evidence for the importance of environmental events. Some people, like Marsha in the case presented earlier, apparently inherit a predisposition to the development of schizophrenia. Among that select group of vulnerable individuals, certain environmental events must determine whether a given person will eventually exhibit the full-blown symptoms of the disorder.

*ADOPTION STUDIES* Studies of children who were adopted away from their biological parents and reared by foster families provide further evidence regarding the impact of genetic and environmental factors. The first adoption study of schizophrenia began by identifying records for a group of 49 children who were born between 1915 and 1945 while their mothers were

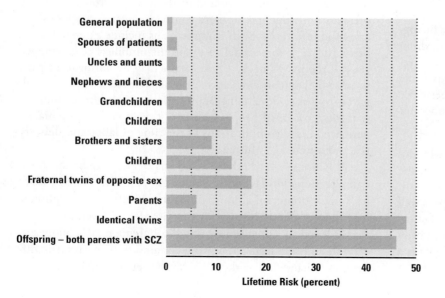

**FIGURE 13.1**

**Rates of schizophrenia among relatives of patients with schizophrenia**

Lifetime risk of developing schizophrenia increases as a function of percent of genes shared with a person who has been diagnosed with the disorder.
*Source:* Based on data from I.I. Gottesman (1991). *Schizophrenia genesis: The origins of madness,* p. 96. Freeman.

hospitalized for schizophrenia (Heston, 1966). All the children were apparently normal at birth and were separated from their mothers within three days of birth. To rule out possible exposure to the environment associated with the mother's psychosis, any child who had been in contact with maternal relatives was excluded from the study. A control group of children was selected using the admission records of foundling homes where many of the target children had originally been placed. These children were matched to the patients' children on a number of variables, including age, sex, type of eventual placement, and amount of time spent in institutions.

Most of the offspring were successfully located and interviewed when they were in their mid-thirties. Five of the adult offspring of schizophrenic mothers received a diagnosis of schizophrenia. Correcting for the fact that most of the participants were still within the period of risk for the disorder, this resulted in a lifetime morbidity risk for schizophrenia of 16.6 percent in the target group, which is almost exactly the rate observed among children of schizophrenic parents who were raised by their biological parents (see Figure 13.1). In contrast, none of the adult offspring in the control group received a diagnosis of schizophrenia. Because the only difference between the two groups was the genetic relationship between the target offspring and their schizophrenic biological mothers, these data indicate that genetic factors play a role in the development of the disorder. Several other adoption studies have been concerned with schizophrenia, and all reach the same conclusion as Heston's original report (Pogue-Geile & Gottesman, 2007).

**THE SPECTRUM OF SCHIZOPHRENIC DISORDERS** Results from adoption and twin studies also provide interesting clues regarding the boundaries of the concept of schizophrenia. Several types of psychotic disorders and personality disorders resemble schizophrenia in one way or another, including schizoaffective disorder, delusional disorder, and schizotypal personality disorder (discussed in Chapter 9). Are these conditions a reflection of the same genetically determined predisposition as schizophrenia, or are they distinct disorders caused by different forces? If they are genetically related, then investigators should find that the biological relatives of schizophrenic adoptees are more likely to exhibit these conditions as well as schizophrenia. The overall pattern of results does suggest that vulnerability to schizophrenia is sometimes expressed as schizophrenia-like personality traits and other types of psychoses (Tarbox & Pogue-Geile, 2011; van Snellenberg & de Candia, 2009).

**MOLECULAR GENETICS** The combined results from twin and adoption studies indicate that genetic factors are involved in the transmission of schizophrenia. This conclusion does not imply, however, that the manner in which schizophrenia develops is well understood. We know little beyond the fact that genetic factors are involved in some way. The mode of transmission has not been identified. Most clinical scientists believe that schizophrenia is a polygenic characteristic, which means that it is the product of a

reasonably large number of genes rather than a single gene (see Chapter 2).

One of the most exciting areas of research on genetics and schizophrenia focuses on molecular genetics (see Research Methods in Chapter 14 for an explanation of this process). Studies of this type are designed to identify specific genes that are responsible for the disorder (or some important components of the disorder). So far, investigators have not been able to identify any genes that account for a major proportion of the heritability of schizophrenia, but they have found several genes that apparently have a very small but measurable impact (Mitchell & Porteous, 2011; Owen, et al., 2010; Sanders, et al., 2008). Supporters of the search for specific genes involved in the transmission of schizophrenia contend that the absence of more definitive discoveries is not surprising when we consider the complexity of this process and the magnitude of the search. They feel that the search for a particular gene that causes schizophrenia will simply take more time (Cannon, 2010).

One specific gene that has attracted considerable research attention is associated with the production of catechol O-methyltransferase (COMT), which is an enzyme that is involved in breaking down the neurotransmitter dopamine. The COMT gene is located on chromosome 22, a region that has been linked to schizophrenia. People who possess a specific form of the COMT gene (called the Val allele) seem to have a small but consistently increased risk for schizophrenia (Glatt, Faraone, & Tsuang, 2003). Scientists believe that this gene may increase risk for schizophrenia by affecting dopamine transmission in the prefrontal cortex of the brain, with the net effect being impaired cognitive ability (Prata, et al., 2009; van Haren, Bakker, & Kahn, 2008) (see later section on working memory and vulnerability to schizophrenia).

**PREGNANCY AND BIRTH COMPLICATIONS** People with schizophrenia are more likely than the general population to have been exposed to various problems during their mother's pregnancy and to have suffered birth injuries. Problems during pregnancy include the mother's contracting various types of diseases and infections. Birth complications include extended labor, breech delivery, forceps delivery, and the umbilical cord wrapped around the baby's neck. These events may be harmful, in part, because they impair circulation or otherwise reduce the availability of oxygen to developing brain regions. Birth records indicate that the mothers of people who later develop schizophrenia experienced more complications at the time of labor and delivery (Cannon, Jones, & Murray, 2002).

It is not clear whether the effects of pregnancy and birth complications interact with genetic factors. They may produce neurodevelopmental abnormalities that result in schizophrenia regardless of family history for the disorder. Conversely, a fetus that is genetically predisposed to schizophrenia may be more susceptible to brain injury following certain kinds of obstetric difficulties (Khandaker, et al., 2013; Walker, et al., 2004).

The devastating consequences of war include severe nutritional deficiencies, such as those suffered in Somalia by this mother and her 4-year-old son. The offspring of women who are pregnant during serious famines may be more likely to develop schizophrenia as they reach adulthood.

Dietary factors may also play a role in the etiology of the disorder. Severe maternal malnutrition in the early months of pregnancy leads to an increased risk of schizophrenia among the offspring. This conclusion is based on a study of medical and psychiatric records of people who were born in the western part of the Netherlands between 1944 and 1946 (Susser, et al., 1996). The German blockade of ports and other supply routes in this area led to a severe famine at the end of World War II. People who were conceived during the worst months of the famine were twice as likely to develop schizophrenia than were people whose mothers became pregnant at other times, including the early months of the famine. These results, coupled with more recent findings, suggest that prenatal nutritional deficiencies may disrupt normal development of the fetal nervous system (Abel et al., 2010; Insel, et al., 2008).

**VIRAL INFECTIONS** Some speculation has focused on the potential role that viral infections may play in the etiology of schizophrenia (Brown & Derkits, 2010). One indirect line of support for this hypothesis comes from studies indicating that people who develop schizophrenia are somewhat more likely than other people to have been born during the winter months (McGrath & Welham, 1999). Some clinicians interpret this pattern to mean that, during their pregnancies, the mothers were more likely to develop viral infections, which are more prevalent during the winter. Exposure to infection presumably interferes with brain development in the fetus. This possibility has received considerable attention in the research literature and remains an important topic of debate (Clarke, et al., 2009).

**NEUROPATHOLOGY** One important step toward understanding the etiology of schizophrenia would be to identify its neurological underpinnings. If people with schizophrenia suffer from a form of neurological dysfunction, shouldn't it be possible to observe differences between the structure of their brains and those of other people? This is a challenging task. Scientists have invented methods to create images of the living human brain (see Chapter 4). Some of these procedures provide static pictures of various brain structures at rest, just as an X-ray provides a photographic image of a bone or some other organ of the body. More recently, sophisticated methods have enabled scientists to create functional images of the brain while a person is performing different tasks. Studies using these techniques have produced evidence indicating that a number of brain areas are involved in schizophrenia (Fitzsimmons, et al, 2013; Reichenberg & Harvey, 2007). You may want to review the description of brain structures in Chapter 2 (Figure 2.3) before reading the next sections of this chapter.

***STRUCTURAL BRAIN IMAGING*** Many investigations of brain structure in people with schizophrenia have employed magnetic resonance imaging (MRI; see Chapter 4 for an explanation of this process). The disorder is not associated with abnormalities in one specific brain region or in one particular type of nerve cell. Rather, it seems to affect many different regions of the brain and the ways in which they connect or communicate with each other (Shepherd, et al., 2012). Most MRI studies have reported a decrease in total volume of brain tissue among schizophrenic patients. Another consistent finding is that some people with schizophrenia have mildly to moderately enlarged lateral ventricles, the cavities on each side of the brain that are filled with cerebrospinal fluid.

These differences seem to reflect a natural part of the disorder rather than a side effect of treatment with antipsychotic medication. In fact, some studies have found enlarged ventricles in young schizophrenic patients before they have been exposed to any form of treatment (Steen, et al., 2006). Some studies have also found enlarged ventricles prior to the onset of symptoms. The structural changes seem to occur early in the development of the disorder and therefore may play a role in the onset of symptoms (DeLisi, 2008; Weinberger & McClure, 2002).

The temporal lobes have also been studied extensively using MRI scans. Several studies have reported decreased size of the hippocampus, the parahippocampus, the amygdala, and the

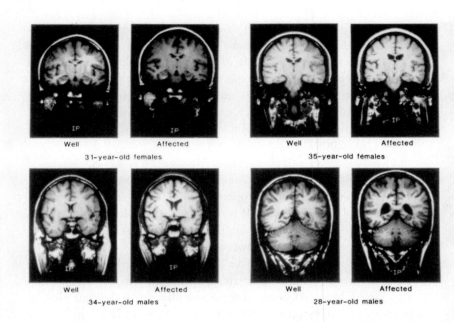

MRI scans from four identical twin pairs discordant for schizophrenia showing varying degrees of increased ventricular size in the twin with the disorder compared to the twin who is well.

Well     Affected
31-year-old females

Well     Affected
35-year-old females

Well     Affected
34-year-old males

Well     Affected
28-year-old males

thalamus, all of which are parts of the limbic system (Price, et al., 2006). These areas of the brain (see Figure 13.2) play a crucial role in the regulation of emotion as well as the integration of cognition and emotion. Decreased size of these structures in the limbic area of the temporal lobes may be especially noticeable on the left side of the brain, which plays an important role in the control of language.

Many questions remain to be answered regarding the relation between structural brain abnormalities and schizophrenia. Does the pattern reflect a generalized deterioration of the brain, or is it the result of a defect in specific brain sites? We don't know. Is the presence of enlarged ventricles and cortical atrophy consistently found in some subset of schizophrenic patients? Some investigators have reported an association between this type of

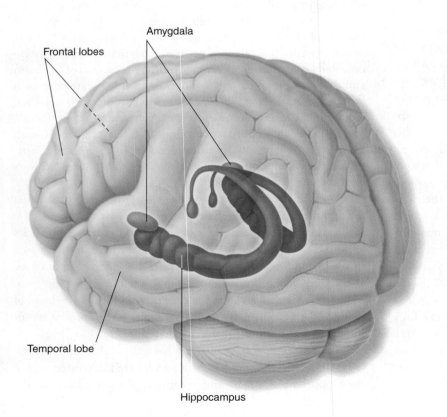

Frontal lobes

Amygdala

Temporal lobe

Hippocampus

### FIGURE 13.2

**Structures of the Brain Implicated in Schizophrenia**
Structural imaging procedures indicate reduced size of temporal lobe structures, such as the hippocampus and amygdala, among some patients with schizophrenia.

neuropathology and other factors, such as negative symptoms, poor response to medication, and absence of family history of the disorder. These are all interesting possibilities, but none has been firmly established.

*FUNCTIONAL BRAIN IMAGING* In addition to static pictures of brain structures, clinical scientists use techniques that provide dynamic images of brain functions. One dynamic brain imaging technique, known as positron emission tomography (PET), can reflect changes in brain activity as the person responds to various task demands. Visual stimulation will produce increased cerebral blood flow in the visual cortex; people performing a simple motor task exhibit increased flow in the motor cortex. Functional MRI is another tool that can be used to observe brain activity. The results of studies using these techniques suggest dysfunction in various neural circuits, including some regions of the prefrontal cortex (see Figure 13.3) and several regions in the temporal lobes (Bonner-Jackson, et al., 2005; Whalley, et al., 2012). The problems seem to involve activities within, as well as integration between, a variety of functional circuits rather than a localized abnormality in one region of the brain.

The role of neurological abnormalities in schizophrenia has been highlighted by a study of identical twins conducted by investigators at the National Institute of Mental Health (NIMH). Participants included 27 pairs of twins discordant for schizophrenia and 13 pairs that were concordant for the disorder. Changes in brain structure, measured by MRI, and changes in brain function, measured by cerebral blood flow, were prominent in the twins who had developed schizophrenia. Their well co-twins also exhibited more neurological impairment than a group of normal control participants, but these abnormalities were less marked than those found in the probands. Among discordant monozygotic pairs, the schizophrenic twin typically had the smaller hippocampus and smaller amygdala. The schizophrenic twins always showed reduced frontal lobe activity compared with their unaffected co-twins. Results for enlarged ventricles were less consistent. In general, neurological dysfunction seemed to be associated with the overall severity of the disorder rather than being indicative of an etiologically distinct subgroup of patients (Bridle, et al., 2002).

*GENERAL CONCLUSIONS* The primary conclusion that can be drawn from existing brain imaging studies is that schizophrenia is associated with diffuse patterns of neuropathology. The most consistent findings point toward structural as well as functional irregularities in the frontal cortex and limbic areas of the temporal lobes, which play an important role in cognitive and emotional processes. The neural network connecting limbic areas with the frontal cortex may be fundamentally disordered in schizophrenia.

Speculation regarding disruptions in neural circuitry must also be tempered with caution. Evidence of neuropathology does not seem to be unique to schizophrenic patients. Many patients with other psychiatric and neurological disorders show similar changes in brain structure and function. Furthermore, a specific brain lesion has not been identified, and it is unlikely that

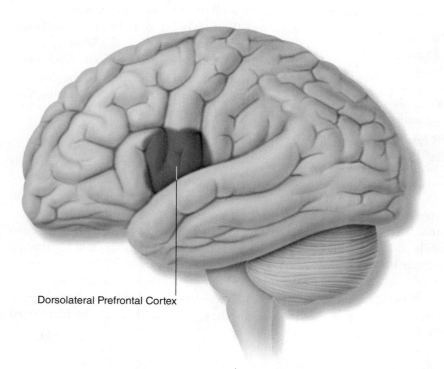

**FIGURE 13.3**

**Areas of Brain Function Implicated in Schizophrenia**
Neural circuits in the dorsolateral prefrontal cortex may function improperly in schizophrenia.

Dorsolateral Prefrontal Cortex

one will be found. It is unlikely that a disorder as complex as schizophrenia will be traced to a single site in the brain. The various symptoms and cognitive deficits that have been observed in schizophrenic patients may be linked to a host of subtle disruptions in neurological functions (Csernansky & Cronenwett, 2008; Green, 2001).

It should also be emphasized that brain imaging procedures are not diagnostically meaningful tests for mental disorders. For example, an MRI showing enlarged ventricles does not prove that a patient has schizophrenia. Brain imaging procedures have identified interesting group differences, but they do not predict the presence of schizophrenia for individuals. The group differences that have been observed are very subtle in comparison to the levels of neuropathology found in disorders such as Alzheimer's disease and Huntington's disease (see Chapter 14). Some schizophrenic patients do not show abnormalities in brain structure or function.

A dramatic example of this point was found in the NIMH study of discordant MZ twins. In one pair, the well twin was a successful businessman who had never had any problems with mental disorder. His twin brother had been severely impaired with schizophrenia for 20 years. The well twin had ventricles that were five times larger than those of the schizophrenic twin. Thus, we should approach all these hypotheses with caution and skepticism.

**NEUROCHEMISTRY** The neurological underpinnings of schizophrenia may not take the form of changes in the size or organization of brain structures. They may be even more subtle, involving alterations in the chemical communications among neurons within particular brain circuits.

*THE DOPAMINE HYPOTHESIS* Scientists have proposed various neurochemical theories to account for the etiology of schizophrenia. The most influential theory, known as the *dopamine hypothesis,* focuses on the function of specific dopamine pathways in the limbic area of the brain. The original version of the dopamine hypothesis proposed that the symptoms of schizophrenia are the product of excessive levels of dopaminergic activity. This hypothesis grew out of attempts to understand how antipsychotic drugs improve the adjustment of many schizophrenic patients. Animals who receive doses of antipsychotic drugs show a marked increase in the production of dopamine. In 1963, it was suggested that antipsychotic drugs block postsynaptic dopamine receptors. The presynaptic neuron recognizes the presence of this blockade and increases its release of dopamine in a futile attempt to override it (Carlsson & Lindqvist, 1963).

If the dopamine system is dysfunctional in schizophrenic patients, what is the specific form of this problem? One possibility is that certain neural pathways have an elevated sensitivity to dopamine because of increased numbers of postsynaptic dopamine receptors. The potency of various types of antipsychotic drugs is specifically related to their ability to block one type of dopamine receptor, known as $D_2$ receptors. Imaging studies of brain functions in patients with schizophrenia have found elevated levels of dopamine functioning in the striatum (Howes et al., 2009).

*INTERACTIONS OF MULTIPLE NEUROTRANSMITTERS* A dysregulation and exaggerated response of certain dopamine pathways is certainly involved in schizophrenia, at least for some patients. On the other hand, experts now agree that several other neurotransmitters also play an important role. A neurochemical model focused narrowly on dopamine fails to explain many different aspects of the disorder, including the following: Some patients do not respond positively to drugs that block dopamine receptors; the effects of antipsychotic drugs require several days to become effective, but dopamine blockage begins immediately; and research studies that examined the by-products of dopamine in cerebrospinal fluid were inconclusive at best.

Current neurochemical hypotheses regarding schizophrenia focus on a broad array of neurotransmitters (Carlsson et al., 2001). Special interest has been focused on serotonin pathways since the introduction of a new class of antipsychotic drugs such as clozapine (Clozaril) that are useful in treating patients who were resistant to standard antipsychotic drugs. (See the section on treatment.) These "atypical" antipsychotics produce a strong blockade of serotonin receptors and only a weak blockade of $D_2$ receptors. This pattern leads to speculation that the neurochemical substrates of schizophrenia may involve a complex interaction between serotonin and dopamine pathways in the brain (Downar & Kapur, 2008).

Brain imaging studies that point to problems in the prefrontal cortex have also drawn attention to glutamate and GABA (gamma-aminobutyric acid), the two principal neurotransmitters in the cerebral cortex (Wassef, Baker, & Kochan, 2003). Glutamate is an excitatory neurotransmitter, and GABA is an inhibitory neurotransmitter. As in the case of serotonin, hypotheses regarding the role of glutamate and GABA focus on their interactions with dopamine pathways, especially those connecting temporal lobe structures with the prefrontal and limbic cortexes.

## Social Factors

There is little question that biological factors play an important role in the etiology of schizophrenia, but twin studies also provide compelling evidence for the importance of environmental events. The disorder is expressed in its full-blown form only when vulnerable individuals experience some type of environmental event, which might include anything from nutritional variables to stressful life events (Howes et al., 2004; Walker, et al., 2004). What sorts of nongenetic events interact with genetic factors and other biological factors to produce schizophrenia? We will review some of the hypotheses that have been proposed and studied.

**SOCIAL CLASS** One general indicator of a person's status within a community's hierarchy of prestige and influence is social class. People from different social classes are presumably exposed to different levels of environmental stress, with those people in the lowest class being subjected to the most hardships. More than 70 years ago, social scientists working in Chicago found that the highest prevalence of schizophrenia was found in neighborhoods of the lowest socioeconomic status (Faris & Dunham, 1939). Many research studies have subsequently confirmed this finding in several other geographic areas (Boydell & Murray, 2003). The evidence supporting an inverse relationship between social class and schizophrenia is substantial.

There are two ways to interpret the relationship between social class and schizophrenia. One holds that harmful events associated with membership in the lowest social classes, which might include many factors ranging from stress and social isolation to poor nutrition, play a causal role in the development of the disorder. This is often called the *social causation* hypothesis. It is also possible, however, that low social class is an outcome rather than a cause of schizophrenia. Those people who develop schizophrenia may be less able than others to complete a higher level education or to hold a well-paying job. Their cognitive and social impairments may cause downward social mobility. In other words, regardless of the social class of their family of origin, many schizophrenic patients may gradually drift into the lowest social classes. This view is sometimes called the *social selection hypothesis*.

Research studies have found evidence supporting both views. The social selection hypothesis is supported by studies that have compared the occupational roles of male schizophrenic patients with those of their fathers. The patients are frequently less successful than their fathers, whereas the opposite pattern is typical of men who do not have schizophrenia (Jones et al., 1993). It is also true, however, that a disproportionately high percentage of the fathers of schizophrenic patients were from the lowest social class (Harrison et al., 2001). This finding is consistent with the social causation hypothesis.

**MIGRANT STUDIES** Higher rates of schizophrenia have also been found repeatedly among people who have migrated to a new country (Cantor-Graae & Selton, 2005). Several influential studies of this sort focused on African Caribbean people who moved to the United Kingdom from Jamaica, Barbados, and Trinidad. Risk for schizophrenia in these migrant groups was found to be several times higher than the risk observed in the native-born U.K. population. It was also much higher than the risk observed among people living in the migrants' countries of origin. Subsequent studies demonstrated that the effect is not unique to the United Kingdom. Larger effects are reported for migrants from developing rather than developed countries, and they are also larger for migrants from countries where the majority population is black. One possible explanation for this phenomenon is that social adversity increases risk for schizophrenia. Migrants tend to settle in urban areas where they may be exposed to discrimination and other forms of disadvantage (Fearon & Morgan, 2006; Weiser et al., 2008).

In general, the evidence regarding socioeconomic status and schizophrenia indicates that the disorder is, to a certain extent,

influenced by social factors. Adverse social and economic circumstances may increase the probability that persons who are genetically predisposed to the disorder will develop its clinical symptoms (van Os & McGuffin, 2003).

## Psychological Factors

Most of the attention devoted to psychological factors and schizophrenia has focused on patterns of behavior and communication within families. Research evidence indicates that family interactions and communication problems are not primarily responsible for the initial appearance of symptoms. Disturbed patterns of communication among family members do not *cause* people to develop schizophrenia. This knowledge is important to parents of schizophrenic patients. They experience enough emotional anguish without also being made to feel that something they did or said was the primary cause of their child's problems.

**EXPRESSED EMOTION** The family environment does have a significant impact on the course (as opposed to the original onset) of schizophrenia. Studies of this effect are concerned with the adjustment of patients who have already been treated for schizophrenic symptoms. This effect was discovered by people who were interested in the adjustment of patients who were discharged after being treated in a psychiatric hospital. Men with schizophrenia were much more likely to return to the hospital within the next nine months if they went to live with their wives or parents than if they went to live in other lodgings or with their siblings. The patients who relapsed seemed to react negatively to some feature of their close relationship with their wives or mothers.

Subsequent research confirmed this initial impression (Vaughn & Leff, 1976). Relatives of schizophrenic patients were

Criticism and hostility can increase the risk of relapse for some patients with schizophrenia. Conversely, warmth and family support can serve as a protective factor.

interviewed prior to the patients' discharge from the hospital, and many of the relatives made statements that reflected negative or intrusive attitudes toward the patient. These statements were used to create a measure of **expressed emotion (EE).** For example, many of the relatives expressed hostility toward the patient or repeatedly criticized the patient's behavior. The following comments, made by the stepfather of a young man with schizophrenia, illustrate generalized, hostile criticisms of the patient's behavior. These comments would be considered to be high in expressed emotion.

> **INTERVIEWER:** What seemed different about Stephen's behavior?
> **STEPFATHER:** Everything and anything. In other words, he's the type of person, you don't tell him, he tells you.
> **INTERVIEWER:** You say that he spent time in a juvenile facility?
> **STEPFATHER:** Yeah. This kid is a genuine con artist, believe me. I spent time in the service and I've been around con artists. This kid is a first-class, genuine con artist, bar none.
> (Leff & Vaughn, 1985, p. 42)

Other family members appeared to be overprotective or too closely identified with the patient. These phenomena are also rated as being high in expressed emotion. Of course, a certain amount of worrying and concern should be expected from a parent whose child has developed a severe disorder such as schizophrenia. In the assessment of expressed emotion, relatives were considered to be emotionally overinvolved if they reported responses such as extreme anxiety or exaggerated forms of self-sacrifice. For example, the following exchange illustrates emotional overinvolvement (high EE) by the mother of a 24-year-old male patient who had his first onset of the disorder when he was 22:

> **MOTHER:** He talked to me a lot—because I was his therapist—the person he shared with more than anybody else. He involves me, ruminates with me, because I allow him to do it.
> **INTERVIEWER:** How frequently?
> **MOTHER:** He would do it constantly. He would do it as much as I would be there with him.
> **INTERVIEWER:** Once or twice a week?
> **MOTHER:** No, it happened daily. All the time I was with him, particularly in the last four or five months. He would talk to me for hours at a time, worrying and sharing how bad he felt, reporting to me every change in mood or feeling from 5-minute to 5-minute period.
> (Leff & Vaughn, 1985, p. 51)

Patients who returned to live in a home with at least one member who was high in EE were more likely than patients from low EE families to relapse in the first nine months after discharge. This result has been replicated many times (Marom et al., 2005). Approximately half of schizophrenic patients live in families that would be rated as being high in EE. Average relapse rates—defined primarily in terms of the proportion of patients who show a definite return of positive symptoms in the first year following hospital discharge—are 52 percent for patients in high EE families and 22 percent for patients in low EE families. Among the various types of comments that can contribute to a high EE rating, criticism is usually most strongly related to patients' relapse (Hooley & Gotlib, 2000).

High EE seems to be related, at least in part, to relatives' knowledge and beliefs about their family member's problems. Relatives find it easier to accept the most obvious positive symptoms as being the product of a mental disorder (Brewin et al., 1991). They show less tolerance toward negative symptoms, such as avolition and social withdrawal, perhaps because the patient may appear to be simply lazy or unmotivated.

**UNDERSTANDING FAMILY ATTITUDES** The influence of expressed emotion is not unique to schizophrenia. Patients with mood disorders, eating disorders, panic disorder with agoraphobia, and obsessive–compulsive disorder are also more likely to relapse following discharge if they are living with a high EE relative (Miklowitz, 2004). In fact, EE is an even better predictor of outcome for mood disorders and eating disorders than it is for schizophrenia (Butzlaff & Hooley, 1998). The extension of this phenomenon to other disorders should not be taken to mean that it is unimportant or that the social context of the family is irrelevant to our understanding of the maintenance of schizophrenia (see Research Methods). It may indicate, however, that this aspect of the causal model is shared with other forms of psychopathology. The specific nature of the person's symptoms may hinge on the genetic predisposition.

Cross-cultural evidence suggests that high EE may be more common in Western or developed countries than in non-Western or developing countries (Kymalainen & Weissman de Mamani, 2008). This observation might help explain why the long-term course of schizophrenia is typically less severe in developing countries. Some speculation has focused on family members' attitudes and beliefs: People in developing countries may be more tolerant of eccentric behavior among their extended family members. These attitudes may create environments similar to those found in low EE homes in the West. An alternative view places greater emphasis on the culturally determined relationships between patients and other members of their families (Aguilera et al., 2010). Studies of Mexican American families suggest that prosocial aspects of interactions between patients and their families can enhance family cohesion and decrease the stigma associated with serious mental disorders. In some cultures, family warmth serves as a protective factor and reduces the probability of patients' relapse (López et al., 2004).

We must be cautious to avoid a narrow view of this phenomenon. The concept of expressed emotion raises extremely sensitive issues for family members, who have too frequently been blamed for the problems of people with schizophrenia. Expressed emotion is not the only factor that can influence the course of a schizophrenic disorder. Some patients relapse in spite of an

## Comparison Groups: What Is Normal?

Research studies in the field of psychopathology typically involve comparisons among two or more groups of participants. One group, sometimes called "cases," includes people who already meet the diagnostic criteria for a particular mental disorder, such as schizophrenia. Comparison groups are composed of people who do not have the disorder in question. This approach is sometimes called the case control design because it depends on a contrast between cases and control participants. If the investigators find a significant difference between groups, they have demonstrated that the dependent variable is correlated with the disorder (see Research Methods in Chapter 2). They hope to conclude that they have identified a variable that is relevant to understanding the etiology of this condition. Causal inferences are risky, however, in correlational research. Our willingness to accept these conclusions hinges in large part on whether the investigators selected an appropriate comparison group.

People conducting correlational research must make every effort to identify and test a group of people who are just like the cases except that they do not have the disorder in question (Gehlbach, 1988). This typically means that the people in both groups should be similar with regard to such obvious factors as age, gender, and socioeconomic background. If the investigators find differences between people who have the disorder and those who do not, they want to attribute those differences to the disorder itself. Two main types of comparison groups are used in psychopathology research: people with no history of mental disorder, sometimes called "normal participants," and people who have some other form of mental disorder, sometimes called "patient controls."

Selecting normal comparison groups is not as simple as it might seem. In fact, researchers must make several basic decisions. Does "normal" mean that the person has never had the disorder in question, or does it mean a complete absence of any type of psychopathology? Should people be included as normal control participants if they have a family history of the disorder, even though they do not have the disorder themselves?

A second research strategy involves comparing patients with one type of disorder to those who have another form of psychopathology. Investigators usually employ this strategy to determine whether the variable in question is specifically related to the disorder that they are studying. Are enlarged lateral ventricles or family communication problems unique to people with schizophrenia? Lack of specificity may raise questions about whether this variable is related to the cause of the disorder. It might suggest that this particular variable is, instead, a general consequence of factors such as hospitalization, which the patient control group has also experienced.

Many of the causal factors that we have discussed in this chapter are not unique to schizophrenia. For example, expressed emotion predicts relapse among patients with mood disorders as well as among those with schizophrenia. Should this result be taken to mean that EE does not play an important role in the development of schizophrenia? Not necessarily. The answer to this question depends on the specific causal model that is being considered (Garber & Hollon, 1991). All forms of psychopathology depend on the interaction of multiple factors spanning biological, social, and psychological systems. Some of these may be specific to the disorder being studied, and others may be general. The development of schizophrenia may depend on a specific genetically determined predisposition. The environmental events that are responsible for eventually causing vulnerable people to express this disorder might be nonspecific. The fact that similar factors influence people with mood disorders should not be taken to mean that EE is not an important factor in the complex chain of events that explain schizophrenia.

---

understanding, tolerant family environment. Furthermore, research studies have shown that the relationship between patients' behavior and relatives' expressed emotion is a transactional or reciprocal process. In other words, patients influence their relatives' attitudes at the same time that relatives' attitudes influence patients' adjustment. Persistent negative attitudes on the part of relatives appear to be perpetuated by a negative cycle of interactions in which patients play an active role (Goldstein et al., 1997).

### Interaction of Biological and Environmental Factors

A useful causal model for schizophrenia must include the interaction of genetic factors and environmental events. The heterogeneous nature of the disorder, in terms of symptoms as well as course, also suggests that schizophrenia should be explained in terms of multiple pathways (Tandon, Keshavan, & Nasrallah, 2008). Some forms of the disorder may be the product of a strong genetic predisposition acting in combination with relatively common psychosocial experiences, such as stressful life events or disrupted communication patterns. For other people, relatively unusual circumstances, such as severe malnutrition during pregnancy, may be responsible for neurodevelopmental abnormalities that eventually lead to the onset of psychotic symptoms in the absence of genetic vulnerability (Gilmore, 2010).

Various kinds of environmental events have been linked to the etiology of schizophrenia. Some may operate in interaction with the genotype for schizophrenia; others may be sufficient to produce the disorder on their own. Considerable speculation has focused recently on biological factors, such as viral infections and nutritional deficiencies. Psychosocial factors, such as adverse economic circumstances, may also be involved. These events may be particularly harmful to people who are genetically predisposed to the disorder.

## The Search for Markers of Vulnerability

Schizophrenia is often a chronic disorder, and it can be difficult to treat. Many clinicians believe that the outcome of treatment programs would be more positive if the intervention could be started earlier, before the person has become severely disturbed and before the disorder has had a prolonged impact on the person's social and educational experiences (Jacobs et al., 2012). One way of approaching that problem would be to focus on the earliest overt signs of the disorder, subtle patterns of disturbed thinking and speaking, which are often accompanied by a progressive pattern of social withdrawal. These behavioral manifestations—symptoms of the prodromal phase—are often evident before the onset of full-blown psychotic symptoms. In fact, the *DSM-5* workgroup considered introducing a new diagnostic category, called attenuated psychosis syndrome, for this purpose (Carpenter & van Os, 2011; Tsuang et al., 2013). It was eventually relegated to Section III of the manual (Conditions for Further Study) because the field trials indicated that it cannot be identified reliably and the research evidence does not support its validity (see Thinking Critically About DSM-5).

## THINKING CRITICALLY about DSM-5

### Attenuated Psychosis Syndrome Reflects Wishful Rather Than Critical Thinking

For many years, mental health professionals have hoped to find a way to intervene early with people who are vulnerable to schizophrenia and prevent the onset of full-blown psychosis. In this spirit, the workgroup on schizophrenia for *DSM-5* considered a proposal for a new disorder to be called attenuated psychosis syndrome (APS) (Carpenter & van Os, 2011; Tsuang et al., 2013). In order to qualify for a diagnosis of APS, the person would need to show at least one psychotic symptom *in an attenuated form*. For example, the person might view other people as being untrustworthy, but he would not have paranoid delusions. He might speak in a vague or unfocused manner without showing disorganized speech. Furthermore, the person would be aware of the difference between the reality and fantasy and able to conform to accepted norms for social behavior (i.e., show "intact reality testing"). What does this definition mean? In layperson's terms, APS describes people who fall somewhere in that poorly defined zone between unusual and psychotic.

The motivation to define APS as a formal diagnostic category was well intentioned. Considerable research has been devoted to identifying prodromal symptoms of schizophrenia and signs of high-risk for the disorder. If we start with a group of people who have already developed full-blown psychosis and follow them back in time, before the development of their obvious symptoms, it's true that their experiences could be described in terms of the defining features of APS (Lencz et al., 2004). But, we also have to ask several other important questions before this disorder could serve any useful purpose. Is it possible to identify reliably the vague level of attenuated symptoms that serve as diagnostic criteria for APS? Based on the results of the *DSM-5* field trials, the answer to that question is clearly "no" (Freedman et al., 2013).

Second, let's assume that we can identify reliably people who show symptoms of APS, how many will go on to develop full-blown symptoms of psychosis (i.e., convert to schizophrenia)? The answer is "some, but not very many" (Fusar-Poli et al., 2013; Phillips, 2013).

Third, if people who qualify for a diagnosis of APS are treated in some way (most likely with the same drugs that are used to treat full-blown psychosis), will their progression to more severe symptoms be prevented? The answer is "occasionally, but not very often"

Finally, what risks are associated with being treated for APS? Several have been considered (Yung, 2011). Of course one form of risk is associated with the negative consequences of labeling (see section on Labeling Theory in Chapter 4). Even more important, however, are the potentially harmful effects of antipsychotic medication. Substantial evidence indicates that there are long-term neurological consequences to taking these drugs (Whitaker, 2010). These include intrusive motor side effects, which are sometimes irreversible, as well as increased risk of obesity and the many health consequences that follow from that condition. Would you want your friend or sibling to be exposed to these risks simply because they are behaving in an unusual way (especially if those behaviors are extremely difficult to identify)?

The proponents of APS based their proposal on wishful thinking rather than sound research data. Perhaps to their credit, the members of the workgroup recommended that APS be relegated to Section III, with other proposed disorders that require further study. But APS should have been omitted from the manual entirely. The danger is that many of the proposals that have been listed in this appendix eventually made their way into the main body of the *DSM-5* (see premenstrual dysphoric disorder and binge eating disorder). The appendix is a staging area where diagnostic fads go to incubate until sufficient pressure can be mobilized to force their incorporation into the main body of the diagnostic manual. APS is a poorly defined diagnostic construct. It could easily lead to much more harm than good, and it doesn't belong anywhere in *DSM-5*.

Another promising option for identifying people before they develop over symptoms of schizophrenia would focus on the genetic predisposition to the disorder. Studies of molecular genetics will obviously be part of that answer, if several genes are found to be responsible for the disorder. The search for more precise ways to identify people before they become psychotic may also hinge on the ability to identify vulnerability markers, which have also been called *endophenotypes* (Gottesman & Gould, 2003; Greenwood et al., 2007). An endophenotype is a component or trait that lies somewhere on the pathway between the genotype, which lays the foundation for the disorder, and full-blown symptoms of the disorder. It can be measured with precise laboratory procedures of many kinds, but it cannot be seen by the unaided eye.

If we are looking for signs of vulnerability—or endophenotypes—that can be detected among individuals who are genetically predisposed to schizophrenia, where should we look? What form will these signs take? Is it possible to detect signs of vulnerability among individuals who approach the threshold for developing schizophrenia spectrum disorders but have not exhibited any kind of overt symptoms? This issue has attracted considerable attention, but we don't have firm answers to these questions.

People who are vulnerable to schizophrenia might be identified by developing measures that could detect the underlying biological dysfunction or by developing sensitive measures of their subtle eccentricities of behavior. The range of possible markers is, therefore, quite large.

Assume that we have selected a specific measure, such as a biochemical assay or a psychological test, and we are interested in knowing whether it might be useful in identifying people who are vulnerable to schizophrenia. What criteria should a **vulnerability marker** fulfill? First, the proposed marker must distinguish between people who already have schizophrenia and those who do not. Second, it should be a stable characteristic over time. Third, the proposed measure of vulnerability should identify more people among the biological relatives of schizophrenic patients than among people in the general population. For example, it should be found among the discordant MZ twins of schizophrenic patients, even if they don't exhibit any symptoms of schizophrenia. Finally, the proposed measure of vulnerability should be able to predict the future development of schizophrenia among those who have not yet experienced a psychotic episode (Braff, Schork, & Gottesman, 2007; Snitz, MacDonald, & Carter, 2006).

Although reliable measures of vulnerability have not been identified, they are being actively pursued by many investigators with a wide variety of measurement procedures. In the following pages we will outline some of the psychological procedures that have been shown to be among the most promising.

**WORKING MEMORY IMPAIRMENT** Many investigators have pursued the search for signs of vulnerability by looking at measures of cognitive performance in which schizophrenic patients differ from other people. Some of these studies have focused on cognitive tasks that evaluate information processing, working memory, and attention/vigilance (Forbes et al., 2009; Green et al., 2004).

Considerable emphasis has been focused on one aspect of cognitive functioning known as *working memory*, or the ability to maintain and manipulate information for a short period of time. Working memory can be broken down into several more specific processes. Some of these involve memory buffers that provide short-term storage for visual and verbal information. The most important processes in working memory involve a *central executive component* that is responsible for the manipulation and transformation of data that are held in the storage buffers. Many studies have reported that people with schizophrenia are impaired in their ability to perform laboratory tasks that depend on this central executive component of working memory (Barch, 2005; Gold et al., 2010).

The identification of deficits in working memory is particularly interesting with regard to schizophrenia because it links to other evidence regarding brain functions and this disorder. Processes that are associated with central executive processing are associated with brain activity located in the dorsolateral area of the prefrontal cortex (see Figure 13.3) which seems to be dysfunctional in schizophrenia. Neurochemical hypotheses regarding schizophrenia are also relevant in this regard because the dopamine neurotransmitter system plays a crucial role in supporting activities involved in working memory (Goldman-Rakic, Muly, & Williams, 2000).

Working memory problems seem to be a stable characteristic of patients with schizophrenia; they do not fluctuate over time (Cannon et al., 2002). Furthermore, these cognitive deficits are found with increased prevalence among the unaffected first-degree relatives of schizophrenic persons, including discordant MZ twins (Sitskoom et al., 2004). Finally, children who later receive a diagnosis of schizophrenia are more likely to have been impaired on tests of verbal working memory than are their siblings who do not develop the disorder. Therefore, measures of working memory fulfill several of the criteria for an index of vulnerability. The research indicates that problems in working memory may be useful signs of vulnerability to schizophrenia (Barch, 2005).

**EYE-TRACKING DYSFUNCTION** Another promising line of work involves impairments in eye movements—specifically, difficulty in tracking the motion of a pendulum or a similarly oscillating stimulus while the person's head is held motionless. When people with schizophrenia are asked to track a moving target, like an oscillating pendulum, with their eyes, a substantial number of them show dysfunctions in smooth-pursuit eye movement (Levy et al., 2010). Instead of reproducing the motion of the pendulum in a series of smooth waves, their tracking records show frequent interruptions of smooth-pursuit movements by numerous rapid movements. Examples of normal tracking records and those of schizophrenic patients are presented in Figure 13.4. Only about 8 percent of normal people exhibit the eye-tracking dysfunctions

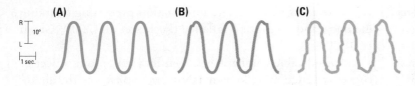

**FIGURE 13.4**

**Eye-Tracking Patterns** This illustration contrasts smooth-pursuit eyetracking patterns of normal subjects with those of schizophrenic patients. Part (A) shows the actual target. Part (B) illustrates the pattern for people without schizophrenia, and part (C) shows the pattern for people with schizophrenia.

*Source:* Based on Levy DL, Holzman PS, Matthysse S, Mendell NR. Eye tracking dysfunction and schizophrenia: A critical perspective. Schizophrenia Bulletin. 1993; 19: 461–536.

illustrated in part (C) of Figure 13.4, although some studies have reported higher figures.

Approximately 50 percent of the first-degree relatives of schizophrenic persons show similar smooth-pursuit impairments (Calkins, Iacono, & Ones, 2008; Hong et al., 2008). The overall pattern of results seen in people with schizophrenia and their families suggests that poor tracking performance may be associated with the predisposition to schizophrenia. That conclusion becomes even more interesting in light of evidence from additional studies suggesting that tracking ability is stable over time, influenced by genetic factors, and found among people who exhibit features associated with schizotypal personality disorder (Gooding, Miller, & Kwapil, 2000; O'Driscoll & Callahan, 2008).

It is not yet possible to identify people who are specifically predisposed to the development of schizophrenia, but research studies have identified potential vulnerability markers. The real test, of course, will center around predictive validity. Can any of these measures, such as working memory deficits or smooth-pursuit eye-tracking impairment, predict the later appearance of schizophrenia in people whose scores indicate possible vulnerability? High-risk studies will be useful in providing this type of evidence.

## Treatment

Schizophrenia is a complex disorder that often must be treated over an extended period of time. Clinicians must be concerned about the treatment of acute psychotic episodes as well as the prevention of future episodes. A multifaceted approach to treatment is typically required. Antipsychotic medication is the primary mode of treatment for this disorder. Because many patients remain impaired between episodes, long-term care must often involve the provision of housing and social support. People with impaired social and occupational skills need special types of training. The treatment of schizophrenia requires attention on all of these fronts and is necessarily concerned with the cooperative efforts of many types of professionals (Lehman et al., 2004). Schizophrenia also takes its toll on families. The Getting Help section at the end of this chapter discusses some of the resources available for patients and families.

### Antipsychotic Medication

The many different forms of medication that are used to treat patients with schizophrenia can be divided into two broad categories. The first generation of drugs began to be introduced in the 1950s, and a second generation swept into practice in the 1990s. Both kinds of medication are in standard use today.

The first generation of antipsychotic drugs—also called classical or traditional antipsychotics—was discovered accidentally in the early 1950s. Early reports of success in treating chronic psychotic patients quickly led to the widespread use of these drugs, such as chlorpromazine (Thorazine), in psychiatric hospitals throughout Europe and the United States (Shen, 1999). This process quickly changed the way in which schizophrenia was treated. Large numbers of patients who had previously been institutionalized could be discharged to community care (but see Chapter 18 on the effects of deinstitutionalization).

Several related types of drugs were developed in subsequent years. They are called **antipsychotic drugs** because they have a relatively specific effect—to reduce the severity of psychotic symptoms. Some beneficial effects on problems such as agitation and hostility may be noticed within a week after the patient begins taking antipsychotic medication, but it usually takes two or three weeks before improvement is seen with regard to psychotic symptoms (Kutscher, 2008). Positive symptoms, such as hallucinations, respond better to antipsychotic medication than negative symptoms, such as alogia and diminished emotional expression. Viewed from the patient's perspective, medication allows them to be less bothered or preoccupied by troublesome thoughts and perceptual experiences. In other words, they are able to distance themselves from their positive symptoms, even though the medication seldom eliminates hallucinations and delusional beliefs completely.

Double-blind, placebo-controlled studies have confirmed the effectiveness of antipsychotic medication in the treatment of patients who are acutely disturbed. Literally thousands of studies have addressed this issue over a period of more than 40 years (Haddad et al., 2009; Sharif et al., 2007). Most studies find that about half of the patients who receive medication are rated as being much improved after four to six weeks of treatment. Further improvements may continue beyond that point for some patients. In contrast, patients treated with placebos exhibit much smaller rates of improvement, and many of them actually deteriorate.

Unfortunately, a substantial minority of schizophrenic patients, perhaps 25 percent, do not improve on antipsychotic drugs (Conley & Kelly, 2001). Another 30 to 40 percent might be considered partial responders: Their condition improves, but they do not show a full remission of symptoms. Investigators have not been able to identify reliable differences between patients who improve on medication and those who do not. Some experts have suggested that treatment-resistant patients may have more prominent negative symptoms, greater disorganization, and more evidence of neurological abnormalities (Elkis, 2007).

**MAINTENANCE MEDICATION** After patients recover from acute psychotic episodes, there is a high probability that they will have another episode. The relapse rate may be as high as 65 to 70 percent in the first year after hospital discharge if patients discontinue medication. Continued treatment with antipsychotic drugs can reduce this rate to approximately 40 percent (Takeuchi et al., 2012). Therefore, patients with schizophrenia are encouraged to continue taking medication after they recover from psychotic episodes, although usually at a lower dose. Unfortunately, may patients stop taking medication, often to avoid unpleasant side effects (Falkai, 2008).

**MOTOR SIDE EFFECTS** Antipsychotic drugs produce several unpleasant side effects. They come in varying degrees and affect different patients in different ways. The most obvious and troublesome are called *extrapyramidal symptoms* (EPS) because they are mediated by the extrapyramidal neural pathways that connect the brain to the motor neurons in the spinal cord. These symptoms include an assortment of neurological disturbances, such as muscular rigidity, tremors, restless agitation, peculiar involuntary postures, and motor inertia. EPS may diminish spontaneously after the first few months of treatment, but some patients continue to experience EPS for many years.

Prolonged treatment with antipsychotic drugs can lead to the development of a more severe set of motor symptoms called *tardive dyskinesia* (TD). This syndrome consists of abnormal involuntary movements of the mouth and face, such as tongue protrusion, chewing, and lip puckering, as well as spasmodic movements of the limbs and trunk of the body. The latter include writhing movements of the fingers and toes and jiggling of the legs, as well as jerking movements of the head and pelvis. Taken as a whole, this problem is quite distressing to patients and their families. The TD syndrome is induced by antipsychotic treatment, and it is irreversible in some patients, even after the medication has been discontinued. In fact, in some patients, TD becomes worse if antipsychotic medication is withdrawn (Eberhard, Lindström, & Levander, 2006; Lauterbach et al., 2001).

**SECOND-GENERATION ANTIPSYCHOTICS** Several additional forms of antipsychotic medication began to be introduced in the 1990s. Although some clinicians hailed their development as a "second revolution" in the care of patients with schizophrenia, many experts now recognize that this claim has been overstated (Lieberman, 2006; Miyamoto et al., 2012). These drugs are frequently called *atypical antipsychotics* because they are less likely than the classical antipsychotics to produce unpleasant motor side effects. The best known of the atypical drugs, clozapine (Clozaril), has been used extensively throughout Europe since the 1970s. The second generation of antipsychotic medications also includes risperidone (Risperdal), olanzapine (Zyprexa), quetiapine (Seroquel), and several other drugs that have recently become available or are waiting for approval by the FDA. Some of these drugs are listed in Table 13.2.

The good news about second-generation antipsychotics is that they are at least as effective as traditional drugs for the treatment of positive symptoms of schizophrenia (Lieberman et al., 2005; Sikich et al., 2008), and they are useful in maintenance treatment to reduce the risk of relapse (Wang et al., 2010). They

**TABLE 13.2**
## Examples of Medications Used to Treat Schizophrenic Disorders

| | | Modes of Action | | | |
|---|---|---|---|---|---|
| | | Selected Side Effects | | Selected Receptors | |
| Drug Class | Generic Name (trade name) | EPS | Weight Gain | $D_2$ | $5HT_{2A}$ |
| First-generation antipsychotics | chlorpromazine (Thorazine) | + + | + | + + | + |
| | haloperidol (Haldol) | + + + + | + | + + + + | + |
| Second-generation Antipsychotics | clozapine (Clozaril) | +/− | + + + + | + + | + + + + |
| | risperidone (Risperdal) | + + | + + | + + + | + + + + + |
| | olanzapine (Zyprexa) | + | + + + + | + + + | + + + + |
| | quetiapine (Seroqul) | +/− | + + | + + | + + + |
| | amisulpride (Solian)* | + | + + | + + + + | − |

$D_2$ = dopamine receptors; $5HT_{2a}$ = serotonin receptors.

*Amisulpride is not available in the United States, but it has been used for more than 15 years in France (Leucht et al., 2002).

*Source*: S. Kapur and G. Remington. 2001. Atypical Antipsychotics: New Directions and New Challenges in the Treatment of Schizophrenia. Annual Review of Medicine; 52: 503–517.

are also less likely to produce tardive dyskinesia. One review of several outcome studies reported that 13 percent of patients taking second-generation antipsychotics developed tardive dyskinesia, compared to 32 percent patients taking first-generation antipsychotics (Correll & Shenk, 2008). The combination of beneficial effects on positive symptoms and reduced motor side effects makes these forms of medication a reasonable choice in the treatment of schizophrenia.

The bad news is that, contrary to initial claims, second-generation antipsychotics are not significantly more effective for treating negative symptoms (Buckley & Stahl, 2007; Murphy et al., 2006). They also produce additional side effects, and some of them are serious. For example, many of the atypical antipsychotics lead to weight gain and obesity (Das et al., 2012). These problems increase the person's risk for additional medical problems, such as diabetes, hypertension, and coronary artery disease. These adverse reactions lead many patients to discontinue their medication, thus increasing risk of relapse. One influential study compared one first-generation antipsychotic with four types of second-generation drugs. The investigators reported that 74 percent of patients stopped taking their prescribed medication before the end of the 18-month treatment period (Lieberman et al., 2005). Poor compliance was found for all of the different drugs. The bottom line is that various kinds of antipsychotic medication are beneficial for patients with schizophrenia, but they all have weaknesses, and none is without adverse side effects.

All antipsychotic medications—both first and second-generation forms—act by blocking dopamine receptors in the cortical and limbic areas of the brain (Factor, 2002). They also affect a number of other neurotransmitters, including serotonin, norepinephrine, and acetylcholine. Table 13.2 includes a comparison of two first-generation and five second-generation antipsychotic drugs in terms of their ability to block specific types of dopamine and serotonin receptors. Most second-generation antipsychotics produce a broader range of neurochemical actions in the brain than do the traditional drugs, which act primarily on dopamine receptors. Clozapine and olanzapine, for example, produce a relatively strong blockade of serotonin receptors and a relatively weaker blockade of dopamine receptors (Richelson, 1999). This increased affinity of some atypical drugs for serotonin receptors might explain why they can have a beneficial effect on symptoms of schizophrenia while producing fewer motor side effects (EPS). This hypothesis is contradicted, however, by the modes of action associated with a newer form of atypical drug, amisulpride, which does not affect serotonin receptors (Leucht, Kissling, & Davis, 2009). Neurochemical differences between different forms of antipsychotic drugs are not completely understood and are currently the topic of interesting debate (Richtand et al., 2007).

Further progress in the pharmacological treatment of schizophrenia will undoubtedly produce new drugs that have varying mechanisms of neurochemical action. The rate of progress in this field is very rapid. You can obtain regularly updated reviews of evidence regarding the treatment of schizophrenia from the Cochrane Library at its website: www.cochrane.org.

## Psychosocial Treatment

Several forms of psychological treatment have proved to be effective for schizophrenic patients. These procedures address a wide range of problems that are associated with the disorder. Psychological treatments have usually concentrated on long-term strategies rather than the resolution of acute psychotic episodes (Kopelowicz, Liberman, & Zarate, 2002). More recently, several investigators have begun to explore the use of psychosocial interventions in combination with antipsychotic medication for first-episode patients (Grawe et al., 2006; Penn et al., 2005).

**FAMILY-ORIENTED AFTERCARE** Studies of expressed emotion have inspired the development of innovative family-based treatment programs. Family treatment programs attempt to improve the coping skills of family members, recognizing the burdens that people often endure while caring for a family member with a chronic mental disorder. Patients are maintained on antipsychotic medication on an outpatient basis throughout this process. There are several different approaches to this type of family intervention. Most include an educational component that is designed to help family members understand and accept the nature of the disorder (see Getting Help on page 376). One goal of this procedure is to eliminate unrealistic expectations for the patient, which may lead to harsh criticism. Behavioral family management also places considerable emphasis on the improvement of communication and problem-solving skills, which may enhance the family members' ability to work together and thereby minimize conflict.

Patients and families respond in many creative ways to the presence of mental disorder. Brandon Staglin (left) has struggled with schizophrenia for several years. His parents founded an annual Music Festival for Mental Health, which has raised millions of dollars for mental health charities and research.

Several empirical studies have evaluated the effects of family interventions. Most have found reductions in relapse rates for people receiving family treatment (Barrowclough & Lobban, 2008; Girón et al., 2010). Family-based treatment programs can delay relapse, but they do not necessarily prevent relapse in the long run. In the case of a disorder such as schizophrenia, which is often chronic, difficult decisions have to be made about priorities and the availability of services. Family-based programs can have a positive effect, but we need to find more efficient and more effective ways to integrate this aspect of treatment into an overall treatment program.

**SOCIAL SKILLS TRAINING** Many patients who avoid relapse and are able to remain in the community continue to be impaired in terms of residual symptoms. They also experience problems in social and occupational functioning. For these patients, drug therapy must be supplemented by psychosocial programs that address residual aspects of the disorder. The need to address these problems directly is supported by evidence that shows that deficits in social skills are relatively stable in schizophrenic patients and relatively independent of other aspects of the disorder, including both positive and negative symptoms.

*Social skills training* (SST) is a structured, educational approach to these problems that involves modeling, role playing, and the provision of social reinforcement for appropriate behaviors (Heinssen, Liberman, & Kopelwicz, 2000). A general description of this type of approach to treatment is provided in Chapter 3. Controlled-outcome studies indicate that, in combination with neuroleptic medication, SST leads to improved performance on measures of social adjustment. It is not clear, however, that SST has any beneficial effects on relapse rates (Pilling et al., 2002b). That result may not be surprising in light of evidence regarding the course of this disorder, which suggests that various aspects of outcome, including symptom severity and social adjustment, tend to be relatively independent.

**COGNITIVE THERAPY** One area of treatment that has received much greater emphasis in recent years is the use of various forms of cognitive therapy for schizophrenia (Rathod & Turkington, 2005; Temple & Ho, 2005). In some cases, these interventions have focused on the use of standard cognitive therapy procedures that are designed to help patients evaluate, test, and correct distorted ways of thinking about themselves and their social environments. Other forms of cognitive treatment have become more specialized and are aimed specifically at cognitive deficits that are particularly evident in schizophrenia.

One example of a specialized treatment program is cognitive enhancement therapy (CET) for schizophrenia (Hogarty et al., 2004). This is a comprehensive, integrated program aimed at the improvement of cognitive abilities, including those that are concerned with performance on laboratory tasks (such as attention, working memory, and problem solving) as well as social cognition

(such as recognizing the perspectives of other people and appraising social contexts). It is designed for use with people who are also taking antipsychotic medication and have already recovered from active symptoms of psychosis but nevertheless continue to exhibit signs of cognitive disability. Patients spend many hours practicing computerized cognitive exercises. Several weeks after beginning cognitive training exercises, they also participate in an extended series of small group exercises (interpreting verbal messages, recognizing others' emotions, maintaining conversations, and so on). One large-scale two-year outcome study compared patients who received cognitive enhancement therapy with patients in a control group who received enhanced supportive therapy. Those who received CET showed more improvement with regard to performance on measures of cognitive performance, social cognition, overall social adjustment, and employment (Eack et al., 2011). Thus, in the context of ongoing treatment with antipsychotic medication, cognitive therapy can be beneficial for patients with schizophrenia.

**ASSERTIVE COMMUNITY TREATMENT** The treatment of a chronic disorder such as schizophrenia clearly requires an extensive range of comprehensive services that should be fully integrated and continuously available. *Assertive community treatment* (ACT) is a psychosocial intervention that is delivered by an interdisciplinary team of clinicians (DeLuca, Moser, & Bond, 2008; Stein & Santos, 1998). They provide a combination of psychological treatments—including education, support, skills training, and rehabilitation—as well as medication. Services are provided on a regular basis throughout the week and during crisis periods (any time of day and any day of the week). The program represents an intensive effort to maintain seriously disordered patients in the community and to minimize the need for hospitalization. It differs from more traditional outpatient services in its assertive

Many people have made remarkable achievements in spite of suffering from schizophrenia. Tom Harrell has been named jazz trumpeter of the year three times by *Downbeat Magazine*. He hears disturbing auditory hallucinations, but they disappear when he is playing music.

approach to the provision of services: Members of an ACT team go to the consumer rather than expecting the consumer to come to them.

Outcome studies indicate that ACT programs can effectively reduce the number of days that patients spend in psychiatric hospitals, while improving their level of functioning (Nordentoft et al., 2010; Thornicroft & Susser, 2001). One study found that only 18 percent of the people in the ACT group were hospitalized during the first year of treatment compared to 89 percent of the people in the control group. ACT is an intensive form of treatment that requires a well-organized and extensive network of professional services. In spite of the expense that is required to maintain this kind of program, empirical studies indicate that it is more cost-effective than traditional services provided by community mental health centers (Lehman et al., 1999). Reduction in costs of inpatient care offsets the expense of the ACT program.

**INSTITUTIONAL PROGRAMS** Although schizophrenic persons can be treated with medication on an outpatient basis, various types of institutional care continue to be important. Most patients experience recurrent phases of active psychosis. Brief periods of hospitalization (usually two or three weeks) are often beneficial during these times.

Some patients are chronically disturbed and require long-term institutional treatment. Social learning programs, sometimes called *token economies*, can be useful for these patients (Dickerson, Tenhula, & Green-Paden, 2005). In these programs specific behavioral contingencies are put into place for all of the patients on a hospital ward. The goal is to increase the frequency of desired behaviors, such as appropriate grooming and participation in social activities, and to decrease the frequency of undesirable behaviors, such as violence or incoherent speech. Staff members monitor patients' behavior throughout the day. Each occurrence of a desired behavior is praised and reinforced by the presentation of a token, which can be exchanged for food or privileges, such as time to watch television. Inappropriate behaviors are typically ignored, but occasional punishment, such as loss of privileges, is used if necessary. Carefully structured inpatient programs, especially those that follow behavioral principles, can have important positive effects for chronic schizophrenic patients.

## getting HELP

Schizophrenia can be a devastating condition for patients and their families. Fortunately, the past two decades have seen many important advances in treatment for this disorder. Perhaps no other disorder requires such an extensive array of services, ranging from medication and short-term inpatient care to long-term residential facilities and psychosocial help for family members. An extremely useful book, *Coping with Schizophrenia: A Guide for Families*, written by Kim Mueser and Susan Gingrich, offers sound advice on a variety of crucial topics. For example, the authors discuss various forms of antipsychotic drugs, their side effects, their use in preventing relapse, and ways to respond to a patient's reluctance to continue taking necessary medication. They outline available community resources that help patients and their families deal with acute episodes, as well as the long-term challenges of residual symptoms, occupational difficulties, and housing needs.

Another excellent resource is *The Family Face of Schizophrenia*, by Patricia Backlar, who is a mental health ethicist and also the mother of a son who suffers from schizophrenia. This book includes a series of seven stories about people who have struggled with this disorder and the often confusing and sometimes inadequate array of mental health services that are available in many communities. Each story is followed by a commentary that includes advice for patients and their families (e.g., how to obtain insurance benefits for treatment, how to find a missing mentally ill family member, how to cope with suicidal risks, and how to navigate legal issues that can arise in caring for someone with a serious mental disorder). Anyone who must cope with a psychotic disorder will benefit from reading these books carefully.

The National Alliance for the Mentally Ill (NAMI) is an extremely influential grassroots support and advocacy organization that has worked tirelessly to improve the quality of life for patients and their families. It has more than 1,000 state and local affiliates throughout the United States. NAMI is committed to increasing access to community-based services such as housing and rehabilitation for people with severe mental disorders. The address for its website is www.nami.org. It is a comprehensive source of information regarding all aspects of severe mental disorders (especially schizophrenia and mood disorders), including referral to various types of support groups and professional service providers.

# 13 Summary

People who meet the diagnostic criteria for **schizophrenia** exhibit symptoms that represent impairments across a broad array of cognitive, perceptual, and interpersonal functions. These symptoms can be roughly divided into three types. **Positive symptoms** include **hallucinations** and **delusions.** **Negative symptoms** include **diminished emotional expression, alogia, avolition,** and social withdrawal. Symptoms of disorganization include verbal communication problems and disorganized behavior.

*DSM-5* requires evidence of a decline in the person's social or occupational functioning, as well as the presence of disturbed behavior over a continuous period of at least six months for a diagnosis of schizophrenia.

Related psychotic disorders include delusional disorder, brief psychotic disorder, and schizoaffective disorder.

The onset of schizophrenia is typically during adolescence or early adulthood. The disorder can follow different patterns over time. Some people recover fairly quickly from schizophrenia, whereas others deteriorate progressively after the initial onset of symptoms.

The lifetime prevalence of schizophrenia is approximately 1 percent in the United States and Europe. Men are 30 to 40 percent more likely than women to be affected by the disorder, and its onset tends to occur at an earlier age in males. Male patients are more likely than female patients to exhibit negative symptoms, and they are also more likely to follow a chronic, deteriorating course.

Genetic factors clearly play a role in the development of schizophrenia. Risk for developing the disorder is between 10 percent and 15 percent among first-degree relatives of schizophrenic patients. Concordance rates are approximately 48 percent in MZ twins compared to only 17 percent in DZ pairs. Twin and adoption studies indicate that the disorder has variable expressions, sometimes called the schizophrenia spectrum. Schizophrenia spectrum disorders include schizotypal personality disorder as well as other psychotic disorders.

A specific brain lesion has not been identified, and it is unlikely that a disorder as complex as schizophrenia will be traced to a single site in the brain. Structural images of schizophrenic patients' brains reveal enlarged ventricles as well as decreased size of parts of the limbic system. Studies of brain metabolism and blood flow have identified functional changes in the frontal lobes, temporal lobes, and basal ganglia in many persons with schizophrenia.

The discovery of antipsychotic medication stimulated interest in the role of neurochemical factors in the etiology of schizophrenia. The dopamine hypothesis provided the major unifying theme in this area for many years, but it is now considered too simple to account for the existing evidence. Current neurochemical hypotheses regarding schizophrenia focus on a broad array of neurotransmitters, with special emphasis on serotonin.

Several social and psychological factors have been shown to be related to the disorder. Social class is inversely related to the prevalence of schizophrenia. People who have migrated to a new country are at greater risk for schizophrenia, suggesting the possible influence of social adversity and discrimination.

Patients from families that are high in **expressed emotion** are more likely to relapse than those from low EE families. Expressed emotion is the product of an ongoing interaction between patients and their families, with patterns of influence flowing in both directions.

The evidence regarding etiology supports a diathesis-stress model. It should be possible to develop **vulnerability markers** that can identify individuals who possess the genetic predisposition to the disorder. Promising research in this area is concerned with a broad range of possibilities, including laboratory measures of working memory and smooth-pursuit eye-tracking movements.

The central aspect of treatment for schizophrenia is antipsychotic medication. These drugs help to resolve acute psychotic episodes. They can also delay relapse and improve the level of patients' functioning between episodes. Unfortunately, they often produce troublesome side effects, and a substantial minority of schizophrenic patients are resistant to antipsychotic medication.

Various types of psychosocial treatments also provide important benefits to schizophrenic patients and their families. Prominent among these are family-based treatment for patients who have been stabilized on medication following discharge from the hospital. Social skills training can also be useful in improving the level of patients' role functioning.

# critical thinking review

**13.1** Why do clinical scientists say that schizophrenia is a "heterogeneous" disorder?

Schizophrenia is a disorder of many faces. It is defined by an extremely diverse set of symptoms that involve distortions of cognition, perception, and emotion. Finally, it can follow many different patterns over time . . . (see page 349).

**13.2** How should long-term outcome be measured in schizophrenia?

It must be viewed from a broad spectrum. Important dimensions include the presence and severity of symptoms, the ability to function socially and occupationally, the need for housing and other social services, and the impact on other family members . . . (see page 358).

**13.3** Why are some personality disorders considered to be schizophrenia spectrum disorders?

Some of the symptoms of schizotypal personality disorders represent less severe forms of psychotic symptoms. The first-degree relatives of patients with schizophrenia are more likely than other people to qualify for a diagnosis of certain types of personality disorders . . . (see page 362).

**13.4** Why can't we use brain imaging to diagnose schizophrenia?

They are useful research tools, but they have not identified any aspects of brain structure or function that are unique to people with this disorder . . . (see pages 363–365).

**13.5** What characteristics would define a useful marker of vulnerability to schizophrenia?

It should be found more frequently among schizophrenic patients and their first-degree relatives, it should be stable over time, and it should be present prior to the onset of psychotic symptoms . . . (see page 371).

**13.6** What aspects of schizophrenia are addressed most directly by psychosocial treatments?

Problems with social cognition (ways of thinking about oneself and others) and interpersonal relationships are often the targets of psychological interventions, which are designed to be used in conjunction with antipsychotic medication . . . (see page 375).

# key terms

anhedonia  354
antipsychotic drugs  372
avolition  354
brief psychotic disorder  357
delusions  352

delusional disorder  357
diminished emotional
 expression  353
disorganized speech  354
expressed emotion (EE)  368

hallucinations  352
negative symptoms  351
positive symptoms  351
prodromal phase  350
schizoaffective disorder  358

schizophrenia  349
vulnerability marker  371

# neurocognitive disorders

14

# The Big Picture

## learning objectives

### 14.1
What is the difference between cognitive problems in anxiety and those seen in major neurocognitive disorders?

### 14.2
In what ways is delirium different from dementia?

### 14.3
Is memory impairment the only indication that a person is developing a major neurocognitive disorder?

### 14.4
Why is depression in an elderly person sometimes confused with dementia?

### 14.5
How could education help to reduce a person's risk for major neurocognitive disorder?

### 14.6
What are the most difficult problems faced by people caring for a person with a major neurocognitive disorder?

Most of us are absent-minded from time to time. We may forget to make a phone call, run an errand, or complete an assignment. Occasional lapses of this sort are part of normal experience. Unfortunately, some people develop severe and persistent memory problems and other types of cognitive dysfunction that disrupt their everyday activities and interactions with other people. Imagine that you have lived in the same house for many years. You go for a short walk, and then you can't remember how to get home. Suppose you are shown a photograph of your parents, and you don't recognize them. These are some of the fundamental cognitive problems discussed in this chapter.

## Overview

Neurocognitive disorders, including dementia and delirium, are the most frequent disorders found among elderly psychiatric patients. Both conditions involve memory impairments, but they are quite different in other ways. **Dementia** is a gradually worsening loss of memory and related cognitive functions, including the use of language, as well as reasoning and decision making. It is a clinical syndrome that involves progressive impairment of many cognitive abilities (Waldemar & Burns, 2009). **Delirium** is a confusional state that develops over a short period of time and is often associated with agitation and hyperactivity. The most important symptoms of delirium are disorganized thinking and a reduced ability to maintain and shift attention (de Lange, Verhaak, & van der Meer, 2013). Delirium and dementia are produced by very different processes. Dementia is a chronic, deteriorating condition that reflects the gradual loss of neurons in the brain. Delirium is usually the result of medical problems, such as infection, or of the side effects of medication. If diagnosed and properly treated, it is typically short-lived. It can, however, result in serious medical complications, permanent cognitive impairment, or death, if the causes go untreated.

Dementia and delirium are listed as Neurocognitive Disorders in *DSM-5*. Cognitive processes, including perception and attention, are related to many types of mental disorders that we have already discussed, such as depression, anxiety, and schizophrenia. In most forms of psychopathology, however, the cognitive problems are relatively subtle—mediating factors that help us understand the process by which clinical symptoms are produced. In the case of depression, for example, self-defeating biases may contribute to the onset of a depressed mood. These cognitive schemas are not used, however, as part of the diagnostic criteria for major depression in *DSM-5*. They are not considered to be the central, defining features of the disorder. Problems in working memory may represent vulnerability markers for schizophrenia, but again, they are not considered symptoms of the disorder. In dementia, memory and other cognitive functions are the most obvious manifestations of the problem. They are its defining features. As dementia progresses, the person's attention span, concentration, judgment, planning, and decision making become severely disturbed.

Dementia is often associated with specific identifiable changes in brain tissue. Many times, these changes can be

Confusion and disorientation are common symptoms of neurocognitive disorders. This elderly woman may not have been aware that she was walking in front of a line of riot police sent to control demonstrators in Moscow.

observed only during autopsy, after the patient's death. For example, in Alzheimer's disease, which is one form of neurocognitive disorder, microscopic examination of the brain reveals the presence of an unusual amount of debris called *plaque* left from dead neurons and neurofibrillary tangles, indicating that the connections between nerve cells had become disorganized. We describe the neuropathology of Alzheimer's disease later in this chapter.

Due to the close link between neurocognitive disorders and brain disease, patients with these problems are often diagnosed and treated by **neurologists**—physicians who deal primarily with diseases of the brain and the nervous system. Multidisciplinary clinical teams study and provide care for people with dementia and amnestic disorders. Direct care to patients and their families is usually provided by nurses and social workers. **Neuropsychologists** have particular expertise in the assessment of specific types of cognitive impairments. This is true for clinical assessments as well as more detailed laboratory studies for research purposes.

The following two case studies illustrate the variety of symptoms and problems that are included in the general category of dementia. The first case describes the early stages of dementia.

### → A Physician's Developing Dementia

Jonathan was a 68-year-old physician who had been practicing family medicine for the past 35 years. His wife, Alice, worked as his office manager. A registered nurse, Kathryn, had worked with them for several years. Four months earlier, Alice and Kathryn both noticed that Jonathan was beginning to make obvious errors at work. On one occasion, Kathryn observed that Jonathan had prescribed the wrong medication for a patient's condition. At about the same time, Alice became concerned when she asked Jonathan about a patient whom he had seen the day before. Much to her surprise, he did not remember having seen the patient, despite the fact that he spent almost half an hour with her, and she was a patient whom he had treated for several years. Jonathan's personality also seemed to change in small but noticeable ways. He seemed uncharacteristically apathetic about daily activities that he and Alice typically enjoyed together. She also found that he had become increasingly self-centered.

Although Alice tried to convince herself that these were isolated incidents, she finally decided to discuss them with Kathryn. Kathryn agreed that Jonathan's memory was failing. He had trouble recognizing patients whom he had known for many years, and had unusual difficulty making treatment decisions. These problems had not appeared suddenly. Over the past year or two, both women had been doing more things for Jonathan than they had ever done in the past. They needed to remind him about things that were parts of his routine practice. As they pieced together various incidents, the pattern of gradual cognitive decline became obvious.

Alice talked seriously to Jonathan about the problems that she and Kathryn had observed. He said that he felt fine, but reluctantly allowed her to make an appointment for him to be examined by a neurologist, who also happened to be a friend. Jonathan admitted to the neurologist that he had been having difficulty remembering things. He believed that he had been able to avoid most problems, however, by writing notes to himself—directions, procedures, and so on. The results of psychological testing and brain imaging procedures, coupled with Jonathan's own description of his experiences and Alice's account of his impaired performance at work, led the neurologist to conclude that Jonathan was exhibiting early signs of dementia, perhaps Alzheimer's disease. He spoke directly to Jonathan regarding his diagnosis and recommended firmly that he retire immediately. A malpractice suit would be devastating to his medical practice. Jonathan agreed to retire.

Although Jonathan was no longer able to cope with his demanding work environment, his adjustment at home was not severely impaired. The changes in his behavior remained relatively subtle for many months. In short conversations, his cognitive problems were not apparent to his friends, who still did not know the real reason for his retirement. His speech was fluent, and his memory for recent events was largely intact, but his comprehension was diminished. Alice noticed that Jonathan's emotional responses were occasionally flat or restricted. At other times, he would laugh at inappropriate times when they watched television programs together. If Alice asked him about his reaction, it was sometimes apparent that Jonathan did not understand the plot of even the simplest television programs.

Alice found that she had to sew labels into Jonathan's collars to distinguish the clothes that he wore to work in the yard from those that he wore if they were going shopping or out to eat. Jonathan had become increasingly literal minded. If Alice asked him to do something for her, she had to spell out every last detail. For example, he began to have trouble selecting his clothes, which had been a source of pride before the onset of his cognitive problems. His judgment about what was appropriate to wear in different situations had disappeared altogether.

It had also become difficult for Jonathan to do things that required a regular sequence of actions or decisions, even if they were quite simple and familiar. Routine tasks took longer than before, usually because he got stuck part of the way through an activity. He had, for example, always enjoyed making breakfast

## MyPsychLab VIDEO CASE

### Dementia

ALVIN

*"That's one of the real difficulties. There's no sign that goes off and says, Yes, he's understanding, or No, he's not understanding it."*

**Watch** the **Video** *Alvin: Dementia* on **MyPsychLab**

As you watch the interview and the day-in-the-life segment, try to identify the various signs of Alvin's cognitive impairment.

for Alice on weekends. After his retirement, Alice once found him standing in the kitchen with a blank expression on his face. He had made a pot of coffee and some toast for both of them, but he ran into trouble when he couldn't find coffee cups. That disrupted his plan, and he was stymied.

••••••••••••••••••••••••••••••••••••••••••••••••••••••••••••

Jonathan's case illustrates many of the early symptoms of dementia, as well as the ways in which the beginnings of memory problems can severely disrupt a person's life. The onset of the disorder is often difficult to identify precisely because forgetfulness increases gradually. Problems are most evident in challenging situations, as in Jonathan's medical practice, and least noticeable in familiar surroundings.

Changes in emotional responsiveness and personality typically accompany the onset of memory impairment in dementia. In some cases, personality changes may be evident before the development of full-blown cognitive symptoms (Duchek et al., 2007). These personality changes may be consequences of cognitive impairment. Jonathan's emotional responses may have seemed unusual sometimes because he failed to comprehend aspects of the environment that were obvious to his wife and other people.

Our next case illustrates more advanced stages of dementia, in which the person can become extremely disorganized. Memory impairment progresses to the point where the person no longer recognizes his or her family and closest friends. People in this condition are unable to care for themselves, and become so disoriented that the burden on others is frequently overwhelming. This case also provides an example of delirium superimposed on dementia. Up to 50 percent of dementia patients admitted to a hospital are also delirious. It is important for the neurologist to recognize the distinction between these conditions because the cause of the delirium (which might be an infection or a change in the patient's medications) must be treated promptly (Young et al., 2008).

### → Dementia and Delirium—A Niece's Terrible Discoveries

Mary was an 84-year-old retired schoolteacher who had grown up in the same small rural community in which she still lived. Never married, she lived with her parents most of her life, except for the years when she was in college. Her parents had died when Mary was in her early sixties. After her retirement at age 65, Mary continued living in her parents' farmhouse. She felt comfortable there, despite its relative isolation, and liked the fact that it had plenty of space for animals, including her dog, which she called "my baby," several cats, and a few cows that were kept in the pasture behind the house. Mary's niece, Nancy, who was 45 years old and lived an hour's drive away, stopped to visit her once every two or three months.

Over the past year, Nancy had noticed that Mary was becoming forgetful, as well as more insistent that her routines remain unchanged. Bills went unpaid—in fact, the telephone had been disconnected for lack of payment—and the mail wasn't brought in from the roadside box. Nancy had suggested to Mary that she might be better off in a nursing home, but Mary was opposed to that idea.

During her most recent visit, Nancy was shocked to find that conditions at Mary's home had become intolerable. Most distressing was the fact that some of her animals had died because Mary forgot to feed them. The dog's decomposed body was tied to its house, where it had starved. Conditions inside the house were disgusting. Almost 30 cats lived inside the house, and the smell was unbearable. Mary's own appearance was quite disheveled. She hadn't bathed or changed her clothes for weeks. Nancy contacted people at a social service agency, who arranged for Mary's admission to a nursing home. Mary became furious, refusing to go and denying that there was anything wrong with her own home. Nancy was soon declared her legal guardian because Mary was clearly not competent to make decisions for herself.

Mary grew progressively more agitated and belligerent during the few weeks that she lived at the nursing home. She was occasionally disoriented, not knowing where she was or what day it was. She shouted and sometimes struck people with her cane. She had trouble walking, a problem that was compounded by visual and spatial judgment difficulties. After she fell and broke her hip, Mary was transferred to a general hospital.

Mary became delirious in the hospital, apparently as a result of medication she was given for her injury. She appeared to be having visual hallucinations and often said things that did not make sense. These periods of incoherence fluctuated in severity throughout the course of the day. During her worse moments, Mary did not respond to her name being spoken, and her speech was reduced primarily to groans and nonsense words. This clouding of consciousness cleared up a few days after her medication was changed. She became less distractible and was once again able to carry on brief conversations. Unfortunately, her disorientation became more severe while she was immobilized in the hospital. When her hip eventually healed, she was moved to a psychiatric hospital and admitted to the geriatric ward.

Although Mary was no longer aware of the date or even the season of the year, she insisted that she did not have any problems with her mind. For the first six weeks at the psychiatric hospital, she would be surprised that she was not in her own home on waking up each morning. Later, she acknowledged that she was in a hospital, but did not know why she was there, and she did not understand that the other patients on the unit were also demented. She didn't recognize hospital staff members from one day to the next. She was completely unable to remember anything that had happened recently. Nevertheless, her memory for events that had happened many years earlier was quite good. Mary repeated stories about her childhood over and over again.

Nurses on the unit were bombarded continuously with her complaints about being removed from her home. Every 20 minutes or so, Mary would approach the nurses' station, waving her cane and shouting, "Nurse, I need to go home. I have to get out of here. I have to go home and take care of my dog." The hospital staff would explain to her that she would have to stay at the hospital, at least for a while longer, and that her dog had died several months earlier. This news would usually provoke sadness, but she seemed unable to remember it long enough to complete the grieving process. Several minutes later, the whole scene would be repeated. Mary also became paranoid, claiming to anyone who would listen that people were trying to steal her things. The most common focus of her concern was her purse. If it was out of her sight, she would announce loudly that someone had stolen it.

In the midst of these obvious problems, Mary retained many other intellectual abilities. She was a well-educated and intelligent woman. Her attention span was reduced, but she was still able to play the piano—pieces that she had practiced over and over again for many years. Poetry had always been one of her special interests, and she was still able to recite some of her favorite poems beautifully from memory. In a quiet room, it was often possible to talk with her and pursue a meaningful conversation. Unfortunately, these lucid periods were interspersed with times of restless pacing and shouting. Her agitation would escalate rapidly unless staff members distracted her, taking her to a quiet room, talking to her, and getting her to read or recite something out loud.

## Symptoms

The symptoms of neurocognitive disorders are often overlooked in elderly patients. It can be difficult to distinguish the onset of dementia from patterns of modest memory decline that are an expected part of the aging process. Different forms of neurocognitive disorder can also be confused with one another. Recognition of these disorders and the distinctions among them carries important treatment implications for patients and their families.

### Delirium

The *DSM-5* criteria for delirium are listed in "DSM-5: Delirium." The primary symptom of delirium is clouding of consciousness in association with a reduced ability to maintain and shift attention. The disturbance in consciousness might also be described as a reduction in the clarity of a person's awareness of his or her surroundings. Memory deficits may occur in association with impaired consciousness and may be the direct result of attention problems. The person's thinking appears disorganized, and he or she may speak in a rambling, incoherent fashion. Fleeting perceptual disturbances, including visual hallucinations, are also common in delirious patients (Gofton, 2011).

The symptoms of delirium follow a rapid onset—from a few hours to several days—and typically fluctuate throughout the day. The person may alternate between extreme confusion and periods in which he or she is more rational and clearheaded. Symptoms are usually worse at night. The sleep/wake cycle is often disturbed. Daytime drowsiness and lapses in concentration are often followed by agitation and hyperactivity at night. If the condition is allowed to progress, the person's senses may become dulled, and he or she may eventually lapse into a coma. The delirious person is also likely to be disoriented with relation to time ("What day, month, or season is it?") or place ("Where are we? What is the name of this place?"). However, identity confusion ("What is your name?") is rare.

It isn't always easy to recognize the difference between dementia and delirium, especially when they appear simultaneously

---

**TABLE 14.1**

## Distinguishing Features of Dementia and Delirium

| Characteristic | Delirium | Dementia |
|---|---|---|
| Onset | Sudden (hours to days) | Slow (months to years) |
| Duration | Brief | Long/lifetime |
| Course | Fluctuating | Stable, with downward trajectory over time |
| Hallucinations | Visual/tactile/vivid | Rare |
| Insight | Lucid intervals | Consistently poor |
| Sleep | Disturbed | Less disturbed |

*Source:* Data from Insel, K.C. and T.A. Badger. 2002. Deciphering the 4Ds: Cognitive Decline, Delirium, Depression, and Dementia A Review. *Journal of Advanced Nursing*; 38: 360–368.

in the same patient. Table 14.1 summarizes several considerations that are useful in making this diagnostic distinction (Insel & Badger, 2002). One important consideration involves the period of time over which the symptoms appear. Delirium has a rapid onset, whereas dementia develops in a slow, progressive manner. In dementia, the person usually remains alert and responsive to the environment. Speech is most often coherent in demented patients, at least until the end stages of the disorder, but is typically confused in delirious patients. Finally, delirium can be resolved, whereas dementia cannot.

## Major Neurocognitive Disorder

*DSM-5* covers dementia under a new diagnostic label, **major neurocognitive disorder** (NCD). Dementia is still used as a term to describe gradually worsening loss of memory and related cognitive functions. The category of major NCD is somewhat broader than the term dementia because it also includes individuals whose cognitive decline is limited to a single domain (formerly known as amnestic disorders). In the following description of symptoms, we focus on symptoms of dementia.

The cases at the beginning of this chapter illustrate the changing patterns that emerge as dementia unfolds. Jonathan's cognitive symptoms were recognized at a relatively early stage of development,because of his occupational situation and his close relationships with other people. Mary's situation was much different, because she lived in a relatively isolated setting without close neighbors or friends. By the time Nancy recognized the full severity of Mary's problems, the cognitive impairment had progressed so far that Mary was no longer able to appreciate the nature of her own difficulties. In the following

pages, we describe in more detail the types of symptoms that are associated with dementia.

**NEUROCOGNITIVE SYMPTOMS** Dementia appears in people whose intellectual abilities have previously been unimpaired. Both of the people in our case studies were bright, well educated, and occupationally successful before the onset of their symptoms. The earliest signs of dementia are often quite vague. They include difficulty remembering recent events and the names of people and familiar objects. These are all problems that are associated with normal aging, but they differ from that process in order of magnitude (see Memory Changes in Normal Aging on the next page). The distinguishing features of dementia include cognitive problems in a number of areas, ranging from impaired memory and learning to deficits in language and abstract thinking. By the final stages of dementia, intellectual and motor functions may disappear almost completely.

*MEMORY AND LEARNING* The diagnostic hallmark of dementia is memory loss. In order to describe the various facets of memory impairment, it is useful to distinguish between old memories and the ability to learn new things. **Retrograde amnesia** refers to the loss of memory for events prior to the onset of an illness or the experience of a traumatic event. **Anterograde amnesia** refers to the inability to learn or remember new material after a particular point in time.

Anterograde amnesia is usually the most obvious problem during the beginning stages of dementia. Consider, for example, the case of Jonathan. Alice eventually noticed that he sometimes could not remember things that he had done the previous day. Mary, the more severely impaired person, could not remember for more than a few minutes that her dog had died. Long-term memories are usually not affected until much later in the course of the disorder. Even in advanced stages of dementia, a person may retain some recollections of the past. Mary was able to remember, and frequently described, stories from her childhood.

*VERBAL COMMUNICATION* Language functions can also be affected in dementia. **Aphasia** is a term that describes various types of loss or impairment in language that are caused by brain damage (Mesulam, 2007). Language disturbance in dementia is sometimes relatively subtle, but it can include many different kinds of problems. Patients often remain verbally fluent, at least until the disorder is relatively advanced. They retain their vocabulary skills and are able to construct grammatical sentences. They may have trouble finding words, naming objects, and comprehending instructions.

In addition to problems in understanding and forming meaningful sentences, the demented person may also have difficulty performing purposeful movements in response to verbal commands, a problem known as **apraxia.** The person possesses

Changes in cognitive abilities are part of the normal aging process. Most elderly adults complain more frequently about memory problems than younger adults do, and they typically perform slower and less efficiently than younger adults on laboratory tests of memory. There are, of course, individual differences in the age at which cognitive abilities begin to decline, as well as in the rate at which these losses take place. Nevertheless, some types of memory impairment are an inevitable consequence of aging (Nilsson, 2003).

In order to understand more clearly the cognitive changes associated with aging, it is useful to distinguish between two general aspects of mental functioning: fluid intelligence and wisdom (Baltes, 1993; Salthouse, 1999). The computer can be used as a metaphor to explain this distinction. Fluid intelligence refers to "the hardware of the mind." These functions are concerned with the speed and accuracy of such basic processes as perception, attention, and working memory. The proficiency of fluid intelligence depends on neurophysiological processes and on the structural integrity of the person's brain.

Nelson Mandela won the Nobel Peace Prize at age 75. His wisdom and courage provide a remarkable example of successful aging.

Wisdom, on the other hand, represents the "culture-based software of the mind." Reading and writing skills, as well as knowledge about the self and ways of coping with environmental challenges, are examples of cognitive abilities that might be included under the general heading of wisdom. These aspects of intelligence represent information about the world that is acquired continually throughout the person's lifetime (Baltes & Smith, 2008).

Fluid intelligence and wisdom follow different trajectories over the normal human life span (Kunzmann & Baltes, 2003). Fluid intelligence develops continuously during childhood and adolescence, reaching a point of optimal efficiency during young adulthood. After that point, it follows a gradual pattern of decline (Bugg et al., 2006). Wisdom also increases throughout adolescence and young adulthood, but it does not become increasingly impaired as the person ages. In fact, it often expands. The erosion of fluid intelligence over time is presumably due to subtle atrophy of brain regions, such as the hippocampus, that take place during normal aging (Head et al., 2008).

The aging mind apparently depends on the coordination of gains and losses. The elderly person strikes a balance through a process that involves selection, optimization, and compensation (Freund & Baltes, 2002). Arthur Rubinstein, the brilliant pianist who performed concerts well into his eighties, provides an example of this process. Rubinstein described three strategies that he employed in his old age: (1) He was selective, performing fewer pieces; (2) he optimized his performance by practicing each piece more frequently; and (3) he compensated for a loss of motor speed by utilizing pieces that emphasized contrast between fast and slow segments so that his playing seemed faster than it really was. Successful aging is based on this dynamic process. The person compensates for losses in fluid intelligence by taking advantage of increased knowledge and information.

The fact that an older person begins to experience a reduction in memory capacity and speed of information processing does not necessarily indicate that he or she is becoming demented. Where can we find the line between normal aging and dementia? Is this distinction simply a matter of degree, or is there a qualitative difference between the expected decline in cognitive mechanics and the onset of cognitive pathology? These issues present an important challenge for future research.

---

the normal strength and coordination to carry out the action and is able to understand the other person's speech. However, he or she is unable to translate the various components into a meaningful action (Ballard, Granier, & Robin, 2008).

**PERCEPTION** Some patients with dementia have problems identifying stimuli in their environments. The technical term for this phenomenon is **agnosia**, which means "perception without meaning." The person's sensory functions are unimpaired, but he or she is unable to recognize the source of stimulation (Bauer & Demery, 2003). Agnosia can be associated with visual, auditory, or tactile sensations, and it can be relatively specific or more generalized. For example, visual agnosia is the inability to recognize certain objects or faces. Some people with visual agnosia can identify inanimate stimuli but are unable to recognize human faces.

It is sometimes difficult to distinguish between aphasia and agnosia. Imagine, for example, that a clinician shows a patient a toothbrush and asks, "What is this object?" The patient may look at the object and be unable to name it. Does that mean that the person cannot think of the word "toothbrush"? Or does it mean that the person cannot recognize the object at all? In this case, the distinction could be made by saying to the person, "Show me what you do with this object." A person suffering from aphasia would take the toothbrush in his hand and make brushing movements in front of his mouth, thereby demonstrating that he recognizes the object but cannot remember its name. A person with agnosia would be unable to indicate how the toothbrush is used.

**ABSTRACT THINKING** Another manifestation of cognitive impairment in dementia is the loss of the ability to think in abstract ways. The person may be bound to concrete interpretations of things that other people say. It may also be difficult for the person to interpret words that have more than one meaning (for example, "pen") or to explain why two objects are alike ("Why are a basketball and a football helmet alike?" Because they are both types of sporting equipment.).

In our opening case, Jonathan became increasingly literal minded in his conversations with other people. After he retired, he had much more time to become involved in routine tasks around the home. Alice found that she had to give him very explicit instructions if she wanted him to do anything. For example, if she asked him to mow the grass, he would do exactly that—nothing more. This was unusual for Jonathan, because he had always enjoyed taking care of their lawn and took great pride in their bushes and flower gardens. Previously, "mowing the grass" would have been taken to include trimming, pulling weeds, raking leaves from under bushes, and all sorts of related details. Now, Jonathan interpreted this instruction in concrete terms.

***JUDGMENT AND SOCIAL BEHAVIOR*** Related to deficits in abstract reasoning is the failure of social judgment and problem-solving skills. In the course of everyday life, we must acquire information from the environment, organize and process it, and then formulate and perform appropriate responses by considering these new data in the light of past experiences. The disruption of short-term memory, perceptual skills, and higher-level cognitive abilities obviously causes disruptions of judgment. Examples from Jonathan's case include problems deciding which clothes to wear for working around his home as opposed to going out in public, as well as his inability to understand the humor in some television programs. Impulsive and careless behaviors are often the product of the demented person's poor judgment. Activities such as shopping, driving, and using tools can create serious problems.

**ASSESSMENT OF NEUROCOGNITIVE IMPAIRMENT** There are many ways to measure a person's level of cognitive impairment. One is the Mini-Mental State Examination outlined in Table 14.2. We include sample items to give you an idea of the types of questions that a clinician might ask in order to elicit the cognitive problems of dementia. Some are directed at the person's orientation to time and place. Others are concerned

John O'Connor suffered from Alzheimer's disease for several years prior to his death in 2009. In his later years, he was unable to remember that he was married to Sandra Day O'Connor, the first woman to serve on the U.S. Supreme Court. He struck up a romance with a fellow patient after moving into an assisted living center. Justice O'Connor said that she was not jealous and simply pleased that he was comfortable.

with anterograde amnesia, such as the ability to remember the names of objects for a short period of time. Agnosia, is addressed by item 3.

**Neuropsychological assessment** can be used as a more precise index of cognitive impairment. This process involves the evaluation of performance on psychological tests to indicate whether a person has a brain disorder (Weintraub et al., 2009). Neuropsychological testing can involve a variety of tasks that are designed to measure sensorimotor, perceptual, and speech functions. For example, in one tactile performance test, the person is blindfolded and then required to fit differently shaped blocks into spaces in a form board. The time needed to perform this test reflects one specific aspect of the person's motor skills. Complete neuropsychological test batteries are rarely used for the diagnosis of dementia because they are too long and time-consuming. It is more common to use specific tasks that focus on abilities that are impaired in patients with dementia.

Some neuropsychological tasks require the person to copy simple objects or drawings. The drawings illustrated in Figure 14.1 demonstrate this process and the type of impairment typically seen in a patient during the relatively early stages

of Alzheimer's disease. The patient was asked to reproduce a drawing. This was done initially while the original figure was still in sight and then repeated after it had been covered up. The performance of the patient indicates two problems associated with the disorder. First, inconsistencies between drawings 1 and 2 reflect perceptual difficulties. Second, the drastic deterioration from drawing 2 to drawing 3 indicates that the patient had a great deal of difficulty remembering the shape of the figure for even a few brief moments.

**PERSONALITY AND EMOTION** Personality changes, emotional difficulties, and motivational problems are frequently associated with dementia. These problems may not contribute to the diagnosis of the disorder, but they do have an impact on the person's adjustment. They can also create additional burdens for people who care for demented patients.

Hallucinations and delusions are seen in at least 20 percent of dementia cases and are more common during the later stages of the disorder (Savva et al., 2009). The delusional beliefs are typically understandable consequences of the person's disorientation or anterograde amnesia. They are most often simple in nature and are relatively short-lived. Mary's frequent insistence that someone had stolen her purse is a typical example. Other common themes are phantom houseguests and personal persecution (Mizrahi et al., 2006).

The emotional consequences of dementia are quite varied. Some demented patients appear to be apathetic or emotionally flat. Their faces are less expressive, and they appear to be indifferent to their surroundings. Alice noticed, for example, that something seemed a bit vacant in Jonathan's eyes. At other times, emotional reactions may become exaggerated and less predictable. The person may become fearful or angry in situations that would not have aroused strong emotion in the past. Changes like this often lead others to believe that the person's personality has changed.

Depression is another problem that is frequently found in association with dementia (Stroud, Steiner, & Iwuagwu, 2008). In many ways, feelings of depression are understandable. The realization that your most crucial cognitive abilities are beginning to fail, that you can no longer perform simple tasks or care for yourself, would obviously lead to sadness and depression. Mary's case illustrates one way in which cognitive impairment can complicate depression: Her inability to remember from one day to the next that her dog had died seemed to interfere with her ability to

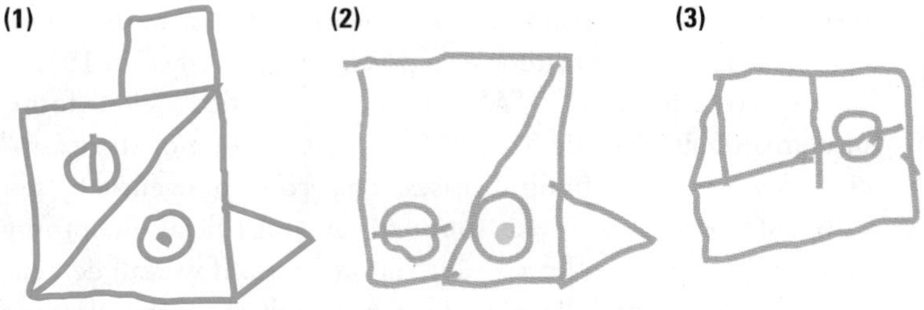

**(1)**        **(2)**        **(3)**

**FIGURE 14.1**

**Neuropsychological Test Performance** These drawings represent part of the neuropsychological test performance of a 75-year-old woman with a diagnosis of Alzheimer's disease. The figure on the left (1) was drawn by the psychologist, who then handed the piece of paper to the patient and asked her to make an exact copy of the figure next to the original. After the patient had completed her replica (2), the piece of paper was turned over and she was asked to draw the figure again, this time from memory. The figure that she drew based on memory is presented on the right (3).

grieve for the loss of her pet. Each time that she was reminded of his death was like the first time that she had heard the news.

**MOTOR BEHAVIORS** Demented persons may become agitated, pacing restlessly or wandering away from familiar surroundings. In the later stages of the disorder, patients may develop problems in the control of the muscles by the central nervous system. Some patients develop muscular rigidity accompanied by painful cramping. Others experience epileptic seizures, which consist of involuntary, rapidly alternating movements of the arms and legs.

Some specific types of dementia are associated with involuntary movements, or dyskinesiatics, tremors, and jerky movements of the face and limbs called chorea. These motor symptoms help to distinguish among different types of dementia. We return to this area later in the chapter when we discuss the classification of differentiated and undifferentiated dementias.

**DEMENTIA VERSUS DEPRESSION** Another condition that can be associated with symptoms of dementia, especially among the elderly, is depression. There are, indeed, many areas of overlap between these disorders, but the nature of the relationship is not yet clear. Approximately 25 percent of patients with a diagnosis of dementia also exhibit symptoms of major depressive disorder (Steffens & Potter, 2008). The symptoms of depression include a lack of interest in, and withdrawal of attention from, the environment. People who are depressed often have trouble concentrating, appear preoccupied, and their thinking is labored. These cognitive problems closely resemble some symptoms of dementia. Some depressed patients exhibit poverty of speech and restricted or unchanging facial expression. A disheveled appearance, due to self-neglect and loss of weight, in an elderly patient may contribute to the impression that the person is suffering from dementia.

Despite the many similarities, there are important differences between depression and dementia. These are summarized in Table 14.3. Experienced clinicians can usually distinguish between depression and dementia by considering the pattern of onset and associated features (Insel & Badger, 2002). In those cases where the distinction cannot be made on the basis of these characteristics, response to treatment may be the only way to establish a differential diagnosis. If the person's condition, including cognitive impairments, improves following treatment with antidepressant medication or electroconvulsive therapy, it seems reasonable to conclude that the person was depressed.

The relationship between depression and dementia has been the topic of considerable debate. Is depression a consequence of dementia, or are the symptoms of dementia a consequence of depression? Some clinicians have used the term *pseudodementia* to describe the condition of patients with symptoms of dementia whose cognitive impairment is actually produced by a major depressive disorder. There is no doubt that cases of this sort exist (Raskind, 1998). In fact, depression and dementia are not necessarily mutually exclusive disorders. We know that these

---

> **TABLE 14.3**
> ## Signs and Symptoms Distinguishing Depression from Dementia
>
> | Depression | Dementia |
> |---|---|
> | Uneven progression over weeks | Even progression over months or years |
> | Complains of memory loss | Attempts to hide memory loss |
> | Often worse in morning, better as day goes on | Worse later in day or when fatigued |
> | Aware of, exaggerates disability | Unaware or minimizes disability |
> | May abuse alcohol or other drugs | Rarely abuses drugs |

*Source:* "Signs and Symptoms Distinguishing Depression from Dementia" from the book THE VANISHING MIND: A Practical Guide to Alzheimer's Disease and Other Dementias, 2E by Leonard L. Heston and June A. White. © 1983, 1991 by W.H. Freeman and Company. Reprinted by permission of Henry Holt, LLC. All rights reserved.

conditions coexist more often than would be expected by chance, but we do not know why (Jorm, 2001).

## Diagnosis

Neurocognitive disorders have been classified by a somewhat different process than most other forms of psychopathology because of their close link to specific types of neuropathology. Description of specific cognitive and behavioral symptoms has not always been the primary consideration. In the following pages, we describe the ways in which these disorders have been defined and some of the considerations that influence the way in which they are classified.

## Brief Historical Perspective

Alois Alzheimer (1864–1915), a German psychiatrist, worked closely in Munich with Emil Kraepelin, who is often considered responsible for modern psychiatric classification (see Chapters 4). Alzheimer's most famous case involved a 51-year-old woman who had become delusional and also experienced a severe form of recent memory impairment, accompanied by apraxia and agnosia. This woman died four years later. Following her death, Alzheimer conducted a microscopic examination of her brain and made a startling discovery: bundles of neurofibrillary tangles and amyloid plaques. Alzheimer presented the case at a meeting of psychiatrists in 1906 and published a three-page paper in 1907. Emil Kraepelin began to refer to this condition as Alzheimer's disease in the eighth edition of his famous textbook on psychiatry, published in 1910.

In early editions of *DSM,* the manual classified various forms of dementia as Organic Mental Disorders because of their association with known brain diseases. That concept eventually fell into disfavor because it was founded on an artificial dichotomy between biological and psychological processes. If we call dementia an organic mental disorder, does that imply that other types of psychopathology are not organically based (Spitzer et al., 1992)? Obviously not. Therefore, in order to be consistent with the rest of the diagnostic manual, and so as to avoid falling into the trap of simplistic mind–body dualism, dementia and related clinical phenomena are now classified as Neurocognitive Disorders in *DSM-5*. These disorders are divided into three major headings: delirium, major NCD, and mild NCD (Blazer, 2013; Ganguli et al., 2011).

**Major neurocognitive disorder** is a new term that includes dementia and related forms of significant cognitive decline (including those that were formerly known as *amnestic disorders,* in which the cognitive impairment is more circumscribed than in dementia). The *DSM-5* criteria for major NCD are listed in "DSM-5: Criteria for Major Neurocognitive Disorder." In order to qualify for a diagnosis of major NCD, the person must exhibit evidence of significant cognitive decline in one or more domain (such as complex attention or learning and memory), and those cognitive deficits must interfere with the person's independence in everyday activities. Finally, *DSM-5* notes that the cognitive problems must be above and beyond anything that could be attributed solely to delirium or another mental disorder, such as major depression or schizophrenia.

Mild NCD is another new diagnostic concept, introduced in *DSM-5*, to recognize less severe forms of neurocognitive disorders. This concept applies to cognitive problems that fall short of the threshold for major NCD but also exceed the losses in fluid intelligence that are characteristic of normal aging (see Memory Changes in Normal Aging earlier in this chapter). By definition, this is an ambiguous clinical phenomenon. The diagnostic criteria for mild NCD are identical to those listed in "DSM-5: Criteria for Major Neurocognitive Disorder," with two exceptions. First, rather than specifying evidence of "significant" cognitive decline, mild NCD requires evidence of "modest" cognitive decline. Second, in mild NCD, these cognitive symptoms must *not* interfere with the person's capacity for independence in everyday activities (criterion "C"). This diagnostic category can be used to describe

people who are still able to live on their own, but who also struggle with cognitive problems. For example, a person may need to use a map to drive to a store where he has shopped for many years. Some people with these problems will progress eventually to meet criteria for major NCD, but others will not. Early identification of these problems might eventually offer an advantage in terms of treatment success, but at the present time, no interventions have been shown to reverse the progression of dementia or even slow its progress substantially. For that reason, and in light of difficulties associated with diagnosing the condition reliably, it remains to be seen whether mild NCD will eventually be seen as a useful addition to the diagnostic manual (Morris, 2012; Remington, 2012).

## Specific Types of Neurocognitive Disorder

Many specific conditions are associated with NCD. They are distinguished primarily on the basis of known neuropathology—specific brain lesions that have been discovered over the past 100 years. According to *DSM-5*, the first step in the diagnostic process is concerned with the generic definition of major or minor NCD. Does the person meet criteria for one of these conditions? If the answer is yes, the clinician must determine whether the person meets a more specific definition of either major or minor NCD due to one of several conditions, such as Alzheimer's Disease (see "DSM-5: Criteria for Major Neurocognitive Disorder"). For example, in order to meet criteria for NCD due to Alzheimer's Disease, several additional criteria must be present. Most importantly, the person must show clear evidence of decline in memory and learning, and the onset of this impairment must follow a steadily progressive pattern. Major NCD due to AD is diagnosed if the person shows problems with memory and learning and at least one other cognitive domain; minor NCD due to AD is diagnosed if the cognitive problems are limited to learning and memory. This process is clearly in flux. Several authoritative groups have proposed

---

criteria for
## Major Neurocognitive Disorder

A. Evidence of significant cognitive decline from a previous level of performance in one or more cognitive domains (complex attention, executive function, learning and memory, language, perceptual-motor, or social cognition) based on:

1. Concern of the individual, a knowledgeable informant, or the clinician that there has been a significant decline in cognitive function; and

2. A substantial impairment in cognitive performance, preferably documented by standardized neuropsychological testing or, in its absence, another quantified clinical assessment.

B. The cognitive deficits interfere with independence in everyday activities (i.e., at a minimum, requiring assistance with complex instrumental activities of daily living such as paying bills or managing medications).

C. The cognitive deficits do not occur exclusively in the context of a delirium.

D. The cognitive deficits are not better explained by another mental disorder (e.g., major depressive disorder, schizophrenia).

# CRITICAL THINKING matters

## How Can Clinicians Establish an Early Diagnosis of Alzheimer's Disease?

The *DSM-5* diagnostic criteria for major and minor NCD due to Alzheimer's Disease represent an interesting example of a point that we have tried to make throughout this book. In the field of psychopathology, diagnostic criteria usually represent a "work in progress." Do not take any of these definitions as being the final word with regard to the identification of a disorder. Prevailing views about the best way to identify mental disorders will continue to evolve as more evidence is collected and evaluated.

One of the most important problems with regard to the diagnosis of Alzheimer's Disease involves the initial identification of the disorder. Symptoms associated with advanced stages of the disorder are obvious. But what are the *earliest* reliable indications that a person has developed the disorder? Are these early signs the same as (although perhaps more subtle than) the symptoms that are present when the disorder has progressed for several years? If the disorder could be identified in its beginning stages, it might be possible to develop more effective treatment procedures.

Do people in the early stages of Alzheimer's Disease show changes specifically in memory performance, or does the disorder have a more generalized impact on many different aspects of cognition, such as reasoning and planning, attention, perception, and use of language? In an effort to answer this question, research studies have been conducted to investigate "mild cognitive impairment"

in elderly persons (Morris, 2012). Investigators have tested people who meet various definitions for this condition. The participants are later followed up and retested, in an effort to determine whether specific kinds of problems do, in fact, indicate that the person will go on to develop a more disabling form of dementia.

The most useful definition of mild cognitive impairment seems to be one that includes evidence of a decline in any area of cognitive performance, not simply memory (Johnson et al., 2009). For example, people who show a decline in *executive functioning* (reasoning and planning) are just as likely to develop DAT three or four years after initial testing. These data suggest that Alzheimer's disease does not always begin as a memory problem.

The definition of mild NCD due to Alzheimer's Disease that is included in *DSM-5* will almost surely be revised when the next edition of the manual is published. Studies of the progression of mild cognitive impairment suggest that, in the earliest stages of the disorder, memory impairment may not be its only symptom. Increased emphasis may be placed on evidence regarding a decline in executive functioning (Storandt, 2008). Longitudinal studies also indicate that more obvious symptoms, such as aphasia, apraxia, and agnosia, are primarily evident during the advanced stages of the disorder. Critical thinking about this kind of evidence will lead to better refined and more useful diagnostic criteria.

---

definitions of Alzheimer's Disease (Arevalo-Rodriguez et al., 2013; McKhann et al., 2011). The one included in *DSM-5* represents a compromise among these alternatives, and it will surely change over the next few years, as further research unfolds with special interest being focused on early signs of the disorder (see Critical Thinking Matters).

**NEUROCOGNITIVE DISORDER DUE TO ALZHEIMER'S DISEASE** The speed of onset serves as the main feature to distinguish **Alzheimer's disease** from the other types of dementia listed in *DSM-5*. In this disorder, the cognitive impairment appears gradually, and the person's cognitive deterioration is progressive (Waldemar & Burns, 2009). If the person meets these criteria, the diagnosis has traditionally made on the basis of excluding other conditions, such as vascular disease, Huntington's disease, Parkinson's disease, or chronic substance abuse. In *DSM-5*, a diagnosis of *probable* Alzheimer's disease is made if the person shows evidence of a genetic mutation associated with Alzheimer's disease, either from family history or genetic testing.

A definite diagnosis of Alzheimer's disease can only be determined by autopsy because it requires the observation of two specific types of brain lesions: neurofibrillary tangles and amyloid

plaques (see Figure 14.2). The brain is composed of millions of neurons. The internal structure of branches that extend from each neuron includes microtubules, which provide structural support for the cell and help transport chemicals used in the production of neurotransmitters (Caselli et al., 2006). These microtubules are reinforced by tau proteins, which are organized symmetrically. Tau proteins are the proteins associated with the assembly and stability of microtubules. In patients with Alzheimer's disease, enzymes loosen tau from their connections to the microtubule, and they break apart. The microtubules disintegrate in the absence of tau proteins, and the whole neuron shrivels and dies. The disorganized tangles of tau left at the end of this process are known as **neurofibrillary tangles**. They are found in both the cerebral cortex and the hippocampus. Neurofibrillary tangles have also been found in adults with Down syndrome and patients with Parkinson's disease.

The other type of lesion in Alzheimer's disease is known as **amyloid plaques**, which consist of a central core of homogeneous protein material known as *beta-amyloid* surrounded by clumps of debris left over from destroyed neurons. These plaques are located primarily in the cerebral cortex. They are found in large numbers in the brains of patients with Alzheimer's disease,

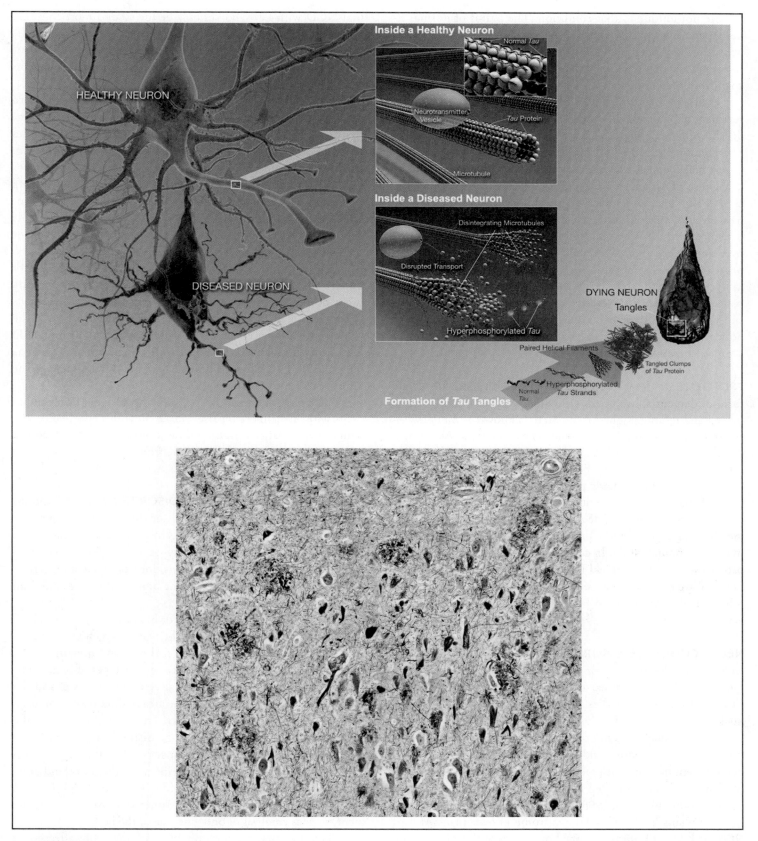

**FIGURE 14.2**

(Top) Brain Damage in Alzheimer's Disease. (Bottom) This photomicrograph of a brain tissue specimen from an Alzheimer's patient shows the characteristic plaques (dark patches) and neurofibrillary tangles (irregular pattern of strand-like fibers).
*Source:* Courtesy of the National Institute of Health.

but are not unique to that condition. The brains of normal elderly people, especially after the age of 75, often contain some neurofibrillary tangles and amyloid plaques. A few widely scattered cells of this type do not appear to interfere with normal cognitive functioning.

Brain imaging procedures offer exciting new tools for the measurement of brain lesions associated with dementia. Scientists have developed a technique to detect amyloid plaques using positron emission tomography (PET imaging) in the living brain. This procedure may eventually replace the need to wait for autopsy to verify a diagnosis of Alzheimer's disease (Koyama et al., 2012; Quigley et al., 2011). Some studies have identified nondemented people who have levels of amyloid plaque that are comparable to levels seen in demented people. When these nondemented people are followed over time, high levels of amyloid plaque predict the subsequent onset of obvious symptoms of dementia (Roe et al., 2013). It is not yet possible to create images of (and measure) neurofibrillary tangles in living brains. Nevertheless, advances in the development and validation of these brain imaging tools promise to transform both research and practice related to dementia and other severe forms of cognitive impairment.

**FRONTOTEMPORAL NEUROCOGNITIVE DISORDER** A rare form of dementia associated with circumscribed atrophy of the frontal and temporal lobes of the brain is known as *frontotemporal neurocognitive disorder*. This syndrome is similar to Alzheimer's disease in terms of both behavioral symptoms and cognitive impairment. Patients with both disorders display problems in memory and language. Early personality changes that precede the onset of cognitive impairment are more common among patients with frontotemporal NCD (Seelaar et al., 2011). Impaired reasoning and judgment are more prominent than anterograde amnesia in frontotemporal NCD. In comparison with Alzheimer patients, patients with frontotemporal NCD are also more likely to engage in impulsive sexual actions, roaming and aimless exploration, and other types of disinhibited behaviors (Mendez, Lauterbach, & Sampson, 2008).

**NEUROCOGNITIVE DISORDER WITH LEWY BODIES** *Lewy bodies* (also called *intracytoplasmic inclusions*) are rounded deposits found in nerve cells. Named after F. H. Lewy, who first described them in 1912, Lewy bodies are often found in the brain-stem nuclei of patients with Parkinson's disease. Neurologists later discovered occasional cases of progressive dementia in which autopsies revealed Lewy bodies widespread throughout the brain. The development of more sensitive staining techniques that can identify cortical Lewy bodies led to greatly increased interest in this phenomenon during the 1990s.

Clinicians have defined a syndrome known in *DSM-5* as **NCD with Lewy bodies**, but the boundaries of this disorder are not entirely clear. It overlaps, both in terms of clinical symptoms and brain pathology, with other forms of dementia such as Alzheimer's disease and Parkinson's disease. Many experts now agree that NCD with Lewy bodies may be the second most common form of dementia, after Alzheimer's disease. Among patients who meet diagnostic criteria for Alzheimer's disease, 30 percent also have evidence of diffuse Lewy bodies in cortical neurons (Andersson et al., 2011).

Symptoms of NCD with Lewy bodies typically begin with memory deficits followed by a progressive decline to dementia (Cummings, 2004). Patients' cognitive impairment includes problems in attention, executive functions, problem solving, and visuospatial performance. Unlike patients with Alzheimer's disease, patients with NCD with Lewy bodies often show a fluctuation in cognitive performance, alertness, and level of consciousness. Their episodic confusional states sometimes resemble delirium. These changes may be evident over a period of hours or several days.

The symptom that is most likely to distinguish NCD with Lewy bodies from Alzheimer's disease and vascular dementia is the presence of recurrent and detailed visual hallucinations (Borroni et al., 2006). The patient usually recognizes that the hallucinations are not real. Many patients who suffer from NCD with Lewy bodies also develop Parkinsonian features, such as muscular rigidity, which appear early in the development of the disorder.

The course of dementia appears to be different between patients with Alzheimer's disease and NCD with Lewy bodies. Patients with the latter condition show a more rapid progression of cognitive impairment, and the time from onset of symptoms to death is also shorter.

**VASCULAR NEUROCOGNITIVE DISORDER** Many conditions other than those that attack brain tissue directly can also produce symptoms of NCD. The central agent in these problems can be either medical conditions or other types of mental disorders. Diseases that affect the heart and lungs, for example, can interfere with the circulation of oxygen to the brain. Substance abuse can also interfere with brain functions.

One cause of NCD is vascular or blood vessel disease, which affects the arteries responsible for bringing oxygen and sugar to the brain (Roman, 2002). A *stroke*, the severe interruption of blood flow to the brain, can produce various types of brain damage, depending on the size of the affected blood vessel and the area of the brain that it supplies. The area of dead tissue produced by the stroke is known as an *infarct*. The behavioral effects of a stroke are usually obvious and can be distinguished from NCD on several grounds: (1) They appear suddenly rather than gradually; (2) they affect voluntary movements of the limbs and gross speech patterns, as well as more subtle intellectual abilities; and (3) they often result in unilateral rather than bilateral impairment, such as paralysis of only one side of the body.

There are instances, however, in which the stroke affects only a very small artery and may not have any observable effect on the person's behavior. If several of these small strokes occur over a period of time, and if their sites are scattered in different areas of the brain, they may gradually produce cognitive impairment. *DSM-5* refers to this condition as **vascular neurocognitive disorder**. The cognitive symptoms of vascular NCD that are listed in the diagnostic manual are similar to those for Alzheimer's disease. However, *DSM-5* does not require a gradual onset for vascular dementia, as it does for dementia of the Alzheimer's type. In addition, the diagnosis of vascular dementia depends on the presence of either focal neurological signs and symptoms associated with the experience of stroke, such as gait abnormalities or weakness in the extremities, or laboratory evidence of blood vessel disease (Paul, Garrett, & Cohen, 2003).

**NEUROCOGNITIVE DISORDER DUE TO TRAUMATIC BRAIN INJURY** Traumatic brain injury (TBI) is caused when the head is involved in a collision, resulting in the displacement of the brain inside the skull. This can occur as a result of many different kinds of injuries, ranging from exposure to explosions during combat to violent collisions during athletic events. Often the person loses consciousness following the trauma and may experience amnesia for the event itself. The severity of the injury can be rated as a function of the duration of loss of consciousness and posttraumatic amnesia as well as the amount of disorientation and confusion experienced immediately following the injury. Individuals who have experienced TBI may be more likely than others to develop dementia later in their lives, but the research evidence is mixed on this issue (Moretti et al., 2012; Wang et al., 2012). Most people who develop dementia do not have a history of TBI, and most survivors of TBI do not develop dementia.

There is no question that some people do develop NCD many years after experiencing TBI. Symptoms include significant problems in a number of cognitive domains, including attention, executive functioning, and memory. Popular media have recently devoted considerable attention to these problems because of soldiers returning from combat experiences and also because of medical problems experienced by many former professional football players. In the case of concussions suffered by football players, the crucial factor may be the number and the frequency of the head injuries that they experience, rather than the severity of any individual blow. The stories problems experienced by returning military veterans and retired athletes will undoubtedly motivate additional research efforts to understand the mechanisms that link TBI and the development of NCD in later life (Dams-O'Connor et al., 2013).

John Mackey (1941–2011) developed frontotemporal dementia several years after the end of his legendary playing career in the NFL. His family's struggle to care for him brought extensive public attention to neurocognitive problems experienced by many former football players.

**HUNTINGTON'S DISEASE** Unusual involuntary muscle movements known as *chorea* (from the Greek word meaning "dance") represent the most distinctive feature of **Huntington's disease**. These movements are relatively subtle at first, with the person appearing to be merely restless or fidgety. As the disorder progresses, sustained muscle contractions become difficult. Movements of the face, trunk, and limbs eventually become uncontrolled, leaving the person to writhe and grimace. A large proportion of Huntington's patients also exhibit a variety of personality changes and symptoms of mental disorders, primarily depression and anxiety. Between 5 and 10 percent develop psychotic symptoms. The symptoms of mental disorder may be evident before the appearance of motor or cognitive impairment (Narding & Janzing, 2003).

The movement disorder and the cognitive deficits are produced by progressive neuronal degeneration in the basal ganglia (Ross & Tabrizi, 2011). This is a group of nuclei, including the caudate nucleus, the putamen, and the globus pallidus, that form a collaborative system of connections between the cerebral cortex and the thalamus (see Figure 14.3).

Neurocognitive disorder appears in all Huntington's disease patients, although the extent of the cognitive impairment and the rate of its progression vary widely. Impairments in recent memory and learning are the most obvious cognitive problems. Patients

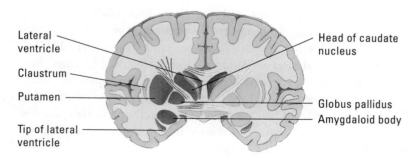

Lateral ventricle — Head of caudate nucleus
Claustrum — 
Putamen — Globus pallidus
Tip of lateral ventricle — Amygdaloid body

**FIGURE 14.3**

**Areas of the Brain Implicated in Huntington's Disease**
Huntington's disease involves deterioration of the basal ganglia (also known as the cerebral nuclei). The primary units of this system are the caudate nucleus, putamen, globus pallidus, and the claustrum.
*Source:* Martini, Frederich H. and Michael J. Timmons. Human Anatomy, 1st Ed., (C) 1995, p. 378. Reprinted and electronically produced by permission of Pearson Education, Inc., Upper Saddle River, NJ.

Boxing legend Muhammed Ali and actor Michael J. Fox joke around before testifying at a government hearing on Parkinson's disease. Both men have the disorder, and they encouraged the committee to increase funds for research.

have trouble encoding new information. Higher-level cognitive functions are typically well preserved, and insight is usually intact. Unlike the pattern of dementia seen in Alzheimer's disease, patients with Huntington's do not develop aphasia, apraxia, or agnosia (Morris, 1995).

The diagnosis of Huntington's disease depends on the presence of a positive family history for the disorder. It is one of the few disorders that are transmitted in an autosomal dominant pattern with complete penetrance. In other words, the person must only inherit one gene—from either parent—to be vulnerable, and an individual who inherits the problematic gene will always develop the disorder (see Research Methods).

**PARKINSON'S DISEASE** A disorder of the motor system, known as *Parkinson's disease,* is caused by a degeneration of a specific area of the brain stem known as the substantia nigra and loss of the neurotransmitter dopamine, which is produced by cells in this area. Typical symptoms include tremors, rigidity, postural abnormalities, and reduction in voluntary movements (Kontakos & Stokes, 1999). Unlike people with Huntington's disease, most patients with Parkinson's disease do not develop symptoms of neurocognitive disorder. Follow-up studies suggest that approximately 20 percent of elderly patients with Parkinson's disease eventually show neurocognitive impairments. Their risk is approximately double the risk of dementia found among people of similar age who do not have Parkinson's disease (Caviness et al., 2011).

## Frequency of Delirium and Major Neurocognitive Disorders

Cognitive disorders represent one of the most pressing health problems in our society. Detailed evidence regarding the prevalence of delirium is not available, but it does seem to be one of the most frequent symptoms of disease among elderly people. At least 15 percent of elderly hospitalized medical patients exhibit symptoms of delirium (Grover et al., 2009). The rate is much higher among nursing home patients, where delirium is often combined with dementia (as in the case study at the beginning of this chapter).

Neurocognitive disorder is an especially important problem among elderly people. Although it can appear in people as young as 40 to 45, the average age of onset is much later. The incidence of dementia will be much greater in the near future, because the average age of the population is increasing steadily (Kukull & Bowen, 2002; Vickland et al., 2010). People over the age of 80 represent one of the fastest growing segments of our population (see Chapter 17). By the year 2030, more than 9 million people in the United States will be affected by Alzheimer's disease. The personal and economic impact of dementia on patients, their families, and our society clearly warrants serious attention from health care professionals, policymakers concerned with health care reform, and clinical scientists seeking more effective forms of treatment.

Epidemiological studies must be interpreted with caution, of course, because of the problems associated with establishing a diagnosis of neurocognitive disorder. Mild cases are difficult to identify reliably. At the earliest stages of the disorder, symptoms are difficult to distinguish from forgetfulness, which can increase in normal aging. Definitive diagnoses depend on information collected over an extended period of time so that the progressive nature of the cognitive impairment, and deterioration from an earlier, higher level of functioning, can be documented. Unfortunately, this kind of information is often not available in a large-scale epidemiological study.

Also bear in mind the fact that the diagnosis of specific subtypes of NCD, such as NCD due to Alzheimer's disease, requires microscopic examination of brain tissue after the person's death or evidence regarding the presence of specific genes. Again, these data are not typically available to epidemiologists. With these limitations in mind, we now consider what is known about the frequency of NCD in the general population.

### Prevalence of Dementia

The incidence and prevalence of dementia increase dramatically with age. Studies of community samples in North America and Europe indicate that the prevalence of dementia in people between the ages of 65 and 69 is approximately 1 percent. For people between the ages of 75 and 79, the prevalence rate is approximately 6 percent, and it increases dramatically in older age groups. Almost 40 percent of people over 90 years of age exhibit symptoms of moderate or severe dementia (Rocca et al., 2011).

Survival rates are reduced among demented patients (Brodaty et al., 2012). In Alzheimer's disease, for example, the average time between onset of the disorder and the person's death is less than six years. There is considerable variability in these figures. Some patients have survived more than 20 years after the first appearance of obvious symptoms.

## RESEARCH methods

### Finding Genes That Cause Behavioral Problems

Behavior genetic studies have demonstrated that most clinical disorders are under some degree of genetic influence. However, it is one thing to say that genetic factors "are involved" in the development of a disorder, and quite another to identify the specific genes involved. Discovery of the genes that are involved in a disorder would be an exciting step toward explaining the etiology of the disorder. It would also have important implications for developing targeted prevention and intervention programs for those people at greatest risk. Rapid advances in the field of molecular genetics are making it possible for scientists to identify specific genes involved in many disorders.

Finding genes involved in complex behavioral disorders has been difficult because there is no straightforward pattern of inheritance. Many genes are thought to be involved, and each of these genes on its own only increases or decreases risk a small amount. In addition, the environment is known to play an important role in the development of most clinical disorders. Whether an individual develops a disorder is a product of the combination of genetic and environmental risk and protective factors that the individual experiences. This has complicated efforts to identify genes involved in psychiatric disorders because the original methods developed for gene identification were based on simple, Mendelian disorders that are caused by a single defective gene. The application of these methods to complex psychiatric disorders led to many early failures and disappointments. Fortunately, new methods have been developed to take into account the complexities introduced when studying psychiatric phenotypes.

Most cells in the human body have 46 chromosomes grouped in 23 pairs. These chromosomes are transferred from the parents to the child during fertilization, with each parent providing 23 chromosomes. These chromosomes contain a chemical sequence called deoxyribonucleic acid (DNA). The characteristics of an individual that are inherited from one generation to the next are controlled by segments of DNA called genes. Any two human beings are about 99.9 percent identical genetically, but this 0.1 percent difference translates to about 3 million differences in our DNA. Some of these differences in DNA sequence contribute to individual differences in many human characteristics, ranging from eye color to personality. Most of these DNA differences are "silent" and don't appear to have any effect. These locations where the DNA comes in different forms can be used as genetic "markers," and they provide a useful way to find genes.

One method to find genes is a strategy called *linkage analysis*. **Genetic linkage** studies focus on families that have multiple members affected with the disorder. Investigators systematically search the entire genome by testing for linkage between genetic markers, evenly spaced across all chromosomes, and the expression of a particular disease or behavior. They are looking for stretches of DNA that are more likely to be shared among the affected individuals and less likely to be found in the unaffected individuals, suggesting that there is a gene in that region that contributes to the disorder. One strength of the linkage analysis approach is that it allows susceptibility genes to be identified when we have no, or limited, knowledge about what causes the disorder. This strategy led to the identification of the gene causing Huntington disease, which is a single-gene, Mendelian disorder (Gusella et al., 1983).

Another strategy that is used to identify genes is case-control *association analysis*. This involves identifying two groups of individuals: One group consists of people affected with the disorder (cases) and the other group consists of people who do not have the disorder (controls). The two groups should be matched on factors such as gender, ethnicity, and age, so they only differ on disease status. The frequency with which particular versions of a gene occur in the two groups is then compared. If a gene is involved in the disorder, the "risk variant" should be more frequent among the affected individuals. This approach is often used to test genes that have been targeted as good candidates for involvement in the disorder for biological reasons (for example, genes involved in serotonin reception are considered good candidates for involvement in depression because antidepressants work by altering serotonin levels) or because they lie within a region of linkage identified in family studies, as described above.

It is currently a very exciting time in gene identification efforts for complex disorders. Genes involved in the predisposition to schizophrenia (O'Donovan, Williams, & Owen, 2003), alcoholism (Dick et al., 2006), and ADHD (Faraone, 2003), among others, have all been recently reported, with replications across multiple studies. Another exciting advance is the incorporation of gene–environment interaction into the study of genetic effects. One important study found that a particular version of the serotonin transporter gene contributes to the development of depression, *but only when the individual also experiences stressful life events* (Caspi et al., 2003). Identifying the specific genes involved in clinical disorders, and how these genes interact with environmental risk factors, promises to enhance dramatically our understanding of the etiology of these disorders.

There are no obvious differences between men and women with regard to the overall prevalence of dementia, broadly defined. It seems, however, that dementia in men is more likely to be associated with vascular disease or to be secondary to other medical conditions or to alcohol abuse. The incidence of Alzheimer's disease is the same in men and women up to age 90; after that, the number of new cases continues to increase for women while it apparently declines for men (Ruitenberg et al., 2001). The incidence of vascular dementia is generally lower in women than in men at all age groups.

## Prevalence by Subtypes of Neurocognitive Disorder

The studies we have already reviewed refer to cross-sectional examinations of populations, which do not allow diagnosis of specific subtypes of dementia. Some clinical studies, based on hospital populations, have allowed investigators to look at the frequency of specific subtypes of NCD. Alzheimer's disease appears to be the most common form (Waldemar & Burns, 2009), accounting for perhaps half of all cases (depending on the diagnostic criteria employed and the geographic location of the study). NCD with Lewy bodies may be the second leading cause of dementia; studies report prevalence rates of approximately 20 percent for NCD with Lewy bodies among patients with primary dementia (Rahkonen et al., 2003). Prevalence rates for vascular NCD are similar to those for NCD with Lewy bodies (Jellinger & Attems, 2010). Frontotemporal NCD is much less common than Alzheimer's disease, vascular dementia, or NCD with Lewy bodies. Huntington's disease is quite rare; it affects only 1 person in every 20,000 (Ross & Tabrizi, 2011).

## Cross-Cultural Comparisons

Several issues make it difficult to collect cross-cultural data regarding the prevalence of dementia. Tests that are used to measure cognitive impairment must be developed carefully to be sure that they are not culturally or racially biased (see Chapter 4 on the validity of assessment procedures). Elderly people in developing countries who have little formal education pose a special challenge, since most cognitive tasks have been developed for use with a different population. Those who follow more traditional ways of life, such as the Australian aboriginal people, may have very different views of old age and its problems. For all these reasons, we must interpret preliminary results on this topic with great caution (Prince et al., 2003).

Prevalence rates for dementia seem to be relatively consistent across various regions of the world (Prince et al., 2013). It is less clear whether there are regional variations with regard to the prevalence of specific types of neurocognitive disorders. For example, Alzheimer's disease may be more common in North America and Europe, whereas vascular NCD may be more common in Japan and China (Chiu et al., 1998). There are also some tentative indications that prevalence rates for dementia may be significantly lower in developing countries than in developed countries. This finding can be misleading, however, because the most common dementias are age-related. As developing countries have much lower life expectancies, they would also be expected to have lower rates of dementia.

## Causes

Delirium and NCD are clearly associated with brain pathology. Damage to various brain structures and neurotransmitter pathways can be the product of various biological and environmental events. In the following pages, we review some of the considerations that guide current thinking about the causes of these disorders.

### Delirium

The underlying mechanisms responsible for the onset of delirium undoubtedly involve neuropathology and neurochemistry (Goldstein, 2003). The incidence of delirium increases among elderly people, presumably because the physiological effects of aging make elderly people more vulnerable to medication side effects and cognitive complications of medical illnesses (Jacobson, 1997). Delirium can be caused by many different kinds of medication, including the following:

1. Psychiatric drugs (especially antidepressants, antipsychotics, and benzodiazepines)

2. Drugs used to treat heart conditions

3. Painkillers

4. Stimulants (including caffeine)

Delirium also develops in conjunction with a number of metabolic diseases, including pulmonary and cardiovascular disorders (which can interfere with the supply of oxygen to the brain), as well as endocrine diseases (especially thyroid disease and diabetes mellitus). Various kinds of infections can lead to the onset of delirium. Perhaps the most common among elderly people is urinary tract infection, which can result from the use of an indwelling urinary catheter (sometimes necessary with incontinent nursing home patients).

### Neurocognitive Disorder

In discussing the classification of NCD, we have touched on many of the factors that contribute to the etiology of these problems. Most of the other disorders listed in *DSM-5* are classified on the basis of symptoms alone. The classification of dementia is sometimes determined by specific knowledge of etiological factors, even though these may be determined only after the patient's death, as in Alzheimer's disease. In the following discussion, we consider in greater detail a few of the specific pathways that are known to lead to dementia.

**GENETIC FACTORS** Neurologists who treat demented patients have recognized for many years that the disorder often runs in

Chuck Jackson was diagnosed at the age of 50 with a rare, early-onset form of Alzheimer's disease. Speaking at a Congressional hearing on the disease, Jackson showed a family photo because he is the fifth generation of his family to have Alzheimer's.

families. Until recently, twin studies have not been used extensively to evaluate the influence of genetic factors in dementia because of the comparatively late age of onset of these disorders. By the time a proband develops symptoms of dementia, his or her co-twin may be deceased. A few studies have capitalized on national samples to find an adequate number of twin pairs. They confirm the impression, based on family studies, that genetic factors play an important role in the development of dementia. One Swedish study, for example, found that the concordance rate in monozygotic twins was over 50 percent, more than double the dizygotic rate (Pedersen et al., 2004). A U.S. study, based on a registry of aging twin veterans of World War II and the Korean War, found an MZ concordance rate of 35 percent in 24 male pairs. None of the 16 DZ pairs was concordant at the time of the report (Breitner et al., 1993).

Most of the research concerned with genetic factors and Alzheimer's disease has focused on gene identification strategies (see Research Methods on page 395). The astounding advances that have been made in molecular genetics have been applied to Alzheimer's disease with fruitful results. Experts now agree that Alzheimer's disease is genetically heterogeneous. In other words, there are several forms of the disorder, and each seems to be

associated with a different gene or set of genes. Three genes (located on chromosomes 21, 14, and 1) have been identified that, when mutated, cause early-onset forms of Alzheimer's disease. A fourth gene, located on chromosome 19, serves as a risk factor for late-onset forms of the disorder (Holmes, 2002; McQueen & Blacker, 2008). The locations of these genes are illustrated in Figure 14.4, along with graphs that indicate the average age of onset for dementia associated with the different genes.

It has been known for many years that amyloid plaques and neurofibrillary tangles are found in the brains of all people who have Down syndrome (see Chapter 15), as well as in people with Alzheimer's disease. This similarity led investigators to search for a link between the gene for Alzheimer's disease and known markers on chromosome 21, because people with Down syndrome possess three copies of chromosome 21 in every cell instead of the normal two. In fact, the gene responsible for producing proteins (amyloid precursor protein, or APP) that serve as precursors to beta-amyloid, found in the core of amyloid plaques, is located on chromosome 21. Several research groups have independently confirmed this association. Therefore, within some families, the gene for Alzheimer's disease is located on chromosome 21.

Mutations on chromosome 14 (presenilin 1, or PS1) and chromosome 1 (presenilin 2, or PS2) have also been found to be associated with early-onset forms of Alzheimer's disease (Plassman & Breitner, 1997). Like the APP gene, both of the presenilin genes are inherited in an autosomal dominant mode of transmission and cause overproduction of beta-amyloid. Mutations in the PS1 gene are probably responsible for 50 percent of early-onset cases of the disorder (which represent less than 3 percent of all patients with Alzheimer's disease).

A fourth gene produces vulnerability to late-onset Alzheimer's disease without having a direct or necessary effect on the development of dementia. In other words, people who carry this gene have an increased risk for Alzheimer's disease, but many people without the gene develop the disorder, and some people who do have the gene do not develop the disorder. The apolipoprotein E (APOE) gene is located on chromosome 19. There are three common alleles (forms) of APOE, called e-2, e-3, and e-4. The APOE-2 allele is correlated with a decreased risk for Alzheimer's disease. People who have the APOE-4 allele at this locus have an increased probability of developing the disorder (Farrer et al., 1997). Although the effect may be weaker in some groups of people (such as Hispanics and African Americans), the finding has been replicated in more than 100 different laboratories. The risk for Alzheimer's disease is between 25 and 40 percent among people who have at least one APOE-4 allele (Mayeux & Ottman, 1998). As most cases of Alzheimer's disease have a late onset, the APOE gene is probably involved in more cases of the disorder than the genes on chromosomes 21, 14, and 1.

Research findings with regard to specific genes and Alzheimer's disease are obviously exciting, but a word of caution is also in

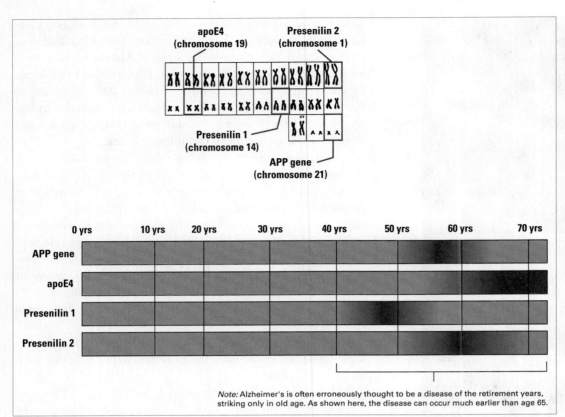

**FIGURE 14.4**

**Genes Associated with Alzheimer's Disease** Four different genes are associated with the creation of plaques found in Alzheimer's disease. The top panel, which illustrates the 23 pairs of human chromosomes, identifies which chromosome carries which AD-related gene. The bottom panel indicates that average age of onset of the disorder depends, in part, on the gene that is involved. The age of first diagnosis is illustrated in red.
*Source: Medina, John J. 1999. What You Need to Know About Alzheimer's. New Harbinger.*

*Note:* Alzheimer's is often erroneously thought to be a disease of the retirement years, striking only in old age. As shown here, the disease can occur much earlier than age 65.

order. Although some important genes have been identified, most people who develop the disorder do *not* posses one of these specific genes. In other words, these genes do increase the risk for the disorder, but most cases of the disorder do not follow this pattern. Many questions remain to be answered about the ways in which specific genes interact with other causal factors.

**NEUROTRANSMITTERS** In patients suffering from dementia, the process of chemical transmission of messages within the brain is probably disrupted, but the specific mechanisms that are involved have not been identified. We know that Parkinson's disease, which is sometimes associated with dementia, is caused by a degeneration of the dopamine pathways in the brain stem. This dysfunction is responsible for the motor symptoms seen in patients with that disorder. It is not entirely clear, however, that the intellectual problems experienced by patients with Parkinson's disease are directly related to dopamine deficiencies.

Other types of dementia have also been linked to problems with specific neurotransmitters. Huntington's disease may be associated with deficiencies in gamma-aminobutyric acid (GABA). A marked decrease in the availability of acetylcholine (ACh), another type of neurotransmitter, has been implicated in Alzheimer's disease. Reductions in ACh levels, especially in the temporal lobes, are correlated with the severity of dementia

symptoms (Kihara & Shimohama, 2004; Raskind & Peskind, 1997).

**VIRAL INFECTIONS** Some forms of primary dementia are known to be the products of "slow" viruses—infections that develop over a much more extended period of time than do most viral infections. Creutzfeldt–Jakob disease is one example. Susceptibility to infection by a specific virus can be influenced by genetic factors. The demonstration that a condition is transmitted in a familial fashion does not rule out the involvement of viral infection. In fact, familial transmission has been demonstrated for the forms of dementia that are known to be associated with a specific virus.

**IMMUNE SYSTEM DYSFUNCTION** The immune system is the body's first line of defense against infection. It employs antibodies to break down foreign materials, such as bacteria and viruses, that enter the body. The regulation of this system allows it to distinguish between foreign bodies that should be destroyed and normal body tissues that should be preserved. The production of these antibodies may be dysfunctional in some forms of dementia, such as Alzheimer's disease. In other words, the destruction of brain tissue may be caused by a breakdown in the system that regulates the immune system.

The presence of beta-amyloid at the core of amyloid plaques is one important clue to the possible involvement of immune

Families often assume overwhelming burdens in caring for patients with neurocognitive disorders. This woman, her husband, and their children moved across the country so that her 83-year old father, who suffers from dementia, could live with them.

system dysfunction. This protein is the breakdown product of a structural component of brain cells. It is made and eliminated constantly as part of normal brain functioning. For some reason, which probably involves genetic factors, some people develop problems with the elimination of beta-amyloid. Clumps of beta-amyloid accumulate. Some clinical scientists believe that immune cells in the brain attempt to destroy these amyloid plaques and inadvertently harm neighboring, healthy brain cells. Some research evidence supports this hypothesis (McGeer & McGeer, 1996; Richardson, 1996).

**ENVIRONMENTAL FACTORS** Epidemiological investigations have discovered several interesting patterns that suggest that some types of dementia, especially Alzheimer's disease, may be related to environmental factors. One example is head injury, which can cause a sudden increase of amyloid plaque. Elderly people who have been knocked unconscious as adults have an increased risk of developing Alzheimer's disease, compared to people with no history of head injury (Holsinger et al., 2002).

Some studies have reported significant relationships between Alzheimer's disease and variables that seem to protect the person from developing dementia. People who have achieved high levels of education are less likely to develop Alzheimer's disease than are people with less education (Sharp & Gatz, 2011). For example, one fascinating study has reported that among elderly Catholic nuns those who graduated from college were much less likely to be cognitively impaired than were those who had less than a college education (Butler, Ashford, & Snowdon, 1996). This finding may be interpreted to mean that increased "brain work" leads to a facilitation of neuronal activation, increased cerebral blood flow, and higher levels of glucose and oxygen consumption in the brain. All of this may increase the density of synaptic connections in the person's cortex and reduce risk for later neuronal deterioration. The discovery of environmental experiences (e.g., going to school) that serve a protective function points to the important role that cultural factors may play in moderating risk for dementia.

## Treatment and Management

The most obvious consideration with regard to treatment of the cognitive disorders is accurate diagnosis (Cummings & Cole, 2002). The distinction between delirium and neurocognitive disorder is important because many conditions that cause delirium can be treated. Delirium must be recognized as early as possible so that the source of the problem, such as an infection or some other medical condition, can be treated (Bourne et al., 2008). Some types of secondary dementia can also be treated successfully. For example, if the patient's cognitive symptoms are the products of depression, there is a relatively good chance that he or she will respond positively to antidepressant medication or electroconvulsive therapy.

When the person clearly suffers from a primary type of dementia, such as NCD due to Alzheimer's disease, a return to previous levels of functioning is extremely unlikely (see Thinking Critically About DSM-5). No form of treatment is presently capable of producing sustained and clinically significant improvement in cognitive functioning for patients with Alzheimer's disease (Tune, 2007). Realistic goals include helping the person to maintain his or her level of functioning for as long as possible despite cognitive impairment and minimizing the level of distress experienced by the person and the person's family. Several treatment options are typically used in conjunction, including medication, management of the patient's environment, behavioral strategies, and providing support to caregivers.

### Medication

Some drugs are designed to relieve cognitive symptoms of dementia by boosting the action of acetylcholine (ACh), a neurotransmitter that is involved in memory and whose level is reduced in patients with Alzheimer's disease. One drug that has been approved for use with Alzheimer's patients—donepezil (Aricept)—increases ACh activity by inhibiting acetylcholinesterase, the enzyme that breaks down ACh in the synapse. Research studies have demonstrated that donepezil can provide temporary symptomatic improvement for some patients (Kumagai et al., 2008; Rojas-Fernandez et al., 2001). Unfortunately, it usually works for only six to nine months and is not able to reverse the relentless progression of the disease. Furthermore, its use has been seriously questioned because of the relatively small effects on memory that it is able to produce (Pryse-Phillips, 1999). A statistically

## Will Patients and Their Families Understand "Mild" Neurocognitive Disorder?

The prognosis for individuals who have already reached the stage of major NCD is rather bleak. Investigators hope that early identification of these problems may eventually allow for the discovery of new, powerful treatments—probably in the form of medication—that can prevent further cognitive decline. In that sense, the addition of mild neurocognitive disorder to *DSM-5* may offer a more optimistic future for patients and their families. But those treatments are not yet available. Is the use of this term premature in clinical practice? It may be misleading in more than one way.

One is simply that the word "mild" may be confusing in this context (Remington, 2012). These symptoms may be mild compared to more advanced stages of NCD, but the diagnosis certainly signals the onset of a serious disorder and the beginning of what will likely become a prolonged struggle for patients and their families. Patients may be more inclined to ignore a diagnosis that is explicitly labeled as being mild. Imagine, for example, that this option was available with regard to the diagnosis of alcohol use disorder. Many people with serious drinking problems deny that they have a problem ("Mind your own business. I can quit whenever I want."). It might be easier to treat drinking problems before they become severe, but would a diagnosis of "mild alcohol use disorder" provide a useful message to patients? We doubt it.

The value of the diagnosis of mild NCD is also open to question from a scientific point of view. Clinicians will have more trouble agreeing on a diagnosis in cases that are, by definition, more ambiguous than cases of major NCD. As in the case of other categories that focus on early stages of a disorder (see Thinking Critically About DSM-5 in Chapter 13), the symptoms of mild neurocognitive disorder are difficult to identify reliably. People experience many changes in cognitive ability across the lifespan (see Memory Changes in Normal Aging). Expected declines in attention and memory can easily be confused with symptoms of NCD, particularly in the absence of neuropsychological testing. Cognitive decline would be easier to evaluate and understand if we all took standardized tests at regular intervals after the age of 50, much like the way people are now encouraged to get a colonoscopy once every 10 years. However, we don't take these tests routinely. It also might be important to measure the presence of biomarkers, such as amyloid plaques and tau, in order to identify the earliest stages of NCD. Scientific advances are being made rapidly in this area, but again, the evidence is not yet available to be used for clinical purposes (Noel-Storr et al., 2012; Roe et al., 2013). For all of these reasons, the value of mild NCD is open to question.

Finally, communication with patients is likely to suffer as a consequence of this addition to *DSM-5*. The meeting in which a physician presents a diagnosis of dementia to a patient can be challenging for everyone. Patients and their families are understandably frightened by the long-term implications of neurocognitive disorder and frequently confused about the symptoms and treatment options. It's important that everyone settle on a common understanding of these issues in order to make plans for the patient's care. Unfortunately, studies of this process suggest people come away from these meetings with different impressions. One study focused on diagnostic discussions that involved a physician, a nurse, the patient being evaluated, and a companion or family member. After the meeting, level of agreement among participants was modest at best (Zaleta et al., 2012). Agreement among sources was particularly low in cases where the symptoms of dementia were mild. This evidence points to another important challenge for physicians who use the diagnosis of mild NCD.

---

significant change in scores on a cognitive task does not necessarily imply a clinically significant improvement in overall clinical condition (see Research Methods in Chapter 6).

New drug treatments are being pursued that are aimed more directly at the processes by which neurons are destroyed (Sabbagh, Richardson, & Relkin, 2008). One possibility involves the use of synthetic peptides and natural proteins that inhibit the formation of amyloid plaques. Others focus on blocking the construction of neurofibrillary tangles by keeping tau protein anchored to microtubules. These alternatives are being developed and tested at a rapid pace. Recent evidence regarding these new treatment options can be obtained on the Web from the Cochrane Library.

Although the cognitive deficits associated with primary dementia cannot be completely reversed with medication, neuroleptic medication can be used to treat some patients who develop psychotic symptoms (Martinez & Kurik, 2006). These are the same drugs that are used to treat schizophrenia. Low doses are preferable because demented patients are especially vulnerable to the side effects of neuroleptics. Care must be taken to avoid use of these drugs with patients suffering from dementia with Lewy bodies because they may experience a severe negative reaction.

## Environmental and Behavioral Management

Patients with dementia experience fewer emotional problems and are less likely to become agitated if they follow a structured and predictable daily schedule. Activities such as eating meals, exercising, and going to bed are easier and less anxiety-provoking if they occur at regular times. The use of signs and notes may be helpful reminders for patients who are in the earlier stages of the disorder. As the patient's cognitive impairment becomes more severe, even simple activities, such as getting dressed or eating a meal, must be broken down into smaller and more manageable steps. Directions have to be adjusted so that they are appropriate to the patient's level of functioning. Patients with apraxia, for example, may not be able to perform tasks in response to verbal instructions. Caregivers need to adjust their expectations and assume increased responsibilities as their patients' intellectual abilities deteriorate.

Severely impaired patients often reside in nursing homes and hospitals. The most effective residential treatment programs combine the use of medication and behavioral interventions with an environment that is specifically designed to maximize the level of functioning and minimize the emotional distress of patients who are cognitively impaired. Several goals guide the design of such an environment (Gauthier et al., 2010). These include considerations that enhance the following aspects of the patient's life.

1. *Knowledge of the environment:* For example, rooms and hallways must be clearly labeled, because patients frequently cannot remember directions.

2. *Negotiability:* In the case of dementia, psychological accessibility is at least as important as physical accessibility. For example, spaces that the person would use (a commons area or the dining room) should be visible from the patient's room if they cannot be remembered.

3. *Safety and health:* For example, access to the setting must be secured so that patients who would otherwise wander away can remain as active as possible.

One important issue related to patient management involves the level of activity expected of the patient. It is useful to help the person remain active and interested in everyday events. Patients who are physically active are less likely to have problems with agitation, and they may sleep better. Engaging in a home-based exercise program can reduce functional dependence and delay institutionalization among patients with dementia (Rockwood & Middleton, 2007). Nevertheless, expectations regarding the patient's activity level may have to be reduced in proportion to

the progression of cognitive impairment. Efforts should be made to preserve familiar routines and surroundings in light of the inevitable difficulties that are associated with learning new information and recalling past events. Helping the person to cope with these issues may minimize the emotional turmoil associated with the increasing loss of cognitive abilities. ⊙ **Watch** the **Video** *Brain Damage in Alzheimer's Disease* on **MyPsychLab**

## Support for Caregivers

A final area of concern is the provision of support to people who serve as caregivers for demented patients. In the United States, spouses and other family members provide primary care for more than 80 percent of people who have dementia of the Alzheimer's type (Ballard, 2007). Their burdens are often overwhelming, both physically and emotionally.

In addition to the profound loneliness and sadness that caregivers endure, they must also learn to cope with more tangible stressors, such as the patient's incontinence, functional deficits, and disruptive behavior (Wolfs et al., 2012). Relationships among other family members and the psychological adjustment of the principal caregiver are more disturbed by caring for a demented person than by caring for someone who is physically disabled. Guilt, frustration, and depression are common reactions among the family members of patients (Kneebone & Martin, 2003).

Some treatment programs provide support groups, as well as informal counseling and ad hoc consultation services, for spouses caring for patients with Alzheimer's disease. These approaches attempt to improve the quality of life for the person with dementia while also helping the caregiver survive the spouse's illness and to postpone the need to place the patient in a nursing home. Results from several randomized controlled outcome studies indicate that these programs are able to improve the quality of life for both patients and their caregivers (Cooper et al., 2012).

## MyPsychLab VIDEO CASE

### Wife of Patient with Alzheimer's Disease

SARAH

*"You kind of have hope whenever you have cancer, (but with) Alzheimer's you die just a little each day . . ."*

⊙ **Watch** the **Video** *Sarah: Wife of Patient with Alzheimer's Disease* on **MyPsychLab**

What are the special challenges faced by family members and those who care for people suffering from Alzheimer's disease?

Many resources are available to help people cope with problems associated with neurocognitive disorders. One particularly useful book, *What You Need to Know About Alzheimer's,* by John Medina, describes the symptoms of the disorder and their progression. It also explains current knowledge of the ways in which brain cells are destroyed by this disease.

When a person learns that he or she has Alzheimer's disease or some other form of neurocognitive disorder, a number of important challenges must be faced. Family members must be informed so that they can help make plans for the future. Decisions must be made about eventual changes in living arrangements and work (if the person is still employed). Perhaps most important, the person must prepare to cope with changes in daily life, as things that were once easy—such as communicating with other people and getting around in the community—become more difficult. The Alzheimer's Association (www.alz.org) maintains a comprehensive Web page that includes advice on all of these topics.

Family members and friends who provide care for patients with major neurocognitive disorders face a very challenging situation. The Alzheimer's Association Web page provides information regarding strategies that can help caregivers prepare for these responsibilities. These include ways to adapt to inevitable changes in the caregivers' relationship with the patient, as well as advice about how to respond to challenging or unexpected behaviors on the part of the patient. The person with Alzheimer's disease will eventually become unable to perform daily tasks, and the caregiver will inevitably be faced with additional responsibility. As the burden mounts, he or she must locate additional sources of support and find ways to take care of his or her own health while also caring for the patient. Support groups and social services are often available locally.

# 14 Summary

Dementia and delirium are listed as neurocognitive disorders in *DSM-5*. Disruptions of memory and other cognitive functions are the most obvious symptoms of these disorders.

**Dementia** is defined as a gradually worsening loss of memory and related cognitive functions, including the use of language as well as reasoning and decision making. **Aphasia** and **apraxia** are among the most obvious problems in verbal communication. Perceptual difficulties, such as **agnosia**, are also common.

**Delirium** is a confusional state that develops over a short period of time and is often associated with agitation and hyperactivity.

**Neurocognitive disorder** (NCD) can be associated with many different kinds of neuropathology. The most common form of NCD is associated with **Alzheimer's disease,** which accounts for approximately half of all diagnosed cases of dementia. **Neurocognitive disorder with Lewy bodies** and vascular NCD each account for 15 to 20 percent of cases. Less common forms of dementia include frontotemporal NCD, as well as NCD associated with **Huntington's disease**, and Parkinson's disease.

A definitive diagnosis of Alzheimer's disease requires the observation of two specific types of brain lesions: **neurofibrillary tangles** and **amyloid plaques**, which are found throughout the cerebral cortex. Neurofibrillary tangles are also found in the hippocampus, an area of the brain that is crucial for memory.

The incidence and prevalence of neurocognitive disorders increase dramatically with age. The annual incidence of dementia is 1.4 percent in people over the age of 65 and 3.4 percent for people over the age of 75. Almost 40 percent of people over 90 years of age exhibit symptoms of moderate or severe dementia.

The causes of neurocognitive disorders include many different factors. Some types of dementia are produced by viral infections and dysfunction of the immune system. Environmental toxins also may contribute to the onset of cognitive impairment.

Considerable research efforts have been devoted to the identification of genes involved in Alzheimer's disease. Within some families, a gene for Alzheimer's disease is located on chromosome 21. Experts now assume that there are several forms of Alzheimer's disease, and each may be associated with a different gene or set of genes.

Delirium can often be resolved successfully by treating the medical condition. The intellectual deficits in primary forms of dementia are progressive and irreversible. Treatment goals in these disorders are more limited and focus on maintaining the person's level of functioning for as long as possible while minimizing the level of distress experienced by the patient and the family. Medication can produce modest cognitive benefits for some patients with neurocognitive disorders, but not all patients respond to such treatment, and the clinical significance of these changes is extremely limited.

Behavioral and environmental management are important aspects of any treatment program for patients with neurocognitive disorder patients. They allow patients to reside in the least restrictive and safest possible settings. Respite programs provide much-needed support to caregivers, usually spouses and other family.

## The Big Picture

# critical thinking review

**14.1** What is the difference between cognitive problems in anxiety and those seen in major neurocognitive disorders?
In anxiety disorders and depression, subtle cognitive factors might play a role in causing the disorder. In dementia, the cognitive problems are the defining features of the disorder . . . (see page 380).

**14.2** In what ways is delirium different from dementia?
The two conditions differ both in terms of their characteristic symptoms and the pattern that the symptoms follow over time . . . (see page 384).

**14.3** Is memory impairment the only indication that a person is developing a major neurocognitive disorder?
No, decline in executive functioning is also closely linked to subsequent development of Alzheimer's disease . . . (see page 390).

**14.4** Why is depression in an elderly person sometimes confused with dementia?
Depressed people can exhibit cognitive symptoms that resemble some aspects of dementia, including lack of interest, trouble concentrating, and poverty of speech . . .(see page 388).

**14.5** How could education help to reduce a person's risk for major neurocognitive disorder?
Higher levels of challenging cognitive activity may increase the density of synaptic connections in the person's cortex and make it less vulnerable to the impact of neuronal degeneration . . . (see page 399).

**14.6** What are the most difficult problems faced by people caring for a person with a major neurocognitive disorder?
Caregivers face prolonged emotional challenges, including loneliness, frustration, and guilt, as well as the overwhelming financial and physical demands of being responsible for a person who becomes increasingly unable to care for himself or herself . . . (see page 401).

# key terms

agnosia  385
Alzheimer's disease  390
amyloid plaque  390
anterograde amnesia  384
aphasia  384
apraxia  384

delirium  380
dementia  380
genetic linkage  395
Huntington's disease  393
major neurocognitive
    disorder  384

neurocognitive disorder with
    Lewy bodies  392
neurofibrillary tangles  390
neurologists  381
neuropsychological
    assessment  387

neuropsychologists  381
retrograde amnesia  384
vascular neurocognitive
    disorder  393

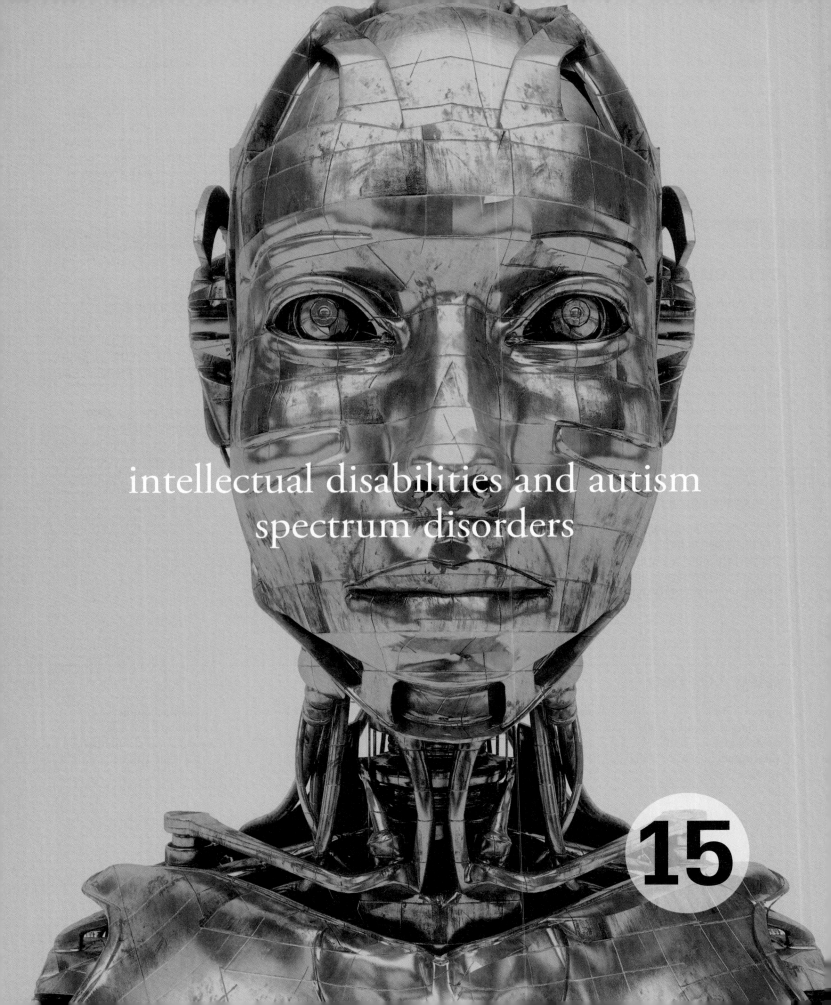

intellectual disabilities and autism
spectrum disorders

15

# The Big Picture

## learning objectives

**15.1**
How are IQ scores like "grading on the curve"?

**15.2**
Did the United States really support human breeding (eugenics)?

**15.3**
How can intellectual disabilities be prevented?

**15.4**
Is there an "epidemic of autism"?

**15.5**
Are children exceptionally intelligent underneath their autism?

**15.6**
What is wrong with psychological theories
of the cause of autism?

In many ways, intellectual disabilities and autism spectrum disorders are very different from one another. Intellectual disabilities (ID) impair academic aptitude. Autism spectrum disorders (ASD) disrupt relationships, behavior, and social communication. Yet the two disorders share key similarities. Both are either present at birth or begin early in life. Both typically lead to difficulties in a wide range of life functioning. And initially, at least, both disorders are a shock to parents who must learn to accept their child's developmental disability, embrace their child's positive qualities, and learn how best to raise a child who is undoubtedly different.

## Overview

**Autism** is perhaps a more familiar term than autism spectrum disorders. *DSM-5* uses ASD to refer to a range of conditions, including autism and **Asperger's disorder** (which you can think of for now as "high functioning autism"). These difficulties had been viewed as related but qualitatively different disorders. As the term "spectrum" indicates, *DSM-5* sees them as differing quantitatively, that is, by a matter of degree, not kind. Which perspective is more accurate? We will consider this question carefully.

Dustin Hoffman played a man with autism in the popular movie *Rain Man*, a largely accurate portrayal—and a reminder that children with autism grow up and often continue to have similar problems. Autism spectrum disorders are distinguished by dramatic, often severe, and unusual symptoms. Socially, the child lives in a world apart. At best, social awkwardness is pronounced; at worst, people are objects, terrifying objects. Severely disturbed children with ASD cannot communicate. Others speak oddly, preferring unusually focused topics of conversation (for example, how mechanical objects work), speaking with subtle oddities in tone and emphasis, or both. In addition, people with ASD are preoccupied with unusual repetitive behavior. In severe cases, they endlessly perform the same action, for example, flapping their hands for hours on end. Even the highest functioning people with ASD struggle to understand emotions and abstractions. And as we will see, there are more and more people with high functioning ASD, because professionals have defined the disorder more broadly in recent years.

In this chapter, we discuss intellectual disabilities before ASD for a simple and important reason: Contrary to some views, most people with ASD also have intellectual disabilities.

## Intellectual Disabilities

Too often, people with intellectual disabilities are defined in terms of what they cannot do. Today, the emphasis is on what the person with an intellectual disability *can* do. People with intellectual disabilities are people first. We emphasize this with the convention of putting the "person first" in our writing. We refer to the "person with an intellectual disability," not to the "intellectually disabled person."

A real-life triumph of ability over disability is Lauren Potter, who plays the character Becky Jackson on the television show, *Glee*. Potter's screen persona tries out for the cheerleading squad, and eventually wins a spot. Interestingly, Potter got her role on *Glee* shortly after failing to make her high school's real-life cheerleading squad. Potter, who also starred in the movie, *Mr. Blue Sky*, was appointed by President Obama to serve on an advisory committee for people with intellectual disabilities.

Academic struggles often are the focus of attention for intellectual disabilities. As the following case illustrates, the disorder also can challenge emotions and life roles.

### ⟶ Should This Mother Raise Her Children?

Karen Cross was a 41-year-old woman with three children when child protective services referred her and her husband, Mark, for a family evaluation. Two months earlier, the Crosses' 16-year-old daughter, Lucy, had called the police following a family fight. Lucy and her mother were arguing about Lucy's excessive use of the telephone. Mr. Cross entered the dispute, and he cuffed Lucy across her mouth in anger. Lucy was not seriously hurt, and the social workers who visited with the Cross family found no history of physical abuse. They were concerned about the adequacy of the Crosses' parenting, however, and the agency strongly recommended an evaluation for the family.

Lauren Potter, who has Down syndrome, is an actress who has appeared in the popular television program, *Glee*, and the film *Mr. Blue Sky*. Here she attends a briefing in Washington, DC, to highlight a report on bullying of children with special needs.

At the time of the referral, Mr. Cross was employed as a custodian at an elementary school where he had been working for 15 years. Testing indicated that he had an IQ of 88, and no serious psychopathology based on a diagnostic interview. Both Mr. Cross and his wife admitted that he had frequent, angry outbursts, but they both denied any history of violence toward the children or Mrs. Cross.

Mrs. Cross was a homemaker who cared for Lucy and a 12-year-old daughter, Sue. The Crosses' 19-year-old son was serving in the Army. Mrs. Cross had a tested IQ of 67. She reported attending special education classes throughout her schooling. She married at the age of 19 and lived a normal life with her husband and children, but their low income barely kept the family out of poverty. Although Mrs. Cross demonstrated many adaptive skills in caring for her family, her coping currently was impaired by a severe depression. Mrs. Cross's speech and body movements were slowed, and she reported feeling constantly tired. She felt unhappy and unable to cope with her children. She was not sure what had caused her troubles, but Mr. Cross traced her problems to her mother's death a year earlier.

Mrs. Cross cried when recalling the loss of her mother. She described her mother as her best friend. They had lived in the same trailer park, and mother and daughter spent most of their days together. Her mother supported Mrs. Cross in many ways, especially in raising the children. Now the children ignored their mother's directions, and Mr. Cross was of little help. Mrs. Cross felt that her husband was too harsh, and she often contradicted him when he tried to punish the girls.

A family interview confirmed the impressions offered by the parents. Lucy looked distracted and bored. Sue frequently looked toward and imitated her older sister. The girls paid more attention briefly when their father got angry, but this ended when Mr. and Mrs. Cross started arguing.

School records indicated that the girls had mostly C grades. Standardized test scores showed that the girls' academic abilities were in the normal range, but below average. Telephone calls to each of their homeroom teachers indicated that Sue was not much of a problem in school, but Lucy had lately become very disruptive.

Based on the data obtained from multiple sources, the psychologists made several recommendations. They suggested antidepressant medication for Mrs. Cross, a referral to the school counselor for Lucy, and family therapy to help the parents agree on a set of rules and enforce discipline with a clear system of rewards and punishments. Therapy also would be an opportunity to monitor Mr. Cross's anger and Mrs. Cross's depression. Finally, they made a referral to a community service agency that could offer Mrs. Cross some parenting support.

The case of Karen Cross raises several issues. A basic one is whether she suffers from an intellectual disability. Her IQ is below the typical cutoff of 70, but she functioned well in her family life with her mother's support. Because of her adaptive skills, many professionals would not consider her to have an intellectual disability. Others might argue that she does because she now needs additional supports as a result of her low IQ, depression, or both. Karen Cross's depression also is important to note. Emotional difficulties often are overlooked among people with intellectual disabilities.

Other issues concern her children. How can we support families like Karen's? When should children be removed from troubled family environments? You may have seen the movie *I Am Sam,* starring Sean Penn, which raised similar concerns. Penn played a loving father with an intellectual disability who fought to get his daughter back after social workers judged him to be an unfit parent. Like Karen Cross's real-life experience, *I Am Sam* portrayed the tensions between supporting parents with disabilities versus protecting children from seriously troubled families. We consider these difficult issues in this chapter (and in Chapter 18 on mental illness and the law), but first we more closely examine the definition of intellectual disability.

## Symptoms of Intellectual Disabilities

The *DSM-5* was influenced by definitions developed by the American Association on Intellectual and Developmental Disabilities (AAIDD), the leading organization for professionals concerned with intellectual and developmental disabilities. The AAIDD dropped the term *mental retardation in favor of intellectual disability* in 2006, and *DSM-5* adopted the same term. Both groups now also agree broadly on the three major criteria for defining **intellectual disability**: (1) deficits in intellectual functions, (2) deficits in adaptive functioning, and (3) onset before the age of 18 (see "DSM-5: Intellectual Disability").

**MEASURING INTELLIGENCE** Deficits in intellectual functions are operationally defined by scores on an individualized *intelligence test,* a standardized measure for assessing intellectual ability. Commonly used intelligence tests include the Wechsler Intelligence Scale for Children, Fourth Edition (WISC-IV), and the Wechsler Adult Intelligence Scale, Fourth Edition (WAIS-IV). Intelligence tests yield a score called the **intelligence quotient (IQ)**, the test's rating of an individual's intellectual ability. An IQ score of approximately 70 or below is the cutoff for an intellectual disability. The number is approximate because testing can be somewhat imprecise and because IQ is measured on a continuum. The difference between an IQ score of 69 and 71 is trivial.

Defining *intelligence* can be controversial, and definitions and measures of intellectual ability have changed over the years. Early intelligence tests derived an IQ by dividing the individual's "mental age" by his or her chronological age. Mental age was determined by comparing an individual's test results with the average obtained for various age groups. For example, someone who answered the same number of items correctly as the average

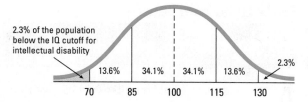

**FIGURE 15.1**

Contemporary IQ tests have a mean of 100 and a standard deviation of 15. The IQ cutoff for an intellectual disability (70) is two standard deviations below the mean.

10 year old would be given a mental age of 10. After mental age was divided by chronological age, the ratio was multiplied by 100 to yield an IQ score. According to this system, an eight-year-old with a mental age of 10 would have an IQ of 125, calculated as 10/8 × 100.

Contemporary intelligence tests instead calculate a *deviation IQ*. According to this system, intellectual ability follows the **normal distribution**, the familiar bell-shaped frequency distribution illustrated in Figure 15.1. The deviation IQ "grades on the curve." Most people score near the average in intelligence; a few people are exceptionally low or exceptionally high. An individual's IQ is determined based on comparisons with his or her age group. Narrow age ranges are used for children, because cognitive abilities and knowledge acquisition change rapidly with age. In contrast, all adults are treated as a part of the same age group.

Intelligence tests are scored to have a *mean* IQ score of 100 and a *standard deviation* of 15 (see Research Methods on p. 408). About two-thirds of the population has an IQ within one standard deviation of the mean—between 85 and 115. The cutoff score for intellectual disability is approximately two standard

---

### criteria for
### Intellectual Disability (Intellectual Developmental Disorder)

**DSM-5**

Intellectual disability (intellectual developmental disorder) is a disorder with onset during the developmental period that includes both intellectual and adaptive functioning deficits in conceptual, social, and practical domains. The following three criteria must be met:

**A.** Deficits in intellectual functions, such as reasoning, problem solving, planning, abstract thinking, judgment, academic learning, and learning from experience, confirmed by both clinical assessment and individualized, standardized intelligence testing.

**B.** Deficits in adaptive functioning that result in failure to meet developmental and sociocultural standards for personal independence and social responsibility. Without ongoing support, the adaptive deficits limit functioning in one or

more activities of daily life, such as communication, social participation, and independent living, across multiple environments, such as home, school, work, and community.

**C.** Onset of intellectual and adaptive deficits during the developmental period.

**Note:** The diagnostic term intellectual disability is the equivalent term for the ICD-11 diagnosis *of intellectual developmental disorders.* Although the term *intellectual disability* is used throughout this manual, both terms are used in the title to clarify relationships with other classification systems. Moreover, a federal statute in the United States (Public Law 111-256, Rosa's Law) replaces the term *mental retardation* with *intellectual disability,* and research journals use the term *intellectual disability.* Thus, *intellectual disability* is the term in common use by medical, educational, and other professions and by the lay public and advocacy groups.

## Central Tendency and Variability: What Do IQ Scores Mean?

We can explain IQ scores more fully by describing a few basic statistics. A *frequency distribution* simply is a way of arranging data according to the frequencies of different scores. For example, we might obtain the following frequency distribution of ages in a group of 10 college students:

| Age | Frequency |
|-----|-----------|
| 17 | 1 |
| 18 | 4 |
| 19 | 1 |
| 20 | 2 |
| 21 | 2 |

The **mean** is the arithmetic average of a distribution of scores, as defined by the formula

$$M = \frac{\text{sum of scores}}{N}$$

where *M* is the mean and *N* is the number of scores. Thus, the mean of the frequency distribution of ages listed above is

$$M = \frac{17 + 18 + 18 + 18 + 18 + 19 + 20 + 20 + 21 + 21}{10} = 19$$

The mean is the most commonly used of various *measures of central tendency,* which are single scores that summarize and describe a frequency distribution.

Other important and commonly used measures of central tendency are the median and the mode. The **median** is the midpoint of a frequency distribution—the score that half of all scores fall above and half of all scores fall below. In the above example, 19 is the median age. The **mode** is the most frequent score in a distribution. In our example, the mode is 18.

Measures of variability also provide useful summary information about a frequency distribution. The *range* is a simple measure that lists the lowest and highest scores. In our example, the range of ages is 17 to 21. As a more complex measure of variability, we may wish to compute the average distance of each individual score from the overall mean (21–19, 17–19, etc.). However, when we subtract each score in a frequency distribution from the mean of the distribution, the positive and negative numbers always add up to zero. (Try this in our example.) As a way of compensating for this inevitability, statisticians created a statistic called the **variance** in which the differences from the mean are squared (to eliminate negative numbers) before they are added together

and divided by their total number. The variance is defined by the following formula:

$$V = \frac{\text{sum of (scores} - M)^2}{N}$$

where *V* is the variance, *M* is the mean, and *N* is the number of scores. The variance in our example is 1.8. Calculate this statistic yourself to aid your understanding.

The variance is an extremely useful measure, but the variance is expressed as a different unit of measurement from the mean because the scores have been squared. This problem is easily solved by taking the square root of the variance, which results in a statistic called the **standard deviation** or the *standard deviation from the mean.* The standard deviation is defined by the formula:

$$SD = \sqrt{V}$$

where *SD* is the standard deviation and *V* is the variance. In our example, the standard deviation is 1.34, or the square root of 1.8 (the variance).

**Standard scores** are created by subtracting each score in a frequency distribution from the mean and dividing the difference by the standard deviation. Standard scores, or *z-scores,* as they are often called, are computed according to the following formula:

$$z = \frac{\text{score} - M}{SD}$$

where *z* is the standard score, *M* is the mean, and *SD* is the standard deviation. Because of the nature of the statistic, *z*-scores always have a mean of zero and a standard deviation of 1. This is a very useful feature of *z*-scores, because it allows us to readily compare or combine scores from different frequency distributions.

This brings us back to the deviation IQ, which is a standard score. IQ scores have a mean of 100 and a standard deviation of 15, simply because the *z*-scores are first multiplied by 15 and then a constant of 100 is added to the product. For example, a standard score of 1 translates into a deviation IQ score of 115 ([1 x 15] + 100) or a standard score of 22 translates into a deviation IQ score of 70 ([−2 x 15] + 100).

The mean and the standard deviation are central to understanding numerous psychological concepts in addition to the deviation IQ. For example, you should now be better able to understand the discussion of standard deviation units in meta-analysis (see Chapter 3). If you are confused, we recommend that you reread this discussion and calculate the statistics yourself.

deviations below the average. (The *DSM-5* says 65-75, because of typical measurement error in IQ testing.) About 2 percent of the population falls below this 70 cutoff (refer back to Figure 15.1).

One potential problem with the deviation IQ is that IQ scores are *rising* across generations, a phenomenon known as the *Flynn effect* (named for James Flynn, who first noted the trend). The Flynn effect can have substantial implications for people near the two standard deviation cutoff, because IQ averages are constantly updated. This means that, even if their intellectual abilities remain unchanged in an *absolute* sense, older people's IQ scores fall *relative* to the rising mean.[1] One calculation puts the drop at over 5 IQ points, a difference that could influence the identification of an intellectual disability for those close to the 70 cutoff (Kanaya, Scullin, & Ceci, 2003).

IQ tests are widely used, and they predict performance in school quite well. Measures of intelligence for very young children are unstable, but IQ scores of children 4 years old and older are good predictors of IQ scores many years later. For those with intellectual disabilities, IQ scores are stable even when accurately assessed among infants and toddlers (Baroff & Olley, 1999; Mash & Wolfe, 2005). An infant with a significantly subaverage IQ is likely to remain below the cutoff for an intellectual disability.

### CONTROVERSIES ABOUT INTELLIGENCE TESTS

Despite their value, IQ tests can be controversial. One key question is whether intelligence tests are "culture-fair." *Culture-fair tests* contain material that is equally familiar to people who differ in their ethnicity, native language, or immigrant status. Tests that are *culturally biased* contain language, examples, or other assumptions that favor one ethnic group over another.

In the United States, the average IQ scores of African Americans and of Latinos are lower than those of Caucasians and Asians. More members of these groups also are classified as having intellectual disabilities (Robinson, Zigler, & Gallagher, 2000). Some of these differences have been attributed to culture bias—some test items seem geared toward the language and the experience of majority groups. However, ethnic differences may have a simpler explanation. Lower IQ is associated with poverty, and a disproportionate number of blacks and Latinos in the United States are poor. Whatever the explanation, the disparity is shrinking (Mash & Wolfe, 2005).

The most basic concern about intelligence tests is: What is intelligence? Intelligence tests measure precisely what their original developer, Alfred Binet, intended them to measure: potential for school achievement. They correlate 0.4 to 0.7 with grades and other achievement measures (Baroff & Olley, 1999). However, performance in school is not the same as "intelligence." Common sense, social sensitivity, and "street smarts" are also part of what most of us would consider intelligence, and they are not measured by IQ tests.

### MEASURING ADAPTIVE SKILLS

Both the AAIDD and DSM recognize that intelligence is more than an IQ score, and require adaptive skill deficits for diagnosing intellectual disability. Like AAIDD (2010), *DSM-5* (2013) uses a practical definition of adaptive skills, that is, whether the individual needs support (see "DSM-5: Intellectual Disability"). Both systems also indicate that adaptive behavior includes conceptual, social, and practical skills. *Conceptual skills* focus largely on community self-sufficiency including communication, self-direction, and health and safety. *Social skills* focus on understanding how to behave in social situations. Finally, *practical skills* focus on the tasks of daily living like self-care, home living, and work.

Adaptive skills are difficult to quantify. How would *you* measure "social intelligence"? The Vineland Adaptive Behavior Scales are one commonly used instrument (see Table 15.1). As with IQ, adaptive skills are judged by age. Among preschoolers, they include the acquisition of motor abilities, language, and self-control. Key skills during the school-age years include developing social relationships with peers. In adult life, adaptive skills

---

**TABLE 15.1**
## Sample Items from the Vineland Adaptive Behavior Scales

**Daily Living Skills**

| | |
|---|---|
| Age 1: | Drinks from a cup. |
| Age 5: | Bathes or showers without assistance. |
| Age 10: | Uses a stove for cooking. |
| Age 15: | Looks after own health. |

**Socialization**

| | |
|---|---|
| Age 1: | Imitates simple adult movements like clapping. |
| Age 5: | Has a group of friends. |
| Age 10: | Watches television about particular interests. |
| Age 15: | Responds to hints or indirect cues in conversation. |

*Source:* Reprinted with permission of NCS Pearson, Inc.

include the ability to manage oneself, live independently, and assume adult interpersonal roles.

Some experts argue that intellectual disability should be defined solely based on intelligence tests, because measures of adaptive skills are imprecise (Detterman & Gabriel, 2007). Moreover, intellectual limitations imply that adaptive skills are likely to be limited (Zigler & Hodapp, 1986). Since 1959, however, deficits in adaptive behavior have been an essential part of the AAIDD's definition (Heber, 1959).

Deficits in adaptive behavior are less stable than IQ, especially as life demands change from school to the more diverse world of work. Thus, an intellectual disability can be "cured" in the sense that adaptive skills can be taught or environmental demands can be shaped to match an individual's unique abilities and experiences.

**ONSET BEFORE AGE 18 YEARS** The third criterion for defining intellectual disability is onset during the developmental period, typically, before 18 years of age. This excludes people whose deficits in intellect and adaptive skills begin later in life as a result of brain injury or disease. Besides differences in cause, the most important aspect of the age criterion is the experience of normal development. People with intellectual disabilities have not lost skills they once had mastered, nor have they experienced a notable change in their condition. Unfortunately, this means that their disability may be perceived as "who they are" and not as something that has "happened to them." This is why we put the "person first" in writing about intellectual disabilities, as a small but constant reminder of the person behind the disorder.

## Diagnosis of Intellectual Disabilities

Many people with mild intellectual disabilities might not have been viewed as disabled in the past. Academic aptitude was less necessary to life in earlier, agrarian societies than in our modern,

This girl with Down syndrome shows that children with intellectual disabilities can join in many normal childhood activities.

technological world. Even today, intellectual disability is defined differently in more industrialized countries than in less industrialized ones because of differing educational and technological requirements for work (Scheerenberger, 1982).

**EARLY EFFORTS** The beginnings of contemporary classifications of intellectual disabilities date to the second half of the nineteenth century. In 1866, the British physician Langdon Down first described a group of children with intellectual disabilities who had a characteristic appearance. Their faces reminded Down of the appearance of Mongolians, who he viewed as inferior, and he used the term *mongolism* to describe them. Despite this offensive terminology, Down's classification turned out to be a valid one. Scientists eventually discovered a specific cause of what we now know as Down syndrome.

The creation of IQ tests helped to improve the classification of intellectual disabilities. The French psychologists Alfred Binet (1856–1911) and Theophile Simon (1873–1961) developed the first successful intelligence test in 1905 in response to a French government effort to identify children in need of special educational services. The Binet scale was refined by the American psychologist Lewis Terman of Stanford University, and these efforts resulted in the Stanford–Binet intelligence tests. The first Wechsler intelligence test was developed by David Wechsler in 1939. Revisions of Wechsler's individualized intelligence tests continue to dominate contemporary intellectual assessment.

There has always been some controversy about what IQ score cutoff should define intellectual disability. Debates reached a climax in 1959. In an attempt to help more people in need of services, the AAIDD shifted the IQ cutoff from two standard deviations below the mean to one standard deviation below the mean. An IQ score of 85 or lower qualified for the diagnosis—almost 15 percent of the population. This well-intentioned change included far too many well-functioning individuals and distracted attention from those most in need of help. Thus, in 1973, the AAIDD returned to the cutoff of 70 (Grossman, 1983).

**CONTEMPORARY DIAGNOSIS** Today, intellectual disabilities can be subdivided according to two different systems, one based on severity and the other on known or presumed etiology. Both approaches are reliable, and each is valid for different purposes. In fact, the two systems illustrate a point we have made repeatedly: Different classification systems may be useful for different purposes.

Intellectual disability traditionally has been divided into four levels based on IQ scores: mild, moderate, severe, and profound. However, AAIDD (2002, 2010) abandoned this approach in favor of individualized assessment. It rates "intensity of needed support" across many different areas of functioning, an effort criticized by some as cumbersome and unreliable. The *DSM-5* compromised. The manual retained the four levels, but defined them generally in terms of conceptual, social, and practical functioning, not by IQ scores. We appreciate individualization and agree that IQ is not everything. Yet, the traditional system is straightforward, reliable,

## TABLE 15.2
## Traditional Levels of Intellectual Disability

| Level | Approximate IQ Range | Adult Mental Age | Typical Adult Support/ Living Circumstances | Percent of Intellectual Disability |
|---|---|---|---|---|
| Mild | 50–55 to 70 | 9 to 12 year old | Some, none/community | 85 |
| Moderate | 35–40 to 50–55 | 6 to 9 year old | Close/community, group | 10 |
| Severe | 20–25 to 35–40 | 3 to 6 year old | Special/family, group | 3–4 |
| Profound | Below 20–25 | 3 year old or younger | Constant/family, group, institution | 1–2 |

and supported by considerable research (Detterman & Gabriel, 2007). We offer a brief summary in Table 15.2.

**LIFE AND DEATH** We appreciate *DSM-5*'s effort to de-emphasize specific IQ scores, which can literally be a life or death issue. Why? In 2002, the United States Supreme Court ruled that the death penalty is "cruel and unusual punishment" for people with intellectual disabilities. In close cases throughout the country, lawyers are now arguing about what IQ defines intellectual disability (Greenspan & Switzy, 2007). The difference between an IQ of 69 and 71 is trivial—except in the courtroom. As we discuss in Chapter 18, because of the magical 70 cutoff, a couple of IQ points can mean the difference between life and death.

### Frequency of Intellectual Disabilities

Theoretically, IQ is distributed according to the normal curve, so 2.3 percent of the population should have IQs of 70 or below. In reality, however, more than 2.3 percent of people have IQs below 70. Very low IQ scores, in particular, are found more often than expected, a result of the various biological conditions that produce intellectual disabilities (Volkmar & Dykens, 2002). We, therefore, can think of there being two IQ distributions. One is the normal distribution of IQ scores. The other is the distribution of IQs of people with biological disorders that can cause intellectual disabilities (Zigler, 1967; see Figure 15.2).

Even though *more* than 2.3 percent of people have IQs below 70, the best estimate is that only 1 percent of the population has an intellectual disability (Volkmar & Dykens, 2002). The prevalence of intellectual disability is lower than the prevalence of IQs below 70 because (1) IQs cannot be adequately assessed among very young children, who, therefore, may be omitted from prevalence figures; (2) many people with low IQs have good adaptive skills; and (3) life expectancy is shorter for certain causes of many intellectual disability. As an indication of these first two facts, twice as many school-age children as preschoolers have intellectual disabilities, but prevalence rates drop again among adults (Grossman, 1983).

Intellectual disabilities in the United States are more common among the poor and, as a result, among certain ethnic groups.

However, the increased prevalence is not found for all subtypes of intellectual disability. An intellectual disability with a specific, known organic cause (for example, Down syndrome) generally has an equal prevalence among all social classes, whereas an intellectual disability of nonspecific cause is more common among families living in poverty (Patton, Beirne-Smith, & Payne, 1990).

### Causes of Intellectual Disabilities

The causes of intellectual disabilities can be grouped into two broad categories: Cases caused by known biological abnormalities and cases resulting from normal variations in IQ (see Figure 15.2). We review known biological causes before considering cases at the tail of the normal IQ distribution.

**BIOLOGICAL FACTORS** About one-half of all cases of intellectual disability are caused by known biological abnormalities (Volkmar & Dykens, 2002). Known biological causes often lead to intellectual disabilities of moderate to profound severity and are associated with physical handicaps. Of the over 250 known biological causes (AAIDD, 2010), we focus only on a few major ones here.

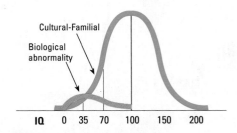

### FIGURE 15.2

**The Two-Curve Model of Intellectual Disabilities** The causes of intellectual disabilities can be grouped into two categories. Cultural-familial intellectual disability includes people with no known disorder. The low IQ of this group is attributable to genetic and environmental variation following the normal curve. The second category includes all known biological causes of intellectual disability. The IQ of this group also follows the normal distribution, but the mean is much lower.
*Source:* Adapted from Familial Mental Retardation: A Continuing Dilemma from Science 155. Reprinted with permission from AAAS.

**CHROMOSOMAL DISORDERS** The most common known biological cause of intellectual disability is the chromosomal disorder **Down syndrome**. People with Down syndrome have a distinctive physical appearance. They have slanting eyes with an extra fold of skin in the inner corner, a small head and short stature, a protruding tongue, and a variety of organ, muscle, and skeletal abnormalities. They also have physical handicaps and limited speech (Thapar et al., 1994).

The cause of Down syndrome is an extra chromosome, resulting from the failure of chromosomes to separate during cell division, a *nondisjunction*. Children with Down syndrome have 47 chromosomes instead of the normal 46. The extra chromosome is attached to the 21st pair; thus the disorder often is referred to as *trisomy 21*.

The incidence of Down syndrome is related to maternal age. For women under the age of 30, about 1 in 1,000 births are Down syndrome infants. The incidence rises to 1 in 750 births for mothers between ages 30 and 34, 1 in 300 between 35 and 39, and over 1 in 100 after age 40. Down syndrome can be detected by testing during pregnancy.

In general, children and adults with Down syndrome function within the moderate to severe range of intellectual disability. They exhibit substantial variation in their intellectual level, however, and research suggests that intensive intervention can lead to higher achievement and greater independence. Institutionalization once was commonly recommended, but home or community care is now the rule. In fact, many experts report that people with Down syndrome are especially sociable, although research on distinctive personality traits is not conclusive (Cicchetti & Beegly, 1990).

By their thirties, the majority of adults with Down syndrome develop brain pathology similar to that found in Alzheimer's disease. About one-third also exhibit the symptoms of dementia (Thase, 1988). Death in mid-adult life is common, although some adults with Down syndrome live into their fifties and sixties.

Several other chromosomal abnormalities have been linked to intellectual disabilities, particularly in the sex chromosomes. *Klinefelter syndrome*, found in about 1 in 1,000 live male births, is characterized by the presence of one or more extra X chromosomes. The most common configuration is XXY. With Klinefelter syndrome, IQ functioning typically is in the low normal to mild range of intellectual disability. Another chromosomal abnormality, *XYY syndrome*, once was thought to increase criminality but is now recognized to be linked with only minor social deviance and a mean IQ about 10 points lower than average. The syndrome occurs in 1 to 2 out of 2,000 male births. *Turner syndrome*, the XO configuration in females, is characterized by a missing X chromosome. Girls with Turner syndrome are small, fail to develop sexually, and generally have intelligence near or within the normal range. The disorder occurs in about 1 in every 2,200 live female births (Thapar et al., 1994).

**GENETIC DISORDERS** Few cases of intellectual disability result from dominant genetic inheritance, because such a mutation is unlikely to remain in the gene pool. One exception is **fragile-X**

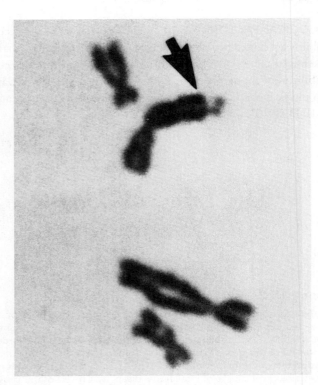

Left: Fragile-X syndrome is now known to be transmitted genetically. Originally, it was identified by a gap or break in the long arm of the X chromosome, as pictured. Right: This adolescent boy suffers from fragile-X syndrome. His elongated face prominent forehead, and large ears are typical characteristics of the disorder.

**syndrome**, the most common known *genetic* cause of intellectual disability (Taylor, Richards, & Brady, 2005). Fragile-X syndrome originally was diagnosed by a weakening or break on one arm of the X sex chromosome (see accompanying photo). The disorder is now known to be transmitted genetically by the FMR1 gene (Fragile-X Mental Retardation), which was discovered in 1991.

Not all children who inherit the FMR1 gene have intellectual disabilities. About 1 in 4,000 male births have the fragile-X mutation, as do about 1 in 6,000 female births. Most boys, but only about one-third of girls with the FMR1 gene, have intellectual disabilities. (Girls have two X chromosomes, one of which may function normally.) About 1 in 800 men and about 1 in 250 women are carriers of the FMR1 gene. Male carriers never pass the gene to their sons but always affect their daughters. Female carriers with only one affected chromosome have a 50/50 chance of passing the disorder on to their sons or daughters.

Among FMR1 carriers with normal intelligence, learning disabilities are common. Most of those with intellectual disabilities have a characteristic facial appearance that includes an elongated face, high forehead, large jaw, and large, underdeveloped ears (Bregman et al., 1987). Children with fragile-X tend to be socially anxious, avoid eye contact, and have stereotypic hand movements. Approximately 15 percent display the symptoms of autism (Rogers, Wehner, & Hagerman, 2001).

Several recessive gene pairings can cause intellectual disabilities. **Phenylketonuria (PKU)** is one of these. Geneticists estimate that about 1 in every 54 normal people carries a recessive gene for PKU, but the two genes are paired only in 1 of every 15,000 live births (NIH, 2000).

PKU is caused by abnormally high levels of the amino acid *phenylalanine*, usually due to the inherited absence of or an extreme deficiency in *phenylalanine hydroxylase*, an enzyme that metabolizes phenylalanine. Children with PKU have normal intelligence at birth. However, as they eat foods containing phenylalanine, the amino acid builds up in their system. This *phenylketonuria* produces brain damage that eventually results in an intellectual disability. Intellectual disability typically progresses to the severe to profound range.

Fortunately, PKU can be detected by blood testing in the first several days after birth. (All states have laws that require routine screening of newborns for PKU.) Early detection is very important, because intellectual and behavioral impairments are diminished dramatically if the child maintains a diet low in phenylalanine. In such cases, the child is likely to have normal to mildly impaired intelligence. In order to maximize the benefits of the diet, the child should be maintained on it for as long as possible—to age 20 and preferably throughout life (Widaman, 2009). It also is very important for adult women with PKU to regulate their diet shortly before and during pregnancy in order to avoid damage to the fetus. Otherwise, high levels of phenylalanine in the mother's bloodstream can damage the developing brain of the fetus and cause intellectual disability (Widaman, 2009). Maintaining a diet low in phenylalanine is very difficult

because phenylalanine is found in most foods and many food additives. Take a look at the labels of some of the foods you have at home (such as diet sodas). You will notice a warning about phenylalanine on many of the labels.

Other relatively rare recessive-gene disorders can also cause intellectual disabilities. *Tay-Sachs disease* is a particularly severe disorder that eventually results in death during the infant or preschool years. The recessive gene that causes Tay-Sachs is particularly common among Jews of Eastern European heritage. *Hurler syndrome,* or *gargoylism,* results in gross physical abnormalities, including dwarfism, humpback, bulging head, and clawlike hands. Children with this disorder usually do not live past the age of 10. *Lesch-Nyhan syndrome* is most notable for the self-mutilation that accompanies the intellectual disability. Children with this disorder bite their lips and fingers, often causing tissue loss. As with Down syndrome and fragile-X syndrome, many of these genetic abnormalities can be detected during pregnancy.

***INFECTIOUS DISEASES*** Intellectual disabilities can also be caused by various infectious diseases. Damaging infections may be contracted during pregnancy, at birth, or in infancy to early childhood. Among the diseases passed from mother to fetus during pregnancy are cytomegalovirus, the most common fetal infection (and one that is usually harmless), and toxoplasmosis, a protozoan infection contracted from ingestion of infected raw meats or from contact with infected cat feces. Toxoplasmosis is rare, which makes routine screening impractical.

*Rubella* (German measles) is a viral infection that may produce a few symptoms in the mother but can cause severe intellectual disability and even death in the developing fetus, especially if it is contracted in the first three months of pregnancy. Fortunately, rubella can be prevented by vaccination of prospective mothers before pregnancy, which is now a part of routine health care.

The *human immunodeficiency virus (HIV)* can be transmitted from an infected mother to a developing fetus. Fortunately, only about one-third of children who contract HIV prenatally develop *acquired immune deficiency syndrome (AIDS)*, but those who do develop AIDS rapidly. The effects on the child are profound, including intellectual disability, visual and language impairments, and eventual death (Baroff & Olley, 1999).

*Syphilis* is a bacterial disease that is transmitted through sexual contact. Infected mothers can pass the disease to the fetus. If untreated, syphilis produces a number of physical and sensory handicaps in the fetus, including intellectual disability. The adverse consequences are avoided by testing the mother and administering antibiotics when an infection has been detected. Because penicillin crosses the placental barrier, treating the mother will also cure the disease in the fetus.

Another sexually transmitted disease, *genital herpes*, can be transmitted to an infant particularly during birth. Herpes is a viral infection that produces small lesions on the genitals immediately following the initial infection and intermittently thereafter. The disease is most likely to be transmitted when the lesions are present. If a pregnant woman has an outbreak of genital lesions at the time of delivery, a cesarean section can be performed. If there is no outbreak, the risk of infecting the infant is exceedingly small and a vaginal delivery is recommended. Infected infants can develop very serious problems, including intellectual disability, blindness, and possible death.

Two infectious diseases that occur after birth, primarily during infancy, can cause intellectual disabilities. *Encephalitis* is an infection of the brain that produces inflammation and permanent damage in about 20 percent of all cases. *Meningitis* is an infection of the *meninges*, the three membranes that line the brain. The inflammation creates intracranial pressure that can irreversibly damage brain tissues. Encephalitis and meningitis can be caused by a variety of infectious diseases. Cases resulting from bacterial infections can usually be treated successfully with antibiotics. In other cases, the outcome of both encephalitis and meningitis is unpredictable. Neuromuscular problems, sensory impairments, and intellectual disabilities are possible.

**TOXINS** Like infectious diseases, toxic chemicals can produce intellectual disabilities when exposure occurs either before or after birth, but exposure during pregnancy creates the greatest risk. Because of its frequent use, alcohol presents the greatest threat. About 1 to 2 of every 1,000 births is a baby with **fetal alcohol syndrome (FAS)**. This disorder is characterized by retarded physical development, a small head, narrow eyes, cardiac defects, and cognitive impairment. Intellectual functioning ranges from mild intellectual disability to normal intelligence accompanied by learning disabilities, particularly difficulties in mathematics (Rasmussen & Bisanz, 2009).

Women who drink heavily during pregnancy (an average of 5 ounces of alcohol per day) are twice as likely to have a child with the syndrome as are women who average 1 ounce of alcohol per day or less (Baroff & Olley, 1999). Controversy continues about the risk for difficulties associated with drinking in the intermediate range. The Surgeon General of the United States recommends that pregnant women abstain from alcohol altogether.

This father adopted three children with fetal alcohol syndrome.

Environmental toxins also present a potential hazard to intellectual development after birth. Mercury poisoning is known to produce severe physical, emotional, and intellectual impairments, but it does not present a major public health problem because few children are exposed to mercury. The mercury compound, thimerosal, formerly was used as a vaccine preservative, and as discussed in Chapter 2, it is not linked to autism despite some hysterical claims that it does. Current concerns about mercury exposure focus on game fish like tuna and swordfish, which contain elevated mercury levels (Hubbs-Tait et al., 2005).

Much more threatening to public health is *lead poisoning*. Until banned by federal legislation, the lead commonly used in paint and produced by automobile emissions exposed hundreds of thousands of children to a potentially serious risk. Although controversy continues about the effects of exposure to low levels of lead, at toxic levels lead poisoning can produce a number of adverse behavioral and cognitive impairments, including intellectual disabilities. Despite federal bans on lead-based paints and leaded gasoline, which greatly reduced children's exposure, lead poisoning continues to pose a risk to children who may eat lead-based paint chips while being reared in dilapidated housing (Hubbs-Tait et al., 2005).

**OTHER BIOLOGICAL ABNORMALITIES** Pregnancy and birth complications also can cause intellectual disabilities. One major complication is Rh incompatibility. The Rh factor is a protein found on the surface of red blood cells, and it is a dominant hereditary trait. People who possess this protein are Rh-positive; people who don't are Rh-negative. Rh incompatibility can occur when the mother is Rh-negative and the father is Rh-positive. In such cases, the mother can develop antibodies that attack the blood cells of her Rh-positive fetus. The antibodies destroy oxygen-carrying red blood cells in the developing fetus, with a number of adverse consequences, including a possible intellectual disability.

Rh-negative women develop antibodies only after exposure to their infant's Rh-positive blood. If this exposure occurs at all, it usually does not happen until delivery. Thus, the risk of Rh incompatibility in first births is minimal; the greatest risk is for subsequent pregnancies. This risk can be largely prevented, however, by the administration of the antibiotic $Rh_o(D)$ Immune Globulin (RhoGAM) to the mother within 72 hours after the birth of the first child. RhoGAM prevents the mother's body from developing internal antibodies against the Rh-positive factors, thus eliminating most of the risk to the fetus during the next pregnancy. In the event that an Rh-negative mother develops antibodies against Rh-positive factors during pregnancy, a fetal blood transfusion must be carried out to replace the destroyed red blood cells.

Another pregnancy and birth complication that can cause intellectual deficits is *premature birth*. Premature birth is defined either as birth before 38 weeks of gestation or a birth weight of less than 5 pounds. There are many potential causes of prematurity: poor maternal nutrition, maternal age of less than 18 years or more than 35 years, maternal hypertension or diabetes, and damage to the placenta. The effects of prematurity on the infant

**TABLE 15.3**

## Correlations Between the IQ Scores of Pairs of Relatives Reared Together or Apart

| Type of Relative | Reared Together | | Reared Apart | |
|---|---|---|---|---|
| | Correlation | (N) | Correlation | (N) |
| Monozygotic twins | .86 | (4,672) | .72 | (65) |
| Dizygotic twins | .60 | (5,546) | – | |
| Biological siblings | .47 | (26,473) | .24 | (203) |
| Adoptive siblings | .34 | (369) | – | |
| Parent–child | .42 | (8,633) | .22 | (814) |
| Adoptive parent–child | .19 | (1,397) | – | |

*Source:* Figure 3 (adapted) from "Familial Studies of Intelligence: A Review" by T. J. Bouchard, Jr. and M. McGue, *Science*, 212 (1981), pp. 1055–1059. Copyright © 1981 by the American Association for the Advancement of Science. Reprinted by permission of the publisher.

vary, ranging from few or no deficits to sensory impairments, poor physical development, and intellectual disability. More serious consequences occur at lower birth weights, and infant mortality is common at very low weights.

Other pregnancy and birth complications that can cause intellectual disabilities include extreme difficulties in delivery, particularly *anoxia*, or oxygen deprivation; severe *malnutrition* (which is rare in the United States but a major problem in less developed countries); and the seizure disorder *epilepsy*. The intellectual difficulties associated with each of these causes vary but are potentially significant.

***Normal Genetic Variation*** Cases of intellectual disabilities of unknown etiology—often referred to as **cultural-familial retardation**—are generally assumed to be variations in the normal distribution IQ (see Figure 15.1 on p. 407). Cultural-familial retardation runs in families and is linked with poverty. A controversial issue is whether this typically mild form of intellectual disability is caused primarily by genes or by psychosocial disadvantage.

Normal genetic variation clearly contributes to individual differences in intelligence (Thapar et al., 1994). As summarized in Table 15.3, numerous family, twin, and adoption studies point to a substantial genetic contribution to intelligence. For example, the

IQs of adopted children are more highly correlated with the IQs of their biological parents than with those of their adoptive ones.

How much of intelligence is inherited? Behavior geneticists calculate an index to measure the extent of genetic contribution to a characteristic, called the *heritability ratio*. Estimates generally indicate that up to 75 percent of the normal range of intelligence is attributable to genetics, but no research specifically identifies the extent of genetic contributions to cultural-familial retardation (Thapar et al., 1994). Moreover, heritability ratios can be misleading, because genes and the environment work together, not separately (Dickens & Flynn, 2001; see Research Methods in Chapter 17).

The concept of *reaction range* better conveys how genes and environment interact to determine IQ (Gottesman, 1963). The reaction range concept proposes that heredity determines the upper and lower limits of IQ, and experience determines the extent to which people fulfill their genetic potential. Figure 15.3 portrays some theoretical reaction ranges for children with Down syndrome, cultural-familial retardation, normal intelligence, and superior intelligence.

**PSYCHOLOGICAL FACTORS** The genetic contributions to intelligence do *not* mean that environment matters little or not at

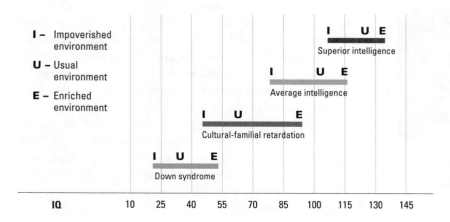

**I –** Impoverished environment

**U –** Usual environment

**E –** Enriched environment

Superior intelligence

Average intelligence

Cultural-familial retardation

Down syndrome

IQ    10  25  40  55  70  85  100  115  130  145

**FIGURE 15.3**

According to the reaction range concept, genes set the limit on IQ and environment determines variation within the limits. Note that the usual environmental contributions to IQ differ for the four groups.

*Source:* Reprinted with permission from Mental Retardation: Nature, Cause and Management by G.S. Barloff (1986). Routledge.

all. Environment does matter. In particular, grossly abnormal environments can produce gross abnormalities in intelligence.

An example is Koluchova's (1972) case study of the effects of the abuse and deprivation experienced by two identical twin boys. Until they were discovered at the age of six, the twins were confined to a closet in almost total isolation. They were beaten regularly throughout their early life. When discovered, the twins could barely walk, had extremely limited speech, and showed no understanding of abstractions, like photographs. Several years of therapy raised their measured intelligence from moderate intellectual disability when first discovered to the normal range by the age of 11.

Fortunately, cases of such torturous abuse are rare. They illustrate the theoretical contribution of experience to intelligence more than the actual contribution. Most children growing up in the United States live in pretty decent environments, if far from perfect ones. As a social ideal, Americans hope to provide all citizens with an equally advantaged environment. In working toward this laudable goal, we can overlook the fact that the influence of genes *increases* as environmental variation *decreases*. In fact, *all* individual differences in IQ would be caused by genes if everyone had exactly the same environmental advantages. Ironically, as we succeed in creating a more nurturing and stimulating world for every child, we run the risk of concluding that "environment doesn't matter." We need to remember our successes—and how truly wretched environments can devastate children's development (see Eugenics: Our History of Shame).

**SOCIAL FACTORS** The range of environments in the United States today still includes many undesirable circumstances for children. Millions of children are reared in psychosocial disadvantage in cities and in the equally unstimulating environments found among the rural poor. In fact, children are the most

impoverished age group in the United States (America's Children, 1999).

Cultural-familial retardation is far more frequent among the poor. Part of this is explained by the fact that lower intelligence causes lower social status. People with a below-average IQ generally make less money. However, poverty and psychosocial disadvantage also lower IQ scores.

Impoverished environments lack the *stimulation* and *responsiveness* that promote children's intellectual development (Floyd, Costigan, & Phillippe, 1997). A stimulating environment challenges children's developing intellectual skills. A responsive environment offers encouragement for their pursuits. Unfortunately, mothers with borderline IQ are less sensitive and positive than other mothers (Fenning et al., 2007).

Studies of adopted children demonstrate the positive effects of stimulating and responsive environments (Turkheimer, 1991). Skodak and Skeels (1949) first demonstrated that children who were adopted away from unfortunate circumstances early in life achieved IQ scores at least 12 points higher than those of their biological mothers. More recent studies find similarly dramatic increases (Capron & Duyme, 1989; Schiff et al., 1982). Many children with cultural-familial retardation could function normally if stimulating and responsive environments helped them to function near the upper end of their potential.

## Treatment: Prevention and Normalization

Three major categories of intervention are essential in the treatment of intellectual disabilities. First, many cases can be prevented through adequate maternal and child health care, as well as early psychoeducational programs. Second, educational, psychological, and biomedical treatments can help people with intellectual disabilities to raise their achievement levels. Third, the lives of people with intellectual disabilities can be normalized through mainstreaming in public schools and promoting care in the community.

**PRIMARY PREVENTION** Good maternal and child health care is one major step toward the primary prevention of intellectual disability. Health care measures include specific actions, such as vaccinations for rubella or the detection and treatment of infectious diseases like syphilis. In addition, an adequate diet and abstinence from alcohol, cigarettes, and other drugs are essential to the health of pregnant women and the welfare of the developing fetus.

Planning for childbearing can also help to prevent intellectual disability. Pregnancy and birth complications are notably more common among mothers younger than 18 and older than 35. Although most babies born to women outside this age range are healthy and normal, many women are aware of the statistical risks and attempt to time their pregnancies accordingly. Children of teenage mothers also are much more likely to face a life of poverty—a pressing issue, given that close to 10 percent of all children in the United States are born to adolescent mothers (America's Children, 1999).

Raymond Hudlow was involuntarily sterilized at the Virginia Colony for Epileptics and Feebleminded in 1942. He was released in 1943 and drafted into the army shortly afterward. Fighting for his country in World War II, Hudlow won the Bronze Star for valor, the Purple Heart, and the Prisoner of War Medal.

## Eugenics: Our History of Shame

**E**ugenics is a movement dedicated to the "genetic improvement" of the human stock. British aristocrat Francis Galton coined the term in 1883 while advocating for "good breeding" among humans. Galton promoted "positive eugenics" by encouraging the elite to intermarry and bear many children. Others took up the mission of "negative eugenics" by putting up barriers to childbearing, as well as undertaking more gruesome efforts to eliminate "undesirables" from the human gene pool (Lombardo, 2001).

You surely are aware that Adolf Hitler embraced eugenic principles while committing genocide in Nazi Germany. You may *not* know that the principles of eugenics were embraced widely in the United States prior to World War II. Eugenic policies in the United States included laws limiting immigration from southern and eastern Europe, prohibiting interracial marriage, and permitting the forced sterilization of so-called defectives: the insane, the diseased, the deformed, the blind, the delinquent, the alcoholic, and primarily the "feebleminded" (Lombardo, 2001). About 60,000 people in the United States were sterilized involuntarily beginning in the 1920s. Most had intellectual disabilities. Despite the decline in the eugenics movement after World War II, forced sterilization continued in some states until the late 1970s (*Los Angeles Times*, May 13, 2002).

The Commonwealth of Virginia was a dubious "leader" in the eugenics movement, second only to California in the number of sterilizations performed. Shockingly, in 1927 the U.S. Supreme Court upheld Virginia's forced sterilization law in the infamous case of *Buck* v. *Bell*. Carrie Buck was a young woman from Charlottesville, Virginia, who had been institutionalized in the Virginia Colony for Epileptics and Feebleminded. To justify her planned sterilization, Buck was portrayed as "morally delinquent" and "feebleminded," although it is doubtful that she was either (Lombardo, 2001). Expert witnesses relied on family pedigrees, family trees indicating intellectual and personality defects across generations, to "prove" that Buck's problems were hereditary (see Figure 15.4).

The U.S. Supreme Court upheld the Virginia law by a vote of eight to one. Buck was sterilized. In a stunning statement, Supreme Court Justice Oliver Wendell Holmes wrote: "It is better for all the world, if instead of waiting to execute degenerate offspring for crime, or to let them starve for their imbecility, society can prevent those who are manifestly unfit from continuing their kind. . . . Three generations of imbeciles are enough" (*Buck* v. *Bell*, 274 U.S. 200, 1927). Seventy-five years later, on May 2, 2002, the governor of Virginia apologized for the state's role in embracing eugenics and sterilizing some 8,000 people from 1927 through 1979 (*Washington Post*, May 3, 2002).

The philosopher George Santayana said, "Those who cannot remember the past are condemned to repeat it." We believe that we must acknowledge and learn from our shameful history of eugenics. We also believe that society can benefit from research on the many genetic contributions to behavior if that evidence is debated vigorously, considered cautiously, and used wisely. Finally, we strongly believe that it is essential to respect the humanity—and the human rights—of people with intellectual disabilities.

**Most Immediate Blood-kin of Carrie Buck.
Showing illegitimacy and hereditary feeblemindedness.**

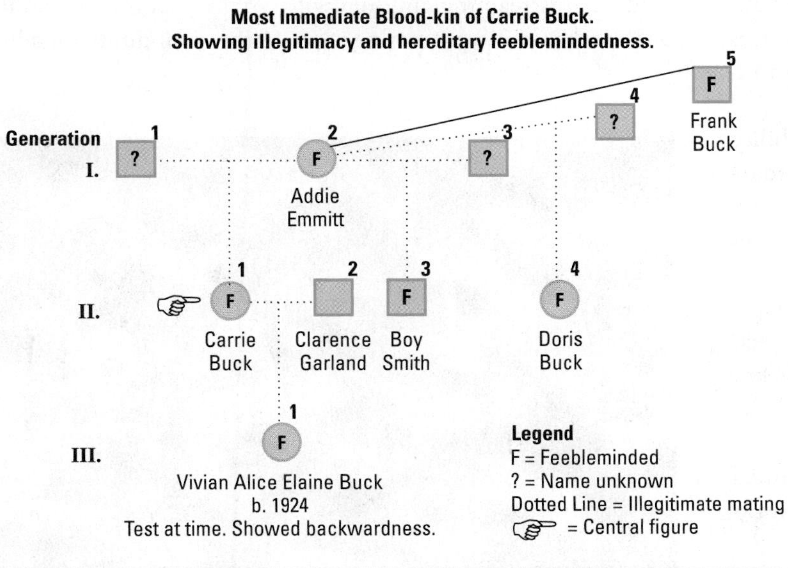

**FIGURE 15.4**

The actual family history used in the U.S. Supreme Court Trial, *Buck* v. *Bell*, which, in 1927, upheld Virginia's mandatory sterilization law.
*Source:* Courtesy of the Harry Truman Library.

A more controversial means of preventing intellectual disability is through diagnostic testing and selective abortion. One diagnostic procedure is *amniocentesis,* in which fluid is extracted from the amniotic sac that protects the fetus during pregnancy. Many chromosomal and genetic defects in the fetus can be detected with amniocentesis, potentially leaving parents with extremely difficult decisions about terminating a pregnancy. In the future, *gene therapy* may instead offer the opportunity for treating the developing fetus.

Older women are particularly likely to consider amniocentesis, given the link between maternal age and Down syndrome. Amniocentesis can cause miscarriage, however. Fortunately, it is now possible to screen for Down syndrome using *ultrasound,* a procedure that uses harmless sound waves to create an image of the fetus (Cuckle, 2001). While not as definitive, ultrasound also has the advantage of being able to detect Down syndrome in the first trimester of pregnancy versus the second trimester with amniocentesis. In fact, the American College of Obstetricians and Gynecologists (2007) now recommends routine ultrasound screening for all interested expecting mothers, not just for women 35 years of age or older.

**SECONDARY PREVENTION** Early intervention can lead to the secondary prevention of cultural-familial retardation. The most important current effort is Head Start, a federal program begun in 1964. Head Start provides preschool children living in poverty with early educational experiences, nutrition, and health care monitoring. Head Start produces short-term increases in IQ (5 to 10 points) and achievement. The academic advantages diminish or disappear within a few years after intervention ends, but data indicate that children who participate in Head Start are less likely to repeat a grade or to be placed in special education classes. They also are more likely to graduate from high school (McKey et al., 1985; Zigler & Styfco, 1993). Head Start undoubtedly reduces the prevalence of cultural-familial retardation through its influence on adaptive behavior if not on IQ itself.

More specific evidence on preventing intellectual disability comes from two research programs—the Carolina Abecedarian Project (Ramey & Bryant, 1982) and the Milwaukee Project (Garber, 1988). Both interventions offered a variety of services to children of mothers with below-average IQs, and both used control groups to assess the effectiveness of intervention. Gains of 20 or more points in IQ were reported in the Milwaukee Project, but questions about this study suggest caution (Baroff & Olley, 1999). More modest gains of 5 to 10 IQ points come from the Abecedarian Project. These projects, together with adoption studies and findings from Head Start, indicate that cases of familial retardation can be prevented by increasing environmental stimulation and responsiveness.

**TERTIARY PREVENTION** Careful assessment early in life is critical to tertiary prevention. Unfortunately, many cases of intellectual disability are not detected early, as the doubling in prevalence during the school years indicates. Public screening of children's academic potential typically is not conducted until school age.

Early intervention can help. Programs for infants typically take place in the home and focus on stimulating the infant, educating parents, and promoting good parent–infant relationships (Shearer & Shearer, 1976). During the preschool years, special instruction may take place in child development centers, which also offer respite care for the parents who need relief from the added demands of rearing a child with an intellectual disability.

Treatment of the social and emotional needs of people with intellectual disabilities may include teaching basic self-care skills during younger ages and various "life-survival" skills at later ages. Children with intellectual disabilities may also be treated for unusual behaviors, such as self-stimulation or aggressiveness. In general, operant behavior therapy is the most effective treatment approach (Bernard, 2002).

Medical care for physical and sensory handicaps also is critical in the treatment of certain types of intellectual disabilities. In addition, medications are helpful in treating comorbid disorders such as epilepsy.

As many as 50 percent of institutionalized people with intellectual disabilities are prescribed medication, often inappropriately, to control their behavior problems (Singh, Guernsey, & Ellis, 1992). Neuroleptics are used commonly to treat aggressiveness and other uncontrolled behavior (Grossman, 1983). In some institutions, these drugs have been used primarily to sedate patients, raising broad questions about their misuse (Scheerenberger, 1982).

**NORMALIZATION** **Normalization** means that people with intellectual disabilities are entitled to live, as much as possible, like other members of society. The major goals of normalization include mainstreaming children with intellectual disabilities into public schools and promoting a role in the community for adults.

The Special Olympics offers three million people with intellectual disabilities a chance to exercise, compete, and excel in sports competitions—and to change attitudes about intellectual disabilities.

Prior to 1975, only about half of all children with intellectual disabilities received an education at public expense. That year Congress passed the Education for All Handicapped Children Act,[1] which affirmed that all children have a right to a free and appropriate education in the "least restrictive environment." Within the limits set by the handicapping condition, services must be provided in a setting that restricts personal liberty as little as possible.

For many children with intellectual disabilities, the least restrictive environment means **mainstreaming** them into regular classrooms, rather than being taught in special classes. Unfortunately, the extent of mainstreaming and the quality of support services vary widely across school districts and across states (Robinson et al., 2000). This is a matter of concern, because children with intellectual disabilities who are mainstreamed into regular classrooms may learn as much as or more than they do in special classes (Taylor et al., 2005).

The *deinstitutionalization* movement that began in mental hospitals in the 1960s also has helped to normalize the lives of many people with intellectual disabilities. Deinstitutionalization has been particularly rapid for those with mild intellectual disability. Of those now living in institutions, 7.1 percent have mild, 13.0 percent have moderate, 24.4 percent have severe, and 55.5 percent have profound levels of intellectual disability (Baroff & Olley, 1999). People with intellectual disabilities who move from institutions to the community receive better care and function at a higher level. These people also contribute to communities through their work and their relationships.

Changing attitudes is ultimately the most effective way to normalize the lives of people with intellectual disabilities and their families. One of our students, whose sister has a profound intellectual disability, offered the following impassioned comments:

In my favorite picture of my family, my parents and I are all looking at the camera, but my sister is smiling expectantly up at me, waiting for me to sing the alphabet. Every time I look at this picture I smile. What makes me angry is that other people don't see why. Other people see a vegetable who will need to be cared for the rest of her life. . . . My sister has been described to me as "damaged," a "tragedy," and a "loss," all by well-meaning psychologists. I've been told that secretly when I look at my sister, I feel disgusted, which is the farthest thing from the truth. . . . I will not lie, when I was in middle school I was disappointed that I didn't have a "normal" sibling who could talk with me or give me advice, but I have now reached the point where I am more upset at the world for not treating her properly and not seeing her the way that I do. This is why I have worked in a summer camp for children with severe and profound disabilities since I was in middle school—this is the only environment I have found where "my kids," as I call them, are embraced, doted over, seen as sweet, cute, and not ever as "tragedies." (Anonymous, 2003)

## Autism Spectrum Disorder

**Autism spectrum disorder (ASD)** begins early in life and involves impairments in social interaction, social communication, and restricted, repetitive behaviors. ASD is a new term that evolved prior to *DSM-5* (Lord & Bailey, 2002). Several disorders once viewed as distinct are now seen as falling on a continuum (a spectrum). The most important of these "separate" disorders are *autism* (where children often cannot communicate and typically have intellectual disabilities) versus *Asperger's disorder* (where intelligence and communication are in the normal range). Even though *DSM-5* changed the language, we occasionally refer to "classic autism" and "Asperger's disorder" to help you understand past research (which typically studied the problems separately) and changing concepts. Terminology is not terribly important, but the underlying question is: Does ASD refer to variations on the same disorder, or has *DSM-5* mistakenly given the same name to different problems?

One thing is not in question. ASD is defined far more broadly in *DSM-5* (2013) than classic autism was defined in DSM-IV (1994). As a result, the symptoms of ASD include far less serious impairments, the prognosis is brighter, comorbid problems like intellectual disabilities are less frequent, and prevalence estimates are far higher. We pay careful attention to changing definitions, and you should too. Many people think that ASD itself has changed, but mostly what has changed is the definition of ASD.

The dictionary definition of autism, "absorption in one's own mental activity," grossly understates the disorder's potentially severe social disturbances. The classic autism—the severe end of the ASD spectrum—is characterized by profound indifference to social relationships, odd, stereotypical behaviors, and severely impaired or nonexistent communication. Even those adults who achieve exceptionally good outcomes show severely disturbed social emotions and social understanding. Consider the remarkable case of Temple Grandin, a woman who achieved what may be the most successful outcome of classic autism on record.

### MyPsychLab VIDEO CASE

#### Asperger's Disorder

DAVID

*"It's gruelling to think about what to say, what not to say."*

⊙ **Watch** the **Video** *David: Asperger's Disorder* on **MyPsychLab**

As you watch the video, observe David's odd behaviors and social problems, but ask yourself if this is a disorder on the same spectrum with autism or something different.

[1]The act, which is reauthorized periodically, was renamed Individuals with Disabilities Education Act (IDEA) in 1990.

Temple Grandin with actress Claire Danes, who won a Golden Globe award for her title role as Grandin in an HBO movie.

## ⟶ Temple Grandin—An Anthropologist on Mars

Temple Grandin, a woman now in her sixties, suffered from the classic symptoms of autism as a young child. She had not developed language by the age of three, and she threw wild tantrums in response to social initiations, even gentle attempts to give her a hug. Grandin spent hours staring into space, playing with objects, or simply rocking or spinning herself. She also engaged in other unusual behaviors, such as repeatedly smearing her own feces. With the extensive help of her parents and teachers, and her own determination, however, Grandin learned strategies to compensate for, and cope with, her severe psychological impairments. She earned a Ph.D. in animal science and has developed widely used techniques for managing cattle. In stark contrast to Grandin, the majority of people with autism in her generation spent most of their life in institutions.

One of Grandin's coping strategies is "computing" how other people feel. Like the characters of Data or Mr. Spock from the *Star Trek* series, with whom she identifies, Grandin does not experience normal human emotions. Rather, she describes herself as "an anthropologist on Mars." She has learned how to relate to the human species through careful observation of "their" behavior. The following is from a book by neurologist Oliver Sacks, who wrote a detailed case study about Grandin.

"I can tell if a human being is angry," she told me, "or if he's smiling." At the level of the sensorimotor, the concrete, the unmediated, the animal, Temple has no difficulty. But what about children, I asked her. Were they not intermediate between animals and adults? On the contrary, Temple said, she had great difficulties with children—trying to talk with them, to join in their games (she could not even play peekaboo with a baby, she said, because she would get the timing all wrong)—as she had had such difficulties herself as a child. Children, she feels, are already far advanced, by the age of three or four, along a path that she, as an autistic person, has never advanced far on. Little children, she feels, already "understand" other human beings in a way she can never hope to. (Sacks, 1985, p. 270)

Grandin finds human touch—hugging—overwhelming, but also comforting. To solve this dilemma, Grandin developed a "squeeze machine," a device that gives her a soothing, mechanical hug. In one of her two autobiographies, *Thinking in Pictures*, Grandin describes her development of her squeeze machine:

From as far back as I can remember, I always hated to be hugged. I wanted to experience the good feeling of being hugged, but it was just too overwhelming. It was like a great all-engulfing tidal wave of stimulation, and I reacted like a wild animal. . . . After visiting my aunt's ranch in Arizona I watched cattle being put in the squeeze chute for their vaccinations, I noticed some of them relaxed. I asked Aunt Ann to press the squeeze sides against me and to close the head restraint bars around my neck. I hoped it would calm my anxiety. At first there were a few moments of sheer panic as I stiffened up and tried to pull away from the pressure. Five seconds later I felt a wave of relaxation. . . . I copied the design and built the first human squeeze machine out of plywood panels when I returned to school. (Grandin, 1995, pp. 62–63)

We know a good deal about the often bizarre behavior of children and adults with severe ASD. But we know little about it on the inside. The sufferer typically is too disturbed to understand or communicate about their experience. Temple Grandin is a compelling exception to this rule. While discussing how the symptoms of severe ASD appear to the outsider, we return to Grandin's words in an effort to better understand the inner world.

## Symptoms of ASD

Judging from physical appearance alone, you would not expect children with ASD to have a serious psychological impairment. Motor milestones may be reached late, and movement may appear awkward or rather uncoordinated (Prior & Ozonoff, 2007).

But most children are normal in physical appearance, and physical growth is generally normal.

**EARLY ONSET** The normal physical appearance is one reason why ASD, which begins early in life[2], may go unrecognized. In retrospect, parents may recall abnormalities that seem to date to birth. For example, a parent may remember that her ASD child was easy as a baby—too easy, perhaps uninterested in attention, cuddling, and stimulation. In 20 percent to 40 percent of cases of severe ASD, the baby develops normally for a time but either stops learning new skills or loses the skills acquired earlier (Volkmar, Chawarska, & Klin, 2005).

The National Institute of Mental Health hopes to improve the early identification of ASD, and researchers are working to identify early warning signs (Volkmar et al., 2005). One clever study used videotapes of one-year-olds' birthday parties in this effort. Normal children were compared with those later diagnosed with classic autism or with an intellectual disability. Infants with classic autism looked at others and oriented to their names less often than infants with an intellectual disability. Both groups used fewer gestures, looked less at objects held by others, and engaged in more repetitive motor movements than normally developing babies (Osterling, Dawson, & Munson, 2002). Findings like this cannot yet be used for early identification, but scientists are searching for more definitive markers (Lord et al., 2012). Problems in social communication skills are one promising focus (Ingersoll, 2011).

**DEFICITS IN SOCIAL COMMUNICATION AND INTERACTION** ASDs are characterized by a range of persistent deficits in social communication and social interaction—a very wide range of deficits. Social communication problems include normal language accompanied by odd "body language" at one extreme to a total absence of verbal and nonverbal communication at the other. Many children with classic autism fail to develop normal speech. Some learn a few words and then suddenly lose their language abilities. About half are mute (Volkmar et al., 1994).

Children with ASD who do acquire language often speak oddly. One example is *dysprosody,* subtle disruptions in the rate, rhythm, and intonation of speech. Another is *echolalia,* uttering phrases back, perhaps repeatedly. When the mother of a 1½-year-old points to herself and says, "Who is this?" normal toddlers respond with "Mama." A 10-year-old child with classic autism and echolalia responds to the same question by repeating, "Who is this?"

Even high-functioning people with ASD have trouble communicating or understanding abstractions. Here is how Temple Grandin describes her struggles:

> Autistics have problems learning things that cannot be thought about in pictures. The easiest words for an autistic child to learn are nouns, because they are directly related to pictures. . . .

A mother with her young daughter, who suffers from autism.

Spatial words such as "over" and "under" had no meaning for me until I had a visual image to fix them in my memory. Even now, when I hear the word "under" by itself, I automatically picture myself getting under the cafeteria tables at school during an air-raid drill, a common occurrence on the East Coast during the early fifties. When I read, I translate written words into color movies or I simply store a photo of the written page to be read later. When I retrieve material, I see a photocopy of the page in my imagination. I can then read it like a TelePrompTer. . . . When I am unable to convert text to pictures, it is usually because the text has no concrete meaning. Some philosophy books and articles about the cattle futures market are simply incomprehensible. (pp. 29–31)

Problems with social communication spill over into many social interactions. Social impairments range from relatively mild problems with social or emotional reciprocity, for example, struggling with back and forth conversation, to extreme difficulties. Some children and adults with severe ASD have no interest in relationships. They treat other people as if they were confusing, foreign objects.

Some have suggested that ASD is characterized by the absence of a *theory of mind*—a failure to appreciate that other people have a different point of reference (Baron-Cohen, Tager-Flusberg, & Cohen, 1993). Theory of mind is illustrated by the "Sally–Ann task" (see Figure 15.5 on p. 422). The child is shown two dolls, Sally, who has a basket, and Ann, who has a box. Sally puts a marble in her basket and then leaves. While Sally is gone, Ann takes the marble out of Sally's basket and puts it into her own box. When Sally returns, the question is: Where will she look for her marble?

Sally should look for the marble in her basket, where she left it, because she did not see Ann hide it. However, children with severe ASD often fail to appreciate Sally's perspective—they lack

---

[2]The DSM-5 does not specify an age cutoff, but indicates that, "Symptoms must be present in the early developmental period…" (p. 50).

**FIGURE 15.5**

Where will Sally (on left) look for the marble? Many children with autism answer "in the box," evidence that they may lack a "theory of mind."

*Source:* Frith, U. 1989. Autism: Explaining the Enigma. Blackwell Publishing, Ltd.

a theory of mind. In one early study, 80 percent of children with severe ASD said Sally would search in Ann's box, whereas only 14 percent of children with Down syndrome made the same error (Baron-Cohen, Leslie, & Frith, 1985).

Theory of mind is not a "core" deficit in ASD, however. Many higher functioning children with ASD do have a theory of mind, while many with intellectual disabilities do not (Prior & Ozonoff, 2007; Tager-Flusberg, 2007). The social interaction deficits in ASD are emotional, not just cognitive (Losh & Capps, 2006). In fact, some children with severe ASD appear to be missing the basic motivation to form attachments. As infants, they do not seek out attachment figures in times of distress, nor are they comforted by physical contact. As children, they show little interest in their peers, failing to engage in social play or to develop friendships. Throughout life, they avoid others in small but significant ways, for example, through *gaze aversion*, actively avoiding eye contact (see photo).

**RESTRICTED, REPETITIVE INTERESTS AND ACTIVITIES**
Another defining symptom of ASD is restricted, repetitive patterns of behavior, interests, or activities. Again, the *DSM-5* provides a wide range of possible symptoms. A high functioning adult with ASD may be unusually fascinated with some activity, perhaps

collecting and endlessly reviewing baseball cards, but hide or no longer engage in the behavior. Children with severe ASD may literally spend most of their day flapping a string in front of their eyes.

Behaviors like string flapping seem to serve no other function than *self-stimulation*. One interpretation is that the child receives too little sensory input, and self-stimulation increases sensation to a more desirable level. We prefer an alternative interpretation. Self-stimulation *reduces* sensory input by making stimulation monotonously predictable. Stereotyped behavior in ASD may help to make a terrifying world more constant and predictable. Temple Grandin's (1996) observations seem consistent with our view:

When left alone, I would often space out and become hypnotized. I could sit for hours on the beach watching sand dribbling through my fingers. I'd study each individual grain of sand as it flowed between my fingers. Each grain was different, and I was like a scientist studying the grains under a microscope. As I scrutinized their shapes and contours, I went into a trance which cut me off from the sights and sounds around me.

Rocking and spinning were other ways to shut out the world when I became overloaded with too much noise. Rocking made me feel calm. It was like taking an addictive drug. The

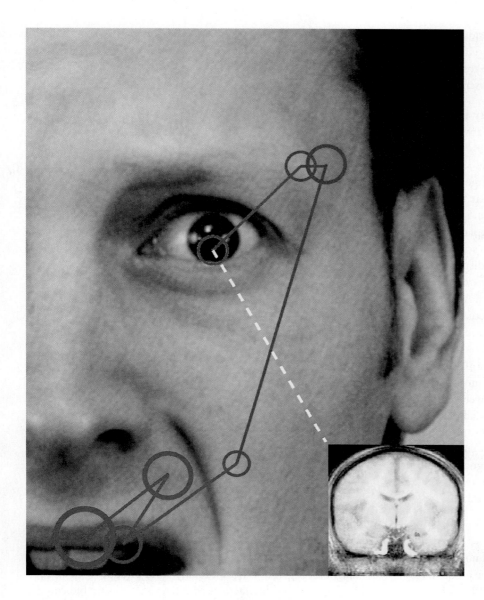

A demonstration of gaze aversion in children with autism using eye tracking technology. The circles show where the subjects gazed. Larger circles indicate longer gaze time, and the straight lines indicate eye movement. The dot in the brain slice shows activation of the subjects' amygdala cluster, indicating emotional arousal due to potential eye contact.

more I did it, the more I wanted to do it. My mother and my teachers would stop me so I would get back in touch with the rest of the world. (pp. 44–45)

**UNUSUAL SENSORY SENSITIVITY** Although not required for the diagnosis,[3] many people with ASD respond to sound, touch, sight, or smell in unusual ways. At the mild end, a child may find certain clothing intolerable, even painful, for example, wearing a leotard. At the severe end, a patient may respond as if he were deaf, even though his hearing is intact, an *apparent sensory deficit* (Lovaas et al., 1971). The sensory deficit is "apparent," because the sense organ is not impaired even though the response suggests otherwise. Even more puzzling, the "deaf" patient may scream in pain in reaction to a much quieter sound like the scratch of chalk on a blackboard. This suggests that the problem lies at some higher level of perception (Prior & Ozonoff, 2007). Temple

Grandin, who called this "sensory jumbling," believes that this symptom is an understudied aspect of autism:

> When I was little, loud noises were also a problem, often feeling like a dentist's drill hitting a nerve. They actually caused pain. I was scared to death of balloons popping, because the sound was like an explosion in my ear. Minor noises that most people can tune out drove me to distraction. When I was in college, my roommate's hair dryer sounded like a jet plane taking off. (p. 67)

**SELF-INJURY** *Self-injurious behavior* is one of the most bizarre and dangerous difficulties that can accompany severe ASD. The most common forms are repeated head banging and biting the fingers and wrists (Rutter, Greenfield, & Lockyer, 1967). Injuries may involve minor bruises, or they can be severe—broken bones,

---

[3]Unusual sensory response is one of the four categories of restricted patterns of behavior, interests, or activities. Two of four are required, so the sensory symptoms are not necessary for diagnosis (see "DSM-5: Autism Spectrum Disorder" on p. 425).

brain damage, and even death. Self-injury is not suicidal behavior. The child with severe ASD does not have enough self-awareness to be truly suicidal. Fortunately, self-injury can be treated effectively with behavior therapy, using techniques we discuss shortly.

**SAVANT PERFORMANCE** A fascinating ability sometimes associated with ASD is the rare child who shows **savant performance**—an exceptional ability in a highly specialized area of functioning. Savant performance typically involves artistic, musical, or mathematical skills. The photo on this page shows the savant abilities of Stephen Wiltshire, who did not speak until age 5. Diagnosed with autism, his first words were "paper" and "pen."

No one has an adequate theory, let alone an explanation, for savant performance. Unfortunately, one thing does seem clear: The existence of savant performance does not indicate that, as many have hoped, children with classic autism really are normal or even superior in intelligence. Most people with severe ASD do not show savant performance, and most have an intellectual disability (Fombonne, 2007). Past research showed that about a quarter of children with classic autism have IQs below 55, about half have IQs between 55 and 70, and only one-fourth have IQs over 70 (Volkmar et al., 1994; see Table 15.4). And for the most part, IQ scores are stable over time (Prior & Ozonoff, 2007). Average IQs are higher in more recent samples—perhaps 50 percent fall below 70. However, this is primarily a result of broader definitions of ASD, a diagnosis that now includes less severely disturbed children. On a more optimistic note, some children are being diagnosed sooner and treated more successfully, so some of the IQ increase may be real (Chakrabarti & Fombonne, 2001; Volkmar & Lord, 2007).

## Diagnosis of ASD

Two psychiatrists independently described ASD at almost the same point in history. Importantly, however, they viewed the problem differently. In 1943, psychiatrist Leo Kanner (1894–1981) of Johns Hopkins University identified a small group of severely disturbed young children with an inability to form relationships, delayed or noncommunicative speech, a demand for sameness in the environment, stereotyped activities, and lack of imagination. Kanner (1943)

Stephen Wiltshire drew this panorama of New York City from memory after a 20 minute helicopter ride. He first displayed his savant ability at age 5, when he was a student in a school for children with autism.

called the problem "early infantile autism." Kanner's patients suffered from what we have called classic autism in this chapter.

At about the same time, Viennese psychiatrist Hans Asperger (1906–1980) described children with similar social problems and stereotyped behavior. But Asperger's (1944) patients had normal intellectual functioning and good communication skills. Asperger's work received little attention until late in the twentieth century when his papers were translated into English. In 1994, *Asperger's disorder* was listed in the DSM for the first time.

In the decade that followed, practitioners began to use broader and broader definitions of Asperger's disorder. At first, links between the new diagnosis and classic autism seemed clear, and the idea of an autism spectrum (ASD) was born. Over time, however, the Asperger's diagnosis began to be given to any child or adult with odd social interactions and highly focused interests. Web sites blossomed, and Albert Einstein, Thomas Jefferson, Sir Isaac Newton, and many others were posthumously diagnosed with Asperger's disorder!

Experts became concerned about overdiagnosis, particularly about a false "epidemic of autism." As we discuss further on,

**TABLE 15.4**
## IQ Scores for Patients with Autism and Other Autistic Spectrum Disorders

| IQ Score | Autism | | Other Autistic Spectrum Disorders | |
| --- | --- | --- | --- | --- |
| | N | Percent | N | Percent |
| >70 | 118 | 26.0 | 122 | 50.8 |
| 55–69 | 197 | 43.4 | 61 | 25.4 |
| <20–54 | 114 | 25.1 | 53 | 22.1 |
| Unspecified | 25 | 5.5 | 4 | 1.7 |

*Source:* Volkmar, FR. Field Trial for Autistic Disorder in DSM-IV. American Journal of Psychiatry. 1994 Sep;151(9):1361-7. Reprinted with permission from the American Journal of Psychiatry (Copyright © 1994). American Psychiatric Association. All Rights Reserved.

increased estimates of the prevalence of ASD reflect inflation of the diagnosis much more than a real increase in the disorder. Vehement debates about how to define ASD in *DSM-5* focused on the benefits versus the costs of containing diagnostic inflation (Huerta et al., 2012; McPartland et al., 2012; Skuse, 2012; Swedo et al., 2012; Tsai, 2012). Should ASD be defined more narrowly and perhaps more accurately? What would happen to people who no longer qualified for the Asperger's disorder diagnosis? Would they be denied services?

In one of its most controversial changes, *DSM-5* embraced the idea of an autism spectrum and of a broad definition of the disorder. Read through the diagnostic criteria in "DSM-5: Autism Spectrum Disorder." The impairments sound severe, and they often are tragic. But also note the *least* severe symptoms that meet diagnostic criteria. If these symptoms fall along a continuum, it is a very long line (see Thinking Critically About DSM-5 on p. 426).

## Frequency of ASD

For decades, classic autism was viewed as a very rare disorder, occurring in perhaps 4 of 10,000 children (Lotter, 1966). However, the diagnosis of ASD exploded after the introduction of Asperger's disorder. The U.S. Centers for Disease Control and Prevention (CDC) now estimates that perhaps 200 in 10,000 children suffer from ASD (Blumberg et al., 2013). This startling 50-fold increase has created an uproar. Many parents and some professionals believe that environmental factors, such as pollution or vaccines, caused an "epidemic of autism." The dramatic increase in the number of cases has been carefully and repeatedly documented (Barbaresi et al., 2005; Baron-Cohen et al., 2009; Fombonne, 2007; Kogan et al., 2009; Newschaffer, Falb, & Gurney, 2005). In fact, the CDC reported an increase of 400 percent in the prevalence of ASD between 1998 and 2007, and another

---

### criteria for
### Autism Spectrum Disorder

### DSM-5

**A.** Persistent deficits in social communication and social interaction across multiple contexts, as manifested by the following, currently or by history (examples are illustrative, not exhaustive; see text):

  **1.** Deficits in social-emotional reciprocity, ranging, for example, from abnormal social approach and failure of normal back-and-forth conversation; to reduced sharing of interests, emotions, or affect; to failure to initiate or respond to social interactions.

  **2.** Deficits in nonverbal communicative behaviors used for social interaction, ranging, for example, from poorly integrated verbal and nonverbal communication; to abnormalities in eye contact and body language or deficits in understanding and use of gestures; to a total lack of facial expressions and nonverbal communication.

  **3.** Deficits in developing, maintaining, and understanding relationships, ranging, for example, from difficulties adjusting behavior to suit various social contexts; to difficulties in sharing imaginative play or in making friends; to absence of interest in peers.

*Specify* current severity:

  **Severity is based on social communication impairments and restricted, repetitive patterns of behavior** (see Table 2).

**B.** Restricted, repetitive patterns of behavior, interests, or activities, as manifested by at least two of the following, currently or by history (examples are illustrative, not exhaustive; see text):

  **1.** Stereotyped or repetitive motor movements, use of objects, or speech (e.g., simple motor stereotypies, lining up toys or flipping objects, echolalia, idiosyncratic phrases).

  **2.** Insistence on sameness, inflexible adherence to routines, or ritualized patterns of verbal or nonverbal behavior (e.g., extreme distress at small changes, difficulties with

transitions, rigid thinking patterns, greeting rituals, need to take same route or eat same food every day).

  **3.** Highly restricted, fixated interests that are abnormal in intensity or focus (e.g., strong attachment to or preoccupation with unusual objects, excessively circumscribed or perseverative interests).

  **4.** Hyper- or hyporeactivity to sensory input or unusual interest in sensory aspects of the environment (e.g., apparent indifference to pain/temperature, adverse response to specific sounds or textures, excessive smelling or touching of objects, visual fascination with lights or movement).

*Specify* current severity:

  **Severity is based on social communication impairments and restricted, repetitive patterns of behavior** (see Table 2).

**C.** Symptoms must be present in the early developmental period (but may not become fully manifest until social demands exceed limited capacities, or may be masked by learned strategies in later life).

**D.** Symptoms cause clinically significant impairment in social, occupational, or other important areas of current functioning.

**E.** These disturbances are not better explained by intellectual disability (intellectual developmental disorder) or global developmental delay. Intellectual disability and autism spectrum disorder frequently co-occur; to make comorbid diagnoses of autism spectrum disorder and intellectual disability, social communication should be below that expected for general developmental level.

**Note:** Individuals with a well-established DSM-IV diagnosis of autistic disorder, Asperger's disorder, or pervasive developmental disorder not otherwise specified should be given the diagnosis of autism spectrum disorder. Individuals who have marked deficits in social communication, but whose symptoms do not otherwise meet criteria for autism spectrum disorder, should be evaluated for social (pragmatic) communication disorder.

## How Far Out on the Autism Spectrum?

IQ is on a continuum. The numbers make it easy to see that. It also is easy to understand that the IQ cutoff for intellectual disability is somewhat arbitrary. You know this. Turning test scores into A's, B's, and so on involves somewhat arbitrary cutoffs. Finally, history tells us that, at times, definitions of intellectual disability reached too far. Changing the IQ threshold from 2 to 1 standard deviations below the mean, from 70 to 85, was well intentioned. But the resulting overdiagnosis created far more problems than it solved. You know this too. If a lot of people flunk a class, the problem is probably the grading, not the students.

These exact same issues apply to the autism spectrum, but they are harder to see. ASD involves symptoms that, unlike IQ, are not nicely quantified. And we do not have the perspective of history. We are smack in the middle of diagnostic upheaval.

We are skeptical about the autism spectrum. We certainly find it impossible to tell you about what is supposed to be the *same* problem, ASD, without repeatedly discussing the no-longer-different problems of autism and Asperger's disorder. True, past definitions of autism and Asperger's disorder did not exactly cut nature at her joints. But prototypical cases of the two disorders sure *look* different. You can see this for yourself. Watch our MyPsychLab videos of David (Asperger's disorder, this chapter) and Xavier (high functioning classic autism, Chapter 2). As you watch David and Xavier, think about whether their disorders seem to differ in kind or only by a matter of degree.

But we want you to consider another issue now. So for the sake of argument, let's assume there is an autism spectrum. Our question is: How far out on the spectrum should we go in defining ASD? Definitions certainly have gyrated in the last two decades. The situation is not unlike when the IQ cutoff was changed from 70 to 85. Should we keep reaching further out to diagnose more and more people? Or should *DSM-5* have reigned in diagnostic inflation?

Consider this. As we discuss in this chapter, *DSM-5* includes much less severe symptoms in defining ASD compared to those that defined classic autism. *DSM-5* even changed the age criterion. According to DSM-IV, classic autism began before age three. According to DSM-5, ASD can be diagnosed later in life. The symptoms may have been "masked" previously or presently (see "DSM-5: Autism Spectrum Disorder").

Or consider this. A recent study estimated the prevalence of ASD to be 2.64 percent, a bit higher than recent CDC estimates (Kim et al., 2011). But *two-thirds* of the identified children were in regular classrooms. They were apparently functioning at least OK, because they had received no previous diagnosis or treatment. Are these children missing out on needed help? Or might we be creating a problem where there is none? One thing we know for sure is that these children were functioning far more adequately than is typical in classic autism. Children with classic autism require near constant treatment, often institutionalization.

Here's something else to ponder. On January 31, 2012, the *New York Times* published a fascinating essay entitled, "I Had Asperger's Syndrome. Briefly." The essay was written by a young man whose mother, a psychology professor and Asperger's disorder expert, featured him as a case study in a video she made about the disorder. Problem was, he didn't suffer from ASD. A quiet teenager who spent a lot of time reading, writing, and playing music, the essayist blossomed when he moved to New York City and found like-minded friends. He had recently published a psychologically minded novel, reflecting social insights missing in ASD. And worrying about what might have happened if he had been diagnosed as a vulnerable child instead of a skeptical teenager, he advocated a narrowing of ASD in *DSM-5*. He wrote, "My experience can't be unique. Under the rules in place today, any nerd, any withdrawn, bookish kid, can have Asperger syndrome."

We do not know how history will judge how we define ASD today. We suspect, however, that history will tell us that our definitions went too far, too often defining quirky as disorder.

---

increase of another 300 percent by 2012 (Blumberg et al., 2013) (see Figure 15.6).

In the minds of many parents, the measles/mumps/rubella (MMR) vaccination, which used to contain *thimerosal,* a mercury-based organic compound, explains the upsurge in ASD. Despite the fear, even hysteria, that vaccines cause autism, no scientific evidence links MMR to ASD (Offit, 2010; see Critical Thinking Matters in Chapter 2). Similarly, no evidence ties environmental pollutants with the upsurge in ASD (Rutter, 2005; Wing & Potter, 2002). Of course, many popular media and Internet sites make claims that are not exactly based on science. Nevertheless, the "epidemic of autism" appears to be more of a reason for celebration than paranoia. Leading experts agree that the increasing prevalence estimates are most likely due to increased awareness and broadened diagnostic criteria (Barbaresi et al., 2005; Charman, 2002; Miles, 2011; Newschaffer et al., 2005; Rutter, 2005; Wing & Potter, 2002). One piece of evidence in support of this interpretation is the declining percentage of children diagnosed with ASD who have comorbid intellectual disabilities. The diagnosis is now being applied to less severely disturbed children (Blumberg et al., 2013).

We need to tackle another myth about the epidemiology of ASD. Parents of children with ASD were once thought to be especially intelligent, a finding that contributed to the mistaken

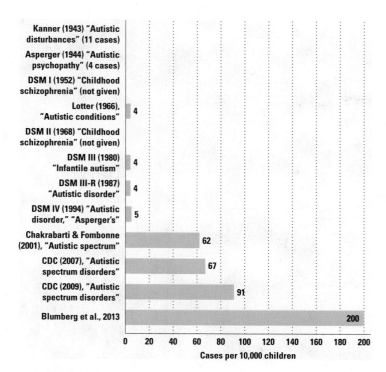

FIGURE **15.6**

**Prevalence of Autistic Spectrum Disorders in Selected Sources 1943–2012**   Recent estimates seem to suggest an "epidemic of autism," but they more likely indicate greater awareness and a broadening definition of autistic spectrum disorder.

*Source:* Authors' compilation from original sources.

Leo Kanner (1896–1981) identified what he called "early infantile autism," now viewed as lying at the severe end of the autism spectrum. In a 1960 interview with Time magazine, Kanner unfortunately and wrongly described the "refrigerator" parents of children with autism as "just happening to defrost long enough to produce a child."

view that children with ASD have superior intelligence. Researchers did repeatedly find that children treated for ASD had especially well-educated parents. However, this is because well-educated parents are vigorous in seeking specialized treatment for their troubled children, so the parents of children *treated* for ASD are more educated than the average parent. In other words, a biased sample created a false correlation (Gillberg & Schaumann, 1982). In the general population, ASD is unrelated to parental education (Schopler, Andrews, & Strupp, 1979).

Two legitimate findings about the prevalence of ASD have inspired research on possible causes. Four times as many boys as girls suffer from ASD, suggesting a gender-linked etiology, as in fragile-X syndrome. ASD also is much more common among siblings of a child with ASD (Ozonoff et al., 2011), suggesting possible genetic causes.

## Causes of ASD

Before discussing evidence on biological contributions to ASD, we first briefly consider—and reject—environmental explanations.

**PSYCHOLOGICAL AND SOCIAL FACTORS**  For many years, parents were blamed for causing ASD in their children. Psychoanalytic speculations said that ASD results from the infant's defense against maternal hostility (Bettelheim, 1967). Behaviorists viewed the disorder as caused by inappropriate parental reinforcement (Ferster, 1961). Both views blamed parents as cold, distant, and

subtly rejecting of their children. In fact, in 1960, *Time* magazine published an account of these "refrigerator parents." The article stated that the parents of children with autism "just happened to defrost long enough to produce a child" (Schreibman, 1988).

Such harmful assertions are simply wrong. Researchers have found no differences in the child-rearing styles of the parents of children with ASD when compared with those of the parents of normal children (Cantwell, Baker, & Rutter, 1979). And even if differences existed, common sense would force us to challenge the "refrigerator parent" interpretation. How could a parent's emotional distance create such an extreme disturbance so early in life? Even heinous abuse does not cause symptoms that approach the form or severity of the problems found in ASD. Moreover, if parents are emotionally distant, could this be a reaction to the child's social disturbance? If an infant shows no normal interest in cuddling or mimicking, is it surprising if a parent grows a bit distant?

Speculation about poor parenting—or vaccines—can never be completely disproved. However, logic and mounting research on biological causes make it unfathomable to think that ASD has a psychological cause. And as we hope you have come to understand, the rules of science require you to prove your hypothesis. Until a proven true, the community of scientists assumes a hypothesis is false. Claims about "refrigerator parents" offer sad testament to the wisdom of this scientific principle.

**BIOLOGICAL FACTORS**  In terms of its cause, ASD does not appear to be one disorder. Like intellectual disabilities, ASD includes several problems that look similar but actually have different biological causes. Known causes include fragile-X syndrome, Rett's disorder, and a handful of other known causes of intellectual disability. Other suspected causes include genetics and brain abnormalities.

**GENETICS** Genetic factors are widely thought to play an important role in ASD. The prevalence of ASD is much greater among siblings of a child with ASD, and several studies have found higher concordance among MZ than DZ twins (Smalley et al., 1988; Smalley & Collins, 1996; Steffenburg et al., 1989). In the largest study to date, concordance rates were 60 percent for MZ twins and 0 percent for DZ twins (Bailey et al., 1995). For a broader spectrum of disturbances, the rates were 92 percent for MZ and 10 percent for DZ twins in the same study.

These results suggest that ASD is strongly genetic, but there is a puzzle. The DZ rates are *too* low. Recall that, in dominant genetic transmission, rates are 100 percent MZ and 50 percent DZ. The anomaly might be explained if ASD is caused by a combination of different genes or perhaps by a spontaneous genetic mutation (Gottesman & Hanson, 2004). Recent research identified a "hot spot" on chromosome 16 (16p.11.2) that is linked with perhaps 1 percent of cases (Weiss et al., 2008). And one analysis suggested that, if all causes are included (such as fragile-X, Rett's, and 16p.11.2), as many as 25 percent of cases of ASD can be attributed to various genetic causes (Miles, 2011). Finally, three different research groups recently reported associations between ASD and spontaneous genetic mutations (Neale et al., 2012; Roak et al., 2012; Sanders et al., 2012).

**NEUROSCIENCE OF ASD** Different causes could lead to similar abnormalities in brain development, structure, or function, thus producing similar symptoms. Some evidence indicates that the brains of children with ASD are larger than average. The problem seems to be developmental. Brain growth appears to be unusually rapid in children with ASD, at least until the age of two or three. Then brain growth is arrested, so that cerebral and cerebellar brain volume are smaller than normal at later ages (Courchesne et al., 2001).

Still, no obvious brain abnormalities have been identified in ASD. Early theorizing about potential brain damage focused on the left cerebral hemisphere, where language is controlled. However, the communication deficits in ASD are more basic, and current thinking focuses more on subcortical brain structures involved in emotion, perception, and social interaction (Waterhouse, Fein, & Modahl, 1996; Wing, 1988). Two likely sites are the cerebellum, where sensorimotor input is integrated, and the limbic system, the area of the brain that regulates emotions (Bauman, 1996; Courchesne et al., 2001; Schreibman, 1988; Waterhouse et al., 1996). Within the limbic system, the amygdalae are a particular focus, and recent evidence indicates that these structures follow the pattern of early rapid then slowed development (Mosconi et al., 2009). The frontal lobe, the site of executive functioning, also may be involved (Moldin, 2003).

Recent theorizing also points to the functioning of *mirror neurons*, neurons that fire both when an individual performs an action and when the individual observes another performing the same

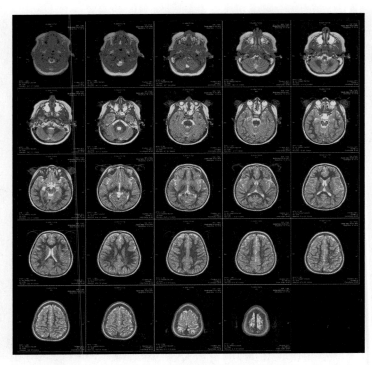

Neuroscientists hope that increasingly sophisticated brain imaging techniques will help to unlock the mysteries of ASD.

action. Mirror neurons were first identified in the 1990s and are known to be involved in many normal abilities that are impaired in ASD including imitation, understanding others' intentions, empathy, and language learning. Research on ASD and the mirror neuron system is in its infancy, but it is exciting because of its potential relevance to several key symptoms (Oberman & Ramachandran, 2007).

The most promising research on neurotransmitters and ASD focuses on endorphins and neuropeptides (Polleux & Lauder, 2004). *Endorphins* are internally produced opioids that have effects similar to externally administered opiate drugs like morphine. One theory suggested that ASD is caused by excess endorphins. According to this speculation, people with ASD are like addicts high on heroin. They lack interest in others, because their excessive internal rewards reduce the value of the external rewards offered by relationships (Panksepp & Sahley, 1987). More recent theorizing has expanded to include various *neuropeptides*, substances that affect the action of neurotransmitters. Oxytocin and vasopressin, which affect attachment and social affiliation in animals, are two neuropetides that are the subject of active investigation (Waterhouse et al., 1996). ASD is widely viewed as a brain disorder, but to date, it has defied explanation in terms of specific abnormalities.

## Treatment of ASD

Controversy exists about the degree to which treatment can help children with ASD. Some researchers are optimistic about new treatments, whereas others are skeptical, especially because a large number of dubious treatments have been promoted (see Critical Thinking Matters). Everyone acknowledges, however, that there is no cure for ASD. Thus, the effectiveness of treatment must

## The Bogus Treatment Called Facilitated Communication

*acilitated communication* is a technique that created excited optimism—and deep skepticism—as a treatment for autism. In facilitated communication, a "facilitator" supports the hand and arm of a disabled individual, thus allowing the child to type on a keyboard. Douglas Biklen (1992) claimed that the technique allows people with autism to communicate, show insight, awareness, and literary talent—and even reveal traumatic experiences that purportedly caused their autism.

In the early 1990s, facilitated communication was touted as a cure for autism throughout the popular media. Eager for a cure, many relatives of people with autism embraced the technique. Unfortunately, but not surprisingly, systematic studies found that facilitated communication offered no benefits (Jacobson, Mulick, & Schwartz, 1995).

For example, Eberlin and coworkers (1993) investigated facilitated communication in 21 adolescents diagnosed with autism and 10 adult facilitators who were enthusiastic about the technique. In the baseline condition, the adolescents with autism were asked

A teacher attempting facilitated communication with a student with autism. Evidence indicates that the technique does not allow us to communicate with people with autism.

questions and allowed to communicate their answers to the best of their abilities. A special alphabetically configured keyboard was used for typing in this and all other conditions. Next, the adolescents responded to the same questions, but they were encouraged to type their answers with the aid of the facilitator, who was screened from hearing or seeing the questions being asked. Later, the adolescents responded to questions with the aid of the facilitator after the facilitator had received 20 hours of training in the technique. In this condition, the facilitator could see and hear the questions being asked. Finally, the adolescents responded to the identical questions as in the first and second conditions with the aid of the facilitator. The facilitators were screened in this last condition.

Results for a few people during sessions where the facilitator heard the questions contrasted dramatically with sessions where the facilitator did not hear the questions. When aided by a facilitator who also heard the question, for example, one uncommunicative autistic now typed "EMOTION ZOMETHIN* FEEL EXPREZ."

Such dramatic improvements surely would be more impressive if we did not know other results. When the facilitators were screened from hearing questions, the autistics performed significantly *worse* than responding on their own. Apparently, some facilitators experienced the Ouija board effect. Their own thoughts subtly influenced the "response" they "facilitated."

The American Psychological Association officially concluded that facilitated communication is ineffective (Jacobson, Mulik, & Schwartz, 1995). Yet, a subsequent study found that 18 percent of service providers still used facilitated communication as a treatment (Myers, Miltenberger, & Studa, 1998). And the documentary, *Autism Is a World*, which purports to show that facilitated communication works (and was coproduced by Biklen) was nominated for an Academy Award in 2005.

In considering these unhappy circumstances, we once again urge you to be an inquiring skeptic. When a real miracle treatment is discovered, it will be easy to demonstrate its effectiveness scientifically. Until then, without critical thinking, you—and desperate mentally ill people and their relatives—are susceptible to false hope and phony treatments.

be compared against the unhappy course and outcome of the disorder.

**COURSE AND OUTCOME** Unfortunately, classic autism is a lifelong disorder. A recent review of 16 follow-up studies concluded that only about 20 percent achieve a "good" outcome, defined as living a somewhat normal and independent life. The outcome is "poor" for 50 percent, who require substantial supervision and support. A major change in more recent

years is that more children and adults with classic autism are cared for in their homes or communities instead of institutions (Howlin, 2007). More recent studies also find somewhat better outcomes, but this may be a result of including higher functioning individuals, not necessarily because of improved care (Howlin, 2007; see Figure 15.7). Asperger's disorder is generally thought to have a much more optimistic prognosis (Gillberg, 1991), but this has not yet been shown empirically (Howlin, 2007).

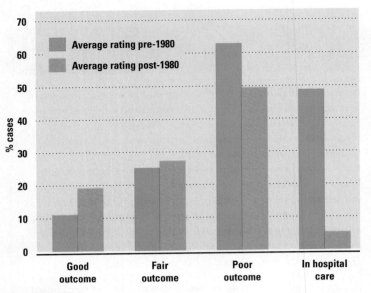

**FIGURE 15.7**

**Adult outcomes for children diagnosed with autism.** Outcomes are somewhat better in more recent studies, but good outcomes are infrequent and poor outcomes remain most common. One major change is that, in recent studies, far fewer adults with autism were cared for in institutions, reflecting increased family and community care.
*Source:* Based on Howlin, P. 2007. Adult outcomes for children diagnosed with autism in Autism and Pervasive Developmental Disorders, 2nd edition. Cambridge University Press.

A more positive prognosis for classic autism is predicted by language skills at the age of five or six (Yirmiya & Sigman, 1996 and higher IQ (Schreibman, 1988). Recent research also shows that *joint attention*, coordinating attention with another person through gestures, social responding, or social initiation, predicts language development from preschool age to age nine (Anderson et al., 2007). Importantly, a quarter or more of young people with classic autism develop seizure disorders as teenagers (Wing, 1988). In adult life, affective disorders are common (Howlin, 2007).

Statistics offer a sobering view of ASD. Can treatment help?

**MEDICATION** A huge variety of medications have been tried for classic autism, ranging from antipsychotics to opiate agonists. Unfortunately, no medication is very effective, although temporary claims of success have fueled false hope more than once.

A cautionary tale can be told about secretin, a "breakthrough" medication in the late 1990s. Secretin is a hormone involved in digestion. It is sometimes used to test for gastrointestinal problems, which are common in classic autism. Widespread interest in the drug was sparked by three case studies of children who reportedly showed remarkable improvement in language and social behavior while taking secretin for a routine gastrointestinal workup (Horvath et al., 1998). Rumors spread on the Internet, and thousands of desperate parents across the country sought secretin for their autistic children.

Scientists quickly responded to the intense interest. Unfortunately, the news was not good. A double-blind study using random assignment found no improvement over placebo in 58 autistic children treated with a single dose of secretin (Sandler

et al., 1999). Several subsequent studies also showed no benefit (Erickson et al., 2007). As with other "miracle" medications, the effects of secretin are not miraculous.

Even more troubling, desperate parents and at least some physicians have been attempting to treat classic autism with *chelation therapy*, administering agents that remove heavy metals from the body (presumably the mercury that does *not* cause ASD). Chelation can be dangerous to children's health, and the National Institutes of Health recently canceled a proposed study of chelation and ASD because the risks far outweighed any potential benefits (*Wall Street Journal*, September 18, 2008). In a similar vein of desperation (and quackery), the *Chicago Tribune* (November 23, 2009) reported that various potentially dangerous substances are being misused to "treat" ASD by attempting to reduce "inflammation" of the brain, an approach legitimate scientists find frightening. About the only mention of this treatment in the scientific literature is a warning not to misinterpret research on brain development and try something like this (Pardo & Eberhart, 2007).

Some legitimate medications are known to help with some symptoms of ASD. Certain antipsychotics, particularly *risperidone*, help in behavior management. Medications used in treating obsessive–compulsive disorder (the SSRIs) may also help with some stereotyped behavior in ASD (Lewis, 1996). However, no medication can be considered to be an effective treatment (Erickson et al., 2007; Lord & Bailey, 2002).

**APPLIED BEHAVIOR ANALYSIS** Intensive behavior modification using operant conditioning techniques called *Applied Behavior Analysis (ABA)* is the most promising approach to treating classic autism. ABA therapists focus on treating specific symptoms, including communication deficits, lack of self-care skills, and self-stimulatory or self-destructive behavior. Even within these different symptom areas, behavior modification emphasizes very specific and small goals. In attempting to teach language, for example, the therapist might spend hours, days, or weeks teaching the pronunciation of a specific syllable. Months of intensive effort may be needed to teach a small number of words and phrases. The lack of imitation among many children with classic autism is one reason why so much effort goes into achieving such modest goals.

If the first goal of ABA is to identify very specific target behaviors, the second is to gain control over these behaviors through the use of reinforcement and punishment. Unlike normal children, who are reinforced by social interest and approval, children with classic autism often do not respond to ordinary praise, or they may find all social interaction unpleasant. For these reasons, the child's successful efforts must be rewarded repeatedly with primary reinforcers such as a favorite food, at least in the beginning phases of treatment.

An example helps to illustrate the level of detail of ABA programs. A common goal in treating echolalia is to teach the child to respond by answering questions rather than repeating them. As an early step in treatment, a target behavior might be to teach the child to respond to the question "What is your name?" with the correct answer "Joshua."

In order to bring this specific response under the control of the therapist, initially it may be necessary to reward the child for simply echoing. Therapist: "What is your name?" Child: "What is your name?" Reward. This first step may have to be repeated hundreds of times over the course of several days.

A logical next step would be to teach the child to echo both the question and the response. Therapist: "What is your name? Joshua." Child: "What is your name? Joshua." Reward. Again, hundreds of repetitions may be necessary.

Gradually, the ABA therapist sets slightly more difficult goals, rewarding only increasingly accurate approximations of the correct response. One such intermediate step might be to echo the question "What is your name?" in a whisper and repeat the response "Joshua" in a normal tone of voice. Over a period of days, even weeks, the child learns to respond "Joshua" to the question "What is your name?"

Similar detailed strategies are used to teach children other language skills. In the hope of speeding the process, some tried teaching sign language to children with classic autism (Carr, 1982). Unfortunately, this was not a breakthrough. The communication deficits are more basic than receptive or expressive problems with spoken language. Children sometimes use *instrumental* gestures to get what they want, but not *expressive* gestures to show how they feel (Frith, 2003). ABA remains a painfully slow process that differs greatly from the way in which children normally learn to speak. The intensity and detail of ABA remind us that normal children come into the world remarkably well equipped to acquire language.

In addition to teaching communication skills, behavior therapists who work with children with ASD concentrate on reducing the excesses of self-stimulation, self-injurious behavior, and general disruptiveness, as well as teaching new skills to eliminate deficits in self-care and social behavior (Schreibman, 1988). ABA programs have successfully eliminated some behavioral excesses, particularly self-injury, but the treatments are controversial because they typically rely on punishment. A gentle slap or a mild electric shock can reduce or eliminate such potentially dangerous behaviors as head banging, but are such aversive treatments justified? This question confronts therapists,

parents, and others concerned with the treatment and protection of children.

Behavior therapists have been fairly successful in teaching self-care skills and less successful in teaching social responsiveness. The struggle with social skills is unfortunate, because treatment outcomes for children with classic autism are especially positive when social responsiveness improves (Koegel, Koegel, & McNerney, 2001). As Schreibman (1988) noted, "It is perhaps prophetic that the behavior characteristic which most uniquely defines autism is also the one that has proven the most difficult to understand and treat" (p. 118).

Although ABA focuses on specific target behaviors, ultimately the important question is: To what extent does treatment improve the entire disorder? Research shows that autistic children can learn specific target behaviors, but do intensive training efforts bring about improvements that are clinically significant?

An optimistic answer to this question was provided by O. Ivar Lovaas (1927–2010), who was a psychologist at UCLA and an acknowledged leader in ABA for classic autism. In a comprehensive report on the efforts of his research team, Lovaas (1987) compared the outcomes of three groups of children with autism: 19 children who received intensive ABA; 19 children who were referred to the program but who received less intensive treatment due to the unavailability of therapists; and 21 children who were treated elsewhere. Children with extremely low IQ scores were excluded, and treatment began before the children were four years of age. The children in the treatment group received the types of interventions described above, including both reinforcement and punishment procedures. In fact, they were treated 40 hours a week for more than two years.

No differences among the three groups of children were found before treatment began. Assessments following treatment were conducted between the ages of six and seven at the time when the children ordinarily would have finished the first grade of school. In the intensive behavior modification group, nine children (47 percent) completed first grade in a normal school. Eight more children (42

**TABLE 15.5**
## Educational Placement and IQ of Children with Autism Following ABA

| Group | Classroom | N | (%) | Mean IQ |
|---|---|---|---|---|
| Intensive Behavior Modification | Normal | 9 | (47) | 107 |
| | Aphasic | 8 | (42) | 74 |
| | Retarded | 2 | (11) | 30 |
| Limited Treatment | Normal | 0 | (0) | — |
| | Aphasic | 8 | (42) | 74 |
| | Retarded | 11 | (58) | 36 |
| No Treatment | Normal | 1 | (5) | 99 |
| | Aphasic | 10 | (48) | 67 |
| | Retarded | 10 | (48) | 44 |

*Source:* From "Behavioral Treatment and Normal Educational and Intellectual Functioning in Young Autistic Children" by O. I. Lovaas, Journal of Consulting & Clinical Psychology, 55 (1987), pp. 3–9. Copyright © 1987, American Psychological Association.

percent) passed first grade in a special class for children who cannot speak. In comparison, only one child (2 percent) in the two control groups completed first grade in a normal classroom, and 18 children (45 percent) completed first-grade classes for aphasic children. Table 15.5 summarizes these outcomes, and also the strong relation between IQ and classroom placement. Note the low mean IQ levels of all the children, despite the investigators' attempts to screen out the most severely impaired children.

These data are reason for considerable optimism. And a follow-up study indicated that many gains continued into late childhood and adolescence (McEachin, Smith, & Lovaas, 1993). Other research shows significant, but notably smaller, gains with very intensive ABA approaches (Smith, Groen, & Wynn, 2000). Recent research indicates that activities designed to encourage joint attention and social coordination improve language learning in ABA treatments (Kasari et al., 2008), at least when children show prior evidence of joint attention (Yoder & Stone, 2006). And a new study provocatively suggests that a very small percentage of people with ASD, especially those with higher social functioning, show essentially no symptoms of the disorder after treatment (Fein et al., 2013).

We applaud the efforts of Lovaas and others who have used ABA to teach skills to children with classic autism. Despite the fact that ASD apparently is caused by neurological abnormalities, the most effective treatment for the disorder is highly structured and intensive ABA (Rutter, 1996). Still, we must raise cautions: Are the children who passed first grade functioning normally in other respects? Because pretreatment IQ predicted outcome (Lovaas, 1987), does ABA work only with children who are high functioning? But perhaps the most important question about ABA is its cost. The children in the intensive ABA group were treated for 40 hours per week for more than two years. The children in the "limited treatment" control group received almost 10 hours of weekly treatment, yet they showed few improvements. The expenses associated with early but effective treatment clearly are far less than those involved in a lifetime of care (Lovaas, 1987). Still, we wonder: How do we justify devoting so many resources to ASD when, in comparison, we neglect intervention with children with intellectual disabilities?

## getting HELP

You may want to learn about getting help for intellectual disabilities or autism spectrum disorders for several reasons. You may have a family member with a disorder. You may want to know more about preventing intellectual disability in your own children when that time comes. Or you may be thinking of a career in special education or related disciplines.

If you have a family member with one of these disorders, you may find it helpful to get some more information. The National Research Council published an authoritative book called *Educating Children with Autism*. The book not only reviews the best approaches, but it also suggests ways of supporting educators and family members. As a way of getting inside this mysterious disorder, try reading one of Temple Grandin's accounts of her life with autism, *Thinking in Pictures* or *Emergence: Labeled Autistic*. A helpful guide for families is Robert and Martha Perske's *Hope for the Families: New Directions for Parents of Persons with Retardation and Other Disabilities*.

Depending on your age and relationship status, you may not yet be interested in learning how to prevent intellectual disability. But you will be highly motivated when the time comes to have a baby. We hope that, even if having a child seems like a distant event, you will pay special attention to our discussion of what you can do to limit risk, for personal as well as academic reasons.

If you are interested in a career in special education, we urge you to follow your dream. Working with children with special needs is a challenging and undervalued career, but it also is enormously important and personally rewarding. Even as a nonprofessional you can help people with intellectual disabilities or ASD. In this chapter, we use language that puts the person first by referring to "person with an intellectual disability" rather than "intellectually disabled person." You can put the person first, too, not only in your language, but through your actions.

How? Watch the language of others around you, particularly those all too familiar pejorative comments that may seem innocent but are demeaning and dehumanizing. You can put the person first in your actions by being friendly, helpful, and inclusive when you meet people with intellectual disabilities in your school, work, and community. You can put the person first by doing volunteer work with children or adults with intellectual disabilities or autism. Volunteers are needed in schools and group homes, as well as in work and recreational settings.

You also can put the person first by supporting and advocating fair policies for people with intellectual disabilities and ASD in schooling, employment, housing, and access to recreational activities. You will find many specific advocacy suggestions at the website of the American Association on Intellectual and Developmental Disabilities. Or if you need more motivation to become an advocate, pick up a copy of *Christmas in Purgatory*, by Burton Blatt and Fred Kaplan, a photographic essay on the horrid conditions under which people with intellectual disabilities live in institutions. After wincing at the pictures in this book, you will want to do something to help.

# 15 Summary

**Intellectual disabilities** are defined by (1) deficits in intellectual functioning, (2) deficits in adaptive skills, and (3) an onset before age 18.

People who have IQs below 70 but function adequately in the world are not considered to have an intellectual disability.

**IQ** tests are reliable and valid (if imperfect) predictors of academic performance.

*DSM-5* divides intellectual disability severity into mild, moderate, severe, and profound but no longer bases this on IQ scores.

**Down syndrome** is caused by an extra chromosome on the 21st pair and is the most common of the known biological causes of intellectual disability. **Fragile-X syndrome** is a genetic disorder that often causes intellectual disabilities, especially in boys. Other known biological causes include **phenylketonuria (PKU)**, an inherited metabolic deficiency; infectious diseases transmitted to the fetus during pregnancy or birth, such as rubella, syphilis, and genital herpes; excessive maternal alcohol consumption or drug use during pregnancy; Rh incompatibility; and malnutrition, premature birth, and low birth weight.

So-called **cultural-familial retardation** typically involves a mild intellectual disability and no known specific cause. It is assumed to represent normal IQ variation.

A major policy goal is **normalization** of the lives of people with intellectual disabilities through **mainstreaming** in public schools and promoting care in the community.

**Autism spectrum disorder (ASD)** involves disturbances in social relationships and communication, as well as stereotyped activities.

*DSM-5* views ASD as a single disorder, and eliminates problems once considered to be different, including **autism**, which typically involves extreme symptoms, including an intellectual disability, and **Asperger's disorder**, characterized by similar but less severe difficulties like those found in autism except without communication problems and with normal intelligence.

Estimates of the prevalence of ASD increased dramatically over the last decade, a trend likely primarily due to increased awareness and a broader diagnosis and not new causes of ASD.

Several known causes of intellectual disabilities may also cause ASD, which appears to be caused by multiple, mostly unidentified biological problems.

Applied behavior analysis is a promising treatment for autism, but the expense and effort involved are considerable.

# The Big Picture

## critical thinking review

**15.1  How are IQ scores like "grading on the curve"?**
Contemporary intelligence tests . . . calculate a "deviation IQ." According to this system, intellectual ability follows the **normal distribution**, the familiar bell-shaped frequency distribution . . . . (see page 407).

**15.2  Did the United States really support human breeding (eugenics)?**
You surely are aware that Adolf Hitler embraced eugenic principles. . . . You may *not* know that the principles of eugenics were embraced widely in the United States prior to World War II . . . . (see page 417).

**15.3  How can intellectual disabilities be prevented?**
Good maternal and child health care is one major step toward the primary prevention of intellectual disability . . . . (see page 416).

**15.4  Is there an "epidemic of autism"?**
Experts became concerned about overdiagnosis, particularly about a false "epidemic of autism." . . . (see page 424).

**15.5  Are children exceptionally intelligent underneath their autism?**
The existence of savant performance does not indicate that, as many have hoped, children with classic autism really are normal or even superior in intelligence. . . . (see page 424).

**15.6  What is wrong with psychological theories of the cause of autism?**
Before discussing evidence on biological contributions to autism, we first briefly consider—and reject—environmental explanations . . . . (see page 427).

# key terms

psychological disorders of childhood

16

# 16

## The Big Picture

### learning objectives

**16.1**
Are children's psychological disorders different from adults'?

**16.2**
Is ADHD different from just being a "bad kid"?

**16.3**
Are children's psychological problems a sign of family problems?

**16.4**
Can medication help children behave—and do better in school?

**16.5**
Can young children be depressed?

**16.6**
Do antidepressants cause teen suicide?

Have you ever fallen to the floor, kicking, screaming, and crying because you did not get your way? Almost certainly. Temper tantrums are normal for frustrated 2-year-old children—but not for 20-year-old college students. Similarly, it is developmentally normal for 4-year-old children to be terrified of imaginary monsters, but not for 14-year-old adolescents. As these examples illustrate, the first question we must ask in evaluating a child's behavior is: How old is the child?

## Overview

At every age, **developmental psychopathology,** understanding abnormal behavior within the context of normal development, is important. Because change is so rapid during the first 18 years of life, the developmental psychopathology approach is absolutely essential for psychological disorders of childhood. Psychologists are concerned only if a child's behavior deviates substantially from **developmental norms,** behavior that is typical for children of a given age.

In an effort to make developmental considerations a part of all disorders, *DSM-5* greatly reorganized its classification of psychological problems usually diagnosed first among children. Childhood disorders formerly grouped together are now scattered across the manual. Diagnoses given more commonly to children are listed first in various *DSM-5* chapters. Also, some "adult" diagnoses include guidance, usually very little, on how to diagonose

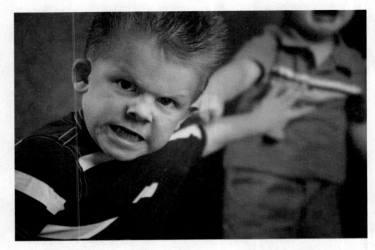

Temper tantrums are a normal, if trying, part of child development during the "terrible twos" (and beyond). Awareness of such developmental norms is essential to evaluating abnormal behavior in children.

children. We think *DSM-5* made a big mistake. Pediatricians, and parents, need to pay special attention to physical illnesses like colic (babies crying for more than three hours a day), "Otitis media" (middle ear infection), and Osgood–Schlatter disease (a painful bump on the knee stemming from rapid growth). The same is true for psychological disorders of childhood.

We introduce and use *DSM-5* terms, but organize developmental issues very differently. Chapter 15 discusses intellectual disabilities and autism spectrum disorders, serious psychological problems either present at birth or beginning early in childhood. Chapter 17 highlights key developmental issues in adult life. This chapter is organized around two long-established and widely recognized dimensions of psychological problems in children. **Externalizing disorders** create difficulties for the child's external world. They are characterized by children's failure to control their behavior according to the expectations of parents, peers, teachers, or legal authorities. **Internalizing disorders** are psychological problems that primarily affect the child's internal world, for example, excessive anxiety or sadness. We also briefly discuss several other psychological problems that commonly begin during childhood but do not fit under these dimensions.

Few children or adolescents identify themselves as needing a therapist. Instead, some adult, often a parent or teacher, decides that the child has a problem. Sometimes, a child is unable to recognize or admit to his or her difficulties. Other times, the problem is as much the adult's as the child's (Yeh & Weisz, 2001). Often, it is challenging to decide where the problem lies, as illustrated in the following case study.

### → Bad Boy, Troubled Boy, or All Boy?

Jeremy W. was eight years old when his mother brought him to a clinical psychologist recommended by his teacher and a school counselor. Mrs. W. was not sure she agreed with the school personnel about Jeremy. In fact, Mrs. W. wasn't sure if she agreed with her husband about what was going on with their son.

Jeremy was constantly in trouble at school. His teacher reprimanded him daily for disrupting the class, not paying attention, and failing to finish his work. But the teacher felt that her discipline had little effect. Sometimes he would listen for a while, but soon he was pestering another child, talking out of turn, or simply staring off into space. His classmates thought of him as a "pain." Lately, Jeremy had begun to talk back, and his teacher sent him to the principal's office several times.

The school psychologist tested Jeremy and found he had an IQ of 108. Yet, he was almost a year behind his grade in reading and arithmetic. The school psychologist suspected a learning disability but thought that Jeremy might instead be emotionally disturbed, as his behavior problems were interfering with his learning. She wanted him to remain in his regular classroom for now. After he got some treatment for behavior problems, she would reevaluate him for possible placement in a special class for students with learning problems.

Mrs. W. was frightened by the suggestion that Jeremy might be "emotionally disturbed" or "learning disabled." She said Jeremy could be difficult to manage at home, but she had never considered the possibility that he needed psychological help. Jeremy had always been a handful, but in her view, he had never been a bad child. Instead, Mrs. W. thought that Jeremy expressed himself better through actions than words. He was the opposite of his 11-year-old sister, who was an A and B student. Mrs. W. was not convinced that Jeremy's teacher was the best person to work with him, but agreed that he was having problems in school. In her mind, he was developing low self-esteem, and many of his actions were attempts to get attention.

According to Mrs. W., Jeremy's father spent very little time with him. Mr. W. worked long hours on his construction job, and was often off with his friends on weekends. She said that her husband was of little help even when he was at home. He would tell his wife that it was her job to take care of the kids—he needed his rest. With tears in her eyes, Mrs. W. said that she needed it too.

Mrs. W. said her husband was not concerned about Jeremy. He thought that Jeremy was just "all boy" and not much of a student—just as Mr. W. had been as a child. He refused to take time off from work to see the psychologist.

Mrs. W. said that she, too, saw a lot of his father in Jeremy—too much of him. She blamed her husband for Jeremy's problems, and was secretly furious with him. She was willing to try anything to help Jeremy, but doubted that she could do anything without her husband's support.

· · · · · · · · · · · · · · · · · · · · · · · · · · · · · · · · · · · · · · · · · ·

Is Jeremy a disobedient child, as his teacher thinks? A learning-disordered child, as suggested by the school psychologist? Suffering from low self-esteem, as his mother fears? Or is he simply "all boy," as his father claims? What about Jeremy? How does he feel about himself, his family, his schoolwork, and his friendships at school?

Mental health professionals who treat children are constantly vexed by such difficult questions. Treatment often begins with an attempt to achieve consensus about the nature of a child's problem (Hawley & Weisz, 2003). Psychologists want an accurate diagnosis, but another goal is to get adults working together. Mr. and Mrs. W. need to present a "united front" to Jeremy. In order to do so, they may need to resolve issues in their marriage. Due to such conflicts, many psychologists prefer to see children in family therapy rather than treat them alone. Many psychologists also work to establish better communication and cooperation between parents and teachers.

Of course, Jeremy is at least part of the problem. If we can trust his teacher's report—and experienced child clinical psychologists do trust teachers—Jeremy clearly has some type of externalizing problem. Perhaps Jeremy's behavior is a reaction to his parents' conflicts; he might act better if they work out their differences. Or perhaps he is a troubled child who is causing some of his parents' conflicts, not just reacting to them. Mr. and Mrs. W. both felt that Jeremy and his father were a lot alike. Could Jeremy have learned or inherited some of his father's characteristics?

## Externalizing Disorders

Children with externalizing disorders often break rules, are angry and aggressive, impulsive, overactive, and inattentive. These troublesome actions tend to occur together; however, different clusters of problems have different implications for the cause, treatment, and course of children's externalizing disorders.

### Symptoms of Externalizing

Many externalizing symptoms involve violations of age-appropriate social rules, including disobeying parents or teachers, annoying peers, and perhaps violating the law. All children break some rules, of course, and we often admire an innocent and clever rule breaker. For example, Calvin of the Calvin and Hobbes cartoons is devilish, but he is not really "bad," and certainly not "sick"!

**RULE VIOLATIONS** However, the rule violations in externalizing disorders are not trivial and are far from "cute." Many schoolteachers lament that they spend far too much time disciplining children, a circumstance that is also unfair to the well-behaved youngsters in the classroom. Even more serious, the Federal Bureau of Investigation reported that 25.9 percent of arrests for violent and 37.1 percent for property offenses—major crimes including murder, forcible rape, and robbery—were of young

**Calvin and Hobbes**　　　　　　　　　　　　by **Bill Watterson**

people under the age of 21 in 2011 (U.S. Department of Justice, 2011). Other evidence indicates that the worst 5 percent of juvenile offenders account for about half of all juvenile arrests (Farrington, Ohlin, & Wilson, 1986). With all our fears about youth violence, you should know, however, that the rate of violent crime among juveniles is falling (Snyder, 2002; see Figure 16.1).

Externalizing behavior is a far greater concern when it is frequent, intense, lasting, and pervasive. That is, externalizing behavior is more problematic when it is part of a *syndrome,* or cluster of problems, than when it is a *symptom* that occurs in isolation. The existence of an externalizing syndrome has been demonstrated consistently by statistical analysis of symptom checklists completed about children by parents or teachers. Moreover, agreement among adult raters typically is fairly high (Duhig et al., 2000).

**CHILDREN'S AGE AND RULE VIOLATIONS**  Children of different ages are likely to violate very different rules (Lahey et al., 2000). A preschooler with an externalizing problem may be disobedient to his parents and aggressive with other children. During the school years, he is more likely to be disruptive in the classroom, uncooperative on the playground, or defiant at home. By adolescence, the problem teenager may be failing in school, ignoring all discipline at home, hanging out with delinquent peers, and violating the law.

Children's age is also important to consider in relation to the timing of rule violations. All children break rules, but those with externalizing problems violate rules at a younger age than is developmentally normal (Loeber, 1988). For example, most young people experiment with smoking, alcohol, or sexuality, but children with externalizing disorders do so at a notably younger age.

**ADOLESCENT-LIMITED OR LIFE-COURSE-PERSISTENT?**  Teenagers often violate the rules laid down by parents, teachers, and society as a means of asserting their independence and perhaps in order to conform to their peer group. Due to this, psychologists distinguish between externalizing behavior that is *adolescent-limited*—that ends along with the teen years—and *life-course-persistent* antisocial behavior that continues into adult life (Moffitt, 1993). In fact, externalizing problems that begin *before* adolescence are more likely to persist into adult life than are problems that begin *during* adolescence. The antisocial behavior of children whose problems begin before the age of 12 is more likely to continue when they have fewer social bonds, including larger, less involved families and troubled peer relationships (van Domburgh et al., 2009).

Can adolescent-limited and life-course-persistent antisocial behavior be distinguished in other ways? Many investigators are searching for symptoms that predict adult *antisocial personality disorder (ASPD)* (Lynam et al., 2007). One early indicator of this lifelong pattern is *callousness* or indifference to the suffering of others. Young people with antisocial tendencies do not readily recognize sadness and fear in other people's facial expressions (Blair et al., 2001). Callousness predicts future ASPD when externalizing disorders are absent, but may not improve prediction when externalizing disorders are present already (Burke, Waldman, & Lahey, 2010; McMahon et al., 2010). Given mixed results, experts are debating whether externalizing problems should be subtyped based on the presence or absence of callousness. *DSM-5* does not include separate diagnoses, but indicates that the presence or absence of callousness should be noted among youth with conduct disorders.

**ANGER AND AGGRESSION**  Children with externalizing problems are often angry and aggressive. Younger children may lose their temper and be argumentative, while adolescents may be hostile and physically injure others. In addition to the actions themselves, motivation is important. We chuckle at the innocent adventures of a Calvin, but we judge children harshly if their *intent* is selfish and they show little *remorse.* You might judge Jeremy W's behavior differently based on whether he is an angry child who cares little about being "bad" or an impulsive child who wants to but just cannot consistently be "good."

Motivation also is a key to *relational aggression,* actions designed to hurt others in more subtle ways, for example, put downs, gossip, and social exclusion. Relational aggression is more common among girls, and has been hypothesized to be a marker of girls' externalizing (Crick, Ostrov, & Werner, 2006). However,

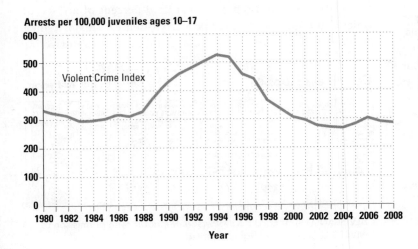

**Arrests per 100,000 juveniles ages 10–17**

Violent Crime Index

Year

**FIGURE 16.1**

**Arrests of Juveniles for Violent Crimes in the United States, 1980–2008**  Despite public fears, youth violence in the United States peaked in the 1990s and has remained comparatively low. *Source:* Puzzanchera, C. Juvenile arrests 2008. Juvenile Justice Bulletin. December, 2009; 5.

In contrast to boys' physical aggression, girls engage in more relational aggression. As illustrated in the movie *Mean Girls*, relational aggression includes put downs, gossip, and social exclusion.

measures of relational aggression add little to the diagnosis of conduct disorder in girls (Keenan et al., 2010).

**IMPULSIVITY** Impulsive children seem unable to control their behavior according to the demands of many situations. They act before they think, failing to wait for their turn, blurting out answers in class, and interrupting others. Often, impulsive children are *trying* to behave. They struggle with *executive functioning,* the internal direction of behavior.

**HYPERACTIVITY** **Hyperactivity** involves squirming, fidgeting, and restless behavior. Hyperactive children are in constant motion. They often have trouble sitting still, even during leisure activities like watching television. Hyperactivity is found across situations, even during sleep, but it is more obvious in structured settings than in unstructured ones (Barkley, 2006). Hyperactive behavior is particularly noticeable in the classroom. Due to this, reports from teachers are critical in identifying hyperactive behavior.

**ATTENTION DEFICITS** **Attention deficits** are characterized by distractibility, frequent shifts from one uncompleted activity to another, careless mistakes, poor organization or effort, and general "spaciness" (for example, not listening well). As with impulsivity, inattention usually is not intentional or oppositional; rather, it reflects an inability to maintain a focus despite an apparent desire to do so. A particular attention problem is "staying on task," or *sustained attention.* Children with ADHD perform substantially worse on the continuous *performance test,* a measure of sustained attention where children must closely monitor long lists of letters presented on a computer screen (Huang-Pollock et al., 2012).

## Diagnosis of Externalizing Disorders

Externalizing disorders are listed at different places in *DSM-5,* one of our objections to the manual's organization. Like most child clinical psychologists, we are primarily concerned with three disorders: attention-deficit/hyperactivity disorder, oppositional defiant disorder, and conduct disorder.

**ATTENTION-DEFICIT/HYPERACTIVITY DISORDER** As its name indicates, **attention-deficit/hyperactivity disorder (ADHD)** is characterized by hyperactivity, attention deficit—and impulsivity. You may have heard ADHD called "hyperactivity" or perhaps "ADD." In fact, hyperactivity and attention deficit each have been viewed as the driving symptom behind ADHD. *DSM-II* called the disorder *hyperkinesis,* a synonym for "hyperactivity." *DSM-III* labeled it *attention-deficit disorder,* or *ADD.* Some experts now view impulsivity as the core symptom (Barkley, 2006; Nigg, 2001). We are not concerned with which symptom gets top billing for a problem with ever-changing names. We are concerned with two facts. First, contrary to what some professionals have argued, hyperactivity is not merely a consequence of inattention, or vice versa (Barkley, 2006). Each is an independent symptom. Second, some children have problems primarily with inattention or overactivity/impulsivity, a difference that can be specified as a part of the *DSM-5* diagnosis. Predominantly inattentive children are more "spacy" than "distractible," and they struggle with learning far more than behavior control (Milich, Balentine, & Lynam, 2001). Predominantly hyperactive/impulsive children may show these behavior problems as early as the preschool years. Often, attention deficits appear or get noticed during the early school years (Hart et al., 1995).

*DSM-5* counts symptoms for the ADHD diagnosis, viewing the underlying problem as dimensional even though the diagnosis

**A.** A persistent pattern of inattention and/or hyperactivity-impulsivity that interferes with functioning or development, as characterized by (1) and/or (2):

1. **Inattention:** Six (or more) of the following symptoms have persisted for at least 6 months to a degree that is inconsistent with developmental level and that negatively impacts directly on social and academic/occupational activities:

   **Note:** The symptoms are not solely a manifestation of oppositional behavior, defiance, hostility, or failure to understand tasks or instructions. For older adolescents and adults (age 17 and older), at least five symptoms are required.

   a. Often fails to give close attention to details or makes careless mistakes in schoolwork, at work, or during other activities (e.g., overlooks or misses details, work is inaccurate).

   b. Often has difficulty sustaining attention in tasks or play activities (e.g., has difficulty remaining focused during lectures, conversations, or lengthy reading).

   c. Often does not seem to listen when spoken to directly (e.g., mind seems elsewhere, even in the absence of any obvious distraction).

   d. Often does not follow through on instructions and fails to finish schoolwork, chores, or duties in the workplace (e.g., starts tasks but quickly loses focus and is easily sidetracked).

   e. Often has difficulty organizing tasks and activities (e.g., difficulty managing sequential tasks; difficulty keeping materials and belongings in order; messy, disorganized work; has poor time management; fails to meet deadlines).

   f. Often avoids, dislikes, or is reluctant to engage in tasks that require sustained mental effort (e.g., schoolwork or homework; for older adolescents and adults, preparing reports, completing forms, reviewing lengthy papers).

   g. Often loses things necessary for tasks or activities (e.g., school materials, pencils, books, tools, wallets, keys, paperwork, eyeglasses, mobile telephones).

   h. Is often easily distracted by extraneous stimuli (for older adolescents and adults, may include unrelated thoughts).

   i. Is often forgetful in daily activities (e.g., doing chores, running errands; for older adolescents and adults, returning calls, paying bills, keeping appointments).

2. Hyperactivity and impulsivity: Six (or more) of the following symptoms have persisted for at least 6 months to a degree that is inconsistent with developmental level and that negatively impacts directly on social and academic/occupational activities:

**Note:** The symptoms are not solely a manifestation of oppositional behavior, defiance, hostility, or a failure to understand tasks or instructions. For older adolescents and adults (age 17 and older), at least five symptoms are required.

a. Often fidgets with or taps hands or feet or squirms in seat.

b. Often leaves seat in situations when remaining seated is expected (e.g., leaves his or her place in the classroom, in the office or other workplace, or in other situations that require remaining in place).

c. Often runs about or climbs in situations where it is inappropriate. (Note: In adolescents or adults, may be limited to feeling restless.)

d. Often unable to play or engage in leisure activities quietly.

e. Is often "on the go," acting as if "driven by a motor" (e.g., is unable to be or uncomfortable being still for extended time, as in restaurants, meetings; may be experienced by others as being restless or difficult to keep up with).

f. Often talks excessively.

g. Often blurts out an answer before a question has been completed (e.g., completes people's sentences; cannot wait for turn in conversation).

h. Often has difficulty waiting his or her turn (e.g., while waiting in line).

i. Often interrupts or intrudes on others (e.g., butts into conversations, games, or activities; may start using other people's things without asking or receiving permission; for adolescents and adults, may intrude into or take over what others are doing).

**B.** Several inattentive or hyperactive-impulsive symptoms were present prior to age 12 years.

**C.** Several inattentive or hyperactive-impulsive symptoms are present in two or more settings (e.g., at home, school, or work; with friends or relatives; in other activities).

**D.** There is clear evidence that the symptoms interfere with, or reduce the quality of, social, academic, or occupational functioning.

**E.** The symptoms do not occur exclusively during the course of schizophrenia or another psychotic disorder and are not better explained by another mental disorder (e.g., mood disorder, anxiety disorder, dissociative disorder, personality disorder, substance intoxication or withdrawal).

Reprinted with permission from the *Diagnostic and Statistical Manual of Mental Disorders*, Fifth Edition, (Copyright 2013). American Psychiatric Association.

is categorical (see "DSM-5: Attention-Deficit/Hyperactivity Disorder"). Several symptoms must begin before the age of 12 for the diagnosis of ADHD, an upward revision from the earlier cutoff of 7 years. *DSM-5* classifies ADHD as a *neurodevelopmental disorder*, a diagnostic grouping that includes intellectual disability, autism spectrum disorder, and specific learning disorder (see What Are Learning Disabilities?).

**OPPOSITIONAL DEFIANT DISORDER Oppositional defiant disorder (ODD)** is defined by a pattern of angry, defiant, and vindictive behavior. As you can see from "DSM-5: Oppositional Defiant Disorder" on p. 442, the rule violations in ODD typically involve minor transgressions, such as refusing to obey adult requests, arguing, and acting angry. Such misbehavior is a cause for concern among school-aged children, and often foreshadows

## What Are Learning Disabilities?

The *DSM-5* diagnosis of *learning disorders*—we prefer the term used by educators, **learning disability (LD)**—is used for students who perform substantially below their ability in a specific area of learning. (Many wonder why learning disorders are included in the *DSM*, a listing of *mental* disorders, when the difficulties are so clearly academic in nature.) LD is defined in many different ways, but all definitions have problems (Waber, 2010). The most common approach has been the *discrepancy definition*, comparing scores on intelligence tests with scores on academic achievement tests. LD can be defined as a difference of one or two standard deviations between aptitude and achievement in a specific area of learning—reading, writing, or mathematics. Thus, a diagnosis of reading disorder (*dyslexia*) would be made if a child scored a standard deviation above the mean on the verbal portion of an intelligence test (an IQ of 115) but a standard deviation below the mean in reading.

Although widely used, both the reliability and validity of the discrepancy definition has been called into question. For example, 30 percent of children diagnosed this way in third grade no longer meet diagnostic criteria in fifth grade (Francis et al., 2005). Parents and politicians have also objected to the definition, arguing that it excludes children who could benefit from special instruction. In fact, federal legislation passed in 2005 prohibited using the discrepancy definition as a way of excluding children from being diagnosed LD, although the method can be used legally to *include* children as LD. The diagnostic method currently in vogue is called "response-to-intervention" (RTI). This approach calls for the use of evidence-based methods to teach children. It defines LD as those children who still fail to learn. Among the many problems with this approach is the absence of evidence-based teaching methods (Reynolds & Shaywitz, 2009; Waber, 2010).

The lack of an evidence base is not the result of a lack of effort to treat LD. In 1975, the U.S. Congress passed the Education for All Handicapped Children Act (now called the Individuals with Disabilities Education Act, or IDEA), a law mandating that local school systems provide special resources for educating handicapped children, including children with LD. The federal legislation dramatically increased the number of children identified as having LD, rising from less than 2 percent in 1976–1977 to over 4 percent in 2002–2003 (Office of Special Education Programs, 2003). However, some commentators wonder whether this reflects overly broad definitions of LD (Lyon, 1996). And it is not clear that the identification of more students has led to more effective education. Intervention attempts include intensive tutoring, individually or in small groups (including teacher-based direct instruction and student-based cooperative learning); behavior therapy programs in which academic success is systematically rewarded; psychostimulant medication; counseling for related problems (for example, low self-esteem); and various special efforts such as training in visual–motor skills. Unfortunately, no treatment has demonstrated consistent success (Swanson, Harris, & Graham, 2003; Waber, 2010).

Another problem is that research has not identified a specific psychological, neurological, or genetic cause of LD (Mash & Wolfe, 2010; Snowling, 2002; Swanson et al., 2003). LD appears to involve disruptions in several aspects of information processing, including perception, attention, language processing, and executive function. Typically, the cause is viewed as biological. Neuroimaging research on reading disabilities identifies activity differences particularly in the temporal-parietal region of the left hemisphere of the brain (Miller, Sanchez, & Hynd, 2003; Shaywitz, Mody, & Shaywitz, 2006). (Recall that language abilities are lateralized in the left hemisphere.) Behavior genetic research shows that LD, like normal reading abilities, is moderately heritable, and genetic linkage analysis suggests possible loci on chromosomes 1, 2, 6, 15, and 18 (Kovas & Plomin, 2007; Thomson & Raskind, 2003). Special attention is currently focused on the *DCDC2*, which appears to affect how neurons function in the left temporal-parietal region (Waber, 2010). While exciting, advances in genetics and imaging are a long way from identifying a specific deficit in LD, let alone leading to more effective treatments.

Perhaps 5 percent of all schoolchildren in the United States do not achieve at a level consistent with their abilities (Waber, 2010). LD is "real" in the sense that these children seem to have the ability and motivation to perform better in school, yet they do not. Despite decades of legislation, special teaching programs, and research, however, controversy is rampant about the definition, cause, and treatment of LD.

---

the development of much more serious antisocial behavior during adolescence and adult life. However, these types of rule violations fall within developmental norms for adolescents, who are typically somewhat rebellious.

*DSM-5* lists ODD in a *different* diagnostic category than ADHD, a real difficulty given the similarity between the two problems. Both are externalizing problems that are likely to be diagnosed for the first time among early school-aged children. In fact, experts have long debated whether ODD and ADHD are really similar or different problems. Intent is a key to the difference between the two problems. Children with ADHD want to "be good," but are impulsive and have trouble behaving. Children with ODD are angrier and intentionally rebellious. The current consensus is that the two disorders are separate but frequently comorbid (Waschbusch, 2002). Approximately half of all children with one disorder also have the other problem (Schachar & Tannock, 2002). About 25 percent of children with each problem also have a learning

**A.** A pattern of angry/irritable mood, argumentative/defiant behavior, or vindictiveness lasting at least 6 months as evidenced by at least four symptoms from any of the following categories, and exhibited during interaction with at least one individual who is not a sibling.

### Angry/Irritable Mood
1. Often loses temper.
2. Is often touchy or easily annoyed.
3. Is often angry and resentful.

### Argumentative/Defiant Behavior
4. Often argues with authority figures or, for children and adolescents, with adults.
5. Often actively defies or refuses to comply with requests from authority figures or with rules.
6. Often deliberately annoys others.
7. Often blames others for his or her mistakes or misbehavior.

### Vindictiveness
8. Has been spiteful or vindictive at least twice within the past 6 months.

**Note:** The persistence and frequency of these behaviors should be used to distinguish a behavior that is within normal limits from a behavior that is symptomatic. For children younger than 5 years, the behavior should occur on most days for a period of at least 6 months unless otherwise noted (Criterion A8). For individuals 5 years or older, the behavior should occur at least once per week for at least 6 months, unless otherwise noted (Criterion A8). While these frequency criteria provide guidance on a minimal level of frequency to define symptoms, other factors should also be considered, such as whether the frequency and intensity of the behaviors are outside a range that is normative for the individual's developmental level, gender, and culture.

**B.** The disturbance in behavior is associated with distress in the individual or others in his or her immediate social context (e.g., family, peer group, work colleagues), or it impacts negatively on social, educational, occupational, or other important areas of functioning.

**C.** The behaviors do not occur exclusively during the course of a psychotic, substance use, depressive, or bipolar disorder. Also, the criteria are not met for disruptive mood dysregulation disorder.

disorder (Rucklidge & Tannock, 2001; Schachar & Tannock, 2002).

**CONDUCT DISORDER** **Conduct disorder (CD)** is a persistent and repetitive pattern of serious rule violations, most of which are illegal as well as antisocial—for example, assault or robbery (see "DSM-5: Conduct Disorder"). There is often a developmental continuity between ODD and CD, as younger rule violators "graduate" to more serious offenses. *DSM-5* places both problems in a new diagnostic category called *Disruptive, Impulse-Control, and Conduct Disorders*. It distinguishes between conduct disorders that begin before or after the age of 10 in recognition of the fact that earlier onset predicts more life-course-persistent antisocial behavior—perhaps antisocial personality disorder. Yet to add to organizational confusion, *DSM-5* lists antisocial personality disorder in yet another diagnostic grouping, personality disorders (see Chapter 9). Perhaps now you are beginning to understand why we consider these three externalizing disorders together in one chapter!

Conduct disorder is roughly equivalent to juvenile delinquency. Most of the symptoms involve *index offenses*—crimes against people or property that are illegal at any age. A few symptoms are comparable to **status offenses**—acts that are illegal only because of the youth's status as a minor, for example, truancy from school. Of course, *juvenile delinquency* is a *legal* classification. Technically, youths are not delinquent until a judge finds them guilty of either a criminal or status offense. Adolescents who repeatedly break the law have conduct disorders regardless of whether they are arrested and convicted. Still, American law traditionally treats the criminal behavior of juveniles differently from crimes committed by adults, viewing it as a psychological problem, not just a legal one.

## Frequency of Externalizing

A study of a nationally representative sample found that fully 19.1 percent of adolescents in the United States had an externalizing disorder at some point in their life (Merikangas et al., 2010; see Research Methods on p. 444). The Centers for Disease Control and Prevention (CDC) reported that 9.5 percent of children in the United States had a lifetime diagnosis of ADHD (CDC, 2010). Diagnostic practice is more conservative in Europe where 1 to 2 percent of children receive an ADHD diagnosis despite similar frequencies of disruptive behavior (Schachar & Tannock, 2002). In contrast, the diagnosis of ADHD actually increased by two-thirds between 2000 and 2010 in the United States (Garfield et al., 2012). And perhaps surprisingly, the diagnosis is given more commonly among the children of *more* affluent parents (Getahun et al., 2013). This may reflect active efforts on the part of wealthier parents to help their children's schooling, while the children of parents with fewer resources may be identified as ODD or CD.

**A.** A repetitive and persistent pattern of behavior in which the basic rights of others or major age-appropriate societal norms or rules are violated, as manifested by the presence of at least three of the following 15 criteria in the past 12 months from any of the categories below, with at least one criterion present in the past 6 months:

### Aggression to People and Animals
1. Often bullies, threatens, or intimidates others.
2. Often initiates physical fights.
3. Has used a weapon that can cause serious physical harm to others (e.g., a bat, brick, broken bottle, knife, gun).
4. Has been physically cruel to people.
5. Has been physically cruel to animals.
6. Has stolen while confronting a victim (e.g., mugging, purse snatching, extortion, armed robbery).
7. Has forced someone into sexual activity.

### Destruction of Property
8. Has deliberately engaged in fire setting with the intention of causing serious damage.
9. Has deliberately destroyed others' property (other than by fire setting).

### Deceitfulness or Theft
10. Has broken into someone else's house, building, or car.
11. Often lies to obtain goods or favors or to avoid obligations (i.e., "cons" others).
12. Has stolen items of nontrivial value without confronting a victim (e.g., shoplifting, but without breaking and entering; forgery).

### Serious Violations of Rules
13. Often stays out at night despite parental prohibitions, beginning before age 13 years.
14. Has run away from home overnight at least twice while living in the parental or parental surrogate home, or once without returning for a lengthy period.
15. Is often truant from school, beginning before age 13 years.

**B.** The disturbance in behavior causes clinically significant impairment in social, academic, or occupational functioning.

**C.** If the individual is age 18 years or older, criteria are not met for antisocial personality disorder.

Reprinted with permission from the *Diagnostic and Statistical Manual of Mental Disorders*, Fifth Edition, (Copyright 2013). American Psychiatric Association.

---

Two to ten times as many boys as girls have externalizing problems (Keenan & Shaw, 1997). Except for the normative increase during adolescence, the prevalence generally declines with age, although it declines at much earlier ages for girls than for boys (Keenan & Shaw, 1997). In fact, the prevalence of life-course-persistent antisocial behavior is far lower among girls than boys, even more so than for other externalizing problems (Earls & Mezzacappa, 2002).

**FAMILY RISK FACTORS** Externalizing disorders are associated with various indicators of family adversity, a fact highlighted by British psychiatrist Michael Rutter, an international authority on the epidemiology of child psychopathology. Rutter's (1989) Family Adversity Index includes six family predictors of behavior problems among children: (1) low income, (2) overcrowding in the home, (3) maternal depression, (4) paternal antisocial behavior, (5) conflict between the parents, and (6) removal of the child from the home. The risk for externalizing problems does not increase substantially when only one family risk factor is present. However, the risk increases fourfold with two factors—and even further with three or more sources of family adversity.

Other findings underscore the relationship between children's externalizing problems and social disadvantage (Earls & Mezzacappa, 2002). For example, externalizing disorders are found among more than 20 percent of children living in inner-city neighborhoods and are associated with divorce and single parenting (National Academy of Sciences, 1989).

## Causes of Externalizing

All children need to learn to control their behavior. If you doubt this, visit any preschool. Children frequently need to be reminded to share, to cooperate, and not to hit, push, scratch, or bite. The natural behavior we observe in children also can be wonderful—preschoolers freely make friends, exchange favors, and show empathy when others are hurt. Still, all children need some discipline (together with a lot of love). Of course, different children need—or receive—more or less guidance. Thus, biological, psychological, and social factors can all contribute to externalizing problems.

**BIOLOGICAL FACTORS** The biological factors involved in externalizing disorders include a difficult temperament, neuropsychological abnormalities, and genetics. Biological risk factors can be a "double whammy," because they affect behavior problems directly and also strain relationships with parents, teachers, and peers.

**TEMPERAMENT** Children differ in their **temperament,** inborn behavioral characteristics including activity level, emotionality,

# RESEARCH methods

## Samples: How to Select the People We Study

Psychologists typically do not use a **representative sample**—a sample that accurately represents some larger group of people. Instead, we often use convenience samples—groups of people who are easily recruited and studied. For many purposes, convenience samples work just fine. For example, we do not need a representative sample to study the effectiveness of alternative treatments for ADHD.

For some purposes, however, obtaining representative samples is essential. For example, many children with externalizing problems in clinical settings come from single-parent families, and some studies of clinical samples have concluded that single parenting causes behavior problems. However, we need to be cautious in generalizing from convenience or clinical samples. These groups are unrepresentative of the population of children and families. Consider this: Pediatricians surely would greatly overestimate the prevalence of ear infections if they generalized from their clinical samples! In fact, when we study representative samples of children from single-parent families, we find that most do not have psychological problems. Most children, and most single parent families, are resilient; they cope successfully with the stressors of single parenting (Emery, 1999a).

How do social scientists (typically sociologists) select representative samples so they can generalize accurately to a larger population? First, the researcher must identify the population of interest, the entire group of people to whom the researcher wants to generalize—for example, children under the age of 18 living in the United States. Second, the researcher must randomly select participants from the population and obtain a large enough sample to ensure that the results are statistically reliable. This allows researchers to make generalizations that sometimes seem remarkable, such as accurately predicting the outcome of a political election from polls of a relatively small number of voters.

Errors can occur in identifying the population of interest or in random selection. One of the most famous errors occurred in 1948, when newspaper headlines heralded Thomas E. Dewey's election over Harry S. Truman in the U.S. presidential election. Actually, Truman won handily. Where did the pollsters go wrong? They made a mistake in identifying the population of voters. The researchers sampled randomly from the U.S. population, but more Democrats went to the polls to vote for Truman than Republicans did for Dewey. (This is one reason why election pollsters now do exit surveys.) The polls also were conducted a week or more before the election, and late voter sentiment swung from Dewey to Truman.

Political scientists have become much more sophisticated in their sampling strategies since 1948. A fortunate trend in psychology is a new collaboration with sociologists in studying normal and abnormal behavior. Many large-scale surveys now follow representative samples of children or families over time and include measures of psychological well-being. Psychological scientists are increasingly using these samples to make sure that the same pattern of findings obtained in intensive studies of small convenience samples are found in representative samples of the population.

---

and sociability (Buss, 1991). Temperament can be classified in various ways, but Thomas and Chess's (1977) grouping into easy, difficult, and slow-to-warm-up is a useful summary. *Easy* children are friendly and obey most rules; *difficult* children are unpredictable and challenging; *slow-to-warm-up* children are shy and withdrawn. A difficult temperament during infancy or toddlerhood predicts the development of later externalizing disorders (Shaw et al., 1997).

***NEUROPSYCHOLOGICAL ABNORMALITIES*** Other biological factors contribute to externalizing disorders, particularly ADHD. Brain damage can produce overactivity and inattention, but *hard*

*signs* of brain damage, such as an abnormal CT scan, are found in less than 5 percent of cases of ADHD (Rutter, 1983). Much more common are neurological *soft signs,* such as delays in fine motor coordination (as may be evident in poor penmanship). However, many children with ADHD do not show soft signs, while many normal children do (Barkley, 2006). Thus, their implications are ambiguous.

Minor anomalies in physical appearance, delays in reaching developmental milestones, maternal smoking and alcohol consumption, and pregnancy and birth complications also are more common among children with ADHD. Still, researchers are yet to discover a specific marker of biological vulnerability.

Preschoolers need to learn to share, cooperate, and generally "be nice." Human nature includes selfish and aggressive motivations (as well as altruistic ones). Inborn variation and the availability and success of socialization both contribute to the development of externalizing disorders.

One candidate is impairment in the prefrontal cortical–striatal network. This area of the brain controls executive functions including attention, inhibition, and emotion regulation (Barkley, 2006), although executive functioning may be a problem only for a subset of cases (Nigg et al., 2004).

**GENETICS AND ADHD** Several studies show that genetic factors strongly contribute to ADHD. For example, a study of almost 4,000 Australian twins found concordance rates among MZ twins of roughly 80 percent, whereas DZ twins had concordance rates of approximately 40 percent (Levy et al., 1997). These rates are close to what one would expect for a *purely* genetic disorder (where the concordances would be 100 percent for MZ and 50 percent for DZ twins). In fact, genetic factors explain 90 percent of the variance in ADHD symptoms, a much higher proportion than for most behavior disorders (Burt, 2010; Nikolas & Burt, 2010). Such evidence has spurred a search for specific genes that may cause ADHD. The dopamine receptor gene (DRD4) has been thought to be involved, but studies often fail to replicate

earlier findings, and many other candidate genes have been (inconsistently) linked to ADHD (Banaschewski et al., 2010; Gizer, Ficks, & Waldman, 2009). Possible explanations for the disappointing results of efforts to identify specific genes include polygenic contributions to ADHD, the existence of as-of-yet unidentified subtypes of ADHD (with different causes), and other complexities such as gene–environment interactions.

Single genes (yet to be identified) may cause some cases of ADHD. However, most cases appear to be polygenic. As we hope you know by now, this means that that ADHD is *not* an "either you have it or you don't" disorder, that is, a problem qualitatively different from normal (see Chapter 2). In fact, the best evidence indicates that variation in attention and activity level is quantitative not qualitative (Barkley, 2006). You cannot be "a little bit pregnant," but you *can* be "a little bit ADHD."

Why is this important? Because people tend to think of "genetic" as meaning you have a "gene for" a given condition. However, like most mental disorders, most cases of ADHD appear to involve many genes. This leaves us with the very important question of deciding where to draw the line dividing "normal" activity or attention struggles and "abnormal" ADHD. The dividing line question is particularly important to consider (as we do shortly) with relation to the "either/or" decision of whether to medicate a child.

### GENE–ENVIRONMENT INTERACTIONS AND ODD

Genes contribute less strongly to ODD than to ADHD (Burt et al., 2001). However, genetic influences are greater for early- than late-onset antisocial behavior (Taylor, Iacono, & McGue, 2000). This is important because genes appear to play a role in the continuity between early-onset ODD and adult antisocial behavior. However, adolescent limited antisocial behavior largely reflects the environment of teen rebellion (Gottesman & Goldsmith, 1994).

If genes contribute to antisocial behavior, an essential question is: What is the inherited mechanism? Hyperactivity or inattention may be directly inherited, but rule violations surely are not (Earls & Mezzacappa, 2002). No one suggests that there is a "crime gene," let alone an "argue with your teacher gene"!

Part of what is inherited may be a tendency to react more negatively to adverse environments. In a much-cited study, the effect of childhood maltreatment on adolescent conduct problems differed depending on the gene producing monoamine oxidase activity (MAOA). (The MAOA gene encodes an enzyme that metabolizes neurotransmitters and renders them inactive.) Child maltreatment predicted significantly more adolescent conduct problems if the boys were genetically predisposed to low rather than high MAOA activity (Caspi et al., 2002). In a similar vein, a recent study linked low SES to increased callousness only among youth with a certain allele for the serotonin transporter (5-HTTLPR) gene (Sadeh et al., 2010). You should know that chance results are common in the fervent search to discover specific genes that influence complex social behaviors (Risch et al., 2009). Still, interactions between genes and the environment undoubtedly contribute to many psychological problems including antisocial behavior.

### SOCIAL FACTORS

*Socialization* is the process of shaping children's behavior and attitudes to conform to the expectations of parents, teachers, and society. Although parental explanation, example, and appropriate discipline typically are most important in socializing children, other influences cannot be ignored. Peer groups exert strong, if sometimes subtle, conformity pressures that increase as children grow older. School and popular media also are powerful socialization agents.

### PARENTING STYLES

Parental love is sometimes mistakenly viewed as the opposite of disciplining children, but warm parent–child relationships make discipline both less necessary and more effective (Shaw & Bell, 1993). In fact, developmental psychologists classify parenting into four styles based on warmth and discipline (see Figure 16.2). *Authoritative parents* are both loving and firm. Their children are well-adjusted. In contrast, *authoritarian* parents lack warmth, and their discipline is often harsh and autocratic. Children of authoritarian parents are generally compliant, but they may also be anxious and perhaps rebellious. *Indulgent* parents are the opposite of authoritarian parents: affectionate but lax in discipline. Their children tend to be impulsive and noncompliant, but not extremely antisocial. Finally, *neglectful* parents are not concerned either with their children's emotional needs or discipline. Children with serious conduct problems often have neglectful parents (Hoeve et al., 2008).

### COERCION

More specific problems in parenting also contribute to children's externalizing. One example is psychologist Gerald Patterson's (1982) concept of **coercion,** which occurs when parents *positively* reinforce a child's misbehavior by giving in to the child's demands. The child, in turn, *negatively* reinforces the parents by ending his or her obnoxious behavior as soon as the parents capitulate. Thus, coercion describes an interaction in which parents and children reciprocally reinforce child misbehavior and parent capitulation, as is illustrated in the following brief case study.

### ➞ I Want Candy!

Ms. B. finally admitted that she had lost all control of her four-year-old son Billy. She was a single parent who was exhausted by her routine of working from 8 to 5:30 every day and managing Billy and the household in the evenings and on weekends. She had no parenting or financial support from Billy's father or anyone else, and Ms. B. was worn down. When it was time to discipline Billy, she usually gave in—either because this was the easiest thing to do or because she felt too guilty to say no.

Ms. B. described many difficult interactions with Billy. One example stood out. Ms. B. often stopped at the grocery store with Billy after work, and he inevitably gave her trouble. Dealing

| | Accepting, Responsive, Child-centered | Rejecting, Unresponsive, Parent-centered |
|---|---|---|
| **Demanding, controlling** | Authoritative | Authoritarian |
| **Undemanding, low in control attempts** | Indulgent | Neglectful |

**FIGURE 16.2**

**Four styles of parenting, based on dimensions of parental warmth and discipline efforts.**

*Source:* E. E. Maccoby and J. A. Martin, 1983, "Socialization in the Context of the Family: Parent–Child Interaction," in E. M. Hetherington (Ed.), Socialization, Personality, and Social Development, Vol. 4, Handbook of Child Psychology, pp. 1–101. New York: Wiley.

with the candy aisle was a particular problem. Billy would ask for some candy when they first approached the aisle. Ms. B. told him no, but in an increasingly loud voice Billy protested, "I WANT CANDY!" Ms. B. would try to be firm, but soon she was embarrassed by the disapproving looks on the faces of other parents. Feeling resentful and resigned, she would grab a bag of M&Ms and give it to Billy. This gave her a few minutes of peace and quiet while she completed her shopping.

........................................................

Clearly, Ms. B. rewarded Billy for his misbehavior. Billy also (negatively) reinforced his mother by quieting down when she gave in to his demands. As both parties were reinforced, the coercive interaction should (and did) continue over time (Patterson, 1982).

The coercion concept has direct, practical implications. Parents need to break the pattern by ignoring the misbehavior, punishing it, or rewarding more positive actions (Herbert, 2002). In Billy's case, the psychologist recommended the use of *time-out,* the technique of briefly isolating a child following misbehavior. The next time Billy acted up in the grocery store, Ms. B. left her shopping cart, and she and Billy went to sit in the car until he quieted down. She then completed her shopping. Two trips to the car were needed the first day, but Billy's behavior improved as a result. He soon was earning rewards for being good—not for being bad—while shopping.

**NEGATIVE ATTENTION** Sometimes children misbehave as a way of getting attention rather than getting what they want. *Negative attention* is the idea that a "punishment" sometimes may actually reinforce misbehavior. For example, a "class clown" may like the attention that comes from getting in trouble. A teacher's attempt at punishment actually serves as a reinforcement. We think it is essential to understand *why* negative attention is reinforcing. Many children do not get enough positive attention—enough love. For them, any attention is better than being ignored. In this case, increasing attention and affection is a better way of treating their externalizing behavior than increasing discipline (Emery, 1992).

**INCONSISTENCY** Inconsistency also is linked with children's externalizing problems (Patterson, DeBaryshe, & Ramsey, 1989). Inconsistency can involve frequent changes in the style and standards of one parent, or two parents may be inconsistent in their rules and expectations. Inconsistency often becomes a problem when parents have conflicts in their own relationship—when they are unhappily married or are divorced (Emery, 1982; Repetti, Taylor, & Seeman, 2002). Some angry parents even deliberately undermine each other.

Yet another problem occurs when parents' actions are inconsistent with their words. For example, consider the contradiction inherent in angry and harsh physical punishment (Gershoff, 2002). On one hand, such discipline tells children to follow the rules. On the other hand, it teaches children that anger and aggression are acceptable means of solving problems. Children often learn from what their parents do, not what they say.

A young boy playing *Grand Theft Auto*. More aggressive children seek out, and are influenced by, the violence found routinely in video games, television shows, and other popular media.

**PEERS, NEIGHBORHOODS, AND MEDIA** Peer groups also can encourage delinquent and antisocial behavior (Dishion, McCord, & Poulin, 1999), and among adolescents, peers may be stronger influences than parents (Walden et al., 2004). In fact, socialized delinquency, in which criminal acts occur in the company of others, may be an important subtype of externalizing disorders (Kazdin, 1995).

Neighborhood and media also contribute to externalizing problems. Television violence is rampant, as is violence in computer games, and research shows that aggressive children both prefer and become more aggressive in response to video violence (Anderson et al., 2010). Youth who witness violence in their communities also are more likely to be violent themselves (Shahinfar, Kupersmidt, & Matza, 2001), and in general, children who grow up in unstable, poor, inner-city neighborhoods are more likely to have externalizing problems (Dupéré et al., 2007; Stouthamer-Loeber et al., 2002).

**SOCIAL FACTORS IN ADHD** There are few theories of how social factors play a role in the development of ADHD (Hinshaw, 1994). Mothers of children with ADHD are more critical, demanding, and controlling compared to the mothers of normal children (Mash & Johnston, 1982). However, research shows that problems primarily are a *reaction* to the children's troubles, not a cause for them. Children with ADHD become more attentive and compliant while medicated, and their mothers' behavior "improves" as well—mothers become less negative and less controlling (Danforth, Barkley, & Stokes, 1991). The improved mothering is due to the medicine's effects on the children—and the children's effects on their mothers. In fact, children's disruptive behavior can strain marriages as well as parenting (Wymbs & Pelham, 2010).

This does not mean that good parenting is unimportant. Ineffective parenting surely intensifies ADHD symptoms (Hinshaw et al., 2000), and, importantly, parents can help to prevent comorbid

ODD from developing out of ADHD (Harvey et al., 2011; Tully et al., 2004). Family and social adversity also contribute to ODD and its comorbidity with ADHD (Burt et al., 2001).

**PSYCHOLOGICAL FACTORS** *Low self-esteem,* feelings of low worth, is sometimes blamed as causing externalizing problems. However, research shows, perhaps surprisingly, that children with ADHD *overestimate* rather than undervalue their competence (Hoza et al., 2004). The best explanation for this positive illusory bias appears to be self-protection, trying to appear more competent to peers and oneself (Owens et al., 2007).

Lack of *self-control,* the internal regulation of behavior, is often linked to externalizing disorders (Denson, DeWall, & Finkel, 2012). A specific problem with self-control is *delay of gratification*—the ability to defer smaller but immediate rewards for larger, long-term benefits, for example, studying for an exam rather than going out with friends. Children with externalizing problems are less able to delay gratification than are other children. They opt for immediate rewards rather than for long-term goals, an impediment to achieving educational and career goals (Nigg, 2001).

Studies by psychologist Ken Dodge and his colleagues also show that aggressive children overinterpret their peers' aggressive intentions (Dodge et al., 2003). They view other children as threatening and may attempt to "get you before you get me." Psychologist Seth Pollak and his colleagues show one way that such biases can develop. Physically abused children see more anger in neutral facial expressions than normal children (Pollak & Tolley-Schell, 2003). This bias may be adaptive when living in a threatening family, but it is maladaptive in other circumstances.

What about the "conscience" of children with externalizing problems? Psychologist Lawrence Kohlberg's (1985) hierarchy of moral reasoning argues that, as they grow older, children use increasingly abstract moral principles (see Table 16.1). A young boy may say that the reason he behaves well is because "Mommy will get mad." An older boy may say "You need to follow the rules." A teenager might explain "It is the right thing to do." Consistent with Kohlberg's theorizing, aggressive children reason more like younger children, focusing on immediate consequences rather

than following principles that guide behavior even when you aren't likely to get caught (Stams et al., 2006).

**INTEGRATION AND ALTERNATIVE PATHWAYS** How can we integrate evidence on the diverse contributions to the development of externalizing behavior? Two conclusions seem clear. First, externalizing disorders have many causes, not one. Various biological vulnerabilities account for most of some children's externalizing. For other children, externalizing stems largely from a lack of discipline or socialization that rewards antisocial, not prosocial, behavior. Second, for many children, biological, psychological, and social factors interact to create externalizing disorders. Temperament theorists note that the *goodness of fit* between a child's temperament and the family environment may be of greatest importance to healthy socialization (Shaw & Bell, 1993). For example, research shows that impulsive youth have unusually high rates of juvenile offending when they grow up in poor versus better-off neighborhoods. However, whether the neighborhood is poor or better off has no effect on offending for nonimpulsive youth (Lynam et al., 2000).

## Treatment of Externalizing Disorders

Numerous treatments have been developed for children's externalizing disorders. Unfortunately, the problems can be difficult to change (Kazdin, 1997). The most promising treatments include psychostimulants for ADHD, behavioral family therapy for ODD, and intensive programs for treating conduct disorders and delinquent youth.

**PSYCHOSTIMULANTS AND ADHD Psychostimulants** are medications that increase central nervous system activity. In appropriate dosages, the medications increase alertness, arousal, and attention. These produce immediate and noticeable improvements in the behavior of about 75 percent of children with ADHD. Before considering their effects further, we first must consider a mistaken view about psychostimulants and ADHD.

***"PARADOXICAL EFFECT"*** Psychostimulants lead to restless, even frenetic, behavior when abused. These effects are accurately

**TABLE 16.1**
## Kohlberg's Stages of Moral Development

| Stage | Approximate Age Range | Description |
|---|---|---|
| Obedience/punishment | Very young child | No difference between doing right and punishment |
| Self-interest | Preschool | Secure greatest benefit for self |
| Conformity | Early school age | Secure approval. "Good boy/girl." |
| Authority and social order | Later school age | Need to follow the law/rules. |
| Social contract | Adolescence | Utilitarian. Legally right is not always morally right. |
| Universal ethics | Adulthood | Morality transcends benefits. |

*"How am I supposed to think about consequences before they happen?"*
© David Sipress/The New Yorker Collection/www.cartoonbank.com

conveyed by a street name for the drugs, "speed." The U.S. psychiatrist Charles Bradley (1937) was one of the first to observe that these medications seem to have a "paradoxical effect" on overactive children: The drug slows them down. For many years, professionals believed that this was proof of abnormal brain functioning in ADHD. The real irony, however, is that the idea of a paradoxical effect was wrong.

One reason for the enduring "paradoxical effect" myth is that it was deemed unethical to give psychostimulants to normal children—even though the medication was given regularly to millions of "abnormal" children with ADHD! A group of researchers at the National Institute of Mental Health (NIMH) eventually found a clever way around the ethical dilemma. They obtained permission from NIMH colleagues to study the effects of psychostimulants on *their* children. The researchers found that the psychostimulants affected the normal children in the same way as ADHD children. The medication improved attention and decreased motor activity (Rapoport et al., 1978). In fact, they have the same effects on *adults* when taken in comparably smaller dosages, which is one reason why the medications are being widely abused among college students (Smith & Farah, 2011). The bottom line is: There is *no* paradoxical effect of psychostimulants on children with ADHD.

**USAGE AND EFFECTS** The most commonly prescribed psychostimulants are known by the trade names of Ritalin, Dexedrine, Cylert, and Adderall. Each has the effect of increasing alertness and arousal. Psychostimulants are usually prescribed by pediatricians, who typically are consulted about a child's difficulties in the early years of school. The fact that behavior problems in school are

the main concern is demonstrated in how psychostimulants are prescribed. A pill is taken in the morning before school, and because the effects of many psychostimulants last only three or four hours, another pill may be taken at the lunch hour.[1] A third pill may or may not be taken after school depending on the child's behavior at home, study demands, and whether the child eats and sleeps well with a third pill. (Decreased appetite and trouble sleeping are two common side effects of psychostimulants.) In any case, the medication is typically not taken on weekends or during school vacations due to concerns about various side effects.

Children take psychostimulants for years, not days or weeks. Traditionally, medication was discontinued in early adolescence because it was believed that the problem was "outgrown" by that age. However, research shows that, while hyperactivity and impulsivity usually improve somewhat by the teen years, problems with inattention often continue (Sibley et al., 2012). Thus, psychostimulants are now taken through the teen years, and perhaps into adulthood. Interest has grown in "adult ADHD," inattention, impulsivity, and, to a lesser extent, overactivity in adults (Barkley, 2006). *DSM-5* formally recognizes this new diagnosis. Adult ADHD requires only five of the six symptoms necessary for the diagnosis in children (see Table 16.1).

Numerous double-blind, placebo-controlled studies show that psychostimulants improve attention and decreases hyperactivity in ADHD (Barkley, 2006). In the largest treatment study to date, the Multimodal Treatment of Study of Children with ADHD (MTA), 579 children with ADHD were randomly assigned to either: (1) controlled medication management, (2) intensive behavior therapy, (3) the two treatments combined, or (4) uncontrolled community care (which typically included medication). A 14-month follow-up assessment showed that the controlled medication and combined treatments produced significantly more improvements in ADHD symptoms than the alternatives. Intensive behavior therapy (part of the combined treatment) resulted in only a slight improvement over medication for ADHD symptoms (see Figure 16.3) but may have modestly helped comorbid aggressive behavior (MTA, 1999; Swanson et al., 2001), parenting (Wells et al., 2006), and minority children and families (Arnold et al., 2003). And more aggressive behavior therapies, including summer treatment programs, may produce more notable benefits (Pelham et al., 2002).

Still, the MTA established psychostimulant medication as the first-line treatment for the behavioral symptoms of ADHD. Importantly, however, the study also found that problems with community care, which typically included medication but was much less effective than controlled medication management. Unfortunately, community care often involves writing a prescription with little ongoing monitoring of ADHD.

Another concern is that psychostimulants improve hyperactivity and impulsivity, but their effects on attention and learning are less certain. Children on medication complete more reading,

[1]Release delivery versions of psychostimulants (trade names Concerta, Adderall XR) are available that release medication in a manner similar to taking three separate pills throughout the day.

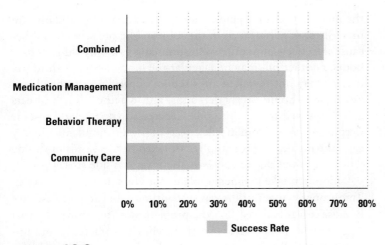

**FIGURE 16.3**

**Success Rates at the End of Treatment in the MTA** Psychostimulants produce notable short-term improvements in ADHD, as long as medication is managed carefully. Community care, which usually included medication, led to much less improvement. Medication outperforms behavior therapy in the short-term, but not in the long term as revealed by MTA follow-up studies (not shown).

*Source:* Based on J. M. Swanson, et al. Clinical Relevance of the Primary Findings of the MTA: Success Rates Based on Severity of ADHD and ODD Symptoms at the End of Treament. The Journal of the American Academy of Child and Adolescent Psychiatry; 40 (2): 168–179.

spelling, and arithmetic assignments with somewhat improved accuracy (Pelham et al., 1985). However, their grades and achievement test scores improve little, if at all (Henker & Whalen, 1989). This pattern of improvement in behavior but not in learning was also observed in the MTA (1999).

An even more troubling and puzzling fact is that psychostimulants have not been found to lead to *long-term* improvements in behavior, learning, or any other areas of functioning (see Table 16.2). For example, an eight-year follow-up of the MTA showed no benefits of psychostimulants (or behavior therapy) on ADHD or other symptoms (Molina et al., 2009). Is this due to failure to take medication consistently over the course of many years, a shortcoming of medication as a treatment for ADHD, or some other issue? No one knows for sure, but continued medication use did not predict greater improvement in the MTA (Molina et al., 2009). Clearly, the difference in short- versus long-term results is a puzzle that needs to be solved.

The important issue with the effectiveness of psychostimulants in treating ADHD preschoolers was investigated in another large-scale clinical trial, the Preschoolers with ADHD Treatment Study (PATS). Randomization and other critical aspects of the design were necessarily compromised because of ethical concerns in treating this young age group. The study produced two clear results: (1) Preschoolers who remain on the medication improve over 10-month follow-up (although there is no control group) and (2) about one-third of preschoolers discontinue medication (Vitiello et al., 2007).

**SIDE EFFECTS** The side effects of psychostimulants can be troubling, including decreased appetite, increased heart rate, and sleeping difficulties. These may be minor problems for children's health, but not for parents who want their children to eat right and go to bed! Other side effects are clearly serious, such as an increase in motor tics in a small percentage of cases.

Evidence that psychostimulants can slow physical growth is also a very important concern. Past research found that children maintained on psychostimulants fell somewhat behind expected gains in height and weight, but the growth effect was interpreted as minor. Moreover, rebounds in growth occur during medication-free periods (Barkley, 2006). (This is why the medication may be discontinued when children are not in school.) Is the slowed growth minor? In the MTA, newly medicated children gained 6 pounds less and grew .8 inches less over three years than never medicated children (Swanson et al., 2007). Whether this is minor may be a matter of interpretation, but in the eyes of school-aged boys, being smaller is *not* a minor matter.

**ARE PSYCHOSTIMULANTS OVERUSED?** Psychostimulants are effective, but parents and professionals still face a basic question: Should we use medication to correct children's misbehavior? Currently, 2.7 million children in the United States—4.8 percent of the school-age population—are treated with psychostimulants for ADHD (CDC, 2010). This startling number generates considerable controversy, as do these facts: (1) Between 1987 and 2008 stimulant use for youth under age 18 increased 300 percent to 700 percent (Zito et al., 2003; see Figure 16.4); (2) the use of psychostimulants tripled among preschoolers during the 1990s (Zito et al., 2000); (3) psychostimulants are used 3 to 10 times more often in the United States than in Europe, Canada, and Australia (Vitiello, 2008); and (4) the United States consumes 90 percent of the psychostimulants produced in the world (LeFever et al., 2003).

Are psychostimulants overused in the United States? Pills can be a "quick fix" not only for troubled children, but also for troubled schools. Many public schools are underfunded, overcrowded,

**TABLE 16.2**

**Short-Term and Long-Term Effects of Psychostimulants on ADHD Symptoms**

| | Hyperactivity/Impulsivity | Inattention/Learning |
| --- | --- | --- |
| Short-term | Dramatic improvements; less active and more focused; fewer social problems | More work completed, but no change in grades or standardized test scores |
| Long-term | No demonstrated benefit | No demonstrated benefit |

© CartoonStock Ltd.

*Strattera,* a norepinephrine reuptake inhibitor, is the only nonstimulant medication approved by the U.S. Food and Drug Administration (FDA) for the treatment of ADHD. Strattera is often prescribed for adults with ADHD, because it has less potential for abuse. Misuse of psychostimulants is common in older ages. For example, as many as 35 percent of college students on psychostimulants are estimated to use or "share" the medication as a study aid or for recreation (Wilens et al., 2008). Unfortunately, Strattera is less effective than psychostimulants, and it can have serious side effects, including increasing suicidal thinking (Bangs et al., 2008; Newcorn et al., 2008).

*Clonidine,* which can lead to decreases in aggressive behavior, is used in combination with psychostimulants in 20 percent or more of cases. Despite this frequent practice, the use of clonidine is controversial. The medication's primary use is for high blood pressure in adults, and only limited research supports its effectiveness for ADHD. Most controversial, there are isolated reports of sudden death among treated children (Hazell & Stuart, 2003).

and inadequately staffed. Do we need to look at the bigger picture of children's lives instead of looking to a pill for a quick fix?

Psychostimulants are an inexpensive and effective treatment for ADHD, especially in comparison with the alternatives (see Critical Thinking Matters on p. 452). Still, the benefits of medication are limited, various side effects are a concern, and there is no bright line between normal and abnormal behavior in diagnosing ADHD. Should mental health professionals in the United States raise the threshold for making the diagnosis and for prescribing medication? We think this is a reasonable question to ask.

**OTHER MEDICATIONS FOR ADHD** Over the last decade, many children have taken antidepressants for ADHD. Although depression and ADHD often co-occur, this is not the reason for the treatment. Rather, antidepressants may affect ADHD symptoms directly for unknown reasons. However, antidepressants clearly are a second-line treatment. Their use is justified only following the failure of psychostimulants (DeVane & Sallee, 1996).

**BEHAVIORAL FAMILY THERAPY FOR ODD** *Behavioral family therapy (BFT)* teaches parents to be very clear and specific about their expectations for children's behavior, to monitor children's actions closely, and systematically reward positive behavior while ignoring or mildly punishing misbehavior. BFT is sometimes used as an adjunct or alternative to medication in treating ADHD, although it offers limited benefits (MTA Cooperative Study, 1999). However, BFT is more promising as a treatment of ODD (Brestan & Eyberg, 1998).

BFT typically begins with *parent training*. Parents are taught to identify specific problematic behaviors such as fighting with siblings, list preferred alternative behaviors like speaking nicely, and set consequences for appropriate and inappropriate behavior. They may also make a "star chart" for recording children's progress and perhaps develop a "daily report card" that the child carries home from school as a way of coordinating discipline in both settings (Scott, 2002).

Parent training also may include teaching parents about punishment strategies, such as time-out. Conventional wisdom holds that punishment should be firm but not angry and that rewards

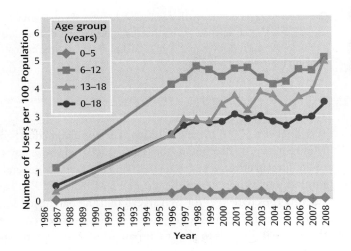

**FIGURE 16.4**

Use of Psychostimulant Medications for Children Increased Dramatically in the United States Between 1987 and 2008. Are Medications Being Overused?

*Source:* S.H. Zuvekas & B. Vitiello. 2012. Stimulant medication use in children: A 12-year perspective. American Journal of Psychiatry; 169: 160-166. Reprinted with permission from the American Journal of Psychiatry (Copyright © 2012). American Psychiatric Association. All Rights Reserved.

# CRITICAL THINKING matters

## ADHD's False Causes and Cures

"We don't know what causes this" and "There is no cure" are not the kind of answers desperate parents want to hear about their psychologically troubled children. Unfortunately, these often are the most honest and scientifically accurate answers. Even more unfortunately, the absence of answers does not prevent many self-appointed experts from responding to parents' questions with partial truths, dubious theories, or pure fantasy. Myths abound for every mental disorder. However, if we were to give a prize for the most misleading information, ADHD might just win.

Self-proclaimed "experts" have blamed the cause of ADHD on everything from fluorescent lights (the lights were installed in schools during a time of increasing rates of ADHD) to sugar (a favorite among teachers and parents—after all, children get "hyper" around Halloween) to a failure to learn to crawl properly before learning to walk (somehow out-of-sequence locomotion is supposed to disrupt developing brain circuitry, a theory we never understood, nor do we wish to try). We hope we do not need to say this, but just in case: There is no evidence to support any of these theories or treatments based on them. We know, for example, that sugar can cause cavities, but increasing dietary sugar does not produce hyperactivity nor does decreasing sugar cure it (Milich, Wolraich, & Lindgren, 1986).

Recently, a number of "experts" blamed the MMR vaccine for causing ADHD along with autism, learning disabilities, and who knows what else (see Critical Thinking Matters in Chapter 2). Some still do,

despite widespread evidence to the contrary. Some even claim that drug companies and the National Institute of Mental Health are conspiring to cover up evidence. We give these worries the same credibility as theories that the government is covering up evidence of extraterrestrials visiting Earth. But saying, "Ridiculous!" to discredited ideas is easy. The trick for you is to be an inquiring skeptic, so you will not fall victim to the next bogus idea.

The past can be an instructive warning about the future. Consider a theory popular in the 1970s—that ADHD is caused by food additives, particularly salicylates, which are commonly found in processed foods. Physician Benjamin Feingold (1975) offered this theory in his immodestly titled book, Why Your Child Is Hyperactive. Feingold recommended a natural-foods diet as an ADHD cure. Hundreds of thousands of parents embraced the Feingold diet. Many reported that their children's symptoms improved. (Do a Web search, and you will still find advocates.) Congress considered banning salicylates. Any problem? Well, the "benefits" were nothing more than a placebo effect. Keeping kids on a natural foods diet requires a lot of work, and parents believed their efforts made a difference. It did—in the parents' minds. Research showed that actual ADHD behavior did not change (Conners, 1980).

Among the other treatments that do not work for ADHD are food supplements (amino acids and megavitamins are two often recommended "treatments"); play therapy (the therapist plays with the child and interprets the play analogous to the way an analyst interprets free association); eye movement desensitization and reprocessing (see Chapter 7); neurofeedback (where patients watch EEG readings and try to alter their brain waves); sensorimotor integration therapy (which may include exercises like watching a pencil as you touch your nose with it); acupuncture (the ancient Chinese procedure); or various homeopathic remedies, including pycnogenol (an organically based substance that advocates claim is as effective as Ritalin—and also helps to cure tennis elbow!). Again, none of these treatments work (Waschbusch & Hill, 2004).

Critical thinking is one thing that will work for you, if you learn to use it. Sure. Watch science fiction movies and suspend disbelief for a couple of hours. But when it comes to real life problems, critical thinking matters.

---

should far outweigh punishments. Some experts believe that parent training should directly emphasize increasing warmth as well as discipline in parent–child relationships (Cavell, 2001). From this perspective, the goal is to teach **authoritative parenting**.

Research supports the short-term effectiveness of BFT (Patterson, 1982), and parent training can be effectively delivered in groups (Webster-Stratton, 1994), to parents of toddlers (Gardner et al., 2007), or even through the popular media (Sanders, Montgomery, & Brechman-Toussaint, 2000). However, evidence on long-term effectiveness is less certain, and benefits generally are limited to children under the age of 12 (Kazdin, 1997). In considering the challenges for BFT, recall that the parents of children with externalizing problems often live in adverse circumstances that make it difficult to alter their parenting (Emery, Fincham, &

Cummings, 1992). Parents can be effective in changing children's behavior, but psychologists need to develop more ways to help parents who live in difficult circumstances (Scott, 2002). In fact, BFT is less effective when parents are unhappily married, depressed, substance abusers, or harsh and critical with their children (Beauchaine, Webster-Stratton, & Reid, 2005). It is more effective when treatment includes efforts to help parents cope with *their* stress (Kazdin & Whitley, 2003).

Some behavioral therapies also include direct training of children as well as parents. *Problem-solving skills training (PSST)* is one technique in which children are taught to slow down, evaluate a problem, and consider alternative solutions before acting. Some evidence indicates that the combination of PSST and parent training leads to more improvement than either therapy alone in treating ODD (Kazdin, Siegel, & Bass, 1992). However, PSST offers no or minimal help to children with ADHD.

Research shows that parent involvement leads to more effective treatment for oppositional-defiant disorder.

**TREATMENT OF CONDUCT DISORDERS** Enthusiastic claims about effective, new programs for treating conduct disorders or juvenile delinquency are often reported in the popular media. You should be skeptical when you learn of a new "solution." Conduct disorders among adolescents are even more resistant to treatment than are externalizing problems among younger children (Kazdin, 1997).

Some BFT approaches have shown promise in treating young people with family or legal problems (Alexander & Parsons, 1982). These treatments are based on principles similar to those in programs for younger children, except that *negotiation*—actively involving young people in setting rules—is central to BFT with adolescents. Negotiation is critical because parents have less direct control over adolescents than younger children. Due to diminishing parental control, an even better strategy is to prevent conduct disorders by treating externalizing problems prior to adolescence.

**MULTISYSTEMIC THERAPY** *Multisystemic therapy (MST)* is a promising intervention with conduct disorders that has received considerable attention (Henggeler & Borduin, 1990). MST combines family treatment with coordinated interventions in other important contexts of the troubled child's life, including peer groups, schools, and neighborhoods. Several studies now document that MST improves family relationships, and to a lesser extent, delinquent behavior and troubled peer relationships (Curtis, Ronan, & Borduin, 2004). A 13-year follow-up study found significantly lower **recidivism,** or repeat offending, among seriously troubled youth treated with MST versus individual therapy. Despite this positive result, you should know that recidivism remained high for both groups: 50 percent following MST versus 81 percent for individual therapy (Schaeffer & Borduin, 2005).

**RESIDENTIAL PROGRAMS AND JUVENILE COURTS** Many adolescents with serious conduct problems or very troubled families are treated in residential programs outside the home. One of the most actively researched residential programs is *Achievement Place,* a group home that operates according to highly structured

behavior therapy principles. Achievement Place homes, like many similar residential programs, are very effective while the adolescent is living in the treatment setting. Unfortunately, the programs do little to prevent recidivism once the adolescent leaves the residential placement (Bailey, 2002; Emery & Marholin, 1977; Kazdin, 1995). Delinquent adolescents typically return to family, peer, and school environments that do not consistently reward prosocial behavior or monitor and punish antisocial behavior.

Many delinquent youths are "treated" in the juvenile justice system, where *rehabilitation* is supposed to be the goal. The philosophy of the juvenile justice system in the United States is based on the principle of *parens patriae*—the state as parent. In theory, juvenile courts are supposed to help troubled youth, not punish them. This lofty goal is belied by research indicating that *diversion*—keeping problem youths out of the juvenile justice system—is an effective "treatment" (Davidson et al., 1987).

Because rehabilitation is so challenging, more juvenile offenders have been treated like adult criminals than troubled youth. In the 1990s, more youth were placed into custody, and more minors were transferred out of the juvenile justice system and tried as adults. However, these trends have declined in recent years (Puzzanchera, Adams, & Sickmund, 2010).

We see the difficulties in treating problem youth as a challenge, not a defeat. Therapists need to work to establish good relationships with troubled youth, an important predictor of treatment outcome for externalizing problems (Shirk & Karver, 2003). Another key is preventing externalizing disorders by easing the family adversity that creates them (Earls & Mezzacappa, 2002), or teaching new ways of coping with adversities that cannot be readily changed (Lochman & Wells, 2004). We need to be realistic about the limited effectiveness of treatment, but if we do not want troubled youth to give up on themselves, we cannot give up on them.

**COURSE AND OUTCOME** Do children "outgrow" externalizing disorders? For ADHD, hyperactivity generally declines during

adolescence. However, attention deficits and impulsivity are more likely to continue, as measured, for example, by higher levels of motor vehicle accidents (Barkley, 2006). The continuity of symptoms into adult life is evident in the growing interest in adult ADHD (Mannuzza et al., 1998).

Importantly, the prognosis for ADHD depends on whether there is comorbid ODD or CD. If so, youth are more likely to develop problems with substance abuse, criminality, and other forms of antisocial behavior (Hinshaw, 1994). In fact, roughly half of all children with ODD or CD continue to have problems with antisocial behavior into adulthood (Hinshaw, 1994; Kazdin, 1995). As we have noted, adolescent-onset antisocial behavior is less likely to continue than childhood-onset antisocial behavior (Moffit, 1993).

## Internalizing and Other Disorders

Teachers cannot ignore disruptive children in the classroom, but they may overlook anxious or depressed children who sit quietly and unhappily alone. The negative effect of externalizing disorders is an important reason why we have focused on these problems, but like schoolteachers, we do not want to overlook children whose troubles are *not* disruptive. We begin with a case study.

### ⟶ Turning the Tables on Tormentors

Mark was 12 years old when his mother took him to a new psychologist. Both Mark and his mother agreed that he had been depressed for well over a year, and nine months of "play therapy" resulted in little improvement. Mark felt sad most of the time, cried often, and felt helpless and hopeless about the future. He had withdrawn from his usual activities, and his straight As had fallen to Bs, Cs, and even a few Ds—despite an IQ of 145. Teasing was a particular problem, one that brought Mark to tears during the first appointment. A group of boys at his school constantly tormented Mark, calling him the "little professor." Their teasing frequently brought Mark to the point of tears.

Mark's family was well functioning, and there was no family history of depression. Mark's mother was a homemaker, and

his father was a police officer. His parents were happily married, and his two younger brothers were doing well. Mark's mother attributed many of his problems to his unusual intelligence and to the fact that Mark had played with few children during the first years of his life. The family had lived in an apartment in an unsafe neighborhood before the birth of his brothers.

The new treatment followed a cognitive behavior therapy approach but began with a careful period of building rapport. Establishing a good therapeutic relationship was very important to Mark who was socially isolated and unhappy with his previous therapy. Treatment eventually focused on social skills training and behavioral activation. Mark was encouraged to rejoin various activities and initiate relationships with his peers. His parents were told to treat him normally. In particular, they were encouraged to hold the same high (but not demanding) expectations for Mark's schoolwork as they did for their other sons.

A special emphasis of treatment was how Mark could deal with his tormentors. As a step, the therapist began to tease Mark playfully—and to encourage teasing back in return. This was viewed both as a way of teaching Mark some skills and of desensitizing him to teasing, which is normal if sometimes vicious among 12-year-old boys. Given the strong therapeutic relationship that had developed, Mark quickly learned not only to play this game but to relish it. With his high IQ, he soon became devastatingly clever in his banter.

The benefits clearly generalized outside of the therapy session. Mark no longer cried when he was teased; instead, he learned retorts that set his tormentors on their heels. In fact, Mark did not limit his self-defense to words. He punched one particularly mean boy in the nose one day—a response that was *not* encouraged in therapy but one that did not upset his father, the police officer (or, privately, the therapist).

Over the course of about three months of therapy, Mark's mood improved considerably. He started getting As again and reengaged in various activities. Teasing was no longer an issue. He remained himself—a quiet, intelligent, and introspective boy—but he learned to have more reasonable expectations, to stay involved, and to handle his tormentors.

## Symptoms of Internalizing Disorders

Mark shows that children can suffer from "adult" disorders like depression. Yet the diagnosis is not always so clear. Imagine if Mark was six years old. He might act and look sad, but he would be less able to express or reflect on his feelings. And even if six-year-old Mark could say that he was sad, the meaning of his words would be difficult to interpret. When does sadness become depression at this young age?

Children's internalizing symptoms include sadness, fears, and social withdrawal. As noted earlier, *DSM-5* includes no separate category of internalizing disorders of childhood, but indicates that children may qualify for "adult" diagnoses of depressive and anxiety disorders. The manual does identify some unique ways in which children may experience symptoms. When diagnosing major depressive disorder, for example, the clinician may substitute irritable mood for depressed mood and failure to make expected weight gain for weight loss.

Accommodations like these are a start, but psychologists need to develop better, developmentally sensitive diagnostic systems. Children's capacity to experience and recognize emotions emerges over the course of development, as does their ability to express—and to mask—their own feelings. This makes it much more difficult for adults to evaluate children's inner distress than it is to observe their externalizing behavior.

**DEPRESSIVE SYMPTOMS** The assessment of depression in children can be particularly difficult. One study of children hospitalized for depression found a correlation of zero between children's and parents' ratings of the children's depression (Kazdin, French, & Unis, 1983). In another study, children's ratings of depression were associated with their hopelessness, low self-esteem, and internal attributions for negative events. Their *parents'* ratings of the children's depression, in contrast, were associated with the parents' ratings of externalizing behavior, not with children's internal distress (Kazdin, 1989). Finally, and perhaps of greatest concern, parents systematically underestimate the extent of depression reported by their children and adolescents (Kazdin & Petti, 1982; Rutter, 1989).

Given parents' and children's widely differing perceptions, psychologists are rightly concerned if *either* a parent *or* a child

Depression becomes much more common during adolescence, especially among teenage girls.

notes problems. In assessing children's internalizing problems, mental health professionals must obtain information from *multiple informants*—parents, teachers, and the children themselves (Harrington, 2002).

When assessing children directly, child clinical psychologists are sensitive to different signs that may indicate depression at different ages (Luby, 2010): unresponsiveness to caregivers under the age of; sad expressions and social withdrawal in preschoolers; somatic complaints in young school-aged children; more direct admission of sad feelings or marked irritability in older school-aged children or early adolescents; and full-blown depression, including suicide risk, among adolescents.

Depression in children also differs from depression in adolescents in its lower prevalence, equal frequency among boys and girls, stronger relation with family dysfunction, and less persistent course (Harrington, 2002).

**CHILDREN'S FEARS AND ANXIETY** *Anxiety* is a general and diffuse emotional reaction that often is linked with anticipation of future, unrealistic threats. In contrast, *fear* is a reaction to real and immediate danger. Children often have trouble identifying their general anxiety, but adults can observe much of children's fearful behavior which is a clear reaction to environmental events. Thus, research on the development of children's fears is more advanced than on their anxiety.

Two findings from fear research are important to note. First, children develop different fears for the first time at different ages, often suddenly and with no apparent cause. Infants typically develop a fear of strangers in the months just before their first birthday; preschoolers develop fears of monsters and the dark between the ages of 2 and 4; and children between ages 5 and 8 often develop fears related to school. (If you ever dreamed of going to school in your underwear, you are not alone!) Thus, different fears are developmentally normal at different ages. Second, fears of monsters, the dark, and so on become less frequent with age (Meltzer et al., 2009). Apparently, children "outgrow" many fears, probably by gradually confronting them in everyday life. Developing and overcoming fears is normal and adaptive, much like getting sick and gaining resistance to physical illness.

**SEPARATION ANXIETY DISORDER AND SCHOOL REFUSAL** Separation anxiety illustrates these developmental findings. *Separation anxiety* is distress expressed following separation from an attachment figure, typically a parent or caregiver. This normal fear develops around a baby's eighth month of life. An infant who easily tolerated separations in the past may suddenly start to cling, cry, and scream whenever a parent tries to leave, even for a brief period. Separation anxiety generally peaks around 15 months and lessens over time. Toddlers and preschoolers typically continue to experience distress upon separation, however, particularly when left in an unfamiliar circumstance.

Although normal at younger ages, separation anxiety can become a serious problem if children fail to "outgrow" it (Silverman &

Dick-Niederhauser, 2004). **Separation anxiety disorder** is defined by symptoms such as persistent and excessive worry for the safety of an attachment figure, fears of getting lost or being kidnapped, nightmares with separation themes, and refusal to be alone.

Separation anxiety disorder is especially problematic when it interferes with school attendance. *School refusal,* also known as *school phobia,* is characterized by an extreme reluctance to go to school and is accompanied by various symptoms of anxiety, such as stomach aches and headaches. Some children are literally school phobic—they are afraid of school or specific aspects of attending school. However, many cases of school refusal can be traced to separation anxiety. Often, parents have trouble separating from their children, and this clearly contributes to the child's separation anxiety. School refusal is a serious problem that has been linked to lower achievement and increased school dropout (Pina et al., 2009).

**TROUBLED PEER RELATIONSHIPS** Children with internalizing problems may have troubles with their peers. One way to evaluate children's relationships is by obtaining information on who is "liked most" and who is "liked least" from a large group of children who know one another (for example, children in a classroom). This *peer sociometric* technique is used to group children into five categories (Coie & Kupersmidt, 1983; Newcomb, Bukowski, & Pattee, 1993):

1. *Popular* children receive many "liked most" and few "liked least" ratings.

2. *Average* children also receive few "liked least" ratings, but they receive fewer "liked most" ratings than popular children.

3. *Neglected* children receive few of either type of rating.

*"I'm not a scaredy-cat—I'm phobic."*

© Barbara Smaller/The New Yorker Collection/www.cartoonbank.com

4. *Rejected* children receive many "liked least" ratings and few "liked most" nominations.

5. *Controversial* children receive many positive and many negative ratings from their peers.

Rejected children are likely to have externalizing problems (Patterson, Kupersmidt, & Griesler, 1990), and peer rejection predicts the development of increased aggression (Dodge et al., 2003). Children with ADHD may be rejected because their symptoms impede social relationships (Greene et al., 2001; Hoza et al., 2005), whereas rejected children with ODD and CD are likely to have a few close friends—friends who, unfortunately, also engage in antisocial behavior (Olweus, 1984).

Not surprisingly, neglected children are likely to have internalizing symptoms such as loneliness (Asher & Wheeler, 1985). An optimistic finding is the neglected status is not particularly stable over time and across situations (Newcomb et al., 1993). Apparently, children who are left out of one social group often succeed in finding friends as they grow older, change schools, and participate in new activities.

## Diagnosis of Internalizing and Other Childhood Disorders

The *DSM-5* defines depressive and anxiety disorders exactly the same for children as for adults, with minor exceptions for some symptoms, as we discussed for major depressive disorder. As we have said, we are troubled that this approach ignores too many developmental considerations. Not only do children show sadness in different ways at different ages, but their cognitive capacities also change in important ways across development. For example, preschoolers do not know that death is permanent, because they lack an understanding of the concept of time. We wonder. Is it possible for a young child to be suicidal when they cannot comprehend death?

**ANXIETY AND DEPRESSIVE DISORDERS** *DSM-5* does include a few internalizing problems that apply mostly to children, but that are listed as anxiety and depressive disorders. *Selective mutism* involves the consistent failure to speak in certain social situations, for example, in preschool, while speech is unrestricted in other situations, for example, at home. Selective mutism is found among less than 1 percent of the children treated for mental health disorders. We do not know of any cases of selective mutism among adults, but like separation anxiety disorder, *DSM-5* places the diagnosis with other anxiety disorders. Disruptive Mood Dysregulation Disorder is a controversial, new diagnosis that applies to children but is listed with depressive disorders (see Thinking Critically about DSM-5).

**OTHER NEURODEVELOPMENTAL DISORDERS** In addition to intellectual disability, autism spectrum disorder, and ADHD, *DSM-5* lists a few other problems as neurodevelopmental

## Disruptive Mood Dysregulation Disorder

For the most part, the *DSM-5* views psychological problems in children as having *homotypic continuity*, that is, an underlying problem looks pretty much the same on the surface for children and adults. This is why *DSM-5* uses essentially the same diagnostic criteria for childhood disorders as for "adult" disorders.

We believe that the diagnosis of childhood disorders needs to be sensitive to development, to the unique ways children experience and express their psychological symptoms. Much will be gained if we can develop diagnostic systems that recognize *heterotypic continuity*, where the same underlying problem is represented in different ways or by different symptoms across childhood and into adult life.

Intelligence is a good example of heterotypic continuity. Reading and math knowledge and abilities change a great deal between the ages of 6 and 18. We would be foolish to give first graders and high school seniors the same tests. Yet, we can predict which first graders are likely to do well in high school by comparing them to age-mates on tests with carefully constructed developmental norms—IQ and achievement tests. The underlying trait, academic aptitude, stays quite stable over time. Yet, knowledge and ability in reading and math changes rapidly across development, so we assess academic aptitude in different ways at different ages. That's heterotypic continuity.

We think it would be wonderful if *DSM-5* diagnoses similarly could account for developmental change. Yet, trying to equate symptoms in children and adults is a tricky business. Efforts to diagnose bipolar disorder in children provide an instructive caution. Beginning in the 1990s, a number of clinicians and researchers argued that many children were being misdiagnosed as having ADHD when, in fact, their real problem would prove to be mania, which would emerge in adult life (Biederman et al., 1998). These experts argued that mania shows heterotypic continuity. They suggested that, in children, unpredictable, brief episodes of intense irritability really were early manifestations of the classic, longer mood swings seen in adults with mania (Biederman et al., 2004; Mick et al., 2005).

As a result of this theorizing, the diagnosis of bipolar disorder in children increased by a factor of 40 (!) between 1994 and 2003 (Moreno et al., 2007). The surge in use of the diagnosis would have been a wonderful step forward—if it turned out that childhood bipolar disorder had been miserably underdiagnosed. Unfortunately, longitudinal research eventually showed that episodic irritability in youth does not preface mania in adult life (Stringaris et al., 2009). There may be heterotypic continuity in bipolar disorder from childhood to adulthood, but these clinicians and theorists did not identify it correctly. As a result, their efforts instead led to the overdiagnosis of childhood bipolar disorder. And many of these children were treated with powerful antipsychotic medications, a questionable approach at very best.[2]

How did the *DSM-5* deal with this issue? It created a brand new diagnosis, *disruptive mood dysregulation disorder*, in an effort to better understand the meaning of episodic irritability in children and adolescents. The main symptom is severe, recurrent temper outbursts, beginning before the age of 10 that are way out of proportion to the situation that provokes them. The diagnosis, which cannot be made before the age of 6, has created a swirl of controversy focused on (1) concerns about pathologizing normal behavior and (2) an absence of research. In fact, the very first study using the *DSM-5* definition was just published. Several existing data sets were re-analyzed using the new diagnosis. The investigators found that the disorder had a fairly low prevalence (about 1–3 percent) and a very high level of comorbidity with other problems, particularly with externalizing disorders (Copeland et al., 2013).

Will disruptive mood dysregulation disorder prove to be a useful diagnosis? Only time will tell. However, you can learn a couple of lessons now. For one, some diagnoses got into the *DSM-5* without much, if any research support. For another, the *DSM-5*, like many classification systems, includes a number of "wastebasket" categories, which mainly serve the purpose of keeping other diagnoses "clean." Finally, while we firmly believe psychological disorders of childhood show heterotypic continuity, psychology does not yet have a reliable and valid system for making developmentally sensitive diagnoses. One reason why we consider childhood disorders separately from adult problems is we want you to recognize where the field needs to go, not just where it is right now.

---

disorders. *Specific Learning Disorder*, which you may know as "learning disability," is a diagnosis for students who perform substantially below their ability in a specific area of learning (see p. 441 What Are Learning Disabilities?). *Tic Disorders* include *Tourette's disorder*, which is a rare problem (4 to 5 cases per 10,000 people) that is characterized by repeated motor and verbal tics.

The tics can be voluntarily suppressed only for brief periods of time and interfere substantially with life functioning. *Developmental coordination disorder* is defined, in large part, as, ". . . slowness and inaccuracy of performance of motor skills (e.g., catching an object, using scissors or cutlery, hand writing, riding a bike, or participating in sports)" (p. 74). We mention developmental

---

[2]Questions are being raised about possible law suits (*New York Times*, October 2, 2010).

coordination disorder to remind you that, too often, *DSM-5* turns normal "issues" into mental disorders. In poking fun at such diagnostic overzealousness, two pediatricians proposed a new diagnostic category called "sports deficit disorder." The major diagnostic criterion is always being the last one chosen for a team (Burke & McGee, 1990).

**TRAUMA- AND STRESSOR-RELATED DISORDERS** *DSM-5* includes two diagnoses in this category that really apply to children. *Reactive attachment disorder* is characterized by withdrawn behavior among very young children around adult caregivers. Observed following neglect, babies or toddlers may fail to seek comfort when distressed and generally show limited emotional responsiveness. *Disinhibited social engagement disorder* also is a reaction to neglect, but in this case, very young children are indiscriminant toward caregivers. They may be overly familiar and willing to go off with anyone, showing no special attachment to anyone. In Chapter 18, we discuss child abuse and neglect as legal issues. Finally, we should note that *DSM-5* created detailed, developmentally sensitive diagnoses for: acute and posttraumatic stress disorder for children under the age of 6. We do think positively, not just critically, about *DSM-5*.

**ELIMINATION DISORDERS** *Encopresis* and *enuresis* refer, respectively, to inappropriately controlled defecation and urination. According to *DSM-5*, enuresis may be considered abnormal beginning at age 5, as most children have developed bladder control by this age. Bedwetting is found among approximately 5 percent of 5-year-olds, 2 to 3 percent of 10-year-olds, and 1 percent of 18-year-olds. Encopresis, a much less common problem, may be diagnosed beginning at age 4. Encopresis is found among approximately 1 percent of all 5-year-olds and fewer older children.

Encopresis and enuresis typically are causes of, not reactions to, psychological distress. Shyness or social anxiety may accompany enuresis or encopresis, but the symptoms generally disappear once children learn to control their bowels and bladders. Encopresis and especially enuresis can be effectively treated with various biofeedback devices. The best-known is the *bell and pad,*

a device that awakens children by setting off an alarm as they begin to wet the bed during the night. The bell and pad is about 75 percent effective in treating bedwetting among young school-aged children (Houts, 1991).

**CONTEXTUAL CLASSIFICATIONS?** As a final note, we remind you that children's behavior is intimately linked with the family, school, and peer contexts. Due to this, some experts have suggested that diagnosing individual children is misleading and misguided. Instead, children's psychological problems could be classified within the context of key relationships, particularly the family (Group for the Advancement of Psychiatry, 1995). As you saw in the case of Jeremy, parents, teachers, and peers often are part of a child's "individual" problem. We discuss contextual classification generally in Chapter 17.

## Frequency of Internalizing Disorders

The prevalence of externalizing disorders decreases as children grow older, but the opposite is true for internalizing disorders. Depression increases dramatically during adolescence, especially among girls (Garber, Keiley, & Martin, 2002; see Figure 16.5). According to one startling estimate, 35 percent of young women and 19 percent of young men experience at least one major depressive episode by the age of 19 (Lewinsohn, Rohde, & Seeley, 1998). Some have claimed that such statistics point to an "epidemic" of teen depression. However, objective evidence suggests that the only thing that has increased is awareness of the problem (Costello et al., 2006).

A recent national estimate found that fully 31.9 percent of adolescents met diagnostic criteria for an anxiety disorder at some time in their life (Merikangas et al., 2010). Another national study estimated that 3.7 percent of boys and 6.3 percent of girls suffered from PTSD during the past six months (Kilpatrick et al., 2003). Estimates of the prevalence of both anxiety and depression are controversial, however, because there is no "gold standard" for diagnosing these problems in children and adolescents (Harrington, 2002). Much lower rates of clinically significant anxiety and depression are suggested by the relatively small numbers of young people in treatment for internalizing

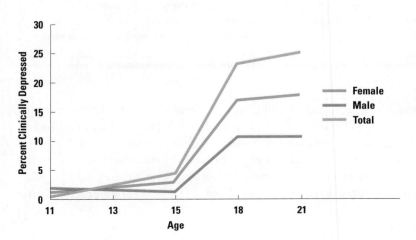

**FIGURE 16.5**

The prevalence of depression increases rapidly during adolescence, particularly among girls.
*Source:* Adapted from B. L. Hankin, et al., 1998, "Development of Depression from Preadolescence to Young Adulthood: Emerging Gender Differences in a 10-Year Longitudinal Study," Journal of Abnormal Psychology, 107, pp. 128–140. Copyright © 1998, American Psychological Association.

problems. Similarly, researchers found severe impairments in less than one-third of adolescents diagnosed with an anxiety disorder in the recent national study (Merikangas et al., 2010).

The fact that younger boys have more externalizing disorders while older girls have more internalizing problems leads to a distinctive pattern in child treatment referrals. Parents, teachers, and other adults seek treatment for children with externalizing problems, especially school-aged boys. The increase in depression among girls—and self-initiated treatment—begins to balance the gender ratio during the teenage years (Lewinsohn et al., 1994). By early adult life, notably more females than males are treated for psychological problems.

**SUICIDE** Adults need to be sensitive to children's internal distress, as evidence on the epidemiology of suicide underscores in a dramatic fashion. Suicide is the third leading cause of death among teenagers, trailing only automobile accidents and natural causes. A recent national survey found that 12.1 percent of adolescents had thought of suicide, and 4.1 percent actually attempted suicide (Nock et al., 2012). Suicide is extremely rare among children under the age of 10 (Shaffer & Gutstein, 2002). However, adolescent suicide rates tripled between 1960 and 1990 (see Figure 16.6). Teen suicide declined 28.5 percent from 1990 to 2003, but increased 8 percent from 2003 to 2004 (CDC, 2007). The increase coincides with a drop in prescribing antidepressants to adolescents based on FDA "black box" warnings. As we discuss later, experts are debating whether antidepressants reduce or increase suicidality.

In comparison with adults, suicide attempts among adolescents are more impulsive, more likely to follow a family conflict, and more often motivated by anger than depression (Shaffer & Gutstein, 2002). *Cluster suicides* can also occur among teenagers. When one teenager commits suicide, his or her peers are at an increased risk. The risk sometimes stems from suicide pacts; the death may also make suicide more acceptable to despondent teenagers who may or may not know the victim.

**CAUSES OF INTERNALIZING DISORDERS** Most research on the causes of mood and anxiety disorders among children is based

Mourners at the funeral of a young person who committed suicide.

on the same theories of etiology we have discussed in relation to adults. Evidence simply is lacking or inadequate on the development of many other psychological problems of childhood. Thus, our discussion of causal factors is limited.

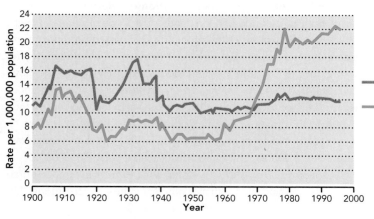

**FIGURE 16.6**

Teen suicide rates tripled between the 1960s and 1990s but have fallen in recent years.
*Source:* Based on Hendin, Herbert. 1996. Suicide in America: New and Expanded Edition. W. W. Norton & Company.

Suicide rate total population

Suicide rate males, ages 15–24

**BIOLOGICAL FACTORS** Except for some research documenting genetic influences on childhood onset obsessive-compulsive disorder (March, Leonard, & Swedo, 1995), few behavior genetic studies have been conducted on children's internalizing disorders. Moreover, existing research once again calls attention to the problems in classifying and assessing anxiety and depression among children. In the few studies completed to date, widely different estimates of genetic contributions are obtained based on children's versus parents' reports (Rutter et al., 1998).

Jerome Kagan and colleagues (Kagan & Snidman, 1991) have conducted important, basic research that suggests a more general, biological predisposition to anxiousness. These psychologists have identified a temperamental style that they call *inhibited to the unfamiliar.* Infants with this temperamental style cry easily and often in response to novel toys, people, or circumstances. Their psychophysiological response (e.g., heart rate acceleration) also indicates fearfulness. About 10 percent of babies consistently show this pattern during the first two years of life (Kagan & Snidman, 1991), and these children are more likely to develop anxiety disorders as they grow older (Klein & Pine, 2002). One prevention study found that the rate of anxiety disorders can be significantly reduced by parent education. The keys are discouraging overprotectiveness, a common reaction to temperamentally inhibited children, and encouraging gradual exposure to the sources of children's fear (Rapee et al., 2005).

**SOCIAL FACTORS: A FOCUS ON ATTACHMENTS** Together with John Bowlby (1969, 1973, 1980), Canadian American psychologist Mary Ainsworth (1913–1999) developed attachment theory, a set of proposals about the normal development of attachments and the adverse consequences of troubled attachment relationships. Troubled attachments may include the failure to develop a selective attachment early in life; the development of an insecure attachment; or multiple, prolonged separations from (or the permanent loss of) an attachment figure.

Extreme parental neglect deprives infants of the opportunity to form a selective attachment. Such neglect can cause *reactive attachment disorder,* or what attachment researchers sometimes call *anaclitic depression*—the lack of social responsiveness found among infants who do not have a consistent attachment figure (Sroufe & Fleeson, 1986). Research on the consequences of extreme neglect for children is strongly buttressed by evidence from animal analogue research. Nonhuman primates who are raised in isolation without a parent or a substitute attachment figure have dramatically troubled social relationships (Suomi & Harlow, 1972).

Attachment theory also predicts that variations in the quality of early attachments are associated with children's psychological adjustment. Attachment quality can be broadly divided into secure (healthy) and anxious attachments. Infants with *secure attachments* separate easily and explore away from their attachment figures, but they readily seek comfort when they are threatened or distressed. Infants with **anxious attachments** are fearful about exploration and are not easily comforted by their attachment figures, who respond inadequately or inconsistently

to the child's needs (Cassidy & Shaver, 2008). Anxious attachments are further subcategorized into (1) *anxious avoidant attachments,* where the infant is generally unwary of strange situations and shows little preference for the attachment figure over others as a source of comfort; (2) *anxious resistant attachments,* where the infant is wary of exploration, not easily soothed by the attachment figure, and angry or ambivalent about contact; and (3) *disorganized attachments,* where the infant responds inconsistently because of conflicting feelings toward an inconsistent caregiver who is the potential source of either reassurance or fear (Cassidy & Shaver, 2008).

A number of longitudinal studies have demonstrated that anxious attachments during infancy foreshadow difficulties in children's social and emotional adjustment throughout childhood. However, an insecure attachment does not seem to result in the development of any particular emotional disorder. Rather, insecure attachments predict a number of internalizing and social difficulties, including lower self-esteem, less competence in peer interaction, and increased dependency on others (Cassidy & Shaver, 2008). Stable, anxious attachments during infancy also predict externalizing behavior at three years of age (Shaw & Vondra, 1995). Thus, anxious attachments are a general rather than a specific risk factor for children's psychological problems.

Finally, separation and loss clearly cause distress among children. In the short run, children move through a four-stage process akin to grief when they are separated from or lose an attachment figure. The process includes (1) numbed responsiveness, (2) yearning and protest, (3) disorganization and despair, and, ultimately (4), reorganization and detachment or loss of interest in the former attachment figure (Bowlby, 1979). However, there is considerable controversy about the long-term consequences of separation and loss. Bowlby (1973) asserted that detachment increases the risk for depression. Critics suggest, however, that what Bowlby called detachment really is adjustment to new circumstances (Rutter, 1981). This interpretation highlights children's **resilience**—their ability to "bounce back" from adversity (Masten, 2001). The resilience interpretation is consistent with research that fails to find a relationship between childhood loss and depression during adult life (Harrington & Harrison, 1999).

**PSYCHOLOGICAL FACTORS Emotion regulation** is the process of learning to identify, evaluate, and control your feelings. As with children's conduct, emotion regulation in children progresses from external to internal control with age. For example, attachment figures soothe the anxiety of infants and toddlers. As they grow older, however, children develop *internal working models* or expectations about relationship security, and these expectations help them to control their own fear. Rumination, repeatedly focusing on distress, appears to be a particular poor form of emotion regulation, one that foreshadows future depression in early adolescence (Abela & Hankin, 2011).

Other research links troubles with emotion regulation to children's internalizing disorders, particularly the guilt felt among children with a depressed parent (Rakow et al., 2011). A related concern is *role reversal,* where children come to care for a parent rather than vice versa. Caretaking children attempt, and inevitably fail, to make a depressed mom or dad happy. This leaves children feeling guilty and responsible (Zahn-Waxler et al., 1990). In fact, adolescent girls who engage in emotional (but not practical) caretaking of a depressed mother are more depressed themselves (Champion et al., 2009).

Of course, it is laudable for a child to feel empathy and concern for a troubled parent. Yet, with their parents' help, children need to learn that taking care of a disturbed parent is not their "job"—not their responsibility. Optimistically, recent research shows that the development of internalizing symptoms in children can be prevented by a psychoeducational program that teaches parenting skills to depressed parents and coping skills to their children. Of note, the program also reduces parents' depressive symptoms (Compas et al., 2009).

## Treatment of Internalizing Disorders

"Adult" treatments have often been used without evidence that they work specifically for depressed children. For example, antidepressant medications are second only to psychostimulants as the most commonly prescribed psychotropic drugs for children and adolescents (Zito et al., 2000). Yet, only fluoxetine (Prozac) has proven effectiveness for children (Whittington et al., 2004).[3]

Fortunately, more research is now focusing on treatments specifically for children, even depressed preschoolers (Luby, Lenze, & Tillman, 2012). One of the best examples is the Treatment for Adolescents with Depression Study (TADS). This multisite clinical trial randomly assigned 439 depressed adolescents to receive either (1) fluoxetine alone, (2) cognitive behavior therapy (CBT), (3) combined medication and CBT, or (4) placebo (TADS, 2004). After 12 weeks of treatment, 71 percent of the patients receiving combined therapy improved, which was statically superior to medication alone, CBT alone, or placebo. Medication alone also was statistically superior to CBT or placebo at 12 weeks (see Figure 16.7; TADS, 2004).

---

**Suicidality and Antidepressant Drugs**

Antidepressants increased the risk compared to placebo of suicidal thinking and behavior (suicidality) in children, adolescents, and young adults in short-term studies of major depressive disorder (MDD) and other psychiatric disorders. Anyone considering the use of [Insert established name] or any other antidepressant in a child, adolescent, or young adult must balance this risk with the clinical need. Short-term studies did not show an increase in the risk of suicidality with antidepressants compared to placebo in adults beyond age 24; there was a reduction in risk with antidepressants compared to placebo in adults aged 65 and older. Depression and certain other psychiatric disorders are themselves associated with increases in the risk of suicide. Patients of all ages who are started on antidepressant therapy should be monitored appropriately and observed closely for clinical worsening, suicidality, or unusual changes in behavior. Families and caregivers should be advised of the need for close observation and communication with the prescriber. [Insert Drug Name] is not approved for use in pediatric patients. [The previous sentence would be replaced with the sentence, below, for the following drugs: Prozac: Prozac is approved for use in pediatric patients with MDD and obsessive compulsive disorder (OCD). Zoloft: Zoloft is not approved for use in pediatric patients except for patients with obsessive compulsive disorder (OCD). Fluvoxamine: Fluvoxamine is not approved for use in pediatric patients except for patients with obsessive compulsive disorder (OCD).] (See Warnings: Clinical Worsening and Suicide Risk, Precautions: Information for Patients, and Precautions: Pediatric Use)

On October 15, 2004, the US. Food and Drug Administration (FDA) ordered drug companies to place this "black box" warning on the labels of antidepressant medications. The warning remains, although some more recent evidence suggests that antidepressants may actually lower teen suicide risk.

Importantly, the results at 36 weeks showed no differences between treatments (see Figure 16.7). (The longer-term results must be qualified because random assignment was broken after 12 weeks.) Of critical importance, however, 14.7 percent of patients in the medication-only group attempted, planned, or thought seriously about suicide at 36 weeks, significantly more than in the combined group (8.4 percent) or with CBT alone (6.3 percent) (TADS, 2007). Together with the superior short-term response, this outcome strongly supports combining medication with CBT in treating depressed adolescents (Reinecke, Curry, & March, 2009).

Evidence that antidepressants increase suicidality in TADS and other studies (Hammand, Laughren, & Racoosin, 2006) led the FDA to require manufacturers to place a "black box" warning on the medications in 2004 (see photo). Prescriptions to children and adolescents declined significantly as a result (Olfson, Marcus,

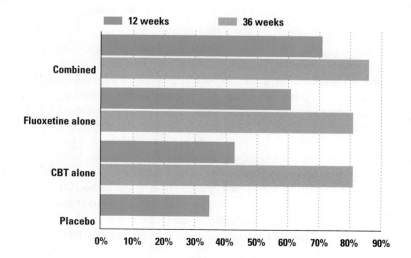

**FIGURE 16.7**

The Treatment of Adolescents with Depression Study (TADS) found that combined fluoxetine and CBT significantly accelerated treatment response (at 12 weeks) compared to all other treatments. Fluoxetine alone worked significantly faster than CBT alone or placebo. No differences were found at 36 weeks. CBT, alone or combined with medication, reduced suicidality (not shown) compared to medication alone.

*Source:* Courtesy of the National Institute of Mental Health.

---

[3]Recent evidence does indicate, however, that about 40 percent of youth are helped by switching antidepressants if the first is ineffective (Walkup, 2010).

& Druss, 2008), but as we noted earlier, adolescent suicide *increased* during this time (CDC, 2007).

What is the wise course given this conflicting information? Some experts argue that while antidepressants increase suicidality for *some* teens, the medications reduce suicidality for *more* adolescents. From this perspective, the benefits of antidepressants outweigh their risks (Bridge et al., 2007; Friedman & Leon, 2007). We generally agree. Our view is that antidepressants are a valuable treatment option for adolescent depression. However, suicide potential needs to be carefully assessed, and if there is any hint of suicide risk, medication should not be used or should be combined with CBT.

Turning to the treatment of children's anxiety, the Child/Adolescent Anxiety Multimodal Study recently reported that the combination of sertraline (an SSRI) and cognitive behavior therapy led to more remission in children's anxiety disorders than either treatment alone (Ginsburg et al., 2011). This clinical trial of 488 children and adolescents clarifies the results of numerous, smaller studies of individual and family treatment of children's anxiety disorders. Family and individual CBT generally are equally effective (Kendall et al., 2008), with benefits evident even six to seven years after treatment (Barrett et al., 2001; Kendall et al., 2004). Other medications also may help. Imipramine in combination with CBT is more effective in treating school refusal than therapy alone (Bernstein et al., 2000). Both clomipramine and SSRIs also are effective in treating children with obsessive-compulsive disorders (Rapoport & Swedo, 2002), although exposure and response prevention, perhaps in combination with medication, is still the treatment of choice for both children and adults (March et al., 2004).

**COURSE AND OUTCOME** Psychologists used to believe that children "outgrew" internalizing problems. However, research shows that some internalizing disorders persist over time. Specific fears tend to be relatively short-lived, but more complex disorders, such as depression (Harrington et al., 1990; Kovacs et al., 1984) and obsessive-compulsive disorder (March et al., 1995), are likely to continue from childhood into adolescence and adult life. Childhood depression predicts a sixfold increase in the risk for suicide in young adults (Harrington, 2002). This prognosis shows the pressing need to develop more effective treatments for children and adolescents with serious internalizing disorders.

## getting HELP

After reading this chapter, you might be wondering about your own mental health during your childhood. If so, your first reaction, as always, should be caution about the "medical student's syndrome": the tendency to diagnose yourself with every new disorder. Most psychological disorders are on a continuum with normal behavior, and most of us struggle at some time with a short attention span, restlessness, difficulty in learning, or moodiness. Still, we urge you to consider getting help if you are deeply concerned that you may have ADHD, a learning disability, or long-hidden depression. Or perhaps you are struggling to come to grips with a very difficult childhood experience, anything from your parents' divorce to abuse. If so, a first step could be to contact your college's counseling center. Or you may want to begin by talking with an advisor, professor, or dean at your school. Many colleges also offer testing for learning disabilities or other academic-related problems.

Or you may be concerned about a younger brother or sister, or perhaps a child you are working with as a volunteer. If so, you may want to begin your search for information and help at the Web site of the National Institute of Child Health and Human Development. An excellent book for working with children with attention-deficit/hyperactivity disorder is Russell Barkley's *Taking Charge of ADHD*. For dealing with children who have ODD, or simply for help with managing children, Rex Forehand and Nicholas Long's book *Parenting the Strong-Willed Child* offers a lot of sound, practical advice. Martin Seligman's engaging book

*The Optimistic Child* focuses on the prevention of depression in children. Katharine Manassis' *Keys to Parenting Your Anxious Child* offers helpful advice about dealing with children who are anxious but not necessarily suffering from an anxiety disorder.

Playing a game with children is something else you can do to help them (and you) understand their feelings. The Feelings Company sells therapeutic games online; simply looking through the games may give you some creative ideas. For example, you and your young friend could make up cards with different feeling words (sad, mad, scared), facial expressions, or leading questions (When was the last time you felt really, really sad?). Turn this into a game, and you may turn the game into a meaningful conversation.

What if you know a child or an adolescent who you think needs professional help? If the young person has confided in you, that's a great start. You can do a lot by being a caring friend or sibling and a good role model. But you also want to encourage a child with an internalizing problem to confide in a parent—if not about the details of the problems, at least about the child's interest in getting help. Or you may know a parent who is looking to find help for a child with an externalizing disorder. In either case, asking for names from a teacher or school counselor is a good place to start. In fact, the child's school may be able to—or required to—provide free services for a troubled student. Another option is the child's pediatrician, who can prescribe medication if appropriate, or make a referral to a mental health professional.

# 16 Summary

Externalizing disorders create difficulties for the child's external world, as children fail to control their behavior according to the expectations of others.

Attention-deficit/hyperactivity disorder (ADHD) is particularly noticeable in school and is characterized by inattention, overactivity, and impulsivity. Oppositional defiant disorder (ODD) is characterized by negative, hostile, and defiant behavior and is also common among school-aged children. Conduct disorder (CD) is similar to ODD, except the rule violations are much more serious and it is more common among adolescents than younger children.

Internalizing disorders primarily affect the child's internal world, for example, excessive anxiety or sadness. DSM-5 does not list special internalizing disorders for children but notes that children may qualify for many "adult" diagnoses, such as anxiety or mood disorders.

DSM-5 no longer includes a special section listing psychological disorders of childhood, although ADHD, learning disorder, autism, and intellectual disability are among the most important "neurodevelopmental disorders." It does include many diagnoses that apply primarily to children, but scatters them across various "adult" diagnostic categories, for example, separation anxiety disorder and disruptive mood dysregulation disorder.

Boys are more likely to have externalizing problems during childhood, but girls have more internalizing in adolescence and early adult life.

Family adversity is an important risk factor for externalizing problems.

Parents are most effective when they are authoritative: loving and firm in disciplining their children.

Coercion is a parenting problem that occurs when parents reinforce children's misbehavior by giving in to their demands.

Biological factors in ADHD include temperament, neuropsychological abnormalities, and especially genetics.

Lack of self-control, a tendency to overattribute aggressive intentions to others, and less-developed moral reasoning are psychological characteristics related to externalizing disorders.

The most promising treatments for externalizing disorders include psychostimulants for attention deficit/hyperactivity disorder (short term benefits only), behavioral family therapy for oppositional defiant disorder, and multisystemic family therapy for conduct disorders and juvenile delinquency.

The causes of internalizing disorders in children have been studied inadequately but may involve problems with attachment relationships.

Recent research shows that antidepressants, cognitive behavior therapy, and especially the combination are effective in treating adolescent mood disorders, where suicide is an important concern. Cognitive behavior therapy and perhaps medication is the treatment of choice for children's anxiety disorders.

## The Big Picture

## critical thinking review

16.1 Are children's psychological disorders different from adults'?
Pediatricians, and parents, need to pay special attention to childhood illnesses like colic (babies crying for more than three hours a day), "Otitis media" (middle ear infection), and Osgood–Schlatter disease (a painful bump on the knee stemming from rapid growth). The same is true for psychological disorders of childhood. . . . (see page 436).

16.2 Is ADHD different from just being a "bad kid"?
. . . experts have long debated whether ODD and ADHD are really the same or different problems. Intent is a key to the difference . . . (see page 441).

16.3 Are children's psychological problems a sign of family problems?
Externalizing disorders are associated with various indicators of family adversity. . . (see page 443).

16.4 Can medication help children behave—and do better in school?
. . .psychostimulants improve hyperactivity and impulsivity, but their effects on attention and learning are less certain. . . An even more troubling and puzzling fact is that psychostimulants have not been found to lead to long-term improvements in behavior, learning, or any other areas of functioning . . . (see page 449).

**16.5** Can young children be depressed?

The assessment of depression in children can be particularly difficult . . . (see page 455).

**16.6** Do antidepressants cause teen suicide?

Evidence that antidepressants increase suicidality in TADS and other studies led the FDA to require manufacturers to place a "black box" warning on the medications in 2004 . . . (see page 461).

# key terms

anxious attachments  460

attention deficit  439

attention-deficit/hyperactivity disorder (ADHD)  439

authoritative parenting  452

coercion  446

conduct disorder (CD)  442

developmental norms  436

developmental psychopathology  436

emotion regulation  460

externalizing disorders  436

hyperactivity  439

learning disability (LD)  441

internalizing disorders  436

oppositional defiant disorder (ODD)  440

psychostimulants  449

recidivism  453

representative sample  444

resilience  460

separation anxiety disorder  456

status offenses  442

temperament  443

# adjustment disorders and life-cycle transitions

17

# The Big Picture

## learning objectives

### 17.1
What problems in living cause some people to seek psychological help?

### 17.2
How does *DSM-5* classify emotional problems that are *not* disorders?

### 17.3
Is the "midlife crisis" a myth?

### 17.4
Is an identity crisis necessary for healthy adult development?

### 17.5
How are family relationships critical to psychological well-being?

### 17.6
Is it depressing to grow older?

People frequently seek guidance from a mental health professional for problems in living or what *DSM-5* calls *adjustment disorders.* These problems are *not* mental disorders, although individual psychological problems like depression may result from—or cause—problems in living. Young people may want a therapist's perspective on struggles associated with becoming an adult, like sorting out values, goals, family issues, or relationship concerns. In midlife, many people seek help for conflicts that arise from an unhappy marriage, a divorce, or lifestyle choices. Older adults sometimes consult therapists about adjusting to later life, including dealing with retirement, loneliness, and bereavement.

## Overview

In fact, half of people receiving treatment do *not* meet diagnostic criteria for a mental disorder (Kessler, Demler, et al., 2005). Many otherwise well-functioning people seek help with life difficulties or *psychological pain,* upsetting but normal emotions that can result from difficult life events, for example, hurt feelings, sadness, anger, or longing (Laumann-Billings & Emery, 2000).

How can we describe the problems in living that bring people into therapy? *DSM-5* uses two approaches. First is the diagnosis *adjustment disorder,* the development of clinically significant symptoms in response to stress that are *not* severe enough to be considered a mental disorder. Second is a list of *other conditions that may be a focus of clinical attention,* a *DSM-5* list that includes things such as a "partner relational problem" and "phase of life problem."

Unfortunately, *DSM-5* only very briefly describes adjustment disorders and other conditions that may be the focus of treatment. There are some good reasons for this shortcoming (Strain & Friedman, 2011). People face an array of life problems. Trying to list every possibility can seem like an impossible task. In fact, experts have only rarely attempted to classify life or relationships struggles, and they disagree about existing proposals.

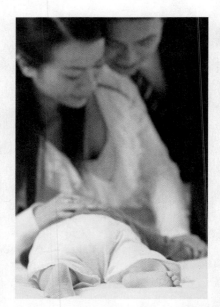

Moving into a new stage of adult life can be a happy time, but many people struggle with the changes brought about by life transitions.

Certainly this enterprise is far behind our (imperfect) efforts to classify mental disorders.

Still, we have learned much about *adult development*, the fairly predictable challenges that occur during adult life in relationships, work, life goals, and personal identity. Several theorists divide adult development into three periods—early, middle, and later life. Consistent with this division, we highlight three major **life-cycle transitions** struggles in moving from one stage of adult development into a new one. The *transition to adult life* is a time for grappling with the major issues related to identity, career, and relationships. *Family transitions*, in the middle adult years may include very happy events like the birth of the first child, or very unhappy ones, like a difficult divorce. The *transition to later life* may involve major changes in life roles such as retirement, grief over the loss of loved ones, and inner conflicts about aging, mortality, and the life one has lived. As an introduction, consider the following case study.

### → Left for Another Man

Chuck was 51 years old when his wife told him she wanted a divorce. Chuck had been married for 27 years, and he was totally unprepared for her announcement. He knew that his marriage was not perfect, but he had thought of his wife's complaints as normal "nagging." Chuck was content in his life, and he could not fathom what his wife was thinking. After serving in the navy for 20 years, Chuck was collecting a pension and working as a technician for an electronics company. His two children were grown, the family was financially secure, and Chuck was planning to retire to Florida in another 10 or 15 years. His life was on the course he had set long ago.

At first, Chuck simply did not believe what was happening. His wife said that she had been unhappy for years, but only recently got the courage to leave him. This account clashed with Chuck's view of their marriage. He openly wondered if the real problem was his wife's menopause, or what he called "her change of life."

Reality began to hit Chuck when his wife moved out of their house and into an apartment. Chuck's wife said that she wanted a friendly divorce, and she telephoned him a few times a week just to talk. Chuck did not want a divorce, but he worked hard to avoid conflict. He said that he wanted to avoid hard feelings. Although he saw no need for it, Chuck consulted a clinical psychologist at his wife's suggestion. She had been seeing a counselor and found their discussions helpful.

Chuck remained stoic during the first several therapy sessions. He freely discussed the events of his life and admitted that he now realized that he had taken his wife for granted. He grudgingly acknowledged that he was a "little upset" and "pretty angry" but he could not or would not describe his emotions with intensity or detail. Mostly, he wanted the therapist to help him to figure out what was wrong with his wife.

A few weeks later, Chuck's feelings came flooding out when his wife told him that she was in love with another man. Chuck raged to the therapist about how he felt used and cheated. He was stunned, but he was not going to let his wife get away with this. He immediately contacted a lawyer. He wanted to make sure that his wife "didn't get a dime" out of the divorce settlement. Chuck also called his children and told them all of the details about what had happened. He seemed bent on revenge.

Chuck admitted that, in addition to anger, he felt intense hurt and pain: real, physical pain, as though someone had just punched him in the chest. When the therapist asked if any of these emotions were familiar to him, Chuck recalled his feelings when he was 17 years old. His father died suddenly that year, and Chuck remembered feeling intense grief over the loss. He had controlled his feelings at the time, so he was surprised by the strong emotions he now felt in recalling the unfortunate event over 30 years later. His current feelings reminded him a lot of his sadness at his father's death, but his present grief was more volatile and he was angrier than before.

Chuck talked more about his intense loneliness and sadness as the therapy continued over the next few months and it became clear that his marriage really was ending. He kept up his daily routine at home and at work, but he said that it seemed as if he were living in a dream. In the midst of his grief, he sometimes wondered if his entire marriage, entire life, had been a sham. How could he have been so blind? Who was this woman he had been married to? What was he supposed to do with himself now?

........................................................................

## Symptoms

Are Chuck's reactions typical "symptoms" of adjustment to divorce?[1] Life-cycle transitions differ greatly, and different people respond to the same event in various ways. Chuck's feelings may have little in common with other people's reactions to divorce, let alone with people who are experiencing other major life changes.

Yet, there are similarities across diverse life-cycle transitions. The psychologist Erik Erikson (1902–1994) highlighted *conflict* as a common theme. Erikson organized each of his eight stages of psychosocial development around a central conflict, or what he termed a "*crisis of the healthy personality*" (Erikson, 1959/1980). According to him, the conflict inherent in change creates both psychological and interpersonal tension, as the comfortable but predictable known is pitted against the fearsome but potentially exciting unknown.

We also view conflict as a commonality across different life-cycle transitions. By definition, transitions involve change, and conflict is a frequent consequence of change. Conflict is not

---

[1]We discuss normal reactions to life-cycle transitions in this chapter but use the terms *symptoms* and *diagnosis* for the sake of consistency with earlier chapters.

necessarily bad; in fact, conflict may be necessary in order for change to occur. Nevertheless, conflict can be distressing. During life-cycle transitions, interpersonal conflicts commonly occur in close relationships. Emotional conflicts include uncertain and difficult feelings. Cognitive conflicts often involve broad doubts about what Erikson (1968) called *identity,* our global sense of self.

*Psychological pain* often is another common "symptom" of life-cycle transitions. What do we mean by psychological pain? People often draw analogies between physical and emotional pain. We talk about hurt feelings, painful memories. Chuck said he felt like he'd been punched in the chest. Well, the analogy may be more than verbal. Many of the same brain systems are involved in both physical and psychological pain (Eisenberger, 2012). Recent research even shows that *acetaminophen,* an over-the-counter pain reliever you have surely taken for a headache, reduces psychological pain—according to both self-report and measured brain activity (DeWall et al., 2010). Emotional pain feels like physical pain, because both activate similar neural processes.

Humans need more than an aspirin to relieve their emotional pain. However, therapy probably is a pain reliever, and this may explain why so many people seek psychological help for problems in living. Difficult transitions like a parental divorce do not typically cause psychopathology, but they almost always are very painful emotionally (Laumann-Billings & Emery, 2000).

## Diagnosis

*DSM-5* includes two ways of classifying problems that are not mental disorders but cause people to seek treatment. **Adjustment disorders** involve clinically significant symptoms in response to stress that are not severe enough to warrant classification as a mental disorder (see "DSM-5: Adjustment Disorder" ). The

limited research on adjustment disorders suggests that they fall in between normal reactions to stress and anxiety or mood disorders, are rarely diagnosed, and often treated with antidepressants (Fernandez et al., 2012). Adjustment disorders are grouped with acute stress disorder (ASD) and posttraumatic disorders (PTSD) in *DSM-5,* because stress causes all three conditions. However, an adjustment disorder can be a reaction to a stressor of *any* severity, not just traumatic stress, and unlike ASD and PTSD, adjustment disorder has no clear symptom pattern (Casey & Doherty, 2012). We consider adjustment disorders in this chapter because of the wide range of life stressors and reactions to them, as well as to complete the developmental psychopathology focus of Chapters 15, 16 and 17.

*DSM-5* also contains a list of *other conditions that may be a focus of clinical attention* (see Table 17.1). This manual offers only very brief descriptions of each problem. Due to *DSM-5's* limited coverage, we focus on other approaches to conceptualizing life-cycle transitions.

**ERIKSON'S PSYCHOSOCIAL DEVELOPMENT** Erik Erikson (1959/1980) was one of the first theorists to highlight that development does not stop at age 18 but continues throughout adult life. His theory of psychosocial development (see Table 2.5) includes four stages of adult development: (1) identity versus role confusion(2) intimacy versus self-absorption(3) generativity versus stagnation and (4) integrity versus despair.

Erikson viewed *identity versus role confusion* as the major challenge of adolescence and young adulthood. The young person's task is to integrate their experiences, goals, and values into a global sense of self. When resolved, the **identity crisis,** a normal period of basic uncertainty about self, provides a comprehensive answer to the question "Who am I?" Erikson viewed this resolution as allowing young adults to embark on a journey toward achieving long-term life goals.

---

| criteria for | |
|---|---|
| **Adjustment Disorder** | **DSM-5** |

**A.** The development of emotional or behavioral symptoms in response to an identifiable stressor(s) occurring within 3 months of the onset of the stressor(s).

**B.** These symptoms or behaviors are clinically significant, as evidenced by one or both of the following:
  **1.** Marked distress that is out of proportion to the severity or intensity of the stressor, taking into account the external context and the cultural factors that might influence symptom severity and presentation.

**2.** Significant impairment in social, occupational, or other important areas of functioning.

**C.** The stress-related disturbance does not meet the criteria for another mental disorder and is not merely an exacerbation of a preexisting mental disorder.

**D.** The symptoms do not represent normal bereavement.

**E.** Once the stressor or its consequences have terminated, the symptoms do not persist for more than an additional 6 months.

**TABLE 17.1**

**DSM-5 Categories and Examples of "Other Conditions That May Be a Focus of Clinical Attention"**

| General Category | Specific Example |
|---|---|
| Relational Problems Within Family | High Expressed Emotion Level |
| Abuse and Neglect | Child sexual abuse |
| Educational and Occupational Problems | Academic or Educational Problem |
| Housing and Economic Problems | Homelessness |
| Other Problems Related to the Social Environment | Phase of Life Problem |
| Problems Related to Crime or Interaction with Legal System | Victim of Crime |
| Other Health Service Encounters for Counseling and Medical Advice | Sex counseling |
| Problems Related to Other Psychosocial, Personal, And Environmental Circumstances | Religious or spiritual problem |
| Other Circumstances of Personal History | Overweight or Obesity |

One life goal is to form an intimate relationship early in adulthood. Erikson's second stage of adult development, *intimacy versus self-absorption,* centers on the conflict between closeness and independence. Self-absorbed people either become dependent in intimate relationships or remain aloof from others. True intimacy is a balance between connectedness and autonomy.

Erikson's third crisis of adult life is *generativity versus stagnation.* Generativity is defined by accomplishments in middle adult life, including career and family achievements. People who stagnate may have both a family and a job, but they live their life without a sense of purpose or direction.

Erikson's last stage involves the conflict between *integrity and despair* in later life. Integrity comes from "the acceptance of one's one and only life cycle as something that had to be and that, by necessity, permitted of no substitutions" (Erikson, 1963, p. 260). Despair comes from the impossible desire to change the past and from yearning for a second chance at life.

**ADULT TRANSITIONS** Erikson focused on the psychological side of psychosocial development, but contemporary theorists often highlight social aspects. Psychologist Daniel Levinson (1986) noted three major (and many minor) transitions between broad "eras" or "seasons" in adult life. The *early adult transition* involves moving away from family and assuming adult roles. The *midlife transition*—often called a "midlife crisis"—is a time for becoming less driven and developing more compassion. The *late adult transition* is characterized by the changing roles and relationships of later life.

As you ponder these models of adult development, you should also consider their limits. History, ethnicity, gender, culture, and values all influence what tasks are "normal." For example, Erikson assumed that normal adult development included forming an enduring intimate heterosexual relationship, an idea that may seem old fashioned given the diverse lifestyles and demographics of our times.

Another caution is that transitions not perfectly predictable. Not every young adult experiences an identity crisis; turning 40 does not automatically mean midlife crisis. And women and men confront different issues in physical aging, relationships, and values (Stewart & Ostrove, 1998). Still, the outlines offered by Erikson and Levinson capture broad commonalities in the experiences of a great many people. Most of us create **social clocks**—age-related goals for ourselves—and we evaluate our achievements to the extent that we are "on time" or "off time."

## The Transition to Adulthood

In the United States, the transition to adult life typically begins in the late teen years, and it may continue into the middle twenties or even later (Furstenberg, 2010). This is the time young adults assume increasing independence, and many leave their family home. By the end of the transition, most young adults have begun life roles in the central areas of adult development: love and work. More subjectively, 90 percent of American 30-year-olds also report that they feel like they have fully reached adulthood (Arnett, 2007).

## Symptoms of the Adult Transition

**IDENTITY CRISIS** Erikson (1959/1980) saw the **identity crisis** as the central psychological conflict of the transition to adult life. Identity conflicts are epitomized by the searching question "Who am I?" He argued that, in order to assume successful and lasting adult roles, young people need a **moratorium,** a time of uncertainty about themselves and their goals. In his words:

> The period can be viewed as a *psychosocial moratorium* during which the individual through free role experimentation may find a niche in some section of his society, a niche which is firmly defined and yet seems to be uniquely made for him. In finding it the young adult gains an assured sense of inner continuity and social sameness which will bridge what he was as a child and what he is about to become, and will reconcile his conception of himself and his community's recognition of him. (pp. 119–120, italics in original)

Erikson's view of identity has broad appeal. A search for identity is a frequent theme in coming of age novels like Khaled Hosseini's *The Kite Runner* or Sue Monk Kidd's *The Secret Life of Bees* and movies such as *Juno* or *Almost Famous.* At this time of change, many of us feel unable to decide on a career, and our choices can be tentative and volatile. We question our values about religion, sex, and morality. We often doubt our ability to succeed in work or in relationships. Significantly, we also lack perspective on our experience. We feel as though we are confronting fundamental questions about who we are, not merely passing through a "stage."

A contemporary approach to identity is the construction of a "life story," an informal autobiography that gives our lives a consistent theme (McAdams, 2013). By creating a life story, we make our new identity concrete and public. Life stories sometimes offer oversimplified answers to the question, "Who am I?" in order to make our narrative clear, concise, and compelling.

A related task is searching for, and finding, "meaning in life." A recent study of high school seniors examined how much young people were searching for meaning in life and the degree to which they had found meaning (Kiang & Fuligni, 2010). Twelfth-graders who were searching for meaning had lower psychological adjustment; those who had found meaning were better adjusted. These patterns held across ethnic groups, although Asian Americans reported higher levels of searching for meaning than either Latin or European Americans. Finding meaning in life accounted for much of the relation between *ethnic identity* and well-being. Ethnic identities may impart meaning in the lives of youth.

**CHANGING ROLES AND RELATIONSHIPS** Young people also grapple with more concrete questions than "Who am I?" and "What's the meaning of life?" They also make very important decisions about whether and where to go to college, how to manage intimate relationships, and what career path to pursue. Such major decisions can permanently alter the course of life. At the same time, young adults and their parents must negotiate new boundaries for their relationship, finding the right balance between autonomy and relatedness (Allen et al., 2002). Conflicts typically increase, as young people interpret parental control as an infringement on their independence (Smetana, 1989). Successfully renegotiating parent–child relationships predicts healthy individual and family adjustment in adult life (Bell & Bell, 2005).

Ego psychologist Karen Horney (1939) theorized that people have competing needs to move toward, to move away from, and to move against others. *Moving toward* others fulfills needs for love and acceptance. *Moving away* from others is a way of establishing independence and efficacy. *Moving against* others meets the individual's need for power and dominance. Horney saw relationship difficulties as conflicts among these three basic needs. Young adults want their parents' support; they also want their own independence; and at the same time, they may also want to outdo their parents.

Conflicts can increase in peer relationships too. Young adults become less certain about their friends as they become less certain about themselves. In fact, a sense of certainty about personal identity is associated with both greater intimacy and less conflict in peer relationships, including loving relationships (Fitch & Adams, 1983). Of course, intimate relationships can take on a new meaning. Young adults may seriously consider making a lifelong commitment, a prospect that puts new pressures on love relationships.

The number of changing roles and relationships suggests that the search for self may be less of an attempt to define a single "me" and more of a struggle to integrate new role identities with old ones. Given all the real and practical changes, it is not surprising that many young adults ask: "Who am I?"

Young people often explore new roles, relationships, and activities as they search for identity during the transition to young adult life.

**EMOTIONAL TURMOIL** Research shows that young people experience intense and volatile emotions (Paikoff & Brooks-Gunn, 1991). In a clever series of studies, psychologists used "beepers" to signal adolescents and adults at various times during the day and night to assess their activities and emotional states. In comparison with adults, young people between the ages of 13 and 18 reported emotions that were more intense, short-lived, and more subject to change (Csikszentmihalyi & Larson, 1984; Larson, Csikszentmihalyi, & Graef, 1980).

Many emotional conflicts during the adult transition stem from uncertainty about relationships. Young people often experience the conflicting feelings of love, sadness, and anger in close relationships (Sbarra & Emery, 2005). Thus, emotional struggles stem both from competing feelings and from the intensity of these emotions.

## Diagnosis of Identity Conflicts

Believe it or not, *DSM-III-R* listed "identity disorder" as a mental disorder(!). *DSM-5* wisely lists identity problems only under "other conditions that may be a focus of clinical attention." The manual includes a one-sentence description: "This category can be used when the focus of clinical attention is uncertainty about multiple issues relating to identity such as long-term goals, career choice, friendship patterns, sexual orientation and behavior, moral values, and group loyalties" (*DSM-5*, 2013).

Alternative classifications of identity conflicts are based on Erikson's concepts. For example, Marcia (1966) proposed several categories:

1. *Identity diffusion:* Young people who have questioned their childhood identities but are not actively searching for new adult roles.

2. *Identity foreclosure:* Young adults who never questioned themselves or their goals but instead proceed along the predetermined course of their childhood commitments.

3. *Identity moratorium:* People who are in the middle of an identity crisis and actively searching for adult roles.

4. *Identity achievement:* Young people who have questioned their identities and who have successfully decided on their own long-term goals.

Some research supports the validity of these categories (Marcia, 1994). For example, the percentage of students classified as identity achievers increases between the first and last years of college (Waterman, Geary, & Waterman, 1974), and the percentage continues to increase in the years after college graduation (Waterman & Goldman, 1976). Consistent with Erikson's theory, identity achievers also are less conforming and more confident in social interaction than others (Adams et al., 1985; Adams, Abraham, & Markstrom, 1987). Moreover, some exciting research on *racial identity* (ethnic identity specifically among African Americans) supports both the four group model and the better adjustment of identity achievers (Seaton, Scottham, & Sellers, 2006). Still, the

expected developmental progression from identity diffusion to identity achievement may not accurately describe many people's growth. Instead, the different identity statuses can reflect differences in personality and cultural expectations (Bosma & Kunnen, 2001; Seaton et al., 2006).

## Frequency of Identity Conflicts

In industrialized countries, young people wait longer in assuming adult roles, even compared to a few decades ago. Erikson wrote of late adolescence as the time of identity conflict. Popular books today focus on the "quarter-life crisis," grappling with becoming an adult around the age of 25. The extended period of *emerging adulthood* is reflected in movies like *Failure to Launch*—and documented by more young people living at home, staying in school, and delaying marriage and childbearing (Settersen & Ray, 2010; see Figure 17.1).

Demographic data tell us that, even without more delays due to education, young people with a high school education or less often have the most trouble transitioning into adult roles (Hendry & Kloep, 2007). In 2008, large numbers of young people aged 16 to 24 in the United States were neither in school nor employed, including 12 percent of white males (13 percent of white females), 21 percent of black males (21 percent of black females), and 15 percent of Hispanic males (26 percent of Hispanic females) (Danziger & Ratner, 2010). These young people, and others working in low-paying jobs, face extremely limited prospects not only for work but also for family life. Nonmarital childbearing and cohabitation (that is unlikely to endure) have become the norm. College-educated young people also live together frequently. However, most college graduates eventually marry, and

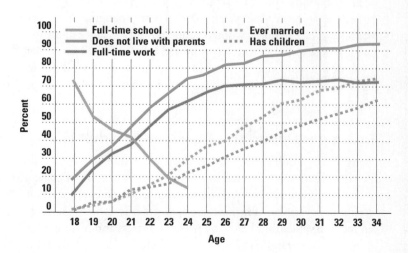

**FIGURE 17.1**

**Roles That Mark the Adult Transition** Percent of young adults in the United States engaged in roles associated with the transition to adult life. Today, young people assume adult roles at an older age than they did a generation or two earlier—and later than young people still do in many less industrialized societies.

*Source:* From the Future of Children, a collaboration of the Woodrow Wilson School of Public and International Affairs at Princeton University and the Brookings Institution.

they generally delay childbearing until after marriage—and until they have completed their education (Furstenberg, 2010). Identity diffusion may be a consequence of unresolved psychological conflicts. However, delays in making commitments to work and family can also result from the limited opportunities available to some members of society.

## Causes of Identity Conflicts

The most successful young adults have parents who strike a balance between supporting and supervising their children—and giving them increasing independence (Hill & Holmbeck, 1986; Sartor & Youniss, 2002). Identity achievers often grow up in such families, whereas identity diffusers may have rejecting and distant families. Identity foreclosers often have overprotective families (Adams & Adams, 1989; Marcia, 1994).

Is the absence of an identity crisis a problem that foreshadows struggles later in life? Cross-cultural considerations suggest that the "storm and stress" of the transition to adult life is a consequence of the affluence, education, and independence of young people in Western, industrialized societies. In other cultures, people's life course may be determined by parental authority or economic necessity, neither of which allows for an identity crisis (Hendry & Kloep, 2007). In the not-too-distant past, people also assumed adult roles at much younger ages in the United States. In some families and socioeconomic groups, they still do.

Gender roles also may influence identity formation, or at least they once did. In the 1980s, Erikson's theories were criticized for focusing on men and work. Women, it was argued, form identities based on their relationships (Gilligan, 1982). This difference suggested that men may form an identity *before* entering a lasting relationship, while women define themselves *in terms of* those relationships. However, gender roles are changing. For practical and social reasons, women today more typically establish a career before entering into a committed relationship. This "quiet revolution" means that women, like men, now are more likely to form their identity in terms of work and outside of relationships (Goldin, 2006).

## Treatment During the Transition to Adult Life

Many young adults seek therapy during the transition to adult life, an observation bolstered by the frequent utilization of college counseling services. However, no research has been conducted on alternative treatments for these young people. Treatment goals often include validating the young person's distress and helping him or her to understand and clarify difficult life choices. In addition, it may be helpful to "normalize" the experience of identity conflict, that is, to conceptualize the individual's struggle as a part of the difficult but normal confusion resulting from the search for self. Finally, many clinicians suggest that supportive, nondirective therapy is a particularly appropriate treatment for young people who are trying to "find themselves." The following brief case illustrates the approach.

### ➡ Samantha's Birth Mother

Samantha was stunned. She was a 21-year-old senior in college when her birth mother contacted Samantha for the first time in her life. Samantha contacted a therapist at her college counseling center to seek advice. She had not yet met her biological mother, and was pretty certain that she did not want to. She had always known that she was adopted, and she deeply loved her parents—parents, not adoptive parents, she insisted. Samantha had never yearned to meet her biological parents, and she did not welcome this unexpected intrusion in her life. She also did not want to do anything that would seem slightly disloyal to her parents, who also were surprised and distraught about the sudden appearance of Samantha's birth mother.

Apart from this recent shock, Samantha was a happy, well-adjusted, and successful young woman. She reported no history of emotional problems, talked at length about her close friends and boyfriend, seemed thoroughly attached to her parents, and was a successful psychology major who maintained a 3.4 GPA. Yet, she was understandably confused and upset about the appearance of her birth mother. She cried at length, but her overall affect was angry. She half-shouted questions at her therapist like, "What right does this stranger have to intrude in my life?"

The therapist encouraged Samantha to give voice to her many feelings. Samantha *was* angry—and guilty, frustrated, and confused. She was also afraid to meet her biological mother, largely because she felt like she might be meeting a part of herself. What if this woman were mean? Ugly? Unpleasant? What if Samantha didn't like her? What if she did? Who would her mother be then? Who would Samantha be?

With the psychologist's support, Samantha explored her feelings and options. She read about other adopted young people who had met their birth parents, and even chatted with some on the Internet. The sharing of their trying experiences "normalized" Samantha's feelings in a much more direct way than the psychologist's reassuring comments.

Eventually, Samantha decided that she did want to meet her birth mother after all. Despite her initial apprehension, Samantha was exuberant afterwards. She *liked* her birth mother, who was apologetic, sad, and eager to get to know Samantha, but understanding of Samantha's ambivalent feelings and not at all pushy. Moreover, her mother, like Samantha herself, was relieved when the known proved to be far less frightening than the unknown. Samantha ended therapy before she had figured out who she was—now. Still, she was confident that she was going to be able to answer that question.

## Family Transitions

Not everyone experiences a midlife crisis, but most adults experience a variety of challenging family transitions during the middle years of adult life. *Family transitions* may involve the addition or loss of members of a family household and include transitions to

**TABLE 17.2**

## The Family Life Cycle

| Stage | Family Developmental Tasks |
|---|---|
| 1. Married Couple | Establishing a mutually satisfying marriage; adjusting to pregnancy and the promise of parenthood; fitting into kin network |
| 2. Childbearing | Having, adjusting to, and encouraging the development of infants; establishing a satisfying home for both parents and infants |
| 3. Preschool Age | Adapting to the critical needs and interests of preschool children in stimulating, growth-promoting ways; coping with energy depletion and lack of privacy as parents |
| 4. School Age | Fitting into the community of school-aged families in constructive ways; encouraging children's educational achievement |
| 5. Teenage | Balancing freedom with responsibility as teenagers mature and emancipate themselves; establishing postparental interests and careers |
| 6. Launching Center | Releasing young adults into work, military service, college, marriage, and so forth with appropriate rituals and assistance; maintaining a supportive home base |
| 7. Middle-Aged Parents | Rebuilding the marriage relationship; maintaining kin ties with older and younger generations |
| 8. Aging Family Members | Coping with bereavement and living alone; closing the family home or adapting to aging; adjusting to retirement |

*Source:* Duvall, *Marriage & Family Development,* 6th, © 1984. Printed and Electronically reproduced by permission of Pearson Education, Inc., Upper Saddle River, New Jersey.

marriage, parenting, and the *empty nest*—the adjustment that occurs when adult children leave the family home. Divorce and remarriage also are common family transitions in the United States today, an observation that underscores the fact that families extend beyond the boundaries of one household.

Social scientists often conceptualize family change in terms of the **family life cycle**—the developmental course of family relationships throughout life. Table 17.2 outlines one view of the family life cycle. This outline, like most, focuses on how families react to major changes in children's development. Of course, the tasks are not the same for all families. Childless families, single-parent families, divorced families, remarried families, gay and lesbian families, and extended family groups all face unique obstacles and opportunities, as do families of different ethnic backgrounds.

## Symptoms of Family Transitions

All family transitions are characterized by change—changes in time demands, changing expectations, and changes in love and power in family relationships. Early in marriage, newlyweds negotiate expectations about time together, emotional closeness, and who will assume responsibility for various tasks inside and outside the household. The roles that couples assume early in their marriage can set a pattern that lasts a lifetime. Still, roles must be renegotiated when children are born. Children place numerous demands on each partner's time, energy, and patience—and between work and family (Cowan & Cowan, 1992). And although it is a joyous event, the birth of the first child also challenges marriages, as the spouses' needs may become a second priority to the

children's. On average, marital satisfaction declines following the birth of the first child and does not rise again until the family nest begins to empty (Gorchaff, John, & Helson, 2008).

As children grow older, the parent–child relationships must evolve. Maintaining warmth while loosening the reins of control is the overriding theme. When children leave the family home, adults must rediscover interests inside their marriage and outside the home. These patterns are again altered by transitions of later life like the birth of grandchildren or retirement.

**FAMILY CONFLICT** Increased conflict is a common consequence of family transitions. Family members may fight about hundreds of issues. However, one analysis suggests that all disputes ultimately involve either power struggles or intimacy struggles (Emery, 1992). *Power struggles* are about dominance. For example, a messy room can be a sign of autonomy, not sloppiness, to a teenager. *Intimacy struggles* are about closeness or love. Impulsively screaming, "I want a divorce!" can be a bid for attention, not an announcement of a plan to get a lawyer.

Psychologists often are more concerned with the process than the content of family conflicts. One of the most consistent findings concerns the *reciprocity*, or social exchange, of cooperation and conflict (Bradbury, Fincham, & Beach, 2000; Gottman & Notarious, 2000). Family members who have happy relationships reciprocate each other's positive actions, but overlook negative behavior. A grouchy remark is dismissed as part of a "bad day," whereas a compliment is readily returned. In contrast, families with troubled relationships get caught in negative cycles of interaction. They ignore positive actions but reciprocate negative

"Do you want to tell him he's taking all the fun out of our marriage or shall I?"

© Robert Weber/The New Yorker Collection/ www.cartoonbank.com

ones. An unhappily married wife might ask her husband to stop reading the paper during dinner. Instead of putting the paper down, he puts her down. In far too many families, such conflict can escalate into family violence (Cordova et al., 1993).

A particular problem in intimate relationships is the *demand* and *withdrawal* pattern, where one partner becomes increasingly demanding and the other withdraws further and further. Evidence indicates that demand and withdrawal interactions predict future marital dissatisfaction, especially among women (Heavey, Christensen, & Malamuth, 1995). Other evidence shows that conflicts in troubled families are more likely to continue over time and spill over into other family relationships (Margolin, Christensen, & John, 1996). For example, marital conflicts may lead to fights between parents and children, as the children become another focus of an ongoing marital dispute.

**EMOTIONAL DISTRESS** Whether family conflict is expressed through explosive outbursts, constant bickering, or the "silent treatment," fighting often causes emotional distress for all family members. Venting a little anger can be a relief, but ongoing conflict and anger can become all-consuming. Moreover, anger often is an "emotional cover-up," masking deeper hurts including loneliness, pain, longing, and grief (Emery, 2004, 2011; MacDonald & Leary, 2005).

Of course, some conflict is natural, even constructive, during family transitions. We solve problems by working through our differences. Interestingly, happily married couples tend to blame their marital disputes on difficult but temporary circumstances. They "get over it." Unhappily married couples blame their

partner's personality, a recipe for *not* solving problems (Bradbury & Fincham, 1990). In fact, the use of the pronoun "you" in couples' interactions predicts marital unhappiness, while the use of the pronoun "I" predicts greater satisfaction (Simmons, Gordon, & Chambless, 2005).

Unresolved conflicts can cause considerable individual distress (Whisman, Sheldon, & Goering, 2000). Ongoing conflict in intimate relationships is closely linked with depression, especially among women (Beach, Sandeen, & O'Leary, 1990) and children (Cummings & Davies, 2010). Emotional turmoil also is a painful part of separation and divorce. The most significant, long-term consequence of divorce for children involves painful feelings and memories, not psychological problems. Even resilient young people report painful feelings many years after their parents' divorce (Laumann-Billings & Emery, 2000).

**COGNITIVE CONFLICTS** Family transitions also can create a new identity crisis. Identity is closely linked with family roles, and changes in those roles can cause us to doubt ourselves. For example, a recently divorced mother no longer is a wife. She may also feel like a failure as a mother. She may wonder, "Who am I—now?" A crisis of identity is not limited to the adult transition, turning 40, or divorce. Getting married, becoming a parent, infertility, or the empty nest also may trigger a search for a new definition of self.

More broadly, family transitions confront people with a fundamental conflict between acceptance and change (Christensen et al., 2006). Our ability to mold children, parents, partners, or ourselves is not limitless. In order to maintain harmony, we must learn to accept those things we cannot change in our loved ones and in ourselves.

## Diagnosis of Troubled Family Relationships

Efforts to classify troubled relationships are in their early stages. The *DSM-5* uses straightforward if limited groupings like

Interpersonal conflict and emotional distress often accompany difficult family transitions.

## Do Psychological Problems Reside within Individuals?

The *DSM-5* makes an assumption so basic that you probably have not even realized it. It diagnoses individuals. This assumes that psychological problems reside within the individual. You are anxious. You have depression.

Some psychologists question this assumption. They view humans as relational beings. Human problems exist *in relation to* something or, more likely, someone else. You are anxious *about* doing well in school and making career choices. You are depressed *about* being in an unhappy relationship. In recognition of our relational nature, these experts argue that we should diagnose troubled relationships, not troubled individuals. At least in the planning stages, a *DSM-5* committee even considered relational diagnoses (First et al., 2002).

Various individuals and groups have proposed systems for making *relational* or *interpersonal diagnoses* (Group for the Advancement of Psychiatry, 1995; Heyman & Slep, 2006; McLemore & Benjamin, 1979). Some classifications focus on categories, like "partner relational problem," which are straightforward but not terribly informative. Other classifications are more theoretical. Psychologist Timothy Leary (1957) proposed the still influential "interpersonal circumplex," which grouped personality types around the two dimensions of power and love. (Leary became even more famous for his advocacy for LSD in the 1960s.) Still other systems are based on interaction patterns. We have discussed two in this chapter. The demand–withdraw pattern is when one partner constantly pursues the other, who distances as if in a dance that moves only in one direction. The family scapegoat unites dysfunctional family members together

against a "common enemy," not unlike the way the United States and the Soviet Union became unlikely allies during World War II in a shared effort to defeat Nazi Germany.

The idea of classifying relationships, not just individuals, is intuitively appealing. We *are* social animals. You surely have wondered how much your happiness is affected by a relationship, or perhaps your college choice. Psychologists often ask their clients, and themselves, similar questions, particularly when working with children (see Chapter 16) or with someone who is stuck in a troubled relationship or life circumstance. Are *they* the problem, or is the real problem their ineffective parents, cold husband, unfeeling boss, or their social isolation?

Unfortunately, the appeal of any current system for classifying troubled relationships is pretty much limited to intuition. No system for classifying relationships is well-supported empirically, and the more interesting systems require us to somehow discern causality in relationships. These are reasons why some experts take a simpler approach, and focus on descriptive categories like "relational problem" or "child maltreatment." (Recall that *DSM-5* also eschews making causal inferences and instead focuses on description.)

Even though the scientific support for relational or interpersonal diagnoses is limited, you still can benefit from stepping back and questioning the assumptions made in *DSM-5*. A simple descriptive approach does seem to sacrifice richness for reliability. And the manual does locate psychological problems within the individual, even though many of our struggles are interpersonal. While we are not there yet, we envision a future that includes the diagnosis of troubled relationships, not just troubled individuals.

---

"partner relational problem," "child physical abuse," and "parenting problem." There is some initial support for the reliability and validity of such diagnoses (Heyman et al., 2009).

Others argue that, as a general rule, diagnostic systems should classify troubled relationships, not just individuals (Beach et al., 2006; Heyman et al., 2009; see Thinking Critically about *DSM-5*). Many psychological problems seem to reside in relationships, so that a system might diagnose "depression in the context of an unhappy marriage" or "conduct problems owing to neglectful parenting." A more complex example is *scapegoating*, where family members all blame one "disturbed" person for everyone else's troubles. While scapegoating and other troubled interactions undoubtedly occur in some families (see Figure 17.2), we can readily identify one of many challenges for such groupings: Establishing that a troubled relationship is the cause of individual distress.

**FIGURE 17.2**

Miguel arranged family members in this way when asked to make a "sculpture" of his family during a family therapy session. Miguel put himself behind the table and apart from his siblings and parents, a clue to his status as the family scapegoat.

*Source:* Gatson, Weisz. Handbook of Structured Techniques in Marriage and Family Therapy. 1986. Routledge.

## Frequency of Family Transitions

Some family transitions are so important that the U.S. Census Bureau and other federal agencies regularly collect information on their frequency. Surveys indicate that over 90 percent of adults in the United States get married during their adult lives. Age at first marriage has increased, however, rising from the early to the later twenties over the last several decades. The average age at first marriage is 25.9 for women and 28.1 for men (U.S. Bureau of the Census, 2010). And over half of all couples today cohabit before marriage (Cherlin, 2009). About five out of every six women in the United States bear a child, but childbirth increasingly is taking place outside of marriage. In 2007, almost 40 percent of births were to unmarried mothers, including 69.9 percent of births to African American mothers, 48.0 percent for Hispanic mothers, and 25.3 percent for white mothers. Contrary to popular perception, nonmarital births to teenagers are declining. Births to teens comprised 50 percent of nonmarital births in 1970, but fell to 23 percent in 2007 (Ventura, 2009).

Although "happily ever after" may be the stuff of fairy tales, at any point in time most people report their marriage as happy. Still, one national study found significant marital discord among 31 percent of couples (Whisman, Beach, & Snyder, 2008). The number of couples who are unhappy with their marriage at some point in time is surely much larger as satisfaction fluctuates through the family life cycle.

Divorce rates increased dramatically in the United States from the late 1960s to the early 1980s but stabilized and fell somewhat since then (see Figure 17.3). Some are heartened by the decline in divorce, but most of the drop is due to increases in nonmarital

childbearing and cohabitation. Those people who are most prone to divorce are less likely to marry today. And estimates indicate that about 40 percent of all existing marriages will still end in divorce. Divorce is likely to be followed by remarriage. About three out of four whites and one out of two blacks remarry following a divorce. Many divorced adults, including divorced parents, cohabit before remarriage or instead of remarrying (Emery, 1999a).

## Causes of Difficulty in Family Transitions

Most theories of the causes of difficulties in family transitions emphasize psychological and social factors. However, individuals also help in making their own environments, which means that environments are partially *heritable* (see Research Methods). Thus, we also must consider biological contributions to family transitions.

**PSYCHOLOGICAL FACTORS** Psychologists often blame family difficulties on problems with *communication*. Communication includes both intended meaning and nonverbal behaviors that can convey subtle or even contradictory meanings. For example, think of the different potential meanings of a simple statement like "You look great today." Depending on tone of voice, emphasis, and nonverbal gestures, the statement might be an honest compliment, a sarcastic insult, a sexual invitation, or a disinterested platitude.

Based on his extensive studies of marital interaction, John Gottman (1994), a clinical psychologist and noted marital interaction researcher, has identified four basic communication troubles. He observed these patterns in studies of married couples, but these communication problems also occur between other intimate partners, parents and children, and even divorced parents:

1. *Criticism* involves attacking someone's personality rather than his or her actions, for example, "You're boring!" instead of "Can we do something different?"

2. *Contempt* is an insult that may be motivated by anger and is intended to hurt the other person, for example, "I never loved you!"

3. *Defensiveness* is a form of self-justification, such as, "I was only trying to help, but I guess my feelings don't matter!"

4. *Stonewalling* is a pattern of isolation and withdrawal, for example, verbally or nonverbally saying, "I don't want to talk about this anymore!"

**SOCIAL FACTORS** Broader family roles also can contribute to distressed family relationships. Many people believe, for example, that pressures to fulfill traditional marital roles—the wife as homemaker and the husband as breadwinner—cause difficulties for some marriages. One study found that *androgynous* couples—husbands and wives who both scored high on measures of masculinity *and* femininity—had marriages that were happier and less distressed than more traditional unions (Baucom et al., 1990). Although nontraditional gender roles may lead to better long-term outcomes, androgyny may create more conflict in the short

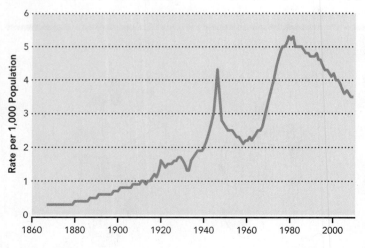

**FIGURE 17.3**

**U.S. Divorce Rates Have Risen for over 100 Years** Divorce rates have trended upward for over a century. The steep rise in the 1960s and 1970s reached a plateau, but the decline since 1980 is misleading. Divorce is declining because couples who are most likely to divorce are cohabiting and/or having children outside of marriage.
*Source:* Based on Emory, Robert. 1999. Marriage, Divorce, and Children's Adjustment. Sage.

# RESEARCH methods

## Genes and the Environment

As twin studies yield information about both genes and environments, behavior geneticists have developed ways of measuring **heritability,** the relative contribution of genes to a characteristic. Researchers often estimate heritability with a statistic called the **heritability ratio,** which can be described according to the following simple formula:

$$\text{Heritability ratio} = \frac{\text{Variance due to genetic factors}}{\text{Total variance}}$$

where Total variance = Variance due to genetic factors + Variance due to environmental factors + Variance due to the interaction of genes and environment.[2]

The heritability ratio is a useful summary when it is interpreted carefully. You should note two cautions. First, any estimate of heritability applies only to a particular sample; the one, true heritability has not been discovered. Consider this. If everyone experienced the same environment, all differences between people would be genetic. You can see this by setting the variance due to the environment to zero in the above equation. In this case, heritability always equals 1.0. The environmental variation found in today's research does not include historical changes that have produced huge increases in life expectancy, education, and material resources. Thus, estimates of heritability in today's samples may be high, in part because there is relatively limited environmental variation (Stoolmiller, 1999)—notwithstanding ongoing social problems like poverty, racism, and sexism.

Our second caution is that genes and environments work together, not separately. Thus, dividing contributions into genetic and environmental components artificially separates them. For example, what is the appropriate heritability for PKU, a cause of mental retardation known to result from the pairing of two recessive genes *combined* with the ingestion of foods containing phenylalanine? PKU is not caused by some percentage of genes and some percentage of the environment. PKU is caused by a critical *gene–environment interaction.*

This brings us to another important point about genes and the environment. Behavior geneticists have emphasized that experience is not random (Scarr & McCartney, 1983). Rather, there is a **gene–environment correlation,** an association between inborn propensities and environmental experience. The gene–environment correlation can be *active,* because different people seek out different environments. For example, risk takers constantly seek thrills, while risk-adverse people seek stable, predictable environments. Gene–environment correlations can also be *passive,* because parents provide children both with genes and a family environment. For example, genetically influenced impulsivity may make people both more likely to divorce and to pass on impulsive traits to their children. Due to gene–environment correlations, family transitions may be partly determined by biology.

Gene–environment correlations are very important to recognize in trying to interpret the effects of environmental experiences. As divorce does not occur at random, for example, children from divorced and married families differ in more ways than their parents' marital status. Thus, researchers who compare children from married and divorced families are comparing apples and oranges. Recent, genetically informed research suggests that this concern is more than theoretical. The internalizing problems found among children from divorced families can be explained by correlated genetic influences, while their externalizing problems are more likely to be true divorce consequences (D'Onofrio et al., 2006).

Genes and the environment are treated as separate in calculating the heritability ratio, but in real life they are connected through gene–environment correlations and gene–environment interactions.

---

run. Androgynous couples must negotiate the terms of their relationship instead of assuming traditional roles. Doing so takes time, effort, and conflict resolution skills.

Numerous other social and cultural influences may contribute to family distress (Karney & Bradbury, 1995). Poverty, unemployment, crowded living conditions, and limited social support all can challenge family life. In fact, many family problems are societal concerns in the United States today. Teenage pregnancy, nonmarital childbirth, divorce, and family violence are pressing social issues, not just psychological ones.

**BIOLOGICAL FACTORS** Biological factors also contribute to problems in families (Booth et al., 2000), which brings us to a central debate: Does family conflict cause individual dysfunction, or do troubled individuals cause relationship problems? For example, people who are divorced are at risk for depression. But this correlation has several potential explanations. Divorce may cause depression, or a happy marriage might protect against it. Or causality may work in the other direction. People who are depressed can be difficult to live with and may be more likely to divorce (South, Turkheimer, & Oltmanns, 2008).

---

[2]The variance due to environments can be further divided into shared and nonshared environmental components. An example of a shared environment is family income; an example of a nonshared environment is your boyfriend or wife.

An important special case of the "correlation does not mean causation" problem is the *gene–environment correlation,* the fact that environmental experience is itself correlated with genetic background (see Critical Thinking Matters ). We know from twin studies, for example, that even divorce is partly genetic (D'Onofrio et al., 2006; McGue & Lykken, 1992). This may seem startling—or foolish—when you first consider it, but if you pause to ponder this puzzle, it will begin to make sense. Divorce—or teen pregnancy or cohabitation or most any family event—does not occur at random. Research, and common sense, tell us that these experiences are more likely when people differ in their background (for example, education and income), personality (for example, tendency toward risk taking or social conformity), and physical characteristics (for example, age at first menarche or physical appearance). To the extent that background, personality, or physical characteristics are influenced by genes, the family experience also is correlated with those genes. That is, there is a gene–environment correlation.

Consider this example. Jane Mendle and colleagues (2006) tested the well-established finding that girls who grow up with an unrelated male in their household (for example, a stepfather) reach menarche at a younger age than other girls. Researchers have struggled to explain this puzzling finding. Some have suggested that this results from an evolutionary adaptation: Stressful family life causes early menarche because it contributes to the reproductive strategy of having more children (Belsky, Steinberg, & Draper, 1991).

However, Mendle and colleagues (2006) found that a gene–environment correlation is responsible for the puzzling correlation. What is the genetic third variable? The *mother's* early age at menarche. Mother's age at menarche strongly determines her daughter's age at menarche (which makes sense; Meyer et al., 1991). Mother's age at menarche also contributes to the likelihood that her daughter will grow up with an unrelated man in the household. How? Early maturing girls, in this case the mother, attract older men who are not particularly good long-term prospects. These men are attracted to younger girls because of the girls prominent secondary sexual characteristics (early breast and hip development)—and surely for other bad reasons. As a result, young age at menarche is likely to be associated with relationship instability, and ultimately with your daughter growing up with an unrelated man in the household.

Researchers are beginning to untangle gene–environment correlations. Doing so is a challenging and exciting area of research. Biology undeniably contributes to family experience (see Critical Thinking Matters).

## Treatment During Family Transitions

Treatments for families include couple and family therapy and various community projects designed to prevent problems. We introduce a few of these many and varied efforts.

**PREVENTION** Programs designed to prevent relationship distress have a long and informal history. Perhaps the most common efforts involve religious groups. Many religions encourage or require couples to attend counseling sessions. Religious and secular marriage education programs lead to better communication and

## CRITICAL THINKING matters

### A Divorce Gene?

Throughout the text, we have noted genetic contributions to various mental disorders. You may be a bit surprised to hear that experience also is genetic. Divorce is one provocative example. Psychologists Matt McGue and David Lykken (1992) of the University of Minnesota found higher concordance rates for divorce among MZ than among DZ twin pairs in a sample of more than 1,500 twin pairs. In fact, the investigators calculated that the heritability of divorce was .525.

How could divorce be genetic? This is where critical thinking is, well, critical. Clearly, there is no divorce gene. But wait. When you read that mood disorders or eating disorders were genetic, maybe you *did* think there was a gene for depression or bulimia. Yet, just like divorce, you should think critically about what *mechanism* might make these mental disorders genetic.

One mechanism that might make divorce genetic is personality, at least that part of personality which is partially shaped by genetics—for example, a tendency toward thrill seeking or a relative insensitivity to social sanctions. However, there are other possibilities. Genes affect physical attractiveness and the age at menarche (Mendle et al., 2006). Physical attractiveness and early sexual maturation, in turn, may set other events into motion: attention for something other than your good character, which attracts less committed potential mates, who ultimately increase the risk of divorce. This would make divorce genetic, but not in the way you typically think "genetic" means.

"Genes" is a common answer to the question, "What causes mental disorders?" But this does not necessarily mean there is a gene for eating disorders, depression, and so on. Rather, the genetic mechanism might be indirect, affecting body type in the case of eating disorders and perhaps family experience in the case of depression. Critical thinking does not change the fact that mental disorders are influenced by genes. However, critical thinking might help us to think more broadly, creatively, and, we hope, more accurately about possible genetic mechanisms.

Many religious groups require couple counseling before marriage. Premarital counseling has some benefits, and some government agencies now encourage it as well.

relationship satisfaction, but demonstrated benefits are limited to middle-income, white samples (Hawkins et al., 2008). Whether such efforts help lower-income and minority group members is an important question for research—and for policy, as the U.S. government has tried to promote marriage in recent years.

An exemplary relationship education program is the Premarital Relationship Enhancement Program (PREP). PREP participants meet in small groups, where they freely discuss their expectations for their relationships, including difficult topics such as sexuality. Couples also learn specific communication and problem-solving skills. One study found that couples randomly assigned to PREP maintained their relationship satisfaction three years later, while the happiness of control couples declined during this time (Markman et al., 1988). Even five years later, PREP couples maintained improved communication and reported lower rates of violence than control couples (Markman et al., 1993). Researchers report similar benefits for a variation on the program implemented in Germany (Hahlweg et al., 1998). Yet, there is a caveat to these positive findings. In two different studies, a small group of women who became extremely positive after PREP reported *more* marital distress five years later (Baucom et al., 2006). This suggests that, while it is important to be supportive in communication, it is unhealthy to become a "Pollyanna." Couples invariably face challenges, and maintaining a happy relationship involves recognizing and addressing important issues.

The success of PREP is encouraging, as are efforts to prevent distress at a critical time in the family life cycle: when a couple's first child is born (Schulz et al., 2006). However, the systematic research conducted on these model programs is of broader importance. Prevention programs have been developed to help families at nearly every transition in the family life cycle. There are childbirth programs, parenting programs, and support groups for parents whose children are infants, preschoolers, school-aged, or teenagers. Courts have programs for helping parents cope with separation, divorce, and remarriage. Creativity in developing programs is not lacking. What is often missing, however, is systematic research on the effectiveness of prevention efforts.

**COUPLE THERAPY AND FAMILY THERAPY** *Couple therapy* and *family therapy* both focus on changing relationships rather than changing individuals (Gurman & Jacobson, 2002). The couple or family therapist acts as an objective outsider who helps family members to identify and voice their disagreements, work on improving communication, solve specific problems, and ultimately change troubled family relationships. This very different approach to therapy is illustrated in the following brief case study.

#### ⟶ Learning to Listen

Jan and Bill sought therapy for long-standing troubles in their marriage. Jan, a homemaker, complained that Bill did not help enough with running the household or raising the couple's three children. More poignantly, Jan felt unloved, because Bill did not seem to enjoy being around her and the children. Bill countered that he loved being with his children, but that Jan was a constant nag who did not appreciate the demands of his job as an insurance salesman. He also said that she was a "bottomless pit" in demanding his love and attention. The couple had been seen for several sessions when the following interaction occurred:

JAN: Bill and I were supposed to be working on a schedule so that he would only call on clients two evenings last week. But just like I knew would happen, Bill didn't follow through. (Jan begins to cry.) I just knew you wouldn't do it! Is that so much to ask? Couldn't you be home a few evenings during the week? Couldn't you at least tell me when you have to go out?

BILL: (in a monotone) I got some new clients this week, and there's a sales push on. I couldn't reschedule. Next week will be better.

JAN: Next week won't be any different! Or the week after that! You aren't going to change. Why should you? You have everything your way!

THERAPIST: I can see you're upset, Jan, but let's give Bill a chance. Do you know your schedule for next week?

BILL: Pretty much, but you never know.

THERAPIST: Do you want to make a commitment to Jan right now about what nights you will be home in the evening next week?

BILL: I suppose I can be home around six or so on Tuesday . . .

JAN: You suppose! Go ahead and . . .

THERAPIST: One second, Jan. OK, Bill. Tuesday is a start, but do you see what your tone of voice says to Jan?

BILL: But she's always complaining about something! I said that I'd be home, OK? What else do you want me to do?

JAN: I want you to want to be home.

THERAPIST: Now we're getting to the real issue. Part of this is about schedules and time together, but part of this is about what these things mean. Jan, when it seems like Bill doesn't want to be around you and the kids, you feel unloved.

JAN: That's what I just said. You heard me, but he didn't.

THERAPIST: Bill, you feel controlled when Jan asks you about your work schedule. You have a lot to balance between work and home, and maybe you really don't want to be with Jan when you feel like she's forcing you to come home.

BILL: That's exactly how I feel.

THERAPIST: I want the two of you to talk with each other about these feelings. Then we will get back to work on a schedule that might help to solve some practical problems. Jan, tell Bill how you feel—and Bill, I only want you to listen to her feelings. Try to understand what she says. Don't worry about rebuttal. In a few minutes, we'll try this the other way around.

Several aspects of couple therapy are evident in this brief exchange. One goal was to help the couple negotiate tricky work and family schedules. Even an imperfect schedule might reduce some conflict. Another goal was to break the couple's negative cycle of interaction and encourage Jan and Bill to talk about deeper feelings. The discussion of emotions should allow the couple to develop a schedule in a way that might alleviate some hurt feelings. If they could mutually agree on a plan, Jan would have one less reason to feel rejected, and Bill would have one less reason to feel controlled.

**RESEARCH ON COUPLE THERAPY** Most research on couple therapy has examined cognitive behavioral approaches. *Cognitive behavioral couple therapy (CBCT)* emphasizes the couple's moment-to-moment interaction, particularly their exchange of positive and negative behaviors, their style of communication, and their strategies for solving problems (Baucom, Epstein, & LaTaillade, 2002). Systematic research on the effectiveness of CBCT indicates that couple therapy leads to significant improvements (Shadish & Baldwin, 2005). Still, approximately half of the couples seen in CBCT do not improve significantly. Relapse at follow-up is also common, and other treatment approaches appear to be about as effective (Alexander, Holtzworth-Munroe, & Jameson, 1994).

There clearly is a need to expand on CBCT and perhaps integrate it with other approaches. Emerging treatment research demonstrates the long-term importance of helping couples to accept each other's imperfections, not just trying to get each other to change (Christensen et al., 2004, 2006). Other evidence-based approaches to couple therapy focus much more on emotion and emotional understanding (Johnson, 2008). Finally, there is also a need to extend research efforts to include treatments for other difficult family transitions, for example, coping with divorce (Emery, 2011).

Couple therapy is increasingly being used not only to improve relationships, but also as an alternative to individual therapy in treating psychological disorders, including depression, anxiety, alcoholism, and psychological disorders of childhood. Research suggests that an improved relationship helps in alleviating individual disorders, particularly depression (Beach, Sandeen, & O'Leary, 1990; Jacobson, Holtzworth-Munroe, & Schmaling, 1989). These findings again underscore the reciprocal nature of individual and family relationships. In some cases, successful couple therapy removes the cause of individual distress. In other cases, it enables others to understand and cope with one person's psychological troubles.

## The Transition to Later Life

Many people think of "old" as beginning at the age of 65 or 70, but aging and the transition to later life do not begin at any particular age. The transition extends over many years and includes a number of changes in appearance, health, family, friendships, work, and living arrangements. The nature, timing, and meaning of the transition may also differ for men and women.

Adults become increasingly aware of aging in their forties and fifties. Middle-aged men often worry about their physical performance in athletics and sex. Men also become more concerned about their physical health, especially as they learn of events like a friend's unexpected heart attack. Women also worry about their physical performance and appearance in middle age, but married women often are more concerned with their husbands' than with their own physical health. Men have a notably shorter life expectancy than women—seven years shorter on average. Thus, even as they encourage their husbands to follow good health practices, many middle-aged wives begin a mental "rehearsal for widowhood" (Neugarten, 1990).

Concerns about physical health increase for both men and women in their sixties, seventies, and eighties. Chronic diseases such as hypertension become common (Federal Interagency

The transition to later life is not a time of despair for most people. Older adults who remain physically active and socially involved have better mental and physical health.

Forum on Aging-Related Statistics [FIFARS], 2010). All five sensory systems decline in acuity, and many cognitive abilities diminish with advancing age (Salthouse, 2004). All these physical changes occur gradually, but the decline in functioning accelerates, on average, around the age of 75. Major social transitions also take place during the later adult years. Most people retire in their early to late sixties, a transition that is eagerly anticipated by many people but dreaded by some. Whether retirement is seen as the end of a valued career or the beginning of a new life, it requires a redefinition of family roles as people have more time and new expectations for themselves and loved ones. Parents also become more of a "friend" to children who are now adults themselves, while many older adults offer children and grandchildren practical support and a sense of continuity in family life. As older adults move through their seventies and into their eighties, children who are now middle-aged increasingly find themselves worrying about and caring for their parents.

Death is an inevitability for all of us. With advancing age, we must face both the abstraction of our own mortality and specific fears about a painful and prolonged death. Bereavement is a part of life for older adults, as friends fall ill and die. Due to differences in life expectancy, women are particularly likely to become widows in their sixties, seventies, and eighties (see Figure 17.4).

Older adults often confront **ageism** misconceptions, and prejudices about aging (Pasupathi, Carstensen, & Tsai, 1995). Young people, even mental health professionals, sometimes view older adults as stubborn, irritable, bossy, or complaining. Adults may become more inwardly focused as they enter later life, but overall, personality is consistent throughout adult life (Magai, 2001). Some older adults *are* stubborn and irritable—much like they were as younger adults. Stereotypes about aging are just that, and older adults can be prejudiced too. In fact, negative stereotypes of aging lead older adults to recover less quickly from disability than those with positive views (Levy et al., 2012).

## Symptoms

Later life encompasses a large age range as well as numerous social and psychological transitions, so we can offer an overview of only a few topics here: changes in physical functioning and health; happiness, work, and relationships; bereavement and grief; and mental health and suicide.

**PHYSICAL FUNCTIONING AND HEALTH** Physical functioning and health decline with age, but the loss of health and vigor is not nearly as rapid as stereotypes suggest. Men and women can and do remain healthy and active well into their seventies and eighties. In fact, physical activity and physical health are among the better predictors of psychological well-being among older adults.

**Menopause** the cessation of menstruation, is an important physical focus for middle-aged women. (Men do not experience a similar change in reproductive functioning.) Women in the United States have their last period at an average age of 51 years, although menstruation typically is erratic for at least two or three years prior to its complete cessation. Many women experience physical symptoms such as "hot flashes" during menopause, and some experience emotional swings as well, for example, crying for no apparent reason. Episodes of depression also increase during menopause.

Declining production of the female sex hormone, *estrogen,* can contribute to emotional volatility during menopause. *Hormone replacement therapy,* the administration of artificial estrogen, alleviates many physical and psychological symptoms. However, it has no direct effect on depression, which is unrelated to estrogen levels during menopause (Rutter & Rutter, 1993). Hormone replacement therapy also reduces the risk for heart and bone disease, but it is a controversial treatment because it increases the risk for cancer.

Some women struggle to redefine their identity as they face changes in their bodies, appearance, and family lives around the time of menopause. Others find the freedom from fear of pregnancy liberating and enjoy the "empty nest." They value the time they now have for themselves and for their partners (Gorchaff et al., 2008).

Menopause is a rather "sudden" event in comparison with other physical changes that occur with age. Visual acuity declines slowly, as does the ability of the lens to accommodate focusing on an object that is near to one that is far away. The eye also adapts to darkness or light more slowly with age. Hearing loss also is gradual throughout adult life, particularly the ability to hear high tones. Sensitivity to taste, smell, and touch also decreases with advancing age. As with vision and hearing, however, decline in these senses are typically gradual until the

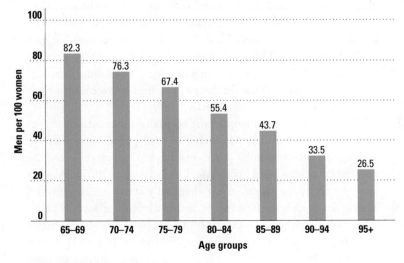

**FIGURE 17.4**

**The Number of Men per 100 Women Among Older Adults** Women live longer than men; therefore, the ratio of men to women shrinks with increasing age.
*Source:* Courtesy of the U.S. Census Bureau.

seventies, when loss of sensitivity may accelerate notably (Fozard & Gordon-Salant, 2001).

Muscle mass declines with age, but, like sensory function, the loss is gradual until advanced age. A 70-year-old retains 80 percent of his or her young adult muscle strength, but the loss may double in the next 10 years. Bone loss also occurs with advancing age, with women experiencing bone loss at twice the rate of men.

After menopause, women are especially susceptible to the development of *osteoporosis,* a condition in which bones become honeycombed and can be broken easily. Many older adults develop other chronic illnesses, especially arthritis, cardiovascular diseases, cancer, and diabetes (FIFARS, 2010). It is often assumed that sleep disorders are epidemic among older adults. After controlling for health and other indirect influences on sleep, however, sleep is generally not a problem for older adults. When it is, evidence shows that "sleep hygiene" interventions are effective in improving sleeping problems among the aged (Vitiello, 2009).

**HAPPINESS, WORK, RELATIONSHIPS, AND SEX** The fact that aging is accompanied by gradual declines in physical health does *not* mean that older adults experience similar declines in

Contrary to stereotypes, sex often remains an important part of intimate relationships for older adults.

psychological well-being. In fact, older adults report more positive relationships and a greater sense of mastery over their environment than do adults who are young or in midlife (Fingerman & Charles, 2010). On the other hand, older adults have less of a sense of purpose in life and less satisfaction with personal growth (Ryff, Kwan, & Singer, 2001).

Older adults report greater job satisfaction than younger people, but this may be a result of self-selection, since people tend to remain in a satisfying occupation. Retirement can be a mixed blessing. It leads to a loss of income and perhaps of status, and these changes can be difficult. On average, however, these costs are outweighed by the added benefits of increased leisure and freedom, especially for people with adequate financial resources (Wang, Henkens, & Solinge, 2011).

Erik Erikson theorized that the conflict between integrity and despair is the central psychological struggle of later life. Many older adults do wonder about the meaning of their lives when they look back from the perspective of their later years. Identity conflicts also may accompany the changes that come from becoming a grandparent or retiring from a long-term occupation (Kaufman & Elder, 2003). Unfortunately, little research has been conducted on Erikson's conceptualization (see Reliving the Past).

People have more friendships as young adults than during later life, but the quality of relationships is more important than the number (Antonucci, 2001). And one reason why older adults have fewer friendships is because they become more selective. Older adults choose to spend time with the people they care for most, perhaps because their time is limited and thus more valuable (Carstensen, Isaacowitz, & Charles, 1999).

Family relationships strongly influence psychological well-being throughout the life span. Later in life, relationships with children become especially important. Sibling relationships may also take on renewed practical and emotional importance (Cohler & Nakamura, 1996). Satisfaction with an enduring intimate relationship increases in later life, and conflicts may become less embedded or intense. This, too, may be related to the foreshortened sense of time. The belief that "this may be the last time" encourages older adults to focus on the positive and overlook or forgive the negative (Fingerman & Charles, 2010).

Sexuality remains important to many older adults. A national survey found that 73 percent of adults aged 57 to 64 were sexually active, as were 53 percent of 65- to 74-year-olds and 26 percent of adults aged 75 to 85 (Lindau et al., 2007). Almost one-quarter of the oldest group of sexually active adults reported having sex once a week or more! Sexual difficulties such as problems with lubrication or erection increase with age—14 percent of older men take medication for erectile dysfunction. Good health predicts more sexual activity, as does (not surprisingly) the presence of a spouse or other intimate partner.

Unfortunately, the loss of loved ones, including the loss of a spouse, is a fact of life for older adults, as illustrated in the following case study.

## Reliving the Past

Researchers are studying a common phenomenon among older adults: *reminiscence*—the recounting of personal memories of the distant past. Reminiscence, sometimes called *life-review* or *nostalgia*, may be helpful in facilitating adjustment during later life, and many senior centers offer life history discussion groups as a part of their services (Coleman, 2005; Sedikides et al., 2008).

All memories of the past are not equal, as suggested by Erikson's conflict between integrity and despair. Older adults may recall their journey through life with pride and acceptance or with disappointment and regret. As a way of studying how memories of the past can mark adjustment, the Canadian psychologists Paul Wong and Lisa Watt outlined six categories of reminiscence.

*Integrative reminiscence* is an attempt to achieve a sense of self-worth, coherence, and reconciliation with the past. It includes a discussion of past conflicts and losses, but it is characterized by an overriding acceptance of events. *Instrumental reminiscence* involves the review of goal-directed activities and attainments. It reflects a sense of control and success in overcoming life's obstacles. *Transitive reminiscence* serves the function of passing on cultural heritage and personal legacy, and it includes both direct moral instruction and storytelling that has clear moral implications. *Escapist reminiscence* is full of glorification of the past and deprecation of the present, a yearning for the "good old days." *Obsessive reminiscence* includes preoccupation with failure and is full of guilt, bitterness, and despair. Finally, *narrative reminiscence* is descriptive rather than interpretive. It involves "sticking to the facts" and does not serve clear intrapsychic or interpersonal functions.

Evidence indicates that integrative reminiscence and instrumental reminiscence are related to successful aging, whereas obsessive reminiscence is associated with less successful adjustment in later life (Wong & Watt, 1991). Other research similarly finds that reminiscence can be positively (focusing on communication or preparing for death) or negatively (reviving old problems, filling the void, or trying to maintain connections with the departed) related to better mental health (Cappeliez, O'Rourke, & Chaudhury, 2005). The next step is to study whether reminiscence can be structured or guided in such a way that it helps older adults review and come to terms with their lives.

---

### ⟶ Mrs. J.'s Loss

Mrs. J. was 78 years old when she consulted a clinical psychologist for the first time in her life. She was physically fit, intellectually sharp, and emotionally vital. However, she remained terribly distressed by her husband's death. Eighteen months earlier, the 83-year-old Mr. J. had suffered a stroke. After a few weeks in the hospital, he was transferred to a nursing home, where his recuperation progressed slowly over the course of several months. According to his wife, Mr. J.'s care in the nursing home bordered on malpractice. He died as a result of infections from pervasive bedsores that he developed lying in the same position for hours on end. The staff was supposed to shift his position frequently in order to prevent bedsores from developing, but according to Mrs. J., they simply ignored her husband.

Mrs. J. was uncertain about how to handle her grief, because she was stricken by many conflicting emotions. She had literally waited a lifetime to find the right man—she had married for the first time at the age of 71 after a long and successful career as a schoolteacher. She had been content throughout her life, but her marriage was bliss. She felt intensely sad over the loss of her husband, and she continued to make him a part of her life. She would talk aloud to his picture when she awoke in the morning, and visited his grave daily except when the weather was very bad.

Mrs. J. cried freely when discussing her loss, but she also chastised herself for not doing better in "getting on with her life."

She had several female friends with whom she played bridge several times a week. Mrs. J. enjoyed the company of her friends, who were also widowed and who seemed more accepting of their losses.

A greater problem than acceptance was the intense anger Mrs. J. often felt but rarely acknowledged. She was furious at the nursing home, and was vaguely considering legal action against the institution. During her career as a teacher, she had never tolerated incompetence, and the failures of the nursing home had robbed her of happiness. She was confused, however, because her minister said that her anger was wrong. He said that she should forgive the nursing home and be happy to know that her husband was in heaven. Mrs. J. wanted to follow her minister's advice, but her emotions would not allow it. She wanted the psychologist to tell her if her feelings were wrong.

Clearly, it was not wrong for Mrs. J. to be distraught over her husband's death, but were some of her other reactions abnormal? Having constant thoughts of another person might seem obsessive in some circumstances, and talking out loud to a picture might indicate delusions or hallucinations. Mrs. J. was showing normal reactions to grief, however, as similar responses are common among other grief-stricken older people. Frequent thoughts of a loved one are a normal part of grief, and it also is normal for intense grief to continue for a year or two, or perhaps longer. But what about Mrs. J.'s anger? Whether she should forgive the nursing home or sue depends on many factors, of course, but she was not wrong—abnormal—for feeling angry. Evidence indicates that anger, too, is a common part of grief (Sbarra & Emery, 2005).

**GRIEF AND BEREAVEMENT** **Grief** is the emotional and social process of coping with a separation or a loss. **Bereavement** is a specific form of grieving in response to the death of a loved one. Grief in bereavement is commonly described as proceeding in a series of stages. For example, Elisabeth Kübler-Ross (1969), who developed a popular model of bereavement from her work with the terminally ill, described grief as occurring in five stages: (1) denial, (2) anger, (3) bargaining, (4) depression, and (5) acceptance.

Kübler-Ross's model is similar to Bowlby's (1979) four-stage outline of children's responses to separation or loss (see Chapter 16). Importantly, Bowlby's attachment theory offers an explanation for why someone might feel angry in the middle of intense sadness over a loss. Yearning and searching (his second stage of grief) is a pursuit of, and a signal to, the missing attachment figure—an attempt to bring about reunion. A child who is separated from a parent cries and screams angrily, and searches for the parent in order to get her or him back. Of course, a reunion is impossible following the death of a loved one, as bereaved people understand intellectually. However, emotions are not rational, particularly at a time of loss.

Stage theories of grief have intuitive appeal, but research shows that few people grieve in a fixed sequence of stages. Rather, mourners vacillate among different emotions—for example, moving back and forth between longing, sadness, and anger (Sbarra & Emery, 2005). Many people do not experience the stages described by Kübler-Ross, and others show few observable reactions—they "suffer in silence." In short, there is no one "right"

Grief is a part of life for older adults.

way to grieve, and people should not be forced to express grief. In fact, research generally indicates that *less* intense bereavement predicts *better* long-term adjustment to loss (Bonanno et al., 2005; Stroebe et al., 2002; Wortman & Silver, 2001). Another predictor of better long-term adjustment is expressing grief selectively depending on whether it is appropriate to the context (Coifman & Bonanno, 2010).

In general, bereavement is more intense when a loss is "off time"—for example, when the loss of a mate occurs early in adult life or when a child dies before a parent (Cohler & Nakamura, 1996). There is no "good" time to lose a loved one, of course, but we are more prepared for the death of aged family members, and we can often find some solace in their long life.

Mrs. J.'s grief was normal, but can grief become abnormal? Perhaps 10 to 15 percent of bereaved people experience especially intense or prolonged grief (Bonanno et al., 2007; Neimeyer & Currier, 2009). "Complicated grief" was proposed (but rejected) as a new diagnostic category in *DSM-5* (Shear et al., 2011). The idea of diagnosing grief is controversial (see "Thinking Critically about *DSM-5*" in Chapter 6). Some experts are concerned about labeling a normal experience as abnormal. "Medicalizing" grief also might undermine social and cultural supports for bereavement.

**MENTAL HEALTH AND SUICIDE** Contrary to some stereotypes, later life is not a time of fear, disappointment, dejection, and despair. Affective disorders are less than half as common among older as among younger adults, and anxiety disorders also are less prevalent (Gatz & Smyer, 2001; IOM, 2012).

Psychological disorders still are an important concern among older adults, especially depression, which can be more profound, lasting, and debilitating (IOM, 2012). Suicide risk is a particular concern; adults over the age of 65 have the highest rate of completed suicide of any age group. The risk for completed suicide is notably higher among older white males. In fact, suicide is one of the top 10 causes of death among older adults (FIFARS, 2010). Many experts view the increase in suicide as a consequence of not only emotional problems, but also as a result of chronic pain, physical disease, and the prospect of a long terminal illness (Wrosch, Schulz, & Heckhausen, 2004). In fact, *rational suicide* is a controversial term for the decision some severely ill older adults make in ending their lives (Gallagher-Thompson & Osgood, 1997).

Even more controversial is *assisted suicide,* a hotly debated procedure where a medical professional helps terminally ill people to end their own lives. In 1997, Oregon became the first state where physicians can legally assist patients to hasten their death. (Assisted suicide is now also legal in Washington and Vermont.) In Oregon, assisted suicide is legal provided the patient is (1) over 18 years old; (2) a resident of Oregon; (3) diagnosed with a terminal illness with a life expectancy of six months or less; and (4) capable of making a reasonable decision (Rosenfeld, 2004). To date, the 596 legally assisted suicides in Oregon involved

## TABLE 17.3
### Assisted Suicides in Oregon

| | 1998 | 1999 | 2000 | 2001 | 2002 |
|---|---|---|---|---|---|
| Number of assisted suicides | 16 | 27 | 27 | 23 | 36 |
| Average age | 70 | 71 | 70 | 68 | 69 |
| Percent female | 50 | 41 | 56 | 62 | 29 |
| Percent white | 100 | 96 | 96 | 95 | 97 |
| Percent cancer | 88 | 63 | 78 | 86 | 84 |

Oregon is one of three states in the United States where assisted suicide is legal. Most assisted suicides involve older whites who are dying of cancer.
*Source:* Based on Rosenfeld, B. 2004. Assisted suicide and the right to die: The interface of social science, public policy, and medical ethics. Washington, DC: American Psychological Association.

patients who were older, white, well educated, and dying of cancer (*New York Times*, August 8, 2012; see Table 17.3).

## Diagnosis of Aging

Experts often classify adults in later life based on their age and health status. In **gerontology** the multidisciplinary study of aging, it is common to distinguish among the young-old, the old-old, and the oldest-old.

The *young-old* are adults roughly between the ages of 65 and 75. However, the category is defined less by age than by health and vigor. Notwithstanding the normal physical problems of aging, the young-old are in good health and are active members of their communities. The majority of older adults belong to this group.

The *old-old* are adults between the ages of approximately 75 and 85 who suffer from major physical, psychological, or social (largely economic) problems. They require some routine assistance in living, although only about 6 percent of Americans in this age group live in a nursing home. Despite advanced age, a healthy and active 80-year-old adult would be considered to be young-old instead of old-old.

Finally, the *oldest-old* are adults 85 years old or older and includes a disproportionate number of widowed women and low-income groups (as a result of male mortality and financial strains, including health care costs). Still, the oldest-old is a diverse group. Some people maintain their vigor; others need constant assistance. Fifteen percent live in nursing homes (FIFARS, 2010).

## Frequency of Aging

In 2008, 13 percent of the U.S. population—39 million people—were 65 years of age or older. Approximately 15 percent are the oldest-old—people 85 years old or older—the fastest growing segment of the population (FIFARS, 2010). Both the proportion and the absolute number of older Americans will increase through the middle of the twenty-first century in what has been called a "silver tsunami" (IOM, 2012). The increase is partly as a result of medical advances but primarily due to the aging of the post–World War II "baby boom" generation (see Figure 17.5).

The proportion of the U.S. population 65 years of age or older should peak around the year 2030. At that time, one out of every five Americans will be at least 65 years old. The number of the oldest-old will increase most dramatically. In fact, the proportion and absolute number of the oldest-old will continue to rise until halfway through the twenty-first century. By the year 2050, the oldest-old should comprise one-fourth of the population of older adults (U.S. Census Bureau, 1996).

One important consequence of gender differences in longevity is that the majority of older men (72 percent) live with a spouse, while only a minority of older women do (42 percent) (FIFARS, 2010). Census data also indicate that poverty rates are higher among older Americans than among younger age groups (except children), and the percentage of older Americans living in poverty increases with advancing age (FIFARS, 2010). This is due, in part, to the lower economic status of widowed women.

A protestor campaigning in favor of legalizing assisted suicide.

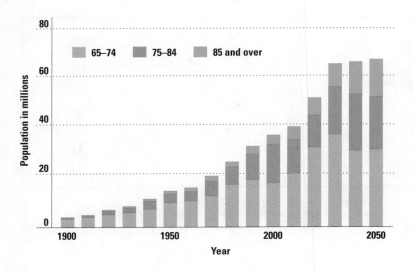

FIGURE **17.5**

**The Growing Number of Older Adults** The actual and projected number of older adults in the United States aged 65 or older. Note the particularly dramatic increase in the oldest-old population.
*Source:* Courtesy of the US Census Bureau.

## Causes of Psychological Problems in Later Life

The most important biological contribution to psychological well-being in later life is good physical health (Cohler & Nakamura, 1996). In fact, a study of adults over the age of 70 found that both men and women listed poor health as the most common contribution to a negative quality of life (Flanagan, 1982). We should note, however, that the relationship between psychological well-being and health also operates in the opposite direction. The experience of positive emotion in later life predicts more successful coping with stress and improved health behavior (Ong, 2010).

*Health behavior* is particularly important to the physical well-being of older adults. Increased vigor and good health are associated with proper diet, continued exercise, weight control, and avoiding cigarette smoking and excessive alcohol use (Leventhal et al., 2001). Many of these health behaviors also are tied to better cognitive functioning among older people (Colcombe &

Kramer, 2003; Hess, 2005). It has even been suggested that the overriding goal of gerontology should be to promote healthy and active lifestyles among older adults, because in industrialized societies, current life expectancies probably are very close to the biological limits of the human species (Fries, 1990). Increasing longevity may be unrealistic, but it is possible to extend the number of vigorous and healthy years of life.

Psychological contributions to adjustment in later life include close relationships and loss. Bereavement and living alone are more strongly related to depression among men than among women (Siegel & Kuykendall, 1990). Among men over the age of 70, the most frequent positive contributions to quality of life include relationships with spouses, friends, and children. As so many women over the age of 70 are widowed, they list relationships with friends and children, as well as general socializing, as most important to their well-being (Flanagan, 1982).

Relationships and physical activity are two keys to healthy adjustment in later life.

Numerous social factors are linked with a happier transition to later life, especially material well-being and participation in recreational activities. Religion is also very important to many older adults, and religious affiliations have been found to moderate the ill effects of bereavement, particularly among men (Siegel & Kuykendall, 1990).

## Treatment of Psychological Problems in Later Life

Good medical care is of great importance to older adults, not only for treating disease but also for promoting physical health and psychological well-being. Because health behavior is critical to the quality of life, experts view health psychology and behavioral medicine as central components of medical care. *Geropsychology* is a growing and needed specialty in a variety of practice settings (Karel, Gatz, & Smyer, 2012).

Similar psychological and biological therapies can be used to treat depression and other emotional problems among older adults, but the aged seek treatment less than younger people. Substantial evidence demonstrates that short-term treatment in primary care settings—the doctor's office—is a convenient and effective alternative (IOM, 2012). Treatments for normal grief offer some small, short-term benefit, but longer-term benefits are no better than the mere passage of time. One exception is therapy for complicated grief (Currier, Neimeyer, & Berman, 2008; Neimeyer & Currier, 2009).

Health care professionals must focus not only on improving quality of life among older adults, but on maintaining integrity in death. *Living wills* are legal documents that direct health care professionals not to perform certain procedures in order to keep a terminally ill or severely disabled patient alive. Older adults often are much better at accepting death than are younger people, and living wills and other efforts to humanize dying allow dignity to be maintained through the end of life (Lawton, 2001; Rosenfeld, 2004).

## getting HELP

The wide range of transitions considered in this chapter makes it difficult to offer many generalizations about getting help. But we can make two broad suggestions. First, self-help and self-education are particularly important and effective in helping yourself, a friend, or family member cope with life-cycle transitions. We suggest that you find out more about the transition you or a loved one may be facing, how other people feel in similar circumstances, what coping strategies others have found helpful, what you can expect might happen as time passes, and where you might end up when you are through this phase of your life. Second, we also urge you—or your friends or family members—not to be shy about seeking professional help if you are stuck, suffering greatly, or just want the support of a caring expert to help you through this time. As we noted at the outset of the chapter, a quarter of the people who see mental health professionals do not have a diagnosable mental disorder, so you will be far from alone in seeking a therapist.

Reading, writing, and talking to friends are three helpful activities when struggling with your goals, relationships, and identity. Erik Erikson's *Childhood and Society* and *Identity and the Life Cycle* are classics that you should find helpful even though they were written half a century ago. Another type of reading may also help—reading literature. Coming of age is a common theme in great (and not-so-great) books, and great writers are also insightful psychologists. Besides reading, keeping a journal is always a good idea, particularly when you are confused. Finally, we urge you to talk about your doubts and uncertainties with fellow students, even with your professors!

There are many resources available in bookstores, on the Internet, or in therapy if you or someone you know is struggling through a family transition. In fact, the biggest problem may not be finding a resource, but finding a *credible* resource. We urge you to look for self-help resources and therapists that offer advice based on psychological science, not just "pop" psychology. As a good start, many of the psychological scientists whose research we have used in this chapter also have written books for the general public. Among the many books we recommend are Carolyn Cowan and Philip Cowan's *When Partners Become Parents*; John Gottman's *The Seven Principles for Making Marriage Work*; and Robert Emery's *The Truth About Children and Divorce*.

An excellent book on aging is George Vaillant's *Aging Well: Surprising Guideposts to a Happier Life*. Mitch Albom's *Tuesdays with Morrie* is another superb book on aging that is partly a self-help book, partly a journal, and partly a work of literature. As with coming of age, coming to grips with aging is another common theme in literature, and it is a genre you may want to explore.

# 17 Summary

- One out of two people who seek psychological treatment do not have a mental disorder. *DSM-5* categorizes their problems either as **adjustment disorders**, clinically significant symptoms in response to stress, or as "other conditions that may be a focus of clinical attention." We prefer to view life problems in terms of **life-cycle transitions**, struggles in moving from one stage of adult development into a new one.

- The experiences associated with life-cycle transitions differ greatly, but conflict is one common theme, including interpersonal, emotional, and cognitive (identity) conflict.

- The transition to adult life begins late in the teen years and may continue through the twenties. The **identity crisis** is a central psychological conflict at this time, as are making major decisions about love and work.

- Family transitions in midlife often involve the addition or loss of members of a family household. Ongoing family conflict is closely linked with individual psychological problems, especially among women and children.

- Gradual declines in physical health do not mean that older adults experience similar declines in psychological well-being. The prevalence of most mental disorders is lower, not higher, among adults 65 years of age and older.

- Most adults view retirement positively, and relationships with children, siblings, and partners take on renewed importance.

- The loss of loved ones, including the loss of a spouse, is a fact of life for older adults, particularly for older women, and leads to **bereavement**, a specific form of **grief**.

- Well-being in later life is linked to good physical health, close relationships, the absence of loss, material well-being, recreation, religion, and community.

## The Big Picture

## critical thinking review

**17.1** What problems in living cause some people to seek psychological help?
People frequently seek guidance from a mental health professional for problems in living or what *DSM-5* calls adjustment disorders . . . (see page 466).

**17.2** How does DSM-5 classify emotional problems that are *not* disorders?
How can we describe the problems in living that bring people into therapy? *DSM-5* uses two approaches. . . . (see page 466).

**17.3** Is the "midlife crisis" a myth?
Not every young adult experiences an identity crisis; turning 40 does not automatically mean midlife crisis. . . . (see page 469).

**17.4** Is an identity crisis necessary for healthy adult development? Is the absence of an identity crisis a problem that foreshadows struggles later in life? . . . (see page 472).

**17.5** How are family relationships critical to psychological well-being?
Whether family conflict is expressed through explosive outbursts, constant bickering, or the "silent treatment," fighting often causes emotional distress for all family members. . . . (see page 474).

**17.6** Is it depressing to grow older?
The fact that aging is accompanied by gradual declines in physical health does *not* mean that older adults experience similar declines in psychological well-being . . . (see page 482).

## key terms

mental health and the law

18

# 18

# The Big Picture

## learning objectives

**18.1**
Is "insanity" the same thing as "mental illness"?

**18.2**
When and why can someone be hospitalized involuntarily?

**18.3**
How can being wrong two times out of three beat a coin flip?

**18.4**
What rights do mental patients retain when hospitalized against their will?

**18.5**
What is deinstitutionalization, and how has it worked?

**18.6**
What custody arrangements are in children's "best interests"?

**18.7**
When must therapists break confidentiality?

The legal definition of insanity is *not* the same as the psychological definition of mental illness. Bizarre acting Jeffrey Dahmer, who killed at least 17 people, chopped them up, and stored the body parts, was sane in the eyes of the law. So was 17-year-old Lee Malvo, who some claim was "brainwashed" by his fellow Beltway sniper, 42-year-old John Muhammad. Psychotically depressed and schizophrenic Andrea Yates, who systematically drowned her five children in a bathtub, was found sane and guilty of murder. That verdict was overturned on appeal, and a retrial jury found her not guilty by reason of insanity. Lorena Bobbitt, infamous for cutting off her husband's penis following an alleged rape, was found not guilty by reason of insanity—in the absence of any major mental illness. The paranoid schizophrenic "unabomber" Ted Kaczynski, who mailed exploding packages to unsuspecting victims, gained fame for *refusing* to use the insanity defense. And as we were writing this, lawyers just entered a plea of not guilty by reason of insanity for James Holmes, charged in the Aurora, Colorado, movie theater shootings in which 12 people were killed and 70 injured.

## Overview

In this chapter we consider a number of topics at the intersection of mental health and the law, including the different concepts, goals, and values of the two professions. We begin with a discussion of criminal law, focusing on the insanity defense.

Next, we consider civil law, particularly the rights of mental patients. The confinement of the mentally ill against their will is a serious action. At best, it protects patients and society; at worst, it strips people of their human rights. Many political dissidents in the former Soviet Union were confined under the guise of "treating" their "mental illnesses." At the other extreme, many seriously mentally ill people in the United States today receive no therapy because they have the right to refuse treatment—a right they may exercise due to mental illness, not philosophical objections.

Later in the chapter, we discuss family law, with an emphasis on child abuse and custody disputes after divorce. Concerns about serious mental illness are the exception, not the rule, in custody and abuse cases. However, predictions about children's emotional well-being often are vital, and the legal decisions have far-reaching implications for children and their families.

Finally, we consider some of the legal responsibilities of mental health professionals, especially professional negligence and confidentiality. These issues, and all the topics in this chapter, are not only of interest to professionals; they also have broad implications for society. Our most basic legal rights and responsibilities are reflected and defined by the manner in which we treat the mentally ill.

We begin with a case study of an infamous and successful use of the insanity defense: the acquittal of John Hinckley. In 1981, Hinckley attempted to assassinate Ronald Reagan, the president of the United States.

### → John Hinckley and the Insanity Defense

On March 30, 1981, John Hinckley stood outside the Washington Hilton hotel, drew a revolver from his raincoat pocket, and fired six shots at President Ronald Reagan. The president and three other men were wounded. The president rapidly recovered from his potentially fatal wound, but the presidential press secretary, James Brady, was permanently crippled by a shot that struck him just above the left eye. Hinckley was charged with attempted assassination, but his trial resulted in a verdict of "not guilty by reason of insanity."

Hinckley, who came from a wealthy family, had never been convicted of a crime. He had a history of unusual behavior, however, and had expressed violent intentions. Hinckley had read several books on famous assassinations and had joined the American Nazi Party. In fact, he was expelled from the Nazi Party in 1979 because of his continual advocacy of violence. A particular oddity was Hinckley's obsession with the actress Jodie Foster, whom he had seen play the role of a child prostitute in the movie *Taxi Driver*. In an attempt to win her favor, Hinckley adopted much of the style of Foster's movie rescuer, Travis Bickle. This included acquiring weapons and stalking the president, much as the movie character had stalked a political candidate. Hinckley repeatedly tried to contact Foster in real life and succeeded a few times, but his approaches were consistently rejected. He came to believe

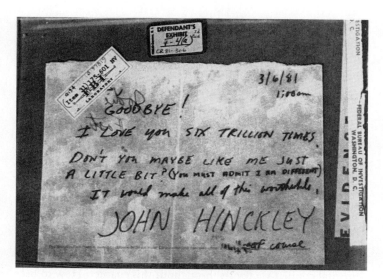

One of several notes that John Hinckley wrote to actress Jodie Foster. Hinckley believed that he could win Foster's love by gaining notoriety, a delusion that apparently motivated him to attempt to assassinate former president Ronald Reagan.

that the only way to win her over was through dramatic action. Less than two hours before he shot the president, he completed a letter to Foster, which said:

> Jodie, I would abandon this idea of getting Reagan in a second if I could only win your heart and live out the rest of my life with you, whether it be in total obscurity or whatever.
>
> I will admit to you that the reason I'm going ahead with this attempt now is because I just cannot wait any longer to impress you. I've got to do something now to make you understand, in no uncertain terms, that I am doing all of this for your sake! By sacrificing my freedom and possibly my life, I hope to change your mind about me. This letter is being written only an hour before I leave for the Hilton Hotel. Jodie, I'm asking you to please look into your heart and at least give me the chance, with this historical deed, to gain your respect and love.

Hinckley's trial centered on the question of his sanity, or as one author put it, whether he was "mad" or merely angry (Clarke, 1990). Both the defense and the prosecution called numerous expert witnesses to determine whether Hinckley was legally sane or insane. All the prosecution's experts concluded that Hinckley was sane; all the defense's experts concluded that Hinckley was insane.

According to the federal law in effect at the time, the prosecution had to prove "beyond a reasonable doubt" that Hinckley was indeed sane. That is, the prosecution had to establish that mental disease had not either (1) created an irresistible impulse that made it impossible for Hinckley to resist attempting to kill the president or (2) so impaired Hinckley's thinking that he did not appreciate the wrongfulness of his actions. (The burden of proof and the definition of insanity in the federal law were changed because of Hinckley's acquittal.)

The prosecution's experts called attention to the fact that Hinckley's actions were planned in advance and to Hinckley's awareness that his actions would have consequences, including possible imprisonment or death. He chose six deadly "devastator" bullets from an abundance of ammunition, and he fired them all accurately in less than three seconds. Defense experts emphasized his erratic behavior, particularly his obsession with Jodie Foster. One psychiatrist suggested, for example, that the president and other victims were merely "bit players" in Hinckley's delusion that through his "historic deed" he would be united with Foster in death.

Hinckley was found not guilty by reason of insanity. The verdict meant that Hinckley received no prison sentence. Instead, he was ordered into a mental hospital to be treated in confinement for an unspecified period of time. As of now, Hinckley remains confined in St. Elizabeth's Hospital, outside Washington, D.C. However, he is allowed to have ten-day, unsupervised visits with his mother outside the hospital. Hinckley could be released permanently if hospital staff concluded that he is no longer dangerous to himself or to others (and the court approves). On the other hand, Hinckley could remain in the hospital for the rest of his life.

John Hinckley obviously was emotionally disturbed, and legally he was determined to be insane. But in other cases, mentally ill defendants are found legally sane (e.g., Jeffrey Dahmer). In still others, mentally healthy defendants are legally insane (e.g., Lorena Bobbitt). What is the basis for such conflicts between psychology and the law?

### Expert Witnesses

One conflict between mental health and the law concerns the role of **expert witnesses**, specialists allowed to testify about matters of opinion (not just fact) that lie within their area of expertise (Cutler & Kovera, 2011). As in the Hinckley case, mental health experts often present conflicting testimony, creating a confusing and sometimes professionally embarrassing "battle of the experts." In fact, some critics believe that mental health professionals should not serve as expert witnesses, because the mental health questions posed by the legal system cannot be answered reliably or validly (Emery, Otto, & O'Donohue, 2005; Faust & Ziskin, 1988).

The law does limit expert testimony to opinion based on established science (Faigman & Monahan, 2005). In *Daubert* v. *Merrell Dow Pharmaceuticals* (1993), the United States Supreme Court ruled that expert opinion must be based on an ". . . inference or assertion . . . derived by the scientific method," and courts must determine "whether the reasoning or methodology underlying the testimony is scientifically valid and . . . whether that reasoning or methodology can be applied to the facts in issue" (p. 2796). As you know, however, experts can and do interpret the same information in different ways. And lawyers "shop" for friendly experts who have a history of interpreting evidence in a way that will help their case (Murrie et al., 2008).

"Shopping for experts" illustrates how the legal system and science differ in defining "truth." Lawyers are duty-bound to present the most convincing case for their side, not the most objective case. As such, it is often said that the law is more concerned with justice than truth. Lawyers expect challenges to their expert witnesses' testimony, and they anticipate that experts for the opposing side will present conflicting testimony (Fitch, Petrella, & Wallace, 1987). One way to limit conflict, and hopefully improve expert testimony, is for courts to appoint neutral experts rather than having each side employ its own "hired gun" (Faigman & Monahan, 2005).

## Free Will Versus Determinism

A more fundamental conflict between the legal and mental health systems involves assumptions about the causes of and responsibility for human behavior. Criminal law assumes that human behavior is the product of *free will*, the capacity to make choices and freely act on them. The assumption of free will makes people responsible for their actions in the eyes of the law. The legal concept of **criminal responsibility** holds that, because people act out of free will, they are accountable for their actions when they violate the law.

In contrast, psychology is based on an assumption of *determinism*, the view that human behavior is determined (or at least constrained) by biological, psychological, and social forces (Seligman, Railton, Baumeister, & Sripada, 2013). Determinism is essential to science. We cannot hope to know what causes human behavior unless it is determined by factors that can be measured and perhaps controlled. This raises a profound question: Are people responsible for their behavior if they have no free will?

Assumptions about free will and determinism collide in the insanity defense. In U.S. law, **insanity** is an exception to criminal responsibility. The law assumes that the legally insane are not acting out of free will. As a result, defendants like John Hinckley are not criminally responsible for their actions. By calling attention to rare exceptions to criminal responsibility, the insanity defense reaffirms the view that people are accountable for their actions.

Thus, debates about the insanity defense often involve a broad conflict of philosophies, not just differences about a given case. Is human behavior a product of free will, or is it determined by biological, psychological, and social forces? Is the truth somewhere in between, and if so, where do we draw the line? Are people with mental disorders responsible for their actions, or are they not responsible?

## Rights and Responsibilities

In the law, rights and responsibilities go hand in hand. When responsibilities are lost, rights are lost, too. When responsibilities are assumed, rights are gained. The profound implications of this simple relationship were most evident in the provocative views of the American psychiatrist Thomas Szasz (1920–2012). Szasz (1963, 1970) asserted that all people—even people with emotional disorders—are responsible for their actions. Consistent with this position, Szasz argued that the insanity defense should be abolished (1963). It also follows from Szasz's view that other exceptions made for mentally disturbed people in the legal system should be eliminated—for example, commitment to mental hospitals against their will (Moore, 1975).

In arguing for a broader concept of responsibility, Szasz also argued for a broader recognition of human dignity and individual rights of the mentally ill. Since rights and responsibilities go hand in hand, one avenue to gaining rights might be to assume more responsibility through the abolition of the insanity defense.

Not surprisingly, Szasz's views generally have been viewed as extreme (Appelbaum, 1994). Nevertheless, they illustrate a fundamental conflict we revisit throughout this chapter: How to balance tradeoffs between rights and responsibilities.

# Mental Illness and Criminal Responsibility

There are three ways in which the law assumes that mental disorders may affect an individual's ability to exercise his or her rights and responsibilities: (1) Defendants who are *not guilty by reason of insanity* are not criminally responsible for their actions; (2) Defendants who are *incompetent to stand trial* are unable to exercise their right to participate in their own defense; and (3) mental illness may be a *mitigating factor* that can lead to a less harsh sentence—or a harsher one.

## The Insanity Defense

The idea behind the **insanity defense**—that mental disability should limit criminal responsibility—dates to ancient Greek and Hebrew traditions. Early English records similarly include cases where kings or judges pardoned murderers because of "madness" or "idiocy" (Slobogin, Rai, & Reisner, 2009). The rationale for these acquittals was not whether the perpetrator suffered from a mental illness. Instead, the issue was whether the defendant lacked the capacity to distinguish "good from evil," the ability to distinguish right from wrong. This ground for the insanity defense was codified in 1843, after Daniel M'Naghten was found not guilty of murder by reason of insanity.

**M'NAGHTEN TEST** M'Naghten was a British subject who claimed that the "voice of God" ordered him to kill Prime Minister Robert Peel, but who mistakenly murdered Peel's private secretary instead. His insanity acquittal raised considerable controversy and caused the House of Lords to devise the following insanity test:

To establish a defense on the ground of insanity, it must be clearly proved that, at the time of the committing of the act,

Serial killer Jeffery Dahmer, who chopped up and stored his victims' bodies, was held to be legally sane. James Holmes, accused of killing 12 and wounding 70 in the July 2012 Aurora, CO movie theater shootings, entered a plea of not guilty by reason of insanity.

the party accused was laboring under such a defect of reason, from disease of the mind, as not to know the nature and quality of the act he was doing; or, if he did know it, that he did not know he was doing what was wrong. [*Regina* v. *M'Naghten*, 8 Eng. Rep. 718, 722 (1843)]

Subsequently known as the *M'Naghten test*, this rule clearly articulated the "right from wrong" principle for determining insanity. If, at the time a criminal act is committed, a mental disease or defect prevents a criminal from knowing the wrongfulness of his or her actions, the criminal can be found to be *not guilty by reason of insanity (NGRI)*. The "right from wrong" ground established in the *M'Naghten* case continues to be the major focus of the insanity

defense in U.S. law today. However, subsequent developments first broadened and later narrowed the grounds for determining insanity.

**IRRESISTIBLE IMPULSE** The *irresistible impulse test* broadened the insanity defense to include defendants who were unable to control their actions because of mental disease. In the 1886 case, *Parsons* v. *State* [81 Ala. 577, 596, 2 So. 854 (1886)], an Alabama court ruled that defendants could be judged insane if they could not "avoid doing the act in question" because of mental disease. The rationale for the irresistible impulse test was that when people are unable to control their behavior, the law can have no effect on deterring crimes. *Deterrence*, the idea that people will avoid committing crimes because they fear being punished for them, is a major public policy goal of criminal law. In the *Parsons* case, the court reasoned that convicting people for acts that they could not control would serve no deterrence purpose, thus a finding of NGRI was justified.

**PRODUCT TEST** A 1954 ruling by the Washington, D.C., federal circuit court in *Durham* v. *United States* further broadened the insanity defense [214 F.2d 862 (D.C. Cir. 1954)]. Known as the *product test*, the Durham opinion indicated that an accused is not criminally responsible if his or her unlawful act was the product of mental disease or defect. The ruling made no attempt to define either *product* or *mental disease*. The terms were intended to be very broad to allow mental health professionals wide discretion in determining insanity and testifying in court.

*Durham* tried to align the definitions of insanity and mental illness, a seemingly reasonable goal. But some mental health professionals considered psychopathy (antisocial personality disorder in *DSM-5*) to be one of the mental diseases that proved insanity. This created a circular problem: Antisocial personality disorder is defined by criminal behavior, yet the same criminal behavior proved the perpetrator was insane (Campbell, 1990). This and related problems came to a halt when the *Durham* decision was overruled in 1972 (Slobogin et al., 2009). (If this had not happened, you can imagine how the product test might have influenced the politics of deciding what disorders were included in *DSM-5*.)

**LEGISLATIVE ACTIONS** In 1955, a year after the *Durham* decision, the American Law Institute drafted model legislation designed to address problems with the previous insanity rules. The model is important, because it subsequently was adopted by the majority of states. The rule indicates that

> A person is not responsible for criminal conduct if at the time of such conduct as a result of mental disease or defect he lacks substantial capacity either to appreciate the criminality [wrongfulness] of his conduct or to conform his conduct to the requirements of the law.

This definition of insanity combines the M'Naghten and irresistible impulse tests, although it softens the requirements somewhat with the term *substantial capacity*. (Compare this with the language used in the M'Naghten test.) The American Law Institute also excluded a history of criminal behavior from the definition of "mental disease or defect." This provision addresses the problem of circularity in the antisocial personality disorder diagnosis.

The most recent major developments most in the law occurred as a result of the acquittal of John Hinckley. Following the controversy over this case, both the American Bar Association and the American Psychiatric Association recommended eliminating the irresistible impulse component of the insanity defense. These organizations judged this strand of the insanity defense to be more controversial and unreliable than the right from wrong standard (Mackay, 1988). Consistent with these recommendations, the federal Insanity Defense Reform Act was passed in 1984 and defined the insanity defense as follows:

> It is an affirmative defense to a prosecution under any federal statute that, at the time of the commission of acts constituting the offense, the defendant, as a result of severe mental disease or defect, was unable to appreciate the nature and quality or the wrongfulness of his acts. Mental disease or defect does not otherwise constitute a defense. (Title 18 of the United States Code)

Several states echoed this change in federal law by enacting similar, more restrictive legislation. Thus, John Hinckley's assassination attempt is one reason why Andrea Yates initially was found sane and therefore guilty of drowning her five children in Texas. Tighter rules also played a role in the legal strategy for Jared Lee Lougher, whose victims in his Tucson, Arizona

A jury declared Andrea Yates (in orange prison garb) legally sane, despite her psychosis. They found her guilty of murdering her five children. The verdict was overturned on appeal, and Yates was found not guilty by reason of insanity.

shooting rampage included U.S. Representative Gabrielle Giffords. He considered the insanity defense, but in the end, simply pleaded guilty. As of this writing, the lawyers for James Holmes, the assailant in the Aurora, Colorado movie theater shootings, were considering using the insanity defense even over their client's objections. In the wake of the *Hinckley* case, the states of Montana, Idaho, Utah, Kansas, and Nevada completely abolished the insanity defense.

**GUILTY BUT MENTALLY ILL** The verdict *guilty but mentally ill (GBMI)* is another attempt to reform the insanity defense (American Bar Association, 1995). Defendants are GBMI if they are guilty of the crime, were mentally ill at the time it was committed, but were not legally insane at that time (see Table 18.1). A defendant found GBMI is sentenced in the same manner as any criminal, but the court can order treatment for the mental disorder as well. The GBMI verdict was designed as a compromise that would reduce NGRI verdicts, hold defendants criminally responsible, but acknowledge mental disorders and the need for treatment (Mackay, 1988). However, the GBMI verdict has not replaced NGRI. Instead, it is most often used in cases in which defendants simply would have been found guilty in the past (Smith & Hall, 1982). Others criticize GBMI for confusing the issues and suggest that interest in GBMI is rightfully declining (Melton et al., 2007).

Recent developments clearly led to a more restrictive insanity defense. The furor surrounding the high-profile *Hinckley* case was not unlike the controversy that surrounded the high profile *M'Naghten* case more than 100 years earlier. Ironically, the *Hinckley* case caused the insanity defense to be revised to resemble the original M'Naghten test (Mackay, 1988). As it was for a time after 1843, the most common contemporary standard for determining legal insanity is the inability to distinguish right from wrong.

**BURDEN OF PROOF** Under U.S. criminal law, a defendant is innocent until proven guilty "beyond a reasonable doubt." The *burden of proof* thus rests with the prosecution, and the *standard of proof* is very high—beyond a reasonable doubt. Who has the burden of proof in insanity cases?

In the Hinckley trial, the prosecution was obliged to prove that Hinckley was sane beyond a reasonable doubt, a case it failed to make. The Insanity Defense Reform Act changed federal law. In federal courts the defense now must prove defendants' insanity rather than the prosecution having to prove their sanity. Insanity must be proven by "clear and convincing evidence," a stringent standard but not as exacting as "beyond a reasonable doubt."

About two-thirds of states also now place the burden of proof on the defense, but the standard of proof typically is less restrictive—"the preponderance of the evidence." Thus, the insanity defense has been narrowed further by shifting the burden of proof from the prosecution to the defense (American Bar Association, 1995).

## TABLE 18.1
## Developments in the Insanity Defense

| Grounds for NGRI | Mental Incapacity at Time of Crime | How Broad? | Brief History of Rule |
|---|---|---|---|
| Right from wrong | Inability to distinguish right from wrong | Narrow | Formalized in 1843 *M'Naghten* case, many states again made this the only ground for NGRI following Hinckley. |
| Irresistible impulse | Unable to control actions | Broader | Dating to 1886, this broader rule remains in effect in some states. |
| Product test | Mental disease or defect | Broadest | Established in 1954 *Durham* case, this very broad rule was eliminated in 1972. |
| American Law Institute definition | Inability to distinguish right from wrong or unable to control actions | Broader | Combination of right from wrong and irresistible impulse tests, this hybrid model law was common before Hinckley. |
| Guilty but mentally ill | Legally responsible for crime but also mentally ill | Alternative | Recent alternative to NGRI. Defendant is not legally insane but may get treatment for mental illness. |

**DEFINING "MENTAL DISEASE OR DEFECT"** An issue of obvious importance to the mental health professions is the precise meaning of the term *mental disease or defect*. The American Law Institute's proposal specifically excluded antisocial personality disorder, but would any other diagnosis listed in *DSM-5* qualify? The 1984 federal legislation indicates that the mental disease must be "severe," but what does this mean?

The question of which mental disorders qualify for the "mental disease or defect" component of the insanity defense is unresolved. Some legal and mental health professionals would allow any disorder listed in *DSM-5* to qualify. Others have argued that especially difficult circumstances—for example, being a victim of repeated violence—should qualify, even if the problems are *not* mental disorders (see The Battered Woman Syndrome as a Defense on p. 496). Still others would sharply restrict the diagnoses qualifying for the insanity defense to intellectual disabilities, schizophrenia, mood disorders, and cognitive disorders (excluding cognitive disorders induced by substance use or abuse) (Appelbaum, 1994).

**USE OF THE INSANITY DEFENSE** Given the intensive media coverage of high-profile cases, you might be surprised to learn that the insanity defense is used in only about 1 percent of all criminal cases in the United States. Only about 25 percent of defendants who offer the defense are actually found to be NGRI (Callahan et al., 1991; Steadman, Pantle, & Pasewark, 1983). Furthermore, over 90 percent of these acquittals result from plea bargains rather than jury trials (Callahan et al., 1991). In addition, the post-Hinckley shift in the burden of proof from the prosecution to the defense has reduced both the frequency and the success rate (Steadman et al., 1993). In England, where the M'Naghten rule still stands, the insanity defense is virtually nonexistent. It is used in only a handful of cases each year (Mackay, 1988).

Do defendants "walk" if they are found NGRI? Some are incarcerated in mental institutions for much shorter periods of time than if they had been sentenced to prison. (Lorena Bobbitt was hospitalized for 45 days.) Others actually are incarcerated for much longer periods of time—yet another reminder that rights are lost when responsibilities are not assumed. On average, NGRI acquittees spend approximately the same amount of time in mental institutions as they would have served in prison (Pantle, Pasewark, & Steadman, 1980). Some state laws actually limit the length of confinement following an NGRI verdict to the maximum sentence the acquittee would have served if convicted. However, the U.S. Supreme Court has ruled that longer confinements are permitted because treatment, not punishment, is the goal of an NGRI verdict (American Bar Association, 1995).

## Competence to Stand Trial

Many more people are institutionalized because of findings of incompetence than because of insanity rulings. **Competence** is a defendant's ability to understand the legal proceedings that are taking place against them and to participate in their own defense. Competence was defined as follows by the U.S. Supreme Court in *Dusky* v. *United States* [363 U.S. 402, 80 S. Ct. 788, 4 L. Ed.2d. 824 (1960)]:

> The test must be whether he [the defendant] has sufficient present ability to consult with his attorney with a reasonable degree of rational understanding and a rational as well as factual understanding of proceedings against him.

You should note several features of the legal definition of competence. First, competence refers to the defendant's current mental state, whereas insanity refers to the defendant's state of mind at the time of the crime. Second, as with insanity, the legal definition of incompetence is not the same as the psychologist's definition of mental illness. Even a psychotic individual may possess enough rational understanding to be deemed competent in the eyes of the law. Third, competence refers to the defendant's

Battered women often remain in an abusive relationship for incomprehensibly long periods of time. To outsiders, their reluctance to leave the relationship can seem foolish, even masochistic. To the battered woman, however, leaving the relationship often seems impossible. She may feel trapped by finances or by concern for her children; chronic abuse may cause her to lose all perspective. Some women eventually escape only by killing their tormentors. According to a report of the American Psychological Association (1995), approximately 1,000 women kill their current or former batterer each year. Is this violence in response to violence ever justified?

The killing of an abuser clearly is justified in U.S. law when the victim's life is in immediate danger. In this case, the action is committed in self-defense. In many cases, however, the killing takes place when the threat of abuse looms in the future but is not immediate. In this situation, a woman still might plead self-defense. The defense may depend heavily on the battered woman syndrome.

The *battered woman syndrome* is a term coined by psychologist Lenore Walker (1979) to describe her observations about the psychological effects of chronic abuse on victims. Two aspects of the syndrome are crucial to its use as a defense. First, Walker postulates a "cycle of violence," that includes three stages: (1) a tension-building phase leading up to violence; (2) the battering incident itself; and (3) a stage of loving contrition, during which the batterer apologizes and attempts to make amends. Second, Walker asserts that the abused woman is prevented from leaving the relationship by learned helplessness. This implies that the battered woman expects to be beaten repeatedly but is immobilized and unable to leave the relationship.

The battered woman syndrome has been used successfully to acquit many battered women or, in other cases, to reduce their sentences. In fact, at least five states enacted statutes explicitly allowing the battered woman syndrome defense (Toffel, 1996). However, a similar defense arising when an abused child kills a parent or stepparent has met with much more resistance (Ryan, 1996).

Not surprisingly, the battered woman defense is controversial. Criminal lawyer Alan Dershowitz (1994) is a notably vocal critic. He writes:

> On the surface, the abuse excuse affects only a few handfuls of defendants. But at a deeper level, the abuse excuse is a symptom of a general abdication of responsibility. It also endangers our collective safety by legitimating a sense of vigilantism. (p. 4)

Some courts have ruled that expert testimony on the battered woman syndrome is inadmissible, but the trend is toward increasing acceptance (Faigman et al., 1997). Given the growing use of the defense, it may surprise you to learn that commentators generally agree about one point: The scientific evidence supporting the battered woman syndrome is weak to nonexistent (Faigman et al., 1997; Schopp, Sturgis, & Sullivan, 1994). One question that has been asked, for example, is: How can someone who is suffering from learned helplessness bring herself to kill?

An alternative defense is *temporary insanity*, which may be more easily proved in court. (The legal definition of insanity refers to a defendant's mental state at the time of committing the criminal act; thus it is possible for a defendant to suffer from "temporary insanity.") An argument for temporary insanity based on the battered woman syndrome would stress that the physical abuse so impaired the battered woman's thinking that either she was unable to appreciate the consequences of her actions, or she was driven to the point where she could no longer control her behavior (Cipparone, 1987).

In cases where women have killed their batterers, temporary insanity pleas are used less frequently than self-defense. Perhaps this is because the temporary insanity defense carries a stigma, as well as the possibility of confinement in a mental institution. More broadly, a successful insanity defense relieves one woman of criminal responsibility for her actions. A successful self-defense makes a broader political statement. Women have a right to take extreme action in the face of chronic battering (Walker, 1989).

A member of the "Framingham Eight," eight women imprisoned for killing their abusers. The women petitioned for early release from prison, claiming they acted in self-defense. The governor of Massachusetts eventually commuted their sentences.

## TABLE 18.2
## Measuring Legal Competence

**A. Legal Understanding**

1. Understanding the roles of defense attorney and prosecutor.
2. Understanding both the act and mental elements of a serious offense.
3. Understanding the elements of a less serious offense.
4. Understanding the role of a jury.
5. Understanding the responsibilities of a judge at a jury trial.
6. Understanding sentencing as a function of the severity of the offense.
7. Understanding the process of a guilty plea.
8. Understanding the rights waived in pleading guilty.

**B. Legal Reasoning**

9. Reasoning about evidence suggesting self-defense.
10. Reasoning about evidence related to criminal intent.
11. Reasoning about evidence of provocation.
12. Reasoning about motivation for one's behavior.
13. Reasoning about the potential impact of alcohol on one's behavior.
14. Capacity to identify information that might inform the decision to plead guilty versus plead not guilty.
15. Capacity to identify both potential costs and potential benefits of a legal decision (e.g., pleading guilty).
16. Capacity to compare one legal option (e.g., accepting a plea bargain) with another legal option (e.g., going to trial) in terms of advantages and disadvantages.

**C. Legal Appreciation**

17. Plausibility of defendant's beliefs about the likelihood of being treated fairly by the legal system.
18. Plausibility of defendant's beliefs about likelihood of being helped by his/her lawyer.
19. Plausibility of defendant's beliefs about whether to disclose case information to his/her attorney.
20. Plausibility of defendant's beliefs about likelihood of being found guilty.
21. Plausibility of defendant's beliefs about likelihood of being punished if found guilty.
22. Plausibility of defendant's beliefs about whether to accept a plea bargain.

*Source:* Items reprinted from the MacCAT-CA. Reprinted by permission of Professor R. Otto, University of South Florida.

ability to understand criminal proceedings, not willingness to participate in them. For example, a defendant who simply refuses to consult with a court-appointed lawyer is not incompetent. Finally, the "reasonable degree" of understanding needed to establish competence is fairly low. Only those who suffer from severe emotional disorders are likely to be found incompetent (Melton et al., 2007).

The legal definition of competence contains no reference to "mental disease or defect." The role of expert witnesses in determining competency is therefore quite different from their role in determining sanity. The evaluation focuses much more on specific behaviors and capacities than on DSM disorders. Table 18.2 summarizes the areas of legal understanding and reasoning necessary for competence as formulated by a distinguished group of experts.

Incompetence to stand trial is the most common finding of incompetence, but the issue may arise around other

Zacarias Moussaoui, the "twentieth terrorist," pleaded guilty to conspiring in the September 11 attacks. His lawyers objected that he was not competent to plead guilty, but he eventually was found competent and his plea was accepted.

aspects of the legal process. Defendants must be competent to understand the *Miranda warning* issued during their arrest. (The Miranda warning details the suspect's rights to remain silent and to have an attorney present during police questioning.) Defendants also must be competent at the time of their sentencing. Finally, recent rulings indicate that defendants sentenced to death must be competent at the time of their execution, or the death sentence cannot be carried out. One issue that is currently working its way through the courts is whether a psychotic death-row inmate retains the right to refuse treatment (discussed shortly) or can be medicated against his wishes for the sole purpose of making him competent to be executed (Slobogin et al., 2009).

Competency hearings generally do not make front-page stories. Typically, a competency finding is accepted by agreement or reached in a relatively informal hearing. An exception arose in the trial of Zacarias Moussaoui, the so-called "twentieth terrorist" who was arrested before September 11 but was accused of being a conspirator in the attacks. Moussaoui first pleaded guilty to the charges against him, but his court-appointed lawyers objected that he was not competent to enter the guilty plea. Although the judge later found Moussaoui competent, she gave him a week to change his plea, which he did. After years of back and forth, a legally competent Moussaoui was found guilty by a jury on May 3, 2006, and sentenced to life in prison.

If defendants are determined to be incompetent, legal proceedings must be suspended until they can be understood by the defendant. Evidence shows that 75 percent of incompetent defendants are restored to competence within six months (Zapf & Roesch, 2011). Among those not restored to competence, many defendants have been confined for periods of time much greater than they would have served if convicted (Zapf & Roesch, 2011). Although there is little doubt that they have severe mental disorders, incompetent defendants do not always receive the same protections as those hospitalized through civil commitment procedures, which we discuss shortly.

## Sentencing and Mental Health

Mental health also is a consideration in sentencing. Mental disorders are one of several potential *mitigating factors* that judges are required to consider before sentencing a guilty party (Slobogin et al., 2009). The presence of a mental illness may justify a less harsh sentence, particularly in death penalty cases. Yet mental illness also can be used to justify longer periods of confinement, particularly for sex offenders.

Because death is the ultimate punishment, judicial scrutiny is particularly intense in death penalty cases. A thorough review of potential mitigating factors, including mental illness and duress at the time of the crime, is a major part of the scrutiny required by the court (Slobogin et al., 2009). *Mitigation evaluations*, which include an assessment for mental disorders, are required in all death penalty cases.

**INTELLECTUAL DISABILITY** In the landmark case of *Atkins* v. *Virginia* (2002), the U.S. Supreme Court ruled that an intellectual disability (formerly called mental retardation) is a mitigating factor that makes the death penalty unconstitutional. Daryl Atkins, a man with an IQ of 59, was found guilty of robbing a 21-year-old man for beer money and subsequently shooting and killing him. According to the court, the death penalty would be cruel and unusual punishment in this case—and for all people with an intellectual disability. Writing for the majority, Justice John Paul Stevens reasoned:

> First, there is serious question whether either justification underpinning the death penalty—retribution and deterrence of capital crimes—applies to mentally retarded offenders. . . . Second, mentally retarded defendants in the aggregate face a special risk of wrongful execution because of the possibility that they will unwittingly confess to crimes they did not commit, their lesser ability to give their counsel meaningful assistance, and the facts that they typically are poor witnesses and that their demeanor may create an unwarranted impression of lack of remorse for their crimes. (536 U.S. 321, 2002, pp. 2–3)

A firestorm of debate about the precise definition of intellectual disability is one practical consequence of the Supreme Court ruling. Whether a defendant has an intellectual disability literally may be a life-or-death question (see Thinking Critically about DSM-5).

The Supreme Court also has ruled that the death penalty is cruel and unusual punishment for another category of defendants: anyone who commits a capital crime when under the age

A surveillance camera captures Daryl Atkins (left) with Eric Nesbitt (center) and an accomplice (right). Atkins and his accomplice later shot Nesbitt for beer money. Atkins was sentenced to death, but in 2002 the U.S. Supreme Court ruled the death penalty is cruel and unusual punishment for someone, like Atkins, who suffers from an intellectual disability.

## Thresholds Can Be a Matter of Life or Death

The *DSM-5* is a categorical classification system. In the end, you either have a disorder or you do not (based on some *threshold*, the number of symptoms required for the diagnosis). At the same time, the *DSM-5* recognizes that many of problems really lie along a dimension. While you (categorically) either do or do not suffer from depression, you (dimensionally) can be a little depressed, extremely depressed, or depressed to varying degrees in between. In fact, the *DSM-5* contains a variety of severity rating scales to call attention to the fact that it often turns dimensions into categories.

Discussions about categories and dimensions may seem abstract and irrelevant—until you consider their tremendous importance when applied in the real world. In the case of intellectual disabilities, it can be a matter of life or death. Intellectual disability is a categorical diagnosis. IQ is very much a dimension. The *DSM-5's* rough threshold for defining an intellectual disability is an IQ of 70 (see Chapter 15).

In *Atkins v. Virginia* (2002) the U.S. Supreme Court outlawed the death penalty for people with intellectual disabilities as "cruel and unusual punishment." Yet, in a 2005 retrial, a Virginia jury ruled that Daryl Atkins no longer suffered from an intellectual disability. The prosecution argued that Atkins' constant contact with his lawyers raised his IQ over 70! He was again sentenced to death. (His sentence was later commuted to life in prison because of prosecutorial misconduct during his first trial.)

A similar debate ended in the death penalty for Teresa Lewis. On September 30, 2010, she became the first woman executed in Virginia since 1912. Lewis had an IQ of 72. She was convicted of being the "mastermind" behind a conspiracy in which she hired two men to kill her husband. Her defenders pointed to the likelihood that she was manipulated, not a mastermind, as her accomplices had much higher IQs.

A 2009 report identified 234 death penalty cases that had raised the intellectual disability defense (Blume, Johnson, & Seeds, 2009). The difference between an IQ of 69 and 72 is trivial, except when it comes to the death penalty.

While less dramatic, other distinctions between categories and dimensions raise various *DSM-5* controversies. For example, the manual dropped the categorical diagnosis of Asperger's disorder in favor of the explicitly dimensional autism spectrum disorder. This created two controversies. First, many people only recently diagnosed with Asperger's (introduced in 1994 in DSM-IV) objected to losing their diagnosis. The manual abandoned a term that offered these socially awkward and misunderstood individuals an explanation, understanding, and support. Second, at least one field trial suggested that *DSM-5's* new diagnostic thresholds would dramatically reduce the number of people meeting criteria for autism spectrum disorder (McPartland, Reichow, & Volkmar, 2012). Children and adults typically must qualify for a diagnosis in order to obtain services from schools, agencies, and insurance, so this concern about thresholds really applies to *every* diagnosis.

You may not realize it, but you, as a student, are very much aware of controversies about dimensions, categories, and thresholds. Will your instructor turn your 89.1 test score average (a dimension) into a B or an A (a category)? When arguing why you deserve the A, maybe you will get extra credit if you mention that the exact same debates were involved in creating the *DSM-5*.

of 18 [*Roper* v. *Simmons*, (03-633) (2005)]. The Supreme Court went one step further in 2010, ruling that a life sentence without the possibility of parole is cruel and unusual punishment for juveniles who commit crimes in which no one was killed [*Graham* v. *Florida*, 560, U.S. (2010)].

**SEXUAL PREDATORS** Intellectual disabilities may mitigate against harsh sentencing, but a history of and potential for sexual violence can lead to harsher sentencing. Several states have passed *sexual predator laws*, designed to keep sexual offenders confined for indefinite periods of time. These laws were challenged in the U.S. Supreme Court case of *Kansas* v. *Hendricks* (521 U.S. 346, 1997). In this case, Leroy Hendricks, who had a long and gruesome history of pedophilia, was about to be released from prison after serving a 10-year term for taking "indecent liberties" with two 13-year-old boys. Before he was released, however, Hendricks was confined indefinitely to a maximum security institution under a new Kansas sexual predator law.

In court, Hendricks admitted that when he "gets stressed out" he "can't control the urge" to molest children. Still, Hendricks argued against his continued confinement on several grounds, including "double jeopardy," that is, being punished twice for the same crime. The Supreme Court ruled in favor of the state of Kansas, however, concluding that Hendricks's indefinite confinement under the sexual predator law did not constitute punishment. Instead, the court viewed Hendricks's continued detention in a maximum security prison as justified on the basis of his dangerousness to others. A recent Supreme Court ruling upheld the extended detention of potential sexual predators in a similar case [*United States* v. *Comstock*, 560 U.S._1951__ (2010)]. While we may feel safer with someone like Hendricks in jail, the court's decision can be questioned. Other classes of criminals—for example, burglars (who commit 60 percent of all rapes in the home)—have notably higher rates of recidivism than sex offenders, yet they are not confined for dangerousness beyond their prison sentences (Slobogin et al., 2009). Moreover, confined sex offenders typically get little or no treatment, a justification for civil commitment, our next topic.

## Civil Commitment

Involuntary hospitalization raises three questions of major importance in civil law: (1) civil commitment, the legal process of hospitalizing people against their will; (2) patients' rights; and (3) deinstitutionalization, treating patients in their communities instead of in mental hospitals. We begin with a brief review of the history of mental hospitals in the United States.

### A Brief History of U.S. Mental Hospitals

In 1842, the famous British author Charles Dickens toured the United States and visited several mental institutions. In *American Notes and Pictures from Italy* (1842/1970), he wrote about one of the institutions that he visited:

> I cannot say that I derived much comfort from the inspection of this charity. The different wards might have been cleaner and better ordered; I saw nothing of that salutary system which had impressed me so favorably elsewhere; and everything had a lounging, listless, madhouse air, which was very painful. The moping idiot, cowering down with long disheveled hair; the gibbering maniac, with his hideous laugh and pointed finger; the vacant eye, the fierce wild face, the gloomy picking of the hands and lips, and munching of the nails: there they were all without disguise, in naked ugliness and horror. In the dining-room, a bare, dull, dreary place, with nothing for the eye to rest on but the empty walls, a woman was locked up alone. She was bent, they told me, on committing suicide. If anything could have strengthened her in her resolution, it would certainly have been the insupportable monotony of such an existence. (p. 93)

Such cruel care of the mentally disturbed has been a problem throughout history. Ironically, many of the large mental institutions that still dot the U.S. countryside were built in the nineteenth century to fulfill the philosophy of *moral treatment,* the laudable but failed movement to alleviate mental illnesses by offering respite and humane care. In 1830, only four public mental hospitals with fewer than 200 patients existed in the United States. By 1880, 75 public mental hospitals housed more than 35,000 residents (Torrey, 1988). As the moral treatment movement faded, these institutions simply became larger and more grotesque human warehouses. The squalid conditions in state mental hospitals did not become a concern until shortly after World War II. Conscientious objectors, who worked in mental hospitals instead of serving in the armed forces, brought the terrible conditions to public attention (Torrey, 1988).

As shown in Figure 18.1, the number of patients in state mental hospitals began to shrink dramatically in the 1950s. This was due to the discovery of antipsychotic medications and to the *deinstitutionalization movement*—the attempt to care for the mentally ill in their communities. This laudable movement, which had the same goal but the opposite solution as the moral treatment movement, also suffered from many problems. Many patients were moved out of large mental institutions and into private mental hospitals, nursing homes, or homelessness.

One more sad irony: Nineteenth-century reformers hoped to get the mentally disturbed out of jails and into hospitals. Today, jails house more and more people with mental illness (Ditton, 1999). In fact, four times as many people with mental illnesses are incarcerated in prisons as are held in state mental hospitals (U.S. Department of Justice, 1999). New "mental health courts," designed to accommodate the mental health needs of the accused and convicted, are one effort to address this problem. Whether they will prove helpful is uncertain (Slobogin et al., 2009).

### Libertarianism Versus Paternalism

What are society's legal and philosophical rationales for hospitalizing people against their will? Debates about involuntary hospitalization highlight the philosophical tension between

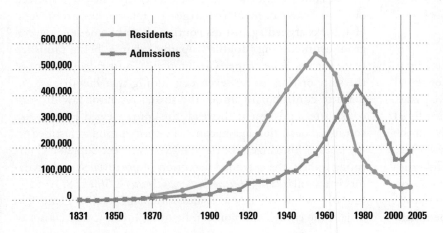

**FIGURE 18.1**

**Residents and Admissions to U.S. Public Mental Hospitals: 1831—2005** The number of patients living in mental hospitals increased from the latter 1800s, when large mental hospitals were built, and declined from the 1950s with the development of antipsychotic medication and deinstitutionalization.

*Source:* Manderscheid, R.W., J.E. Atay, and R.A. Crider. Changing Trends in State Psychiatric Hospital Use from 2002 to 2005. Psychiatric Services 60. 2001; 1.

libertarianism, which emphasizes the protection of individual rights, and paternalism, which emphasizes the state's duty to protect its citizens. The involuntary hospitalization of someone who appears dangerous serves a protective, paternalistic goal. Yet *preventive detention*—confinement before a crime is committed—can lead to substantial abuse. Our laws prohibit the confinement of someone simply on the suspicion that he or she will commit a crime, with a single exception: **civil commitment**, the involuntary hospitalization of the mentally ill.

The conflict between libertarian and paternalistic philosophies is very much alive. A major swing toward libertarianism began in the 1960s. Since at least 1990, however, the pendulum has swung in the direction of paternalism. Interest is increasing in aggressive, sometimes coercive, interventions with the seriously mentally ill (Appelbaum, 1994).

## Involuntary Hospitalization

U.S. law contains two broad rationales for involuntary hospitalization. The first is based on the state's *parens patriae* authority, the philosophy that the government has a humanitarian responsibility to care for its weaker members. (The literal translation of the Latin phrase *parens patriae* is the "state as parent.") Under the *parens patriae* authority, civil commitment may be justified when the mentally disturbed are either dangerous to themselves or unable to care for themselves (Myers, 1983–1984). The concept of *parens patriae* also is used to justify the state's supervision of minors and physically incapacitated adults.

The second rationale is based on the state's police power—its duty to protect public safety, health, and welfare. Our government restricts individual liberties for the public good in many ways. We cannot yell "Fire!" in a crowded theater or drive at 100

Seung-Hui Cho showed frightening, erratic behavior long before he shot and killed 32 people and wounded many others on the Virginia Tech campus on April 16, 2007. He had been treated intermittently for mental health problems and declared a danger to himself by a Virginia court two years earlier. Can such horrors be prevented by more aggressive civil commitment and mandated treatment?

miles an hour. The civil commitment of people who are dangerous to others is justified by similar rationales.

**GROUNDS AND PROCEDURES** Most states distinguish emergency and formal civil commitment procedures. *Emergency commitment* is when an acutely disturbed individual is temporarily confined, typically for no more than a few days. Physicians, mental health professionals, or even police officers may be allowed to institute emergency commitment. Such actions are taken only when the risk to self or others appears to be very high.

*Formal commitment* can be ordered only by a court. A hearing must be available to patients who object to involuntary hospitalization, in order to protect their due process rights. Following involuntary commitment, cases must be reviewed after a set period of time—for example, every six months.

The specific grounds for involuntary hospitalization vary from state to state. Still, three grounds dominate: (1) inability to care for self, (2) dangerousness to self, and (3) dangerousness to others. *Inability to care for self* is a broad criterion used for people unable to care for themselves or who have no family or friends to care for them. The intention of this standard is benevolent, but it has been abused in some cases, violating patient rights (Appelbaum, 1994; Durham & LaFond, 1988). Debates continue in courtrooms and in state legislatures. Should we be paternalistic and sacrifice some individual rights by involuntarily committing mental patients who do not want, but who clearly need, inpatient treatment? Or do we run the danger of trampling on civil liberties if we hospitalize nondangerous people against their will?

Few civil libertarians object to hospitalizing people against their will when they clearly are either *dangerous to self* or *dangerous to others*, provided that the danger is "imminent." Thus, a commonly accepted standard for civil commitment is "clear and convincing evidence of imminent danger to oneself or others." However, a case we discussed earlier, *Kansas* v. *Hendricks* (1997), created controversy about the *imminent* standard. Leroy Hendricks's risk of sexual molestation of minors was not imminent, but more general. Still, the Supreme Court ruled that civil commitment is justified for individuals "who suffer from a volitional impairment rendering them dangerous beyond their control." This vague position may signal a new trend, one that some fear will lead to overreaching in civil commitment cases (Falk, 1999).

**PREDICTING DANGEROUSNESS** The stakes are high in predicting a patient's dangerousness. False positives—wrongly hospitalizing someone who is not dangerous to others or suicidal—unfairly restrict civil rights. False negatives—releasing someone who is dangerous to self or others—put lives at stake. Unfortunately, the prediction of violence is far from perfect. One certainty is that mental health professionals *will* make errors.

***DANGEROUSNESS TO OTHERS*** Research shows that mental illness is linked with an increased risk for violence (Douglas, Guy, & Hart, 2009). However, the public greatly overestimates that

## Violence and Mental Illness

Are mentally disturbed people dangerous? Especially following incidents like the Sandy Hook massacre of school children and teachers, the obvious answer seems to be: "Yes!" In one survey, 61 percent of the respondents agreed that people with schizophrenia were "somewhat" or "very" likely to do something violent to others (Pescosolido et al., 1999). People recall dramatic, frightening, and terribly sad cases like Sandy Hook, the Virginia Tech shootings, or Kendra Webdale, a talented 32-year-old woman who was pushed in front of a subway train and killed in New York City. Her assailant, a complete stranger with schizophrenia, did this because "an overwhelming force took over him."

### TABLE 18.3
### Mental Illness and Violence

| Diagnosis | Percentage Violent |
|---|---|
| No disorder | 2.1 |
| Schizophrenia | 12.7 |
| Major depression | 11.7 |
| Mania or bipolar disorder | 11.0 |
| Alcohol abuse/dependence | 24.6 |
| Substance abuse/dependence | 34.7 |

*Source:* Monahan, John. Mental disorder and violent behavior: Perceptions and evidence. American Psychologist. April 1992; 47(4): 511–521.

The rate of violence is about five times higher among people diagnosed with a major mental disorder than those with no diagnosis. People who abuse alcohol or drugs are even more likely to engage in violent behavior (see Table 18.3). Substance abuse symptoms actually increase the risk of violence in both former psychiatric inpatients and in the general community (Steadman et al., 1998).

Does this evidence support confining the seriously mentally ill based on their dangerousness? The answer is no, for several reasons. First, the risk for violence is far lower than publicly perceived. Approximately 90 percent of the mentally disturbed have *no* history of violence (Douglas et al., 2009; Monahan & Steadman, 2009). Second, family and friends, not strangers in the street, are the victims of over 85 percent of violent acts perpetrated by the mentally ill (Monahan et al., 2001a). Third, *current* psychotic symptoms predict violence, but a *past* history of psychosis does not (Link, Cullen, & Andrews, 1990).

Most importantly, numerous factors other than mental illness predict an increased risk for violence, but they obviously do not justify preventive detention. For example, people who live in poverty or who have a history of criminal behavior are more likely to be violent. But we would not consider confining the poor or those who have paid their debt to society based on their increased statistical risk. Basic civil liberties are at stake. And except in extreme circumstances, our society must accord the same rights to the mentally ill.

risk: The vast majority of people with a psychological disorder are *not* violent (see Critical Thinking Matters). If mental illness is a poor predictor of violence, can individual assessments improve prediction? Well, clinical predictions that someone will be violent are *wrong* approximately two out of three times (Monahan, 1981; Yang, Wong, & Coid, 2010). That is, the false-positive rate is about 67 percent. Some argue that it is unethical for mental health experts to offer specific predictions about dangerousness, because prediction is so inaccurate (Melton et al., 2007).

Prediction is better in the short term than in the long run, a key distinction because most research examines long-term outcomes (Monahan, 1981). For example, two out of three people who are hospitalized involuntarily are not violent after they are released. Would these people have been violent without the commitment? We cannot know for certain, but we do know that (1) clinicians commit patients only when they strongly believe that the risk of violence is imminent, and (2) clinicians release the same patients only if they believe that the patient no longer

is a risk. Such urgent, real-life decisions confound research. No one will ever do the unequivocal experiment: release or confine potentially violent people at random and compare clinical predictions with actual acts of violence.

U.S. Supreme Court Justice Harry Blackmun wrongly claimed that a coin flip would be more accurate than a clinical prediction that is wrong two out of three times (Slobogin et al., 2009). When predicting a very infrequent event (like violence), however, a false-positive rate of two-thirds is, in fact, much better than chance (Lidz, Mulvey, & Gardner, 1993). This is because you must take **base rates**—population frequencies—into account (see Research Methods).

***ASSESSING SUICIDE RISK*** The clinical prediction of suicide risk also involves very high false-positive rates (Pokony, 1983). Yet, concerns about inaccurate prediction are allayed by the fact that suicidal patients typically are committed only when they clearly and directly indicate an imminent likelihood of harming themselves.

# RESEARCH methods

## Base Rates and Prediction: Justice Blackmun's Error

The prediction of violence seems worse than chance: Clinicians are wrong two-thirds of the time when they predict violence will occur. However, predicting rare events is flawed for mathematical reasons. *Base rates*, population frequencies, strongly contribute to errors (Meehl & Rosen, 1955).

Consider a hypothetical example. Assume that (1) future, serious violence has a base rate of 3 percent; (2) clinicians predict that violence will occur among 6 percent of the population; and (3) the clinical prediction of violence is wrong two-thirds of the time. These assumptions are portrayed in the following table:

| | Actually Violent | Actually Not Violent |
|---|---|---|
| **Predicted Violent** | 2% (true positive) | 4% (false positive) |
| **Predicted Not Violent** | 1% (false negative) | 93% (true negative) |

A quick check of the table will confirm our assumptions: The base rate of violence is 3 percent, the clinicians predict violence in 6 percent of the cases, and the prediction is wrong two-thirds of the time. But examine the table more closely. Even though they were wrong in predicting violence two-thirds of the time, the clinicians correctly detect 67 percent of violent patients and 96 percent of nonviolent patients in our example.

Now compare these figures with another hypothetical example: U.S. Supreme Court Justice Harry Blackmun's claim that a coin flip is more accurate than clinicians predictions. Justice Blackmun assumed that a coin flip would be right half of the time while clinical prediction was right only one-third of the time. But the statistics are not so simple. Assume that (1) the base rate

of violence remains at 3 percent, (2) the coin predicts violence (heads) 50 percent of the time, and (3) the coin flip is random. These assumptions are portrayed in the following table:

| | Actually Violent | Actually Not Violent |
|---|---|---|
| **Predicted Violent** | 1.5% | 48.5% |
| **Predicted Not Violent** | 1.5% | 48.5% |

Sorry, Justice Blackmun, but a coin flip does *not* beat clinical prediction. The coin flip correctly detects only 50 percent of violent patients (versus 67 percent) and 50 percent of nonviolent patients (versus 96 percent). The percentage of false positives using Justice Blackmun's method is 48.5%, but using clinical prediction it is 4%. In our first example, the clinical prediction of violence was wrong 67 percent of the time. Justice Blackmun's coin flip was wrong 97 percent of the time [48.5/(48.5 + 1.5)].

A key to understanding Justice Blackmun's error is to recognize the influence of base rates. The base rate of predicting violence using the clinical method (6 percent) was close to the actual base rate (3 percent). However, the base rate of predicting violence using the coin flip (50 percent) was much higher. The statistical potential for accurate prediction is maximized when the predictor and the outcome have more similar base rates (Meehl & Rosen, 1955).

Violence is a low-frequency event, and for statistical reasons alone, this makes it difficult to predict (Meehl & Rosen, 1955). The clinical prediction of violence is far from perfect, but it is better than chance. Justice Blackmun did not understand the influence of base rates. We hope that you do now.

---

In predicting either suicidal risk or dangerousness to others, it is wise and just to include the patient in this process. Many patients freely admit their intention to commit suicide or harm others. Even if they object to involuntary hospitalization, these patients will be more accepting when they are respectfully included in the decision making (Lidz et al., 1995; Monahan et al., 1999).

**ABUSES OF CIVIL COMMITMENT** The police power rationales for civil commitment have been invoked throughout history. Even in colonial times the "furiously insane" could be detained in order to prevent them from doing harm to others (Myers, 1983–1984). In contrast, *parens patriae* rationales for commitment have been overused and abused.

You may also be surprised to learn, for example, that a husband once could have his wife committed to a mental hospital, and a father (or a mother) still can. The first circumstance was changed through the efforts of Mrs. Elizabeth Parsons Ware Packard (Myers, 1983–1984). Mrs. Packard was committed to a mental hospital by her husband under an Illinois law that allowed a man to commit his children or his wife to a mental hospital against their will and without the usual evidence of mental illness. The commitment was questionable at best. In presenting evidence in favor of her commitment, for example, one doctor noted that Mrs. Packard was rational but she was a "religious bigot" (Slobogin et al., 2009). An apparent problem was that her religious beliefs differed from those of her preacher husband. After three years in a mental hospital, her suit for freedom was successful. A jury ruled her to be legally sane after only seven minutes of deliberation. Mrs. Packard subsequently campaigned to revise commitment standards to prevent such abuses.

Parents still have the right to commit children to hospitals. According to the 1979 U.S. Supreme Court ruling in *Parham* v. *J.R.* [442 U.S. 584 (1979)], minors, unlike adults, are not entitled to a full hearing before they can be committed to a mental hospital. State laws may add requirements, but parents can commit minors against their wishes as long as an independent fact finder agrees (Weithorn, 1988). Most children and adolescents in mental hospitals therefore are "voluntary" patients. They were voluntarily committed by their parents.

Libertarians argue that this practice is potentially abusive and want increased recognition of children's rights. Perhaps their strongest point is that many minors are committed because they are troublesome to their parents (Weithorn, 1988). On the other hand, paternalists are reluctant to interfere with parents' rights and family autonomy. Many also are concerned that mentally ill adolescents are particularly bad judges about what is best for them.

## The Rights of Mental Patients

Several important court cases clarified the rights of patients committed to a mental hospital. These include the right to treatment, the right to treatment in the least restrictive environment, and the right to refuse treatment. These libertarian developments offer protections against abuses, yet as you will see, some paternalists think they have gone too far.

**RIGHT TO TREATMENT** Two significant cases established that hospitalized mental patients have a constitutional right to treatment: *Wyatt* v. *Stickney* and *O'Connor* v. *Donaldson*.

**WYATT V. STICKNEY** *Wyatt* v. *Stickney* (1972) began as a dispute over the dismissal of 99 employees from Bryce Hospital in Tuscaloosa, Alabama. The state mental hospital was built in the 1850s and housed nearly 5,000 patients when much-needed staff members were released due to budget cuts. All accounts indicate that conditions in the hospital were very bad even before the layoffs. The buildings were fire hazards, the food was inedible, sanitation was neglected, avoidable sickness was rampant, abuse of patients was frequent, and patients were regularly confined with no apparent therapeutic goal.

Litigation was filed on behalf of Ricky Wyatt, a resident in the institution, as part of a class action suit against the Alabama mental health commissioner, Dr. Stonewall B. Stickney. The suit argued that Bryce Hospital failed to fulfill institutionalized patients' right to treatment. The commissioner was in the unusual position of supporting a suit against him. He wanted to improve care but was faced with budget problems. The case was tried and appealed several times. The patients' suit eventually was upheld.

The victory forced the state of Alabama to provide services, but *Wyatt* had a broader impact. The judicial rulings established that hospitalized mental patients have a right to treatment. Specifically, a federal district court ruled that, at a minimum, public mental institutions must provide (1) a humane psychological and physical environment, (2) qualified staff in numbers sufficient to administer adequate treatment, and (3) individualized treatment plans [334 F. Supp. 1341 (M.D. Ala. 1971) at 1343]. The court also ordered that changes needed to fulfill patients' rights could not be delayed until funding was available.

The *Wyatt* decision helped focus national attention on the treatment of patients in public mental institutions. Numerous "right to treatment" cases were filed. The threat of litigation impelled mental hospitals to improve patient care and helped spur the *deinstitutionalization movement*, which we discuss shortly.

**O'CONNOR V. DONALDSON** The U.S. Supreme Court acknowledged mental patients' right to treatment in another landmark case, *O'Connor* v. *Donaldson* [422 U.S. 563 (1975)]. Kenneth Donaldson was confined in a Florida mental hospital for nearly 15 years. He repeatedly requested release, claiming that he was not mentally ill, was not dangerous to himself or others, and was receiving no treatment. Eventually, he sued the hospital's superintendent, Dr. J. B. O'Connor, for release, asserting that he had been deprived of his constitutional right to liberty.

The evidence presented at the trial indicated that Donaldson was not and never had been dangerous to himself or others. Testimony also revealed that reliable individuals and agencies in the community had made several offers to care for Donaldson, but Superintendent O'Connor repeatedly rejected them. O'Connor insisted that Donaldson could be released only to the custody of his parents, who were very old and unable to care for him. O'Connor's position on Donaldson's supposed inability to care for himself was puzzling, because Donaldson was employed and had lived on his own for many years before being committed to the hospital. Other evidence documented that Donaldson had received nothing but custodial care while he was hospitalized.

After a series of trials and appeals, the Supreme Court ruled that Donaldson was not dangerous either to himself or others. It further ruled that a state could not confine him as being in need of treatment and yet fail to provide him with that treatment. Specifically, it ordered that "the State cannot constitutionally confine a nondangerous individual who is capable of surviving safely in freedom by himself or with the help of willing and responsible family members or friends." Thus, *O'Connor* not only underscored a patient's right to treatment but also set limitations on civil commitment standards. Commitment based on dangerousness to self or others remained unquestioned, but commitment based on inability to care for self became much more controversial, especially if institutionalization offered little treatment or therapeutic benefit.

**LEAST RESTRICTIVE ALTERNATIVE ENVIRONMENT** The patient's right to be treated in the least restrictive alternative environment was first developed in the 1966 case of *Lake* v. *Cameron* [364 F. 2d 657 (D.C. Cir. 1966)]. Catherine Lake was 60 years old when she was committed to St. Elizabeth's Hospital because of "a chronic brain syndrome associated with aging." A particular problem was her tendency to wander away from her home, which posed a threat to her life through exposure to the elements and other dangers.

In contesting the commitment, Mrs. Lake did not object to her need for treatment, but she argued that appropriate treatment was available in a less restrictive setting. The court agreed, suggesting several less restrictive alternatives to institutionalization. These alternatives ranged from having Mrs. Lake carry an identification card to treating her in a public nursing home.

Several cases following *Lake* firmly established the doctrine of the least restrictive alternative. Legislation in numerous states incorporated the right to treatment in the least restrictive alternative environment into their mental health statutes (Hoffman & Foust, 1977). Although the concept was quickly embraced, no one was or is absolutely certain what the expression "least restrictive alternative" means.

In theory, the least restrictive alternative is an attempt to balance paternalistic and libertarian concerns. The state provides mandatory care, but restricts individual liberties to the minimal degree possible. But questions arise about how to implement the theory. Who should determine what alternative is the least restrictive? Should the court monitor the consideration of alternatives? Should an independent party supervise these decisions?

Perhaps the most important issue is the problem that developed in the *Lake* case: Less restrictive alternatives to hospitals often are not available. No suitable community care was found for Mrs. Lake, who was returned to the institution. Thus, *Lake* both established patients' right to treatment in the least restrictive alternative environment and foreshadowed the problem of insufficient alternative treatments in the community. This is especially unfortunate, because community treatment can be more effective than inpatient care (Kiesler, 1982).

**OLMSTEAD V. L.C.** A 1999 U.S. Supreme Court case, *Olmstead* v. *L.C.* (527 US 581 [1999]), upheld the goals of placement in the least restrictive alternative environment but also accepted that the states face problems in providing community care. The case was brought against Tommy Olmstead, the Georgia commissioner of human resources, on behalf of two women with intellectual disabilities and mental illness, L.C. and E.W., who were confined in a Georgia state hospital. The professionals who treated L.C. and E.W. agreed that the women should be treated in the community; however, no community placements were available. The suit was filed under the 1990 Americans with Disabilities Act (ADA), which, among other things, holds that public agencies must provide services to individuals with disabilities, including mental disabilities, "in the most integrated

Lois Curtis was "L.C." in Olmstead v L.C. Her successful U.S. Supreme Court case for placement in the least restrictive alternative environment allowed Lois to eventually move from a state hospital to community care. Here she sings at a peer support facility where she frequently spends daytime hours.

setting appropriate to the needs of qualified individuals with disabilities."

The Supreme Court upheld the ruling of lower courts indicating that Georgia had failed to comply with the ADA. The ruling held that states must demonstrate their efforts to find appropriate community placements, unless doing so would fundamentally alter the state's services and programs for the mentally disabled. *Olmstead* led to further litigation and some legislative change. As with *Lake*'s least restrictive alternative goal, however, progress toward implementing *Olmstead*'s mandate has been slow and limited by the narrow interpretation of subsequent cases (Mathis, 2001; Slobogin et al., 2009). For their part, both L.C. and E.W. were placed in their communities and have remained there for several years. According to the Legal Aid Society of Atlanta, which brought the suit on their behalf, their psychological well-being and quality of life improved immeasurably as a result.

**RIGHT TO REFUSE TREATMENT** The third and most recent development in the rights of mental patients is the *right to refuse treatment*, particularly the right to refuse psychoactive medication. Several courts and state legislatures have concluded that mental health patients have the right to refuse treatment under certain conditions, although this right is on increasingly shaky ground.

The very concept of a committed patient refusing treatment is problematic. After all, the patient who is committed to a mental hospital has refused inpatient treatment but is receiving it anyway. On what grounds can subsequent treatment decisions be refused? Many experts argue that patients lose their right to refuse treatment once they are involuntarily hospitalized (Appelbaum, 1994; Gutheil, 1986; Torrey, 2008). After all, a mental health professional is in an awkward position if a patient is committed to a hospital for treatment yet retains the right to refuse medication.

The question of the right to refuse treatment often turns on the issue of informed consent (Hermann, 1990). **Informed consent** requires that (1) a clinician tell a patient about a procedure and its associated risks, (2) the patient understands the information and freely consents to the treatment, and (3) the patient is competent to give consent. When the patient's competence is in question, a common approach is to appoint an independent guardian who offers a *substituted judgment*, deciding not what is best for the patient but what the patient would do if he or she were competent (Gutheil, 1986).

The rationales for and parameters of patients' right to refuse treatment are still being debated. Several courts have ruled that patients retain their competence to make treatment decisions even if they have been committed through civil procedures. Half the states have recognized the right to refuse psychoactive medications provided that patients are not dangerous to themselves or others (Hermann, 1990). The U.S. Supreme Court first ruled on this topic in the 1990 case of *Washington* v. *Harper* [110 S. Ct. 1028 (1990)]. This case involved a Washington state prison that overrode a patient's refusal of psychoactive medications. The Court decided in favor of the prison, ruling that the prison's review process sufficiently protected the patient's right to refuse treatment. The process stipulated that the patient's wishes could be overruled only after review by a three-member panel consisting of a psychologist, a psychiatrist, and a deputy warden.

In the subsequent case of *Riggins* v. *Nevada* [504 U.S. 127 (1992)], the Court *upheld* the right of a defendant who was being tried for murder to refuse an extremely high dose of antipsychotic medication. The medication ostensibly was being given to ensure the competence of the defendant to stand trial. In *Sell* v. *United States* [123 U.S. 2174 (2003)], the Supreme Court again upheld the right of a defendant to refuse medication when the purpose was to establish competence to stand trial. However, the court signaled that it might have been permissible to medicate the same patient involuntarily if the purpose had been to reduce dangerous behavior (Slobogin et al., 2009). Thus, a patient's right to refuse treatment may be limited if the rationale is to protect the patient or the public, but the right to refuse treatment trumps the state's interest when the purpose is to move prosecution forward for a nondangerous individual.

**ALMOST A REVOLUTION** The libertarian cases and legislation of the 1960s, 1970s, and 1980s defined key patients' rights, producing what one commentator called "almost a revolution" (Appelbaum, 1994). The revolution ended in the 1990s, with the rise of paternalistic concerns. This new paternalism focuses especially on two issues: (1) treating severely disturbed patients who lack insight into their condition and (2) protecting the public from the violently mentally ill.

A newer, assertive approach to treating patients who lack insight is **outpatient commitment**, that is, mandatory, court-ordered treatment in the community (e.g., mandated therapy and/or medication). Outpatient commitment orders must be based on the same legal standards as inpatient commitment, that is, dangerousness and, in some states, inability to care for self. Because it involves less infringement on civil liberties, however, outpatient commitment criteria may be applied less stringently (Melton et al., 2007; Monahan et al., 2001a). In practice, for example, outpatient commitment is sometimes used to prevent future as opposed to imminent dangerousness. Other forms of "leverage" also may be used to get the seriously mentally ill to comply with treatment recommendations, including the threat of jail or help with obtaining public assistance (Monahan et al., 2005). Outpatient treatment of sufficient length reduces the rate of subsequent hospitalization; thus, the coercive procedure can help the seriously mentally ill to receive help in a less restrictive environment (Swartz et al., 2001).

An even newer innovation is the use of **advance psychiatric directives**. Patients can use these legal instruments to declare their treatment preferences, or appoint a surrogate to make decisions for them, should they become psychotic or otherwise are unable to make sound decisions. Advance medical directives are used commonly among the aged, particularly for stating preferences about end of life medical treatments. This new use with severely disturbed patients nicely balances paternalist and libertarian concerns, and initial evidence indicates they greatly reduce the need for more coercive interventions (Monahan, 2010).

Concerns about public protection have been fueled by the Virginia Tech shootings. Tech student Seung-Hui Cho had a history of anxiety, depression, and unusual, threatening behavior long before he shot and killed 32 people on April 16, 2007. In fact, a Virginia court declared him to be "an imminent danger to himself as a result of mental illness" in 2005. Unfortunately, the only outcome was an order for Cho to seek outpatient treatment. Could this horror have been prevented by more definitive action? No one knows. But perhaps foreshadowing a new paternalistic trend, Virginia altered its civil commitment law in 2008. The revised statute extends the time frame of potential dangerousness from "imminent" to "in the near future" (Cohen, Bonnie, & Monahan, 2008).

## Deinstitutionalization

The **deinstitutionalization** movement embraced the philosophy that many patients can be better cared for in their community than in large mental hospitals. In 1963, Congress passed the Community Mental Health Centers (CMHC) Act with the strong support of President John F. Kennedy.[1] The act provided for the creation of community care facilities for the seriously

---

[1]President Kennedy had a special interest in mental health because of his sister Rosemary. She was mildly mentally retarded as a child, but she became psychotic as a young adult and underwent a failed lobotomy that left her so impaired that she had to be confined to a nursing home.

These contrasting images illustrate how mental patients often are neglected both inside and outside of institutions. The photo on the left, taken several decades ago, shows some of the depressing and dehumanizing conditions that characterized many institutions for the mentally ill. The photo on the right depicts the contemporary problem of homelessness. Many homeless people are deinstitutionalized mental patients.

mentally ill as alternatives to institutional care. This law began a broad change in the way mental health services are delivered in the United States.

Deinstitutionalization occurred in dramatic fashion. In 1955, there were 558,239 beds in public mental hospitals in the United States. By 2005, that number had shrunk to 52,539 beds (Torrey et al., 2008). The effects of deinstitutionalization are even greater than these numbers suggest because of population growth. Nearly 900,000 people would be in institutions today if the 1955 proportion of inpatients to the total population had remained unchanged (Torrey, 2008).

Unfortunately, CMHCs have not achieved many of their goals. In fact, the needed numbers of CMHCs were never built, and many in existence do not focus on serious mental illness. Some CMHCs do not even offer emergency treatment or inpatient care, despite the fact that they are mandated to do so by legislation (Torrey, 1997). Other community resources, such as halfway houses, simply have not been implemented in adequate numbers.

Other problems with deinstitutionalization are evident. As public hospitalization has declined, the number of mental patients living in nursing homes and other for-profit institutions has grown. More people with a mental illness also are being confined in jail. In fact, 16 percent of the prison population suffers from a serious mental illness (Ditton, 1999). In addition, a *revolving door* phenomenon has developed in which more patients are admitted to psychiatric hospitals more frequently but for shorter periods of time. For example, one study found that 24 percent of inpatients in New York City had 10 or more previous admissions (Karras & Otis, 1987). Moreover, the deinstitutionalized mentally ill constitute a large part of the homeless population (Torrey, 2008). One study found that 31 percent of the homeless were in need of mental health services (Roth & Bean, 1986).

**MORE PATERNALISM?** Some of the problems of deinstitutionalization are compounded by restrictive civil commitment laws.

One commentary graphically described the situation as one in which patients are "rotting with their rights on" (Appelbaum & Gutheil, 1980).

Advanced psychiatric directives and outpatient commitment can balance some paternalistic concerns against the libertarian fears of restricted freedom. Others support more paternalism in civil commitment laws but argue that a broader reorientation is needed. Most mental health professionals treat "worried well." Perhaps new incentives are needed to direct more of their efforts toward helping the seriously mentally ill (Torrey, 2008).

## Mental Health and Family Law

Family law issues typically involve people whose problems are far less severe than we find in mental health law. This is evident in the major issues that form the focus of family law: divorce, spousal abuse, foster care, adoption, juvenile delinquency, child custody disputes, and child abuse and neglect. These problems can involve serious psychopathology, but they more commonly affect family members who are only mildly disturbed or are functioning normally.

We consider family law and mental health law together in this chapter, because mental health professionals frequently play a role in both areas. However, family and mental health laws are distinct in the legal system and have different historical roots. Much of mental health law is based on the state's police power; virtually all of family law is premised on *parens patriae* duties. Attorneys may specialize in one or the other area, but rarely both. In fact, family law cases typically are tried in separate courts, known variously as "juvenile courts," "domestic relations courts," or "family courts."

According to *parens patriae* theory, family courts are supposed to help and protect children and families, a goal that is psychological as well as legal. Psychological issues carry great weight in family court because of this philosophy—and because family law often is vague. For example, the guiding principle in custody and abuse cases is that judges must make decisions according to the "child's best interest." This may sound laudable, but the law does not clearly define "best." This leaves family court judges in a position of making very difficult decisions with very little legal guidance. As law professor Robert Mnookin (1975) has pointed out:

Deciding what is best for a child poses a question no less ultimate than the purposes and values of life itself. Should the judge be primarily concerned with the child's happiness? Or with the child's spiritual and religious training? Should the judge be concerned with the economic "productivity" of the child when he grows up? Are the primary values of life in warm interpersonal relationships, or in discipline and self-sacrifice? Is stability and security for a child more desirable than intellectual stimulation? These questions could be elaborated endlessly. And yet, where is the judge to look for the set of values that should inform the choice of what is best for the child? (pp. 260–261)

Judges look to the law to outline the values that define "best," but few answers can be found there. As a result, courts frequently turn to mental health professionals for guidance in trying to decide what might be best for a given child in a custody dispute or an abuse/neglect proceeding, the two issues we briefly consider.

## Child Custody Disputes

About 40 percent of children in the United States today will experience their parents' divorce, a circumstance that can lead to a custody dispute (Emery, 1999a, 2011). Child custody disputes also may occur between cohabiting couples and even between extended family members. For example, the case of Elian Gonzalez involved a Cuban boy whose mother died while trying to come to the United States. A national debate focused on whether Elian should be returned to live with his father in Cuba (the parents were divorced) or stay in the United States with distant relatives. He eventually was returned to live with his father.

Although the legal terminology differs from state to state, **child custody** involves two issues: *physical custody,* or where the children will live at what times; and *legal custody,* or how the parents will make decisions about their children's lives. *Sole custody* refers to a situation in which only one parent retains physical or legal custody of the children; in *joint custody* both parents retain legal or physical custody or both.

Parents make the majority of custody decisions outside of court, often with the assistance of attorneys. A growing number of parents are making decisions themselves, often with the help of a *mediator*—a neutral third party who facilitates the parents' discussions. Only a small percentage of custody disputes are decided in court by a judge (Maccoby & Mnookin, 1992). Mental health professionals may provide recommendations during attorney

Kenneth Miller, a Mennonite pastor, leaves a federal courthouse with his wife after being sentenced in his conviction for aiding international parental kidnapping. His religious beliefs against homosexuality led Miller to help a mother flee the country with her child to avoid sharing custody with her former lesbian partner.

negotiations, they may offer expert testimony in court, or they may act as mediators.

**EXPERT WITNESSES IN CUSTODY DISPUTES** The law directs judges to consider only very general factors in evaluating a child's best interests, including the quality of the child's relationship with each parent, the family environment provided by each parent, each parent's mental health, the relationship between the parents, and the child's expressed wishes, if any (Emery, Sbarra, & Grover, 2005). Evaluating these broad family circumstances and drawing implications for child custody is a precarious task. In fact, some commentators have argued that, because of inexact scientific knowledge, mental health professionals should refrain from ever conducting custody evaluations (O'Donohue & Bradley, 1999).

Others suggest that the problem lies in the system for determining child custody (Emery et al., 2005). The "child's best interests" standard can increase conflict between parents, because the directive is so vague. Virtually any information that makes one parent look bad and the other look good may be construed as helping a parent's case—and people who have been married have much private and potentially damaging information about each other. This is a problem, because conflict between parents is strongly related to maladjustment among children following divorce (Cummings & Davies, 2010; Emery, 1982, 1999b; Grych & Fincham, 1990). Many mental health and legal experts believe they serve children and the legal system better if they help settle custody disputes outside of court (Emery et al., 2005).

**DIVORCE MEDIATION** In *divorce mediation,* parents meet with a neutral third party, who may be a mental health or legal professional, who helps them to identify, negotiate, and ultimately resolve their disputes. The role of mediator is very different from the evaluation role of mental health professionals, and mediation also is a major change in the practice of the law. Mediators adopt a cooperative approach to dispute resolution, treating separated parents as parents rather than as legal adversaries (Emery, 1994, 2011).

Mediation reduces custody hearings, helps parents reach decisions more quickly, and is viewed more favorably by parents than litigation (Emery, 1994; Emery, Matthews, & Kitzmann, 1994; Emery et al., 2005). One randomized trial found that five to six hours of mediation causes nonresidential parents to remain far more involved in their children's lives and work together better *12 years later* (Emery et al., 2001; Sbarra & Emery, 2008). Many states now require mediation as a more "family friendly" forum for dispute resolution. Consider the following brief case study.

### ⟶ Not Fighting for Your Children

Jim and Suzanne had been divorced for two years when they first came to a mediator. The parents were disputing custody of their 8-year-old daughter, Ellen, and 10-year-old son, Will. The parents had maintained an uneasy joint physical custody arrangement. Every other week the children alternated between each of their parents' homes. However, Suzanne recently decided to sue for sole custody. She said she was worried about Will's increasingly difficult behavior and Ellen's lack of activities with her father. Jim argued that Ellen's real concern was his recent remarriage. He said that he was eager to get on with his life with his new wife, Adriana, but Suzanne would not accept her.

Suzanne and Jim were referred to mediation by their lawyers, who urged their clients to avoid renewing the long and contentious negotiations that had surrounded their divorce. Suzanne and Jim had decided on joint custody as a last-minute compromise. They reached this decision literally on the courthouse steps.

The mediator urged Suzanne and Jim to take their children's perspective and, for the children's sake, to try to cooperate as parents even though they were not "friends." In private, the mediator also encouraged Suzanne to face her fears of losing her children to Jim's new family. Speaking to Jim alone, the mediator bluntly told him that, while he may have "moved on," Suzanne would always be a part of his life as the children's mother.

Following several frank discussions about their feelings, preferences, and past problems with joint custody, Suzanne and Jim reached a settlement. They would return to the week-to-week joint physical custody schedule but with a new commitment to communicate better, to support each other's efforts in parenting, and to make the children's routines more consistent across their homes. Adriana came for one of the last mediation sessions. All the adults agreed that Adriana would be an important part of raising Will and Ellen. Still, no one could or wanted to replace Suzanne or Jim as the children's parents.

## Child Abuse

**Child abuse** involves the accidental or intentional infliction of harm to a child due to acts or omissions on the part of an adult responsible for the child's care. Such abuse of children was "discovered" to be a problem only relatively recently. The first child protection efforts in the United States did not begin until 1875. A much publicized case of foster parents who physically beat a young girl in their care led to the founding of the New York Society for the Prevention of Cruelty to Children. The society was given the power to police child abuse, and other states rapidly established similar organizations and legislation (Lazoritz, 1990).

Still, public attention did not consistently focus on child abuse until 1962, when the physician Henry Kempe wrote about the "battered child syndrome." Kempe documented tragic cases of child abuse in which children suffered repeated injuries, fractured bones, and, in a substantial number of cases, death

Over 3 million reports of child abuse or neglect are made in the U.S. every year.

(Kempe et al., 1962). Kempe's influential article prompted legislation that defined child abuse and required physicians to report suspected cases. This reporting requirement continues today, and in most states it extends to include mental health professionals, schoolteachers, and others who have regular contact with children. In fact, mental health professionals not only can, but they must also, break the confidentiality if they suspect child abuse (Melton & Limber, 1989).

Four forms of child abuse generally are distinguished: physical abuse, sexual abuse, neglect, and psychological abuse (American Psychological Association, 1995). *Physical child abuse* involves the intentional use of physically painful and harmful actions. The definition of physical abuse is complicated by the fact that corporal punishments like spanking are widely accepted discipline practices (Emery & Laumann-Billings, 1998; Gershoff, 2002).

*Child sexual abuse* involves sexual contact between an adult and a child. Reports of child sexual abuse have increased astronomically in recent years, as the problem has been fully recognized only since the 1980s (Glaser, 2002; Haugaard & Reppucci, 1988). Although exact estimates are difficult to make, the sexual abuse of children is now known to be far more prevalent than would have been believed a short time ago.

*Child neglect*, the most commonly reported form of child abuse, places children at risk for serious physical or psychological harm by failing to provide basic and expected care. Some children are severely neglected, and they experience extreme failure in their growth and development as a result (Wolfe, 1987). Some children also suffer *psychological abuse*—repeated denigration in the absence of physical harm.

*Munchausen-by-proxy syndrome (MBPS)* is a unique, rare, but potentially very harmful form of physical child abuse that merits special note. In MBPS, a parent feigns, exaggerates, or induces illness in a child. In benign cases, the parent simply fabricates the child's illness; in more serious cases, the parent actually induces illness. One study used covert video surveillance to monitor parents suspected of MBPS (Southall et al., 1997). Of 39 children, video recordings captured 30 parents trying to harm their children through such extreme acts as attempting suffocation, trying to break a child's arm, and attempted poisoning with a disinfectant. Alarmingly, of the 41 siblings of the children, 12 had previously died suddenly and unexpectedly. These results clearly illustrate that MBPS can be a severe and ultimately deadly form of child abuse.

The number of reported cases of child abuse has increased dramatically in the United States since the 1970s and through today. As indicated in Figure 18.2, the number of reports of child abuse made to social service agencies climbed from 669,000 in 1976 to over 3,600,000 in 2009. However, over two-thirds of all reports of abuse are found to be unsubstantiated. One reason for this, according to some critics, is that the concept of abuse and neglect is applied too broadly by primarily white, middle-class

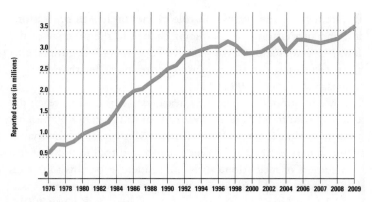

**FIGURE 18.2**

Reports of child abuse made to social service agencies have increased sharply. Experts disagree about what has increased—actual abuse or the awareness and reporting of abuse.

*Source:* Courtesy of the National Center on Child Abuse Prevention and Research.

social workers who are evaluating primarily black, low-income families (Besharov, 1992).

When an allegation of abuse is substantiated, one of the major questions is whether to remove the child from the home. Each year over 100,000 maltreated children are placed in *foster care*, where they live temporarily with another family. Foster care protects children who are in physical danger, but as many as half of all children placed in foster care are in no immediate danger of physical injury (Besharov, 1988). Stable foster care may offer psychological benefits, as well as physical protection (Wald, Carlsmith, & Leiderman, 1988). However, half the children placed in foster care remain there for at least two years, almost one-third are separated from their parents for over six years, and a substantial proportion live in many different foster homes during this time (Besharov, 1998).

Recent federal legislation encourages the adoption of children who are likely to be placed in foster care for long periods of time. However, this raises an even more controversial issue, the *termination of parental rights*, that is, the removal of any right a parent has to care for and supervise his or her child. Obviously, this is an extreme step, and one that the courts take only with great reluctance.

As with child custody, judicial determinations about the disposition of child abuse cases are guided by the child's best interest standard. Psychologists frequently play a role in these legal proceedings by investigating allegations of abuse, making recommendations to the court, and providing treatment to children and families (Becker et al., 1995).

Some have argued that too much effort is devoted to identifying families as abusive, while not enough resources are available to help these families in need (Huntington, 2007). The definition of abuse is applied broadly; consequently, the child protective service system is overwhelmed with investigating report after report (Emery & Laumann-Billings, 2002). In order to allow child protection agencies to offer more support to stressed families, many states are dividing reports of suspected abuse into more and less serious cases. More serious cases are investigated as usual, but social workers offer troubled parents support, counseling, and referral in less serious cases (Emery & Laumann-Billings, 1998). This more family-friendly approach does *not* increase the risk for future abuse. In fact, it reduces recurrence, is liked better by parents, and saves agencies time and money (Loman & Siegel, 2005).

Other evidence shows that multisystemic therapy (see Chapter 16) for child abuse and neglect leads to better child mental health, improved parenting, and fewer out-of-home placements when compared to outpatient treatment (Swenson et al., 2010). Structured interventions that leave maltreated children in the home while supporting effective parenting also show promise for helping families and reducing subsequent abuse (Jouriles et al., 2010). Unless abuse or neglect is serious, we do much better if we try to help distraught families, instead of just policing, labeling, and judging them.

## Professional Responsibilities and the Law

Psychiatrists, clinical psychologists, and social workers all have **professional responsibilities,** obligations to meet the ethical standards of their profession and to uphold the laws of the states in which they practice. The duties of mental health professionals are numerous and varied. Here we focus on two important examples: negligence and confidentiality.

### Professional Negligence and Malpractice

Negligence occurs when a professional fails to perform in a manner that is consistent with the level of skill exercised by other professionals in the field. Simply put, negligence is substandard professional service. Malpractice refers to situations in which professional negligence results in harm to clients or patients. In the law, malpractice is demonstrated when (1) a professional has a duty to conform to a standard of conduct, (2) the professional is negligent in that duty, (3) the professional's client experiences damages or loss, and (4) it is reasonably certain that the negligence caused the damages (Slobogin et al., 2009). When professionals are found to be guilty of malpractice, they are subject to disciplinary action both from their professional organizations and through state licensing boards, as well as to civil suits and possibly criminal actions.

The inappropriate use of medication and negligent treatment are two of the more common reasons for malpractice claims against mental health professionals. Another is the existence of a sexual relationship between therapists and their clients. The ethical codes of the American Psychological Association

and the American Psychiatric Association both prohibit sexual relationships between therapists and their clients. Other claims of professional negligence stem from the failure to prevent suicide, failure to prevent violence against others, and violations of confidentiality. In the future, a new area of professional negligence may become more important: the failure to inform clients about effective treatment alternatives.

### INFORMED CONSENT ON ALTERNATIVE TREATMENTS
Patients may be given a wide range of alternative treatments for the same mental disorder. Unfortunately, the choice of treatment hinges, in part, on chance factors such as the professional's "theoretical orientation" (see Chapter 3). Should mental health professionals be required to reduce this element of chance by informing their patients about alternative treatments and research on their effectiveness?

This issue was raised in *Osheroff* v. *Chestnut Lodge* [62 Md. App. 519, 490 A. 2d. 720 (Md. App. 1985)]. In 1979, Dr. Rafael Osheroff, an internist, admitted himself to Chestnut Lodge, a private psychiatric hospital in Maryland that had long been famous as a center for psychoanalytic psychotherapy. Dr. Osheroff had a history of depression and anxiety, problems that previously had been treated on an outpatient basis with some success using tricyclic antidepressant medication. Apparently, Dr. Osheroff had not been taking his medication prior to his admission to Chestnut Lodge, and his condition had worsened. He was diagnosed by hospital staff as suffering primarily from a narcissistic personality disorder and secondarily from manic–depressive illness (Klerman, 1990b; Malcolm, 1987).

Hospital staff did not offer medication to Dr. Osheroff during his hospitalization. They hoped that, through therapy, he could achieve what they viewed as "more basic" changes in his personality. Dr. Osheroff was seen in individual psychoanalytic psychotherapy four times a week, and he participated in group therapy as well. During Dr. Osheroff's seven months of hospitalization, his condition did not improve and actually may have deteriorated somewhat. After this time, his family discharged him from Chestnut Lodge and admitted him to another private psychiatric hospital, Silver Hill in Connecticut. At Silver Hill, Dr. Osheroff was diagnosed as suffering from a psychotic depressive reaction, and he was treated with phenothiazines and tricyclic antidepressants. He began to improve within three weeks after treatment began, and he was discharged from the hospital within three months. Although he continued to experience some problems following his discharge, Dr. Osheroff was able to resume his medical practice with the help of outpatient psychotherapy and antidepressants (Klerman, 1990b; Malcolm, 1987).

In 1982, Dr. Osheroff sued Chestnut Lodge for negligence. His claim stated that Chestnut Lodge had misdiagnosed his condition, failed to offer appropriate treatment, and failed to offer him informed consent about treatment alternatives (Malcolm, 1987). He argued that research available in 1979 provided clear support for the use of medication in the treatment of severe depression but offered no support for the use of psychoanalytic psychotherapy in the treatment of either depression or narcissistic personality disorder. As required by state law in Maryland, the matter was first heard by an arbitration panel. The panel initially awarded Dr. Osheroff $250,000 in damages, but it later reduced the amount of the award. Both sides appealed the decision of the arbitration board, but the matter was eventually settled out of court (Klerman, 1990b).

The private settlement of this case limits its precedent-setting value. Nevertheless, it suggests that mental health professionals will be held to increasingly higher standards in offering alternative treatments, or at least in informing patients about the risks and benefits of various treatments. As researchers demonstrate that certain approaches are more or less effective in treating particular disorders, offering informed consent about treatment alternatives is likely to become a routine practice for mental health professionals. *Informed consent* includes providing accurate information about risks and benefits in an understandable and noncoercive manner.

## Confidentiality

**Confidentiality**—the ethical obligation not to reveal private communications—is basic to psychotherapy. The therapist's guarantee of privacy is essential to encouraging clients to disclose difficult information, and the maintenance of confidentiality with past clients is essential to gaining the trust of future clients. For these reasons, confidentiality standards are a part of the professional ethics of all of the major mental health professions.

Despite the overriding importance of confidentiality, mental health professionals sometimes may be compelled by law to reveal confidential information. For example, all states require mental health professionals to break confidentiality and report suspected cases of child abuse. This requirement can create dilemmas for therapists (Smith & Meyer, 1985). Must a therapist make the limits on confidentiality clear before beginning therapy? If therapists tell their clients that their disclosures of child abuse will be reported, does this encourage clients to be something less than honest? Does reporting child abuse undermine the therapeutic relationship that might benefit an abused child?

Confidentiality also must be broken when clients are dangerous to themselves or others, so that civil commitment can proceed. The influential case of *Tarasoff* v. *Regents of the University of California* [551 P.2d 334 (1976)] identified another obligation that therapists may assume when a client expresses violent intentions: the duty to warn the potential victim.

**THE DUTY TO PROTECT** On October 27, 1969, a young woman named Tatiana Tarasoff was killed by Prosenjit Poddar, a foreign student at the University of California at Berkeley. Poddar had pursued a romantic relationship with Tarasoff, but after having been repeatedly rejected by her, he sought treatment at the Berkeley student health facility. Poddar was diagnosed as suffering from paranoid schizophrenia, and the clinical psychologist who treated Poddar concluded that he was dangerous to himself and others. After consulting with two psychiatrists, the psychologist decided to pursue civil commitment. He notified the campus police of his concerns and asked them to detain Poddar for the purpose of an emergency commitment. The police concluded that Poddar was not dangerous, however, and released him after he agreed to stay away from Tarasoff. Poddar subsequently discontinued therapy, and no one notified Tarasoff that Poddar posed a threat to her life. Poddar had never mentioned Tatiana Tarasoff by name, but the information he relayed to the psychologist was sufficient to deduce her identity. Two months after the police had questioned him, Poddar murdered Tarasoff after being rejected by her once more.

Tarasoff's parents sued the university, the therapists, and the police for negligence. The California Supreme Court ruled that the defendants were liable for failing to warn the woman of the impending danger. Subsequent California cases and legislation altered the *duty to warn* potential victims to a more general *duty to protect*, which may involve warning but alternatively might involve protective actions like hospitalizing the potentially dangerous patient (Weinstock et al., 2006).

The *Tarasoff* case prompted many states to enact laws outlining therapists' duty to protect potential victims of violence (Appelbaum, 1994). Still, the issues raised by *Tarasoff* are far from resolved. If he or she has a client with AIDS, must a psychologist warn unwitting sexual partners about the risk? In the case of the duty to protect, as with other issues in psychology and the law, psychologists sometimes must walk a thin line between their professional responsibilities and their legal obligations.

Tatiana Tarasoff and Prosenjit Poddar, the man who killed her. The California Supreme Court ruled that Poddar's therapist should have warned Tarasoff that her life might be in danger.

Getting help for people with emotional disorders sometimes involves challenging societal and legal obstacles. Advocacy can be a way of giving help as well as ensuring that you and those you care for can get help when it is needed. For serious mental illness, the National Alliance for the Mentally Ill (NAMI) is the largest and most effective national advocacy organization. In addition to its national efforts, you may be able to find a local chapter of NAMI in your community. Another advocacy group is the Judge David L. Bazelon Center for Mental Health Law. The Bazelon Center tracks funding, legislation, and litigation, and it offers legal advice and assistance in selected cases. The center's website gives information on a number of their pressing priorities such as mental health and gun violence, improving mental health treatment systems, and increasing the availability of services for underserved populations (children, the aged). The American Bar Association's Commission on Mental and Physical Disability Law also collects and offers a wealth of information on mental health law and the rights of people disabled by mental illness.

An excellent book on these topics is *The Rights of People with Mental Disabilities: The Authoritative ACLU Guide to the Rights of People with Mental Illness and Mental Retardation*, by Robert Levy and Leonard Rubenstein. Another book (and author) that we highly recommend is E. Fuller Torrey's *Out of the Shadows: Confronting America's Mental Illness Crisis*.

Mental health advocacy involves individual as well as organized efforts. We encourage you to advocate directly in any number of small ways. You can educate yourself and others about the needs of the mentally ill. In everyday interactions, you can stand up for what you believe is right and just in our society's response to the immense problem of mental illness. You can respond receptively to agencies and individuals in your community. Advocacy, like therapy, begins by recognizing that the person with a psychological disorder is, first and foremost, a person.

# 18 Summary

The **insanity defense** says that you are not legally responsible for your actions, usually based on one of two grounds: A mental disease or defect either (a) prevents you from knowing the wrongfulness of your actions or (b) an irresistible impulse makes it impossible to control your actions.

**Competence** is the defendant's ability to understand legal proceedings and to participate in his or her own defense.

**Civil commitment** generally is based on three grounds: (1) inability to care for self, (2) dangerous to self, and (3) dangerous to others.

The right to treatment indicates that hospitalized patients must receive therapy and not just custodial care.

The right to treatment in the least restrictive environment indicates that therapy should be provided in community settings when it is possible and appropriate.

The right to refuse treatment indicates that patients cannot be forced to receive certain treatments without **informed consent** or a careful substituted judgment.

**Deinstitutionalization** involves caring for many of the mentally ill and intellectually disabled in their community rather than in large mental hospitals.

**Outpatient commitment** may help to balance concerns about requiring treatment while protecting liberties.

**Advance psychiatric directives** are legal instruments where patients declare their treatment preferences, or appoint a surrogate to make decisions for them, should they become psychotic or otherwise are unable to make sound decisions.

**Child custody** decisions involve determinations about both physical custody, where children will live, and legal custody, how parents will make childrearing decisions.

**Child abuse** may involve physical abuse, sexual abuse, neglect, or psychological abuse.

**Confidentiality** is a key **professional responsibility** for mental health professionals, who must meet the ethical standards of their profession and to uphold the law.

## The Big Picture

# critical thinking review

**18.1** Is "insanity" the same thing as "mental illness"?
The idea behind the insanity defense—that mental disability should limit criminal responsibility—dates to ancient Greek and Hebrew traditions . . . (see page 492).

**18.2** When and why can someone be hospitalized involuntarily?
U.S. law contains two broad rationales for involuntary hospitalization. The first is based on . . . the philosophy that the government has a humanitarian responsibility to care for its weaker members. . . . The second rationale is based on the state's police power . . . (see page 501).

**18.3** How can being wrong two times out of three beat a coin flip?
U.S. Supreme Court Justice Harry Blackmun wrongly claimed that a coin flip would be more accurate than a clinical prediction that is wrong two out of three times . . . (see page 502).

**18.4** What rights do mental patients retain when hospitalized against their will?
Several important court cases clarified the rights of patients committed to a mental hospital. These include the right to treatment, the right to treatment in the least restrictive environment, and the right to refuse treatment . . . (see page 504).

**18.5** What is deinstitutionalization, and how has it worked?
The deinstitutionalization movement embraced the philosophy that many patients can be better cared for in their community than in large mental hospitals . . . (see page 506).

**18.6** What custody arrangements are in children's "best interests"?
The guiding principle in custody and abuse cases is that judges must make decisions according to the "child's best interest." This may sound laudable, but the law does not clearly define "best" . . . (see page 508).

**18.7** When must therapists break confidentiality?
Despite the overriding importance of confidentiality, mental health professionals sometimes may be compelled by law to reveal confidential information . . . (see page 512).

# key terms

advance psychiatric
  directives  506
base rates  502
child abuse  509
child custody  508

civil commitment  501
competence  495
confidentiality  512
criminal responsibility  492
deinstitutionalization  507

expert witness  491
informed consent  506
insanity  492
insanity defense  492
outpatient commitment  506

professional
  responsibilities  511

# glossary

## A

**Abnormal psychology** The application of psychological science to the study of mental disorders. Includes investigation of the causes and treatment of psychopathological conditions.

**Acquired immune deficiency syndrome (AIDS)** A disease caused by the human immunodeficiency virus (HIV) that attacks the immune system and leaves the patient susceptible to unusual infections.

**Actuarial interpretation** Analysis of test results based on an explicit set of rules derived from empirical research.

**Acute stress disorder (ASD)** A category of mental disorder in DSM-5 that is defined as a reaction occurring within four weeks of a traumatic event and is characterized by dissociative symptoms, reexperiencing, avoidance, and marked anxiety or arousal. Contrasts with posttraumatic stress disorder, which either lasts longer or has a delayed onset.

**Adjustment disorder** A DSM-5 classification designating the development of clinically significant symptoms in response to stress in which the symptoms are not severe enough to warrant classification as another mental disorder.

**Advance psychiatric directives** A legal instrument that can be used by someone suffering from a mental illness to declare their treatment preferences, or to appoint a surrogate to make decisions for them, should they become psychotic or otherwise are unable to make sound decisions.

**Affect** The pattern of observable behaviors that are associated with subjective feelings. People express affect through changes in their facial expressions, the pitch of their voices, and their hand and body movements.

**Ageism** A number of misconceptions and prejudices about aging and older adults.

**Agnosia** ("perception without meaning") The inability to identify objects. The person's sensory functions are unimpaired, but he or she is unable to recognize the source of stimulation.

**Agoraphobia** An exaggerated fear of being in situations from which escape might be difficult. Literally means "fear of the marketplace" and is sometimes described as fear of public spaces.

**Alcohol use disorder** A problematic pattern of alcohol use leading to clinically significant impairment or distress.

**Allegiance effect** A characterization of psychotherapy outcome research such that investigators commonly find the most effective treatment is the one to which they hold a theoretical allegiance.

**Alzheimer's disease** A form of dementia in which cognitive impairment appears gradually and deterioration is progressive. A definite diagnosis of Alzheimer's disease requires the observation of two specific types of brain lesions: neurofibrillary tangles and senile plaques.

**Amyloid plaques** A central core of homogeneous protein material know as beta-amyloid found in large numbers in the cerebral cortex of patients with Alzheimer's disease, but they are not unique to that condition.

**Analogue study** A research procedure in which the investigator studies behaviors that resemble mental disorders or isolated features of mental disorders. Usually employed in situations in which the investigator hopes to gain greater experimental control over the independent variable.

**Anhedonia** The inability to experience pleasure. In contrast to blunted affect, which refers to the lack of outward expression, anhedonia is a lack of positive subjective feelings.

**Anorexia nervosa** A type of eating disorder characterized by the refusal to maintain a minimally normal body weight along with other symptoms related to body image.

**Anterograde amnesia** The inability to learn or remember new material after a particular point in time.

**Antipsychotic drugs** Various forms of medication that have a beneficial effect on positive symptoms (hallucinations and delusions) of psychosis and psychotic disorganization (e.g., disorganized speech). The effect of first generation antipsychotic drugs depends largely on the blockade of receptors in dopamine pathways in the brain. Second-generation antipsychotics have a much broader effect on different neurotransmitters. All antipsychotic drugs have negative side effects, including motor side effects such as tardive dyskinesia.

**Antisocial personality disorder** A pervasive and persistent disregard for, and frequent violation of, the rights of other people. Also known as *psychopathy*. In DSM-5, it is defined in terms of a persistent pattern of irresponsible and antisocial behavior that begins during childhood or adolescence and continues into the adult years.

**Anxiety** A diffuse emotional reaction that is out of proportion to threats from the environment. Rather than being directed toward the person's present problems, anxiety is typically associated with the anticipation of future problems.

**Anxious attachments** Insecure relationships in which infants or children show ambivalence about seeking reassurance or security from attachment figures.

**Aphasia** The loss or impairment of previously acquired abilities in language comprehension or production that cannot be explained by sensory or motor defects or by diffuse brain dysfunction.

**Apraxia** The loss of a previously acquired ability to perform purposeful movements in response to verbal commands. The problem cannot be explained by muscle weakness or simple incoordination.

**Asperger's disorder** A subtype of pervasive developmental disorder that is identical to autism (oddities in social interaction, stereotyped behavior) with the exception that there is no clinically significant delay in language.

**Assessment** The process of gathering and organizing information about a person's behavior.

**Attachments** Selective bonds that develop between infants and their caregivers, usually their parents, and are theorized to be related to later development. Analogous to the process of imprinting, which has been observed in many animals.

**Attention-deficit/hyperactivity disorder (ADHD)** A psychological disorder of childhood characterized by hyperactivity, inattention, and impulsivity. Typically has an onset by the early school years.

**Attributions** Perceived causes; people's beliefs about cause–effect relations.

**Authoritative parenting** A style of parenting that is both loving and firm and is often used by parents of well-adjusted children.

**Autism spectrum disorder (ASD)** A range of psychological problems that share characteristics with autism, including problems in social relationships, communication, and unusual preferences and behaviors. Autistic spectrum disorders, called Pervasive Developmental Disorders in DSM-5-TR, have an onset at birth or very early in life.

**Autonomic nervous system** The division of the peripheral nervous system that regulates the functions of various bodily organs such as the heart and stomach. The actions of the autonomic nervous system are largely involuntary, and it has two branches, the sympathetic and parasympathetic nervous systems.

**Avoidant personality disorder** An enduring pattern of thinking and behavior that is characterized by pervasive social discomfort, fear of negative evaluation, and timidity. People with this disorder tend to be socially isolated outside of family circles. They want to be liked by others, but are easily hurt by even minimal signs of disapproval from other people.

**Avolition** A psychological state characterized by general lack of drive or motivation to pursue meaningful goals. One of the negative symptoms of schizophrenia. The person may have little interest in social or occupational activities.

## B

**Barbiturates** Drugs that depress activities of the central nervous system; used mostly for sedation.

**Base rates** Population frequencies. Relative base rates set statistical limits on the degree to which two variables can be associated with each other.

**Behavioral medicine** A multidisciplinary field concerned with studying and treating the behavioral components of physical illness.

**Behavior genetics** The study of broad genetic influences on individual differences in normal and abnormal behavior, usually by studying twins or other family members who differ in terms of shared genes and/or experience. Behavior genetic studies also provide information on environmental contributions to behavior.

**Benzodiazepines** Group of drugs that have potent hypnotic, sedative, and anxiolytic action (also called *antianxiety drugs*).

**Bereavement** Grieving in response to the death of a loved one.

**Binge eating** Eating an amount of food in a fixed period of time that is clearly larger than most people would eat under similar circumstances. One part of the eating disorder of bulimia nervosa.

**Binge eating disorder** A controversial diagnosis defined by repeated episodes of binge eating but in the absence of compensatory behavior; included in an appendix of DSM-5.

**Biofeedback** Behavioral medicine treatment that uses laboratory equipment to monitor physiological processes (that generally occur outside of conscious awareness) and provide feedback about them. Hypothesized to help patients to gain conscious control over problematic physiological processes such as hypertension.

**Biopsychosocial model** A view of the etiology of mental disorders that assumes that disorders can best be understood in terms of the interaction of biological, psychological, and social systems.

**Bipolar disorder** A form of mood disorder in which the person experiences episodes of mania as well as episodes of depression.

**Body dysmorphic disorder** A type of somatoform disorder characterized by constant preoccupation with some imagined defect in physical appearance.

**Body image** A cognitive and affective evaluation of one's weight and shape, often a critical one.

**Borderline personality disorder** An enduring pattern of thinking and behavior whose essential feature is a pervasive instability in mood, self-image, and interpersonal relationships. Manifestations of this disorder include frantic efforts to avoid real or imagined abandonment. People who fit this description frequently hold opinions of significant others that vacillate between unrealistically positive and negative extremes.

**Brief psychotic disorder** A diagnostic category in DSM-5 that includes people who exhibit psychotic symptoms for at least one day but no more than one month. After the symptoms

are resolved, the person returns to the same level of functioning that had been achieved prior to the psychotic episode.

**Bulimia nervosa** A type of eating disorder characterized by repeated episodes of binge eating followed by inappropriate compensatory behaviors (such as self-induced vomiting) together with other symptoms related to eating and body image.

## C

**Cardiovascular disease (CVD)** A group of disorders that affect the heart and circulatory system. Hypertension (high blood pressure) and coronary heart disease are the most important forms of CVD.

**Case study** A careful description and analysis of the problems experienced by one person.

**Categorical approach to classification** A view of classification based on the assumption that there are qualitative differences between normal and abnormal behavior as well as between one form of abnormal behavior and other forms of abnormal behavior.

**Cerebral cortex** The uneven surface of the brain that lies just underneath the skull and controls and integrates sophisticated memory, sensory, and motor functions.

**Cerebral hemispheres** The two major structures of the forebrain and the site of most sensory, emotional, and cognitive processes. The functions of the cerebral hemispheres are lateralized. In general, the left cerebral hemisphere is involved in language and related functions, and the right side is involved in spatial organization and analysis.

**Child abuse** A legal decision that a parent or other responsible adult has inflicted damage or offered inadequate care to a child; may include physical abuse, sexual abuse, neglect, and psychological abuse.

**Child custody** A legal decision, especially common in separation and divorce, that involves determining where children will reside and how parents will share legal rights and responsibilities for child rearing.

**Chromosomes** Chainlike structures found in the nucleus of cells that carry genes and information about heredity. Humans normally have 23 pairs of chromosomes.

**Civil commitment** The involuntary hospitalization of the mentally ill; the decision typically is justified based on dangerousness to self or others (or inability to care for self).

**Classical conditioning** Pavlov's form of learning through association. A conditioned response eventually is elicited by a conditioned stimulus after repeated pairings with an unconditioned stimulus (which produces an unconditioned response).

**Classification system** A system for grouping together objects or organisms that share certain

properties in common. In psychopathology, the set of categories in DSM-5 that describes mental disorders.

**Client-centered therapy** Carl Rogers's humanistic therapy that follows the client's lead. Therapists offer warmth, empathy, and genuineness, but clients solve their own problems.

**Clinical depression** A syndrome of depression in which a depressed mood is accompanied by several other symptoms, such as fatigue, loss of energy, difficulty in sleeping, and changes in appetite. Clinical depression also involves a variety of changes in thinking and overt behavior.

**Clinical psychology** The profession and academic discipline that is concerned with the application of psychological science to the assessment and treatment of mental disorders.

**Coercion** A pattern of interaction in which unwitting parents positively reinforce children's misbehavior (by giving in to their demands), and children negatively reinforce parents' capitulation (by ending their obnoxious behavior).

**Cognitive behavior therapy** The expansion of the scope of behavior therapy to include cognition and research on human information processing. Includes various general techniques, such as Beck's cognitive therapy and Ellis's RET.

**Cognitive therapy** A psychotherapy technique and important part of cognitive behavior therapy that was developed by Aaron Beck specifically as a treatment. Beck's cognitive therapy involves challenging negative cognitive distortions through a technique called *collaborative empiricism*.

**Cohort** A group whose members share some feature in common, particularly their date of birth.

**Cohort effects** Differences that distinguish one cohort from another. Cohorts share some feature in common, especially their date of birth, and cohort effects often distinguish people born in one time period (e.g., the 1960s) from those born in another.

**Comorbidity** The simultaneous manifestation of more than one disorder.

**Competence** Defendants' ability to understand legal proceedings and act rationally in relation to them. Competence evaluations can take place at different points in the legal process, but competence to stand trial (the ability to participate in one's own defense) is particularly important.

**Compulsions** Repetitive, ritualistic behaviors that are aimed at the reduction of anxiety and distress or the prevention of some dreaded event. Compulsions are considered by the person to be senseless or irrational. The person feels compelled to perform the compulsion; he or she attempts to resist but cannot.

**Concordance rate** The rate, often a percentage, at which two related individuals are found to both have a disorder or problem or neither has a disorder or problem, i.e., they are concordant. In discordant pairs, only one individual is disordered. Concordance rates often are computed for twin pairs.

**Conduct disorder (CD)** A psychological disorder of childhood that is defined primarily by behavior that is illegal as well as antisocial.

**Confidentiality** The ethical obligation not to reveal private communications in psychotherapy and in other professional contacts between mental health professionals and their clients.

**Construct validity** The overall strength of the network of relations that have been observed among variables that are used to define a construct. The extent to which the construct possesses some systematic meaning.

**Control group** The group of participants in an experiment that receives no treatment or perhaps a placebo treatment. Participants in the control group are compared with participants in the experimental group (who are given an active treatment).

**Conversion disorder** A type of somatoform disorder characterized by physical symptoms that often mimic those found in neurological diseases, such as blindness, numbing, or paralysis. The symptoms often make no anatomic sense.

**Coronary heart disease (CHD)** A group of diseases of the heart that includes angina pectoris (chest pain) and myocardial infarction (heart attack).

**Correlational study** A scientific research method in which the relation between two factors (their co-relation) is studied in a systematic fashion. Has the advantage of practicality, as correlations between many variables can be studied in the real world, but also has the disadvantage that "correlation does not mean causation."

**Correlation coefficient** A number that always ranges between −1.00 and +1.00 and indicates the strength and direction of the relation between two variables. A higher absolute value indicates a stronger relation, while a correlation coefficient of 0 indicates no relation. The sign indicates the direction of the correlation.

**Cortisol** A corticosteroid secreted by the adrenal cortex. Cortisol is known as the "stress hormone" because its release is so closely linked with stress.

**Couple therapy** Partners who are involved in an intimate relationship are seen together in psychotherapy; sometimes called *marital therapy* or *marriage counseling*. Improving communication and negotiation are common goals.

**Criminal responsibility** A legal concept that holds a person responsible for committing a crime if he or she (a) has been proven to have committed the act and (b) was legally sane at the time.

**Cross-cultural psychology** The scientific study of ways that human behavior and mental processes are influenced by social and cultural factors.

**Cross-sectional study** A research design in which subjects are studied only at one point in time. (Contrast with *longitudinal study*.)

**Culture** The shared way of life of a group of people; a complex system of accumulated knowledge that helps the people in a particular society adapt to their environment.

**Cultural-familial retardation** Typically, mild mental retardation that runs in families and is linked with poverty. Thought to be the most common cause of mental retardation. There is controversy about the relative roles of genes or psychosocial disadvantage.

**Cultural concepts of distress** Patterns of erratic or unusual thinking and behavior that have been identified in diverse societies around the world and do not fit easily into the other diagnostic categories that are listed in the main body of DSM-5.

**Cyclothymia** A chronic, less severe form of bipolar disorder. The bipolar equivalent of dysthymia.

# D

**Defense mechanisms** Unconscious processes that service the ego and reduce conscious anxiety by distorting anxiety-producing memories, emotions, and impulses—for example, projection, displacement, or rationalization.

**Deinstitutionalization** The movement to treat the mentally ill and mentally retarded in communities rather than in large mental hospitals.

**Delayed Ejaculation** A form of sexual dysfunction, in which it takes an extended period of sexual stimulation for a man to reach orgasm. Some men with this condition are unable to ejaculate at all.

**Delirium** A confusional state that develops over a short period of time and is often associated with agitation and hyperactivity. The primary symptom is clouding of consciousness or reduced awareness of one's surroundings.

**Delusions** Obviously false and idiosyncratic beliefs that are rigidly held in spite of their preposterous nature.

**Delusional disorder** Describes persons who do not meet the full symptomatic criteria for schizophrenia, but who are preoccupied for at least one month with delusions that are not bizarre.

**Dementia** A gradually worsening loss of memory and related cognitive functions, including the use of language as well as reasoning and decision making.

**Dementia with Lewy bodies (DLB)** A form of progressive dementia in which the central feature is progressive cognitive decline, combined with three additional defining features: (1) pronounced "fluctuations" in alertness and attention, such as frequent drowsiness, lethargy, lengthy periods of time spent staring into space, or disorganized speech; (2) recurrent visual hallucinations; and (3) parkinsonian motor symptoms, such as rigidity and the loss of spontaneous movement.

**Dependent personality disorder** An enduring pattern of dependent and submissive behavior. These people are exceedingly dependent on other people for advice and reassurance. Often unable to make everyday decisions on their own, they feel anxious and helpless when they are alone.

**Dependent variable** The outcome that is hypothesized to vary according to manipulations of the independent variable in an experiment.

**Depersonalization/derealization disorder** A type of dissociative disorder characterized by severe and persistent feelings of being detached from oneself (depersonalization experiences). For example, the repeated and profound sensation of floating above your body and observing yourself act.

**Depressed mood** Depressed feelings such as of disappointment and despair, but which are not yet necessarily part of a clinical syndrome.

**Depression** Can refer to a *symptom* (subjective feelings of sadness), a *mood* (sustained and pervasive feelings of despair), or to a clinical *syndrome* (in which the presence of a depressed mood is accompanied by several additional symptoms, such as fatigue, loss of energy, sleeping difficulties, and appetite changes).

**Depressive Disorders** A category of psychopathology that includes various conditions that involve episodes of depressed mood and associated symptoms that include cognitive symptoms (such as feelings of guilt, difficulty concentrating, and thoughts of suicide) and somatic symptoms (such as changes in appetite, sleep problems, and loss of energy).

**Detoxification** The process of short-term medical care (medication, rest, diets, fluids, etc.) during removal of a drug upon which a person has become dependent. The aim is to minimize withdrawal symptoms.

**Developmental deviation** Significant departures from age-appropriate norms in some specific area of functioning. Some developmental deviations are considered disorders in their own right.

**Developmental norms** Behavior that is typical for children of a given age.

**Developmental psychopathology** An approach to abnormal psychology that emphasizes the importance of normal development to understanding abnormal behavior.

**Developmental stages** Distinct periods of development focused on certain central "tasks" and marked by boundaries defined by changing age or social expectations.

**Diagnosis**  The process of determining the nature of a person's disorder. In the case of psychopathology, deciding that a person fits into a particular diagnostic category, such as schizophrenia or major depressive disorder.

**Diathesis**  A predisposition to disorder. Also known as *vulnerability*. A diathesis only causes abnormal behavior when it is combined with stress or a challenging experience.

**Dimensional approach to classification**  A view of classification based on the assumption that behavior is distributed on a continuum from normal to abnormal. Also includes the assumption that differences between one type of behavior and another are quantitative rather than qualitative in nature.

**Diminished emotional expression (also known as blunted affect)**  A flattening or restriction of the person's nonverbal display of emotional responses. Blunted patients fail to exhibit signs of emotion or feeling. One of the negative symptoms of schizophrenia.

**Disorganized speech**  (also known as *formal thought disorder*) Severe disruptions of verbal communication, involving the form of the person's speech.

**Dissociation**  The separation of mental processes such as memory or consciousness that normally are integrated. Normal dissociative experiences include fleeting feelings of unreality and *déjà vu* experiences—the feeling that an event has happened before. Extreme dissociative experiences characterize dissociative disorders.

**Dissociative amnesia**  A type of dissociative disorder characterized by the sudden inability to recall extensive and important personal information. The onset often is sudden and may occur in response to trauma or extreme stress.

**Dissociative disorders**  A category of psychological disorders characterized by persistent, maladaptive disruptions in the integration of memory, consciousness, or identity. Examples include dissociative fugue and dissociative identity disorder (multiple personality).

**Dissociative fugue**  A rare dissociative disorder characterized by sudden, unplanned travel, the inability to remember details about the past, and confusion about identity or the assumption of a new identity. The onset typically follows a traumatic event.

**Dissociative identity disorder (DID)**  An unusual dissociative disorder characterized by the existence of two or more distinct personalities in a single individual (also known as *multiple personality disorder*). At least two personalities repeatedly take control over the person's behavior, and some personalities have limited or no memory of the other.

**Dizygotic (DZ) twins**  Fraternal twins produced from separate fertilized eggs. Like all siblings, DZ twins share an average of 50 percent of their genes.

**Dominance**  The hierarchical ordering of a social group into more and less powerful members. Dominance rankings are indexed by the availability of uncontested privileges.

**Down syndrome**  A chromosomal disorder that is the most common known biological cause of mental retardation. It is caused by an extra chromosome (usually on the 21st pair) and associated with a characteristic physical appearance.

**Dualism**  The philosophical view that the mind and body are separate. Dates to the writings of the philosopher René Descartes, who attempted to balance the dominant religious views of his times with emerging scientific reasoning. Descartes argued that many human functions have biological explanations, but some human experiences have no somatic representation. Thus, he argued for a distinction—a dualism—between mind and body.

**Dysphoric**  An unpleasant or uncomfortable mood, often associated with disorders such as major depression, dysthymia, and various forms of anxiety disorders. The opposite of euphoric.

**Dysthymia**  One of the mood disorders; a form of mild depression characterized by a chronic course (the person is seldom without symptoms).

# E

**Eating disorders**  A category of psychological disorders characterized by severe disturbances in eating behavior, specifically anorexia nervosa and bulimia nervosa.

**Ego**  One of Freud's three central personality structures. In Freudian theory, the ego must deal with reality as it attempts to fulfill id impulses as well as superego demands. The ego operates on the reality principle, and much of the ego resides in conscious awareness.

**Electroconvulsive therapy (ECT)**  A treatment that involves the deliberate induction of a convulsion by passing electricity through one or both hemispheres of the brain. Modern ECT uses restraints, medication, and carefully controlled electrical stimulation to minimize adverse consequences. Can be an effective treatment for severe depression, especially following the failure of other approaches.

**Emotions**  States of arousal that are defined by subjective feeling states, such as sadness, anger, and disgust. Emotions are often accompanied by physiological changes, such as in heart rate and respiration rate.

**Emotion-focused coping**  Internally oriented coping in an attempt to alter one's emotional or cognitive responses to a stressor.

**Emotion regulation**  The process of learning to control powerful emotions according to the demands of a situation. Children learn to regulate their emotions initially through interactions with their parents and others in their social world, and eventually learn to regulate emotions on their own.

**Empathy**  Emotional understanding. Empathy involves understanding others' unique feelings and perspectives. Highlighted by Rogers but basic to most forms of psychotherapy.

**Endocrine system**  A collection of glands found at various locations throughout the body, including the ovaries or testes and the pituitary, thyroid, and adrenal glands. Releases hormones that sometimes act as neuromodulators and affect responses to stress. Also important in physical growth and development.

**Endorphins**  The term is a contraction formed from the words *endogenous* (meaning "within") and *morphine*. Endorphins are relatively short chains of amino acids, or neuropeptides, that are naturally synthesized in the brain and are closely related to morphine (an opioid) in terms of their pharmacological properties.

**Epidemiology**  The scientific study of the frequency and distribution of disorders within a population.

**Erectile Dysfunction**  A form of sexual dysfunction in men, involving persistent or recurrent inability to attain, or maintain until completion of sexual activity, an adequate erection.

**Etiology**  The causes or origins of a disorder.

**Eugenics**  The very controversial and widely discredited movement to improve the human stock by selectively breeding "desirable" characteristics (or individuals or races) and preventing "undesirable" characteristics (or individuals or races) from reproducing.

**Euphoria**  An exaggerated feeling of physical and emotional well-being, typically associated with manic episodes in bipolar mood disorder.

**Evolutionary psychology**  The application of the principles of evolution to understanding the mind and behavior and identifying species-typical characteristics, that is, genetically influenced traits that people or animals share as a part of their nature. Evolutionary psychologists assume that animal and human psychology, like animal and human anatomy, have evolved and share similarities.

**Exhibitionistic disorder**  One of the paraphilic disorders, characterized by recurrent, intense sexual urges involving exposing one's genitals to an unsuspecting stranger.

**Experiment**  A powerful scientific method that allows researchers to determine cause-and-effect relations. Key elements include random assignment, the manipulation of the independent variable, and careful measurement of the dependent variable.

**Experimental group**  The group of participants in an experiment who receives a treatment that is hypothesized to cause some measured effect. Participants in the experimental group are compared with untreated participants in a control group.

**Expert witness** An individual stipulated as an expert on some subject matter who, because of his or her expertise, is allowed to testify about matters of opinion and not just matters of fact. For example, mental health professionals may serve as expert witnesses concerning a defendant's sanity.

**Expressed emotion (EE)** A concept that refers to a collection of negative or intrusive attitudes sometimes displayed by relatives of patients who are being treated for a disorder. If at least one of a patient's relatives is hostile, critical, or emotionally overinvolved, the family environment typically is considered high in expressed emotion.

**Externalizing disorders** An empirically derived category of disruptive child behavior problems that create problems for the external world (e.g., attention-deficit/hyperactivity disorder).

**Extinction** The gradual elimination of a response when learning conditions change. In classical conditioning, extinction occurs when a conditioned stimulus no longer is paired with an unconditioned stimulus. In operant conditioning, extinction occurs when the contingent is removed between behavior and its consequences.

# F

**Factitious disorder** A feigned condition that, unlike malingering, is motivated by a desire to assume the sick role, not by a desire for external gain.

**Family life cycle** The developmental course of family relationships throughout life; most family life cycle theories mark stages and transitions with major changes in family relationships and membership.

**Family therapy** Treatment that might include two, three, or more family members in the psychotherapy sessions. Improving communication and negotiation are common goals, although family therapy also may be used to help well members adjust to a family member's illness.

**Fear** An unpleasant emotional reaction experienced in the face of real, immediate danger. It builds quickly in intensity and helps to organize the person's responses to threats from the environment.

**Fetal alcohol syndrome** A disorder caused by heavy maternal alcohol consumption and repeated exposure of the developing fetus to alcohol. Infants have retarded physical development, a small head, narrow eyes, cardiac defects, and cognitive impairments. Intellectual functioning ranges from mild mental retardation to intelligence with learning disabilities.

**Fetishistic disorder** One form of paraphilic disorder, in which the individual experiences recurrent, intense sexual urges involving touching and rubbing against a nonconsenting person; the associated problem behaviors often take place in crowded trains, buses, and elevators

**Fight-or-flight response** A response to a threat in which psychophysiological reactions mobilize the body to take action against danger.

**Flashbacks** Reexperienced memories of past events, particularly as occurs in posttraumatic stress disorder or following use of hallucinogenic drugs.

**Fragile-X syndrome** The second most common known biological cause of mental retardation. Transmitted genetically and indicated by a weakening or break on one arm of the X sex chromosome.

**Frotteuristic disorder** One of the paraphilic disorders, characterized by recurrent, intense sexual urges involving touching and rubbing against a nonconsenting person; it often takes place in croded trains, buses, and elevators.

# G

**Gender identity** A person's sense of himself or herself as being either male or female.

**Gender roles** Roles associated with social expectations about gendered behavior, for example, "masculine" or "feminine" activities.

**Gene–environment correlation** The empirical and theoretical observation that experience often, perhaps always, is correlated with genetic makeup. Genes influence personality and other characteristics, and these traits affect the environment parents provide children and the environments people seek or responses they elicit from others. Therefore, experience is associated with genes, and studies of environments are confounded by this correlation.

**Gene–environment interaction** Genetic risk and an environmental experience working together to produce a given outcome. Many psychological disorders are assumed to be caused by such combinations of genetic risk and difficult experience.

**General adaptation syndrome (GAS)** Selye's three stages in reaction to stress: alarm, resistance, and exhaustion.

**Generalization** Making accurate statements that extend beyond a specific sample to a larger population.

**Generalized anxiety disorder (GAD)** One of the anxiety disorders, which is characterized by excessive and uncontrollable worry about a number of events or activities (such as work or school performance) and associated with symptoms of arousal (such as restlessness, muscle tension, and sleep disturbance).

**Genes** Ultramicroscopic units of DNA that carry information about heredity. Located on the chromosomes.

**Genetic linkage** A close association between two genes, typically the genetic locus associated with a disorder or a trait and the locus for a known gene. Two loci are said to be linked when they are sufficiently close together on the same chromosome.

**Genotype** An individual's actual genetic structure, usually with reference to a particular characteristic.

**Gerontology** The multidisciplinary study of aging and older adults.

**Gender dysphoria (previously known as Gender Identity Disorder)** A marked incongruence between the person's experienced gender (being male or female) and assigned gender.

**Gestalt therapy** A variation of the humanistic approach to psychotherapy that underscores affective awareness and expression, genuineness, and experiencing the moment (living in the "here and now").

**Grief** The emotional and social process of coping with a separation or a loss, often described as proceeding in stages.

**Group therapy** The treatment of three or more people in a group setting, often using group relationships as a central part of therapy.

# H

**Hallucinations** A perceptual experience in the absence of external stimulation, such as hearing voices that aren't really there.

**Hallucinogens** Drugs that produce hallucinations.

**Harmful dysfunction** A concept used in one approach to the definition of mental disorder. A condition can be considered a mental disorder if it causes some harm to the person and if the condition results from the inability of some mental mechanism to perform its natural function.

**Hashish** The dried resin from the top of the female cannabis plant. Ingestion of hashish leads to a feeling of being "high" (see *Marijuana*).

**Health behavior** A wide range of activities that are essential to promoting good health, including positive actions such as proper diet and the avoidance of negative activities such as cigarette smoking.

**Health psychologist** A psychologist who specializes in reducing negative health behavior (e.g., smoking) and promoting positive health behavior (e.g., exercise). Health psychology is a part of the interdisciplinary field of behavioral medicine.

**Heritability** The variability in a behavioral characteristic that is accounted for by genetic factors.

**Heritability ratio** A statistic for computing the proportion of variance in a behavioral characteristic that is accounted for by genetic factors in a given study or series of studies.

**High-risk research design** A longitudinal study of persons who are selected from the general population based on some identified risk factor that has a fairly high risk ratio.

**Histrionic personality disorder** An enduring pattern of thinking and behavior that is characterized by excessive emotionality and attention-seeking behavior. People with this disorder are self-centered, vain, and demanding. Their emotions tend to be shallow and may vacillate erratically.

**Homeostasis** The tendency to maintain a steady state. A familiar concept in biology that also is widely applicable in psychology.

**Hormones** Chemical substances that are released into the bloodstream by glands in the endocrine system. Hormones affect the functioning of distant body systems and sometimes act as neuromodulators.

**Human Immunodeficiency Virus (HIV)** The virus that causes AIDS and attacks the immune system, leaving the patient susceptible to infection, neurological complications, and cancers that rarely affect those with normal immune function.

**Humanistic psychotherapy** An approach that assumes that the most essential human quality is the ability to make choices and freely act on them (free will). Promoted as a "third force" to counteract the deterministic views of psychodynamic and the behavioral approaches to psychotherapy.

**Huntington's disease** A primary, differentiated dementia characterized by the presence of unusual involuntary muscle movements. Many Huntington's patients also exhibit a variety of personality changes and symptoms of mental disorders, including depression and anxiety.

**Hyperactivity** A symptom of attention-deficit/hyperactivity disorder (ADHD), often manifested as squirming, fidgeting, or restless behavior. Particularly notable in structured settings.

**Hypnosis** An altered state of consciousness during which hypnotized subjects are particularly susceptible to suggestion. There is considerable debate as to whether hypnosis is a unique state of consciousness or merely a form of relaxation.

**Hypoactive sexual desire** Diminished desire for sexual activity and reduced frequency of sexual fantasies.

**Hypomania** An episode of increased energy that is not sufficiently severe to qualify as a full-blown manic episode.

**Hypothalamus** A part of the limbic system that plays a role in sensation, but more importantly that it controls basic biological urges, such as eating, drinking, and activity, as well as much of the functioning of the autonomic nervous system.

**Hypothesis** A prediction about the expected findings in a scientific study.

**Hypothetical construct** A theoretical device that refers to events or states that reside within a person and are proposed to help understand or explain a person's behavior.

**Hysteria** An outdated but influential diagnostic category that included both somatoform and dissociative disorders. Attempts to treat hysteria had a major effect on Charcot, Freud, and Janet, among others. In Greek, *hysteria* means "uterus," a reflection of ancient speculation that hysteria was restricted to women and caused by frustrated sexual desires.

## I

**Iatrogenesis** The creation of a disorder by an attempt to treat it.

**Id** One of Freud's three central personality structures. In Freudian theory, the id is present at birth and is the source of basic drives and motivations. The id houses biological drives (such as hunger), as well as Freud's two key psychological drives, sex and aggression.

**Identity** Erikson's term for the broad definition of self; in his view, identity is the product of the adolescent's struggle to answer the question "Who am I?"

**Identity crisis** Erikson's period of basic uncertainty about self during late adolescence and early adult life. A consequence of the psychosocial stage of identity versus role confusion.

**Impulse control disorders** Disorders characterized by failure to resist an impulse or a temptation to perform some pleasurable or tension-releasing act that is harmful to oneself or others; examples are pathological gambling, setting fires, and stealing.

**Incidence** The number of new cases of a disorder that appear in a population during a specific period of time.

**Independent variable** The variable in an experiment that is controlled and deliberately manipulated by the experimenter (e.g., whether a subject receives a treatment). Affects the dependent variable.

**Informed consent** A legal and ethical safeguard concerning risks in research and treatment. Includes (a) accurate information about potential risks and benefits, (b) competence on the part of subjects/patients to understand them, and (c) the ability of subjects/patients to participate voluntarily.

**Inhibited sexual arousal** Difficulty experienced by a woman in achieving or maintaining genital responses, such as lubrication and swelling, that are necessary to complete sexual intercourse.

**Insanity** A legal term referring to a defendant's state of mind at the time of committing a crime. An insane individual is not held legally responsible for his or her actions because of a mental disease or defect.

**Insanity defense** An attempt to prove that a person with a mental illness did not meet the legal criteria for sanity at the time of committing a crime. The inability to tell right from wrong and an "irresistible impulse" are the two most common contemporary grounds for the defense.

**Insight** Self-understanding; the extent to which a person recognizes the nature (or understands the potential causes) of his or her disorder. In psychoanalysis, insight is the ultimate goal, specifically, to bring formerly unconscious material into conscious awareness.

**Intellectual disability** Formerly known as *mental retardation*, an intellectual disability is characterized by significantly subaverage IQ, deficits in adaptive behavior, and onset before the age of 18.

**Intelligence quotient (IQ)** A measure of intellectual ability that typically has a mean of 100 and a standard deviation of 15. An individual's IQ is determined by comparisons with norms for same-aged peers.

**Internalizing disorders** An empirically derived category of psychological problems of childhood that affect the child more than the external world (e.g., depression).

**Interpersonal therapy (IPT)** An evidence-based approach to treatment emphasizing the historical importance of close relationships to the development of both normal and problematic emotions and patterns of relating to others. Used particularly in the treatment of depression, IPT uses the past to better understand and directly make changes in the present.

**Interpretation** A tool in psychotherapy and psychoanalysis in which the therapist suggests new meanings about a client's accounts of his or her past and present life.

## L

**Lateralized** Functions or sites that are located primarily or solely in one hemisphere of the brain (the left or the right).

**Learning disability (LD)** Educational problem characterized by academic performance that is notably below academic aptitude.

**Life-cycle transitions** Movements from one social or psychological "stage" of adult development into a new one; often characterized by interpersonal, emotional, and identity conflict.

**Life-span development** The study of continuities and changes in behavior, affect, and cognition from infancy through the last years of life.

**Limbic system** A variety of brain structures, including the thalamus and hypothalamus, that are central to the regulation of emotion and basic learning processes.

**Longitudinal study** A type of research design in which subjects are studied over a period of time (contrasts with the cross-sectional approach of studying subjects only at one point in time). Longitudinal studies attempt to establish whether hypothesized causes precede their putative effects in time.

## M

**Major Neurocognitive Disorder** A broad category in DSM-5 that subsumes diagnoses previously called dementia, delirium, and amnestic disorders.

**Mainstreaming** The educational philosophy that children with intellectual disabilities should be taught, as much as possible, in regular classrooms rather than in "special" classes.

**Malingering** Pretending to have a psychological disorder in order to achieve some external gain such as insurance money or avoidance of work.

**Mania** A disturbance in mood characterized by such symptoms as elation, inflated self-esteem, hyperactivity, and accelerated speaking and thinking. An exaggerated feeling of physical and emotional well-being.

**Marijuana** The dried leaves and flowers of the female cannabis plant. "Getting high" on marijuana refers to a pervasive sense of well-being and happiness.

**Mean** The arithmetic average of a distribution of scores; the sum of scores divided by the number of observations.

**Median** The midpoint of a frequency distribution; half of all subjects fall above and half fall below the median.

**Melancholia** A particularly severe type of depression. In DSM-5, melancholia is described in terms of a number of specific features, such as loss of pleasure in activities and lack of reactivity to events in the person's environment that are normally pleasurable.

**Menopause** The cessation of menstruation and the associated physical and psychological changes that occur among middle-aged women (the so-called "change of life").

**Meta-analysis** A statistical technique that allows the results from different studies to be combined in a standardized way.

**Mode** The most frequent score in a frequency distribution.

**Modeling** A social learning concept describing the process of learning through imitation. Contrasts with the broader concept of identification.

**Monoamine oxidase inhibitors (MAOIs)** A group of antidepressant drugs that inhibit the enzyme monoamine oxidase (MAO) in the brain and raise the levels of neurotransmitters, such as norepinephrine, dopamine, and serotonin.

**Monozygotic (MZ) twins** Identical twins produced from a single fertilized egg; thus MZ twins have identical genotypes.

**Mood** A pervasive and sustained emotional response that, in its extreme, can color the person's perception of the world.

**Mood disorders** A broad category of psychopathology that includes depressive disorders and bipolar disorders. These conditions are defined in terms of episodes in which the person's behavior is dominated by either clinical depression or mania.

**Moratorium** A period of allowing oneself to be uncertain or confused about identity. Erikson advocated a moratorium as an important step in the formation of an enduring identity.

**Multiple personality disorder** An unusual dissociative disorder characterized by the existence of two or more distinct personalities in a single individual (called *dissociative identity disorder* in DSM-5).

# N

**Narcissistic personality disorder** An enduring pattern of thinking and behavior that is characterized by pervasive grandiosity. Narcissistic people are preoccupied with their own achievements and abilities.

**Negative symptoms** (of schizophrenia) Include flat or blunted affect, avolition, alogia, and anhedonia.

**Neurofibrillary tangles** A type of brain lesion found in the cerebral cortex and the hippocampus in patients with Alzheimer's disease. A pattern of disorganized neurofibrils, which provide structural support for the neurons and help transport chemicals that are used in the production of neurotransmitters.

**Neurocognitive Disorder with Lewy Bodies (also known as dementia with Lewy bodies)** A form of progressive dementia in which the central feature is progressive cognitive decline, combined with three additional defining features: (1) pronounced "fluctuations" in alertness and attention, such as frequent drowsiness, lethargy, lengthy periods of time spent staring into space, or disorganized speech; (2) recurrent visual hallucinations; and (3) parkinsonian motor symptoms, such as rigidity and the loss of spontaneous movement.

**Neurologists** Physicians who have been trained to diagnose and treat disorders of the nervous system, including diseases of the brain, spinal cord, nerves, and muscles.

**Neurons** The nerve cells that form the basic building blocks of the brain. Each neuron is composed of the soma or cell body, the dendrites, the axon, and the terminal buttons.

**Neuropsychological assessment** Assessment procedures focused on the examination of performance on psychological tests to indicate whether a person has a brain disorder. An example is the Halstead-Reitan Neuropsychological Test Battery.

**Neuropsychologists** Psychologists who have particular expertise in the assessment of specific types of cognitive impairment, including those associated with dementia and amnestic disorders.

**Neurotransmitters** Chemical substances that are released into the synapse between two neurons and carry signals from the terminal button of one neuron to the receptors of another.

**Nonshared environment** The component of a sibling's environment inside or outside the family that is unique to that sibling, for example, being a favorite child or one's best friend.

Contrasts with the shared environment, family experiences that are common across siblings.

**Normal distribution** A frequency distribution represented by a bell-shaped curve—the normal curve—that is important for making statistical inferences. Many psychological characteristics (e.g., intelligence) are assumed to follow the normal distribution.

**Normalization** The philosophy that mentally retarded or mentally ill people are entitled to live as much as possible like other members of the society. Often with deinstitutionalization in providing custodial care and mainstreaming in education.

**Null hypothesis** The prediction that an experimental hypothesis is not true. Scientists must assume that the null hypothesis holds until research contradicts it.

# O

**Obesity** Excess body fat, a circumstance that roughly corresponds with a body weight 20 percent above the expected weight.

**Obsessions** Repetitive, unwanted, intrusive cognitive events that may take the form of thoughts, images, or impulses. Obsessions intrude suddenly into consciousness and lead to an increase in subjective anxiety.

**Obsessive–compulsive personality disorder** An enduring pattern of thinking and behavior that is characterized by perfectionism and inflexibility. These people are preoccupied with rules and efficiency. They are excessively conscientious, moralistic, and judgmental.

**Operant conditioning** A learning theory asserting that behavior is a function of its consequences. Specifically, behavior increases if it is rewarded, and it decreases if it is punished.

**Operational definition** A procedure that is used to measure a theoretical construct.

**Opiates** (sometimes called *opioids*) Drugs that have properties similar to opium. The main active ingredients in opium are morphine and codeine.

**Oppositional defiant disorder (ODD)** A psychological disorder of childhood characterized by persistent but relatively minor transgressions, such as refusing to obey adult requests, arguing, and acting angry.

**Orgasmic disorder** A sexual disorder in which the person has recurrent difficulties reaching orgasm after a normal sexual arousal.

**Outpatient commitment** Outpatient commitment generally requires the same dangerousness standards as inpatient commitment, but the patient is court-ordered to comply with treatment in the community (e.g., making regular office visits, taking medication). Outpatient commitment is permitted by 39 states, and because it involves less infringement on civil liberties, commitment criteria may be applied less stringently for outpatient versus inpatient commitment.

# P

**Pain disorder**   A type of somatoform disorder characterized by preoccupation with pain, and complaints are motivated at least in part by psychological factors.

**Panic attack**   A sudden, overwhelming experience of terror or fright. While anxiety involves a blend of several negative emotions, panic is more focused.

**Panic disorder**   A form of anxiety disorder in which a person experiences recurrent, unexpected panic attacks. At least one of the attacks must have been followed by a period of one month or more in which the person has either persistent concern about having additional attacks, worry about the implications of the attack or its consequences, or a significant change in behavior related to the attacks. Panic disorder is divided into two subtypes, depending on the presence or absence of agoraphobia.

**Paradigm**   A set of assumptions both about the substance of a theory and about how scientists should collect data and test theoretical propositions. The term was applied to the progress of science by Thomas Kuhn, an influential historian and philosopher.

**Paranoid personality disorder**   An enduring pattern of thinking and behavior characterized by a pervasive tendency to be inappropriately suspicious of other people's motives and behaviors. People who fit the description for this disorder expect that other people are trying to harm them, and they take extraordinary precautions to avoid being exploited or injured.

**Paraphilias**   Forms of sexual disorder that involve sexual arousal in association with unusual objects and situations, such as inanimate objects, sexual contact with children, exhibiting their genitals to strangers, and inflicting pain on another person.

**Paraphilic disorder**   A paraphilia that is currently causing distress or impairment to the individual or a paraphilia whose satisfaction has entailed personal harm, or risk of harm, to others.

**Pedophilic disorder**   One of the paraphilic disorders, characterized by marked distress over, or acting on urges involving sexual activity with a prepubescent child.

**Persistent depressive disorder (also known as dysthymia)**   A mild form of depressive disorder characterized by a chronic course (the person is seldom without symptoms)

**Personality**   The combination of persistent traits or characteristics that, taken as a whole, describe a person's behavior. In DSM-5, personality is defined as "enduring patterns of perceiving, relating to, and thinking about the environment and oneself, which are exhibited in a wide range of important social and personal contexts."

**Personality disorder**   Inflexible and maladaptive patterns of personality that begin by early adulthood and result in either social or occupational problems or distress to the individual.

**Personality inventory**   Sometimes called an *objective personality test,* it consists of a series of straightforward statements that the person is required to rate or endorse as being either true or false in relation to himself or herself.

**Phenotype**   The observed expression of a given genotype or genetic structure, for example, eye color.

**Phenylketonuria (PKU)**   A cause of mental retardation transmitted by the pairing of recessive genes that results in the deficiency of the enzyme that metabolizes phenylalanine. Infants have normal intelligence at birth, but the ingestion of foods containing phenylalanine causes phenylketonuria and produces brain damage. Can be prevented with a phenylalanine-free diet.

**Phobias**   Persistent and irrational narrowly defined fears that are associated with a specific object or situation.

**Placebo effect**   The improvement in a condition produced by a placebo (sometimes a substantial change). An overriding goal of scientific research is to identify treatments that exceed placebo effects.

**Polygenic**   Caused by more than one gene. Characteristics become normally distributed as more genes are involved in the phenotypic expression of a trait.

**Positive symptoms**   (of schizophrenia) Include hallucinations, delusions, disorganized speech, inappropriate affect, and disorganized behavior.

**Posttraumatic stress disorder (PTSD)**   A psychological disorder characterized by recurring symptoms of numbing, reexperiencing, and hyperarousal following exposure to a traumatic stressor.

**Premature ejaculation**   A type of sexual disorder, in which a man is unable to delay ejaculation long enough to accomplish intercourse.

**Premorbid history**   A pattern of behavior that precedes the onset of an illness. Adjustment prior to the disorder.

**Preparedness model**   The notion that organisms are biologically prepared, on the basis of neural pathways in their central nervous systems, to learn certain types of associations (also known as *biological constraints on learning*).

**Prevalence**   An epidemiological term that refers to the total number of cases that are present within a given population during a particular period of time.

**Probands**   Index cases. In behavior genetic studies, probands are family members who have a disorder, and the relatives of the index cases are examined for concordance.

**Problem-focused coping**   Externally oriented coping in an attempt to change or otherwise control a stressor.

**Prodromal phase**   Precedes the active phase of schizophrenia and is marked by an obvious deterioration in role functioning. Prodromal signs and symptoms are less dramatic than those seen during the active phase of the disorder.

**Professional responsibilities**   A professional's obligation to follow the ethical standards of his or her profession and to uphold the laws of the states in which he or she practices, for example, confidentiality.

**Prognosis**   Predictions about the future course of a disorder with or without treatment.

**Projective tests**   Personality tests, such as the Rorschach inkblot test, in which the person is asked to interpret a series of ambiguous stimuli.

**Psychiatry**   The branch of medicine that is concerned with the study and treatment of mental disorders.

**Psychoanalysis**   Freud's orthodox form of psychotherapy that is practiced rarely today because of its time, expense, and questionable effectiveness in treating mental disorders. Freud viewed the task of psychoanalysis as promoting insight by uncovering the unconscious conflicts and motivations that cause psychological difficulties.

**Psychoanalytic theory**   A paradigm for conceptualizing abnormal behavior based on the concepts and writings of Sigmund Freud. Highlights unconscious processes and conflicts as causing abnormal behavior and emphasizes psychoanalysis as the treatment of choice.

**Psychodynamic psychotherapy**   An "uncovering" form of psychotherapy in which the therapist typically is more engaged and directive; the process is considerably less lengthy than in psychoanalysis.

**Psychomotor retardation**   A generalized slowing of physical and emotional reactions. The slowing of movements and speech; frequently seen in depression.

**Psychomotor stimulants**   Drugs such as amphetamine and cocaine that produce their effect by simulating the effects of certain neurotransmitters, specifically norepinephrine, dopamine, and serotonin.

**Psychoneuroimmunology (PNI)**   Research on the effects of stress on the functioning of the immune system.

**Psychopathology**   The manifestations of (and the study of the causes of) mental disorders. Generally used as another term to describe abnormal behavior.

**Psychopathy**   Another term for *antisocial personality disorder.* Usually associated with Cleckley's definition of that concept, which included features such as disregard for the truth, lack of empathy, and inability to learn from experience.

**Psychopharmacology** The study of the effects of psychoactive drugs on behavior. Clinical psychopharmacology involves the expert use of drugs in the treatment of mental disorders.

**Psychophysiology** The study of changes in the functioning of the body that result from psychological experiences.

**Psychosis** A term that refers to several types of severe mental disorder in which the person is out of contact with reality. Hallucinations and delusions are examples of psychotic symptoms.

**Psychostimulants** Medications that heighten energy and alertness when taken in small dosages, but lead to restless, even frenetic, behavior when misused. Often used in the treatment of attention-deficit/hyperactivity disorder.

**Psychotherapy** The use of psychological techniques in an attempt to produce change in the context of a special, helping relationship.

**Purging** An intentional act designed to eliminate consumed food from the body. Self-induced vomiting is the most common form.

## R

**Random assignment** Any of several methods of ensuring that each subject has a statistically equal chance of being exposed to any level of an independent variable.

**Rating scale** An assessment tool in which the observer is asked to make judgments that place the person somewhere along a dimension.

**Reactivity** The influence of an observer's presence on the behavior of the person who is being observed.

**Receptors** Sites on the dendrites or soma of a neuron that are sensitive to certain neurotransmitters.

**Recidivism** Repeat offending in violating the law.

**Reductionism** The scientific perspective that the whole is the sum of its parts and that the task of scientists is to divide the world into its smaller and smaller components.

**Relapse** The reappearance of active symptoms following a period of remission (such as a return to heavy drinking by an alcoholic after a period of sustained sobriety).

**Reliability** The consistency of measurements, including diagnostic decisions. One index of reliability is agreement among clinicians.

**Remission** A stage of disorder characterized by the absence of symptoms (i.e., symptoms that were previously present are now gone).

**Representative sample** A sample that accurately represents the larger population of an identified group (e.g., a representative sample of all children in the United States).

**Resilience** The ability to "bounce back" from adversity despite life stress and emotional distress.

**Retrograde amnesia** The loss of memory for events prior to the onset of an illness or the experience of a traumatic event.

**Reuptake** The process of recapturing some neurotransmitters in the synapse before they reach the receptors of another cell and returning the chemical substances to the terminal button. The neurotransmitter then is reused in subsequent neural transmission.

**Reverse causality** Indicates that causation could be operating in the opposite direction: Y could be causing X instead of X causing Y. A threat to interpretation in correlational studies, and a basic reason why correlation does not mean causation.

**Risk factors** Variables that are associated with a higher probability of developing a disorder.

## S

**Savant performance** An exceptional ability in a highly specialized area of functioning typically involving artistic, musical, or mathematical skills.

**Schizoaffective disorder** A disorder defined by a period of disturbance during which the symptoms of schizophrenia partially overlap with a major depressive episode or a manic episode.

**Schizoid personality disorder** An enduring pattern of thinking and behavior characterized by pervasive indifference to other people, coupled with a diminished range of emotional experience and expression. People who fit this description prefer social isolation to interactions with friends or family.

**Schizophrenia** A type of (or group of) psychotic disorders characterized by positive and negative symptoms and associated with a deterioration in role functioning. The term was originally coined by Eugen Bleuler to describe the *splitting of mental associations,* which he believed to be the fundamental disturbance in schizophrenia (previously known as *dementia praecox).*

**Schizotypal personality disorder** An enduring pattern of discomfort with other people coupled with peculiar thinking and behavior. The latter symptoms take the form of perceptual and cognitive disturbances. Considered by some experts to be part of the schizophrenic spectrum.

**Seasonal affective disorder** A type of mood disorder (either unipolar or bipolar) in which there has been a regular temporal relation between onset (or disappearance) of the person's episodes and a particular time of the year. For example, the person might become depressed in the winter.

**Selective serotonin reuptake inhibitors (SSRIs)** A group of antidepressant drugs that inhibit the reuptake of serotonin into the pre-synaptic nerve endings and therefore promote neurotransmission in serotonin pathways.

**Self-control** Appropriate behavior guided by internal (rather than external) rules.

**Sensate focus** A procedure for the treatment of sexual dysfunction that involves a series of simple exercises in which the couple spends time in a quiet, relaxed setting, learning to touch each other.

**Separation anxiety disorder** A psychological disorder of childhood characterized by persistent and excessive worry for the safety of an attachment figure and related fears such as getting lost, being kidnapped, nightmares, and refusal to be alone. Distinct from normal separation anxiety, which typically develops shortly before an infant's first birthday.

**Sexual dysfunctions** Forms of sexual disorder that involve inhibitions of sexual desire or interference with the physiological responses leading to orgasm.

**Sexual masochism disorder** A form of paraphilic disorder, in which sexual arousal is associated with the act of being humiliated, beaten, bound, or otherwise made to suffer. This diagnosis would not be assigned unless the pattern of arousal is currently causing distress or impairment to the person, or unless it causes harm, or risk of harm to others.

**Sexual sadism disorder** A form of paraphilic disorder, in which sexual arousal is associated with desires to inflict physical or psychological suffering, including humiliation, on another person. This diagnosis would not be assigned unless the pattern of arousal is currently causing distress or impairment to the person, or unless it causes harm, or risk of harm to others.

**Shared environment** The component of the family environment that offers the same or highly similar experiences to all siblings, for example, socioeconomic status. Stands in contrast to the nonshared environment, experiences inside and outside the family that are unique to one sibling.

**Sleep-Wake Disorders** Disorders where sleep is the primary complaint.

**Social anxiety disorder (also known as social phobia)** A form of anxiety disorder in which the person is persistently fearful of social situations that might expose him or her to scrutiny by others, such as fear of public speaking.

**Social clocks** Age-related goals people set for themselves and later use to evaluate life achievements.

**Social support** The emotional and practical assistance received from others.

**Social work** A profession whose primary concern is how human needs can be met within society.

**Somatic symptom disorder** A mood disorders where symptoms are related to basic physiological or bodily functions, including fatigue, aches and pains, and serious changes in appetite and sleep patterns.

**Specific phobia** Marked and persistent fear of clearly apparent, circumscribed objects or situations, such as snakes, spiders, heights, or small enclosed spaces. Exposure to the stimulus leads to an immediate increase in anxiety, and the phobic stimulus is avoided (or endured with great discomfort).

**Standard deviation**   A measure of dispersion of scores around the mean. Technically, the square root of the variance.

**Standard scores**   A standardized frequency distribution in which each score is subtracted from the mean and the difference is divided by the standard deviation.

**Statistically significant**   A statistical statement that a research result has a low probability of having occurred by chance alone. By convention, a result is said to be statistically significant if the probability is 5 percent or less that it was obtained by chance. This probability is often written as $p = .05$.

**Status offenses**   Acts that are illegal only because of a youth's status as a minor, for example, running away from home, truancy from school.

**Stigma**   A negative stamp or label that sets the person apart from others, connects the person to undesirable features, and leads others to reject the person.

**Stress**   An event that creates physiological or psychological strain for the individual. Stress has been defined differently by various scientists.

**Substance use disorders**   Problems that involve excessive use of, or addiction to, chemical substances that alter consciousness and lead to significant substance-related problems including craving, patterns of compulsive and risky use, tolerance or withdrawal, and eventually a variety of serious social and interpersonal consequences. Combines two diagnostic categories, substance abuse and substance dependence, from previous versions of the DSM.

**Superego**   One of Freud's three central personality structures, roughly equivalent to the "conscience." In Freudian theory, the superego contains societal standards of behavior, particularly rules that children learn from identifying with their parents. The superego attempts to control id impulses.

**Synapse**   A small gap filled with fluid that lies between the axon of one neuron and a dendrite or soma of another neuron.

**Syndrome**   A group of symptoms that appear together and are assumed to represent a specific type of disorder.

**Systematic desensitization**   A treatment for overcoming fears and phobias developed by Joseph Wolpe. Involves learning relaxation skills, developing a fear hierarchy, and systematic exposure to imagined, feared events while simultaneously maintaining relaxation.

**Systems theory**   An innovation in the philosophy of conceptualizing and conducting science that emphasizes interdependence, cybernetics, and especially holism—the idea that the whole is more than the sum of its parts. Often traced to the biologist and philosopher Ludwig von Bertalanffy.

## T

**Temperament**   Characteristic styles of relating to the world that are often conceptualized as inborn traits. Generally emphasizes the "how" as opposed to the "what" of behavior.

**Tend and befriend**   An alternative response to stress hypothesized to be more common among females. Tending involves caring for offspring in a way that protects them from harm and also alters the offspring's neuroendocrine responses in a healthful manner. Befriending is responding to threat with social affiliation, thereby reducing the risk of physical danger and encouraging the exchange of resources.

**Therapeutic alliance**   The emotional bond of confidence and trust between a therapist and client believed to facilitate therapy.

**Third variable**   An unmeasured factor that may account for a correlation observed between any two variables. A threat to interpretation in correlational studies, and a basic reason why correlation does not mean causation.

**Tolerance**   The process through which the nervous system becomes less sensitive to the effects of a psychoactive substance. As a result, the person needs to consume increased quantities of the drug to achieve the same subjective effect.

**Transvestic disorder**   One form of paraphilic disorder, in which the individual experiences intense sexual arousal associated with dressing in the clothing of the opposite gender

**Traumatic stress**   A catastrophic event that involves real or perceived threat to life or physical well-being.

**Tricyclics (TCAs)**   A group of antidepressant drugs that block the uptake of neurotransmitters, such as norepinephrine and dopamine, from the synapse.

**Type A behavior pattern**   A characterological response to challenge that is competitive, hostile, urgent, impatient, and achievement-striving. Linked to an increased risk for coronary heart disease.

## V

**Validity**   The meaning or systematic importance of a construct or a measurement.

**Variance**   A measure of dispersion of scores around the mean. Technically, the average squared difference from the mean (see also *standard deviation*).

**Vascular neurocognitive disorder (also known as vascular dementia)**   A type of dementia associated with vascular disease. The cognitive symptoms of vascular neurocognitive disorder are the same as those for Alzheimer's disease, but a gradual onset is not required.

**Ventricles**   Four connected chambers in the brain filled with cerebrospinal fluid. The ventricles are enlarged in some psychological and neurological disorders.

**Voyeuristic disorder**   One of the paraphilic disorders, characterized by recurrent, intense sexual urges involving the observation of unsuspecting people (usually strangers) while they are undressing or engaging in sexual activities.

**Vulnerability marker**   A specific measure, such as a biochemical assay or a psychological test, that might be useful in identifying people who are vulnerable to a disorder such as schizophrenia.

## W

**Weight set points**   Fixed weights or small ranges of weight around which the body regulates weight, for example, by increasing or decreasing metabolism.

**Withdrawal**   The constellation of symptoms that are experienced shortly after a person stops taking a drug after heavy or prolonged use.

**Worry**   A relatively uncontrollable sequence of negative, emotional thoughts and images that are concerned with possible future threats or danger.

# A

Abel, K. M., Wicks, S., Susser, E. S., Dalman, C., Pedersen, M. G., Mortensen, P., & Webb, R. T. (2010). Birth weight, schizophrenia, and adult mental disorder: Is risk confined to the smallest babies? *Archives of General Psychiatry, 67*(9), 923–930.

Abela, J. R. Z., & Hankin, B. L. (2011). Rumination as a vulnerability factor to depression during the transition from early to middle adolescence: A multiwave longitudinal study. *Journal of Abnormal Psychology, 120,* 259–271.

Abraído-Lanza, A. F., Vásquez, E., & Echeverría, S. E. (2004). En las manos de dios [in God's Hands]: Religious and other forms of coping among Latinos with arthritis. *Journal of Consulting and Clinical Psychology, 72,* 91–102.

Abramowitz, J. S. (1997). Effectiveness of psychological and pharmacological treatments for obsessive-compulsive disorder: A quantitative review. *Journal of Consulting and Clinical Psychology, 65,* 44–52.

Abramowitz, J. S. (1998). Does cognitive-behavioral therapy cure obsessive-compulsive disorder? A meta-analytic-evaluation of clinical significance. *Behavior Therapy, 29,* 339–355.

Abramowitz, J. S. (2006). The psychological treatment of obsessive-compulsive disorder. *Canadian Journal of Psychiatry, 51,* 407–416.

Abramowitz, J. S., Tolin, D. F., & Street, G. P. (2001). Paradoxical effects of thought suppression: A meta-analysis of controlled studies. *Clinical Psychology Review, 21,* 683–703.

Abrams, R. (2002). *Electroconvulsive therapy* (4th ed.). New York: Oxford University Press.

Adam, Y., Meinlschmidt, G., Gloster, A. T., & Lieb, R. (2012). Obsessive–compulsive disorder in the community: 12-month prevalence, comorbidity and impairment. *Social Psychiatry and Psychiatric Epidemiology, 47,* 339–349.

Adams, G. R., & Adams, C. M. (1989). Developmental issues. In L. K. G. Hsu & M. Hersen (Eds.), *Recent Developments in Adolescent Psychiatry* (pp. 13–30). New York: Wiley.

Adams, G. R., Abraham, K. G., & Markstrom, C. A. (1987). The relation among identity development, self-consciousness and self-focusing during middle and late adolescence. *Developmental Psychology, 23,* 292–297.

Adams, G. R., Ryan, J. H., Hoffman, J. J., Dobson, W. R., & Nielsen, E. C. (1985). Ego identity status, conformity behavior and personality in late adolescence. *Journal of Personality and Social Psychology, 47,* 1091–1104.

Addis, M. E., & Mahalik, J. R. (2003). Men, masculinity, and the contexts of help seeking. *American Psychologist, 58,* 5–14.

Adler, R. (2001). Psychoneuroimmunology. *Current Directions in Psychological Science, 10,* 94–98.

Adler, A. B., Bliese, P. D., McGurk, D., Hoge, C. W., & Castro, C. A. (2009). Battlemind debriefing and battlemind training as early interventions with soldiers returning from Iraq: Randomization by platoon. *Journal of Consulting and Clinical Psychology, 77,* 928–940.

Agras, W. S., Walsh, T., Fairburn, C. G., Wilson, G. T., & Kraemer, H. C. (2000). A multicenter comparison of cognitive-behavioral therapy and interpersonal psychotherapy for bulimia nervosa. *Archives of General Psychiatry, 57*(5), 459–466.

Agrawal, A., & Lynskey, M. T. (2008). Are there genetic influences on addiction: Evidence from family, adoption and twin studies.*Addiction, 103,* 1069–1081.

Agrawal, A., Dick, D. M., Bucholz, K. K., Madden, P. A. F., Cooper, M. L., Sher, K. J., & Heath, A. C. (2008). Drinking expectancies and motives: A genetic study of young adult women. *Addiction, 103,* 194–204.

Agrawal, A., Heath, A. C., & Lynskey, M. T. (2011). DSM-IV to DSM-5: The impact of proposed revisions on diagnosis of alcohol use disorders. *Addiction, 106,* 1935–1943.

Aguilera, A., López, S. R., Breitborde, N. K., Kopelowicz, A., & Zarate, R. (2010). Expressed emotion and sociocultural moderation in the course of schizophrenia. *Journal of Abnormal Psychology, 119,* 875–885.

Ainsworth, M. D. S., Blehar, M., Waters, E., & Wall, S. (1978). *Patterns of attachment.* Hillsdale, NJ: Erlbaum.

Akagi, H., & House, A. (2001). Epidemiology of conversion hysteria. In P. Halligan, C. Bass, & J. Marshall (Eds.), *Contemporary approaches to the study of hysteria* (pp. 73–86). Oxford, UK: Oxford University Press.

Akiskal, H. S. (1992). Borderline: An adjective still in search of a noun. In D. Silver & M. Rosenbluth (Eds.), *Handbook of Borderline Disorders* (pp. 155–176). Madison, CT: International Universities Press.

Akyuz, G., Dogan, O., Sar, V., Yargic, L. I., & Tutkun, H. (1999). Frequency of dissociative identity disorder in the general population in Turkey. *Comprehensive Psychiatry, 40,* 151–159.

Alarcon, R. D. (2005). Cross-cultural issues. In J. M. Oldham & A. E. Skodol (Eds.), *American Psychiatric Publishing Textbook of Personality Disorders* (pp. 561–578). Washington, DC: American Psychiatric Publishing.

Albarracín, D., Durantini, M. R., & Earl, A. (2006). Empirical and theoretical conclusions of an analysis of outcomes of HIV-prevention interventions. *Current Directions in Psychological Science, 15,* 73–78.

Albarracín, D., Gillette, J. C., Earl, A. N., Glasman, L. R., Durantini, M. R., & Ho, M. (2005). A test of major assumptions about behavior change: A comprehensive look at the effects of passive and active HIV-prevention interventions since the beginning of the epidemic. *Psychological Bulletin, 131,* 856–897.

Aldridge-Morris, R. (1989). *Multiple personality: An exercise in deception.* Hillsdale, NJ: Erlbaum.

Alexander, F., & French, T. M. (1946). *Psychoanalytic therapy: Principles and application.* Oxford, England: Ronald Press.

Alexander, J. F., & Parsons, B. V. (1982). *Functional Family Therapy.* Monterey, CA: Brooks/Cole.

Alexander, J. F., Holtzworth-Munroe, A., & Jameson, P. B. (1994). The process and outcome of marital and family therapy: Research, review, and evaluation. In A. E. Bergin & S. L. Garfield (Eds.), *Handbook of Psychotherapy and Behavior Change* (4th ed., pp. 595–630). New York: Wiley.

Allen, A. (2006). Cognitive-behavior therapy and other psychosocial interventions in the treatment of obsessive-compulsive disorder. *Psychiatric Annals, 36,* 474–479.

Allen, J. P., et al. (2002). Attachment and autonomy as predictors of the development of social skills and delinquency during midadolescence. *Journal of Consulting and Clinical Psychology, 70,* 56–66.

Allen, J. P., Marsh, P., McFarland, C., McElhaney, K. B., Land, D. J., Jodl, K. M., et al. (2002). Attachment and autonomy as predictors of the development of social skills and delinquency during midadolescence. *Journal of Consulting and Clinical Psychology, 70,* 56–66.

Allen, L. A., Escobar, J. I., Lehrer, P. M., Gara, M. A., & Woolfolk, R. L. (2002). Psychosocial treatments for multiple unexplained symptoms: A review of the literature. *Psychosomatic Medicine, 64,* 939–950.

Alloy, L. B., Abramson, L. Y., Walshaw, P. D., & Neeren, A. M. (2006). Cognitive vulnerability to unipolar and bipolar mood disorders. *Journal of Social and Clinical Psychology, 25,* 726–754.

Alloy, L. B., Bender, R. E., Wagner, C. A., Abramson, L. Y., & Urosevic, S. (2009). Longitudinal predictors of bipolar spectrum disorders: A behavioral approach system perspective. *Clinical Psychology: Science and Practice, 16,* 206–226.

Almeida, D. M. (2005). Resilience and vulnerability to daily stressors assessed via diary methods. *Current Directions in Psychological Science, 14,* 64–68.

Al-Sawaf, M., & Al-Issa, I. (2000). Sex and sexual dysfunction in an Arab-Islamic society. In I. Al-Issa (Ed.), *Mental illness in the Islamic World* (pp. 295–311). Madison, CT: International Universities Press.

Altemus, M. (2006). Sex differences in depression and anxiety disorders: Potential biological determinants. *Hormones and Behavior, 50,* 534–538.

Amato, L., Davoli, M., Vecchi, S., Ali, R., Farrell, M., Faggiano, F., et al. (2011). Cochrane systematic reviews in the field of addiction: What's there and what should be. *Drug and Alcohol Dependence, 113*(2–3), 96–103.

Amato, P. R. (2010). Research on divorce: Continuing trends and new developments. *Journal of Marriage and Family, 72,* 650–666.

American Bar Association. (1995). *Mental Disability Law* (5th ed.). Washington, DC: Author.

American Psychiatric Association. (2000). *Diagnostic and statistical manual of mental disorders* (DSM-IV-TR) (4th edition, text revision). Washington, DC: Author.

American Psychological Association. (1995). *Violence in the family.* Washington, DC: Author.

Andersen, A. E. (1995). Eating disorders in males. In K. D. Brownell & C. G. Fairburn (Eds.), *Eating disorders and obesity: A comprehensive handbook* (pp. 177–182). New York: Guilford.

Anderson, A. E. (2002). Eating disorders in males. In C. G. Fairburn & K. D. Brownell (Eds.), *Eating disorders and obesity* (2nd ed., pp. 188–192). New York: Guilford.

Anderson, B. L., Kiecolt-Glaser, J. K., & Glaser, R. (1994). A biobehavioral model of cancer stress and disease course. *American Psychologist, 49,* 389–404.

Anderson, C. A., Shibuya, A., Ihori, N., Swing, E. L., Bushman, B. J., Sakamoto, A., et al. (2010). Violent video game effects on aggression, empathy, and prosocial behavior in eastern and western countries: A meta-analytic review. *Psychological Bulletin, 136,* 151–173.

Anderson, D. K., Lord, C., Risi, S., DiLavore, P. S., Shulman, C., Thurm, A., et al. (2007). Patterns of growth in verbal abilities among children with autism spectrum disorder. *Journal of Consulting and Clinical Psychology, 75,* 594–604.

Anderson, I. (2006). The new guidelines from the British Association for Psychopharmacology for anxiety disorders. *International Journal of Psychiatry in Clinical Practice, 10*(Suppl. 3), 10–17.

Anderson, P. (1996, May 21). Obsessive compulsion and tics linked to sore throats. *The Medical Post.* Retrieved October 18, 2008, from www.mentalhealth.com/mag1/p5m-ocd1.html

Andersson, M. M., Zetterberg, H. H., Minthon, L. L., Blennow, K. K., & Londos, E. E. (2011). The cognitive profile and CSF biomarkers in dementia with Lewy bodies and Parkinson's disease dementia. *International Journal of Geriatric Psychiatry, 26,* 100–105.

Andreasen, N. C. (2001). *Brave new brain: Conquering mental illness in the era of the genome.* New York: Oxford University Press.

Andrews, G. (1996). Comorbidity and the general neurotic syndrome. *British Journal of Psychiatry, 168,* 76–84.

Andrews, G. G., Goldberg, D. P., Krueger, R. F., Carpenter, W. R., Hyman, S. E., Sachdev, P. P., et al. (2009). Exploring the feasibility of a meta-structure for DSM-V and ICD-11: Could it improve utility and validity? *Psychological Medicine, 39,* 1993–2000.

Andrews, G., MacMahon, S. W., Austin, A., & Byrne, D. G. (1984). Hypertension: Comparison of drug and non-drug treatments.*British Medical Journal, 284,* 1523–1530.

Angst, J., Sellaro, R., & Merikangas, K. R. (2000). Depressive spectrum diagnoses. *Comprehensive Psychiatry, 41,* 39–47.

Anthony, J. C., & Helzer, J. E. (1991). Syndromes of drug abuse and dependence. In L. N. Robins & D. A. Regier (Eds.), *Psychiatric disorders in America: The Epidemiologic Catchment Area Study* (pp. 116–154). New York: Free Press.

Anthony, J. C., Warner, L. A., & Kessler, R. C. (1994). Comparative epidemiology of dependence on tobacco, alcohol, controlled substances, and inhalants: Basic findings from the National Comorbidity Survey. *Experimental and Clinical Psychopharmacology, 2,* 1–24.

Antoni, M. H., Lechner, S. C., Kazi, A., Wimberly, S. R., Sifre, T., Urcuyo, K. R., et al. (2006). How stress management improves quality of life after treatment for breast cancer. *Journal of Consulting and Clinical Psychology, 74,* 1143–1152.

Antonucci, T. C. (2001). Social relations. In J. E. Birren & K. W. Schaie (Eds.), *Handbook of the Psychology of Aging* (5th ed., pp. 427–453). San Diego, CA: Academic Press.

Appelbaum, P. S. (1994). *Almost a revolution: Mental health law and the limits of change.* New York: Oxford University Press.

Appelbaum, P. S., & Gutheil, T. G. (1980). The Boston State Hospital case: "Involuntary mind control," the constitution, and the "right to rot." *American Journal of Psychiatry, 137*(6), 720–723.

Arevalo-Rodriguez, I., Pedraza, O. L., Rodríguez, A., Sánchez, E., Gich, I., Solà, I., et al. (2013). Alzheimer's disease dementia guidelines for diagnostic testing: A systematic review. *American Journal of Alzheimer's Disease and Other Dementias, 28,* 111–119.

Arnett, J. J. (2007). Emerging adulthood: What is it, and what is it good for? *Child Development Perspectives, 1,* 68–73.

Arnold, L. E., Elliot, M., Sachs, L., Bird, H., Kraemer, H. C., Wells, K. C., et al. (2003). Effects of ethnicity on treatment attendance, stimulant response/dose, and 14-month outcome in ADHD. *Journal of Consulting and Clinical Psychology, 71*(4), 713–727.

Arntz, A. A. (2003). Cognitive therapy versus applied relaxation as treatment of generalized anxiety disorder. *Behaviour Research and Therapy, 41,* 633–646.

Asher, S. R., & Wheeler, V. A. (1985). Children's loneliness: A comparison of rejected and neglected peer status. *Journal of Consulting and Clinical Psychology, 53,* 500–505.

Atalay, F., & Atalay, H. (2006). Gender differences in patients with schizophrenia in terms of sociodemographic and clinical characteristics. *German Journal of Psychiatry, 9,* 41–47.

Atkinson, D. R., Morten, G., & Sue, D. W. (1993). *Counseling American minorities: A cross-cultural perspective* (4th ed.). Madison, WI, and England: Brown & Benchmark and Wm. C. Brown Publishers.

Attia, E., & Roberto, C. A. (2009). Should amenorrhea be a diagnostic criterion for anorexia nervosa? *International Journal of Eating Disorders, 42,* 581–589.

Averill, P. M., Reas, D. L., Shack, A., Shah, N. N., Cowan, K., Krajewski, K., et al. (2004). Is schizoaffective disorder a stable diagnostic category? A retrospective examination. *Psychiatric Quarterly, 75,* 215–227.

Ayres, J. J. B. (1998). Fear conditioning and avoidance. In W. T. O'Donohue (Ed.), *Learning and Behavior Therapy* (pp. 122–145). Boston: Allyn and Bacon.

# B

Baardseth, T. P., Goldberg, S. B., Pace, P. T., Wislocki, A. P., Frost, N. D., Siddiqui, J. R., Lindemann, A. M., Kivlighan, D. M., Laska, K. M., Del Re, A. C., Minami, T., & Wampold, B. E. (2013). Cognitive-behavioral therapy versus other therapies: Redux. *Clinical Psychology Review, 33,* 395–405.

Babor, T., & Del Boca, F. (2003). *Treatment matching in alcoholism.* New York: Cambridge University Press.

Bach, A. K., Brown, T. A., & Barlow, D. H. (1999). The effects of false negative feedback on efficacy expectancies and sexual arousal in sexually functional males. *Behavior Therapy, 30,* 79–95.

Bachar, K., & Koss, M. P. (2001). From prevalence to prevention: Closing the gap between what we know about rape and what we do. In C. M. Renzetti & J. L. Edleson (Eds.), *Sourcebook on violence against women* (pp. 117–142). Thousand Oaks, CA: Sage.

Baer, J. S. (2002). Student factors: Understanding individual variation in college drinking. *Journal of Studies on Alcohol* (Supp. 14), 40–53.

Bailey, A., Le Couteur, A., Gottesman, I., Bolton, P., Simonoff, E., Yuzda, E., et al. (1995). Autism as a strongly genetic disorder: Evidence from a British twin study. *Psychological Medicine, 25,* 63–77.

Bailey, S. (2002). Treatment of delinquents. In M. Rutter & E. Taylor (Eds.), *Child and Adolescent Psychiatry* (4th ed., pp. 1019–1037). Oxford, England: Blackwell.

Baker, T. B., McFall, R. M., & Shoham, V. (2008). Current status and future prospects of clinical psychology: Toward a scientifically principled approach to mental and behavioral health care. *Psychological Science in the Public Interest, 9,* 67–103.

Baldwin, S. A., Berkeljon, A., Atkins, D. C., Olsen, J. A., & Nielsen, S. L. (2009). Rates of change in naturalistic psychotherapy: Contrasting dose-effect and good-enough level models of change. *Journal of Consulting and Clinical Psychology, 77,* 203–211.

Baldwin, S. A., Wampold, B. E., & Imel, Z. E. (2007). Untangling the alliance-outcome correlation: Exploring the relative importance of therapist and patient vulnerability in the alliance. *Journal of Consulting and Clinical Psychology, 75,* 842–852.

Ballard, E. (2007). Support groups: Meeting the needs of families caring for persons with Alzheimer's disease. In C. B. Cox (Ed.), *Dementia and social work practice: Research and interventions* (pp. 321–337). New York: Springer Publishing Co.

Ballard, K. J., Granier, J. P., & Robin, D. A. (2008). Understanding the nature of apraxia of speech: Theory, analysis, and treatment. *Neuropsychological Trends, 4,* 7–44.

Ballenger, J. C. (2001). Overview of different pharmacotherapies for attaining remission in generalized anxiety disorder. *Journal of Clinical Psychiatry, 62*(Suppl. 19), 11–19.

Baltes, P., & Smith, J. (2008). The fascination of wisdom: Its nature, ontogeny, and function. *Perspectives on Psychological Science, 3,* 56–64.

Banaschewski, T., Becker, K., Scherag, S., Franke, B., & Coghill, D. (2010). Molecular genetics of attention-deficit/hyperactivity disorder: An overview. *European Child & Adolescent Psychiatry, 19,* 237–257.

Bancroft, J., & Vukadinovic, Z. (2004). Sexual addiction, sexual compulsivity, sexual impulsivity, or what? Toward a theoretical model. *Journal of Sex Research, 41,* 225–234.

Bandura, A., & Walters, R. H. (1963). *Social learning and personality development.* New York: Ronald Press.

Bangs, M. E., Tauscher-Wisniewski, S., Polzer, J., Zhang, S., Acharya, N., Desaiah, D., Trzepacz, P. T., et al. (2008). Meta-analysis of suicide-related behavior events in patients with atomoxetine. *Journal of the Academy of Child & Adolescent Psychiatry, 47,* 209–218.

Bankier, B., Aigner, M., & Bach, M. (2001). Alexithymia in DSM-IV disorder: Comparative evaluation of somatoform disorder, panic disorder, obsessive-compulsive disorder, and depression. *Psychosomatics, 42,* 235–240.

Barbaree, H. E., & Seto, M. C. (1997). Pedophilia: Assessment and treatment. In D. R. Laws & W. T. O'Donohue (Eds.), *Handbook of sexual deviance: Theory and application.* New York: Guilford.

Barbaresi, W. J., Katusic, S. K., Colligan, R. C., Weaver, A. L., & Jacobsen, S. J. (2005). The incidence of autism in Olmsted County, Minnesota, 1976–1997: Results from a population-based study. *Archives of Pediatric & Adolescent Medicine, 159,* 37–44.

Barber, C. (2008, February 27). The medicated Americans: Antidepressant prescriptions on the rise. *Scientific American Mind.*

Barch, D. M. (2005). The cognitive neuroscience of schizophrenia. *Annual Review of Clinical Psychology, 1,* 321–353.

Barel, E., Van IJzendoorn, M. H., Sagi-Schwartz, A., & Bakermans-Kranenburg, M. J. (2010). Surviving the Holocaust: A meta-analysis of the long-term sequelae of a genocide. *Psychological Bulletin, 136,* 677–698.

Bargh, J. A., & Morsella, E. (2008). The unconscious mind. *Perspectives on Psychological Science, 3,* 73–79.

Barkley, R. A. (Ed.). (2006). *Attention-Deficit Hyperactivity Disorder* (3rd ed.). New York: Guilford Press.

Barlow, D. H. (1997). Cognitive-behavioral therapy for panic disorder: Current status. *Journal of Clinical Psychiatry, 58*(Suppl. 2), 32–37.

Barlow, D. H. (2004). *Anxiety and its disorders: The nature and treatment of anxiety and panic* (2nd ed.). New York: Guilford.

Barlow, D. H. (Ed.). (2008). *Clinical handbook of psychological disorders* (4th ed.). New York: Guilford.

Barlow, D. H., Brown, T. A., & Craske, M. G. (1994). Definitions of panic attacks and panic disorder in the DSM-IV: Implications for research. *Journal of Abnormal Psychology, 103,* 553–564.

Barlow, D. H., Pincus, D. B., Heinrichs, N., & Choate, M. L. (2003). Anxiety disorders. In G. Stricker & T. Widiger (Eds.), *Handbook of psychology: Clinical psychology* (Vol. 8, pp. 119–147). New York: Wiley.

Barlow, D. H., Raffa, S. D., & Cohen, E. M. (2002). Psychosocial treatments for panic disorders, phobias, and generalized anxiety disorder. In P. E. Nathan & J. M. Gorman (Eds.), *A guide to treatments that work* (2nd ed., pp. 301–336). New York: Oxford.

Barnier, A. J. (2002). Posthypnotic amnesia for autobiographical episodes: A laboratory model of functional amnesia? *Psychological Science, 13,* 232–237.

Baroff, G. S., & Olley, J. G. (1999). *Mental retardation* (3rd ed.). Philadelphia: Brunner/Mazel.

Baron-Cohen, S., Leslie, A. M., & Frith, U. (1985). Does the autistic child have a "theory of mind"? *Cognition, 21,* 37–46.

Baron-Cohen, S., Scott, F. J., Allison, C., Williams, J., Bolton, P., Matthews, F. E., & Brayne, C. (2009). Prevalence of autism-spectrum conditions: UK school-based population study. *The British Journal of Psychiatry, 194,* 500–509.

Baron-Cohen, S., Tager-Flusberg, H., & Cohen, D. J. (Eds.). (1993). *Understanding other minds.* Oxford: Oxford University Press.

Barondes, S. H. (1993). *Molecules and Mental Illness.* New York: Scientific American.

Barrett, J. E., Williams, J. W., Jr., Oxman, T. E., Frank, E., Katon, W., Sullivan, M., et al. (2001). Treatment of dysthymia and minor depression in primary care: A randomized trial in patients aged 18 to 59 years. *Journal of Family Practice, 50,* 405–412.

Barrowclough, C., & Lobban, F. (2008). Family intervention. In *Clinical handbook of schizophrenia* (pp. 214–225). New York: Guilford Press.

Bartz, J. A., & Hollander, E. (2006). Is obsessive compulsive disorder an anxiety disorder? *Progress in Neuro-Psychopharmacology & Biological Psychiatry, 30,* 338–352.

Baskin, T. W., Tierney, S. C., Minami, T., & Wampold, B. E. (2003). Establishing specificity in psychotherapy: A meta-analysis of structural equivalence of placebo controls. *Journal of Consulting and Clinical Psychology, 71,* 973–979.

Basoglu, M., Mineka, S., Paker, M., Aker, T., Livanou, M., & Gok, S. (1997). Psychological preparedness for trauma as a protective factor in survivors of torture. *Psychological Medicine, 27,* 1421–1433.

Bass, C., Peveler, R., & House, A. (2001). Somatoform disorders: Severe psychiatric illnesses neglected by psychiatrists. *British Journal of Psychiatry, 179,* 11–14.

Bass, E., & Davis, L. (1988). *The courage to heal.* New York: Harper & Row.

Bass, J. K., Eaton, W. W., Abramowitz, S., & Sartorius, N. (2012). Global mental health issues: Culture and psychopathology. In W. W. Eaton (Ed.), *Public mental health* (pp. 41–57). New York: Oxford University Press.

Basson, R. (2002). A model of women's sexual arousal. *Journal of Sex & Marital Therapy, 28,* 1–10.

Basson, R., & Brotto, L. A. (2009). Disorders of sexual desire and subjective arousal in women. In R. Balon, R. Segraves, R. Balon, & R. Segraves (Eds.), *Clinical manual of sexual disorders* (pp. 119–159). Arlington, VA: American Psychiatric Publishing.

Basson, R., Berman, J., Burnett, A., Derogatis, L., Ferguson, D., Fourcroy, J., et al. (2000). Report of the international consensus development conference on female sexual dysfunction: Definitions and classification. *Journal of Urology, 163,* 888–896.

Basson, R., Brotto, L. A., Laan, E., Redmond, G., & Utian, W. H. (2005). Assessment and management of women's sexual dysfunctions: Problematic desire and arousal. *Journal of Sexual Medicine, 2,* 291–300.

Bastiani, A. M., Rao, R., Weltzin, T., & Kaye, W. H. (1995). Perfectionism in anorexia nervosa. *International Journal of Eating Disorders, 17,* 147–152.

Batelaan, N. M., Spijker, J., de Graaf, R., & Cuijpers, P. (2012). Mixed anxiety depression should not be included in *DSM-5*. *Journal of Nervous and Mental Disease, 200,* 495–498.

Bates, J. E., Wachs, T. D., & Emde, R. N. (1994). Toward practical uses for biological concepts of temperament. In J. E. Bates & T. D. Wachs (Eds.), *Temperament: Individual differences at the interface of biology and behavior* (pp. 275–306). Washington, DC: American Psychological Association.

Baucom, D. H., & Epstein, N. (1990). *Cognitive-behavioral marital therapy.* New York: Brunner/Mazel.

Baucom, D. H., Epstein, N., & LaTaillade, J. J. (2002). Cognitive-behavioral couple therapy. In A. Gurman & N. Jacobson (Eds.), *Clinical Handbook of Couple Therapy* (3rd ed., pp. 26–58). New York: Guilford.

Baucom, D. H., Hahlweg, K., Atkins, D. C., Engl, J., & Thurmaier, F. (2006). Long-term prediction of marital quality following a relationship education program: Being positive in a constructive way. *Journal of Family Psychology, 20,* 448–455.

Baucom, D. H., Notarius, C. I., Burnett, C. K., & Haefner, P. (1990). Gender differences and sex-role identity in marriage. In F. D. Fincham & T. N. Bradbury (Eds.), *The Psychology of Marriage: Basic Issues and Applications* (pp. 150–171). New York: Guilford.

Bauer, M. S., & Mitchner, L. (2004). What is a "mood stabilizer"? An evidence-based response. *American Journal of Psychiatry, 161,* 3–18.

Bauer, R. M., & Demery, J. A. (2003). Agnosia. In K. M. Heilman & E. Valenstein (Eds.), *Clinical neuropsychology* (4th ed., pp. 236–295). London: Oxford University Press.

Baum, A., Davidson, L. M., Singer, J. E., & Street, S. W. (1987). Stress as a psychophysiological response. In A. Baum & J. E. Singer (Eds.), *Handbook of psychology and health stress* (Vol. 5, pp. 1–24). Hillsdale, NJ: Erlbaum.

Bauman, M. L. (1996). Neuroanatomic observations of the brain in pervasive developmental disorders. *Journal of Autism and Developmental Disorders, 26,* 199–203.

Baumeister, R. F. (1990). Suicide as escape from self. *Psychological Review, 97,* 90–113.

Baumeister, R. F. (1997). Identity, self-concept, and self-esteem: The self lost and found. In R. Hogan, J. Johnson, & S. Briggs (Eds.), *Handbook of personality psychology* (pp. 681–710). San Diego, CA: Academic Press.

Baumeister, R. F., & Butler, J. L. (1997). Sexual masochism. In D. R. Laws & W. T. O'Donohue (Eds.), *Handbook of sexual deviance: Theory and application.* New York: Guilford.

Baumeister, R. F., Campbell, J. D., Krueger, J. L., & Vohs, K. D. (2003). Does high self-esteem cause better performance, interpersonal success, happiness, or healthier lifestyles? *Psychological Science in the Public Interest, 4,* 1–44.

Bay-Cheng, L. Y., Zucker, A. N., Stewart, A. J., & Pomerleau, C. S. (2002). Linking femininity, weight concern, and mental health among Latina, Black and White women. *Psychology of Women Quarterly, 26,* 36–45.

Beach, S. R. H., Sandeen, E. E., & O'Leary, K. D. (1990). *Depression in Marriage: A Model for Etiology and Treatment.* New York: Guilford.

Beach, S. R. H., Wamboldt, M. Z., Kaslow, N. J., Heyman, R. E., & Reiss, D. (2006). Describing relationship problems in *DSM-V*: Toward better guidance for research and clinical practice. *Journal of Family Psychology, 20,* 359–368.

Beauchaine, T. P., Webster-Stratton, C., & Reid, M. J. (2005). Mediators, moderators, and predictors of 1-year outcomes among children treated for early-onset conduct problems: A latent growth curve analysis. *Journal of Consulting and Clinical Psychology, 73,* 371–388.

Bechtoldt, H., Norcross, J. C., Wyckoff, L. A., Pokrywa, M. L., & Campbell, L. F. (2001). Theoretical orientations and employment settings of clinical and counseling psychologists: A comparative study. *The Clinical Psychologist, 54,* 3–6.

Beck, A. T. (1967). *Depression: Clinical, experimental, and theoretical aspects.* New York: Harper & Row.

Beck, A. T. (1976). *Cognitive therapy and the emotional disorders.* New York: International Universities Press.

Beck, A. T., Rush, A. J., Shaw, B. F., & Emery, G. (1979). *Cognitive therapy of depression.* New York: Guilford.

Becker, C. B., Bull, S., Schaumberg, K., Cauble, A., & Franco, A. (2008). Effectiveness of peerled eating disorders prevention: A replication trial. *Journal of Consulting and Clinical Psychology, 76,* 347–354.

Becker, J. V., & Johnson, B. R. (2009). Gender identity disorders and paraphilias. In J. A. Bourgeois, R. E. Hales, J. S. Young, & S. C. Yudofsky (Eds.), *The American Psychiatric Publishing Board Review Guide for Psychiatry* (pp. 425–435). Arlington, VA: American Psychiatric Publishing.

Becker, J. V., Alpert, J. L., BigFoot, D. S., Bonner, B. L., Geddie, L. F., Henggeler, S. W., et al. (1995). Empirical research on child abuse treatment: Report by the Child Abuse and Neglect Treatment Working Group, American Psychological Association. *Journal of Clinical Child Psychology, 24,* 23–46.

Beesdo-Baum, K. K., Knappe, S. S., Fehm, L. L., Höfler, M. M., Lieb, R. R., Hofmann, S. G., & Wittchen, H. U. (2012). The natural course of social anxiety disorder among adolescents and young adults. *Acta Psychiatrica Scandinavica, 126,* 411–425.

Behan, C., Kennelly, B., & O'Callaghan, E. (2008). The economic cost of schizophrenia in Ireland: A cost of illness study. *Irish Journal of Psychological Medicine, 25*(3), 80–87.

Bell, L. G., & Bell, D. C. (2005). Family dynamics in adolescence affect midlife well-being. *Journal of Family Psychology, 19,* 198–207.

Belsky, J., & Pluess, M. (2009). Beyond diathesis stress: Differential susceptibility to environmental influences. *Psychological Bulletin, 135,* 885–908.

Belsky, J., Steinberg, L., & Draper, P. (1991). Childhood experience, interpersonal development and reproductive strategy: An evolutionary theory of socialization. *Child Development, 62,* 647–670.

Bender, R. E., & Alloy, L. B. (2011). Life stress and kindling in bipolar disorder: Review of the evidence and integration with emerging biopsychosocial theories. *Clinical Psychology Review, 31,* 383–398.

Benitez, C. I. P., Smith, K., Vasile, R. G., Rende, R., Edelen, M. O., & Keller, M. B. (2008). Use of benzodiazepines and selective serotonin reuptake inhibitors in middle-aged and older adults with anxiety disorders. *American Journal of Geriatric Psychiatry, 16,* 5–13.

Berenbaum, H., & Barch, D. (1995). The categorization of thought disorder. *Journal of Psycholinguistic Research, 24,* 349–376.

Berg, K. C., Crosby R. D., Cao L, Peterson, C. B., Engel S. G., Mitchell J. E., & Wonderlich S. A. (2013). Facets of negative affect prior to and following binge-only, purge-only, and binge/purge events in women with bulimia nervosa. *Journal of Abnormal Psychology, 122,* 111–118.

Berman, A. L., & Jobes, D. A. (1994). Treatment of the suicidal adolescent. In A. A. Leenaars, J. T. Maltsberger, & R. A. Neimeyer (Eds.), *Treatment of suicidal people* (pp. 89–100). Washington, DC: Taylor & Francis.

Berman, J. R., Berman, L. A., Werbin, T. J., Flaherty, E. E., Leahy, N. M., & Goldstein, I. (1999). Clinical evaluation of female sexual function: Effects of age and estrogen status on subjective and physiologic sexual responses. *International Journal of Impotence Research, 11*(Suppl. 1), 31–38

Bernard, S. H. (2002). Services for children and adolescents with severe learning disabilities (mental retardation). In M. Rutter & E. Taylor (Eds.), *Child and adolescent psychiatry* (4th ed., pp. 1114–1127). Oxford: Blackwell.

Bernlef, J. (1988). *Out of mind.* London: Faber.

Bernstein, G. A., Borchardt, C. M., Perwien, A. R., Crosby, R. D., Kushner, M. G., Thuras, P. D., et al. (2000). Imipramine plus cognitive-behavioral therapy in the treatment of school refusal. *Journal of the Academy of Child & Adolescent Psychiatry, 39,* 276–283.

Berry, J. W., Poortinga, Y. H., Segall, M. H., & Dasen, P. R. (2002). *Cross-cultural psychology: Research and applications* (2nd ed.). New York: Cambridge University Press.

Bertelson, A., Harvald, B., & Hauge, M. (1977). A Danish twin study of manic-depressive disorders. *British Journal of Psychiatry, 130,* 330–351.

Besharov, D. J. (1988). How child abuse programs hurt poor children: The misuse of foster care. *Clearinghouse Review, 20,* 219–227.

Besharov, D. J. (1992). A balanced approach to reporting child abuse. *Child, Youth, and Family Services Quarterly, 15,* 5–7.

Bettleheim, B. (1967). *The empty fortress.* New York: Free Press.

Beutler, L. E., Clarkin, J. F., Crago, M., & Bergan, J. (1991). Client-therapist matching. In C. R. Snyder & D. R. Forsyth (Eds.), *Handbook of social and clinical psychology* (pp. 699–716). Elmsford, NY: Pergamon Press.

Beutler, L. E., Machado, P. P. P., & Neufeldt, S. A. (1994). Therapist variables. In A. E. Bergin & S. L. Garfield (Eds.), *Handbook of psychotherapy and behavior change* (4th ed., pp. 229–269). Oxford England: John Wiley & Sons.

Beynon, C. M., McVeigh, J., & Roe, B. (2007). Problematic drug use, ageing and older people. *Ageing & Society, 27,* 799–810.

Biederman, J., Faraone, S. V., Wozniak, J., Mick, E., Kwon, A., & Aleardi, M. (2004). Further evidence of unique developmental phenotypic correlates of pediatric bipolar disorder: Findings from a large sample of clinically referred preadolescent children assessed over the last 7 years. *Journal of Affective Disorders, 82,* S45–S58.

Biederman, J., Klein, R. G., Pine, D. S., & Klein, D. F. (1998). Resolved: Mania is mistaken for ADHD in prepubertal children. *Journal of the American Academy of Child & Adolescent Psychiatry, 37,* 1091–1096.

Binik, Y. M. (2005). Should dyspareunia be retained as a sexual dysfunction in DSM-V? *Archives of Sexual Behavior, 34,* 11–21.

Birditt, K. S., & Antonucci, T. C. (2007). Relationship quality profiles and well-being among married adults. *Journal of Family Psychology, 21,* 595–604.

Bishop, S. J. (2007). Neurocognitive mechanisms of anxiety: An integrative account. *Trends in Cognitive Sciences, 11,* 307–316.

Bisson, J. I., Ehlers, A., Matthews, R., Pilling, S., Richards, D., & Turner, S. (2007). Psychological treatments for chronic post-traumatic stress disorder: Systematic review and meta-analysis. *British Journal of Psychiatry, 190,* 97–104.

Black, D. W., Kehrberg, L. D., Flumerfelt, D. L., & Schlosser, S. S. (1997). Characteristics of 36 subjects reporting compulsive sexual behavior. *American Journal of Psychiatry, 154,* 243–250.

Black, D. W., McCormick, B., Losch, M. E., Shaw, M., Lutz, G., & Allen, J. (2012). Prevalence of problem gambling in Iowa: Revisiting Shaffer's adaptation hypothesis. *Annals of Clinical Psychiatry, 24,* 279–284.

Black, P. H., & Garbutt, L. D. (2002). Stress, inflammation and cardiovascular disease. *Journal of Psychosomatic Research, 52,* 1–23.

Black, S. A., Gallaway, M. S., Bell, M. R., & Ritchie, E. C. (2011). *Military Psychology, 23,* 433–451.

Blair, R. J. R. et al. (2001). A selective impairment in the processing of sad and fearful expressions in children with psychopathic tendencies. *Journal of Abnormal Child Psychology, 29,* 491–498.

Blanchard, E. B. (1994). Behavioral medicine and health psychology. In A. E. Bergin & S. L. Garfield (Eds.), *Handbook of psychotherapy and behavior change* (4th ed., pp. 701–733). New York: Wiley.

Blanchard, E. B. (Ed.). (1992). Special issue on behavioral medicine. *Journal of Consulting and Clinical Psychology, 60,* 493–498.

Blanchard, J., Cohen, A., & Carreño, J. (2007). Emotion and schizophrenia. In *Emotion and psychopathology: Bridging affective and clinical science* (pp. 103–122). Washington, DC: American Psychological Association.

Blanchard, R. (2010). The DSM diagnostic criteria for pedophilia. *Archives of Sexual Behavior, 39,* 304–316.

Blashfield, R. (2000). Growth of the literature on the topic of personality disorders. *American Journal of Psychiatry, 157,* 472–473.

Blazer, D. (2013). Neurocognitive disorders in DSM-5. *American Journal of Psychiatry, 170,* 585–587.

Blazer, D. G. (2004). The epidemiology of depressive disorders in late life. In S. P. Roose & H. A. Sackheim (Eds.), *Late-life depression* (pp. 3–11). New York: New York University Press.

Bleiberg, K. L., & Markowitz, J. C. (2008). Interpersonal psychotherapy for depression. In D. H. Barlow (Ed.), *Clinical handbook of psychological disorders: A step-by-step treatment manual* (4th ed., pp. 306–327). New York, NY: The Guilford Press.

Bloemers, J., van Rooij, K., Poels, S., Goldstein, I., Everaerd, W., Koppeschaar, H., et al. (2013). Toward personalized sexual medicine (Part 1): Integrating the "dual control model" into differential drug treatments for hypoactive sexual desire disorder and female sexual arousal disorder. *Journal of Sexual Medicine, 10*, 791–809.

Blumberg, S. J., et al. (2013). Changes in prevalence of parent-reported autism spectrum disorder in school-aged U.S. children: 2007–2011–2012. *National Health Statistics Reports; No 65.* Hyattsville, MD: National Center for Health Statistics.

Blume, J. H., Johnson, S. L., & Seeds, C. (2009). An empirical look at *Atkins v. Virginia* and its application in capital cases. *Tennessee Law Review, 76*, 625–639.

Blundell, J. E. (1995). The psychobiological approach to appetite and weight control. In K. D. Brownell & C. G. Fairburn (Eds.), *Eating disorders and obesity: A comprehensive handbook* (pp. 13–20). New York: Guilford.

Bogg, T., & Roberts, B. W. (2004). Conscientiousness and health-related behaviors: A meta-analysis of the leading behavioral contributors to mortality. *Psychological Bulletin, 130*, 887–919.

Bohus, M., Haaf, B., Simms, T., Limberger, M. F., Schmahl, C., Unckel, C., et al. (2004). Effectiveness of inpatient dialectical behavioral therapy for borderline personality disorder: A controlled trial. *Behaviour Research & Therapy, 42*, 487–499.

Bolla, K. I., Cadet, J., & London, E. D. (1998). The neuropsychiatry of chronic cocaine abuse. *Journal of Neuropsychiatry and Clinical Neurosciences, 10*, 280–289.

Bonanno, G. A. (2004). Loss, trauma, and human resilience: Have we underestimated the human capacity to thrive after extremely aversive events? *American Psychologist, 59*, 20–28.

Bonanno, G. A., Neria, Y., Mancini, A., Coifman, K. G., Litz, B., & Insel, B. (2007). Is there more to complicated grief than depression and posttraumatic stress disorder? A test of incremental validity. *Journal of Abnormal Psychology, 116*, 342–351.

Bonanno, G. A., Papa, A., Lalande, K., Westphal, M., & Coifman, K. (2004). The importance of being flexible: The ability to both enhance and suppress emotional expression predicts long-term adjustment. *Psychological Science, 15*, 482–487.

Bonanno, G. A., Papa, A., Lalande, K., Zhang, N., & Noll, J. G. (2005). Grief processing and deliberate grief avoidance: A prospective comparison of bereaved spouses and parents in the United States and the People's Republic of China. *Journal of Consulting and Clinical Psychology, 73*, 86–98.

Bonanno, G. A., Westphal, M., & Mancini, A. D. (2011). Resilience to loss and potential trauma. *Annual Review of Clinical Psychology, 7*, 1.1–1.25.

Bonner-Jackson, A., Haul, K., Csernansky, J., & Barch, D. (2005). The influence of encoding strategy on episodic memory and cortical activity in schizophrenia. *Biological Psychiatry, 58*, 47–55.

Booth, A., et al. (2000). Biosocial perspectives on the family. *Journal of Marriage and the Family, 62*, 1018–1034.

Borkovec, T. D., Alcaine, O. M., & Behar, E. (2004). Avoidance theory of worry and generalized anxiety disorder. In R. G. Heimberg & C. L. Turk (Eds.), *Generalized anxiety disorder: Advances in research and practice* (pp. 77–108). New York: Guilford.

Borkovec, T. D., Newman, M. G., Pincus, A. L., & Lytle, R. (2002). A component analysis of cognitive-behavioral therapy for generalized anxiety disorder and the role of interpersonal problems. *Journal of Consulting and Clinical Psychology, 70*, 288–298.

Borroni, B., Agosti, C., Gipponi, S., & Padovani, A. (2006). Dementia with Lewy bodies with and without hallucinations: A clue to different entities? *International Psychogeriatrics, 18*, 355–360.

Bosma, H. A., & Kunnen, E. S. (2001). Determinants and mechanisms in ego identity development: A review and synthesis. *Developmental Review, 21*, 39–66.

Bourne, R., Tahir, T., Borthwick, M., & Sampson, E. (2008). Drug treatment of delirium: Past, present and future. *Journal of Psychosomatic Research, 65*, 273–282.

Bouton, M. E., Mineka, S., & Barlow, D. (2001). A modern learning theory perspective on the etiology of panic disorder. *Psychological Review, 108*, 4–32.

Bower, G. H. (1990). Awareness, the unconscious, and repression: An experimental psychologist's perspective. In J. L. Singer (Ed.), *Repression and dissociation* (pp. 209–232). Chicago: University of Chicago Press.

Bowie, C. R., Depp, C., McGrath, J. A., Wolyniec, P., Mausbach, B. T., Thornquist, M. H., et al. (2010). Prediction of real-world functional disability in chronic mental disorders: A comparison of schizophrenia and bipolar disorder. *American Journal of Psychiatry, 167*(9), 1116–1124.

Bowker, G. C., & Star, S. L. (1999). *Sorting things out: Classification and its consequences.* Cambridge, MA: MIT Press.

Bowlby, J. (1980). *Loss: Sadness and Depression.* New York: Basic Books.

Bowlby, J. (1969). *Attachment.* New York: Basic Books.

Bowlby, J. (1973). *Separation: Anxiety and Anger.* New York: Basic Books.

Bowlby, J. (1979). *The Making and Breaking of Affectional Bonds.* London: Tavistock.

Boydell, J., & Murray, R. (2003). Urbanization, migration and risk of schizophrenia. In R. M. Murray & P. B. Jones (Eds.), *The epidemiology of schizophrenia* (pp. 49–67). New York: Cambridge University Press.

Boysen, G. A., & VanBergen, A. (2013). A review of published research on adult dissociative identity disorder: 2000–1010. *Journal of Nervous and Mental Disease, 201*, 5–11.

Bradbury, T. N., & Fincham, F. D. (1990). Attributions in marriage: Review and critique. *Psychological Bulletin, 107*, 3–33.

Bradbury, T. N., Fincham, F. D., & Beach, S. R. H. (2000). Research on the nature and determinants of marital satisfaction: A decade in review. *Journal of Marriage and the Family, 62*, 964–980.

Bradford, J. M. W. (2001). The neurobiology, neuropharmacology, and pharmacological treatment of the paraphilias and compulsive sexual behaviour. *Canadian Journal of Psychiatry, 46*, 26–34.

Bradford, J. M. W., & Pawlak, A. (1993). Double-blind placebo cross-over study of cyproterone acetate in the treatment of paraphilias. *Archives of Sexual Behavior, 22*, 383–402.

Bradley, C. (1937). The behavior of children receiving benzedrine. *American Journal of Psychiatry, 94*, 577–585.

Brady, K. T., Back, S. E., & Coffey, S. F. (2004). Substance abuse and posttraumatic stress disorder. *Current Directions in Psychological Science, 13*, 206–209.

Braff, D., Schork, N., & Gottesman, I. (2007). Endophenotyping schizophrenia. *American Journal of Psychiatry, 164*, 705–707.

Bramlett, M. D., & Mosher, W. D. (2001). *First marriage dissolution, divorce, and remarriage: United States* (Advance Data From Vital and Health Statistics No. 323). Hyattsville, MD: National Center for Health Statistics.

Braun, B. G. (1989). Psychotherapy of the survivor of incest with a dissociative disorder. *Psychiatric Clinics of North America, 12*, 307–324.

Braun, D. L., Sunday, S. R., & Halmi, K. A. (1994). Psychiatric comorbidity in patients with eating disorders. *Psychological Medicine, 24*, 859–867.

Brébion, G., Ohlsen, R., Pilowsky, L., & David, A. (2008). Visual hallucinations in schizophrenia: Confusion between imagination and perception. *Neuropsychology, 22*(3), 383–389.

Breggin, P. R. (2004). Recent U.S. Canadian and British regulatory agency actions concerning antidepressant-induced harm to self and others: A review and analysis. *International Journal of Risk and Safety in Medicine, 16*, 247–259.

Bregman, J. D., Dykens, E., Watson, M., Ort, S. I., & Leckman, J. F. (1987). Fragile-X syndrome: Variability of phenotypic expression. *Journal of the American Academy of Child and Adolescent Psychiatry, 26*, 463–471.

Breitner, J. C. S., Gatz, M., Bergem, A. L. M., Christian, J. C., Mortimer, J. A., McClearn, G. E., et al. (1993). Use of twin cohorts for research in Alzheimer's disease. *Neurology, 43*, 261–267.

Bremner, J. D. (2005). *Brain imaging handbook.* New York: Norton.

Brent, D. A. (2004). Antidepressants and pediatric depression—The risk of doing nothing. *New England Journal of Medicine, 351*, 1598–1601.

Brent, D. A., & Bridge, J. (2003). Firearms availability and suicide: Evidence, interventions, and future directions. *American Behavioral Scientist, 46*, 1192–1210.

Breslau, N., Kessler, R. C., Chilcoat, H. D., Schultz, L. R., Davis, G. C., & Andreski, P. (1998). Trauma and post traumatic stress disorder in the community: The 1996 Detroit Area Survey of Trauma. *Archives of General Psychiatry, 55*, 626–632.

Breslau, N., Peterson, E. L., & Schultz, L. R. (2008). A second look at prior trauma and the posttraumatic stress disorder effects of subsequent trauma: A prospective epidemiological study. *Archives of General Psychiatry, 65*, 431–437.

Brestan, E. V., & Eyberg, S. M. (1998). Effective psychosocial treatments of conduct-disordered children and adolescents: 29 years, 82 studies, and 5,272 kids. *Journal of Clinical Child Psychology, 27*, 180–189.

Brewin, C. R., Andrews, B., & Gotlib, I. H. (1993). Psychopathology and early experience: A reappraisal of retrospective reports. *Psychological Bulletin, 113*, 82–98.

Brewin, C. R., MacCarthy, B., Duda, K., & Vaughn, C. E. (1991). Attributions and expressed emotion in the relatives of patients with schizophrenia. *Journal of Abnormal Psychology, 100*, 546–554.

Brezo, J., Klempan, T., & Turecki, G. (2008). The genetics of suicide: A critical review of molecular studies. *Psychiatric Clinics of North America, 31*, 179–203.

Bridge, J. A., Iyengar, S., Salary, C. B., Barbe, R. P., Birmaher, B., Pincus, H. A., et al. (2007). Clinical response and risk for reported suicidal ideation and suicide attempts in pediatric antidepressant treatment: A meta-analysis of randomized control trials. *Journal of the American Medical Association, 297*, 1683–1696.

Brodaty, H., Seeher, K., & Gibson, L. (2012). Dementia time to death: A systematic literature review on survival time and years of life lost in people with dementia. *International Psychogeriatrics, 24*, 1032–1045.

Broderick, G. (2006). Premature ejaculation: On defining and quantifying a common male sexual dysfunction. *Journal of Sexual Medicine, 3*, 295–302.

Bromet, E. J., & Susser, E. (2012). The burden of mental illness. In E. Susser, S. Schwarz, A. Morabia, E. J. Bromet, M. D. Begg, J. M. Gorman, & M. King (Eds.), *Psychiatric epidemiology: Searching for the causes of mental disorders.* New York: Oxford University Press.

Bromet, E., Naz, B., Fochtmann, L., Carlson, G., & Tanenberg-Karant, M. (2005). Long-term diagnostic stability and outcome in recent first-episode cohort studies of schizophrenia. *Schizophrenia Bulletin, 31*, 639–649.\

Brothers, B. M., Yang, H., Strunk, D. R., & Andersen, B. L. (2011). Cancer patients with major depressive disorder: Testing a biobehavioral/cognitive behavior intervention. *Journal of Consulting and Clinical Psychology, 79*, 253–260.

Brown, A. S., & Derkits, E. J. (2010). Prenatal infection and schizophrenia: A review of epidemiologic and translational studies. *American Journal of Psychiatry, 167*(3), 261–280.

Brown, C. H., Wyman, P. A., Brinales, J. M., & Gibbons, R. D. (2007). The role of randomized trials in testing interventions for the prevention of youth suicide. *International Review of Psychiatry, 19*, 1–15.

Brown, G. W. (2002). Social roles, context and evolution in the origins of depression. *Journal of Health and Social Behavior, 43,* 255–276.

Brown, G. W., & Harris, T. O. (1978). *Social origins of depression: A study of psychiatric disorder in women.* London: Tavistock.

Brown, R. J. (2004). Psychological mechanisms of medically unexplained syndromes: An integrative conceptual model. *Psychological Bulletin, 130,* 793–812.

Brown, S. L., Nesse, R. M., Vinokur, A. D., & Smith, D. M. (2003). Providing social support may be more beneficial than receiving it: Results from a prospective study of mortality. *Psychological Science, 14,* 320–327.

Brown, T. A., & Barlow, D. H. (2009). A proposal for a dimensional classification system based on the shared features of the DSM-IV anxiety and mood disorders: Implications for assessment and treatment. *Psychological Assessment, 21,* 256–271.

Brownell, K. D., & Fairburn, C. G. (Eds.). (1995). *Eating disorders and obesity: A comprehensive handbook.* New York: Guilford.

Browning, C. R., & Laumann, E. O. (1997). Sexual contact between children and adults: A life course perspective. *American Sociological Review, 62,* 540–560.

Bruch, H. (1982). Anorexia nervosa: Therapy and theory. *American Journal of Psychiatry, 132,* 1531–1538.

Bryant, R. A., Friedman, M. J., Spiegel, D., Ursano, R., & Strain, J. (2010). A review of acute stress disorder in DSM-5. *Depression and Anxiety, 0,* 1–16.

Bryant, R. A., & Guthrie, R. M. (2005). Maladaptive appraisals as a risk factor for posttraumatic stress: A study of trainee firefighters. *Psychological Science, 16,* 749–752.

Bryant, R. A., & Harvey, A. G. (2000). *Acute stress disorder: A handbook of theory assessment and treatment.* Washington, DC: American Psychological Association.

Bryant, R. A., Moulds, M. L., & Nixon, R. D. V. (2003). Cognitive behaviour therapy of acute stress disorder: A four-year follow-up. *Behaviour Research and Therapy, 41,* 489–494.

Bryant, R. A., Moulds, M. L., Nixon, R. D. V., Mastrodomenico, J., Felmingham, K., & Hopwood, S. (2006). Hypnotherapy and cognitive behaviour therapy of acute stress disorder: A 3-year follow-up. *Behaviour Research and Therapy, 44,* 1331–1335.

Bryne, S. M. (2002). Sport, occupation, and eating disorders. In C. G. Fairburn & K. D. Brownell (Eds.), *Eating disorders and obesity* (2nd ed., pp. 256–259). New York: Guilford.

Buchanan, R. (2007). Persistent negative symptoms in schizophrenia: An overview. *Schizophrenia Bulletin, 33,* 1013–1022.

Buckley, P., & Stahl, S. (2007). Pharmacological treatment of negative symptoms of schizophrenia: Therapeutic opportunity or cul-de-sac? *Acta Psychiatrica Scandinavica, 115,* 93–100.

Budney, A. J., & Lile, J. A. (2009). Moving beyond the cannabis controversy into the world of the cannabinoids. *International Review of Psychiatry, 21,* 91–95.

Bugg, J., Zook, N., DeLosh, E., Davalos, D., & Davis, H. (2006). Age differences in fluid intelligence: Contributions of general slowing and frontal decline. *Brain and Cognition, 62,* 9–16.

Buhlmann, U., Glaesmer, H., Mewes, R., Fama, J. M., Wilhelm, S., Brähler, E., & Rief, W. (2010). Updates on the prevalence of body dysmorphic disorder: A population-based survey. *Psychiatry Research, 178,* 171–175.

Buka, S. L., & Gilman, S. E. (2002). Psychopathology and the life course. In J. E. Helzer & J. J. Hudziak (Eds.), *Defining psychopathology in the 21st century* (pp. 129–142). Washington, DC: erican Psychiatric Press.

Bulik, C. M., Sullivan, P. F., Tozzi, F., Furberg, H., Lichtenstein, P., & Pedersen, N. L. (2006). Prevalence, heritability, and prospective risk factors for anorexia nervosa. *Archives of General Psychiatry, 63,* 305–312.

Burke, B. L., & McGee, D. P. (1990). Sports deficit disorder. *Pediatrics, 85,* 1118.

Burke, J. D., Waldman, I., & Lahey, B. B. (2010). Predictive validity of childhood oppositional defiant disorder and conduct disorder: Implications for the DSM-V. *Journal of Abnormal Psychology, 119,* 739–751.

Burlingame, M. (1994). *The inner world of Abraham Lincoln.* Urbana and Chicago: University of Illinois Press.

Burns, J. (2006). Psychosis: A costly by-product of social brain evolution in Homo sapiens. *Progress in Neuro-Psychopharmacology & Biological Psychiatry, 30,* 797–814.

Burt, S. A. (2010). Are there shared environmental influences on attention-deficit/hyperactivity disorder? Reply to Wood, Buitelaar, Rijsdijk, Asherson, and Kunsti (2010). *Psychological Bulletin, 136,* 341–343.

Burt, S. A., Krueger, R. F., McGue, M., & Iancono, W. G. (2001). Sources of covariation among attention-deficit/hyperactivity disorder, oppositional defiant disorder, and conduct disorder: The importance of shared environment. *Journal of Abnormal Psychology, 110,* 516–525.

Buss, A. (1991). The EAS theory of temperament. In J. Strelau & A. Angleitner (Eds.), *Explorations in Temperament.* New York: Plenum.

Buss, D. M. (2009). How can evolutionary psychology successfully explain personality and individual differences? *Perspectives on Psychological Science, 4,* 359–366.

Butcher, J. N. (2006). *MMPI-2: A practitioner's guide.* Washington, DC: American Psychological Association.

Butler, S. M., Ashford, J., & Snowdon, D. A. (1996). Age, education, and changes in the Mini-Mental State Exam scores of older women: Findings from the nun study. *Journal of the American Geriatrics Society, 44,* 675–681.

Butzlaff, R. L., & Hooley, J. M. (1998). Expressed emotion and psychiatric relapse. *Archives of General Psychiatry, 55,* 547–552.

Byrne, C. A., Kilpatrick, D. G., Howley, S. S., & Beatty, D. (1999, September). Female victims of partner versus nonpartner violence: Experiences with the criminal justice system. *Criminal Justice and Behavior, 26*(3), 275–292. doi: 10.1177/0093854899026003001

## C

Cadieux, R. J. (1996). Azapirones: An alternative to benzodiazepines for anxiety. *American Family Physician, 53,* 2349–2353.

Cadoret, R. J., Yates, W. R., Troughton, E., Woodworth, G., & Stewart, M. A. (1995). Genetic-environmental interaction in the genesis of aggressivity and conduct disorders. *Archives of General Psychiatry, 52,* 916–924.

Cafri, G., Yamamiya, Y., Brannick, M., & Thompson, J. K. (2005). The influence of sociocultural factors on body image: A meta-analysis. *Clinical Psychology: Science and Practice, 12,* 421–433.

Cahill, S. P., & Foa, E. B. (2007). Psychological theories of PTSD. In M. J. Friedman, T. M. Keane, & P. A. Resick (Eds.), *Handbook of PTSD: Science and practice* (pp. 55–77). New York: The Guilford Press.

Calkins, M. E., Iacono, W. G., & Ones, D. S. (2008). Eye movement dysfunction in first-degree relatives of patients with schizophrenia: A meta-analytic evaluation of candidate endophenotypes. *Brain and Cognition, 68,* 436–461.

Callaghan, G. M., Chacon, C., Coles, C., Botts, J., & Laraway, S. (2009). An empirical evaluation of the diagnostic criteria for premenstrual dysphoric disorder: Problems with sex specificity and validity. *Women & Therapy, 32,* 1–21.

Callahan, L. A., Steadman, H. J., McGreevy, M. A., & Robbins, P. C. (1991). The volume and characteristics of insanity defense pleas: An eight-state study. *Bulletin of the American Academy of Psychiatry and the Law, 19,* 331–338.

Campbell, E. (1990). The psychopath and the definition of "mental disease of defect" under the model penal code test of insanity: A question of psychology or a question of law? *Nebraska Law Review, 69,* 190–229.

Campbell, R. (2008). The psychological impact of rape victims' experiences with the legal, medical, and mental health systems. *American Psychologist, 63,* 702–717.

Campbell-Sills, L., Barlow, D. H., Brown, T. A., & Hofmann, S. G. (2006). Acceptability and suppression of negative emotion in anxiety and mood disorders. *Emotion, 6,* 587–595.

Canino, G. J., Bird, H. R., Shrout, P. E., Rubio-Stipec, M., Bravo, M., Martinez, R., et al. (1987). Prevalence of specific psychiatric disorders in Puerto Rico. *Archives of General Psychiatry, 44,* 727–735.

Canli, T. (2009). Individual differences in human amygdala function. In P. J. Whalen, E. A. Phelps, P. J. Whalen, & E. A. Phelps (Eds.), *The human amygdala* (pp. 250–264). New York, NY US: Guilford Press.

Cannon, M., Jones, P. B., & Murray, R. M. (2002). Obstetric complications and schizophrenia: Historical and meta-analytic review. *American Journal of Psychiatry, 159,* 1080–1092.

Cannon, T. D. (2010). Candidate gene studies in the GWAS era: The MET proto-oncogene, neurocognition, and schizophrenia. *American Journal of Psychiatry, 167,* 369–372.

Cannon, T. D., Kaprio, J., Loennqvist, J., Huttunen, M., & Koskenvuo, M. (1998). The genetic epidemiology of schizophrenia in a Finnish twin cohort: A population-based modeling study. *Archives of General Psychiatry, 55,* 67–74.

Cantor-Graae, E., & Selten, J. (2005). Schizophrenia and migration: A meta-analysis and review. *American Journal of Psychiatry, 162,* 12–24.

Cantwell, D. P., Baker, L., & Rutter, M. (1979). Families of autistic and dysphasic children: I. Family life and interactions pattern. *Archives of General Psychiatry, 36,* 682–687.

Cappeliez, P., O'Rourke, N., & Chaudhury, H. (2005). Functions of reminiscence and mental health in later life. *Aging & Mental Health, 9,* 95–301.

Capron, C., & Duyme, M. (1989). Assessment of effects of socioeconomic status on IQ in a full cross-fostering study. *Nature, 340,* 552–554.

Cardno, A. G., Jones, L. A., Murphy, K. C., Sanders, R. D., Asherson, P., Owen, M. J., et al. (1998). Sibling pairs with schizophrenia or schizoaffective disorder: Associations of subtypes, symptoms and demographic variables. *Psychological Medicine, 28,* 815–823.

Carlat, D. J., Camargo, C. A., & Herzog, D. B. (1997). Eating disorders in males: A report on 135 patients. *American Journal of Psychiatry, 154,* 1127–1132.

Carlsson, A., & Lindqvist, M. (1963). Effect of chlorpromazine and haloperidol on the formation of 3-methoxytyramine and normetanephrine in mouse brain. *Acta Pharmacology, 20,* 140.

Carlsson, A., Waters, N., Holm-Waters, S., Tedroff, J., Nilsson, M., & Carlsson, M. L. (2001). Interactions between monoamines, glutamate, and GABA in schizophrenia: New evidence. *Annual Review of Pharmacology and Toxicology, 41,* 237–260.

Carmen, B., Angeles, M., Munoz, A., & Amate, J. (2004). Efficacy and safety of naltrexone and acamprosate in the treatment of alcohol dependence: A systematic review. *Addiction, 99,* 811–823.

Carmin, C., & Ownby, R.L. (2010). Assessment of anxiety in older adults. In P.A. Lichtenberg (Ed.), *Handbook of assessment in clinical gerontology* (pp. 45–60). Burlington, MA: Elsevier.

Carney, R. M., Freeland, K. E., Rich, M. W., & Jaffe, A. S. (1995). Depression as a risk factor for cardiac events in established coronary heart disease: A review of possible mechanisms. *Annals of Behavioral Medicine, 17,* 142–149.

Carpenter, W. T. & van Os, J. (2011). Should attenuated psychosis syndrome be a DSM-5 diagnosis? *American Journal of Psychiatry, 168,* 460–463.

Carr, E. G. (1982). *How to teach sign language to developmentally disabled children.* Lawrence, KS: H & H Enterprises.

Carstensen, L. L., Isaacowitz, D. M., & Charles, S. T. (1999). Taking time seriously: A theory of socioemotional selectivity. *American Psychologist, 54,* 165–181.

Carter, J. C., & Fairburn, C. G. (1998). Cognitive-behavioral self-help for binge eating disorder: A controlled effectiveness study. *Journal of Consulting and Clinical Psychology, 66,* 616–623.

Carter, R. (1999) *Mapping the mind.* Berkeley: University of California Press.

Carvalheira, A. A., Brotto, L. A., & Leal, I. (2010). Women's motivations for sex: Exploring the diagnostic and statistical manual, fourth edition, text revision criteria for hypoactive sexual desire and female sexual arousal disorders. *Journal of Sexual Medicine, 7,* 1454–1463.

Carver, C. S., & Scheier, M. F. (1999). Optimism. In C. R. Snyder (Ed.), *Coping: The psychology of what works* (pp. 182–204). New York: Oxford University Press.

Casas, J. M. (1995). Counseling and psychotherapy with racial/ethnic minority groups in theory and practice. In B. M. Bongar & L. E. Beutler (Eds.), *Comprehensive textbook of psychotherapy: Theory and practice* (pp. 311–335). New York: Oxford University Press.

Caselli, R., Beach, T., Yaari, R., & Reiman, E. (2006). Alzheimer's disease a century later. *Journal of Clinical Psychiatry, 67,* 1784–1800.

Casey, P. (2001). Multiple personality disorder. *Primary Care Psychiatry, 7,* 7–11.

Casey, P., & Doherty, A. (2012). Adjustment disorder: Implications for ICD-11 and DSM-5. *British Journal of Psychiatry, 201,* 90–92.

Cash, T. F., & Henry, P. E. (1995). Women's body images: The results of a national survey in the U.S.A. *Sex Roles, 33,* 19–28.

Cash, T. F., Morrow, J. A., Hrabosky, J. I., & Perry, A. A. (2004). How has body image changed? A cross-sectional investigation of college women and men from 1983-2001. *Journal of Consulting and Clinical Psychology, 72,* 1081–1089.

Caspi, A. Sugden, K., Moffitt, T. E., Taylor, A., Craig, I. W., Harrington, H., et al. (2003). Influence of life stress on depression: Moderation by a polymorphism in the 5-HTT gene. *Science, 301,* 386–389.

Caspi, A., & Shiner, R. (2008). Temperament and personality. In M. Rutter, D. Bishop, D. Pine, S. Scott, J. Stevenson, E. Taylor, A. Thapar (Eds.), *Rutter's child and adolescent psychiatry* (5th ed., pp. 182–198). Hoboken, NJ: Wiley-Blackwell.

Caspi, A., Hariri, A. R., Holmes, A., Uher, R., & Moffitt, T. E. (2010). Genetic sensitivity to the environment: The case of the serotonin transporter gene and its implications for studying complex diseases and traits. *American Journal of Psychiatry, 167,* 509–527.

Caspi, A., Henry, B., McGee, R. O., Moffitt, T. E., et al. (1995). Temperamental origins of child and adolescent behavior problems: From age three to fifteen. *Child Development, 66,* 55–68.

Caspi, A., McClay, J., Moffitt, T. E., Mill, J., Martin, J., Craig, I. W., et al. (2002). Role of genotype in the cycle of violence in maltreated children. *Science, 297,* 851–854.

Cassidy, J., & Mohr, J. J. (2001). Unsolvable fear, trauma, and psychopathology: Theory, research, and clinical considerations related to disorganized attachment, across the life span. *Clinical Psychology: Science and Practice, 8,* 275–298.

Cassidy, J., & Shaver, P. R. (Eds.). (2008). *Handbook of attachment: Theory, research, and clinical applications* (2nd ed.). New York: The Guilford Press.

Castonguay, L. G., Boswell, J. F., Constantino, M. J., Goldfried, M. R., & Hill, C. E. (2010). Training implications of harmful effects of psychological treatments. *American Psychologist, 65,* 34–49.

Cavell, T. A. (2001). Updating our approach to parent training. I: The case against targeting noncompliance. *Clinical Psychology: Science and Practice, 8,* 299–318.

Caviness, J. N., Lue, L., Adler, C. H., & Walker, D. G. (2011). Parkinson's disease dementia and potential therapeutic strategies. *CNS Neuroscience & Therapeutics, 17,* 32–44.

CDC. (2010). Increasing prevalence of parent-reported attention-deficit/hyperactivity disorder among children–United States, 2003 and 2007. *Morbidity and Mortality Weekly Report, 59,* 1439–1443.

Center for Disease Control and Prevention. (2013). Suicide among adults aged 35-64 years—United States, 1999-2010. *Morbidity and Mortality Weekly Report, 62,* 321–325.

Centers for Disease Control and Prevention. (2007). Suicide trends among youths and young adults aged 10-24 years—United States, 1990-2004. *Morbidity and Mortality Weekly Report, 56,* 905–908.

Chakrabarti, S., & Fombonne, E. (2001). Pervasive developmental disorders in preschool children. *Journal of the American Medical Association, 285,* 3093–3099.

Chaloupka, F. (2005). Explaining recent trends in smoking prevalence. *Addiction, 100,* 1394–1395.

Chambless, D. L., & Ollendick, T. H. (2000). Empirically supported psychological interventions. Controversies and evidence.*Annual Review of Psychology, 52,* 685–716.

Champagne, F. A., & Mashoodh, R. (2009). Genes in context: Gene-environment interplay and the origins of individual differences in behavior. *Current Directions in Psychological Science, 18,* 127–131.

Champion, J. E., Jaser, S. S., Reeslund, K. L., Simmons, L., Potts, J. E., Shears, A. R., & Compas, B. E. (2009). Caretaking behaviors by adolescent children of mothers with and without a history of depression. *Journal of Family Psychology, 23,* 156–166.

Charman, T. (2002). The prevalence of autism spectrum disorders: Recent evidence and future challenges. *European Child & Adolescent Psychiatry, 11,* 249–256.

Chassin, L., & Handley, E. D. (2006). Parents and families as contexts for the development of substance use and substance use disorders. *Psychology of Addictive Behaviors, 20,* 135–137.

Chassin, L., Ritter, J., Trim, R. S., & King, K. M. (2003). Adolescent substance use disorders. In E. J. Mash & R. A. Barkley (Eds.), *Child psychopathology* (2nd ed., pp. 199–230). New York: Guilford.

Chen, C., & Yin, S. (2008). Alcohol abuse and related factors in Asia. *International Review of Psychiatry, 20,* 425–433.

Chen, R. T., & DeStefano, R. (1998). Vaccine adverse events: Causal or coincidental? *Lancet, 351,* 611–612.

Chen, S., Boucher, H. C., & Tapias, M. P. (2006). The relational self revealed: Integrative conceptualization and implications for interpersonal life. *Psychological Bulletin, 132,* 151–179.

Chen, W., Landau, S., & Sham, P. (2004). No evidence for links between autism, MMR and measles virus. *Psychological Medicine, 34,* 545–553.

Cherlin, A. J. (2009). *The Marriage Go-round: The State of Marriage and the Family in America Today.* New York: Knopf.

Cherry, D. K., Woodwell, D. A., & Rechtsteiner, E. A. (2007). *National ambulatory medical care survey: 2005 summary* (Advance Data from Vital and Health Statistics; No 387). Hyattsville, MD: National Center for Health Statistics.

Chiu, H. F. K., Lam, L. C. W., Chi, I., Leung, T., Li, S. W., Law, W. T., et al. (1998). Prevalence of dementia in Chinese elderly in Hong Kong. *Neurology, 50,* 1002–1009.

Christensen, A., Atkins, D. C., Berns, S., Wheeler, J., Baucom, D. H., & Simpson, L. E. (2004). Traditional versus integrative behavioral couple therapy for significantly and chronically distressed married couples. *Journal of Consulting and Clinical Psychology, 72,* 176–191.

Christensen, A., Atkins, D. C., Yi, J., Baucom, D. H., & George, W. H. (2006). Couple and individual adjustment for 2 years following a randomized clinical trial comparing traditional versus integrative behavioral therapy. *Journal of Consulting and Clinical Psychology, 74,* 1180–1191.

Christensen, B. S., Grønbæk, M., Osler, M., Pedersen, B. V., Graugaard, C., & Frisch, M. (2011). Sexual dysfunctions and difficulties in Denmark: Prevalence and associated sociodemographic factors. *Archives of Sexual Behavior, 40,* 121–132.

Christoforou, A. A., McGhee, K. A., Morris, S. W., Thomson, P. A., Anderson, S. S., McLean, A. A., & Evans, K. L. (2011). Convergence of linkage, association and GWAS findings for a candidate region for bipolar disorder and schizophrenia on chromosome 4p. *Molecular Psychiatry, 16,* 240–242.

Ciarnello, R. D., Aimi, J., Dean, R. R., Morilak, D. A., Porteus, M. H., & Cicchetti, D. (1995). Fundamentals of molecular neurobiology. In D. Cicchetti & D. Cohen (Eds.), *Developmental Psychopathology* (pp. 109–160). New York: Wiley.

Cicchetti, D., & Beegly, M. (1990). *Children with Down syndrome: A developmental perspective.* New York: Cambridge University Press.

Cicchetti, D., & Cohen, D. (Eds.).(1995). *Developmental psychopathology* (Vols. 1 & 2). New York: Wiley.

Cipparone, R. C. (1987). The defense of battered women who kill. *University of Pennsylvania Law Review, 135,* 427–452.

Clancy, S. A. (2010). *The trauma myth: The truth about the sexual abuse of children-and its aftermath.* New York: Basic Books.

Clark, D. M. (1986). Cognitive therapy for anxiety. *Behavioral Psychotherapy, 14,* 283–294.

Clark, D. M., Salkovskis, P. M., Hackmann, A., Wells, A., Ludgate, J., & Gelder, M. (1999). Brief cognitive therapy for panic disorder: A randomized controlled trial. *Journal of Consulting and Clinical Psychology, 67,* 583–589.

Clark, L. A. (1999). Dimensional approaches to personality disorder assessment and diagnosis. In C. R. Cloninger (Ed.), *Personality and psychopathology* (pp. 219–244). Washington, DC: American Psychiatric Press.

Clark, D. C., & Goebel-Fabbri, A. E. (1999). Lifetime risk of suicide in major affective disorders. In D. G. Jacobs et al. (Eds.), *The Harvard medical school guide to suicide assessment and intervention* (pp. 270–286). San Francisco: Jossey-Bass.

Clark, D. M., Salkovskis, P. M., Hackmann, A., Wells, A., Fennell, M., Ludgate, J., et al. (1998). Two psychological treatments for hypochondriasis: A randomised controlled trial. *British Journal of Psychiatry, 173,* 218–225.

Clark, L. A. (2007). Assessment and diagnosis of personality disorder: Perennial issues and an emerging reconceptualization.*Annual Review of Psychology, 58,* 227–257.

Clarke, J. W. (1990). *On Being Mad or Merely Angry: John W. Hinckley, Jr., and Other Dangerous People.* Princeton University Press.

Clarke, M. C., Tanskanen, A., Huttunen, M., Whittaker, J. C., & Cannon, M. (2009). Evidence for an interaction between familial liability and prenatal exposure to infection in the causation of schizophrenia. *The American Journal of Psychiatry, 166*(9), 1025–1030.

Clarkin, J. F., Foelsch, P. A., Levy, K. N., Hull, J. W., Delaney, J. C., & Kernberg, O. F. (2001). The development of a psychodynamic treatment for patients with borderline personality disorder: A preliminary study of behavioral change. *Journal of Personality Disorders, 15,* 487–495.

Clayton, A. (2007). Epidemiology and neurobiology of female sexual dysfunction. *Journal of Sexual Medicine, 4,* 260–268.

Clayton, A. H., & West, S. G. (2003). The effects of antidepressants on human sexuality. *Primary Psychiatry, 10,* 62–70.

Cleckley, H. (1976). *The Mask of Sanity* (5th ed.). St. Louis, MO: Mosby.

Clemans, K. H., DeRose, L. M., Graber, J. A., & Brooks-Gunn, J. (2010). Gender in adolescence: Applying a person-in-context approach to gender identity and roles. In J. C. Chrisler & D. R. McCreary (Eds.), *Handbook of gender research in psychology,: Gender research in general and experimental psychology* (Vol. 1, pp. 527–557). New York: Springer.

Clifton, A., Turkheimer, E., & Oltmanns, T. F. (2004). Contrasting perspectives on personality problems: Descriptions from the self and others. *Personality and Individual Differences, 36,* 1499–1514.

Coan, J. A., Schaefer, H. S., & Davidson, R. J. (2006). Lending a hand: Social regulation of the neural response to threat.*Psychological Science, 17,* 1032–1039.

Coccaro, E. F., Posternak, M. A., & Zimmerman, M. (2005). Prevalence and features of intermittent explosive disorder in a clinical setting. *Journal of Clinical Psychiatry, 66,* 1221–1227.

Cohen, A. N., Hammen, C., Henry, R. M., & Daley, S. E. (2004). Effects of stress and social support on recurrence in bipolar disorder. *Journal of Affective Disorders, 82,* 143–147.

Cohen, B. J., Bonnie, R. J., & Monahan, J. (2008). *Understanding and applying Virginia's new statutory civil commitment criteria.* Unpublished manuscript, University of Virginia, Charlottesville, VA.

Cohen, L. J., & Galynker, I. I. (2002). Clinical features of pedophilia and implications for treatment. *Journal of Psychiatric Practice, 8,* 276–289.

Cohen, P., Chen, H., Crawford, T. N., Brook, J. S., & Gordon, K. (2007). Personality disorders in early adolescence and the development of later substance use disorders in the general population. *Drug and Alcohol Dependence, 88,* S71–S84.

Cohen, P., Crawford, T. N., Johnson, J. G., & Kasen, S. (2005). The children in the community study of developmental course of personality disorder. *Journal of Personality, 19,* 466–486.

Cohen, S., Kaplan, J. R., Cunnick, J. E., Manuck, S. B., & Rabin, B. S. (1992). Chronic social stress, affiliation, and cellular immune response in nonhuman primates. *Psychological Science, 3,* 301–304.

Cohen, S., & Pressman, S. D. (2006). Positive affect and health. *Current Directions in Psychological Science, 15,* 122–125.

Cohen, S., & Williamson, G. M. (1991). Stress and infectious disease in humans. *Psychological Bulletin, 109,* 5–24.

Cohler, B. J., & Nakamura, J. E. (1996). In J. Sadavoy, L. W. Lazarus, L. F. Jarvik, & G. T. Grossberg (Eds.), *Comprehensive Review of Geriatric Psychiatry II* (pp. 153–194). Washington, DC: American Psychiatric Press.

Coid, J., Yang, M., Tyrer, P., Roberts, A., & Ullrich, S. (2006). Prevalence and correlates of personality disorder among adults aged 16 to 74 in Great Britain. *British Journal of Psychiatry, 188,* 423–431.

Coie, J., & Kupersmidt, J., (1983). A behavioral analysis of emerging social status in boys' groups. *Child Development, 54,* 1400–1416.

Coifman, K. G., & Bonanno, G. A. (2010). When distress does not become depression: Emotion context sensitivity and adjustment to bereavement. *Journal of Abnormal Psychology, 119,* 479–490.

Colcombe, S., & Kramer, A. F. (2003). Fitness effects on the cognitive function of older adults: A meta-analytic study. *Psychological Science, 14,* 125–130.

Cole, W. (1992). Incest perpetrators: Their assessment and treatment. *Psychiatric Clinics of North America, 15,* 689–670.

Cole, S. W. (2009). Social regulation of human gene expression. *Current Directions in Psychological Science, 18,* 132–137.

Coleman, P. G. (2005). Uses of reminiscence: Functions and benefits. *Aging & Mental Health, 9,* 291–294.

Comas-Diaz, L. (2000). An ethnopolitical approach to working with people of color. *American Psychologist, 55,* 1319–1325.

Compas, B. E., Forehand, R., Keller, G., Champion, J. E., Rakow, A., Reeslund, K. L., et al. (2009). Randomized controlled trial of a family cognitive-behavioral preventive intervention for children of depressed parents. *Journal of Consulting and Clinical Psychology, 77,* 1007–1020.

Compton, W. M., Thomas, Y. F., Stinson, F. S., & Grant, B. F. (2007). Prevalence, correlates, disabilities, and comorbidities of DSM-IV drug abuse and dependence in the United States. *Archives of General Psychiatry, 64,* 566–576.

Confer, J. C., Easton, J. A., Fleischman, D. S., Goetz, C. D., Lewis, D. M. G., Perilloux, C., et al. (2009). Evolutionary psychology: Controversies, questions, prospects, and limitations. *American Psychologist, 65,* 110–126.

Conley, R. R., & Kelly, D. L. (2001). Management of treatment resistance in schizophrenia. *Biological Psychiatry, 50,* 898–911.

Conners, C. K. (1980). Artificial colors and the diet of disruptive behavior: Current status of research. In R. M. Knights & D. J. Bakker (Eds.), *Treatment of Hyperactive and Learning Disabled Children.* Baltimore: University Park Press.

Constable, N. (2004). *This is cocaine (addiction).* New York: Sanctuary Publishing.

Contrada, R. J., Ashmore, R. D., Gary, M. L., Coups, E., Egeth, J. D., Sewell, A., et al. (2001). Ethnicity-related sources of stress and their effects on well-being. *Current Directions in Psychological Science, 9,* 136–139.

Cook, J. M., Riggs, D. S., Thompson, R., Coyne, J. C., & Sheikh, J. I. (2004). Posttraumatic stress disorder and current relationship functioning among World War II ex-prisoners of war. *Journal of Family Psychology, 18,* 36–45.

Coombs, R. H., Howatt, W. A., & Coombs, K. (2005). Addiction recovery tools. In R. H. Coombs (Ed.), *Addiction counseling review* (pp. 425–446). Mahwah, NJ: Erlbaum.

Coons, P. M., & Bowman, E. S. (2001). Ten-year follow-up study of patients with dissociative identity disorder. *Journal of Trauma and Dissociation, 2,* 73–89.

Cooper, C., Mukadam, N., Katona, C., Lyketsos, C. G., Ames, D., Rabins, P., et al. (2012). Systematic review of the effectiveness of non-pharmacological interventions to improve quality of life of people with dementia. *International Psychogeriatrics, 24,* 856–870.

Cooper, M. H. (1994). Regulating tobacco: Can the FDA break America's smoking habit? *CQ Research, 4,* 843–858.

Coovert, D. L., Kinder, B. N., & Thompson, J. K. (1989). The psychosexual aspects of anorexia nervosa and bulimia nervosa: A review of the literature. *Clinical Psychology Review, 9,* 169–180.

Copeland, W. E., Angold, A., Costello, E. J., & Eger, H. (2013). Prevalence, comorbidity, and correlates of DSM-5 proposed disruptive mood dysregulation disorder. *American Journal of Psychiatry, 170,* 173–179.

Corbitt, E. M. (2002). Narcissism from the perspective of the five-factor model. In P. T. Costa, Jr. & T. A. Widiger (Eds.), *Personality disorders and the five-factor model of personality* (2nd ed., pp. 293–298). Washington, DC: American Psychological Association.

Cordova, J. V., Jacobson, N. S., Gottman, J. M., Rushe, R., & Cox, G. (1993). Negative reciprocity and communication in couples with a violent husband. *Journal of Abnormal Psychology, 102,* 559–564.

Cornelius, J. R., Reynolds, M., Martz, B. M., Clark, D. B., Kirisci, L., & Tarter, R. (2008). Premature mortality among males with substance use disorders. *Addictive Behaviors, 33,* 156–160.

Correll, C., & Schenk, E. (2008). Tardive dyskinesia and new antipsychotics. *Current Opinion in Psychiatry, 21,* 151–156.

Coryell, W., Solomon, D., Turvey, C., Keller, M., Leon, A. C., Endicott, J., et al. (2003). The long-term course of rapid-cycling bipolar disorder. *Archives of General Psychiatry, 60,* 914–920.

Coser, L. A. (1977). *Masters of sociological thought: Ideas in historical and social context.* San Diego, CA: Harcourt Brace Jovanovich.

Costello, E. J., Erkanli, A., & Angold, A. (2006). Is there an epidemic of child or adolescent depression? *Journal of Child Psychology and Psychiatry, 47,* 1263–1273.

Costigan, C L.; Floyd, F J.; Harter, K S. M.; & McClintock, J C. (1997). Family process and adaptation to children with mental retardation: Disruption and resilience in family problem-solving interactions. Journal of Family Psychology, 11, 515–529.

Courchesne, E., Karns, C. M., Davis, H. R., Ziccardi, R., Carper, R. A., Tigue, Z. D., et al. (2001). Unusual brain growth patterns in early life in patients with autistic disorder: An MRI Study. *Neurology, 57,* 245–254.

Couture, S. M., & Penn, D. L. (2003). Interpersonal contact and the stigma of mental illness. A review of the literature. *Journal of Mental Health, 12,* 291–305.

Covault, J., Gelernter, J., Hesselbrock, V., Nellissery, M., & Kranzler, H. R. (2004). Allelic and haplotypic association of GABRA2 with alcohol dependence. *American Journal of Medical Genetics (Neuropsychiatric Genetics), 129B,* 104–109.

Cowan, C. P., & Cowan, P. A. (1992). *When Partners Become Parents.* New York: Basic Books.

Cox, W. T. L., Abramson, L. Y., Devine, P. G., & Hollon, S. D. (2012). Stereotypes, prejudice, and depression: The integrated perspective. *Perspectives on Psychological Science, 7,* 427–449.

Coyne, J. C., Thombs, B. D., Stefanek, M., & Palmer, S. C. (2009). Time to let go of the illusion that psychotherapy extends the survival of cancer patients: Reply to Kraemer, Kuchler, & Spiegel (2009). *Psychological Bulletin, 135,* 179–182.

Craighead, W. E., & Miklowitz, D. J. (2000). Psychosocial interventions for bipolar disorder. *Journal of Clinical Psychiatry, 61*(Suppl. 13), 58–64.

Cramer, P. (2000). Defense mechanisms in psychology today: Further processes for adaptation. *American Psychologist, 55,* 637–646.

Craske, M. G., & Rowe, M. K. (1997). Nocturnal panic. *Clinical Psychology: Science and Practice, 4,* 153–174.

Crawford, T. N., Cohen, P., & Brook, J. S. (2001). Dramatic-erratic personality disorder symptoms: I. Continuity from early adolescence into adulthood. *Journal of Personality Disorders, 15,* 319–335.

Crean, R. D., Crane, N. A., & Mason, B. J. (2011). An evidence-based review of acute and long-term effects of cannabis use on executive cognitive functions. *Journal of Addiction Medicine, 5,* 1–8.

Creed, F., & Barsky, A. (2004). A systematic review of the epidemiology of somatisation disorder and hypochondriasis. *Journal of Psychosomatic Research, 56,* 391–408.

Crick, N. R., Ostrov, J. M., & Werner, N. E. (2006). A longitudinal study of relational aggression, physical aggression, and children's social-psychological adjustment. *Journal of Abnormal Child Psychology, 34,* 131–142.

Crick, N. R., & Zahn-Waxler, C. (2003). The development of psychopathology in females and males: Current progress and future challenges. *Development and Psychopathology, 15,* 719–742.

Crimlisk, H. L., Bhatia, K., Cope, H., David, A., Marsden, C. D., & Ron, M. A. (1998). Slater revisited: 6-year follow-up study of patients with medically unexplained motor symptoms. *British Medical Journal, 316,* 582–586.

Crits-Christoph, P. (1998). Psychosocial treatments for personality disorders. In P. E. Nathan & J. M. Gorman (Eds.), *A guide to treatments that work* (pp. 544–553). New York: Oxford University Press.

Cronbach, L. J., & Meehl, P. E. (1955). Construct validity in psychological tests. *Psychological Bulletin, 52,* 281–302.

Crow, S. J., Peterson, C. B., Swanson, S. A., Raymond, N. C., Specker, S., Eckert, E. D., & Mitchell, J. E. (2009). Increased mortality in bulimia nervosa and other eating disorders. *American Journal of Psychiatry, 166,* 1342–1346.

Csernansky, J. G., & Cronenwett, W. J. (2008). Neural networks in schizophrenia. *American Journal of Psychiatry, 165,* 937–939.

Csikszentmihalyi, M., & Larson, R. (1984). *Being Adolescent.* New York: Basic Books.

Cuckle, H. (2001). Time for a total shift to first trimester screening for down syndrome. *The Lancet, 358,* 1658–1659.

Cuellar, A. K., Johnson, S. L., & Winters, R. (2005). Distinctions between bipolar and unipolar depression. *Clinical Psychology Review, 25,* 307–339.

Cuijpers, P., Reynolds, C., Donker, T., Li, J., Andersson, G., & Beekman, A. (2012). Personalized treatment of adult depression: Medication, psychotherapy, or both? A systematic review. *Depression and Anxiety, 29,* 855–864.

Culbert, K. M., Burt, S. A., McGue, M., Iacono, W. G., & Klump, K. L. (2009). Puberty and the genetic diathesis of disordered eating attitudes and behaviors. *Journal of Abnormal Psychology, 118,* 788–796.

Cummings, E. M., & Davies, P. T. (2010). *Marital Conflict and Children: An Emotional Security Perspective.* New York: Guilford.

Cummings, J. L. (2004). Dementia with Lewy bodies: Molecular pathogenesis and implications for classification. *Journal of Geriatric Psychiatry and Neurology, 17,* 112–119.

Cummings, J. L., & Cole, G. (2002). Alzheimer disease. *Journal of the American Medical Association, 287,* 2335–2338.

Cunningham, J., Yonkers, K., O'Brien, S., & Eriksson, E. (2009). Update on research and treatment of premenstrual dysphoric disorder. *Harvard Review of Psychiatry, 17,* 120–137.

Currier, D., & Mann, J. J. (2008). Stress, genes and the biology of suicidal behavior. *Psychiatric Clinics of North America, 31,* 247–269.

Currier, J. M., Neimeyer, R. A., & Berman, J. S. (2008). The effectiveness of psychotherapeutic interventions for bereaved persons: A comprehensive review. *Psychological Bulletin, 134,* 648–661.

Curtis, N. M., Ronan, K. R., & Borduin, C. M. (2004). Multisystemic treatment: A meta-analysis of outcome studies. *Journal of Family Psychology, 18*(3), 411–419.

Cutler, B. L., & Kovera, M. B. (2011). Expert psychological testimony. *Current Directions in Psychological Science, 20,* 53–57.

Cyranowski, J. M., & Frank, E. (2006). Targeting populations of women for prevention and treatment of depression. In C. M. Mazure & G. Keita (Eds.), *Understanding depression in women: Applying empirical research to practice and policy* (pp. 71–112). Washington, DC: American Psychological Association.

## D

Dell'Osso, B., Nestadt, G., Allen, A., & Hollander, E. (2006). Serotonin-norepinephrine reuptake inhibitors in the treatment of obsessive-compulsive disorder: A critical review. *Journal of Clinical Psychiatry, 67,* 600–610.

D'Onofrio, B. M., Turkheimer, E., Emery, R. E., Maes, H. H., Silberg, J., & Eaves, L. J. (2007). A children of twins study of parental divorce and offspring psychopathology. *Journal of Child Psychology and Psychiatry, 48,* 667–675.

D'Onofrio, B., Turkheimer, E., Emery, R., Slutske, W., Heath, A., Madden, P., & Martin, N. (2006). A genetically informed study of the processes underlying the association between parental marital instability and offspring life course patterns. *Developmental Psychology, 42,* 486–499.

da Rocha, F. F., Correa, H., & Teixeira, A. L. (2008). Obsessive-compulsive disorder and immunology: A review. *Progress in Neuro-Psychopharmacology & Biological Psychiatry, 32,* 1139–1146.

Dalenberg, C. J., Brand, B. L., Gleaves, D. H., Dorahy, M. J., Loewenstein, R. J., Cardeña, E., et al. (2012). Evaluation of the evidence for the trauma and fantasy models of dissociation. *Psychological Bulletin, 138,* 550–588.

Weiss, L. A., Shen, Y., Korn, J. M., Arking, D. E., Miller, D. T., Fossdal, R., et al. for the Autism Consortium . (2008). Association between microdeletion and microduplication at 16p11.2 and autism. *The New England Journal of Medicine, 358,* 1–9.

Dams-O'Connor, K., Gibbons, L. E., Bowen, J. D., McCurry, S. M., Larson, E. B., & Crane, P. K. (2013). Risk for late-life re-injury, dementia and death among individuals with traumatic brain injury: A population-based study. *Journal of Neurology, Neurosurgery & Psychiatry, 84,* 177–182.

Danforth, J. S., Barkley, R. A., & Stokes, T. F. (1991). Observations of parent-child interactions with hyperactive children: Research and clinical implications. *Clinical Psychology Review, 11,* 703–727.

Danziger, S., & Ratner, D. (2010). Labor market outcomes and the transition to adulthood. *The Future of Children, 20,* 133–158.

Darcangelo, S. (2008). Fetishism: Psychopathology and theory. In D. Laws & W. T. O'Donohue (Eds.), *Sexual deviance: Theory, assessment, and treatment* (2nd ed., pp. 108–118). New York: Guilford Press.

Dar-Nimrod, I., & Heine, S. J. (2011). Genetic essentialism: On the deceptive determinism of DNA. *Psychological Bulletin, 137,* 800–818.

Das, C., Mendez, G., Jagasia, S., & Labbate, L. A. (2012). Second-generation antipsychotic use in schizophrenia and related weight gain: A critical review and meta-analysis behavioral and pharmacologic treatments. *Annals of Clinical Psychiatry, 24,* 225–239.

Das-Munshi, J., Goldberg, D., Bebbington, P. E., Bhugra, D. K., Brugha, T. S., Dewey, M. E., et al. (2008). Public health significance of mixed anxiety and depression: Beyond current classification. *British Journal of Psychiatry, 192,* 171–177.

Davidson, J. R., DuPont, R. L., Hedges, D., & Haskins, J. T. (1999). Efficacy, safety, and tolerability of venlafaxine extended release and buspirone in outpatients with generalized anxiety disorder. *Journal of Clinical Psychiatry, 60,* 528–535.

Davidson, R. J., Pizzagalli, D., Nitschke, J. B., & Putnam, K. (2002). Depression: Perspectives from affective neuroscience. *Annual Review of Psychology, 53,* 545–574.

Davidson, W. S., Redner, R., Blakely, C. H., Mitchell, C. M., & Emshoff, J. G. (1987). Diversion of juvenile offenders: An experimental comparison. *Journal of Consulting and Clinical Psychology, 55,* 68–75.

Davis, D., & Herdt, G. (1997). Cultural issues and sexual disorders. In T. A. Widiger, A. J. Frances, H. A. Pincus, R. Ross, M. B. First, & W. Davis (Eds.), *DSM-IV source-book* (Vol. 3, pp. 951–958). Washington, DC: American Psychiatric Press.

Davis, H. J., & Reissing, E. D. (2007). Relationship adjustment and dyadic interaction in couples with sexual pain disorders: A critical review of the literature. *Sexual & Marital Therapy, 22,* 245–254.

Dawood, K., Kirk, K. M., Bailey, J., Andrews, P. W., & Martin, N. G. (2005). Genetic and environmental influences on the frequency of orgasm in women. *Twin Research, 8,* 27–33.

de Lange, E. E., Verhaak, P. M., & van der Meer, K. K. (2013). Prevalence, presentation and prognosis of delirium in older people in the population, at home and in long term care: A review. *International Journal of Geriatric Psychiatry, 28,* 127–134.

De Silva, P., & Rachman, S. (2004). *Obsessive–compulsive disorders: The facts* (3rd ed.). Oxford: Oxford University Press.

Delgado, P. L., & Moreno, F. A. (2006). Neurochemistry of mood disorders. In D. J. Stein, D. J. Kupfer, & A. F. Schatzberg (Eds.), *The American psychiatric publishing textbook of mood disorders* (pp. 101–116). Washington, DC: American Psychiatric Publishing.

DeLisi, L. (2008). The concept of progressive brain change in schizophrenia: Implications for understanding schizophrenia. *Schizophrenia Bulletin, 34,* 312–321.

DeLuca, N., Moser, L., & Bond, G. (2008). Assertive community treatment. In *clinical handbook of schizophrenia* (pp. 329–338). New York: Guilford Press.

Denis, C., Fatséas, M., & Auriacombe, M. (2012). Analyses related to the development of DSM-5 criteria for substance use related disorders: 3. An assessment of Pathological Gambling criteria. *Drug and Alcohol Dependence, 122,* 22–27.

Denson, T. F., DeWall, C. N., & Finkel, E. J. (2012). Self-control and aggression. *Current Directions in Psychological Science, 21,* 20–25.

DePaulo, J. R., & Horvitz, L. A. (2002). *Understanding depression: What we know and what you can do about it.* New York: Wiley.

DeRogatis, L. R., & Burnett, A. L. (2008). The epidemiology of sexual dysfunctions. *Journal of Sexual Medicine, 5,* 289–300.

DeRubeis, R. J., Brotman, M. A., & Gibbons, C. J. (2005). A conceptual and methodological analysis of the nonspecific argument. *Clinical Psychology: Science and Practice, 12,* 174–183.

Detera-Wadleigh, S., & McMahon, F. J. (2004). Genetic association studies in mood disorders: Issues and promise. *International Review of Psychiatry, 16,* 301–310.

Detterman, D. K., & Gabriel, L. (2007). Look before you leap: Implications of the 1992 and 2002 definitions of mental retardation. In H. N. Switzky & S. Greenspan (Eds.), *What is mental retardation? Ideas for an evolving disability in the 21st century* (pp. 133–144). Washington: AAIDD.

DeVane, C. L., & Sallee, F. R. (1996). Serotonin selective reuptake inhibitors in child and adolescent psychopharmacology: A review of published evidence. *Journal of Clinical Psychiatry, 57,* 55–66.

DeWall, C. N., MacDonald, G., Webster, G. D., Masten, C. L., Baumeister, R. F., Powell, C., et al. (2010). Acetaminophen reduces social pain: Behavioral and neural evidence. *Psychological Science, 21,* 931–937.

Diamond, M. (2009). Clinical implications of the organizational and activational effects of hormones. *Hormones and Behavior, 55,* 621–632.

Dick, D. M. (2007). Identification of genes influencing a spectrum of externalizing psychopathology. *Current Directions in Psychological Science, 16,* 331–335.

Dick, D. M., & Foroud, T. (2003). Candidate genes for alcohol dependence: A review of genetic evidence from human studies. *Alcoholism: Clinical and Experimental Research, 5,* 868–879.

Dick, D. M., Jones, K., Saccone, N., Hinrichs, A. L., Wang, J. C., Goate, A., et al. (2006). Endophenotypes successfully lead to gene identification: Results from the collaborative study on the genetics of alcoholism. *Behavior Genetics, 36,* 112–126.

Dick, D. M., Pagan, J. L., Holliday, C., Viken, R., Pulkkinen, L., Kaprio, J., & Rose, R. J. (2007). Gender differences in friends' influences on adolescent drinking: A genetic epidemiological study. *Alcoholism: Clinical and Experimental Research, 31,* 2012–2019.

Dickens, W. T., & Flynn, J. R. (2001). Heritability estimates versus large environmental effects: The IQ paradox resolved. *Psychological Review, 108,* 346–369.

Dickerson, F., Tenhula, W., & Green-Paden, L. (2005). The token economy for schizophrenia: Review of the literature and recommendations for future research. *Schizophrenia Research, 75,* 405–416.

Dishion, T. J, McCord, J., & Poulin, F. (1999). When interventions harm: Peer groups and problem behavior. *American Psychologist, 54,* 755–764.

Distel, M. A., Willemsen, G., Ligthart, L., Derom, C. A., Martin, N. G., Neale, M. C., et al. (2010). Genetic covariance structure of the four main features of borderline personality disorder. *Journal of Personality Disorders, 24,* 427–444.

Ditton, P. M. (1999). *Mental health and treatment of inmates and probationers.* Washington, DC: Bureau of Justice Statistics.

Dobbs, D. (2009, April 13). Soldiers' stress: What doctors get wrong about PTSD. *Scientific American.* Retrieved from http://www.scientificamerican.com/article.cfm?id=post

Dobson, K. S. (2008). Cognitive therapy for depression. In M. A. Whisman (Ed.), *Adapting cognitive therapy for depression: Managing complexity and comorbidity* (pp. 3–35). New York: Guilford.

Docherty, N. M., DeRosa, M., & Andreasen, N. C. (1996). Communication disturbances in schizophrenia and mania. *Archives of General Psychiatry, 53,* 358–364.

Dodge, K. A., Lansford, J. E., Burks, V. S., Bates, J. E., Pettit, G. S., Fontaine, R., et al. (2003). Peer rejection and social information-processing factors in the development of aggressive behavior problems in children. *Child Development, 74*(2), 374–393.

Dohrenwend, B. P. (2006). Inventorying stressful life events as risk factors for psychopathology: Toward resolution of the problem of intracategory variability. *Psychological Bulletin, 132,* 477–495.

Dolan-Sewell, R. T., Krueger, R. F., & Shea, M. T. (2001). Co-occurrence with syndrome disorders. In W. J. Livesley (Ed.), *Handbook of personality disorders: Theory, research, and treatment* (pp. 84–104). New York: Guilford.

Dominguez, M., Saka, M., Lieb, R., Wittchen, H., & van Os, J. (2010). Early expression of negative/disorganized symptoms predicting psychotic experiences and subsequent clinical psychosis: A 10-year study. *American Journal of Psychiatry, 167,* 1075–1082.

Doss, B. D. (2004). Changing the way we study change in psychotherapy. *Clinical Psychology: Science and Practice, 11,* 368–386.

Dougherty, D. D., & Rauch, S. L. (2007). Somatic therapies for treatment-resistant depression: New neurotherapeutic interventions. *Psychiatric Clinics of North America, 30,* 1–7.

Douglas, K. S., Guy, L. S., & Hart, S. D. (2009). Psychosis as a risk factor for violence to others: A meta-analysis. *Psychological Bulletin, 135,* 679–706.

Downar, J., & Kapur, S. (2008). Biological theories. In *clinical handbook of schizophrenia* (pp. 25–34). New York: Guilford Press.

Dozier, M., Stovall-McClough, K., & Albus, K. E. (2008). Attachment and psychopathology in adulthood. In J. Cassidy

& P. R. Shaver (Eds.), *Handbook of attachment: Theory, research, and clinical applications* (2nd ed., pp. 718–744). New York: Guilford Press.

Draguns, J. G. (2006). Culture in psychopathology—psychopathology in culture: Taking a new look at an old problem. In T. G. Plante (Ed.), *Mental disorders of the new millennium: Public and social problems* (Vol. 2, pp. 215–233). Westport, CT: Praeger Publishers/Greenwood Publishing Group.

Draguns, J. G., & Tanaka-Matsumi, J. (2003). Assessment of psychopathology across and within cultures: Issues and findings. *Behaviour Research & Therapy, 41,* 755–776.

Drevets, W. C. (2002). Neuroimaging studies of mood disorders. In J. E. Helzer & J. J. Hudziak (Eds.), *Defining psychopathology in the 21st century: DSM-IV and beyond* (pp. 71–106). Washington, DC: American Psychiatric Press.

Dreyfuss, R. (1996). Tobacco, enemy number 1. *Mother Jones, 21,* 42–48.

Duchek, J., Balota, D., Storandt, M., & Larsen, R. (2007). The power of personality in discriminating between healthy aging and early-stage Alzheimer's disease. *Journals of Gerontology: Series B: Psychological Sciences and Social Sciences, 62B,* P353–P361.

Duhig, A. M., Renk, K., Epstein, M. K., & Phares, V. (2000). Interparental agreement on internalizing, externalizing, and total behavior problems: A metaanalysis. *Clinical Psychology: Science and Practice, 7,* 435–453.

Duke, D. C., Keeley, M. L., Geffken, G. R., & Storch, E. A. (2010). Trichotillomania: A current review. *Clinical Psychology Review, 30,* 181–193.

Dupéré, V., Lacourse, é., Willms, J. D., Vitaro, F., & Tremblay, R. E. (2007). Affiliation to youth gangs during adolescence: The interaction between childhood psychopathic tendencies and neighborhood disadvantage. *Journal of Abnormal Child Psychology, 35,* 1035–1045.

Durazzo, T. C., Pathak, V., Gazdzinski, S., Mon, A., & Meyerhoff, D. J. (2010). Metabolite levels in the brain reward pathway discriminate those who remain abstinent from those who resume hazardous alcohol consumption after treatment for alcohol dependence. *Journal of Studies on Alcohol and Drugs, 71,* 278–289.

Durham, M. L., & LaFond, J. Q. (1988). A search for the missing premise of involuntary therapeutic commitment: Effective treatment of the mentally ill. *Rutgers Law Review, 40,* 303–368.

Durkheim, E. (1897/1951). *Suicide: A study in sociology.* New York: Free Press.

Dusseldorp, E., van Elderen, T., Maes, S., Meulman, J., & Kraaij, V. (1999). A meta-analysis of psychoeducational programs for coronary heart disease patients. *Health Psychology, 18,* 506–519.

Dutere, E., Segraves, T., & Althof, S. (2007). Psychotherapy and pharmacotherapy for sexual dysfunctions. In P. E. Nathan & J. M. Gorman (Eds.), *A Guide to Treatments That Work* (3rd ed, pp. 531–560). New York: Oxford University Press.

Dykas, M. J., & Cassidy, J. (2011). Attachment and the processing of social information across the life span: Theory and evidence. *Psychological Bulletin, 137,* 19–46.

# E

Eack, S. M., Hogarty, G. E., Greenwald, D. P., Hogarty, S. S., & Keshavan, M. S. (2011). Effects of cognitive enhancement therapy on employment outcomes in early schizophrenia: Results from a 2-year randomized trial. *Research on Social Work Practice, 21,* 32–42.

Earl, A., Albarracín, D., Durantini, M. R., Gunnoe, J. B., Leeper, J., & Levitt, J. H. (2009). Participation in counseling programs: High-risk participants are reluctant to accept HIV-prevention counseling. *Journal of Consulting and Clinical Psychology, 77,* 668–679.

Earls, F., & Mezzacappa, E. (2002). Conduct and oppositional disorders. In M. Rutter & E. Taylor (Eds.), *Child and adolescent Psychiatry* (4th ed., pp. 419–436). Oxford, England: Blackwell.

Eaton, N. R., South, S. C., & Krueger, R. F. (2009). The cognitive-affective processing system (CAPS) approach to personality and the concept of personality disorder: Integrating clinical and social-cognitive research. *Journal of Research in Personality, 43,* 208–217.

Eaton, W. W., Alexandre, P., Bienvenu, O., Clarke, D., Martins, S. S., Nestadt, G., & Zablotsky, B. (2012). The burden of mental disorders. In W. W. Eaton (Ed.), *Public mental health* (pp. 3–30). New York: Oxford University Press.

Eberhard, J., Lindström, E., & Levander, S. (2006). Tardive dyskinesia and antipsychotics: A 5-year longitudinal study of frequency, correlates and course. *International Clinical Psychopharmacology, 21,* 35–42.

Eberhart, N. K., Auerbach, R. P., Bigda-Peyton, J., & Abela, J. Z. (2011). Maladaptive schemas and depression: Tests of stress generation and diathesis-stress models. *Journal of Social and Clinical Psychology, 30,* 75–104.

Eddy, K. T., Keel, P. K., Dorer, D. J., Delinsky, S. S., Franko, D. L., & Herzog, D. B. (2002). Longitudinal comparison of anorexia nervosa subtypes. *International Journal of Eating Disorders, 31,* 191–201.

Edwards, D., Hackett, G., Collins, O., & Curram, J. (2006). Vardenafil improves sexual function and treatment satisfaction in couples affected by erectile dysfunction (ED): A randomized, double-blind, placebo-controlled trial in PDE5 inhibitor-naïve men with ED and their partners. *Journal of Sexual Medicine, 3,* 1028–1036.

Edwards, R. R., Campbell, C., Jamison, R. N., & Wiech, K. (2009). The neurobiological underpinnings of coping with pain. *Current Directions in Psychological Science, 18,* 237–241.

Edwards, W., & Hensley, C. (2001). Contextualizing sex offender management legislation and policy: Evaluating the problem of latent consequences in community notification laws. *International Journal of Offender Therapy and Comparative Criminology, 45,* 83–101.

Ehlers, A., & Clark, D. M. (2000). A cognitive model of persistent posttraumatic stress disorder. *Behavior Research and Therapy, 38,* 319–345.

Ehlers, A., Mayou, R. A., & Bryant, B. (1998). Psychological predictors of chronic posttraumatic stress disorders after motor vehicle accidents. *Journal of Abnormal Psychology, 107,* 508–519.

Eifert, G. H., Zvolensky, M. J., & Lejuez, C. W. (2000). Heart-focused anxiety and chest pain: A conceptual and clinical review. *Clinical Psychology: Science and Practice, 7,* 403–417.

Eisenberger, N. I. (2012). Broken hearts and broken bones: A neural perspective on the similarities between social and physical pain. *Current Directions in Psychological Science, 21,* 42–47.

Eliason, M. J., & Amodia, D. S. (2007). An integral approach to drug craving. *Addiction Research & Theory, 15,* 343–364.

Elkis, H. (2007). Treatment-resistant schizophrenia. *Psychiatric Clinics of North America, 30,* 511–533.

Ellis, A. (1962). *Reason and emotion in psychotherapy.* New York: Lyle Stuart.

Ellis, B. J., & Boyce, W. T. (2008). Biological sensitivity to context. *Current Directions in Psychological Science, 17,* 183–187.

Emery, R. E. (1982). Interparental conflict and the children of discord and divorce. *Psychological Bulletin, 92,* 310–330.

Emery, R. E. (1992). Family conflict and its developmental implications: A conceptual analysis of deep meanings and systemic processes. In C. U. Shantz & W. W. Hartup (Eds.), *Conflict in Child and Adolescent Development* (pp. 270–298). London: Cambridge University Press.

Emery, R. E. (1994). *Renegotiating family relationships: Divorce, child custody, and mediation.* New York: Guilford.

Emery, R. E. (1999a). *Marriage, Divorce, and Children's Adjustment* (2nd ed.). Thousand Oaks, CA: Sage.

Emery, R. E. (1999b). Changing the rules for determining child custody in divorce cases. *Clinical Psychology: Science and Practice, 6,* 323–327.

Emery, R. E. (2004). *The Truth About Children and Divorce: Dealing with the Emotions So You and Your Children Can Thrive.* New York: Viking/Penguin.

Emery, R. E. (2011). *Renegotiating family relationships: Divorce, child custody, and mediation* (2nd ed.). New York: Guilford.

Emery, R. E., & Laumann-Billings, L. (1998). An overview of the nature, causes, and consequences of abuse family relationships: Toward differentiating maltreatment and violence. *American Psychologist, 53,* 121–135.

Emery, R. E., & Laumann-Billings, L. (2002). Child abuse. In M. Rutter & E. Taylor (Eds.), *Child and adolescent psychiatry* (4th ed., pp. 325–339). Oxford, England: Blackwell.

Emery, R. E., & Marholin, D. (1977). An applied behavior analysis of delinquency: The irrelevancy of relevant behavior. *American Psychologist, 32,* 860–873.

Emery, R. E., Fincham, F. D., & Cummings, E. M. (1992). Parenting in context: Systemic thinking about parental conflict and its influence on children. *Journal of Consulting and Clinical Psychology, 60,* 909–912.

Emery, R. E., Laumann-Billings, L., Waldron, M., Sbarra, D. A., & Dillon, P. (2001). Child custody mediation and litigation: Custody, contact, and co-parenting 12 years after initial dispute resolution. *Journal of Consulting and Clinical Psychology, 69,* 323–332.

Emery, R. E., Matthews, S., & Kitzmann, K. (1994). Child custody mediation and litigation: Parents' satisfaction and functioning a year after settlement. *Journal of Consulting and Clinical Psychology, 62,* 124–129.

Emery, R. E., Otto, R. K., & O'Donohue, W. (2005). A Critical Assessment of Child Custody Evaluations: Limited Science and a Flawed System. *Psychological Science in the Public Interest, 6*(1).

Emery, R. E., Sbarra, D. S., & Grover, T. (2005). Divorce mediation: Research and reflections. *Family Court Review, 43,* 22–37.

Emery, R. E., Shim, H. J., & Horn, E. (2012). Examining divorce consequences and policies and the question: Is marriage more than a piece of paper? In L. Campbell & T. J. Loving (Eds.), *Close relationships: An interdisciplinary integration* (pp. 227–250). Washington: American Psychological Association.

Emmons, R. A. (1997). Motives and goals. In R. Hogan, J. Johnson, & S. Briggs (Eds.), *Handbook of personality psychology* (pp. 486–512). San Diego, CA: Academic Press.

Emrick, C. D. (1999). Alcoholics anonymous and other 12-step groups. In M. Galanter & H. D. Kleber (Eds.), *Textbook of substance abuse treatment* (2nd ed., pp. 403–411). Washington, DC: American Psychiatric Press.

Epperson, C., Steiner, M., Hartlage, S., Eriksson, E., Schmidt, P. J., Jones, I., & Yonkers, K. A. (2012). Premenstrual dysphoric disorder: Evidence for a new category for DSM-5. *American Journal of Psychiatry, 169,* 465–475.

Epstein, S. (1994). Integration of the cognitive and the psychodynamic unconscious. *American Psychologist, 49,* 709–724.

Erdelyi, M. H. (1990). Repression, reconstruction, and defense: History and integration of the psychoanalytic and experimental frameworks. In J. L. Singer (Ed.), *Repression and dissociation* (pp. 1–32). Chicago: University of Chicago Press.

Erickson, C. A., Stigler, K. A., Posey, D. J., & McDougle, C. J. (2007). Psychopharmacology. In F. R. Volkmar (Ed.), *Autism and pervasive developmental disorders* (pp. 221–253). New York: Cambridge University Press.

Erikson, E. H. (1959/1980). *Identity and the Life Cycle.* New York: Norton.

Erikson, E. H. (1963). *Childhood and Society* (rev. ed.). Harmondsworth, England Penguin.

Erikson, E. H. (1968). *Identity: Youth and Crisis.* New York: Norton.

Escobar, J., Cook, B., Chen, C. N., Gara, M., Alegria, M., Interian, A., et al. (in press). Whether medically unexplained or not, three or more concurrent somatic symptoms predict psychopathology and service use in community populations. *Journal of Psychosomatic Research.*

Esterberg, M. L., Goulding, S. M., & Walker, E. F. (2010). Cluster a personality disorders: Schizotypal, schizoid and paranoid personality disorders in childhood and adolescence.

*Journal of Psychopathology and Behavioral Assessment, 32,* 515–528.

Bridle, N., Pantelis, C., Wood, S., Coppola, R., Velakoulis, D., McStephen, M., et al. (2002). Thalamic and caudate volumes in monozygotic twins discordant for schizophrenia. *Australian and New Zealand Journal of Psychiatry, 36,* 347–354.

Etkin, A., & Wager, T. D. (2007). Functional neuroimaging of anxiety: A meta-analysis of emotional processing in PTSD, social anxiety disorder, and specific phobia. *American Journal of Psychiatry, 164,* 1476–1488.

Evans, D. L., Leserman, J., Perkins, D. O., Stern, R. A., Murphy, C., Zheng, B., et al. (1997). Severe life stress as a predictor of early disease progression in HIV infection. *American Journal of Psychiatry, 154,* 630–634.

Evans, G. W. (2004). The environment of childhood poverty. *American Psychologist, 59,* 7–92.

Evans, G. W., & Kim, P. (2012). Childhood poverty and young adults' allostatic load: The mediating role of childhood cumulative risk exposure. *Psychological Science, 23,* 979–983.

Eysenck, H. J. (1992, ). The effects of psychotherapy: An evaluation. *Journal of Consulting and Clinical Psychology, 60*(5), 659–663. (Originally in *Journal of Consulting Psychology,* 1952, *16,* 319–324.)

# F

Fabian, J. (2011). Paraphilias and predators: The ethical application of psychiatric diagnoses in partisan sexually violent predator civil commitment proceedings. *Journal of Forensic Psychology Practice, 11*(1), 82–98.

Factor, S. A. (2002). Pharmacology of atypical antipsychotics. *Clinical Neuropharmacology, 25,* 153–157.

Fagan, P. J., Wise, T. N., Schmidt, C. W., & Berlin, F. S. (2002). Pedophilia. *Journal of the American Medical Association, 288,* 2458–2465.

Faigman, D. L., & Monahan, J. (2005). Psychological evidence at the dawn of the law's scientific age. *Annual Review of Psychology, 56,* 631–659.

Faigman, D. L., Kaye, D. H., Saks, M. J., & Sanders, J. (1997). *Modern scientific evidence: The law and science of expert testimony.* St. Paul, MN: West.

Fairburn, C. G. (1996). *Overcoming binge eating.* New York: Guilford.

Fairburn, C. G. (2002). Cognitive-behavioral therapy for bulimia nervosa. In C. G. Fairburn & K. D. Brownell (Eds.), *Eating disorders and obesity* (2nd ed., pp. 302–307). New York: Guilford.

Fairburn, C. G., & Beglin, S. J. (1990). Studies of the epidemiology of bulimia nervosa. *American Journal of Psychiatry, 147,* 401–480.

Fairburn, C. G., & Brownell, K. D. (Eds.). (2002). *Eating disorders and obesity* (2nd ed.). New York: Guilford.

Fairburn, C. G., Jones, R., Peveler, R. C., Carr, S. J., Solomon, R. A., O'Connor, M. E., et al. (1991). Three psychological treatments for bulimia nervosa: A comparative trial. *Archives of General Psychiatry, 48,* 463–469.

Fairburn, C. G., Jones, R., Peveler, R. C., Hope, R. A., & O'Connor, M. (1993). Psychotherapy and bulimia nervosa: Longer-term effects of interpersonal psychotherapy, behavior therapy, and cognitive behavior therapy. *Archives of General Psychiatry, 50,* 419–428.

Fairburn, C. G., Stice, E., Cooper, Z., Doll, H. A., Norman, P. A., & O'Connor, M. E. (2003). Understanding persistence in bulimia nervosa: A 5-year naturalistic study. *Journal of Consulting and Clinical Psychology, 71,* 103–109.

Fairburn, C. G., Welch, S. L., Doll, H. A., Davies, B. A., & O'Connor, M. E. (1997). Risk factors for bulimia nervosa: A community-based case-control study. *Archives of General Psychiatry, 54,* 509–517.

Falk, A. J. (1999). Sex offenders, mental illness, and criminal responsibility: The constitutional boundaries of civil commitment after *Kansas v. Hendricks. American Journal of Law and Medicine, 25,* 117–147.

Falkai, P. (2008). Limitations of current therapies: Why do patients switch therapies? *European Neuropsychopharmacology, 18,* S135–S139.

Fallon, P., Katzman, M. A., & Wooley, S. C. (1994). *Feminist perspectives on eating disorders.* New York: Guilford.

Faraone, S. V. (2003). Report from the 4th international meeting of the attention deficit hyperactivity disorder molecular genetics netw4ork. *American Journal of Medical Genetics, 121B,* 55–59.

Faraone, S. V., Tsuang, M. T., & Tsuang, D. W. (1999). *Genetics of mental disorders.* New York: Guilford.

Faris, R. E. L., & Dunham, H. W. (1939). *Mental disorders in urban areas: An ecological study of schizophrenia and other psychoses.* Chicago: University of Chicago Press.

Farquhar, J. W., Maccoby, N., Wood, P. D., Alexander, J. K., Breitrose, H., Brown, B. W., Jr., et al. (1977). Community education for cardiovascular health. *Lancet, 1,* 1192–1195.

Farrer, L. A., Cupples, A., Haines, J. L., Hyman, B., Kukull, W. A., Mayeux, R., et al. (1997). Effects of age, sex, and ethnicity on the association between apolipoprotein E genotype and Alzheimer disease: A meta-analysis. *Journal of the American Medical Association, 278,* 1349–1356.

Farrington, D. P. (2006). Family background and psychopathy. In C. J. Patrick (Ed.). *Handbook of Psychopathy* (pp. 229–250). New York: Guilford.

Farrington, D., Ohlin, L., & Wilson, J. Q. (1986). *Understanding and Controlling Crime.* New York: Springer.

Faust, D., & Ziskin, J. (1988). The expert witness in psychology and psychiatry. *Science, 241,* 31–35.

Fawzy, F. I., Fawzy, N. W., Hyun, C. S., Gutherie, D., Fahey, J. L., & Morton, D. (1993). Malignant melanoma. Effects of an early structured psychiatric intervention, coping, and affective state on recurrence and survival six years later. *Archives of General Psychiatry, 50,* 681–689.

Fearon, P., & Morgan, C. (2006). Environmental factors in schizophrenia: The role of migrant studies. *Schizophrenia Bulletin, 32,* 405–408.

Federal Interagency Forum on Aging-Related Statistics. Older Americans 2010: Key Indicators of Well-Being. (2010, July). Federal Interagency Forum on Aging-Related Statistics. Washington, DC: U.S. Government Printing Office.

Fedoroff, J. P. (2003). The paraphilic world. In S. B. Levine & C. B. Risen (Eds.), *Handbook of clinical sexuality for mental health professionals* (pp. 333–356). New York: Brunner-Routledge.

Fein, D. (2013). Optimal outcome in individuals with a history of autism. *Journal of Child Psychology and Psychiatry, 54,* 195–205.

Feingold, A., & Mazzella, R. (1998). Gender differences in body image are increasing. *Psychological Science, 9,* 190–195.

Feingold, B. F. (1975). *Why Your Child Is Hyperactive.* New York: Random House.

Fenning, R. M., Baker, J. K., Baker, B. L., & Crinic, K. A. (2007). Parenting children with borderline intellectual functioning: A unique risk population. *American Journal on Mental Retardation, 112,* 107–121.

Fenton, W. S. (2000). Heterogeneity, subtypes, and longitudinal course in schizophrenia. *Psychiatric Annals, 30,* 638–644.

Fernandez, A., et al., (2012). Adjustment disorders in primary care: Prevalence, recognition and use of services. *British Journal of Psychiatry, 201,* 137–142.

Fernando, B. P., & Robbins, T. W. (2010). Animal models of neuropsychiatric disorders. *Annual Review of Clinical Psychology, 6,* 1–24.

Fernandez, H. (1998). *Heroin.* Center City, MN: Hazeldon.

Ferster, C. B. (1961). Positive reinforcement and behavioral deficits of autistic children. *Child Development, 32,* 437–456.

Field, A. E., & Kitos, N. (2010). Eating and weight concerns in eating disorders. In W. S. Agras (Ed.), *The oxford handbook of eating disorders* (pp. 206–222). New York: Oxford University Press.

Figley, C. R. (1978). *Stress disorders among Vietnam veterans.* New York: Brunner/Mazel.

Fingarette, H. (1988). *Heavy drinking: The myth of alcoholism as a disease.* Berkeley: University of California Press.

Fingerman, K. L., & Charles, S. T. (2010). It takes two to tango: Why older people have the best relationships. *Current Directions in Psychological Science, 19,* 172–176.

Fink, H. A., MacDonald, R., Rutks, I. R., Nelson, D. B., and Wilt, T. J. (2002). Sildenafil for male erectile dysfunction: A systematic review and meta-analysis. *Archives of Internal Medicine, 162,* 1349–1360.

Finney, J. W., & Moos, R. H. (2002). Psychosocial treatments for alcohol use disorders. In P. E. Nathan & J. M. Gorman (Eds.), *A guide to treatments that work* (2nd ed., pp. 157–168). New York: Oxford.

Finney, J. W., Moos, R. H., & Humphreys, K. (1999). A comparative evaluation of substance abuse treatment. II. Linking proximal outcomes of 12-step and cognitive-behavioral treatment to substance use outcomes. *Alcoholism: Clinical and Experimental Research, 23,* 537–544.

First, M. (2002). Personality Disorders and Relational Disorders: A research Agenda for Addressing Crucial Gaps in DSM. In D. J. Kupfer, M. B. First, & D. A. Regier, *A research agenda for DSM-V* (pp. 123–200). Washington: American Psychiatric Association.

First, M., Bell, C., Cuthbert, B., Krystal, J., Malison, R., Offord, D., et al. (2002). Personality disorders and relational disorders: A Research Agenda for Addressing Crucial Gaps in DSM. In D. Kupfer, M. First, & D. Regier (Eds.), *A Research Agenda for DSM–V* (pp. 123–200). Washington, DC: American Psychiatric Association.

Fishbain, D. A., Cutler, R. B, Rosomoff, H. L., Rosomoff, R., & Steele, R. (1998). Do antidepressants have an analgesic effect in psychogenic pain and somatoform pain disorder? A meta-analysis. *Psychosomatic Medicine, 60,* 503–509.

Fitch, S. A., & Adams, G. R. (1983). Ego-identity and intimacy status: Replication and extension. *Developmental Psychology, 19,* 839–845.

Fitch, W. L., Petrella, R. C., & Wallace, J. (1987). Legal ethics and the use of mental health experts in criminal cases. *Behavioral Sciences and the Law, 5,* 105–117.

Fitzsimmons, J., Kubicki, M., & Shenton, M. E. (2013). Review of functional and anatomical brain connectivity findings in schizophrenia. *Current Opinion in Psychiatry, 26,* 172–187.

Flanagan, J. C. (1982). *New Insights to Improve the Quality of Life at Age 70.* Palo Alto, CA: American Institutes for Research.

Floyd, F. J., Costigan, C. L., & Phillippe, K. A. (1997, May). Developmental change and consistency in parental interactions with school-age children who have mental retardation. *American Journal on Mental Retardation, 101*(6), 579–594.

Foa, E. B. & Street, G. P. (2001). Women and traumatic events. *Journal of Clinical Psychiatry, 62,* 29–34.

Foa, E. B., Gillihan, S. J., & Bryant, R. A. (2013). Challenges and successes in dissemination of evidence-based treatments for posttraumatic stress: Lessons learned from prolonged exposure therapy for PTSD. *Psychological Science in the Public Interest, 14,* 65–111.

Foa, E. B., Hembree, E. A., Cahill, S. P., Rauch, S. A. M., Riggs, D. S., Feeny, N. C., et al. (2005). Randomized trial of prolonged exposure for posttraumatic stress disorder with and without cognitive restructuring: Outcome at academic and community clinics. *Journal of Consulting and Clinical Psychology, 73,* 953–964.

Foley, S. (2009). The complex etiology of delayed ejaculation: Assessment and treatment implications. *Journal of Family Psychotherapy, 20,* 261–282.

Fombonne, E. (2007). Epidemiological surveys of pervasive developmental disorders. In F. R. Volkmar (Ed.), *Autism and pervasive developmental disorders* (pp. 33–68). New York: Cambridge University Press.

Fonagy, P., & Bateman, A. (2008). The development of borderline personality disorder—a mentalizing model. *Journal of Personality Disorders, 22,* 4–21.

Forbes, N. F., Carrick, L. A., McIntosh, A. M., & Lawrie, S. M. (2009). Working memory in schizophrenia: A meta-analysis. *Psychological Medicine: A Journal of Research in Psychiatry and the Allied Sciences, 39*(6), 889–905.

Fornari, V., Wlodarczyk-Bisaga, K., Matthews, M., Sandberg, D., Mandel, F. S., & Katz, J. L. (1999). Perception of family functioning and depressive symptomatology in individuals with anorexia nervosa or bulimia nervosa. *Comprehensive Psychiatry, 40,* 434–444.

Fountoulakis, K. N., Thessaloniki, T., Grunze, H., Panagiotidis, P., & Kaprinis, G. (2008). Treatment of bipolar depression: An update. *Journal of Affective Disorders, 109,* 21–34.

Fournier, J. C., DeRubeis, R. J., Shelton, R. C., Gallop, R., Amsterdam, J. D., & Hollon, S. D. (2008). Antidepressant medications v. cognitive therapy in people with depression with or without personality disorder. *British Journal of Psychiatry, 192,* 124–129.

Fowles, D. C., & Dindo, L. (2006). A dual-deficit model of psychopathy. In C. J. Patrick (Ed.), *Handbook of psychopathy* (pp. 14–34). New York: Guilford.

Fozard, J. L., & Gordon-Salant, S. (2001). Changes in vision and hearing with aging. In J. E. Birren & K. W. Schaie (Eds.), *Handbook of the Psychology of Aging* (5th ed., pp. 241–266). San Diego, CA: Academic Press.

Frances, A. (2013). *Saving Normal: An insider's revolt against out-of-control psychiatric diagnosis, DSM-5, Big Pharma, and the Medicalization of Ordinary Life.* New York: William Morrow.

Frances, A. J., & Widiger, T. (2012). Psychiatric diagnosis: Lessons from the DSM-IV past and cautions for the DSM-5 future. *Annual Review of Clinical Psychology, 8,* 109–130.

Frances, A., First, M. B., & Pincus, H. A. (1995). *DSM-IV guidebook.* Washington, DC: American Psychiatric Press.

Francis, D. J., Fletcher, J. M., Stuebing, K. K., Lyon, G. R., Shaywitz, B. A., & Shaywitz, S. E. (2005). Psychometric approaches to the identification of LD: IQ and achievement scores are not sufficient. Journal of Learning Disabilities, 38, 98–108.

Frank, E. (2005). *Treating bipolar disorder: A clinician's guide to interpersonal and social rhythm therapy.* New York: Guilford.

Frank, J. D. (1973). *Persuasion and healing: A comparative study of psychotherapy.* Baltimore, MD: Johns Hopkins University Press.

Franklin, M. E., & Foa, E. B. (2002). Cognitive behavioral treatments for obsessive compulsive disorder. In P. E. Nathan & J. M. Gorman (Eds.), *A guide to treatments that work* (2nd ed., pp. 367–386). London: Oxford University Press.

Frasure-Smith, N., & Lespérance, F. (2005). Depression and coronary heart disease: Complex synergism of mind, body, and environment. *Current Directions in Psychological Science, 14,* 39–43.

Frasure-Smith, N., & Prince, R. (1985). Long-term follow-up of the ischemic heart disease life stress monitoring program. *Psychosomatic Medicine, 51,* 485–513.

Fredrickson, B. L., & Losada, M. (2005). Positive emotions and the complex dynamics of human flourishing. *American Psychologist, 60,* 678–686.

Freedman, R., Lewis, D. A., Michels, R., Pine, D. S., Schultz, S. K., Tamminga, C. A., et al. (2013). The initial field trials of DSM-5: New blooms and old thorns. *American Journal of Psychiatry, 170,* 1–5.

Freud, S. (1924/1962). The aetiology of hysteria. In J. Strachey (Ed. and Trans.), *The standard edition of the complete psychological works of Sigmund Freud* (Vol. 3, pp. 191–221). London: Hogarth Press.

Freund, A. M., & Baltes, P. B. (2002). Life-management strategies of selection, optimization, and compensation: Measurement by self-report and construct validity. *Journal of Personality and Social Psychology, 82,* 642–662.

Freund, K., & Blanchard, R. (1993). Erotic target location errors in male gender dysphorics, paedophiles, and fetishists. *British Journal of Psychiatry, 162,* 558–563.

Freund, K., & Seto, M. C. (1998). Preferential rape in the theory of courtship disorder. *Archives of Sexual Behavior, 27,* 433–445.

Friedman, J. H., & LaFrance, C., Jr. (2010). Psychogenic disorders: The need to speak plainly. *Archives of Neurology, 67,* 753–755.

Friedman, M. J., & Davidson, J. R. T. (2007). Pharmacotherapy for PTSD. In M. J. Friedman, T. M. Keane, & P. A. Resick (Eds.), *Handbook of PTSD: Science and practice* (pp. 376–405). New York: The Guilford Press.

Friedman, M. J., Resick, P. A., & Keane, T. M. (2007). PTSD: Twenty-five years of progress and challenges. In M. J. Friedman, T. M. Keane, & P. A. Resick (Eds.), *Handbook of PTSD: Science and practice* (pp. 3–18). New York: The Guilford Press.

Friedman, M., Thoresen, C. E., Gill, J. J., Ulmer, D., Powell, L. H., Price, V. A., et al. (1986). Alteration of Type A behavior and its effect on cardiac recurrences in post-myocardial infarction patients: Summary results of the recurrent coronary prevention project. *American Heart Journal, 112,* 653–665.

Friedman, R. A., & Leon, A. C. (2007). Expanding the black box—Depression, antidepressants, and the risk of suicide. *New England Journal of Medicine, 356,* 2343–2346.

Fries, J. F. (1990). Medical perspectives upon successful aging. In P. B. Baltes & M. M. Baltes (Eds.), *Successful Aging: Perspectives from the Behavioral Sciences* (pp. 35–49). Cambridge, UK: Cambridge University Press.

Frith, U. (2003). *Autism: Explaining the enigma* (2nd ed.). Oxford, England: Blackwell.

Froehlich, J. (1997). Opioid peptides. *Alcohol Health & Research World, 21,* 132–136.

Frost, R. O., Steketee, G., & Tolin, D. F. (2012). Diagnosis and assessment of hoarding disorder. *Annual Review of Clinical Psychology, 8,* 219–242.

Fuller, R. K., & Gordis, E. (2004). Does disulfiram have a role in alcoholism treatment today? *Addiction, 99,* 21–24, 115–135.

Furr, R. M., & Funder, D. C. (2007). Behavioral observation. In R. C. Fraley & R. F. Krueger (Eds.), *Handbook of research methods in personality psychology* (pp. 273–291). New York: Guilford.

Furstenberg, F. F., Jr. (2010). On a new schedule: Transitions to adulthood and family change. *The Future of Children, 20,* 67–87.

Fusar-Poli, P. P., & Van Os, J. J. (2013). Lost in transition: Setting the psychosis threshold in prodromal research. *Acta Psychiatrica Scandinavica, 127,* 248–252.

## G

Gabbard, G. O. (2000). Psychodynamic psychotherapy of borderline personality disorder: A contemporary approach. *Bulletin of the Menninger Clinic, 65,* 41–57.

Gadde, K. M., & Krishnan, R. R. (1997). Recent advances in the pharmacologic treatment of bipolar illness. *Psychiatric Annals, 27,* 496–506.

Galea, S., Ahern, J., Resnick, H., Kilpatrick, D., Bucuvalas, M., Gold, J., et al. (2002). Psychological sequelae of the September 11 terrorist attacks. *New England Journal of Medicine, 346,* 982–987.

Gallagher-Thompson, D., & Osgood, N. J. (1997). Suicide in later life. *Behavior Therapy, 28,* 23–41.

Ganguli, M., Blacker, D., Blazer, D. G., Grant, I., Jeste, D. V., Paulsen, J. S., et al. (2011). Classification of neurocognitive disorders in DSM-5: A work in progress. *American Journal of Geriatric Psychiatry, 19,* 205–209.

Garb, H. N. (2005). Clinical judgment and decision making. *Annual Review of Clinical Psychology, 1,* 67–89.

Garb, H. N., Klein, D. F., & Grove, W. M. (2002). Comparison of medical and psychological tests. *American Psychologist, 57,* 137–138.

Garb, H. N., Wood, J. M., Lilienfeld, S. O., & Nezworski, M. T. (2005). Roots of the Rorschach controversy. *Clinical Psychology Review, 25,* 97–118.

Garber, H. I. (1988). *The Milwaukee project: Preventing mental retardation in children at risk.* Washington, DC: American Association on Mental Retardation.

Garber, J., & Hollon, S. D. (1991). What can specificity designs say about causality in psychopathology research? *Psychological Bulletin, 110,* 129–136.

Garber, J., Keiley, M. K., & Martin, N. C. (2002). Developmental trajectories of adolescents' depressive symptoms: Predictors of change. *Journal of Consulting and Clinical Psychology, 70*(1), 79–95.

Gardner, F., Shaw, D. S., Dishion, T. J., Burton, J., & Supplee, L. (2007). Randomized prevention trial for early conduct problems: Effects on proactive parenting and links to toddler disruptive behavior. *Journal of Family Psychology, 21,* 398–406.

Garfield, C. F., et al., (2012). Trends in attention deficit hyperactivity disorder ambulatory diagnosis and medical treatment in the United States, 2000-2010. *Academic Pediatrics, 12,* 110–116.

Garfinkel, P. E., & Garner, D. M. (1982). *Anorexia nervosa: A multidimensional perspective.* New York: Basic Books.

Garfinkel, P. E., Kennedy, S. H., & Kaplan, A. S. (1995). Views on classification and diagnosis of eating disorders. *Canadian Journal of Psychiatry, 40,* 445–456.

Garner, D. M., & Needleman, L. D. (1996). Stepped-care and decision-tree models for treating eating disorders. In J. K. Thompson (Ed.), *Body image, eating disorders, and obesity* (pp. 225–252). Washington, DC: American Psychological Association.

Garner, D. M., Garfinkel, P. E., Schwartz, D., & Thompson, M. (1980). Cultural expectations of thinness in women. *Psychological Reports, 47,* 483–491.

Garratt, G., Ingram, R. E., Rand, K. L., & Sawalani, G. (2007). Cognitive processes in cognitive therapy: Evaluation of the mechanisms of change in the treatment of depression. *Clinical Psychology: Science and Practice, 14,* 224–239.

Gatchel, R. J., Peng, Y. B., Peters, M. L., Fuchs, P. N., & Turk, D. C. (2007). The biopsychosocial approach to chronic pain: Scientific advances and future directions. *Psychological Bulletin, 133,* 581–624.

Gatz, M., & Smyer, M. A. (2001). Mental health and aging at the outset of the twenty-first century. In J. E. Birren & K. W. Schaie (Eds.), *Handbook of the Psychology of Aging* (5th ed., pp. 523–544). San Diego, CA: Academic Press.

Gaulin, S. J. C., & McBurney, D. H. (2001). *Psychology: An evolutionary approach.* Upper Saddle River, NJ: Prentice-Hall.

Gauthier, S., Cummings, J., Ballard, O., Brodaty, H., Grossberg, G., Robert, P., et al. (2010). Management of behavioral problems in Alzheimer's disease. *International Psychogeriatrics, 22,* 346–372.

Geddes, J. R., Burgess, S., Hawton, K., Jamison, K., & Goodwin, G. M. (2004). Long-term lithium therapy for bipolar disorder: Systematic review and meta-analysis of randomized controlled studies. *American Journal of Psychiatry, 161,* 217–222.

Gehlbach, S. H. (1988). *Interpreting the medical literature: Practical epidemiology for clinics* (2nd ed.). New York: Macmillan.

Geisbrecht, T., Lynn, S. J., Lilienfeld, S., & Merckelbach, H. (2008). Cognitive processes in dissociation: An analysis of core theoretical assumptions. *Psychological Bulletin, 134,* 617–647.

Geraerts, E., Schooler, J. W., Merckelbach, H., Jelicic, M., Hauer, B. J. A., & Ambadar, Z. (2007). The reality of recovered memories: Corroborating continuous and discontinuous memories of childhood sexual abuse. *Psychological Science, 18,* 564–568.

Gershoff, E. T. (2002). Corporal punishment by parents and associated child behaviors and experience: A meta-analytic and theoretical review. *Psychological Bulletin, 128,* 539–579.

Gershon, E. S., Alliey-Rodriguez, N., & Liu, C. (2011). After GWAS: Searching for genetic risk for schizophrenia and bipolar disorder. *American Journal of Psychiatry, 168,* 253–256.

Getahun, D., et al. (2013). Recent trends in childhood attention-deficit/hyperactivity disorder. *JAMA Pediatrics, 167,* 282–288.

Ghanem, H., & El-Sakka, A. (2007). Sex and sexual dysfunctions in the Middle Eastern culture. In *Sexual health: Moral and cultural foundations* (Vol. 3, pp. 279–295). Westport, CT: Praeger Publishers/Greenwood Publishing Group.

Gianoulakis, C., DeWaele, J. P., & Thavundayil, J. (1996). Implications of the endogenous opioid system in excessive ethanol consumption. *Alcohol, 13,* 19–23.

Gibbons, M. B. C., Crits-Christoph, P., Barber, J. P., Stirman, S. W., Gallop, R., Goldstein, L. A., et al. (2009). Unique and common mechanisms of change across cognitive and dynamic psychotherapies. *Journal of Consulting and Clinical Psychology, 77,* 801–813.

Gibbons, R. D., Brown, C. H., Hur, K., Marcus, S. M., Bhaumik, D. K., & Mann, J. J. (2007). Relationship between antidepressants and suicide attempts: An analysis of the Veterans Health Administration data sets. *American Journal of Psychiatry, 164,* 1044–1049.

Gibbs, N. A., South, S. C., & Oltmanns, T. F. (2003). Attentional coping style in obsessive-compulsive personality disorder: A test of the intolerance of uncertainty hypothesis. *Personality and Individual Differences, 33,* 1205–1222.

Gilbert, D. L., & Kurlan, R. (2009). PANDAS: Horse or zebra? *Neurology, 73,* 1252–1253.

Gilbert, P. (2006). Evolution and depression: Issues and implications. *Psychological Medicine, 36,* 287–297.

Gilbertson, M. W., Shenton, M. E., Ciszewski, A., Kasai, K., Lasko, N. B., Orr, S. P., et al. (2002). Smaller hippocampal predicts pathologic vulnerability to psychological trauma. *Nature Neuroscience, 5,* 1242–1247.

Gillberg, C. (1991). Outcome in autism and autistic-like conditions. *Journal of the American Academy of Child & Adolescent Psychiatry, 30*(3), 375–382.

Gillberg, C., & Schaumann, H. (1982). Social class and infantile autism. *Journal of Autism and Developmental Disorders, 12,* 223–228.

Gilligan, C. (1982). *In a Different Voice.* Cambridge, MA: Harvard University Press.

Gilmore, J. H. (2010). Understanding what causes schizophrenia: A developmental perspective. *American Journal of Psychiatry, 167,* 8–10.

Ginsburg, G. S., et al. (2011). Remission after acute treatment in children and adolescents with anxiety disorders: Findings from the CAMS. *Journal of Consulting and Clinical Psychology, 79,* 806–813.

Giraldi, A., Rellini, A. H., Pfaus, J., & Laan, E. (2013). Female sexual arousal disorders. *Journal of Sexual Medicine, 10,* 58–73.

Girón, M. M., Fernández-Yañez, A. A., Mañá-Alvarenga, S. S., Molina-Habas, A. A., Nolasco, A. A., & Gómez-Beneyto, M. M. (2010). Efficacy and effectiveness of individual family intervention on social and clinical functioning and family burden in severe schizophrenia: A 2-year randomized controlled study. *Psychological Medicine, 40,* 73–84.

Gizer, I. R., Ficks, C., & Waldman, I. D. (2009). Candidate gene studies of ADHD: A meta analytic review. *Human Genetics, 126,* 51–90.

Gladis, M. M., Gosch, E. A., Dishuk, N. M., & Crits-Christoph, P. (1999). Quality of life: Expanding the scope of clinical significance. *Journal of Consulting and Clinical Psychology, 6,* 320–331.

Glaser, D. (2002). Child sexual abuse. In M. Rutter & E. Taylor (Eds.), *Child and adolescent psychiatry* (4th ed., pp. 340–358). Oxford, England: Blackwell.

Glasner-Edwards, S., & Rawson, R. (2010). Evidence-based practices in addiction treatment: Review and recommendations for public policy. *Health Policy, 97,* 93–104.

Glatt, S. J., Faraone, S. V., & Tsuang, M. T. (2003). Association between a functional catechol O-methyltransferase gene polymorphism and schizophrenia: Meta-analysis of case-control and family-based studies. *American Journal of Psychiatry, 160,* 469–476.

Gleaves, D. H. (1996). The sociocognitive model of dissociative identity disorder: A reexamination of the evidence. *Psychological Bulletin, 120,* 42–59.

Gleaves, D. H., Smith, S. M., Butler, L. D., & Spiegel, D. (2004). False and recovered memories in the laboratory and clinic: A review of experiment and clinical evidence. *Clinical Psychology: Science & Practice, 11,* 3–28.

Glied, S. A., & Frank, R. G. (2009). Better but not best: Recent trends in the well-being of the mentally ill. *Health Affairs, 28,* 637–648.

Gofton, T. (2011). Delirium: A review. *Canadian Journal of Neurological Sciences/Le Journal Canadien Des Sciences Neurologiques, 38,* 673–680.

Gold, J. M., Hahn, B., Zhang, W., Robinson, B. M., Kappenman, E. S., Beck, V. M., & Luck, S. J. (2010). Reduced capacity but spared precision and maintenance of working memory representations in schizophrenia. *Archives of General Psychiatry, 67,* 570–577.

Gold, M. S., Tabrah, H., & Frost-Pineda, K. (2001). Psychopharmacology of MDMA (Ecstasy). *Psychiatric Annals, 31,* 675–681.

Goldberg, J. F., & Truman, C. J. (2003). Antidepressant-induced mania: An overview of current controversies. *Bipolar Disorders, 5,* 407–420.

Goldberg, J., True, W. R., Eisen, S. A., & Henderson, W. G. (1990). A twin study of the effects of the Vietnam War on posttraumatic stress disorder. *Journal of the American Medical Association, 263,* 2725–2729.

Golden, R. N., Gaynes, B. N., Ekstrom, R., Hamer, R. M., Jacobsen, F. M., Suppes, T., & Nemeroff, C. B. (2005). The efficacy of light therapy in the treatment of mood disorders: A review and meta-analysis of the evidence. *American Journal of Psychiatry, 162,* 656–662.

Goldin, C. (2006). The quiet revolution that transformed women's employment, education, and family. *American Economic Review, 96,* 1.

Goldman-Rakic, P. S., Muly, E. C., & Williams, G. V. (2000). D1 receptors in prefrontal cells and circuits. *Brain Research Review, 31,* 295–301.

Goldsmith, S. K. (2001). *Risk Factors for Suicide.* Washington, DC: National Academy Press.

Goldstein, G. (2003). Delirium, dementia, and amnestic and other cognitive disorders. In M. Hersen & S. M. Turner (Eds.), *Adult Psychopathology and Diagnosis* (4th ed., pp. 153–191). New York: Wiley.

Goldstein, I. (2004). Epidemiology of erectile dysfunction. *Sexuality & Disability, 22,* 113–120.

Goldstein, J. J., Rosenfarb, I., Woo, S., & Nuechterlein, K. (1997). Transactional processes which can function as risk or protective factors in the family treatment of schizophrenia. In H. D. Brenner & W. Boeker (Eds.), *Towards a comprehensive therapy for schizophrenia* (pp. 147–157). Kirkland, WA: Hogrefe & Huber.

Goldstein, J. M., Buka, S. L., Seidman, L. J., & Tsuang, M. T. (2010). Specificity of familial transmission of schizophrenia psychosis spectrum and affective psychoses in the New England family study's high-risk design. *Archives of General Psychiatry, 67,* 458–467.

Goldstein, R. B., Dawson, D. A., Chou, S., & Grant, B. F. (2012). Sex differences in prevalence and comorbidity of alcohol and drug use disorders: Results from wave 2 of the national epidemiologic survey on alcohol and related conditions. *Journal of Studies on Alcohol and Drugs, 73,* 938–950.

Golier, J. A., Legge, J., & Yehuda, R. (2007). Pharmacological treatment of posttraumatic stress disorder. In P. E. Nathan & J. M. Gorman (Eds.), *A Guide to Treatments That Work* (3rd ed., pp. 475–512). New York: Oxford University Press.

Good, B., & Kleinman, A. (1985). Culture and anxiety: Cross-cultural evidence for the patterning of anxiety disorders. In A. H. Tuma & J. Maser (Eds.), *Anxiety and the Anxiety Disorders.* Hillsdale, NJ: Erlbaum.

Gooding, D. G., Miller, M. D., & Kwapil, T. R. (2000). Smooth pursuit eye tracking and visual fixation in psychosis-prone individuals. *Psychiatry Research, 93,* 41–54.

Goodman, G. S., Ghetti, S., Quas, J. A., Edelstein, R. S., Alexander, K. W., Redlich, A. D., et al. (2003). A prospective study of memory for child sexual abuse: New findings relevant to the repressed-memory controversy. *Psychological Science, 14,* 113–118.

Goodman, L. A., Koss, M. P., & Russo, N. F. (1993). Violence against women: Physical and mental health effects. Part i. Research findings. *Applied and Preventive Psychology, 2,* 79–89.

Goodman, W. K., Price, L. H., Rasmussen, S. A., Mazure, C., Fleischman, R. L., Hill, C. L., et al. (1989). The Yale-Brown Obsessive-Compulsive Scale. 1. Development, use, and reliability. *Archives of General Psychiatry, 46,* 1006–1011.

Gorchaff, S. M., John, O. P., & Helson, R. (2008). Contextualizing change in marital satisfaction during middle age: An 18-year longitudinal study. *Psychological Science, 19,* 194–1200.

Gosselin, C. C., & Wilson, G. D. (1980). *Sexual variations.* London: Faber & Faber.

Gotlib, I. H., & Hamilton, J. P. (2008). Neuroimaging and depression: Current status and unresolved issues. *Current Directions in Psychological Science, 17,* 159–163.

Gotlib, I. H., & Hammen, C. (1992). *Psychological Aspects of Depression: Toward a Cognitive-Interpersonal Integration.* New York: Wiley.

Gotlib, I. H., & Joormann, J. (2010). Cognition and depression: Current status and future directions. *Annual Review of Clinical Psychology, 6,* 285–312.

Gotlib, I. H., Joormann, J., Minor, K. L, & Hallmaer, J. (2008). HPA axis reactivity: A mechanism underlying the associations among 5-HTLPR, stress, and depression. *Biological Psychiatry, 63,* 847–851.

Gottesman, I. G. (1963). Genetic aspects of intelligent behavior. In N. Ellis (Ed.), *The handbook of mental deficiency: Psychological theory and research* (pp. 253–296). New York: McGraw-Hill.

Gottesman, I. I. (1987). The psychotic hinterlands or, the fringes of lunacy. *British Medical Bulletin, 43,* 1–13.

Gottesman, I. I. (1991). *Schizophrenia genesis: The origins of madness.* New York: Freeman.

Gottesman, I. I., & Goldsmith, H. H. (1994). Developmental psychopathology of antisocial behavior: Inserting genes into its ontogenesis and epigenesis. In C. A. Nelson (Ed.), *Threats to Optimal Development: Integrating Biological, Psychological, and Social Risk Factors* (pp. 69–104). Hillsdale, NJ: Erlbaum.

Gottesman, I. I., & Gould, T. D. (2003). The endophenotype concept in psychiatry: Etymology and strategic intentions. *American Journal of Psychiatry, 160,* 636–645.

Gottesman, I. I., & Hanson, D. R. (2005). Human Development: Biological and Genetic Processes. Annual Review of Psychology, 56, 263–286.

Gottman, J. M. (1994). *Why Marriages Succeed or Fail.* New York: Simon & Schuster.

Gottman, J. M. (1997). *Why Marriages Succeed or Fail: And How You Can Make Yours Last.* London: Bloomsbury, 1997.

Gottman, J. M., & Notarius, C. I. (2000). Decade review: Observing marital interaction. *Journal of Marriage and the Family, 62,* 927–947.

Gottman, J., Notarius, C., Gonso, J., & Markman, H. (1976). *A Couple's Guide to Communication.* Champaign, IL: Research Press.

Grabe, S., & Shibley-Hyde, J. (2006). Ethnicity and body dissatisfaction among women in the United States: A meta-analysis. *Psychological Bulletin, 132,* 622–640.

Grabe, S., Ward, L. M., & Hyde, J. S. (2008). The role of the media in body image concerns among women: A meta-analysis of experimental and correlational studies. *Psychological Bulletin, 134,* 460–476.

Grant, B. F., Stinson, F. S., Dawson, D. A., Chous, S. P., & Ruan, W. J. (2005). Co-occurrence of DSM-IV personality disorders in the United States: Results from the National Epidemiologic Survey on Alcohol and Related Conditions. *Comprehensive Psychiatry, 46,* 1–5.

Grawe, R., Falloon, I., Widen, J., & Skogvoll, E. (2006). Two years of continued early treatment for recent-onset schizophrenia: A randomised controlled study. *Acta Psychiatrica Scandinavica, 114,* 328–336.

Grant, B. F., Stinson, F. S., Dawson, D. A., Chous, S. P., Dufour, M. C., Compton, W., Pickering, R. P., & Kaplan, K. (2006). Prevalence and co-occurrence of substance use disorders and independent mood and anxiety disorders: Results from the National Epidemiologic Survey on Alcohol and Related Conditions. *Alcohol Research & Health, 29,* 107–120.

Grant, B. F., Stinson, F. S., Dawson, D. A., Chous, S. P., Dufour, M. C., Compton, W., et al. (2004). Prevalence and co-occurrence of substance use disorders and independent mood and anxiety disorders: Results from the national epidemiologic survey on alcohol and related conditions. *Archives of General Psychiatry, 61,* 807–816.

Grant, D. M., Beck, J. G., Marques, L., Palyo, S. A., & Clapp, J. D. (2008). The structure of distress following trauma: Posttraumatic stress disorder, major depressive disorder, and generalized anxiety disorder. *Journal of Abnormal Psychology, 117,* 662–672.

Grant, J. E., & Potenza, M. N. (2006). Compulsive aspects of impulse-control disorders. *Psychiatric Clinics of North America, 29,* 539–551.

Greaves, G. B. (1980). Multiple personality disorder: 165 years after Mary Reynolds. *Journal of Nervous and Mental Disease, 168,* 577–596.

Green, B. L., Epstein, S. A., Krupnick, J. L., & Rowland, J. H. (1997). Trauma and medical illness: Assessing trauma-related disorders in medical settings. In J. P. Wilson & T. M. Keane (Eds.), *Assessing Psychological Trauma and PTSD.* New York: Guilford.

Green, M. F. (2001). *Schizophrenia revealed: From neurons to social interactions.* New York: Norton.

Green, M. F., Nuechterlein, K. H., Gold, J. M., Barch, D. M., Cohen, J., Essock, S., et al. (2004). Approaching a consensus cognitive battery for clinical trials in schizophrenia: The NIMH-MATRICS conference to select cognitive domains and test criteria. *Biological Psychiatry, 56,* 301–307.

Greenberg, R. P., Bornstein, R. F., Zborowski, M. J., Fisher, S., & Greenberg, M. D. (1994). A meta-analysis of fluoxetine outcome in the treatment of depression. *Journal of Nervous and Mental Disease, 182,* 547–551.

Greene, R. L. (2006). Social impairment in girls with ADHD: Patterns, gender comparisons, and correlates. *Journal of the American Academy of Child and Adolescent Psychiatry, 40,* 704–710.

Greene, R. L. (2006). Use of the MMPI-2 in outpatient mental health settings. In J. N. Butcher (Ed.), *MMPI-2: A practitioner's guide* (pp. 253–271). Washington, DC: American Psychological Association.

Greene, R. W., Biederman, J., Faraone, S. V., Monuteaux, M. C., Mick, E., & DuPre, E. P. (2001). Social impairment in girls with ADHD: Patterns, gender comparisons, and correlates. *Journal of the American Academy of Child and Adolescent Psychiatry, 40,* 704–710.

Greenspan, S., & Switzky, H. N. (2007). Lessons from the Atkins decision for the next AAMR manual. In H. N. Switzky & S. Greenspan (Eds.), *What is mental retardation? Ideas for and evolving disability in the 21st century* (pp. 281–300). Washington: AAIDD.

Greenwood, T. A., Braff, D. L., Light, G. A., Cadenhead, K. S., Calkins, M. E., Dobie, D. J., et al. (2007). Initial heritability analyses of endophenotypic measures for schizophrenia: The consortium on the genetics of schizophrenia. *Archives of General Psychiatry, 64,* 1242–1250.

Griffin, M. G., Resick, P. A., & Mechanic, M. B. (1997). Objective assessment of peritraumatic dissociation: Psychophysiological indicators. *American Journal of Psychiatry, 154,* 1081–1088.

Grob, G. N. (2011). *The mad among us: A history of the care of America's mentally ill.* New York: Free Press.

Grossman, H. J. (1983). *Classification in mental retardation.* Washington, DC: American Association on Mental Deficiency.

Group for the Advancement of Psychiatry. (1995). A model for the classification and diagnosis of relational disorders. *Psychiatric Services, 46,* 926–931.

Grover, S., Subodh, B. N., Avasthi, A., Chakrabarti, S., Kumar, S., Sharan, P., et al. (2009). Prevalence and clinical profile of delirium: A study from a tertiary-care hospital in North India. *General Hospital Psychiatry, 31,* 25–29.

Grucza, R. A., Bucholz, K. K., Rice, J. P., & Bierut, L. J. (2008). Secular trends in the lifetime prevalence of alcohol dependence in the United States: A re-evaluation. *Alcoholism: Clinical and Experimental Research, 32,* 763–770.

Grych, J. H., & Fincham, F. D. (1990). Marital conflict and children's adjustment: A cognitive-contextual framework. *Psychological Bulletin, 101,* 267–290.

Guarnaccia, P., & Pincay, I. M. (2008). Culture-specific diagnoses and their relationship to mood disorders. In S. Loue & M. Sajatovic (Eds.), *Diversity issues in the diagnosis, treatment and research of mood disorders* (pp. 32–53). New York: Oxford University Press.

Gunderson, J. (1984). *Borderline personality disorder.* Washington, DC: American Psychiatric Press.

Gunderson, J. G. (1994). Building structure for the borderline construct. *Acta Psychiatrica Scandinavica, 89*(Suppl. 379), 12–18

Gunderson, J. G. (2010). Revising the borderline diagnosis for DSM-V: An alternative proposal. *Journal of Personality Disorders, 24,* 694–708.

Gureje, O., Simon, G. E., Ustun, T. B., & Goldberg, D. P. (1997). Somatization in cross-cultural perspective: A world health organization study in primary care. *American Journal of Psychiatry, 154,* 989–995.

Gurman, A. S., & Jacobson, N. S. (2002). *Clinical Handbook of Couple Therapy* (3rd ed.). New York: Guilford.

Gusella, J. F., Wexler, N. S., Conneally, P. M., Naylor, S. L., Anderson, M. A., Tanzi, R. E., et al. (1983). A polymorphic DNA marker genetically linked to Huntington's disease. *Nature, 306,* 234–238.

Gutheil, T. G. (1986). The right to refuse treatment: Paradox, pendulum and the quality of care. *Behavioral Sciences and the Law, 4,* 265–277.

Gutierrez-Lobos, K., Schmid-Siegel, B., Bankier, B., & Walter, H. (2001). Delusions in first-admitted patients: Gender, themes, and diagnoses. *Psychopathology, 34,* 1–7.

# H

Haddad, P. M., Taylor, M., & Niaz, O. S. (2009). First-generation antipsychotic long-acting injections v. oral antipsychotics in schizophrenia:Systematic review of randomised controlled trials and observational studies. *British Journal of Psychiatry, 195*(Suppl 52), s20–s28.

Haefner, H., Heiden, W., Behrens, S., Gattaz, W. F., Hambrecht, M., Loeffler, W., et al. (1998). Causes and consequences of the gender difference in age at onset of schizophrenia. *Schizophrenia Bulletin, 24,* 99–113.

Hafner, H., Maurer, K., Loffler, W., an der Heiden, W., Hambrecht, M., & Schultze-Lutter, F. (2003). Modeling the early course of schizophrenia. *Schizophrenia Bulletin, 29,* 325–340.

Hagedoorn, M., Sanderman, R., Bolks, H. N., Tuinstra, J., & Coyne, J. C. (2008). Distress in couples coping with cancer: A meta-analysis and critical review of role and gender effects. *Psychological Bulletin, 134,* 1–30.

Hahlweg, K., Fiegenbaum, W., Frank, M., Schroeder, B., & Witzleben, I. (2001). Short- and long-term effectiveness of an empirically supported treatment for agoraphobia. *Journal of Consulting and Clinical Psychology, 69,* 375–382.

Hahlweg, K., Markman, H. J., Thurmaier, F., Engl, J., & Eckert, V. (1998). Prevention of marital distress: Results of a German prospective longitudinal study. *Journal of Family Psychology, 12,* 543–556.

Halbreich, U., Alarcon, R. D., Calil, H. I., Douki, S., Gaszner, P., Jadresic, E., et al. (2007). Culturally-sensitive complaints of depressions and anxieties in women. *Journal of Affective Disorders, 102,* 159–176.

Hall, B. J., Tolin, D. F., Frost, R. O., & Steketee, G. (2013). An exploration of comorbid symptoms and clinical correlates of clinically significant hoarding symptoms. *Depression and Anxiety, 30*(1), 67–76.

Hall, G. C. N. (2001). Psychotherapy research with ethnic minorities: Empirical, ethical, and conceptual issues. *Journal of Consulting and Clinical Psychology, 69,* 502–510.

Hall, W., & Pacula, R. L. (2003). *Cannabis use and dependence: Public health and public policy.* Cambridge, UK: Cambridge University Press.

Halligan, S. L., Michael, T., Clark, D. M., & Ehlers, A. (2003). Posttraumatic stress disorder following assault: The role of cognitive processing, trauma memory, and appraisals. *Journal of Consulting and Clinical Psychology, 71,* 419–431.

Halliwell, E., & Dittmar, H. (2004). Does size matter? The impact of model's body size on women's body-focused anxiety and advertising effectiveness. *Journal of Social & Clinical Psychology, 23,* 104–122.

Halmi, K. A. (1997). Models to conceptualize risk factors for bulimia nervosa. *Archives of General Psychiatry, 54,* 507–509.

Halmi, K. A. (2010). Psychological comorbidity of eating disorders. In W. S. Agras (Ed.), *The Oxford handbook of eating disorders* (pp. 292–303). New York: Oxford University Press.

Hammand, T. A., Laughren, T., & Racoosin, J. (2006). Suicidality in pediatric patients treated with antidepressant drugs.*Archives of General Psychiatry, 63,* 332–339.

Hammen, C. (2005). Stress and depression. *Annual Review of Clinical Psychology, 55,* 11.1–11.27.

Hammen, C., & Garber, J. (2001). Vulnerability to depression across the lifespan. In *Vulnerability to Psychopathology: Risk Across the Lifespan* (pp. 258–267). New York: Guilford Press.

Hankin, B. L., & Abramson, L. Y. (2001). Development of gender differences in depression: An elaborated cognitive vulnerability-transactional stress theory. *Psychological Bulletin, 127,* 773–796.

Hansen, N. B., Lambert, M. J., & Forman, E. M. (2002). The psychotherapy dose–response effect and its implications for treatment service delivery. *Clinical Psychology: Science and Practice, 9,* 329–343.

Hare, R. D. (1993). *Without conscience: The disturbing world of the psychopaths among us.* New York: Pocket Books.

Harford, T. C., Yi, H., & Grant, B. F. (2010). The five-year diagnostic utility of "diagnostic orphans" for alcohol use disorders in a national sample of young adults. *Journal of Studies on Alcohol and Drugs, 71,* 410–417.

Harkness, K. L., & Stewart, J. G. (2009). Symptom specificity and the prospective generation of life events in adolescence.*Journal of Abnormal Psychology, 118,* 278–287.

Harkness, K. L., Alavi, N., Monroe, S. M., Slavich, G. M., Gotlib, I. H., & Bagby, R. M. (2010). Gender differences in life events prior to onset of major depressive disorder: The moderating effect of age. *Journal of Abnormal Psychology, 119,* 791–803.

Harkness, K. L., & Wildes, J. E. (2002). Childhood adversity and anxiety versus dysthymia co-morbidity in major depression. *Psychological Medicine, 32,* 1239–1249.

Harpur, T. J., & Hare, R. D. (1994). Assessment of psychopathy as a function of age. *Journal of Abnormal Psychology, 103,* 604–609.

Harrington, A. (2008). *The cure within: A history of mind-body medicine.* New York: W. W. Norton & Company.

Harrington, R. (2002). Affective disorders. In M. Rutter & E. Taylor (Eds.), *Child and Adolescent Psychiatry* (4th ed., pp. 463–485). Oxford, England: Blackwell.

Harrington, R. C., & Harrison, L. (1999). Unproven assumptions about the impact of bereavement on children. *Journal of the Royal Society of Medicine, 92,* 230–233.

Harrington, R., Fudge, H., Rutter, M., Pickles, A., & Hill, J. (1990). Adult outcomes of childhood and adolescent depression. I. Psychiatric status. *Archives of General Psychiatry, 47,* 465–473.

Harris, G. T., & Rice, M. E. (2006). Treatment of psychopathy: A review of empirical findings. In C. J. Patrick (Ed.), *Handbook of psychopathy* (pp. 555–572). New York: Guilford.

Harrison, G., Gunnell, D., Glazebrook, C., Page, K., & Kwiecinski, R. (2001). Association between schizophrenia and social inequality at birth: Case control study. *British Journal of Psychiatry, 179,* 346–350.

Hart, A. B., Craighead, W. E., & Craighead, L. W. (2001). Predicting recurrence of major depressive disorder in young adults: A prospective study. *Journal of Abnormal Psychology, 110,* 633–643.

Hart, C., McCance-Katz, E. F., & Kosten, T. R. (2001). Pharmacotherapies used in common substance use disorders. In F. M. Tims & C. G. Leukefeld (Eds.), *Relapse and recovery in addictions* (pp. 303–333). New Haven, CT: Yale University Press.

Hart, E. L., Lahey, B. B., Loeber, R., Applegate, B., & Frick, P. J. (1995). Developmental change in attention-deficit hyperactivity disorder in boys: A four-year longitudinal study. *Journal of Abnormal Child Psychology, 23,* 729–750.

Hart, S. D., & Hare, R. D. (1997). Psychopathy: Assessment and association with criminal conduct. In D. M. Stoff, J. Breiling, & J. Maser (Eds.), *Handbook of antisocial behavior* (pp. 22–35). New York: Wiley.

Hartlage, S., Freels, S., Gotman, N., & Yonkers, K. (2012). Criteria for premenstrual dysphoric disorder: Secondary analyses of relevant data sets. *Archives of General Psychiatry, 69,* 300–305.

Harvey, A. G., Bryant, R. A., & Dang, S. T. (1998). Autobiographical memory in acute stress disorder. *Journal of Consulting and Clinical Psychology, 66,* 500–506.

Harvey, A. G., & Tang, N. K. Y. (2012, January). (Mis) perception of sleep in insomnia: A puzzle and a resolution. *Psychological Bulletin, 138*(1), 77–101. doi: 10.1037/a0025730

Harvey, E. A., et al., (2011). The role of family experience and ADHD in the early development of oppositional defiant disorder.*Journal of Consulting and Clinical Psychology, 79,* 784–795.

Hasin, D. S., Stonson, F. S., Ogburn, E., & Grant, B. F. (2007). Prevalence, correlates, disability, and comorbidity of DSM-IV alcohol abuse and dependence in the United States. *Archives of General Psychiatry, 64,* 830–842.

Haugaard, J. J., & Reppucci, N. D. (1988). *The sexual abuse of children.* San Francisco: Jossey-Bass.

Hawkins, A. J., Blanchard, V. L., Baldwin, S. A., & Fawcett, E. B. (2008). Does marriage and relationship education work? A meta-analytic study. *Journal of Consulting and Clinical Psychology, 76,* 723–734.

Hawley, K. M., & Weisz, J. R. (2003). Child, parent, and therapist (dis)agreement on target problems in outpatient therapy: The therapist's dilemma and its implications. *Journal of Consulting and Clinical Psychology, 71*(1), 62–70.

Hawton, K., Casañas i Comabella, C., Haw, C., & Saunders, K. (2013). Risk factors for suicide in individuals with depression: A systematic review. Journal of Affective Disorders,

Hay, P. J., & Claudino, A. D. M. (2010). Evidence-based treatment for the eating disorders. In W. S. Agras (Ed.), *The oxford handbook of eating disorders* (pp. 452–479). New York: Oxford University Press.

Hayes, S. C. (2004). Acceptance and commitment therapy, relational frame theory, and the third wave of behavioral and cognitive therapies. *Behaviour Therapy, 35,* 639–665.

Hayes, R. D. (2011). Circular and linear modeling of female sexual desire and arousal. *Journal of Sex Research, 48,* 130–141.

Hayes, R. D., Dennerstein, L., Bennett, C. M., & Fairley, C. K. (2008). What is the "true" prevalence of female sexual dysfunctions and does the way we assess these conditions have an impact? *Journal of Sexual Medicine, 5,* 777–787.

Hayes, S. L., Storch, E. A., & Berlanga, L. (2009). Skin picking behaviors: An examination of the prevalence and severity in a community sample. *Journal of Anxiety Disorders, 23,* 314–319.

Haynes, S. G., & Feinleib, M. (1980). Women, work, and coronary heart disease: Prospective findings from the Framingham heart study. *American Journal of Public Health, 70,* 133–141.

Hazell, P. L., & Stuart, J. E. (2003). A randomized controlled trial of clonidine added to psychostimulant medication for hyperactive and aggressive children. *Journal of the American Academy of Child and Adolescent Psychiatry, 42*(8), 886–894.

Hazlett-Stevens, H., & Craske, M. G. (2009). Breathing retraining and diaphragmatic breathing techniques. In W. T. O'Donohue & J. E. Fisher (Eds.), *General Principles and Empirically Supported Techniques of Cognitive Behavior Therapy* (pp. 167–172). Hoboken, NJ: John Wiley & Sons.

Head, D., Rodrigue, K., Kennedy, K., & Raz, N. (2008). Neuroanatomical and cognitive mediators of age-related differences in episodic memory. *Neuropsychology, 22*(4), 491–507.

Heaner, M. K. & Walsh, T. B. (2013). A history of the identification of the characteristic eating disturbances of Bulimia Nervosa, Binge Eating Disorder and Anorexia Nervosa. *Appetite, 65,* 185–188.

Heath, A. C., Bucholz, I. I., Madden, P. A. F., Dinwiddie, S. H., Slutske, W. S., Bierut, L. J., et al. (1997). Genetic and environmental contributions to alcohol dependence risk in a national twin sample: Consistency of findings in women and men.*Psychological Medicine, 27,* 1381–1396.

Heatherton, T. F., & Polivy, J. (1992). Chronic dieting and eating disorders: A spiral model. In J. Crowther, S. E. Hobfall, M. A. P. Stephens, & D. L. Tennenbaum (Eds.), *The Etiology of Bulimia: The individual and familial context* (pp. 135–155). Washington, DC: Hemisphere.

Heavey, C. L., Christensen, A., & Malamuth, N. M. (1995). The longitudinal impact of demand and withdrawal during marital conflict. *Journal of Consulting and Clinical Psychology, 63,* 797–801.

Heber, R. (1959). A manual on terminology and classification in mental retardation. *American Journal on Mental Deficiency, 64*(Monograph Suppl.).

Heerey, E. A., & Kring, A. M. (2007). Interpersonal consequences of social anxiety. *Journal of Abnormal Psychology, 116,* 125–134.

Heiman, J. R. (2002). Psychologic treatments for female sexual dysfunction: Are they effective and do we need them? *Archives of Sexual Behavior, 31,* 445–450.

Heisel, M. (2008). Suicide. In *clinical handbook of schizophrenia* (pp. 491–504). New York: Guilford Press.

Helgeland, M. I., & Torgersen, S. (2004). Developmental antecedents of borderline personality disorder. *Comprehensive Psychiatry, 45,* 138–147.

Helgeson, V. S., Reynolds, K. A., & Tomich, P. L. (2006). A meta-analytic review of benefit finding and growth. *Journal of Consulting and Clinical Psychology, 74,* 797–816.

Helzer, J. E., Bucholz, K. K., & Gossop, M. (2008). A dimensional option for the diagnosis of substance dependence in DSM-V. In J. E. Helzer, H. Kraemer, R. F. Krueger, H. Wittchen, P. J. Sirovatka, D. A. Regier, … D. A. Regier (Eds.), *Dimensional approaches in diagnostic classification: Refining the research agenda for DSM-V* (pp. 19–34). Washington, DC: US American Psychiatric Association.

Helzer, J. E., Kraemer, H. C., & Krueger, R. F. (2006). The feasibility and need for dimensional psychiatric diagnoses. *Psychological Medicine, 36,* 1671–1680.

Hendry, L. B., & Kloep, M. (2007). Conceptualizing emerging adulthood: Inspecting the emperor's new clothes? *Child Development Perspectives, 1,* 74–79.

Henggeler, S. W., & Borduin, C. M. (1990). *Family Therapy and Beyond: A Multisystemic Approach to Treating the Behavior Problems of Children and Adolescents.* Pacific Grove, CA: Brooks/Cole.

Henker, B., & Whalen, C. K. (1989). Hyperactivity and attention deficits. *American Psychologist, 44,* 216–223.

Herbener, E. S., & Harrow, M. (2002). The course of anhedonia during 10 years of schizophrenic illness. *Journal of Abnormal Psychology, 111,* 237–248.

Herbenick, D., Reece, M., Schick, V., Sanders, S. A., Dodge, B., & Fortenberry, J. (2010). Sexual behavior in the United States: Results from a national probability sample of men and women ages 14-94. *Journal of Sexual Medicine, 7*(Suppl. 5), 255–265

Herbert, J. D., & Forman, E. M. (2011). *Acceptance and Mindfulness in Cognitive Behavior Therapy.* United Kingdom: John Wiley and Sons Ltd.

Herbert, M. (2002). Behavioural therapies. In M. Rutter & E. Taylor (Eds.), *Child and Adolescent Psychiatry* (4th ed., pp. 900–920). Oxford, England: Blackwell.

Hermann, D. H. J. (1990). Autonomy, self determination, the right of involuntarily committed persons to refuse treatment, and the use of substituted judgment in medication decisions involving incompetent persons. *International Journal of Law and Psychiatry, 13,* 361–385.

Herpertz, S. C., Werth, U., Lucas, G., Qunaibi, M., Schuerkens, A., Kunert, H., et al. (2001). Emotion in criminal offenders with psychopathy and borderline personality disorders. *Archives of General Psychiatry, 58,* 737–745.

Hess, T. M. (2005). Memory and aging in context. *Psychological Bulletin, 131,* 383–406.

Heston, L. L. (1966). Psychiatric disorders in foster home reared children of schizophrenic mothers. *British Journal of Psychiatry, 112,* 819–825.

Heyman, R. E., & Slep, A. M. S. (2006). Creating and field-testing diagnostic criteria for partner and child maltreatment.*Journal of Family Psychology, 20,* 379–408.

Heyman, R. E., Slep, A. M. S., Beach, S. R. H., Wamboldt, M. Z., Kaslow, N. J., & Reiss, D. (2009). Relationship problems and the DSM: Needed improvements and suggested solutions. *World Psychiatry, 8,* 7–14.

Hiatt, K. D., & Newman, J. P. (2006). Understanding psychopathy: The cognitive side. In C. J. Patrick (Ed.), *Handbook of psychopathy* (pp. 334–352). New York: Guilford.

Higgins, D. M. et al. (in press). Binge eating behavior among a national sample of overweight and obese veterans. *Obesity.*

Hill, A., Briken, P., Kraus, C., Strohm, K., & Berner, W. (2003). Differential pharmacological treatment of paraphilias and sex offenders. *International Journal of Offender Therapy, 47,* 407–421.

Hill, J., & Holmbeck, G. (1986). Attachment and autonomy during adolescence. In G. Whitehurst (Ed.), *Annals of Child Development* (Vol. 3, pp. 145–189). Greenwich, CT: JAI.

Hill, P. C., & Pargament, K. I. (2003). Advances in the conceptualization and measurement of religion and spirituality: Implications for physical and mental health research. *American Psychologist, 58*(1), 64–74.

Hilliard, R. B., & Spitzer, R. L. (2002). Change in criterion for paraphilias in DSM-IV-TR. *American Journal of Psychiatry, 159,* 12–49.

Hinde, R.A. (1992). Developmental psychology in the context of other behavioral sciences. *Developmental Psychology, 28,* 1018–1029.

Hines, M. (2004). Psychosexual development in individuals who have female pseudohermaphroditism. *Child and Adolescent Psychiatric Clinics of North America, 13,* 641–656.

Hinshaw, S. P. (1994). *Attention Deficits and Hyperactivity in Children.* Thousand Oaks, CA: Sage.

Hinshaw, S. P., et al. (2000). Family processes and treatment outcome in the MTA: Negative/ineffective parenting practices in relations to multimodal treatment. *Journal of Abnormal Child Psychology, 28,* 555–568.

Hirschfeld, R. M. A. (2001). Antidepressants in the United States: Current status and future needs. In M. M. Weissman (Ed.),*Treatment of Depression: Bridging the 21st Century* (pp. 123–134). Washington, DC: American Psychiatric Press.

Hobfoll, S. E., Canetti-Nisim, D., & Johnson, R. J. (2006). Exposure to terrorism, stress-related mental health symptoms, and defensive coping among Jews and Arabs in Israel. *Journal of Consulting and Clinical Psychology, 74,* 207–218.

Hoek, H. W. (2002). Distribution of eating disorders. In C. G. Fairburn & K. D. Brownell (Eds.), *Eating disorders and obesity* (2nd ed., pp. 233–237). New York: Guilford.

Hoek, H. W., & Van Hoeken, D. (2003). Review of the prevalence and incidence of eating disorders. *International Journal of Eating Disorders, 34,* 383–396.

Hoeve, M., Blokland, A., Dubas, J. S., Loeber, R., Gerris, J. R. M., & van der Laan, P. H. (2008). Trajectories of delinquency and parenting styles. *Journal of Abnormal Child Psychology, 36,* 223–235.

Hofer, M. A. (2010). Evolutionary concepts of anxiety. In D. J. Stein, E. Hollander, B. O. Rothbaum, D. J. Stein, E. Hollander, B. O. Rothbaum (Eds.), *Textbook of Anxiety Disorders* (2nd ed., pp. 129–145). Arlington, VA: American Psychiatric Publishing.

Hoffman, P. B., & Foust, L. L. (1977). Least restrictive treatment of the mentally ill: A doctrine in search of its senses.*San Diego Law Review, 14,* 1100–1154.

Hofmann, S. G., Asnaani, A., Vonk, I. J., Sawyer, A. T., & Fang, A. (2012). The efficacy of cognitive behavioral therapy:

A review of meta-analyses. *Cognitive Therapy and Research, 36,* 427–440.

Hogarty, G. E., Flesher, S., Ulrich, R., Carter, M., Greenwald, D., Pogue-Geile, M., et al. (2004). Cognitive enhancement therapy for schizophrenia: Effects of a 2-year random- ized trial on cognition and behavior. *Archives of General Psychiatry, 61,* 866–876.

Hoge, E. A., Tamraker, S. M., Christian, K. M., Mahara, N., Nepal, M. K., Pollack, M. H., et al. (2006). Cross-cultural differences in somatic presentation in patients with general- ized anxiety disorder. *Journal of Nervous and Mental Disease, 194,* 962–966.

Hollander, E., & Stein, D. J. (Eds.). (2006). *Clinical manual of impulse-control disorders.* Arlington, VA: American Psychiatric Publishing.

Hollon, S. D., Stewart, M. O., & Strunk, D. (2006). Enduring effects for cognitive behavior therapy in the treatment of depression and anxiety. *Annual Review of Psychology, 57,* 285–315.

Hollon, S. D., Thase, M. E., & Markowitz, J. C. (2002). Treatment and prevention of depression. *Psychological Science in the Public Interest, 3,* 39–77.

Holmes, C. (2002). Genotype and phenotype in Alzheimer's disease. *British Journal of Psychiatry, 180,* 131–134.

Holsinger, T., Steffens, D. C., Phillips, C., Helms, M. J., Havlik, R. J., Breitner, J. C. S., et al. (2002). Head injury in early adulthood and the lifetime risk of depression. *Archives of General Psychiatry, 59,* 17–22.

Honda, H., Shimizu, Y., & Rutter, M. (2005). No effect of MMR withdrawal on the incidence of autism: A total popu- lation study. *Journal of Child Psychology and Psychiatry, 46,* 572–579.

Hong, L., Turano, K., O'Neill, H., Hao, L., Wonodi, I., McMahon, R., et al. (2008). Refining the predictive pursuit endophenotype in schizophrenia. *Biological Psychiatry, 63,* 458–464.

Hooley, J. M., & Gotlib, I. H. (2000). A diathesis-stress con- ceptualization of expressed emotion and clinical outcome. *Applied and Preventive Psychology, 9,* 135–151.

Hopper, K., Harrison, G., Janca, A., & Sartorius, N. (2007). *Recovery from schizophrenia: An international perspective: A report from the WHO collaborative project, the international study of schizophrenia.* New York: Oxford University Press.

Hopwood, C. J., Thomas, K. M., Markon, K. E., Wright, A. C., & Krueger, R. F. (2012). DSM-5 personality traits and DSM–IV personality disorders. *Journal of Abnormal Psychology, 121,* 424–432.

Horevitz, R., & Loewenstein, R. J. (1994). The rational treat- ment of multiple personality disorder. In S. J. Lynn & J. W. Rhue (Eds.), *Dissociation: Clinical and Theoretical Perspectives* (pp. 289–316). New York: Guilford.

Horley, J. (2001). Frotteurism: A term in search of an underly- ing disorder? *Journal of Sexual Aggression, 7,* 51–55.

Horn, E. E., Xu, Y., Beam, C. R., Turkheimer, E., & Emery, R. E. (in press). Accounting for the physical and mental health benefits of entry into marriage: A genetically- informed study of selection and causation. *Journal of Family Psychology.*

Horney, K. (1939). *New Ways in Psychoanalysis.* New York: International Universities Press.

Horvath, K., Stefanatos, G., Sokolski, K. N., Wachtel, R., Nabors, L., & Tildon, J. T. (1998). Improved social and language skills after secretin administration in patients with autistic spectrum disorders. *Journal of the Association of the Academy of Minority Physicians, 9,* 9–15.

Horwitz, A. V., & Wakefield, J. C. (2007). *The Loss of Sadness: How Psychiatry Transformed Normal Sorrow into Depressive Disorder.* New York: Oxford University Press.

Houezec, J. L. (1998). Pharmacokinetics and pharmacodynam- ics of nicotine. In J. Snel & M. M. Lorist (Eds.), *Nicotine, caffeine and social drinking: Behaviour and brain function* (pp. 3–20). Amsterdam: Harwood.

Houts, A. C. (1991). Nocturnal enuresis as a biobehavioral problem. *Behavior Therapy, 22,* 133–151.

Howard, K. J., Kopta, S. M., Krause, M. S., & Orlinsky, D. E. 1986, The Dose–Effect Relationship in Psychotherapy.

*American Psychologist, 41,* 159–164. © 1996 by American Psychological Association.

Howes, O. D., McDonald, C., Cannon, M., Arseneault, L., Boydell, J., & Murray, R. M. (2004). Pathways to schizophrenia: The impact of environmental factors. *International Journal of Neuropsychopharmacology, 7* (Suppl 1), S7–S13.

Howes, O. D., Montgomery, A. J., Asselin, M., Murray, R. M., Valli, I., Tabraham, P., et al. (2009). Elevated striatal dopamine function linked to prodromal signs of schizophre- nia. *Archives of General Psychiatry, 66,* 13–20.

Howlin, P. (2007). The outcome in adult life for people with ASD. In F. R. Volkmar (Ed.), *Autism and pervasive devel- opmental disorders* (pp. 269–306). New York: Cambridge University Press.

Hoza, B., et al. (2005). What aspects of peer relationships are impaired in children with attention-deficit/hyperactivity disorder? *Journal of Consulting and Clinical Psychology, 73,* 411–423.

Hoza, B., Gerdes, A. C., Hinshaw, S. P., Arnold, L. E., Pelham, W. E., Jr., Molina, B. S. G, et al. (2004). Self- perceptions of competence in children with ADHD and comparison children. *Journal of Consulting and Clinical Psychology, 72,* 382–391.

Huang-Pollock, C. L., et al., (2012). Evaluating vigilance defi- cits in ADHD: A meta-analysis of CPT performance. *Journal of Abnormal Psychology, 121,* 360–371.

Hubbs-Tait, L., Nation, J. R., Krebs, N. F., & Bellinger, D. C. (2005). Neurotoxicants, micronutrients, and social environ- ments: Individual and combined effects on children's develop- ment. *Psychological Science in the Public Interest, 6,* 57–121.

Hucker, S. J. (1997). Sexual sadism: Theory and psychopathol- ogy. In D. R. Laws & W. T. O'Donohue (Eds.), *Handbook of sexual deviance: Theory and application.* New York: Guilford.

Hucker, S. J. (2008). Sexual masochism: Psychopathology and theory. In D. Laws, W. T. O'Donohue, D. Laws, & W. T. O'Donohue (Eds.), *Sexual deviance: Theory, assessment, and treatment* (2nd ed., pp. 250–263). New York: Guilford Press.

Hudson, J. I., Hiripi, E., Pope, H. G., Jr., & Kessler, R. C. (2007, February). The prevalence and correlates of eating disorders in the national comorbidity survey replication. *Biological Psychiatry, 61*(3), 348–358. doi: 10.1016/j.bio- psych.2006.03.040

Huerta, M., Bishop, S. L., Duncan, A., Hus, V., & Lord, C. (2012). Application of DSM-5 criteria for autism spectrum disorder to three samples of children with DSM-IV diagnoses of pervasive developmental disorders. American Journal of Psychiatry, 169, 1056–1064.

Huettel, S. A., Song, A. W., & McCarthy, G. (2004). *Functional magnetic resonance imaging.* Sunderland, MA: Sinauer.

Hughes, C. C. (1998). The glossary of culture-bound syn- dromes in DSM-IV: A critique. *Transcultural Psychiatry, 35,* 413–421.

Hughes, J. R. (2007). Measurement of the effects of abstinence from tobacco: A qualitative review. *Psychology of Addictive Behaviors, 21,* 127–137.

Huntington, C. (2007). Mutual independence in child welfare. *Notre Dame Law Review, 82,* 1485–1536.

Hurt, S. W., Reznikoff, M., & Clarkin, J. F. (1991). *Psychological assessment, psychiatric diagnosis, and treatment planning.* New York: Brunner/Mazel.

Husak, D. N. (2002). *Legalize this! The case for decriminalizing drugs.* New York: Verso.

Husted, D. S., Shapira, N. A., & Goodman, W. K. (2006). The neurocircuitry of obsessive-compulsive disorder and disgust. *Progress in Neuro-Psychopharmacology & Biological Psychiatry, 30,* 389–399.

Hviid, A., Stellfeld, M., Wohlfahrt, J., & Melbye, M. (2003). Association between thimerosal-containing vaccine and autism. *Journal of the American Medical Association, 290,* 1763–1766.

Hwang, W. (2006). The psychotherapy adaptation and modifi- cation framework: Application to Asian Americans. *American Psychologist, 61,* 702–715.

Hwang, W., Myers, H. F., Abe-Kim, J., & Ting, J. Y. (2008). A conceptual paradigm for understanding culture's impact on mental health. *Clinical Psychology Review, 28,* 211–227.

Hyman, S. E., & Malenka, R. C. (2001). Addiction and the brain: The neurobiology of compulsion and its persistence. *Nature Reviews Neuroscience, 2,* 695–703.

## I

Ingersoll, B. (2011). Recent advances in early identification and treatment of autism. *Current Directions in Psychological Science, 20,* 335–339.

Ingram, R. E., & Ritter, J. (2000). Vulnerability to depres- sion: Cognitive reactivity and parental bonding in high-risk individuals. *Journal of Abnormal Psychology, 109,* 588–596.

Insel, B. J., Schaefer, C. A., McKeague, I. W., Susser, E. S., & Brown, A. S. (2008). Maternal iron deficiency and the risk of schizophrenia in offspring. *Archives of General Psychiatry, 65*(10), 1136–1144.

Insel, K. C., & Badger, T. A. (2002). Deciphering the 4 D's: Cognitive decline, delirium, depression and dementia—a review. *Journal of Advanced Nursing, 38,* 360–368.

IOM (Institute of Medicine). (2012). *The mental health and substance use workforce for older adults: In whose hands?* Washington, DC: The National Academies Press.

## J

Jablensky, A. (1985). Approaches to the definition and clas- sification of anxiety and related disorders in European psy- chiatry. In A. H. Tuma & J. Maser (Eds.), *Anxiety and the anxiety disorders (pp. 735–758).* Hillsdale, NJ: Erlbaum.

Jacobi, C., & Fittig, E. (2010). Psychosocial risk factors for eat- ing disorders. In W. S. Agras (Ed.), *The Oxford handbook of eating disorders* (pp. 123–136). New York: Oxford University Press.

Jacobi, C., Hayward, C., de Zwaan, M., Kraemer, H. C., & Agras, W. S. (2004). Coming to terms with risk factors for eat- ing disorders: Application of risk terminology and suggestions for a general taxonomy. *Psychological Bulletin, 130,* 19–65.

Jacobs, E., Kline, E., & Schiffman, J. (2012). Defining treat- ment as usual for attenuated psychosis syndrome: A survey of community practitioners. *Psychiatric Services, 63,* 1252–1256.

Jacobson, J. W., Mulick, J. A., & Schwartz, A. A. (1995). A history of facilitated communication: Science, pseudoscience, and antiscience. *American Psychologist, 50,* 750–765.

Jacobson, N. S., & Christensen, A. (1996). *Integrative couple therapy: Promoting acceptance and change.* New York: Norton.

Jacobson, N. S., & Truax, P. (1991). Clinical significance: A statistical approach to defining meaningful change in psychotherapy research. *Journal of Consulting and Clinical Psychology, 59,* 12–19.

Jacobson, S. A. (1997). Delirium in the elderly. *Psychiatric Clinics of North America, 20,* 91–110.

Jaffe, J. H. (1995). Pharmacological treatment of opioid depen- dence: Current techniques and new findings. *Psychiatric Annals, 25,* 369–375.

Jaffe, J. H., & Jaffe, A. R. (1999). Neurobiology of opiates/ opioids. In M. Galanter & H. D. Kleber (Eds.), *Textbook of substance abuse treatment* (2nd ed., pp. 11–20). Washington, DC: American Psychiatric Press.

James, J. E., & Keane, M. A. (2007). Caffeine, sleep and wakefulness: Implications of new understanding about withdrawal reversal. *Human Psychopharmacology: Clinical and Experimental, 22,* 549–558.

Janet, P. (1914/1915). Psychoanalysis. *Journal of Abnormal Psychology, 1*(35), 187–253.

Janssen, E. (2002). Psychophysiological measurement of sexual arousal. In M. W. Wiederman & B. E. Whitley, Jr. (Eds.), *Handbook for conducting research on human sexuality* (pp. 139–171). Mahwah, NJ: Erlbaum.

Jefferson, J. W. (1997). Antidepressants in panic disorder. *Journal of Clinical Psychiatry, 58*(Suppl. 2), 20–24.

Jellinger, K. A., & Attems, J. (2010). Prevalence and pathology of vascular dementia in the oldest-old. *Journal of Alzheimer's Disease, 21*(4), 1283–1293.

Jenkins, C. D. (1988). Epidemiology of cardiovascular diseases. *Journal of Consulting and Clinical Psychology, 56,* 324–332.

Jiang, W., Babyak, M., Krantz, D. S., Waugh, R. A., Coleman, R. E., Hanson, M. M., et al. (1996). Mental stress-induced myocardial ischemia and cardiac events. *Journal of the American Medical Association, 275,* 1651–1656.

Joannides, P. (2012). The challenging landscape of problematic sexual behaviors, including "sexual addiction" and "hypersexuality." In P. J. Kleinplatz (Ed.), *New directions in sex therapy: Innovations and alternatives* (2nd ed., pp. 69–83). New York: Routledge/Taylor & Francis Group.

Johansson, A., Sundbom, E., Höjerback, T., & Bodlund, O. (2010). A five-year follow-up study of Swedish adults with gender identity disorder. *Archives of Sexual Behavior, 39*(6), 1429–1437.

Johnson, D. K., Storandt, M., Morris, J. C., & Galvin, J. E. (2009). Longitudinal study of the transition from healthy aging to Alzheimer disease. *Archives of Neurology, 66,* 1254–1259.

Johnson, J. G., Cohen, P., Brown, J., Smailes, E. M., & Bernstein, D. P. (1999). Childhood maltreatment increases risk for personality disorders during early adulthood. *Archives of General Psychiatry, 56,* 600–606.

Johnson, P. (1989). Hemingway: Portrait of the artist as an intellectual. *Commentary, 87,* 49–59.

Johnson, S. L., Leedom, L. J., & Muhtadie, L. (2012). The dominance behavioral system and psychopathology: Evidence from self-report, observational, and biological studies. *Psychological Bulletin, 138,* 692–743.

Johnson, S. M. (2008). Emotionally focused couple therapy. In A. S. Gurman (Ed.), *Clinical Handbook of Couple Therapy* (4th ed., pp. 107–137). New York: Guilford Press.

Johnson, T. P. (2007). Cultural-level influences on substance use and misuse. *Substance Use & Misuse, 42,* 305–316.

Johnston, D. W. (1989). Prevention of cardiovascular disease by psychological methods. *British Journal of Psychiatry, 154,* 183–194.

Joiner, T. (2005). *Why people die by suicide.* Cambridge, MA: Harvard University Press.

Joiner, T. E., Jr., Brown, J. S., & Wingate, L. R. (2005). The psychology and neurobiology of suicidal behavior. *Annual Review of Psychology, 56,* 287–314.

Jones, K. (2012). A critique of the DSM-5 field trials. *Journal of Nervous and Mental Disease, 200,* 517–519.

Jones, C. M., Mack, K. A., & Paulozzi, L. J. (2013). Pharmaceutical overdose deaths, United States, 2010. *Journal of the American Medical Association, 309,* 657–659.

Jones, B. T., Corbin, W., & Fromme, K. (2001). A review of expectancy theory and alcohol consumption. *Addiction, 96,* 57–72.

Jones, E., Thomas, A., & Ironside, S. (2007). Shell shock: An outcome study of a First World War "PIE" unit. *Psychological Medicine, 37,* 215–223.

Joormann, J. (2010). Cognitive inhibition and emotion regulation in depression. *Current Directions in Psychological Science, 19*(3), 161–166.

Jones, J. H. (1997). *Alfred C. Kinsey: A public/private life.* New York: Norton.

Jones, R. T., & Ollendick, T. H. (2002). The impact of residential fire on children and their families. In A. La Greca, W. Silverman, E. Vernberg, & M. Roberts (Eds.), *Helping children cope with disasters: Integrating research and practice* (pp. 175–202). Washington, DC: American Psychological Association Books.

Jorm, A. F. (2001). History of depression as a risk factor for dementia: An updated review. *Australian and New Zealand Journal of Psychiatry, 35,* 776–781.

Jouriles, E. N., McDonald, R., Rosenfield, D., Norwood, W. D., Spiller, L., Stephens, N., et al. (2010). Improving parenting in families referred for child maltreatment: A randomized controlled trial examining effects of project support. *Journal of Family Psychology, 24,* 328–338.

Julien, R. M., Advokat, C. D., & Comaty, J. (2010). *Primer of drug action* (12th ed.). New York: Worth.

## K

Kafka, M. P. (2010). Hypersexual disorder: A proposed diagnosis for DSM-V. *Archives of Sexual Behavior, 39,* 377–400.

Kagan, J. (1998). *Three seductive ideas.* Cambridge, MA: Harvard University Press.

Kagan, J. (2007). A trio of concerns. *Perspectives on Psychological Science, 2,* 361–376.

Kagan, J., & Snidman, N. (1991). Temperamental factors in human development. *American Psychologist, 46,* 856–862.

Kahneman, D. (2003). A perspective on judgment and choice: Mapping bounded rationality. *American Psychologist, 58,* 697–720.

Kajantie, E. (2008). Physiological stress response, estrogen, and the male-female mortality gap. *Current Directions in Psychological Science, 17,* 348–352.

Kalueff, A. V., & Nutt, D. J. (2007). Role of GABA in anxiety and depression. *Depression and Anxiety, 24,* 495–517.

Kamarck, T., & Jennings, J. R. (1991). Biobehavioral factors in sudden cardiac death. *Psychological Bulletin, 109,* 42–75.

Kanaya, T., Scullin, M. H., & Ceci, S. J. (2003). The Flynn effect and U.S. policies: The impact of rising IQ scores on American society via mental retardation diagnoses. *American Psychologist, 58*(10), 778–790.

Kangas, M., Henry, J. L., & Bryant, R. A. (2005). A prospective study of autobiographical memory and posttraumatic stress disorder following cancer. *Journal of Consulting and Clinical Psychology, 73*(2), 293–299.

Kangas, M., Bovbjerg, D. H., & Montgomery, G. H. (2008). Cancer-related fatigue: A systematic and meta-analytic review of non-pharmacological therapies for cancer patients. *Psychological Bulletin, 134,* 700–741.

Kaptchuk, T. J., Kelly, J. M., Conboy, L. A., Davis, R. B., Kerr, C. E., Jacobson, E. E., et al. (2008). Components of placebo effect: Randomised controlled trial in patients with irritable bowel syndrome. *British Medical Journal, 336,* 998–1003.

Kapusta, N. D., Etzersdorfer, E., Krall, C., & Sonneck, G. (2007). Firearm legislation reform in the European Union: Impact on firearm availability, firearm suicide and homicide rates in Austria. *British Journal of Psychiatry, 19,* 253–257.

Karasek, R. A., Theorell, T. G., Schwartz, J., Pieper, C., & Alfredsson, L. (1982). Job, psychological factors and coronary heart disease: Swedish prospective findings and U.S. prevalence findings using a new occupational inference method. *Advances in Cardiology, 29,* 62–67.

Karel, M. J., Gatz, M., & Smyer, M. (2012). Aging and mental health in the decade ahead: What psychologists need to know. *American Psychologist, 67,* 184–198.

Karg, K., Burmeister, M., Shedden, K., & Sen, S. (2011). The serotonin transporter promoter variant (5-HTTLPR), stress, and depression meta-analysis revisited: Evidence of genetic moderation. *Archives of General Psychiatry, 68,* 1–11.

Karney, B. R., & Bradbury, T. N. (1995). The longitudinal course of marital quality and stability: A review of theory, method, and research. *Psychological Bulletin, 118,* 3–34.

Karras, A., & Otis, D. B. (1987). A comparison of inpatients in an urban state hospital in 1975 and 1982. *Hospital and Community Psychiatry, 38,* 963–967.

Kasari, C., Paparella, T., Freeman, S., & Jahromi, L. B. (2008). Language outcome in autism: Randomized comparison of joint attention and play interventions. *Journal of Consulting and Clinical Psychology, 76,* 125–137.

Kashdan, T. B., Ferssizidis, P., Collins, R. L., & Muraven, M. (2010). Emotion differentiation as resilience against excessive alcohol use: An ecological momentary assessment in underage social drinkers. *Psychological Science, 21,* 1341–1347.

Kaskutas, L. A., Turk, N., Bond, J., & Weisner, C. (2003). The role of religion, spirituality and alcoholics anonymous in sustained sobriety. *Alcoholism Treatment Quarterly, 21,* 1–16.

Katz, R. J., DeVeaugh-Geiss, J., & Landau, P. (1990). Clomipramine in obsessive-compulsive disorder. *Biological Psychiatry, 28,* 401–414.

Kaufman, G., & Elder, G. H., Jr. (2003). Grandparenting and age identity. *Journal of Aging Studies, 17,* 269–282.

Kaye, W. H., Weltzin, T. E., Hsu, L. K. G., McConahan, C. W., & Bolton, B. (1993). Amount of calories retained after binge eating and vomiting. *American Journal of Psychiatry, 150,* 969–971.

Kaysen, S. (2001). *The camera my mother gave me.* New York: Knopf.

Kazak, A. E., Hoagwood, K., Weisz, J. R., Hood, K., Kratochwill, T. R., Vargas, L. A., et al. (2010). A meta-systems approach to evidence-based practice for children and adolescents. *American Psychologist, 65,* 85–97.

Kazdin, A. E. (1989). Identifying depression in children: A comparison of alternative selection criteria. *Journal of Abnormal Child Psychology, 17,* 437–455.

Kazdin, A. E. (1995). *Conduct Disorders in Childhood and Adolescence* (2nd ed.). Thousand Oaks, CA: Sage.

Kazdin, A. E. (1997). Parent management training: Evidence, outcomes, and issues. *Journal of the American Academy of Child and Adolescent Psychiatry, 36,* 1349–1365.

Kazdin, A. E. (2008). Evidence-based treatment and practice: New opportunities to bridge clinical research and practice, enhance the knowledge base, and improve patient care. *American Psychologist, 63,* 146–159.

Kazdin, A. E., & Petti, T. A. (1982). Self-report and interview measures of childhood and adolescent depression. *Journal of Child Psychology and Psychiatry, 23,* 437–457.

Kazdin, A. E., & Whitley, M. K. (2003). Treatment of parental stress to enhance therapeutic change among children referred for aggressive and antisocial behavior. *Journal of Consulting and Clinical Psychology, 71*(3), 504–515.

Kazdin, A. E., French, N. H., & Unis, A. S. (1983). Child, mother, and father evaluations of depression in psychiatric inpatient children. *Journal of Abnormal Child Psychology, 11,* 167–180.

Kazdin, A. E., Siegel, T. C., & Bass, D. (1992). Cognitive problem-solving skills training and parent management training in the treatment of antisocial behavior in children. *Journal of Consulting and Clinical Psychology, 60,* 753–747.

Keane, T. M., Marshall, A. D., & Taft, C. T. (2006). Posttraumatic stress disorder: Etiology, epidemiology, and treatment outcome. *Annual Review of Clinical Psychology, 2,* 161–197.

Keefe, F. J., Lumley, M., Anderson, T., Lynch, T., & Carson, K. L. (2001). Pain and emotion: New research directions. *Journal of Clinical Psychology, 57,* 587–607.

Keel, P. K. (2010). Epidemiology and course of eating disorders. In W. S. Agras (Ed.), *The Oxford handbook of eating disorders* (pp. 25–32). New York: Oxford University Press.

Keel, P. K., & Heatherton, T. F. (2010). Weight suppression predicts maintenance and onset of bulimic syndromes at 10-year follow-up. *Journal of Abnormal Psychology, 119,* 268–275.

Keel, P. K., & Klump, K. L. (2003). Are eating disorders culture-bound syndromes? Implications for conceptualizing their etiology. *Psychological Bulletin, 129,* 747–769.

Keel, P. K., & Mitchell, J. E. (1997). Outcome in bulimia nervosa. *American Journal of Psychiatry, 154,* 313–321.

Keel, P. K., Baxter, M. G., Heatherton, T. F., & Joiner, T. E., Jr. (2007). A 20-year longitudinal study of body weight, dieting, and eating disorder symptoms. *Journal of Abnormal Psychology, 116,* 422–432.

Keel, P. K., Forney, J., Brown, T. A., & Heatherton, T. F. (2013). Influence of college peers on disordered eating in women and men at 10-year follow-up. *Journal of Abnormal Psychology, 122,* 105–110.

Keenan, K., & Shaw, D. (1997) Developmental and social influences on young girls' early problem behavior. *Psychological Bulletin, 121,* 95–113.

Keenan, K., Wroblewski, K., Hipwell, A., Loeber, R., & Stouthamer-Loeber, M. (2010). Age of onset, symptom threshold, and expansion of the nosology of conduct disorder for girls. *Journal of Abnormal Psychology, 119,* 689–698.

Keesey, R. E. (1995). A set-point model of body weight regulation. In K. D. Brownell & C. G. Fairburn (Eds.), *Eating disorders and obesity: A comprehensive handbook* (pp. 46–50). New York: Guilford.

Kellner, R. (1985). Functional somatic symptoms in hypochondriasis. *Archives of General Psychiatry, 42,* 821–833.

Kelly, M. P., Strassberg, D. S., & Turner, C. M. (2004). Communication and associated relationship issues in female anorgasmia. *Journal of Sex & Marital Therapy, 30,* 263–276.

Kelly, T. A. (1990). The role of values in psychotherapy: A critical review of process and outcome effects. *Clinical Psychology Review, 10,* 171–186.

Kelly, T., Soloff, P. H., Cornelius, J., George, A., Lis, J. A., & Ulrich, R. (1992). Can we study (treat) borderline patients? Attrition from research and open treatment. *Journal of Personality Disorders, 6,* 417–433.

Kempe, C. H., Silverman, F., Steele, B., Droegueller, W., & Silver, H. (1962). The battered child syndrome. *Journal of the American Medical Association, 181,* 17–24.

Kendall, P. C., Hudson, J. L., Gosch, E., Flannery-Schroeder, E., & Suveg, C. (2008). Cognitive-behavioral therapy for anxiety disordered youth: A randomized clinical trial evaluating child and family modalities. *Journal of Consulting and Clinical Psychology, 76,* 282–297.

Kendall, P. C., Safford, S., Flannery-Schroeder, E., & Webb, A. (2004). Child anxiety treatment: Outcomes in adolescence and impact on substance use and depression at 7.4-year follow-up. *Journal of Consulting and Clinical Psychology, 72*(2), 276–287.

Kendell, R., & Jablensky, A. (2003). Distinguishing between the validity and utility of psychiatric diagnoses. *American Journal of Psychiatry, 160,* 4–12.

Kendler, K. S., & Prescott, C. A. (2006). *Genes, environment, and psychopathology: Understanding the causes of psychiatric and substance use disorders.* New York: Guilford.

Kendler, K. S., Aggen, S. H., Knudsen, G., Røysamb, E., Neale, M. C., & Reichborn-Kjennerud, T. (2011). The structure of genetic and environmental risk factors for syndromal and subsyndromal common DSM-IV axis I and all axis II disorders. *American Journal of Psychiatry, 168,* 29–39.

Kendler, K. S., Eaves, L. J., Loken, E. K., Pedersen, N. L., Middeldorp, C. M., Reynolds, C., & Gardner, C. O. (2011). The impact of environmental experiences on symptoms of anxiety and depression across the life span. *Psychological Science, 22,* 1343–1352.

Kendler, K. S., Hettema, J. M., Butera, F., Gardner, C. O., & Prescott, C. A. (2003). Life event dimensions of loss, humiliation, entrapment, and danger in the prediction of onsets of major depression and generalized anxiety. *Archives of General Psychiatry, 60,* 789–796.

Kendler, K. S., MacLean, C., Neale, M., Kessler, R., Heath, A., & Eaves, L. (1991). The genetic epidemiology of bulimia nervosa. *American Journal of Psychiatry, 148,* 1627–1637.

Kendler, K. S., Myers, J., & Zisook, S. (2008). Does bereavement-related major depression differ from major depression associated with other stressful life events? *The American Journal of Psychiatry, 165,* 1449–1455.

Kenrick, D. T., Griskevicius, V., Neuberg, S. L., & Schaller, M. (2010). Renovating the pyramid of needs: Contemporary extensions built upon ancient foundations. *Perspectives on Psychological Science, 5,* 292–314.

Kernberg, O. F. (1967). Borderline personality organization. *Journal of the American Psychoanalytic Association, 15,* 641–685.

Kernberg, O. F. (1975). *Borderline conditions and pathological narcissism.* New York: Aronson.

Kerns, J. G., & Berenbaum, H. (2002). Cognitive impairments associated with formal thought disorder in people with schizophrenia. *Journal of Abnormal Psychology, 111,* 211–224.

Kessler, R. C. (2006). The epidemiology of depression among women. In C. L. M. Keyes & S. H. Goodman (Eds.), *Women and depression* (pp. 22–40). New York: Cambridge University Press.

Kessler, R. C., Demier, O., Frank, R. G., Olfson, M., Pincus, H., Walters, E. E., et al. (2005). U.S. prevalence and treatment of mental disorders, 1990 to 2003. *The New England Journal of Medicine, 352,* 2515–2523.

Kessler, R. C., Demier, O., Frank, R. G., Olfson, M., Pincus, H., Walters, E. E., et al. (2005). Prevalence and treatment of mental disorders, 1990 to 2003. *The New England Journal of Medicine, 352,* 2515–2523.

Kessler, R. C., Demler, O., Frank, R. G., Olfson, M., Pincus, H. A., Walters, E. E., et al. (2005). Prevalence and treatment of mental disorders, 1990 to 2003. *New England Journal of Medicine, 352,* 2515–2523.

Kessler, R. C., Gruber, M., Hettema, J. M., Hwang, I., Sampson, N., & Yonkers, K. A. (2008). Co-morbid major depression and generalized anxiety disorders in the National Comorbidity Survey follow-up. *Psychological Medicine, 38,* 365–374.

Kessler, R. C., McGonagle, K. A., Zhao, S., Nelson, C. R., Highes, M., Eshleman, S., et al. (1994). Lifetime and 12-month prevalence of DSM-III-R psychiatric disorders in the United States: Results from the National Comorbidity Survey. *Archives of General Psychiatry, 51,* 8–19.

Kessler, R. C., Merikangas, K. R., & Wang, P. S. (2007). Prevalence, comorbidity, and service utilization for mood disorders in the United States at the beginning of the twenty-first century. *Annual Review of Clinical Psychology, 3,* 137–158.

Kessler, R. C., & Wang, P. S. (2008). The descriptive epidemiology of commonly occurring mental disorders in the United States. *Annual Review of Public Health, 29,* 115–129.

Kessler, R. C., Ruscio, A., Shear, K., & Wittchen, H. (2009). Epidemiology of anxiety disorders. In M. M. Antony & M. B. Stein, M. M. Antony, M. B. Stein (Eds.), *Oxford Handbook of Anxiety and Related Disorders* (pp. 19–33). New York: Oxford University Press.

Kessler, R. C., Sonnega, A., Bromet, E., Hughes, M., & Nelson, C. B. (1995). Posttraumatic stress disorder in the National Comorbidity Survey. *Archives of General Psychiatry, 52,* 1048–1060.

Kessler, R., & Stafford, D. (2008). Primary care is the de facto mental health system. In R. Kessler & D. Stafford, R. Kessler, D. Stafford (Eds.), Collaborative medicine case studies: Evidence in practice (pp. 9–21). New York, NY: Springer Science + Business Media.

Keteyian, A. (1986, March 10). The straight-arrow addict: Compulsive gambling of A. Schlichter. *Sports Illustrated,* 74–77.

Keyes, C. M. (2009). The mental health continuum: From languishing to flourishing in life (2002). In B. F. Gentile & B. O. Miller (Ed.), *Foundations of psychological thought: A history of psychology* (pp. 601–617). Thousand Oaks, CA: Sage Publications, Inc.

Keyes, K. M., Geier, T., Grant, B. F., & Hasin, D. S. (2009). Influence of a drinking quantity and frequency measure on the prevalence and demographic correlates of DSM-IV alcohol dependence. *Alcoholism: Clinical and Experimental Research, 33,* 761–771.

Keys, A., Brozek, J., Henschel, A., Mickelsen, O., & Taylor, H. L. (1950). *The biology of human starvation* (2). Minneapolis: University of Minnesota Press.

Khalid, N., Atkins, M., Tredget, J., Giles, M., Champney-Smith, K., & Kirov, G. (2008). The effectiveness of electroconvulsive therapy in treatment-resistant depression: A naturalistic study. *Journal of ECT, 24,* 141–145.

Khandaker, G. M., Zimbron, J. J., Lewis, G. G., & Jones, P. B. (2013). Prenatal maternal infection, neurodevelopment and adult schizophrenia: A systematic review of population-based studies. *Psychological Medicine, 43,* 239–257.

Kiang, L., & Fuligni, A. J. (2010). Meaning in life as a mediator of ethnic identity and adjustment among adolescents from Latin, Asian, and European American backgrounds. *Journal of Youth and Adolescence, 39,* 1253–1264.

Kiecolt-Glaser, J. K., Bane, C., Glaser, R., & Malarkey, W. B. (2003). Love, marriage, and divorce: Newlyweds' stress hormones foreshadow relationship changes. *Journal of Consulting and Clinical Psychology, 71,* 176–188.

Kiecolt-Glaser, J. K., Malarkey, W. B., Chee, M., Newton, T., Cacioppo, J. T., Mao, H., et al. (1993). Negative behavior during marital conflict is associated with immunological down-regulation. *Psychosomatic Medicine, 55,* 395–409.

Kiecolt-Glaser, J. K., & Newton, T. L. (2001). Marriage and health: His and hers. *Psychological Bulletin, 127,* 472–503.

Kiesler, C. (1982). Mental hospitals and alternative care: Coninstitutionalization as potential public policy for mental patients. *American Psychologist, 37,* 349–360.

Kihara, T., & Shimohama, S. (2004). Alzheimer's disease and acetylcholine receptors. *Acta Neurobiologiae Experimentalis, 64,* 99–105.

Kihlstrom, J. F. (1998). Dissociations and dissociation theory in hypnosis: A comment on Kirch and Lynn (1998). *Psychological Bulletin, 123,* 186–191.

Kihlstrom, J. F. (1998a). Exhumed memory. In S. J. Lynn & K. M. McConkey (Eds.), *Truth in Memory* (pp. 3–31). New York: Guilford.

Kihlstrom, J. F. (2005). Dissociative disorders. *Annual Reviews in Clinical Psychology, 1,* 10.1–10.27

Kihlstrom, J. F., & Hastie, R. (1997). Mental representations of persons and personality. In R. Hogan, J. Johnson, & S. Briggs (Eds.), *Handbook of personality psychology* (pp. 712–735). San Diego, CA: Academic Press.

Kilmann, P. R., Sabalis, R. F., Gearing, M. L., Bukstel, L. H., & Scovern, A. W. (1982). The treatment of sexual paraphilias: A review of the outcome research. *Journal of Sex Research, 18,* 193–252.

Kihlstrom, J. F., Glisky, M. L., & Angiulo, M. J. (1994). Dissociative tendencies and dissociative disorders. *Journal of Abnormal Psychology, 103,* 117–124

Kilmann, P. R., et al. (1982). The treatment of sexual paraphilias: A review of the outcome research. *Journal of Sex Research, 18,* 193–252.

Kilpatrick, D. G., & Acierno, R. (2003). Mental health needs of crime victims: Epidemiology and outcomes. *Journal of Traumatic Stress, 16,* 119–132.

Kilpatrick, D. G., Edmunds, C. N., & Seymour, A. K. (1992). *Rape in America: A Report to the Nation.* Arlington, VA: National Victim Center

Kilpatrick, D. G., Ruggiero, K. J., Acierno, R., Saunders, B. E., Resnick, H. S., & Best, C. L. (2003). Violence and risk of PTSD, major depression, substance abuse/dependence, and comorbidity: Results from the national survey of adolescents. *Journal of Consulting and Clinical Psychology, 71,* 692–700.

Kilpatrick, D. G., Saunders, B. E., Amick-McMullan, A., Best, C. L., Veronen, L. J., & Resnick, H. S. (1989). Victim and crime factors associated with the development of crime-related posttraumatic stress disorder. *Behavior Therapy, 20,* 199–214.

Kim, Y. S., Leventhal, B. L., Koh, Y. J., Fombonne, E., Laska, E., & Lim, E. C. (2011). Prevalence of autism spectrum disorders in a total population sample. *American Journal of Psychiatry, 168,* 904–912.

Kim, et al., (2011). Prevalence of autism spectrum disorders in a total population sample. *American Journal of Psychiatry, 168,* 904–912.

Kim, H. S., Sherman, D. K., & Taylor, S. E. (2008). Culture and social support. *American Psychologist, 63,* 518–526.

Kimble, G. A. (1989). Psychology from the standpoint of a generalist. *American Psychologist, 44,* 491–499.

Kim-Cohen, J., & Gold, A. L. (2009). Measured gene-environment interactions and mechanisms promoting resilient development. *Current Directions in Psychological Science, 18,* 138–142.

Kimmel, S. B., & Mahalik, J. R. (2005). Body image concerns of gay men: The roles of minority stress and conformity to masculine norms. *Journal of Consulting and Clinical Psychology, 73,* 1185–1190.

King, R. A., Segman, R. H., & Anderson, G. M. (1994). Serotonin and suicidality: The impact of acute fluoxetine administration. I. Serotonin and suicide. *Israel Journal of Psychiatry and Related Sciences, 31,* 271–279.

Kinsey, A. C., Pomeroy, W. B., & Martin, C. E. (1948). *Sexual behavior in the human male.* Philadelphia: Saunders.

Kirisci, L., Tarter, R., Mezzich, A., & Vanyukov, M. (2007). Developmental trajectory classes in substance use disorder etiology. *Psychology of Addictive Behaviors, 21,* 287–296.

Kirmayer, L. J. (2001). Cultural variations in the clinical presentation of depression and anxiety: Implications for diagnosis and treatment. *Journal of Clinical Psychiatry, 62* (Suppl. 13), 22–28

Kirmayer, L. J. (2006). Beyond the new cross-cultural psychiatry: Cultural biology, discursive psychology and the ironies of globalization. *Transcultural Psychiatry, 43,* 126–144.

Kirmayer, L. J., Robbins, J. M., & Paris, J. (1994). Somatoform disorders: Personality and the social matrix of somatic distress. *Journal of Abnormal Psychology, 103,* 125–136.

Kirsch, I., & Lynn, S. J. (1998). Dissociation theories of hypnosis. *Psychological Bulletin, 123,* 100–115.

Klein Hofmeijer-Sevink, M., Batelaan, N. M., van Megen, H. M., Penninx, B. W., Cath, D. C., van den Hout, M. A., & van Balkom, A. M. (2012). Clinical relevance of comorbidity in anxiety disorders: A report from the Netherlands Study of Depression and Anxiety (NESDA). *Journal of Affective Disorders, 137,* 106–112.

Klein, D. F. (1999). Harmful dysfunction, disorder, disease, illness, and evolution. *Journal of Abnormal Psychology, 108,* 421–429.

Klein, R. G., & Pine, D. S. (2002). Anxiety disorders. In M. Rutter & E. Taylor (Eds.), *Child and Adolescent Psychiatry* (4th ed., pp. 486–509). Oxford, England: Blackwell.

Kleinman, A. (1988). *Rethinking psychiatry: From cultural category to personal experience.* New York: Free Press.

Kleinman, A. (2004). Culture and depression. *New England Journal of Medicine, 352,* 951–953.

Klerman, G. (1990b). The psychiatric patient's right to effective treatment: Implications of Osheroff vs. Chestnut Lodge. *American Journal of Psychiatry, 147,* 409–418.

Klonsky, E. D. (2007). The functions of deliberate self-injury: A review of the evidence. *Clinical Psychology Review, 27,* 226–239.

Klonsky, E. D., Oltmanns, T. F., & Turkheimer, E. (2003). Deliberate self-harm in a nonclinical population: Prevalence and psychological correlates. *American Journal of Psychiatry, 160,* 1501–1508.

Klump, K. L., & Culbert, K. M. (2007). Molecular genetic studies of eating disorders: Current status and future directions. *Current Directions in Psychological Science, 16,* 37–41.

Klump, K. L., McGue, M., & Iacono, W. G. (2000). Age differences in genetic and environmental influences on eating attitudes and behaviors in preadolescent and adolescent female twins. *Journal of Abnormal Psychology, 109,* 239–251.

Klump, K. L., Suisman, J. L., Burt, S. A., McGue, M., & Iacono, W. G. (2009). Genetic and environmental influences on disordered eating: An adoption study. *Journal of Abnormal Psychology, 118,* 797–805.

Kluznik, J. C., Speed, N., Van Valkenburg, C., & Magraw, R. (1986). Forty-year follow-up of United States prisoners of war. *American Journal of Psychiatry, 143,* 1443–1446.

Kneebone, I., & Martin, P. (2003). Coping and caregivers of people with dementia. *British Journal of Health Psychology, 8,* 1–17.

Knight, R. A. (2010). Is a diagnostic category for paraphilic coercive disorder defensible? *Archives of Sexual Behavior, 39,* 419–426.

Knight, R. A., & Guay, J. P. (2006). The role of psychopathy in sexual coercion against women. In C. J. Patrick (Ed.), *Handbook of psychopathy* (pp. 512–532). New York: Guilford.

Knop, J., Penick, E., Jensen, P., Nickel, E., Gabrielli, W., Mednick, S., et al. (2003). Risk factors that predicted problem drinking in Danish men at age thirty. *Journal of Studies on Alcohol, 64,* 745–755.

Kochanek, K. D., Murphy, S. L., Anderson, R. N., & Scott, C. (2004). *Deaths: Final Data for 2002.* National Vital Statistics Reports. DHHS Publication No. (PHS) 2005–1120, *53* (5). Hyattsville, MD: National Center for Health Statistics.

Koegel, R. L., Koegel, L. K., & McNerney, E. K. (2001). Pivotal areas intervention for autism. *Journal of Clinical Child Psychology, 30,* 19–32.

Koenen, K. C., Moffitt, T. E., Caspi, A., Gregory, A., Harrington, H., & Poulton, R. (2008). The developmental mental-disorder histories of adults with posttraumatic stress disorder: A prospective longitudinal birth cohort study. *Journal of Abnormal Psychology, 117,* 460–466.

Koenen, K. C., Stellman, J. M., Stellman, S. D., & Sommer, J. F. (2003). Risk factors for course of posttraumatic stress disorder among Vietnam veterans: A 14-year follow-up of American Legionnaires. *Journal of Consulting and Clinical Psychology, 71,* 980–986.

Koenigsberg, H. W., Reynolds, D., Goodman, M., New, A. S., Mitropoulou, V., Trestman, R. L., et al. (2003). Risperidone in the treatment of schizotypal personality disorder. *Journal of Clinical Psychiatry, 64,* 628–634.

Koenigsberg, H. W., Woo-Ming, A., & Siever, L. J. (2002). Pharmacological treatments for personality disorders. In P. E. Nathan & J. M. Gorman (Eds.), *A guide to treatments that work* (2nd ed., pp. 625–641). New York: Oxford University Press.

Kogan, M. D., Blumberg, S. J., Schieve, L. A., Boyle, C. A., Perrin, J. M., Ghandour, R. M., et al. (2009). Prevalence of parent-reported diagnosis of autism spectrum disorder among children in the US, 2007. *Pediatrics, 124,* 1–9.

Kohlberg, L. (1985). *The Psychology of Moral Development.* San Francisco: Harper & Row.

Kolassa, I., & Elbert, T. (2007). Structural and functional neuroplasticity in relation to traumatic stress. *Current Directions in Psychological Science, 16,* 321–325

Kong, L. L., Allen, J. J. B., & Glisky, E. L. (2008). Interidentity memory transfer in dissociative identity disorder. *Journal of Abnormal Psychology, 117,* 686–692.

Kontakos, N., & Stokes, J. (1999). Parkinson's disease—Recent developments and new directions. *Chronic Diseases in Canada, 20,* 58–76

Koob, G. F. (2006). Neurobiology of addiction: A neuroadaptational view relevant for diagnosis. *Addiction, 101*(Suppl. 1), 23–30

Koons, C. R., Robins, C. J., Tweed, J. L., Lynch, T. R., Gonzales. A. M., Morse, J. Q., et al. (2001). Efficacy of dialectical behavior therapy in women veterans with borderline personality disorder. *Behavior Therapy, 32,* 371–390.

Kop, W. J. (1999). Chronic and acute psychological risk factors for liar clinical manifestations of coronary artery disease. *Psychosomatic Medicine, 61,* 476–487.

Kopelowicz, A., Liberman, R. P., & Zarate, R. (2002). Psychosocial treatments for schizophrenia. In P. E. Nathan & J. M. Gorman (Eds.), *A guide to treatments that work* (2nd ed., pp. 201–228). London: Oxford University Press.

Koranyi, E. K. (1989). Physiology of stress reviewed. In S. Cheren (Ed.), *Psychosomatic medicine: Theory, physiology, and practice* (Vol. 1, pp. 241–278). Madison, CT: International Universities Press.

Korda, J. B., Goldstein, S. W., & Goldstein, I. (2010). The role of androgens in the treatment of hypoactive sexual desire disorder in women. In S. R. Leiblum & S. R. Leiblum (Eds.), *Treating sexual desire disorders: A clinical casebook* (pp. 201–218). New York: Guilford Press.

Koskenvuo, M., Kaprio, J., Rose, R. J., Kesaniemi, A., Sarna, S., Heikkila, K., et al. (1988). Hostility as a risk factor for mortality and ischemic heart disease in men. *Psychosomatic Medicine, 50,* 330–340

Kovacs, M., Feinberg, T. L., Crouse-Novak, M. A., Paulaukas, S., Pollock, M., & Finkelstein, R. (1984). Depressive disorders in childhood. II. A longitudinal study of the risk for a subsequent major depression. *Archives of General Psychiatry, 41,* 643–649.

Kovas, Y., & Plomin, R. (2007). Learning abilities and disabilities: Generalist genes, specialist environments. *Current Directions in Psychological Science, 16,* 284–288.

Kowalski, K. M. (1998). The dangers of alcohol. *Current Health, 24,* 6–13.

Koyama, A., Okereke, O. I., Yang, T., Blacker, D., Selkoe, D. J., & Grodstein, F. (2012). Plasma amyloid-β as a predictor of dementia and cognitive decline: A systematic review and meta-analysis. *Archives of Neurology, 69,* 824–831.

Kozak, M. J., Liebowitz, M. R., & Foa, E. G. (2000). Cognitive behavior therapy and pharmacotherapy for obsessive-compulsive disorder: The NIMH-sponsored collaborative study. In W. K. Goodman & M. V. Rudorfer

(Eds.), *Obsessive-Compulsive Disorder: Contemporary Issues in Treatment* (pp. 501–530). Mahwah, NJ: Erlbaum.

Kozlowski, L. T., Henningfield, J. E., & Brigham, J. (2001). *Cigarettes, nicotine, and health: A biobehavioral approach.* Thousand Oaks, CA: Sage Publications.

Kraemer, H. C. (2008). DSM categories and dimensions in clinical and research contexts. In J. E. Helzer, H. C. Kraemer R. F. Krueger, H. Wittchen, & P. J. Sirovotka et al. (Eds.), *Dimensional approaches in diagnostic classification: Refining the research agenda for DSM-V* (pp. 5–17). Washington, DC: American Psychiatric Publishing.

Kraemer, H., Kupfer, D. J., Clarke, D. E., Narrow, W. E., & Regier, D. A. (2012). DSM-5: How reliable is reliable enough? *American Journal of Psychiatry, 169,* 13–15.

Kraemer, H., Kupfer, D. J., Narrow, W. E., Clarke, D. E., & Regier, D. A. (2010). Moving toward DSM-5: The field trials. *American Journal of Psychiatry, 167,* 1158–1160.

Krakow, B., Hollifield, M., Johnston, L., Koss, M., Schrader, R., Warner, T. D., et al. (2001). Imagery rehearsal therapy for chronic nightmares in sexual assault survivors with posttraumatic stress disorder: A randomized clinical trial. *Journal of the American Medical Association, 286,* 537–545.

Krantz, D. S., Contrada, R. J., Hill, D. R., & Friedler, E. (1988). Environmental stress and biobehavioral antecedents of coronary heart disease. *Journal of Consulting and Clinical Psychology, 56,* 333–341.

Krantz, D. S., Gabbay, F. H., Hedges, S. M., Leach, S. G., Gottdiener, J. S., & Rozanski, A. (1993). Mental and physical triggers of silent myocardial ischemia: Ambulatory studies using self-monitoring diary methodology. *Annals of Behavioral Medicine, 15,* 33–40.

Kroenke, K. (2007). Efficacy of treatment for somatoform disorders: A review of randomized controlled trials. *Psychosomatic Medicine, 69,* 881–888.

Kroenke, K., Sharpe, M., & Sykes, R. (2007). Revising the classification of somatoform disorders: Key questions and preliminary recommendations. *Psychosomatics, 48,* 277–285

Kroska, A., & Harkness, S. K. (2006). Stigma sentiments and self-meanings: Exploring the modified labeling theory of mental illness. *Social Psychology Quarterly, 69,* 325–348.

Krueger, A. B., & Stone, A. A. (2008). Assessment of pain: A community-based diary survey in the USA. *The Lancet, 371,* 1519–1525.

Krueger, R. B. (2010). The DSM diagnostic criteria for sexual masochism. *Archives of Sexual Behavior, 39,* 346–356.

Krueger, R. F. (2002). Psychometric perspectives on comorbidity. In J. E. Helzer & J. J. Hudziak (Eds.), *Defining psychopathology in the 21st century* (pp. 41–54). Washington, DC: American Psychiatric Press.

Krueger, R. F., Eaton, N. R., Clark, L., Watson, D., Markon, K. E., Derringer, J., et al. (2011). Deriving an empirical structure of personality pathology for DSM-5. *Journal of Personality Disorders, 25,* 170–191.

Krueger, R. F., & Markon, K. E. (2006). Understanding psychopathology: Melding behavior genetics, personality, and quantitative psychology to develop an empirically based model. *Current Directions in Psychological Science, 15,* 113–117.

Kübler-Ross, E. (1969). *On Death and Dying.* New York: Macmillan.

Kubzansky, L. D., Sparrow, D., Vokonas, P., & Kawachi, I. (2001). Is the glass half empty or half full? A prospective study of optimism and coronary heart disease in the normative aging study. *Psychosomatic Medicine, 63,* 910–916.

Kuehn, B. M. (2010). Military probes epidemic of suicide: Mental health issues remain prevalent. *Journal of the American Medical Association, 304,* 1427–1430.

Kuehner, C. (2003). Gender differences in unipolar depression: An update of epidemiological findings and possible explanations. *Acta Psychiatrica Scandinavica, 108,* 163–174.

Kuhn, T. S. (1962). *The structure of scientific revolutions.* Chicago: University of Chicago Press.

Kukull, W. A., & Bowen, J. D. (2002). Dementia epidemiology. *Medical Clinics of North America, 86,* 573–590.

Kumagai, R., Matsumiya, M., Tada, Y., Miyakawa, K., Ichimiya, Y., & Arai, H. (2008). Long-term effect of donepezil for Alzheimer's disease: Retrospective clinical evaluation of drug efficacy in Japanese patients. *Psychogeriatrics, 8*, 19–23.

Kunzmann, U., & Baltes, P. (2003). Wisdom-related knowledge: Affective, motivational, and interpersonal correlates. *Personality and Social Psychology Bulletin, 29*, 1104–1119.

Kupfer, D. J., & Frank, E. (2001). The interaction of drug- and psychotherapy in the long-term treatment of depression. *Journal of Affective Disorders, 62*, 131–137.

Kupfer, D. J., & Regier, D. A. (2011). Neuroscience, clinical evidence, and the future of psychiatric classification in DSM-5. *American Journal of Psychiatry, 168*, 672–674.

Kupfer, D. J., Regier, D. A., & Kuhl, E. A. (2008). On the road to DSM-V and ICD-11. *European Archives of Psychiatry and Clinical Neuroscience, 258*(Suppl. 5), 2–6

Kurlan, R., & Kaplan, E. L. (2004). The pediatric autoimmune neuropsychiatric disorders associated with streptococcal infection (PANDAS) etiology for tics and obsessive-compulsive symptoms: Hypothesis or entity? *Pediatrics, 113*, 883–886.

Kushner, M. G., Sher, K. J., & Erickson, D. J. (1999). Prospective analysis of the relation between DSM-III anxiety disorders and alcohol use disorders. *American Journal of Psychiatry, 156*, 723–732.

Kutscher, E. (2008). *Antipsychotics. Clinical handbook of schizophrenia* (pp. 159–167). New York: Guilford.

Kwapil, T. R. (1998). Social anhedonia as a predictor of the development of schizophrenia-spectrum disorders. *Journal of Abnormal Psychology, 107*, 558–565.

Kymalainen, J., & Weisman de Mamani, A. (2008). Expressed emotion, communication deviance, and culture in families of patients with schizophrenia: A review of the literature. *Cultural Diversity and Ethnic Minority Psychology, 14*, 85–91.

# L

LaCroix, A. Z., & Haynes, S. G. (1987). Gender differences in the stressfulness of workplace roles: A focus on work and health. In R. Barnett, G. Baruch, & L. Biener (Eds.), *Gender and stress* (pp. 96–121). New York: Free Press.

Lagopoulos, J. (2010). Evolution of brain imaging in neuropsychiatry: Past, present and future. *Acta Neuropsychiatrica, 22*, 152–154.

Lahey, B. B., Schwab-Stone, M., Goodman, S. H., Waldron, I. D., Canino, G., Rathouz, P. J., et al. (2000). Age and gender differences in oppositional behavior and conduct problems: A cross-sectional household study of middle childhood and adolescence. *Journal of Abnormal Psychology, 109*, 488–503.

Lake, C., & Hurwitz, N. (2007). Schizoaffective disorder merges schizophrenia and bipolar disorders as one disease—There is no schizoaffective disorder. *Current Opinion in Psychiatry, 20*, 365–379.

Lam, R. W., Levitt, A., Levitan, R. D., Enns, M. W., Morehouse, R., Michalak, E., & Tam, E. M. (2006). The Can-SAD Study: A randomized controlled trial of the effectiveness of light therapy and fluoxetine in patients with winter seasonal affective disorder. *American Journal of Psychiatry, 163*, 805–812

Lambert, M. J., & Bergin, A. E. (1994). The effectiveness of psychotherapy. In A. E. Bergin & S. L. Garfield, *The Effectiveness of Psychotherapy and Behavior Change* (4th ed.). Oxford, England: John Wiley & Sons.

Lambert, M. J., Hansen, N. B., & Bauer, S. (2008). Assessing the clinical significance of outcome results. In A. M. Nezu & C. Nezu (Eds.), *Evidence-based Outcome Research: A Practical Guide to Conducting Randomized Controlled Trials for Psychosocial Interventions* (pp. 359–378). New York: Oxford University Press.

Landis, D., Gaylord-Harden, N. K., & Malinowski, S. L. (2007). Urban adolescent stress and hopelessness. *Journal of Adolescence, 30*, 1051–1070.

Lanfumey, L., Mongeau, R., & Cohen-Salmon, C. (2008). Corticosteroid-serotonin interactions in the neurobiological mechanisms of stress-related disorders. *Neuroscience & Biobehavioral Reviews, 32*, 1174–1184.

Lang, F. U., Kösters, M. M., Lang, S. S., Becker, T. T., & Jäger, M. M. (2013). Psychopathological long-term outcome of schizophrenia—A review. *Acta Psychiatrica Scandinavica, 127*, 173–182.

Langevin, R. (1992). Biological factors contributing to paraphilic behavior. *Psychiatric Annals, 22*, 307–314.

Långström, N. (2010). The DSM diagnostic criteria for exhibitionism, voyeurism, and frotteurism. *Archives of Sexual Behavior, 39*, 317–324.

Lara, M. E., & Klein, D. N. (1999). Psychosocial processes underlying the maintenance and persistence of depression: Implications for understanding chronic depression. *Clinical Psychology Review, 19*, 553–570.

Larsen, R. J., & Buss, D. J. (2002). *Personality Psychology.* New York: McGraw-Hill.

Larson, R., Csikszentmihalyi, M., & Graef, R. (1980). Mood variability and the psychosocial adjustment of adolescents. *Journal of Youth and Adolescence, 9*, 469–490.

Latendresse, S. J., Rose, R. J., Viken, R. J., Pulkkinen, L., Kaprio, J., & Dick, D. M. (2008). Parenting mechanisms in links between parents' and adolescents' alcohol use behaviors. *Alcoholism: Clinical and Experimental Research, 32*, 322–330.

Lau, J. F., & Eley, T. C. (2010). The genetics of mood disorders. *Annual Review of Clinical Psychology, 6*, 313–337.

Laumann, E. O., Das, A., & Waite, L. J. (2008). Sexual dysfunction among older adults: Prevalence and risk factors from a nationally representative U.S. probability sample of men and women 57-85 years of age. *Journal of Sexual Medicine, 5*, 2300–2311.

Laumann, E. O., Gagnon, J. H., Michael, R. T., & Michaels, S. (1994). *The Social Organization of Sexuality: Sexual practices in the United States.* Chicago: University of Chicago Press.

Laumann-Billings, L. & Emery, R. E. (2000). Distress among young adults from divorced families. *Journal of Family Psychology, 14*, 671–687.

Lauterbach, E. C., Carter, W. G., Rathke, K. M., Thomas, B. H., Shillcutt, S. D., Vogel, R. L., et al. (2001). Tardive dyskinesia—Diagnostic issues, subsyndromes, and concurrent movement disorders. *Schizophrenia Bulletin, 27*, 601–614.

Lawton, M. P. (2001). Quality of life and the end of life. In J. E. Birren & K. W. Schaie (Eds.), *Handbook of the Psychology of Aging* (5th ed., pp. 592–616). San Diego, CA: Academic Press.

Lazarus, R. S. (2000). Toward better research on stress and coping. *American Psychologist, 55*, 665–673.

Lazarus, R. S., & Folkman, S. (1984). *Stress, appraisal, and coping.* New York: Springer.

Lazoritz, S. (1990). What ever happened to Mary Ellen? *Child Abuse and Neglect, 14*, 143–149.

Le Grange, D., & Hoste, R. R. (2010). Family therapy. In W. S. Agras (Ed.), *The Oxford handbook of eating disorders* (pp. 373–385). New York: Oxford University Press.

Leary, T. (1957). Interpersonal diagnosis of personality: A functional theory and methodology for personality evaluation. New York: Ronald Press.

Leckman, J. F., King, R. A., Gilbert, D. L., Coffey, B. J., Singer, H. S., Dure, L., et al. (2011). Streptococcal upper respiratory tract infections and exacerbations of tic and obsessive-compulsive symptoms: A prospective longitudinal study. *Journal of the American Academy of Child & Adolescent Psychiatry, 50*, 108–118

LeDoux. J. E. (2000). Emotion circuits in the brain. *Annual Review of Neuroscience, 23*, 155–184.

Leenaars, A. A. (2004). Altruistic suicide: A few reflections. *Archives of Suicide Research, 8*, 1–7.

LeFever, G. B., et al., (2003). ADHD among American school-children: Evidence of overdiagnosis and over-medication. *The Scientific Review of Mental Health Practice, 2.*

Leff, J. P. (1988). *Psychiatry Around the Globe: A Transcultural View.* London: Royal College of Psychiatrists.

Lehman, A. F., Dixon, L. B., Hoch, J. S., DeForge, B., Kernan, E., & Frank, R. (1999). Cost-effectiveness of assertive community treatment for homeless persons with severe mental illness. *British Journal of Psychiatry, 174*, 346–352.

Lehman, A. F., Kreyenbuhl, J., Buchanan, R. W., Dickerson, F. B., Dixon, L. B., Goldberg, R., et al. (2004). The schizophrenia patient outcomes research team (PORT): Updated treatment recommendations. *Schizophrenia Bulletin, 30*, 193–217.

Leor, J., Poole, W. K., & Kloner, R. A. (1996). Sudden cardiac death triggered by an earthquake. *New England Journal of Medicine, 334*(7), 413–419.

Leiblum, S. R. (1995). Relinquishing virginity: The treatment of a complex case of vaginismus. In R. C. Rosen, S. R. Leiblum (Eds.), *Case studies in sex therapy* (pp. 250–263). New York: Guilford Press.

Leichsenring, F., & Rabung, S. (2008). Effectiveness of long-term psychodynamic psychotherapy: A meta-analysis. *Journal of the American Medical Association, 300*, 1551–1565.

Lejoyeux, M., McLoughlin, M., & Ades, J. (2006). Pyromania. In E. Hollander & D. J. Stein (Eds.), *Clinical manual of impulse-control disorders* (pp. 229–250). Arlington,, VA: American Psychiatric Publishing.

Lencz, T., Smith, C. W., Auther, A., Correll, C. U., & Cornblatt, B. (2004). Nonspecific and attenuated negative symptoms in patients at clinical high-risk for schizophrenia. *Schizophrenia Research, 68*, 37–48.

Lenzenweger, M. F. (1999). Schizophrenia: Refining the phenotype, resolving endophenotypes. *Behaviour Research and Therapy, 37*, 281–295.

Lenzenweger, M. F., Lane, M. C., Loranger, A. W., & Kessler, R. C. (2007). DSM-IV personality disorders in the National Comorbidity Survey Replication. *Biological Psychiatry, 62*, 553–564.

Leon, G. R., Fulkerson, J. A., Perry, C. L., & Early-Zald, M. B. (1995). Prospective analysis of personality and behavioral vulnerabilities and gender influences in the later development of disordered eating. *Journal of Abnormal Psychology, 104*, 140–149.

Leon, G., Fulkerson, J. A., Perry, C. L., & Cudeck, R. (1993). Personality and behavioral vulnerabilities associated with risk status for eating disorders in adolescent girls. *Journal of Abnormal Psychology, 102*, 438–444.

Leonard, K. E., Eiden, R. D., Wong, M. M., Zucker, R. A., Puttler, L. I., Fitzgerald, H. E., et al., (2000). Developmental perspectives on risk and vulnerability in alcoholic families. *Alcoholism: Clinical and Experimental Research, 24*, 238–240.

Leong, F. T. L. (2007). Cultural accommodation as method and metaphor. *American Psychologist, 62*, 916–927.

Lesch, O., Walter, H., Wetschka, C., Hesselbrock, M., & Hesselbrock, V. (2011). *Alcohol and tobacco: Medical and sociological aspects of use, abuse and addiction.* New York, NY: US Springer-Verlag Publishing.

Leserman, J., Jackson, E. D., Petitto, J. M., Golden, R. N., Silva, S. G., Perkins, D. O., et al. (1999). Progression to AIDS: The effects of stress, depressive symptoms, and social support. *Psychosomatic Medicine, 61*, 397–406.

Lesser, J., & O'Donohue, W. (1999). What is a delusion? Epistemological dimensions. *Journal of Abnormal Psychology, 108*, 687–694.

Lester, D. (2002). The effectiveness of suicide prevention and crisis intervention services. In D. Lester (Ed.), *Crisis Intervention and Counseling by Telephone* (2nd ed., pp. 289–298). Springfield, IL: Charles C Thomas.

Leucht, S. S., Kissling, W. W., & Davis, J. M. (2009). Second-generation antipsychotics for schizophrenia: Can we resolve the conflict? *Psychological Medicine, 39*, 1591–1602.

LeVay, S., & Valente, S. M. (2003). *Human sexuality.* Sunderland, MA: Sinauer Associates.

Levenkron, S. (2006). *Cutting: Understanding and Overcoming Self-Mutilation.* New York: W. W. Norton.

Levenson, M. R. (1992). Rethinking psychopathy. *Theory and Psychology, 2*, 51–71.

Levenson, R. W., & Miller, B. L. (2007). Loss of cells—loss of self: Frontotemporal lobar degeneration and human emotion. *Current Directions in Psychological Science, 16*, 289–294.

Leventhal, H., et al. (2001). Heath risk behaviors and aging. In J. E. Birren & K. W. Schaie (Eds.), *Handbook of the Psychology of Aging* (5th ed., pp. 186–214). San Diego, CA: Academic Press.

Levin, R. (2008). Critically revisiting aspects of the human sexual response cycle of Masters and Johnson: Correcting errors and suggesting modifications. *Sexual and Relationship Therapy, 23,* 393–399.

Levine, H. G. (1978). The discovery of addiction: Changing conceptions of habitual drunkenness in America. *Journal of Studies on Alcohol, 39,* 143–174.

Levine, S. B. (2010). What is sexual addiction? *Journal of Sex & Marital Therapy, 36,* 261–275.

Levine, S. B., Risen, C. B., & Althof, S. E. (1990). Essay on the diagnosis and nature of paraphilia. *Journal of Sex and Marital Therapy, 16,* 89–102.

Levinson, D. J. (1986). A conception of adult development. *American Psychologist, 41,* 3–13.

Levy, B. R., Slade, M. D., Murphy, T. E., & Gill, T. M. (2012). Association between Positive Age Stereotypes and Recovery from Disability in Older Persons. *JAMA, 308,* 1972–1973.

Levy, D. L., Sereno, A. B., Gooding, D. C., & O'Driscoll, G. A. (2010). Eye tracking dysfunction in schizophrenia: Characterization and pathophysiology. In N. R. Swerdlow & N. R. Swerdlow (Eds.), *Behavioral neurobiology of schizophrenia and its treatment* (pp. 311–347). New York: Springer-Verlag.

Levy, F., Hay, D. A., McStephen, M., Wood, C., & Waldman, I. (1997). Attention-deficit/hyperactivity disorder: A category or a continuum? Genetic analysis of a large-scale twin study. *Journal of the American Academy of Child and Adolescent Psychiatry, 36,* 737–744.

Lewinsohn, P. M., Holm-Denoma, J. M., Small, J. W., Seeley, J. R., & Joiner, T. E. (2008). Separation anxiety disorder in childhood as a risk factor for future mental illness. *Journal of the American Academy of Child & Adolescent Psychiatry, 47,* 548–555.

Lewinsohn, P. M., Roberts, R. E., Seely, J. R., Rohde, P., Gotlib, I. H., & Hops, H. (1994). Adolescent psychopathology. II. Psychosocial risk factors for depression. *Journal of Abnormal Psychology, 103,* 302–315.

Lewinsohn, P. M., Rohde, P., & Seeley, J. R. (1998). Major depressive disorder in older adolescents: Prevalence, risk factors, and clinical implications. *Clinical Psychology Review, 18,* 765–794.

Lewis, C. M., Ng, M. Y., Butler, A. W., Cohen-Woods, S., Uher, R., Pirlo, K., & McGuffin, P. (2010). Genome-wide association study of major recurrant depression in the U.K. population. *American Journal of Psychiatry, 167,* 949–957.

Lewis-Fernández, R., Guarnaccia, P. J., Martínez, I. E., Salmán, E., Schmidt, A., & Liebowitz, M. (2002). Comparative phenomenology of ataques de nervios, panic attacks, and panic disorder. *Culture, Medicine and Psychiatry, 26,* 199–223.

Lewis, M. H. (1996). Psychopharmacology of autism spectrum. *Journal of Autism and Developmental Disorders, 26,* 231–235.

Leykin, Y., & DeRubeis, R. J. (2009). Allegiance in psychotherapy outcome research: Separating association from bias. *Clinical Psychology: Science and Practice, 16,* 54–65.

Li, S. (2003). Biocultural orchestration of developmental plasticity across levels: The interplay of biology and culture in shaping the mind and behavior across the life span. *Psychological Bulletin, 129,* 171–194.

Lidz, C. W., Hoge, S. K., Gardner, W., Bennett, N. S., Monahan, J., Mulvey, E. P., & Roth, L. H. (1995). Perceived coercion in mental hospital admission: Pressures and process. *Archives of General Psychiatry, 52,* 1034–1039.

Lidz, C. W., Mulvey, E. P., & Gardner, W. (1993). The accuracy of predictions of violence to others. *Journal of the American Medical Association, 269,* 1007–1011.

Lieberman, J. (2006). Comparative effectiveness of antipsychotic drugs. *Archives of General Psychiatry, 63,* 1069–1072.

Lieberman, J., Stroup, T., McEvoy, J., Swartz, M., Rosenheck, R., Perkins, D., ... Clinical Antipsychotic Trials of Intervention Effectiveness (CATIE) Investigators. (2005). Effectiveness of antipsychotic drugs in patients with chronic schizophrenia. *New England Journal of Medicine, 353,* 1209–1223.

Lilienfeld, S. O. (1992). The association between antisocial personality and somatization disorders: A review and integration of theoretical models. *Clinical Psychology Review, 12,* 641–662.

Lilienfeld, S. O. (1994). Conceptual problems in the assessment of psychopathy. *Clinical Psychology Review, 14,* 17–38.

Lilienfeld, S. O. (2007). Psychological treatments that cause harm. *Perspectives on Psychological Science, 2,* 53–70.

Lilienfeld, S. O., Lynn, S. J., & Lohr, J. M. (2003). *Science and Pseudoscience in Clinical Psychology.* New York: Guilford.

Susser, E., Neugebauer, R., Hoek, H. W., Brown, A. S., Lin, A. S., Labovitz, D., & Gorman, J. M. (1996). Schizophrenia after prenatal famine: Further evidence. *Archives of General Psychiatry, 53,* 25–31.

Lincoln, T. M. (2007). Relevant dimensions of delusions: Continuing the continuum versus category debate. *Schizophrenia Research, 93,* 211–220.

Lindau, A. T., Schumm, L. P., Laumann, E. O., Levinson, W., O'Muircheartaigh, C. A., & Waite, L. J. (2007). A study of sexuality and health among older adults in the United States. *The New England Journal of Medicine, 357,* 762–774.

Lindsay, D. S., Hagen, L., Read, J. D., Wade, K. A., & Garry, M. (2004). True photographs and false memories. *Psychological Science, 15,* 149–154.

Linehan, M. M. (1993). *Cognitive-Behavioral Treatment of Borderline Personality Disorder.* New York: Guilford.

Linehan, M. M., Cochran, B. N., & Kehrer, C. A. (2001). Dialectical behavior therapy for borderline personality disorder. In D. H. Barlow (Ed.), *Clinical handbook of psychological disorders: A step by step treatment manual* (3rd ed., pp. 470–522). New York: Guilford.

Linehan, M. M., Kanter, J. W., & Comtois, K. A. (1999). Dialectical behavior therapy for borderline personality disorder: Efficacy, specificity, and cost effectiveness. In D. S. Janowsky (Ed.), *Psychotherapy indications and outcomes* (pp. 93–118). Washington, DC: American Psychiatric Press.

Linehan, M. M., Tutek, D. A., Heard, H. L., & Armstrong, H. E. (1994). Interpersonal outcome of cognitive-behavioral treatment for chronically suicidal borderline patients. *American Journal of Psychiatry, 151,* 1771–1776.

Link, B., Cullen, F., & Andrews, H. (1990, August). *Violent and illegal behavior of current and former mental patients compared to community controls.* Paper presented at the meeting of the Society for the Study of Social Problems.

Link, B. G., & Phelan, J. C. (2010). Labeling and stigma. In T. L. Scheid & T. N. Brown (Eds.), *A handbook for the study of mental health: Social contexts, theories, and systems* (2nd ed., pp. 571–587). New York, NY US: Cambridge University Press.

Linley, P. A., & Joseph, S. (2005). The human capacity for growth through adversity. *American Psychologist, 60,* 262–264.

Linney, Y. M., Murray, R. M., Peters, E. R., MacDonald, A. M., Rijskijk, F., & Sham, P. (2003). A quantitative genetic analysis of schizotypal personality traits. *Psychological Medicine, 33,* 803–816.

Linscott, R. J., Allardyce, J., & van Os, J. (2010). Seeking verisimilitude in a class: A systematic review of evidence that the criterial clinical symptoms of schizophrenia are taxonic. *Schizophrenia Bulletin, 36,* 811–829.

Lipowski, Z. J. (1988). Somatization: The concept and its clinical applications. *American Journal of Psychiatry, 145,* 1358–1368.

Lipsey, M.W., & Wilson, D.B. (1993). The efficacy of psychological, educational, and behavioral treatment: Confirmation from meta-analysis. *American Psychologist, 48*(12), 1181–1209.

Lisanby, S. H. (2007). Electroconvulsive therapy for depression. *New England Journal of Medicine, 357,* 1939–1945.

Lisanby, S. H., Maddox, J. H., Prudic, J., Devanand, D. P., & Sackheim, H. A. (2000). The effects of electroconvulsive therapy on memory of autobiographical and public events. *Archives of General Psychiatry, 57,* 581–590.

Litz, B. T. (Ed.) (2004). *Early Intervention for Trauma and Traumatic Loss.* New York: Guilford.

Livesley, J. (2008). Toward a genetically-informed model of borderline personality disorder. *Journal of Personality Disorders, 22,* 42–71.

Livesley, W. (2012). Disorder in the proposed DSM-5 classification of personality disorders. *Clinical Psychology & Psychotherapy, 19,* 364–368.

Llera, S. J., & Newman, M. G. (2010). Effects of worry on physiological and subjective reactivity to emotional stimuli in generalized anxiety disorder and nonanxious control participants. *Emotion, 10,* 640–650.

Lochman, J. E., & Wells, K. C. (2004). The coping power program for preadolescent aggressive boys and their parents: Outcome effects at the 1-year follow-up. *Journal of Consulting and Clinical Psychology, 72*(4), 571–578.

Lock, J., Le Grange, D., Agras, S., Moye, A., Bryson, S. W., & Jo, B. (2010). Randomized clinical trial comparing family-based treatment with adolescent-focused individual therapy for adolescents with anorexia nervosa. *Archives of General Psychiatry, 67,* 1025–1032.

Loeb, K. L., Walsh, B. T., Lock, J., le Grange, D., Jones, J., Marcus, S., et al. (2007, July). Open trial of family-based treatment for full and partial anorexia nervosa in adolescene. Evidence of Successful Dissemination. *Journal of the American Academy of Child & Adolescent Psychiatry, 46*(7), 792–800. doi: 10.1097/chi.0b013e318058a98e

Loeb, T. B., Williams, J. K., Carmona, J. V., Rivkin, I., Wyatt, G. E., Chin, D., & Asuan-O'Brien, A. (2002). Child sexual abuse: Associations with the sexual functioning of adolescents and adults. *Annual Review of Sex Research, 13,* 307–345.

Loeber, R. (1988). Natural histories of conduct problems, delinquency, and associated substance use: Evidence for developmental progression. In B. B. Lahey & A. E. Kazdin (Eds.), *Advances in Clinical Child Psychology* (Vol. 11, pp. 73–118). New York: Plenum.

Loftus, E. F. (2003). Make-believe memories. *American Psychologist, 58,* 867–871.

Loftus, E. F. (2004). Memories of things unseen. *Current Directions in Psychological Science, 13,* 145–147.

Loftus, E. F., & Klinger, M. R. (1992). Is the unconscious smart or dumb? *American Psychologist, 47*(6), 761–765.

Loman, L. A., & Siegel, G. (2005). Alternative response in Minnesota: Findings of the program evaluation. *Protecting Children, 20,* 78–92.

Lombardo, P. A. (2001). Carrie Buck's pedigree. *Journal of Laboratory and Clinical Medicine, 138,* 278–282.

Looper, K. J., & Kirmayer, L. J. (2002). Behavioral medicine approaches to somatoform disorders. *Journal of Consulting and Clinical Psychology, 70,* 810–827.

Lopez, A. D., Mathers, C. D., Ezzati, M., Jamison, D. T., & Murray, C. J. L. (2006). *Global burden of disease and risk factors.* Washington, DC: The World Bank and Oxford University Press.

Lopez, S. R., & Guarnaccia, P. J. (2000). Cultural psychopathology: Uncovering the social world of mental illness. *Annual Review of Psychology, 51,* 571–598.

Lopez, S. R., Concepcion, B., Kopelowicz, A., & Vega, W. A. (2012). From documenting to eliminating disparities in mental health care for Latinos. *American Psychologist, 67,* 511–523.

López, S., Nelson Hipke, K., Polo, A. J., Jenkins, J. H., Karno, M., Vaughn, C., & Snyder, K. S. (2004). Ethnicity, expressed emotion, attributions, and course of schizophrenia: Family warmth matters. *Journal of Abnormal Psychology, 113,* 428–439.

Lorains, F. K., Cowlishaw, S., & Thomas, S. A. (2011). Prevalence of comorbid disorders in problem and pathological gambling: Systematic review and meta-analysis of population surveys. *Addiction, 106,* 490–498.

Lord, C., & Bailey, A. (2002). Autism spectrum disorders. In M. Rutter & E. Taylor (Eds.), *Child and adolescent psvchiatry* (4th ed., pp. 636–663). Oxford, England: Blackwell.

Lord, C., Luyster, R., Guthrie, W., & Pickles, A. (2012). Patterns of developmental trajectories in toddlers with autism spectrum disorder. *Journal of Consulting and Clinical Psychology, 80,* 477–489.

Losh, M., & Capps, L. (2006). Understanding of emotional experience in autism: Insights from the personal accounts of high-functioning children with autism. *Developmental Psychology, 42,* 809–818.

Lotter, V. (1966). Epidemiology of autistic conditions in young children. *Social Psychiatry, 1,* 124–137.

Lovaas, O. I. (1987). Behavioral treatment and normal educational and intellectual functioning in young autistic children. *Journal of Consulting and Clinical Psychology, 55,* 3–9.

Luborsky, L., Barber, J. P., & Beutler, L. (1993). Introduction to Special Section: A briefing on curative factors in dynamic psychotherapy. *Journal of Consulting and Clinical Psychology, 61*(4), 539–541.

Luborsky, L., Diguer, L., Seligman, D. A., Rosenthal, R., Krause, E. D., Johnson, S., Halperin, G., Bishop, M., Berman, J. S., & Schweizer, E. (1999). The researcher's own therapy allegiances: A "wild card" in comparisons of treatment efficacy. *Clinical Psychology: Science and Practice, 6*(1), 95–106.

Luby, J. L. (2010). Preschool depression: The importance of identification of depression early in development. *Current Directions in Psychological Science, 19,* 91–95.

Luby, J., Lenze, S., & Tillman, R. (2012). A novel early intervention for preschool depression: Findings from a pilot randomized controlled trial. *Journal of Child Psychology and Psychiatry, 53,* 313–322.

Lussier, P., & Piché, L. (2008). Frotteurism: Psychopathology and theory. In D. Laws & W. T. O'Donohue (Eds.), *Sexual deviance: Theory, assessment, and treatment* (2nd ed., pp. 131–149). New York: Guilford Press.

Lynam, D. R., & Vachon, D. D. (2012). Antisocial personality disorder in DSM-5: Missteps and missed opportunities. *Personality Disorders: Theory, Research, and Treatment, 3,* 483–495.

Lynam, D. R., Caspi, A., Moffitt, T. E., Loeber, R., & Stouthamer-Loeber, M. (2007). Longitudinal evidence that psychopathy scores in early adolescence predict adult psychopathy. *Journal of Abnormal Psychology, 116,* 155–165.

Lynam, D. R., et al. (2000). The interaction between impulsivity and neighborhood context on offending: The effects of impulsivity are stronger in poor neighborhoods. *Journal of Abnormal Psychology, 109,* 563–574.

Lynn, S. J., Lilienfeld, S. O., Merckelbach, H., Giesbrecht, T., & van der Kloet, D. (2012). Dissociation and dissociative disorders: Challenging conventional wisdom. *Current Directions in Psychological Science, 21,* 48–53.

Lyon, G. R. (1996). Learning disabilities. *Future of Children, 6,* 54–76.

Lyons, M. J. (1995). Epidemiology of personality disorders. In M. T. Tsuang, M. Tohen, & G. E. P. Zahner (Eds.), *Textbook in psychiatric epidemiology* (pp. 407–436). New York: Wiley.

# M

Maccoby, E. E. (1998). *The Two Sexes: Growing Up Apart, Coming Together.* Cambridge, MA: Belknap Press.

Maccoby, E. E., & Mnookin, R. H. (1992). *Dividing the child: Social and legal dilemmas of custody.* Cambridge, MA: Harvard University Press.

MacCoun, R. J., Reuter, P., & Wolf, C. (2001). *Drug war heresies: Learning from other vices, times, and places (RAND studies in policy analysis).* New York: Cambridge University Press.

MacDonald, G., & Leary, M. R. (2005). Why does social exclusion hurt? The relationship between social and physical pain. *Psychological Bulletin, 131,* 202–223.

Mackay, R. D. (1988). Post-Hinckley insanity in the U.S.A. *Criminal Law Review,* 88–96.

MacKillop, J., McGeary, J. E., & Ray, L. A. (2010). Genetic influences on addiction: Alcoholism as an exemplar. In D. Ross, H. Kincaid, D. Spurrett, P. Collins, D. Ross, H. Kincaid, … P. Collins (Eds.), *What is addiction?* (pp. 53–98). Cambridge, MA: MIT Press.

MacLeod, C., Rutherford, E., Campbell, L., Ebsworthy, G., & Holker, L. (2002). Selective attention and emotional vulnerability: Assessing the causal basis of their association through the experimental manipulation of attentional bias. *Journal of Abnormal Psychology, 111,* 107–123.

Magai, C. (2001). Emotions over the life span. In J. E. Birren & K. W. Schaie (Eds.), *Handbook of the Psychology of Aging* (5th ed., pp. 399–426). San Diego, CA: Academic Press.

Mahe, V., & Balogh, A. (2000). Long-term pharmacological treatment of generalized anxiety disorder. *International Clinical Psychopharmacology, 15,* 99–105.

Maher, B. A. (2001). Delusions. In P. B. Sutker & H. E. Adams (Eds.), *Comprehensive handbook of psychopathology* (3rd ed., pp. 309–339). New York: Kluwer Academic/Plenum.

Maier, S. F., Watkins, L. R., & Fleshner, M. (1994). Psychoneuroimmunology: The interface between behavior, brain, and immunity. *American Psychologist, 49,* 1004–1017.

Maier, T. (2009). *Masters of sex: The life and times of William Masters and Virginia Johnson, the couple who taught America how to love.* New York: Basic Books.

Maimon, D., & Kuhl, D. C. (2008). Social control and youth suicidality: Situating Durkheim's ideas in a multilevel framework. *American Sociological Review, 73,* 921–943.

Malcolm, J. G. (1987). Treatment choices and informed consent in psychiatry: Implications of the Osheroff case for the profession. *Journal of Psychiatry and the Law, 15,* 9–81.

Malcolm, R. (2003). Pharmacologic treatments manage alcohol withdrawal, relapse prevention. *Psychiatric Annals, 33,* 593–601.

Maldonado, J. R., Butler, L. D., & Spiegel, D. (2001). Treatments for dissociative disorders. In P. E. Nathan & J. M. Gorman (Eds.), *A Guide to Treatments That Work* (pp. 463–469). London: Oxford University Press.

Maletzky, B. M. (2002). The paraphilias: Research and treatment. In P. E. Nathan & J. M. Gorman (Eds.), *A guide to treatments that work* (2nd ed., pp. 525–557). London: Oxford University Press.

Mann, K., Lehert, P., & Morgan, M. Y. (2004). The efficacy of acamprosate in the maintenance of abstinence in alcohol-dependent individuals: Results of a meta-analysis. *Alcoholism: Clinical & Experimental Research, 28,* 51–63.

Mannuzza, S., et al. (1998). Adult psychiatric status of hyperactive boys grown up. *American Journal of Psychiatry, 155,* 493–498.

March, J. S., Leonard, H. L., & Swedo, S. E. (1995). Obsessive-compulsive disorder. In J. S. March (Ed.), *Anxiety Disorders in Children and Adolescents* (pp. 251–275). New York: Guilford.

March, J. S., Silva, S., Petrycki, S., Curry, J., Wells, K., Fairbank, J., et al. (2004). Fluoxetine, cognitive-behavioral therapy, and their combination for adolescents with depression: Treatment for Adolescents With Depression Study (TADS) randomized control trial. *Journal of the American Medical Association, 292,* 807–820.

Marcia, J. E. (1994). The empirical study of ego identity. In H. A. Bosma, T. L. G. Graafsma, H. D. Grotevant, & D. J. de Levita (Eds.), *Identity and Development* (pp. 67–80). Thousand Oaks, CA: Sage.

Marcia, J. E., (1966), Development and validation of ego identity status. *Journal of Personality and Social Psychology, 3,* 551–558.

Marcus, M. D. & Wildes, J. E. (2009). Obesity: Is it a mental disorder? *International Journal of Eating Disorders, 42,* 739–753.

Margolin, G., Christensen, A., & John, R. S. (1996). The continuance and spillover of everyday tensions in distressed and nondistressed families. *Journal of Family Psychology, 10,* 304–321.

Markman, H. J., Floyd, F. J., Stanley, S. M., & Storaasli, R. D. (1988). Prevention of marital distress: A longitudinal investigation. *Journal of Consulting and Clinical Psychology, 56,* 210–217.

Markman, H. J., Renick, M. J., Floyd, F. J., Stanley, S. M., & Clements, M. (1993). Preventing marital distress through communication and conflict management training: A 4- and 5-year follow-up. *Journal of Consulting and Clinical Psychology, 61,* 70–77.

Marks, I. M., & Nesse, R. M. (1994). Fear and fitness: An evolutionary analysis of anxiety disorders. *Ethology and Sociobiology, 15,* 247–261.

Marks, I. M., Swinson, R. P., Basoglu, M., Kuch, K., Noshirvani, H., O'Sullivan, G., et al. (1993). Alprazolam and exposure alone and combined in panic disorder with agoraphobia: A controlled study in London and Toronto. *British Journal of Psychiatry, 162,* 776–787.

Marks, P. A., Seeman, W., & Haller, D. L. (1974). *The Actuarial Use of the MMPI with Adolescents and Adults.* New York: Oxford University Press.

Marlatt, G. A., Blume, A. W., & Parks, G. A. (2001). Integrating harm reduction therapy and traditional substance abuse treatment. *Journal of Psychoactive Drugs, 33,* 13–21.

Marom, S., Munitz, H., Jones, P., Weizman, A., & Hermesh, H. (2005). Expressed emotion: Relevance to rehospitalization in schizophrenia over 7 years. *Schizophrenia Bulletin, 31,* 751–758.

Marques, J. K. (1999). How to answer the question "Does sexual offender treatment work? *Journal of Interpersonal Violence, 14,* 437–451.

Marques, J. K., Day, D. M., Nelson, C., & West, M. A. (1993). Findings and recommendations from California's experimental treatment program. In G. C. N. Hall, R. Hirschman, J. R. Graham, & M. S. Zaragoza (Eds.), *Sexual aggression: Issues in etiology, assessment, and treatment* (pp. 197–214). Washington, DC: Hemisphere.

Marshall, W. L. (1989). Intimacy, loneliness, and sexual offenders. *Behaviour Research and Therapy, 27,* 491–503.

Marshall, W. L. (2007). Diagnostic issues, multiple paraphilias, and comorbid disorders in sexual offenders: Their incidence and treatment. *Aggression and Violent Behavior, 12,* 16–35.

Marshall, W. L., Bryce, P., Hudson, S. M., Ward, T., & Moth, B. (1996). The enhancement of intimacy and the reduction of loneliness among child molesters. *Journal of Family Violence, 11,* 219–236.

Marshall, W. L., Eccles, A., & Barbaree, H. E. (1991). The treatment of exhibitionists: A focus on sexual deviance versus cognitive and relationship features. *Behaviour Research and Therapy, 29,* 129–135.

Martin, R. L., Roberts, W. V., & Clayton, P. J. (1980). Psychiatric status after hysterectomy: A one-year prospective follow-up. *Journal of the American Medical Association, 244,* 350–353.

Martinez, M., & Kurik, M. E. (2006). The role of pharmacotherapy for dementia patients with behavioral disturbances. In S. M. LoboPrabhu, V. A. Molinari, J. W. Lomax, *Supporting the Caregiver in Dementia: A Guide for Caregivers* (pp. 151–157). Baltimore, MD: Johns Hopkins Press

Martire, L. M., & Schulz, R. (2007). Involving family in psychosocial interventions for chronic illness. *Current Directions in Psychological Science, 16,* 90–94.

Mash, E. J., & Johnston, C. (1982). A comparison of the mother-child interactions of younger and older hyperactive and normal children. *Child Development, 53,* 1371–1381.

Mash, E. J., & Wolfe, D. A. (2005). *Abnormal child psychology* (3rd ed.). Belmont, CA: Thomson Wadsworth.

Mash, E. J., & Wolfe, D. A. (2010). *Abnormal Child Psychology,* 4th ed. Belmont, CA: Wadsworth, Cengage Learning.

Mashour, G. A., Walker, E. E., & Martuza, R. L. (2005). Psychosurgery: Past, present, and future. *Brain Research Reviews, 48,* 409–419.

Masten, A. S. (2001). Ordinary magic: Resilience processes in development. *American Psychologist, 56,* 227–238.

Masters, W. H., & Johnson, V. E. (1970). *Human sexual inadequacy.* Boston: Little, Brown.

Mathews, A., & MacLeod, C. (2005). Cognitive vulnerability to emotional disorders. *Annual Review of Clinical Psychology, 1,* 167–195

Mathis, J. (2001). Community integration of individuals with disabilities: An update on Olmstead implementation. *Journal of Poverty Law and Policy, 23,* 395–410.

Matthysse, S., & Pope, A. (1986). The neuropathology of psychiatric disorders. In P. Berger & K. H. Brodie (Eds.), *American Handbook of Psychiatry* (Vol. 8, 2nd ed., 151–159). New York: Basic Books.

Mavissakalian, M. R., & Ryan, M. T. (1998). Rational treatment of panic disorder with antidepressants. *Annals of Clinical Psychiatry, 10,* 185–195.

Mayeux, R., & Ottman, R. (1998). Alzheimer's disease genetics: Home runs and strikeouts. *Annals of Neurology, 44,* 716–719.

McAdams, D. P. (2013). The psychological self as actor, agent, and author. *Perspectives on Psychological Science, 8,* 272–295.

McAdams, D., & Pals, J. L. (2006). A new big five: Fundamental principles for an integrative science of personality. *American Psychologist, 61,* 204–217.

McCabe, M. P. (2005). The role of performance anxiety in the development and maintenance of sexual dysfunction in men and women. *International Journal of Stress Management, 12,* 379–388.

McCabe, M. P., & Wauchope, M. (2005). Behavioral characteristics of men accused of rape: Evidence for different types of rapists. *Archives of Sexual Behavior, 34,* 241–253.

McCarroll, J. E., Ursano, R. J., Fullerton, C. S., Liu, X., & Lundy, A. (2002). Somatic symptoms in Gulf War mortuary workers. *Psychosomatic Medicine, 64,* 29–33.

McCabe, P. M., Gonzales, J. A., Zaias, J., Szeto, A., Kumar, M., Herron, A. J., et al. (2002). Social environment influences the progression of atherosclerosis in the Watanabe heritable hyperlipidemic rabbit. *Circulation, 105,* 354–359.

McCarthy, B. W. (1989). Cognitive-behavioral strategies and techniques in the treatment of early ejaculation. In S. R. Leiblum & R. C. Rosen (Eds.), *Principles and practice of sex therapy* (2nd ed.). New York: Guilford.

McCarthy, B. W. (2004). An integrative cognitive-behavioral approach to understanding, assessing, and treating female sexual dysfunction. *Journal of Family Psychotherapy, 15,* 19–35.

McConaghy, N. (1999). Methodological issues concerning evaluation of treatment for sexual offenders: Randomization, treatment dropouts, untreated controls, and within-treatment studies. *Sexual Abuse: Journal of Research and Treatment, 11,* 183–193.

McCrae, R. R., & Costa, P. T. (2013). Introduction to the empirical and theoretical status of the five-factor model of personality traits. In T. A. Widiger & P. T. Costa (Eds.), *Personality disorders and the five-factor model of personality* (3rd ed., pp. 15–27). Washington: American Psychological Association.

McCullough, J. P., Jr., Klein, D. N., Borian, F. E., Howland, R. H., Riso, L. P., Keller, M. B., et al. (2003). Group comparisons of DSM-IV subtypes of chronic depression: Validity of the distinctions, Part 2. *Journal of Abnormal Psychology, 112,* 614–622.

McDonagh, A., Friedman, M., McHugo, G., Ford, J., Sengupta, A., Mueser, K., et al. (2005). Randomized trial of cognitive-behavioral therapy for chronic posttraumatic stress disorder in adult female survivors of childhood sexual abuse. *Journal of Consulting and Clinical Psychology, 73,* 515–524.

McEachin, J. J., Smith, T., & Lovaas, O. I. (1993). Long-term outcome for children with autism who received early intensive behavioral treatment. *American Journal on Mental Retardation, 97*(4), 359–372.

McElroy, S. L., Guerdjikova, A. I., O'Melia, A. M., Mori, N., & Keck, P. E., Jr. (2010). Pharmacotherapy of the eating disorders. In W. S. Agras (Ed.), *The Oxford handbook of eating disorders* (pp. 417–451). New York: Oxford University Press.

McFall, R. M. (2005). Theory and utility—key themes in evidence-based assessment. *Psychological Assessment., 17,* 312–323.

McGeer, P. L., & McGeer, E. G. (1996). Anti-inflammatory drugs in the fight against Alzheimer's disease. *Annals of the New York Academy of Sciences, 777,* 213–220.

McGlashan, T. (1986). The Chestnut Lodge follow-up study: III. Long-term outcome of borderline personalities. *Archives of General Psychiatry, 43,* 20–30.

McGlashan, T. H. (1998). The profiles of clinical deterioration in schizophrenia. *Journal of Psychiatric Research, 32,* 133–141.

McGlashan, T. H., & Fenton, W. S. (1991). Classical subtypes for schizophrenia: Literature review for DSM-IV. *Schizophrenia Bulletin, 17,* 609–623.

McGrath, J. (2005). Myths and plain truths about schizophrenia epidemiology—The NAPE lecture 2004. *Acta Psychiatrica Scandinavica, 111,* 4–11.

McGrath, J. J., & Welham, J. L. (1999). Season of birth and schizophrenia: A systematic review and meta-analysis of data from the Southern Hemisphere. *Schizophrenia Research, 35,* 237–242.

McGue, M., & Iacono, W. G. (2008). The adolescent origins of substance use disorders. *International Journal of Methods in Psychiatric Research, 17*(Suppl. 1), S30–S38

McGue, M., & Lykken, D. T. (1992). Genetic influence on risk of divorce. *Psychological Science, 3,* 368–373.

McGue, M., Iacono, W., Legrand, L., & Elkins, I. (2001). Origins and consequences of age at first drink: II. Familial risk and heritability. *Alcoholism: Clinical and Experimental Research, 25,* 1166–1173.

McGuffin, P., & Farmer, A. E. (2005). Are there phenotype problems? In C. F. Zorumski & E. H. Rubin (Eds.), *Psychopathology in the Genome and Neuroscience Era* (pp. 65–84). Washington, DC: American Psychiatric Publishing.

McGuffin, P., Katz, R., Watkins, S., & Rutherford, J. (1996). A hospital-based twin register of the heritability of DSM-IV unipolar depression. *Archives of General Psychiatry, 53,* 129–136.

McGuffin, P., Rijsdijk, F., Andrew, M., Sham, P., Katz, R., & Cardno, A. (2003). The heritability of bipolar affective disorder and the genetic relationship to unipolar depression. *Archives of General Psychiatry, 60,* 497–502.

McHugh, R. K., & Barlow, D. H. (2010). The dissemination and implementation of evidence-based psychological treatments: A review of current efforts. *American Psychologist, 65,* 73–84.

McKenna, M. C., Zevon, M. A., Corn, B., & Rounds, J. (1999). Psychosocial factors and the development of breast cancer: A meta-analysis. *Health Psychology, 18,* 520–531.

McKey, R. H., Condelli, L., Granson, H., Barrett, B., McConkey, C., & Plantz, M. (1985, June). *The impact of Head Start on children, families, and communities. Final report of the Head Start evaluation, synthesis and utilization project.* Washington, DC: Corporate Social Responsibility.

McKhann, G. M., Knopman, D. S., Chertkow, H., Hyman, B. T., Jack, C. R., Kawas, C. H., et al.. (2011). The diagnosis of dementia due to Alzheimer's disease: Recommendations from the National Institute on Aging-Alzheimer's Association workgroups on diagnostic guidelines for Alzheimer's disease. *Alzheimer's & Dementia, 7,* 263–269.

McKim, W. (2000). *Drugs and behavior: An introduction to behavioral pharmacology* (4th ed.). Upper Saddle River, NJ: Prentice Hall.

McKim, W. A. (2006). *Drugs and behavior: An introduction to behavioral pharmacology* (6th ed.). Upper Saddle River, NJ: Prentice Hall.

McLaughlin, K. A., & Hatzenbuehler, M. L. (2009). Stressful life events, anxiety sensitivity, and internalizing symptoms in adolescents. *Journal of Abnormal Psychology, 118,* 659–669.

McLaughlin, K., Borkovec, T., & Sibrava, N. (2007). The effects of worry and rumination on affect states and cognitive activity. *Behavior Therapy, 38,* 23–38.

McLemore, C. W., & Benjamin, L. A. (1979). Whatever happened to interpersonal diagnosis? A psychosocial alternative to DSM-III. *American Psychologist, 34,* 17–34.

McMahon, R. J., Witkiewitz, K., Kotler, J. S., & The Conduct Problems Prevention Research Group. (2010). Predictive validity of callous-unemotional traits measured in early adolescence with respect to multiple antisocial outcomes. *Journal of Abnormal Psychology, 119,* 752–763.

McManus, F., Surawy, C., Muse, K., Vazquez-Montes, M., & Williams, J. M. G. (2012). A randomized clinical trial of mindfulness-based cognitive therapy versus unrestricted services for health anxiety (hypochondriasis). *Journal of Consulting and Clinical Psychology, 80,* 817–828.

McNally, R. J. (1994). Cognitive bias in panic disorder. *Current Directions in Psychological Science, 3,* 129–132.

McNally, R. J. (2003). Recovering memories of trauma: A view from the laboratory. *Current Directions in Psychological Science, 12,* 32–35.

McNally, R. J. (2007). Mechanisms of exposure therapy: How neuroscience can improve psychological treatments for anxiety disorders. *Clinical Psychology Review, 27,* 750–759.

McNally, R. J., Bryant, R. A., & Ehlers, A. (2003). Does early psychological intervention promote recovery from posttraumatic stress? *Psychological Science in the Public Interest, 4,* 45–79.

McPartland, J. C., Reichow, B., & Volkmar, F. R. (2012). Sensitivity and specificity of proposed DSM-5 diagnostic criteria for autism spectrum disorder. *Journal of the American Academy of Child and Adolescent Psychiatry, 51,* 368–383.

McQueen, M., & Blacker, D. (2008). *Genetics of Alzheimer's Disease. Psychiatric Genetics: Applications in Clinical Practice* (pp. 177–193). Arlington, VA: American Psychiatric Publishing, Inc.

Medico. (2011). America's state of mind. *New York Times* (September 25, 2012). A call for caution on antipsychotic drugs.

Meehl, P. E. (1973). *Psychodiagnosis: Selected papers.* Oxford England: U. Minnesota Press.

Meehl, P. E. (1993). The origins of some of my conjectures concerning schizophrenia. In L. J. Chapman, J. P. Chapman, & D. Fowles (Eds.), *Progress in experimental personality and psychopathology research* (pp. 1–11). New York: Springer.

Meehl, P. E., & Rosen, A. (1955). Antecedent probability and the efficiency of psychometric signs, patterns, or cutting scores. *Psychological Bulletin, 52,* 194–216.

Meichenbaum, D. (1977). *Cognitive-Behavior Modification: An Integrative Approach.* New York: Plenum Press.

Melman, A., & Tiefer, L. (1992). Surgery for erectile disorders: Operative procedures and psychological issues. In R. C. Rosen & S. R. Leiblum (Eds.), *Erectile disorders: Assessment and treatment* (pp. 255–282). New York: Guilford.

Melton, G. B., & Limber, S. (1989). Psychologists' involvement in cases of child maltreatment: Limits of roles and expertise. *American Psychologist, 44,* 1225–1233.

Melton, G. B., Petrila, J., Poythress, N. G., & Slobogin, C. (1997). *Psychological evaluations for the courts* (2nd ed.). New York: Guilford.

Melton, G. B., Petrila, J., Poythress, N. G., & Slobogin, C. (2007). *Psychological evaluations for the courts: A handbook for mental health professionals and lawyers* (3rd ed.). New York: Guilford Press.

Meltzer, H., Vostanis, P., Dogra, N., Doos, L., Ford, T, & Goodman, R. (2009). Children's specific fears. *Child Care, Health, & Development, 35,* 781–789.

Mendez, M., Lauterbach, E., & Sampson, S. (2008). An evidence-based review of the psychopathology of frontotemporal dementia: A report of the ANPA committee on research. *Journal of Neuropsychiatry & Clinical Neurosciences, 20,* 130–149.

Mendle, J., Turkheimer, E., D'Onofrio, B. M., Lynch, S. K., Emery, R. E., Slutske, W. S., & Martin, N. G. (2006). Family structure and age at menarche: A children-of-twins approach. *Developmental Psychology, 42,* 533–542.

Mendlewicz, J., Souery, D., & Rivelli, S. K. (1999). Short-term and long-term treatment for bipolar patients: Beyond the guidelines. *Journal of Affective Disorders, 55,* 79–85.

Menzies, L., Chamberlain, S. R., Laird, A. R., Thelen, S. M., Sahakian, B. J., & Bullmore, E. T. (2008). Integrating evidence from neuroimaging and neuropsychological studies of obsessive-compulsive disorder: The orbitofronto-striatal model revisited. *Neuroscience and Biobehavioral Reviews, 32,* 525–549.

Merckelbach, H., Muris, P., & Schouten, E. (1996). Pathways to fear in spider phobic children. *Behaviour Research and Therapy, 34,* 935–938.

Merikangas, K. R., He, J., Burstein, M., Swanson, S. A., Avenevoli, S., Cui, L., et al. (2010). Lifetime prevalence of mental disorders in U.S. adolescents: Results from the National Comorbidity Survey Replication-Adolescent Supplement (NCS-A). *Journal of the American Academy of Child & Adolescent Psychiatry, 49,* 980–989.

Merkin, D. (1996, February 26 and March 4). Unlikely obsession: Confronting a taboo. *The New Yorker*, pp. 98–115.

Mervielde, I., DeClercq, B., DeFruyt, F., & Van Leeuwen, K. (2005). Temperament, personality, and developmental psychopathology as childhood antecedents of personality disorders. *Journal of Personality Disorders, 19*, 171–201.

Messias, E., Chen, C., & Eaton, W. (2007). Epidemiology of schizophrenia: Review of findings and myths. *Psychiatric Clinics of North America, 30*, 323–338.

Meston, C. M., & Rellini, A. (2008). Sexual dysfunction. In W. E. Craighead, D. J. Miklowitz, & L. W. Craighead (Eds.), *Psychopathology: History, diagnosis, and empirical foundations* (pp. 544–564). Hoboken, NJ: Wiley.

Meston, C. M., Rellini, A. H., & McCall, K. (2010). The sensitivity of continuous laboratory measures of physiological and subjective sexual arousal for diagnosing women with sexual arousal disorder. *Journal of Sexual Medicine, 7*, 938–950.

Meston, C. M., Trapnell, P. D., & Gorzalka, B. B. (1996). Ethnic and gender differences in sexuality: Variations in sexual behavior between Asian and non-Asian university students. *Archives of Sexual Behavior, 25*, 33–72.

Mesulam, M. (2007). Primary progressive aphasia: A 25-year retrospective. *Alzheimer Disease & Associated Disorders, 21*, S8–S11.

Metz, M. E., & Epstein, N. (2002). Assessing the role of relationship conflict in sexual dysfunction. *Journal of Sex and Marital Therapy, 28*, 139–164.

Metz, M. E., & Pryor, J. L. (2000). Premature ejaculation: A psychophysiological approach for assessment and management. *Journal of Sex and Marital Therapy, 26*, 293–320.

Metzl, J. M. (2004). Voyeur nation? Changing definitions of voyeurism, 1950-2004. *Harvard Review of Psychiatry, 12*, 127–131.

Meuret, A. E., Ritz, T., Wilhelm, F. H., & Roth, W. T. (2005). Voluntary hyperventilation in the treatment of panic disorder. *Clinical Psychology Review, 25*, 285–306.

Meyer, G. J., & Archer, R. P. (2001). The hard science of Rorschach research: What do we know and where do we go? *Psychological Assessment, 13*, 486–502.

Meyer, G. J., & Viglione, D. J. (2008). An introduction to Rorschach assessment. In R. P. Archer & S. R. Smith (Eds.), *Personality assessment* (pp. 281–336). New York, NY: Routledge/Taylor & Francis Group.

Meyer, G. J., Finn, S. E., Eyde, L. D., Kay, G. G., Moreland, K. L., Dies, R. R., et al. (2001). Psychological testing and psychological assessment: A review of evidence and issues. *American Psychologist, 56*, 128–165.

Meyer, I. H. (2003). Prejudice, social stress, and mental health in lesbian, gay, and bisexual populations: Conceptual issues and research evidence. *Psychological Bulletin, 129*, 674–697.

Meyer, J. M., Eaves, L. J., Heath, A. C., & Martin, N. G. (1991). Estimating genetic influences on the age-at-menarche: A survival analysis approach. *American Journal of Medical Genetics, 39*, 148–154.

Mezzich, J. E., Berganza, C. E., & Ruiperez, M. A. (2001). Culture in DSM-IV, ICD-10, and evolving diagnostic systems. *Psychiatric Clinics of North America, 24*, 407–419.

Michelini, S., Cassano, G. B., Frare, F., & Perugi, G. (1996). Long-term use of benzodiazepines: Tolerance, dependence and clinical problems in anxiety and mood disorders. *Pharmacopsychiatry, 29*, 127–134.

Mick, E., Spencer, T., Wozniak, J., & Biederman, J. (2005). Heterogeneity of irritability in attention-deficit/hyperactivity disorder subjects with and without mood disorders. *Biological Psychiatry, 58*, 576–582.

Mickelson, K. D., Kessler, R. C., & Shaver, P. R. (1997). Adult attachment in a nationally representative sample. *Journal of Personality and Social Psychology, 73*, 1092–1106.

Middleton, L. S., Kuffel, S. W., & Heiman, J. R. (2008). Effects of experimentally adopted sexual schemas on vaginal response and subjective sexual arousal: A comparison between women with sexual arousal disorder and sexually healthy women. *Archives of Sexual Behavior, 37*, 950–961.

Mihura, J. L., Meyer, G. J., Dumitrascu, N., & Bombel, G. (2013). The validity of individual Rorschach variables:

Systematic reviews and meta-analyses of the comprehensive system. *Psychological Bulletin, 139*, 548–605.

Miklowitz, D. (2004). The role of family systems in severe and recurrent psychiatric disorders: A developmental psychopathology view. *Development and Psychopathology, 16*, 667–688.

Miklowitz, D. J. (2007). The role of the family in the course and treatment of bipolar disorder. *Current Directions in Psychological Science, 16*, 192–196.

Miklowitz, D. J., & Johnson, S. L. (2009). Social and familial factors in the course of bipolar disorder: Basic processes and relevant interventions. *Clinical Psychology: Science and Practice, 16*, 281–296.

Miklowitz, D. J., Otto, M. W., & Frank, E. (2007). Intensive psychosocial intervention enhances functioning in patients with bipolar depression: Results from a 9-month randomized controlled trial. *American Journal of Psychiatry, 164*, 1340–1347.

Miles, J. H. (2011). Autism spectrum disorders—A genetics review. *Genetics in Medicine, 13*, 278–294

Milich, R., Balentine, A. C., & Lynam, D. R. (2001). ADHD combined type and ADHD predominantly inattentive type are distinct and unrelated disorders. *Clinical Psychology: Science and Practice, 8*, 463–488.

Milich, R., Wolraich, M., & Lindgren, S. (1986). Sugar and hyperactivity: A critical review of empirical findings. *Clinical Psychology Review, 6*, 493–513.

Miller, T. Q., Smith, T. W., Turner, C. W., Guijarro, M. L., & Hallet, A. J. (1996). A meta-analytic review of research on hostility and physical health. *Psychological Bulletin, 119*, 322–348.

Miller, C. J., Sanchez, J., & Hynd, G. W. (2003). Neurological correlates of reading disabilities. In H. L. Swanson, K. R. Harris, & S. Graham (Eds.), *Handbook of Learning Disabilities* (pp. 242–255). New York: Guilford.

Miller, G. A., & Keller, J. (2000). Psychology and neuroscience: Making peace. *Current Directions in Psychological Science, 9*, 212–215.

Miller, G. E., Chen, E., & Parker, K. J. (2011). Psychological stress in childhood and susceptibility to the chronic diseases of aging: Moving toward a model of behavior and biological mechanisms. *Psychological Bulletin, 137*, 959–997.

Miller, S. L., Maner, J. K. (2011). Sick bodyvigilant mind: the biological immune system activates the behavioral immune system. *Psychological Science221*467–1471.

Miller, T., & Swartz, L. (1990). Clinical psychology in general hospital settings: Issues in interprofessional relationships. *Professional Psychology: Research and Practice, 21*(1), 48–53.

Miller, T. W. (1989). *Stressful life events*. Madison, CT: International Universities Press.

Miller, W. R. (1995). Increasing motivation for change. In R. K. Hester & W. R. Miller (Eds.), *Handbook of alcoholism treatment approaches* (2nd ed., pp. 89–104). Boston: Allyn & Bacon.

Miller, W. R., & Longabaugh, R. (2003). Summary and conclusions. In T. F. Babor & F. K. Del Boca (Eds.), *Treatment matching in alcoholism* (pp. 207–221). New York: Cambridge University Press.

Miller, W. R., & Rose, G. S. (2009). Toward a theory of motivational interviewing. *American Psychologist, 64*, 527–537.

Miller-Johnson, S., Emery, R. E., Marvin, R. S., Clarke, W., Lovinger, R., & Martin, M. (1994). Parent-child relationships and the management of insulin-dependent diabetes mellitus. *Journal of Consulting and Clinical Psychology, 62*, 603–610.

Millon, T., & Martinez, A. (1995). Avoidant personality disorder. In W. J. Livesley (Ed.), *The DSM-IV personality disorders* (pp. 218–233). New York: Guilford.

Milosevic, A., & Ledgerwood, D. M. (2010). The subtyping of pathological gambling: A comprehensive review. *Clinical Psychology Review, 30*, 988–998.

Mineka, S., & Kihlstrom, J. F. (1978). Unpredictable and uncontrollable events: A new perspective on experimental neurosis. *Journal of Abnormal Psychology, 87*(2), 256–271.

Mineka, S., & Oehlberg, K. (2008). The relevance of recent developments in classical conditioning to understanding

the etiology and maintenance of anxiety disorders. *Acta Psychologica, 127*, 567–580.

Mineka, S., & Zinbarg, R. (1998). Experimental approaches to the anxiety and mood disorders. In J. G. Adair & D. Belanger (Eds.), *Advances in Psychological Science*, Vol. 1: *Social, Personal, and Cultural Aspects* (pp. 429–454). Hove, England: Psychology Press/Erlbaum (UK) Taylor & Francis.

Minino, A. M., & Smith, B. L. (2001). Deaths: Preliminary data for 2000. *National Vital and Statistics Report, 49*(12). Hyattsville, MD: National Center for Health Statistics.

Minuchin, S., Rosman, B. L., & Baker, L. (1978). *Psychosomatic families*. Cambridge, MA: Harvard University Press.

Mitchell, J. (1982). When disaster strikes . . . The critical incident stress debriefing process. *Journal of Emergency Medical Services, 8*, 36–39.

Mitchell, J. E., & Crow, S. J. (2010). Medical comorbidities of eating disorders. In W. S. Agras (Ed.), *The Oxford handbook of eating disorders* (pp. 259–266). New York: Oxford University Press.

Mitchell, J. E., Pyle, R. L., Eckert, E. D., Hatsukami, D., Pomeroy, C., & Zimmerman, R. (1990). A comparison study of antidepressants and structured intensive group psychotherapy in the treatment of bulimia nervosa. *Archives of General Psychiatry, 47*, 149–157.

Mitchell, J. E., Raymond, N., & Specker, S. (1993). A review of controlled trials of pharmacotherapy and psychotherapy in the treatment of bulimia nervosa. *International Journal of Eating Disorders, 14*, 229–247.

Mitchell, J., & Dyregrov, A. (1993). Traumatic stress in disaster workers and emergency personnel. In J. P. Wilson & B. Raphael (Eds.), *International Handbook of Traumatic Stress Syndromes* (pp. 905–914). New York: Plenum.

Mitchell, K. J., & Porteous, D. J. (2011). Rethinking the genetic architecture of schizophrenia. *Psychological Medicine, 41*, 19–32.

Mitchell, K., & Graham, C. A. (2008). Two challenges for the classification of sexual dysfunction. *Journal of Sexual Medicine, 5*, 1552–1558.

Miyamoto, S. S., Miyake, N. N., Jarskog, L. F., Fleischhacker, W. W., & Lieberman, J. A. (2012). Pharmacological treatment of schizophrenia: A critical review of the pharmacology and clinical effects of current and future therapeutic agents. *Molecular Psychiatry, 17*, 1206–1227.

Mizrahi, R., Starkstein, S. E., Jorge, R., & Robinson, R. G. (2006). Phenomenology and clinical correlates of delusions in Alzheimer disease. *American Journal of Geriatric Psychiatry, 14*, 573–581.

Moffitt, T. E. (1993). Adolescence-limited and life-course-persistent antisocial behavior: A developmental taxonomy. *Psychological Review, 100*, 674–701.

Moffitt, T. E. (2007). A review of research on the taxonomy of life-course persistent versus adolescence-limited antisocial behavior. In D. J. Flannery, A. T. Vazsonyi, & I. D. Waldman (Eds.), *The Cambridge handbook of violent behavior and aggression* (pp. 47–74). New York: Cambridge University Press.

Moffitt, T. E., Caspi, A. A., Taylor, A. A., Kokaua, J. J., Milne, B. J., Polanczyk, G. G., & Poulton, R. R. (2010). How common are common mental disorders? Evidence that lifetime prevalence rates are doubled by prospective versus retrospective ascertainment. *Psychological Medicine, 40*, 899–909.

Mojtabai, R., & Olfson, M. (2008). National trends in psychotherapy by office-based psychiatrists. *Archives of General Psychiatry, 65*, 962–970.

Moldin, S. O. (2003). Neurobiology of autism: The new frontier. *Genes, Brain and Behavior, 2*, 253–254.

Molina, B. S. G., Hinshaw, S. P., Swanson, J. M., Arnold, E., Vitiello, B., Jensen, P. S., et al. (2009) The MTA at 8 years: Prospective follow-up of children treated for combined type ADHD in a multisite study. *Journal of the American Academy of Child & Adolescent Psychiatry, 48*, 484–500.

Monahan, J. (1981). *The clinical prediction of violent behavior*. Rockville, MD: National Institute of Mental Health.

Monahan, J. (2010). Mandated psychiatric treatment in the community: Forms, prevalence, outcomes, and controversies.

In Kallert, T., Mezzich, J., & Monahan, J. (Eds.), *Coercive treatment in psychiatry: Clinical, legal, and ethical aspects* (in press). London: Wiley-Blackwell.

Monahan, J., & Steadman, H. J. (2009). Extending violence reduction principles to justice-involved persons with mental illness. In Dvoskin, J., Skeem, J., Novaco, R., & Douglas, K. (Eds.), *Applying social science to reduce violent offending* (in press). New York: Oxford University Press.

Monahan, J., Bonnie, R. J., Appelbaum, P. S., Hyde, P. S., Steadman, H. J., & Swartz, M. S. (2001). Mandated community treatment: Beyond outpatient commitment. *Psychiatric Services, 52,* 1198–1205.

Monahan, J., Lidz, C. W., Hoge, S. K., Mulvey, E. P., Eisenberg, M., Roth, L. H., et al. (1999). Coercion in the provision of mental health services: The MacArthur studies. In J. P. Morrissey & J. Monahan (Eds.), *Research in community and mental health* (pp. 13–29). Greenwich, CT: JAI.

Monahan, J., Redlich, A. D., Swanson, J., Robbins, P. C., Appelbaum, P. S., Petrila, J., et al. (2005). Use of leverage to improve adherence to psychiatric treatment in the community. *Psychiatric Services, 56,* 37–44.

Money, J. (2002). *A first person history of pediatric psychoendocrinology.* New York: Kluwer Academic/Plenum Publishers.

Monroe, S. M., & Harkness, K. L. (2005). Life stress, the "kindling" hypothesis, and the recurrence of depression: Considerations from a life stress perspective. *Psychological Review, 112,* 417–445.

Monroe, S. M., & Reid, M. W. (2009). Life stress and major depression. *Current Directions in Psychological Science, 18,* 68–72.

Monson, C. M., Schnurr, P. P., Resick, P. A., Friedman, M. J., Young-Xu, Y., & Stevens, S. P. (2006). Cognitive processing therapy for veterans with military-related posttraumatic stress disorder. *Journal of Consulting and Clinical Psychology, 74,* 898–907.

Montgomery, H. A., Miller, W. R., & Tonigan, J. S. (1993). Differences among AA groups: Implications for research. *Journal of Studies on Alcohol, 54,* 502–504.

Moore, M. (1975). Some myths about "mental illness." *Inquiry, 18,* 233–240.

Moos, R. H., Finney, J. W., Ouimette, P. C., & Suchinsky, R. T. (1999). A comparative evaluation of substance abuse treatment. I. Treatment orientation, amount of care, and 1-year outcomes. *Alcoholism: Clinical and Experimental Research, 23,* 529–536.

Moreno, C., Laje, G., Blanco, C., Jiang, H., Schmidt, A. B., & Olfson, M. (2007). National trends in the outpatient diagnosis and treatment of bipolar disorder in youth. *Archives of General Psychiatry, 64,* 1032–1039.

Moretti, L., Cristofori, I., Weaver, S. M., Chau, A., Portelli, J. N., & Grafman, J. (2012). Cognitive decline in older adults with a history of traumatic brain injury. *Lancet Neurology, 11,* 1103–1112.

Morgentaler, A. (2003). *The Viagra Myth: The surprising impact on love and relationships.* New York: Jossey-Bass.

Moriarty, P. J., Lieber, D., Bennett, A., White, L., Parrella, M., Harvey, P. D., & Davis, K. L. (2001). Gender differences in poor outcome patients with lifelong schizophrenia. *Schizophrenia Bulletin, 27,* 103–113.

Morin, C. M., Bootzin, R. R., Buysse, D. J., Edinger, J. D., Espie, C. A., & Lichstein, K. L. (2006). Psychological and behavioral treatment of insomnia: Update of the recent evidence (1998–2004) *Sleep, 29*(11), 1398–1414.

Morokoff, P. J. (1989). Sex bias and POD. *American Psychologist, 73*–75.

Morris, J. (1995). Dementia and cognitive changes in Huntington's disease. In W. J. Weiner & A. E. Lang (Eds.), *Behavioral neurology of movement disorders. Advances in neurology* (Vol. 65, pp. 187–200). New York: Raven Press.

Morris, J. C. (2012). Revised criteria for mild cognitive impairment may compromise the diagnosis of Alzheimer disease dementia.*Archives of Neurology, 69,* 700–708.

Morrison, J., & Herbstein, J. (1988). Secondary affective disorder in women with somatization disorder. *Comprehensive Psychiatry, 29,* 433–440.

Mosconi, M. W., Cody-Hazlett, H., Poe, M. D., Gerig, G., Gimpel-Smith, R., & Piven, J. (2009).

Moser, C. (2001). Paraphilia: A critique of a confused concept. In P. J. Kleinplatz (Ed.), *New directions in sex therapy: Innovations and alternatives* (pp. 91–108). Philadelphia: Brunner-Routledge.

Moser, C. (2011). Hypersexual disorder: Just more muddled thinking. *Archives of Sexual Behavior, 40,* 227–229.

Moskovitz, R. A. (1996). *Lost in the mirror: An inside look at borderline personality disorder.* Dallas, TX: Taylor Publishing.

Moss, A. C., & Albery, I. P. (2009). A dual-process model of the alcohol-behavior link for social drinking. *Psychological Bulletin, 135,* 516–530.

Moussavi, S., Chatterji, S., Verdes, E., Tandon, A., Patel, V., & Ustun, B. (2007). Depression, chronic diseases, and decrements in health: Results from the World Health Surveys. *Lancet, 370,* 851–858.

MTA Cooperative Group. (1999). A 14-month randomized clinical trial of treatment strategies for attention-deficit/hyperactivity disorder. *Archives of General Psychiatry, 56,* 1073–1086.

Mueser, K. T., & Bellack, A.S. (2007). Social skills training: Alive and well? *Journal of Mental Health, 16,* 549–552.

Jacobson, N. S., Holtzworth-Munroe, A., & Schmaling, K. B. (1989). Marital therapy and spouse involvement in the treatment of depression, agoraphobia, and alcoholism. *Journal of Consulting and Clinical Psychology, 57,* 5–10.

Murphy, B. P., Chung, Y., Park, T., & McGorry, P. D. (2006). Pharmacological treatment of primary negative symptoms in schizophrenia: A systematic review. *Schizophrenia Research, 88,* 5–25.

Murphy, D. (2006). *Psychiatry in the scientific image.* Cambridge, MA: The MIT Press.

Murphy, D. A., Armistead, L., Marelich, W. D., Payne, D. L., & Herbeck, D. M. (2011). Pilot trial of a disclosure intervention for HIV + mothers: The TRACK program. *Journal of Consulting and Clinical Psychology, 79,* 203–214.

Murphy, W. D. (1997). Exhibitionism: Psychopathology and theory. In D. R. Laws & W. T. O'Donohue (Eds.), *Handbook of sexual deviance: Theory and application.* New York: Guilford.

Murphy, W. D., & Page, I. (2008). Exhibitionism: Psychopathology and theory. In D. Laws & W. T. O'Donohue (Eds.), *Sexual deviance: Theory, assessment, and treatment* (2nd ed., pp. 61–75). New York: Guilford Press.

Murray, C. J. L., & Lopez, A. D. (1997). Global mortality, disability, and the contribution of risk factors: Global Burden of Disease Study. *Lancet, 349,* 1436–1442.

Jones, P. B., Bebbington, P., Foerster, A., Lewis, S. W., Murray, R. M., Russell, A., et al. (1993). Premorbid social underachievement in schizophrenia: Results from the Camberwell Collaborative Psychosis Study. *British Journal of Psychiatry, 162,* 65–71.

Murrie, D. C., Boccaccini, M. T., Johnson, J. T., & Janke, C. (2008). Does interrater (dis)agreement on Psychopathy Checklist scores in sexual violent predator trials suggest partisan allegiance in forensic evaluations? *Law and Human Behavior, 32,* 352–362.

Myers, J. E. B. (1983–1984). Involuntary civil commitment of the mentally ill: A system in need of change. *Villanova Law Review, 29,* 367–433.

Myers, T. C., Miltenberger, R. G., & Studa, K. T. (1998). A survey of the use of facilitated communication, in community agencies serving persons with developmental disabilities. *Behavioral Interventions, 13*(3), 135–146.

## N

Najman, J. M., Dunne, M. P., Purdie, D. M., Boyle, F. M., & Coxeter, P. D. (2005). Sexual abuse in childhood and sexual dysfunction in adulthood: An Australian population-based study. *Archives of Sexual Behavior, 34,* 517–526.

Nanni, V., Uher, R., & Danese, A. (2012). Childhood maltreatment predicts unfavorable course of illness and treatment outcome in depression: A meta-analysis. *American Journal of Psychiatry, 169,* 141–151.

Narding, P., & Janzing, J. G. E. (2003). The neuropsychiatric manifestations of Huntington's disease. *Current Opinion in Psychiatry, 16,* 337–340.

Nathan, D. (2012). *Sybil Exposed.* New York: Free Press.

Nathan, P. E. (1993). Alcoholism: Psychopathology, etiology, and treatment. In P. B. Sutker & H. E. Adams (Eds.), *Comprehensive handbook of psychopathology* (2nd ed., pp. 451–476). New York: Plenum.

Nathan, P. E., & Gorman, J. M. (Eds.). (2007). *A guide to treatments that work* (3rd ed.). New York: Oxford.

Nathan, P. E., & Langenbucher, J. (2003). Diagnosis and classification. In G. Stricker, T. A. Widiger, et al. (Eds.), *Handbook of psychology: Clinical psychology* (Vol. 8, pp. 3–26). New York: Wiley.

National Academy of Sciences, Institute of Medicine. (1989). *Research on Children & Adolescents with Mental, Behavioral, and Developmental Disorders.* Washington, DC: National Academy Press.

National Research Council. (2013). *U.S. health in international perspective: Shorter lives, poorer health.* Washington: National Academies Press.

Neale, B. M., et al. (2012). Patterns and rates of exonic *de novo* mutations in autism spectrum disorders. *Nature, 485,* 242–245.

Neimeyer, R. A., & Currier, J. M. (2009). Grief therapy: Evidence of efficacy and emerging directions. *Current Directions in Psychological Science, 18,* 352–356.

Neisser, U., & Harsch, N. (1992). Phantom flashbulbs: False recollections of hearing the news about *Challenger.* In E. Winograd & U. Neisser (Eds.), *Affect and accuracy in recall: Studies of "Flashbulb" memories* (pp. 9–31). New York: Cambridge University Press.

Nemeroff, C. (1998). The neurobiology of depression. *Scientific American, 278,* 42–49.

Neria, Y., & Galea, S. (2007). Post-traumatic stress disorder following disasters: A systematic review. *Psychological Medicine, 28,* 467–480.

Nes, R. B., Røysamb, E., Reichborn-Kjennerud, T., Harris, J. R., & Tambs, K. (2007). Symptoms of anxiety and depression in young adults: Genetic and environmental influences on stability and change. *Twin Research and Human Genetics, 10,* 450–461.

Nesse, R. M. (1999). Proximate and evolutionary studies of anxiety, stress and depression: Synergy at the interface. *Neuroscience and Biobehavioral Reviews, 23,* 895–903.

Neugarten, B. L. (1990). The changing meanings of age. In M. Bergener & S. I. Finkel (Eds.), *Clinical and Scientific Psychogeriatrics: The Holistic Approachs* (pp. 1–6). New York: Springer.

Newcomb, A. F., Bukowski, W. M., & Pattee, L. (1993). Children's peer relations: A meta-analytic review of popular, rejected, neglected, controversial, and average sociometric status. *Psychological Bulletin, 113,* 99–128.

Newcorn, J. H., Kratochvil, C. J., Allen, A. J., Casat, C. D., Ruff, D. D., Moore, R. J., et al. (2008). Atomoxetine/methylphenidate comparative study group: Atomoxetine and osmotically released methylphenidate for the treatment of attention deficit hyperactivity disorder: Acute comparison and differential response. *American Journal of Psychiatry, 165,* 721–730.

Newman, M. G., & Llera, S. J. (2011). A novel theory of experiential avoidance in generalized anxiety disorder: A review and synthesis of research supporting a contrast avoidance model of worry. *Clinical Psychology Review, 31,* 371–382.

Newport, D. J., & Nemeroff, C. B. (2000). Neurobiology of posttraumatic stress disorder. *Cognitive Neuroscience, 10,* 211–218.

Newschaffer, C. J., Falb, M. D., & Gurney, J. G. (2005). National autism prevalence trends from United States special education data. *Pediatrics, 115*(3), e277–e282.

Nichols, D. S. (2006). The trials of separating bath water from baby: A review and creitique of the MPPI-2 restructured clinical scales. *Journal of Personality Assessment, 87,* 121–138.

Nicolai, J., Demmel, R., & Moshagen, M. (2010). The Comprehensive Alcohol Expectancy Questionnaire:

Confirmatory factor analysis, scale refinement, and further validation. *Journal of Personality Assessment, 92,* 400–409.

Nigg, J. T. (2001). Is ADHD a disinhibitory disorder? *Psychological Bulletin, 127,* 571–598.

Nigg, J. T., Blaskey, L. G., Stawicki, J. A., & Sachek, J. (2004). Evaluating the endophenotype model of ADHD neuropsychological deficit: Results for parents and siblings of children with ADHD combined and inattentive subtypes. *Journal of Abnormal Psychology, 113*(4), 614–625.

Nikolas, M. A., & Burt, S. A. (2010). Genetic and environmental influences on ADHD symptom dimensions of inattention and hyperactivity: A meta-analysis. *Journal of Abnormal Psychology, 119,* 1–17.

Nilsson, L. (2003). Memory function in normal aging. *Acta Neurologica Scandinavica, 107,* 7–13.

Ninan, P. T., & Dunlop, B. W. (2005). Neurobiology and etiology of panic disorder. *Journal of Clinical Psychiatry, 66*(Suppl. 4), 3–7.

Nisbett, R. E., & Wilson, T. D. (1977). Telling more than we can know: Verbal reports on mental processes. *Psychological Review, 84,* 231–259.

Nobre, P. J., & Pinto-Gouveia, J. (2006). Dysfuncitonal sexual beliefs as vulnerability factors for sexual dysfunction. *Journal of Sex Research, 43,* 68–75.

Nock M. K. (2013). Prevalence, correlates, and treatment of lifetime suicidal behavior among adolescents. *JAMA Psychiatry,70,* 300–310.

Nock, M. K., & Kessler, R. C. (2006). Prevalence of and risk factors for suicide attempts versus suicide gestures: Analysis of the National Comorbidity Survey. *Journal of Abnormal Psychology, 115,* 616–623.

Nock, M. K., Deming, C. A., Chiu, W., Hwang, I., Angermeyer, M., Borges, G., et al. (2012). Mental disorders, comorbidity, and suicidal behavior. In M. K. Nock, G. Borges, & Y. Ono (Eds.), *Suicide: Global perspectives from the WHO world mental health surveys* (pp. 148–163). New York: Cambridge University Press.

Noel-Storr, A. H., Flicker, L., Ritchie, C. W., Nguyen, G., Gupta, T., Wood, P., et al. (2012). Systematic review of the body of evidence for the use of biomarkers in the diagnosis of dementia. *Alzheimer's & Dementia, 9,* e96–e105.

Nolen-Hoeksema, S. (1990). *Sex differences in depression.* Stanford, CA: Stanford University Press.

Nolen-Hoeksema, S. (1994). An interactive model for the emergence of gender differences in depressive in adolescence. *Journal of Research on Adolescence, 4,* 519–534.

Nolen-Hoeksema, S. (2000). The role of rumination in depressive disorders and mixed anxiety/depressive symptoms. *Journal of Abnormal Psychology, 109,* 504–511.

Norcross, J. C., & Hill, C. E. (2004). Empirically supported therapy relationships. *The Clinical Psychologist, 57,* 19–25.

Nordentoft, M. M., Øhlenschlaeger, J. J., Thorup, A. A., Petersen, L. L., Jeppesen, P., & Bertelsan, M. M. (2010). Deinstitutionalization revisited: A 5-year follow-up of a randomized clinical trial of hospital-based rehabilitation versus specialized assertive intervention (OPUS) versus standard treatment for patients with first-episode schizophrenia spectrum disorders. *Psychological Medicine, 40,* 1619–1626.

Norris, F. H., Murphy, A. D., Baker, C. K., Perilla, J. L., Rodriguez, F. G., & Rodriguez, J. J. (2003). Epidemiology of trauma and posttraumatic stress disorder in Mexico. *Journal of Abnormal Psychology, 112,* 646–656.

Nunes, E. V., Frank, K. A., & Kornfeld, J. (1987). Psychologic treatment for the type a behavior pattern and for coronary heart disease: A meta-analysis of the literature. *Psychosomatic Medicine, 48,* 159–173.

## O

O'Behan, C., Kennelly, B., & O'Callaghan, E. (2008). The economic cost of schizophrenia in Ireland: A cost of illness study.*Irish Journal of Psychological Medicine, 25*(3), 80–87.

O'Brien, C. P., & McKay, J. (2002). Pharmacological treatments for substance use disorders. In P. E. Nathan &

J. M. Gorman (Eds.), *A guide to treatments that work* (2nd ed., pp. 125–156). London: Oxford University Press.

O'Connor, D. W. (2006). Do older Australians truly have low rates of anxiety and depression? A critique of the 1997 National Survey of Mental Health and Well-being. *Australian and New Zealand Journal of Psychiatry, 40,* 623–631.

O'Donohue, W. T., Swingen, D. N., Dopke, C. A., & Regev, L. G. (1999). Psychotherapy for male sexual dysfunction: A review.*Clinical Psychology Review, 19,* 591–630.

O'Donohue, W., & Bradley, A. R. (1999). Conceptual and empirical issues in child custody evaluations. *Clinical Psychology: Sciences and Practice, 6,* 310–322.

O'Donovan, M. C., Williams, N. M., & Owen, M. J. (2003). Recent advances in the genetics of schizophrenia. *Human Molecular Genetics, 12*(Spec. no 2), R125–133.

O'Driscoll, G. A., & Callahan, B. L. (2008). Smooth pursuit in schizophrenia: A meta-analytic review of research since 1993.*Brain and Cognition, 68,* 359–370.

Oltmanns, T. F., & Balsis, S. (2011). Personality disorders in later life: Questions about the measurement, course, and impact of disorders. *Annual Review of Clinical Psychology, 7,* 321–349.

O'Roak, B. J., et al., (2012). Sporadic autism exomes reveal a highly interconnected protein network of *de novo* mutations. *Nature, 485,* 246–250.

Oberman, L. M., & Ramachandran, V. S. (2007). The simulating social mind: The role of the mirror neuron system and simulation in the social and communicative deficits of autism spectrum disorders. *Psychological Bulletin, 133,* 310–327.

Oei, T. P. S., Lim, B., & Hennessy, B. (1990). Psychological dysfunction in battle: Combat stress reactions and post-traumatic stress disorder. *Clinical Psychology Review, 10,* 355–388.

Office of Special Education Programs. (2003). *Implementation of the Individuals with Disabilities Act: 25th Annual Report to Congress.* Washington, DC: U.S. Office of Education.

Offit, P. (2010). *Autism's false prophets.* New York: Columbia University Press.

Offit, P. A. (2008). Vaccines and Autism revisited—The Hannah Poling case. *New England Journal of Medicine, 358,* 2089–2091.

Ogden, C. L., Carroll, M. D., Curtin, L. R., McDowell, M. A., Tabak, C. J., & Flegal, K. M. (2006). Prevalence of overweight and obesity in the United States, 1999–2004. *JAMA, 295,* 1549–1555.

Öhman, A. (1996). Preferential preattentive processing of threat in anxiety: Preparedness and attentional biases. In R. M. Rapee (Ed.), *Current controversies in the anxiety disorders* (pp. 253–290). New York: Guilford.

Öhman, A., & Mineka, S. (2001). Fears, phobias, and preparedness: Toward an evolved module of fear and fear learning. *Psychological Review, 108,* 483–522.

Öhman, A., & Mineka, S. (2003): The malicious serpent: Snakes as a prototypical stimulus for an evolved module of fear. *Current Directions in Psychological Science, 12,* 5–9.

Okrent, D. (2010). *Last call: The rise and fall of prohibition.* New York: Scribner.

Olfson, M., & Marcus, S. C. (2009). National patterns in antidepressant medication treatment. *Archives of General Psychiatry, 66,* 848–856.

Olfson, M., Marcus, S. C., & Druss, B. G. (2008). Effects of food and drug administration warnings on antidepressant use in a national sample. *Archives of General Psychiatry, 65,* 94–101.

Olsson, S., & Moller, A. R. (2003). On the incidence and sex ratio of transsexualism in Sweden, 1972-2002. *Archives of Sexual Behavior, 32,* 381–386.

Oltmanns, T. F. (1988). Defining delusional beliefs. In T. F. Oltmanns & B. A. Maher (Eds.), *Delusional beliefs.* New York: Wiley.

Oltmanns, T. F., & Powers, A. D. (2012). Knowing our pathology. In S. Vazire, T. D. Wilson (Eds.), *Handbook of self-knowledge* (pp. 258–273). New York: Guilford Press.

Oltmanns, T. F., & Turkheimer, E. (2009). Person perception and personality pathology. *Current Directions in Psychological Science, 18,* 32–36.

Olvera, R. L. (2002). Intermittent explosive disorder: Epidemiology, diagnosis and management. *CNS Drugs, 16,* 517–526.

Olweus, D. (1984). Aggressors and their victims: Bullying at school. In N. Frude & H. Gault (Eds.), *Disruptive Behavior in Schools* (pp. 57–76). New York: Wiley.

Ong, A. D. (2010). Pathways linking positive emotion and health in later life. *Current Directions in Psychological Science, 19,* 358–362.

Orne, M. T., Dingers, D. F., & Orne, E. C. (1984). On the differential diagnosis of multiple personality in the forensic context.*International Journal of Clinical and Experimental Hypnosis, 32,* 118–169.

Orth, U., & Wieland, E. (2006). Anger, hostility, and post-traumatic stress disorder in trauma-exposed adults: A meta-analysis.*Journal of Consulting and Clinical Psychology, 74,* 698–706.

Öst, L. (2008). Efficacy of the third wave of behavioral therapies: A systematic review and meta-analysis. *Behaviour Research and Therapy, 46,* 296–321.

Osterling, J. A., Dawson, G., & Munson, J. A. (2002). Early recognition of 1-year-old infants with autism spectrum disorder versus mental retardation. *Development and Psychopathology, 14,* 239–251.

Otto, J. W., Smits, J. A. J., & Reese, H. E. (2004). Cognitive-behavioral therapy for the treatment of anxiety disorders.*Journal of Clinical Psychiatry, 65*(Suppl. 5), 34–41.

Otto, J. W., Smits, J. A. J., & Reese, H. E. (2005). Combined psychotherapy and pharmacotherapy for mood and anxiety disorders in adults: Review and analysis. *Clinical Psychology: Science and Practice, 12,* 72–86.

Otto, M. W., Wilhelm, S., Cohen, L. S., Harlow, B. L. (2001). Prevalence of body dysmorphic disorder in a community sample of women. *American Journal of Psychiatry, 158,* 2061–2063.

Owen, M. J., Craddock, N., & O'Donovan, M. C. (2010). Suggestion of roles for both common and rare risk variants in genome-wide studies of schizophrenia. *Archives of General Psychiatry, 67,* 667–673.

Owen, P. R., & Laurel-Seller, E. (2000). Weight and shape ideals: Thin is dangerously in. *Journal of Applied Social Psychology, 30,* 979–990.

Owens, J. S., Goldfine, M. E., Evangelista, N. M., Hoza, B., & Kaiser, N. M. (2007). A critical review of self-perceptions and the positive illusory bias in children with ADHD. *Clinical Child and Family Psychology Review, 10,* 335–351.

Ozer, E. J., & Weiss, D. S. (2004). Who develops posttraumatic stress disorder? *Current Directions in Psychological Science, 13,* 169–172.

Ozer, E. J., Best, S. R., Lipsey, T. L., & Weiss, D. S. (2003). Predictors of posttraumatic stress disorder and symptoms in adults: A meta-analysis. *Psychological Bulletin, 129,* 52–73.

Ozonoff, S., et al. (2011). Recurrence risk for autism spectrum disorders: A baby siblings research consortium study. *Pediatrics, 128,* 488–495.

## P

Paap, M. S., Kreukels, B. C., Cohen-Kettenis, P. T., Richter-Appelt, H., de Cuypere, G., & Haraldsen, I. R. (2011). Assessing the utility of diagnostic criteria: A multisite study on gender identity disorder. *Journal of Sexual Medicine, 8,* 180–190.

Padilla, A. M. (2001). Issues in culturally appropriate assessment. In L. A. Suzuki, J. G. Ponterotto, & P. J. Metter (Eds.),*Handbook of multicultural assessment: Clinical psychological and educational applications* (2nd ed.). San Francisco: Jossey-Bass.

Paikoff, R. L., & Brooks-Gunn, J. (1991). Do parent-child relationships change during puberty? *Psychological Bulletin, 110,* 47–66.

Pallanti, S., & Sandner, C. (2007). Treatment of depression with selective serotonin inhibitors: The role of fluvoxamine.*International Journal of Psychiatry in Clinical Practice, 11,* 233–238.

Pally, R. (2002). The neurobiology of borderline personality disorder: The synergy of "nature and nurture." *Journal of Psychiatric Practice, 8,* 133–142.

Palmer, R. L. (1995). Sexual abuse and eating disorders. In K. D. Brownell & C. G. Fairburn (Eds.), *Eating disorders and obesity: A comprehensive handbook* (pp. 230–233). New York: Guilford.

Panksepp, J. (2005). Why does separation distress hurt? Comment on MacDonald and Leary. *Psychological Bulletin, 131,* 224–230.

Panksepp, J., & Biven, L. (2012). *The archaeology of the mind: Neuroevolutionary origins of human emotions.* New York: Norton.

Panksepp, J., & Sahley, T. L. (1987). Neurobiological issues in autism. In E. Schopler & G. B. Mesibov, Gary B. (Eds.), Current issues in autism (pp. 357–372). New York: Plenum Press.

Pantle, M., Pasewark, R., & Steadman, H. (1980). Comparing institutionalization periods and subsequent arrests of insanity acquittees and convicted felons. *Journal of Psychiatry and the Law, 8,* 305–316.

Pardo, C. A., & Eberhart, C. G. (2007). The neurobiology of autism. *Brain Pathology, 17,* 434–447.

Pargament, K. I., & Park, C. L. (1995). Merely a defense? The variety of religious means and ends. *Journal of Social Issues, 51,* 13–32.

Paris, J. (2003). Personality disorders over time: Precursors, course and outcome. *Journal of Personality Disorders, 17,* 479–488.

Park, C. L. (2010). Making sense of the meaning literature: An integrative review of meaning making and its effects on adjustment to stressful life events. *Psychological Bulletin, 136,* 257–301.

Parker, G., Fink, M., Shorter, E., Taylor, M., Akiskal, H., Berrios, G., et al. (2010). Issues for DSM-5: Whither melancholia? The case for its classification as a distinct mood disorder. *American Journal of Psychiatry, 167,* 745–747.

Parker, G., Roussos, J., Mitchell, P., Wilhelm, K., Austin, M. P., Hadzi-Pavlovic, D. (1997). Distinguishing psychotic depression from melancholia. *Journal of Affective Disorders, 42,* 155–167.

Parks, F. M. (2003). The role of African American folk beliefs in the modern therapeutic process. *Clinical Psychology: Science and Practice, 10,* 456–467.

Pascual-Leone, A., & Greenberg, L. S. (2007). Emotional processing in experiential therapy: Why "the only way is through."*Journal of Consulting and Clinical Psychology, 75,* 875–887.

Pasupathi, M., Carstensen, L. L., & Tsai, J. L. (1995). Ageism in interpersonal settings. In B. Lott & D. Maluso (Eds.), *The Social Psychology of Interpersonal Discrimination* (pp. 160–182). New York: Guilford.

Patrick, C. J., & Zempolich, K. A. (1998). Emotion and aggression in the psychopathic personality. *Aggression and Violent Behavior, 3,* 303–338.

Patterson, C. J., Kupersmidt, J. B., & Griesler, P. C. (1990). Children's perceptions of self and of relationships with others as a function of sociometric status. *Child Development, 61,* 1335–1349.

Patterson, C. M., & Newman, J. P. (1993). Reflectivity and learning from aversive events: Toward a psychological mechanism for the syndromes of disinhibition. *Psychological Review, 100,* 716–736.

Patterson, G. R., DeBaryshe, B. D., & Ramsey, E. (1989). A developmental perspective on antisocial behavior. *American Psychologist, 44,* 329–335.

Patterson, G.R. (1982). *Coercive Family Process.* Eugene, OR: Castalia.

Patterson, D. R. (2004). Treating pain with hypnosis. *Current Directions in Psychological Science, 13,* 252–255.

Patton, J. R., Beirne-Smith, M., & Payne, J. S. (1990). *Mental retardation* (3rd ed.). Columbus, OH: Merrill.

Paul, G. L., & Lentz, R. J. (1977). *Psychosocial treatment of chronic mental patients: Milieu versus social-learning programs.* Cambridge, MA: Harvard University Press.

Paul, R., Garrett, K., & Cohen, R. (2003). Vascular dementia: A diagnostic conundrum for the clinical neuropsychologist. *Applied Neuropsychology, 10,* 129–136.

Pauli, P., & Alpers, G. W. (2002). Memory bias in patients with hypochondriasis and somatoform pain disorder. *Journal of Psychosomatic Research, 52,* 45–53.

Pavlov, I. P. (1928). Experimental psychology and psychopathology in animals. In I. P. Pavlov & W. H. Gantt (Trans.), *Lectures on conditioned reflexes: Twenty-five years of objective study of the higher nervous activity (behaviour) of animals.* (pp. 47–60). New York, NY: Liverwright Publishing Corporation. doi: 10.1037/11081-001

Pedersen, N. L., Gatz, M., Berg, S., & Johansson, B. (2004). How heritable is Alzheimer's disease late in life? Findings from Swedish twins. *Annals of Neurology, 55,* 180–185.

Pelham, W. E., et al. (1985). Methylphenidate and children with attention deficit disorder: Dose effects on classroom academic and social behavior. *Archives of General Psychiatry, 42,* 948–952.

Pelham, W. E., et al. (2002). Effects of methylphenidate and expectancy on children with ADHD: Behavior, academic performance, and attributions in a summer treatment program and regular classroom settings. *Journal of Consulting and Clinical Psychology, 70,* 320–335.

Penn, D., Waldheter, E., Perkins, D., Mueser, K., & Lieberman, J. (2005). Psychosocial treatment for first-episode psychosis: A research update. *American Journal of Psychiatry, 162,* 2220–2232.

Perkins, D., Miller-Andersen, L., & Lieberman, J. (2006). Natural history and predictors of clinical course. In *The American psychiatric publishing textbook of schizophrenia* (pp. 289–301). Arlington, VA: American Psychiatric Publishing.

Pertusa, A., Frost, R. O., Fullana, M. A., Samuels, J., Steketee, G., Tolin, D., et al. (2010). Refining the diagnostic boundaries of compulsive hoarding: A critical review. *Clinical Psychology Review, 30,* 371–386.

Pescosolido, B., Monahan, J., Link, B. G., Stueve, A., & Kikuzawa, S. (1999). The public's view of the competence, dangerousness, and need for legal coercion among persons with mental illness. *American Journal of Public Health, 89,* 1339–1345.

Peters, K. D., Kochanek, K. D., & Murphy, S. L. (1998). Deaths: Final data for 1996. *National Vital Statistics Reports, 47*(9). Hyattsville, MD: National Center for Health Statistics.

Petrie, K. J., & Weinman, J. (2012). Patients' perceptions of their illness: The dynamo of volition in health care. *Current Directions in Psychological Science, 21,* 60–65.

Petry, N. M. (2006). Should the scope of addictive behaviors be broadened to include pathological gambling? *Addiction, 101*(Suppl. 1), 152–160

Pfohl, B., Blum, N., & Zimmerman, M. (1995). *Structured interview for DSM-IV personality (SIDP-IV).* Iowa City: University of Iowa.

Phelan, J. C., & Link, B. G. (1999). The labeling theory of mental disorder (I): The role of social contingencies in the application of psychiatric labels. In A. V. Horwitz & T. L. Scheid (Eds.), *A handbook for the study of mental health: Social contexts, theories, and systems* (pp. 139–150). New York: Cambridge University Press.

Phillips, E. L., Phillips, E. A., Fixsen, D. L., & Wolf, M. M. (1973). Behavior shaping works for delinquents. *Psychology Today, 7*(1), 74–79.

Phillips, J. (2013). Conceptual issues in the classification of psychosis. *Current Opinion in Psychiatry, 26,* 214–218.

Phillips, J., Frances, A., Cerullo, M. A., Chardavoyne, J., Decker, H. S., First, M. B., & Zachar, P. (2012). The six most essential questions in psychiatric diagnosis: A pluralogue part 1: Conceptual and definitional issues in psychiatric diagnosis.*Philosophy, Ethics, and Humanities in Medicine, 7,* 1–29.

Phillips, K. A. (1991). Body dysmorphic disorder: The distress of imagined ugliness. *American Journal of Psychiatry, 148,* 1138–1149.

Phillips, K. A., Albertini, R. S., & Rasmussen, S. A. (2002). A randomized placebo-controlled trial of fluoxetine in body dysmorphic disorder. *Archives of General Psychiatry, 59,* 381–388.

Phillips, K. A., Wilhelm, S., Koran, L. M., Didie, E. R., Fallon, B. A., Feusner, J., et al. (2010). Body dysmorphic disorder: Some key issues for DSM-V. *Depression and Anxiety, 27,* 573–591.

Phillips, N. K., Hammen, C. L., Brennan, P. A., Najman, J. M., & Bor, W. (2005). Early adversity and the prospective prediction of depressive and anxiety disorders in adolescents. *Journal of Abnormal Child Psychology, 33,* 13–24.

Pilling, S., Bebbington, P., Kuipers, E., Garety, P., Geddes, J., Orbach, G., & Morgan, C. (2002). Psychological treatments in schizophrenia: II. Meta-analyses of family intervention and cognitive behavior therapy. *Psychological Medicine, 32,* 763–782.

Pina, A. A., Zerr, A. A., Gonzales, N. A., & Ortiz, C. D. (2009). Psychosocial interventions for school refusal behavior in children and adolescents. *Child Development Perspectives, 3,* 11–20.

Pincus, T., & Morley, S. (2001). Cognitive-processing bias in chronic pain: A review and integration. *Psychological Bulletin, 127,* 599–617.

Pinheiro, A. P., et al., (2007). Patterns of menstrual disturbance in eating disorders. *International Journal of Eating Disorders, 40,* 424–434.

Pinheiro, A. P., Thornton, L. M., Plotonicov, K. H., Tozzi, F., Klump, K. L., Berrettini, W. H., et al. (2007). Patterns of menstrual disturbance in eating disorders. *International Journal of Eating Disorders, 40,* 424–434.

Pinker, S. (1997). *How the mind works.* New York: Norton.

Pintar, J., & Lynn, S. J. (2008). *A brief history of hypnosis.* New York: Wiley-Blackwell.

Pinto, C., Dhavale, H. S., Nair, S., Patil, B., & Dewan, M. (2000). Borderline personality disorder exists in India. *Journal of Nervous and Mental Disease, 188,* 386–388.

Piper, A., & Merskey, H. (2004a). The persistence of folly: A critical examination of dissociative identity disorder. Part I. The excesses of an improbable concept. *Canadian Journal of Psychiatry, 49,* 592–600.

Piper, A., & Merskey, H. (2004b). The persistence of folly: A critical examination of dissociative identity disorder. Part II. The defence and decline of multiple personality or dissociative identity disorder. *Canadian Journal of Psychiatry, 49,* 678–683.

Plassman, B. L., & Breitner, J. C. S. (1997). The genetics of dementia in late life. *Psychiatric Clinics of North America, 20,* 59–76.

Plomin, R., DeFries, J. C., McClearn, G. E., & McGuffin, P. (2008). *Behavioral genetics* (5th ed.). New York: Worth.

Pogue-Geile, M., & Gottesman, I. (2007). Schizophrenia: Study of a genetically complex phenotype. In *Neurobehavioral genetics: Methods and applications* (2nd ed., pp. 209–226). Boca Raton, FL: CRC Press.

Pohl, J., Olmstead, M. C., Wynne-Edwards, K. E., Harkness, K., & Menard, J. L. (2007). Repeated exposure to stress across the childhood-adolescent period alters rats' anxiety and depression-like behaviors in adulthood. *Behavioral Neuroscience, 121,* 462–474.

Pokony, A. (1983). Prediction of suicide in psychiatric patients: A prospective study. *Archives of General Psychiatry, 40,* 249–257.

Pole, N. (2007). The psychopathology of posttraumatic stress disorder: A meta-analysis. *Psychological Bulletin, 133,* 725–749.

Pole, N., Gone, J. P., & Kulkarni, M. (2008). Posttraumatic stress disorder among ethnoracial minorities in the United States.*Clinical Psychology: Science and Practice, 15,* 35–61.

Polivy, J., & Herman, C. P. (2002). Causes of eating disorders. *Annual Review of Psychology, 53,* 187–213.

Pollak, S. D., & Tolley-Schell, S. A. (2003). Selective attention to facial emotion in physically abused children. *Journal of Abnormal Psychology, 112*(3), 323–338.

Polleux, F., & Lauder, J. M. (2004). Toward a developmental neurobiology of autism. *Mental Retardation and Developmental Disabilities Research Reviews, 10,* 303–317.

Poole, D. A., Lindsay, D. S., Memon, A., & Bull, R. (1995). Psychotherapy and the recovery of memories of childhood sexual abuse: U.S. and British practitioners' opinions, practices, and experiences. *Journal of Consulting and Clinical Psychology, 63,* 426–437.

Pope, H. G., Poliakoff, M. B., Parker, M. P., Boynes, M., & Hudson, J. I. (2007). Is dissociative amnesia a culture-bound syndrome? Findings from a survey of historical literature. *Psychological Medicine, 37,* 225–233.

Pope, H. R., & Yurgelun-Todd, D. (2004). Residual cognitive effects of long-term cannabis use. In D. Castle, R. Murray (Eds.),*Marijuana and madness: Psychiatry and neurobiology* (pp. 198–210). New York, NY: Cambridge University Press.

Posner, M. I., & DiGirolamo, G. J. (2000). Cognitive neuroscience: Origins and promise. *Psychological Bulletin, 126,* 873.

Poulton, R., & Menzies, R. G. (2002). Non-associative fear acquisition: A review of the evidence from retrospective and longitudinal research. *Behaviour Research and Therapy, 40,* 127–149.

Powell, L. H., Shahabi, L., & Thoresen, C. E. (2003). Religion and spirituality: Linkages to physical health. *American Psychologist, 58*(1), 36–52.

Prata, D. P., Mechelli, A., Fu, C. Y., Picchioni, M., Toulopoulou, T., Bramon, E., et al. (2009). Epistasis between the DAT 3' UTR VNTR and the COMT val-158met SNP on cortical function in healthy subjects and patients with schizophrenia. *Proceedings of the National Academy of Sciences, 106,* 13600–13605.

Prentky, R. A. (1997). Arousal reduction in sexual offenders: A review of antiandrogen interventions. *Sexual Abuse: Journal of Research and Treatment, 9,* 335–347.

Prentky, R., Lee, A., Knight, R., & Cerce, D. (1997). Recidivism rates among child molesters and rapists: A methodological analysis. *Law and Human Behavior, 21,* 635–659.

Presnell, K. & Stice, E. (2003). An experimental test of the effect of weight-loss dieting on bulimic pathology: Tipping the scales in a different direction. *Journal of Abnormal Psychology, 112,* 166–170.

Presta, S., Marazziti, D., Dell'Osso, L., Pfanner, C., Pallanti, S., & Cassano, G. B. (2002). Kleptomania: Clinical features and comorbidity in an Italian sample. *Comprehensive Psychiatry, 43,* 7–12.

Price, G., Cercignani, M., Bagary, M., Barnes, T., Barker, G., Joyce, E., & Ron, M. A. (2006). A volumetric MRI and magnetization transfer imaging follow-up study of patients with first-episode schizophrenia. *Schizophrenia Research, 87,* 100–108.

Price, J. S., Gardner, R., Jr., & Erickson, M. (2004). Can depression, anxiety and somatization be understood as appeasement displays? *Journal of Affective Disorders, 79,* 1–11.

Prigerson, H. G., Maciejewski, P. K., & Rosenbeck, R. A. (2002). Population attributable fractions of psychiatric disorders and behavioral outcomes associated with combat exposure among U.S. men. *American Journal of Public Health, 92,* 59–63.

Prince, M., Acosta, D., Chiu, H., Scazufca, M., & Varghese, M. (2003). Dementia diagnosis in developing countries: A cross-cultural validation study. *Lancet, 361,* 909–917.

Prince, M., Bryce, R., Albanese, E., Wimo, A., Ribeiro, W., & Ferri, C. P. (2013). The global prevalence of dementia: A systematic review and metaanalysis. *Alzheimer's & Dementia, 9,* 63–75.

Prior, M., & Ozonoff, S. (2007). Psychological factors in autism. In F. R. Volkmar (Ed.), *Autism and pervasive developmental disorders* (pp. 69–128). New York: Cambridge University Press.

Prochaska, J. O., & Norcross, J. C. (2006). *Systems of psychotherapy: A transtheoretical analysis.* Belmont, CA: Wadsworth.

Pryse-Phillips, W. (1999). Do we have drugs for dementia? *Archives of Neurology, 56,* 735–737.

Purdon, C. (2004). Empirical investigations of thought suppression in OCD. *Journal of Behavior Therapy & Experimental Psychiatry, 35,* 121–136.

Puzzanchera, C., Adams, B., & Sickmund, M. (2010). *Juvenile court statistics 2006-2007.* Pittsburgh, PA: National Center for Juvenile Justice.

## Q

Quadagno, D., Sly, D. F., Harrison, D. F., Eberstein, I. W., & Soler, H. R. (1998). Ethnic differences in sexual decisions and sexual behavior. *Archives of Sexual Behavior, 27,* 57–75.

Quigley, H., Colloby, S. J., & O'Brien, J. T. (2011). PET imaging of brain amyloid in dementia: A review. *International Journal of Geriatric Psychiatry, 26,* 991–999.

## R

Rachman, S. (1991). *Fear and courage* (2nd ed.). San Francisco: Freeman.

Rachman, S. (2002). *Anxiety* (2nd ed.). New York: Psychology Press (Taylor and Francis Group).

Rachman, S., & de Silva, P. (1978). Abnormal and normal obsessions. *Behaviour Research and Therapy, 16,* 233–248.

Racine, S. E., Burt, S. A., Iacono, W. G., McGue, M., & Klump, K. L. (2011). Dietary restraint moderates genetic risk for binge eating. *Journal of Abnormal Psychology, 120,* 119–128.

Radel, M., Vallejo, R. L., Iwata, N., Aragon, R., Long, J. C., Virkkunen, M., et al. (2005). Haplotype-based localization of an alcohol dependence gene to the 5q34 gamma-aminobutyric acid type A gene cluster. *Archives of General Psychiatry, 62,* 47–55.

Rahkonen, T., Eloniemi-Sulkava, U. U., Rissanen, S. S., Vatanen, A. A., Viramo, P. P., & Sulkava, R. R. (2003). Dementia with Lewy bodies according to the consensus criteria in a general population aged 75 years or older. *Journal of Neurology, Neurosurgery & Psychiatry, 74,* 720–724.

Raichle, M. E. (2001). Bold insights. *Nature, 412,* 128–130.

Rakow, A., et al. (2011). Use of parental guilt induction among depressed parents. *Journal of Family Psychology, 25,* 147–151.

Ramey, C. T., & Bryant, D. (1982). Evidence for primary prevention of developmental retardation. *Journal of the Division of Early Childhood, 5,* 73–78.

Ramsawh, H. J., Raffa, S. D., Edelen, M., Rende, R. R., & Keller, M. B. (2009). Anxiety in middle adulthood: Effects of age and time on the 14-year course of panic disorder, social phobia, and generalized anxiety disorder. *Psychological Medicine, 39,* 615–624.

Rapee, R. M., et al. (2005). Prevention and early intervention of anxiety disorders in inhibited preschool children. *Journal of Consulting and Clinical Psychology, 73,* 488–497.

Raphael, B., Wilson, J., Meldrum L., & McFarlane, A. C. (1996). Acute preventive interventions. In B. A. van der Kolk, A. C. McFarlane, & L. Weisaeth (Eds.), *Traumatic stress* (pp. 463–479). New York: Guilford.

Rapoport, J. L., Buchsbaum, M. S., Zahn, T. P., Weingartner, H., Ludlow, C., & Mikkelsen, E. J. (1978). Dextroamphetamine: Cognitive and behavioral effects in normal prepubertal boys. *Science, 199,* 560–563.

Rapoport, J., & Swedo, S. (2002). Obsessive-compulsive disorders. In M. Rutier & E. Taylor (Eds.), *Child and Adolescent Psychiatry* (4th ed., pp. 571–592). Oxford, England: Blackwell.

Raskind, M. A. (1998). The clinical interface of depression and dementia. *Journal of Clinical Psychiatry, 59*(Suppl. 10), 9–12.

Raskind, M. A., & Peskind, E. R. (1997). Neurotransmitter abnormalities and the psychopharmacology of Alzheimer's disease. In L. Heston (Ed.), *Progress in Alzheimer's disease and similar conditions (pp. 245–257).* Washington, DC: American Psychiatric Press.

Rasmussen, C., & Bisanz, J. (2009). Exploring mathematics difficulties in children with fetal alcohol spectrum disorders.*Child Development Perspectives, 3,* 125–130.

Rastam, M., Gillberg, C., & Gillberg, C. (1995). Anorexia nervosa 6 years after onset. Part II. Cormorbid psychiatric problems.*Comprehensive Psychiatry, 36,* 70–76.

Rathod, S., & Turkington, D. (2005). Cognitive-behaviour therapy for schizophrenia: A review. *Current Opinion in Psychiatry, 18,* 159–163.

Ratliff, K. A., & Nosek, B. A. (2010). Creating distinct implicit and explicit attitudes with an illusory correlation paradigm.*Journal of Experimental Social Psychology, 46,* 721–728.

Ratner, C., & Hui, L. (2003). Theoretical and methodological problems in cross-cultural psychology. *Journal for the Theory of Social Behaviour, 33,* 67–94.

Regier, D. A., Narrow, W. E., Clarke, D. E., Kraemer, H. C., Kuramoto, S., Kuhl, E. A., et al. (2013). DSM-5 field trials in the United States and Canada, part II: Test-retest reliability of selected categorical diagnoses. *American Journal of Psychiatry, 170,* 59–70.

Rehm, J., Mathers, C., Popova, S., Thavorncharoensap, M., Teerawattananon, Y., & Patra, J. (2009). Global burden of disease and injury and economic cost attributable to alcohol use and alcohol-use disorders. *The Lancet, 373,* 2223–2233.

Reichenberg, A., & Harvey, P. D. (2007). Neuropsychological impairments in schizophrenia: Integration of performance-based and brain imaging findings. *Psychological Bulletin, 133*(5), 833–858.

Reid, R. C., Carpenter, B. N., Hook, J. N., Garos, S., Manning, J. C., Gilliland, R., et al. (2012). Report of findings in a DSM-5 field trial for hypersexual disorder. *Journal of Sexual Medicine, 9,* 2868–2877.

Reinares, M., Rosa, A. R., Franco, C., Goikolea, J., Fountoulakis, K., Siamouli, M., et al. (2013). A systematic review on the role of anticonvulsants in the treatment of acute bipolar depression. *International Journal of Neuropsychopharmacology, 16,* 485–496.

Reinecke, M. A., Curry, J. F., & March, J. S. (2009). Findings from the Treatment for Adolescents with Depression Study (TADS): What have we learned? What do we need to know? *Journal of Clinical Child & Adolescent Psychology, 38,* 761–767.

Reis, H. T., Collins, W. A., & Berscheid, E. (2000). The relationship context of human behavior and development. *Psychological Bulletin, 6,* 844–872.

Reissing, E. D., Binik, Y. M., Khalife, S., Cohen, D., & Amsel, R. (2004). Vaginal spasm, pain, and behavior: An empirical investigation of the diagnosis of vaginismus. *Archives of Sexual Behavior, 33,* 5–17.

Rekhborn-Kjennerud, T. T., Czajkowski, N. N., Røysamb, E. E., Ørstavik, R. E., Neale, M. C., Torgersen, S. S., & Kendler, K. S. (2010). Major depression and dimensional representations of DSM-IV personality disorders: A population-based twin study.*Psychological Medicine, 40,* 1475–1484.

Remington, R. (2012). Neurocognitive diagnostic challenges and the DSM-5: Perspectives from the front lines of clinical practice.*Issues in Mental Health Nursing, 33,* 626–629.

Repetti, R. L., Taylor, S. E., & Seeman, T. E. (2002). Risky families. Family social environments and the mental and physical health of offspring. *Psychological Bulletin, 128,* 330–366.

Resick, P. A., Monson, C. M., & Gutner, C. (2007). Psychosocial treatments for PTSD. In M. J. Friedman, T. M. Keane, & P. A. Resick (Eds.), *Handbook of PTSD: Science and practice (330–358).* New York: The Guilford Press.

Resnick, P. A., Williams, L. F., Suvak, M. K., Monson, C. M., & Gradus, J. L. (2012). Long-term outcomes of cognitive-behavioral treatments for posttraumatic stress disorder among female rape survivors. *Journal of Consulting and Clinical Psychology, 80,* 201–210.

Ressler, K. J., & Mayberg, H. S. (2007). Targeting abnormal neural circuits in mood and anxiety disorders: From the laboratory to the clinic. *Nature neuroscience, 10,* 1116–1124.

Reynolds, C. R., & Shaywitz, S. E. (2009). Response to intervention: Prevention and remediation, perhaps. Diagnosis, no. *Child Development Perspectives, 3,* 44–47.

Rhee, S. H., Hewitt, J. K., Young, S. E., Corley, R. P., Crowley, T. J., & Stallings, M. C. (2003). Genetic and environmental influences on substance initiation, use, and problem use in adolescents. *Archives of General Psychiatry, 60,* 1256–1264.

Ricciardelli, L. A., & McCabe, M. P. (2004). A biopsychoso-cial model of disordered eating and the pursuit of muscular-ity in adolescent boys. *Psychological Bulletin, 130,* 179–205.

Richardson, S. (1996). The besieged brain: Immune cells in brain may further progression of Alzheimer's disease. *Discover, 17,* 30–32.

Richelson, E. (1999). Receptor pharmacology of neuroleptics: Relation to clinical effects. *Journal of Clinical Psychiatry, 60*(Suppl. 10), 5–14.

Richmond, K., Carroll, K., & Denboske, K. (2010). Gender identity disorder: Concerns and controversies. In J. C. Chrisler & D. R. McCreary (Eds.), *Handbook of gender research in psychology: Gender research in social and applied psychology* (Vol. 2, pp. 111–131). New York: Springer Science + Business Media.

Richtand, N., Welge, J., Logue, A., Keck, P., Strakowski, S., & McNamara, R. (2007). Dopamine and serotonin receptor binding and antipsychotic efficacy. *Neuropsychopharmacology, 32,* 1715–1726.

Richters, J. E. (1993). Community violence and children's development: Toward a research agenda for the 1990s. *Psychiatry, 56,* 3–6.

Rief, W., Hiller, W., & Margraf, J. (1998). Cognitive aspects of hypochondriasis and the somatization syndrome. *Journal of Abnormal Psychology, 107,* 587–595.

Rietkerk, T., Boks, M., Sommer, I., Liddle, P., Ophoff, R., & Kahn, R. (2008). The genetics of symptom dimensions of schizophrenia: Review and meta-analysis. *Schizophrenia Research, 102,* 197–205.

Rind, B., Tromovitch, P., & Bauserman, R. (1998). A meta-ana-lytic examination of assumed properties of child sexual abuse using college samples. *Psychological Bulletin, 124,* 22–53.

Risch, N., Herrell, R., Lehner, T., Liang, K. Y., Eaves, L., Hoh, J., et al. (2009). Interaction between the serotonin transporter gene (5-HTTLPR), stressful life events, and risk of depression: A meta-analysis. *Journal of the American Medical Association, 301,* 2462–2471.

Ritterband, L. M., Thorndike, F. P., Gonder-Frederick, L. A., Magee, J. C., Bailey, E. T., Saylor, D. K., et al. (2010). Efficacy of an internet-based behavioral intervention for adults with insomnia. In T. Lee-Chiong (Ed.), *Best of sleep medicine 2010: An annual collection of scientific lit-erature* (pp. 89–91). CreateSpace Independent Publishing Platform.

Ro, E., & Clark, L. A. (2009). Psychosocial functioning in the context of diagnosis: Assessment and theoretical issues. *Psychological Assessment, 21,* 313–324.

Roberts, L. J., & Marlatt, G. A. (1999). Harm reduction. In P. J. Ott, R. E. Tarter, & R. T. Ammerman (Eds.), *Sourcebook on substance abuse: Etiology, epidemiology, assess-ment, and treatment* (pp. 389–398). Boston: Allyn & Bacon.

Robins, E., & Guze, S. (1989). Establishment of diagnostic validity in psychiatric illness. In L. N. Robins & J. E. Barrett (Eds.), *The validity of psychiatric diagnosis* (pp. 177–197). New York: Raven Press.

Robins, L. N. (1966). *Deviant children grown up: A sociologi-cal and psychiatric study of sociopathic personality.* Baltimore: Williams & Wilkins.

Robins, L. N., & Regier, D. A. (1991). *Psychiatric disorders in America: The epidemiologic catchment area study.* New York: Free Press.

Robinson, N. M., Zigler, E., & Gallagher, J. J. (2000). Two tails of the normal curve: Similarities and differences in the study of mental retardation and giftedness. *American Psychologist, 55,* 1413–1424.

Robinson, P. (1976). *The modernization of sex: Havelock Ellis, Alfred Kinsey, William Masters and Virginia Johnson.* New York: Harper & Row.

Rocca, W. A., Petersen, R. C., Knopman, D. S., Hebert, L. E., Evans, D. A., Hall, K. S., et al. (2011). Trends in the incidence and prevalence of Alzheimer's disease, dementia, and cognitive impairment in the United States. *Alzheimer's & Dementia, 7,* 80–93.

Rockwood, K., & Middleton, L. (2007). Physical activity and the maintenance of cognitive function. *Alzheimer's & Dementia, 3,* S38–S44.

Rodebaugh, T. L., Gianoli, M., Turkheimer, E., & Oltmanns, T. F. (2010). The interpersonal problems of the socially avoidant: Self and peer shared variance. *Journal of Abnormal Psychology, 119,* 331–340.

Roe, C. M., Fagan, A. M., Grant, E. A., Hassenstab, J., Moulder, K. L., Dreyfus, D., et al. (2013). Amyloid imaging and CSF biomarkers in predicting cognitive impairment up to 7.5 years later. *Neurology, 80,* 1784–1791.

Roelofs, K., Hagenaars, M. A., & Stins, J. (2010). Facing freeze: Social threat induces bodily freeze in humans. *Current Directions in Psychological Science, 21,* 1575–1581.

Rogers, S., Wehner, E. A., & Hagerman, R. (2001). The behavioral phenotype in fragile X: Symptoms of autism in very young children with fragile X syndrome, idiopathic autism, and other developmental. *Journal of Developmental & Behavioral Pediatrics,22,* 409–417.

Rogers, C. R. (1951). *Client-centered therapy.* Boston: Houghton-Mifflin.

Rohrbaugh, M. J., Mehl, M. R., Shoham, V., Reilly, E. S., & Ewy, G. A. (2008). Prognostic significance of spouse we talk in couples coping with heart failure. *Journal of Consulting and Clinical Psychology, 76,* 781–789.

Rohan, K. J., Roecklein, K. A., Lindsey, K. T., Johnson, L. G., Lippy, R. D., Lacy, T. J., et al. (2007). A randomized controlled trial of cognitive-behavioral therapy, light therapy, and their combination for seasonal affective disorder. *Journal of Consulting and Clinical Psychology, 75,* 489–500.

Rohrbaugh, M. J., Shoham, V., Coyne, J. C., Cranford, J. A., Sonnega, J. S., & Nicklas, J. M. (2004). Beyond the "self?" in self-efficacy: Spouse confidence predicts patient survival following heart failure. *Journal of Family Psychology, 18,* 184–193.

Roisman, G. I. (2005). Conceptual clarifications in the study of resilience. *American Psychologist, 60,* 264–265.

Rojas-Fernandez, C. H., Lanctot, K. L., Allen, D. D., & MacKnight, C. (2001). Pharmacotherapy of behavioral and psychological symptoms of dementia: Time for a different paradigm? *Pharmacotherapy, 21,* 74–102.

Roman, G. C. (2002). Vascular dementia revisited: Diagnosis, pathogenesis, treatment, and prevention. *Medical Clinics of North America, 86,* 477–499.

Ronningstam, E., & Gunderson, J. (1991). Differentiating borderline personality disorder from narcissistic personality disorder.*Journal of Personality Disorders, 5,* 225–232.

Room, R. (2007). Cultural and societal influences on substance use diagnoses and criteria. In J. B. Saunders, M. A. Schuckit, P. J. Sirovatka, & D. A. Regier (Eds.), *Diagnostic issues in substance use disorders* (pp. 45–60). Washington,, DC: American Psychiatric Press.

Rosen, J. C., Reiter, J., & Orosan, P. (1995). Cognitive-behavioral body image therapy for body dysmorphic disorder. *Journal of Consulting and Clinical Psychology, 63,* 263–269.

Rosen, R. C. (2000). Medical and psychological interventions for erectile dysfunction: Toward a combined treatment approach.*In Principles and Practice of Sex Therapy,* pp. 276–304.

Rosen, R. C., & Leiblum, S. R. (1995). Treatment of sexual disorders in the 1990s: An integrated approach. *Journal of Consulting and Clinical Psychology, 63,* 877–890.

Rosen, R. C., Weigel, M., & Gendrano, N. (2007). Sexual dysfunction, sexual psychophysiology, and psychophar-macology: Laboratory studies in men and women. In E. Janssen (Ed.), *The psychophysiology of sex* (pp. 381–409). Bloomington: Indiana University Press.

Rosenfeld, B. (2004). *Assisted Suicide and the Right to Die.* Washington, DC: American Psychological Association.

Rosenhan, D. L. (1973). On being sane in insane places. *Science, 179*(4070), 250–258.

Rosler, A., & Witztum, E. (1998). Treatment of men with paraphilia with a long-acting analogue of gonadotropin-releasing hormone.*New England Journal of Medicine, 338,* 416–422.

Ross, C. A. (1991). Epidemiology of multiple personality dis-order and dissociation. *Psychiatric Clinics of North America, 14,* 503–516.

Ross, C. A. (2009). Errors of logic and scholarship concerning dissociative identity disorder. *Journal of Child Sexual Abuse, 18,* 221–231.

Ross, C. A., & Tabrizi, S. J. (2011). Huntington's disease: From molecular pathogenesis to clinical treatment. *The Lancet Neurology, 10,* 83–98.

Ross, C. A., Duffy, C. M., & Ellason, J. W. (2002). Prevalence, reliability, and validity of dissociative disorders in an inpatient setting. *Journal of Trauma and Dissociation, 3,* 7–17.

Roth, D., & Bean, J. (1986). New perspectives on homeless-ness: Findings from a statewide epidemiological study. *Hospital and Community Psychiatry, 37,* 712–723.

Roth, W. T., Wilhelm, F. H., & Pettit, D. (2005). Are cur-rent theories of panic falsifiable? *Psychological Bulletin, 131,* 171–192.

Rousseau, G. (2009). "Splitters and lumpers": Samuel Johnson's tics, gesticulations and reverie revisited. *History of Psychiatry, 20,* 72–86.

Roy-Byrne, P. P., & Cowley, D. S. (2002). Pharmacological treatments for panic disorder, generalized anxiety disorder, specific phobia, and social anxiety disorder. In P. E. Nathan & J. M. Gorman (Eds.), *A guide to treatments that work* (2nd ed., pp. 337–365). London: Oxford University Press.

Rozanski, A., Blumenthal, J. A., & Kaplan, J. (1999). Impact of psychological factors on the pathogenesis of cardiovas-cular disease and implications for therapy. *Circulation, 99,* 2192–2217.

Rubio, G., & Lopez-Ibor, J. J. (2007). Generalized anxiety disorder: A 40-year follow-up study. *Acta Psychiatrica Scandinavica, 115,* 372–379.

Rucklidge, J. J., & Tannock, R. (2001). Psychiatric, psy-chosocial, and cognitive functioning of female adolescents with ADHD.*Journal of the American Academy of Child and Adolescent Psychiatry, 40,* 530–540.

Ruitenberg, A., Ott, A. L., van Swieten, J. C., Hofman, A., & Breteler, M. M. B. (2001). Incidence of dementia: Does gender make a difference? *Neurobiology of Aging, 22,* 575–580.

Ruscio, A. M., Stein, D. J., Chiu, W. T., & Kessler, R. C. (2010). The epidemiology of obsessive-compulsive disorder in the National Comorbidity Survey Replication. *Molecular Psychiatry, 15,* 53–63.

Ruscio, J. (2004). Diagnoses and the behaviors they denote: A critical evaluation of the labeling theory of mental illness.*The Scientific Review of Mental Health Practice, 3,* 5–22.

Russell, C. J. & Keel, P. K. (2002). Homosexuality as a specific risk factor for eating disorders in men. *International Journal of Eating Disorders, 31,* 300–306.

Rutter, M. (1983). Introduction: Concepts of brain dys-function syndromes. In M. Rutter (Ed.), *Developmental Neuropsychiatry* (pp. 1–14). New York: Guilford.

Rutter, M. (1989). Isle of Wight revisited: Twenty-five years of child psychiatric epidemiology. *Journal of the American Academy of Child & Adolescent Psychiatry, 28,* 633–653.

Rutter, M. (1996). Autism research: Prospects and priori-ties. *Journal of Autism and Developmental Disorders, 26,* 257–275.

Rutter, M. (2005). Incidence of autism spectrum disorders: Changes over time and their meaning. *Acta Paediatrica, 94*(1), 2–15.

Rutter, M. (2007). Proceeding from observed correlation to causal inference: The use of natural experiments. *Perspectives on Psychological Science, 2,* 377–395.

Rutter, M. L. (1981). *Maternal Deprivation Reassessed* (2nd ed.). London: Penguin.

Rutter, M., & Garmezy, N. (1983). Developmental psycho-pathology. In E.M. Hetherington (Ed.), *Handbook of Child Psychology* (Vol. 4, pp. 775–912). New York: Wiley.

Rutter, M., & Rutter, M. (1993). *Developing Minds.* New York: Basic Books.

Rutter, M., & Silberg, J. (2002). Gene-environment interplay in relation to emotional and behavior disturbance. *Annual Review of Psychology, 53,* 463–490.

Rutter, M., Greenfield, D., & Lockyer, L. (1967). A five- to fifteen-year follow-up study of infantile psychosis: II. Social and behavioral outcome. *British Journal of Psychiatry, 113,* 1187–1199.

Rutter, M., Moffitt, T. E., & Caspi, A. (2006). Gene-environment interplay and psychopathology: Multiple varieties but real effects. *Journal of Child Psychology and Psychiatry, 47,* 226–261.

Rutter, M., Pickles, A., Murray, R., & Eaves, L. (2001). Testing hypotheses on specific environmental causal effects on behavior. *Psychological Bulletin, 127,* 291–324.

Ryan, C. S. (1996). Battered children who kill: Developing an appropriate legal response. *Notre Dame Journal of Law, Ethics, and Public Policy, 10,* 301–339.

Ryff, C. D., Kwan, C. M. L., & Singer, B. H. (2001). Personality and aging: Flourishing agendas and future challenges. In J. E. Birren & K. W. Schaie (Eds.), *Handbook of the Psychology of Aging* (5th ed., pp. 477–499). San Diego, CA: Academic Press.

## S

Sabbagh, M., Richardson, S., & Relkin, N. (2008). Disease-modifying approaches to Alzheimer's disease: Challenges and opportunities—Lessons from donepezil therapy. *Alzheimer's & Dementia, 4,* S109–S118.

Sackeim, H. A., Prudic, J., & Devanand, D. P. (2000). A prospective, randomized, double-blind comparison of bilateral and right unilateral electroconvulsive therapy at different stimulus intensities. *Archives of General Psychiatry, 57,* 425–434.

Sacks, O. (1985). *The Man Who Mistook His Wife for a Hat and Other Clinical Tales.* New York: Summit.

Sadeh, N., Javdani, S., Jackson, J. J., Reynolds, E. K., Potenza, M. N., Gelernter, J. & Lejuez, C. W. (2010). Serotonin transporter gene associations with psychopathic traits in youth vary as a function of socioeconomic resources. *Journal of Abnormal Psychology, 119,* 604–609.

Saha, S., Chant, D., & McGrath, J. (2008). Meta-analyses of the incidence and prevalence of schizophrenia: Conceptual and methodological issues. *International Journal of Methods in Psychiatric Research, 17,* 55–61.

Saha, S., Welham, J., Chant, D., & McGrath, J. (2006). Incidence of schizophrenia does not vary with economic status of the country: Evidence from a systematic review. *Social Psychiatry and Psychiatric Epidemiology, 41,* 338–340.

Salkovskis, P. M., & Harrison, J. (1984). Abnormal and normal obsessions—A replication. *Behaviour Research and Therapy, 22,* 549–552.

Salthouse, T. A. (1999). Pressing issues in cognitive aging. In N. Schwarz & D. C. Park (Eds.), *Cognition, Aging, and Self-Reports* (pp. 185–198). Hove, England: Psychology Press/Erlbaum.

Salthouse, T. A. (2004). What and when of cognitive aging. *Current Directions in Psychological Science, 13,* 140–144.

San Miguel, V., Guarnaccia, P. J., Shrout, P. E., Lewis-Fernández, R., Canino, G. J., & Ramírez, R. R. (2006). A quantitative analysis of ataque de nervios in Puerto Rico: Further examination of a cultural syndrome. *Hispanic Journal of Behavioral Sciences, 28,* 313–330.

Sanders, A. R., Duan, J., Levinson, D. F., Shi, J., He, D., Hou, C., et al. (2008). No significant association of 14 candidate genes with schizophrenia in a large European ancestry sample: Implications for psychiatric genetics. *American Journal of Psychiatry, 165,* 497–506.

Sanders, M. R., Montgomery, D. T., & Brechman-Toussaint, M. L. (2000). The mass media and the prevention of child behavior problems: The evaluation of a television series to promote better child and parenting outcomes. *Journal of Child Psychology and Psychiatry, 41,* 939–948.

Sanders, S. J., et al. (2012). *De novo* mutations revealed by whole-exome sequencing are strongly associated with autism. *Nature, 485,* 237–241.

Sandler, A. D., Sutton, K. A., DeWeese, J., Giradi, M. A., Sheeppard, V., & Bodfish, J. W. (1999). Lack of benefit of a single does of synthetic human secretin in the treatment of autism and pervasive developmental disorder. *New England Journal of Medicine, 341,* 1801–1806.

Sapolsky, R. M. (1992). Neuroendocrinology of the stress response. In J. B. Becker, S. M. Breedlove, & D. Crews (Eds.), *Behavioral endocrinology* (pp. 288–324). Cambridge, MA: MIT Press.

Sapolsky, R. M. (2003). Taming stress. *Scientific American, 286,* 86–95.

Sartor, C. E., & Youniss, J. (2002). The relationship between positive parental involvement and identity achievement during adolescence. *Adolescence, 37,* 221–234.

Sartorius, N. (2007). Twenty-five years of WHO-Coordinated activities concerning schizophrenia. In *Recovery from schizophrenia: An international perspective: A report from the WHO collaborative project, the international study of schizophrenia* (pp. 3–9). New York: Oxford University Press.

Savva, G. M., Zaccai, J., Matthews, F. E., Davidson, J. E., McKeith, I., & Brayne, C. (2009). Prevalence, correlates and course of behavioural and psychological symptoms of dementia in the population. *British Journal of Psychiatry, 194,* 212–219.

Sayette, M. A., Shiffman, S., Tiffany, S. T., Niaura, R. S., Martin, C. S., & Shadel, W. G. (2000). The measurement of drug craving. *Addiction, 95*(Suppl. 2), S189–S210.

Sbarra, D. A., & Emery, R. E. (2008). Deeper into divorce: Using actor-partner analyses to explore systemic differences in coparenting following mediation and litigation of custody disputes. *Journal of Family Psychology, 22,* 144–152.

Sbarra, D. S., & Emery, R. E. (2005). The emotional sequelae of non-marital relationship dissolution: Descriptive evidence from a 28-day prospective study. *Personal Relationships, 12,* 213–232.

Scarr, S., & McCartney, K. (1983). How people make their own environments: A theory of genotype-environment effects. *Child Development, 54,* 424–435.

Scepkowski, L. A., Wiegel, M., Bach, A. K., Weisberg, R. B., Brown, T. A., & Barlow, D. H. (2004). Attributions for sexual situations in men with and without erectile disorder: Evidence from a sex-specific attributional style measure. *Archives of Sexual Behavior, 33,* 559–569.

Schachar, R., & Tannock, R. (2002). Syndromes of hyperactivity and attention deficit. In M. Rutter & E. Taylor (Eds.), *Child and Adolescent Psychiatry* (4th ed., pp. 399–418). Oxford, England: Blackwell.

Schacter, D. L. (1987). Implicit memory: History and current status. *Journal of Experimental Psychology: Learning, Memory, and Cognition, 13,* 501–518.

Schaeffer, C. M. & Borduin, C. M. (2005). Long-term follow-up to a randomized clinical trial of multisystemic therapy with serious and violent juvenile offenders. *Journal of Consulting and Clinical Psychology, 73,* 445–453.

Schalock, R. L. et al., (2010). *Intellectual Disability: Definition, Classification, and Systems of Supports* (Eleventh edition). Washington: AAIDD.

Scheerenberger, R. C. (1982). Public residential services, 1981: Status and trends. *Mental Retardation, 20,* 210–215.

Schell, T. L., Marshall, G. N., & Jaycox, L. H. (2004). All symptoms are not created equal: The prominent role of hyperarousal in the natural course of posttraumatic psychological distress. *Journal of Abnormal Psychology, 113,* 189–197.

Schiavi, R. C., & Segraves, R. T. (1995). The biology of sexual function. *Psychiatric Clinics of North America, 18,* 7–23.

Schiavi, R. C., Stimmel, B. B., Mandeli, J., & White, D. (1995). Chronic alcoholism and male sexual function. *American Journal of Psychiatry, 152,* 1045–1051.

Schiff, M., Duyme, M., Dumaret, A., & Tomkiewicz, S. (1982). How much could we boost scholastic achievement and IQ scores? A direct answer from a French adoption study. *Cognition, 12,* 165–196.

Schiller, J. S., Martinez, M., Hao, C., & Barnes, P. (2005). *Early release of selected estimates based on data from the January–September 2004 National Health Interview Survey.* National Center for Health Statistics. Retrieved from www. cdc.gov/nchs/nhis.htm

Schnall, E., Wassertheil-Smoller, S., Swencionis, C., Zemon, V., Tinker, L., O'Sullivan, M. J., et al. (2008). The relationship between religion and cardiovascular outcomes

and all-cause mortality in the women's health initiative observational study. *Psychology and Health, 25,* 249–263.

Schneiderman, N., Chesney, M. A., & Krantz, D. S. (1989). Biobehavioral aspects of cardiovascular disease: Progress and prospects. *Health Psychology, 8,* 649–676.

Schneiderman, N., Ironson, G., & Siegel, S. D. (2004). Stress and health: Psychological, behavioral, and biological determinants. *Annual Review of Clinical Psychology, 1,* 19.1–19.22.

Schneidman, E. S. (1996). *The Suicidal Mind.* New York: Oxford.

Schopler, E. M., Andrews, C. E., & Strupp, K. (1979). Do autistic children come from upper-middle-class parents? *Journal of Autism and Developmental Disorders, 9,* 139–152.

Schopp, R. F., Sturgis, B. J., & Sullivan, M. (1994). Battered woman syndrome, expert testimony, and the distinction between justification and excuse. *University of Illinois Law Review, 54,* 45–113.

Schott, R. L. (1995). The childhood and family dynamics of tranvestites. *Archives of Sexual Behavior, 24,* 309–328.

Schreibman, L. (1988). *Autism.* Beverly Hills, CA: Sage.

Schuckit, M. A. (2005). *Drug and alcohol abuse: A clinical guide to diagnosis and treatment* (6th ed.). New York: Springer.

Schuckit, M. A. (2010). *Drug and alcohol abuse: A clinical guide to diagnosis and treatment* (6th ed.). New York: Springer.

Schuckit, M. A., & Smith, T. L. (2011). Onset and course of alcoholism over 25 years in middle class men. *Drug and Alcohol Dependence, 113,* 21–28.

Schuepbach, W. M. M., Adler., R. H., & Sabbioni, M. E. E. (2002). Accuracy of clinical diagnosis of psychogenic disorders in the presence of physical symptoms suggesting a general medical condition: A 5-year follow-up in 162 patients. *Psychotherapy and Psychosomatics, 71,* 11–17.

Schulz, M. S., Cowan, C. P., & Cowan, P. A. (2006). Promoting healthy beginnings: A randomized controlled trial of a preventive intervention to preserve marital quality during the transition to parenthood. *Journal of Consulting and Clinical Psychology, 74,* 20–31.

Schuyler, D. (1991). *A Practical Guide to Cognitive Therapy.* New York: Norton.

Schwartz, C. E., Covino, N., Morgenstaler, A., & DeWolf, W. (2000). Quality of life after penile prosthesis placed at radical prostatectomy. *Psychology & Health, 15,* 651–661.

Schwartz, G. E. (1982). Testing the biopsychosocial model: The ultimate challenge facing behavioral medicine. *Journal of Consulting and Clinical Psychology, 50,* 1040–1053.

Scott, S. (2002). Parent training programs. In M. Rutter & E. Taylor (Eds.), *Child and Adolescent Psychiatry* (4th ed., pp. 949–967). Oxford, England: Blackwell.

Sczesny, S., Bosak, J., Diekman, A. B., & Twenge, J. (2008). Dynamics of sex-role stereotypes. In Y. Kashima, K. Fiedler, & P. Freytag (Eds.), *Stereotype dynamics: Language-based approaches to the formation, maintenance, and transformation of stereotypes* (pp. 135–161). Mahwah, NJ: Lawrence Erlbaum Associates.

Seaton, E. K., Scottham, K. M., & Sellers, R. M. (2006). The status model of racial identity development in African American adolescents: Evidence of structure, trajectories, and well-being. *Child Development, 77,* 1416–1426.

Sedikides, C., Wildschut, T., Arndt, J., & Routledge, C. (2008). Nostalgia: Past, present, and future. *Current Directions in Psychological Science, 17,* 304–307.

Seelaar, H., Rohrer, J. D., Pijnenburg, Y. L., Fox, N. C., & van Swieten, J. C. (2011). Clinical, genetic and pathological heterogeneity of frontotemporal dementia: A review. *Journal of Neurology, Neurosurgery & Psychiatry, 82,* 476–486.

Seeman, M. (2008). Gender. In *Clinical handbook of schizophrenia* (pp. 575–580). New York: Guilford Press.

Seery, M. D. (2011). Resilience: A silver lining to experiencing adverse life events? *Current Directions in Psychological Science, 20,* 390–394.

Segal, D. L., June, A., & Marty, M. A. (2010). Basic issues in interviewing and the interview process. In D. L. Segal, M. Hersen, D. L. Segal, & M. Hersen (Eds.), *Diagnostic interviewing* (pp. 1–21). New York, NY: Springer Publishing Co.

Segerstrom, S. C. (2007). Stress, energy, and immunity: An ecological view. *Current Directions in Psychological Science, 16,* 326–330.

Segerstrom, S. C., & Sephton, S. E. (2010). Optimistic expectancies and cell-mediated immunity: The role of positive affect.*Psychological Science, 21,* 448–455.

Segraves, R., Balon, R., & Clayton, A. (2007). Proposal for changes in diagnostic criteria for sexual dysfunctions. *Journal of Sexual Medicine, 4,* 567–580.

Seidman, B. T., Marshall, W. L., Hudson, S. M., & Robertson, P. J. (1994). An examination of intimacy and loneliness in sex offenders. *Journal of Interpersonal Violence, 9,* 518–534.

Self, D., & Tamminga, C. A. (2004). Drug dependence and addiction: Neural substrates. *American Journal of Psychiatry, 161,* 223.

Selfe, L. (1977). *Nadia: A case of extraordinary drawing ability in an autistic child.* London: Academic Press.

Seligman, M. E. P. (2007). *What you can change and what you can't: The complete guide to successful self-improvement.* New York: Vintage.

Selye, H. (1956). *The stress of life.* New York: McGraw-Hill.

Seligman, M. E. P., Railon, P., Baumeister, R. F., & Sripada, C. (2013). Navigating the future or driven by the past.*Perspectives on Psychological Science, 8,* 119–141.

Seligman, M. P. (1995). *What You Can Change, and What You Can't: The Complete Guide to Successful Self-Improvement.* New York: Fawcett Books.

Serdula, M. K., Collins, M. E., Williamson, D. F., Anda, R. F., Pamuk, E. R., & Byers, T. E. (1993). Weight control practices of U.S. adolescents and adults. *Annals of Internal Medicine, 119,* 667–671.

Seto, M. C., & Barbaree, H. E. (2000). Paraphilias. In V. B. Van Hasselt & M. Horsen (Eds.), *Aggression and violence: An introductory text.* Boston: Allyn and Bacon.

Settersen, R. A., Jr., & Ray, B. (2010). What's going on with young people today? The long and twisting path to adulthood.*The Future of Children, 20,* 19–41.

Seyfried, L. S., & Marcus, S. M. (2003). Postpartum mood disorders. *International Review of Psychiatry, 15,* 231–242.

Shadish, W. R., & Baldwin, S. A. (2005). Effects of behavioral marital therapy: A meta-analysis of randomized controlled trials.*Journal of Consulting and Clinical Psychology, 73,* 6–14.

Shaffer, D., & Gutstein, J. (2002). Suicide and attempted suicide. In M. Rutter & E. Taylor (Eds.), *Child and Adolescent Psychiatry* (4th ed., pp. 529–554). Oxford, England: Blackwell.

Shahinfar, A., Kupersmidt, J. B., & Matza, L. S. (2001). The relation between exposure to violence and social information processing among incarcerated adolescents. *Journal of Abnormal Psychology, 110,* 136–141.

Shalev, A. Y. (1996). Stress versus traumatic stress: From acute homeostatic reactions to chronic psychopathology. In B. A. Van der Kolk, A. C. McFarlane, & L. Weisaeth (Eds.), *Traumatic stress* (pp. 77–101). New York: Guilford.

Shalev, A. Y., Peri, T., Caneti, L., & Schreiber, S. (1996). Predictors of PTSD in injured trauma survivors. *American Journal of Psychiatry, 53,* 219–224.

Shankman, S. A., & Klein, D. N. (2003). The relation between depression and anxiety: An evaluation of the tripartite, approach-withdrawal and valence-arousal models. *Clinical Psychology Review, 23,* 605–637.

Sharif, Z., Bradford, D., Stroup, S., & Lieberman, J. (2007). Pharmacological treatment of schizophrenia. In P. E. Nathan & J. M. Gorman (Eds.), *A guide to treatments that work* (3rd ed., pp. 203–241). New York: Oxford University Press.

Shapiro, D. (1965). *Neurotic styles.* New York: Basic Books.

Shariff, A. F., & Tracy, J. L. (2011). What are emotion expressions for? *Current Directions in Psychological Science, 20,* 395–399.

Sharp, E., & Gatz, M. (2011). Relationship between education and dementia: An updated systematic review. *Alzheimer Disease and Associated Disorders, 25,* 289–304.

Shavelson, L. (2001). *Hooked: Five addicts challenge our misguided drug rehab system.* New York: New Press.

Shaw, D. S., & Bell, R. Q. (1993). Developmental theories of parental contributors to antisocial behavior. *Journal of Abnormal Child Psychology, 21,* 493–518.

Shaw, D. S., & Vondra, J. I. (1995). Infant attachment security and maternal predictors of early behavior problems: A longitudinal study of low-income families. *Journal of Abnormal Child Psychology, 23,* 335–357.

Shaw, D. S., Winslow, E. B., Owens, E. B., Vondra, J. I., Cohn, J. F., & Bell, R. Q. (1997). The development of early externalizing problems among children from low-income families: A transformational perspective. *Journal of Abnormal Child Psychology, 26,* 95–107.

Shaywitz, S. E., Mody, M., & Shaywitz, B. A. (2006). Neural mechanisms in dyslexia. *Current Directions in Psychological Science, 15,* 278–281.

Shear, M. K., et al. (2011). Complicated grief and related bereavement issues for DSM-5 *Depress and Anxiety, 28,*103–117.

Shearer, D. E., & Shearer, M. S. (1976). The Portage project: A model for early childhood intervention. In T. D. Tjossem (Ed.),*Intervention strategies for high risk infants and young children.* Baltimore: University Park Press.

Shedler, J., Mayman, M., & Manis, M. (1993). The illusion of mental health. *American Psychologist, 48,* 1117–1131.

Shedler, J. (2010). The efficacy of psychodynamic psychotherapy. *American Psychologist, 65,* 98–109.

Shen, W. W. (1999). A history of antipsychotic drug development. *Comprehensive Psychiatry, 40,* 407–417.

Shepherd, A. M., Laurens, K. R., Matheson, S. L., Carr, V. J., & Green, M. J. (2012). Systematic meta-review and quality assessment of the structural brain alterations in schizophrenia. *Neuroscience and Biobehavioral Reviews, 36,* 1342–1356.

Sher, K. J., Grekin, E. R., & Williams, N. A. (2005). The development of alcohol use disorders. *Annual Review of Clinical Psychology, 1,* 493–523.

Shiffman, S., Paty, J. A., Gnys, M., Kassel, J. A., et al. (1996). First lapses to smoking: Within-subjects analysis of real-time reports. *Journal of Consulting and Clinical Psychology, 64,* 366–379.

Shih, J. H., & Eberhart, N. K. (2010). Gender differences in the associations between interpersonal behaviors and stress generation.*Journal of Social and Clinical Psychology, 29,* 243–255.

Shirk, S. R., & Karver, M. (2003). Prediction of treatment outcome from relationship variable in child and adolescent therapy: A meta-analytic review. *Journal of Consulting and Clinical Psychology, 71*(3), 452–464.

Shorter, E. (1992). *From Paralysis to Fatigue: A History of Psychosomatic Illness in the Modern Era.* New York: Free Press.

Showalter, E. (1997). *Hystories: Hysterical Epidemics and Modern Medicine.* New York: Columbia University Press.

Shulman, M., & Redmond, J. (2008). Access to psychoanalytic ideas in American undergraduate institutions. *Journal of the American Psychoanalytic Association.*

Shyn, S. I., Shi, J., Kraft, J. B., Potash, J. B., Knowles, J. A., Weissman, M. M., et al. (2011). Novel loci for major depression identified by genome-wide association study of sequenced treatment alternatives to relieve depression and meta-analysis of three studies. *Molecular Psychiatry, 16,* 202–215.

Sibley, M. H. et al., (2012). Diagnosing ADHD in adolescence. *Journal of Consulting and Clinical Psychology, 80,* 139–150.

Siegel, J. M., & Kuykendall, D. H. (1990). Loss, widowhood, and psychological distress among the elderly. *Journal of Consulting and Clinical Psychology, 58,* 519–524.

Siegel, S. (2005). Drug tolerance, drug addiction, and drug anticipation. *Current Directions in Psychological Science, 14,* 296–300.

Siev, J., & Chambless, D. L. (2007). Specificity of treatment effects: Cognitive therapy and relaxation for generalized anxiety and panic disorders. *Journal of Consulting and Clinical Psychology, 75,* 513–522.

Sikich, L., Frazier, J. A., McClellan, J., Findling, R. L., Vitiello, B., Ritz, L., et al. (2008). Double-blind comparison of first- and second-generation antipsychotics in early-onset schizophrenia and schizoaffective disorder: Findings from the treatment of early-onset schizophrenia spectrum disorders

(TEOSS) study. *American Journal of Psychiatry, 165*(11), 1420–1431.

Silverman, W. K., & Dick-Niederhauser, A. (2004). Separation anxiety disorder. In T. L. Morris & J. S. March (Eds.), *Anxiety Disorders in Children and Adolescents* (2nd ed., pp. 164–188). New York: Guilford.

Simmons, R. A., Gordon, P. C., & Chambless, D. L. (2005). Pronouns in marital interaction: What do "You" and "I" say about marital health? *Psychological Science, 16,* 932–936.

Simon, G. E. (2002). Management of somatoform and factitious disorders. In P. E. Nathan & J. M. Gorman (Eds.), *A Guide to Treatments That Work* (2nd ed., pp. 447–461). New York: Oxford.

Simon, J., Pilling, S., Burbeck, R., & Goldberg, D. (2006). Treatment options in moderate and severe depression: Decision analysis supporting a clinical guideline. *British Journal of Psychiatry, 189,* 494–501.

Singer, M. T., & Lalich, J. (1996). *"Crazy" Therapies.* San Francisco: Jossey-Bass.

Singh, N. N., Guernsey, T. F., & Ellis, C. R. (1992). Drug therapy for persons with developmental disabilities: Legislation and litigation. *Clinical Psychology Review, 12,* 665–679.

Sitskoom, M. M., Aleman, A., Ebisch, S. J. H., Appels, M. C. M., & Kahn, R. S. (2004). Cognitive deficits in relatives of patients with schizophrenia: A metaanalysis. *Schizophrenia Research, 71,* 285–295.

Sizemore, C. C., & Pittillo, E. S. (1977). *I'm Eve!* New York: Doubleday.

Skinner, B. F. (1956). A case history in scientific method. *American Psychologist, 11,* 221–234.

Skodak, M., & Skeels, H. (1949). A final follow-up study of one hundred adopted children. *Journal of Genetic Psychology, 75,* 85–125.

Skodol, A. E., & Bender, D. S. (2003). Why are women diagnosed borderline more than men? *Psychiatric Quarterly, 74,* 349–360.

Skodol, A. E., Clark, L., Bender, D. S., Krueger, R. F., Morey, L. C., Verheul, R., et al. (2011). Proposed changes in personality and personality disorder assessment and diagnosis for DSM-5 part I: Description and rationale. *Personality Disorders: Theory, Research, and Treatment, 2,* 4–22.

Skodol, A. E., Johnson, J. G., Cohen, P., Sneed, J. R., & Crawford, T. N. (2007). Personality disorder and impaired functioning from adolescence to adulthood. *British Journal of Psychiatry, 190,* 415–420.

Skoog, G., & Skoog, I. (1999). A 40-year follow-up of patients with obsessive-compulsive disorder. *Archives of General Psychiatry, 56,* 121–127.

Skuse, D. H. (2012). DSM-5's conceptualization of autistic disorders. *Journal of the American Academy of Child and Adolescent Psychiatry, 51,* 344–346.

Slater, E. (1965). Diagnosis of hysteria. *British Medical Journal, 1,* 1395–1399.

Sloane, R. B., Staples, A. H., Cristo, N. J., & Whipple, K. (1975). In *Psychotherapy versus Behavior Therapy* (pp. 237–240). Cambridge, MA: Harvard University Press.

Slobogin, C., Rai, A., & Reisner, R. (2009). *Law and the mental health system: Civil and criminal aspects* (5th ed.). St. Paul, MN: West Group.

Sloman, L., Gardner, R., & Price, J. (1989). Biology of family systems and mood disorders. *Family Process, 28,* 387–398.

Smalley, S. L., & Collins, F. (1996). Brief report: Genetic, prenatal, and immunologic factors. *Journal of Autism and Developmental Disorders, 26,* 195–197.

Smalley, S. L., Asarnow, R. F., & Spence, M. A. (1988). Autism and genetics: A decade of research. *Archives of General Psychiatry, 45,* 953–961.

Smetana, J. G. (1989). Adolescents' and parents' reasoning about actual family conflict. *Child Development, 60,* 1052–1067.

Smith, E. (1991). First person account: Living with schizophrenia. *Schizophrenia Bulletin, 17,* 689–691.

Smith, G. T., & Combs, J. (2010). Issues of construct validity in psychological diagnoses. In T. Millon, R. F. Krueger, &

E. Simonsen (Eds.), *Contemporary directions in psychopathology: Scientific foundations of the DSM-V and ICD-11* (pp. 205–222). New York, NY: Guilford Press.

Smith, G. R., Monson, R. A., & Ray, D. C. (1986). Psychiatric consultation in somatization disorder: A randomized controlled study. *New England Journal of Medicine, 314,* 1407–1413.

Smith, G. T., Goldman, M. S., Greenbaum, P. E., & Christiansen, A. (1995). Expectancy for social facilitation from drinking: The divergent paths of high-expectancy and low-expectancy adolescents. *Journal of Abnormal Psychology, 104,* 32–40.

Smith, G., & Hall, M. (1982). Evaluating Michigan's guilty but mentally ill verdict: An empirical study. *University of Michigan Journal of Law Reform, 16,* 77–114.

Smith, M. E., & Farah, M. J. (2011). Are prescription stimulants "smart pills"? The epidemiology and cognitive neuroscience of prescription stimulant use by normal healthy individuals. *Psychological Bulletin, 137,* 717–741.

Smith, M. L., & Glass, G. V. (1977). Meta-analysis of psychotherapy outcome studies. *American Psychologist, 32(9),* 752–760.

Smith, R. C., Gardiner, J. C., Lyles, J. S., Sirbu, C., Dwamena, F. C., Hodges, A., et al. (2005). Exploration of DSM-IV criteria in primary care patients with medically unexplained symptoms. *Psychosomatic Medicine, 67,* 123–129.

Smith, S. M., & Moynan, S. C. (2008). Forgetting and recovering the unforgettable. *Psychological Science, 19,* 462–468.

Smith, S. R., & Meyer, R. G. (1985). Child abuse reporting laws and psychotherapy: A time for reconsideration. *International Journal of Law and Psychiatry, 7,* 351–366.

Smith, T., Groen, A. D., & Wynn, J. W. (2000). Randomized trial of intensive early intervention for children with pervasive developmental disorder. *American Journal of Mental Retardation, 105,* 269–285.

Smith, T. W., & Ruiz, J. M. (2002). Psychosocial influences on the development and course of coronary heart disease: Current status and implications for research and practice. *Journal of Consulting and Clinical Psychology, 70,* 548–568.

Snitz, B., MacDonald, A., & Carter, C. (2006). Cognitive deficits in unaffected first-degree relatives of schizophrenia patients: A meta-analytic review of putative endophenotypes. *Schizophrenia Bulletin, 32,* 179–194.

Snorrason, I., Belleau, E. L., & Woods, D. W. (2012). How related are hair pulling disorder (trichotillomania) and skin picking disorder? A review of evidence for comorbidity, similarities and shared etiology. *Clinical Psychology Review, 32,* 618–629.

Snowden, L. R. (2012). Health and mental health policies' role in better understanding and closing African American-white American disparities in treatment access and quality of care. *American Psychologist, 67,* 523–531.

Snowling, M. J. (2002). Reading and other learning difficulties. In M. Rutter & E. Taylor (Eds.), *Child and Adolescent Psychiatry* (4th ed., pp. 682–696). Oxford, England: Blackwell.

Snyder, D. K. (1999). Affective reconstruction in the context of a pluralistic approach to couple therapy. *Clinical Psychology: Science and Practice, 6,* 348–365.

Snyder, H. N. (2002, September). Juvenile arrests 2002. *Juvenile Justice Bulletin,* pp. 1–12.

Sohn, M., & Bosinski, H. A. G. (2007). Gender identity disorders: Diagnostic and surgical aspects. *Journal of Sexual Medicine, 4,* 1193–1208.

Solomon, A. (2001). *The Noonday Demon: An atlas of depression.* New York: Scribner.

Solomon, K., Manepalli, J., Ireland, G. A., & Mahon, G. M. (1993). Alcoholism and prescription drug abuse in the elderly: St. Louis University grand rounds. *Journal of the American Geriatrics Society, 41,* 57–69.

Somerfield, M. R., & McCrae, R. R. (2000). Stress and coping research: Methodological challenges, theoretical advances, and clinical applications. *American Psychologist, 55,* 620–625.

Song, C., & Leonard, B. E. (2000). *Fundamentals of psychoneuroimmunology.* New York: Wiley.

South, S. C., & Krueger, R. F. (2008). Marital quality moderates genetic and environmental influences on the internalizing spectrum. *Journal of Abnormal Psychology, 117,* 826–837.

South, S. C., Reichborn-Kjennerud, T., Eaton, N. R., & Krueger, R. F. (2012). Behavior and molecular genetics of personality disorders. In T. A. Widiger (Ed.), *The Oxford handbook of personality disorders* (pp. 143–165). New York: Oxford University Press.

South, S. C., Turkheimer, E., & Oltmanns, T. F. (2008). Personality disorder symptoms and marital functioning. *Journal of Consulting and Clinical Psychology, 76,* 769–780.

Southall, D. P., Plunkett, M. C., Banks, M. W., Falkov, A. F., & Samuels, M. P. (1997). Covert video recordings of life-threatening child abuse: Lessons for child protection. *Pediatrics, 100,* 735–774.

Spanagel, R., Bartsch, D., Brors, B., Dahmen, N., Deussing, J., Eils, R., et al. (2010). An integrated genome research network for studying the genetics of alcohol addiction. *Addiction Biology, 15,* 369–379.

Spanos, N. P., Weekes, J. R., & Bertrand, L. D. (1985). Multiple personality: A social psychological perspective. *Journal of Abnormal Psychology, 94,* 362–376.

Spiegel, D. A., & Bruce, T. J. (1997). Benzodiazepines and exposure-based cognitive behavior therapies for panic disorder: Conclusions from combined treatment trials. *American Journal of Psychiatry, 154,* 773–781.

Spiegel, D., & Cardena, E. (1991). Disintegrated experience: The dissociative disorders revisited. *Journal of Abnormal Psychology, 100,* 366–378.

Spirito, A., & Esposito-Smythers, C. (2006). Attempted and completed suicide in adolescence. *Annual Review of Clinical Psychology, 2,* 237–266.

Spitzer, R. L., First, M. B., Williams, J. B. W., Kendler, K., Pincus, H. A., & Tucker, G. (1992). Now is the time to retire the term "organic mental disorders." *American Journal of Psychiatry, 149,* 240–244.

Sroufe, L. A., & Fleeson, J. (1986). Attachment and the construction of relationships. In W. W. Hartup & Z. Rubin (Eds.), *Relationships and Development* (pp. 51–72). Hillsdale, NJ: Erlbaum.

Stack, S. (2004). Emile Durkheim and altruistic suicide. *Archives of Suicide Research, 8,* 9–22.

Stahl, S., & Buckley, P. (2007). Negative symptoms of schizophrenia: A problem that will not go away. *Acta Psychiatrica Scandinavica, 115,* 4–11.

Stams, G.J., Brugman, D., Dekovic, M., Rosmalen, L.V., van der Laan, P., & Gibbs, J.C. (2006). The moral judgment of juvenile delinquents: A meta-analysis. *Journal of Abnormal Child Psychology, 34,* 697–713.

Stanton, A. L., & Low, C. A. (2012). Expressing emotions in stressful contexts: Benefits, moderators, and mechanisms. *Current Directions in Psychological Science, 21,* 124–128.

Stanton, A. L., Danoff-Burg, S., Cameron, C. L., Bishop, M., Collins, C. A., Kirk, S. B., et al. (2000). Emotional expressive coping predicts psychological and physical adjustment to breast cancer. *Journal of Consulting and Clinical Psychology, 68,* 875–882.

Steadman, H. J., Mulvey, E. P., Monahan, J., Robbins, P. C., Appelbaum, P. S., Grisso, T., et al. (1998). Violence by people discharged from acute psychiatric inpatient facilities and by others in the same neighborhoods. *Archives of General Psychiatry, 55,* 393–401.

Steadman, H., Margaret, A. M., Joseph, P. M., & Lisa, A. C. (1993). *Before and after Hinckley. Evaluating insanity defense reform.* New York: Guilford.

Steen, R., Mull, C., McClure, R., Hamer, R., & Lieberman, J. (2006). Brain volume in first-episode schizophrenia: Systematic review and meta-analysis of magnetic resonance imaging studies. *British Journal of Psychiatry, 188,* 510–518.

Steffenburg, S., Gillberg, C., Hellgren, L., Andersson, L., Gillberg, I., Jakobsson, G., et al. (1989). A twin study of autism in Denmark, Finland, Iceland, Norway and Sweden. *Journal of Child Psychology and Psychiatry, 30,* 405–416.

Steffens, D., & Potter, G. (2008). Geriatric depression and cognitive impairment. *Psychological Medicine, 38,* 163–175.

Steggall, M. J., Gann, S. Y., & Chinegwundoh, F. I. (2004). Sexual dysfunction screening: The advantages of a culturally sensitive joint assessment clinic. *Sexual & Relationship Therapy, 19,* 179–189.

Stein, D. J. (2008). Classifying hypersexual disorders: Compulsive, impulsive, and addictive models. *Psychiatric Clinics of North America, 31,* 587–591.

Stein, D. J., Phillips, K. A., Bolton, D. D., Fulford, K. M., Sadler, J. Z., & Kendler, K. S. (2010). What is a mental/psychiatric disorder? From DSM-IV to DSM-V. *Psychological Medicine, 40,* 1759–1765.

Stein, L. I., & Santos, A. B. (1998). *Assertive community treatment of persons with severe mental illness.* New York: Norton.

Steinhausen, H. C. (2002). The outcome of anorexia nervosa in the 20th century. *International Journal of Eating Disorders, 159,* 1284–1293.

Stevens, S. E., Hynan, M. T., & Allen, M. (2000). A metaanalysis of common factor and specific treatment effects across the outcome domains of the phase model of psychotherapy. *Clinical Psychology: Science and Practice, 7,* 273–290.

Stevens, V. J., Obarzanek, E., Cook, N. R., Lee, I. M., Appel, L. J., Smith West, D., et al. (2001). Long-term weight loss and changes in blood pressure: Results of the Trials of Hypertension Prevention, Phase II. *Annals of Internal Medicine, 134,* 1–11.

Stewart, A. J., & Ostrove, J. M. (1998). Women's personality in middle age: Gender, history, and midcourse corrections. *American Psychologist, 53,* 1185–1194.

Stice, E. (2001). A prospective test of the dual-pathway model of bulimic pathology: Mediating effects of dieting and negative affect. *Journal of Abnormal Psychology, 110,* 124–135.

Stice, E. (2002). Risk and maintenance factors for eating pathology: A meta-analytic review. *Psychological Bulletin, 128,* 825–848.

Stice, E., & Fairburn, C. G. (2003). Dietary and dietary-depressive subtypes of bulimia nervosa show differential symptom presentation, social impairment, comorbidity, and course of illness. *Journal of Consulting and Clinical Psychology, 71,* 1090–1094.

Stice, E., & Shaw, H. (2004). Eating disorder prevention programs: A meta-analytic review. *Psychological Bulletin, 130,* 206–227.

Stice, E., Davis, K., Miller, N. P., & Marti, C. N. (2008). Fasting increases risk for onset of binge eating and bulimic pathology: A 5-year prospective study. *Journal of Abnormal Psychology, 117,* 941–946.

Stice, E., Rohde, P., Gau, J., & Shaw, H. (2009). An effectiveness trial of a dissonance-based eating disorder prevention program for high-risk adolescent girls. *Journal of Consulting and Clinical Psychology, 77,* 825–834.

Stice, E., Rohde, S. D., & Shaw, H. (2012). A preliminary trial of a prototype internet dissonance-based eating disorder prevention program for young women with body image concerns. *Journal of Consulting and Clinical Psychology, 80,* 907–916.

Stice, E., Shaw, H., Burton, E., & Wade, E. (2006). Dissonance and healthy weight eating disorder prevention programs: A randomized efficacy trial. *Journal of Consulting and Clinical Psychology, 74,* 263–275.

Stice, E., Spangler, D., & Agras, W. S. (2001). Exposure to media-portrayed thin-ideal images adversely affects vulnerable girls: A longitudinal experiment. *Journal of Social & Clinical Psychology, 20,* 270–288.

Stockard, J., & O'Brien, R. M. (2002). Cohort effects on suicide rates: International variations. *American Sociological Review, 67,* 854–872.

Stockmeier, C. A. (2003). Involvement of serotonin in depression: Evidence from postmortem and imaging studies of serotonin receptors and the serotonin transporter. *Journal of Psychiatric Research, 37,* 357–373.

Stokols, D. (1992). Establishing and maintaining healthy environments: Toward a social ecology of health promotion. *American Psychologist, 47,* 6–22.

Stoller, R. J. (1991). *Pain and passion: A psychoanalyst explores the world of S & M.* New York: Plenum.

Stone, E. A., Lin, Y., & Quartermain, D. (2008). A final common pathway for depression? Progress toward a general conceptual framework. *Neuroscience and Biobehavioral Reviews, 32,* 508–524.

Stone, M. H. (1993). Long-term outcome in personality disorders. *British Journal of Psychiatry, 162,* 299–313.

Stoolmiller, M. (1999). Implications of the restricted range of family environments for estimates of heritability and non-shared environment in behavior-genetic adoption studies. *Psychological Bulletin, 125,* 392–409.

Storandt, M. (2008). Cognitive deficits in the early stages of Alzheimer's disease. *Current Directions in Psychological Science, 17,* 198–202.

Storch, E. A., Murphy, T. K., Geffken, G. R., Mann, G., Adkins, J., Merlo, L. J., et al. (2006). Cognitive-behavioral therapy for PANDAS-related obsessive-compulsive disorder: Findings from a preliminary waitlist controlled open trial. *Journal of the American Academy of Child and Adolescent Psychiatry, 45,* 1171–1177.

Stouthamer-Loeber, M., Loeber, R., Wei, E., Farrington D. P., & Wilkstrom, P. H. (2002). Risk and promotive effects in the explanation of persistent serious delinquency in boys. *Journal of Consulting and Clinical Psychology, 70*(1), pp. 111–123.

Strain, J. J., & Friedman, M. J. (2011). Considering adjustment disorders as stress response syndromes for DSM_5. *Depression and Anxiety, 28,* 818–823.

Stratton, K., Ford, A., Rusch, E., & Clayton, E. W. (2011). *Adverse effects of vaccines: Evidence and causality.* Washington, DC: National Academies Press.

Strauss, M. E., & Smith, G. T. (2009). Construct validity: Advances in theory and methodology. *Annual Review of Clinical Psychology,* 51–25.

Stricker, G., & Gold, J. R. (1999). The Rorschach: Toward a nomothetically based, idiographically applicable configurational model. *Psychological Assessment, 11,* 240–250.

Striegel-Moore, R. H., & Bulik, C. M. (2007). Risk factors for eating disorders. *American Psychologist, 62,* 181–198.

Striegel-Moore, R. H., & Smolak, L. (2001). *Eating disorders: Innovative directions in research and practice.* Washington, DC: American Psychological Association.

Striegel-Moore, R. H., Silberstein, L. R., & Rodin, J. (1993). The social self in bulimia nervosa: Public self-consciousness, social anxiety, and perceived fraudulence. *Journal of Abnormal Psychology, 102,* 297–303.

Stringaris, A., Cohen, P., Pine, D. S., & Leibenluft, E. (2009). Adult outcomes of adolescent irritability: A 20-year community follow-up. *American Journal of Psychiatry, 166,* 1048–1054.

Stroebe, M., Stroebe, W., Schut, H., Zech, E., & van den Bout, J. (2002). Does disclosure of emotions facilitate recovery from bereavement? Evidence from two prospective studies. *Journal of Consulting and Clinical Psychology, 70,* 169–178.

Stroud, J., Steiner, V., & Iwuagwu, C. (2008). Predictors of depression among older adults with dementia. *Dementia: The International Journal of Social Research and Practice, 7,* 127–138.

Subramaniam, M., Abdin, E., Vaingankar, J., & Chong, S. (2012). Obsessive–compulsive disorder: Prevalence, correlates, help-seeking and quality of life in a multiracial Asian population. *Social Psychiatry and Psychiatric Epidemiology, 47,* 2035–2043.

Sue, S. (1998). In search of cultural competence in psychotherapy and counseling. *American Psychologist, 53*(4), 440–448.

Sue, S., Cheng, J. K. Y., Saad, C. S., & Chu, J. P. (2012). Asian American mental health: A call to action. *American Psychologist, 67,* 532–544.

Sugarman, S. D. (2007). Cases in vaccine court—legal battles over vaccines and autism. *New England Journal of Medicine, 357,* 1275–1277.

Suomi, S. J., & Harlow, H. F. (1972). Social rehabilitation of isolate-reared monkeys. *Developmental Psychology, 6,* 487–496.

Surgeon General. (2001). *Mental health: Culture. Race, and ethnicity.* Washington, DC: Department of Health and Human Services.

Susser, E., Varma, V. K., Mattoo, S. K., Finnerty, M., Mojtabi, R., Tripathi, B. M., et al. (1998). Long-term course of acute brief psychosis in a developing country setting. *British Journal of Psychiatry, 173,* 226–230.

Sutker, P. B., Davis, J. M., Uddo, M., & Ditta, S. R. (1995). War zone stress, personal resources, and PTSD in Persian Gulf War returnees. *Journal of Abnormal Psychology, 104,* 444–452.

Swann, W. B., Jr., Chang-Schneider, C., McClarty, K. L. (2007). Do people's self-views matter? Self-concept and self-esteem in everyday life. *American Psychologist, 62,* 84–94.

Swanson, H. L., Harris, K. R., & Graham S. (Eds.), (2003). *Handbook of Learning Disabilities.* New York: Guilford.

Swanson, J. M., et al. (2001). Clinical relevance of the primary findings of the MTA: Success rates based on severity of ADHD and ODD symptoms at the end of treatment. *Journal of the American Academy of Child and Adolescent Psychiatry, 40,* 168–179.

Swanson, J., Elliott, G. R., Greenhill, L. L., Wigal, T., Arnold, E., Vitiello, B., et al. (2007). Effects of stimulant medication on growth rates across 3 years in the MTA follow-up. *Journal of the American Academy of Child & Adolescent Psychiatry, 46,* 1015–1027.

Swartz, M. S., Hughes, D., Blazer, D. G., & George, L. K. (1987). Somatization disorder in the community: A study of diagnostic concordance among three diagnostic systems. *Journal of Nervous and Mental Disease, 175,* 26–33.

Swartz, M. S., Swanson, J. W., Hiday, V. A., Wagner, H. R., Burns, B. J., & Borum, R. (2001). Randomized controlled trial of outpatient commitment in North Carolina. *Psychiatric Services, 52,* 325–329.

Swedo, S. E., & Grant, P. J. (2005). Annotation: PANDAS: A model for human autoimmune disease. *Journal of Child Psychology & Psychiatry, 46,* 227–234.

Swedo, S. E., et al. (2012). Commentary from the DSM-5 workgroup on neurodevelopmental disorders. *Journal of the American Academy of Child and Adolescent Psychiatry, 51,* 347–349.

Swedo, S. E., Leonard, H. L., Garvey, M., Mittleman, B., Allen, A. J., Perlmutter, S., et al. (1998). Pediatric autoimmune neuropsychiatric disorders associated with streptococcal infections: Clinical description of the first 50 cases. *American Journal of Psychiatry, 155,* 264–271.

Swendsen, J. D., & Merikangas, K. R. (2000). The comorbidity of depression and substance use disorders. *Clinical Psychology Review, 20,* 173–189.

Swenson, C. C., Schaeffer, C. M., Henggeler, S. W., Faldowski, R., & Mayhew, A. M. (2010). Multisystemic therapy for child abuse and neglect: A randomized effectiveness trial. *Journal of Family Psychology, 24,* 497–507.

Symonds, T., Roblin, D., Hart, K., & Althof, S. (2003). How does premature ejaculation impact a man's life? *Journal of Sex & Marital Therapy, 29,* 361–370.

Szasz, T. (1963). *Law, liberty, and psychiatry: An inquiry into the social uses of mental health practices.* New York: Macmillan.

## T

TADS. (2004). Fluoxetine, cognitive-behavioral therapy, and their combination for adolescents with depression: Treatment for Adolescents with Depression Study (TADS) randomized controlled trial. *Journal of the American Medical Association, 292,* 807–820.

TADS. (2007). The Treatment for Adolescents with Depression Study: Long-term effectiveness and safety outcomes. *Archives of General Psychiatry, 64,* 1132 1143.

Taft, C. T., Murphy, C. M., King, L. A., Dedeyn, J. M., & Musser, P. H. (2005). Posttraumatic stress disorder symptomatology among partners of men in treatment for relationship abuse. *Journal of Abnormal Psychology, 114,* 259–268.

Tager-Flusberg, H. (2007). Evaluating the theory-of-mind hypothesis of autism. *Current Directions in Psychological Science, 16,* 311–315.

Takeuchi, H., Suzuki, T., Uchida, H., Watanabe, K., & Mimura, M. (2012). Antipsychotic treatment for schizophrenia in the maintenance phase: A systematic review of the guidelines and algorithms. *Schizophrenia Research, 134,* 219–225.

Tandon, R., Keshavan, M., & Nasrallah, H. (2008). Schizophrenia, "just the facts" what we know in 2008. 2. Epidemiology and etiology. *Schizophrenia Research, 102,* 1–18.

Tarbox, S. I., & Pogue-Geile, M. F. (2011). A multivariate perspective on schizotypy and familial association with schizophrenia: A review. *Clinical Psychology Review, 31,* 1169–1182.

Tarrier, N., Taylor, K., & Gooding, P. (2008). Cognitive-behavioral interventions to reduce suicide behavior: A systematic review and meta-analysis. *Behavior Modification, 32,* 77–108.

Tarter, R. E., & Vanyukov, M. M. (2001). Theoretical and operational framework for research into the etiology of substance use disorders. *Journal of Child and Adolescent Substance Abuse, 10,* 1–12.

Tarter, R. E., Vanyukov, M., & Kirisci, L. (2008). Etiology of substance use disorder: Developmental perspective. In Y. Kaminer & O. G. Bukstein (Eds.), *Adolescent substance abuse: Psychiatric comorbidity and high-risk behaviors* (pp. 5–27). New York: Routledge/Taylor & Francis.

Taylor, C. B., & Luce, K. H. (2003). Computer- and Internet-based psychotherapy interventions. *Current Directions in Psychological Science, 12,* 18–22.

Taylor, F., Huffman, M. D., Macedo, A. F., Moore, T. H., Burke, M., Davey Smith, G., et al. (2011). Statins for the primary prevention of cardiovascular disease. *Cochrane Database of Systematic Reviews, 1,* CD004816.

Taylor, J., Iacono, W. G., & McGue, M. (2000). Evidence for a genetic etiology of early-onset delinquency. *Journal of Abnormal Psychology, 109,* 634–643.

Taylor, M. A., & Fink, M. (2008). Restoring melancholia in the classification of mood disorders. *Journal of Affective Disorders, 105,* 1–14.

Taylor, P., Gooding, P., Wood, A. M., & Tarrier, N. (2011). The role of defeat and entrapment in depression, anxiety, and suicide. *Psychological Bulletin, 137,* 391–420.

Taylor, R. L., Richards, S. B., & Brady, M. P. (2005). *Mental retardation: Historical perspectives, current practices, and future directions.* New York: Pearson Education.

Taylor, R., & Langdon, R. (2006). Understanding gender differences in schizophrenia: A review of the literature. *Current Psychiatry Reviews, 2,* 255–265.

Taylor, S. E. (1990). Health psychology: The science and the field. *American Psychologist, 45,* 40–50.

Taylor, S. E. (1995). *Health psychology* (3rd ed.). New York: McGraw-Hill.

Taylor, S. E., Lerner, J. S., Sherman, D. K., Sage, R. M., & McDowell, N. K. (2003). Portrait of the self-enhancer: Well adjusted and well liked or maladjusted and friendless? *Journal of Personality & Social Psychology, 84,* 165–176.

Taylor, S. E., Welch, W. T., Kim, H. S., & Sherman, D. K. (2007). Cultural differences in the impact of social support on psychological and biological stress responses. *Psychological Science, 18,* 831–837.

Teachman, B. A. (2006). Aging and negative affect: The rise and fall and rise of anxiety and depression symptoms. *Psychology and Aging, 21,* 201–207.

Teachman, B. A., Marker, C. D., & Smith-Janik, S. B. (2009). Automatic associations and panic disorder: Trajectories of change over the course of treatment. *Journal of Consulting and Clinical Psychology, 76,* 988–1002.

Teachman, B. A., Smith-Janik, S. B., & Saporito, J. (2007). Information processing biases and panic disorder: Relationships among cognitive and symptom measures. *Behaviour Research and Therapy, 45,* 1791–1811.

Tedeschi, R. G., & McNally, R. J. (2011). Can we facilitate posttraumatic growth in combat veterans? *American Psychologist, 66,* 19–24.

Temple, S., & Ho, B. (2005). Cognitive therapy for persistent psychosis in schizophrenia: A case-controlled clinical trial. *Schizophrenia Research, 74,* 195–199.

Testa, M., Fillmore, M. T., Norris, J., Abbey, A., Curtin, J. J., Leonard, K. E., et al. (2006). Understanding alcohol expectancy effects: Revisiting the placebo condition. Alcoholism. *Clinical and Experimental Research, 30*, 339–348.

Thakker, J., & Ward, T. (1998). Culture and classification: The cross-cultural application of the DSM-IV. *Clinical Psychology Review, 18*, 501–529.

Thapar, A., Gottesman, I. I., Owen, M. J., O'Donovan, M. C., & McGuffin, P. (1994). The genetics of mental retardation. *British Journal of Psychiatry, 164*, 747–758.

Thase, M. (1988). The relationship between Down syndrome and Alzheimer's disease. In L. Nadel (Ed.), *The psychobiology of Down syndrome*. Cambridge, MA: MIT Press.

Thase, M. E. (2003). Achieving remission and managing relapse in depression. *Journal of Clinical Psychiatry, 64* (Suppl. 118), 3–7.

Thase, M. E. (2006). Preventing relapse and recurrence of depression: A brief review of therapeutic options. *CNS Spectrums, 11* (Suppl. 15), 12–21.

Thase, M. E., Ripu, J., & Howland, R. H. (2002). Biological aspects of depression. In I. H. Gotlib and C. L. Hammen (Eds.), *Handbook of Depression*. New York: Guilford.

The American College of Obstetricians and Gynecologists. (2007, January 2). *New recommendations for Down syndrome call for screening of all pregnant women*. Retrieved January 4, 2007, from http://www.acog.org/from_home/publications/press_releases/nr01-02-07-1.cfm

Thibaut, F., De LaBarra, F., Gordon, H., Cosyns, P., & Bradford, J. W. (2010). The World Federation of Societies of Biological Psychiatry (WFSBP) guidelines for the biological treatment of paraphilias. *World Journal of Biological Psychiatry, 11*, 604–655.

Thomas, A., & Chess, S. (1977). *Temperament and Development*. New York: Brunner/Mazel.

Thomas, E. (1996, May 27). A matter of honor. *Newsweek*, 24–29.

Thomas, V. H., Melchert, T. P., & Banken, J. A. (1999). Substance dependence and personality disorders: Comorbidity and treatment outcome in an inpatient treatment population. *Journal of Studies on Alcohol, 60*, 271–277.

Thompson, J., Pogue-Geile, M., & Grace, A. (2004). Developmental pathology, dopamine, and stress: A model for the age of onset of schizophrenia symptoms. *Schizophrenia Bulletin, 30*(4), 875–900.

Thompson-Brenner, H., Glass, S., & Westen, D. (2003). A multidimensional meta-analysis of psychotherapy for bulimia nervosa. *Clinical Psychology, 10*, 269–287.

Thomson, J. B., & Raskind, W. H. (2003). Genetic influences on reading and writing disabilities. In H. L. Swanson, K. R. Harris, & S. Graham (Eds.), *Handbook of Learning Disabilities* (pp. 256–270). New York: Guilford.

Thoresen, C. E., & Powell, L. H. (1992). Type a behavior pattern: New perspectives on theory, assessment, and intervention. *Journal of Consulting and Clinical Psychology, 60*, 595–604.

Thornicroft, G., & Susser, E. (2001). Evidence-based psychotherapeutic interventions in the community care of schizophrenia. *British Journal of Psychiatry, 178*, 2–4.

Thornton, D. (2010). Evidence regarding the need for a diagnostic category for a coercive paraphilia. *Archives of Sexual Behavior, 39*, 411–418.

Tiefer, L. (2001). The "consensus" conference on female sexual dysfunction: Conflicts of interest and hidden agendas. *Journal of Sex and Marital Therapy, 27*, 227–236.

Tienari, P., Wynne, L., Läksy, K., Moring, J., Nieminen, P., & Sorri, A. (2003). Genetic boundaries of the schizophrenia spectrum: Evidence from the Finnish Adoptive Family Study of Schizophrenia. *American Journal of Psychiatry, 160*, 1587–1594.

Tienari, P., Wynne, L., Läksy, K., Moring, J., Nieminen, P., Sorri, A., et al. (2003). Genetic boundaries of the schizophrenia spectrum: Evidence from the Finnish Adoptive Family Study of Schizophrenia. *American Journal of Psychiatry, 160*, 1587–1594.

Tilburt, J. C., Emanuel, E. J., Kaptchuk, T. J., Curlin, F. A., & Miller, F. G. (2008). Prescribing "placebo treatments": Results of national survey of US internists and rheumatologists. *British Medical Journal, 337*, 1–5.

Timpano, K. R., Exner, C., Glaesmer, H., Rief, W., Keshaviah, A., Brahler, E., et al. (2011). The epidemiology of the proposed DSM-5 hoarding disorder: Exploration of the acquisition specifier, associated features, and distress. *Journal of Clinical Psychiatry, 72*, 780–786.

Toffel, H. (1996). Crazy women, unharmed men, and evil children: Confronting the myths about battered people who kill their abusers, and the argument for extending battering syndrome self-defenses to all victims of domestic violence. *Southern California Law Review, 70*, 337–380.

Tolin, D. F., & Foa, E. B. (2006). Sex differences in trauma and posttraumatic stress disorder: A quantitative review of 25 years of research. *Psychological Bulletin, 132*, 959–992.

Tolin, D. F., Meunier, S. A., Frost, R. O., & Steketee, G. (2010). Course of compulsive hoarding and its relationship to life events. *Depression and Anxiety, 27*, 829–838.

Tomkins, D. M., & Sellers, E. M. (2001). Addiction and the brain: The role of neurotransmitters in the cause and treatment of drug dependence. *Canadian Medical Association Journal, 164*, 817–821.

Tonigan, J. S., Connors, G. J., & Miller, W. R. (2003). Participation and involvement in Alcoholics Anonymous. In T. F. Babor & F. K. Del Boca (Eds.), *Treatment Matching in Alcoholism* (pp. 184–204). New York: Cambridge University Press.

Torres, A. R., Prince, M. J., Bebbington, P. E., Bhugra, D., Brugha, T. S., Farrell, M., et al. (2006). Obsessive-compulsive disorder: Prevalence, comorbidity, impact, and help-seeking in the British National Psychiatric Morbidity Survey of 2000. *American Journal of Psychiatry, 163*, 1978–1985.

Torrey, E. F. (1988). *Nowhere to go: The tragic Odyssey of the homeless mentally ill*. New York: Harper & Row.

Torrey, E. F. (1997). *Out of the shadows*. New York: Wiley.

Torrey, E. F. (2008). *The insanity offense: How America's failure to treat the seriously mentally ill endangers its citizens*. New York: Norton.

Torrey, E. F., Entsminger, K., Geller, J., Stanley, J., & Jaffe, D. J. (2008). *The shortage of public hospital beds for mentally ill persons: A report of the Treatment Advocacy Center*. Arlington, VA: Treatment Advocacy Center.

Triandis, H. C. (1994). Culture and social behavior. In W. J. Lonner & R. S. Malpass (Eds.), *Psychology and culture* (pp. 169–174). Boston: Allyn & Bacon.

Truax, C., & Carkhuff, R. (1967). *Toward Effective Counseling and Psychotherapy: Training and Practice*. Hawthorne, NY: Aldine Publishing.

True, W. R., Rice, J., Eisen, S. A., Heath, A. C., Goldberg, J., Lyons, M. J., et al. (1993). A twin study of genetic and environmental contributions to liability for posttraumatic stress symptoms. *Archives of General Psychiatry, 50*, 257–264.

Trull, T. J., Jahng, S., Tomko, R. L., Wood, P. K., & Sher, K. J. (2010). Revised NESARC personality disorder diagnoses: Gender, prevalence, and comorbidity with substance dependence disorders. *Journal of Personality Disorders, 24*, 412–426.

Trull, T. J., Stepp, S. D., & Solhan, M. (2006). Borderline personality disorder. In F. Andrasik (Ed.), *Comprehensive handbook of personality and psychopathology* (Vol. 2, pp. 299–315). Hoboken, NJ: Wiley.

Tsai, L. Y. (2012). Sensitivity and specificity: DSM-IV versus DSM-5 criteria for autism spectrum disorder. *American Journal of Psychiatry, 169*, 1009–1011.

Tschudin, S., Bertea, P., & Zemp, E. (2010). Prevalence and predictors of premenstrual syndrome and premenstrual dysphoric disorder in a population-based sample. *Archives of Women's Mental Health, 13*, 485–494.

Tsuang, M. T., Van Os, J., Tandon, R., Barch, D. M., Bustillo, J., Gaebel, W., & ... Carpenter, W. (2013). Attenuated psychosis syndrome in DSM-5. *Schizophrenia Research*,

Tuckey, M. R. (2007). Issues in the debriefing debate for the emergency services: Moving research outcomes forward. *Clinical Psychology: Science and Practice, 14*, 106–116.

Tully, L. A., Arseneault, L., Caspi, A., Moffitt, T. E., & Morgan, J. (2004). Does maternal warmth moderate the

effects of birth weight on twins' attention-deficit/hyperactivity disorder (ADHD) symptoms and low IQ? *Journal of Consulting and Clinical Psychology, 72*(2), 218–226.

Tune, L. (2007). Treatments for dementia. In *A Guide to Treatments That Work* (3rd ed., pp. 105–143). New York: Oxford University Press.

Turkheimer, E. (1991). Individual and group differences in adoption studies of IQ. *Psychological Bulletin, 110*, 392–405.

Turkheimer, E. (1998). Heritability and biological explanation. *Psychological Review, 105*, 782–791.

Tyrer, P. (2012). Diagnostic and statistical manual of mental disorders: A classification of personality disorders that has had its day. *Clinical Psychology & Psychotherapy, 19*, 372–374.

Tyrer, P., Crawford, M., Mulder, R., Blashfield, R., Farnam, A., Fossati, A., et al. (2011). The rationale for the reclassification of personality disorder in the 11th revision of the international classification of diseases (ICD-11). *Personality and Mental Health, 5*, 246–259.

## U

U.S. Bureau of the Census. (1996). Sixty-five plus in the United States. *Current Population Reports* (pp. 23–190). Washington, DC: U.S. Government Printing Office.

U.S. Bureau of the Census. (2010). Family and living arrangements characteristics: Estimated median age at first marriage, by sex: 1890 to the present. *Historical Time Series, Table MS-2*. Washington, DC: U.S. Government Printing Office.

U.S. Census Bureau. (2012). *Statistical abstract of the United States*. Washington, DC: U.S. Census Bureau.

U.S. Department of Justice, Bureau of Justice Statistics. (1999). *Special report: Mental health and treatment of inmates and probationers*. Washington, DC: National Criminal Justice.

Uchino, B. N. (2009). Understanding the links between social support and physical health: A life-span perspective with emphasis on the separability of perceived and received support. *Perspectives on Psychological Science, 4*, 236–255.

Uchiyama, T., Kurosawa, M., & Inaba, Y. (2007). MMR-vaccine and regression in autism spectrum disorders: Negative results presented from Japan. *Journal of Autism and Developmental Disorders, 37*, 210–217.

UK ECT Review Group. (2003). Efficacy and safety of electroconvulsive therapy in depressive disorders: A systematic review and meta-analysis. *Lancet, 361*, 799–808.

Updegraff, J. A., & Taylor, S. E. (2000). From vulnerability to growth: Positive and negative effects of stressful life events. In J. H. Harvey & E. D. Miller (Eds.), *Loss and Trauma: General and Close Relationship Perspectives* (pp. 3–28). Philadelphia: Brunner-Routledge.

Uttal, W. R. (2001). *The new phrenology: The limits of localizing cognitive processes in the brain*. Cambridge, MA: MIT Press.

## V

Vaillant, G. (2003). A 60-year follow-up of alcoholic men. *Addiction, 98*, 1043–1051.

Vaillant, G. E. (1995). *The natural history of alcoholism revisited*. Cambridge, MA: Harvard University Press.

Valenstein, E. S. (1973). *Brain control*. New York: Wiley.

Valenstein, E. S. (1998). *Blaming the Brain*. New York: Free Press.

Valente, J. (1996, January). A long road to daylight: Football player's gambling problems. *People Weekly, 15*, 811.

Van de Velde, S., Bracke, P., & Levecque, K. (2010). Gender differences in depression in 23 European countries. Cross-national variation in the gender gap in depression. *Social Science & Medicine, 71*, 305–313.

Van der Kloet, D., Merckelbach, H., Giesbrech, T., & Lynn, S. J. (2012). Fragmented sleep, fragmented mind: The role of sleep in dissociative symptoms. *Perspectives on Psychological Science, 7*, 159–175.

van der Kolk, B. A., & McFarlane, A. C. (1996). The black hole of trauma. In B. A. van der Kolk, A. C. McFarlane, & L. Weisaeth (Eds.), *Traumatic Stress* (pp. 3–23). New York: Guilford.

van der Made, F., Bloemers, J., Yassem, W. E., Kleiverda, G., Everaerd, W., van Ham, D., et al. (2009). The influence of testosterone combined with a PDE5-inhibitor on cognitive, affective, and physiological sexual functioning in women suffering from sexual dysfunction. *Journal of Sexual Medicine, 6,* 777–790.

Van Domburgh, L., Loeber, R., Bezemer, D., Stallings, R., & Stouthamer-Loeber, M. (2009). Childhood predictors of desistance and level of persistence in offending in early onset offenders. *Journal of Abnormal Child Psychology, 37,* 967–980.

van Haren, N., Bakker, S., & Kahn, R. (2008). Genes and structural brain imaging in schizophrenia. *Current Opinion in Psychiatry, 21,* 161–167.

Van Orden, K. A., Witte, T. K., Gordon, K. H., Bender, T. W., & Joiner, T. E. (2008). Suicidal desire and the capability for suicide: Tests of the interpersonal-psychological theory of suicidal behavior among adults. *Journal of Consulting and Clinical Psychology, 76,* 72–83.

Van Os, J., & McGuffin, P. M. (2003). Can the social environment cause schizophrenia? *British Journal of Psychiatry, 182,* 291–292.

Van Snellenberg, J. X., & de Candia, T. (2009). Meta-analytic evidence for familial coaggregation of schizophrenia and bipolar disorder. *Archives of General Psychiatry, 66*(7), 748–755.

Vandereycken, W. (1995). The families of patients with an eating disorder. In K. D. Brownell & C. G. Fairburn (Eds.), *Eating disorders and obesity: A comprehensive handbook* (pp. 219–223). New York: Guilford.

Vanin, J. R. (2008). Psychopharmacotherapy. In J. R. Vanin & J. D. Helsley (Eds.). *Anxiety Disorders: A Pocket Guide for Primary Care* (pp. 63–112). Totowa, NJ: Humana Press.

Vaughn, C. E., & Leff, J. P. (1976). The influence of family and social factors on the course of psychiatric illness: A comparison of schizophrenic and depressed neurotic patients. *British Journal of Psychiatry, 129,* 125–137.

Ventura, S. J. (2009). *Changing Patterns of Nonmarital Childbearing in the United States.* NCHS data brief, no 18. Hyattsville, MD: National Center for Health Statistics.

Verheul, R. (2012). Personality disorder proposal for DSM-5: A heroic and innovative but nevertheless fundamentally flawed attempt to improve DSM-IV. *Clinical Psychology & Psychotherapy, 19,* 369–371.

Verheul, R., van den Bosch, L. M. C., Koeter, M. W. J., de Ridder, M. A. J., Stijnen, T., & van den Brink, W. (2003). Dialectical behaviour therapy for women with borderline personality disorder: 12-month, randomized clinical trial in The Netherlands.*British Journal of Psychiatry, 182,* 135–140.

Verma, K., Khaitan, B., & Singh, O. (1998). The frequency of sexual dysfunctions in patients attending a sex therapy clinic in North India. *Archives of Sexual Behavior, 27,* 309–314.

Vickland, V., McDonnell, G., Werner, J., Draper, B., Low, L., & Brodaty, H. (2010). A computer model of dementia prevalence in Australia: Foreseeing outcomes of delaying dementia onset, slowing disease progression, and eradicating dementia types.*Dementia and Geriatric Cognitive Disorders, 29,* 123–130.

Viken, R. J., Treat, T. A., Nosofsky, R. M., McFall, R. M., & Palmeri, T. J. (2002). Modeling individual differences in perceptual and attentional processes related to bulimic symptoms. *Journal of Abnormal Psychology, 111,* 598–609.

Visintainer, M. A., Seligman, M. E. P., & Volpicelli, J. R. (1982). Tumor rejection in rats after inescapable or escapable electric shock. *Science, 216,* 437–439.

Vitiello, B. (2008). An international perspective on pediatric psychopharmacology. *International Review of Psychiatry, 20,* 121–126.

Vitiello, B., Abikoff, H. B., Chuang, S. Z., Kollins, S. H., McCracken, J. T., Riddle, M. A., et al. (2007). Effectiveness of methylphenidate in the 10-month continuation phase of the Preschoolers with ADHD Treatment Study (PATS). *Journal of Child and Adolescent Psychopharmacology, 17,* 593–603.

Vitiello, M. V. (2009). Recent advances in understanding sleep and sleep disturbances in older adults: Growing older does not mean sleeping poorly. *Current Directions in Psychological Science, 18,* 316–320.

Vögele, C., & Gibson, E. L. (2010). Mood, emotions, and eating disorders. In W. S. Agras (Ed.), *The Oxford handbook of eating disorders* (pp. 180–205). New York: Oxford University Press.

Volkmar, F. R., & Lord, C. (2007). Diagnosis and definition of autism and other pervasive developmental disorders. In F. R. Volkmar (Ed.), *Autism and pervasive developmental disorders* (pp. 1–31). New York: Cambridge University Press.

Volkmar, F. R., Klin, A., Siegel, B., Szatmari, P., Lord, C., Campbell, M., et al. (1994). Field trial for autistic disorder in DSM-IV. *American Journal of Psychiatry, 151,* 1361–1367.

Volkmar, F., & Dykens, E. (2002). Mental retardation. In M. Rutter & E. Taylor (Eds.), *Child and adolescent psychiatry* (4th ed., pp. 697–710). Oxford, England: Blackwell.

Volkmar, F., Chawarska, K., & Klin, A. (2005). Autism in infancy and early childhood. *Annual Review of Psychology, 56,* 315–336.

Von Korff, M., Crane, P., Lane, M., Miglioretti, D. L., Simon, G., Saunders, K., et al. (2005). Chronic spinal pain and physical-mental comorbidity in the United States: Results from the National Comorbidity Survey Replication. *Pain, 113,* 331–339.

von Wolff, A. A., Hölzel, L. P., Westphal, A. A., Härter, M. M., & Kriston, L. L. (2013). Selective serotonin reuptake inhibitors and tricyclic antidepressants in the acute treatment of chronic depression and dysthymia: A systematic review and meta-analysis.*Journal of Affective Disorders, 144,* 7–15.

# W

Waber, D. P. (2010). *Rethinking learning disabilities: Understanding children who struggle in school.* New York: The Guilford Press.

Waber, R. L., Shiv, B., Carmon, Z., & Ariely, D. (2008). Commercial features of placebo and therapeutic efficacy. *Journal of the American Medical Association, 299,* 1016–1017.

Wade, T. D. (2010). Genetic influences on eating and the eating disorders. In W. S. Agras (Ed.), *The Oxford handbook of eating disorders* (pp. 103–122). New York: Oxford University Press.

Wager, T. D. (2005). The neural bases of placebo effects in pain. *Current Directions in Psychological Science, 14,* 175–179.

Wahl, R. L. (Ed.). (2002). *Principles and practice of positron emission tomography.* Philadelphia: Lippincott Williams and Wilkins.

Waite, L. J., & Gallagher, M. (2000). *The Case for Marriage: Why Married People are Happier, Healthier, and Better off Financially.* New York: Doubleday.

Wakefield, A. J., Murch, S, H., Anthony, A., Linnell, J. Casson, D. M., Malik, M., et al. (1998). Ileal lymphoid nodular hyperplasia, non-specific colitis, and regressive developmental disorder in children. *Lancet, 351,* 637–641.

Wakefield, A. J., Murch, S, H., Anthony, A., Linnell, J. Casson, D. M., Malik, M., Berelowitz, M., Dhillon, A. P., Thomson, M. A., Harvey, P., Valentine, A., Davies, S. E., Walker-Smith, J. A. (1998). Ileal lymphoid nodular hyperplasia, non-specific colitis, and regressive developmental disorder in children.*Lancet, 351,* 637–641.

Wakefield, J. C. (1999). The measurement of mental disorder. In A. V. Horwitz & T. L. Scheid (Eds.), *A handbook for the study of mental health: Social contexts, theories, and systems.* Cambridge, UK: Cambridge University Press.

Wakefield, J. C. (2011). DSM-5 proposed diagnostic criteria for sexual paraphilias: Tensions between diagnostic validity and forensic utility. *International Journal of Law and Psychiatry, 34,* 195–209.

Wakefield, J. C. (2012). The *DSM-5*'s proposed new categories of sexual disorder: The problem of false positives in sexual diagnosis. *Clinical Social Work Journal, 40,* 21–23.

Wald, M. S., Carlsmith, J. M., & Leiderman, P. H. (1988). *Protecting abused and neglected children.* Stanford, CA: Stanford University Press.

Waldemar, G., & Burns, A. (2009). *Alzheimer's disease.* New York: Oxford University Press.

Walden, B., McGue, M., Iacono, W. G., Burt, S. A., & Elkins, I. (2004). Identifying shared environmental contributions to early substance use: The respective roles of peers and parents. *Journal of Abnormal Psychology, 113*(3), 440–450.

Waldinger, M. D. (2009). Delayed and premature ejaculation. In R. Balon & R. Segraves (Eds.), *Clinical manual of sexual disorders* (pp. 273–304). Arlington, VA: American Psychiatric Publishing.

Waldman, I. D., & Rhee, S. H. (2006). Genetic and environmental influences on psychopathy and antisocial behavior. In C. J. Patrick (Ed.), *Handbook of psychopathy* (pp. 205–228). New York: Guilford.

Walker, E., Davis, D., & Baum, K. (1993). Social withdrawal. In C. G. Costello (Ed.), *Symptoms of schizophrenia* (pp. 227–260). New York: Wiley.

Walker, E., Kestler, L., Bollini, A., & Hochman, K. M. (2004). Schizophrenia: Etiology and course. *Annual Review of Psychology, 55,* 401–430.

Walker, L. (1989). Psychology and violence against women. *American Psychologist, 44,* 695–702.

Wallace, J. F., & Newman, J. P. (2004). A theory-based treatment model for psychopathy. *Cognitive and Behavioral Practice, 11,* 178–189.

Walsh, B. T., Kaplan, A. S., Attia, E., Olmsted, M., Parides, M., Carter, J. C., et al. (2006). Fluoxetine after weight restoration in anorexia nervosa: A randomized controlled trial. *Journal of the American Medical Association, 295,* 2605–2612.

Walsh, B. T., Fairburn, C. G., Mickley, D., Sysko, R., & Parides, M. K. (2004). Treatment of bulimia nervosa in a primary care setting. *American Journal of Psychiatry, 161,* 556–561.

Walsh, T., Wilson, G. T., Loeb, K. L., Devlin, M. J., Pike, K. M., Roose, S. P., et al. (1997). Medication and psychotherapy in the treatment of bulimia nervosa. *American Journal of Psychiatry, 154,* 523–531.

Walters, G. D. (1999). *The addiction concept: Working hypothesis or self-fulfilling prophesy?* Boston: Allyn & Bacon.

Wampold, B. E. (2007). Psychotherapy: The humanistic (and effective) treatment. *American Psychologist, 62,* 857–873.

Wandersman, A., & Florin, P. (2003). Community interventions and effective prevention. *American Psychologist, 2003,* 441–448.

Wang, C., Xiang, Y., Cai, Z., Weng, Y., Bo, Q., Zhao, J., et al. (2010). Risperidone maintenance treatment in schizophrenia: A randomized, controlled trial. *American Journal of Psychiatry, 167*(6), 676–685.

Wang, H., Lin, S., Sung, P., Wu, M., Hung, K., Wang, L., et al. (2012). Population based study on patients with traumatic brain injury suggests increased risk of dementia. *Journal of Neurology, Neurosurgery & Psychiatry, 83,* 1080–1085.

Wang, M., Henkens, K., & van Solinge, H. (2011, February 21). Retirement adjustment: A review of theoretical and empirical advancements. *American Psychologist, 66,* 204–213.

Warnock, J. K. (2002). Female hypoactive sexual desire disorder: Epidemiology, diagnosis and treatment. *CNS Drugs, 16,* 745–753.

Waschbusch, D. A. (2002). A meta-analytic examination of comorbid hyperactive-impulsive-attention problems and conduct problems.*Psychological Bulletin, 128*(1), 118–150.

Waschbusch, D. A., & Hill, G. P. (2004). Empirically supported, promising, and unsupported treatments for children with Attention-Deficit/Hyperactivity Disorder. In S. O. Lilienfeld et al. (Eds.), *Science and Pseudoscience in Clinical Psychology* (pp. 333–362). New York: Guilford.

Wassef, A., Baker, J., & Kochan, L. D. (2003). GABA and schizophrenia: A review of basic science and clinical studies. *Journal of Clinical Psychopharmacology, 23,* 601–640.

Waterhouse, L., Fein, D., & Modahl, C. (1996). Neurofunctional mechanisms in autism. *Psychological Review, 103,* 457–489.

Waterman, A. S., & Goldman, J. A. (1976). A longitudinal study of ego identity development at a liberal arts college. *Journal of Youth and Adolescence, 5,* 361–369.

Waterman, G., Geary, P., & Waterman, C. (1974). Longitudinal study of changes in ego identity status from the freshman to the senior year at college. *Developmental Psychology, 10,* 387–392.

Watkins, J. G. (1984). The Bianchi (L.A. Hillsdale Strangler) case: Sociopath or multiple personality. *International Journal of Clinical and Experimental Hypnosis, 32,* 67–101.

Watts, C., & Zimmerman, C. (2002). Violence against women: Global scope and magnitude. *Lancet, 359,* 1232–1237.

Webster-Stratton, C. (1994). Advancing videotape parent training: A comparison study. *Journal of Consulting and Clinical Psychology, 62,* 583–593.

Wegner, D. M. (1994). Ironic processes of mental control. *Psychological Review, 101,* 34–52.

Wehr, T. A. (1989). Seasonal affective disorder: A historical overview. In N. E. Rosenthal & M. C. Blehar (Eds.), *Seasonal Affective Disorders and Phototherapy.* New York: Guilford.

Weinberger, D. R., & McClure, R. K. (2002). Neurotoxicity, neuroplasticity, and magnetic resonance imaging morphometry: What is happening in the schizophrenic brain? *Archives of General Psychiatry, 59,* 553–558.

Weiner, I. B., & Meyer, G. J. (2009). Personality assessment with the Rorschach Inkblot Method. In J. N. Butcher & J. N. Butcher (Eds.), *Oxford handbook of personality assessment* (pp. 277–298). New York, NY: Oxford University Press.

Weintraub, S., Salmon, D., Mercaldo, N., Ferris, S., Graff-Radford, N. R., & Chui, H. (2009). The Alzheimer's disease centers' uniform data set (UDS): The neuropsychologic test battery. *Alzheimer Disease and Associated Disorders, 23,* 91–101.

Weinstein, Y., Gleason, M. J., & Oltmanns, T. F. (2012). Borderline but not antisocial personality disorder symptoms are related to self-reported partner aggression in late middle-age. *Journal of Abnormal Psychology, 121,* 692–698.

Weinstock, R., Vari, G., Leong, G. B., & Silva, J. A. (2006). Back to the past in California: A temporary retreat to a Tarasoff duty to warn. *Journal of the American Academy of Psychiatry and the Law, 34,* 523–528.

Weiser, M. M., Werbeloff, N. N., Vishna, T. T., Yoffe, R. R., Lubin, G. G., Shmushkevitch, M. M., & Davidson, M. M. (2008). Elaboration on immigration and risk for schizophrenia. *Psychological Medicine, 38,* 1113–1119.

Weissman, M. M., Markowitz, J. C., & Klerman, G. L. (2000). *Comprehensive Guide to Interpersonal Psychotherapy.* New York: Basic Books.

Weithorn, L. A. (1988). Mental hospitalization of troublesome youth: An analysis of skyrocketing admission rates. *Stanford Law Review, 40,* 773–838.

Welch, S. L., & Fairburn, C. G. (1996). Childhood sexual and physical abuse as risk factors for the development of bulimia nervosa: A community-based case control study. *Child Abuse & Neglect, 20*(7), 633–642.

Wells, K. C., Chi, T. C., Hinshaw, S. P., Epstein, J. N., Pfiffner, L., Nebel-Schwalm, M., et al. (2006). Treatment-related changes in objectively measured parenting behaviors in the Multimodal Treatment Study of children with attention-deficit/hyperactivity disorder. *Journal of Consulting and Clinical Psychology, 74,* 649–657.

Welte, J. W., Barnes, G. M., Tidwell, M. O., & Hoffman, J. H. (2008). The prevalence of problem gambling among U.S. adolescents and young adults: Results from a national survey. *Journal of Gambling Studies, 24,* 119–133.

Werneke, U., Northey, S., & Bhugra, D. (2006). Antidepressasnts and sexual dysfunction. *Acta Psychiatric Scandinavica, 114,* 384–397.

Werner, J. S., & Smith, R. S. (1992). *Vulnerable but Invincible: A Longitudinal Study of Resilient Children and Youth.* New York: McGraw-Hill.

Westen, D., & Bradley, R. (2005). Empirically supported complexity: Rethinking evidence-based practice in psychotherapy. *Current Directions in Psychological Science, 14,* 266–271.

Weston, D., Novotny, C. M., & Thompson-Brenner, H. (2004). The empirical status of empirically supported psychotherapies: Assumptions, findings, and reporting in controlled clinical trials. *Psychological Bulletin, 130,* 631–663.

Westrin, A., & Lam, R. W. (2007). Seasonal affective disorder: A clinical update. *Annals of Clinical Psychiatry, 19,* 239–246.

Whaley, A. L. (2001). Cultural mistrust and the clinical diagnosis of paranoid schizophrenia in African American patients. *Journal of Psychopathology and Behavioral Assessment, 23,* 93–100.

Whaley, A. L., & Hall, B. N. (2009). Effects of cultural themes in psychotic symptoms on the diagnosis of schizophrenia in African Americans. *Mental Health, Religion & Culture, 12*(5), 457–471.

Whalley, H. C., Papmeyer, M., Sprooten, E., Lawrie, S. M., Sussmann, J. E., & McIntosh, A. M. (2012). Review of functional magnetic resonance imaging studies comparing bipolar disorder and schizophrenia. *Bipolar Disorders, 14,* 411–431.

Whisman, M. A., Beach, S. R. H., & Snyder, D. K. (2008). Is marital discord taxonic and can taxonic status be assessed reliably? Results from a national, representative sample of married couples. *Journal of Consulting and Clinical Psychology, 76,* 745–755.

Whisman, M. A., Sheldon, C. T., & Goering, P. (2000). Psychiatric disorders and dissatisfaction with social relationships: Does type of relationship matter? *Journal of Abnormal Psychology, 109,* 803–808.

Whisman, M. A., Tolejko, N., & Chatav, Y. (2007). Social consequences of personality disorders: Probability and timing of marriage and probability of marital disruption. *Journal of Personality Disorders, 21,* 690–695.

Whitaker, R. (2010). *Anatomy of an epidemic: Magic bullets, psychiatric drugs, and the astonishing rise of mental illness in America.* New York: Crown Publishers.

Whittington, C. J., et al. (2004). Selective serotonin reuptake inhibitors in childhood depression: Systematic review of published versus unpublished data. *Lancet, 363,* 1341–1345.

Whybrow, P. C. (1997). *A Mood Apart: The Thinker's Guide to Emotion and Its Disorders.* New York: HarperCollins.

Widaman, K. F. (2009). Phenylketonuria in children and mothers. *Current Directions in Psychological Science, 18,* 48–52.

Widiger, T. A. (2006). Psychopathy and DSM-IV psychopathology. In C. J. Patrick (Ed.), *Handbook of psychopathy* (pp. 156–171). New York: Guilford.

Widiger, T. A., Costa, P. R., & McCrae, R. R. (2013). Diagnosis of personality disorder using the five-factor model and the proposed DSM-5. In T. A. Widiger & P. R. Costa (Eds.), *Personality disorders and the five-factor model of personality* (3rd ed.) (pp. 285–310). Washington: American Psychological Association.

Wiederman, M. W. (1997). Pretending orgasm during sexual intercourse: Correlates in a sample of young adult women. *Journal of Sex and Marital Therapy, 23,* 131–139.

Wiegel, M., Scepkowski, L. A., & Barlow, D. H. (2007). Cognitive-affective processes in sexual arousal and sexual dysfunction. In E. Janssen (Ed.), *The psychophysiology of sex* (pp. 143–165). Bloomington: Indiana University Press.

Wiehe, V. R., & Richards, A. L. (1995). *Intimate betrayal: Understanding and responding to the trauma of acquaintance rape.* Thousand Oaks, CA: Sage.

Wildes, J. E., Emery, R. E., & Simons, A. D. (2001). The roles of ethnicity and culture in the development of eating disturbance and body dissatisfaction: A meta-analytic review. *Clinical Psychology Review, 21,* 521–551.

Wilens, T. E., Adler, L. A., Adams, J., Sgambati, S., Rotrosen, J., Sawtelle, R., et al. (2008). Misuse and diversion of stimulants prescribed for ADHD: A systematic review of the literature. *Journal of the American Academy of Child and Adolescent Psychiatry, 47,* 21–31.

Wilfley, D. E., Bishop, M. E., Wilson, G. T., & Agras, W. S. (2008). Classification of eating disorders: Toward DSM-V. *International Journal of Eating Disorders, 40,* S123–S129.

Williams, K. D., & Nida, S. A. (2011). Ostracism: Consequences and coping. *Current Directions in Psychological Science, 20,* 71–75.

Williams, L. M., & Finkelhor, D. (1990). The characteristics of incestuous fathers: A review of recent studies. In W. L. Marshall, D. R. Laws, & H. E. Barbaree (Eds.), *Handbook of sexual assault: Issues, theories, and treatment of the offender* (p. 231). New York: Plenum.

Williams, R. B., Barefoot, J. C., Califf, R. M., Haney, T. L., Saunders, W. B., et al. (1992). Prognostic importance of social and economic resources among medically treated patients with angiographically documented coronary artery disease. *Journal of the American Medical Association, 267,* 520–524.

Williams, L. M. (1994). Recall of childhood trauma: A prospective study of women's memories of child sexual abuse. *Journal of Consulting and Clinical Psychology, 62,* 1167–1176.

Wilson, D. (2010, October 2). Side effects may include lawsuits. *New York Times.* Retrieved March 15, 2011, from http://www.nytimes.com/2010/10/03/business/03psych.html

Wilson, G. (2010). Eating disorders, obesity and addiction. *European Eating Disorders Review, 18,* 341–351.

Wilson, G. T. (2010). Cognitive behavioral therapy for eating disorders. In W. S. Agras (Ed.), *The Oxford handbook of eating disorders* (pp. 331–347). New York: Oxford University Press.

Wilson, G. T., Grilo, C. M., & Vitousek, K. M. (2007). Psychological treatment of eating disorders. *American Psychologist, 62,* 199–216.

Wilson, G. T., Loeb, K. L., Walsh, B. T., Labouvie, E., Petkova, E., Liu, X., et al. (1999). Psychological versus pharmacological treatments of bulimia nervosa: Predictors and processes of change. *Journal of Consulting & Clinical Psychology, 67,* 451–459.

Wilson, T. D. (2002). *Strangers to Ourselves: Discovering the Adaptive Unconscious.* New York: Belknap.

Wilson, T. D., & Linville, P. W. (1982). Improving the academic performance of college freshmen: Attribution therapy revisited. *Journal of Personality and Social Psychology, 42*(2), 367–376.

Wimberly, S. R., Carver, C. S., Laurenceau, J. P., Harris, S. D., Antoni, M. H., et al. (2005). Perceived partner reactions to diagnosis and treatment of breast cancer: Impact on psychosocial and psychosexual adjustment. *Journal of Consulting and Clinical Psychology, 73,* 300–311.

Wincze, J. P. (1989). Assessment and treatment of atypical sexual behavior. In S. R. Lieblum & R. C. Rosen (Eds.), *Principles and practice of sex therapy* (2nd ed., pp. 382–404). New York: Guilford.

Wincze, J. P., Bach, A. K., & Barlow, D. H. (2008). Sexual dysfunction. In D. H. Barlow (Ed.), *Clinical handbook of psychological disorders: A step-by-step treatment manual* (4th ed., pp. 615–661). New York: Guilford.

Wing, L. (1988). Autism: Possible clues to the underlying pathology: 1. Clinical facts. In L. Wing (Ed.), *Aspects of autism: Biological research* (pp. 11–18). London: Gaskell.

Wing, L., & Potter, D. (2002). The epidemiology of autistic spectrum disorders: Is the prevalence rising? *Mental Retardation and Developmental Disabilities Research Reviews, 8*(3), 151–161.

Winter, D. G., John, O. P., Stewart, A. J., Klohnen, E. C., & Duncan, L. E. (1998). Traits and motives: Toward an integration of two traditions in personality research. *Psychological Review, 105,* 230–250.

Wirth, J. H., & Bodenhausen, G. V. (2009). The role of gender in mental-illness stigma: A national experiment. *Psychological Science, 20,* 169–173.

Wiseman, C. V., Gray, J. J., Mosimann, J. E., & Ahrens, A. H. (1992). Cultural expectations of thinness in women: An update. *International Journal of Eating Disorders, 11,* 85–89.

Witkiewitz, K., Marlatt, G. A., & Walker, D. (2005). Mindfulness-based relapse prevention for alcohol and substance use disorders. *Journal of Cognitive Psychotherapy, 19,* 221–228.

Wittchen, H., Schuster, P., & Lieb, R. (2001). Comorbidity and mixed anxiety-depressive disorder: Clinical curiosity or pathophysiological need? *Human Psychopharmacology, 16* (Suppl. 1), S21–S30.

Witvliet, C., Ludwig, T. W., & Vander Laan, K. L. (2001). Granting forgiveness or harboring grudges: Implications for emotion, physiology, and health. *Psychological Science, 12,* 117–124.

Wolfe, D. (1987). *Child abuse: Implications for child development and psychopathology.* Beverly Hills, CA: Sage.

Wolfs, C. G., Kessels, A., Severens, J. L., Brouwer, W., de Vugt, M. E., Verhey, F. J., & Dirksen, C. D. (2012).

Predictive factors for the objective burden of informal care in people with dementia: A systematic review. *Alzheimer Disease and Associated Disorders, 26*, 197–204.

Wonderlich, S. A., Joiner, Jr., T. E., Keel, P. K., Williamson, D. A., & Corsby, R. D. (2007). Eating disorder diagnoses: Empirical approaches to classification. *American Psychologist, 62*, 167–180.

Wong, P. T., & Watt, L. M. (1991). What types of reminiscence are associated with successful aging? *Psychology and Aging, 6*, 272–279.

Wood, J. M., Nezworski, M. T., Lilienfeld, S. O., & Garb, H. N. (2003). *What's wrong with the Rorschach?* San Francisco: Jossey-Bass.

Woods, S. W., Addington, J., Cadenhead, K. S., Cannon, T. D., Cornblatt, B. A., Heinssen, R., et al. (2009). Validity of the prodromal risk syndrome for first psychosis: Findings from the North American prodrome longitudinal study. *Schizophrenia Bulletin, 35*, 894–908.

Woodside, D. B., Garfinkel, P. E., Lin, E., Goering, P., & Kaplan, A. S. (2001). Comparisons of men with full or partial eating disorders, men without eating disorders, and women with eating disorders in the community. *American Journal of Psychiatry, 158*, 570–574.

Woody, E., & Sadler, P. (1998). On reintegrating dissociated theories: Comment on Kirsch and Lynn (1998). *Psychological Bulletin, 123*, 192–197.

Woody, S. R., Steketee, G., & Chambless, D. L. (1995). Reliability and validity of the Yale-Brown obsessive-compulsive scale. *Behaviour Research and Therapy, 33*, 597–605.

Woody, S. R., Weisz, J. R., & McLean, C. (2005). Empirically supported treatments: 10 years later. *The Clinical Psychologist, 58*, 5–11.

Woolfolk, R. L., Allen, L. A., & Tiu, J. E. (2007). New direction in the treatment of somatization. *Psychiatric Clinics of North America, 30*, 621–644.

Wortman, C. B., & Silver, R. C. (2001). The myths of coping with loss revisited. In M. S. Stroebe et al. (Eds.), *Handbook of Bereavement Research* (pp. 405–429). Washington, DC: American Psychological Association.

Wright, S. (2010). Depathologizing consensual sexual sadism, sexual masochism, transvestic fetishism, and fetishism. *Archives of Sexual Behavior, 39*, 1229–1230.

Wrosch, C., Schulz, R., & Heckhausen, J. (2004). Health stresses and depressive symptomatology in the elderly: A control-process approach. *Current Directions in Psychological Science, 13*, 17–20.

Wu, E., Birnbaum, H., Shi, L., Ball, D., Kessler, R., Moulis, M., & Aggarwal, J. (2005). The economic burden of schizophrenia in the United States in 2002. *Journal of Clinical Psychiatry, 66*(9), 1122–1129.

Wylie, K., & Machin, A. (2007). Erectile dysfunction. *Primary Psychiatry, 14*, 65–71.

Wymbs, B. T., & Pelham, W. E., Jr. (2010). Child effects on communication between parents of youth with and without attention-deficit/hyperactivity disorder. *Journal of Abnormal Psychology, 119*, 366–375.

## Y

Yanez, B., Edmondson, D., Stanton, A. L., Park, C. L., Kwan, L., Ganz, P. A., & Blank, T. O. (2009). Facets of spirituality as predictors of adjustment to cancer: Relative contributions of having faith and finding meaning. *Journal of Consulting and Clinical Psychology, 77*, 730–741.

Yang, J., McCrae, R. R., Costa, P. T., Yao, S., Dai, X., Cai, T., et al. (2000). The cross-cultural generalizability of Axis-II constructs: An evaluation of two personality disorder assessment instruments in the People's Republic of China. *Journal of Personality Disorders, 14*, 249–263.

Yang, L., Kleinman, A., Link, B. G., Phelan, J. C., Lee, S., & Good, B. (2007). Culture and stigma: Adding moral experience to stigma theory. *Social Science & Medicine, 64*, 1524–1535.

Yang, M., Wong, S. C. P., & Coid, J. (2010). The efficacy of violence prediction: A meta-analytic comparison of nine risk assessment tools. *Psychological Bulletin, 136*, 740–767.

Yates, W. R., Cadoret, R. J., & Troughton, E. P. (1999). The Iowa adoption studies: Methods and results. In M. C. LaBuda & E. L. Grigorenko (Eds.), *On the way to individuality: Current methodological issues in behavioral genetics* (pp. 95–125). Huntington, NY: Nova Science Publishers.

Yeh, M., & Weisz, J. R. (2001). Why are we here at the clinic? Parent-child (dis)agreement on referral problems at outpatient treatment entry. *Journal of Consulting and Clinical Psychology, 69*, 1018–1025.

Yehuda, R. (2002). Current concepts: Posttraumatic stress disorder. *New England Journal of Medicine, 346*, 108–114.

Yeung, P. P., & Greenwald, S. (1992). Jewish Americans and mental health: Results of the NIMH Epidemiologic Catchment Area Study. *Social Psychiatry and Psychiatric Epidemiology, 27*, 292–297.

Yirmiya, N., & Sigman, M. D. (1996). High functioning individuals with autism: Diagnosis, empirical findings, and theoretical issues. *Clinical Psychology Review, 11*(6), 669–683.

Yoder, P., & Stone, W. L. (2006). Randomized comparison of two communication interventions for preschoolers with autism spectrum disorders. *Journal of Consulting and Clinical Psychology, 74*, 426–435.

Young, J., Leentjens, A., George, J., Olofsson, B., & Gustafson, Y. (2008). Systematic approaches to the prevention and management of patients with delirium. *Journal of Psychosomatic Research, 65*, 267–272.

Young, M. (2013). Statistics, scapegoats and social control: A critique of pathological gambling prevalence research. *Addiction Research & Theory, 21*, 1–11.

Younglove, J. A., & Vitello, C. J. (2003). Community notification provisions of "Megan's law" from a therapeutic jurisprudence perspective: A case study. *American Journal of Forensic Psychology, 21*, 25–38.

Yudofsky, S. C. (2005). *Fatal flaws: Navigating destructive relationships with people with disorders of personality and character.* Washington, DC: American Psychiatric Publishing.

Yung, A. R., Wood, S. J., McGorry, P. D., & Pantelis, C. C. (2011). Commentary on 'Should the diagnostic boundaries of schizophrenia be expanded?' *Cognitive Neuropsychiatry, 16*, 107–112.

## Z

Zahn-Waxler, C., Kochanska, G., Krupnick, J., & McKnew, D. (1990). Patterns of guilt in children of depressed and well mothers. *Developmental Psychology, 26*, 51–59.

Zaleta, A. K., Carpenter, B. D., Porensky, E. K., Xiong, C., & Morris, J. C. (2012). Agreement on diagnosis among patients, companions, and professionals after a dementia evaluation. *Alzheimer Disease and Associated Disorders, 26*, 232–237.

Zanarini, M. C., & Frankenburg, F. R. (2001). Olanzapine treatment of female borderline personality disorder patients: A double-blind, placebo-controlled pilot study. *Journal of Clinical Psychiatry, 62*, 849–854.

Zanarini, M. C., Frankenburg, F. R., Hennen, J., Reich, D. B., & Silk, K. R. (2006). Prediction of the 10-year course of borderline personality disorder. *The American Journal of Psychiatry, 163*, 827–832.

Zapf, P. A., & Roesch, R. (2011). Future directions in the restoration of competency to stand trial. *Current Directions in Psychological Science, 20*, 43–47.

Zautra, A. J., Johnson, L. M., & Davis, M. C. (2005). Positive affect as a source of resilience for women in chronic pain. *Journal of Consulting and Clinical Psychology, 73*, 212–220.

Zigler, E. (1967). Familial mental retardation: A continuing dilemma. *Science, 155*, 292–298.

Zigler, E., & Hodapp, R. M. (1986). *Understanding mental retardation.* New York: Cambridge University Press.

Zigler, E., & Styfco, S. J. (1993). Using research and theory to justify and inform Head Start expansion. *Social Policy Report for the Society Research in Child Development, 7*(2), 1–20.

Zilbergeld, B. (1995). The critical and demanding partner in sex therapy. In R. C. Rosen & S. R. Leiblum (Eds.), *Case studies in sex therapy* (pp. 311–330). New York: Guilford.

Zimmerman, M. (2012). Is there adequate empirical justification for radically revising the personality disorders section for DSM-5? *Personality Disorders: Theory, Research, and Treatment, 3*, 444–457.

Zito, J. M., Safer, D. J., dosReis, S., Gardner, J. F., Boles, M., & Lynch, F. (2000). Trends in the prescribing of psychotropic medications to preschoolers. *Journal of the American Medical Association, 283*, 1025–1030.

Zito, J. M., Safer, D. J., dosReis, S., Gardner, J. F., Magder, L. S., Soeken, K., et al. (2003). Psychotropic practice patterns for youth: A 10-year perspective. *Archives of Pediatrics and Adolescent Medicine, 157*, 17–25.

Zoccolillo, M., & Cloninger, C. R. (1986). Somatization disorder: Psychologic symptoms, social disability, and diagnosis. *Comprehensive Psychiatry, 27*, 65–73.

Zorn, C. A. (1998). My private disorder. *Groton School Quarterly*, 19–21.

Zucker, K. J., & Blanchard, R. (1997). Tranvestic fetishism: Psychopathology and theory. In D. R. Laws & W. T. O'Donohue (Eds.), *Handbook of sexual deviance: Theory and application.* New York: Guilford.

Zuckerman, M. (1991). *Psychobiology of Personality.* New York: Cambridge University Press.

Zuckerman, M. (1999). *Vulnerability to psychopathology: A biosocial model.* Washington, DC: American Psychological Association Press.

# Photo Credits

**Cover**
Terry Vine/Getty Images

**Chapter 1**
**page 1:** Kelly Redinger/Design Pics Inc./Alamy; **page 4:** Raymond Depardon/Magnum Photos, Inc.; **page 5 (bottom):** Pearson Education, Inc.; **page 5 (top left):** Richard Drew/AP Images; **page 11:** SuperStock/Getty Images; **page 12:** Rob/Fotolia; **page 16:** Worcester Historical Museum; **page 16:** Bettmann/Cobis; **page 20:** Historical/Corbis

**Chapter 2**
**page 24:** LaCozza/Fotolia; **page 27 (top left):** Photo Researchers/Alamy; **page 27 (bottom right):** Mary Evans Picture Library/Alamy; **page 32 (top right):** Kzenon/Fotolia; **page 32 (bottom):** Robert E. Emery; **page 35:** CALVIN AND HOBBES © Bill Watterson. Reprinted with permission of UNIVERSAL UCLICK. All rights reserved.; **page 41:** Robert E. Emery; **page 42:** Pictorial Press Ltd/Alamy; **page 44:** Wim Van Den Heever/Tetra Images/Alamy; **page 45:** Michael Luckett/Fotolia; **page 45 (top left):** Carolita Johnson/The New Yorker Collection/www.cartoonbank.com; **page 46:** Charles Barsotti/The New Yorker Collection/www.cartoonbank.com; **page 47:** Jenner/Fotolia; **page 49 (top):** Photoedit, Inc.; **page 49 (bottom):** Pearson Education, Inc.

**Chapter 3**
**page 52:** EV203/Image Source/Alamy; **page 58:** Bettmann/Corbis; **page 59:** Danny Shanahan/The New Yorker Collection/www.cartoonbank.com; **page 61:** Tony/Fotolia; **page 63:** Pearson Education, Inc.; **page 64:** Asiseeit/E+/Getty Images; **page 66:** Manuel Litran/Paris Match Archive/Getty Images; **page 70:** WavebreakmediaMicro/Fotolia; **page 72:** Jack Ziegler/The New Yorker Collection/www.cartoonbank.com; **page 73:** Nancy Sheehan/Photoedit, Inc.; **page 74:** Phillip Bond/Alamy

**Chapter 4**
**page 77:** Okeyphotos/Getty Images; **page 80:** Bezikus/Shutterstock; **page 82:** Mandel Ngan/Newscom; **page 84:** Rogelio V. Solis/AP Images; **page 89:** Trekandshoot/Shutterstock; **page 90:** Alexsokolov/Fotolia; **page 91:** Mary Hockenbery/Flickr/Getty Images; **page 93:** Pearson Education, Inc.; **page 95:** Raymond Stott/The Image Works; **page 98:** Michael Maslin/The New Yorker Collection/www.cartoonbank.com; **page 99:** Pearson Education, Inc.; **page 102:** NASA Earth Observatory; **page 100:** Mark Harmel/The Image Bank/Getty Images

**Chapter 5**
**page 105:** F1 Online/SuperStock; **page 109:** Shutterstock; **page 110:** Flint/Cardinal/Corbis; **page 113:** Yuri Arcurs Media/SuperStock; **page 115:** Pearson Education, Inc.; **page 116:** Lakov Filimonov/Shutterstock; **page 117:** Monkey Business Images/Shutterstock; **page 118 (bottom):** Pearson Education, Inc.; **page 120:** Themba Hadebe/AP Images; **page 121:** Pearson Education, Inc.; **page 123:** Moodboard/Corbis; **page 130:** Barbara Smaller/The New Yorker Collection/www.cartoonbank.com; **page 132:** James D. Wilson/Aurora Photos; **page 133:** TWPhoto/Corbis; **page 134:** Andrea Comas/Reuters/Landov; **page 135:** Elena Dorfman/Redux Pictures; **page 136:** Terry Schmitt/UPI/Landov

**Chapter 6**
**page 143:** Ikon Images/SuperStock; **page 146 (bottom left):** Carsten Peter/National Geographic Image Collection/Getty Images; **page 146 (top right):** Wally Santana/AP Images; **page 147 (top):** Pearson Education, Inc.; **page 147:** Pearson Education, Inc.; **page 150 (bottom):** Pearson Education, Inc.; **page 150 (top):** OjoVertical/Fotolia; **page 152:** William Casey/Fotolia; **page 159:** Olly/Fotolia; **page 162:** Joe Dator/The New Yorker Collection/www.cartoonbank.com; **page 163:** Fernando Madeira/Fotolia; **page 166:** Michael Maloney/San Francisco Chronicle/Corbis

**Chapter 7**
**page 174:** F1 Online/SuperStock; **page 175:** Andrew Gombert/Newscom; **page 177:** Bettmann/Corbis; **page 182 (bottom):** Pearson Education, Inc.; **page 183:** Boston Globe/Getty Images; **page 184 (top):** Pearson Education, Inc.; **page 184 (bottom):** Jason Hornick/The Potomac News/AP Images; **page 187:** SPL/Science Source; **page 188:** Jerry Torrens/AP Images; **page 189:** Erin Painter/Midland Daily News/AP Images; **page 190:** Neville Elder/Corbis; **page 191:** Lois Bernstein Photography; **page 192:** Gabriel Utasi; **page 196:** The Mankato Free Press/AP Images; **page 199:** Mike Kemp/RubberBall/Alamy; **page 200:** Rich Legg/E+/Getty Images; **page 202:** Mary Evans Picture Library/The Image Works

**Chapter 8**
**page 206:** B. Wylezich/Fotolia; **page 208 (middle right):** Laurence Gough/Shutterstock; **page 208 (bottom left):** Kaphotokevm1/Fotolia; **page 210:** Vitaly Titov & Maria Sidelnikova/Shutterstock; **page 213:** Meckes/Ottawa/Science Source; **page 215:** Lefteris Pitarakis/AP Images; **page 219 (top left):** Paula Lerner/Aurora Photos/Alamy; **page 219 (bottom right):** Noboru Hashimoto/Sygma/Corbis; **page 221(top left):** Monkey Business/Fotolia; **page 221 (bottom right):** Bernd Leitner/Fotolia; **page 222:** Bridge/Glow Images; **page 223:** Alamy **page 225:** Edward Koren/The New Yorker Collection/www.cartoonbank.com; **page 226:** Shaun Best/Reuters/Landov; **page 227 (bottom left):** Edward Koren/The New Yorker Collection/www.cartoonbank.com; **page 227 (top right):** Paul Wood/Alamy

**Chapter 9**
**page 231:** Ocean/Corbis; **page 234:** Edward Frascino/The New Yorker Collection/www.cartoonbank.com; **page 235:** Firma V/Shutterstock; **page 239 (bottom right):** Pat Benic/Bettmann/Corbis; **page 239 (bottom left):** Pearson Education, Inc.; **page 240:** Peter Dejong/AP Images; **page 242:** Shutterstock; **page 246:** Everett Collection; **page 247:** Alexander Zemlianichenko/AP Images; **page 251:** Tim James/The Gray Gallery/Alamy; **page 255:** Newscom; **page 258:** Newscom

**Chapter 10**
**page 262:** Image Source Plus/Alamy; **page 263:** Bloomberg/Getty Images; **page 264:** Bill Greenblatt/UPI/Landov; **page 266:** Flash&Partners/Reuters/Landov; **page 267:** Wallace Kirkland/Time & Life Pictures/Getty Images; **page 270:** Pearson Education, Inc.; **page 271:** Pearson Education, Inc.; **page 272:** Jackson Lee/Splash News/Newscom; **page 273:** Emilio Flores/Everett Collection; **page 274:** Pictorial Press Ltd./Alamy; **page 275:** Trinity Mirror/Mirrorpix/Alamy; **page 277:** Frank Trapper/Corbis; **page 278:** L'Equipe Agence/Reuters/Landov; **page 281:** Sylvain Gaboury/AP Images; **page 281:** Rebecka Silvekroon/www.swedishmannequins.com

**Chapter 11**
**page 284:** SGM/AGE Fotostock/SuperStock; **page 288:** Pearson Education, Inc.; **page 289:** Michaela Begsteiger/Getty Images; **page 292:** Kuzma/

Shutterstock; **page 295:** Yuri K/Fotolia; **page 296:** Bettmann/Corbis; **page 299:** Joel Ryan/Invision/AP Images; **page 302:** www.cartoonbank.com; **page 303:** Bill Aron/Photoedit, Inc.; **page 309:** Andres Rodriguez/Fotolia; **page 309:** Fotolia; © Pearson Education, Upper Saddle River, New Jersey; **page 313:** Ronald Markowitz/The New Yorker Collection/www.cartoonbank.com

## Chapter 12

**page 318:** Beyond Fotomedia GmbH/Alamy; **page 319:** Apops/Fotolia; **page 321:** Ortenstone Delattre Fine Art; **page 323:** Corbis; **page 328:** Radius Images/Alamy; **page 330:** Dann Tardif/LWA/Corbis; **page 331:** Alex Gregory/The New Yorker Collection/www.cartoonbank.com; **page 334:** Donna Svennevik/American Broadcasting Companies, Inc.; **page 334:** Brand X Pictures/Getty Images; **page 335:** Margarita Borodina/Shutterstock; **page 336:** Pearson Education, Inc.; **page 337:** Yoshikazu Tsumo/AFP/Getty Images/Newscom; **page 343 (top left):** SIPA/Newscom; **page 343 (bottom right):** Dylan Martinez/Reuters/Landov; **page 345:** Pearson Education, Inc.

## Chapter 13

**page 348:** Alexei Gridenko/Fotolia; **page 350:** National Library of Medicine; **page 351:** Stokkete/Fotolia; **page 352:** Pearson Education, Inc.; **page 358 (top right):** Pearson Education, Inc.; **page 358 (top left):** Damian Dovarganes/AP Images; **page 359:** Barbara Smaller/www.cartoonbank.com; **page 363:** Mike Goldwater/Alamy; **page 364 (top):** National Institute of Mental Health; **page 367:** Corbis; **page 374:** Eric Risberg/AP Images; **page 375:** JazzSign/Lebrecht/The Image Works

## Chapter 14

**page 379:** Jeffrey Blackler/Alamy; **page 380:** Olga Shalygin/AP Images; **page 381:** Pearson Education, Inc.; **page 385:** Heiko Junge/AP Images; **page 386:** CD1 WENN Photos/Newscom; **page 393:** Steve Ruark/AP Images; **page 394:** Kenneth Lambert/AP Images; **page 397:** Jose Luis Magana/AP Images; **page 399:** Ed Kashi/VII/Corbis; **page 401:** Pearson Education, Inc.

## Chapter 15

**page 404:** LaCozza/Fotolia; **page 406:** MWH WENN Photos/Newscom; **page 410:** Elaine Rebman/Science Source; **page 412 (bottom left):** American Medical Association; **page 412 (bottom right):** American Medical Association; **page 414:** Michael Conroy/AP Images; **page 416:** Andres R. Alonso/AP Images; **page 418:** Jeff Greenberg/Alamy; **page 419:** Pearson Education, Inc.; **page 420:** Everett Collection; **page 421:** John Birdsall/The Image Works; **page 423:** University of Wisconsin Madison; **page 424:** Jeffrey Neira/CBS/Landov; **page 427:** Kelly Hertz/AP Images; **page 428:** Kondor83/Fotolia; **page 429:** Alan Carey/The Image Works

## Chapter 16

**page 435:** Okeyphotos/Getty Images; **page 436:** Crestajohnson/Fotolia; **page 437:** CALVIN AND HOBBES © Bill Watterson. Reprinted with permission of UNIVERSAL UCLICK. All rights reserved.; **page 439:** Moviestore Collection Ltd/Alamy; **page 444:** Frank Cancellare/Bettmann/Corbis; **page 445:** Mary Kate Denny/Photoedit, Inc.; **page 446:** US Food and Drug Administration FDA; **page 447:** Alex Segre/Alamy; **page 449:** David Sipress/The New Yorker Collection/www.cartoonbank.com; **page 451:** CartoonStock Ltd.; **page 452:** Gemphotography/Fotolia; **page 453:** Lisa F. Young/Alamy; **page 454:** Pearson Education, Inc.; **page 455:** Jpaget/Alamy; **page 456:** Barbara Smaller/The New Yorker Collection/www.cartoonbank.com; **page 459:** Marmaduke St. John/Alamy

## Chapter 17

**page 464:** Robert Kneschke/Fotolia; **page 465:** Wolfman57/Shutterstock; **page 466 (bottom right):** Darren Baker/Fotolia; **page 466 (bottom left):**

Monashee Frantz/OJO Images Ltd/Alamy; **page 466 (bm):** Alamy; **page 470:** Digital Vision/Getty Images; **page 474 (top left):** Robert Weber/The New Yorker Collection/www.cartoonbank.com; **page 474 (bottom right):** MBI/Stockbroker/Alamy; **page 479:** Con Tanasiuk/Design Pics Inc./Alamy; **page 480:** Bob Daemmrich/The Image Works; **page 482:** Luke Jarvis/Corbis; **page 484:** Ckellyphoto/Fotolia; **page 485:** Charles Dhara Pak/AP Images; **page 486:** Blend Images/Alamy

## Chapter 18

**page 489:** Ocean/Corbis; **page 491:** Bettmann/Corbis; **page 493 (top):** Eugene Garcia/AP Images; **page 493 (middle):** RJ Sangosti/AFP/Getty Images/Newscom; **page 496:** Marilyn Humphries photography; **page 497:** Dana Verkouteren/AP Images; **page 498:** MCT/Newport News Daily Press/Landov; **page 501:** Newscom; **page 505:** Robin Nelson/ZUMApress/Newscom; **page 507 (top right):** Jerry Cooke/Science Source; **page 507 (top middle):** VILevi/Fotolia; **page 508:** Toby Talbot/AP Images; **page 509:** Firma V/Shutterstock; **page 512:** AP Images

# Text Credits

## Chapter 1

**page 6:** Wakefield, J. C. 2010. Taking disorder seriously: A critique of psychiatric criteria for mental disorders from the harmful-dysfunction perspective. In T. Millon, R. F. Krueger, & E. Simonsen (Eds.), Contemporary directions in psychopathology: Scientific foundations of the DSM-V and ICD-11/75–300. New York: Guilford Press.

## Chapter 2

**page 31:** Lord Byron (1788–1824).

## Chapter 4

**page 98:** Marks, P.A., William Seeman, Deborah L. Haller. 1974. The actuarial use of the MMPI with adolescents and adults. Lippincott Williams & Wilkins.

## Chapter 5

**page 107:** Solomon, A. 2001. The Noonday Demon. Scribner; **page 109:** Solomon, A. 2001. The Noonday Demon. Scribner; **page 109:** Jamison, K.R. 1995. An Unquiet Mind: A Memoir of Moods and Madness. Vintage Books; **page 110:** Jamison, K.R. 1995. An Unquiet Mind: A Memoir of Moods and Madness. Vintage Books; **page 116:** Jamison, K.R. 1995. An Unquiet Mind: A Memoir of Moods and Madness. Vintage Books; **page 131:** US Food and Drug Administration.

## Chapter 6

**page 169:** Belkin, Lisa. Can You Catch Obsessive-Compulsive Disorder? New York Times. 2005 May 22.

## Chapter 7

**page 188:** Bass, E. and Laura Davis. 1998. The Courage to Heal. William Morrow & Company; **page 190:** Based on Grann, David. "Which Way Did He Run?" New York Times. January 13, 2002; **page 191:** Sizemore, C. 1998. A Mind of Her Own. William Morrow & Company;

## Chapter 8

**page 213:** The Serenity Prayer by Reinhold Niebuhr.

## Chapter 9

**page 239:** Brief Case Studies: Borderline Personality Disorder and Schizotypal Personality Disorder © 1993 BJP: 162,299-313; **page 244:** Corbitt, E. M. (2002). Narcissism from the perspective of the five-factor model. In P. T. Costa, Jr., & T. A. Widiger (Eds.), Personality Disorders and the Five-Factor Model of Personality (2nd ed., pp. 293–298). Washington, DC: American Psychological Association; **page 249:** Brief Case Studies: Borderline Personality Disorder and Schizotypal Personality Disorder © 1993 BJP: 162,299-313; **page 251:** Brief Case Studies: Borderline Personality Disorder and Schizotypal Personality Disorder © 1993 BJP: 162,299-313; **page 252:** Moskovitz,Richard. 1996. Lost in the Mirror: An Inside Look at Borderline Personality Disorder. Taylor Trade Publishing, pp. 5–6; **page 255:** Hare, R. D. 1993. Without Conscience: The Disturbing World of the Psychopaths Among Us. New York: Pocket Books; **page 257:** Moffitt. T.E. Adolescence-limited and life-course-persistent antisocial behavior: a developmental taxonomy. Psychological Reviews 1993 Oct;100(4):674-701.

## Chapter 10
**page 266:** Courtesy of the authors; **page 279:** Zorn, C. A. 1998. My private disorder. Groton School Quarterly: 19–21.

## Chapter 11
**page 286:** Reprinted from COMMENTARY, February 1989, by permission;copyright © 1989 by Commentary, Inc.; **page 287:** Vaillant, G. E. 1995. The Natural History of Alcoholism Revisited. Cambridge, MA: Harvard University Press; **page 292:** Fernandez, H. 1998. Heroin. Center City, MN: Hazeldon; **page 302:** Solomon, K., Manepalli, J., Ireland, G. A., & Mahon, G. M. 1993. Alcoholism and prescription drug abuse in the elderly: St. Louis University grand rounds. Journal of the American Geriatrics Society; 41: 57–69; **page 310:** Shavelson, L. 2001. Hooked: Five Addicts Challenge Our Misguided Drug Rehab System. New York: New Press.

## Chapter 12
**page 320:** McCarthy, B. W. 1989. Cognitive-behavioral strategies and techniques in the treatment of early ejaculation. In S. R. Leiblum & R. C. Rosen (Eds.), Principles and Practice of Sex Therapy (2nd ed.). New York: Guilford; **page 324:** Zilbergeld, Bernie. 1995. Men and Sex. Guilford;

**page 326:** Morokoff, P. J. Sex bias and POD. American Psychologist. Jan 1989: 44(1); 73-75; **page 326:** Kaysen, S. 2001. The Camera My Mother Gave Me. Alfred A. Knopf; **page 329:** Case Studies in Sex Therapy. 1995. Raymond C. Rosen and Sandra R. Leiblum (eds). Guilford Press; **page 333:** Levine et. al. Diagnosis and Nature of Paraphilia. Journal of Sex & Marital Therapy. Feb 1990; 16(2):89-102; **page 335:** Merkin, D. Unlikely Obsession: Confronting a taboo. The New Yorker. 1996, February 26 and March 4: 98–115.

## Chapter 13
**page 368:** Leff, J., & Vaughn, C. 1985. Expressed Emotion in Families: Its Significance for Mental Illness. New York: Guilford; **page 353:** Payne, R. L. 1992. First person account: My schizophrenia. Schizophrenia Bulletin; 18: 725–728.

## Chapter 15
**page 419:** Anonymous student; **page 420:** Sacks, O. 1985. The Man Who Mistook His Wife for a Hat and Other Clinical Tales. New York: Summit; **page 420:** Grandin, Temple. 2010. My Life with Autism. Vintage Books; **page 422:** Grandin, Temple. 2010. My Life with Autism. Vintage Books.

## Chapter 17
**page 470:** Erikson, E. 1963. Youth: Change and Challenge. Basic Books.

## Chapter 18
**page 492:** Regina v. M'Naghten, 8 Eng. Rep. 718, 722 (1843); **page 493:** Model Penal Code. Copyright © 1985 by the American Law Institute. Reproduced with permission. All rights reserved; **page 494:** Title 18 United States Code; **page 498:** 536 U.S. 321 (2002); **page 500:** Dickens, Charles. 1902. American Notes and Pictures from Italy. Harper; **page 508:** Mnookin, R. Child Custody Aadjudication: Judicial Functions in the Face of Indeterminacy, 39 Law and Contemporary Problem. 1975; 226; **page 496:** Dershowitz, Alan. 1994. The Abuse Excuse: And Other Cop-Outs, Sob Stories, and Evasions of Responsibility. Hachette Book Group.

# name index

Bone loss, elderly women and, 482
Boot camps, 65t
Borderline personality disorder, 251–255
　case study, 240, 251
　causes, 253–254, 254f
　criteria for, 253
　definition of, 240
　diagnostic criteria, 253, 253t
　historical background, 251, 252
　symptoms, 252–253, 253t
　treatment, 254–255
Bowlby, John, 44, 60, 460
Bradley, Charles, 449
Brain
　cerebral hemispheres, 38
　changes
　　in amnestic disorders, 380–381
　　in dementia, 380
　chemical imbalances in, 35
　damage, hard signs of, 444
　dopamine, reward pathways and, 304–305, 304f, 305f
　growth, in autism, 428
　healthy, 36
　neurobiology, of anxiety disorders, 157–158, 158f
　psychopathology and, 37f, 38
　regions associated with obsessive-compulsive disorder, 100–102, 101f
　structures, major, 36–37, 36f–37f
　unhealthy, 37f
Brain imaging. See also specific brain imaging techniques
　advantages, 101
　disadvantages, 102
　functional, in schizophrenic disorders, 365, 365f
　structural, in schizophrenic disorders, 363–365, 364f
　studies, of mood disorders, 120, 121f, 122, 125–126
　techniques for, 100–101
Brain stem, 36f
Brainstorming, 63
Breathing-related sleep disorders, 221
Breathing retraining, for anxiety disorders, 160
Breuer, Joseph, 58
Brief psychotic disorder, 357–358
Briquet's syndrome, 198
Broader approach, mood depression, 111
Buck v. Bell, 417, 417f
Bulimia nervosa
　age of onset, 273–274
　case study, 10, 267–268
　causes, 274–277, 276f
　comorbidity, 268, 269
　course, 280
　criteria for, 271
　definition of, 263
　diagnosis, DSM-IV-TR criteria, 271t
　differences and similarities of anorexia nervosa, 268t
　frequency of, 271–274
　incidence/prevalence, 14, 263, 271–272, 271t
　in males, 265
　and medical complications, 269
　nonpurging-type, 270, 271t
　outcome, 280
　prevention, 280–281, 281f

　purging-type, 270t, 271–272
　risk in women, 272f
　symptoms of, 267–269
　treatment, 279–280

## C

Campral (acamprosate), 309
Cancer, psychological factors in, 218–219
Cannabis (cannabinoids)
　short-term vs. long-term effects, 294
　symptoms, 294
　types of, 285
Cannon, Walter, 211
Carbamazepine (Tegretol), for bipolar disorder, 130
Carcinogens, 219
Cardiovascular disease (CVD), 221–228
　causes, 222–226
　diagnosis, 222
　frequency, 222
　integration and alternative pathways, 226
　prevention
　　primary, 226
　　secondary, 226–228
　　tertiary, 228
　risk factors, 222
　and social factors, 225–226
　treatment, 226–228
Caregiver support, 401
Carolina Abcedarian Project, 418
Case studies
　adjustment disorder, 467
　alcoholism, 286–287, 302
　amnesia for September 11, 190
　anorexia nervosa, 265
　antisocial personality disorder, 233–234, 255
　autistic spectrum disorder, 420
　bipolar mood disorder, 108
　body dysmorphic disorder, 199
　borderline personality disorder, 240, 251
　bulimia nervosa, 10, 267–268
　child custody dispute, 509
　of coercion, 446–447
　conversion disorder, 197–198
　couple therapy, 479–480
　death of spouse, 483
　definition of, 18
　delirium, 382–383
　dementia, 381–382, 382–383
　depression, 53–54
　disorganized schizophrenia, 351
　dissociative fugue, 186–187
　erectile dysfunction, 324
　externalizing disorder, 436–437
　gambling disorder, 314
　genital pain, 326
　heart attack, 207–208
　heroin abuse, 292–293
　heroin use relapse, 310
　hyperactivity with learning disability, 25–26
　insanity defense, 490–491
　internalizing disorders, 454
　limitations of, 18–20
　major depression, 107
　masochism, 335–336
　multiple personality disorder, 191
　narcissism, 244–245
　obsessions/compulsions, 78–79

　obsessive-compulsive disorder, 163–164, 169–170
　panic disorder with agoraphobia, 144–145
　paranoid schizophrenia, 2–3, 350
　schizotypal personality disorder, 249
　sexual assault and PTSD, 176
　sexual communication, 320
　suicide, 132–133
　treatment for "finding oneself,", 472
　uses of, 18–20
　vaginismus and alcohol dependence, 329–330
Catastrophic misinterpretation, in anxiety disorders, 155
Catatonic behavior, 355
Catechol-O-methyltransferase (COMT), 362
Categorical approach to classification, 80
Cathartic therapies, 202
Causal attributions, 122
Causality, 31–32
Causation, vs. correlation, 33
CBCT (cognitive behavioral couple therapy), 480
CBT. See Cognitive behavioral therapy
CD. See Conduct disorder
CDC. See Centers for Disease Control and Prevention (CDC)
Centers for Disease Control and Prevention (CDC), 219–220
Central nervous system (CNS), 100
Central nervous system depressants, 285
Cerebellum, 36f, 37
Cerebral cortex, 38
CET (cognitive enhancement therapy), for schizophrenia, 375
Change, and life events, 209t
Charcot, Jean-Martin, 27, 187
CHD. See Coronary heart disease; Coronary heart disease (CHD)
Checking, compulsive, 165
Chelation therapy, 430
Chemical imbalances, in brain, 35
Child abuse
　battered child syndrome, 509
　borderline personality disorder and, 253, 254f
　forms of, 510
　reporting, 509–511, 510f
　sexual, 305, 510
Child custody, 508–509
Childhood adversity, anxiety disorders and, 153
Childhood bipolar disorder, 457
Child molesters, 337, 343
Child neglect, 510
Child protective service system, 510–511, 510f
Child's best interest standard, 508, 510
Child sexual abuse, 275
Chlorpromazine (Thorazine), 372, 373t
CHMC (Community Mental Health Centers Act), 506–507
Cho, Seung-Hui, 501, 506
Chromosomal disorders, causing intellectual disabilities, 412
Chromosome 14 mutations, in Alzheimer's disease, 397
Chromosomes, 39
Chronological age, vs. mental age, 407
Cialis (tadalafil), 331

Cingulotomy, 58
Circadian rhythm sleep disorder, 221
CISD (critical incident stress debriefing), 184
Civil commitment, 500–507
　abuses of, 503–504
　defined, 501
　grounds/procedures for, 501
　history of mental hospitals in U.S., 500, 500f
　involuntary hospitalization, 501–504
　libertarianism vs. paternalism., 500–501
　rights of mental patients and, 504–506
Classical conditioning
　of anxiety disorders, 154
　definition of, 30
Classification, of psychopathology, 78–90
　anxiety disorders, 148–150
　categorical approach, 80
　culture and, 83–84
　by descriptive features, 81, 82
　dimensional approach, 80
　labeling theory, 82
　need for, 81
　suicide, 133–135
Classification systems. See also specific classification system
　definition of, 80
　Diagnostic and Statistical Manual (DSM-5), 81–83, 83t
　evaluation of, 85–90
　International Classification of Diseases (ICD), 81
Cleaning, compulsive, 164
Client-centered therapy, 64
Clinical assessment. See Assessment
Clinical depression, definition of, 107
Clinical psychologists, number in United States, 14t
Clinical psychology, 14
Clinical research methods, 20–21, 20t
Clinical significance, 62
Clinton, Bill, 9
Clomipramine (Anafranil), for anxiety disorders, 170
Close relationships, abnormal behaviour and, 48
Clozapine (Clozaril), 366, 373, 373t, 374
Cluster suicides, 459
Cocaine abuse, short-term vs. long-term effects, 291–292
Coercion, in parenting, 446–447
Cognition, 45
Cognitive behavioral couple therapy (CBCT), 480
Cognitive-behavioral paradigm, 29–30, 30t
Cognitive behavioral therapy (CBT)
　for bulimia nervosa, 267
　vs. other treatments, 54t, 55
　for paraphilias, 341–342
　for posttraumatic stress disorder, 185
　for substance use disorders, 310–311
Cognitive conflicts, 468, 474
Cognitive distortions/errors, depression and, 122
Cognitive enhancement therapy (CET), for schizophrenia, 375
Cognitive factors, in anxiety disorders, 154–155

Cognitive perspectives, personality disorders and, 235
Cognitive restructuring, 330, 341–342
Cognitive slowness, in mood disorders, 110
Cognitive symptoms, in mood disorders, 110
Cognitive techniques, 63
Cognitive therapy
  for anxiety disorders, 160
  for depression disorder, 128
  for schizophrenia, 375
Cognitive vulnerability, 122
Cohort, 271
Cohort effects, 271
Combat neurosis, 177
Common elements, in suicide, 136, 137
Communication
  as cause of difficult family transitions, 476
  deficits in social, 421–422
  training, in sexual dysfunction treatment, 331
Community Mental Health Centers Act (CHMC), 506–507
Community notification laws, 343
Community psychology, 74
Comorbidity
  definition of, 13, 89
  depression and, 111
  disease burden and, 13, 13f
  interpretation of, 89
Comorbid psychological disorders, 269
Comparison groups, 369
Competence, to stand trial, 495–498, 497t
Competitive sports, "making weight" in, 264
Compulsions, in anxiety disorders, 163–165
Computerized tomography (CT), 101
COMT (catechol-O-methyltransferase), 362
Conceptual skills, 409
Concordance rates, 40, 41t
Concurrent validity, 87
Conditioned response, 30, 154
Conditioned stimulus, 30, 154
Conduct disorder (CD)
  causes, 443–448, 446f
  diagnosis, 442, 443t
  family risk factors, 443
  frequency, 442
  treatment, 453–454
Confidentiality, 512
Conflict
  cognitive, 474
  family, 473–474
  in life-cycle transitions, 467
  resolution of, 72
  unresolved, 474
Confounds, 62
Consciousness, altered state of, 189
Construct validity, 325
Consumer Reports study, on psychotherapy effectiveness, 68
Contempt, in family transition difficulties, 476
Context, and personality, 237
Contingency, 61
Contingency management, 62–63
Continuous performance test, 439
Control
  issues of

in anorexia nervosa, 266
  eating disorders and, 275
  perception of, in anxiety disorders, 155
  predictability and, 213–214
Control group, 62
Convenience sample, 444
Conversion disorder
  case study, 197–198
  definition of, 196
  symptoms, 197, 197f
Coping, with stress, 213–214
Coping skills training, for substance use disorders, 310
Coping with Schizophrenia: A Guide for Families (Mueser & Gingrich), 376
Coronary heart disease (CHD)
  anxiety and, 225
  behavior and, 224
  definition of, 221
  depression and, 225
  hostility and, 224–225
  risk factors, 222
  type A behavior and, 224–225
Coronary occlusion, 222–223
Correlation, vs. causation, 33
Correlational method, 62
Correlational research, 369
Correlational study, 33
Correlation coefficient, 33
Cortex, 36f
Corticotrophin-releasing factor (CRF), 211
Cortisol (stress hormone), 211
Counselors, number in United States, 14t
Countertransference, 59
Couple therapy, 72–73, 479–480
Course specifiers, 115
Creutzfeld-Jakob disease, 398
CRF. See Corticotrophin-releasing factor (CRF)
Criminal responsibility
  definition of, 492
  mental illness and, 492–500, 495t
Crisis centers, 138
Crisis of healthy personality, 467
Critical incident stress debriefing (CISD), 65t, 184
Criticism, in family transition difficulties, 476
Cross-cultural issues
  comparisons
    anxiety disorders, 152
    of personality disorders, 248
    in schizophrenic disorders, 360
  differences, in mood disorders, 118–119
  identity crisis as, 472
Cross-cultural psychology, 248
Cross-cultural studies, of mental disorders, 14
Cross-sectional study, 223
CT (computerized tomography), 101
Cultural-familial retardation, 415, 415f
Culture
  classification of psychopathology and, 83–84
  definition of, 7
  diagnostic practice and, 7–9
  personality and, 247–248
  somatic symptom disorders and, 200
  substance use and, 299

validity of assessment procedures and, 92
Culture-bound syndromes, 83–84
Culture-fair intelligence tests, 409
"Culture of thinness," 272, 273, 275
CVD. See Cardiovascular disease (CVD)
Cyclothymia, 115
Cytomegalovirus, 413

**D**

Dangerousness, to self or others
  as civil commitment criterion, 501–502
  prediction of, 501
DARE programs, 65t
Daubert v. Merrell Down Pharmaceuticals, 491
DBT (dialectical behavior therapy), 64, 254–255
Death
  alcohol-related, 290, 290f
  of spouse, case study, 483
Decatastrophizing, of anxiety disorders, 160
Defense mechanisms, 29, 29t, 59
"Defensive deniers,", 214
Defensiveness, in family transition difficulties, 476
Defensive style, 55
Deinstitutionalization movement
  historical background, 500, 504
  problems with, 506–507
Deinstitutionalization movement
  historical background, 419
Delay of gratification, 448
Delirium
  case study, 382–383
  causes, 396
  frequency, 396
  symptoms, 382–383, 383t
  treatment/management, 399–401
Delusional beliefs, 352–353
Delusional disorder, 357
Delusions, in dementia, 387
Demand and withdrawal pattern, in intimate relationships, 474
Dementia
  case study, 381–382, 382–383
  causes, 396–399, 398f
  vs. depression, 388, 388t
  prevalence
    cross-cultural comparisons, 396
    by subtype, 396
  pseudodementia, 388
  resources, 402
  symptoms, 382–383, 383t
    emotional responsiveness, 387
    judgment, 386–388
    loss of abstract thinking, 386
    memory and learning, 384
    motor behaviors, 388
    neurocognitive, 384
    perception, 385–386
    personality changes, 387
    social behavior, 386
    verbal communication, 384–385
  treatment/management, 399–401
Dendrites, 34
Denial, 29t, 55
Depakene (valproic acid), 130
Department of Veterans Affairs study (VA study), 311
Dependent personality disorder, 241

Dependent variable, 62
Depersonalization, 177, 189
Depersonalization disorder, symptoms, 190
Depressants, 285
Depressed mood, definition of, 106
Depression
  alcoholism and, 111
  and anxiety, 225
  bipolar. See Bipolar disorder
  brain and, 35
  brain imaging studies, 125–126, 126f
  case study, 53–54, 107
  causes, 119–128
    biological, 122–127, 124f, 125f
    integration of social, psychological and biological factors, 127–128
    psychological, 119
    psychological factors, 121–122
    social factors, 119–121, 120f
    stressful life events, 119–120, 120f
  clinical
    definition of, 107
    vs. normal sadness, 108t
  comorbidity, 111
    with anorexia nervosa, 266–267
    with anxiety disorders, 151
    with bulimia nervosa, 269
  coronary heart disease and, 225
  cross-cultural differences, 118–119
  definition of, 106
  dementia and, 387, 388, 388t
  diagnosis, 111–116, 113t
  disability from, 106, 106t
  distorted perceptions of reality and, 46
  eating disorders and, 275–276
  gender differences, 118
  incidence/prevalence, 458, 458f
  internalizing disorders and, 455
  lifetime prevalence, 117–118, 118f
  major, course of, 116, 116f
  neurotransmitters in, 126–127
  postpartum onset, 115
  with psychotic features, 115
  resources for, 139
  symptoms, 109–111, 113t
  treatments, 128–132
Depressive triad, 110
Derealization, in ASD and PTSD, 177
Descriptive approach, 28
Determinants of Outcome of Severe Mental Disorders (DOS), 360
Determinism, vs. free will, 492
Deterrence, 493
Detoxification, 308
Development, stages of, 46–48, 47t
Developmental norms, 436
Developmental psychopathology, definition of, 33, 436
Developmental transitions, 47–48
Deviant Children Grown Up (Robbins), 255
Deviation IQ, 407, 407f
Dexamethasone suppression test (DST), 124
Diagnosis
  causal analysis and, 78
  definition of, 78
  by exclusion, 200–201
Diagnostic and Statistical Manual (DSM), 81
Diagnostic and Statistical Manual (DSM-IV), 8

Exaggerated startle response, in ASD and PTSD, 177
Excitement, sexual, 319
Excoriation disorder, 166t, 167, 168
Executive functioning, 439
Exhaustion stage, of general adaptation syndrome, 213
Exhibitionism, 337, 340, 341
Exhibitionistic disorder, 336–337
Experiential system, 189
Experimental group, 62
Experimental hypothesis, 19
Experimental method, 61, 62
Expert witnesses, 491–492, 508
Explicit memory, 189
Exposure and response prevention, for anxiety disorders, 170
Exposure therapies, 61
Expressed emotion (EE), 367–368
Externalizing disorders, 149
    ADHD. *See* Attention-deficit/ hyperactivity disorder
    case study, 436–437
    causes, 443–448
        biological factors, 443
        coercion, 446–447
        gene–environment interactions and ODD, 446
        genetics and ADHD, 445–446
        inconsistency, 447
        integration and alternative pathways, 448
        negative attention, 447
        neuropsychological abnormalities, 444–445
        parenting styles, 446
        peers, neighborhood and media, 447
        psychological factors, 448
        social factors, 446
        social factors in ADHD, 447–448
        temperament, 443–444
    CD. *See* Conduct disorder
    definition, 436
    diagnosis, 439–442, 440t, 442t–444t
        attention-deficit/hyperactivity disorder (ADHD), 439–442
        conduct disorder (CD), 442
    frequency, 442–443
        family risk factors, 443
    *vs.* internalizing disorders, 149
    ODD. *See* Oppositional defiant disorder
    outgrowing of, 453
    symptoms, 437–439
        adolescent-limited and life-course-persistent, 438
        anger and aggression, 438–439
        attention deficits, 439
        chilren's age and rule violations, 438
        hyperactivity, 439
        impulsivity, 439
        rule violations, 437–438
    treatment, 448–454
        behavioral family therapy, 451–453
        family court, 453
        multisystemic therapy, 453
        psychostimulants, 448–451, 450f
        residential programs, 453
External validity, 62
Extinction, 30
Extrapyramidal symptoms, 373

Eye movement desensitization and reprocessing (EMDR), 186
Eysenck, Hans, 67

# F

Facilitated communication, 65t, 66, 429
Factitious disorder, 199
*Failure to Launch* (movie), 471
False memory syndrome, 188
Family attitudes, in schizophrenic disorders, 368–369
Family conflict, 473–474
Family incidence studies, 40
Family law
    child custody disputes, 508–509
    mental health and, 507–511, 510f
Family life cycle, 473, 473t
Family-oriented aftercare, for schizophrenia, 374–375
Family relationships
    later life transitions and, 482
    troubled
        diagnosis of, 474–475
        eating disorders and, 274–275
Family studies, *of* schizophrenia, 361, 361f
Family therapy, 73, 479–480
Family transitions
    causes of difficulty in, 476–478
    family life cycle and, 467, 473, 473t
    frequency of, 476, 476f
    symptoms, 473
    treatment during, 478–480
Fatalistic suicide, 134
Fatigue, cancer-related, 219
FDA (Food and Drug Administration) tobacco product regulations, 301
Fear
    adaptive and maladaptive, in anxiety disorders, 152–153
    definition of, 146
    of failure, sexual dysfunction and, 329
    of gaining weight, 266
    internalizing disorders and, 455
Fear conditioning, 157
Feingold diet, 452
Female orgasmic disorder, 8, 323t, 325–326
Female sexual arousal disorder, 323t, 324–325
Female sexual dysfunctions, causes of, 329
Female stress response, 211
"Female Viagra," 332
Feminist therapies, 278
Fetal alcohol syndrome, 414
Fetishism, 334
Fetishistic disorder, 334–335
Fever therapy, 18t
Fight anxiety, 28
Fight-or-flight response, 211
"Finding oneself," case study, 472
Firearms, suicide and, 138
Five-factor model of personality, 235, 236t
Flashbacks, in ASD and PTSD, 176
Flashbulb memories, 188
Flight anxiety, 28
Flooding, 61
Fluid intelligence, 385
Fluoxetine, 170
Fluvoxamine, 170
Flynn effect, 409

FMR1 gene, 413
FMRI (functional magnetic resonance imaging), 101
Food additives, ADHD and, 452
Food and Drug Administration (FDA), 301
Forebrain, 37
Formal commitment, 501
Foster care, 510
Fournier, Jan, 26–27
Fragile X syndrome, 413
Framingham Heart study, 224
Frances, Allen, 192–193
Frank, Jerome, 71
Fraternal twins (dizygotic), 40–41, 41t
Free association, 58
Freeman, Walter, 58
Free will, *vs.* determinism, 492
Frequency, of OCD and related disorders, 168
Frequency distribution, 408
Freud, Sigmund
    hysteria and, 187
    psychodynamic paradigm and, 27–29
    stages of development, 46–48, 47t
Freudian psychoanalysis, 58
Freudian slips, 58
Frontal lobe, 36f, 38
Frontotemporal neurocognitive disorder, 392
Frotteurism, 337
Frotteuristic disorder, 337
Frustration, outlets of, 214
Functional magnetic resonance imaging (fMRI), 101
Functional neurological symptoms, 201

# G

GABA (gamma-aminobutyric acid), 158, 160, 398
GABA interneuron, 305f
GAD. *See* Generalized anxiety disorder
Gambling disorder, 312–314
    case studies, 314
    diagnosis, 314
    frequency, 314
    symptoms, 313–314
Gamma-aminobutyric acid (GABA), 158, 160, 398
Gargoylism, 413
GAS (general adaptation syndrome), 213
Gaze aversion, 422, 423f
GBMI (guilty but mentally ill), 494, 495t
Gender
    differences
        in alcohol abuse and dependence prevalence, 299–300, 300f
        anxiety disorders, 151
        in lifetime prevalence, 11–12, 12f
        in personality disorders, 246
        in schizophrenia, 359, 360t
        in stressful life events, 120
    psychopathology and, 48–49
    somatic symptom disorders and, 200
Gender dysphoria (gender identity disorder)
    causes, 344–345
    definition of, 343
    frequency, 344
    resources, 345
    symptoms, 343–344
    with transvestic disorder, 335
    treatment, 345

Gender identity, 343
Gender identity disorder (gender dysphoria). *See* Gender dysphoria (gender identity disorder)
Gender roles, 48–49, 472
Gene-environment correlation
    *vs.* causation, 478
    description of, 42
    in ODD, 446
General adaptation syndrome (GAS), 213
Generalized anxiety disorder (GAD)
    definition of, 150
    twin studies, 156–157
Generalizing, 444
General paresis, 26
Generativity *vs.* stagnation, 468
Genes
    associated, with Alzheimer's disease, 397
    behavioral problems, 395
    definition of, 39
    environment and, 42
Gene therapy, 418
Genetic disorders
    causing intellectual disabilities, 412–413
    dominant inheritance, 39, 40f
    polygenic inheritance, 39–40, 40f
    recessive, 39, 40f
    recessive inheritance, 39, 40f
Genetic factors
    in alcoholism, 303–304
    in anxiety disorders, 156–157
    in attention-deficit/hyperactivity disorder, 445–446
    in autism, 428
    in divorce, 478
    in eating disorders, 277
    neurocognitive disorder, 396–398, 398f
    in schizophrenic disorders, 361–362
    in substance use disorders, 308
Genetic linkage, 395
Genetics
    field of, 39
    mood disorders and, 123, 123f
    psychopathology and, 41–42
    risk for mood disorders, 124, 124f
Genetic variation, normal, intellectual disabilities and, 415, 415f
Genetic vulnerability, to depression, 124, 124f
Genital herpes, 413
Genital pain, case study, 326
Genito-Pelvic pain disorder, 326
Genotype, 39
German measles (rubella), 413
Gerontology, 485
Global Burden of Disease Study, 13
Glutamate, 366
Goodness of fit, 448
*Graham v. Florida,* 499
Grandin, Temple, 419–423
Graves' disease, 39
Greek tradition, in medicine, 15–16
Grief, 484
Group therapy, 73–74
Guilt feelings, in mood disorders, 110
Guilty but mentally ill (GBMI), 494

# H

Hair-pulling disorder. *See also* Trichotillomania
    and OCD, 167
    and skin-picking, 167

in mood disorders, 121–122
in pain disorder, 220
in paraphilias, 341
in posttraumatic stress disorder, 183–184
in schizophrenia, 367–369
in sexual dysfunction, 330–331
in sleep-wake disorders, 220–221
in somatoform disorders, 201, 202f
and stress, 223
in substance use disorders, 306–307
in suicide, 136
Psychological interventions, for anxiety disorders, 158–160
Psychological pain, 466–468
Psychological problems in later life, causes of, 487
Psychological treatments, for sexual dysfunction, 330–331
Psychomotor retardation, 111
Psychomotor stimulants, 57t, 291
Psychoneuroimmunology (PNI), 212
Psychopathology
  assessment. See Assessment; (See Assessment)
  brain structures and, 36–37, 36f–37f
  classification. See Classification, of psychopathology
  definition of, 2
  gender/gender roles and, 48–49
  genetics and, 41–42
  in historical context, 15–18
  history of, lessons from, 17–18
  marital status and, 48
  neurotransmitters and, 35–36
  poverty and, 49
  prejudice and, 49
  prevention, 74
  psychophysiology and, 39
  social relationships and, 48
  society and, 49
Psychopathy, 255
  symptoms of, 257t
Psychopharmacology, 55–57, 57t
Psychophysiological responses to stress, 211–213
Psychophysiology
  adoption studies, 40, 41
  autonomic nervous system and, 39
  behavior genetics and, 39, 41–42
  definition of, 38
  endocrine system and, 38–39
  psychopathology and, 39
  twin studies, 40–41, 41t
Psychosexual development, 29
Psychosis, definition of, 4
Psychosocial rehabilitation (PSR), 15
Psychosocial rehabilitation providers, number in United States, 14t
Psychosocial treatment, for schizophrenia, 374–376
Psychosomatic disorders, 207
Psychostimulants
  for ADHD, 448–451, 450f
  overuse, 450–451
  paradoxical effect, 448–449
  short-term vs. long-term effects, 450t
  side effects, 450
  usage and effects, 449–450
Psychosurgery, 58
Psychotherapist, social influence of, 71
Psychotherapy
  active ingredients, 72
  for anorexia nervosa, 278

for bipolar disorder, 130–131
common factors, 69–71, 71t
definition of, 53
definitions of, 69t
for depression, 130
effectiveness of, 67–68
efficacy, 67
ethnic minorities in, 70
harmful, 65t
hoaxes, 66
improvement from, 68, 69f
outcome research, 65–69
placebos, 280
process research, 69–72
research on, 65–72
  as social influence, 71
  as social support, 71
  for specific disorders, 72
  for suicidal people, 138–139
Psychotic features, 115
Psychotic symptoms (positive symptoms)
  in depression, 115
  in schizophrenic disorders, 352–353
Psychotropic medications, 55, 57t
PTSD. See Posttraumatic stress disorder
PTSD Checklist (PCL), 185
Punishment, 30
Purging, 268
Pycnogenol, 452
Pyromania, 252

## Q

Quetiapine (Seroqul), 373, 373t

## R

Racial identity, 471
Random assignment, 62
Random selection, 444
Range, 408
Rape, 338–340, 338f
Rapid cycling, 115
Rapists
  nonsadistic, 339
  opportunistic, 340
  sadistic, 338
  vindictive, 339–340
Rating scale, 95
Rational-emotive therapy (RET), 63
Rationalization, 29, 29t, 55
Rational suicide, 484
Rational system, 189
Reaction formation, 29t
Reaction range, 415
Reactive attachment disorder, 458, 460
Reality principle, 29
Rebirthing therapy, 65t, 66
Receptors, 34
Recessive genetic disorders, 40f, 42
Recessive inheritance, 39, 40f
Recidivism, 453
Reciprocal causality, 32
Reciprocity, in family transitions, 473
Recovered memories, 65t, 188, 190
Reductionism, 29–30
"Refrigerator parents," 427, 427f
Rehabilitation, 453
Reinforcement, 201
Relapse
  definition of, 116
  prevention, for substance use disorders, 310
Relational aggression, motivation and, 438–439

Relational selves, 46
Relationships
  in adult transition, 470
  later life transitions and, 482–484
Relaxation therapy, for anxiety disorders, 160
Reliability, 28
  definition of, 85
  evaluation of, 85
  vs. validity, 86–87
Religion, in coping with stress, 214
Reminiscence, 483
Remission, 116
Representative sample, 444
Repression, 29t, 214
Research
  methods
    comparison groups, 369
    for sexual arousal, 325
    studies of at-risk populations, 307
  on psychotherapy, 65–72
Residential treatment programs, for conduct disorder, 453
Residual phase, of schizophrenia, 350, 351
Resilience, 181, 214–215, 460
Resistance
  definition of, 59
  as stage in general adaptation syndrome, 213
Resistant attachment, 460
Response-to-intervention (RTI), 441
Responsibilities, individual, 492
Reston, Ana Carolina, 273, 278
RET (rational-emotive therapy), 63
Reticular activating system, 37
Retrograde amnesia, 58, 384
Retrospective reports, 195
Rett's disorder, 427–428
Reuptake, 36
Reverse anorexia, 264
Reverse causality, 33
Reverse tolerance, 294
Revolving door phenomenon, 507
Reward pathways, 304–305, 304f, 305f
Rh incompatibility, 414
RhoGAM, 414
Riggins v. Nevada, 506
Right from wrong principle, 493, 495t
Rights, individual, 492
Right to refuse treatment, 505–506
Risk factors, 32, 307
Risperidone (Risperdal), 373, 373t, 430
Role changes, in adult transition, 470
Role playing, 63, 228
Role reversal, 461
Roper v. Simmons, 499
Rorschach test, 99
RTI (response-to-intervention), 441
Rubella (German measles), 413
Rule violations, in externalizing disorder, 437–438
Rumination disorder, 269
Ruminative style, 122
Rush, Benjamin, 16

## S

Sadness, normal, vs. clinical depression, 108t
Sak, Elyn, 358
Salicylates, ADHD and, 452
Sally-Ann task, 421, 422f
Savant performance, 424, 424t
Scapegoating, 475, 475f

Scared straight, 65t
Scheduling, in sexual dysfunction treatment, 330
Schizoaffective disorder, 358
Schizoid personality disorder, 239
Schizophrenia
  age of onset, 350
  brain structures and, 36–37, 36f–37f
  causes, interaction of biological and environmental factors, 369–370
  course, 358–359
  diagnosis
    DSM-5, 355–356, 356t
    subtypes, 356–357
  family members and, 349
  impact
    on family, 358–359
    on society, 349
  outcome, 358–359
  prodromal phase, 350
  as psychosis, 4
  related psychotic disorders, 357–358
  resources for, 376
  symptoms, 351–355
  vulnerability markers, 370–372, 372f
Schizophrenic disorders
  causes, 360–372
    biological factors, 360–366, 361f, 364f, 365f
    interaction of biological and environmental factors, 369–370
    psychological factors, 367–369
    social factors, 366–367
  diagnosis, 355–359
  frequency, 359–360, 360t
  interaction of biological and environmental factors, 369–370
  spectrum of, 362
  symptoms, 351–355
    negative, 353–354
    positive, 352–353
Schizophreniform disorder, 356
Schizotypal personality disorder, 239, 249
  case study, 249
  causes, 250
  definition of, 229
  diagnostic criteria, 249, 250t
  schizophrenia and, 249
  structured interviews, 93, 94t
  symptoms, 249–250
  treatment, 250–251
Schlichter, Art, 252, 314
School refusal (school phobia), 456
Scientific evidence, proving, 19
Scientific research, importance of, 17
Scientific study methods, for mental disorders, 18–21
Search finding, in PTSD, 183
Seasonal affective disorder, 116, 132
Secondary gain, 201
Secondary hypertension, 222
Secondary prevention, 74
Secretin, 430
Secure attachment, 460
Sedative hypnotics, 57t
Sedatives, 285, 293–294
Selective amnesia, 190
Selective mutism, 456
Selective serotonin reuptake inhibitors (SSRIs), 128–129, 129t
  for acute stress disorder, 186
  for anxiety disorders, 162

Selective serotonin (*continued*)
for depression, 129, 129*t*
for OCD, 170
for suicidal people, 138–139
violent behaviour and, 131
Self, sense of, 46, 468
Self-control, 46
Self-control, lack of, 448
Self-defeating biases, 122
Self-destructive ideas, in mood
disorders, 110
Self-disclosure, 64
Self-esteem
definition of, 46
low, 275–276, 448
Self-fulfilling prophesy, 48
Self-help groups, 73, 309–310
Self-help resources, 21
Self-injury, 423–424
Self-injury, nonsuicidal, 134–135
Self-instruction training, 63
Self-monitoring, 96
Self-report inventories, 96–98, 97*t*
Self-report measures, limitations, 234
Self-stimulation, 422
Self-talk, 156
*Sell v. United States,* 506
Selye, Hans, 213
Sensate focus exercises, 330
Sentencing, mental health and, 498–500
Separation anxiety
anxiety disorders and, 153–154
school refusal and, 455–456
Separation/loss, internalizing disorders
and, 460
September 11, 2001 terrorist attacks
amnesia for, case study, 190
flashbulb memories, 190
posttraumatic stress disorder and,
175, 180
trauma victims, emergency help for, 184
"twentieth terrorist," 498
Seroqul (quetiapine), 373*t*
Serotonin
abnormal behavior and, 35, 36
impulsive personality characteristics
and, 137
mood and, 126–127
Serotonin transporter genes
5-HTT, 124, 124*f*
5-HTTLPR, 446
Sertraline, 170
Sex, later life transitions and, 482
Sex education, 331
Sex-reassignment surgery, 345
Sexual addiction, 9
Sexual assault, 338–340
PTSD and, case studies, 176
trauma of, 180
Sexual behavior
across life span, 327–328
cross-cultural comparisons, 328
historical perspective, 321
Sexual communication, case study, 320
Sexual compulsion, 9
Sexual dysfunctions, 321–332. *See also*
specific sexual dysfunctions
causes, 328–330
definition of, 321
diagnosis, 323–327, 323*t*
frequency, 327–328
incidence/prevalence, 327–328, 327*f*
medications for, 331, 332
paraphilas. *See* Paraphilias

resources for, 345
symptoms, 321–323
treatment, 330–332
Sexuality Information and Education
Council of the United Sates
(SIECUS), 345
Sexual masochism disorder, 335–336
Sexual predator laws, 343, 499
Sexual response, 319–320, 322*f*
Sexual sadism disorder, 336
Sexual selection, 44
Shared environment, 41
Shell shock neurosis, 177
*Shutter Island,* 58
Sick role, learning, 201
SIECUS (Sexuality Information and
Education Council of the
United Sates), 345
Sildenafil (Viagara), 331
Simon, Theophile, 410
Situational exposure, for anxiety
disorders, 159
Situational orgasmic difficulties, 325
Skinner, B. F., 30, 32
Skinner box, 30
Skin-picking. *See also* Excoriation
disorder
case study, 167
and OCD, 168
Sleep disorders, stress and, 220–221
breathing-related, 221
circadian rhythm, 221
Sleeping problems, in mood disorders,
110–111
Sleep terror disorder, 221
Sleepwalking disorder, 221
Slinical syndrome, 106
Slips of the tongue, 58
Slow-to-warm-up children, 444
Social behavior, in dementia, 386–388
Social class, in schizophrenic disorders,
366–367
Social clocks, 469
Social cognition, 45
Social exchange, in family transitions, 473
Social factors
in abnormal behavior, 48
in acute stress disorder, 182
in alcoholism, 302–303
in anorexia and bulimia, 274–275
in antisocial personality disorder, 258
in anxiety disorders, 153–154
in attention deficit/hyper activity
disorder, 447–448
in autism, 427
bipolar disorders and, 120–121
in cardiovascular disease, 225–226
causing intellectual disabilities, 416
in dissociative disorders, 195–196
in drug abuse, 302–303
in externalizing disorder, 446
in family transition difficulties, 476–477
in internalizing disorders, 460
in mood disorders, 119–121, 120*f*
in paraphilias, 340–341
in posttraumatic stress disorder, 182
in schizophrenic disorders, 366–367
in somatoform disorders, 201–202
in successful life transition, 487
in suicide, 137–138
Social influence, in psychotherapy, 71
Socialization, 46, 446
Social motivation, personality disorders
and, 234–235

Social phobia
anxious apprehension and, 156, 156*f*
definition of, 148–149
Social problem solving, 63
Social Readjustment Rating Scale
(SRRS), 209, 209*t*, 210*t*
Social relationships, psychopathology
and, 48
Social selection hypothesis, 367
Social skills, 409
Social skills training (SST), 63, 375
Social support
for cancer victims, 219
implicit *vs.* explicit, 216
psychotherapy as, 71
Social values, psychiatric, 8–9
Social work, 14
Social workers, number in United
States, 14
Society, psychopathology and, 48
Socioeconomic status, somatoform
disorders and, 200
Sole custody, 508
Solian (amisulpride), 373*t*
Soma, 34
Somatic nervous system, 39
Somatic symptom disorders, 196–203,
220
causes of, 200–202
comorbidity, 200
culture, 200
definition of, 196
diagnosis, 197–199
diagnostic criteria, 198
frequency, 199–200
gender and, 200
resources, 203
socioeconomic status and, 200
symptoms, 196–197, 198
treatment, 202–203
treatment of, 202–203
Somatic symptoms, in mood disorders,
110–111
Somatic (bodily) treatment, 18, 18*t*
Somatization disorder, 198
Specific gene, of mood disorders, 123
Specific phobia, 148
Speech, poverty of, 354
Speedball, 292
Spiritual/religious tradition, of
psychological treatment, 55–57
Split-half reliability, 91
"Splitters," 149
Splitting, 251, 355
Spontaneous remission, 67
SRRS. *See* Social Readjustment Rating
Scale (SRRS)
SSRIs. *See* Selective serotonin reuptake
inhibitors (SSRIs)
SST (social skills training), 63, 375
Standard deviation, 65, 407, 408
Standard scores, 408
State-dependent learning, 195
Statistical norms, abnormal behavior
and, 5
Statistical significance, 62, 161
Status offenses, 442
Sterilization, planned, 417
Stigma, 82
Stonewalling, in family transition
difficulties, 476
Strattera, 451
Strep infections, obsessive-compulsive
disorder and, 169

Stress
acquired immune deficiency
syndrome and, 219–221
as appraisal of life events, 210–211,
210*t*
cardiovascular disease and. *See*
Cardiovascular disease
cardiovascular reactivity to, 224
causes, illness, 217
chronic, illness and, 213
coping with, 213–214
and death, 218*f*
definition, 32, 208–209
diagnosis, 217–218
generation, 121
health behavior and, 215–216, 215*f*
as life event, 209
male *vs.* female response, 211
management programs, 226
pain management and, 220, 220*f*
pathways, 212*f*
and psychological influences,
223–224
psychophysiological responses to,
211–213
resources for, 228
response, neuroendocrine system and,
124–125
sensitivity, risk for mood disorders,
124, 124*f*
sleep disorders and, 220–221
symptoms, 210–217
traumatic, 175
Stressful life events, anxiety disorders
and, 153
Stressor-related disorders, 177
Stroke, 37*f,* 38
Structured Interview for DSM-IV
Personality Disorders, 93, 94*t*
Structured interviews
advantages, 93
limitations, 94
for schizotypal personality disorder,
93, 94*t*
Stuporous state, 355
Sublimation, 29*t*
Substance dependence
comorbidity, with anxiety disorders,
151
definition of, 285
development, 299
*DSM-5,* 296–297, 297*t*
resources for, 312
treatment outcome results, 311–312
Substance use
dependence development, 299
drugs associated with, 286
Substance use disorders. *See also* specific
substance use disorders
addictions, disorders associated with,
298
case study, 286–287
causes, 302–308
integrated systems, 307–308
course, 297–298
definition, 285
diagnosis, 295–298, 297*t*
frequency, 298–302, 300*f*
outcome, 297–298, 298*f*
symptoms, 288–295, 289*f*
treatment, 308–312
Substantial capacity, 493
Substituted judgment, 506
Sudden cardiac death, 222